DUMBARTON OAKS TEXTS

XII

# THE TAKTIKA
# OF LEO VI

CORPUS FONTIUM
HISTORIAE BYZANTINAE

CONSILIO SOCIETATIS INTERNATIONALIS
STUDIIS BYZANTINIS PROVEHENDIS
DESTINATAE EDITUM

VOLUMEN XLIX

# LEONIS VI TACTICA

EDIDIT, ANGLICE VERTIT, ADNOTAVIT
GEORGE DENNIS

SERIES WASHINGTONIENSIS,
EDIDIT JOHN DUFFY

In aedibus Dumbarton Oaks
Washingtoniae, D.C.

MMXIV

# THE TAKTIKA
# OF LEO VI

TEXT, TRANSLATION, AND COMMENTARY

*by*

GEORGE DENNIS

REVISED EDITION

DUMBARTON OAKS

RESEARCH LIBRARY AND COLLECTION

WASHINGTON, D.C.
2014

original edition ©2010,
revised paperback edition ©2014
Dumbarton Oaks
Trustees for Harvard University
Washington, D.C.
Printed in the United States of America.

19  18  17  16  15  14        1  2  3  4  5  6

LIBRARY OF CONGRESS CATALOGING-IN-PUBLICATION DATA
Leo VI, Emperor of the East, 866–912.
[Tactica. English & Greek]
The Taktika of Leo VI / text, translation,
and commentary by George Dennis. — 1st ed.
p. cm. — (Dumbarton Oaks texts ; 12)
Greek text and English translation on facing pages;
notes and commentary in English.
Includes bibliographical references and index.

ISBN 978-0-88402-359-3 (hardcover : alk. paper)
ISBN 978-0-88402-394-4 (revised paperback : alk. paper)

1. Military art and science—Early works to 1800.
2. Tactics—Early works to 1800.
3. Military art and science—Byzantine Empire.
4. Byzantine Empire—History, Military—527–1081.
I. Dennis, George T.    II. Title.
U101.L42313  2010
355.4'2—dc22
2009075248

*In accordance with the rules adopted by the*
*International Commission*
*for the Edition of Sources of Byzantine History,*
*the text and translation of this volume have been verified*
*by John Duffy, John Haldon, and Alice-Mary Talbot.*

# CONTENTS

# PREFACE TO THE CORRECTED EDITION

Fr. George Dennis's edition and translation of Leo VI's *Taktika* has met with great success. In the three years since its publication, all copies have been sold, making evident the need to keep an affordable version in print. Preparing for a new paperback edition brought with it the opportunity to make corrections. Instrumental in this effort were Everett Wheeler and John Haldon. Professor Wheeler provided numerous suggestions for improvement, nearly all touching on the *apparatus fontium* and the notes to the English translation. Those corrections that allowed us to remain faithful to the 2010 page and line numbers were accommodated; those that could not were taken into consideration by Professor Haldon in his *A Critical Commentary on the Taktika of Leo VI*, Dumbarton Oaks Studies 44 (Washington, DC, 2014), which is referred to occasionally in this edition.

Very few changes have been made to the Greek text (pr.60, 94 [capitalization]; 20.101 [MS reading]). The great majority of alterations touch on typographical errors and the identification of Leo's sources, which are frequently difficult to pinpoint. Fr. Dennis intended to steer the reader to the chief primary sources without implying the specific nature of Leo's text reuse. Hence, corrections to the *apparatus fontium* and footnotes are intended to adhere to his original design; for greater specificity the reader is advised to consult Haldon, *Commentary*. The few footnotes where it was necessary to depart from the numbering of the 2010 edition (Constitutions 4, 6, 14, 17, 20) are marked with an asterisk.

# PREFACE

My dissertation director, Raymond-J. Loenertz, OP, once told me that, in old age, one should not undertake a critical edition of a Greek text. Perhaps I should have followed his advice. When I began work on the present edition, however, old age was off in the distant future and I could still distinguish an acute accent from a grave. But, owing to unforeseen circumstances, the work took much longer than I had anticipated and I came to realize the pertinence of Fr. Loenertz's cautionary advice. Despite our best efforts, there surely remain imperfections and mistakes. That they are not too numerous is due largely to the careful, time-consuming work of John Duffy in reading and correcting my typescript. To him I express my heartfelt thanks. My thanks also to John Haldon for his helpful suggestions and, among other things, his corrections of the equine terminology. My sincere thanks go to Alice-Mary Talbot, of Dumbarton Oaks, for her kind and constant support and for expediting the production of this book. My thanks, as well, to Joel Kalvesmaki, a former student, who so efficiently presided over the editorial process, and to Lionel Yaceczko who moved that process along carefully and professionally.

I must, as any scholar must, acknowledge the gracious, professional assistance of the librarians at Biblioteca Medicea Laurenziana, Biblioteca Apostolica Vaticana, Biblioteca de El Escorial, Biblioteca Ambrosiana, as well as those at Dumbarton Oaks, The Catholic University of America, and Santa Clara University.

*Los Gatos, California*
*George T. Dennis, S.J.*
*September, 2009*

# INTRODUCTION

Although he probably never set foot on a battlefield, the Byzantine emperor Leo VI (r. 886–912) appears to have had a lively interest in military matters and the conduct of war. He was after all the supreme commander of the Byzantine or, as he would prefer, Roman armed forces. Successor to Caesar Augustus, Trajan, Constantine, and Justinian, he was expected to be victorious in war and to subject barbarian peoples to the authority of Rome. He soon realized that he could not do this without a solid knowledge of military equipment and practice. This is precisely what Leo set about to acquire. The Byzantines had inherited a voluminous series of military treatises from antiquity: diagrams of battle formations and instructions for improving one's archery, for besieging or defending a city, and for nearly every aspect of warfare. Leo went through all this, summarized it, and presented what he considered to be an elementary handbook for his officers on how to prepare soldiers for war and how to move them about on campaign and on the battlefield. The *Tactical Constitutions*, or *Taktika*, were the result.

Preceded by a prologue and concluding with an epilogue, the twenty Constitutions, or chapters, offer little that is original. But the Byzantines were not interested in original compositions; they revered the authority of the ancients. Apart, then, from sections devoted to the Saracens and to naval warfare, the *Taktika* consist largely of adaptations and paraphrases of previous authors, the most obvious of which are Onasander (first century A.D.), Aelian (second century A.D.), and Maurice (ca. A.D. 600). Leo must have compiled the *Taktika* during his reign as emperor, for he refers to his father, Basil I, as deceased. As with any work attributed to an emperor, it is not clear how much was written by Leo himself (although there are some very personal remarks) and how much by his secretaries or research assistants. At any rate, copies were made and, sometime before the death of his son, Constantine VII, in 959, it was incorporated into a large volume of Greek military treatises, a sort of military encyclopedia, and deposited in the imperial library. This, or a copy of it, is the mid-tenth-century codex Mediceo-Laurentianus graecus, 55, 4 (**M**).

This manuscript, written by one hand on good parchment, has been the subject of several detailed studies.[1] Alphonse Dain claims that it exemplifies the first manuscript family, which he designates as the authentic tradition. In its present state, it is made up of 404 folios, mostly quaternions, although some folios are now missing, as will be noted *suo loco*. Each page measures 32.5 × 26 cm., 32 lines to a page. The script is a clear and somewhat elegant minuscule, with the titles in semi-uncial. The ink is dark brown, fading in places, with red ink used for the titles, which are preceded by ornamental bands.

It seems that not many copies were made of **M**, and much of its subsequent history is not clear. Early in the fifteenth century, it was owned by a high-ranking army officer in the service of Emperor Manuel II Palaiologos, Demetrios Laskaris Leontares, who made use of blank spaces to record births and deaths in his family from 1408 to 1439. His grandson, also named Demetrios, made further notations for the years 1448 to 1450.[2] After the fall of Constantinople, in 1453, the volume found its way to Thessaly, where it was purchased in 1491 by Janus Laskaris and brought to Florence.

The *Tactical Constitutions*, beginning on folio 281, originally consisted of sixteen constitutions, which were followed by an assortment of maxims; an epilogue; and three treatises on surprise attacks, siege warfare, and naval warfare. These three treatises, as well as a collection of concise sayings, were soon incorporated into the main body of the work, as can be seen in the codex Vindobonensis phil. graecus 275 (**W**), resulting in the following order for the final sections: Constitution XIV, The Day of Battle; XV, Siege Warfare; XVI, The Day after Battle; XVII, Surprise Attacks; XVIII, Customs of Different Nations; XIX, Naval Warfare; XX, Concise Sayings; Epilogue. This is the plan, perhaps the original plan, given in the prologue (lin. 103–19). One should also note that, in the manuscripts, Constitutions III and IV are in reverse order.

In addition to the above changes in the order of the chapters, **W** made a few other changes, mostly minor ones, indicated below. It is, in essence, an expand-

---

1. A. M. Bandini, *Catalogus codicum manuscriptorum graecorum Bibliothecae Laurentianae* (Florence, 1768), 1:218–38; Dain, "Stratégistes," 382–85, with bibliography; also his *Histoire*, 183–85.

2. P. Schreiner, *Die byzantinischen Kleinchroniken*, 3 vols. (Vienna, 1975), 1:641–49.

ed copy of **M**, a sort of second edition. Although mutilated in the beginning and at the end, and missing several folios, it must be consulted to establish the authentic text of the *Taktika*. **W** is a small (octavo) parchment volume consisting presently of 249 folios. The script is clear, 24 lines to a page, although the ink has faded in several places. Especially in the earlier chapters, there are numerous brief, crudely written marginal notations, perhaps by a later hand, often without diacritical marks (reproduced as such in this edition), meant to clarify certain terms in the text. When **W** was written is not clear, probably early in the second half of the tenth century.

A thorough study of the two manuscripts indicates that **W** may have been copied directly from **M** or, at least, from a manuscript very closely linked to it. The differences between the two are minimal, and a survey of the first fourteen chapters reveals some 220 common errors, such as κουτουβέρνιν and τόλδον (see p. xiii below). And, of course, each manuscript has some unique errors, with **W** having a few more than **M**, including some omissions. Both seem to regard indicative and subjunctive as interchangeable, o ↔ ω, ει ↔ η. **M** tends to present numerals as such, whereas **W** tends to spell them out, e.g., ιβ′ versus δώδεκα. Both prefer o to ω in words such as κουρσάτορες. In a few instances, **W** has the correct reading whereas **M** does not, but these are usually due to simple scribal corrections of mistakes in **M**. **W** generally adds final ν before a word beginning with κ or τ.

The second family of manuscripts, as identified by scholars, is headed by codex Ambrosianus B 119 sup. (139) (**A**), a parchment manuscript consisting of 347 folios, mostly quaternions, 29.5 × 22.5 cm, with 31 lines to a page.[3] The *Taktika* of Leo begins on folio 189. The manuscript has been dated to early in the second half of the tenth century.[4] The text, however, is not the same as that found in **M** and **W**, but is a paraphrase, with words often transposed. One cannot therefore speak of common or unique errors in **A** with any precision. While it cannot be ignored, it is, for the most part, not very helpful in reconstituting the original text; on occasion, when **M** is faulty or lacking, **A** provides the correct reading. A glance at the apparatus of this edition, however, makes it obvious that **A** has

3. A. Martini and D. Bassi, *Catalogus codicum graecorum Bibliothecae Ambrosianae* (Milan, 1906), 1:157–60. See now B. Leoni, *La Parafrasi Ambrosiana dello Strategicon di Maurizio: l'arte della guerra a Bisanzio* (Milan, 2003).

4. C. Mazzuchi, "Dagli anni di Basilio Parakimomenos (Cod. Ambros. B 119 sup.)," *Aevum* 52 (1978): 267–318.

much more in common with the third manuscript family than with the first, although it is difficult to be more exact about their relationship. Whether it is a paraphrase based directly on **M** or on a common ancestor, or on perhaps a sibling, is not clear.

The third family includes the largest number of manuscripts, but only three are relevant to our study of the text. Codex Vaticanus graecus 1164 (**V**) is a parchment manuscript, 23 × 31 cm, with 33 lines to a page, composed of quaternions, and written in a careful, regular minuscule. Only 281 of its original 392 folios remain. Consisting of ancient and medieval military treatises, its copy of the *Taktika* begins only at the end of Constitution V. This manuscript is very closely related to Parisinus graecus 2442 (**P**) and Neapolitanus graecus 284 (**N**). All three were produced in the same scriptorium, that of Ephrem, in Constantinople, at about the same time, probably around 1020.[5]

**P** and the codex Barberinianus graecus II 97 (276) (**B**) originally formed one manuscript, but the separation was poorly done and several quaternions were mixed up in both.[6] It is written in a careful minuscule, "Perlschrift," on parchment, 125 folios in **P** and 240 in **B**, quaternions, 34 × 26 cm, with 36 lines to a page. It was produced perhaps a bit later than **V**. The *Tactical Constitutions* of Leo begin in **B** at folio 130.

The third manuscript from the same scriptorium, also divided in two, is formed by **N** and the codex Scorialensis graecus Y-III-11 (**E**). It is a parchment manuscript, consisting of quaternions, 22.5 × 14 cm, with 38 lines to a page. In their present states, **N** consists of 101 folios that do not include the *Taktika*, and **E** of 308, with the *Taktika* beginning on folio 160. The derivation of this manuscript has been disputed, but there are reasons to think that **N E** was copied from **V**.

Other manuscripts containing complete or partial texts of the *Taktika* continued to be produced through the sixteenth century—Vári counted 88 of them.[7] They are, however, of no use in reconstituting the original text.

The *Taktika* has been wholly or partially edited before this. A few pages of

5. J. Irigoin, "Pour une étude des centres de copies byzantins," *Scriptorium* 12 (1958): 208–27; 13 (1959): 177–209.

6. Ibid. See also H. A. Omont, *Inventaire sommaire des manuscrits grecs de la Bibliothèque nationale et des autres bibliothèques de Paris et des Départements*, vol. 2, *Ancien fonds grec: Droit, histoire, sciences* (Paris, 1888), 262.

7. R. Vári, *Leonis imperatoris Tactica*, 2 vols. (Budapest, 1917–1922) (= **Va**), 1:xv–xxix.

Constitution IV, as found in codex Monacensis graecus 244, were printed in Venice, in 1552. The entire work, as found in three secondary manuscripts, was first published by Joannes Meurs (Leyden, 1612). After some mistakes were corrected and the text compared with **M**, it was again published by J. Lami (Florence, 1745). This edition, in turn, was incorporated by J.-P. Migne into his Patrologia graeca, vol. 107, cols. 672–1094 (= **PG**). Finally, a critical edition of the prologue and Constitutions I–XIV (to line 228) was published by Vári (see n. 7). At the top of each page are printed the sources utilized by the author, and at the bottom the paraphrase of Nikephoros Ouranos under the title *recensio constantiniana*. He also published Constitution XVIII, together with a Hungarian translation.[8]

It is clear that any scholarly edition of the *Taktika* must be based on **M**, along with what is found in **W**. And such is the rationale of the present edition. **A**, although a paraphrase, sometimes provides the correct reading or helps to clarify the terminology of **M**. It has therefore been included in the apparatus. For the same reasons, the readings of **V B E,** although of less help, have also been included. We have indicated the folio numbers of **M** in the margin and, where that is missing, those of **W** or **A**. In general, we have retained its arrangement of paragraphs and its orthography, including some inconsistencies, such as τάφρος ↔ τράφος. There are some exceptions, such as the sequence of the books, noted above, and the spelling of some words. For example, instead of κουτουβέρνιν of **MW**, we have preferred κοντουβέρνιν (-ιον) of the other manuscripts (a better reflection of the Latin original *contubernium*), and τοῦλδον rather than the incorrect τόλδον of **MW**. There are very few other changes and the reasons for them should be clear from the apparatus.

### TRANSLATION

Byzantine military writers, just like their modern counterparts, made no effort to write in an imaginative or sophisticated manner. In fact, they explicitly tell us that they have made no pretense of fine writing, of producing literary masterpieces. Leo's *Taktika* is no exception (cf. Epilogue, 70). Intended for practical use, it is written in a straightforward and generally uncomplicated Greek. We have tried to render this in the same kind of English. A very literal, word-for-word

---

8. "Böles Leo Hadi Taktikájának XVIII Fejezete" in *A Magyar Honfoglalás Kútföi*, edited by G. Pauler and S. Szilágyi (Budapest, 1900) (= **Va,Hung.**).

translation may have some advantages, but it would not be readable. Sometimes, therefore, we have altered sentence structure, omitted several Greek particles (γάρ, μέν, δέ), and added a few words in < >, all in an effort to make the text easier to read and to understand. We believe that the present translation, while not perfect, is nonetheless an accurate, idiomatic rendition of the Greek original.

Words that have no exact equivalent in English would be awkward if translated literally and so have been left in transliterated Greek, e.g., *bandon, tagma, pentarch, dekarch, merarch*. This has special relevance to the names given to the units and officers of the Byzantine army. Company and regiment are not the same as *tagma* or *meros*; a *merarch* is not really a colonel. One exception is the plural of *meros*: "divisions" seems preferable to *mere* or *meroses*. In the manuscripts some numbers are written as numerals and others are spelled out. These have been regularized in the translation: round numbers and numbers up to one hundred are spelled out (e.g., ιβ′ becomes "twelve"); all others are rendered in Arabic numerals.

In an effort to clarify some terms and to identify some citations or references, we have appended a few brief notes to the translation. An extended commentary by John Haldon is in preparation at Dumbarton Oaks.

# SELECT BIBLIOGRAPHY

| Abbreviation | Texts |
|---|---|
| Aelian | Aelianus' Theorie der Taktik. In *Griechische Kriegsschriftsteller*. Edited by H. Köchly and W. Rüstow. 2 vols. Leipzig, 1855. vol.2, pt.1. |
| CampOrg | Anonymous. "Campaign Organization and Tactics." In *Three Byzantine Military Treatises*. Edited and translated by G. Dennis. 241–335. CFHB 25. Washington, DC, 1985. |
| | Anonymous. "Chapitres peu connus de l'*Apparatus bellicus*." Edited by C. Zuckerman. *TM* 12 (1994): 359–89. |
| | Anonymous. "De arcus usu." In *Griechische Kriegsschriftsteller*. Edited by H. Köchly and W. Rüstow, 2.2: 198–209. Leipzig, 1855. |
| Skirmishing | Anonymous. "Skirmishing." In *Three Byzantine Military Treatises*. Edited and translated by G. Dennis, 137–239. CFHB 25. Washington, DC, 1985. |
| Arrian | *Arriani Tactica et Mauricii Artis militaris libri duodecim*. Edited by J. Scheffer. Uppsala, 1664. |
| Asclepiodotus | "Tactics." In *Aeneas Tacticus, Onasander, Asclepiodotus*. Edited and translated by the Illinois Greek Club, 229–340. Cambridge, MA, 1928. |
| *DAI* | Constantine Porphyrogenitus. *De administrando imperio*. Vol. 1, Greek text edited by G. Moravcsik. Rev. edition and translation by R. J. Jenkins. CFHB 1. Washington, DC, 1967. Vol. 2, *Commentary*. Edited by Jenkins. London, 1962. |
| *ImpExp* | Constantine Porphyrogenitus. *Three Treatises on Imperial Military Expeditions*. Edited and translated by J. Haldon. CFHB 28. Vienna, 1990. |
| | *De cerimoniis aulae byzantinae*. Edited by J. Reiske. 2 vols. Bonn, 1929–30. |
| *Siegecraft* | Heron of Byzantium. *Two Tenth Century Instructional Manuals*. Edited and translated by D. Sullivan. Washington, DC, 2000. |

Kekaumenos        *Soviety: Raskazy Kekavmena.* Edited by G. Litavrin. Moscow, 1972.

                  *Raccomandazioni e consigli di un galantumoma: Στρατηγικόν.*
                  Edited by M. D. Spadaro. Alessandria, 1998.

                  Leo the Deacon. *Leonis diaconi Caloensis historiae libri decem.*
                  Edited by C. B. Hase. Bonn, 1828.

                  ———. *The History of Leo the Deacon.* Translated by A.-M. Talbot
                  and D. Sullivan. Washington, DC, 2005.

                  Leo VI. *Leonis imperatoris Tactica.* Edited by R. Vári. 2 vols. Buda-
                  pest, 1917–22; complete in PG 107. [Contains Constitutions I–XIV]

Strat.            Maurice. *Das Strategikon des Maurikios.* Edited by G. Dennis with
                  Germ. translation by E. Gamillscheg. CFHB 17. Vienna, 1981.

                  ———. *Maurice's Strategikon.* Engl. translation by G. Dennis.
                  Philadelphia, 1984.

                  *Naumachica.* Edited by A. Dain. Paris, 1943.

                  Nikephoros Phokas, *Le traité sur la guérilla de Nicéphore Phocas.*
                  Edited and translated by G. Dagron and H. Mihaescu. Paris, 1986

Onas.             "The General." In *Aeneas Tacticus, Onasander, Asclepiodotus.*
                  Edited and translated by the Illinois Greek Club, 341–527. Cambridge,
                  MA, 1928.

                  *Oracles chaldaïques.* Edited and translated by E. des Places. Paris,
                  1971.

Polyaen.          Polyaenus. *Strategematon libri VIII.* Edited by K. Woelfflin and
                  I. Melber. Stuttgart, 1970.

                  ———. *Polyaenus: Stratagems of War.* Translated by P. Krentz and
                  E. Wheeler. Chicago, 1994.

Skylitzes         John Skylitzes. *Ioannis Scylitzae Synopsis historiarum.* Edited by
                  J. Thurn. CFHB 5. Berlin, 1973.

Suda              *Suidae Lexicon.* Edited by A. Adler. 5 vols. Leipzig, 1928–38.

                  *Sylloge tacticorum.* Edited by A. Dain. Paris, 1938.

SyrMag            Syrianes (magistros). "Strategy." In *Three Byzantine Military
                  Treatises.* Edited and translated by G. Dennis, 1–136. CFHB 25.
                  Washington, DC, 1985.

                  *Theophanis Chronographia.* Edited by C. de Boor. Vol. 1. Leipzig,
                  1863.

                  *Theophanis Continuatus.* Edited by I. Bekker. Bonn, 1838.

*Secondary Works*

Ahrweiler, H. *Byzance et la Mer.* Paris, 1966.

Amatuccio, G. *Peri Toxeias: L'arco da guerra nel mondo bizantino e tardoantico.* Bologna, 1996.

Carile, A., and S. Cosentino. *Storia della marineria bizantina.* Bologna, 2004.

Cheynet, J. C. "Les Phocas." In Nikephoros Phokas, *Traité*, 289–315.

Christides, V. "Ibn al-Manqali (Mangli) and Leo VI: New Evidence on Arab-Byzantine Ship Construction and Naval Warfare." In *Stephanos, Studia byzantina ac Slavica Vladimiro Vavrinek dedicata = BSl* 56 (1995): 83–96.

Cosentino, S. "The Syrianos Strategikon: A Ninth Century Source?" *Bizantinistica. Rivista di studi bizantini e slavi* 2 (2000): 248–61.

Dagron, G. "Byzance et le modèle islamique au Xe siècle à propos des constitutions tactiques de l'empereur Léon VI." *Comptes rendus de l'Acad. des Inscript. et Belles-Lettres* (1983): 219–42.

Dain, A. *Histoire du texte d'Elien le Tacticien.* Paris, 1946.

———. "Les stratégistes byzantins." *TM* 2 (1967): 317–92.

———. "Touldos et Touldon dans les traités militaires." In *Mélanges Henri Grégoire* (Brussels, 1950) 2:161–69.

Dennis, G. T. "Byzantine Battle Flags." *ByzF* 8 (1982): 51–59.

———. "Byzantine Heavy Artillery: The Helepolis." *GRBS* 39 (1998): 99–115.

———. "The Byzantines in Battle." In *Byzantium at War.* Edited by K. Tsinakes. 165–78. Athens, 1997.

———. "Religious Services in the Byzantine Army." *ΕΥΛΟΓΗΜΑ: Studies in Honor of Robert Taft, S.J.* Studia Anselmiana 110. Edited by E. Carr et al. 107–17. Rome, 1993.

———. "Some Reflections on Byzantine Military Theory." *John K. Zeender: A Festschrift.* Edited by R. Calinger and T. West. 1–18. Maplecrest, NY, 2007.

Dufrenne, S. "Aux sources des gonfanons." *Byzantion* 43 (1973): 51–60.

Eickhoff, E. *Seekrieg und Seepolitik zwischen Islam und Abendland.* Berlin, 1966.

Greatrex, G., et al. "Urbicius' *Epitedeuma*: An Edition, Translation and Commentary." *BZ* 98 (2005): 35–74.

Grosdidier de Matons, J. "Trois études sur Léon VI." *TM* 5 (1973): 229–42.

Grosse, R. "Die Fahnen in der römisch-byzantinischen Armee des 4.–10. Jahrhunderts." *BZ* 24 (1924): 359–72.

Haldon, J. F. *Byzantine Praetorians: An Administrative, Institutional and Social Survey of the Opsikion and Tagmata, c. 580–900.* Bonn, 1984.

———. *The Byzantine Wars: Battles and Campaigns of the Byzantine Era.* Gloucestershire, 2001.

———. *A Critical Commentary on the Taktika of Leo VI.* Dumbarton Oaks Studies 44. Washington, DC, 2014.

———. *Recruitment and Conscription in the Byzantine Army c. 550–950: A Study of the Origins of the Stratiotika Ktemata.* Vienna, 1979.

———. "Some Aspects of Byzantine Military Technology from the Sixth to the Tenth Centuries." *BMGS* 1 (1975): 11–47.

———. "Theory and Practice in Tenth Century Military Administration: Chapters II, 45 and 46 of the Book of Ceremonies." *TM* 13 (2000): 201–352.

———. *Warfare, State and Society in the Byzantine World, 565–1204.* London, 1999.

Haldon, J. F., and M. Byrne. "A Possible Solution to the Problem of Greek Fire." *BZ* 70 (1977): 91–99.

Hild, F., and M. Restle. *Tabula imperii byzantini.* Vol. 2, *Kappadokien.* Vienna, 1981.

Hunger, H. *Die hochsprachliche profane Literatur der Byzantiner.* 2 vols. Munich, 1978.

Kaegi, W. *Some Thoughts on Byzantine Military Strategy.* Brookline, MA, 1983.

Kazhdan, A., et al., eds. *Oxford Dictionary of Byzantium.* 3 vols. New York, 1991.

Kolias, T. G. "The Taktika of Leo VI the Wise and the Arabs." *Graeco-Arabica* 3 (1984): 129–35.

———. *Byzantinische Waffen.* Vienna, 1988.

Korres, T. Ὑγρὸν πῦρ· ἕνα ὅπλο τῆς Βυζαντινῆς ναυτικῆς τακτικῆς. 3rd ed. Thessalonike, 1995.

Kučma, V. "Iz istorij vizantijskogo voennogo." *Vizantijskij Vremmenik* 38 (1977): 94–101.

Kuhn, H. J. *Die byzantinische Armee im 10. und 11. Jahrhundert.* Vienna, 1991.

*Lexikon zur byzantinischen Gräzität.* Edited by E. Trapp et al. Vienna, 1994.

Luttwak, E. *The Grand Strategy of the Byzantine Empire.* Cambridge, MA, 2009.

Maliaras, N. "Die Musikinstrumente des byzantinischen Heers vom 6. bis zum 12. Jahrhundert." *JÖB* 51 (2001): 94–95.

McGeer, E. *Sowing the Dragon's Teeth: Byzantine Warfare in the Tenth Century.* Washington, DC, 1995.

———. "Menaulion—Menaulatoi." *Diptycha* 4 (1986–87): 53–57.

———. "Tradition and Reality in the Taktika of Nikephoros Ouranos." *DOP* 45 (1991): 29–40.

Moravcsik, G. *Byzantinoturcica*. 2nd ed. 2 vols. Berlin, 1958.

Pryor, J., and E. Jeffreys. *The Age of the Dromon: the Byzantine Navy ca. 500–1204*. Leiden–Boston, 2006.

Rance, P. "Drungus, drouggos, and drouggisti: A Gallicism and Continuity in Late Roman Cavalry Tactics." *Phoenix* 58 (2004): 96–130.

———. "Tactics and Tactica in the Sixth Century." PhD diss., University of St Andrews, 1993.

Schilbach, E. *Byzantinische Metrologie*. Munich, 1970.

Vári, R. "Zur Überlieferung mittelgriechischer Taktikern." *BZ* 15 (1906): 47–87.

———. "Böles Leo Hadi Taktikájának XVIII Fejezete." In *A Magyar Honfoglalás Kútföi*. Edited by G. Pauler and S. Szilágyi. Budapest, 1900.

Vasiliev, A. A. *Byzance et les Arabes*. 2 vols. Brussels, 1935–50.

Wiita, J. E. "The Ethnika in Byzantine Military Treatises." PhD diss., University of Minnesota, 1977.

Zuckerman, C. "The Military Compendium of Syrianus Magister." *JÖB* 40 (1990): 216.

# ACRONYMS

For bibliographical abbreviations see above, Select Bibliography.

| | |
|---|---|
| *BMGS* | *Byzantine and Modern Greek Studies* |
| *BSl* | *Byzantinoslavica* |
| *ByzF* | *Byzantinische Forschungen* |
| *BZ* | *Byzantinische Zeitschrift* |
| CFHB | Corpus Fontium Historiae Byzantinae |
| *DOP* | *Dumbarton Oaks Papers* |
| *GRBS* | *Greek, Roman, and Byzantine Studies* |
| *JÖB* | *Jahrbuch der Österreichischen Byzantinistik* |
| *LBG* | *Lexikon zur byzantinischen Gräzität* |
| *ODB* | *Oxford Dictionary of Byzantium* |
| PG | Patrologiae cursus completus, series graeca, edited by J.-P. Migne 161 vols. (Paris, 1855–67) |
| *REB* | *Revue des études byzantines* |
| *TM* | *Travaux et Mémoires* |

# SIGLA

M     *Codex Mediceo-Laurentianus graecus 55, 4.*

W     *Codex Vindobonensis phil. graecus 275.*

A     *Codex Ambrosianus B 119 sup. (139).*

V     *Codex Vaticanus graecus 1164.*

B     *Codex Barberinianus graecus II 97 (276).*

E     *Codex Scorialensis graecus Y-III-11.*

Dain     *Naumachica*, edited by A. Dain (Paris, 1943).

Onas.     *Strategikos*, in *Aeneas Tacticus, Onasander, Asclepiodotus,* edited and translated by the Illinois Greek Club (Cambridge, MA, 1928), 341–527.

Strat.     *Das Strategikon des Maurikios*, edited by G. Dennis with Germ. translation by E. Gamillscheg (Vienna, 1981).

Va     R. Vári, *Leonis imp. Tactica*, 2 vols. (Budapest 1917–22).

Va,Hung.     R. Vári, "Böles Leo Hadi Taktikájának XVIII Fejezete," In *A Magyar Honfoglalás Kútföi,* edited by G. Pauler and S. Szilágyi (Budapest, 1900). (= Const. XVIII; see Introduction).

PG     Patrologiae cursus completus, series graeca, edited by J.-P. Migne, 161 vols. (Paris, 1857–66), 107:672–1094.

De     G. Dennis.

Du     J. Duffy.

| | |
|---|---|
| < > | suppleta ab editore. |
| ci. | coniecit. |
| corr. | correxit. |
| des. | desinit. |
| fol. | folium. |
| inc. | incipit. |
| mg. | in margine. |
| om. | omisit, omiserunt. |
| scr. | scripsit. |
| trsp. | transposuit, transposuerunt. |

# THE TAKTIKA
# OF LEO VI

# ΛΕΟΝΤΟΣ ΕΝ ΧΡΙΣΤΩι ΑΥΤΟΚΡΑΤΟΡΟΣ ΤΩΝ ΕΝ ΠΟΛΕΜΟΙΣ ΤΑΚΤΙΚΩΝ ΣΥΝΤΟΜΟΣ ΠΑΡΑΔΟΣΙΣ

1. Ἐν ὀνόματι τοῦ Πατρὸς καὶ τοῦ Υἱοῦ καὶ τοῦ Ἁγίου Πνεύματος, τῆς ἁγίας καὶ ὁμοουσίου καὶ προσκυνητῆς Τριάδος, τοῦ ἑνὸς καὶ μόνου ἀληθινοῦ Θεοῦ

5 ἡμῶν, Λέων, ὁ εἰρηνικὸς ἐν Χριστῷ αὐτοκράτωρ, πιστός, εὐσεβής, ἀεισέβαστος, αὔγουστος.

2. Οὐ βασιλικὴ δορυφορία καὶ ἐξουσία, οὐ τῆς ἐξουσίας δυναστεία καὶ περιουσία, οὐ τῆς περιουσίας ἐπίδειξις καὶ ἀπόλαυσις, οὐδὲν ὅσα τῶν ἐν ἀνθρώ- ποις ἐφετῶν καὶ τιμίων τὴν ἡμετέραν οὕτως εὐφραίνει βασιλείαν ὡς ἡ τῶν

10 ὑπηκόων εἰρήνη καὶ εὐημερία καὶ τῶν πολιτικῶν πραγμάτων ἡ δι᾽ αὐτῶν ἐπὶ τὸ κρεῖττον κατάστασίς τε καὶ ἐπανόρθωσις. ὥσπερ τὸ ἐναντίον οὐδὲν οὕτω τὴν ἡμῶν καρδίαν ἀνιᾷ καὶ λυπεῖ ὡς ἡ τῶν ὑπὸ χεῖρα δυσπραγία καὶ τῶν περὶ αὐτοὺς ἀγαθῶν ἡ δι᾽ ἀμελείας ἐλάττωσις καὶ κατάπτωσις. εἰ γὰρ ἑνὸς ἀνδρὸς τῆς ἡμῶν ἠξιωμένου προνοίας ἡ μὲν ἐπὶ τὸ κρεῖττον ἀνάνευσις ἄφατον ἡμῖν

15 εὐφροσύνην ἐργάζεται, ἡ δ᾽ ἐπὶ τὸ χεῖρον ἀπόνευσις ἀλγηδόνα ψυχῆς ἀνυπέρ- βλητον, τί οὐκ ἂν πάθοιμεν τοσούτων μυριάδων τῆς ἡμῶν μετὰ Θεὸν ἠρτημέ- νων προνοίας ὧν τὴν φροντίδα καὶ ἐπιμέλειαν χρεωστοῦντες, νύκτωρ μὲν ἐπαγρυπνοῦμεν, ἡμέρας δὲ διαμελετῶμεν πάσης μὲν ἀηδίας καὶ βλάβης ἐλευθέ- ρους διατηρεῖσθαι, πάσης δὲ χαρᾶς καὶ εὐημερίας προσηκόντως ἐπαπολαύειν;

20 3. Ἀλλὰ τῶν μὲν ἄλλων περὶ τὴν πολιτείαν πραγμάτων μικράν τινα δεξα- μένων ἴσως ἐλάττωσιν οὐ τοσαύτην κατανοοῦμεν τὴν βλάβην, τῆς δὲ στρατη- γικῆς μεθόδου διαπεσούσης τοσούτῳ κατόπιν τὰ Ῥωμαίων συνηλάθη πράγμα- τα, ὅσον ἡ πεῖρα τοῦ νῦν χρόνου πᾶσιν ἅπαντα κατ᾽ ὀφθαλμοὺς ὁρώμενα παρί- στησι πρόδηλα.

25 4. Ἔδει μὲν γὰρ ἀνθρώπους ἅπαντας, εἰκόνι Θεοῦ καὶ λόγῳ τετιμημένους τὴν εἰρήνην ἀσπάζεσθαι καὶ τὴν εἰς ἀλλήλους περιθάλπειν ἀγάπην καὶ μὴ

---

M W (mut.) A B E    Va    PG 107:672

1–6 λέοντος...αὔγουστος M om. ABE    9 ἐφετῶν M ἐπιθυμητῶν ABE    11 τε καὶ ἐπανόρθωσις MA om. BE    15 δ᾽ M δὲ ABE | ἀλγηδόνα M ὀδύνην ABE    16 πάθοιμεν M πάθωμεν ABE    16–17 ἠρτημένων M ἐκκρεμαμένων ABE    17 καὶ MA καὶ τὴν BE | νύκτωρ M νυκτὸς ABE    22 τοσούτῳ MA τοσοῦτον BE | κατόπιν...συνηλάθη MA τὰ ῥωμαίων συνηλάθη κατόπιν BE    23 νῦν MA om. BE

# LEO IN CHRIST AUTOKRATOR,
# SUMMARY TRANSMISSION OF THE TACTICS
# EMPLOYED IN WAGING WAR

1. In the name of the Father and of the Son and of the Holy Spirit, the holy, consubstantial, and worshipful Trinity, our one and only true God, Leo, peaceful autokrator in Christ, faithful, pious, ever revered Augustus.

2. It is not the imperial pageantry and authority, not the power and extent of that authority, not the display and enjoyment of all that. It is not any of those things sought after and esteemed by men that brings such joy to Our Majesty as does the peace and prosperity of our subjects and the setting aright and the constant improvement in those matters that affect our citizens. On the contrary, nothing so grieves and pains our heart as the misfortunes of our subjects and any decrease or failure <in their attaining> the good things due them, because of <someone's> negligence. Now, if an improvement in the condition of just one person who has been entrusted to our care causes us ineffable happiness and the worsening of his condition brings us unsurpassed grief of soul, what would we not suffer with so many tens of thousands depending, after God, on our providence? Mindful of our obligation to take thought and to be concerned about them, we stay up at night, and during the day we deliberate on how to preserve them free of all unpleasantness and harm and on how they may enjoy all the happiness and prosperity that are rightfully theirs.[1]

3. When other matters affecting the state deteriorate to some small degree, we do not consider the damage to be excessive. But everyone can clearly see, with his own eyes, how the collapse of strategic knowledge has cast all the affairs of the Romans down to such a degree as we experience at this very moment.

4. For honored by the image and word of God, all men ought to embrace peace and foster love for one another instead of taking up murderous weapons

---

1. Leo and other emperors employ similar words to articulate their overwhelming concern, "night and day," for the welfare of their subjects. See H. Hunger, *Prooimion: Elemente der byzantinischen Kaiseridee in den Arengen der Urkunden* (Vienna, 1964), 97–99.

χεῖρας φονίους κατὰ τῶν ὁμογενῶν καθοπλίζειν. ἐπειδὴ δὲ ὁ ἀπ᾽ ἀρχῆς ἀνθρω-
ποκτόνος διάβολος καὶ τοῦ γένους ἡμῶν ἐχθρὸς διὰ τῆς ἁμαρτίας ἰσχύσας κατὰ
τῆς ἰδίας φύσεως ἀντιστρατεύεσθαι τοὺς ἀνθρώπους παρεσκεύασεν, πᾶσα ἀ| 283ᵛ
30 νάγκη ταῖς αὐτοῦ γινομέναις διὰ τῶν ἀνθρώπων μηχαναῖς ἀνθρώπους ἀντιστρατεύεσθαι καὶ τοῖς ἐθέλουσι πολέμους ἔθνεσι μὴ εὐχειρώτους καθίστασθαι.
ἀλλὰ ταῖς στρατηγικαῖς μεθόδοις τὴν σωτηρίαν πορίζεσθαι καὶ δι᾽ αὐτῶν
φυλάττεσθαι μὲν ἀπὸ τῶν ἐπερχομένων πολεμίων, δρᾶν δὲ κατ᾽ αὐτῶν ὅσα
παθεῖν ἐκεῖνοι ἂν εἶεν ἄξιοι ὡς ἂν ἐκκοπέντος τοῦ διὰ τῶν πονηρῶν ἐγχειρουμέ-
35 νου κακοῦ καὶ πάντων τὴν οἰκείαν σωτηρίαν ἀσπαζομένων ἡ εἰρήνη παρὰ πᾶσι
στερχθείη καὶ πολιτεύοιτο.
    5. Ἕως μὲν γάρ, ὡς ἔοικε, τὰ κατὰ πολέμους Ῥωμαίοις ἐν εὐταξίᾳ ὄντα ἐτύγ-
χανε, τῆς τε ἐπ᾽ οὐκ ὀλίγους χρόνους θείας ἀπέλαυε βοηθείας τὸ κράτος καὶ τῇ
εὐταξίᾳ κιρνώμενος τῶν ἀριστέων ὁ πόνος, τὸ λαμπρὸν τῆς νίκης ἐπὶ πλέον
40 ἐταινιοῦτο. νῦν δὲ τῆς τακτικῆς τε καὶ στρατηγικῆς καταστάσεως ἐπ᾽ οὐκ
ὀλίγους χρόνους ἀμελουμένης, ἵνα μὴ λέγω καὶ εἰς παντελῆ περιελθούσης
λήθην, ὡς μηδὲ αὐτὰ τὰ πρόχειρα τοὺς στρατηγεῖν ἐγχειροῦντας ἐπίστασθαι,
πολλὰ δυσχερῆ διαφόρως ὁρῶμεν συμβαίνοντα. τῆς γὰρ πολλῶν ἀγαθῶν
προξένου ἐπιστήμης διαπεσούσης, ὅσων δι᾽ αὐτῆς ἡ Ῥωμαίων πάλαι πολιτεία
45 εὐμοίρησε, τοὐναντίον ὁρῶμεν τὴν θείαν ἀποῦσαν εὐμένειαν καὶ τὴν συνήθη
τῆς Ῥωμαίων πολιτείας νίκην τῶν ἀγωνιζομένων ἀφιπταμένην. κατὰ μικρὸν γὰρ
ἀμελουμένης τῆς κατὰ πολέμους εὐταξίας καὶ γυμνασίας συνημελήθη, ὡς ἔοικε,
καὶ τῶν ἀριστέων ἡ εὐψυχία. εἶτα ποτὲ μὲν ἀγυμνασίαν ἢ ἀνανδρίαν αἰτιώμεθα
στρατιωτῶν, ποτὲ δὲ ἀπειρίαν ἢ δειλίαν καταμεμφόμεθα στρατηγῶν, ἐνίοτε δὲ
50 <δι᾽> ἀσάφειαν τῆς τῶν ἀρχαίων τακτικῶν διαγνώσεως ἀμελοῦμεν. ταύτην οὖν

---

44 ab δι᾽ αὐτῆς inc. W

---

27–28 Ioan. 8:44.   40–78 Strat., praef.10–35.

27 χεῖρας φονίους M φονικὰς χεῖρας ABE   28 διάβολος ABE διαβολικὸς M | ἰσχύσας MA
ἰσχυρᾶς BE   33 δρᾶν M πράττειν ABE   34 παθεῖν…εἶεν M ἐκεῖνοι παθεῖν εἰσίν ABE
35 πᾶσι M πάντων ABE   36 στερχθείη M ἀγαπηθῇ ABE   37–38 ὡς…ἐτύγχανε M οἱ
ρωμαϊκοὶ πόλεμοι ἐν εὐταξίᾳ ἐγίνοντο (ἐγένοντο BE) ABE   38 τε…χρόνους M om. ABE |
ἀπέλαυε MAB ἀπέλαβε E   38–40 καὶ…ἐταινιοῦτο M om. ABE   39 ἀριστέων Va
ἀριστείων codd.   40 τε M om. ABE   40–41 ἐπ᾽…χρόνους M ἐπὶ χρόνους οὐκ ὀλίγους
ABE   42 τὰ ABE om. M   45 εὐμοίρησε MABE εὐμοίρησεν W | τοὐναντίον MW τὸ
ἐναντίον ABE   47 ὡς ἔοικε MW om. ABE   48 ἀγυμνασίαν…αἰτιώμεθα MW αἰτιώμεθα
ἀγυμνασίᾳ ἢ ἀνανδρίᾳ ABE   49 ἐνίοτε MW πολλάκις ABE   50 δι᾽ ci. Du om. codd. |
ἀσάφειαν…ἀμελοῦμεν MW τὴν τῶν ἀρχαίων τακτικῶν διάγνωσιν ὡς ἀσαφῆ καὶ δύσκολον
παρορῶμεν ABE | τακτικῶν WABE om. M

in their hands to use against their own people. But since the devil, the killer of men from the beginning,[2] the enemy of our race, has made use of sin to bring men to the point of waging war against their own kind, it becomes entirely necessary for men to wage war making use of contrivances of the devil, developed through men and, without flinching, to take their stand against those nations that want war. They must then make provision for their security by military means, employing them to defend themselves against the onslaughts of the enemy, to take action against them, and to make them suffer what they may well deserve. In this way, the evil brought about by those wicked people will be excised. With everyone embracing his own safety, peace will be cherished by all and will become a way of life.

5. For, so it seems, as long as the armed forces of the Romans were in good order, the state enjoyed divine assistance for not a few years, and the toil of the most valorous was mingled with discipline and, for the most part, was crowned with the splendor of victory. But, for many years now, the pursuit of tactics and strategy has been neglected, not to say fallen so completely into oblivion that those assuming the command of an army do not understand even the most obvious matters.[3] We may observe that this leads to quite a number of different problems. For with the disappearance of this knowledge, productive of so many good things, and by means of which the commonwealth of the Romans flourished of old, we behold the opposite; divine favor is absent and the accustomed triumph of the Roman commonwealth has flown away from its fighting men. For, along with the gradual neglect of military discipline and training, the courage of our brave warriors, so it would seem, has also declined. Sometimes we attribute the cause to the lack of training and the cowardice of the soldiers; sometimes we place the blame on the inexperience and timidity of their commanders; and sometimes we neglect the clear teaching of the ancient tacticians because of its obscurity. Wishing, therefore, with God's help, to restore

2. John 8:44.
3. See *Strat.*, Preface 10–35.

τὴν ὀνησιμωτάτην ἐπιστήμην ἀνασώσασθαι σὺν Θεῷ καὶ οἵαν ἀπωσθεῖσαν ἐκ
τῆς Ῥωμαϊκῆς ἡμῶν πολιτείας ἀνακαλέσασθαι βουλόμενοι, οὐκ ὠκνήσαμεν
σπουδῇ τοσαύτῃ ἀναδέξασθαι μὲν ἰδίως πόνον, κοινὴν δὲ τοῖς ὑπηκόοις χαρί-
σασθαι τὴν ὠφέλειαν.

55    6. Ταῖς γὰρ ἀρχαίαις καὶ δὴ καὶ ταῖς νεωτέραις στρατηγικαῖς τε καὶ τακτικαῖς
ἐμφιλοχωρήσαντες μεθόδοις καὶ ταῖς ἄλλαις καταλογάδην ἐντυχόντες ἱστορίαις, καὶ εἴ τι κατὰ χεῖρας ἔδοξε χρήσιμον τῶν ἐν πολέμοις ἀναγκαίων, ἐκεῖθεν
ἀναλεξάμενοι καὶ οἷον ἐρανισάμενοι, ὅσα καὶ διὰ μετρίας πείρας ἐπὶ τῶν ἔργων
αὐτῶν ἀνεμάθομεν τῷ καθ᾽ ἡμᾶς καιρῷ καὶ τῇ νῦν καταστάσει πρόσφορά τε καὶ
60 ἁρμόδια, ταῦτα ὑμῖν κατὰ τὸ δυνατὸν σύντομόν τε καὶ | ἁπλῆν τὴν ὠφέλειαν ἐπὶ   284
τῶν πραγμάτων ἔχοντα ὡς ἄλλον Πρόχειρον Νόμον παραδιδόαμεν, ἐν πράξεσι
μᾶλλον ἢ λέξεσι τὸ σεμνὸν καὶ χρειῶδες παρεχόμενοι, οἷον εἰσαγωγήν τινα
τακτικὴν τοῖς ἡμετέροις ὑποστρατήγοις καὶ τὰς πολεμικὰς ἐμπεπιστευμένοις
χρείας, δι᾽ ὑμῶν ὑπαγορεύοντες ὡς εὔκολον ἐντεῦθεν εἶναι τοῖς βουλομένοις
65 καὶ ἐπὶ τὰ μείζω τῶν παλαιῶν ἐκείνων τακτικῶν καὶ ἀρχαίων <θεωρημάτων>
τάξει τινὶ καὶ βαθμῷ προϊέναι, φράσεως μὲν ἀκριβοῦς ἢ κόμπου ῥημάτων
οὐδεμίαν ποιησάμενοι φροντίδα, πραγμάτων δὲ μᾶλλον καὶ σαφηνείας λόγου
καὶ λέξεως ἁπλῆς πεφροντικότες. ὅθεν ταύτας παλαιὰς τῆς τακτικῆς πολλάκις
Ἑλληνικὰς μὲν ἐσαφηνίσαμεν λέξεις, Ῥωμαϊκὰς δὲ διερμηνεύσαμεν, καί τισιν
70 ἑτέραις στρατιωτικῇ συνηθείᾳ λελεγμέναις ἐχρησάμεθα λέξεσιν ἕνεκεν τῆς
σαφοῦς καταλήψεως τῶν ἐντυγχανόντων, μόνον τῶν οὐκ ἀναγκαίων διατάξεων
ἐξῃρημένων διά τε τὸ περιττὸν καὶ τὴν ἀχρηστίαν καὶ τὴν τῶν συγγραμμάτων
ἀσάφειαν, ἵν᾽ ἔχοιεν εὐσύνοπτον οἱ βουλόμενοι στρατηγεῖν πολλὴν τῶν κατὰ

---

51 ὀνησιμωτάτην MW ὠφελιμωτάτην ABE | ἀπωσθεῖσαν MW ἀποδιωχθεῖσαν ABE   55 καὶ
δὴ MW om. ABE   56 ἐμφιλοχωρήσαντες MW φιλοπόνως ἐντυχόντες ABE   56–57 ταῖς…
ἱστορίαις MW τὰς ἄλλας ἱστορίας ἀνερευνήσοντες AB τὰς ἄλλας καταλογάδην ἐντυχόντες E
| scr. mg. αρριανου αιλιανου πελοπος ονησανδρου μηνᾶ πολυαίνου συριανοῦ πλουτάρχου W
57 εἴ τι WBE εἴτε MA   | κατὰ χεῖρας MW om. ABE | ἔδοξε χρήσιμον MW trsp. ABE
58 ἀναλεξάμενοι MWA ἐπιλεξάμενοι BE | καὶ¹…ἐρανισάμενοι MW om. ABE | ὅσα καὶ MW
trsp. ABE | διὰ μετρίας MW δι᾽ ὀλίγης ABE   60 σύντομόν ABE συντόμως MW   61 ὡς…
νόμον ABE προχείρου τάξιν νόμου MW   62 εἰσαγωγήν MW εἴσοδον ABE   63 πολεμικὰς
MW πολιτικὰς ABE   65 μείζω MW μείζονα ABE | θεωρημάτων ci. Va om. codd.
66 προιέναι MW προχωρεῖν ABE | φράσεως…ῥημάτων MW κάλλους μὲν λόγου ABE
67 ποιησάμενοι φροντίδα MW trsp. ABE   67–68 σαφηνείας…ταύτας MW(ὅθεν καὶ)
συντόμου καὶ εὐκόλου διηγήσεως φροντίσαντες διὰ τοῦτο ABE   68 τῆς…πολλάκις MW
λέξεις τῆς τακτικῆς ABE   69–71 καί…ἐντυγχανόντων MW καὶ ἑτέραις λέξεσιν ἐχρησάμεθα
ἐν στρατιωτικῇ συνηθείᾳ λεγομέναις πρὸς τὸ εὔκολον εἶναι τὴν διήγησιν τοῖς ἐντυγχάνουσιν
ABE   71–78 μόνον…τάξιν MW om. ABE

this most profitable knowledge and, after it had been almost driven out of our Roman commonwealth, to call it back into being, we have not hesitated, with great seriousness, to take up this task ourselves and, in this way, to graciously bestow a common benefit upon our subjects.

6. After devotedly giving our attention to the ancient, as well as to the more recent, strategic and tactical methods, and having read about further details in other accounts, if we came across anything in those sources that seemed useful for the needs of war, we have, as it were, gathered it up and collected it.[4] Those things, moreover, that we have learned from our own limited experience of active duty and that are applicable and serviceable in our day and in the present situation, we now pass on to you as best we can. We offer them as a modest assistance in these matters, succinctly, as another *Procheiros Nomos*, presenting in practice rather than in words what is useful and worthy of respect. It is a sort of introductory book on tactics for our subcommanders and those who have been entrusted with the responsibilities of combat.[5] We assure you that this should make it easier for those who wish to advance in an orderly manner and by degrees to a better knowledge of those old tactical authors and ancient theories. We have paid no heed to the strictures of good diction or fine-sounding words. Our concern, rather, has been with practicality, clarity of expression, and simplicity of style. With this in mind, we have frequently clarified the ancient Greek tactical terms and we have translated the Latin ones into their Greek equivalents. We have also employed certain other expressions in common military usage to make it easier for the reader to understand them. The only thing we have done away with are formations that are no longer needed because they are superfluous, useless, and their description is not clear. Thus, those who desire to command troops may have ready access to a great store of experience concerning the requirements for combat and military campaigns. This manual

4. In the margin of W, someone (perhaps the scribe) has written the names of Arrian, Aelian, Pelops, Onasander, Menas, Polyaenus, Syrianus, Plutarch.

5. Subcommander: hypostrategos, also lieutenant general (see 4.8–9). At one time all generals were called lieutenant generals, the emperor being considered the one supreme general, with the others as his delegates. In Leo's time, the term was applied to the senior merarch.

πολέμους καὶ ἐκστρατείας ἀναγκαίων τὴν πεῖραν, οὐ λόγῳ μόνον τὸ χρήσιμον
75 ἔχουσαν, ἀλλὰ δὴ καὶ αὐτοῖς ἔργοις παρὰ τῶν παλαιῶν ἐγγυμνασθεῖσαν καὶ
ἄχρις ἡμῶν, εἰ καὶ μὴ ἔργοις αὐτοῖς οἷς τὰ Ῥωμαίων ἐπὶ μέγα ἤρθη δυνάμεως,
παραπεμφθεῖσαν, ἀλλ᾽ οὖν τοῖς λόγοις δι᾽ ὧν ἀναλαμβάνεται καὶ ἀναμιμνήσκε-
ται τὰ λήθη παραπεμφθέντα καὶ εἰς τὴν ἀρχαίαν πάλιν ἀποκαθίστασθαι τάξιν.

7. Ἀλλ᾽ ἐφ᾽ ὅσῳ μὲν ἐν τοῖς ῥηθησομένοις τὸ εὔχρηστον ἀναδειχθῇ, χάρις
80 τῷ πάντων ἀγαθῶν δοτῆρι Χριστῷ, τῷ βασιλεῖ τοῦ παντὸς καὶ Θεῷ ἡμῶν, τῷ
καὶ τοῖς ἡμετέροις λόγοις δωρησαμένῳ τὴν χάριν. εἰ δέ τις καὶ ἕτερος δι᾽ αὐτῆς
τῆς ἐπιμελείας καὶ πείρας κρείττονα τούτων ἐφεύρῃ, χάρις καὶ οὕτως τῷ πανα-
γάθῳ Θεῷ, συγγνώμη δὲ ἡμῖν τῆς προθυμίας ἕνεκεν.

8. Πάντως δὲ χρή, εἴτε ἐπὶ πλέον εἴτε ἐπ᾽ ἔλαττον, τοὺς βουλομένους στρα-
85 τηγεῖν ταῖς τακτικαῖς τε καὶ στρατηγικαῖς ἐνδιατρίβειν μελέταις. οὐδὲ γάρ, ὥς
τινες τῶν ἀπείρων ἔχουσι, διὰ πλήθους ἀνδρῶν καὶ θράσους οἱ πόλεμοι κρίνον-
ται, ἀλλὰ δι᾽ εὐμενείας Θεοῦ καὶ στρατηγίας καὶ τάξεως, ἧς μᾶλλον ἐπιμελητέον
ἢ συλλογῆς πλήθους ἀκαίρου· ἡ μὲν γὰρ καὶ ἀσφάλειαν καὶ ὠφέλειαν ἄγει τοῖς
καλῶς αὐτῇ κεχρημένοις, ἡ δὲ καὶ συντριβὴν καὶ ἐπιζήμιον δαπάνην.

90 9. Ὥσπερ γὰρ οὐκ ἔστιν ὁλκάδα πελάγη διαπορθμεύεσθαι κυβερνητικῆς
ἐπιστήμης | χωρίς, οὕτως οὐδὲ πολεμίους καταγωνίζεσθαι τάξεως καὶ στρατη- 284ᵛ
γίας ἐκτός, δι᾽ ἧς οὐ μόνον τοῦ ἰσορροποῦντος πλήθους τῶν πολεμίων περιγενέσθαι σὺν Θεῷ δυνατόν ἐστιν, ἀλλὰ καὶ τοῦ πολλῷ πλέον τῷ ἀριθμῷ <ὑπερ>-
βάλλοντος. ὥσπερ οὖν ἄλλον τινὰ Πρόχειρον Νόμον ὑμῖν, ὡς εἴρηται, στρατη-
95 γικὸν τὴν παροῦσαν πραγματείαν ὑπαγορεύοντες προσεχῶς τε καὶ ἐπιπόνως
ἀκούειν ἡμῶν παρακελευόμεθα.

10. Χρεὸν τοίνυν πρότερον μὲν ὑπογράψαι τὴν ἐν πολέμοις τακτικήν, καὶ τί
ἐστι στρατηγός, εἶτα τίνα καὶ ὁποῖον τὸν στρατηγὸν εἶναι δεῖ καὶ ὅπως δέον
βουλεύεσθαι, ἑξῆς δὲ τὴν εἰς ἄρχοντας καὶ ἀρχομένους τοῦ στρατοῦ διαθεῖναι
100 διαίρεσιν, τήν τε ἄλλην ἀποσκευὴν καὶ τῶν ὅπλων κατασκευὴν καὶ τὴν ἑκάστου

---

90–96 *Strat.*, 7.A.1.

---

79 ἐφ᾽…ἀναδειχθῇ MW εἰ μὲν χρήσιμα τὰ παρ᾽ ἡμῶν ῥηθησόμενα φανῶσι ABE    82 καὶ
πείρας MWA om. BE | ἐφεύρῃ MWA om. BE | οὕτως MWA οὕτω BE    83 δὲ MWA om. BE
86 τινες…ἔχουσι MW τῶν ἀπείρων ὑπολαμβάνουσι τινὲς A ὑπολαμβάνουσι τινὲς τῶν
ἀπείρων BE    87 δι᾽ εὐμενείας MW διὰ φιλανθρωπίας ABE | ἐπιμελητέον MW ἐπιμελεῖσθαι
χρή ABE    88 ἄγει MWBE ἔχει A    90 ὁλκάδα MW πλοῖον ABE.| διαπορθμεύεσθαι MW
διαπερᾶν ABE    90–91 κυβερνητικῆς…χωρίς MW χωρὶς κυβερνητικῆς ἐπιστήμης ABE
92 ἰσορροποῦντος W ἰσορροποιοῦντος M ἴσου ABE    93–94 πλέον…βάλλοντος MW
πλείονος ABE ὑπερ suppl. Lami (PG)    94 νόμον ABE om. MW    95 προσεχῶς ABE νόμον
προσεχῶς MW    97 χρεὸν MW χρεία ABE    98 τὸν MWA om. BE

derives its usefulness not only from what has been written down but also from the fact that it has been put into practice by ancient authorities and has been transmitted down to our own day. Even if it had not been accompanied by those actions that had raised the situation of the Romans to great power, at least the words that had been consigned to oblivion have been brought back to life, remembered, and again restored to their ancient position.

7. To the extent that something useful may be discovered in what we are about to say, thanks be to Christ, the giver of all good things, the king of all and our God, who has bestowed his favor upon our words. If anyone else, through his own diligence and experience, should improve upon these words, likewise, thanks be to the all-good God, and may we be pardoned for being so enthusiastic.

8. It is absolutely essential, to a greater or less degree, that men who intend to command troops should spend their time in tactical and strategic exercises. For it is not true, as some inexperienced persons may hold, that wars are decided by a multitude of men and courage, but by the favor of God and by generalship and discipline; one must be concerned about this rather than assembling an unreasonable multitude. For the former brings safety and advantage to those who make good use of it, while the latter brings trouble and harmful expenditure.

9. Just as it is not possible to sail a ship over the sea without knowledge of navigation, neither is it possible to overcome the enemy without discipline and generalship.[6] Whereas, with these, and with God's help, not only is it possible to prevail over an enemy force of equal strength but also over one which greatly outnumbers yours. We submit the present treatise on generalship, as we have said, like another *Procheiros Nomos* and we earnestly advise you to listen to us attentively and very seriously.

10. First, it is necessary to outline the tactics employed in warfare. Then, what is a general? Who and what sort of person should he be? How should he make his plans? After that, explain the division of the army into officers and the troops they command, as well as their equipment, the weapons provided them,

6. Cf. *Strat.* 7.A.1.

τῶν μαχομένων ὅπλισιν, πρὸς τούτοις τὴν πρὸ τῶν ἀληθινῶν ἀγώνων τοῦ στρατοῦ γυμνασίαν, ἔπειτα δὲ καὶ τὰ κείμενα ὑπαναγνωσθῆναι ἐπιτίμια. εἶτα περὶ ὁδοιπορίας εἰπεῖν τῆς τε ἐν τῇ ἰδίᾳ καὶ τῆς ἐν τῇ πολεμίᾳ, περί τε τοῦ λεγομένου τούλδου καὶ δὴ καὶ περὶ ἁπλίκτων τῆς τε προκατασκευῆς καὶ παραγ-
105 γελίας. καὶ τί δεῖ γενέσθαι πρὸ τῆς τοῦ πολέμου ἡμέρας καὶ ὅσα ἐν τῇ τοῦ πολέμου ἡμέρᾳ ἐποφείλεται; καὶ ἔτι περὶ πολιορκίας, εἶτα καὶ τὰ μετὰ τὸν πόλεμον ὀφειλόμενα καὶ τὰς δι’ ἐνέδρων ἀδοκήτους ἐφόδους τῶν τε ἡμετέρων καὶ τῶν πολεμίων. καὶ ἐπὶ τούτοις διαφόρων παρατάξεων μελέτας ἐθνικῶν τε καὶ Ῥωμαϊκῶν. εἶτα πρὸς τοῖς εἰρημένοις καὶ περὶ ναυμαχίας διατάξαι μετρίως.
110 καὶ ἐπὶ τούτοις ἅπασι γνώμας τινὰς τακτικάς τε καὶ στρατηγικὰς ἰδίως ἐν ἐκθέ-σει συναγαγεῖν, ὅσας δηλονότι κατὰ χώραν ἐντάξαι τὸ εὐσύνοπτον καὶ πρόχει-ρον τῶν διατάξεων οὐ συγχωρεῖ, ἀφ’ ὧν ὁρμώμενον σοφὸν ὄντα καὶ ὀξὺν τῇ διανοίᾳ τὸν στρατηγὸν σοφώτερον γενέσθαι ἐλπίζομεν.

    11. Καὶ πρῶτον μὲν ἀρκτέον ἐντεῦθεν. |

---

105 ad γενέσθαι des. W | inter ff. 2 et 3 remanet fol. pars exigua, in qua legitur: recto: πρὸ τῆ<ς>…ὅσα ἐ<ν>…ἐποφε<ίλεται>…<πολι>ορκίας…πόλ<εμον>…δι’ ἐ<νέδρων>…τῶν… ων…π…τε. verso: <στ>ρατηγοῦ…πολεμικῶν…πολεμικαὶ…<αἱ> δὲ κατὰ…<στρατηγι>κὴ… καὶ κι<νήσεων>…ἀγα<θῶν>…<μελ>έτη…<στρατηγημάτ>ων.

---

112–113 Prov. 1:5.

---

101 τῶν¹ MWAB om. E | πρὸ τῶν MWA πρὸς τὸν BE   102 στρατοῦ Va στρατηγοῦ codd.
103 πολεμίᾳ MWAB πολεμίᾳ γῆ E   104 καὶ δὴ MW om. ABE   106 ἐποφείλεται W ὑποφείλεται MABE | τὰ MA om. BE   107 ἐνέδρων M ἐγκρυμμάτων ABE | ἀδοκήτους M ἀπροσδοκήτους A ἀπροσδοκήτως BE   108 μελέτας MBE μελέταις A   109 πρὸς M ἐπὶ ABE | καὶ περὶ ABE om. M | διατάξαι μετρίως M εἰπεῖν ABE   110 ἅπασι M om. ABE
110–112 ἰδίως…συγχωρεῖ M ἐκθεῖναι ABE

and the armament of each one of the fighting men. In addition, the training of the army before actual combat. Then, the official reading of the penalties in force. There follows a discussion about the army on the march, both in our own and in hostile territory, and about the so-called baggage train and, of course, about preparation and instructions regarding encampments. What must be done the day before battle and what has to be done on the day of battle? Further, about siege warfare. Then, what is to be done after battle? What about unexpected attacks and ambushes both of our own troops and of the enemy? In addition to these, training in various battle formations, foreign and Roman. Our compilation is then followed by a limited exposition of naval warfare. Concluding all this, certain tactical and strategic maxims have been collected and set forth individually, those, that is, that the summary, handbook nature of the chapters does not permit to insert in their place. We hope that the study of these will lead the wise and sharp-witted commander to become even wiser.[7]

11. We must first begin here.

7. Proverbs 1:5.

## Περὶ τακτικῆς καὶ στρατηγοῦ

1. Τακτική ἐστιν ἐπιστήμη πολεμικῶν κινήσεων· κινήσεις δὲ πολεμικαὶ
διτταί, αἱ μὲν κατὰ γῆν, αἱ δὲ κατὰ θάλασσαν.

5  2. Τακτική ἐστι τέχνη στρατηγικὴ παρατάξεων καὶ ὁπλισμῶν καὶ κινήσεων
στρατιωτικῶν.

3. Στρατηγικὴ δέ ἐστι στρατηγῶν ἀγαθῶν συνάσκησις ἤγουν μελέτη καὶ
γυμνασία μετὰ στρατηγημάτων ἤτοι τροπαίων συναθροισμός.

4. Σκοπὸς τῇ τακτικῇ διὰ τῶν ἐνδεχομένων ἐπιβολῶν καὶ πράξεων νικῆσαι
10  τοὺς πολεμίους.

5. Χρήσιμον δέ ἐστι τῇ τακτικῇ τὸ δι' εὐτάκτου <ἐπι>θέσεως συμπλέκεσθαι
τοῖς πολεμίοις.

6. Τέλος τῇ τακτικῇ κατὰ ἐνδεχόμενον ἀνεπιλήπτως διατάξαι τὸ στράτευμα.

7. Αἱ δὲ εἰς τοὺς πολέμους τέλειαι παρετοιμασίαι δύο εἰσίν· ἡ μὲν κατὰ γῆν
15  πεζική, ἡ δὲ κατὰ θάλασσαν ναυτική. περὶ μὲν οὖν τῆς ναυτικῆς ὕστερον ἐροῦμεν. τῶν δὲ κατὰ γῆν ἐπὶ πολέμους ἀθροιζομένων ἀνδρῶν τὸ πλῆθος, τὸ μέν
ἐστι μάχιμον ἤγουν πολεμικόν, τὸ δὲ διὰ τὰς τούτου χρείας συνερχόμενον
ἄμαχον. καὶ πολεμικὸν μὲν τὸ παρατασσόμενον πρὸς τοὺς πολεμίους στρατιω-
τικόν· ἄμαχον δὲ τὸ λοιπόν, οἷον ἰατρῶν, δούλων, ἐμπόρων, καὶ ἄλλων, ὅσοι διὰ
20  τὰς ὑπηρεσίας ἐπακολουθοῦσιν. τοῦ δὲ μαχίμου μέρους ἤγουν πολεμικοῦ στρατοῦ τὸ μέν ἐστι πεζικόν, τὸ δὲ καβαλλαρικόν. καὶ τὸ μὲν ἰδίως πεζικὸν τὸ ἐπὶ γῆς
ἱστάμενον, τὸ δὲ καβαλλαρικὸν τὸ ἐπὶ τῶν ἵππων ὀχούμενον. ἢν δέ ποτε καὶ ἐπὶ
ἁρμάτων ἁπλῶν καὶ ἁρμάτων δρεπανηφόρων καὶ ἐπὶ ἐλεφάντων πύργους

---

MABE   Va   PG 107:680

3–25 Aeliani Tact. Theoria, 2.1.

1 πολεμικῶν παρασκευῶν ΜΑ om. ΒΕ | α' ΜΒ πρώτη ΑΕ   4 διτταί Μ δύο ΑΒΕ   5 ἐστι
ΜΑ ἐστιν ΒΕ   9 νικῆσαι De κινῆσαι codd.   11 ἐστι ΜΑ ἐστιν ΒΕ | ἐπιθέσεως De θέσεως
codd.   13 ἀνεπιλήπτως Μ ἀμέμπτως ΑΒΕ   14 πολέμους Α πολεμίους ΜΒΕ   19 οἷον ΜΑ
οἷοι ΒΕ | ἰατρῶν…ἄλλων De ἰατρῶν δούλων ἐμπείρων καὶ ἄλλων Μ ἰατροὶ δοῦλοι ἔμποροι
καὶ ἄλλοι Α ἰατροὶ δοῦλοι ἐμπείροι καὶ ἄλλοι ΒΕ   20 ἐπακολουθοῦσιν Μ ἐπακολουθοῦσι
ΑΒΕ   21 καβαλλαρικόν ΑΒΕ καβαλλάριον Μ   23 καὶ¹ Μ καὶ ἐπὶ ΑΒΕ

# PREPARATION FOR WAR, CONSTITUTION I

## About Tactics and the General

1. Tactics is the science of movement in warfare. Movements in warfare are twofold, those on land and those on sea.[1]

2. Tactics is the military skill <that is concerned with> battle formations, armament, and troop movements.

3. Strategy is how good commanders put their military training into practice, their drilling with stratagems, and putting together ways of defeating <the enemy>.[2]

4. The aim of tactics is to defeat the enemy by all possible means of assaults and actions.

5. The usefulness of tactics lies in engaging the enemy in combat by means of a well disciplined attack.

6. The purpose of tactics is, inasmuch as possible, to draw up the army in an unassailable formation.

7. Complete preparation for warfare is twofold: infantry on land and naval forces at sea. About naval warfare we will discourse later. Of the mass of men mobilized for warfare on land, one part consists of fighting men or warriors, the other of non-combatants who are to see to their needs. The fighting men are drawn up as an army confronting the enemy. The rest are noncombatants such as doctors, slaves, merchants, and others, all those who follow along to provide services. Of the fighting units, that is, the army in the field, some are infantry and some cavalry. The infantry, specifically, take their stand on the ground, the cavalry are mounted on horses. There was a time when war involved plain chariots and chariots armed with scythes, as well as elephants carrying towers

---

1. Much of this chapter is derived from Aelian, *Tactical Theory*, 2.1. See also SyrMag 14.
2. SyrMag 4–5.

φερόντων πλήρεις ἀνδρῶν, ἀλλὰ τούτων οὐδεὶς ἡμῖν λόγος νῦν διά τε τὴν
25 ἀχρηστίαν καὶ τὴν παντελῆ ἀργίαν τῶν τοιούτων παρασκευῶν.

8. Τῆς οὖν τακτικῆς μετρίως πως οὕτως ὑπογραφείσης δεῖ καὶ τὸν στρατηγὸν ἀναδειχθῆναι. τί τέ ἐστι καὶ τίς ὁ τῆς τοιαύτης ἐγχειρήσεως ἄξιος;

9. Στρατηγὸς τοίνυν ἐστὶν ὁ τῆς ὑπ᾽ αὐτὸν ἁπάσης ἐπαρχίας μείζονα πάντων
ἐξουσίαν ἔχων μετὰ τὸν βασιλέα.

30 10. Στρατηγός ἐστιν ὁ τοῦ ὑπὸ χεῖρα στρατιωτικοῦ θέματος κορυφαῖος
ἄρχων, | ἐκ βασιλέως μὲν προχειριζόμενος, τοὺς δὲ ὑπ᾽ αὐτὸν ἄρχοντας τοὺς μὲν 285ᵛ
ψήφῳ τῇ ἑαυτοῦ, ἐκ βασιλέως δὲ καταπεμπομένους, τοὺς δὲ ἐξουσίᾳ ἰδίᾳ
προβαλλομένους.

11. Ἴδιον δὲ στρατηγοῦ τὸ κρείττονα εἶναι πάντων τῶν ὑπὸ χεῖρα φρονήσει
35 καὶ ἀνδρίᾳ καὶ δικαιοσύνῃ καὶ σωφροσύνῃ, τὸ εἰς αὐτὸν ἀναφέρεσθαι τῆς κατ᾽
αὐτὸν ἐπαρχίας τὰς διοικήσεις, ὅσαι τε στρατιωτικαὶ καὶ ὅσαι ἰδιωτικαὶ καὶ
δημόσιοι, τὸ παραλαβόντα στρατὸν ἄτακτον ἐκτάξαι δεόντως κατὰ τὴν ἁρμό-
ζουσαν τῷ καιρῷ τακτικὴν διάταξιν.

12. Σκοπὸς δὲ στρατηγῷ τὸ μὲν ὑπ᾽ αὐτὸν θέμα αὐξῆσαι καὶ ἀβλαβὲς ἀπό τε
40 πολεμίων καὶ τῶν ἄλλων ἀδικημάτων καὶ δὴ καὶ ἀταξιῶν καὶ στάσεων διαφυλά-
ξαι, τοὺς δὲ πολεμίους παντὶ τρόπῳ, ἢ πολέμῳ ἢ ἐφόδοις ἀδοκήτοις, ταπει-
νῶσαι, καὶ ἅπερ ποιήσει κατὰ τῶν ἐχθρῶν, ταῦτα φυλάξασθαι, μὴ παθεῖν ἀπ᾽
αὐτῶν.

13. Τέλος τῷ στρατηγῷ τῷ εὐδοκιμήσαντι διὰ πάντων τῆς τε θείας καὶ
45 βασιλικῆς ἀπολαύειν εὐνοίας ἢ κατολιγωρήσαντι τῶν πρεπόντων καὶ ἁρμοζόν-
των πραγμάτων τεύξεσθαι τοῦ ἐναντίου. οὕτω τοίνυν καὶ τῆς τοῦ στρατηγοῦ
προτυπωθείσης εἰκόνος δεῖ καθάπερ διὰ χρωμάτων ἡμᾶς ἀναζωγραφῆσαι τὴν
τούτου ποιότητα καὶ δεῖξαι φανερῶς τίς καὶ ποταπὸς εἶναι ὀφείλει καὶ ὁποῖος
εἶναι ὁ τῆς τοιαύτης ἐξουσίας προχειριζόμενος ἄρχων.

---

26 οὖν τακτικῆς M trsp. ABE | πως ME om. AB | οὕτως ABE οὕτω M   27 ἐστι MA ἐστιν
BE | τῆς BE om. MA   28 ὁ ABE om. M | ἐπαρχίας ABE ὑπαρχίας M   30 στρατηγός ἐστιν
ABE ἐστι M   31 ἄρχοντας De ἄρχοντες codd.   32 ἑαυτοῦ M αὐτοῦ ABE | κατα-
πεμπομένους ABE καταπεμπόμενος M   33 προβαλλομένους De προβαλλόμενος codd.
34 τὸ κρείττονα MA τῷ κρείττω BE | εἶναι πάντων MA trsp. BE   40 ἀδικημάτων καὶ M om.
ABE   44 τῷ εὐδοκιμήσαντι BE τὸ εὐδοκιμῆσαι τὰ M τὸ εὐδοκιμήσαντα A
45 κατολιγωρήσαντι Va κατολιγωρήσαντα codd.   46 τεύξεσθαι τοῦ ἐναντίου Va τεύξασθαι
τοῦ ἐναντίου M τὰ ἐναντία παθεῖν ABE | οὕτω M οὕτως ABE   47 χρωμάτων BE χρημάτων
MA   48 καὶ ποταπὸς εἶναι ABE om. M   48–49 καὶ ὁποῖος εἶναι M om. ABE   49 ὁ MA ὁ
εἰς BE | τῆς τοιαύτης ἐξουσίας M τὴν τοιαύτην ἐξουσίαν ABE

filled with men. But we will not discuss these now because such armament is no longer employed and has gone completely out of use.

8. After this more or less brief outline of tactics, it is necessary to present the general. What is he? Who is fit for such an undertaking?

9. The general is the person who, after the emperor, has greater authority than anyone else over the entire province subject to him.

10. The general is the chief officer of the military theme under his command. He is appointed by the emperor; as far as the officers under him are concerned, some are promoted by his decision, although sent to him by the emperor, and others directly on his own authority.

11. It is characteristic of the general that he be superior to all under his command in practical wisdom, bravery, righteousness, and discretion, reserving to himself the administration of the province assigned to him, including military, private, and public matters. Having received an undisciplined army, he must dutifully dispose it for battle according to the tactical formation suited to the occasion.

12. The goal of the general is to strengthen the theme under his command and to preserve it free from harm caused by enemies and from other wrongdoing, especially from disorder and mutiny. He is to bring down the enemy by every means, whether by battle or by unexpected attacks. Whatever action he will take against the enemy, he must be on his guard so that he does not suffer the same thing from them.

13. The ultimate objective of the highly esteemed general is to enjoy in all things the divine and the imperial favor rather than, by paying little account to fitting and suitable matters, to arrive at the opposite. So then, having made this preliminary sketch of the general, we must now paint his qualities as though it were a portrait in color. We must demonstrate clearly who and what sort of person he ought to be and what should characterize the officer who has been entrusted with such authority.

# ΠΟΛΕΜΙΚΩΝ ΠΑΡΑΣΚΕΥΩΝ ΔΙΑΤΑΞΙΣ Β΄

## Περὶ τοῦ οἷον εἶναι δεῖ τὸν στρατηγόν

1. Κελεύομεν τοίνυν εἶναι τὸν στρατηγὸν σώφρονα περὶ τὸ σῶμα, περὶ τὴν
δίαιταν ἐγκρατῆ, νηφάλιον καὶ ἐγρήγορον, λιτὸν καὶ ἀπέριττον περὶ τὰς χρείας,
5 φερέπονον περὶ τοὺς ἐπικόπους καμάτους, νοήμονα καὶ φρόνιμον, μισοῦντα
φιλαργυρίαν, ἔνδοξον περὶ τὴν φήμην, μήτε νέον μήτε γέροντα, ἱκανὸν δὲ καὶ
πρὸς τὸ λέγειν ἀπὸ στόματος ἐν μέσῳ λαοῦ, ἂν τύχῃ δέ, καὶ πατέρα παίδων, μὴ
ἐμπορείας φιλοῦντα ἤ τι τοιοῦτον, μηδὲ μικρόψυχον, ὡς καὶ τῶν σμικρῶν
πραγμάτων ἐπιθυμεῖν, καὶ ἁπλῶς εὐγενῆ τῇ ψυχῇ, εἰ δυνατόν, καὶ τῷ σώματι καὶ
10 ἐν ἅπασι μεγαλόψυχον.

2. Σώφρονα μὲν ἵνα | μὴ ταῖς τῆς φύσεως κατασυρόμενος ἡδοναῖς ἀπολείπῃ  286
τὴν περὶ τῶν ἀναγκαίων φροντίδα καὶ ἐπιμέλειαν.

3. Ἐγκρατῆ δὲ ἐπειδὴ τηλικαύτης ἀρχῆς μέλλει τυγχάνειν. αἱ γὰρ ἀκρατεῖς
καὶ ἀκόλαστοι ὁρμαί, ὅτ᾽ ἂν προσλάβωσι δύναμιν κατ᾽ ἐξουσίαν τοῦ ποιεῖν ἃ
15 βούλονται, ἀκράτητοι γίνονται πρὸς τὰς ἐπιθυμίας.

4. Νηφάλιον δὲ καὶ ἐγρήγορον ὅπως ἐπαγρυπνῇ ἐν ταῖς μεγίσταις πράξεσιν.
ἐν νυκτὶ γάρ, ὅτ᾽ ἂν ἡ ψυχὴ ἠρεμῇ μάλιστα, πολλάκις ἡ τοῦ στρατηγοῦ γνώμη
καὶ ἀπευθύνεται καὶ τελειοῦται.

5. Λιτὸν δὲ καὶ ἀπέριττον περὶ τὰς χρείας· καὶ γὰρ καταδαπανῶσιν αἱ πολυ-
20 τελεῖς καὶ πολλαὶ θεραπεῖαι καὶ χρόνον ἄπρακτον καὶ ἀναγκαίας ἐξόδους εἰς
τὴν τῶν ἀρχόντων τρυφήν.

---

M W (mut.) A B E   Va   PG 107:681

---

3–70 Onas. 1.1–14.

---

1 β΄ MBE δευτέρα A   4 νηφάλιον M νηφαλέον ABE | καὶ ἀπέριττον M om. ABE
5 φερέπονον M ὑπομένοντα ABE | περὶ…καμάτους M τοὺς πόνους ABE   6 περὶ…φήμην
M om. ABE   8 ἐμπορείας M πραγματείας ABE | φιλοῦντα M ἀγαπῶντα ABE | σμικρῶν M
μικρῶν ABE   9 τῇ ψυχῇ M τὴν ψυχὴν ABE | τῷ σώματι M τὸ σῶμα ABE   12 περὶ MA om.
BE   14 δύναμιν MA δυνάμ<ε>ις BE | κατ᾽…ποιεῖν M trsp. ABE   16 νηφάλιον M
νηφαλέον ABE   19 καὶ ἀπέριττον M om. ABE

# PREPARATION FOR WAR, CONSTITUTION II

## About the Qualities Required in the General

1. We insist that the general should be discreet in bodily matters and exercise self-control in his mode of life. He should be sober and vigilant, frugal and unpretentious when it comes to necessities, bearing up under the toil of heavy labor. He should be endowed with intelligence and practical wisdom, a man who hates avarice and is of excellent repute, neither a youth nor an old man. He should be capable of speaking extemporaneously in the midst of his troops. Let him also be, when it so turns out, a father of children. He should not be overly fond of commerce or anything of that sort, nor should he be niggardly, as if setting his heart on petty matters.[1] Quite simply, he should be noble in soul and, if possible, in body and, in every respect, greathearted.

2. Let him be discreet and not so dragged down by physical pleasures that he neglects to attend to necessary matters and shows no concern about them.

3. As a man entrusted with such great authority, he will exercise self-control. Unrestrained and licentious impulses, when combined with the power and ability to do whatever one wants, become uncontrollable in seeking gratification.

4. Let him be sober and vigilant so that he may remain alert when dealing with truly important projects. It is often at night, when the soul is more at rest, that the plans of the general assume their final, definitive shape.

5. Let him be frugal and unpretentious regarding his needs. Very costly and continual attendance upon the luxurious tastes of commanders wastes time without accomplishing anything and eats away at necessary expenses.

---

1. For this constitution cf. Onasander 1.1–14.

6. Φερέπονον δὲ ἵνα μὴ πρῶτος τῶν στρατευομένων τὰς ἀναπαύσεις ἐπιζητῇ, ἀλλὰ γίνεται αὐτοῖς μᾶλλον εἰκὼν πρὸς τὸ γενναίως ὑποφέρειν τοὺς πόνους.

25    7. Νοήμονα δὲ καὶ φρόνιμον· ὀξὺν γὰρ εἶναι δεῖ τὸν στρατηγόν, πανταχοῦ περιστρέφοντα τὸν σκοπὸν διὰ ταχυτῆτα ψυχῆς. πολλάκις γὰρ ἀνυπονόητοι ταραχαὶ προσπεσοῦσαι παρευθὺ τὸ συμφέρον ἐπινοεῖν ἀναγκάζουσιν.

8. Ἀφιλάργυρον δέ· καὶ γὰρ ἡ ἀφιλαργυρία τοῦ στρατηγοῦ δοκιμάζεται, ὅτ' ἂν ἀδωροδοκήτως καὶ μεγαλοφρόνως προΐσταται τῶν πραγμάτων καὶ δι' ἀρε-
30    τὴν μόνην δωρεὰν προβάλληται τὰς ἀρχὰς τοῦ ὑπ' αὐτὸν θέματος. πολλοὶ γάρ, κἂν ἀνδρεῖοί εἰσι τῇ ψυχῇ καὶ ῥωμαλέοι τῷ σώματι κατὰ τῶν ἐχθρῶν, ἀλλ' ὅτ' ἂν ἀντιβλέψωσι πρὸς χρυσόν, ἀμαυροῦνται καὶ σκοτίζονται. δεινὸν γὰρ ὅπλον κατὰ στρατηγοῦ <ἢ> φιλαργυρία καὶ δραστήριον εἰς τὸ νικῆσαι τοῦτον καὶ καταβαλεῖν.

35    9. Οὔτε δὲ νέον εἶναι οὔτε γέροντα, ἐπειδὴ ὁ μὲν νέος ἄπιστον ἔχει καὶ εὐκλόνητον τὸ φρόνημα διὰ τὴν νεότητα, ὁ δὲ γέρων ἀσθενής ἐστι τῷ σώματι, καὶ οὐδέτερος αὐτῶν ἀσφαλής. ὁ μὲν ἵνα μή τι πταίσῃ διὰ τὴν ἀλόγιστον τόλμαν ὥσπερ θρασύς, ὁ δὲ γέρων ἵνα μὴ διὰ τὴν φυσικὴν ἀσθένειαν ἐλλείπῃ εἰς τὰ δέοντα τῶν πραγμάτων. κρατίστη δὲ ἐκλογὴ τοῦ μέσου, μήτε νέου ὄντος μήτε
40    γέροντος. καὶ γὰρ τὸ δυνατὸν καὶ ῥωμαλέον ἐν τῷ μέσῳ γεγηρακότι, τὸ δὲ φρόνιμον καὶ σταθηρὸν ἐν τῷ μὴ πάνυ νεάζοντι. οἵτινες γὰρ ἢ ἰσχὺν σώματος ἄνευ φρονήσεως θαυμάζουσι ψυχικῆς ἢ πάλιν ψυχὴν φρόνιμον ἄνευ σωματικῆς δυνάμεως, οὐδὲν ἐνόησαν | πέρας ἀγαθόν. καὶ γὰρ ἡ ὑστερήσασα δυνάμεως    286ᵛ
φρόνησις οὐδὲν διενοήθη κρεῖττον ἢ ἐλλείπουσα φρονήσεως δύναμις οὐδὲν
45    ἐτελείωσεν.

---

37 ad διὰ de novo inc. W | scr. mg. απροσχω W

---

22 φερέπονον δὲ Μ ὑπομένοντα τοὺς πόνους ΑΒΕ    23 γίνεται Μ γένηται Α γίνηται ΒΕ
25 δὲ ΜΑΒ om. Ε    26 περιστρέφοντα Μ περιφέροντα ΑΒΕ | ἀνυπονόητοι ΑΒΕ
ἀνυπονόηται Μ    27 ἀναγκάζουσιν Μ ἀνακάζουσι ΑΒΕ    28 τοῦ ΑΒΕ om. Μ    31 κἂν ΜΑ
καὶ ΒΕ    33 ἢ ci. Va om. codd. | δραστήριον Μ ἐνεργέστατον ΑΒΕ    35 ἔχει ΜΑΒ ἔχειν Ε
36 εὐκλόνητον Μ ἄστατον ΑΒΕ    37 οὐδέτερος Va οὐδεὶς codd. | τι ΜΑΕ om. Β
39 κρατίστη ΜW καλλίστη ΑΒΕ    40 ῥωμαλέον ΜW ἰσχυρὸν ΑΒΕ    41 σταθηρὸν ΜWΒΕ
σταθερὸν Α | νεάζοντι ΑΒΕ νεάζοντι καὶ μέντοι ΜW | γὰρ ΑΒΕ om. ΜW    43 πέρας ΜW
τέλος ΑΒΕ | ἡ ΜW ἡ φρόνησις ΑΒΕ    44 οὐδὲν διενοήθη ΜW οὐδὲν ὠφέλησεν ΑΒΕ |
ἐλλείπουσα...δύναμις ΜW δύναμις στερηθεῖσα φρονήσεως ΑΒΕ    45 ἐτελείωσεν ΜWΑ
ἐτελείωσε ΒΕ

6. Let him endure toil and not be the first among the soldiers to seek rest. Rather, let him be a model to them in nobly bearing up under hard labor.

7. Let him be intelligent and wise. The general must be sharp-witted, fast-thinking, with his gaze turned in every direction. Unsuspected disorders frequently arise and force him, on the spur of the moment, to come up with a way to remedy the situation.

8. Let him be free of avarice. In particular, the commander's freedom from avarice is tested and proven whenever he presides over affairs in an incorruptible and magnanimous manner and makes appointments to positions of command in his theme freely and on the basis of virtue alone. Many men, even though courageous in spirit and strong of body in facing the foe, find that, when they gaze upon gold, their sight is darkened and they become blind. Avarice is a terrible weapon when used against the general and very effective in defeating and overthrowing him.

9. He should not be a young man or an old man. A young man's mind lacks confidence and is easily confused because of his youth, whereas the old man's body is feeble. Neither of them offers security. The young man is impulsive and may err by reckless daring. The old man is weak physically and may neglect something that has to be done. The ideal choice is between the two, neither young nor old. Vigor and strength characterize the man who has not yet grown old, while wisdom and stability mark the man who is not too young. There are those who marvel at physical strength that exists without mental discretion or, on the other hand, who are impressed by a wise mind but one lacking in bodily strength. In their reasoning these people have not reached a correct conclusion. A mind deficient in physical strength has never conceived anything worthwhile; neither has strength deprived of intelligence ever accomplished anything.

10. Καὶ φιλούμενον δὲ παρὰ τῶν ὑπηκόων τὸν στρατηγὸν εὐδοκιμώτερον ἴσμεν γίνεσθαι· καὶ γὰρ μεγάλα τοὺς ἀρχομένους ὠφελήσειεν. ὅντινα γὰρ ἄνθρωποι φιλοῦσι, τούτῳ ἐπιτάττοντι μὲν ταχὺ πείθονται, λέγοντι δὲ καὶ συντιθεμένῳ οὐκ ἀπιστοῦσι, κινδυνεύοντι δὲ συναγωνίζονται. τοιοῦτον γὰρ ἡ
50 ἀγάπη, τὸ τιθέναι τὴν ψυχὴν ὑπὲρ τοῦ φιλουμένου.

11. Πατέρα δὲ παίδων προκρίνομεν μᾶλλον ἢ ἄπαιδα, οὐδὲ τὸν ἄνευ παίδων παραιτούμενοι ἐὰν ἀγαθός ἐστι· καὶ γὰρ ὁ παῖδας ἔχων στρατηγός, εἰ μὲν νηπίους, θερμότερος γίνεται περὶ τὴν σπουδὴν τῶν ἐν βίῳ πραγμάτων ὑπὲρ τῆς τῶν παίδων φιλίας καὶ εὐπραγίας ἀγωνιζόμενος. εἰ δὲ τέλειοί εἰσι τὴν ἡλικίαν,
55 σύμβουλοι καὶ συστράτηγοι καὶ πιστοὶ ὑπηρέται γενόμενοι συγκατορθοῦσι τῷ πατρὶ τὰ μεταχειριζόμενα ὑπὲρ κοινῆς σωτηρίας πράγματα· δι' ὧν μᾶλλον δοκεῖ τοῦ ἄπαιδος ὁ παῖδας ἔχων προτιμότερος εἶναι.

12. Λέγειν δὲ καὶ δημηγορεῖν ἱκανόν· ἡγοῦμαι γὰρ τὰ μέγιστα ὠφελεῖν διὰ τοῦτο τὸ στράτευμα, ἐάν τε γὰρ παρατάσσεται πρὸς μάχην στρατηγός, διὰ τῆς
60 τοῦ λόγου παρακελεύσεως, τῶν μὲν γὰρ δεινῶν πολλάκις καὶ αὐτοῦ θανάτου ποιεῖ καταφρονεῖν, τῶν δὲ καλῶν καὶ ἡδέων ἐπιθυμεῖν. οὐχ οὕτως γὰρ ἐνηχοῦσα σάλπιγξ ἀκοαῖς ἐξεγείρει ψυχὰς εἰς κίνησιν μάχης ὡς λόγος μετὰ φρονήσεως λεγόμενος προτρέπεται εἰς ἀρετὴν καὶ ἐναγωνίους ποιεῖ τοὺς ἀκούοντας καὶ ἐξανιστᾷ πρὸς τὰ δεινὰ τὴν διάνοιαν. ἐὰν δέ τι συμβῇ πταῖσμα περὶ τὸ στρατό-
65 πεδον, ἡ τοῦ λόγου παρηγορία τὰς ψυχὰς ἀναρρωννύει. καὶ πολὺ δὴ χρησιμώτερός ἐστι στρατηγοῦ λόγος δυνατὸς ὥστε παραμυθήσασθαι στρατοπέδου συμφοράς, μᾶλλον τῶν ἐπιμελουμένων τὰ τραύματα ἰατρῶν. οἱ μὲν γὰρ ἐκείνους μόνους τοὺς τραυματίας θεραπεύουσι ταῖς ἰατρείαις καὶ διὰ χρόνου τάχα πλείονος, ὁ δὲ παρευθὺ καὶ τοὺς πονοῦντας καὶ τοὺς κάμνοντας εὐθυμοτέρους
70 ποιεῖ, καὶ τοὺς ἐρρωμένους ἀνιστᾷ πρὸς ἀνδρίαν καὶ εὐψυχίαν.

---

59 cum στρατη des. W (fol. desideratur)

---

50 Ioan. 15:13.

---

46 φιλούμενον MW ἀγαπώμενον ABE    47 ἴσμεν MW οἴδαμεν ABE | καὶ…ὠφελήσειεν MW om. ABE    48 φιλοῦσι MBE φιλοῦσιν WA    49 συντιθεμένῳ MW ὑπισχνουμένῳ ABE
51 ἢ ἄπαιδα MW om. ABE | ἄνευ παίδων MW μὴ ἔχοντα παῖδας ABE    52 ἀγαθός ἐστι M ἀγαθός ἐστιν W trsp. ABE    53 ἐν MWAB ἐν τῷ E    55 γενόμενοι MW γινόμενοι ABE
57 ἄπαιδος MW παῖδας μὴ ἔχοντος ABE    59 παρατάσσεται MW παρατάσσηται ABE
60 γὰρ MBE om. A | αὐτοῦ M αὐτοῦ τοῦ ABE    61 ἡδέων Va ἠθέων M γλυκέων ABE
62 ἀκοαῖς…μάχης M ταῖς ἀκοαῖς ἐγείρει ψυχὰς εἰς μάχην ABE    64 τι MA om. BE    65 δὴ
M om. ABE    67 τραύματα MA πράγματα BE    68 τραυματίας M τραυματισθέντας ABE
70 ἐρρωμένους Va ἐρρουμένους M ἰσχυροὺς ABE

10. We know that a general who is loved by his subjects will be more highly regarded and be very helpful to the men under his command. When men love someone, they are quick to obey his commands, they do not distrust his words and promises and, when he is in danger, they will fight along with him. For love is like this: to lay down one's life on behalf of the person one loves.[2]

11. We prefer a man who is a father of children rather than a childless one, although I would not turn away a childless one if he is a good man. The general who has children, if they are infants, becomes more enthused and serious about life's concerns as he struggles out of love for his children and their welfare. If they are adults, on the other hand, they become advisors and colleagues in command and faithful servants; they help in bringing to a successful conclusion the tasks on behalf of our common salvation entrusted to their father. For these reasons, it seems better that a man who has children is to be preferred to him who has none.

12. He should be capable of speaking and exhorting in public. I think that this ability is of the greatest benefit to the army. If the general, when he is drawing up his troops for battle, should encourage them by his words, he will often induce them to despise the terrors, even death itself. At the same time, he makes them eager to obtain the good and pleasant rewards. A trumpet blast echoing in one's ears does not stir the soul to move into battle as effectively as a speech, delivered in high spirits, urges one to valor, instills a martial spirit in its hearers, and arouses them to face terrible dangers. Moreover, if some calamity should befall the army, an encouraging speech will give new strength to the men's spirits. A skillful address by the general is far more useful in providing consolation for a defeated army than the care of the doctors for the wounded. For the physicians provide medical treatment only for the wounded, and it might take a long time, whereas the speech immediately raises the morale of the weary and disabled and arouses bravery and courage in the healthy.

2. John 15:13.

13. Ἔνδοξον δέ φαμεν, ἐπειδὴ ἀηδίζεται καὶ ἀσχάλλει ἐν τοῖς ἀδόξοις τὸ πλῆθος ὑποταττόμενον. οὐδεὶς γὰρ ἐθέλων ὑπομένει τὸν χείρονα κύριον ἑαυτοῦ ἀναδέχεσθαι καὶ ἡγεμόνα. δοκεῖ δέ μοι ὅτι πᾶσα ἀνάγκη τὸν τοιοῦτον εὑρισκό- μενον | στρατηγόν, ὥστε ἔχειν ἀρετὰς τοσαύτας ὅσας εἴρηκα στρατηγοῦ καὶ    287
75 ἔνδοξον εἶναι. ἡ γὰρ τοσαύτη ἀρετὴ ἄσημον ἄνθρωπον διαμένειν ἐπιπολὺ οὐ καταλιμπάνει.

14. Φάμεν δὲ καὶ μήτε πλούσιον, ἐὰν μὴ ἔχῃ τὰς τοῦ στρατηγοῦ ἀρετάς, προχειρίζεσθαι στρατηγὸν διὰ τὰ χρήματα, μήτε τὸν πένητα, ἐὰν ἀγαθός ἐστι, παραιτεῖσθαι διὰ τὴν πενίαν καὶ ἔνδειαν. οὐ μὴν δὲ τὸν πλούσιον ἀποδοκιμά-
80 ζομεν ὅτι πλούσιος, ἀλλ᾽ ἐὰν τὰς τῷ στρατηγῷ πρεπούσας μὴ κέκτηται ἀρετάς· οὐδὲ τὸν πένητα αἱρούμεθα ὅτι πένης, ἀλλ᾽ ὅτι στρατηγικήν τε καὶ γενναίαν ἔχει ψυχήν. οὐδέτερον γὰρ διὰ τὴν τύχην ἀποδοκιμάζομεν, ἀλλὰ μᾶλλον διὰ τὸν τρόπον ἀμφοτέρους προβαλούμεθα. οὐδὲ πλούσιος ἀγαθὸς ὢν τοσούτῳ διαφέρει τοῦ γενναίου πένητος ὅσον αἱ ἐπάργυροι καὶ κατάχρυσοι πανοπλίαι
85 τῶν καταχάλκων καὶ σιδηρῶν· αἱ μὲν γὰρ τῷ λαμπρῷ κόσμῳ πλεονεκτοῦσιν, αἱ δὲ ἐν αὐτῷ τῷ δραστηρίῳ διαγωνίζονται. πένητα δέ φημι γενναῖον ἐὰν μὴ χρηματιστής ἐστι καὶ δωρολήπτης· τὸν γὰρ χρηματιστὴν οὐδ᾽ ἂν πλουσιώτατος ὢν τύχῃ συμφέρει ποτὲ προχειρίζεσθαι στρατηγόν. ἀλλὰ μηδὲ μικρόλογον τινὰ καὶ ὀβολολόγον περὶ τὰ κέρδη ἢ ἔμπορον ἢ παραπλήσιόν τι τοιοῦτον πράτ-

---

80 ab ται ἀρετάς de novo inc. W

---

71–113 Onas. 1.17–25.

---

71 φαμεν Μ λέγομεν ABE | ἀηδίζεται…ἐν Μ ἀγανακτεῖ ABE  71–72 τοῖς…πλῆθος Μ trsp. ABE  72 ὑποταττόμενον Μ ὑποτασσόμενον ABE | ἐθέλων Μ θέλων ABE | ἑαυτοῦ Μ αὐτοῦ ABE  74 εἴρηκα στρατηγοῦ Μ εἰρήκαμεν AVa  75 ἄσημον Μ ἀφανῆ καὶ ἄγνωστον BE  81 ὅτι¹ MW ἐστι ABE  82 οὐδέτερον MW οὐδένα ABE | ἀποδοκιμάζομεν MW ἀποβάλλομεν ABE scr. mg. ἀδόκιμον καὶ ἀπόβλητον λογιζόμεθα W  82–83 τὸν τρόπον MW τὴν ἀρετὴν ABE  83 προβαλούμεθα Va προσκαλούμεθα MWA προκαλούμεθα BE | οὐδὲ Μ ὁ δὲ WABE | τοσούτῳ MW τοσοῦτον ABE  85 σιδηρῶν ABE σιδηρέων MW | αἱ¹ MWAE om. B | ad πλεονεκτοῦσιν scr. mg. ὑπερέχουσιν W  86 ad δραστηρίῳ scr. mg. τῷ δυναμενω ἐνεργ<εῖν> W | φημι MW λέγω ABE  87–88 χρηματιστής…τύχη MW ἔστιν δωρολήπτης μηδὲ κερδαίνειν ἀπὸ κακῶν βουλόμενος τὸν γὰρ τοιοῦτον οὐδὲ ἐάν ἐστι ABE  87 ad χρηματιστής scr. mg. χρημάτων ἐπι<μελούμενος> W | ad χρηματιστὴν scr. mg. χρήματα συνάγων W  88–92 μικρόλογον…ἐπιτηδευμάτων MW καταπραγματευόμενον τοῦ οἰκείου λαοῦ καὶ περὶ τὰ κέρδη σπουδάζοντα ἀνάγκη γὰρ τὸν τοιοῦτον μικρόφωνον (τοὺς τοιούτους μικρόφωνας Β τὸν τοιοῦτον μικρόφωνα Ε) εἶναι καὶ περὶ τὸ κέρδος σπουδάζοντα καὶ περὶ τὴν συλλογὴν τῶν χρημάτων ἀγαθὸν ἐπιτηδεύεσθαι ABE  88 ad μικρόλογον scr. mg. aliquid nunc evanidum W  89 τοιοῦτον Μ τὸν αὐτὸν W

13. We call for a man of good reputation.[3] An army becomes disgusted and angry when placed under the command of a man who is not respected. Nobody is willing to submit to or accept a master or a leader who is a worse man than oneself. It is absolutely necessary, in my opinion, that the general be recognized as such a man and that he should possess all those character traits of a general that I have listed, and be of good repute. Truly great virtue does not permit a man to remain unnoticed for long.

14. We say that a wealthy man must not be appointed general because of his riches unless he possesses the virtuous qualities of a general. Neither should a poor man, if he is a good man, be excluded because of his poverty and need. Indeed, we do not reject a rich man because he is rich, but only if he lacks the good qualities befitting a general. Neither do we select a poor man because he is poor, but because he has the noble soul expected of a general. We do not reject either one because of his fortune in life, but we promote both because of their manner of life. A wealthy general who is good differs from a poor but noble one only to the degree that armor inlaid with gold and silver differs from that of bronze and iron. The former has the advantage of brilliant ornamentation, the latter proves superior in action. We consider a poor man to be noble if he is not a dealer in money and greedy for gain. It is better never to promote a financier to the rank of general, even though he be the richest man around. Neither should he be a miserly man or one making a profit with petty cash or a

3. Sections 13–16 derive from Onasander 1.17–25.

90 τοντα. ἀνάγκη γὰρ τοὺς τοιούτους μικρόφρονας εἶναι καὶ περὶ τὸ κέρδος
ἐπτοημένους καὶ μεμεριμνημένους περὶ τὴν συλλογὴν τῶν χρημάτων καὶ μηδὲν
ἔχοντας τῶν καλῶν ἐπιτηδευμάτων.

15. Ἐὰν δὲ προγόνων ἐστὶ λαμπρῶν καὶ περιδόξων ἀπόγονος ἀγαπᾶν μὲν δεῖ
τοῦτο, οὐ μὴν δὲ πάντως ἐπιζητεῖν τὴν τοιαύτην εὐγένειαν ἀποῦσαν· οὐδὲ διὰ
95 ταύτην κρίνειν ἀνάξιον τὸν στρατηγόν, ἐὰν τὸ στρατηγεῖν καλῶς κέκτηται.
ὥσπερ γὰρ τὰ ζῷα ἀπὸ τῶν ἰδίων πράξεων καὶ ἠθῶν ἐξετάζομεν εὐγενῆ ἢ δυσ-
γενῆ, οὕτω χρὴ σκοπεῖν καὶ τὴν τῶν ἀνθρώπων εὐγένειαν, οὐκ ἀπὸ τῶν προγόνων, ἀλλ᾽ ἀπὸ τῶν ἰδίων πράξεων καὶ κατορθωμάτων. καὶ πῶς γὰρ οὐκ
ἀπρεπὲς καὶ ἀπαίδευτον τοὺς μὲν λιτοὺς στρατιώτας διὰ τὰς ἰδίας ἀριστείας καὶ
100 τοὺς ἀγῶνας τιμᾶν, οὐ τοὺς ἐκ προγόνων λαμπρούς, ἀλλὰ τοὺς αὐτοχειρίᾳ τι
λαμπρὸν ἔργον πεποιηκότας, τοὺς δὲ στρατηγοὺς διὰ τοὺς προγόνους ἐπιλέγεσθαι, κἂν εἰσιν ἄχρηστοι, ἀλλὰ μὴ διὰ τὴν ἰδίαν αὐτῶν ἀρετήν, κἂν μὴ ἀπὸ τοῦ
γένους λαμπρύνεται; προσόντων μὲν δὴ τούτῳ καὶ προγόνων λαμπρῶν εὐτυχὴς
ὁ στρατηγός, ἀπόντων δὲ τῶν ἀρετῶν, κἂν παρῇ ταῦτα, ἄπρακτος.
105 16. Τάχα δέ τις ἐλπίσει | καὶ κρείττονας ἔσεσθαι στρατηγοὺς τοὺς οὐκ ἔχον- 287ᵛ
τας ἀπὸ τῶν προγόνων σεμνύνεσθαι. οἱ μὲν γὰρ ἐπὶ γονεῦσι δοξαζόμενοι καὶ
τὴν ἀπ᾽ ἐκείνων ἔχοντες εὔκλειαν πολλάκις ῥαθυμότερον καὶ ἀμελέστερον
διοικοῦσιν· οἱ δὲ μηδεμίαν δόξαν προγόνων ἔχοντες, οὗτοι τὴν ἐκ πατέρων
ἐλάττωσιν ἐθέλοντες ἀναπληρῶσαι τῇ ἰδίᾳ προθυμίᾳ φιλοκινδυνότερον ἐπὶ τὰς
110 πράξεις κινοῦνται. καὶ καθάπερ οἱ πενέστεροι ἐπιπονώτερον μᾶλλον τῶν εὐπο-

---

96–102 Cf. Arist. Pol., 1.6.1255b.

---

90 μικρόφρονας M μικρόφονος WABE   93 περιδόξων MW ἐνδόξων ABE | ἀπόγονος MW
om. ABE   93–94 δεῖ τοῦτο MW καὶ τοῦτον ABE   94 μὴν…πάντως MW πάντως δὲ ABE |
ἀποῦσαν MW ἐὰν μὴ πρόσεστιν ABE scr. mg. μὴ οὖσαν W   95 κρίνειν ἀνάξιον M κρίνειν
ἄξιον W ἀνάξιον κρίνειν ABE | κέκτηται MWA κέχρηται BE   96 καὶ ἠθῶν MW om. ABE
96–97 δυσγενῆ ABE δυσχερῆ MW   97 οὕτω MWAB οὕτως E | τῶν² BE om. MWA
98 ἀπὸ MW ἐκ ABE   100 ἀγῶνας MW τὰ ἀνδραγαθήματα ABE | οὐ MW καὶ μὴ ABE |
λαμπρούς MW λαμπρῶν ABE | αὐτοχειρίᾳ MW om. ABE | scr. mg. δια των ιδιων χειρων W
100–101 τι…ἔργον MW ἔργον τι λαμπρὸν ABE   101 δὲ MWA δὲ μὴ BE   103 ad
προσόντων scr. mg. ηγουν εχοντος στρατηγοῦ και προγονους λαμπρ<ούς> W   104 ad κἂν
scr. mg. κἂν εὐγενῆ υπαρχη W | ad ἄπρακτος scr. mg. αδοκιμος W   105 ad τοὺς scr. mg. τους
μη δυναμένους ἐγκαυχασθαι εἰς εὐγένειαν W   106 ad γονεῦσι scr. mg. οἱ θαρρουντες
ἐγκαυχώμεν<οι> εἰς το γενος W   107 ad εὔκλειαν scr. mg. δοξαν W   108 διοικοῦσιν MW
διάκεινται ABE   108–109 τὴν…ἐλάττωσιν MW τὴν τῶν πατέρων ἀδοξίαν ABE
109 ἐθέλοντες ἀναπληρῶσαι MW ἀναπληρῶσαι θέλοντες ABE   110 κινοῦνται MW
ἔρχονται ABE | καὶ MWA om. BE | πενέστεροι MWA πένητες BE

merchant or man engaged in any business of that kind. Men such as these are bound to have petty minds; they are excited by the prospect of gain and anxious about collecting money, and they are without any noble habits.

15. If the man is descended from illustrious and highly regarded ancestors, then this must be in his favor but, if this is lacking, we should certainly not require such noble birth. Neither should we use this as a criterion to judge a man unworthy of being general if he clearly possesses the ability to assume that position. For just as we evaluate the good or bad pedigrees of animals by their individual performance and disposition, so we must also view the noble lineage of men, not from the perspective of their forefathers, but from that of their own performance and accomplishments.[4] Is it not improper, even stupid, on the one hand to honor simple soldiers for their individual valor in combat who are not from illustrious families but who have performed a brilliant deed by their own effort, and, on the other hand, to select a general because of his ancestry, even though he is incompetent, and not because of his individual virtue, even if he does not come from an illustrious family? Of course, if a general has a brilliant lineage in addition to these other qualities, he is fortunate. Still, even if he is of good birth, without the virtuous qualities he is useless.

16. Perhaps one might expect that those who cannot take pride in their ancestors would become even better generals, for men who glory in their forefathers and appropriate their good reputation to themselves often prove to be careless and negligent administrators, whereas those who have no ancestral renown desire to make up for the obscurity of their lineage by their own enthusiasm and are moved to undertake more dangerous activities. Just as poor men

---

4. Cf. Aristotle, *Politics* 1.6.1255b.

ρωτέρων ἐπὶ τὴν τοῦ βίου κτῆσιν ὁρμῶνται, τὸ ἐλλεῖπον ἀνταναπληρῶσαι τῆς
τύχης σπουδάζοντες, οὕτως οἱ μὴ ἐκ πατέρων κληρονομήσαντες δόξαν διὰ τῶν
ἰδίων πράξεων σπουδάζουσιν οἰκειώσασθαι δόξαν.

17. Διὰ ταῦτα οὖν προχειριζέσθω μὲν στρατηγὸς ἀγαθός, εὐγενής, πλούσι-
115 ος, μὴ ἀποδοκιμαζέσθω δὲ πένης μετὰ ἀρετῆς, εἰ καὶ μὴ ἀπὸ λαμπρῶν καὶ ἐνδό-
ξων προγόνων κατάγει τὸ γένος.

18. Κεφάλαιον δὲ εἰπεῖν, χρὴ τὸν στρατηγόν, εἰ δυνατὸν εἴη, καὶ τὸ σῶμα
εὐπρεπῆ καὶ ῥωμαλέον καὶ φιλόπονον καὶ ὀξύτατον καὶ τὴν γνώμην ἀνδρεῖον
καὶ φιλότιμον καὶ σπουδαῖον καὶ φιλοκίνδυνον καὶ μάλιστα τοῦ θείου καὶ περὶ
120 τὰ θεῖα πράγματα ἐπιμελέστατον, ἡδονῶν δὲ τῶν μὲν τοῦ σώματος ἐγκρατῆ,
τῶν δὲ τῆς γνώμης ἄπληστόν τε καὶ ἀκόρεστον ἐπὶ τῷ ἐπαίνῳ τῶν ἀγαθῶν
πράξεων, συνιδεῖν δὲ τὸ δέον ἔτι ἐν τῷ ἀφανεῖ, ἂν δεινόν τε καὶ ὀξύν, ἐκ τῶν
φαινομένων τὰ κεκρυμμένα στοχάζεσθαι ἐπιτυχέστατον, τάξαι δὲ στρατὸν καὶ
ὁπλίσαι καὶ κοσμῆσαι ἔμπειρον, λόγοις δὲ ἀνιστᾶν τὰ πεπτωκότα φρονήματα
125 τοῦ στρατοῦ καὶ ἐλπίδων ἐμπλῆσαι ἀγαθῶν καὶ ἑτοίμους πρὸς κινδύνους
παρασκευάσαι δυνατόν, καὶ τὰ συντιθέμενα δὲ ἢ ὁμολογούμενα φυλάξαι
βεβαιότερον, μὴ ἁλῶναι δὲ παρὰ τῶν ἐν λόγοις δυνατῶν, οἷς ἐκεῖνοι παρέλκειν
τοῦ καθήκοντος ἐθέλουσιν. εἶναι δεῖ ἀσφαλῆ, χρημάτων δὲ εἰς μὲν ἡδονὰς τὰς

---

114-120 Cf. Onas. 1.1.   114-116 Onas. 2.1.

---

111 ad ἐπὶ scr. mg. επι το κτησιν εὐποριαν W | ἀνταναπληρῶσαι MW ἀναπληρῶσαι ABE
112 οὕτως MWAB οὕτω E   113 ἰδίων MWA οἰκείων BE   114 οὖν...μὲν MW μὲν οὖν
προχειριζέσθω ABE   115 ἀποδοκιμαζέσθω MW ἀποβαλλέσθω ABE scr. mg. αποβλητος και
αδοκιμος λογιζεσθω W   117 εἴη MW ἐστιν ABE   118 ῥωμαλέον MW ἀνδρεῖον ABE
118-119 ἀνδρεῖον...φιλότιμον MW γενναῖον ABE scr. mg. τὸν φιλοῦντα et alia evanida W
119 τοῦ θείου MW θεοσεβῆ ABE   120 τῶν μὲν MWA om. BE   121 τῶν[1]...τῆς ABE τῆς
δὲ MW   121-122 ἄπληστόν...πράξεων ABE ἐπαίνου ἀληθοῦς ἐπὶ πράξεσιν ἀγαθαῖς
ἄπληστόν τε καὶ ἀκόρεστον MW   122 συνιδεῖν MW διανοήσασθαι ABE scr. mg. προνοησαι
συμφερον του καιρου W | ἂν MW ὃ BE om. A | scr. mg. δυνατόν W | ὀξύν WABE ὀξὺ M
123 στοχάζεσθαι ἐπιτυχέστατον MW εὐστόχως στοχαζόμενον ABE | τάξαι δὲ MW ἔμπειρον
δὲ τάξαι ABE   124 ἔμπειρον MW om. ABE | λόγοις...ἀνιστᾶν MW δυνατὸν δὲ διὰ λόγων
διεγείρειν ABE | τὰ BE om. MWA   125 τοῦ ABE om. MW | πρὸς MW πρὸς τοὺς ABE
126 ad ὁμολογούμενα scr. mg. τὴν κυρωθεῖσαν βουλὴν W   127 ἁλῶναι MW παρασύρεσθαι
ABE scr. mg. ἤγουν μὴ ἁ...τᾶσθαι παρὰ δυνάμεως et alia evanida W | παρὰ MW ὑπὸ ABE |
οἷς MW δι' ὧν ABE | παρέλκειν MW παρέλκειν αὐτὸν ABE   128 καθήκοντος MW
προσήκοντος ABE | ἐθέλουσιν MW θέλουσιν ἀλλ' ABE   128-129 ἡδονὰς...ἑαυτοῦ MW
τὰς ἑαυτοῦ ἡδονὰς ABE

will endure more than rich men in their quest to obtain a living and in their eagerness to supply what fortune has not provided, so men who have not inherited ancestral glory strive to achieve glory on their own by their own deeds.

17. For the above reasons, then, that man is to be appointed as general who is good, well born, and wealthy, although a qualified poor man is not to be rejected even if he is not descended from illustrious and renowned ancestors.[5]

18. To sum it up, the general must, inasmuch as possible, be physically impressive, strong and hardworking, very quick in action, courageous, respected, serious, and ready to face danger.[6] He should especially be most attentive to divine matters and his relationship to God. When it comes to bodily pleasures, he should exercise self-control. But in matters of the mind he is insatiable and never satisfied in his efforts to bring about successful actions. While the situation is still unclear, he realizes what has to be done. Clever and quick witted, he is always right on target in estimating what is hidden from what is visible. He is experienced in arming and drawing up an army in battle array. His words are able to resurrect the morale of the army when it is low, fill it with fine expectations, and prepare it to confront dangers. He should be very strict in observing agreements or promises, not swayed by clever speakers who want to drag him away from his duty. He must be steadfast, parsimonious in expenditures on his

5. Onasander 2.1.
6. Cf. Onasander 1.1.

ἑαυτοῦ φειδωλόν τε καὶ ὀλιγαρκῆ, εἰς δὲ σύμπνοιαν τῶν πλησίον καὶ μάλιστα
130 τῆς ὑπὲρ τοῦ κοινοῦ δαπάνης ἄφθονόν τε καὶ ἡπλωμένον.

19. Τοιοῦτον τοίνυν ὄντα τὸν προχειριζόμενον στρατηγόν, οἷον ὁ λόγος
ὑπέγραψεν τῇ τε φύσει καὶ τοῖς ἤθεσί τε καὶ ἐπιτηδεύμασι, δεῖ τῆς ἀρχῆς ἐπειλημμένον ἔτι καὶ χρηστὸν εἶναι, εὐπροσήγορον, ἕτοιμον, ἀτάραχον, μὴ οὕτως
ἐπιεικῆ τε καὶ πρᾶον ὥστε καταφρονεῖσθαι, μήτε μὴν οὕτω | φοβερὸν ὥστε   288
135 μισεῖσθαι, ἵνα μήτε διὰ μειλιχίας ἐκλύσῃ τὸ στρατόπεδον καὶ πάντα τὸν ὑπὸ
χεῖρα λαόν, μήτε διὰ τὸν φόβον τῆς αὐτοῦ ἀγάπης ἀλλοτριώσῃ.

20. Τὰ δ᾽ ἄλλα ὅσα χρὴ τοῦτον ἐπιτηδεύειν ἐν ταῖς ἀεὶ κατὰ μέρος ἐμπιπτού-
σαις ἐπικαίροις διοικήσεσι καὶ ὧν παραφυλάττεσθαι, νῦν μὲν διὰ τὸ πλῆθος
συνεστείλαμεν, ἐν δὲ τῷ πλάτει τῆς παρ᾽ ἡμῶν ἐκτιθεμένης τακτικῆς καθ᾽
140 ἕκαστα μνημονεύσομεν, ὅσῃ δύναμις.

21. Τοιοῦτον δὲ ὄντα καὶ οὕτω διατηρούμενον τὸν παρὰ τῆς βασιλείας ἡμῶν
προχειριζόμενον στρατηγόν, ἐλπίζομεν αὐτὸν καὶ τῆς τοῦ Θεοῦ ἀπολαύειν
εὐμενείας καὶ τῆς ἡμετέρας εὐνοίας καὶ τῆς τοῦ κοινοῦ σωτηρίας καὶ τῆς παρὰ
πάντων εὐφημίας καὶ τῆς κατὰ τὸν βίον εὐημερίας ἐν Χριστῷ τῷ μόνῳ τῶν
145 ὅλων αἰωνίῳ καὶ ἀδιαδόχῳ βασιλεῖ. ἀλλ᾽ οὕτω μὲν τὴν τοῦ στρατηγοῦ κατάστασιν ἀπαρτίσαντες, φέρε τοῦτον οἱονεὶ κατ᾽ ὀφθαλμοὺς τῆς ἡμετέρας παραστη-
σάμενοι βασιλείας—τὰ εἰκότα καὶ πρόσφορα τῇ στρατηγικῇ τε καὶ τακτικῇ
ἐπιστήμῃ—διὰ τῆς ἐφεξῆς ἡμῶν παρακελεύσεως παραινέσωμεν.

---

131–136 Onas. 2.2.

---

129 φειδωλόν τε MW φειδόμενον ABE | ὀλιγαρκῆ MW ἐν ὀλίγοις ἀρκούμενον ABE |
σύμπνοιαν…πλησίον MW τὸ εὐεργετεῖν τοὺς ὑπ᾽ αὐτὸν ABE   130 τῆς MW εἰς τὴν ABE |
δαπάνης MW δαπάνην ABE   132 ὑπέγραψεν MWA ὑπέγραψε BE | τε² MW om. ABE |
ἐπιτηδεύμασι MABE ἐπιτηδεύμασιν W | τῆς ἀρχῆς MW εἰς τὴν ἀρχὴν ABE scr. mg. ἤγουν τὰ
τοῦ στρατηγοῦ διοικοῦντα W   132–133 ἐπειλημμένον MW προχειρισθέντα ABE
133 χρηστὸν MW ἀγαθὸν ABE scr. mg. <μενο>ν εν ταις ιδιαις W   134 τε MW om. ABE |
μήτε MWBE μὴ δὲ A | μὴν MW om. ABE | οὕτω MW οὕτως ABE   135 διὰ μειλιχίας Va δι᾽
ἀμελείας MW διὰ τὴν ἀμελείαν ABE | στρατόπεδον MW στράτευμα καὶ εἰς καταφρόνησιν
ἀγάγῃ ABE   135–136 καὶ…λαόν MW om. ABE   136 τῆς…ἀλλοτριώσῃ MW μισεῖν
αὐτὸν παρασκευάσῃ ABE   137 δ᾽ MW δὲ ABE | χρὴ MW προσήκει ABE | ἀεὶ…μέρος MW
om. ABE   137–138 ἐμπιπτούσαις MW παρεμπιπτούσαις ABE   138 ὧν MW ὅσα ABE |
παραφυλάττεσθαι MW παραφυλάττεσθαι χρὴ ABE   141 οὕτω MW οὕτως ABE
144–145 τῶν ὅλων MW om. ABE   145 οὕτω MW οὕτως ABE | μὲν M μὲν καὶ WABE
146 ἀπαρτίσαντες MW τελειώσαντες ABE scr. mg. τελειωσα<ντες> W | οἱονεὶ MW ὥσπερ
ABE | κατ᾽ ὀφθαλμοὺς MW πρὸ ὀφθαλμῶν ABE   147 εἰκότα MW πρέποντα ABE |
πρόσφορα MW ἁρμόζοντα ABE scr. mg. τὰ ἁρμοζο<ντα> W | τε MW om. ABE

own pleasures, and satisfied with very little. He must be ungrudging and straightforward in working together with his neighbor, especially in expenditures for the common good.

19. The man to be appointed as general, therefore, should be such as this tractate has sketched regarding his nature, his character, and his way of life.[7] Having assumed command, he must in addition be trustworthy, approachable, <always> prepared, and unperturbed; he should not be so lenient and gentle as to be despised or so severe as to be hated. Otherwise, his kindness might loosen the discipline of the army and all the troops under his command, and fear of him might turn the army away from loving him.

20. All the other things that he must put into practice in his timely management of the details that always devolve upon him, as well as the things he must be on his guard against, on account of their great number, we have here summarized. In particular sections of this compilation of ours we will, as best we can, discuss them in greater detail.

21. We hope that the general promoted by Our Majesty will indeed be such a man and that he will remain such. We hope that he will enjoy the favor of God and our own goodwill, that he will share in our common salvation and will be highly regarded by everyone, as well as find happiness in his life. May he find all this in Christ, the only eternal and unchanging emperor of all things. Having thus brought to an end our discussion of the condition of the general, let us now advise him and offer the following recommendations—placing him as it were in front of Our Majesty—in those matters that are applicable and relevant to strategic and tactical science.

7. Cf. Onasander 2.2.

22. Πρὸ μὲν τῶν ἄλλων ἁπάντων, ὦ στρατηγέ, πρώτην σοι ταύτην παρακέλ-
150 ευσίν τε καὶ παραίνεσιν ποιούμεθα, ὥστε θεοφιλείας καὶ δικαιοσύνης ἐπιμελεῖσθαι καὶ οἷον ὁρᾶν διηνεκῶς πρὸ ὀφθαλμῶν τὸν Θεὸν καὶ φοβεῖσθαι αὐτὸν καὶ
ἀγαπᾶν ἐξ ὅλης τῆς καρδίας σου καὶ ἐξ ὅλης τῆς ψυχῆς σου καὶ μετ' ἐκεῖνον
ἡμᾶς, καὶ τὰς αὐτοῦ ἐκτελεῖν ἐντολὰς καὶ τὴν ἐκείνου εὐμένειαν ἐντεῦθεν
προσλαμβάνεσθαι ἵνα—εἰ καὶ τολμηρότερον εἴπω—ἐν καιρῷ περιστάσεως ὡς
155 φίλος φίλῳ τῷ κοινῷ δεσπότῃ θαρρῶν πεποιθότως προσεύχῃ καὶ τῆς σωτηρίας
τὰς ἐλπίδας ἔχων ταύτην παρ' αὐτοῦ φιλίως ἐξαπαιτῇς. ἀψευδὴς γάρ ἐστιν ὁ
εἰπών· θέλημα τῶν φοβουμένων αὐτὸν ποιήσει κύριος καὶ τῆς δεήσεως αὐτῶν
εἰσακούεται καὶ σώσει αὐτούς.
23. Ἴσθι γὰρ ὅτι θείας εὐμενείας ἐκτὸς οὐκ ἔστι καλῶς κατορθωθῆναι βου-
160 λὴν κἂν φρόνιμος εἶναι δόξῃς. οὐκ ἔστι πολεμίων περιγενέσθαι, κἂν ἀσθενεῖς
ἐκεῖνοι νομίζωνται, διὰ τὸ πάντα ἐν τῇ προνοίᾳ τοῦ Θεοῦ κεῖσθαι καὶ αὐτὰ τὰ
ἐλάχιστα δοκοῦντα τὴν αὐτοῦ πρόνοιαν διοικεῖσθαι.
24. Ὥσπερ γὰρ κυβερνήτης πλοίου, κἂν πάνυ ἄριστός ἐστι, τῶν ἀνέμων
αἰσίως μὴ πνεόντων ἄπρακτον ἔχει τὴν τέχνην. ἐὰν δὲ τούτους προσλάβηται καὶ
165 τὴν τέχνην ἔχει συμπράττουσαν, διπλοῦν τὸν δρόμον | τοῦ πλοίου σὺν ἀσφα-     288ᵛ
λείᾳ ποιεῖται· οὕτω καὶ ἄριστος στρατηγός, ἐὰν τὴν εὐμένειαν τοῦ Θεοῦ ἐνδύσηται καὶ τῇ τάξει καὶ τῇ στρατηγίᾳ σὺν ἀγρυπνίᾳ καὶ ἐπιμελείᾳ χρήσηται

---

149–192 Strat., praef.36–69.    152 Deut. 6:5; Matt. 22:37.    157–158 Ps. 144 (145): 19.
161–162 Matt. 6:25–28; Luc. 12:22–26.

---

149–150 πρὸ…ποιούμεθα MW παρακελευόμεθα οὖν σοι ὦ στρατηγὲ πρώτην ταύτην
παρακέλευσιν καὶ παραίνεσιν ABE    150 θεοφιλείας MW πρὸ τῶν ἄλλων ἁπάντων
θεοσεβείας ABE    151 οἷον…θεὸν MW τὸν θεὸν ἔχειν πρὸ ὀφθαλμῶν ABE
152–153 καὶ²…ἡμᾶς MW om. ABE    153 ἐντεῦθεν MW ἐκ τούτου ABE    154 εἰ…εἴπω
MW om. ABE    155 φίλῳ MW φίλῳ εἰ καὶ τολμηρὸν ABE | πεποιθότως MW om. ABE
156 ἔχων…ἐξαπαιτῇς MW εἰς αὐτὸν ἔχων τὴν αὐτοῦ βοήθειαν ἐπισπάσῃ ABE    157 κύριος
MWA om. BE    159 ἴσθι MW γίνωσκε ABE scr. mg. <γ>ινωσκε W | ὅτι WABE τι M |
θείας…ἐκτὸς MW om. ABE | ἔστι MABE ἔστιν W    159–160 βουλὴν MW βουλὴν χωρὶς τῆς
θείας φιλανθρωπίας τε καὶ χρηστότητος ABE    160 ἔστι MABE ἔστιν W    161 προνοίᾳ…
κεῖσθαι MW τοῦ θεοῦ κεῖσθαι προνοίᾳ ABE    161–162 αὐτὰ…πρόνοιαν MW παρ' αὐτοῦ
διοικεῖσθαι καὶ αὐτὰ τὰ ἐλάχιστα ABE    162 διοικεῖσθαι ABE διοικεῖν MW    163 πλοίου
MW om. ABE    164 αἰσίως W αἰτίως M καλῶς ABE scr. mg. ἐπιτηδείως W
164–165 καὶ…ἔχει MW ἔχει δὲ καὶ τὴν τέχνην ABE    165 συμπράττουσαν MW
συνεργοῦσαν αὐτῷ ABE    166 οὕτω MW οὕτως οὖν ABE | εὐμένειαν…θεοῦ MW τοῦ θεοῦ
φιλανθρωπίαν ABE    166–167 ἐνδύσηται MW ἔχει καὶ τὴν βοήθειαν ABE    167 καὶ¹…
στρατηγίᾳ MW τάξῃ δὲ καλῶς τὸ στράτευμα καὶ ABE | ἐπιμελείᾳ MW ἐπιμελείᾳ τῇ
στρατηγίᾳ ABE

22. Before everything else, O general, we propose this to you as our very first subject of exhortation and advice:[8] be concerned about the love of God and righteousness in such manner that you constantly have God before your eyes. Fear him. Love him with all your heart and all your soul and, after him, us.[9] Keep his commandments and, in turn, you will receive his favor, so that—if I may speak rather boldly—in difficult situations you may with confidence and trust pray to our common Lord as a friend to a friend and you may request the salvation you hope for from him as from a friend. That one is not a liar who said: The Lord will do the will of those who fear him and he will hear their prayer and save them.[10]

23. For you must realize that, apart from God's favor, it is not possible to bring any plan to a successful conclusion, however intelligent you may seem to be; it is not possible to overcome the enemy, however weak they may be thought. Everything lies in the providence of God, that providence that takes care of even those things that appear to be the least.[11]

24. Aboard ship, now, a helmsman, even the best, finds that his skill is useless when the winds are not blowing favorably, but when he has them with him and also puts his skill to use, he has no difficulty in doubling the ship's run. So it is with the best general. He will be clad with the favor of God and, ever alert and diligent, he will make good use of his tactical and strategic skills. He

8. Cf. *Strat.*, Preface 36–69.
9. Deuteronomy 6:5; Matthew 22:37.
10. Psalms 144 (145): 19.
11. Matthew 6:25–28; Luke 12:22–26. But cf. Haldon, *Commentary*.

καλῶς, καὶ τὸν πιστευόμενον αὐτῷ στρατὸν ἀσφαλῶς διοικήσει καὶ τῇ ποικίλῃ
γνώμῃ τῶν ἐχθρῶν ἀντιστρατεύεσθαι δύναται. ἡ γὰρ τοῦ Θεοῦ πρόνοια τὰ μὲν
170 διδάξει πρὸς τὸ συμφέρον, τὰ δὲ πρὸς ἀγαθὸν πέρας ἀποτελέσει. τοιοῦτος
τοίνυν, εὐσεβὴς μὲν περὶ τὴν πίστιν, δίκαιος δὲ περὶ τὰς πράξεις ὑπάρχων,
ὥσπερ θεμελίῳ ἀγαθῷ καὶ ἀσαλεύτῳ ἐποικοδομεῖ καὶ τὰ ἄλλα ἀγαθά.

25. Πρᾶος γενοῦ καὶ ἀτάραχος τοῖς ἐντυγχάνουσι· τὸ γὰρ ἄγριον τοῦ ἤθους
μισητὸν καὶ φευκτόν. λιτός τε καὶ ἁπλοῦς περὶ τὴν δίαιταν καὶ τὸ ἔνδυμα· ἡ γὰρ
175 πολυτέλεια καὶ ποικιλία τῶν βρωμάτων καὶ ἐνδυμάτων τὰς ἀναγκαίας δαπάνας
εἰς μάταιον ἐξαντλεῖ. ἀγρύπνως δὲ καὶ ἐπιμελῶς τοῖς ἀναγκαίοις πράγμασιν
ἐπιβάλλων, καὶ μὴ ῥαθύμως καὶ ἀμελῶς· ἡ γὰρ ἐπιμέλεια καὶ ἡ ἐπιμονὴ καὶ τὰ
πάνυ δυσχερῆ τῶν πραγμάτων ῥᾳδίως κατορθοῖ· καὶ ὁ καταφρονῶν πράγματος
καταφρονηθήσεται ὑπ’ αὐτοῦ.

180 26. Ἐπὶ δὲ τοῖς μεγάλοις καὶ ἀναγκαίοις τῶν πραγμάτων μηδὲν χωρὶς βουλῆς
διαπράττου. εἰ τάχα δὲ καὶ βραδέως βουλεύσῃ, ἀλλὰ τὸ βουλευθὲν συντόμως
καὶ ἀσφαλῶς, ὡς δυνατόν, ἐπιτέλει, ὥσπερ ἐπὶ τῶν νοσημάτων οἱ ἰατροί.

27. Ἀλλὰ καὶ τοῖς ἀρχομένοις ἴσως προσφέρου, μηδὲν κατὰ προσωποληψίαν
ἐργαζόμενος, ἀλλὰ πᾶσιν ἴσως κατὰ τὴν τοῦ δικαίου φύσιν ὑπεξερχόμενος.

185 28. Μηδὲ χαύνως καὶ ῥαθύμως διάκεισο ἐπὶ τοῖς ἀπὸ κακίας ἢ ἀμελείας
ἁμαρτανομένοις διὰ τὸ δοκεῖν εἶναι καλόν. οὐδὲ γὰρ καλόν ἐστι τὸ συνεργεῖν
κακίᾳ καὶ ῥαθυμίᾳ, μάλιστα ἐπὶ τῶν καιρίων καὶ ἀναγκαίων πραγμάτων. μηδὲ
πάλιν δι’ ἔνδειξιν αὐστηρίας προπετῶς καὶ ἀδιακρίτως τὰς ἐπεξελεύσεις ποιοῦ.
ἐκεῖνο μὲν γὰρ περιφρόνησιν καὶ ἀπείθειαν φέρει, τοῦτο δὲ μῖσος εὔλογον καὶ

---

172 Cf. Matt. 7:24.   178–179 Prov. 13:13.

---

168 καλῶς MW om. ABE   169 γνώμῃ…ἐχθρῶν MW trsp. ABE | δύναται MW δυνήσεται
AE δυνήσηται B   170 πέρας MW τέλος ABE   172 ἐποικοδομεῖ…ἀγαθά MW καὶ τὰ ἄλλα
ἀγαθὰ ἐποικοδομεῖ ABE   173 ἐντυγχάνουσι MABE ἐντυγχάνουσιν W   174 μισητὸν…
φευκτόν MW καὶ μισεῖται καὶ ἀποστρέφεται ABE | δίαιταν…ἔνδυμα MW τροφὴν καὶ τὴν
ἔνδυσιν ABE | ad δίαιταν scr. mg. τροφὴν W | ad ἔνδυμα scr. mg. την ενδυσιν W   175 ad
πολυτέλεια scr. mg. <ἐ>ν ταις τρυφαῖς καὶ <ταῖ>ς ἐνδύσεσι πολυε<ῐδ>ον W | καὶ ἐνδυμάτων
ABE om. MW   176 ἐξαντλεῖ Va ἐξαντλᾷ MW καταναλίσκει ABE   177 ἐπιβάλλων MW
ἐγχειρῶν ABE   178 ad δυσχερῆ scr. mg. <δ>υσκολα W | ῥᾳδίως MW εὐκόλως ABE quod
etiam scr. mg. W   180 ἐπὶ…μηδὲν MW μηδὲν δὲ τῶν μεγάλων καὶ ἀναγκαίων πραγμάτων
ABE   181 βουλευθὲν MWA βουλευθὲν καὶ δόξαν εἶναι συμφέρον BE | συντόμως MWA
συντόμως ἐπιτελεῖ BE   182 ὥσπερ…ἰατροί MW om. ABE   183 ἀρχομένοις MW
ὑποχειρίοις ABE | ἴσως MW ἴσως πᾶσι A πᾶσιν ἐπίσης BE   184 τοῦ MWA om. BE
185 τοῖς MW τοῖς ἁμαρτήμασι τοῖς ABE   186 καλόν[1] MW καλὸς ABE   187 κακίᾳ…
ῥαθυμίᾳ MW τῇ ῥαθυμίᾳ καὶ τῇ κακίᾳ ABE | καιρίων W καιρῶν M μεγάλων ABE   188 ad
ἐπεξελεύσεις scr. mg. τας τιμωριας W   189–190 καὶ[1]…κρεῖττον MW om. ABE

will safely manage the army entrusted to him and will be able to counter the various machinations of the enemy. The providence of God will teach him those things that are beneficial and will bring them to a successful conclusion. He should be the kind of man who is orthodox in his faith and just in his deeds. As on a firm and unshakable foundation he will build the other good qualities.[12]

25. You should be gentle and untroubled to those you encounter, for a savage temperament is hateful and to be avoided. You should be plain and simple in matters of food and clothing. Extravagance and ostentation in food and raiment squander the funds for necessary items to no purpose. The general should be tireless and painstaking in attending to necessary matters, not slack or careless; care and persistence will easily carry him through the most difficult situations. If he shows no concern for a problem, that problem will show no concern for him.[13]

26. You should take no action regarding serious, unavoidable problems without deliberation. You may perhaps be slow in coming to a decision, but once you have made your decision, carry it out quickly and safely, as far as possible, just as physicians do in treating illness.

27. You should appear even tempered to those under your command, doing nothing in respect of persons, but going out to meet everyone on an equal basis, as expected of a just man.

28. You should not be lackadaisical and too easygoing in dealing with those who have committed offenses out of wickedness or carelessness in order to give the impression of being a good commander, for it is not good to cooperate with wicked and careless men, especially in emergencies and perilous situations. On the other hand, you should not punish hastily and without due investigation in order to show how strict you are. The first leads to contempt and disobedience,

12. Cf. Matthew 7:24.
13. Proverbs 13:13.

190 τοὺς ἐξ αὐτοῦ καρπούς. κρεῖττον γὰρ ὁ μετὰ δικαιοσύνης φόβος καὶ ἡ μετὰ τὴν
γύμνωσιν τῆς αἰτίας εὔλογος ἐπεξέλευσις, ἥτις οὐ κόλασις ἀλλὰ σωφρονισμὸς
τοῖς εὐφρονοῦσι λογίζεται.

29. Πρὸ πάντων δὲ ἐπὶ πολέμους ὁπλιζόμενος ἀποσκόπει δικαίαν εἶναι τὴν
ἀρχὴν τοῦ τοιούτου πολέμου καὶ μὴ χεῖρας ἀδίκους ἐπίβαλέ ποτε κατὰ πολεμί-
195 ων εἰ μὴ πρότερον ἐκεῖνοι διὰ τῆς συνήθους αὐτῶν ἀσεβείας ἐκστρατεύειν
ἀπαρξάμενοι τὴν ἡμετέραν καταδράμωσιν. |

30. Ἡμῶν γὰρ ἀεὶ τὴν εἰρήνην καὶ πρὸς τοὺς ὑπηκόους καὶ πρὸς τοὺς 289
βαρβάρους διὰ Χριστὸν τὸν καθ᾽ ὅλου βασιλέα καὶ Θεὸν ἀσπαζομένων, ἐὰν καὶ
τὰ ἔθνη τοῦτο φιλοῦσι τοῖς ἰδίοις ἐγχαλινούμενα ὅροις καὶ μηδὲν ἀδικεῖν
200 ἐπαγγελλόμενα καὶ αὐτὸς σὺ κατ᾽ αὐτῶν τὰς χεῖρας σύστειλον καὶ αἵμασι τὴν
γῆν μήτ᾽ ἐμφυλίοις μήτε βαρβαρικοῖς κατάχραινε. ἃ γὰρ ἐγκαλέσεις τοῖς ἐχθροῖς
ἤγουν μὴ ἀπάρχεσθαι χειρῶν ἀδίκων οὐδὲν ὑπὸ σοῦ ἀδικουμένους, ταῦτα ἄρα
καὶ αὐτοί, μηδὲν ἐναντίον δρῶντες κατὰ τῶν ὑπηκόων τῆς ἡμῶν βασιλείας, ἀλλ᾽
εἰρηνεύοντες ἐγκαλέσουσί σοι. δεῖ γὰρ ἡμᾶς ἀεὶ τούς, εἰ δυνατὸν τὸ ἐξ ἡμῶν,
205 μετὰ πάντων ἀνθρώπων εἰρηνεύοντας, τοῖς εἰρηνεύειν βουλομένοις ἔθνεσι καὶ
μηδὲν ἀδικεῖν τοὺς ὑποχειρίους ἡμῶν, ὡς τὴν εἰρήνην ἀεὶ τῶν ἄλλων προτιμῶν-
τας ἁπάντων, συνειρηνεύειν ἐκείνοις καὶ πολέμων ἀπέχεσθαι.

31. Εἰ δέ γε μὴ σωφρονεῖ τὸ ἀντίπαλον, ἀλλ᾽ αὐτοὶ τῆς ἀδικίας ἀπάρξονται
τὴν ἡμετέραν κατατρέχοντες γῆν, τότε ἄρα δικαίως αἰτίας προκειμένης ὡς καὶ
210 ἀδίκου πολέμου παρὰ τῶν ἐναντίων ἀπαρχομένου, θαρσαλέως καὶ σὺν προθυ-

---

190–192 Strat., praef.65–68

190 γὰρ ὁ Μ οὖν ὁ W ὁ γὰρ ΑΒΕ    190–191 τὴν γύμνωσιν MW φανέρωσιν ΑΒΕ
191 ἐπεξέλευσις ΑΒΕ ὑπεξέλευσις MW    192 εὐφρονοῦσι MW καλῶς φρονοῦσι ΑΒΕ
193 ἀποσκόπει MW ἀπόβλεπε Α ἀπέβλεπε ΒΕ    194 ἐπίβαλέ MW ἐπίβαλλε ΑΒΕ
196 ἡμετέραν MW ἡμετέραν χώραν ΑΒΕ | καταδράμωσιν ΜΑΒΕ καταδραμοῦνται W
197 εἰρήνην MW εἰρήνην ἀσπαζομένων ΑΒΕ    198 καθ᾽ ὅλου MW τῶν ὅλων ΑΒΕ |
ἀσπαζομένων MW om. ΑΒΕ    199 τοῦτο φιλοῦσι Μ τοῦτο ἀγαπῶσι W ταύτην ἀγαπῶσι
ΑΒΕ | ἐγχαλινούμενα ὅροις MW ὅροις ἐμμένοντα ΑΒΕ scr. mg. ὡρ<αῖον> W    201 μήτ᾽
MW μήτε ΑΒΕ | κατάχραινε MW καταμόλυνε ΑΒΕ scr. mg. μὴ μόλυνε W | ἐγκαλέσεις MW
ἐγκαλέσεις σὺ ΑΒΕ    202 ἤγουν…ἀδίκων MW om. ΑΒΕ | ad ἀπάρχεσθαι scr. mg. μὴ
πρῶτος πρὸς πόλεμον ὁρμᾷ W | οὐδὲν…ἀδικουμένους MW ἀδικοῦσι μηδὲν ἀδικομένοις ὑπὸ
σου ΑΒΕ | ἄρα MW om. ΑΒΕ    203 δρῶντες MW ποιοῦντες ΑΒΕ idem scr. mg. W | ad
ὑπηκόων scr. mg. ὑπὸ τῶν ὑπὸ χεῖρα W | ἡμῶν βασιλείας MW trsp. ΑΒΕ | ἀλλ᾽ MW om. ΑΒΕ
204 ἐγκαλέσουσί ΜΑΒΕ ἐγκαλέσουσιν W | εἰ…ἡμῶν MW om. ΑΒΕ    205 ἔθνεσι ΜΒΕ
ἔθνεσιν WA    208 γε…ἀντίπαλον MW οἱ ἐναντίοι μὴ σωφρονοῦσιν ΑΒΕ scr. mg. ηγουν οι
πολεμιοι W    209 κατατρέχοντες γῆν MW γῆν καταβλάπτοντες ΑΒΕ scr. mg. κουρσευοντες
W | ἄρα δικαίως MW εὐλόγου καὶ δικαίας ΑΒΕ | καὶ MW om. ΑΒΕ scr. mg. ἐνθάρσως W

the second to well-deserved hatred with its consequences. The better course is to join fear with justice; after proof of guilt, impose a fitting punishment. Reasonable men regard this not as chastisement but as correction.[14]

29. Above all, when mobilizing for war, make sure that the cause of this war is just and never take up arms against the enemy unjustly unless they, because of their accustomed impiety, have first initiated hostilities and are invading our land.

30. We must always embrace peace for our own subjects, as well as for the barbarians, because of Christ, the emperor and God of all. If the nations also share these sentiments and stay within their own boundaries and promise that they will not take unjust action against us, then you too refrain from taking up arms against them. Do not stain the ground with the blood of your own people or that of the barbarians. For while you are making accusations against the enemy, saying that they who have not been injured by you should not begin to take up arms unjustly, they may bring the same charges against you, claiming that they have not engaged in any hostile act against the subjects of Our Majesty but have been living in peace with them. We must always, if it is possible on our part, be at peace with all men, especially with those nations who desire to live in peace and who do nothing unjust to our subjects. We must always prefer peace above all else and we should be at peace with those nations and refrain from war.

31. But if our adversary should act unwisely, initiate unjust hostilities, and invade our territory, then you do indeed have a just cause, inasmuch as an unjust war has been begun by the enemy. With confidence and enthusiasm take

14. *Strat.*, Preface 65–68.

μία τοῦ κατ᾽ αὐτῶν ἐγχείρει πολέμου, ὡς ἐκείνων τὰς αἰτίας παρασχομένων καὶ
ἀδίκους χεῖρας κατὰ τῶν ὑποτελῶν ἡμῖν ἀραμένων· καὶ θάρρει τότε ὡς καὶ τὸν
τῆς δικαιοσύνης Θεὸν ἕξεις βοηθόν, καὶ τοὺς ὑπὲρ ἀδελφῶν ἀναδεχόμενος
ἀγῶνας πανστρατιᾷ τὴν νίκην ἕξεις. διὰ τοῦτο οὖν προτρεπόμεθα τὴν σὴν
215 ἐνδοξότητα διὰ πάντων ἀποσκοπεῖν δικαίας ποιεῖσθαι τὰς ἀρχὰς τοῦ πολέμου,
καὶ τότε τὰς χεῖρας ὁπλίζειν κατὰ τῶν ἀδικούντων.

32. Διὰ πάντων δὲ καὶ ἐν ἅπασι κρείττονα σεαυτὸν τῶν ὑποχειρίων ἀναδεῖ-
ξαι διαγωνίζου καὶ κατ᾽ ἐξαίρετον εἷς τε τὴν εἰς Θεὸν πίστιν καὶ τὴν εὐσέβειαν
καὶ τὰς λοιπὰς ἀρετάς. τοῖς γὰρ τῶν ἀρχόντων φρονήμασι φιλεῖ πως συνδιατί-
220 θεσθαι τὸ ἀρχόμενον, ὡς ἂν κατὰ τὴν παροιμίαν· μὴ ἔλαφοι λεόντων ἄρχουσιν
ἀλλὰ λέοντες ἐλάφων.

33. Καὶ ταῦτα μέν σοι, ὦ στρατηγέ, ὡς ἐν συνόψει τῆς βασιλικῆς ἡμῶν
διατάξεως παραγγέλματα, ἅπερ τὸ τῆς συντομίας χρειῶδες ἐπὶ πλέον τέως οὐκ
ἐᾷ παρεκτείνεσθαι. ἔξεστι δέ σοι ταῖς τε παρ᾽ ἡμῶν ἐκτεθειμέναις ἰδίᾳ γνώμαις
225 ἐν τῷδε τῷ συντάγματι καὶ προσέτι ταῖς κατὰ πλάτος συνειλεγμέναις ἡμῖν ἐν τῇ
παραλλήλῳ τῶν τακτικῶν μονοβίβλῳ τὴν ἐκεῖθεν τῶν ζητουμένων πλείονα καὶ
ἀρκοῦσαν πορίσασθαι ὠφέλειαν. |

34. Τούτων οὖν ἐχόμενος αὔξειν καὶ προστιθέναι τοῖς ἀγαθοῖς ἔργοις 289ᵛ
προθυμήθητι, ἵνα πολλαπλασιάζων τῇ σπουδαίᾳ γνώμῃ τὰ κελευόμενα, πρῶτα
230 μὲν Θεὸν ἕξῃς ἐπαινέτην τῶν πράξεων, ἔπειτα δὲ καὶ τὸ ἡμέτερον κράτος, γέρα
τῶν πόνων ἐπάξια δι᾽ ἀμφοῖν κομιζόμενος.

---

220–221 Plut. *Mor.*, 187D; cf. Theognis *Eleg.*, 1.949; 2.1278c.

211 ἐγχείρει MW ἀπάρχου ABE | τὰς αἰτίας MWA ταῖς αἰτίαις BE    212 ὑποτελῶν ἡμῖν
MW ὑποχειρίων ἡμῶν ABE | θάρρει MW θάρσει ABE    214 ἀγῶνας MABE ἀγῶνος W |
πανστρατιᾷ MW τὴν στρατιὰν ABE | τὴν¹…ἕξεις MW νικήσεις ABE    218 εἷς ABE om.
MW    219 ad τοῖς scr. mg. <ἤ>γουν οἷος ὁ ἀρχων <ἔ>στι φιλοῦσι και οἱ <ἀρ>χόμενοι
ὁμοιοῦσθαι W | φιλεῖ MW ἀεὶ ABE    219–220 συνδιατίθεσθαι MW συνδιατίθεται ABE
220 ἄρχουσιν MW ἄρχωσιν ABE    222 σοι MWPE τοι A | βασιλικῆς MW om. ABE
223–224 οὐκ ἐᾷ MW οὐ συγχωρεῖ ABE    224 ἐκτεθειμέναις…γνώμαις MW ἰδίᾳ ἐκτεθεῖσαι
γνώμαις ABE    225 συνειλεγμέναις MW συνηθροισμέναις A συνηδροισμέναις BE
227 πορίσασθαι MW συναγαγεῖν ABE    228 ἐχόμενος MWA ἐχόμενα BE    229 ἵνα ABE
ὡς ἂν MW | πολλαπλασιάζων MW ἐπαυξάνων ABE | σπουδαίᾳ MW σπουδαίᾳ σου ABE
230–231 γέρα…ἐπάξια MW τιμὰς ἐπαξίας τῶν πόνων ABE scr. mg. αμοιβας και τιμας W
231 δι᾽ ἀμφοῖν MW ἐξ ἀμφοτέρων ABE

up arms against them. It is they who have provided the cause by unjustly raising their hands against those subject to us. Take courage then. You will have the God of justice on your side. Taking up the struggle on behalf of your brothers, you and your whole force will be victorious. For this reason, therefore, we call upon Your Excellency always to make sure that the causes of war are just. Only then take up arms against men who act unjustly.

32. At all times and in all circumstances you should work hard to show yourself superior to those under your command, especially in your faith in God, your reverent worship, and the other virtues. Subjects somehow tend to be affected by the resolute spirit of their leaders. As the proverb has it: Deer ought not to rule over lions, but lions over deer.[15]

33. And so, O general, we present you in summary form with these instructions of our imperial constitution, about which the practical form of a summary does not, at this time, permit further elaboration. For questions <that may arise> you can obtain for yourself further and sufficient help both from the precepts that we have set out individually in the present compilation and from those that we have collected in greater detail in the corresponding single volume of the Tactics.[16]

34. Holding fast to these precepts, then, be eager to add to your successes, so that, by your seriousness of purpose and by building upon these ordinances of ours, you might first have God praising your deeds and then our own authority and, from both, you will receive the rewards merited by your labors.

---

15. Cf. Plutarch, *Mor.* 187D; Theognis, *Elegies* 1.949; 2.1278c.
16. Undoubtedly refers to the *Sylloge tacticorum.*

## Περὶ τοῦ πῶς χρὴ βουλεύεσθαι

1. Ἐπειδὴ δὲ πρὸ πάσης πράξεως βουλὴν ἡγεῖσθαι χρεόν—διοίκησις γὰρ ἀπροβούλευτος οὐκ ἀσφαλής, κἂν ἐκ τοῦ παραχρῆμά τις αὐχῇ πολλάκις κατορ-
5 θῶσαί τι ὡς ἅμα καὶ βουλευσάμενος καὶ πράξας, ἀλλ᾽ οὐ νόμος τὸ σπάνιον—, διὰ τοῦτο καὶ πρὸ τῶν ἄλλων παρακελευόμεθά σοι πάσης πράξεως ἀναγκαίας καὶ μάλιστα πολεμικῆς βουλεύεσθαί σε πρότερον μετὰ τῶν δοκούντων σοι ἱκανῶν περὶ ταύτην ἀρχόντων, οἷον τουρμάρχων καὶ τῶν ἐφεξῆς, ἐπὰν δὲ τὸ δοκοῦν ἐπὶ βεβαίου λόγου στῇ, τότε τὸ ἔργον δι᾽ ὅπερ ἐβουλεύσω, σπουδῇ καὶ
10 ἐπιμελείᾳ μεταχειρισάμενος εἰς πέρας ἀγαγεῖν, εἴγε μηδὲν ἀπαντήσοι ἐναντίον, ὡς τὰ πολλὰ εἴωθε, προθυμήθητι. τῆς δὲ βουλῆς τὸ εἶδος τί τέ ἐστιν καὶ ὡς κατορθώσεις ταύτην ἀσφαλῶς ἤδη σοι διατάξομαι. |

2. Βουλή ἐστι διάσκεψις περὶ τοῦ πρᾶξαί τι ἢ μὴ πρᾶξαι. καὶ εἰ μὲν μὴ πρᾶξαι,   295 σιγὴ τὸ ἐντεῦθεν. εἰ δὲ πρᾶξαι, πῶς πρᾶξαι ἤγουν τὸν τρόπον τῆς πράξεως, ποῦ
15 πρᾶξαι ἤγουν τὸν τόπον τῆς πράξεως, πότε πρᾶξαι ἤγουν τὸν καιρὸν τῆς πρά- ξεως, τί πρᾶξαι ἤγουν τὸ πρᾶγμα τὸ πραττόμενον, τίς πρᾶξαι ἤγουν τὸ πρόσω- πον τὸ μέλλον τὴν βουλὴν εἰς πέρας πράξεως ἀγαγεῖν, διὰ τί πρᾶξαι ἤγουν τὴν αἰτίαν δι᾽ ἣν ἡ πρᾶξις ὀφείλει γενέσθαι.

---

M W A B E    Va    PG 107:695

---

1 Constitutionem tertiam constitutio quarta in codd. antecedit. edd. praevios secutus transposui et ego. | πολεμικῶν παρασκευῶν ΜΑ om. WBE | γ΄ Va PG δ΄ codd.   3 χρεόν W χρεών Μ χρὴ ΑΒΕ scr. mg. χρήσιμον ἀπαιτοῦν W   3–4 διοίκησις…ἀπροβούλευτος ΜW ἡ γὰρ προβούλευτος (ἀπροβούλευτος Α) διοίκησις ΑΒΕ   4–5 ἐκ…τι ΜW καυχωτό (καυχᾶταί Α) τις συντόμως τι κατορθῶσαι ΑΒΕ   6 πράξεως ἀναγκαίας ΜW trsp. ΑΒΕ   8 περὶ… ἀρχόντων ΜW ἐν ταῖς βουλαῖς εἶναι ΑΒΕ | ἐφεξῆς ἐπὰν ΜW λοιπῶν ἐπειδὰν ΑΒΕ scr. mg. ἤγουν ὅταν ἡ βουλὴ κυρωθῇ W   9 δοκοῦν ΜW κινούμενον ΑΒΕ | ἐπὶ…στῇ ΜW βεβαιωθῇ ὡς συμφέρον ἐστὶ ΑΒΕ | τὸ…ἐβουλεύσω ΜW om. ΑΒΕ   9–10 σπουδῇ…ἐπιμελείᾳ ΜW μετὰ σπουδῆς καὶ ἐπιμελείας ΑΒΕ   10 μεταχειρισάμενος ΜW om. ΑΒΕ | πέρας ΜW τέλος Α πέλαγος ΒΕ scr. mg. εἰς τέλος W | ἀγαγεῖν ΜW ἄγειν αὐτὸ ΑΒΕ   10–11 εἴγε… προθυμήθητι (ὡς W ὥστε Μ) ΜW om. ΑΒΕ scr. mg. ὡς πολλάκις συμβαίνει W   13 πρᾶξαί ΜWΑ πρᾶξαι πῶς ΒΕ | μὴ² ΜWΑ om. ΒΕ   14 ἤγουν…πράξεως ΜWΑ om. ΒΕ   16–17 τὸ³…μέλλον ΜWΑ τὸ μέλλον πρόσωπον ΒΕ   17 πέρας ΜW τέλος ΑΒΕ scr. mg. εἰς τέλος W | πράξεως ΜW om. ΑΒΕ

# PREPARATION FOR WAR, CONSTITUTION III

## About How It Is Necessary to Make Plans

1. Before every action it is necessary to consider a plan. It is not safe to carry out anything that has not been planned ahead of time, even if some individual might claim to have straightened things out several times on the spot, making his plans and putting them into action at the same time.[1] But what happens rarely is not a law. For these reasons, above all else, we strongly recommend to you that before every necessary action, especially a military one, you deliberate about it with those officers whom you consider qualified, such as tourmarchs and those next in rank. When your opinions result in a firm decision, then seriously and carefully take in hand the action that you have been deliberating about and, if you should encounter no obstacle, which is usually the case, exert yourself to bring it to fulfillment. But now I shall set before you the nature of deliberation, what it is and how you can bring it to a successful conclusion.

2. Deliberation is an investigation about whether to do something or not to do it. If the decision is not to do it, there is no further discussion. If to do it, then how to do it or the manner of doing it, where to do it or the place in which it will be done, when to do it or the time of doing it, what to do or the action to be taken, who is to do it or the person who is to bring the planned action to its conclusion, why do it or the reason for which the action ought to be taken.

---

1. Cf. infra, Const. 5, n. 7. For identification of sources for this section and the following, see Haldon, *Commentary.*

3. Ὁ δὲ βουλευόμενος καθ᾽ ἑαυτὸν ἐξ ἀνάγκης πρῶτον τὴν διάνοιαν ἐλευθέ-
20 ραν ἐχέτω τῶν ἄλλων ἁπάντων, μάλιστα δὲ τῶν ἀνηκόντων εἰς τὸ πρᾶγμα περὶ
οὗ βουλεύεται, εἴτε ἔχθρας ἢ φιλίας ἤ τινος ἄλλου πάθους.

4. Εἶτα μηδὲ μόνον τὸ εὔκολον δοκοῦν ἐκλέγου καὶ τοῦτο πρόσεχε, ἀλλὰ
πάντα τὰ δυνατὰ γενέσθαι πρόβλεπε· ἴσως τῶν πραγμάτων αὐτῶν μετὰ τὴν
ἔναρξιν ὑποβαλλομένων καὶ ἄλλων ὑποβαλλόντων καὶ ἄλλο τι συμφορώτερον
25 ὅπερ παρέλιπες.

5. Εἰ δὲ μὴ ἰδίως βουλεύσασθαι ἀλλὰ καὶ ἑτέρους παραλαβεῖν πρὸς τὴν
διάσκεψιν βουληθείης, σεαυτὸν ὁμοίως ἑτοίμασον ἀπαθῆ, ὡς εἴρηται, ὥσπερ εἰ
καὶ καθ᾽ ἑαυτὸν ἐβουλεύσω, τοὺς δὲ συμβούλους παραλάμβανε ἐμπείρους τοῦ
πράγματος, προορατικοὺς καὶ στοχαστικούς, συμπαθεῖς καὶ ὀξεῖς εἰς τὸ νοῆσαι
30 καὶ ἀσφαλεῖς, οὔτε σοί, τῷ βουλευσομένῳ, ὑπείκοντας κατὰ χάριν, οὔτε τῷ
κυρίῳ τοῦ πράγματος οὔτε ἀλλήλοις, λέγοντας δὲ τὸ φαινόμενον, ἀκεραίους τε
τὰς γνώμας καὶ ἀπροσκλινεῖς καὶ μηδεμίαν ἐπιβολὴν ἐξ ἑαυτῶν παρέχοντας,
ἀλλὰ τῇ αὐτῇ ὥρᾳ τὸ συμφορώτερον δοκιμάσαντας.

6. Εἰσὶ γάρ τινες ἑαυτοῖς τι ἐνορῶντες ἴδιον συμφέρον ἢ ἑτέροις οὓς ἀγαπῶ-
35 σιν ἢ κήδονται καὶ ἐπισκοποῦνται τὴν κρίσιν τοῦ πράγματος καὶ πολλάκις οὐκ
ἐνδιδόντες παρατρέπουσι τὴν γνώμην εἰς ὃ βούλονται.

7. Ἐπὶ δὲ τῶν ἀπορρήτων καὶ κρυπτῶν πραγμάτων καὶ πιστοὺς παραλάμβανε καὶ ἐγκρατεῖς καὶ μυστηρίων φύλακας καὶ μὴ ὑπὸ τὴν ἑτέρων ἐξουσίαν

---

ad **19–20** ἐλευθέραν scr. mg. ἤγουν ἐλευθέραν ἐχέτω ἀπὸ ἔχθρας ἢ φιλίας W    **20** τῶν[1]…
ἁπάντων MW πάντων τῶν ἄλλων ABE    **21** τινος ἄλλου MW trsp. ABE    **22** τὸ…δοκοῦν
MW τὸ δοκοῦν εὔκολον ABE | τοῦτο MW τούτῳ A τούτων BE    **23** ἴσως MWAE om. B |
αὐτῶν MWAE τῶν B    **24** ὑποβαλλομένων…ἄλλων ABE om. MW | ἄλλο τι MW ἄλλα τινὰ
ABE | συμφορώτερον Va συμφερώτερον MW συμφέροντα ABE    **25** ὅπερ MW ἅπερ ABE
**26** βουλεύσασθαι MWE βουλεύσασθαι θέλεις AB    **27** βουληθείης σεαυτὸν MW σεαυτὸν
μὲν ABE | ad ἀπαθῆ scr. mg. ἵνα μηδὲν ποιήσῃς δι᾽ ἔχθραν ἢ φιλίαν W | ὥσπερ MWA καθὼς
BE    **30** βουλευσομένῳ MWE βουλευσαμένῳ A βουλευομένῳ B    **31** τε MWBE om. A
**32** ἀπροσκλινεῖς MW μὴ προσπαθοῦντας ABE scr. mg. μὴ ῥέποντας πρός τινας μηδὲ
προσπαθοῦντας W | ἐπιβολὴν…παρέχοντας  (ἐπιβουλὴν A) MWA ἐξ αὐτῶν παρέχοντας
ἐπιβολὴν BE    **33** συμφορώτερον Va συμφερώτερον MWA συμφερότερον BE
**34** ἑαυτοῖς…συμφέρον MW ἢ ἴδιον ἑαυτοῖς συμφέρον προορῶντα ABE    **34–35** ἀγαπῶσιν
MWA ἀγαπῶσι BE    **35** ἢ…πράγματος MW om. ABE    **36** ἐνδιδόντες WABE ἐνδιδοῦντες
M | γνώμην MW βουλὴν ABE    **37** ἀπορρήτων…κρυπτῶν MW κρυπτῶν καὶ μυστικῶν ABE
**38** τὴν MW om. ABE

3. The person responsible for devising the plan must necessarily begin by freeing his mind of everything else, especially whatever may be connected with the action that he is deliberating about, whether of enmity or friendship or any other feeling he might have.

4. You should not limit your choice to what seems easy and concentrate on that, but consider all the possibilities. After getting under way, perhaps the course of action itself will give rise to suggestions. Others too may make suggestions about some other more suitable procedure that you may have neglected.

5. If you do not make plans by yourself but wish to include others in your deliberations, you must still keep yourself indifferent, as was said, as though you were devising the plans by yourself. To assist in planning, employ men who have some experience of the matter, men who can look ahead and form a good estimate, who interact well, and who are quick-witted and trustworthy. They should not give in to you as you go about your deliberations or to the one in charge of the action or to one another simply to curry favor. But they should express their opinions and be objective in their views, not inclined one way or the other, not presenting any proposals of their own but, at the same time, giving their approval to what is more beneficial.

6. There are some who look at what is beneficial only for themselves or for others whom they love or care about, and they make this the deciding factor in considering the proposal. Frequently, unwilling to give in, they alter the plan to what they want.

7. In the case of secret and covert projects, invite men who are trustworthy, possessed of self-control, and who can keep secrets. They should not be under

42    Constitution 3

ὄντας, ἄλλως τε μηδὲ τῆς χρείας ταύτης πλήθους δεομένης διὰ τὸ μυστικώτε-
40 ρον.

8. Καὶ βουλεύου μὲν βραδέως, εἰ μή τις χρεία τὸ τάχος ἀπαιτεῖ. τὰ δὲ βουλευθέντα σοι, εἰ μηδὲν ἐμποδίζει, ταχέως ἐπιτέλει.

9. Καιρὸν δέ, ὡς εἴρηται, καὶ τόπον ὁμοίως ἐκλέγου καὶ κατασκεύαζε τῷ
πράγματι οἰκεῖον, πλὴν μὴ ἐπί σοι μόνῳ | ἀνάφερε τὴν περὶ τούτων κρίσιν, ἀλλ᾽  295ᵛ
45 ἐπὶ πάντας τοὺς κοινωνοῦντας ἅμα σοί. καὶ τί μὲν δέον σε πρᾶξαι σκέπτου καὶ
μετὰ πλειόνων βουλεύου, ἃ δὲ πρᾶξαι βουλεύσῃ σὺν ὀλίγοις. τὴν δὲ καλλίονα
γνώμην ἐπιλεξάμενος κάτεχε παρὰ σεαυτῷ, ἵνα μὴ τοῖς ἐναντίοις καταφανὴς
καὶ εὐεπιβούλευτος γένηται.

10. Τὰ δὲ πράγματα πλείονας χορηγοῦσι τοὺς σκοπούς· ἴσως τις περίστασις
50 ἐκ πάντων τῶν μερῶν φανερὰ γενήσεται τοῖς συγκεκλημένοις ἐν τῇ βουλῇ,
συμβαλλομένη τῇ γνώμῃ τῆς συμβουλῆς.

11. Πάντας δὲ χρὴ ῥέπειν καὶ συντρέχειν εἰς φιλαλήθη καὶ ἀπαθῆ συζήτησιν
καὶ κηδεμονίαν καὶ πρόνοιαν τοῦ συγκαλέσαντος.

12. Τέλος δὲ τῆς βουλῆς ἔστω σοι τὸ εὑρεθῆναι εἰ τί πράξεις καὶ πῶς πράξεις
55 καὶ ποῦ καὶ πότε, εἰ δὲ μὴ πράξεις, καὶ διὰ τί ἄρα οὐ πράξεις.

13. Ἐν οἷς δὲ βουλεύσῃ καὶ ἐν τοῖς ἐμπίπτουσι τῇ βουλῇ σκοποῖς συντρέχειν
δεῖ ἅμα καὶ τὸ δυνατὸν καὶ τὸ συμφέρον· τούτων γὰρ εἶναι μὴ δυναμένων
ἀσθενὴς ἡ βουλὴ καὶ ματαία αὐτόθεν οὖσα κατανοεῖται καὶ ὥσπερ ἐν ὄψει ἡ
αὐτῆς ἀλογία βλέπεται.

60 14. Εἰ γὰρ μὴ συμφέρει σοι ὅπερ ἂν βουλεύσῃ, οὐ μόνον οὐκ ὠφελήσεις
ἀλλὰ μᾶλλον καὶ βλάψεις. εἰ δ᾽ αὖ πάλιν οὐ δύνασαι τὰ βουλευθέντα πρᾶξαι,

---

41–42 *Strat.*, 8.1.5.   43–48 *Strat.*, 8.2.23.

---

39–40 ἄλλως…μυστικώτερον bis scr. MW πλὴν οὐδὲ ἡ χρεία αὕτη πλείστους δέχεται διὰ τὸ μυστικώτεραν εἶναι ABE scr. mg. ἤγουν ὅτι οὐδὲν συμφέρει πολλοὺς εἶναι διὰ τὸ φυλάττεσθαι τὸ μυστήριον W   41 εἰ MW ἐὰν ABE | τὸ…ἀπαιτεῖ κατεπείγῃ συντόμως βουλεύσασθαι ABE   43–44 τῷ πράγματι MWAE τῶν πραγμάτων B   44 μὴ…ἀνάφερε MW om. ABE | κρίσιν MW κρίσιν μὴ ἐπί σοι μόνῳ ἀνάφερε ABE   47 καταφανὴς MW φανερὰ ABE   48 καὶ …γένηται MW γένηται καὶ εὐκόλως ἐπιβουλευθῇ ABE   49 χορηγοῦσι…σκοπούς MW trsp. ABE | ἴσως MW καὶ τάχα ABE   50 φανερὰ MWA φανερὰ συμβαλλομένη τῇ βουλῇ BE | γενήσεται MABE γένηται W | συγκεκλημένοις… βουλῇ MW ἐν τῇ βουλῇ (συμβουλὴ B) συγκαλουμένοις ABE   51 συμβαλλομένη… συμβουλῆς MW om. ABE   52 πάντας MWAE πάντα B | ῥέπειν…συζήτησιν MW καὶ συντρέχειν εἰς ἀπαθῆ καὶ ἀληθῆ (ἀληθῆ καὶ ἀπαθῆ A) συζήτησιν ῥέπειν ABE   53 κηδεμονίαν MW εἰς φροντίδα ABE   54 τὸ εὑρεθῆναι MWA om. BE | εἰ W εἰς M εἰ ὅλως ABE   55 εἰ M ἢ WABE | δὲ MW om. ABE   57 εἶναι MW οἶμαι ABE   61 δ᾽ αὖ MW δὲ ABE

the authority of others, and there should not be many of them, the better to keep matters secret.

8. Take your time in making your plans, unless some necessity requires immediate action.[2] But once you have decided on something, unless there is an obstacle, carry it out quickly.

9. In like manner, as was said, select the time and place and make preparations appropriate to the action.[3] Still, do not refer the decision about these things to yourself alone, but to all who are privy to the action together with yourself. Investigate and deliberate with a large number about what it is necessary for you to do, but make your plans about what you are actually going to do with only a few. Once you have opted for the better proposal, keep it to yourself lest it become manifest and exposed to counteraction by the enemy.

10. The affairs themselves furnish many points of view. Perhaps some circumstance from all the parts will clarify matters for those called together for the consultation, contributing to the resolution of the discussion.

11. It is necessary for everyone to be favorably inclined to take an active part in the truth-loving and unbiased inquiry, as well as the concern and foresight of the one who has called them together.

12. Let the purpose of the deliberation be for you to discover if you will do something, how you will do it, and where and when, but if you will not do it, then for what reason will you not do it.

13. In the matters on which you are deliberating and in the objectives that form part of your deliberation, it is necessary for the possible and the beneficial to concur. A deliberation about things that are not possible has no strength and, for that very reason, is rejected as useless, and its irrationality is seen at a glance.

14. If whatever you may be deliberating about is not beneficial for you, not only will you not be helpful; rather, you will cause harm. Again, if you are not

2. Cf. *Strat.* 8.1.5.
3. Cf. *Strat.* 8.2.23.

ματαία ἡ διάσκεψις εἰς ἀνόνητον τέλος διὰ τὴν ἀδυναμίαν καταντῶσα. μάλιστα δὲ χρὴ φυλάττεσθαι τὰς προχείρως ἐμφερομένας ἐν τοῖς πράγμασι βλάβας. καὶ γὰρ οἱ πολλοὶ ἕτοιμοί εἰσι ταῖς μὲν φροντίσιν εὐφραίνειν ἑαυτούς, τὸ δὲ ἐμπί-
65 πτον τῆς βλάβης μὴ προβλέπειν.

15. Χρησιμωτάτη οὖν ἐστιν ἐνταῦθα ἡ πανταχόθεν περίσκεψις καὶ πάντων τῶν γενέσθαι δυνατῶν ὁ περὶ τὴν σκέψιν ἀναλογισμός. οὐ γὰρ προδώσεις σεαυτὸν προπετείᾳ τυφλῇ οὐδὲ ταῖς ἐπιθυμίαις τῶν πράξεων γλιχόμενος εἰς προδήλους κινδύνους ἐμπέσῃς.

70 16. Πάλιν δὲ τὸ δειλὸν τοῦ θάρσους χωρὶς οὐκ ἔστιν ἀβλαβές· φοβούμενος γὰρ τὰ ἄλογα παραπτώματα καὶ τὰ ἐναντία σοι δοκοῦντα παραλόγως πραγμα-τευόμενος πολλάκις τῶν συμφερόντων σοι πραγμάτων κατημέλησας καὶ τῆς αὐτῶν ἀπέστης πράξεως.

17. Οὕτω μὲν οὖν σοι διὰ βραχέων, ὦ στρατηγέ, περὶ βουλῆς διεξελθόντες
75 ἑξῆς καὶ τῆς τῶν πολεμικῶν ἔργων τε καὶ πράξεως τακτικῆς ἀπαρξώμεθα.

---

62 ἀνόνητον MW ἀνωφελὲς ABE idem scr. mg. W    63 ἐμφερομένας MW ἐμφαινομένας ABE    67 γενέσθαι δυνατῶν MW trsp. ABE    68 σεαυτὸν ABE ἑαυτὸν MW | τυφλῇ MW τυφλῇ καὶ ἀπερισκέπτω ABE | γλιχόμενος MW om. ABE    70 τοῦ W καὶ MABE 70–75 χωρὶς…ἀπαρξώμεθα MABE om. sed scr. mg. ἤγουν φοβούμενος πάλιν ἀμέτρως τὸ μὴ ἀλόγως περιπεσεῖν εἰς κίνδυνον καὶ ποιῶν W 71 ἄλογα Μ παράλογα ABE 71–72 πραγματευόμενος ΜΑ πραγματευόμενα ΒΕ    72 κατημέλησας ΜΑ καταμέλησις ΒΕ 73 ἀπέστης ΜΑΒ ἀπάτης Ε 75 τε Μ om. ABE | ἀπαρξώμεθα Μ ἀπαρξόμεθα Α ἀπαρξόμενα ΒΕ

able to turn your plans into action, deliberating about them serves no purpose and, because of the impossibility, ends up accomplishing nothing. It is particularly necessary to guard against the damages that readily occur in taking action. Many are prepared to find happiness in their thoughts but not to foresee the onset of harm.

15. In these matters, then, the examination of every aspect is absolutely essential, as well as a reconsideration regarding the examination of everything that can possibly occur. For <in that way> you will not give yourself up to blind and headlong haste, nor in your great eagerness for action will you fall into obvious dangers.

16. Again, fear without courage is not without harm. By fearing irrational mistakes and unreasonably busying yourself with matters that you think are contrary to your interests, frequently you will have neglected matters which are really in your best interests and you will have turned away from putting them into action.

17. So then, O general, we have briefly gone through the subject of deliberation, and we will begin next about the tactics of military works and action.

Περὶ διαιρέσεως στρατοῦ καὶ καταστάσεως ἀρχόντων

1. Κελεύομεν τοίνυν τῇ σῇ ἐνδοξότητι κατὰ τὴν ἄνωθεν καὶ ἐξ ἀρχῆς συνήθειαν τοὺς στρατιώτας καὶ τοὺς ἄρχοντας αὐτῶν ἐπιλέξασθαι, οὓς ἂν δοκιμάσῃς
5 ἱκανοὺς εἶναι πρὸς τὴν τοῦ πολέμου χρείαν. ἐκλέξῃ δὲ στρατιώτας ἀπὸ παντὸς
τοῦ ὑπό σε θέματος, μήτε παῖδας μήτε γέροντας, ἀλλὰ ἀνδρείους, εὐρώστους,
εὐψύχους, εὐπόρους, ὥστε αὐτοὺς ἐν τῷ ἐξπεδίτῳ ἤγουν ἐν τῇ συναγωγῇ τοῦ
φοσσάτου εἰς τὴν ἰδίαν στρατείαν ἀσχολουμένους ἔχειν ἐν τοῖς ἰδίοις οἴκοις
ἑτέρους, τοὺς γεωργοῦντας καὶ τὰ πρὸς ἀπαρτισμὸν καὶ ἐξόπλισιν τοῦ στρατιώ-
10 του χορηγεῖν δυναμένους, δηλονότι ἐλευθέρους τοὺς οἴκους ἔχοντας τῶν
ἄλλων ἁπασῶν τοῦ δημοσίου δουλειῶν. οὐ γὰρ βουλόμεθα τὸν ἡμέτερον
συστρατιώτην—οὕτω γὰρ ἐγὼ καλῶ τὸν ἀριστεύειν μέλλοντα ὑπέρ τε τῆς ἡμῶν
βασιλείας καὶ τῆς φιλοχρίστου τῶν Ῥωμαίων πολιτείας ἐν τοῖς κατὰ πόλεμον
ἔργοις—πλὴν μόνον τοῦ δημοσίου τέλους ἑτέρᾳ ὑποκεῖσθαι οἱᾳδήποτε δουλείᾳ.
15 2. Διαιρείσθω τοίνυν ὁ πᾶς ὑπό σε στρατὸς εἰς τάγματα ἤγουν τὰ λεγόμενα
βάνδα διάφορα καὶ ἔτι ὑποδιαιρείσθω εἰς δεκαρχίας, καὶ καταστησάτωσαν εἰς
τὰ λεγόμενα κοντουβέρνια. ταῦτα δὲ γινέσθωσαν καὶ ἀπὸ πέντε πολλάκις καὶ
ἀπὸ δέκα ἀνδρῶν ἤγουν κατὰ δεκαρχίαν ἢ ἐν κοντουβέρνιν ἢ δύο.
3. Καὶ ὁ μὲν στρατὸς ὅλος διαιρείσθω οὕτως εἰς τάγματα καὶ εἰς δεκαρχίας.
20 ἐπιστήτωσαν δὲ αὐτοῖς ἄρχοντες κατὰ βάνδα καὶ δρούγγους καὶ τούρμας καὶ
τὰς ἄλλας δεούσας ἀρχὰς οἱ ἱκανώτατοι ἤγουν ὅσοι καὶ πιστοὶ καὶ εὐγνώμονες
φαίνονται τῇ Ῥωμαϊκῇ ἡμῶν πολιτείᾳ, μαρτυροῦνται δὲ καὶ ἀνδρειότεροι. οὐδὲν
δὲ κωλύει καὶ εὐπορωτάτους αὐτοὺς εἶναι καὶ εὐγενεῖς κατά τε τὸ γένος καὶ τὴν

M W A B E   Va   PG 107:697

19–29 Onas. 2.3–5.

1 πολεμικῶν…διάταξις γ′ (τρίτη A) MWA διάταξις γ′ περὶ πολεμικῶν παρασκευῶν BE (περὶ
om. E) | δ′ Va PG γ′ codd.  6 εὐρώστους MW ἰσχυροὺς ABE  7 ad εὐψύχους scr. mg.
προθύμους τολμηρούς W.  10 δηλονότι ἐλευθέρους bis scr. MW trsp. ABE  11 ἁπασῶν
MW πασῶν ABE  12 οὕτω MW οὕτως ABE  16 καταστησάτωσαν MW καταστήτωσαν
ABE  17 κοντουβέρνια MABE κουτουβέρνια W  18 κοντουβέρνιν M κουτουβέρνιν W
κοντουβέρνιον AE κουντουβέρνιον B  20 καὶ τούρμας MW om. ABE  22 ἡμῶν πολιτείᾳ
MWA πολιτείᾳ ὑμῶν B πολιτείᾳ ἡμῶν E  23 αὐτοὺς εἶναι MWAE trsp. B

# PREPARATION FOR WAR, CONSTITUTION IV

## About the Division of the Army and the Appointment of Officers

1. We order Your Excellency, in keeping with the custom going way back to the beginning, to select the soldiers and their officers whom you judge qualified to meet the requirements of warfare. Select soldiers from the entire theme under your command, neither boys nor old men, but men who are brave, vigorous, courageous, and financially well off. While these men are occupied with their own military service on the campaign or, rather, the assembling of the army, they must have others in their households who do the farm work and who are able to provide the required items for the complete equipping and arming of a soldier. This means that the heads of those households should be free from all other services owed the state. For we do not wish our fellow soldier—thus I call the man who goes forth to strive valiantly in warlike deeds on behalf of Our Majesty and the Christ-loving commonwealth of the Romans—with the sole exception of the public tax,[1] to be subject to any imposition whatsoever.

2. Let the entire army under your command be divided into various tagmata, also called banda. Let it be further divided into dekarchies. Then let the so-called squads be set up. These may often be composed of five men, as well as of ten, so that each dekarchy will have one or two squads.

3. In this manner, let the entire army be divided into tagmata and into dekarchies.[2] Let officers be put in charge of them according to banda, droungoi, and tourmai, and the other appropriate units. They should all be extremely competent, faithful, and loyal to our Roman state; they should also give evidence of bravery that is above average. There is nothing to prevent their being very

---

1. See *OBD*, s.v. "demosion."
2. Onasander 2.3–5.

τῆς ψυχῆς ἀρετήν· τὴν μὲν εὐγένειαν ἔχειν, ἵνα εἰσὶ πρόχειροι ἐν ὀξύτητι καιροῦ
25 περὶ τὰς κελευομένας αὐτοῖς πράξεις, τὴν δὲ εὐπορίαν, ἵνα δύνωνται τοῖς στρα| 290
τιώταις ἐκ περιουσίας πολλάκις, εἰ δεήσοι, χορηγεῖν. καὶ γὰρ καὶ ὀλίγη τάχα
χορηγία ἀπὸ τῶν ἡγουμένων ἀρχόντων πρὸς τοὺς ὑποταττομένους γινομένη
εὐνούστατα καὶ φίλια πρὸς αὐτοὺς παρασκευάζει τὰ πλήθη καὶ συναγωνίζεσθαι
—καὶ μέχρι καὶ τέλους—ἐν τοῖς, ὡς εἰκός, ἐμπίπτουσι κινδύνοις.
30   4. Οἱ δὲ μείζονες αὐτῶν καὶ ἐντιμότατοι καὶ συνεδρεύσουσι τῷ στρατηγῷ, οἳ
δὲ καὶ παρέσονται καὶ μεθέξουσι σὺν αὐτῷ πάσης βουλῆς καὶ κοινωνήσουσί που
καὶ γνώμης, εἰ τύχοι, καὶ ἀπορρήτου καὶ κρυπτῆς. καὶ γάρ τις τάχα καὶ ἄριστος
ὢν ἐννοεῖ μέν τι χρήσιμον, βεβαίως δὲ τὰ ἑαυτοῦ μόνος οὐκ οἰκειοῦται. γνώμη
γὰρ ἢ βουλὴ ἑκάστη, ἡ μὲν ἀβοήθητος οὖσα περὶ τὴν ἰδίαν εὕρεσιν μόνην
35 ἀποβλέπει, ἡ δὲ ὑπὸ καὶ ἄλλων πολλῶν ἐπιμαρτυρηθεῖσα πιστοῦται καὶ ἀναφαίνεται μηδὲν ἔχουσα σφαλερόν.
   5. Πρέπον οὖν ἐστιν εἶναι τὸν στρατηγόν—ἵνα καὶ πάλιν σοι περὶ τῶν αὐτῶν
παραινέσωμεν—μήτε οὕτως ἄστατον τὴν διάνοιαν ἵνα αὐτὸς ἑαυτῷ παντελῶς
ἀπιστῇ, μήτε οὕτως αὐθάδη καὶ μονώτατον ὡς μὴ βούλεσθαι παρ' ἑτέρων κάλ-
40 λιόν τι νοηθὲν ἀναμαθεῖν. ἀνάγκη γὰρ αὐτὸν ἢ πᾶσι τοῖς ἄλλοις κατὰ πάντα
προσέχοντα καὶ κατὰ μηδὲν ἑαυτῷ πιστεύοντα πολλάκις πολλὰ καὶ ἀσύμφορα
πράττειν, ἢ μηδὲν ὀλίγων ἀκούοντα πάντα δὲ ἑαυτῷ καταπιστεύοντα, πολλὰ

---

30–36 Onas. 3.1–3.

24 εἰσὶ MWA ὦσι BE   25 δύνωνται MABE δύνανται W | τοῖς WABE om. M   26 δεήσοι
MW δεήσει ABE | καὶ² MW om. ABE   26–27 τάχα χορηγία MW δόσις ABE
27 ἡγουμένων MW om. ABE | ὑποταττομένους MW ὑποχειρίους ABE   28 εὐνούστατα...
πλήθη MW εὔνοιαν καὶ ἀγάπην τοῦ πλήθους ἀπεργάζεται ABE scr. mg. ἀγαπητικὰ
εὐγνώμονα W   29 καὶ¹ MABE om. W | καὶ τέλους MW θανάτου ABE | ὡς...κινδύνοις MW
κινδύνοις παρασκευάζει ABE   30 συνεδρεύσουσι MW συγκάθεδροι ἔσονται ABE
31 παρέσονται...σὺν MW συγκοινωνήσουσιν ABE | αὐτῷ MWAB αὐτῶν E | ad
κοινωνήσουσί scr. mg. <ἢ>γουν ἵνα ὦσι καὶ αὐτοὶ σύμβουλοι καὶ εἰς τὰς κρυφιωτέρας βουλὰς
W   32 καὶ¹...τύχοι MW om. ABE | καὶ²...κρυπτῆς MW μυστικῆς τε καὶ ἀποκρύφου ABE |
καὶ⁴...καὶ⁵ MW κἂν ABE   33 ὢν...χρήσιμον MW ὢν ὁ στρατηγὸς ἐννοεῖ μέν τι καὶ
βουλεύεται χρήσιμον ABE | βεβαίως...οἰκειοῦται MW τὴν δὲ ἰδίαν βουλὴν βεβαιῶσαι οὐ
δύναται ABE   34 ἢ...ἑκάστη MW om. ABE   34–35 περὶ...ἀποβλέπει MW σφάλλεται
περὶ τὴν ἰδίαν εὕρεσιν ABE   35 ὑπὸ καὶ MW καὶ ὑπὸ AE καὶ ἀπὸ B   37–38 εἶναι...παρ-
αινέσωμεν MW om. ABE   38 διάνοιαν MW διάνοιαν εἶναι τὸν στρατηγὸν ABE   39 καὶ
μονώτατον Va καὶ μονώτατος MW om. ABE   41 προσέχοντα MWA προσέχοντι BE | μηδὲν
MWA μηδένα BE | πιστεύοντα MWA πιστεύοντι BE | πολλάκις MWBE om. A | πολλὰ
MWA om. BE   42 πράττειν MWA πράττεσθαι BE | μηδὲν M μηδὲ WE μὴ δὲ AB | ἑαυτῷ
MWA αὐτῷ BE | καταπιστεύοντα MWA καταπιστεύοντι BE

wealthy or noble as far as their birth and virtue of soul is concerned. If they should be of noble birth, at crucial moments they will be quick to put into action what they have been ordered to do; if they should be wealthy, then, when called for, from their abundance they will often be able to devote some funds to the soldiers. Even a small expenditure made by a commanding officer for the benefit of his troops renders the rank and file much better disposed and friendly toward him and ready to fight along with him, even to the end, in the dangers likely to confront them.

4. The higher-ranking and most respected officers should sit in council with the general; they should be at hand and participate with him in every deliberation and somehow share in his decision, even if it might be kept hidden and secret.[3] For an individual, the very best perhaps, may think of something beneficial, but one man alone should certainly not limit himself to his own opinions. Every decision or deliberation that is unsupported looks only at its author's ingenuity, but the decision that has the additional testimony of many others is reliable and may be presented without any uncertainty.

5. It is, therefore, fitting for the general to be—we are still giving you advice about the same matters—neither so indecisive in mind that he has absolutely no confidence in himself nor so opinionated and self-centered that he is unwilling to learn from others anything that has been better thought out. The man who always pays attention to everyone else and never relies on himself will surely make many and frequent errors in practice, whereas the one who never listens,

3. Onasander 3.1–3.

πολλάκις καὶ μεγάλα διαμαρτάνειν. τούτων δὲ οὕτως ἐχόντων πρότερον μὲν ἐξονομάσομέν σοι ἁπλῶς τοὺς καθισταμένους ἄρχοντας, εἶθ᾽ οὕτως καὶ τὰ
45  γνωρίσματα αὐτῶν ὡς ἐν συντόμῳ εἰπεῖν διορισόμεθα.

6. Πρώτη κεφαλὴ ὁ στρατηγός, καὶ μετ᾽ αὐτὸν οἱ μεράρχαι καὶ οἱ τουρμάρχαι, εἶτα δρουγγάριοι, εἶτα οἱ κόμητες, ἤγουν οἱ τῶν λεγομένων βάνδων ἄρχοντες, εἶτα οἱ κένταρχοι, ἐφεξῆς οἱ δέκαρχοι, ἤγουν οἱ πρῶτοι τῶν λεγομένων ἀκιῶν, εἶτα οἱ πεντάρχαι καὶ ἐφεξῆς οἱ τετράρχαι, οἵτινες καὶ διὰ τὸ ἐσχάτους
50  τοῦ στίχου τοῦ κατὰ τὸ βάθος ἤτοι τὸ πάχος τῆς παρατάξεως τάσσεσθαι αὐτοὺς καὶ οὐραγοὶ ἐκαλοῦντο. ὁ γὰρ ἔσχατος τοῦ ὅλου στίχου ἤγουν τῆς ἀκίας ὡς ἐπὶ τῆς οὐρᾶς αὐτῆς οὕτως ἵσταται.

7. Καὶ αὗται μὲν αἱ ὀνομασίαι τῶν ἀρχόντων. εἰσὶ δὲ καὶ ἕτεροι καθ᾽ ἕκαστον τάγμα ἤτοι βάνδον διωρισμένοι, οἷον βανδοφόροι, σαλπιγκταὶ ἤτοι βουκινά-
55  τορες, θεραπευταὶ ἢ ἰατροὶ οἱ καὶ δεποτάτοι, καὶ μανδάτωρες καὶ παρακλήτορες, οἱ διὰ λόγων διεγείροντες τὸν στρατὸν πρὸς τοὺς ἀγῶνας, οὓς οἱ πρὸ ἡμῶν, νεώτεροι δὲ τῶν ἄλλων, τακτικοὶ Ῥωμαϊστὶ καντάτωρες | ἐκάλουν· καὶ ἕτεροί   290ᵛ
τινες πρὸς τὰς ἀνακυπτούσας χρείας ἀφωρισμένοι, οἷον σκρίβωνες καὶ οἱ λοιποί. πάντα γὰρ τῇ νῦν πολιτείᾳ γνωρίζεται τὰ ὀνόματα τῶν παλαιῶν σιγηθέν-
60  των, ἅπερ κατὰ χώραν ὑπομνήσομεν.

8. Στρατηγὸς τοίνυν προσαγορεύεται ὁ τοῦ παντὸς στρατοῦ κορυφαῖός τε καὶ ἡγεμών, ὑποστράτηγος δὲ ὁ τὴν δευτέραν τούτῳ τάξιν ἐκπληρῶν. οἶμαι δὲ ὡς οἱ παλαιότεροι ἡμῶν ὑποστρατήγους μὲν ἐκάλουν τοὺς στρατηγοὺς διὰ τὸ στρατηγὸν ἁπάντων κυρίως εἶναι τὸν βασιλέα, ἐκ προσώπου δὲ αὐτοῦ εἶναι
65  καθ᾽ ἕκαστον θέμα τὸν στρατηγόν, καὶ διὰ τὴν τοιαύτην αἰτίαν ὁ στρατηγὸς ὑποστράτηγος ἐκαλεῖτο, στρατηγὸς δὲ κυρίως ἐλέγετο ὁ ἐκ προσώπου τοῦ βασιλέως πάντων κεφαλὴ ἀποστελλόμενος, ἔχων ὑποστρατήγους τοὺς τῶν θεμάτων στρατηγούς, ὅπερ ἐστὶν ἄριστον.

9. Νῦν δὲ ὑποστράτηγος οὐ γνωρίζεται, εἰ μή τι ὁ καλούμενος μεράρχης.

70  10. Καὶ τουρμάρχης ἐστὶν ὅ ποτε καλούμενος μεράρχης ἤτοι ὁ τοῦ μέρους τὴν ἀρχὴν ἐμπεπιστευμένος.

---

61–122 *Strat.*, 1.3–5.

---

46–47 καὶ²…τουρμάρχαι MW om. ABE    49 ad ἀκιῶν scr. mg. τῶν ὀρδίνων W | τὸ MWAE τοῦ B    54 διωρισμένοι MWAE διωρισμένον B | σαλπιγκταὶ MWAB σαλπηγηταὶ E | ἤτοι² MWAE ἤγουν A    55 ἢ MWA om. BE | δεποτάτοι MW διποτάται AE δαιποτάτοι B    56–57 οὓς…ἐκάλουν MW om. ABE    60 ἅπερ…ὑπομνήσομεν MW om. ABE    62 τούτῳ τάξιν MWAE trsp. B | οἶμαι MW ὑπολαμβάνω ABE    64–65 εἶναι²…ἕκαστον MWAE trsp. B    69 τι MW om. ABE | μεράρχης MWAB μενάρχης E    70 καὶ…μεράρχης MW om. ABE    71 τὴν ἀρχὴν MWA τῆς ἀρχῆς BE

even to a few others, but trusts only himself is likewise bound to make many costly mistakes. This is how these matters stand. Now, we will first simply give you the titles of the officers to be appointed; then we will define, in summary fashion, their characteristics.

6. At the very top is the general and, after him, the merarchs and the tourmarchs, then the droungarioi, then the counts, that is, the officers of the so-called banda, then the kentarchs and, in order, the dekarchs, that is, the first of the so-called files, then the pentarchs and, after them, the tetrarchs who, because they are lined up last in the row, according to the depth or the thickness of the battle line, are also called ouragoi, for the last man of the whole row or file is positioned as though at its tail.

7. These, then, are the titles of the officers, but there are also other men assigned to each tagma or bandon. Such are the standard-bearers, the trumpeters or buglers, the medical attendants or doctors who are also called deputies, the heralds and the exhorters whose task it is to exhort and arouse the army for combat, whom those before us, the more recent tactical writers, called by the Latin term cantatores.[4] Other men are assigned to various needs as they occur. Such are the skribones and the rest.[5] These names, about which the ancient authors are silent, are those recognized by the modern state and which we will discuss in due order.

8. First, the head and leader of the whole army is called the general.[6] The man who ranks second after him is the lieutenant general. I am aware that our predecessors used the term lieutenant general for general since the general who commands everyone is specifically the emperor, and the general for each theme is his delegate. For this reason the general was called lieutenant general. General then became the title for that man who was exclusively designated as the delegate of the emperor, the head of all the troops, and the generals of the themes became his lieutenant generals, all of which is excellent.

9. But, at present, the term lieutenant general is not acknowledged except for the one called merarch.

10. The tourmarch is the officer formerly referred to as merarch, that is, the one entrusted with the command of a meros.

4. See *Strat.* 2.19.
5. Also called skribantes, cf. infra, n. 7.
6. *Strat.* 1.3–5.

11. Δρουγγάριος δὲ λέγεται ὁ μιᾶς μοίρας ἄρχων, ἥτις ὑπὸ τὸ μέρος τοῦ τουρμάρχου τάττεται. μέρος γάρ ἐστιν ἡ τοῦρμα, τὸ ἐκ τριῶν μοιρῶν ἤγουν δρούγγων συγκείμενον ἄθροισμα, μοῖρα δέ ἐστιν ἤτοι δροῦγγος τὸ ἐκ ταγμά-
75 των ἤτοι ἀριθμῶν ἢ βάνδων τῶν λεγομένων κομήτων συγκείμενον πλῆθος.

12. Κόμης δέ ἐστιν ὁ τοῦ ἑνὸς τάγματος ἤτοι βάνδου ἀφηγούμενος.

13. Κένταρχος δέ ἐστιν ὁ ἑκατὸν ἀνδρῶν ἄρχων ἤτοι ἑκατοντάρχης, ὅστις καὶ ὑπὸ τὸν κόμητα τέτακται.

14. Δεκάρχης δέ ἐστιν ὁ τῶν δέκα πρῶτος, ὥσπερ καὶ πεντάρχης ὁ τῶν
80 πέντε, ὅστις καὶ μέσος ἵσταται τῆς ἀκίας.

15. Τετράρχης δέ ἐστιν ὁ καὶ φύλαξ, ὁ λεγόμενος οὐραγὸς καὶ τελευταῖος ἱστάμενος τῆς ἀκίας. ὁ γὰρ πυκνότερος τῶν ἀρχόντων διαμερισμὸς καὶ πλείονας δεικνύει τοὺς γενναίους καὶ ἀνδρείους στρατιώτας, καὶ εὐχερῶς ὑπακούειν καὶ ἐκτελεῖν ποιεῖ τὰ κελευόμενα.

85 16. Καὶ βανδοφόρος μέν ἐστιν ὁ τὸ σημεῖον τοῦ βάνδου βαστάζων.

17. Δηποτάτοι δὲ προσηγορεύοντο πάλαι οἱ νῦν λεγόμενοι σκριβῶνες, οἵτινες παρακολουθοῦντες τῇ παρατάξει τοὺς ἐν τῇ μάχῃ τραυματίας γενομένους ἀναλαμβάνονται ὡς ἰατροὶ καὶ περιποιοῦνται.

18. Μανδάτωρες δέ εἰσιν οἱ τὰ μανδάτα ἀπὸ τῶν ἀρχόντων πρὸς τοὺς
90 στρατιώτας ὀξέως διακομίζοντες. |

19. Λοχαγὸς δὲ λέγεται ὁ πρῶτος τοῦ στίχου ἤγουν τοῦ ὀρδίνου κατὰ τὸ 291 βάθος· ὁ αὐτὸς δὲ λέγεται καὶ πρῖμος καὶ πρωτοστάτης.

20. Σεκοῦνδος δὲ λέγεται ὁ δεύτερος τῆς ἀκίας, ὁ λεγόμενος ἐπιστάτης.

21. Οὐραγὸς δὲ λέγεται ὁ ὀπίσω τοῦ ὅλου στίχου ἤγουν τῆς οὐρᾶς τοῦ
95 ὀρδίνου ἱστάμενος.

22. Κούρσωρες δὲ λέγονται ἤγουν πρόμαχοι οἱ προτρέχοντες τῆς παρατάξεως ἐν τῇ συμβολῇ τοῦ πολέμου καὶ τοῖς φεύγουσιν ἐχθροῖς ὀξέως ἐπιτιθέμενοι οὓς καλοῦσι προκλάστας.

23. Διφένσωρες δὲ οἱ τούτους μὲν ἐπακολουθοῦντες, μὴ ἐκτρέχοντες δὲ καὶ
100 λύοντες τὴν τάξιν, ἀλλὰ συντεταγμένως περιπατοῦντες πρὸς ἐκδίκησιν τῶν

---

72 τὸ μέρος MWA τοῦ μέρους BE   73 τάττεται MW τάσσεται ABE   75 ἀριθμῶν... βάνδων Va ἀνδρῶν codd.   77 ἑκατοντάρχης MWA ἑκατόνταρχος BE   79 δεκάρχης MWA δέκαρχος BE | καὶ MWA om. BE | πεντάρχης MWAB πένταρχος E   80 ἀκίας MWAB ἀκακίας E   86 δηποτάτοι MW δαιποτάτοι B διποτάτοι AE | πάλαι MW τὸ παλαιὸν ABE   87 τραυματίας MW τραυματιζομένους ABE   87–88 γενομένους WBE γινομένους M om. A   91 δὲ AB om. MWE   92 πρωτοστάτης ABE ἐπιστάτης MW   93 ad τῆς ἀκίας scr. mg. τοῦ ὀρδίνου W   94 δὲ BE om. MWA | λέγεται MWA om. BE   100 πρὸς ἐκδίκησιν MABE προσεδίκησιν W

11. Droungarios is the term for the commander of one moira, that takes its position below the meros of the tourmarch. Meros is the tourma that is composed of a grouping of three moirai or droungoi. A moira or droungos is the total unit made up of tagmata, arithmoi, or banda, <whose commanders> are called counts.

12. The count is commander of one tagma or bandon.

13. Kentarch is the officer over a hundred men, also called hekatontarch, and is ranked just below the count.

14. Dekarch is the first over ten men, just as the pentarch is over five and takes his position in the middle of the file.

15. Tetrarch, also known as the guard, is called ouragos and stands last in the file. This rather detailed division of officers results in a larger number of noble and brave soldiers and readily makes for obedience and the implementation of commands.

16. The standard-bearer is the one who carries the standard of the bandon.

17. The term deputy was previously used for those now called skribones.[7] They follow behind the battle line and, like doctors, recover and look after those wounded in battle.

18. Heralds are the men who quickly convey the commands of the officers to the troops.

19. Group leader is the term for the first man in the row or the line according to its depth; he is also referred to as primos and protostates.

20. Sekoundos is the term for the second man of the file, also called epistates.

21. Ouragos is the term for the man behind the whole row, whose position is at the end of the line.

22. Assault troops, also called promachoi, are those who move out ahead of the line when battle is joined and swiftly bear down upon the retreating enemy; they are also called proklastai.

23. Defenders are those who follow after them, not charging out or breaking

---

7. Medical corpsmen, cf. *Strat.* 2.9. Deputy (Lat. deputatus). Greek transliteration varies: δεποτάτος , δηπ-, διπ-, δαιπ-. Skribon, skribas (kribas), is from Lat. scriba, a scribe. Cf. *Sylloge tacticorum*, 35.1; *LBG, s.v.* (forthcoming). The *Suda* (Σ 696) claims that the Latins use the term for "foremost among the bodyguards."

κουρσώρων, εἴπερ αὐτούς, ὡς εἰκός, τραπῆναι συμβαίη, οὕσπερ δικαίως ἄν τις καλέσοι ἐκδίκους.

24. Μίνσωρες δὲ λέγονται οἱ τὰ ἄπλικτα ἤτοι τὰ φοσσάτα μετροῦντες καὶ καθιστῶντες οὓς μινσοράτωρας νῦν καλοῦσιν.

105    25. Ἀντικένσωρας δὲ ἄλλους τινὰς ἔλεγον οἱ παλαιοὶ Ῥωμαῖοι οὕς, ὡς οἶμαι, νῦν τοῖς μινσοράτωρσι συντάσσοντες ἰδίως οὐκ ὀνομάζουσιν. οὗτοι δέ εἰσιν οἱ προλαμβάνοντες ἐν ταῖς ὁδοιπορίαις καὶ τὰς ἐπιτηδείας ὁδοὺς καὶ τοὺς τόπους ἀνερευνῶντες ἐν οἷς τὰ ἄπλικτα γίνεσθαι ὀφείλουσι καὶ ταύτας, ὁποῖαί εἰσι, κατανοοῦντες.

110    26. Σκουλκάτωρες δὲ οἱ κατάσκοποι λέγονται οἵτινες μανθάνοντες τὰ τῶν ἐχθρῶν ἀπαγγέλλουσιν.

27. Πλαγιοφύλακες δέ εἰσιν οἱ πρὸς φυλακὴν τῶν πλαγίων τῆς πρώτης τάξεως ταττόμενοι.

28. Ὑπερκερασταὶ δὲ οἱ πρὸς τὸ περιλαβεῖν τὸ τῶν πολεμίων κέρας ταττό-
115    μενοι.

29. Ἔνεδροι δὲ οἱ πρὸς ἐγκρύμματα κατὰ τῆς παρατάξεως τῶν ἐχθρῶν ἑτοιμαζόμενοι.

30. Νωτοφύλακες δὲ οἱ ὀπίσω τῆς παρατάξεως πάσης τασσόμενοι περιπατεῖν.

120    31. Καὶ τοῦλδόν ἐστιν ἡ ἀποσκευὴ καὶ χρεία πᾶσα τῶν στρατιωτῶν, τοῦτ᾽ ἔστιν παῖδές τε καὶ ὑποζύγια καὶ τὰ λοιπὰ ζῷα, καὶ εἴ τι ἕτερον πρᾶγμα πρὸς ὑπηρεσίαν τοῦ φοσσάτου ἐπισύρεται.

32. Ἔστι δὲ καὶ ἡ τοῦ στρατηγοῦ προέλευσις εἴς τινας ἄρχοντας διαιρουμένη, οἷον τόν τε κόμητα τῆς κόρτης αὐτοῦ καὶ τὸν τοῦ θέματος δομέστικον καί,
125    ἁπλῶς εἰπεῖν, εἰς τοὺς λοιποὺς ἐξ ἔθους τῆς προελεύσεως αὐτοῦ ὑπηρέτας, οὓς περιττὸν ἡγούμεθα καταλέγειν.

---

101 συμβαίη W συμβαίνη Μ συμβῇ ΑΒΕ    102 καλέσοι MW καλέσει ΑΒΕ    103 οἱ... ἄπλικτα MW om. ΑΒΕ    104 μινσοράτωρας Α μινσοράτορας MW μινσαράτωρας ΒΕ    105 παλαιοὶ MWA πάλαι ΒΕ | ὡς MWA om. ΒΕ | οἶμαι MW ὑπολαμβάνω ΑΒΕ    108 ὀφείλουσι MABE ὀφείλουσιν W    111 ἀπαγγέλλουσιν WA ἀπαγγέλλουσι Μ ἀπαγγέλουσι ΒΕ    113 ταττόμενοι MW τασσόμενοι ΑΒΕ    114 περιλαβεῖν MWAE λαβεῖν Β scr. mg. κυκλῶσαι W    114–115 ταττόμενοι W τασσόμενοι ΑΒΕ    116 πρὸς MW πρὸς τὰ ΑΒΕ    120–121 τοῦτ᾽ ἔστιν Μ τουτέστιν WAE τουτέστι Β    121 ad παῖδές scr. mg. δοῦλοι W | ad ὑποζύγια scr. mg. ἄλογα σαγμάρια W    122 ὑπηρεσίαν WA ὑπερεσίαν MBE    125 εἰς MWAB εἰ Ε | ὑπηρέτας MABE ὑπηρέτους W    126 περιττὸν MW περισσὸν ΑΒΕ | καταλέγειν MW καταριθμεῖν ΑΒΕ

ranks, but marching in good order to provide support for the assault troops in case they should happen to fall back; one might justly call them avengers.

24. Surveyors is the term for those who measure and set up the camps or the encampments and whom they now call minsoratores.

25. The ancient Romans called certain other men antikensores, who, as I am aware, are now lined up with the minsoratores and are not given a special name. When the army is on the march, they go ahead to assess the condition of the roads and to search for ones that are suitable and for places in which to pitch camp.

26. Spies are called skoulkatores; they learn what is going on with the enemy and inform us.

27. Flank guards are the troops assigned to guard the flanks of the first line.

28. Outflankers are the troops assigned to envelop the enemy's wings.

29. Ambushers are the troops prepared to set up ambushes against the battle line of the enemy.

30. Rear guard designates the troops assigned to march behind the entire battle line.

31. The baggage train consists of the supplies and everything else needed for the soldiers, that is, servants, pack animals, and the other beasts, as well as anything else that is brought along for the service of the army.

32. The entourage of the general is composed of certain officers, such as the count of his tent, the domestic of the theme and, to put it succinctly, the rest of the assistants ordinarily in his entourage, but we believe it is superfluous to list them.

33. Ὁ γὰρ πρωτονοτάριος τοῦ θέματος καὶ ὁ χαρτουλάριος, προσέτι δὲ καὶ ὁ
πραίτωρ ἤγουν ὁ τοῦ θέματος δικαστής—ὁ μὲν τῆς πολιτικῆς ἐστι διοικήσεως
ἄρχων, ὁ δὲ πρὸς τὴν τοῦ στρατοῦ καταγραφήν | τε καὶ ἀναζήτησιν, ὁ δὲ τὰς    291ᵛ
130 δίκας τῶν δικαζομένων διαλύει—οὓς εἰ καὶ τῷ στρατηγῷ ἔν τισιν ὑποτάττεσθαι
χρή, ἀλλ᾽ οὖν τοὺς λόγους τῶν ἰδικῶν αὐτῶν διοικήσεων πρὸς τὴν βασιλείαν
ἡμῶν ἀφορᾶν, ὥστε δι᾽ αὐτῶν μανθάνειν τάς τε τῶν πολιτικῶν καὶ τῶν στρατιωτικῶν πραγμάτων καταστάσεις καὶ διοικήσεις ἀσφαλέστερον ἡγούμεθα.

34. Τὸν μὲν οὖν στρατὸν ὅλον, ὦ στρατηγέ, διαιρήσεις εἰς διάφορα τάγματα
135 καὶ ἐπιστήσεις αὐτοῖς, ὡς εἴρηται, ἄρχοντας φρονίμους καὶ ἀνδρείους καὶ
προσφόρους αὐτοῖς.

35. Ἀπὸ δὲ τοῦ τάγματος ἤτοι βάνδου τοὺς ἑκατοντάρχας ἐπιλέγου φρονίμους καὶ γενναίους εἰς ἀνδρείαν, εἶτα τοὺς δεκάρχας καὶ αὐτοὺς γενναίους καὶ
αὐτόχειρας, εἰ δυνατὸν δὲ καὶ τοξεύειν εἰδότας· καὶ μετὰ τοὺς δεκάρχας καὶ
140 πεντάρχας καὶ τετράρχας ὁμοίως· καὶ τότε τοὺς φύλακας τῶν ἀκιῶν ἤγουν τῶν
κατὰ τὸ πάχος τῆς παρατάξεως ὀρδίνων, οἳ καὶ δεκαρχίαι καλοῦνται, δύο ἀπὸ
ἑκάστης ἀκίας, ὡς γίνεσθαι τοὺς ἐπιλέκτους ἑκάστης ἀκίας ἄνδρας πέντε· καὶ
τοὺς ἀπομένοντας ὀρδινεῦσαι εἰς τὰς ἀκίας, παλαιούς τε καὶ νέους, ἀναμίκτους,
ὅσοι ἄν εἰσι κατὰ τὸ μέτρον τοῦ πλήθους τοῦ στρατοῦ.

145 36. Στήσας δὲ καὶ τούτους τοὺς ἀπομένοντας τότε τοὺς ἐπιλέκτους ἐπιβαλεῖς κατὰ διαφορὰν πρὸς τὴν ἑκάστου ποιότητα ἤγουν φύσιν καὶ δύναμιν, τοὺς
μὲν κρείττονας ἔμπροσθεν, τοὺς δὲ λοιποὺς ἀναλόγως ὄπισθέν τε καὶ διὰ μέσου.

37. Δύο δὲ μανδάτωρας ἀγρύπνους καὶ φρονίμους ἐπιλεγῆναι δέον καὶ δύο
βανδοφόρους ἀπὸ ἑκάστου τάγματος, τὴν δὲ τοιαύτην ἐπιλογὴν καὶ ὀρδινείαν
150 ποιεῖσθαι ἐν τοῖς κοντουβερνίοις, τοῦτ᾽ ἔστιν ἐν ταῖς ἀκίαις.

---

127–136 *Strat.*, 1.4.    137–154 *Strat.*, 1.5.

---

128 πραίτωρ ἤγουν MWA πραίτω ρηγοῦν BE | ad δικαστής scr. mg. κρίτης W | μὲν MWAE
μέν ἐστι B    129 ἄρχων MWA ὁ ἄρχων BE | ὁ¹...ἀναζήτησιν MWAE om. B | στρατοῦ
MWAB στρατηγοῦ E    130 ὑποτάττεσθαι MW ὑποτάσσεσθαι ABE    131 ad ἰδικῶν scr. mg.
ὦν ἕκαστος διοικεῖ W    132–133 καὶ...στρατιωτικῶν MWA om. BE    136 προσφόρους
MW ἁρμόζοντας ABE    137 ἀπὸ...τάγματος MWA om. BE | βάνδου MWA om. BE |
ἑκατοντάρχας MWA ἐκτάρχος BE    138 καὶ¹ MWA om. BE | εἰς ἀνδρείαν MWA om. BE |
δεκάρχας ABE δεκάρχους MW    139 αὐτόχειρας MW ἰσχυροὺς ABE scr. mg. ευτολμους W |
δεκάρχας ABE δεκάρχους MW    140 καὶ² M τοὺς WABE    144 εἰσι MBE εἰσιν WA
145–146 ἐπιβαλεῖς Du ἐπιβάλει MW ἐπίβαλον BE om. A    147 ἀναλόγως MWA ἀλόγως
BE    148 ad δέον scr. mg. ἁρμόζον W    150 κοντουβερνίοις MWAE κουντουβερνίοις B

33. Then there is the protonotary of the theme and the chartoularios and, in addition, the praetor, who is the chief legal officer of the theme.[8] The first is an official in the civil administration; the second sees to the registration and inspection of the army; the third adjudicates the penalties of those who are accused. Even if they must necessarily be subject to the general in some things, nonetheless they are obliged to give an account of their own administration to Our Majesty. We believe that through them we will more surely learn about the condition and administration of civil and military affairs.

34. You will divide the entire army, O general, into various units and over them, as was said, you will appoint intelligent, brave, and competent officers.

35. From the tagma or bandon select hekatontarchs, men of sound judgment, courageous, and brave, then the dekarchs, courageous and good at hand-to-hand fighting and, if possible, good shots with the bow.[9] After the dekarchs, in like manner, the pentarchs and tetrarchs. Then the guards for the files or of the rows, that are called dekarchies, according to the thickness of the battle line. There should be two of these for each file, resulting in five specially rated men in each file. The rest of them, veterans and recruits together, that is, all the men, should be assigned places in the files, depending on the size of the assembled army.

36. After placing these men in their positions, assign the specially rated troops, keeping in mind the different qualities of each man, that is, his nature and ability. The better men should be in front and then the rest in relative order behind and in the middle.

37. Two alert and intelligent men must be selected as heralds and two as standard-bearers from each tagma. Selection and assignment of this sort ought to be made in the squads, that is, in the files.

*8. Sections 33–34 derive from *Strat.* 1.4.
*9. Sections 35–38 derive from *Strat.* 1.5.

38. Καὶ ἔνθα, ὡς εἰκός, παῖδες οὐκ εἰσί, τοὺς ὑποδεεστέρους τῶν στρατιωτῶν εἰς τὰ σαγμάρια ἀφορίζειν, τοῦτ᾽ ἔστιν εἰς τρία ἢ τέσσαρα σαγμάρια ἄνδρα
ἕνα, καὶ ἕτερόν τινα τῶν ἐλλογίμων ἐξ αὐτῶν στρατιωτῶν χρήσιμον μετὰ
σημείου, ᾧτινι τὸ ὅλον τοῦλδον ἤγουν τὰ σαγμάρια ἀκολουθεῖν ὀφείλουσιν.

155    39. Ὁρίσεις δὲ καὶ τὰς ἀκίας, πόσαι καὶ ποῖαι ὀφείλουσι δεξιᾷ τοῦ βάνδου
τάττεσθαι καὶ πόσαι καὶ ποῖαι ἀριστερᾷ αὐτοῦ.

40. Τάξεις δὲ καὶ τὰ κοντουβέρνια ἢ κατὰ πέντε, ὡς εἴρηται, ἢ δέκα ἄνδρας ἢ
κατὰ τέσσαρας ἢ ὀκτὼ ἢ δεκαέξ, ὡς ἂν γινώσκῃς τὸ κατὰ καιρὸν χρήσιμον, ἵνα
τῇ συνηθείᾳ δεσμούμενοι καὶ ὑπὲρ ἀλλήλων ἐν ταῖς μάχαις ἀγωνιζόμενοι
160    χρησιμώτεροι πρὸς ἀνδρείαν γένωνται. | ἔχειν δὲ αὐτοὺς κοινὴν καὶ τὴν χρείαν    292
καθ᾽ ἕκαστον κοντουβέρνιον, ὡς ἤδη προδιωρισάμεθα.

41. Φρονιμώτερον δὲ ποιήσεις ἐὰν τάξῃς, εἰ τύχοι, ἀδελφοὺς μετὰ ἀδελφῶν
καὶ φίλους μετὰ φίλων, μάλιστα ἐν ταῖς τῆς μάχης παρατάξεσιν. ὅτ᾽ ἂν γάρ ἐστι
τῷ κινδυνεύοντι ὁ πλησίον προσφιλέστατος, ἀνάγκη τὸν ἀγαπῶντα φιλοκιν-
165    δυνότερον ὑπὲρ τοῦ πλησίον καὶ φιλουμένου ἀγωνίζεσθαι. καὶ δή τις αἰδούμενος μὴ ἀποδοῦναι χάριν τῷ φίλῳ ὧν πέπονθε φιλικῶν, αἰσχύνεται καταλιπεῖν
τὸν εὐεργετήσαντα καὶ πρῶτος αὐτὸς ἄρξασθαι φυγῆς.

42. Τὰ δὲ κοντουβέρνια, ὡς ἤδη εἴπομεν, διὰ τοῦτο ἀπὸ παλαιῶν καὶ νέων
στρατιωτῶν δεῖ γίνεσθαι, ἵνα μηδὲ οἱ παλαιοὶ καθ᾽ ἑαυτοὺς τασσόμενοι ἀσθε-
170    νεῖς εἰσι καὶ ἀδύνατοι, μηδὲ οἱ νεώτεροι ἄτακτοι εὑρεθῶσιν ὡς ἀπείραστοι. οἱ
μὲν γάρ, εἰ καὶ γηραῖοι ἀλλὰ πεπειραμένοι, οἱ δὲ εἰ καὶ νεάζοντες καὶ ἀνδρεῖοι
ἀλλὰ ἄπειροί εἰσιν.

43. Οὕτως οὖν τῶν ταγμάτων ἤγουν βάνδων διαιρουμένων ἐφ᾽ ἑαυτά, χρὴ
ἐπιστῆναι αὐτοῖς ἄρχοντας τοὺς λεγομένους κόμητας, συνίστασθαι δὲ ἕκαστον
175    τάγμα ἀπὸ ἀνδρῶν τριακοσίων κατὰ τὸν μέσον τόπον. μήτε δὲ πλέον τετρα-

---

162–167 Onas. 24.    168–172 *Strat.*, 2.7.    173–209 *Strat.*, 1.4.

---

152 ἢ MWA εἰς E ἢ εἰ B    154 ἤγουν…σαγμάρια MW om. ABE    155 πόσαι ABE ποιῆσαι
MW    156 τάττεσθαι MW τάσσεσθαι ABE    157 κοντουβέρνια MA κουτουβέρνια W
κουντουβέρνια B κοντοῦ βέρνια E    159 καὶ ABE om. MW    160 αὐτοὺς WABE αὐτοῖς M
161 κοντουβέρνιον MWAE κουντουβέρνιον B | προδιωρισάμεθα MWAE προδιωρισόμεθα B
162 εἰ τύχοι MWE om. AB    165 ad δή τις scr. mg. ηγουν εντρεπομενος την αγαπην ην εχει
προς αὐτὸν ὁ φιλος αὐτοῦ W    165–166 αἰδούμενος MW αἰσχυνόμενος ABE    166 φιλικῶν
MWA φιλῶν BE    167 αὐτὸς Va αὐτοῦ MW om. ABE | ἄρξασθαι φυγῆς MW φυγεῖν ABE
168 κοντουβέρνια MAE κουτουβέρνια W κουντουβέρνια B | ἤδη MW om. ABE    170 εἰσι
MWA ὦσι BE    171 γηραῖοι MW γέροντες ABE    173 ἐφ᾽ ἑαυτά MW om. ABE
175 τριακοσίων MWA τ′ BE

38. Then, in the likely event that no servants are present, the poorer soldiers should be detailed to the pack animals, that is, one man to three or four animals. Another man from among the soldiers, highly regarded and able to carry the standard, should be chosen, whom the whole baggage train or the pack animals must follow.

39. The commander must then determine how many and which files are to form on the right of the standard and how many and which on the left.

40. Arrange the squads, as was said, by five men, by ten, by four, by eight, or by sixteen, however you think useful at the time. As a result, bound by close ties and struggling in battle on behalf of one another, they will prove more efficient and valiant. They should have common duties in each squad, as we have already decreed.

41. You will act very wisely if you line up, depending on the situation, brothers with brothers and friends with friends, especially in combat formations.[10] For whenever the very close friend is near his friend who is in danger, he will feel compelled to embrace danger himself to fight on behalf of his friend next to him. Indeed, a man is ashamed not to return a favor to his friend for those he has received out of friendship, and he is ashamed to abandon his benefactor and be the first to take flight.

42. The squads, as we have already said, should be made up of old and young soldiers so that the old men in formation by themselves may not be weak and powerless, and the younger men may not turn out to be inexperienced and disorganized.[11] The former, even if they are old, have a good deal of experience, while the latter, even if young and brave, still have no real experience.

43. Once the various tagmata or banda have been properly lined up, it is necessary to appoint officers, called counts, over them.[12] Each tagma should consist, on the average, of three hundred men. You should insist that the tagma

*10. Onasander 24.
*11. *Strat.* 2.7.
*12. *Strat.* 1.4.

κοσίων ἀνδρῶν τὸ τάγμα ἔχειν ὁρίσῃς, κἂν πάνυ πολὺν στρατὸν ἔχεις, μήτε
ὑποκάτω τῶν διακοσίων, κἂν ἔστιν ὀλίγος ὁ στρατός.

44. Ταῦτα δὲ τὰ τάγματα συνάξεις εἰς χιλιαρχίας ἤτοι μοίρας τὰς λεγομένας
δρούγγους, καὶ ἐπιστήσεις αὐτοῖς μοιράρχας χρησίμους ἀνδρείᾳ καὶ φρονήσει
180 καὶ εὐταξίᾳ, εἰ δυνατόν, καὶ εὐγενείᾳ καὶ εὐπορίᾳ τοὺς λεγομένους δρουγγαρίους οὕς ποτε χιλιάρχους ἐκάλουν οἱ παλαιοί.

45. Τὰς δὲ μοίρας ταύτας ἤτοι τοὺς δρούγγους συνάξεις εἰς μέρη ἤγουν
τούρμας καὶ ἐπιστήσονται αὐτοῖς γνώμῃ τῆς βασιλείας ἡμῶν μεράρχαι, οἱ
λεγόμενοί ποτε καὶ στρατηλάται, νῦν δὲ τῇ συνηθείᾳ καλούμενοι τουρμάρχαι·
185 καὶ τούτους φρονίμους καὶ εὐτάκτους εἶναι καὶ ἐναρέτους καὶ ἐμπείρους, εἰ
δυνατόν, εἰδότας καὶ γράμματα, καὶ μάλιστα τὸν τοῦ μέσου μέρους, τὸν λεγόμενον ὑποστράτηγον, ὀφείλοντα, εἰ χρεία γένηται, ἐν πᾶσι τὸν τοῦ στρατηγοῦ
τόπον ἀναπληροῦν.

46. Ταῦτα δὲ τὰ μέρη τρία συστῆναι, ἐφ' οἷς καὶ τρεῖς ἐπιστήσονται τουρ-
190 μάρχαι, εἷς ἕκαστος ἰδίου μέρους ἄρχων, ὥστε εἶναι τοῦ παντὸς στρατοῦ τὴν
ἀνωτάτην τομὴν τρία ἰσάριθμα μέρη ἤγουν τούρμας, τοῦτ' ἔστι | μέσον, ἀριστε- 292ᵛ
ρὸν καὶ δεξιόν· ταῦτα δὲ ποιεῖ τὴν πᾶσαν τάξιν τὴν ὑπὸ τῷ στρατηγῷ τεταγμέ-
νην.

47. Χρὴ δέ, ὡς εἴρηται, μήτε τάγμα πλέον τῶν τετρακοσίων ἀνδρῶν γίνε-
195 σθαι ἤγουν τὸ τοῦ κόμητος βάνδον, μήτε δροῦγγον πλέον τῶν τρισχιλίων μήτε
τοῦρμαν πλέον τῶν ἑξακισχιλίων.

48. Εἰ δὲ συμβῇ πλέον τοῦ λεχθέντος μέτρου εἶναι τὸν στρατόν, κάλλιόν
ἐστι ἔξωθεν τῶν μερῶν ἤτοι τῶν τουρμαρχιῶν ἐν δευτέρᾳ τάξει καθίστασθαι,
ἤγουν ἐν τῇ ὄπισθεν τῆς προμάχου τάξεως παραταγῆναι ἐν ὑποβοηθείᾳ καὶ εἰς
200 φυλακὴν τῶν πλαγίων μερῶν καὶ εἰς νωτοφύλακας καὶ εἰς ἐνέδρας ἤτοι ἐγκρύμματα καὶ εἰς κυκλώσεις τῶν πολεμίων.

49. Καὶ μήτε τὰς τούρμας μήτε τοὺς δρούγγους μείζους ποιεῖν, ἵνα μὴ ὡς
μεγάλα καὶ ἐπιπολὺ ἐκτεινόμενα ἀπειθῆ πρὸς τὰ παραγγέλματα καὶ συγκεχυ-
μένα εὑρεθῶσιν.

205 50. Ἀλλὰ καὶ ἕτερόν σοι χρήσιμον παραινέσω, ὥστε μὴ πάντα τὰ τάγματα
ἤτοι βάνδα ἐπιτηδεύεις πάντως ἴσα ποιεῖν, ἵνα μὴ ἐκ τοῦ ἀριθμοῦ τῶν βάνδων

178 συνάξεις MWBE συντάξεις A   180 εὐπορίᾳ MW εὐπορία διαφέροντες ABE
182 συνάξεις BE συντάξεις MWA   189 οἷς MWA ᾧ BE   191 ἀνωτάτην τομὴν MW
πρώτην καὶ μεγίστην διαίρεσιν ABE | ἰσάριθμα μέρη MW trsp. ABE | τούρμας PG τούρμαι
codd. | ἔστι MABE ἔστιν W   191–192 ἀριστερὸν MWA ἀριστερόν τε BE
198 τουρμαρχιῶν MWAB τουρμαχιῶν E   199 παραταγῆναι Du παραταγῇ codd.
202 μείζους MW μείζονας ABE   205 μὴ MWAB μὴ πάντως ἵνα ποιεῖν E

should not have more than four hundred men, even if you have a very large army, and not below two hundred, even if your army is small.

44. You should bring these tagmata together into chiliarchies or moirai, also called droungoi, and place over them competent moirarchs, noted for bravery, good judgment, discipline and, if possible, also noble birth and wealth. These, whom the ancient authors called chiliarchs, are now called droungarioi.

45. You should bring these moirai or droungoi together into divisions or tourmai and let merarchs be appointed over them, with the approval of Our Majesty. These officers were formerly called stratelatai but now are usually called tourmarchs. They should be men of good judgment, disciplined, virtuous, experienced and, if possible, able to read and write. This is particularly important for the commander of the second meros, called lieutenant general, who has to, if it becomes necessary, assume all the duties of the general.

46. There should be three of these divisions and over them three tourmarchs should be appointed, each one the commander of his own division. As a result, the topmost division of the whole army is that of three divisions or tourmai of equal strength, that is, center, left, and right. These then make up the entire formation that is lined up under the general.

47. It is necessary, as was said, that the tagma, the bandon of the count, should not be more than four hundred men or the droungos more than three thousand or the tourma more than six thousand.

48. But if the army should happen to exceed the aforesaid size, it is better to station those men outside the divisions or tourmarchies in the second line, that is, behind the main battle line as a support force and also to guard the divisions on the flanks, and as rear guards and for ambushes or traps and for encircling the enemy.

49. Do not make the tourmai or the droungoi too large. Otherwise, as they become larger and much more extended, they may end up confused and inattentive to the commands.

50. Let me give you another useful bit of advice. Be sure that you do not bring all the tagmata or banda up to the same strength. Otherwise, the enemy

εὐαρίθμητος τοῖς ἐχθροῖς ὁ στρατὸς γένηται, ὅπερ πολλάκις μεγάλας προξενεῖ
τὰς βλάβας. ἀλλὰ τοῦτο φυλάττειν, μηδὲ τῶν τετρακοσίων ἀνδρῶν, ὡς εἴπομεν,
πλέον μηδὲ τῶν διακοσίων ἀνδρῶν ὀλιγώτερα γίνεσθαι αὐτά.

210　51. Διὸ πολλάκις καὶ καθ᾽ ἕκαστον τάγμα ἐὰν δύο βάνδα εὐτρεπίζῃς ἀναδείκνυσθαι ἐν τῷ καιρῷ τῆς τοῦ πολέμου συμβολῆς οὐκ ἄχρηστον εἰς τὸ κατα-
πλῆξαι τοὺς πολεμίους.

52. Χρὴ δὲ ἀφορισθῆναι ἀπὸ ἑκάστου βάνδου εἰς τὰς ἀναγκαίας χρείας, ὡς
εἴρηται, τοὺς μανδάτωρας ἀγρύπνους καὶ συνετοὺς καὶ γοργοὺς καὶ εὐφώνους,
215　εἰδότας, εἰ δυνατόν, καὶ διαφόροις γλώσσαις λαλεῖν, καὶ βουκινάτωρας οἵτινες
ἐν καιρῷ τὰ συνήθη σαλπίσουσι, σαμιάτωρας, τοξοποιούς, σαγιττοποιοὺς καὶ
τοὺς λοιποὺς πρὸς τὴν ἐξ ἔθους διατύπωσιν.

53. Προσαφορίσεις δὲ καί τινας τοὺς ὀφείλοντας τὰ εὑρισκόμενα τῶν
ἀπολλυμένων συνάγειν καὶ ἀποδιδόναι τοῖς κυρίοις αὐτῶν.

220　54. Ὥσπερ δὲ ἐπὶ τοῦ τούλδου τῶν καβαλλαρίων ἀναγκαῖον ὁρίσαι τοὺς
ὀφείλοντας ἐπιστῆναι ἄρχοντας, οὕτως καὶ ἐπὶ τοῦ τούλδου ἤτοι τῶν ἁμαξιῶν
τῆς πεζικῆς τάξεως ἀφορίσεις τινάς, οἷς ὀφείλουσι πείθεσθαι οἱ τοῦ λεγομένου
καραγοῦ.

55. Καραγὸς γὰρ λέγεται ὁ διὰ τῶν ἁμαξῶν καὶ τριβόλων καὶ τῶν ἄλλων μη| 293
225　χανῶν γινόμενος περιορισμὸς εἰς ἀσφάλειαν τοῦ στρατοῦ.

56. Καὶ καθ᾽ ἕκαστον μέρος ἕνα πρῶτον τὸν ἄρχειν ὀφείλοντα καὶ σημεῖον,
ὡς ἐπὶ τῶν ἵππων, ἐντεθῆναι εἰς τὰς βοῦς, ἴδιον ἑκάστου ἀριθμοῦ ἵνα εἰσὶν
εὔδηλοι καὶ φανεραὶ τοῖς ἰδίοις.

57. Καλῶς δὲ καὶ τῆς πεζικῆς τάξεως ἐπεμνήσθημεν. δεῖ γὰρ καὶ ταύτης τὴν
230　διαίρεσιν ὑπογράψαι καὶ τοὺς ἐν αὐτῇ τατομένους ἄρχοντάς τε καὶ ἄλλους
ἡγεμόνας μικρούς τε καὶ μεγάλους καταστῆναι καὶ τὰς αὐτῶν δηλῶσαι ὀνομα-

---

213–312 Strat., 12.B.7–8.

---

207 τοῖς ἐχθροῖς MW om. ABE | στρατὸς ABE στρατηγὸς MW　208 τετρακοσίων MWA υ′
BE　210–211 ἀναδείκνυσθαι MW ἀναφαίνεσθαι ABE　212 πολεμίους MABE ἐναντίους
W　214–215 γοργοὺς…εἰδότας MW ἐγρηγόρους καὶ καλλιφώνους γινώσκοντας ABE
215 διαφόροις γλώσσαις MW trsp. ABE　216 ἐν MW ἐν τῷ ABE | σαλπίσουσι MW
σαλπίζουσι BE σαλπίζουσιν A　218 προσαφορίσεις MW ἀφορίσεις AE ἀφορήσεις B
221 οὕτως MW οὕτω ABE | ἤτοι…ἁμαξιῶν MW om. ABE　222 οἱ MWA ὁ BE
223 καραγοῦ MW καραγοῦ ἤτοι τῶν ἁμαξιῶν ABE　224 γὰρ MWA δὲ BE　227 ἵππων
MWA ἱππέων BE | ἐντεθῆναι AB ἐντεθεῖναι MW ἐντιθῆναι E　227–228 εἰσὶν…καὶ MW ἐκ
τῆς χρόας τοῦ σημείου AE ἐκ τῆς χρείας τοῦ σημείου B　228 ἰδίοις MW ἰδίοις ἕκασται
γίνονται AE ἰδίοις ἕκαστοι γίνωνται B　230 τατομένους MW τασσομένους ABE | ἄλλους
ABE ἄλλως MW

can easily estimate the size of the army by counting standards, often resulting in serious harm. However, carefully observe our prescription that they should not consist of more than four hundred men or fewer than two hundred.

51. If you arrange to have each tagma frequently display two standards at the time when battle is about to be joined, it will be helpful in confusing the enemy.

52. In each bandon men must be set apart for necessary chores, as was said, including two heralds, alert and intelligent, with vigorous, pleasant voices and who, if possible, know how to speak several languages.[13] Trumpeters who sound the customary signals at the proper time, weapon makers, bow makers, arrow makers, and the rest according to the customary regulations.

53. You should also assign certain men the duty of collecting whatever lost articles have been found and returning them to their owners.

54. Just as in the cavalry baggage train it was necessary to decree that officers had to be placed in charge, so for the baggage or wagon train of the infantry formation you should designate certain officers whom the men in the baggage train, also called karagos, must obey.

55. Karagos is the term for the barrier formed by the wagons, caltrops, and other devices for the protection of the army.

56. In each division one man should be first in command. Just as with the horses, a special mark should identify the oxen which belong to each arithmos so the men can easily recognize them as their own.

57. It is well that we have kept the infantry in mind. For it is necessary to describe its various units and to appoint the officers assigned to that arm as well as the other leaders, both of higher and lower rank, and to make clear their

*13. *Strat.* 12.B.7–8 .

σίας, ὅπως τε περὶ αὐτῆς ἐκ τῶν παλαιῶν παρελάβομεν τακτικῶν καὶ ὅπως οἱ
νεώτεροι μέχρις ἡμῶν τὴν αὐτῶν ἔκταξίν τε καὶ κατάστασιν παρεπέμψαντο.

58. Οἱ μὲν γὰρ ἀρχαῖοι πολυπληθίας εὐποροῦντες ἴσως στρατευμάτων τῶν
235 ποτε λεγομένων ὁπλιτῶν, νῦν δὲ σκουτάτων καλουμένων, μᾶλλον δὲ καὶ αὐτοῦ
τοῦ ὀνόματος διὰ τὴν ἄγαν τῆς τακτικῆς μελέτης καὶ πράξεως ἀμελείας παρὰ
μικρὸν παρὰ πάντων ἀγνοουμένου, ταῦτα οὖν τὰ τάγματα τῶν σκουτάτων ἀπὸ
δεκαὲξ ἀκιῶν ἐποίουν, ἀνδρῶν διακοσίων νϛ´, τοῦτ᾿ ἔστιν, ἑκάστην ἀκίαν
ἀνδρῶν ιϛ´ ὑπὸ τετραγώνῳ ἀριθμῷ. εὑρίσκεται δὲ ἐν ἐκείνοις ἡ φάλαγξ πεζῶν
240 ἀνδρῶν ͵δϛ´, ἣν ἐκάλουν στρατηγίαν καὶ τὸν ἐφιστάμενον αὐτῇ στρατηγόν.

59. Τὴν δὲ τελείαν παράταξιν ἐποίουν ταγμάτων ξδ´, ἀκιῶν χιλίων κδ´,
ἀνδρῶν μυρίων ͵ϛτπδ´, ψιλῶν δὲ τῶν λεγομένων σαγιττατώρων καὶ ἀκοντιστῶν
καὶ σφενδοβολιστῶν, ἀνδρῶν ͵ηρϙβ´ ἤγουν ἡμίσειαν τῶν ψιλῶν εἶναι τὴν τάξιν
τῶν λεγομένων ὁπλιτῶν ἤτοι σκουτάτων. τῶν δὲ σὺν αὐτοῖς παραταττομένων
245 ἱππέων ἤτοι συμμίκτων τῇ πεζικῇ τάξει ἀνδρῶν καβαλλαρίων ͵δϛ´. καὶ τούτων
ὁ ἡγούμενος ἐλέγετο στρατηγός.

60. Καὶ ταῦτα μὲν ἐμέριζον οὕτως· τὰ δὲ τάγματα τῶν σκουτάτων ἔμπροσθεν εἰς πρόμαχον τάξιν παρέτασσον κατὰ τῶν ἐναντίων καὶ ταύτην εἰς δ´
ἴσα μέρη ἐποίουν, δεξιόν, ἀριστερόν, μέσον ἀριστερόν, μέσον δεξιόν.

250 61. Τὰ δὲ τῶν ψιλῶν τάγματα ἰδίᾳ, διὰ τὸ γοργοὺς εἶναι καὶ ἐλαφροὺς ἢ
ἔμπροσθεν εἰς ἐπιδίωξιν τῶν ἐχθρῶν ἔταττον ἢ εἰς τὰ πλάγια ἢ ἐπὶ τοῦ νώτου
τῆς πρώτης παραταγῆς ἢ ὡς ἡ χρεία ἠπαίτει, περὶ ὧν κατὰ χώραν ἐροῦμεν.

---

232 ὅπως τε MW ὡς ABE    233 μέχρις ἡμῶν ṀW om. ABE | τε MW om. ABE | κατάστασιν
MW    κατάστασιν    μέχρις    ἡμῶν    ABE    234 πολυπληθίας...ἴσως W    πολυπληθίας
ὑποποροῦντες ἴσως M    πολὺ πλῆθος ἔχοντες ABE    236 ἄγαν...ἀμελείας MW παντελῆ
ἀμέλειαν τῆς τακτικῆς ABE    237 παρὰ MWA παρὰ τοῦ BE | ταῦτα MWA ταῦτ᾿ BE | τὰ
MWBE τὰ τὰ A    238 δεκαὲξ MW ιϛ´ ABE | ἀκιῶν MW ἀκιῶν ἤγουν λόχων ABE | νϛ´ MW
σνϛ´ ABE    239 ἐν MWA om. BE    239–240 πεζῶν ἀνδρῶν MW trsp. ABE    240 ͵δϛ´
MWBE τετρακισχιλίων ἐνενήκοντα A | ἐφιστάμενον αὐτῇ MW ταύτης ἡγούμενον ABE
241 χιλίων κδ´ MABE ͵ακδ´ W    242 ͵ϛτπδ´ MW ἑξακισχιλίων τετρακοσίων ὀγδοήκοντα
τεσσάρων A ἑξακισχιλίων τετρακοσίων πδ´ BE    243 σφενδοβολιστῶν MW σφενδονήτων A
σφενδονιστῶν BE | ͵ηρϙβ´ MW ὀκτακισχιλίων ἑκατὸν ἐνενήκοντα δύο A ὀκτακισχιλίων ρϙβ´
B ὀκτακισχιλίων ἑκατὸν ρϙβ´ E | τῶν...εἶναι MWA trsp. BE    245 ͵δϛ´ MW τετρακισχιλίων
ἐνενήκοντα ἓξ A δϛ´ BE    246 ὁ MWA om. BE | ἐλέγετο MWAE ἐλέγετο ὁ B    248 δ´
MWBE τέσσαρα A    249 ἴσα μέρη MW trsp. ABE | μέσον ἀριστερόν MWA om. BE
250 τάγματα MWA ταγμάτων BE    251 ἔταττον MWA ἔτασσον BE | τὰ MWA om. BE |
ἐπὶ...νώτου MW ὀπίσω ABE    252 παραταγῆς MW παρατάξεως ABE | ἠπαίτει Va ἠπέτει
MW ἀπήτει ABE | κατὰ χώραν MW ἐν τῷ ἁρμόζοντι τόπῳ ABE scr. mg. ηγουν εις τον τόπον
αυτ<ῆς> W

titles. We have taken the material about this and about their deployment and formation from that which the ancient tactical authors and the more recent ones up to our own time have transmitted.[14]

58. The ancients were fortunate enough to have large numbers of men in their armies, especially those once called hoplites and now called skoutatoi. Actually, nobody even knows those terms because of the grave neglect of the study and practice of tactics. Those authorities formed the tagmata of heavy infantry from sixteen files, 256 men, that is, each file of sixteen men making up a foursquare body of troops. Among those the phalanx of foot soldiers is numbered at 4,096; it was also called a strategia and was commanded by a general.

59. The ancient writers formed the complete battle line of 64 tagmata or 1,024 files, for a force of 16,384 men, in addition to 8,192 light-armed troops, such as archers, javelin throwers, and slingers. They assigned half of the light infantry to the formation of the heavy infantry, <once> called hoplites or skoutatoi. The horsemen lined up in formation with them or mixed in with the infantry formation came to 4,096 cavalry. The leader of these was called general.

60. This is how they divided the units. They stationed the heavy infantry companies in a forward position as a first line of battle against the enemy, and they divided this into four equal divisions, right, left, right center, left center.

61. They stationed the light infantry companies off by themselves, because they were lightly armed and fast, either out in front to pursue the enemy or on the flanks or to the rear of the first battle line or wherever need dictated. We will speak about these in the proper place.

*14. Especially Aelian and Arrian.

62. Τοὺς δὲ καβαλλαρίους εἰς δύο μέρη διελόντες κατὰ τὰ πλάγια τῆς τῶν πεζῶν παρατάξεως ἔταττον | βοηθοὺς καὶ ὀξέως ἐπιτιθεμένους τοῖς ἐναντίοις.   293ᵛ

255  63. Ἵνα οὖν μὴ καθ᾽ ἕκαστον λέγω ἐπὶ λεπτῷ τῶν τε λόχων καὶ τῶν τάξεων καὶ τῶν ἐφισταμένων αὐτοῖς τότε ἀρχόντων τὰς ὀνομασίας διὰ τὴν νῦν αὐτῶν ἀχρηστίαν καὶ παρὰ πᾶσι τοῖς στρατευομένοις σχεδόν που αὐτῶν ἀσάφειάν τε καὶ ἀκαταληψίαν, καὶ ἵνα μὴ ἀκαίρως δαπανῶμεν τὸν καιρόν, τῶν ἀναγκαιοτέρων ὡς σαφεστέρων καὶ συντομωτέρων ἐπιλήψομαι. ἐκεῖνα μὲν γάρ, ὡς
260  ἔοικε, τά τε τῶν καβαλλαρίων διατάγματα καὶ τὰ τῶν πεζῶν, πλήθους ἦν στρατιᾶς, ὥστε καὶ τοσούτους καὶ γενναίους κατ᾽ ἀνδρείαν εὑρίσκεσθαι στρατιώτας.

64. Νῦν δέ, ὦ στρατηγέ, εὐαριθμήτων ὄντων καὶ μηδὲ ἴσον ἐχόντων τὸ μέτρον, μᾶλλον δὲ καὶ πολὺ ἔλαττον, οὐκ ἔστιν εὐχερὲς ὁρίσαι τὸ μέτρον τοῦ τάγματος οὔτε ἐν τοῖς καβαλλαρίοις οὔτε ἐν τοῖς πεζοῖς, ἵνα μή, ὡς εἰκός, ἢ <οἱ>
265  περιττεύοντες τοῦ ποσοῦ τῶν σνς´ ἀνδρῶν ἀργήσωσιν ἢ πάλιν, ἐὰν ἀκαίρως ἄλλοις τάγμασι προστεθῶσιν, ὡς ἄτακτοι ἀνωφελεῖς εὑρεθῶσιν.

65. Ἀλλὰ τὰ μὲν τάγματα ποιεῖν εἰς ἕκαστον ἀριθμὸν ὡς ἀπαντήσει ἡ τοῦ πλήθους χρεία καὶ τὸ ποσὸν τῶν προσόντων ἀνδρῶν κατὰ τὴν δύναμιν τοῦ κατὰ τὸν καιρὸν εὑρισκομένου λαοῦ· καὶ βάνδον ἔχειν ἴδιον ἕκαστον αὐτῶν καὶ
270  ἄρχοντα ἤτοι κόμητα γενναῖον καὶ φρόνιμον καὶ ἀνδρεῖον καὶ κατὰ χεῖρα μάχεσθαι δυνάμενον.

66. Τὰς μέντοι ἀκίας ἑκάστου τάγματος τῶν πεζῶν παραφυλάττειν ἀπὸ δεκαὲξ ἀνδρῶν ὀρδινεύεσθαι εἰς τὸν τῆς μάχης κάματον, τὴν δὲ παράταξιν πρὸς τὸ μέτρον τοῦ εὑρισκομένου στρατοῦ ποιεῖν.

---

253 διελόντες W ἑλόντες M διαχωρίζοντες ABE   255 λέγω…λεπτῷ ABE λέγων ἐπιλεπτῶ MW | λόχων…τῶν² WABE λόχων τε καὶ M scr. mg. τῶν ὀρδίνων W   255–256 καὶ… ἀρχόντων MWA om. BE   256 ἐφισταμένων WABE ἀφισταμένων M   256–257 τὴν… ἀχρηστίαν MW τὸ ἄχρηστα εἶναι αὐτὰ νῦν ABE scr. mg. το ειναι νῦν ἀνενέργητον W   257–259 παρὰ…ἐπιλήψομαι MW μὴ δὲ παρά τινος τῶν στρατευομένων γινώσκεσθαι τὰ ἀναγκαιότερα καὶ σαφέστερα καὶ συντομώτερα λέξω ABE   257 ad ἀσάφειάν scr. mg. ηγουν δια το ἀδιαγνωστον W   259 ad σαφεστέρων scr. mg. ηγουν εκεινα ως γνωριμώτερα λεγειν W   259–260 ὡς ἔοικε MW om. ABE scr. mg. ὡς φαίνεται W   260–261 στρατιᾶς BE στρατείας MWA   261 κατ᾽ MWAE κατὰ B   262 εὐαριθμήτων MW ὀλίγων ABE scr. mg. ολιγων W   263 μᾶλλον…καὶ MW ἀλλὰ καὶ A ἀλλὰ BE | εὐχερὲς MW εὔκολον ABE   264 ad εἰκός scr. mg. ὡς ἐστιν ἐνδεχομενον W | οἱ ci. Va om. codd.   265 περιττεύοντες MW περισσεύοντες ABE | ἀργήσωσιν MWAE ἀρχήσωσιν B | ἀκαίρως MW om. ABE   266 ὡς… εὑρεθῶσιν MW ἀκαίρως ἀνωφελεῖς εὑρεθῶσιν ὡς ἄτακτοι ABE   268 τὸ ποσὸν MW ἡ ποσότης ABE   269 τὸν MWA om. BE   270 κατὰ χεῖρα MW ἀπὸ χειρὸς ABE   271 μάχεσθαι δυνάμενον MW trsp. ABE   272 παραφυλάττειν MW om. ABE   273 δεκαὲξ MW ις´ ABE | ὀρδινεύεσθαι MW ὀρδινεύειν ABE   274 μέτρον MW μέρος ABE

62. They divided the cavalry into two groups and stationed them along the flanks of the infantry line to support it and to launch rapid attacks against the enemy.

63. Now then, in order that I may not have to discuss in detail the nomenclature formerly in use for the files and the formations and the officers who were placed over them, because they are not in use today and practically nobody serving in the armed forces has any clear understanding of them, and in order not to waste time inopportunely, I will touch upon the other essential matters very clearly and succinctly. For, so it seems, those companies of cavalry and infantry existed when the armies were large and the soldiers proved to be numerous, noble, and brave.

64. But now, O general, if our units are small and not even equal in strength, indeed much less, it is not easy to fix a definite number for a tagma, whether among the cavalry or among the infantry—it could end up with a number of men in excess of 256 having nothing to do or, if inappropriately assigned to serve in other tagmata, they might turn out to be disoriented and useless.

65. It is better to form the companies for each unit in accord with the needs of the army and the manpower at hand, depending, of course, on the capabilities of the troops available at that time. Each unit should have its own standard and officer or count, a noble man of sound judgment, brave, and good at hand-to-hand fighting.

66. Make sure that the files of each infantry tagma are sixteen deep, with the men organized according to their duties in combat. Form the battle line in proportion to the numerical strength of the army as it is found there.

275    67. Ταύτην δὲ εἰς τέσσαρα ἴσα μέρη διανέμειν, ἐξ ὅσων ἀπαντήσει ταγμάτων καὶ ἀκιῶν, ὡς εἴρηταί μοι καὶ ἄνωθεν, τοῦτ' ἔστιν εἰς δεξιὸν οὗ ἄρχει ὁ δεξιὸς μεράρχης ἤτοι στρατηλάτης ὃν τουρμάρχην καλοῦμεν, εἰς ἀριστερὸν οὗ ἄρχει ὁ εὐώνυμος τουρμάρχης, καὶ εἰς τὰ ἕτερα δύο μέσα μέρη ὁμοίως, ἐν οἷς ἵσταται καὶ τὸ τοῦ στρατηγοῦ βάνδον.

280    68. Δέον δέ ἐστιν ἐκ περισσοῦ τῆς παρατάξεως φυλάττειν ὀλίγους καὶ σκουτάτους καὶ ψιλοὺς ἐν ὑποβοηθείᾳ καὶ ἄρχοντα ἔχειν ἴδιον ἢ παρά σου τότε καθιστάμενον ἵνα, ἐὰν χρεία γένηται, εἰς τὰ ἄκρα τῆς παραταγῆς ἔξωθεν τῶν καβαλλαρίων ἢ εἰς τὰς ἁμάξας ἢ εἰς ἑτέρους τόπους μετὰ τῶν ἰδικῶν αὐτῶν ἀρχόντων συντρέχοντες βοηθῶσιν.

285    69. Χρὴ δέ, ἐὰν ὀλιγώτερός ἐστιν ὁ στρατὸς τῶν | κδ' χιλιάδων πεζῶν, μὴ  294
ποιεῖν δ' μέρη τὴν παράταξιν, ἀλλά γ', ἐν τῷ μέσῳ δὲ μέρει τάσσεσθαι τὸ τοῦ στρατηγοῦ βάνδον, ᾧ καὶ πείθεσθαι τὰ λοιπὰ βάνδα ὀφείλουσιν.

70. Πρότερον δὲ χωρίσεις εἰς ψιλοὺς τοὺς εἰδότας τοξεῦσαι ἢ καὶ μαθεῖν δυναμένους, καὶ γοργοὺς καὶ νεωτέρους, ἱκανοὺς πηδᾶν ὅπου βούλονται. ἐὰν
290    μὲν ὑπὲρ τὰς κδ' χιλιάδας εἰσὶ τὸ ἥμισυ μέρος, εἰ δὲ ὀλιγώτερος τῶν κδ' χιλιάδων, τὸ τρίτον μέρος ἐν ἑκάστῳ ἀριθμῷ καὶ τότε ὀρδινευθῆναι αὐτούς, ὥς που καὶ ἀνωτέρω εἴπομεν, εἰς δεκαρχίας καὶ ἐπιστῆναι αὐτοῖς δεκάρχας χρησίμους καὶ ἄρχοντα ἕνα, τὸν λεγόμενον ἀρχισαγιττάτωρα ἤγουν ἀρχιτοξότην.

71. Τὸ δὲ μένον δίμοιρον μέρος ἢ ἥμισυ διανεῖμαι εἰς ἀκίας ἀπὸ ἀνδρῶν ιη',
295    παλαιῶν τε καὶ νέων. ἀκίαι δὲ λέγονται, ὥς μοι εἴρηται, τὰ λεγόμενα κοντου-βέρνια. καὶ τοὺς μὲν δύο αὐτῶν, τοὺς ὑποδεεστέρους ἤτοι τοὺς πλείονας τῶν ις', εἰς τὰς ἁμάξας καὶ εἰς ἑτέρας, ὡς εἰκός, χρείας ἀσχολεῖσθαι, τοὺς δεκαὲξ δὲ

275 εἰς τέσσαρα MWAB δ' E | διανέμειν MW διαχωρίζει ABE scr. mg. διαμερίζειν W | ἀπαντήσει MW ἂν ἀπαντήσῃ ABE    276 ὡς…ἄνωθεν MW καθὼς ἀνωτέρω εἴρηται ABE    278 δύο μέσα MW μέσα δύο AB μέσα β' E    280 ad δέον scr. mg. αρμοζον W | δέ MWA om. BE    281 καὶ² MW om. ABE | ἔχειν MW ἔχοντα ABE    282 παραταγῆς MW παρατάξεως ABE    283 ἰδικῶν MW ἰδίων ABE    284 συντρέχοντες βοηθῶσιν MWAB συντρέχοντος βοηθῶσι E    285 ἐστιν MWA ὑπάρχῃ BE    286 δ' MW τέσσαρα ABE | γ' MWBE τρία A    287 ᾧ MW ᾧτινι ABE    288–290 πρότερον…μέρος MW ἐὰν μὲν οὖν ὑπὲρ τὰς κδ' χιλιάδας εἰσὶν (ὦσιν BE) οἱ στρατευόμενοι τὸ ἥμισυ μέρος χωρίσεις εἰς ψιλοὺς τοὺς εἰδότας τοξεῦσαι ἢ καὶ μαθεῖν δυναμένους γοργοὺς καὶ νεωτέρους ἱκανοὺς πηδᾶν ὅπου βούλονται ABE    290–291 χιλιάδων MW χιλιάδων εἰσὶν A χιλιάδων εἰσὶ BE    291–292 ὥς…εἴπομεν MW om. ABE    293 ἄρχοντα MWA ἄρχοντας BE    294 μένον MW ὑπολιμπανόμενον ABE | ἢ ABE om. MW | διανεῖμαι MW διαμερίσαι ABE | ἀπὸ MWA om. BE    295 τε ABE om. MW | ὥς…εἴρηται MW om. ABE    295–296 κοντουβέρνια MAE κουτουβέρνια W κουντουβέρνια B    296 δύο MWAB β' E | ἤτοι…ις' MW ἑκάστης ἀκίας ABE    297 ὡς εἰκός MW om. ABE | δεκαὲξ MWBE δὲ ις' A    297–298 δὲ στῆναι MW ἵστασθαι ABE

67. Divide this line composed of all the tagmata and files present into four equal units, as I mentioned above, that is, right under the command of the right merarch or stratelates, whom we refer to as tourmarch, left under the command of the left tourmarch, and likewise for the other two middle divisions, in which the standard of the general is flown.

68. A few soldiers, both heavy and light infantry, not really needed in the battle line, with their own officer or one to be designated by you at the time, should be held in reserve so that, if it becomes necessary, together with their own officers, they may hasten to the support of either of the flanks on the line beyond the cavalry or the wagons or other places.

69. If the army consists of less than twenty-four thousand foot soldiers, you must not form the battle line into four divisions but into three. In the center meros raise the general's standard, which the others should use as a guide.

70. First, for the light-armed troops, you should select men who know how to shoot with a bow or who are able to learn, young and vigorous men, capable of leaping wherever they wish. If there are more than twenty-four thousand men, the archers should be half in each company; if fewer than twenty-four thousand, then a third. They should be organized, as we mentioned someplace above, into dekarchies with competent dekarchs placed over them and one commander known as the chief archer or chief bowman.

71. Divide the remaining half or two thirds into files of eighteen men, both veterans and recruits. Files, as I have said, are also called squads. Two of those men, somewhat less qualified, that is, in addition to the other sixteen, should be assigned to the wagons or to other tasks as needed. Have the remaining sixteen

στῆναι ἐν τῇ παρατάξει καὶ ἐπιστῆναι αὐτοῖς τοὺς λοχαγοὺς λεγομένους, γενναίους καὶ χρησίμους.

300    72. Ἐκ τούτων δὲ τῶν ις′ <τοὺς> χρησιμωτέρους ὀκτὼ ἔμπροσθεν ἢ ὄπισθεν
τῆς ἀκίας ἤτοι τοῦ λόχου καταστῆναι—τὴν γὰρ τῶν ις′ ἀνδρῶν ἀκίαν λόχον
ἐκάλουν οἱ παλαιοί—στῆσαι δὲ αὐτοὺς εἰς τὸν πρῶτον τόπον καὶ εἰς τὸν
δεύτερον καὶ εἰς τὸν τρίτον καὶ εἰς τὸν τέταρτον καὶ εἰς τὸν ἑξκαιδέκατον καὶ εἰς
τὸν πεντεκαιδέκατον καὶ εἰς τὸν τεσσαρισκαιδέκατον καὶ εἰς τὸν τρισκαιδέκα-
305    τον, ἵνα καὶ μέχρι τεσσάρων ἀνδρῶν μεριζομένου τοῦ βάθους ἤτοι τοῦ πάχους
τῆς ἀκίας ἐν δυνάμει ἐστὶ καὶ ἡ οὐρὰ αὐτῆς καὶ τὸ μέτωπον. τοὺς δὲ λοιπούς,
τοὺς ὑποδεεστέρους, ἐν τῷ μέσῳ αὐτῆς τάξαι.

73. Τούτους δὲ τοὺς ις′ ὀνομάσαι ἕνα παρ᾽ ἕνα ἀπὸ πρίμων καὶ σεκούνδων
ἤτοι πρωτοστατῶν καὶ ἐπιστατῶν. τοὺς δὲ δύο ἐν αὐτοῖς διωνύμους εἶναι, καὶ
310    τὸν μὲν πρῶτον καλεῖσθαι λοχαγὸν καὶ πρῖμον ἤγουν πρωτοστάτην, τὸν δὲ
δεύτερον δεκάρχην καὶ σεκοῦνδον ἤγουν ἐπιστάτην, καὶ ἑξῆς ὁμοίως ὥστε εἶναι
τὸν ὅλον στίχον ἐκ πρωτοστατῶν καὶ ἐπιστατῶν συγκείμενος.

74. Ἵνα δὲ καὶ ἄρχεσθαι εὐχερῶς δύνανται καὶ ἁρμοδίως συνδιάγειν ἀλλήλοις, κάλλιόν ἐστι μᾶλλον τούτους εἰς δύο μόνα κοντουβέρνια γίνεσθαι, ἵνα οἱ
315    μὲν πρῖμοι ἤγουν οἱ πρωτοστάται εἰσὶ μετὰ τοῦ λοχαγοῦ, οἱ δὲ σεκοῦνδοι ἤγουν
ἐπιστάται μετὰ τοῦ δεκάρχου· οὕτω μέντοι ὥστε, κἂν ἐν τῇ διαγωγῇ | διήρηνται,    294ᵛ
ἀλλ᾽ οὖν ἐν τῇ τάξει ἡνωμένοι ὄντες, οἱ δεκαὲξ τῇ βουλῇ καὶ γνώμῃ τοῦ λοχαγοῦ πείθονται· ἐντεῦθεν γὰρ καὶ ἡ τάξις φυλάττεται καὶ εὐκόλως ἄρχεσθαι
δύνανται.

---

300 ις′ MABE δεκαὲξ W | τοὺς ci. Va om. codd.    301 τῆς…ἤτοι MW om. ABE | ad λόχου
scr. mg. του ορδινου W    302 αὐτοὺς MABE αὐτοῖς W    303 ἑξκαιδέκατον AE ις′ B
ἐνκαιδέκατον MW    304 τεσσαρισκαιδέκατον MWAE ιδ′ B    304–305 τρισκαιδέκατον
MWAE ιγ′ B    305 μέχρι MWAB μέχρι τῶν E    306 ἐστὶ καὶ MA ἐστὶν καὶ W ὑπάρχη BE
308 ις′ MWBE δεκαὲξ A    309 δύο MWAB β′ E | διωνύμους εἶναι MW ἀπὸ δύο (β′ BE)
ἔχειν ὀνομάτων ABE    310 πρῖμον ἤγουν MW om. ABE    311 σεκοῦνδον ἤγουν MW om.
ABE | καὶ²…ὁμοίως MW om. ABE    313 εὐχερῶς MW εὐκόλως ABE | δύνανται MWA
δύνανται BE | ἁρμοδίως MW ἁρμοζόντως ABE    314 ἐστι MAB ἐστιν WE | δύο μόνα MWA
β′ μόνα B β′ μόνα E | κοντουβέρνια AE κουτουβέρνια MW κουντουβέρνια B
315 πρῖμοι…οἱ¹ MW om. ABE | εἰσὶ MW ὦσι ABE | τοῦ MWAE om. B | σεκοῦνδοι ἤγουν
MW om. ABE    316 οὕτω…ὥστε MW om. ABE | κἂν MW κἂν γὰρ ABE | διήρηνται Va
διείρηνται MW διηρημένοι εἰσὶν AB διαιρημένοι εἰσὶν E scr. mg. ηγουν καν εν τη
συναναστροφῇ διακεχωρισμενοι ωσιν W    317 τάξει MW παρατάξει ABE | δεκαὲξ MAE ις′
WB | καὶ MWBE καὶ τῇ A    318 φυλάττεται MWA φυλάσσεται BE    319 δύνανται MWA
δύνωνται BE

take their place in the battle line and appoint courageous and competent men, called group leaders, over them.

72. Of these sixteen, station the eight most competent in the front and in the rear of the file or lochos—the ancients called the file of sixteen men a lochos[15]—station them in positions one, two, three, four; and sixteen, fifteen, fourteen, thirteen. In this way, even if the depth or thickness of the file is reduced to four, its front and rear will still be strong. Line up the remaining men, the weaker ones, in the middle of the file.

73. Designate these sixteen men one by one as primoi or sekoundoi or protostatai and epistatai. Two should bear a double designation, that is, call the first one leader and primos or protostates, call the second dekarch and sekoundos or epistates. Likewise, in due order, the whole row will be made up of protostatai or epistatai.

74. To make it easier to command them and get them to operate more harmoniously with one another, it is really better to arrange them in two squads. The primoi or protostatai go with the group leader and the sekoundoi or epistatai with the dekarch. In this manner, even though they are separated by this arrangement, still these sixteen soldiers are united in formation and are subject to the decisions and will of the group leader. As a result, good order is maintained and the men can be easily commanded.

*15. "Lochos" originally meant an ambush, a group of bandits. Their chief, "lochagos," is here translated as group leader.

320    75. Χρήσιμον δέ ἐστιν, ἐάν ἐστι δυνατόν, μὴ μόνον κατὰ ποιότητα ἤγουν
εὐψυχίαν ὀρδινεύειν τοὺς ις΄ καθ᾽ ἑκάστην ἀκίαν τῶν σκουτάτων, ἀλλὰ καὶ κατὰ
ἡλικίαν, ἵνα οἱ μακρότεροι ἔμπροσθεν τασσόμενοι εὐτακτοτέραν τὴν παράταξιν
ἀποδείξωσιν. εἰ δὲ μὴ ἀπαντᾷ πρὸς ἡλικίαν καὶ ἀνδρείαν, πάντως, ὡς εἴπομεν,
τοὺς εὐψυχοτέρους καὶ γενναιοτέρους ἑκάστης ἀκίας δέον ἐστὶν εἰς τοὺς
325    ἔμπροσθεν καὶ ὄπισθεν τόπους τάσσεσθαι, τοὺς δὲ ὑποδεεστέρους εἰς τὸ μέσον
αὐτῶν, καθ᾽ ὃν εἰρήκαμεν τρόπον.

76. Ὥστε οὖν διὰ τοῦτο καὶ οἱ ἀρχαῖοι ἀπὸ ις΄ ἀνδρῶν πεζῶν τὸ βάθος τῶν
ἀκιῶν ἤτοι τῶν ὀρδίνων ὥρισαν ἐν ταῖς μάχαις, ἐπειδὴ καὶ τὸ μέτρον ἀρκοῦν
ἐστιν, ὅπερ ὑπερβαίνειν οὐ χρή. καὶ ἐν ταῖς χρείαις εὐτάκτως καὶ συντόμως
330    μερίζεται καὶ λεπτύνεται μέχρις ἑνὸς ἀνδρός. τοσαῦτα μὲν οὖν καὶ περὶ τῆς τοῦ
στρατοῦ διαιρέσεώς τε καὶ καταστάσεως καὶ τῶν ἐπὶ τούτοις τεταγμένων ἀρχόν-
των μικρῶν τε καὶ μεγάλων διωρισάμεθα. |

320 ἐστι δυνατόν MW ἐνδέχεται ABE    320–321 ποιότητα…εὐψυχίαν MW ἀνδρίαν ABE
scr. mg. ευτολμιαν W    321 καθ᾽…σκουτάτων MW om. ABE | ἀκίαν WABE ἀκιῶν M
322 εὐτακτοτέραν Va εὐτακτωτέραν MW (corr. ω in ο W) φοβερωτέραν AE φοβεροτέραν B
323 ἀπαντᾷ πρὸς MW ἐνδέχεται καὶ κατὰ ABE | καὶ ἀνδρείαν MW καὶ κατὰ ἀνδρίαν τούτους
τάσσεσθαι ABE    324 εὐψυχοτέρους MW προθυμοτέρους ABE | δέον ἐστὶν MW om. ABE
325 τάσσεσθαι MW om. ABE    326 εἰρήκαμεν τρόπον MW trsp. ABE    327 ὥστε…τοῦτο
MW διὰ τοῦτο δὲ ABE | ις΄ MABE δεκαὲξ W    327–328 τῶν…ἤτοι MW om. ABE
328 ὥρισαν MW ὡρίσαντο ABE | ἐν…μάχαις MW om. ABE    329 ὑπερβαίνειν MWA
βαίνειν BE | εὐτάκτως MWBE συμμέτρως A | καὶ συντόμως MW om. ABE    331 τούτων M
τούτω WBE τοῦτο A

75. It is useful, when possible, to arrange the sixteen men in each file of heavy infantry not only according to their qualifications and good attitudes but also according to stature. By stationing the taller men in front, the whole battle line will look much better ordered. But if it cannot be done according to stature and bravery, then certainly it is necessary, as we have said, to station the more motivated and valiant men of each file in the front and rear positions, with the weaker ones in the middle, in the manner we have sketched.

76. For this reason, therefore, the ancients fixed the depth of the infantry files or rows in combat at sixteen men. This provides an adequate number of troops that should not be exceeded, and in emergencies it can be divided quickly and in an orderly fashion and reduced to only one man. These, therefore, are what we have determined concerning the division of the army and the assignment of both higher and lower ranking officers to be lined up with it.

## Περὶ ὅπλων

1. Κελεύομεν τοίνυν τῇ ὑμῶν ἐνδοξότητι τῶν εἰς τοὺς πολέμους συντεινόν-
των ὅπλων τε καὶ ἀποσκευῶν πεζικῇ τε καὶ καβαλλαρικῇ στρατιᾷ φροντίσαι,
5 ὥστε ταῦτα διαμένειν ἀδιάληπτα καὶ πρὸς τὴν κατεπείγουσαν τῷ καιρῷ χρείαν
ἕτοιμα, τοῦτο δὲ ποιεῖν—τὸ μὲν διά σου αὐτοῦ, τὸ δὲ διὰ τῶν ὑπό σε ἀρχόντων
μικρῶν καὶ μεγάλων—εἰς ὅπλισιν καὶ ὑπηρεσίαν τοῦ ὑπὸ τὸ σὸν θέμα μαχίμου
στρατοῦ.

2. Οἷον τοξάρια μετὰ θηκαρίων αὐτῶν, σαγίττας μετὰ κουκούρων, σπαθία
10 ἠκονημένα καὶ σεσαμιωμένα, σκουτάρια καὶ ἕτερα σκουτάρια μεγάλα, ἅπερ
λέγονται θυρεοί, ἕτερα σκουταρίσκια τῶν πεζῶν τά ποτε λεγόμενα πέλται,
ἕτερα σκουτάρια σιδηρᾶ, στρογγύλα, σεσαμιωμένα, κοντάρια μικρά, ὀκτάπηχα
—ἦσαν δέ ποτε Ῥωμαίοις καὶ Μακεδόσι κοντάρια ἄχρι πηχῶν δεκαὲξ ἅπερ ἡ
νῦν χρεία οὐ καλεῖ, τὸ γὰρ κατὰ τὴν ἑκάστου τῶν μεταχειριζομένων δύναμιν
15 ὅπλον σύμμετρόν τε καὶ χρήσιμον—ῥικτάρια, τζικούρια καὶ ἕτερα τζικούρια
ἀμφίστομα, ἐφ' ἓν μέρος οἱονεὶ σπαθίον, ἐπὶ δὲ τὸ ἕτερον οἷον ξίφος κονταρίου,
μετὰ θηκαρίων αὐτῶν δερματίνων καὶ βασταγίων, παραμήρια, μαχαίρας μεγάλας μονοστόμους.

3. Λωρίκια μέχρι στραγάλου, ἀνασυρόμενα διὰ λωρίων καὶ κρικελλίων, μετὰ
20 τῶν θηκαρίων αὐτῶν δερματίνων καί, εἰ δυνατόν, πάντα ἀλυσιδωτά, εἰ δὲ μήγε,
τινὰ αὐτῶν καὶ διὰ κερατίνης ὕλης ἢ βουβαλείων καταξήρων δερμάτων· ἐπιλω-
ρικὰ ἱμάτια, κλιβάνια σιδηρᾶ ἢ καὶ ἐξ ἑτέρας ὕλης, ὡς εἴρηται, κασσίδας τελείας,

---

M W A V (mut.) B E    Va    PG 107:717

9–30 Cf. *Strat.*, 1.2.    12–15 Cf. Anon. Strat., 16.31–39.

1 πολεμικῶν παρασκευῶν MWA om. BE | ε′ MWA om. BE    3 ὑμῶν MWAE ἡμῶν B
4 καί² MWBE καὶ τῇ A    5 τῶ καιρῶ MW τοῦ καιροῦ ABE    6 τοῦτο MWAB τοῦ E
9 θηκαρίων MWAE θηκάρια B    11 σκουταρίσκια MWA σκουτάρια BE    13 ἦσαν MWAB
ἢ ἦσαν E | δεκαὲξ M δέκα καὶ ἒξ W ις′ ABE    14 οὐ καλεῖ MW οὐκ ἀπαιτεῖ ABE    15
ῥικτάρια MW ῥιπτάρια ABE | καὶ MWA om. BE    16 ἓν μέρος MWA ἑνὸς μέρους BE |
σπαθίον ABE σπαθίου MW    17 μετὰ MWA μετὰ τῶν BE    19 στραγάλου MW
ἀστραγάλου ABE    21 καὶ…ὕλης MW ἐκ κεράτων ABE | βουβαλείων Va βουβαλίων MW
βουβαλικῶν ABE | καταξήρων δερμάτων MW trsp. ABE

# PREPARATION FOR WAR, CONSTITUTION V

## About Weapons

1. Now then, we command Your Excellency to turn your attention to the weapons you must employ in war, as well as to the equipment for the infantry and the cavalry forces.[1] There should be a steady supply of them and they should be ready at hand for whatever pressing needs may arise. You are to see to the armament and service of the combat troops from your theme, some of it by yourself and some by your subordinate officers, higher and lower in rank.

2. Such are bows with their carrying cases, arrows with their quivers, swords sharpened and brightly shining, regular shields as well as the larger ones called thyreoi, other small shields, formerly called peltasts, for the foot soldiers, other shields of iron, round and well polished. <They should have> small spears eight pecheis long. At one time, though, the Romans and the Macedonians had spears up to sixteen pecheis long, but those are not called for in the present circumstances.[2] A weapon is appropriate and serviceable if it matches the strength of the person who is to wield it. Also small throwing spears, regular axes as well as double-bladed axes, like a sword on one side and like the point of a spear on the other, together with their leather carrying cases and other packs. Daggers. Large, single-bladed swords.

3. Body armor down to the ankles that can be caught up with straps and rings, as well as leather carrying cases for them. If possible, the armor should be made completely of chain mail, but if not, some of it may be of horn or dry cowhide. Surcoats over the armor. Breastplates of iron or of some other material, as mentioned. Full helmets, foot coverings, and gauntlets of iron or some other

---

1. See also *Strat.* 1.2. On weapons and armament, see T. Kolias, *Byzantinische Waffen* (Vienna, 1988).

2. Eight pecheis is about 3.74 m; sixteen comes to 7.48 m. Cf. also SyrMag 16.31–39.

ποδόψελλα, χειρόψελλα σιδηρὰ ἢ καὶ ἐξ ἑτέρας ὕλης, διὰ τοὺς μὴ ἔχοντας
περιτραχήλια ἀλυσιδωτὰ σιδηρά, ἐνδεδυμένα ἔσωθεν ἀπὸ κεντούκλου καὶ
25 ἔξωθεν δὲ ἀπὸ ρινοῦ, νευρικὰ τὰ ἀπὸ κεντούκλων διπλῶν γινόμενα καὶ αὐτὰ
ἀντὶ λωρικίων τοῖς μὴ ἔχουσι σιδηρά, κέντουκλα φαρδέα, ἐνδύοντα τὸν στρατιώτην μετὰ τῶν ὅπλων, σωληνάρια μετὰ μικρῶν σαγιττῶν καὶ κουκούρων αὐτῶν,
σφενδόβολα, σελλοπούγγια μεγάλα, πυρέκβολα καὶ ἴσκας, λωρόσοκκα, πέδη-
κλα σεληναῖα σιδηρᾶ μετὰ καρφίων αὐτῶν, ρινία, σουβλία, προμετώπια | ἵππων,    296ᵛ
30 στηθάρια ἵππων ἢ σιδηρᾶ ἢ ἀπὸ κεντούκλων, περιτραχήλια ἵππων ὁμοίως.

4. Φλάμουλα μεγάλα, φλαμουλίσκια τῶν κονταρίων, βάνδα διαφόρως
βεβαμμένα, βούκινα μικρὰ καὶ μεγάλα, δρέπανα, ἀξίνας, φαλκίδια, πελέκια,
σκέπαρνα, τριβόλους ἀναδεδεμένας σφηκώμασι δεδεμένοις εἰς ἥλους τελείους.

5. Ἁμάξας εὐσταλεῖς, φερούσας ἑτοίμως τὴν ἀναγκαίαν εἰς χρείαν ἀποσκευ-
35 ήν, οἷον τά τε εἰρημένα ἔργα, καὶ χειρομύλια καὶ πριόνια καὶ ὄρυγας καὶ σφύρας,
πτυάρια, κοφίνους, κιλίκια, καὶ εἴ τι ἄλλο πρὸς φοσσάτου ἔξωθεν φυλακὴν καὶ
περιβολὴν ἐπινοηθείη τῷ στρατηγῷ δι' ἐλαφροτέρας ὕλης μεμηχανημένον.

6. Ἑτέρας ἁμάξας ἐχούσας τοξοβολίστρας, μαγγανικὰ ἀλακάτια ἑκατέρωθεν
στρεφόμενα, βαλιστάριους ἐμπείρους ἤτοι μαγγαναρίους λεπτουργούς, χαλκεῖς
40 μετὰ τῶν ἐργαλείων αὐτῶν, ἑτέρας ἁμάξας λόγῳ ἀρμαμέντου, ἑτέρας ἁμάξας
τὰς φερούσας διατροφὰς καὶ τὰ ἐκ περισσοῦ ἄρματα, ὅσα ἡ χρεία καλεῖ, καὶ ἔτι
ὑποζύγια καὶ ἵππους, σαγμάρια, σκευοφόρα καὶ αὐτὰ καὶ τὰ ἄλλα πάντα ὄργανα, ὅσα ἡ συνήθεια τοῦ φοσσάτου παρακελεύεται.

7. Πρὸς δὲ πολιορκίας καὶ μαγγανικὰ διάφορα καὶ σκάλας ξυλίνας συστελ-
45 λομένας καὶ ἕτερα μηχανικὰ ὄργανα, ὅσα ἐπινοήσεις.

---

42 ad πάντα inc. V

---

23  ποδόψελλα A ποδόψελα MW ποδοψέλλια BE | χειρόψελλα Va χειρόψελα MW om. ABE
24  ἔσωθεν MW ἔσωθεν μὲν ABE | κεντούκλου ABE ἐρίου MW    25  δὲ ἀπὸ ABE om. MW |
ρινοῦ De λίνου codd. | κεντούκλων διπλῶν ABE κενδούκλων MW    26 κέντουκλα ABE
κένδουκλα MW    28 πυρέκβολα MA παρέκβολα BE | ἴσκας MWA ἴσακας BE    29 σουβλία
ABE σουγλία MW    30 ἢ σιδηρᾶ WABE om. M | κεντούκλων ABE κενδούκλων MW
32 πελέκια MWAB πελέκας E    34  εὐσταλεῖς MW ἐλαφρὰς ABE scr. mg. ἐλαφρας ευκολως
συντιθεμενας W    35 χειρομύλια MW χειρόμυλα ABE | ὄρυγας MW ὀρύγια ABE
37 ἐπινοηθείη MW ἐπινοηθῇ ABE    38 τοξοβολίστρας MW τοξοβαλλίστρας ABE | ἀλα-
κάτια MW ἡλακάτια ABE    39 βαλιστάριους MW τοξοβαλλίστας ABE | ἤτοι MW om. ABE
40 λόγῳ ABE λόγου MW    42 ad ὑποζύγια scr. mg. μουλικά W | σκευοφόρα MWA
σκευοφόρια BE    42–43 ὄργανα MW ἔργα AVBE

material. Let those who do not have neck pieces of iron chain mail be protected by those made of quilted material on the inside and leather on the outside. Men who do not have iron body armor should have in its place an outer garment made of two layers of quilted material, broad quilting, that the soldier puts on with his weapons. Also arrow guides with short arrows and their quivers.[3] Slings as well, large saddlebags, flint and tinder, lasso with thong, hobble, crescent-shaped iron horseshoes with their nails, small files and awls, armor for the heads of the horses, breastplates of iron or quilting for the horses, and similar coverings for their necks.

4. Large pennants, as well as smaller ones for the lances, flags in various colors, large and small trumpets, sickles, axes, scythes, hatchets, adzes, caltrops tied together with cords and hardened into very sharp points.

5. Light wagons ready to transport the essential equipment that will be needed, such as the items mentioned. Also hand mills, saws, picks, hammers, shovels, baskets, goatskin matting, and whatever else the commander might think of getting ready, using lighter materials, to protect the encampment and its perimeter from the outside.

6. Other wagons carrying bow ballistai, windlass artillery called alakatia that swivel in both directions, experienced artillery crews, that is, carpenters specialized in artillery, and metal workers with their equipment.[4] Some wagons for the field armory. Others will transport food as well as the extra weapons that might be needed. Pack animals, moreover, and horses, other beasts of burden to bear equipment and all the other implements that are usually required for an army on campaign.

7. Diverse machines for siege warfare, wooden ladders ready for action, and as many other mechanical devices as you will think of.

---

3. Wooden half-tubes (σωληνάρια), through which small arrows were shot. It is difficult to describe them more precisely. See Kolias, *Waffen*, 239–253; G. Dennis, "Flies, Mice, and the Byzantine Crossbow," *BMGS* 7 (1981): 1–5; D. Nishimura, "Crossbows, Arrow-guides, and the *Solenarion*," *Byzantion* 58 (1988): 22–36.

4. See Dennis, "Byzantine Heavy Artillery."

8. Εἰ δὲ πρὸς ποταμοὺς ἢ λίμνας καὶ ναυκέλλια ἤγουν πλοῖα μικρὰ ἢ ἀπὸ βυρσῶν κατεσκευασμένα ἢ κατὰ φύσιν φροντίσεις δὲ καὶ ἑτοιμάσεις καὶ τὰς λεγομένας τέντας καὶ ἀτεγίας μετὰ τῆς αὐτῶν ἐξοπλίσεως, ἐν αἷς καὶ ὑετῶν καὶ καυμάτων, ὅτε χρεία, ἕξεις ἐλευθερίαν.

50    9. Τοῖς δὲ ναυμάχοις στρατηγοῖς καὶ ναῦς παρασκευάζειν ἐξωπλισμένας, τὰς μὲν μαχίμους, τὰς δὲ ἱππαγωγούς, τὰς δὲ σκευοφόρους, ἅμα τῇ περὶ αὐτὰς ἁπάσῃ χρειώδει πανοπλίᾳ καὶ ἀποσκευῇ παρακελευόμεθα.

10. Τῶν δὲ ἀπηριθμημένων σοι παρασκευῶν ἀνωτέρω, τῶν καὶ ὀφειλόντων τινῶν μὲν παρά σου, τινῶν δὲ παρὰ τῶν ὑπό σε ἀρχόντων καὶ στρατιωτῶν 55    πορίζεσθαι, τὰ μὲν ὅπλα ἕξεις εἰς ἄμυναν τῶν πολεμίων, τὰ δὲ εἰς φυλακὴν τῶν μαχομένων στρατιωτῶν, τὰ δὲ εἰς τὴν ἄλλην χρείαν αὐτῶν καὶ ὑπηρεσίαν.

11. Καὶ μάλιστα τῶν πολεμικῶν ὅπλων ἐπιμελήσῃ, ὡς ἂν διαφυλάττωνται πάντοτε λαμπρὰ καὶ τεθηγμένα πρὸς τὴν κατάπληξιν τῶν πολεμίων. ταῦτα πάντα | προευτρεπίσεις, ἵνα ἐν ἑτοίμῳ εἰσὶν εἰς χρείαν τοῖς ὑπὲρ ἀρετῆς χεῖρας    297
60    ὁπλίζουσι κατὰ τῶν πολεμίων, καὶ μὴ τὸν παρατάξεως καιρὸν παρασκευῆς καιρὸν ἀναγκάζῃ ποιεῖσθαι. ταῦτα δὲ καὶ ἄλλα ὅσα ἡμῖν παραλέλειπται διὰ λήθην ἐξ ἀνάγκης ὀφείλεις παρασκευάζειν. εἰ δέ τι πλέον εἰς ὅπλων παρασκευὴν ἐπινοήσεις τῷ Θεῷ χάρις καὶ τῇ σῇ ἀγχινοίᾳ.

12. Πρὸ δὲ πάντων καὶ μετὰ πάντων φόβον Θεοῦ καὶ διάνοιαν ὀξεῖαν καὶ 65    σπουδαίαν γνώμην ἐν παντὶ ἔχειν καιρῷ καὶ τόπῳ καὶ πράγματι, καὶ πρὸς ἅπαντα ἕτοιμον εἶναι παρακελευόμεθα.

---

59–61 Cf. γ΄.3–5.

---

47 κατεσκευασμένα MWA κατασκευασμένα VBE | ἢ…φύσιν MWVBE om. A    48 τέντας MW τένδας AVBE | ἐν αἷς MW αἵτινες AVBE | ὑετῶν MW βροχὰς AVBE    49 καυμάτων… ἐλευθερίαν MW καύματα ἀπαντήσουσιν AVBE    50 ad ναυμάχοις scr. mg. τοις ἐν πλοιοις μαχομενοις W ad 50–51 τὰς μὲν scr. mg. προς το μαχεσθαι επιτηδειας W    51 ad ἱππαγωγούς scr. mg. ιππους φερους<ας> W | ad σκευοφόρους scr. mg. τα σκευη και τας χρειας φερουσας W    53 ἀπηριθμημένων MWA ἀπαριθμημένων VBE | ὀφειλόντων MW ὀφειλουσῶν AVBE    58 τεθηγμένα MW ἠκονημένα AVBE | τὴν MW om. AVBE    59 εἰσὶν MWA ὦσιν VBE    59–60 τοῖς…πολεμίων MW τῶν κατὰ τῶν πολεμίων ἀγωνιζομένων AVBE    60–61 παρατάξεως…καιρὸν MW καιρὸν τῆς παρατάξεως καιρὸν ἑτοιμασίας καὶ παρασκευῆς A καιρὸν ἑτοιμασίας καὶ παρασκευῆς VBE    61 ταῦτα MWAVE ταύτας B | ἄλλα MW om. AVBE    61–62 παραλέλειπται…λήθην MW trsp. AVBE    63 ἀγχινοίᾳ MW φρονήσει AVBE scr. mg. ὀξύτητι τῆς διανοιας W    64 πάντων[1] MWVBE πάντα A | πάντων[2] MW πάντα AVBE | θεοῦ MW θεοῦ ἔχειν AVBE    65 ἔχειν MW om. AVBE

8. If you come to rivers or lakes, you will take care to get ready the skiffs or small boats, constructed either of leather hides or of ordinary materials, as well as what we call tents and shelters with their equipment in which, when necessary, you will find relief from rain and heat.[5]

9. We command that those generals assigned to fighting at sea are to prepare fully armed ships, some for combat, others to transport horses, and others to transport equipment, together with all their required weaponry and equipment.[6]

10. Of all the preparatory tasks enumerated above some are to be carried out directly by you and others by the officers and soldiers under your command. You will see to weapons that ward off the enemy and others that protect the troops in battle, as well as those that cover their other needs and services.

11. Devote particular attention to the weapons needed in battle. Make sure that they are always maintained polished and sharpened, so as to terrify the enemy. You will prepare all these things beforehand so they will be ready for use by those who, because of their valor, engage the enemy in close combat. By so doing, you will not be forced to turn the time of taking battle stations into a time of preparation.[7] The other matters that we may have omitted, out of forgetfulness, must necessarily be your responsibility. And if you think of something more regarding the preparation of weapons, thanks be to God and your own shrewdness.

12. We order you, above all and with all, to have the fear of God, a sharp mind, and serious intent in every time, place, and affair, as well as to be ready for every eventuality.

5. Tent: generally written as τέντα in **MW**, and in modern Greek, instead of the variant τένδα. The *Suda* (T 307) defines it as οἰκία ἐκ λίνων, "a house [made] of linen."

6. See Const. 19 on naval warfare.

7. Cf. Const. 3, n. 1.

13. Περὶ μὲν οὖν τῆς τῶν ὅπλων παρασκευῆς, ὦ στρατηγέ, καθόσον ἡμῖν τέως ἐχωρήγησεν ἡ μνήμη, ὑπεθέμεθα τῇ σῇ ἐνδοξότητι· ἑξῆς δὲ περὶ μὲν πεζικῆς καὶ συμμίκτου τάξεως ὕστερον ἐροῦμεν. νῦν δὲ ὅπως ὁπλίσῃς τὸν 70 καθένα ἄνδρα καβαλλάριον στρατιώτην ἔν τε ταῖς γυμνασίαις καὶ τὸ τέλειον ἐν καιρῷ πολέμου, καὶ ὅποια κατὰ τὸ ἀναγκαῖον εἴδη φέρειν παρασκευάσεις ἤδη ἐροῦμεν.

---

67 στρατηγέ MW στρατηγὲ ὑπερεθέμεθα τῇ σῇ ἐνδοξότητι AVBE    68 ἐχωρήγησεν...
μνήμῃ MW trsp. AVBE | τῇ...ἐνδοξότητι MW om. AVBE    69 τάξεως MWA παρατάξεως
VBE    69–70 τὸν καθένα MW ἕκαστον AVBE    70 τέλειον MAVBE τέλεον W
71–72 παρασκευάσεις...ἐροῦμεν MWA om. VBE

13. Therefore, O general, we have set before Your Excellency everything that our memory has provided for us about the preparation of weapons. Subsequently, we will treat of infantry and mixed formations. But for now we shall speak about how you are to arm each mounted soldier, both for drill and, ultimately, for time of battle, and the necessary equipment you should prepare for them to carry.

# ΠΟΛΕΜΙΚΩΝ ΠΑΡΑΣΚΕΥΩΝ ΔΙΑΤΑΞΙΣ ϛ′

## Περὶ ὁπλίσεως καβαλλαρίων καὶ πεζῶν

1. Δεῖ τοίνυν ὁπλισθῆναι τοὺς στρατιώτας διὰ τῶν ἰδίων αὐτῶν ἀρχόντων
καὶ τὰ ἐπιτήδεια <ἐν> τῷ καιρῷ εἴτε παραχειμαδίου εἴτε φοσσάτου παρασκευ-
5 άζεσθαι, τὰ πρὸς <τὰς> ἀναγκαίας χρείας τῆς ἐκστρατείας, καὶ ἔχειν <αὐτὰ>
πάντας ἀναλόγως ἄρχοντάς τε καὶ ἀρχομένους, πρὸς τὴν ἑκάστου ποιότητά τε
καὶ δύναμιν, καὶ μάλιστα τοὺς ἄρχοντας αὐτῶν ἀπό τε τουρμάρχου καὶ μέχρι
κεντάρχου καὶ τετράρχου καὶ κατεξαίρετον σεαυτὸν καὶ τὴν ὑπό σε προέλευσιν.
2. Ἔχειν δὲ αὐτοὺς δεῖν τὸν καθένα ἄνδρα ὅπλισιν τοιαύτην· ζάβας τελείας
10 μέχρι τοῦ ἀστραγάλου, ἀνασυρομένας δὲ διὰ λωρίων καὶ κρικελλίων, μετὰ τῶν
θηκαρίων αὐτῶν. ἔχειν δὲ καὶ κασσίδας σιδηρᾶς, στιλπνάς, διὰ παντὸς ἐχούσας
ἄνωθεν εἰς τὰς κορυφὰς τουφία μικρά. τοξάρια δὲ ἕκαστον κατὰ τὴν ἰδίαν ἰσχὺν
καὶ οὐχ ὑπὲρ αὐτήν, μᾶλλον δὲ καὶ ἁπαλώτερα, ἔχοντα θηκάρια πλατέα, ἵνα ἐν
καιρῷ δυνατόν ἐστι τεταμένα χωρεῖν τὰ τοξάρια ἐν αὐτοῖς. ἔχειν δὲ καὶ κόρδας
15 ἐκ περισσοῦ ἐν τοῖς πουγγίοις αὐτῶν, κούκουρα μετὰ σαγιττῶν καὶ | σκεπασμά-   297ᵛ
των αὐτῶν ἐπιτήδεια, χωροῦντα ἀπὸ λ′ ἢ μ′ σαγιττῶν. ἐν δὲ τοῖς τοξοζωνίοις
ῥινία καὶ σουβλία. ἔχειν δὲ καὶ κοντάρια καβαλλαρικὰ μικρά, ἔχοντα λωρία
κατὰ τὸ μέσον, μετὰ φλαμούλων. ἔχειν δὲ καὶ σπαθία ἀποκρεμάμενα τῶν ὤμων
αὐτῶν κατὰ τὴν Ῥωμαϊκὴν τάξιν, καὶ ἕτερα παραμήρια ἤτοι μαχαίρας διεζωσμέ-
20 νους.

---

M W A V B E   Va   PG 107:721

3–106 *Strat.*, 1.2.

---

1 διαταξις MWA τάξις VBE | ϛ′ MWVBE ἕκτη A   3 αὐτῶν MWVBE om. A   4 ἐν ci. Va
om. codd.   5 τὰς ci. Va om. codd. | ἐκστρατείας MWA ἐγκρατείας VBE   5–6 αὐτὰ πάντας
Va ἅπαντας codd.   9 αὐτοὺς MW om. AVBE | καθένα MW ἕκαστον AVBE   10 δὲ MW
om. AVBE   11 στιλπνάς MW λαμπρὰς A καὶ λαμπρὰς VBE | διὰ παντὸς MW om. AVBE
14 ἐστι MA ἐστιν W ἢ VBE | τεταμένα AVE τεταγμένα MBW | αὐτοῖς AVBE ἑαυτοῖς MW
16 ἐπιτήδεια MWA ἐπιτηδείων VBE | λ′ MWVBE τριάκοντα A | μ′ MW τεσσαράκοντα
AVBE   17 σουβλία AVBE σουγλία MW | δὲ MWA τε VBE | καβαλλαρικὰ μικρά MWA
trsp. VBE

# PREPARATION FOR WAR, CONSTITUTION VI

## About Armament for the Cavalry and the Infantry

1. Now then, it is necessary for the soldiers to receive their armament from their own officers.[1] While in winter quarters or in camp they are to be provided with the proper equipment they will need on campaign. All the soldiers, both officers and enlisted men, should have equipment corresponding to their rank and strength, particularly the officers from tourmarch to kentarch and tetrarch, with special attention to yourself and the troops marching along with you.

2. Each man should have the following armament. Full coats of mail reaching to their ankles, fastened with thongs and rings, along with their carrying cases. They should also have iron helmets, polished and always with small plumes on their crests. Each man should have a bow suited to his own strength and not above it, more indeed on the weaker side, and cases broad enough so that, when necessary, the strung bows can fit in them. They should also have spare bow strings in their saddle bags, suitable quivers, too, with their covers, holding about thirty or forty arrows. Small files and awls in their baldrics. They should also have short cavalry lances with small thongs in the middle of the shaft and with pennons. In addition, they should have swords hanging from their shoulders, in the Roman manner, as well as daggers or large knives on their belts.[2]

---

1. The first 19 sections derive from *Strat.* 1.2. On weaponry, see Kolias, *Byzantinische Waffen.*

2. Kolias, 133–160. In the 'Roman manner' the soldier carried his sword on his left side.

3. Ὅσοι δὲ μὴ οἴδασι τοξεύειν νεώτεροι, ἐχέτωσαν κοντάρια μετὰ σκουταρίων τελείων· εἰ δὲ καὶ χειρομάνικα σιδηρᾶ, ἃ λέγεται χειρόψελλα, τινὲς κτήσωνται, λίαν χρήσιμον. ἔχειν δὲ καὶ μικρὰ τουφία κατὰ τῶν ὀπισθελλινῶν τῶν ἵππων καὶ φλάμουλα μικρὰ ἐπάνω τῶν ζαβῶν κατὰ τῶν ὤμων. ὅσον γάρ ἐστιν
25 εὔσχημος ἐν τῇ ὁπλίσει αὐτοῦ ὁ στρατιώτης, τοσοῦτον καὶ αὐτῷ προθυμία προσγίνεται καὶ τοῖς ἐχθροῖς δειλία.

4. Εἰ δυνατὸν δὲ καὶ θώρακας ἔχειν, οἵτινες καλοῦνται νῦν κλιβάνια, καὶ αὐτὰ στιλπνὰ καὶ λαμπρά· καὶ περικνημῖδας, ἅτινα λέγεται νῦν ποδόψελλα, καὶ πτερνιστῆρας ἐνίοτε. ἔχειν δὲ καὶ ἐπιλώρικα, ὅτε χρεία, ἐπενδυόμενα.

30 5. Πάντας δὲ τοὺς νεωτέρους Ῥωμαίους ἄχρι μ´ ἐτῶν ἀναγκάζεσθαι, εἴτε κατὰ λόγον οἴδασι τοξεῦσαι, εἴτε καὶ μετρίως, τοῦ πάντως τοξοφάρετρα φορεῖν. τῆς γὰρ τοξείας παντελῶς ἀμεληθείσης καὶ διαπεσούσης ἐν τοῖς Ῥωμαίοις τὰ πολλὰ νῦν εἴωθε σφάλματα γίνεσθαι.

6. Ἔχειν δὲ καὶ κοντάρια δύο, ἵνα τοῦ ἑνός, ὡς εἰκός, ἀστοχοῦντος ἔχῃ τὸ
35 ἄλλο εἰς χρῆσιν. τοὺς δὲ ἀπειροτέρους ἁπαλώτερα ἔχειν τοξάρια· κἂν γὰρ οὐκ οἴδασι τοξεύειν, τῷ χρόνῳ ἐπιτηδεύουσι μαθεῖν, ὅπερ τῶν ἀναγκαίων ἐστίν.

7. Εἰ δὲ δυνατόν, καὶ ἀκόντια ἤτοι ρικτάρια ἔχειν ἕως δύο, ἵνα ἐν καιρῷ καὶ ἀκοντίσοι προχείρως κατὰ τοῦ πολεμίου, καὶ τὸν μὲν ἱππέα στρατιώτην οὕτως ὁπλίσεις.

40 8. Τοὺς δὲ ἵππους καὶ μάλιστα τῶν ἀρχόντων καὶ τῶν λοιπῶν ἐπιλέκτων προμετώπια ἔχειν καὶ στηθάρια ἢ σιδηρᾶ ἢ ἀπὸ κεντούκλων, οἷον νευρικά. καὶ σκέπεσθαι τὰ στήθη καὶ τοὺς τραχήλους αὐτῶν, εἰ δυνατόν, καὶ τὰς κοιλίας διὰ μικρῶν ἀποκρεμασμάτων ἀπὸ τῶν λεγομένων ἀφελέτρων τῆς σέλλας. μεγάλων γὰρ ταῦτα κινδύνων πολλάκις τοὺς ἵππους διασώζουσι, καὶ δι᾽ αὐτῶν τοὺς ἐπ᾽

---

22 λέγεται MWA λέγονται VBE    22–23 τινὲς κτήσωνται MW κτήσονται τινὰς AB κτήσονται τινὲς VE    23 λίαν MW πάνυ ἐστὶ A πάνυ ἐστὶν VBE | ὀπισθελλινῶν Va ὀπιστελλίνων MW ὀπισθελινῶν A ὄπισθεν λινῶν VBE    24 ζαβῶν MW λωρικίων AVBE    25 εὔσχημος MW εὔσχημος καὶ εὔστολος A εὔσχημος καὶ εὔοπλος VBE    27 καὶ¹ MWA om. VBE | θώρακας MWAB θώρακος VE    29 πτερνιστῆρας MWA ὑπερνιστῆρας B ὑπερνιστῆρας VE | ἐνίοτε...δὲ MW πολλάκις δὲ ἔχειν AVBE | ὅτε...ἐπενδυόμενα MW ἐπενδυόμενα A ἐπενδυόμενα ὅτε χρεία γένηται VBE    30 μ´ MW τεσσαράκοντα AVBE    31 κατὰ λόγον MWA κατ᾽ ὀλίγον VBE    32 τὰ MW om. AVBE    33 εἴωθε MWVBE εἴωθεν A    34 δύο MWA β´ VBE    35 ἄλλο MWAB ἄλλον VE    37 ρικτάρια W ῥηκτάρια M ῥιπτάρια AVBE | δύο MWA β´ VBE    38 ἀκοντίσοι MW ἀκοντίσῃ AVBE | τοῦ πολεμίου MW τῶν πολεμίων AVBE | στρατιώτην MWAB στρατιῶν VE    41 κεντούκλων AVBE κενδούκλων MW    43 μικρῶν MWA μακρῶν VBE | ἀφελέτρων MWA ἀφελέτρας VBE    44 διασώζουσι MWVBE διασώζουσιν A

3. All the recruits who do not know how to shoot should have lances and full shields. It will be very useful if some can afford iron gauntlets, called cheiropsella. They should have small tassels on the hindquarters of the horses as well as small pennons over the armor around their shoulders. For the more handsome the soldier is in his armament, the more confidence he gains in himself and the more fear he inspires in the foe.

4. If possible, they should wear breastplates, polished and shiny, that are now called klibania.[3] Also greaves, now called podopsella, and sometimes spurs. Also surcoats to put on when needed.

5. All the Roman recruits, up to the age of forty, must definitely be required to carry bow and quiver, whether they be expert archers or just average. The fact that archery has been completely neglected and fallen into disuse among the Romans has caused a great deal of harm nowadays.

6. They should possess two lances so as to have a spare one at hand in case the first one misses. Inexperienced men should employ lighter bows. With enough time, even men who do not know how to shoot will manage to learn, for it is an essential skill.

7. If possible, they should also have at least two javelins or throwing weapons so that, at the proper moment, they may readily hurl them against the enemy. That is how you shall arm the cavalryman.

8. The horses, especially those of the officers and the other special troops, should have protective armor of iron or of padding, such as cowhide, over their heads and breasts. Their breasts and necks and, if possible, their abdomens will be covered by small pieces of what is called quilting, hanging from the saddles. These have often preserved the horses as well as those riding on them from great

3. Klibanion meant a baking oven and may well suggest how the soldier felt wearing such armor. But the etymology is not certain: see Kolias, 44–50.

45 αὐτῶν ὀχουμένους. ταῦτα δὲ ἔχειν καὶ μάλιστα τοὺς προτασσομένους ἐν τῇ μάχῃ.

9. Καὶ αἱ σέλλαι δὲ ἐχέτωσαν ἐπισέλλια δασέα καὶ μεγάλα, καὶ τὰ χαλινάρια αὐτῶν ἐπιτήδεια ἔστωσαν καὶ ἰσχυρά.

10. Εἰς δὲ τὰς σέλλας τὰς δύο σιδηρᾶς σκάλας | καὶ λωρόσοκκον καὶ πέδι- 298
50 κλον καὶ σελλοπούγγιν, ἐν ᾧ καιροῦ καλοῦντος δυνατόν ἐστι κἂν τριῶν ἢ τεσσάρων ἡμερῶν δαπάνην χωρῆσαι, καὶ τουφία δὲ εἰς τὰς ὀπισθελλίνας τέσσα-ρα, καὶ κορυφάδιν τοῦ ἵππου τουφὶν καὶ ὑπὸ γένειον ὁμοίως.

11. Πάντως δὲ ἔχειν δεῖ τὸν καβαλλάριον στρατιώτην καὶ τζικούριν δί-στομον, τὸ ἓν στόμα τάξιν σπαθίου ἐπίμηκες καὶ τὸ ἕτερον τάξιν ξίφους κον-
55 ταρίου μακρὸν καὶ ὀξύ, ἀποκρεμάμενον μετὰ θηκαρίου δερματίνου ἐν τῇ σέλλᾳ.

12. Τὰ δὲ ἱμάτια τῶν στρατιωτῶν, εἴτε λινᾶ εἰσιν εἴτε ἐξ ἐρίου εἴτε ἑτέρας ὕλης, πλατέα δεῖ εἶναι, ἵνα ἐν τῷ καβαλλικεύειν μὴ ἐμποδίζωνται, ἀλλὰ καὶ σκέπωνται δι' αὐτῶν τὰ γόνατα αὐτῶν καὶ εὔσχημοι φαίνωνται.

13. Χρὴ δὲ καὶ κέντουκλα ἔχειν πλατέα πάνυ, ἔχοντα μανίκια πλατέα, ἵνα ἐν
60 τῷ ὁπλισθῆναι αὐτοὺς καὶ φορεῖν τὰς ζάβας καὶ τὰ τοξάρια, ἐάν, ὡς εἰκός, συμβῇ βροχὴν γενέσθαι ἢ ὑγρότερον τὸν ἀέρα ἐκ τῆς δρόσου, φοροῦντες αὐτὰ ἐπάνω τῶν ζαβῶν καὶ τῶν τοξαρίων φυλάττωσι τὸ ἅρμα αὐτῶν καὶ οὐκ ἐμποδί-ζωνται, εἴτε τοῖς τοξαρίοις εἴτε τοῖς κονταρίοις αὐτῶν βουληθῶσι χρήσασθαι. ἔστι δὲ καὶ ἄλλως πως ἀναγκαῖα τὰ κέντουκλα ἐν ταῖς σκούλκαις ἤγουν ταῖς
65 βίγλαις· οὐ διαφαίνονται γὰρ μήκοθεν τοῖς πολεμίοις αἱ ζάβαι ὑπ' αὐτῶν σκεπό-μεναι, ἀντέχουσι δὲ καὶ πρὸς τὰς βολὰς τῶν σαγιττῶν.

14. Προστάσσομεν δὲ καθ' ἕκαστον κοντουβέρνιν καὶ δρέπανα καὶ ἀξίνας ἔχειν αὐτοὺς διὰ τὸ ἀναγκαῖον τῆς χρείας.

49 δύο MWA β′ VBE | λωρόσοκκον Meursis teste Va λωρόσοκον MW λωρόσωκον A λωρόσοκα VBE    50 σελλοπούγγιν M σελοπούγγιν W σελλοπούγγιον AVBE | καιροῦ AVBE καιρῶ MW | ἐστι MAVBE ἐστιν W | κἂν Va καὶ codd.    51–52 τέσσαρα MWA δ′ VBE    52 κορυφάδιν MW εἰς τὸ κορυφάδιον AVBE | τουφὶν MW τουφίον AVBE | ὑπὸ γένειον Va ὑπογένειον MW εἰς τὸ ὑπογένειον AVBE    53 τζικούριν MW τζικούριον AVBE    54 τάξιν¹ MW δίκην AVBE | τάξιν² MW δίκην AVBE    56 εἰσιν MWA om. VBE | ἐξ ἐρίου MW ἐκ μαλλίου πεποιημένα AVBE | εἴτε³ AVBE ἢ MW    57 δεῖ MWA δὲ VBE | καὶ MWA om. VBE    59 καὶ MWA om. VBE | κέντουκλα AVBE κένδουκλα MW | ἔχειν MWA ἔχον VBE | μανίκια MW μανιάκια AVBE    60 ζάβας Va ζώνας codd.    62 φυλάττωσι MAVBE φυλάττωσιν W | καὶ² MWA om. VBE    63 κονταρίοις Va σκουταρίοις codd.    64 ἔστι AVBE ἔστιν MW | κέντουκλα AVBE κένδουκλα MW | σκούλκαις…ταῖς² MW om. AVBE    65 τοῖς…ζάβαι MWA trsp. VBE | ὑπ' MWAVE ἀπ' B    66 ἀντέχουσι MW ἀπαντῶσι AVBE    67 προστάσσομεν MWA προτάσσομεν VBE | κοντουβέρνιν M κουτουβέρνιν W κοντουβέρνιον AVBE

dangers. In particular, the men stationed in the front line of battle should have these items.

9. Let the saddles have large and thick cloths, and let there be strong bridles of good quality.

10. Two iron stirrups should be attached to the saddles along with a lasso with thong, a hobble, a saddlebag large enough, when the situation so demands, to hold three or four days' rations. There should be four tassels on the haunch strap; likewise, one on the horse's brow and one under the chin.

11. By all means, the cavalry soldier must have a double-sided axe, one side having the long form of a sword and the other the large and sharp form of the point of a spear.[4] It should be hanging from the saddle in a leather case.

12. The clothing of the soldiers, whether of linen, wool, or other material, should be loose fitting so they may not be impeded as they ride along; it should cover their knees and give a neat appearance.

13. They should have a loose, padded mantle with very broad sleeves so that in arming themselves and wearing the body armor with the bow if, perchance, it should rain or the dew cause the air to become quite humid, then by wearing these over their body armor and bow, they may both protect their armament and not be impeded when they want to make use of the bow or the lance. These padded mantles may also be necessary in another way on patrol or reconnaissance. When the body armor is covered by them its brightness will not be seen far off by the enemy and they will also provide protection against being hit by arrows.

14. We also order that each squad should carry sickles and axes to meet their unavoidable needs.

4. See Kolias, 167–169.

15. Τοὺς δὲ τῶν ταγμάτων ἄρχοντας ἢ στρατιώτας καὶ τῶν θεματικῶν
70 βάνδων τοὺς δυνατωτέρους ἀναγκάζεσθαι χρὴ παῖδας ἑαυτοῖς δούλους ἢ ἐλευθέρους καὶ ἐπιμελῶς ἐν τῷ καιρῷ τῆς τε ῥόγας καὶ τοῦ ἀδνουμίου καὶ τοὺς
παῖδας αὐτῶν καὶ τὸ ἄρμα ἀπογράφεσθαι καὶ καταζητεῖσθαι, ἵνα μὴ περιφρονοῦντες τῶν δουλευόντων ἐν καιρῷ πολέμου ἀναγκάζωνται ἐξ αὐτῶν τῶν στρατιωτῶν ἀφορίζεσθαι εἰς τὸ τοῦλδον καὶ ὀλίγοι γίνονται οἱ κοπιῶντες ἐν τῇ
75 μάχῃ. εἰ δέ τινες, ὡς εἰκός, μὴ εὐποροῦσι κτήσασθαι παῖδας, ἀναγκαῖόν ἐστιν εἰς
τοὺς κατωτέρους στρατιώτας τρεῖς ἢ τέσσαρας ἕνα παῖδα, τὸν ὑπηρετεῖν αὐτοῖς
μέλλοντα, ἐπινοεῖν. τὸν ὅμοιον δὲ τρόπον ποιεῖν καὶ εἰς τὰ σαγμάρια, ὧν χρεία
κατὰ τὸ ἀναγκαῖον διὰ τὰς ζάβας καὶ τὰς τέντας αὐτῶν.

16. Προστάσσομεν δὲ καὶ τὰς κεφαλὰς τῶν βάνδων ἑκάστου τάγματος
80 ὁμοχρόους γίνεσθαι, | καὶ τὰ φλάμουλα ἑκάστης τούρμας ἢ δρούγγου ἰδιόχροα    298ᵛ
εἶναι, ἵνα δὲ καὶ τὸ καθ᾿ ἕκαστον τάγμα εὐκόλως ἐπιγινώσκῃ τὸ ἴδιον βάνδον.
δεῖ ἕτερα ἰδικὰ σημεῖα προστιθέναι ταῖς κεφαλαῖς τῶν βάνδων, ἐγνωσμένα τοῖς
στρατιώταις, ὥστε ἐκ τούτου ἐπιγινώσκεσθαι αὐτὰ καὶ κατὰ τὰς τούρμας καὶ
κατὰ τοὺς δρούγγους καὶ κατὰ τὰ βάνδα. πάντως δὲ τὰ τῶν τουρμάρχων <βάν-
85 δα> ἐνηλλαγμένα δεῖ εἶναι καὶ πρόδηλα, ἵνα ἐκ πολλοῦ διαστήματος ἐπιγινώ-
σκωνται τοῖς ὑπ᾿ αὐτοῖς τεταγμένοις.

17. Κελεύομεν δέ σοι, ὦ στρατηγέ, καὶ ἄρμα ἐπιφέρεσθαι ἐκ περισσοῦ διὰ
βασταγῆς καὶ μάλιστα τοξάρια καὶ σαγίττας, ἵνα τοῖς, ὡς εἰκός, ἀστοχοῦσιν
ὅπλοις ἐξ αὐτῶν ἀντεισάγηται.

90    18. Ἔξωθεν δὲ τῶν βοΐνων θηκαρίων τῶν ζαβῶν ἔχειν τοὺς στρατιώτας ἀπὸ
δερμάτων θηκάρια ἕτερα ἐλαφρά, ὅπως ἢ ἐν καιρῷ πολέμου ἢ ἐν καιρῷ κούρ-
σου ὄπισθεν τῶν ὀπισθοκουρβίων κατὰ τὰς ψύας τῶν ἵππων βαστάζωνται, καὶ
ἐὰν συμβῇ, ὡς πολλάκις—ὃ μὴ γένοιτο—τροπῆς γινομένης, πρὸς μίαν ἡμέραν

71 τε MW om. AVBE 72–73 περιφρονοῦντες MWA καταφρονοῦντες VBE
73 δουλευόντων MW δουλεύειν καὶ ὑπηρετεῖν αὐτοῖς ὀφειλόντων παίδων AVBE | πολέμου
AVBE πολέμων MW 74 γίνονται MW καταλιμπάνωνται A καταλιμπάνονται VBE
74–75 κοπιῶντες…μάχῃ MW πολεμοῦντες AVBE 78 τέντας MW τένδας AVBE
80 ἰδιόχροα MWA ἰδιόχρονα VBE 81 καὶ…ἕκαστον De καὶ τὸ καθέκαστον MW δὲ
καθέκαστον A ἕκαστον VBE | ἴδιον MWAVE ἕτερον B 82 ἕτερα MWAVE ἕτερα βάνδα B |
σημεῖα MWAVE σημαίνει B | ταῖς κεφαλαῖς MWAVE τὰς κεφαλὰς B 83 τούτου MW
τούτων AVBE 84–85 βάνδα² ci. Va om. codd. 85 πρόδηλα MW πρόχειρα AVBE
86 ὑπ᾿ αὐτοῖς M ὕπαυτοὺς W ὑπ᾿ αὐτοὺς AVE ὑπ᾿ αὐτοῦ B 87 σοι MWA om. VBE
90 βοΐνων MWVBE βοείων A 93 ὡς MW om. AVBE | γινομένης MW γενομένης AVBE

15. The officers and enlisted men of the regular units as well as the more affluent soldiers in the thematic companies must be required to have their own servants, slave or free. At the time of distributing pay and mustering, care must be taken to register and inquire about the servants and weapons. Should they pay no attention to the servants, then, in time of battle they might be forced to detail some of the soldiers themselves to the baggage train, which means fewer men fighting in the ranks. But if it should turn out that some of the men are unable to afford servants, it is necessary for three or four of the lower-ranking soldiers to provide for one servant who will be at their disposition. A similar arrangement should be followed for the pack animals that are needed for their body armor and their tents.

16. We also order that the fields of the flags of each unit should be of the same color, and the streamers of each tourma or droungos should have their own color, so that each individual unit may easily recognize its own standard.[5] Other distinctive devices known to the soldiers should be imposed on the fields of the flags; they will thus be recognized according to tourma and droungos and bandon. The standards of the tourmarchs should be particularly distinctive and conspicuous so that they may be recognized by their troops at a great distance.

17. We order you, O general, to have your supply train carry extra arms, especially bows and arrows, to replace those weapons likely to be lost.

18. Apart from the leather cases for the body armor, the soldiers should have other light ones of hide. During battle or on raids they may be carried behind the cantle across the horse's hindquarters. If, as may well be the case, they should suffer a reversal—may it not happen—and the men guarding the

---

5. See R. Grosse, "Die Fahnen in der römisch-byzantinischen Armee des 4.–10. Jahrhundert," *BZ* 24 (1924): 359–372; Dennis, "Byzantine Battle Flags"; Haldon, *ImpEx*, 270–274.

ἀφανεῖς γενέσθαι τοὺς τὴν παρασκευὴν ἔχοντας, μή εἰσι γυμναὶ αἱ ζάβαι καὶ
95 φθείρωνται, μήτε καὶ κοποῦσι τοὺς στρατιώτας διηνεκῶς ἐπικείμεναι αὐτοῖς.

19. Οὐδὲ τοῦτο δὲ παραλείψομεν ἐν τῇδε τῇ διατάξει, ἵνα οἱ ἄρχοντες
ἑκάστου τάγματος διαγνώσεις ποιῶσιν ἐν τῷ καιρῷ τοῦ παραχειμαδίου ἢ ἐν
ἑτέρῳ ἀργίας καιρῷ, ὥστε, ἐὰν μὴ εὐπορῶσιν οἱ στρατιῶται κατὰ τὴν χώραν
ἀγοράσαι τὰ ἐπιτήδεια, φανερὸν γίνεσθαι, πόσων ἵππων καὶ ποίου εἴδους καὶ
100 ποίου ἄρματος δέονται τῶν στρατιωτῶν ἕκαστος, ἵνα παρασκευάζῃς, ὦ
στρατηγέ, ταῦτα ἐν τῷ δέοντι καιρῷ εὐτρεπίζεσθαι πρὸς ἀγορασίαν αὐτοῖς ἀπὸ
ἐμπόρων τινῶν, καὶ μήτε ἐντεῦθεν οἱ ἐντόπιοι οἰκήτορες βλάπτωνται, μήτε οἱ
στρατιῶται τῶν ἀναγκαίων εἰδῶν καὶ ὅπλων, εἰ οὕτω τύχοι, ὑστερούμενοι
ἀπορῶσιν. ἐπεὶ οὖν τὸν καβαλλάριον στρατιώτην ἐξωπλίσαμεν, ἑξῆς καὶ ὅπως
105 χρή σε καὶ τῶν πεζῇ μαχομένων στρατιωτῶν τὴν δέουσαν ποιήσασθαι ὅπλισιν
ἤδη λέξομεν.

20. Τῆς πεζικῆς τοίνυν τοῦ στρατοῦ τάξεως πάλαι μὲν εἰς τρία διῃρημένης
παρὰ τοῖς ἀρχαίοις τακτικοῖς, οἷον εἰς ὁπλίτας, οὓς οἱ νεώτεροι σκουτάτους
ἐκάλεσαν, εἰς ψιλούς, οὓς καὶ νῦν ψιλοὺς τῷ αὐτῷ καλοῦσιν ὀνόματι, καὶ εἰς
110 πέλτας, ὦν οἱ καθ᾽ ἡμᾶς οὐ γινώσκουσι μὲν τὴν κλῆσιν, δοκεῖ μοι δὲ τοῖς ψιλοῖς
αὐτοὺς | συγκαταλέξαντας δύο μόνας τάξεις πεζικοῦ μνημονεῦσαι στρατοῦ,  299
ὁπλιτῶν τε καὶ ψιλῶν. περὶ τούτων οὖν ἡμεῖς διαλαβόντες τῶν τάξεων διορισόμεθα.

21. Ὁπλίσεις μὲν οὖν τὸν πεζὸν σκουτάτον, τὸν πάλαι καλούμενον ὁπλίτην,
115 ὥστε ἔχειν σπάθην, κοντάριν, σκουτάριν, ὅτε μὲν χρεία καλεῖ, ἐπίμηκες, μέγα, ὃ

---

107–133 *Strat.*, 12.B.4–5.

---

94 τὴν παρασκευὴν MW τὰς χρείας AVBE scr. mg. ἀποσκευὴν W | εἰσι MWA ὦσιν B ὦσι
VE    95 μήτε De εἶτα codd. | κοποῦσι A σκέπωσι M σκέπουσι W κοπῶσι VBE | τοὺς
στρατιώτας MWAVE τοῦ στρατιώτου B | ἐπικείμεναι MWA ἐπικειμένου VBE    96 οὐδὲ…
διατάξει MW om. AVBE | ἵνα MW ἵνα δὲ καὶ AVBE    97 διαγνώσεις MW διαγνώσεις καὶ
ἀπογραφὰς AVBE    98 εὐπορῶσιν MWA ἐκπορῶσιν VBE    99 ἀγοράσαι MWA om. VBE
102 ἐμπόρων MW πραγματευτῶν AVBE    103 τῶν MW om. AVBE | οὕτω τύχοι MWVBE
οὕτως τύχῃ A    104 ἀπορῶσιν MWAVE ἀποροῦσιν B | ἑξῆς MW ἑξῆς ἐροῦμεν AVBE
105 δέουσαν MW om. AVBE | ποιήσασθαι WAVBE ποιήσας M    106 ἤδη λέξομεν MW om.
AVBE scr. mg. sup. περὶ τῆς τῶν πεζῶν ἐξοπλίσεως W    107 τρία MWA γ′ VBE | ad
διῃρημένης scr. mg. διακεχωρισμένης W    109 οὓς…ὀνόματι MW οὓς καὶ νῦν φίλους A om.
VBE    110 πέλτας MW πελταστὰς AVBE    111 συγκαταλέξαντας MW συνκαταριθ-
μήσαντες A συγκαταριθμήσαντες VBE | δύο MWA β′ VBE | πεζικοῦ MAVBE πεζικῆς W
112 οὖν MWA om. VBE | διαλαβόντες MW om. AVBE    114 ὁπλίτην MW ὁπλίτην οὕτως
AVBE    115 σπάθην MW σπαθίον AVBE | κοντάριν MW κονδάριον AVBE | σκουτάριν
MW σκουτάριον AVE σκουτάριον κοντάριον B

equipment should be missing for a day, the body armor will not be left out in the open and ruined and the soldiers will not be worn out by the constant weight of the armor.

19. In this constitution we will not omit the following. While in winter quarters or at some other period of leisure, the officers of each unit should make an assessment, so that it becomes clear how many horses, what sort of equipment, and what sort of armament is needed for each one of the soldiers and so that, in case the soldiers cannot easily purchase supplies in the region, you, O general, at the requisite time might arrange for these things to be made available for sale to them by certain merchants. As a result, the local inhabitants will not be harmed and, if this is done, the soldiers will not be left helpless, deprived of necessary equipment and weapons. Therefore, now that we have armed the cavalry soldier, our next topic will be about your obligation to see to the proper armament of the soldiers who fight on foot.

20. The ancient tacticians long ago divided the infantry contingents of the army in three.[6] <Heavy-armed troops or> hoplites, called skoutatoi by more re-cent tacticians; second, light-armed troops, whom they now call by that very name. Then there were peltai, a term not recognized by our contemporaries.[7] I believe that they classified them together with the light-armed troops, recording only two divisions of the infantry army, <heavy-armed> hoplites and light-armed troops. Having, therefore, made this distinction, we will now lay down regulations affecting them.

21. You shall equip the infantry skoutatos, formerly called hoplite, with a sword, a lance, and, when necessary, a shield of the kind called thyreos, large

6. See *Strat.*, 12.B.
7. Kolias, 90.

καλεῖται θυρεός, πάντως δὲ στρογγύλον τέλειον. τὰ δὲ σκουτάρια ὁμόχροα πάντων ἢ κατὰ ἀριθμὸν ἢ κατὰ τάγμα. ἔχειν δὲ καὶ κασσίδα τουφὶν μικρὸν ἔχουσαν ἄνωθεν, σφενδόβολα, τζικούρια δίστομα, τὸ μὲν ἓν στόμα ὡς σπάθην, τὸ δὲ ἕτερον ὡς κονταρίου ξίφος, ἀναβασταζόμενα μετὰ θηκαρίων δερματίνων
120 ἢ τζικούρια ἕτερα, ἔχοντα τὸ μὲν ἓν στόμα κόπτον, τὸ δὲ ἕτερον στρογγύλον ἢ ἕτερα τζικούρια δίστομα τάξιν πελεκίων, τοὺς δὲ ἐπιλέκτους τῆς ἀκίας ἔχειν καὶ ζάβας ἤτοι λωρίκια, εἰ μὲν δυνατόν, ὅλους, ἐπεί, κἂν δύο, τοὺς πρώτους τῶν ἀκιῶν, κατὰ δὲ τῶν μήλων ἤτοι τῶν ὤμων τῆς ζάβας φλαμουλίσκια μικρά. ἔχειν δὲ καὶ χειρομάνικα τὰ λεγόμενα μανικέλλια ἢ χειρόψελλα, σιδηρᾶ ἢ ξύλινα, καὶ
125 περικνημῖδας ὁμοίως, ἃ λέγεται ποδόψελλα ἢ χαλκότουβα, μάλιστα τοὺς ἐν ταῖς κεφαλαῖς καὶ οὐραῖς τῶν ἀκιῶν τεταγμένους.

22. Καὶ τοὺς μὲν σκουτάτους οὕτως ὁπλίσεις, ὡς εἴρηται. τοὺς δὲ λεγο-μένους ψιλοὺς τὸν τρόπον τοῦτον· τοξοφάρετρα ἐπὶ τῶν ὤμων ἀναβασταζό-μενα, ἔχοντα κούκουρα μεγάλα, χωροῦντα ἀνὰ λ΄ ἢ μ΄ σαγιττῶν, σωληνάρια
130 ξύλινα μετὰ μικρῶν σαγιττῶν καὶ κουκούρων μικρῶν, ἅπερ καὶ ἐπὶ πολὺ διά-στημα ῥίπτονται διὰ τῶν τοξαρίων, καὶ τοῖς ἐχθροῖς ἄχρηστά εἰσι, βηρύττας, ἃ λέγεται ῥικτάρια, τοὺς ἀπείρως πρὸς τὴν τοξείαν ἔχοντας ἢ καὶ λειπομένους, ὡς εἰκός, τόξων. ἔχειν δὲ καὶ σκουτάρια μικρά, στρογγύλα, σφενδόβολα καὶ τζικού-ρια, ὅμοια τῶν εἰρημένων, ἀναβασταζόμενα καὶ αὐτὰ εἰς θηκάρια δερμάτινα. τὰ
135 δὲ ἱμάτια τῶν πεζῶν ἁπάντων ἔστωσαν κοντὰ μέχρι τῶν γονάτων αὐτῶν. ἐὰν δυνατόν, αὐτοὺς ἔχειν καὶ ἐπιλώρικα. τὰ δὲ ὑποδήματα αὐτῶν μὴ ἔχειν ὀξείας <μύτας> ἔμπροσθεν, ἀναγκαῖον δὲ καὶ ὀλίγοις μικροῖς ἥλοις καθηλοῦσθαι αὐτὰ ἤγουν καρφίοις, πρὸς πλείονα ὑπουργίαν. χρήσιμα γὰρ ταῦτα καὶ ἐν ταῖς ὁδοι-πορίαις μάλιστα. καὶ τὰς κουρὰς δὲ αὐτῶν κοντὰς γίνεσθαι καὶ μὴ ἀφεῖναι
140 αὐτοῖς τελείας τρίχας χρήσιμόν ἐστιν.

---

133–139 *Strat.*, 12.B.1.

---

116 πάντως MWAE πάντα VB    117 κασσίδα MWA κασσίδας VBE    118 ἄνωθεν MW ἄνωθεν τουφίον μικρὸν AVBE | ὡς σπάθην MW δίκην σπαθίου ἐπίμηκες AVBE    122 ἐπεί MW εἰ δὲ μὴ AVBE    123 τῶν¹…ἤτοι MW om. AVBE | τῶν ὤμων MW τοὺς ὤμους AVBE 124 ἢ¹ MW ἢ καὶ AVBE    129 λ΄…μ΄ MWVBE τριάκοντα ἢ τεσσαράκοντα A 130 κουκούρων MWVBE κούρων A    131 καὶ…εἰσι MW om. AVBE | ad ἄχρηστα scr. mg. οὐ χρησιμευουσιν W    132 ῥικτάρια MW ῥιπτάρια AVBE    135 κοντὰ AVBE κονδὰ MW 136 αὐτοὺς ἔχειν MW trsp. AVBE    136–137 μὴ…ὀλίγοις MW ἀναγκαῖον ἐστὶ A ἀναγκαῖον ἐστιν VBE    137 μύτας ci. Va om. codd. | ἥλοις MW καρφίοις AVBE 137–138 αὐτὰ…καρφίοις MW om. AVBE    139 κοντὰς MWA κόμας VBE    140 τελείας MW μακρὰς AVBE

and oblong in shape but altogether completely curved.[8] All the shields in each arithmos or tagma should be of the same color. The men should also have helmets with small plumes on top, slings, double-bladed axes, one side shaped like a sword, the other like the point of a spear, to be carried in leather cases. Other axes with one blade for cutting and the other rounded, still other double-bladed axes shaped like the pelekus.[9] The picked men of the file should have body armor or mail, all the men, if possible, but at least the first two of the file. Across the plates or the shoulders of the body armor <attach> small pennons. They should also have gauntlets, called manikellia or cheiropsella, made of iron or wood, and in like manner greaves, called podopsella or chalkotouba, especially the men stationed in the front and in the rear of the file.

22. You will arm all the skoutatoi in the aforesaid manner, but the so-called light-armed troops as follows. They should carry bows on their shoulders with large quivers holding up to thirty or forty arrows. Also grooved wooden tubes with short arrows in small quivers, that can be fired a great distance with the bows and which cannot be used by the enemy.[10] Small javelins, called riktaria, for men inexperienced in archery or who do not happen to have bows. They should also have small round shields, slings, and axes, similar to those mentioned, and those too carried in leather cases. Let the tunics of all the foot soldiers be short, reaching to their knees. If possible, they should also have surcoats. Their shoes should not have sharp points in front; but they must be studded with a few small rivets or nails for greater durability. These are particularly suitable when marching.[11] Their hair should be cut short; it is better if it is not allowed to grow long.

8. Kolias, 91.
9. Kolias, 169–170.
10. Cf. Const. 5, n. 3.
11. *Strat.* 12.B.1.

23. Ἀλλ' οὕτω μὲν τοὺς πεζοὺς στρατιώτας ἐνδύσεις καὶ περιφράξεις δι'
ὅπλων. πρὸς δὲ τὴν ὑπηρεσίαν αὐτῶν καὶ φυλακὴν | ἀμάξας παρασκευάσεις 299ᵛ
εὐσταλεῖς ἤγουν ἐλαφρὰς καὶ γοργὰς κατὰ δεκαρχίαν ἤτοι κοντουβέρνιν, μίαν
καὶ μὴ πλέον, ἵνα μὴ πολλοὶ εἰς αὐτὰ ἀσχολούμενοι ἀργῶσιν. ἐχέτω δὲ ἑκάστη
145 τῶν ἀμαξῶν χειρομύλιν, ἀξίνην, πελέκιν, σκέπαρνον, πριόνιν, ὄρυγας δύο,
σφῦραν, πτυάρια δύο, κόφινον, κιλίκια, φαλκίδιν, τζικούρια, βαρδούκια, ματζούκια—ἴσως κἂν τούτων χρεία γένηται τοῖς στρατιώταις—τριβόλους ἀναδεδεμένας διὰ λεπτῶν σφηκωμάτων καὶ ἐν ἥλῳ σιδηρῷ ἀποκρατουμένας διὰ τὸ
ἑτοίμως συνάγεσθαι αὐτάς· ἑτέρας ἀμάξας ἐχούσας τοξοβολίστρας καὶ σαγίττας
150 αὐτῶν, καὶ βαλίστρας ἤτοι μαγγανικά, τὰ λεγόμενα ἀλακάτια, στρεφόμενα
κυκλόθεν, καὶ μαγγαναρίους, λεπτουργούς, χαλκεῖς, καὶ τούτοις ἴδιον ἄρχοντα
ἐπιστῆσαι. ἑτέρας ἀμάξας φερούσας τὸ ἀρμαμέντον ἑκάστου ἀριθμοῦ τῶν
στρατιωτῶν· ἑτέρας ἀμάξας, ὡς δέκα ἢ καὶ εἴκοσι, βασταζούσας πίστον καὶ
παξαμάτιν καὶ σαγίττας καὶ τοξάρια ἐκ περισσοῦ.
155 24. Ἵππους σαγματαρίους ἢ ὑποζύγια, εἰ μὲν ἐνδέχεται, καθ' ἕκαστον κοντουβέρνιν, εἰ δὲ μήγε, εἰς τὰ δύο κοντουβέρνια ἕνα, ἵνα, εἰ γένηται καιρὸς
χωρισθῆναι τοὺς πεζοὺς ἐκ τῶν ἀμαξῶν καὶ προκαταλαβεῖν τόπον, βαστάζειν
ὀκτὼ ἢ δέκα ἡμερῶν δαπάνην καὶ ἀκολουθεῖν μέχρις οὗ ἐπιφθάσωσιν αἱ ἄμαξαι
ἀργότερον περιπατοῦσαι.
160 25. Οὐκ ἄχρηστον δέ μοι δοκεῖ μνημονεῦσαι, κἂν ἐν μικρῷ, καὶ τῆς ἀρχαίας
ὁπλίσεως τῶν πεζῶν καὶ τῶν καβαλλαρίων, καθὼς Αἰλιανός τε καὶ οἱ λοιποὶ τῶν

---

142–149 *Strat.*, 12.B.6.    160–168 Aelian., 2; Arrian., 4.

---

141 οὕτω MW οὕτως AVBE | καὶ WAVBE om. M    143 εὐσταλεῖς ἤγουν MW om. AVBE |
κοντουβέρνιν M κουτουβέρνιν W κοντουβέρνιον AVE κοντουβέρνια B    144 ἀργῶσιν
MWA ἀργῶσι VBE    145 τῶν ἀμαξῶν MW ἄμαξα AVBE | χειρομύλιν W χειρομύλιον M
χειρόμυλον AVBE | πριόνιν Va πριώνιν MW πρίονα AVBE | δύο MWA β' VBE    146 δύο
MWA β' VBE | κόφινον AVBE κοφίνην MW | φαλκίδιν Va φαλκίαν MW φαλκίδιον A
φαλκίδα VBE | βαρδούκια MW om. AVBE    147–148 ἀναδεδεμένας MWAVE
ἀναδεδεγμένας B    149 τοξοβολίστρας    W τοξοβαλλίστρας A τοξοβαλίστρας VBE
150 βαλίστρας ἤτοι MW om. AVBE | ἀλακάτια MW ἠλακάτια AVBE
150–151 στρεφόμενα κυκλόθεν MW om. AVBE    151 τούτοις MWAVE τούτους B |
ἄρχοντα MWAVE ἄρχοντας B    152 τὸ ἀρμαμέντον MWA τὸ ἄρμα μὲν τὸν VE τῷ ἄρματι
μὲν τὸν B | ἀριθμοῦ MWA ἀριθμὸν VBE    154 παξαμάτιν Va παξαμάδα MW παξαμάτιον
AVBE    155–156 κοντουβέρνιν M κουτουβέρνιν W κοντουβέρνιον ἕνα AVBE    156 δύο
MWA β' VBE | κοντουβέρνια MAVBE κουτουβέρνια W    158 ὀκτὼ…ἡμερῶν MWA η'
ἡμερῶν ἢ καὶ δέκα B η' ἡμερῶν ἢ δέκα VE | ἐπιφθάσωσιν MWA ἐπιφθάσουσιν VBE scr. mg.
περὶ τῆς ἀρχαίας ἐξοπλίσεως τῶν πεζῶν W    160 οὐκ ἄχρηστον MWA εὔχρηστον VBE |
κἂν…μικρῷ MW πρὸς ὀλίγον AVBE

23. In this manner, then, you will clothe the foot soldiers and provide them with armor and weapons. Then, for their service and protection, you will get ready easily managed, that is, light and fast, wagons, one to each dekarchy or squad, no more lest many of the men become so busy with them that they neglect <other matters>. Let each of the wagons contain a hand mill, an axe, a hatchet, an adze, a saw, two picks, a hammer, two shovels, a basket, some goat-hair matting, a scythe, other axes, maces and clubs, for the soldiers may have need of these too. Also caltrops tied together with light cords attached to an iron peg so they can be easily collected.[12] Other wagons carrying bow ballistai and bolts for them, as well as ballistai or artillery pieces of the type called alakatia, that revolve in all directions.[13] Also artillery crews, carpenters, metal workers, all under their own commander. Other wagons bearing the armament for the soldiers of each arithmos. Another ten or even twenty wagons to transport flour and hardtack as well as extra bows and arrows.[14]

24. Pack horses or asses, if it can be worked out, for each squad; if not, then one for two squads. If the opportunity arises for the infantry to be separated from the wagons to seize some position, these beasts may transport rations for eight or ten days, accompanying the men until the wagons, moving more slowly, should arrive.

25. I do not think it unprofitable to call to mind, even briefly, the ancient armament of the infantry and the cavalry, as Aelian and the other authors on

12. *Strat.* 12.B.6.

13. Ballista is a term used primarily for torsion and tension weapons but often designated any artillery piece. Toxobolistra was a torsion weapon that fired bolts or arrows. See Dennis, "Byzantine Heavy Artillery," 99–101.

14. Hardtack: dry, twice-baked bread, δίπυρος ἄρτος (*Suda* Π 254). See A. Dalby, *Flavours of Byzantium* (Totnes, Devon, 2003), 99–100.

τακτικῶν συγγραφεῖς ὑπηγόρευσαν. παρὰ γὰρ τοῖς ἀρχαίοις τὴν μὲν ἱππικὴν τάξιν εἰς δύο διαφορὰς ὁπλίσεων ἐποίουν οἱ στρατηγοί, μίαν μὲν κατάφρακτον λεγομένην καὶ τὴν ἑτέραν οὐ κατάφρακτον.

165    26. Ὥπλιζον δὲ τὸν μὲν κατάφρακτον καβαλλάριον πανταχόθεν αὐτόν τε καὶ τὸν ἵππον αὐτοῦ. καὶ τὸν μὲν ἄνδρα λωρικίοις καὶ κλιβανίοις ἢ σιδηροῖς ἢ ἐκ κεράτων ἐπιπεπλεγμένοις καὶ παραμηρίοις, τοὺς δὲ ἵππους κατέφραττον παραπλευριδίοις καὶ προμετωπιδίοις, ἤγουν τὰ πλευρὰ καὶ τὰς κεφαλάς, καὶ τοὺς τραχήλους τῶν ἵππων διὰ κλιβανίων ἢ λωρικίων ἢ ἄλλης ὕλης κατέσκεπον.

170    27. Τούτων δὲ πάντων, τῶν τε καταφράκτων καβαλλαρίων καὶ τῶν μὴ καταφράκτων, οἱ μὲν εἶχον κοντάρια, οἱ δὲ τὰ λεγόμενα νῦν μέναυλα, ἅπερ οἱ ἀρχαῖοι λόγχας | ἐκάλουν· οἵτινες καὶ κατάφρακτοι ὄντες χεῖρας συνέβαλλον    300 τοῖς πολεμίοις, οἱ δὲ μακρόθεν ἦσαν ἀκοντίζοντες, οὓς καὶ ἔλεγον ἀκροβολιστάς. τῶν δὲ τὰ κοντάρια ἢ τὰς λόγχας ἐχόντων οἱ μέν, ὡς εἴρηται, ἦσαν οἱ τοῖς 175    πολεμίοις συμπλεκόμενοι καὶ πλησίον διὰ τῶν δοράτων ἤτοι τῶν κονταρίων μαχόμενοι. τούτων δὲ τῶν συμπλεκομένων ἐν τῇ μάχῃ οἱ μὲν θυρεοὺς εἶχον ἤτοι σκουτάρια ἐπιμήκη μεγάλα, οἱ δὲ χωρὶς τῶν θυρεῶν μόνοις τοῖς κονταρίοις ἐμάχοντο. καὶ οἱ μὲν ἐκαλοῦντο θυρεοφόροι, οἱ δὲ ἰδίως δορατοφόροι· δόρυ γὰρ τὸ κοντάριν ἔλεγον.

180    28. Ἀκροβολιστὰς δὲ τῶν καβαλλαρίων ἐκάλουν <τοὺς πόρρωθεν ἀκροβολισμοῖς διαχρωμένους> ἤγουν τοὺς μακρόθεν βάλλοντάς τε καὶ μαχομένους. τούτων δὲ οἱ μὲν δορατίοις ἤγουν ρικταρίοις ἐκέχρηντο, οἱ δὲ τόξοις· καὶ οἱ μὲν αὐτῶν μακρόθεν ἔρριπον τὰ ρικτάρια ἢ ἐπ᾿ εὐθείας ἐρχόμενοι ἢ κύκλῳ περιτρέχοντες, οὓς ἐκάλουν ἱππακοντιστάς, οἱ δὲ τοῖς τόξοις ἔβαλλον οὓς ἐκάλουν 185    ἱπποτοξότας. τινὲς δὲ αὐτῶν ἐλαφροῖς κονταρίοις ἐχρῶντο καὶ μίαν ἢ δεύτερον

---

168–178 Aelian., 2.12.    178–189 Aelian., 2.13; Arrian., 2.7.

163 ὁπλίσεων MWA ὁπλίσεως VBE | κατάφρακτον MWAB κατάφρικτον VE
164 κατάφρακτον MWA κατάφρικτον VBE    167 ἐπιπεπλεγμένοις MWA ἐπιλεγομένοις
VBE    168 προμετωπιδίοις MW προμετωπίοις AVBE    170 τε MWVBE om. A
171 καταφράκτων MWA καταφράκτων καὶ VBE    172 συνέβαλλον MWA συνέβαλον VBE
173 ἦσαν ἀκοντίζοντες MW ἠκόντιζον AVBE    174 τὰς λόγχας MW τὰ μέναυλα AVBE
175 πολεμίοις MWA πολέμοις VBE    176 συμπλεκομένων MWAB συμπλεκομαίων VE | ἐν
AVBE om. MW    177–178 οἱ…δορατοφόροι MW οἱ δὲ δορατοφόροι A om. VBE
179 κοντάριν MW κοντάριον AVBE    180–181 τοὺς…διαχρωμένους Va ex Arriano
181 τε MW om. AVBE    182 δορατίοις ἤγουν MW om. AVBE    182–183 ρικταρίοις…τὰ
MWA om. VBE    182 ρικτάριοις Va ρηκτάριοις MW ριπταρίοις A    183 ἔρριπον MW
ἔρριπτον AVBE | ρικτάρια Va ρηκτάρια MW ριπτάρια AVBE    184 ἱππακοντιστάς WAVBE
ἱπποκοντιστὰς M | ἐκάλουν² MW ἔλεγον AVBE

tactics have described it.[15] Among the ancients, the commanders divided the cavalry force according to two different kinds of armament, the one called heavy armed and the other not heavy armed.

26. They armed the heavy-armed cavalryman and his horse completely. The men wore cuirasses and breastplates, either of iron or horn fitted together, as well as thigh armor. They protected the horses with body and head armor, that is, they covered the sides and heads and necks of the horses with lamellar armor or mail or some other material.

27. Of all these, then, the heavy-armed cavalry as well as the not heavy-armed, the first carried lances, the others the weapons now called menaula, which the ancients called spears.[16] The ones with heavy armor engaged in close combat with the enemy; the others, whom they called akrobolistai, hurled their weapons from a distance. Of the men who carried lances or spears, some, as mentioned, were fighting at close quarters, engaged directly against the enemy with their spears and lances. Some of those engaged in close combat had thyreoi or long, large shields. The soldiers without thyreoi fought with lances alone. The first were called thyreophoroi and the others specifically spearbearers, for they called the lance a spear.

28. The cavalrymen who employed missile weapons from a distance, that is, the men shooting and fighting from far off, were called akrobolistai. Some of them made use of small spears or javelins, others of arrows. Some hurled their javelins from a great distance, either advancing in a straight line or else running around in a circle. These they called hippakontistai; those who shot arrows they called hippotoxotai. Some of them made use of light spears and, after first

15. Aelian 2; Arrian, 4.

16. Menaulon was a heavy spear, a form of pike. See E. McGeer, "Menaulion-Menaulatoi," *Diptycha* 4 (1986–87): 53–57; M. Anastasiadis, "On Handling the Menavlion," *BMGS* 18 (1994): 1–10.

προεξακοντίσαντες τὸ λοιπὸν συνεπλέκοντο τοῖς πολεμίοις ἢ τοῖς δορατίοις οἷς
εἶχον ὑπολειπομένοις ἤγουν τοῖς ἐλαφροῖς κονταρίοις ἢ τοῖς σπαθίοις αὐτῶν
διαχρώμενοι· καὶ τούτους ἐκάλουν ἐλαφρούς. τινὲς δὲ αὐτῶν καὶ πελέκεις
μικροὺς ἔφερον πανταχόθεν ἔχοντας ἀκωκὰς ὀξείας ὡς ὀδόντας ἠκονημένους.
190 καὶ τὴν μὲν καβαλλαρικὴν τάξιν οὕτως ὥπλιζον οἱ παλαιοί, ὅσον ἐν συντόμῳ
εἰπεῖν.

29. Τὴν δὲ πεζικὴν παρὰ τὴν τῶν ἀρχαίων τάξιν οὕτως εὕρομεν. τριχῶς μὲν
γὰρ αὐτῆς διεμέριζον τὴν ὅπλισιν, ὡς ἀνωτέρω εἴρηται ἡμῖν. καὶ τὴν μὲν ἐκάλουν ὁπλίτας, τὴν δὲ πελταστάς, τὴν δὲ ψιλούς.

195 30. Καὶ τὴν μὲν τῶν λεγομένων ὁπλιτῶν βαρυτάτην παρὰ πάντας τοὺς
πεζοὺς ἐποίουν κατὰ τὸν Μακεδονικὸν τρόπον ἤγουν καθ' ὃν Ἀλέξανδρος, ὁ
τῶν Μακεδόνων, ἐχρήσατο. καὶ γὰρ σκουτάρια ἐποίουν αὐτοῖς στρογγύλα,
μεγάλα, παραμήκη, ἃ ἔλεγον θυρεούς· καὶ μαχαίρας ἤγουν παραμήρια, καὶ
θώρακας καὶ κράνη ἤγουν λωρίκια καὶ κλιβάνια καὶ κασσίδας καὶ μανικέλλια
200 καὶ χαλκότουβα, ἅπερ οἱ παλαιοὶ περικνημίδας ἐκάλουν, καὶ κοντάρια μακρότερα. τοὺς μὲν οὖν ὁπλίτας λεγομένους οὕτως ὥπλιζον.

31. Τοὺς δὲ ψιλοὺς πάντων ἐλαφροτάτῃ ὥπλιζον τῇ παρασκευῇ. οὔτε γὰρ
θώρακας ἤγουν κλι|βάνια ἢ λωρίκια οὔτε περικνημίδας ἤγουν ποδόψελλα ἢ  300ᵛ
χαλκότουβα οὔτε θυρεοὺς ἢ ἀσπίδας βαρείας ἤγουν τὰ μεγάλα σκουτάρια,
205 ἀλλὰ διὰ τῶν μακρόθεν βαλλομένων ὅπλων ἐμάχοντο, οἷον ἢ τοξεύοντες ἢ
ρικτάρια ρίπτοντες ἢ λίθους βάλλοντες, τοὺς μὲν διὰ χειρός, τοὺς δὲ διὰ σφεν-
δόνης. στολὰς δὲ εἶχον στερεὰς καὶ πηκτὰς ἀντὶ λωρικίων καὶ κλιβανίων καὶ
τῶν ἄλλων.

---

192–201 Aelian., 2.7.   200–211 Aelian., 2.8.

186–187 δορατίοις…εἶχον MW om. AVBE   187 ὑπολειπομένοις MWA ὑπολιμπανομένοις
VBE | ἤγουν τοῖς MW om. AVBE | σπαθίοις MWAB παθίοις VE   188 διαχρώμενοι MW
om. AVBE   189 ἔχοντας AVBE ἔχουσας MW | ἀκωκὰς Va ἀκοκὰς MW om. AVBE scr. mg.
τὸ ὀξύτατον τοῦ σιδήρου W | ὀξείας…ὀδόντας MW ὡς ὀδόντας ὀξεῖς AVBE   190 μὲν
MWA om. VBE | ὅσον ὅσον MW ὡς AVBE   192 δὲ MWA om. VBE | τὴν MW om. AVBE
| τριχῶς MW εἰς τρία A εἰς γ' VBE   193 εἴρηται ἡμῖν MW εἰρήκαμεν AVBE | τὴν² MWA τῇ
VBE   198–199 καὶ²…λωρίκια MW om. AVBE   200–201 μακρότερα MWA μικρότερα
VBE   202 τῇ παρασκευῇ MW ὁπλίσει AVBE   203 θώρακας ἤγουν κλιβάνια MW om.
AVBE | ἢ¹ MWA οὔτε VBE | περικνημίδας ἤγουν MW om. AVBE   204 χαλκότουβα MW
χειρόψελλα AVBE   204–206 ἀσπίδας…βάλλοντες MW σκουτάρια βαρέα ἀλλ' ἢ ἐτόξευον
ἢ ριπτάρια ἔρριπον ἢ λίθους ἔβαλλον AVBE   206 ρικτάρια Va ρηκτάρια MW ριπτάρια
AVBE   207 στερεὰς MW ἰσχυρὰς AVBE

hurling one or two javelins, they engaged the enemy in close fighting. Others made use of the spears they still had left or of their light spears or of their swords. They called these men light troops. Some of them also carried small axes with points like sharpened teeth on all sides. To the extent that we can summarize it, that is how the ancients armed their cavalry forces.

29. We have found that the ancients ordered their infantry as follows.[17] They divided its armament into three parts, as we mentioned above: one force they called hoplites, another peltastai, another light armed.

30. They made the men they called hoplites the most heavily armed of all the foot soldiers, in the Macedonian manner, that which Alexander, who was <the commander> of the Macedonians, employed. They made shields for them that were large, rounded, oval in shape, that they called thyreoi. Also knives or daggers, cuirasses and helmets, that is, body armor, breastplates, and helmets, as well as gauntlets and greaves that the ancients called shin guards, and longer spears. That is how they armed the troops they called hoplites.

31. They armed the light-armed troops with the lightest equipment of all.[18] For they did not have cuirasses or breastplates or body armor or leg coverings or podopsella or greaves or thyreoi or heavy shields or large shields. But they fought with weapons thrown from a great distance, loosing arrows, hurling missiles, or throwing stones, some by hand, some with slings. In place of body armor, breastplates, and the rest, they had clothing that was stiff and compacted.

*17. Sections 29–30 derive from Aelian 2.7.
*18. Aelian 2.8.

32. Τὸ δὲ τῶν πελταστῶν λεγομένων εἶδος, ὅπερ οἱ νεώτεροι τῶν τακτικῶν
210 οὐκ ἐδήλωσαν—οἶμαι δέ, ὡς ἄνω μοι εἴρηται, τοῖς ψιλοῖς αὐτὸ συμμίξαντες—
καὶ αὐτὸ μὲν εἶχεν ὁπλισμὸν ἐλαφρότερον δὲ τῶν ἄλλων. εἶχε γὰρ πέλτην, ὅ ἐστι
σκουτάριον μικρόν, καὶ τὰ δόρατα αὐτῶν ἤγουν τὰ κοντάρια πολὺ τῶν λεγομένων σαρισῶν παρὰ τοῖς παλαιοῖς κοντότερα. αἱ δὲ σάρισαι ἦσαν κοντάρια
μακρὰ ἕως πηχῶν ιδ΄ καὶ ἄχρι πηχῶν ις΄. ταῦτα δὲ ἦσαν μάλιστα τῆς Μακεδονι-
215 κῆς ὁπλίσεως. ἐδόκει δὲ ἡ τῶν πελταστῶν ὅπλισις μέσην ἔχειν τάξιν τῶν τε
ψιλῶν καὶ τῶν ἰδίως λεγομένων ὁπλιτῶν, βαρυτέρα μὲν οὖσα τῶν ψιλῶν, ἐλα-
φροτέρα δὲ τῶν ὁπλιτῶν.

33. Ἦν δὲ παρὰ τοῖς ὁπλίταις καὶ ἀσπὶς Μακεδονικὴ χαλκῆ, οὐ λίαν κοίλη,
ἤγουν σκουτάριον στρογγύλον, μέγα, ἁπαλωτέραν ἔχον τὴν κοιλότητα, τὸ δὲ
220 μέτρον αὐτῆς σπιθαμῶν τριῶν. ἦν δὲ καὶ κοντάριον οὐ μικρότερον πηχῶν η΄, τὸ
δὲ μακρότερον μέχρι τοῦ δύνασθαι ἄνδρα κρατοῦντα κινεῖν αὐτὸ εὐκόλως.

34. Ἡ δὲ Μακεδονικὴ φάλαγξ ἐκείνη ἤγουν ἡ παραταγὴ ἐδόκει τοῖς πολεμίοις ἀνυπόστατος εἶναι διὰ τὴν ἐν ταῖς τάξεσι κατασκευήν. ἵστατο γὰρ ὁ ἀνὴρ
ἐξωπλισμένος ἐν τῷ τοῦ ἀγῶνος τῆς συμβολῆς καιρῷ καταπυκνουμένης τῆς
225 παραταγῆς ἐν τῇ ἑκάστου στάσει εἰς πήχεις δύο, κατέχων τὴν σάρισαν ἤγουν τὸ
μακρὸν κοντάριον, ὅπερ, ὡς μέν τινες ἔφασαν, πηχῶν ἑξκαίδεκα, κατὰ δὲ τὴν
ἀλήθειαν πηχῶν δεκατεσσάρων. τούτων δὲ τέσσαρες μὲν πήχεις ἀφαιρεῖ τὸ
μεταξὺ τῶν χειρῶν εἰς τὸ ὀπίσω, οἱ δὲ λοιποὶ δέκα πήχεις εἰς τὸ ἔμπροσθεν
ἐκτείνονται πρὸ τῶν σωμάτων.

---

218–221 Aelian., 12.1.    222–229 Aelian., 14.1.

---

210 οἶμαι...εἴρηται MW om. AVBE | αὐτὸ MW αὐτὸ ὡς ὑπολαμβάνω AVBE
213 κοντότερα AVBE κονδότερα MW    214 μακρὰ MWA μικρὰ VBE | ιδ΄ MWAVE ιε΄ B
214–215 ταῦτα...ὁπλίσεως MWA om. VBE    216–217 βαρυτέρα...ὁπλιτῶν MWA om.
VBE    218 ad κοίλη scr. mg. βαρεια W    219 σκουτάριον MWA σκουτάριον τὸ VBE |
ἁπαλωτέραν Va ἁπλοτέραν MWA ἁπλωτέραν VBE    220 τριῶν MA γ΄ WVBE
221 μακρότερον MW μακρότατον AVBE    222 δὲ μακεδονικὴ MAVBE trsp. W | φάλαγξ
WAVBE φάλαξ M    223 ad ἀνυπόστατος scr. mg. ἀναπάντητος W | ὁ MWA om. VBE
224 τοῦ...καιρῷ MW καιρῷ τῆς τοῦ πολέμου συμβολῆς AVBE    225 ἑκάστου στάσει MW
στάσει ἑκάστου A στάσει ἑκάστου ἀνδρὸς VBE | δύο MWA β΄ VBE    226 ὅπερ ὡς MWA ὃ
πρῶτον B ὁ πρῶτος VE | ἔφασαν MWA εἶπον VBE | ἑξκαίδεκα MW ις΄ AVBE
227 δεκατεσσάρων W ιδ΄ MAVBE | τέσσαρες MW δ΄ A τέσσαρας VBE | μὲν MWA om. VBE

32. The class of those called peltasts has not been described by more recent tactical writers, because, as I have already stated, it is my opinion that they confused it with the light-armed troops. Its armament was indeed lighter than the others. For it had a pelta, that is, a small shield. Its spears or lances were much shorter than the so-called pikes used by the ancients. The pikes were long spears from fourteen to sixteen pecheis that were the specialties of the Macedonian armament.[19] It seems that the armament of the peltasts held a middle place between that of the light-armed troops and that of those specifically called hoplites, heavier than that of the light-armed but lighter than that of the hoplites.

33. The hoplites also had a bronze, Macedonian shield, not too concave, or else <they had> a round shield, large, with less curvature, and measuring three spithamai.[20] The spear was not smaller than eight pecheis nor so large that a man carrying it could not easily move it.[21]

34. The Macedonian phalanx was a formation that appeared irresistible to the enemy because of its system of lining up.[22] At the moment of close combat, as the battle line became tighter, the heavily armored men took their stand, each in his own place, two pecheis <apart>. They wielded the pike, or the large spear that, according to some, measured sixteen pecheis, but was really fourteen. Four of these pecheis covered the space from the man's hands to the space behind him and the other ten pecheis stretched out in front of his body.

[19]. 6.55 m to 7.84 m. Cf. Aelian 14.1.

[20]. 73 cm. Aelian 12.1; Asclepiodotus 5.1.

[21]. 3.74 m.

[22]. The formation was sixteen deep. See Aelian 14.1; SyrMag 16.

230   35. Τοσαῦτα μὲν οὖν καὶ περὶ τῆς καθ᾿ ἕνα ἄνδρα στρατιώτην ὁπλίσεως ἔκ τε τῶν παλαιῶν καὶ τῶν νεωτέρων τακτικῶν ἀναλεξάμενοι διεταξάμεθά τε καὶ διωρισάμεθα, ἵνα ἔχων αὐτῶν τὴν γνῶσιν ἐκλέγῃ τὸ χρήσιμον. |

---

230 στρατιώτην MW στρατιωτῶν A om. VBE   230–231 ὁπλίσεως… νεωτέρων MWA om. VBE   231–232 ἀναλεξάμενοι…διωρισάμεθα MW συνελεξάμεθα διωρισάμεθά τε καὶ διεταξάμεθα A συνελεξάμεθα διωρίσαμέν τε καὶ διεταξάμεθα VBE   232 γνῶσιν MW γνώμην AVBE

35. This much, then, about the armament of each individual soldier we have read in the ancient and more recent tacticians. We have organized it and defined it so that, possessing this knowledge, you may choose what is beneficial.

## Περὶ γυμνασίας καβαλλαρικῆς καὶ πεζικῆς

1. Ἑξῆς δὲ καὶ περὶ τῆς αὐτῶν γυμνασίας πρὸ τῶν πολεμικῶν ἀγώνων ὀφειλούσης γίνεσθαι μετρίως σοι καὶ συντόμως ὑπαγορεύσομεν, ὦ στρατηγέ, ἵνα
5 προπαρασκευάζῃς αὐτοὺς ἐθίζεσθαι πρὸς τοὺς ἀληθεῖς κινδύνους διὰ τῶν ἐν
γυμνασίᾳ κινδύνων. τὸ γὰρ ἀγύμναστον παντελῶς ἀμαθὲς καὶ τυφλὸν πρὸς τὰς
ἀθρόας καὶ ἀμελετήτους ἐγχειρήσεις εὑρίσκεται.

2. Ἡ γὰρ ἐν καιρῷ χειμῶνος ἢ ἐν ἑτέρῳ καιρῷ, ἐν ᾧ ἐστιν ἀνοχὴ πολέμου ἢ
τινων ἐπελεύσεων κατὰ πολεμίας γῆς ἄνεσις, γυμνάζειν σε χρὴ τὰ στρατόπεδα
10 καὶ ποιεῖν τοὺς στρατιώτας πολεμικοὺς καὶ ὥσπερ συντρόφους τῶν πόνων διὰ
τοῦ ἐθισμοῦ καὶ μὴ ἀφίῃς αὐτοὺς ἀργεῖν μήτε ῥαθυμεῖν. καὶ γὰρ ἡ ἀργία μαλακὰ
καὶ ἀσθενῆ ποιεῖ τὰ σώματα, ἡ δὲ ῥαθυμία δειλὰς καὶ ἀνάνδρους τὰς ψυχὰς
παρασκευάζει. αἱ γὰρ ἡδοναὶ τὸ καθ᾽ ἡμέραν δελεάζουσαι καὶ τὸν εὐτολμότατον διαφθείρουσι. καὶ ὅτ᾽ ἂν ἐπὶ μακρὸν χρόνον ἀνεθέντες πάλιν ἐπὶ τοὺς
15 πόνους ἔλθωσιν, οὔτε ἡδέως ἐξίασιν, οὔτε ἐπιπολὺ καρτερήσουσιν, ἀλλ᾽ εὐθέως
φεύγουσιν, πρὶν ἢ καὶ πεῖραν λαβεῖν τῶν πολεμικῶν πόνων. εἰ δὲ καὶ εἰς πεῖραν
ἐπὶ μικρὸν ἔλθωσιν, ταχέως ἀποχωρήσονται, φέρειν τοὺς πόνους καὶ κινδύνους
οὐ δυνάμενοι. διόπερ καὶ ἀγαθὸν ἐγὼ κρίνω στρατηγόν, ὅτ᾽ ἂν τὰ χρήσιμα τότε
σκευάζῃ καὶ διατάττῃ καὶ ἔργα καὶ πράγματα ὅτε οὐ κατεπείγουσιν αἱ τῶν
20 πολεμικῶν πόνων ἀνάγκαι.

---

M W A V B E    Va    PG 107:733

**8–20** Onas. 9.2; 10.1.

**1** πολεμικῶν παρασκευῶν MWA. om. VBE | ζʹ MWVBE ἑβδόμη A   **3–4** ὀφειλούσης MW
ὀφειλούσης σοι AVBE   **4** σοι MW om. AVBE   **11** ἀφίῃς MW ἀφὴς AVBE | ad μαλακὰ scr.
mg. χαυνα W   **13** τὸ MWVE om. AB | δελεάζουσαι MWA δελεάζουσι VBE
**13–14** εὐτολμότατον MAVBE διαφθείρουσιν W   **14** ἀνεθέντες MWA
ἀνεθέντας VBE scr. mg. ἤγουν ἐκ τῶν κόπων καὶ πονων ἀργησαντες W   **15** ἐξίασιν Va
ἔξουσιν codd.   **16** φεύγουσιν MW φεύγουσι AVBE | ἢ καὶ MW om. AVBE | πόνων
MWAVE πόνων ἀνάγκαι Β   **17** ἔλθωσιν MWA ἔλθωσι VBE | ἀποχωρήσονται Va
ἀποχωρίζονται codd.   **18** τὰ χρήσιμα MW om. AVBE   **19** σκευάζῃ MW προκατασκευάζῃ
AVBE | ὅτε VBE ὅτ᾽ ἂν MWA | κατεπείγουσιν MAB οὐ κατεπείγωσιν W οὐκεπείγουσιν VE
**19–20** αἱ…πολεμικῶν MWAVE om. Β   **20** πόνων MWAVE καὶ διαπόνων Β

# PREPARATION FOR WAR, CONSTITUTION VII

## About Training for the Cavalry and the Infantry

1. Next, O commander, in a general, summary fashion, we propose for your consideration the training of the men that ought to take place before they engage the enemy. This will help you in preparing them to become accustomed to actual danger by facing dangers in training. Untrained men turn out to be totally ignorant and blind in the face of sudden and unexpected actions.

2. In winter or at other times when there is a respite from war or a halt in expeditions into hostile territory, it is necessary for you to exercise the army and to make the soldiers skilled in war by getting them used to it, as though they were raised on hard labor.[1] Do not permit them to become idle or to relax. Idleness makes the body soft and weak, while relaxation renders the soul cowardly and unmanly. For daily pleasures entrap and corrupt even the most courageous man. Whenever they have been at rest for a long time and then once more return to their labors, they do not go willingly nor will they persevere very long, but they will quickly take to flight before they have experienced the hardships of war. Even if they do acquire a little experience, they swiftly retreat, unable to bear the labor and the dangers. For this reason I judge that man to be a good commander who prepares what will prove helpful and who organizes work and activities during that period when the unavoidable labors of war are not pressing.

---

1. Cf. Onasander 9.2, 10.1.

3. Γύμναζε δὲ τὸν στρατὸν τοιούτοις τρόποις καὶ ἐπιτηδεύμασι· πρῶτον μὲν τὸν καθένα στρατιώτην ὡς ἐν μελέτῃ, τοὺς μὲν ὁπλίτας σκουτάτους πεζῇ ἤγουν τοὺς φοροῦντας τὴν πανοπλίαν εἰς μονομαχίας μετὰ σκουταρίων καὶ βεργίων ἀντὶς ἀλλήλων, εἰς τὸ ῥῖψαι μήκοθεν ῥικτάριν καὶ μαρτζυβάρβουλον, ὃ λέγεται
25 νῦν σαλίβα, καὶ τζικούριν. τοὺς δὲ λεγομένους ψιλοὺς οὕτω γυμνάσεις· εἰς τοξείαν σύντομον κατὰ κονταρίου ὑψηλοῦ ἀπὸ διαστήματος, εἰς τὸ ῥίπτειν μήκοθεν ῥικτάριν καὶ σφενδόβολον, εἰς πηδήσεις καὶ δρόμους κατά τε ὁμαλῶν τόπων καὶ ἀνωμάλων.

4. Τοὺς δὲ καβαλλαρίους γυμνάσεις εἰς τὸ τοξεύειν συντόμως· ἡ γὰρ ταχύ-
30 της καὶ ἐκτινάσσεσθαι παρασκευάζει τὴν σαγίτταν καὶ ἰσχυρῶς βάλλεσθαι, ὅπερ τῶν | ἀναγκαίων ἐστί, καὶ τοῖς ἐπὶ ἵππων ὀχουμένοις χρήσιμον. καὶ ἔτι εἰς  301ᵛ
τὸ τοξεύειν πεζῇ ἀπὸ διαστήματος συντόμως, εἴτε κατὰ κονταρίου εἴτε κατὰ ἑτέρου σημείου. εἰς τὸ τοξεύειν ἐπάνω ἵππου τρέχοντος συντόμως ἔμπροσθεν, ὄπισθεν, δεξιᾷ, ἀριστερᾷ· εἰς τὸ πηδᾶν ἐφ᾽ ἵππους· εἰς τὸ τοξεύειν συντόμως
35 ἐπάνω ἵππου τρέχοντος μίαν ἢ καὶ δευτέραν σαγίτταν καὶ ἀποτίθεσθαι τὸ τόξον τεταμένον ἐν τῷ θηκαρίῳ, ἐὰν πλατύ ἐστιν, ἢ ἐν ἄλλῳ ἡμιθηκίῳ ἐπὶ τούτῳ γινομένῳ εὐκαίρως· καὶ ἐπιλαμβάνεσθαι τοῦ κονταρίου ἐκ τοῦ ὤμου βασταζο-
μένου. καὶ εἰς τὸ ἔχειν μὲν τὸ τόξον τεταμένον ἐν τῷ θηκαρίῳ, κρατεῖν δὲ τὸ κοντάριν καὶ συντόμως ἀποτίθεσθαι αὐτὸ ἐν τῷ ὤμῳ, ἐπιλαμβάνεσθαι δὲ τοῦ
40 τόξου.

5. Εἰς τὸ ἐπέρχεσθαι ἀλλήλοις ἄνδρας δύο καὶ ὑποχωρεῖν καὶ πάλιν ἐπε-
λαύνειν καὶ ἐξελίσσειν κατὰ τὸν τύπον τοῦ λεγομένου παρακοντακίου. τινὰς δὲ αὐτῶν καλόν ἐστι καὶ ἐν τῷ ὁδοιπορεῖν τοὺς στρατιώτας γυμνάζεσθαι ἐν τῇ ἰδίᾳ χώρᾳ καὶ ἐπιτηδεύειν αὐτὰ ἐπάνω τῶν ἵππων ποιεῖν. ἐκ τούτου γὰρ καὶ ἡ ὁδὸς
45 ἀνεμποδίστως ἐκτελεῖται καὶ οἱ ἵπποι οὐ συντρίβονται.

---

21–53 *Strat.*, 1.1.

---

21 γύμναζε MWAVE γυμνάζεσθαι B | τρόποις AVBE πόνοις MW    22 τὸν καθένα MW ἕνα ἕκαστον AVBE    23 μονομαχίας MWAB μοναχίας VE    24 ἀντὶς MW ἐξ ἐναντίας AVBE scr. mg. απεναντι W | ῥικτάριν Va ῥηκτάριν W ῥηκτάριον M ῥιπτάριον AVBE | μαρτζυβάρβουλον A ματζυάρβουλον MW ματζοβάρβουλον VBE | ὃ MW ὅπερ AVBE 25 καὶ MW ἢ A ἢ καὶ VBE | τζικούριν MW τζικούριον AVBE | οὕτω MW οὕτως AVBE 27 ῥικτάριν M ῥηκτάριν W ῥιπτάριον AVBE    29 εἰς τὸ MW om. AVBE    31 ἐπὶ MW ἐπὶ τῶν A ἐφ᾽ VBE | ἔτι MWVBE ἔστι A    32 κατὰ¹ MWA om. VBE    34 εἰς¹…ἵππους MWA om. VBE | συντόμως AVBE συντόνως MW    36 ἐὰν MWA εἰ VBE | ἐστιν WAVBE om. M 39 κοντάριν MW κοντάριον AVBE    41 ἀλλήλοις MWAVE ἀλλήλους B | δύο MWA β′ VBE    43 ἐστι MAVBE ἐστιν W    45 ἐκτελεῖται MW τελεῖται AVBE

3. Train the army in the following ways and practices.[2] Begin by drilling the individual soldier, the heavy-armed foot soldiers with their shields, that is, men who are fully armed, in single combat with shields and staffs against one another, in hurling from a long distance the short javelin and the lead-pointed dart, now called the saliba, as well as the axe. You shall train the so-called light-armed troops as follows. In rapid shooting with a bow, using a lance set up a good distance away as a target. In throwing the small javelin a long distance and using the sling. In jumping and running on level as well as rough ground.

4. Train the cavalrymen to shoot rapidly. Speed is important in releasing the arrow and discharging it with force. This is useful, even essential, for men mounted on horses. They should, moreover, practice shooting rapidly on foot from a distance, either against a spear or some other target. The trooper on horseback should also shoot rapidly on the run, to the front, to the rear, to the right, to the left. Leaping onto the horse. While racing on horseback he should loose one or two arrows rapidly and put the strung bow away in its case, if it is wide enough, or in another half-case specially designed for it. Then grab the spear he has been carrying on his shoulder. While the strung bow is in its case, he should grasp the spear and quickly replace it on his shoulder and grab hold of the bow.

5. Two men should charge against one another and then withdraw; again, ride forward and then wheel about, according to the model called parakontakiou.[3] It is good for some of the soldiers to practice these drills, while marching along on horseback in their own country. For they can continue marching without obstacle and the horses do not become worn out.

2. For sections 3–6 cf. *Strat.* 1 and Haldon, *Commentary*.

3. Parakontakiou may be a mistake for para kontariou (by the spear), following Lami's reading (PG 107:737), or a corruption of the Latin, *per contrarium* (by the opposite), as Vári thought.

6. Ἐὰν δὲ συμβῇ καὶ χρονίσαι τὸ στράτευμα ἐν ἐξπεδίτῳ ἤγουν ἔνθα συνάγεται κατὰ τὸν ἴδιον καιρὸν ὅλος ὁ στρατός, μὴ ἀργοὺς εἶναι τὸν καθένα, ἀλλ᾽
ἐθίζεσθαι αὐτούς, ὡς εἴρηται, πονεῖν. καὶ ποτὲ μὲν γυμνάζεσθαι πονεῖν κατὰ τὸν
εἰρημένον τρόπον, ποτὲ δὲ ὡς ἐν παρατάξει καὶ ἐν ἀλλήλοις, ποτὲ δὲ εἰς ὅπλων
50 ἐργασίας ἀπασχολεῖσθαι. ἡ γὰρ ἀργία οὐ μόνον νωθροὺς καὶ ἀνάνδρους ποιεῖ,
ἀλλὰ καὶ κενά τινα καὶ στασιώδη μελετᾶν αὐτοὺς παρασκευάζει καὶ παρεξάγει·
γυμναζόμενοι δὲ πρὸς τοὺς ἑκουσίους πόνους, εὐκόλως ἄρα καὶ τοὺς ἀκουσί-
ους ὑπενέγκωσι καὶ πρὸς τὰ παραγγελλόμενα αὐτοῖς ὑπακούειν ἐθισθῶσιν.

7. Καὶ οὐ μόνον καθ᾽ ἕνα γυμνάσεις αὐτούς, ἀλλ᾽ ἐθίσεις καὶ καθόλου
55 γινώσκειν τὰς ἰδίας τάξεις καὶ μένειν ἐν αὐταῖς, καὶ ταῖς ὄψεσι καὶ τοῖς ὀνόμασι
συνήθεις ἀλλήλοις γίνεσθαι. καὶ τίς στρατιώτης ὑπὸ τίνα ἐστὶν ἄρχοντα καὶ ἐν
ποίῳ βάνδῳ καὶ μετὰ ποσῶν ἀνδρῶν τάττεται· γινώσκειν δὲ τὰ ὀξέα παραγγέλματα μετὰ τάξεως παρὰ τῶν ἀρχόντων γινόμενα, οἷον τὰς ἐκτάσεις εἴτε κατὰ
πλάτος εἴτε κατὰ μῆκος τῆς παρατάξεως, ὁμοίως δὲ καὶ τὰς συστολὰς ἤγουν
60 σφίγξεις εἰς πύκνωσιν, καὶ τὰς κλίσεις ἐπὶ τὰ ἀριστερὰ καὶ ἐπὶ τὰ δεξιά, καὶ τὰς
τῶν ὀρδίνων μετα|ποιήσεις καὶ τὰ διαστήματα τῶν στάσεων ἀπὸ ἀνδρὸς εἰς    302
ἄνδρα, καὶ τὰς μερικὰς αὐτῶν πυκνώσεις ἢ ἀραιώσεις, καὶ τὰς δι᾽ ἀλλήλων
ἀπαντήσεις καὶ ἀντιδιαβάσεις ἥ τε ἐρχομένων ἢ ἀπερχομένων, καὶ τὰς κατὰ τὰς
ἀκίας ἤγουν τοὺς ὀρδίνους διαιρέσεις αὐτῶν καὶ μερισμοὺς καὶ κατατάξεις.
65 8. Καὶ τὴν <ἐπὶ> φάλαγγα ἤγουν τὴν ὅλην παραταγήν, ὅτ᾽ ἄν, ὡς εἴρηται, ἐπὶ
βάθος συστέλληται καὶ ὅτ᾽ ἂν ἐπὶ μῆκος ἐκτείνηται, καὶ τὴν λεγομένην ἀντίστο-
μον ἤγουν δίστομον μάχην, ὅτ᾽ ἂν οἱ λεγόμενοι οὐραγοὶ ἤτοι οἱ ὄπισθεν τῶν
ὅλων ἀκιῶν ἐπιστρέψαντες πρὸς τοὺς κυκλοῦντας κατὰ πρόσωπον μάχωνται ὡς
πρωτοστάται, καὶ ὄπισθεν αὐτῶν ὁμοίως αὐτοῖς ἀντιστρέψῃ τὸ ἥμισυ τῆς ἀκίας·

---

54–97  Onas. 10. 1–6.

---

46  καὶ MW om. AVBE | ἐξπεδίτῳ A ἐν ἐξπεδήτῳ MW ἐξπεδίῳ VBE    47  τὸν καθένα MW
τοὺς στρατιώτας AVBE    48  πονεῖν[1] MWA om. VBE    50  οὐ μόνον MWAVE οὐ μόνον οὐ
μόνον B | ἀνάνδρους MW ἀνάνδρους τοὺς στρατιώτας AVBE    51  καὶ[1]…τινα MW om.
AVBE    52  ἑκουσίους MWAB ἑκουσίως VE | ἄρα MW om. AVBE    53  ὑπενέγκωσι MAVE
ὑπενέγκωσιν W ὑπενέγκουσι B    55  ὀνόμασι MWVBE ὀνόμασιν A    56  ἀλλήλοις MW
ἀλλήλους AVBE    57  ποσῶν ἀνδρῶν MW πόσους ἄνδρας AVBE | τάττεται MW τάσσεται
AVBE    58  ad ἐκτάσεις scr. mg. ἤγουν ὅταν ὀφείλωσι παρεκταθῆναι W    59  δὲ MWA om.
VBE    60  εἰς MWA om. VBE | καὶ[2] AVBE om. MW    61  καὶ AVBE τὰ W om. M | εἰς
MWAVE om. B    62–63  ἀραιώσεις…ἀπαντήσεις MWA om. VBE    63  ἀντιδιαβάσεις MW
διαβάσεις AVBE | ἥ τε MW εἴτε AVBE | ἢ MW εἴτε AVE om. B | ἀπερχομένων MWAVE om.
B    64  διαιρέσεις MWA διαιρήσεις VBE | καὶ κατατάξεις MWAVE om. B    65  ἐπὶ[1] ci. De
om. codd. | παραταγήν MW παράταξιν AVBE    66  συστέλληται AVBE συστέλλεται MW |
ἐκτείνηται A ἐκτείνεται MW ἐκτείνονται VBE    67  οἱ[2] MWAVE om. B

6. If the expeditionary army should happen to be encamped for a long time or the entire army should be assembled in one place at the same time, do not let all the men take it easy but get them accustomed, as mentioned, to hard work. At times, drill them hard in the way already mentioned, at other times, as though lined up for battle against one another, at yet other times let them devote themselves to working on their weapons. Leisure not only makes them sluggish and cowardly, but prepares the way and misleads them into useless and seditious thoughts. If they are exercised in tasks they are willing to do, they will easily bear up under those they are unwilling to do, and they will become accustomed to obey the orders given to them.

7. Not only shall you drill them individually, but you will get them used to recognizing in its entirety their own formations and to maintain them and to become familiar with the faces and the names of one another.[4] Each soldier <must know> which officer he is under and in what bandon and with how many men he is stationed. He must know the exact commands given by the officers about formations, such as open order, either according to the width of the battle line or its depth. Also, in like manner, close order or the tightening up into close order. Turning to the left and to the right. Re-forming the columns and the distances in the positions of one man from another. Their partial closing up and broadening. The passing and repassing of files through one another, both advancing and retreating. Their divisions according to files or columns and their distribution and arrangement.

8. Also, whenever, as mentioned, the phalanx or the entire battle formation is drawn together in depth or when it is extended in length. And what is called face-to-face battle or one on two fronts, when the men who are called the last of the file or those behind the entire file turn toward those circling about and fight facing forward as protostatai do, and behind them, in like fashion, half of the file

---

4. Sections 7–14 derive from Onasander 10.1–6.

70 καὶ πάλιν τὰς ἐκ τῶν τοιούτων μεταβολῶν ἀνακλήσεις καὶ ἀποκαταστάσεις
ἵππων.

9. Οἱ γὰρ πρὸς ταῦτα πάντα ἐθιζόμενοι στρατιῶται διὰ τάχους, ὡς εἰπεῖν, καὶ
αὐτόματοι φέρονται πρὸς τὴν τάξιν, οἱ δὲ τούτων ἀνέθιστοι καὶ ἀπαίδευτοι διὰ
ταράχου πολλοῦ καὶ μόλις ἀποκαθίστανται εἰς τὰς κατεπειγούσας τῆς τάξεως
75 χρείας.

10. Διαμερίσας δὲ τὰ στρατεύματα πρὸς ἀλλήλους ἀσιδήρῳ μάχῃ συμβαλλέ-
τωσαν ἤτοι διὰ κονταρίων ἄνευ ξιφῶν ἢ σαγιττῶν ὁμοίως ἤ, ὡς εἴπομεν, ἀντὶ
σπαθίων βεργία ἢ νάρθηκας ἢ καλάμους ἀντὶ κονταρίων ἀναδιδούς. ἐὰν δὲ καὶ
βώλους ἔχῃ ἡ γῆ ἐν ᾗ γυμνάζωνται, τούτους βάλλειν κέλευε κατ' ἀλλήλων ἐν τῇ
80 γυμνασίᾳ τῆς συμβολῆς. ποτὲ δὲ καὶ τὰ λεγόμενα χαρζάνια ἢ τούτοις ὅμοιά
τινα χρήσθωσαν ἐν τῇ μάχῃ. δείξας δὲ αὐτοῖς καὶ βουνοὺς ὀρθίους κέλευε σὺν
δρόμῳ ἀναβαίνειν καὶ καταλαμβάνειν αὐτούς, ἔχοντας δηλονότι τοὺς βουνοὺς
ἐκείνους ἑτέρους στρατιώτας ἐφεστῶτας ἐπ' αὐτῶν.

11. Καὶ ὅτ' ἄν τινας τῶν στρατιωτῶν γυμνάσῃς, πάλιν ἐκείνους ἐκβαλὼν
85 ἑτέροις ἐπιδώσεις τὰ εἰρημένα ὅπλα. καὶ τοὺς μὲν μείναντας καὶ ἀνδραγαθήσαντας ἐν τῇ γυμνασίᾳ ἐπαινέσεις, τοὺς δὲ ἀφυῶς ἐλθόντας καὶ ἀνάνδρως
παραθήξεις καὶ παροτρυνεῖς εἰς τὸ τὰ ἐλαττώματα αὐτῶν ἀνορθωθῆναι.

12. Ἐκ γὰρ τῆς τοιαύτης μελέτης καὶ γυμνασίας οὐ μόνον ἐθίζεται πρὸς τοὺς
πόνους τὸ στράτευμα, ἀλλὰ καὶ ὑγιαίνει καὶ πᾶσαν τροφὴν ἡδέως ἐσθίει καὶ
90 πίνει, κἂν λιτή ἐστιν, ὑπὲρ τὰς πολυτελεῖς τροφάς. γίνεται δὲ αὐτῶν τὸ σῶμα καὶ
στερρόν, καὶ συνεθίζεται τοῖς μέλλουσι πόνοις, ἱδρῶτι καὶ θάλπει καὶ καύματι
ἀσκιάστῳ | καὶ κρυμοῖς καὶ χειμῶσι συγγυμναζόμενον.                    302ᵛ

13. Ὁμοίως δὲ γυμνάσεις καὶ τοὺς καβαλλαρίους ἐρίζειν αὐτοῖς ποιῶν καὶ
ἁμιλλᾶσθαι καὶ διώξεις ποιεῖν καὶ συμπλοκὰς καὶ ἀκροβολισμοὺς ἤγουν τοξείας
95 ἢ ἀκοντίσεις. καὶ ὅσα ἐξῆς σοι πλατύτερον δηλώσω.

---

70 ἀποκαταστάσεις AVBE ἀποκαταστήσεις MW    71 ἵππων W om. MAVBE    72 ταῦτα
πάντα MWVBE τὰ παρόντα A    76–77 πρὸς…συμβαλλέτωσαν MW παρακελεύου πρὸς
ἀλλήλους συμβάλλειν μάχην χωρὶς σιδήρου AVBE    78 βεργία AVBE βεργίοις MW |
ἀναδιδούς MW ἐπιδιδοὺς AVBE    80 καὶ τὰ MWAB κατὰ VE    81 χρήσθωσαν MWB
ἐχέτωσαν AVE | κέλευε MWVBE κέλευσον A    83 ἐφεστῶτας MWA ἐστῶτας VBE
86 ἐλθόντας…ἀνάνδρως MW καὶ ἀνάνδρως διατεθέντας AVBE    87 παραθήξεις MW
διεγείρεις AVBE | παροτρυνεῖς MW παρορμήσεις AVBE | εἰς…ἀνορθωθῆναι MW τὰ αὐτῶν
ἀνορθῶσαι ἐλαττώματα AVBE    90 ἐστιν MW ἐστιν καὶ εὐτελὴς A καὶ εὐτελὴς ἤ VBE |
τροφάς AVBE τρυφὰς MW    91 στερρόν MW ἰσχυρὸν AVBE    92 συγγυμναζόμενον WAB
γυμναζόμενον M συγγυμναζόμενοι VE    93 αὐτοῖς MW αὐτοὺς AVBE    94 ἁμιλλᾶσθαι
MW om. AVBE | συμπλοκὰς MWA πλοκὰς VBE | ἀκροβολισμοὺς ἤγουν MW om. AVBE
95 ἢ MW καὶ AVBE

should turn about. Again, <sound> the calls to bring such wheeling about to an end and to bring the horses back into formation.

9. The soldiers who quickly become accustomed to all these are, so to say, brought into formation spontaneously, whereas men without instruction and unaccustomed to these exercises are totally confused and barely able to bring themselves back to the pressing needs of the battle line.

10. Divide the army in two parts, then have them come together in a mock battle, the lances and, likewise, the arrows without points or, as we said, with staffs instead of swords. Or instead of lances distribute staves or reeds. If the ground on which they are drilling has clods of earth, order them to throw these at each other in practicing for battle. At times let them make use of what are called charzania or similar items in their battles. Point out to the men steep hills and order them to ascend them on the run and seize them. Of course, you will have other soldiers in position on top of those hills.

11. After you drill one group of soldiers, then dismiss those troops and give the weapons we spoke of to others. You will praise those who stood firm and acted courageously in the drill, but those who turned out unfit and cowardly you will admonish and exhort them to correct their failures.

12. As a result of practice and drilling of this sort, not only is the army accustomed to hard labor, but it stays healthy, eating and drinking everything, even plain fare, more heartily than gourmet meals. Their bodies become harder and they will get used to future labors since they have done their training sweating and panting in the heat under the open sky and in the icy cold of winter.

13. In like manner you shall drill the cavalry forces, making them compete and vie with one another and engage in pursuits, close combat, and shooting of missiles, either arrows or javelins, as well as in other ways that I will subsequently explain to you at greater length.

14. Ταῦτα δὲ ποιεῖν καὶ ἐν ἐπιπέδοις τόποις καὶ περὶ αὐτὰς τὰς ῥίζας τῶν βουνῶν, ἐφ᾽ ὅσον δυνατόν ἐστιν αὐτοὺς καὶ τῶν τραχέων ἐγγίζειν τόπων.

15. Καὶ τοῦτο μὲν τοῖς παλαιοῖς ἔδοξεν· ἐμοὶ δὲ δοκεῖ μὴ μόνον εἰς δρόμους ἐν τοῖς ὁμαλοῖς τόποις ἐθίζεσθαι τοὺς ἵππους ἀναγκαῖον εἶναι, ἀλλὰ καὶ εἰς
100 ὑψηλοὺς καὶ δασεῖς καὶ τραχεῖς, ὥστε σὺν ἐλασίᾳ τούτους διαβαίνειν, ὁμοίως δὲ καὶ εἰς τοὺς κατωφερεῖς. ἐὰν γὰρ εἰς τοὺς τοιούτους ἐθίζωνται, οὐκέτι οὐδὲ τοὺς ἄνδρας οὐδὲ τοὺς ἵππους ξενίζει τόπος ἢ ἀδικεῖ. ἀλλὰ καὶ ἐν τῷ καιρῷ τοῦ θέρους μὴ ἐπιτηδεύειν πυκνῶς τοὺς ἵππους ποτίζειν. διὸ οὐδὲ χρήσιμόν ἐστι πλησίον ποταμῶν ἀπληκεύειν. καὶ παρατάσσεσθαι δὲ εἰς τοὺς δυσχερεῖς καὶ
105 δυσβάτους τόπους καὶ ἐπιτρέπειν, ὡς ἔστι<ν ἐν τάξει> τὸ βάνδον, καθὼς φθάσει ὁ τόπος ἑκάστῳ σὺν ἐλασίᾳ ἀνέρχεσθαι ὁμοίως δὲ καὶ κατέρχεσθαι. ὅσοι τοίνυν φειδόμενοι τῶν ἵππων αὐτῶν περιφρονοῦσι τῆς τοιαύτης αὐτῶν γυμνασίας, ἑαυτοῖς ἐπιβουλεύουσιν.

16. Ἐπὶ τούτοις δέον ἐστίν, εἰ καὶ μετρίως ὅμως καὶ ἐν ὀλίγοις, ὑποδεῖξαί σοι,
110 καθὼς προϋπεθέμεθα, πλατύτερον τὰς τῶν ἀρχαίων κινήσεις καὶ τὰ λεγόμενα παραγγέλματα, ἵνα προγυμνάζῃς καὶ ἐν τούτοις τὸ στράτευμα καὶ διεγείρῃς αὐτοὺς καὶ διὰ λόγων καὶ δι᾽ ἔργων πρὸς τὰς πολεμικὰς μεθόδους. μετὰ γὰρ τὴν γυμνασίαν τοῦ καθένα στρατιώτου πεζοῦ καὶ καβαλλαρίου δεῖ σε καὶ ἕκαστον τάγμα ἤτοι βάνδον γυμνάζειν καθ᾽ ἑαυτὸ οὕτως. τοῦ βάνδου τῶν καβαλλαρίων
115 ἀπὸ τῶν λεγομένων ἀκιῶν ἤτοι ὀρδίνων συνεστῶτος καὶ συντεταγμένως ἱσταμένου παραγγέλλει ὁ μανδάτωρ τὰ προστεταγμένα, οἷον·

17. <Σιγή,> ὅτ᾽ ἂν ἡ συμβολὴ γένηται. μηδεὶς ἀφήσῃ. μηδεὶς προλάβῃ <τὸ βάνδον>, ἕως ἂν διώξῃς τὸν ἐχθρόν. ἐὰν ἐκβῇς ἀπὸ τῆς τοῦ μετώπου ὄψεως, βλέπε τὸ βάνδον. δίωκε μὴ ὡς στρατιώτης δειλός, ἀλλ᾽ ὡς στρατιώτης ἀνδρεῖος,
120 καὶ μὴ κατὰ παράκλησιν ἐάσῃς μήτε ἄλλῳ τρόπῳ. φύλαττε, στρατιῶτα, τὴν

---

98–108 *Strat.*, 7.B.17.   117–248 *Strat.*, 3.5.

96 ἐπιπέδοις MW ὁμαλοῖς AVBE scr. mg. ἐν πεδίνοις καὶ ὁμαλοῖς W | αὐτὰς MW om. AVBE | τὰς ῥίζας MW τὰ κατώτερα μέρη AVBE   97 ἐφ᾽…τόπων MW ἀναβαίνειν δὲ αὐτοὺς καὶ ἐπὶ τῶν τραχέων τόπων ὅσον ἐστὶ δυνατόν AVBE   100 ὑψηλοὺς MW ὑψηλοὺς τόπους AVBE 103 πυκνῶς MW συχνῶς AVBE   104 ἀπληκεύειν AVBE ἀποκελεύειν Μ ἀπλικεύειν W | δὲ MWAVE om. Β   104–105 τοὺς…τόπους MW τόπους δυσχερεῖς καὶ διαβάτους AVBE 105 ἐν τάξει *Strat.* om. codd. | φθάσει MW λάχῃ AVBE   107 αὐτῶν¹ MWA om. VBE | περιφρονοῦσι MW καταφρονοῦσι AVBE | αὐτῶν² MW om. AVBE   109 ἐστίν…καὶ¹ MW ἐστὶ AVBE | ὅμως…ὀλίγοις MW om. AVBE   110 καθὼς…πλατύτερον MW om. AVBE 113 τοῦ καθένα MW ἑκάστου AVBE | καὶ¹ MWVBE om. A   115 συνεστῶτος MWA συνεστῶτας Β συνεστῶτος VE   117 σιγή *Strat.* om. codd.   117–118 τὸ βάνδον *Strat.* om. codd.   120 ἄλλῳ τρόπῳ MWA ἄλλον τρόπον VBE

14. Carry out these maneuvers in the plain and around the very roots of the hills, as far as they are able to advance in broken country.

15. While the ancient tacticians regarded this merely as good, I consider it essential to accustom the horses not only to rapid maneuvers in level terrain but also over hilly, dense, and rough ground so they may learn to ride quickly though such areas, as well as in steep terrain.[5] If they get used to such terrain, then no place will surprise or trouble either the men or the horses. Even in the heat of summer be careful not to water the horses too much; for this reason it is helpful not to camp too close to rivers. Have them line up in rough and difficult terrain and turn about. When the bandon is in formation, each man should gallop over the ground as he finds it before him and return the same way. The men who spare their horses and neglect drills of this sort are conspiring against themselves.

16. In addition to these, it is necessary to teach you in greater detail, albeit moderately and briefly, the maneuvers of the ancients and the words of their commands, as we previously proposed, so that you may use these to drill the army beforehand and you may stir them up by words and by deeds for military exercises. After the training of each individual soldier, horse and foot, you must drill each tagma or bandon by itself in the following manner. When the cavalry bandon forms up in what are called files or columns and is standing together in proper order, the herald proclaims the prescribed orders as follows.

17. <"Silence,"> when the battle begins. "Nobody fall back.[6] Nobody go ahead of the standard until you are pursuing the enemy. If you lose sight of the front, look at the standard. Follow <it> not as a cowardly soldier but as a brave soldier. Do not allow yourself to be distracted or <to act> in another manner.

---

5. Cf. *Strat.* 7 B.17.
6. *Strat.* 3.5.

τάξιν σου, φύλαττε καὶ σύ, βανδοφόρε, ὅτ᾽ ἂν καταπολε|μίσῃς, ἵνα ἀκολουθῇς 303
τὸν ἐχθρόν. εἰ δὲ ἐκβῇς τὴν ὄψιν τῆς παραταγῆς, μὴ ἐλάσῃς ἰσχυρῶς ἐν τῷ
κάμπῳ ἵνα μὴ σκορπίσῃς τὴν σὴν τάξιν.

18. Ἡ δὲ καθ᾽ ἑαυτὴν τοῦ τάγματος γυμνασία τῶν καβαλλαρίων αὕτη, ὥστε
125 κινεῖν συντεταγμένως ὡς ἐν παραταγῇ ἢ μετὰ δρόμου ἐπί τι σημεῖον καὶ οὕτως
ἵστασθαι. καὶ ὅτ᾽ ἂν θέλῃ κινῆσαι σημαίνειν δέον μονῇ τῇ φωνῇ ἢ τῷ βουκίνῳ ἢ
νεύματι φλαμούλου, καὶ κινεῖν οὕτως· ὅτ᾽ ἂν δὲ θέλῃ στῆναι, σημαίνειν ἢ τῇ
φωνῇ στα ἢ τῷ ἤχῳ τοῦ σκουταρίου ἢ τῇ τούβᾳ, ἣν νῦν λέγουσι βούκινον, ἢ τῇ
ταυρέᾳ. καὶ αὕτη μὲν μία κίνησις.

130 19. Ἑτέρα δέ, ὥστε ἴσα περιπατεῖν ἐν ἀραιοτέροις πρῶτον διαστήμασι, καὶ
παραγγέλλει· ἐξ ἴσου περιπατεῖτε.

20. Ἑτέρα δέ, ὥστε σφίγγεσθαι κατὰ πλευρὰν μάλιστα πρεπόντως, ὁμοίως
δὲ σφίγγεσθαι καὶ κατ᾽ οὐράν. τὸ δὲ σφίγγεσθαί ἐστι τὸ πυκνοῦσθαι, ἵνα καὶ
κατὰ πλευρὰς καὶ κατὰ ὦμον ἀλλήλοις ἐγγίζωσι. παραγγέλλει δέ· κατὰ πλευρὰν
135 σφίγγε, τοῦτ᾽ ἔστι, δεκάρχαι πρὸς δεκάρχας, πεντάρχαι πρὸς πεντάρχας, τετράρχαι πρὸς τετράρχας. καὶ σφίγγονται πάντες, ὡς εἴρηται, πλευρὰν πρὸς
πλευρὰν ἐγγίζοντες. οὐκ ἐπὶ ἑνὸς δὲ μέρους σφίγγονται, ἀλλ᾽ ἐπὶ τὸν μέσον
τόπον, τοῦτ᾽ ἔστι, τὸν βανδοφόρον, ὥστε ἔνθεν κἀκεῖθεν αὐτοῦ γίνεσθαι.
συντόμως γὰρ καὶ εὐτάκτως ἡ τοιαύτη γίνεται σφίγξις. ὥσπερ δὲ οἱ δεκάρχαι
140 ἰσοῦνται ἐν ἀλλήλοις κατὰ μέτωπον, οὕτως πρέπει καὶ τοὺς τετράρχας ἤγουν
τοὺς οὐραγοὺς ἰσοῦσθαι ὀπίσω τοῦ ὀρδίνου. αὐτῶν γὰρ σφιγγομένων κατὰ
λόγον, κἂν λιποτακτήσωσιν ἐν ταῖς συμβολαῖς οἱ ἔμπροσθεν, κωλύονται ὑπ᾽
αὐτῶν εἰς τὰ ὀπίσω τρέπεσθαι.

21. Ἑτέρα δέ, ὅτ᾽ ἂν σφίγγωνται κατ᾽ οὐράν. οὐ γὰρ μόνον τὸ πλάτος τῆς
145 παραταγῆς δέον σφίγγεσθαι, ἀλλὰ καὶ τὸ πάχος αὐτῆς, πολλάκις ἀλλήλοις κατὰ
τοὺς ὤμους ἐγγίζοντες.

---

121 βανδοφόρε MWA βανδιφόρε VBE    122 τὸν ἐχθρόν MW τῶ ἐχθρῶ AVBE
126 σημαίνειν δέον MW trsp. AVBE    127 κινεῖν οὕτως M trsp. WAVBE | ἢ AVBE om.
MW    128 στα AVBE om. MW | ἤχω MW κτύπω AVBE | νῦν λέγουσι M νῦν λέγουσιν W
λέγουσι νῦν AVBE    128–129 ἢ³…ταυρέα MW om. AVBE    130 διαστήμασι MAVE
διαστήμασιν W διαστήματι B    131 ἐξ MWAB om. VE    133 τὸ¹…τὸ² MW (ἔστιν W) ὅ ἐστι
AVBE    134 κατὰ¹…ὦμον MW ὄπισθεν καὶ ἐκ πλαγίου AVBE | ἐγγίζωσι MB ἐγγίζωσιν WA
ἐγγίζουσι VE | δέ MWAVE δὲδὲ B    135 σφίγγε AVBE σφίγγεσθαι MW | ἔστι MAVBE
ἔστιν W    136–137 πλευρὰν…πλευρὰν AVBE πλευρὰ πρὸς πλευρὰ M πλευρὰ πρὸς
πλευρὰν W    137 ἐπὶ ἑνὸς AVBE ἐπιθενὸς M ἐπι.ενὸς W (sic)    137–138 τὸν…τόπον MW
τῶν μέσων τόπων AVBE    138 τὸν M τῶν WAVBE    140 ἐν MW om. AVBE    143 ὀπίσω
M τοὺς ὀπίσω WAVBE    144 κατ᾽ M καὶ κατ᾽ WAVBE    145 καὶ MWAB καὶ καὶ VE |
ἀλλήλοις MWVBE ἀλλήλους A    146 ἐγγίζοντες MWA ἐγγίζοντας VBE

Soldier: keep to your assigned position. Standard-bearer: keep to yours also. When you are fighting and pursuing the enemy, if you leave the front of the battle line, do not charge out impetuously and cause your ranks to be broken up."

18. An individual cavalry tagma should be drilled as follows. At a given signal to move in proper order as in a battle line or on the run; then come to a halt. When the commander wants them to move, he must give the signal for "Move" by voice, by bugle, or by a movement of the flag.[7] And they move as ordered. When he wants them to stop, he signals: "Stand." <He does this by voice>, by banging on the shield or by the tuba, which they now call the trumpet, or else by the horn. And this is one maneuver.

19. Another one. To march in line, first, over a rather broad area, he commands: "In line. March."

20. Still another. Specifically to close ranks in proper order from the flanks and, likewise, to close ranks from the rear. To close ranks is the same as to tighten up, so that the men come close to one another by their sides and shoulders. The command for this is: "By the flank. Close up." This means that the dekarchs come close to the dekarchs, the pentarchs to the pentarchs, the tetrarchs to the tetrarchs. And they all close up, as said, getting closer side by side. They close in not on one section but upon the center, that is, the standard-bearer so as to be on this side and that side of him. This kind of closing up is to be done quickly and in good order. As the dekarchs align themselves with each other along the front, so should the tetrarchs or fileclosers align themselves at the rear of the column. When they close ranks as prescribed, they effectively keep the troops in front of them from deserting in combat and heading to the rear.

21. Another one. When they close up from the rear. Not only must the width of the battle line be closed up but also its thickness, as they come ever closer to one another, shoulder to shoulder.

7. Greek μονη is a mistranscription of Latin *move* (move) and στα is the same as Latin *sta* (stand). Cf. *Strat.* 3.5.11-12.

22. Ἑτέρα δὲ κίνησις, ὥστε μετὰ τὴν ἀκριβῆ πύκνωσιν τῆς κατὰ πλευρὰν μάλιστα σφίγξεως πεπυκνωμένους περιπατεῖν, ὅτ' ἂν ἡ τοξεία ἄρχεται γίνεσθαι, καὶ παραγγέλλει· πάταξον. καὶ ἐπικλινομένων τῶν δεκάρχων καὶ πεντάρχων ἐπὶ
150 τὰ ἔμπροσθεν καὶ σκεπόντων τὰς ἑαυτῶν κεφαλὰς καὶ μέρος τῶν τραχήλων τῶν ἵππων μετὰ τῶν σκουταρίων αὐτῶν καὶ τὰ κοντάρια ἀναβασταζόντων ἐπὶ τοὺς ὤμους καὶ ὑποκρυπτομένων | μετὰ τῶν σκουταρίων ἐπελαύνειν εὐτάκτως 303ᵛ τριπόδῳ μόνῳ ἤγουν κινήματι συμμέτρῳ, τῷ λεγομένῳ κάλπα, καὶ μὴ βιαίως τρέχειν, ἵνα μὴ τῇ ὀξύτητι τῆς ἐλασίας διαλυθῇ ἡ τάξις πρὸ μίξεως χειρῶν, ὅπερ
155 ἐστὶν ἐπικίνδυνον. τοὺς δὲ ὄπισθεν, ὅσοι τοξόται εἰσί, τοξεύειν.

23. Ἑτέρα δὲ κίνησις ὥστε ἐπιδιώκειν ὁτὲ μὲν σὺν ἐλασίᾳ ὡς κούρσωρας, οὓς οἱ νῦν προκλάστας λέγουσιν, ὁτὲ δὲ συντεταγμένως ὡς διφένσωρας, οὓς ἡμεῖς καλοῦμεν ἐκδίκους. καὶ εἰ μὲν ὡς κούρσωρας χρὴ κινεῖν, παραγγέλλει· δρόμῳ ἔλα. καὶ ἕως ἑνὸς μιλίου ἀποκινοῦσι σὺν ἐλασίᾳ. ἐὰν δὲ ὡς διφένσωρας, παραγ-
160 γέλλει· μετὰ τῆς τάξεως ἀκολούθει. καὶ ἀκολουθοῦσι συντεταγμένως.

24. Ἑτέρα δὲ κίνησις ὥστε ὑποχωρεῖν ὀλίγον καὶ πάλιν ἀντιστρέφεσθαι. καὶ ὅτε μὲν θέλει ὑποχωρῆσαι ὁ κούρσωρ, κράζει· τύπτε. καὶ ὑποχωρεῖ σὺν ἐλασίᾳ ὡς ἓν ἢ δεύτερον σαγιττοβόλον ἐπὶ τοὺς διφένσωρας. πάλιν κράζει· στράφου, ἔλα. καὶ ἀνθυποστρέφουσιν ὡς ἂν εἰ κατὰ τῶν ἐναντίων. καὶ τοῦτο ποιεῖν
165 πολλάκις μὴ μόνον ἐπὶ τὰ πρόσω, ἀλλὰ καὶ δεξιᾷ καὶ ἀριστερᾷ, καὶ πάλιν ὡς ἂν εἰ ἐπὶ τὴν δευτέραν τάξιν. καὶ ποτὲ μὲν ἐν αὐτῷ τῷ διαλείμματι ταύτης, ποτὲ δὲ ἐν τῷ μεταξὺ αὐτῆς ἐξελίσσεσθαι καὶ ἅμα δρουγγιστὶ ἤγουν ὁμοῦ ὁρμᾶν κατὰ τῶν ἐχθρῶν. ἐν δὲ ταῖς γυμνασίαις τὰ κοντάρια ἀναβασταζόμενα ἔχειν δεῖ καὶ μὴ εἰς πλάγιον, ἵνα μὴ οἱ ἵπποι ἐν τῇ ἐλασίᾳ ἐμποδίζωνται.

170 25. Ἑτέρα δὲ κίνησις ὥστε μετατίθεσθαι συντεταγμένως ἀριστερᾷ καὶ δεξιᾷ, ὅπερ ἁρμόζει πλαγιοφύλαξιν καὶ ὑπερκερασταῖς ἤγουν τοῖς ἐπὶ τὸ κυκλῶσαι τὴν τῶν πολεμίων παράταξιν τεταγμένοις ἐπὶ τοῦ δεξιοῦ μέρους, ὥσπερ κέρας. καὶ

---

148 πεπυκνωμένους MW περιπατεῖν πεπυκνωμένως A περιπατεῖν πεπυκνωμένος VBE
149 ἐπικλινομένων WAVBE ἐπικλιμένων M  150 τὰ AVBE om. MW  152 ὤμους
MWAVE ἵππους B | ἐπελαύνειν WAVBE ἐπελαύνει M | εὐτάκτως MW εὐτάκτω A ἀτάκτω
VBE  153 τριπόδω...ἤγουν MW om. AVBE | κινήματι συμμέτρω MW trsp. AVBE | βιαίως
MW ἰσχυρῶς AVBE  158 παραγγέλλει VBE παραγγέλλειν MWA  159 διφένσωρας AVE
διφένσορας MW διφένσωρα B  159–160 παραγγέλλει MW παραγγέλλειν AVBE
160 ἀκολούθει MWA ἀκολουθεῖν VBE  163 πάλιν MW ὅτε δὲ θέλει πάλιν ἐπὶ τοὺς
ἐναντίους ὑπστρέψαι AVBE | στράφου MWAB στάφου VE  165 πρόσω MW ἔμπροσθεν
AVBE  166 διαλείμματι MW διαχωρίσματι AVBE  166–168 ταύτης...ἐχθρῶν MW τῆς
αὐτῆς δευτέρας παρατάξεως δρουγγιστὶ ἤγουν (ἢ γὰρ V) ὁμοῦ ἐξελίσσεσθαι ποτὲ δὲ ἐν τῷ
μεταξὺ τῶν (τῆς B) δύο (β′ VBE) παρατάξεων (παρατάξεως B) διαστήματι AVBE
171 πλαγιοφύλαξιν MW πλαγιοφύλαξι AVBE  172 τεταγμένοις MWAVE τεταγμένους B

22. Another maneuver. With the troops marching in close formation, particularly after they have closed in tightly from the flanks, as they come within range of the <enemy> archers, and the command is given: "Strike." The dekarchs and pentarchs then lean forward, cover their heads and part of their horses' necks with their shields, hold their lances at shoulder height and, protected by their shields, they advance in good order, not too fast but at a canter, a measured gait, the so-called kalpa, so that the impetus of their charge might not break up their ranks before coming to blows with the enemy, a very risky action. All the archers to the rear are then to open fire.

23. Another maneuver. In pursuing <the enemy> sometimes they race along as assault troops, now called proklastai, or sometimes together in close order as defenders, now called ekdikoi. If it is necessary to move as assault troops, the commander gives the order: "Charge on the run." And they ride along at this rate for about a mile. If they move as defenders, he commands: "Follow in formation." And they follow in close ranks.

24. Another maneuver. To fall back a little and then wheel about. When the commander wants the assault troops to fall back, he shouts: "Give way." And they speedily withdraw a bowshot or two toward the defenders. Again he shouts: "Turn. Charge." They wheel about as though to face the enemy. Do this frequently, not only forward but also to the right and to the left, and again as though toward the second line. They should maneuver, sometimes in the intervals of that line, sometimes in the space between the lines. All together, in irregular formation, they then charge against the enemy. While drilling, the lances should be held up and not down to their sides, so as not to impede the free movement of the horses.

25. Another maneuver. To change front around to the left or to the right in an orderly fashion and in coordination with the flank guards and the outflankers, that is, the men lined up on the right side, like a horn, for the purpose of encircling the battle line of the enemy. If the commander wants them

παραγγέλλει, εἰ μὲν ἀριστερᾷ μετατίθεσθαι βούλεται· κατάφερε πρὸς τὰ ἀριστερά. εἰ δὲ δεξιᾷ μετατίθεσθαι· κατάφερε πρὸς τὰ δεξιά. καὶ οὕτως μετατίθεσθαι.
175 ἐὰν μὲν ἓν βάνδον ἐστί, τὸ ἕν, εἰ δὲ πλείονα, ὁμοίως τοῦ ἑνὸς μέρους μετατιθεμένου. καὶ τὰ λοιπὰ ὡσαύτως κατὰ ἓν βάνδον ποιοῦσιν.

26. Ἑτέρα δὲ κίνησις ὥστε μεταβάλλεσθαι ποτὲ μὲν ἐν οἷς ἵστανται τόποις,
ποτὲ δὲ καὶ τὸ μέτωπον τῆς παρατάξεως ἀλλάσσοντες. ἐὰν μὲν γὰρ αἰφνιδια-
σμός τις γένηται ὑπὸ ἐχθρῶν κατὰ νώτου ἤγουν ὄπισθεν ἐπιφερομένων, παραγ-
180 γέλλει· μετασχημάτισον. καί, ὡς ἵστανται ἐν τοῖς τόποις αὐτῶν, ἐπὶ οὐρὰν ὄπισθεν βλέπουσι τῶν βανδοφόρων μόνων μετὰ τῶν ἀρχόντων εἰς τὸ κατὰ οὐρὰν
μέτωπον | ἐρχομένων. εἰ δὲ πλῆθος ἐχθρῶν ἐπιφανῇ ὄπισθεν, παραγγέλλει·  304
μετάλλαξον. καὶ τότε μετατίθενται κατὰ βάνδον.

27. Οὐ μόνον δὲ ἐπὶ μῆκος ὀρδινεύειν καὶ γυμνάζειν ἀναγκαῖόν ἐστιν, ἀλλὰ
185 καὶ δρουγγιστὶ τάσσοντας γυμνάζειν καὶ ἐξελαύνειν ἐπ᾽ εὐθείας, καὶ κύκλους
διαφόρους, πρῶτον μὲν διὰ τὰς ὑποχωρήσεις καὶ ἀντιστροφάς, εἶτα διὰ τὰς
αἰφνιδίους κατὰ τῶν ἐχθρῶν ἐφόδους, λοιπὸν δὲ καὶ διὰ τὸ συντόμως τοῖς
δεομένοις ἐπιβοηθεῖν. εἰ γὰρ οὕτως ἐθισθῶσι τὰ τάγματα, ἑτοίμως ἔχουσι καὶ εἰς
κούρσωρας ἤγουν προκλάστας ἢ προμάχους καὶ εἰς διφένσωρας ἤγουν ἐκδί-
190 κους ἢ βοηθούς, καὶ εἰς ἑκάστην χρείαν τάσσεσθαι.

28. Καὶ τῆς τοιαύτης οὖν γυμνασίας κατορθουμένης εἰς τὰ πλείονα, εἰ καὶ μὴ
πάντα, δεῖ γινώσκειν τοὺς στρατιώτας. οὐ γὰρ δεῖ <πάντα> πουβλικίζεσθαι διὰ
τὸ μὴ τοῖς ἐχθροῖς γινώσκεσθαι. διὰ γὰρ τῶν εἰρημένων τούτων ἐννέα κινήσεων
πρὸς πᾶσαν χρείαν ἕτοιμα γίνονται τὰ αὐτῶν τάγματα, καὶ εἰς κούρσωρας καὶ
195 εἰς διφένσωρας καὶ εἰς πλαγιοφύλακας καὶ εἰς ὑπερκεραστάς, ὅτε χρεία γένηται,
ἀφορισθῆναί τινας αὐτῶν, ἐν συνηθείᾳ πάσης τάξεως γενόμενα.

29. Ἀναγκαῖον δέ ἐστι λοιπὸν καὶ τὴν πρὸς ἄλληλα τὰ βάνδα συμφωνίαν καὶ
τάξιν ἐθίζεσθαι, ὡς ἐπὶ παρατάξεως, ἀλλ᾽ ἵνα, ὡς εἴρηται, μὴ φανερὰ γίνηται ἡ
πᾶσα ἔκταξις τοῖς ἐχθροῖς. οὐδέποτε γὰρ <χρὴ> πρὸ τῆς μάχης τὴν πᾶσαν τάξιν

---

173-174 μετατίθεσθαι…ἀριστερά    MWA    om.    VBE    174 κατάφερε…μετατίθεσθαι²
MWAVE om. B    175 βάνδον MWVBE βάδον A | ἐστί MA ἐστὶν W ἢ VBE    179 τις MW
τίς VBE τι A | κατὰ…ἤγουν MW om. AVBE | ἐπιφερομένων MW ἐπερχομένων AVBE
181 βλέπουσι M βλέπουσιν WAVBE    184–185 ἀναγκαῖόν…γυμνάζειν MWAVE om. B
188 ἔχουσι MAVBE ἔχουσιν W    190 εἰς MWA om. VBE    191 καὶ¹ WAVBE om. M
192 στρατιώτας MW om. AVBE | πάντα² ci. Va om. codd. | πουβλικίζεσθαι MW φαυλίζεσθαι
καὶ δημοσιεῦσθαι AVBE    193 γὰρ AVBE om. MW    194 γίνονται MWVBE γίγνονται A
197 ἐστι MA ἐστὶν WVBE    198 γίνηται MWA γένηται VBE    199 χρὴ Strat. πρέπει AVBE
om. MW | τὴν MWA τῆς VBE

to change to the left, he orders: "Turn around to the left." If the change is to the right: "Turn around to the right." This is how they change front. If just one bandon is involved, then that one <changes front>, if several, one unit changes front in like manner, and the rest do so in conformity with the one bandon.

26. Another maneuver. To turn the formation around, sometimes changing the position in which the men stand, at other times changing the front of the battle line around. If there is a sudden movement of the enemy attacking from the rear or from behind, the commander gives the order: "Change position." Remaining in place they face behind, toward the rear, with only the officers and the standard-bearers actually moving to the <new> front, <which had been> the rear. If a large enemy force appears behind them, he commands: "Change place." Then they move about by bandon.

27. Not only is it necessary to have them draw up in linear formation and be drilled, but they should also be drilled in irregular formations, in charging out straight ahead, and in various circular movements. At first, they fall back and wheel about, they then make surprise attacks against the enemy and, finally, give prompt support to units in trouble. If the tagmata become habituated to such <maneuvers> they will be prepared <to operate> as assault troops, that is, as proklastai or promachoi, or as defenders, that is, as ekdikoi or support troops, and to adopt a formation for every contingency.

28. By the proper performance of such drills, the soldiers will necessarily become familiar with almost all of them, even if not all. There is no need to make them all public; if you do so, the enemy may learn about them. By means of the above-mentioned nine maneuvers the tagmata are prepared to face any situation, whether some are assigned to be assault troops or defenders, or flank guards, or outflankers, as need may require, for they will have become accustomed to all the formations.

29. It is essential, moreover, that the banda become used to drawing up and cooperating with one another, as in the battle line, but in such a way, as mentioned, that all our formations do not become apparent to the enemy. Before

200 ἐν τῷ ἅμα, τοῦτ᾽ ἔστιν, εἰς πρώτην καὶ δευτέραν παράταξιν διὰ γυμνασίαν μόνην
τάσσειν, ἢ πλαγιοφύλακας ἢ τοὺς ὑπερκεραστὰς λεγομένους ἢ τοὺς δρουγγιστὶ
καὶ λανθανόντως προσπίπτοντας ἢ ἐνέδρας ἤγουν ἐγκρύμματα. τὰ γὰρ τοιαῦτα
στρατηγίας μᾶλλον ἐπιτηδεύματα εἶναι κατὰ τῶν ἐχθρῶν ἢ τάξεως, ἅπερ
προπουβλικίζεσθαι ἐν ταῖς γυμνασίαις οὐ συμφέρει, ἀλλὰ τότε πρὸς τὸ παρὸν
205 κατὰ τὴν ἀπαντῶσαν χρείαν ποιεῖν.
    30. Πρέπον οὖν, εἴτε καθ᾽ ἑαυτὸ τοῦ κόμητος τὸ βάνδον εἴτε δροῦγγος εἴτε
τοῦρμα εἴτε καὶ προπαράταξις πολλοῦ στρατοῦ ἐστιν, ἐν τρισὶ μέρεσι τάσσειν
τοὺς γυμναζομένους. καὶ εἰ μὲν βάνδον ἐστὶ τὸ καθ᾽ ἑαυτὸ γυμναζόμενον, τοὺς
πλείους αὐτοῦ ἐν τάξει κουρσώρων ποιεῖν ἀπὸ δέκα καβαλλαρίων ἐπὶ ἁπλῆς
210 ἀκίας ἔνθεν κἀκεῖθεν, αὐτοὺς ἰσομετώπους τάσσειν ἐν τάξει διφενσώρων,
ἄλλους δὲ ὀλίγους καβαλλαρίους ἄχρι δέκα τάσσειν δι᾽ ὄψεως ἐναντίους, ὥστε
τὴν συμβολὴν πρὸς αὐτοὺς εἰκάζεσθαι. |                                          304ᵛ
    31. Κινούντων δὲ αὐτῶν ὡς ἐπὶ μάχην ἐξέρχεσθαι σὺν ἐλασίᾳ τοὺς κούρ-
σωρας καὶ χωρίζεσθαι τῶν διφενσώρων, καὶ τρέχοντας ἐπ᾽ εὐθείας ὡς ἓν ἢ
215 δεύτερον μίλιν ὑποστρέφειν ἕως τοῦ ἡμίσεως ἐκείνου διαστήματος καὶ ἐκκλί-
νοντάς ποτε μὲν δεξιᾷ, ποτὲ δὲ ἀριστερᾷ, τρέχειν. οὕτως δὲ ποιεῖν καὶ τρίτον καὶ
τέταρτον, εἶτα πάλιν κυκλοειδῶς ἐλαύνειν καὶ μετὰ ταῦτα προστρέχοντας ἐν τῷ
μεταξὺ τόπῳ τῶν διφενσώρων, ὅθεν καὶ ἐξῆλθον, μετὰ τῶν ὡς ἐν τάξει διφενσώρων ἐλαύνειν ὡς εἰς ἀπάντησιν τῶν καταδιωκόντων αὐτούς.
220 32. Οὕτως δὲ ποιεῖν καὶ δρούγγου γυμναζομένου· καὶ τὰ μὲν τῶν βάνδων
αὐτοῦ τάσσειν κούρσωρας, τὰ δὲ διφένσωρας, καὶ πάλιν ἐναλλάσσειν αὐτά, ὁτὲ
τοὺς κούρσωρας διφένσωρας ποιεῖν, ὁτὲ τοὺς διφένσωρας κούρσωρας, ὥστε
πρὸς τὴν δοκοῦσαν χρείαν ἑτοίμους αὐτοὺς εἶναι.

200 ἐν τῷ MWAVE om. B | δευτέραν MWAVE β′ B | γυμνασίαν MWAVE γυμνασίας B
201 λεγομένους MWAVE λεγομένου B    203 ἐπιτηδεύματα MW καὶ ἐπιτηδευμάτων AVBE
204 προπουβλικίζεσθαι MW προφαυλίζεσθαι AVBE    205 ἀπαντῶσαν Strat. ἀπαντοῦσαν Μ
ἀπαιτοῦσαν WAVBE    207 στρατοῦ MWA λαοῦ VBE    208 βάνδον MWAVE om. B | ἐστὶ
MAVBE ἐστὶν W    209 πλείους MW πλείονας AVBE | αὐτοῦ Strat. αὐτῶν codd. | δέκα
MWA ι′ VBE | καβαλλαρίων WAVBE καβαλλαρίους Μ    210 ἀκίας MW ἀκίας καὶ AVBE |
αὐτοὺς MW αὐτῶν AVE αὐτῷ B | διφενσώρων AVE διφενσόρων MW διφένσωρας B
211 δι᾽…ἐναντίους MW κατέναντι αὐτῶν ὡς ἐναντίους AB κατ᾽ ἔναντι αὐτῶν ἐναντίοις VE
213–214 τοὺς κούρσωρας Va τοὺς κούρσορας MA τοῦ κούρσορος W κούρσωρας VBE
215 μίλιν MW μίλιον AVBE    217 προστρέχοντας MWA προτρέχοντας VBE
218–219 ὅθεν…διφενσώρων² MWAVE om. B    218 μετὰ τῶν MW μετ᾽ αὐτῶν AVBE
220 δὲ MWAVE om. B    221–222 καὶ…διφένσωρας¹ MWAVE om. B    221 ὁτὲ Va ὥστε
codd.    223 χρείαν MWA om. VBE | ἑτοίμους…εἶναι MW ἕτοιμοι ὦσιν A ἕτοιμοι ὦσι VBE

battle, never draw up the entire line all at the same time, but form <the army> into first and second battle lines only for drilling. The same goes for flank guards or those called outflankers or with those in irregular formation or hiding ready to fall upon <the enemy> from ambuscades or ambushes. These dispositions are matters of strategy against the enemy rather than of tactics, and they ought not to be made known ahead of time during drill but should be decided on the spot to meet a specific need.

30. Whether an individual bandon, under its count, or a droungos or a tourma or even the whole front line of a large army is being drilled, it should be drawn up in three parts. If a single bandon is to be drilled by itself, form most of the men as assault troops. On the same front with them about ten horsemen should be drawn up as defenders in a single file on each flank. Station a few other horsemen, say ten, out in front and opposing them so that they can form some idea of the course of the attack.

31. On moving out, as though advancing rapidly to battle, the assault troops separate from the defenders. They ride steadily forward for a mile or two, then turn back about half that distance. Then they turn and ride, first to the right and then to the left. They do this three or four times and circle back again. After this they ride to their original position in the space among the defenders. Then, in formation as defenders, they ride out as if to encounter a force pursuing them.

32. The droungos should be drilled in the same way. Draw up some of its banda as assault troops and some as defenders. Then have them exchange roles. The assault troops become defenders and the defenders become assault troops. As a result, they will be prepared for whatever need must be faced.

33. Ὁμοίως δὲ ποιεῖν καὶ τούρμας γυμναζομένης καὶ παρατάξεως πρώτης
225 καὶ παρατάξεως δευτέρας. ἐπισκέψαι δὲ εἰς τὰς κυκλοειδεῖς ἐλασίας τῶν κουρσώρων, ὅπου διάφορα βάνδα εὑρίσκονται, ὥστε εἰς δύο ἀρχὰς ταῦτα μερίζεσθαι
καὶ ἐλαύνειν τὴν ἐναντίαν ἀλλήλων, καὶ ὑπαντᾶν τὰς ἀρχὰς τὴν μὲν μίαν ἔξω,
τὴν δὲ δευτέραν ἐσωτέρω τρέχειν, ἵνα μὴ προσκρούματα τῶν καβαλλαρίων
γίνωνται.
230    34. Δέον δὲ καὶ πλαγιοφύλακας καὶ ὑπερκεραστὰς ἤγουν τοὺς τὰς κυκλώσεις ἀπὸ τοῦ δεξιοῦ μέρους ποιοῦντας ἰδίως μετ᾽ αὐτῶν δρουγγιστὶ ἤγουν
πυκνοὺς καὶ ὁμοῦ ἐμπιπτόντας γυμνάζειν, λανθάνοντας δὲ δι᾽ ἣν ἀνωτέρω
εἴπομεν αἰτίαν, ὥστε εἰς μὲν τὰς μακροτέρας παρατάξεις τῶν ἐναντίων ἰσοῦσθαι
καὶ μὴ ἐμπεριλαμβάνεσθαι ὑπ᾽ αὐτῶν, κατὰ δὲ τῶν κοντοτέρων εἰς τὸ τὰς
235 κυκλώσεις ποιεῖσθαι, ἀντιτασσομένων αὐτοῖς ὀλίγων καβαλλαρίων ἐπὶ ἁπλῆς
ἀκίας ἄχρι ἑνὸς ἢ δευτέρου βάνδου ὡς ἐναντίων, ἵνα πρὸς αὐτοὺς κανονίζωσιν
οἱ ὑπερκερασταὶ πρότερον ὑπερκερᾶν αὐτοὺς ἤτοι κυκλοῦν· εἶθ᾽ οὕτως οἱ
συνόντες αὐτοῖς δρουγγιστὶ ἤγουν ὡς μᾶζα, ὁμοῦ, λανθανόντως αὐτοὶ μόνοι
ἄφνω ὑπεξερχόμενοι μετὰ ἐλασίας ὀξείας τῷ νώτῳ ἤγουν κατὰ τὰ ὄπισθεν τῶν
240 ἐναντίων ἐπιτίθενται.
35. Αὗται οὖν αἱ γυμνασίαι ἁπλαῖ εἰσι. καὶ κοινῶς δὲ πολλὰ τάγματα καὶ
ἰδίως πάλιν ἓν τάγμα τι ἁρμοδίως γυμνάζουσι, καὶ τοῖς ἐχθροῖς ἄγνωστος ἡ
τάξις φυλάττεται. καὶ δέον σε, ὦ στρατηγέ, ταύτας τὰς γυμνασίας ἐγγράφως | 305
δοῦναι καὶ τοῖς ὑπό σε τουρμάρχαις καὶ τοῖς ἄλλοις τοῖς ἰδίᾳ γυμναζομένοις
245 τάγμασιν, ἐθίζειν δὲ τὰς τοιαύτας γυμνασίας μὴ μόνον ἐν ὁμαλοῖς, ἀλλὰ καὶ ἐν
δυσβάτοις τόποις καὶ εἰς ὑψηλοὺς καὶ εἰς κατωφερεῖς. καὶ ἐν καιρῷ δὲ καύσωνος
καλόν ἐστι γυμνάζειν καὶ ἐθίζειν τὸν στρατόν· οὐδεὶς γὰρ οἶδεν πότε συμβήσεται μάχη καὶ τί συμβήσεται.

---

224 καὶ² WAVBE om. M    226–228 διάφορα…δευτέραν MWAVE διφένσωρα κούρσωρας
ἵνα πρὸς τὴν δοκοῦσαν ἕτοιμοι ὦσι ὅπως τὴν δευτέραν ἔσω Β    227 ἀρχὰς MW ἀρχὰς καὶ
AVBE    228 ἐσωτέρω Va ἐσωτέραν MW ἔσω AVBE | προσκρούματα MWVE
προσκρούσματα ΑΒ    231 μετ᾽ αὐτῶν AVE μεταυτῶν Β μετὰ αὐτῶν MW    232 πυκνοὺς
MWAVE πυκνῶς Β | δὲ MWA om. VBE    232–233 δι᾽…αἰτίαν MW διὰ τὸ μὴ φαυλίζεσθαι
τοῖς πολεμίοις AVBE    233 ἐναντίων MWA πολεμίων VBE | ἰσοῦσθαι AVBE ἵνα ἰσοῦνται
MW    234 ἐμπεριλαμβάνεσθαι AVBE ἐμπεριλαμβάνονται MW    235 αὐτοῖς MWA αὐτῶν
VBE    236 κανονίζωσιν MWAVE κανονίζουσιν Β    237 ἤτοι MWAVE ἤγουν Β    238 ὡς
μᾶζα MW om. AVBE    239 τῷ…ὄπισθεν MW ὀπίσω AVBE    241 εἰσι WVBE εἰσιν ΜΑ
242 τι W om. MAVBE | γυμνάζουσι Strat. γυμνάζωσι MWVE γυμνάζεσθαι ΑΒ | ἄγνωστος
MWA εὔγνωστος VBE    244 τοῖς¹ AVBE τοὺς MW | τουρμάρχαις AVBE τουρμάρχας MW
247 οἶδεν MW οἶδε AVBE

33. Act in like fashion in drilling the tourma, as well as the first and second battle lines. <Practice> encircling charges by assault troops that involve different banda divided into two commands and riding in the opposite direction to one another, with one division advancing on the inside and the second on the outside, in order to avoid collisions among the horsemen.

34. The flank guards and the outflankers, that is, those making circling movements from the right side, must be drilled separately, along with those irregular troops who had been hiding, for reasons explained above, and who attack all at once in a mass, so that when the enemy lines extend beyond ours, they keep our line even and guard it against envelopment by the enemy, whereas when their lines are shorter than ours, they can make use of encircling movements. A few horsemen, say one or two banda, should line up opposite them in a single line as though they were the enemy, so that the outflankers, conforming to the length of their line, may first outflank or encircle them. Then the men who had been hiding can suddenly and swiftly charge out by themselves, in irregular formation or like a lump, and fall upon the rear, that is, behind the enemy.

35. These exercises are simple and can easily be practiced by several tagmata together or, again, by a single tagma, without disclosing our order of battle to the enemy. It is your obligation, O general, to give these exercises in writing to the tourmarchs and others under your command involved in drilling individual tagmata. They should get used to these exercises not only on level ground but also in difficult terrain, among hills and steep inclines. Even in hot weather it is a good idea to drill and get the army used to it. For nobody knows when battle will take place and what will happen.

36. Χρὴ γὰρ οὕτως τὴν γυμνασίαν ποιεῖσθαι ὡς ἐπὶ αὐτοῦ τοῦ πολέμου, διὸ
250 καὶ ἡμεῖς διὰ τὸ χρήσιμον καὶ τὰ ἐν καιρῷ πολέμου ἐνταῦθα εἰρήκαμεν. τὸ γὰρ
πρὸς τοὺς κινδύνους ἐθίζεσθαι ἀνδρειοτέρους τοὺς στρατιώτας ποιεῖ.

37. Ἐπεὶ δὲ τὴν τῶν καβαλλαρίων γυμνασίαν ἐκ μέρους διεταξάμεθα, χρεόν
ἐστιν ὁμοίως καὶ τὴν τῶν πεζικῶν ταγμάτων γυμνασίαν σοι διορίσασθαι, ὅσον
ἐκ τῶν ἀρχαίων τακτικῶν καὶ ὅσον ἐκ τῶν νέων παρειλήφαμεν. ὁρίζονται τοίνυν
255 αἱ ἀκίαι πρῶτον τοῦ πεζικοῦ τάγματος, καθὼς ἄνω που ἐσημάναμεν, ὥστε
τάσσεσθαί τινας μὲν αὐτῶν ἀριστερᾷ, τινὰς δὲ δεξιᾷ τοῦ βάνδου ἤτοι τοῦ
ἄρχοντος. καὶ προπορευομένου τοῦ ἄρχοντος ἅμα τῷ βανδοφόρῳ καὶ τῷ
μανδάτωρι καὶ βουκινάτωρι ἐπακολουθοῦσιν ὡς ὡρίσθησαν οἱ λοχαγοὶ ἤγουν οἱ
πρωτοστάται ἢ δέκαρχοι, πρῶτον οἱ τοῦ ἀριστεροῦ μέρους καὶ τότε τοῦ δεξιοῦ.

260 38. Γινομένων δὲ αὐτῶν ἐν τῷ τῆς γυμνασίας τόπῳ ἢ τῆς παρατάξεως,
ἵσταται ὁ ἄρχων καὶ μετ’ αὐτὸν ὁ βανδοφόρος καὶ εἴ τις ἕτερος κατὰ συνήθειαν.
καὶ παρατάσσονται αὐτοῖς ἔνθεν καὶ ἐκεῖθεν αἱ ἀκίαι, ὡς ὡρίσθησαν, πρῶτον ἐν
ἀραιοτέρῳ διαστήματι, ἵνα μὴ συντρίβωνται ὑπ’ ἀλλήλων, ἀπὸ ις΄ τὸ βάθος
ἤγουν τὸ πάχος, ἔχουσαι καὶ τοὺς ψιλοὺς ὄπισθεν, τὰ δὲ ξίφη τῶν κονταρίων
265 ἄνω βλέποντα ἵνα μὴ ἐμποδίζωνται ὑπ’ αὐτῶν. ἔμπροσθεν δὲ τοῦ μετώπου
περιπατοῦσιν ὁ μανδάτωρ, ὁ καμπιδούκτωρ ἤγουν ὁ ὁδηγὸς τῶν τόπων, ὁ μὲν
τοὺς τόπους ἀνερευνῶν καὶ ὁδηγῶν, ὁ δὲ τὰ μανδάτα γνώμῃ τοῦ ἄρχοντος
διδούς.

39. Καὶ εἰ μὲν τάγμα ἐστὶ τὸ γυμναζόμενον, τὸν τοῦ τάγματος ἄρχοντα
270 ἔμπροσθεν περιπατεῖν μετὰ μανδάτωρος καὶ καμπιδούκτωρος, εἰ δὲ τοῦρμα
γυμνάζεται, μηδένα ἔμπροσθεν περιπατεῖν εἰ μὴ τουρμάρχην καβαλλάριον μετὰ
μανδατώρων δύο, καμπιδουκτώρων δύο, στράτωρος α΄ καὶ σπαθαρίου ἑνὸς ἤτοι

---

254–461 Strat., 12.B.11–16.

---

252 χρεόν MW χρεία AVBE    253 πεζικῶν MW πεζῶν AVBE    253–254 ὅσον…τακτικῶν
MW ὅσην ἐκ τῶν τακτικῶν τῶν ἀρχαίων AVBE    254 ὅσον MW ὅσην AVBE    255 ἀκίαι
MWAVE ἀχίαι B | καθὼς MWA καθὸ VBE | ἄνω που MW ἀνωτέρω AVBE | ὥστε MW ὡς
AVBE    256 αὐτῶν MW ἐν AVBE | δὲ MW δὲ ἐν AVBE    258 βουκινάτωρι A βουκινάτορι
MW βουκινιάτωρι VBE    259 δέκαρχοι MWA δέκαρχαι VBE | οἱ MW om. AVBE
260 γινομένων W γενομένων MAVBE    261 αὐτὸν MWVBE αὐτῶν A scr. mg. ἤγουν
δεύτερος ἐκείνου W    262 αὐτοῖς AVBE αὐτοὶ MW    263 ις΄ VBE κ΄ MW δεκαέξ A
266 περιπατοῦσιν…μανδάτωρ scr. mg. <…> οὐκ ἀπέχουσα στρατιω…ος…απεχ…ιου W
267 μανδάτα MW παραγγέλματα AVBE | γνώμῃ MW προτροπῇ AVBE    269 ἐστὶ MAVBE
ἐστιν W | γυμναζόμενον MW γυμναζόμενον καὶ AVBE    271 τουρμάρχην MWVE
τουρμάχην A τουρμάχης B    272 δύο¹ MWA β΄ VBE | δύο² MA β΄ WVBE | α΄ MW ἑνὸς
AVBE | σπαθαρίου AVBE σπαθάτου MW

36. It is necessary to perform these drills as though you were actually at war. We have, therefore, addressed ourselves herein to what is useful in time of war. Being accustomed to its dangers makes the soldiers more courageous.

37. Since we have set down specific guidelines for drilling the cavalry, it is necessary in like manner to give you instructions concerning the training of the infantry tagmata, based on what we have derived from the ancient tacticians as well as the modern ones.[8] First, the files of the infantry tagma must be organized, as we indicated above, so that some should be drawn up to the left, some to the right of the standard or of the commanding officer. The commander then moves forward together with the standard-bearer and the herald and the trumpeter. The group leaders, that is, the protostatai or dekarchs, follow in their assigned positions, first those on the left side, then those on the right.

38. On arriving at the site of the drill or of the battle line, the commanding officer halts with the standard-bearer behind him and with his customary entourage. The files draw up on both sides of them in their assigned positions, at first a good distance apart to avoid bumping into one another, at a depth or thickness of sixteen, with the light-armed troops to the rear. They hold the points of their spears on high so they will not be impeded by them. The herald and the field guide, that is, the guide of the places, march before the front line, the one for reconnaissance and guide duty, the other to transmit orders from the commander.[9]

39. If a tagma is being drilled, the commanding officer should march in front with the herald and the field guide. If a tourma is being drilled, nobody should march in front except the tourmarch, mounted, with two heralds, two field guides, one strator, and one spatharios, that is, the man bearing the

---

8. *Strat.* 12.B.11–16.

9. Kampidouktor, although translated as drillmaster (*Strat.* 12.B.7.4; Engl. trans. p. 140), Feldwebel (Germ. trans. p. 425), Exerziermeister (*LBG*), in the *Taktika* (7.38; 14.59) reflects its Latin origin (*campus, ductor*), indicating a field guide, who may also have been in charge of drilling the troops.

τοῦ τὰ ὅπλα τοῦ ἄρχοντος | φέροντος, ἕως οὗ πλησίον τῆς συμβολῆς γένηται ἡ    305ᵛ
παραταγή. τότε δὲ ἐν τῇ παραταγῇ ἀσφαλῶς εἰσέρχεται, ἐν ᾧ τόπῳ τὸ βάνδον
275  αὐτοῦ τέτακται.

40. Μὴ συμπλέκεσθαι δὲ αὐτὸν τοῖς ἐναντίοις μηδὲ βούκινον λέγειν εἰς
ἕκαστον μέρος πλὴν τοῦ μεράρχου, εἴτε μίαν τοῦρμαν ἔχει τὸ μέρος εἴτε δύο εἴτε
πλείονας, κἂν εἰ συμβῇ πολλὰ εἶναι τὰ βούκινα, ἵνα μὴ θορύβου γενομένου
κωλύωνται τὰ μανδάτα ἐξακούεσθαι. καὶ οἱ μὲν ὁπλῖται πεζοὶ ἤγουν οἱ σκουτά-
280  τοι τάσσονται οὕτως. οἱ δὲ ψιλοὶ κατὰ διαφόρους τρόπους τάσσονται ἤγουν οἱ
ἀκροβολισταὶ μὲν πάλαι καλούμενοι, νῦν δὲ τοξόται ἢ σαγιττάτωρες· ποτὲ μὲν
γὰρ ὄπισθεν ἑκάστης ἀκίας πρὸς τὸ μέτρον τῶν ὄντων, τοῦτ' ἔστιν εἰς τοὺς ιϛ'
σκουτάτους δ' ψιλοί, ἵνα καὶ μέχρι δ' μεριζομένης τῆς τῶν σκουτάτων ἀκίας
εὑρεθῇ εἰς τοξότης ὄπισθεν αὐτῆς, ποτὲ δὲ ἐν τῷ βάθει τῶν ἀκιῶν εἰς παρ' εἶς
285  σκουτάτος καὶ τοξότης, ποτὲ δὲ καὶ ἐν ταῖς ἀκίαις καὶ ἐν τοῖς κέρασιν ἤγουν
ταῖς ἐξοχαῖς τῶν παρατάξεων, τοῦτ' ἔστιν ἐσωτέρω τῶν καβαλλαρίων, πολλάκις
δὲ καὶ ἐξωτέρω αὐτῶν, ἀπὸ μικροῦ διαστήματος μετὰ καὶ ὀλίγων σκουτάτων εἰς
τὸ ἐκδικεῖσθαι τοὺς εἰς τὸ ἐξώτερον ἑστῶτας καβαλλαρίους, ἐὰν πολλοί εἰσιν οἱ
ψιλοί.

290  41. Οἱ δὲ τὰ ρικτάρια ἢ τζικούρια ἢ βαρδούκια ἔχοντες ἢ ὄπισθεν τῶν ἀκιῶν
τῶν σκουτάτων ἢ εἰς τὰ ἄκρα τῆς παρατάξεως καὶ οὐκ ἐν τῷ μέσῳ· οἱ δὲ σφενδοβολισταὶ πάντως εἰς τὰ ἄκρα τῆς παρατάξεως. νῦν δὲ τάξομεν τοὺς τοξότας
καὶ λοιποὺς ἀκοντιστὰς ὄπισθεν τῶν ἀκιῶν πρὸς τὴν γυμνασίαν ἢ ὡς ἀπαιτεῖ ἡ
χρεία αὐτῆς.

295  42. Τοὺς δὲ καβαλλαρίους εἰς τὰ ἄκρα τῆς πεζικῆς παρατάξεως τάξεις, ὅσα
δὲ αὐτῶν ἀνδρειότερα τάγματα μετὰ τῶν ἀρχόντων αὐτῶν ἐξωτέρω. καὶ εἰ μὲν
πολλοί εἰσιν οἱ καβαλλάριοι, τοῦτ' ἔστι, πλέον τῶν ιβ' χιλιάδων, ἀπὸ δέκα τὸ
βάθος τούτων γίνεσθαι, εἰ δὲ καὶ ὀλιγωτέρους τοῦ μέτρου τούτου, ἀπὸ πέντε.
εἶναι δὲ ἐκ περισσοῦ τινας ὄπισθεν ἐν ὑποβοηθείᾳ αὐτῶν ἐξωτέρω τῶν ἁμαξῶν
300  ἵνα, ἐὰν μὲν διὰ τῶν ὄπισθέν τινες τῶν ἐχθρῶν φθάνωσιν, ἀποσοβήσωσιν

---

273 ἄρχοντος MWAB ἄρχοντα VE    276 μὴ WA μὴ δὲ MVBE    277 δύο MWAVE β' B
278 κἂν MWA καὶ VBE    280–281 ἤγουν…σαγιττάτωρες MW om. AVBE    283 δ'¹
MWVBE τέσσαρες A | δ'² MWVBE τεσσάρων A    288 ἐκδικεῖσθαι MWA ἐκδικεῖσθαι VBE |
τὸ² WAVBE τοὺς M | εἰσιν MWA ὦσιν VBE    290 ρικτάρια Va ῥηκτάρια MW ριπτάρια
AVBE | βαρδούκια MW ματζούκια AVBE    291 μέσῳ MW μέσῳ ταχθήσονται AVBE
291–292 σφενδοβολισταὶ MW σφενδονῆται A σφενδονίται VE σφενδωνίται B    292 τοὺς
AVBE om. MW    297 ιβ' MWVBE δώδεκα A    298 μέτρου MWA μέρους VBE | πέντε
MWAVE ε' B    299 ὄπισθεν MWAVE ὄπιθεν B    300 ἀποσοβήσωσιν Va ἀποσωβήσωσιν
MW ἀπαντῶσιν AVBE

commander's weapons. <They remain there> until the battle line is close to engaging. Then they safely enter back into the battle line, to the place where the standard is located.

40. The commander should not personally fight against the enemy. No trumpet should sound in each meros except that of the merarch, whether the meros has one tourma or two or more, even if there should be many trumpets. Otherwise the resulting noise may prevent the orders from being heard. This is how the heavy infantry, the heavy-armed troops, should be organized. The light-armed troops are formed in various manners. They were formerly called akrobolistai, but now bowmen or archers. Sometimes to the rear of each file in proportion to their numbers, four light-armed troops for sixteen heavy-armed men, so that if the heavy-armed file is reduced to four deep there will be one archer behind it. Sometimes <they are placed> in the depths of the files, one heavy-armed soldier alternating with one archer; sometimes, both in the files and in the horns, that is, the extremities of the battle line, on the inside of the cavalry. Frequently, if there is a large number of light-armed troops, <they are posted> a short distance to the outside of the cavalry, along with a few heavy-armed men, to defend the cavalry stationed outside.

41. The troops carrying missile weapons, axes, or maces should be either behind the heavy infantry files or on the extremities of the battle line and not in the middle. The slingers are always at its extremities. At present we form the archers and the others with missile weapons behind the files for drill or as need requires.

42. Station the cavalry on the extremities of the infantry battle line, the bravest units with their officers further out. If the cavalry force is large, that is, over twelve thousand men, they should be about ten deep. If they number less than that, about five deep. There should be extra troops in the rear, outside the wagons, to support them, so they may scare off any of the enemy who shows up

αὐτούς, εἰ δὲ μή γε, προστεθῶσι τοῖς πλαγίοις καὶ αὐτοί. τάσσονται δὲ καὶ αὐτοὶ
ἐν ἀραιοτέρῳ πρότερον δια|στήματι ἵνα, ἐὰν γένηται καιρὸς εἰς τὸ χρῄζειν 306
μεταβάλλεσθαι, μὴ ἐμποδίζωνται.

43. Παραγγείλῃς δὲ τοὺς καβαλλαρίους μὴ κατατρέχειν τῶν ἐχθρῶν μηδὲ
305 ἀφίστασθαι τῆς πεζικῆς παρατάξεως ὡς ἐπὶ πολὺ διάστημα, κἂν τάχα τραπῶσιν
οἱ ἐχθροί, ἵνα μὴ ἐγκρύμματός τινος παρ’ αὐτῶν γενομένου, εἴπερ ἀπὸ διαστήματός εἰσιν οἱ πεζοί, γυμνούμενοι τῆς παρατάξεως ἐπηρεασθῶσιν ὡς ὀλιγώτεροι ἢ ἀσθενέστεροι. ἀλλὰ καὶ ἐὰν βιασθῶσιν, ὡς εἰκός, παρὰ τῶν ἐναντίων,
ὄπισθεν τῆς παρατάξεως προσφεύγειν καὶ μὴ παρέρχεσθαι τὰς ἁμάξας, τὰς
310 ὀπίσω τῆς παρατάξεως τῶν πεζῶν ὀφειλούσας εἶναι πρὸς φυλακὴν αὐτῶν. εἰ δὲ
μηδὲ οὕτως ἀντέχουσι, κατέρχεσθαι αὐτοὺς ἐκ τῶν ἵππων καὶ οὕτως πεζῇ ἑαυτοὺς ἐκδικεῖν.

44. Ἐὰν δὲ παρατάξασθαι μὲν θέλῃ ὁ στρατός, μὴ συμβαλεῖν δὲ κατὰ τὴν
αὐτὴν ἡμέραν, καὶ ὁρμήσωσιν οἱ ἐχθροὶ κατὰ τῶν καβαλλαρίων καὶ μὴ βαστά-
315 ζωσιν αὐτούς, μὴ ἀναμένωσιν αὐτοὺς ἱστάμενοι εἰς τὰ κέρατα τῆς παρατάξεως,
ἀλλ’ ὄπισθεν μᾶλλον ἔλθωσιν <τῶν πεζῶν>, τοῦτ’ ἔστιν μέσον τῆς παρατάξεως
καὶ τῶν ἁμαξῶν. εἰ δὲ τοῦτο γένηται, χρεία μείζονος τοῦ ἐν τῷ μέσῳ διαστήματος, ἵνα μεταβαλλομένων, ὡς εἰκός, τῶν καβαλλαρίων μὴ στενοχωρηθῶσι μηδὲ
αἱ τῶν ἐχθρῶν σαγίτται βλάψωσιν αὐτούς.

320 45. Ταῦτα δεῖ μάλιστα καὶ ἐν καιρῷ μάχης γίνεσθαι· διὰ ταύτην γὰρ καὶ ἡ
γυμνασία μεταχειρίζεται.

46. Τούτων οὖν τῶν διατάξεων εἰρημένων πρέπον ἡμῖν καὶ τὰ σχήματα καὶ
τὰ παραγγέλματα τῆς πεζικῆς τάξεως, ὥσπερ καὶ τῆς ἱππικῆς, ἐμφανίσαι σοι καὶ
διασαφῆσαι.

325 47. Ὅτ’ ἂν γὰρ παραστῶσι πρὸς τὴν γυμνασίαν τὰ μέρη τῆς παραταγῆς τῶν
ταγμάτων τοῦ στρατοῦ, παραγγέλλει ὁ μανδάτωρ ταῦτα· "μετὰ σιγῆς πάντες τὰ
παραγγέλματα πληρώσατε. μὴ ταραχθῆτε. τὴν τάξιν ὑμῶν φυλάξατε. τῷ βάνδῳ

301 αὐτούς MW αὐτοὺς καὶ ἀποδιώκωσιν AVE αὐτοὺς καὶ ἀποδιώκουσιν B | προστεθῶσι
MAVBE προστεθῶσιν W　302 εἰς…χρῄζειν MW om. AVBE　303 μεταβάλλεσθαι MW
μεταβαλέσθαι αὐτούς AVBE　305 ὡς MW om. AVBE　306 παρ’…γενομένου MWA trsp.
VBE　306–307 εἴπερ…παρατάξεως MW μακρὰν τῆς παρατάξεως τῶν πεζῶν εὑρισκόμενοι
AVBE　307 ἐπηρεασθῶσιν MWAB ἐπηρεαθῶσιν VE　309 παρέρχεσθαι WAVBE
ἐπέρχεσθαι M　311 ἀντέχουσι M ἀντέχουσιν W ἀπαντῶσιν A ἀπαντῶσι VBE
313 συμβαλεῖν AVBE συμβάλλειν MW　313–314 τὴν αὐτὴν MW trsp. AVBE
314 ὁρμήσωσιν MWAVE ὁρμήσουσιν B　316 ἀλλ’…παρατάξεως MWA om. VBE | τῶν
πεζῶν Strat. om. codd. | μέσον A om. MWVBE　318 στενοχωρηθῶσι MAVBE
στενοχωρηθῶσιν W　320 δεῖ PG δὲ codd.　323 ἱππικῆς MWA πεζικῆς VBE
325 παραστῶσι AVBE παραστῶσιν M diff. lectu W　327 φυλάξατε MAVBE πληρώσατε W

in the rear. If there is no <such need> they join in support of the flanks. They should first draw up in a very wide space so that, if the time comes for wheeling about, they do not get in each other's way.

43. Order the cavalry not to race after the enemy or to get too far away from the infantry line, even if the enemy quickly turns to flight. Otherwise, they might run into an ambush and, with the infantry far off, without the support of the battle line, weakened, and few in numbers they might be badly beaten. But if, as may happen, they should be driven back by the enemy, let them seek refuge to the rear of the battle line, but not go beyond the wagons, which ought to be behind the infantry battle line to protect it. If they still cannot hold out, they should dismount and defend themselves on foot.

44. If the army wants to draw up for battle, but not engage in fighting that day, and the enemy charges against our cavalry, and they cannot hold them off, they should not wait for them in their position on the horns of the battle line, but rather ride in behind the infantry, that is, between the line and the wagons. If this happens, there will be a need for more room in that middle area so that the cavalry may not be forced into a narrow space, which is possible, and be injured by the enemy's arrows.

45. These things occur especially in time of battle; it is with this in mind that we devote time to drilling.

46. Now that we have covered these arrangements, it is fitting for us to explain and make clear to you the formations and the commands for the infantry units, as <we did> for the cavalry.

47. When the various divisions are lined up and the units of the army get into position for their drills, the herald gives the following commands. "In silence, everyone observe the commands. Do not be confused. Stay in your

ἐπακολουθήσατε. μηδεὶς ἀφήσῃ τὸ βάνδον καὶ τοὺς ἐχθροὺς διώξατε." καὶ
τούτων εἰρημένων κινοῦσι πράως τε καὶ ἡσύχως, ὥστε μηδὲ ψιθυρισμὸν γίν-
330 εσθαι παρά τινος.

48. Ἐθίζεσθαι δὲ αὐτοὺς πρὸς ταῦτα φωνῇ ἢ νεύματι, διὰ σημείου τινός, οἷον
κινεῖν καὶ ἵστασθαι. λεπτύνεσθαι ἤγουν μερίζεσθαι τὸ βάθος τῶν ἀκιῶν, περιπατεῖν ἴσως καὶ συντεταγμένως ἐπὶ στόμα ἤγουν ἐπ᾽ εὐθείας. καὶ κατὰ ποικίλους
τρόπους καὶ διαφόρους πυκνοῦσθαι ἤτοι σφίγγεσθαι κατὰ βάθος καὶ μῆκος.
335 φούλκῳ περιπατεῖν. συμβάλλειν ὡς ἐν τάξει μάχης μετὰ σχήματος, ποτὲ μὲν
μετὰ βεργίων, ποτὲ δὲ μετὰ γυμνῶν σπαθίων.

49. Γυμνάζεσθαι δὲ καὶ οὕτως· | μερίζεσθαι πρὸς διφαλαγγίαν καὶ πάλιν   306ᵛ
ἀποκαθίστασθαι. δεξιᾷ καὶ ἀριστερᾷ κλίνεσθαι καὶ περιπατεῖν ἐπὶ κέρας ἤγουν
τὸ δεξιὸν μέρος. προάγειν ἔμπροσθεν καὶ πάλιν ἀποκαθίστασθαι. φυλάττεσθαι
340 ἀμφιστόμως ἑκατέρωθεν καὶ πάλιν ἀποκαθίστασθαι. μετατίθεσθαι δεξιᾷ καὶ
ἀριστερᾷ. ἀραιοῦσθαι καὶ πλατύνεσθαι. <βαθύνεσθαι> ἤτοι διπλοῦσθαι τὸ
βάθος τῶν ἀκιῶν. μεταβάλλεσθαι κατὰ νώτου καὶ πάλιν ἀποκαθίστασθαι.

50. Γίνονται δὲ τὰ σχήματα ταῦτα διὰ τὰς διαφόρους ἀνακυπτούσας αἰτίας
φωνῇ τοίνυν ἢ νεύματι, διὰ σημείου τινός, κινοῦσι καὶ ἵστανται. ὅτε δὲ θέλει
345 κινῆσαι, σημαίνει ἢ βουκίνῳ ἢ τῇ ταυρέᾳ ὁ καμπιδούκτωρ ἢ τῇ φωνῇ, καὶ
κινοῦσιν. εἰ δὲ στῆσαι θέλει, ἢ τῇ τούβᾳ, ὅ ἐστι μικρὸν βούκινον, ἢ τῇ φωνῇ ἢ
νεύματι τῆς χειρός, καὶ ἵστανται. διὰ δὲ τοῦτο φωνῇ καὶ σημασίᾳ ἐθίζεσθαι
ἀναγκαῖόν ἐστι διὰ τὸν τοῦ ἅρματος θόρυβον ἢ κονιορτὸν ἢ ὁμίχλην ἐπιγινομένην.

350    51. Λεπτύνονται ἤτοι μερίζονται αἱ ἀκίαι ὅτ᾽ ἂν ἀπὸ ις΄ ἀνδρῶν τὸ βάθος
αὐτῶν ἐστι καὶ θέλεις μᾶλλον τὸ μῆκος τῶν παρατάξεων ἐκτεῖναι διὰ κόμπον ἢ
διὰ τὸ ἰσωθῆναι τῇ τῶν ἐναντίων παρατάξει· καὶ παραγγέλλει· "<ἀπὸ ὀκτὼ>
ἔξελθε." καὶ ἐξέρχονται εἰς παρ᾽ ἕνα μεριζόμενοι, καὶ λεπτύνεται μὲν τὸ βάθος

---

328 καὶ¹…διώξατε MW om. AVBE    329 κινοῦσι AVBE κινήσουσι MW    329–330 γίνεσθαι MWVBE γενέσθαι A    331 αὐτοὺς MW αὐτοὺς δέον AVBE    335 φούλκῳ AVBE
φούλκων MW | συμβάλλειν…σχήματος MW ἤγουν τοὺς ὀπίσω σκέποντας τὰς τῶν
ἔμπροσθεν κεφαλὰς τοῖς σκουταρίοις καὶ οἱονεὶ κεραμωθέντας περιπατεῖν AVBE    337 καὶ¹
MWA om. VBE    341 βαθύνεσθαι Strat. πλατύνεσθαι W om. MAVBE | διπλοῦσθαι AVBE
διαπλοῦσθαι MW    342 κατὰ νώτου MW ὀπίσω AVBE    343 διαφόρους MWA διαφόρως
VBE    344 κινοῦσι MAVBE κινοῦσιν W    345 ταυρέᾳ Va ταυρίᾳ MW σάλπιγγι AVBE
347 ἵστανται MWA ἵσταται VBE | δὲ τοῦτο MW trsp. AVBE | σημασίᾳ MW σημείῳ AVBE
348 ἐστι MAVBE ἐστιν W | τὸν…ἅρματος MW τε τὸν κτύπον τῶν ἁρμάτων AVBE | ἢ¹ MW
καὶ τὸν AVBE    348–349 ἢ²…ἐπιγινομένην MW ἢ καὶ τὴν ἐπιγινομένην ὁμίχλην AVBE
351 ἐστι M ἐστιν WA ἢ VBE | διὰ κόμπον MW ἢ διὰ φαντασίαν AVBE    352 παρατάξει
AVBE τάξει MW | ἀπὸ ὀκτὼ Va om. codd.

position. Follow after the standard. Let nobody leave the standard and pursue the enemy." When this has been said, they move at a steady pace and in silence, without anyone even whispering.

48. They should become accustomed to these movements so that at a spoken command, a nod, or some other signal, they march or halt, reduce or divide the depth of the files, march evenly and in good order out in front or in a straight line, and in a great variety of ways thicken or tighten ranks according to depth and width. March in a foulkon. In battle formation engage in a mock battle, sometimes using staffs and sometimes unsharpened swords.

49. Drill them also in this way. Divide into a double phalanx and then resume normal formation. Face to the right and to the left. March to the flank, that is, to the section on the right. Advance in front and again back to their original position. Defend on a double front from both sides and then return to their original position. Change front to the right and to the left, open files and extend the formation, deepen or double the depths of the files, change their front to the rear and then back again.

50. These maneuvers are set in motion by various means as they present themselves. At a spoken command, a gesture, or some other signal the troops march or halt. When he wants them to march, the field guide signals by trumpet, horn, or voice, and they march. If he wants them to halt, then by tuba, which is a small trumpet, by voice, or by a hand gesture, and they halt.[10] It is essential that the troops become accustomed to these commands by voice or signal because of the confusion caused by the clash of arms, the dust, or the fog settling in.

51. The files may be thinned or divided when they are sixteen men deep and you want rather to extend the width of the battle line to make it look more impressive or to make it equal to the enemy line. Give the command: "March out <by eights>." They divide up with every other man stepping out of line, and

10. In Classical as well as Byzantine Greek, the word for trumpet was σάλπιγξ. In the *Taktika*, however, the common term is boukinon (Latin, *bucina*), which came in several sizes (*supra*, Const. 5 §4), was spiral in shape, and was sounded to begin marching. The small boukinon, also known as tuba, gave the signal to halt; this too came in various sizes and shapes; *The Oxford Latin Dictionary* defines it as a trumpet with a straight tube. Another type of boukinon was the taurea (Lat. *cornu*). See also Vegetius, *Epitoma rei militaris*, 3.5. A "count of the trumpets" (κόμης τῶν βουκίνων) is listed in CampOrg, 1.120. Cf. N. Maliaras, "Die Musikinstrumente des byzantinischen Heers vom 6. bis zum 12. Jahrhundert," *JÖB* 51 (2001): 94–95.

τῶν ἀκιῶν, προστίθεται δὲ τὸ μῆκος τῆς παρατάξεως, καὶ γίνεται τὸ βάθος ἀπὸ
355 η΄. εἰ δὲ θέλει ἀπὸ τεσσάρων, πάλιν λέγει· ἔξελθε. καὶ ἐξέρχονται ὁμοίως πάντες
εἰς ἓν μέρος, δεξιᾷ ἢ ἀριστερᾷ. τοῦτο δὲ χρεία παραφυλάττειν, ἵνα πάντες εἰς ἓν
μέρος καὶ εἰσέρχονται καὶ ἐξέρχονται.

52. Περιπατεῖν ἴσως καὶ συντεταγμένως ὅτ᾽ ἄν τινες τῆς παρατάξεως προκύψωσι καὶ ἀνίσως περιπατοῦσι, καὶ παραγγέλλει· ἴσον τὸ μέτωπον, καὶ ἰσοῦται τὸ
360 μέτωπον.

53. Πυκνοῦνται ἤγουν σφίγγονται, ὅτ᾽ ἄν ὡς ἀπὸ β΄ ἢ γ΄ σαγιττοβόλων τῆς
τῶν ἐχθρῶν παρατάξεως γίνεται ἡμῶν ἡ παράταξις καὶ μέλλη συμβάλλειν.
παραγγέλλει· "ζεῦξον." καὶ πυκνούμενοι σφίγγονται πρὸς τὸν μέσον τόπον
κατὰ βάθος καὶ μῆκος τοσοῦτον, ἵνα οἱ μὲν ἔμπροσθεν τεταγμένοι καὶ ἐκ πλαγί-
365 ου εἰς τὰ ἄρματα ἀλλήλοις ἐγγίζωσιν, οἱ δὲ ὄπισθεν κατὰ νώτου ἀλλήλοις
ὥσπερ κεκόλληνται. τοῦτο δὲ τὸ σχῆμα γίνεσθαι δύναται καὶ περιπατούσης καὶ
ἱσταμένης τῆς παρατάξεως. | χρὴ δὲ τοὺς οὐραγοὺς παραγγέλλεσθαι καὶ ἐκ τῶν 307
ὄπισθεν προωθεῖν καὶ ἀπορθοῦν αὐτοὺς εἰς τὴν χρείαν ἵνα μὴ ἐναπομένωσί
τινες, ὡς εἰκός, δειλιῶντες.

370    54. Φούλκῳ δὲ περιπατεῖν λέγεται ὅτ᾽ ἄν ἐγγιζουσῶν τῶν παρατάξεων, τῆς
τε ἡμετέρας καὶ τῆς τῶν ἐναντίων, μέλλη ἄρχεσθαι ἡ τοξεία γίνεσθαι καὶ οὐ
φοροῦσιν οἱ ἐν τῷ μετώπῳ τεταγμένοι ζάβας ἤτοι λωρίκια. καὶ παραγγέλλει·
"πύκνωσον." καὶ τῶν ἔμπροσθεν κατὰ τὸ μέτωπον τεταγμένων πυκνούντων τὰ
σκουτάρια αὐτῶν μέχρι τοῦ ἐγγίζειν ἀλλήλοις, κατασκέποντες προσπεπλασ-
375 μένως τὰς γαστέρας αὐτῶν μέχρι τῆς κνήμης ἤγουν τοῦ λεγομένου σκέλους, οἱ
παρεστῶτες αὐτοῖς ὄπισθεν ὑπερανέχοντες τὰ σκουτάρια αὐτῶν καὶ ἀναπαύον-

---

355 η΄ MWVBE ὀκτὼ A | θέλει MAVBE θέλῃ W | τεσσάρων MWA δ΄ VBE
358–359 προκύψωσι MVBE προκύψωσιν WA    359 περιπατοῦσι M περιπατοῦσιν W
περιπατῶσιν A περιπατῶσι VBE    361 ἤγουν MAVBE ἤτοι W | β΄ MWVBE δύο A | γ΄
MWVBE τριῶν A | σαγιττοβόλων MWAVE om. B | τῆς WAVBE om. M    362 γίνεται
MWB γένηται AVE | ἡμῶν MWB trsp. AVE | συμβάλλειν MWA συμβάλλει VBE
363 παραγγέλλει AVBE λέγει M om. W | ζεῦξον MW σφίγξον AVBE    366 κεκόλληνται
MW κολλῶνται AVBE | γίνεσθαι δύναται MWA trsp. VBE    367 καὶ MWA om. VBE
368 ἐναπομένωσί MW ἐναπομείνωσι A ἀπομείνωσι VBE    371 ἡμετέρας MWAB ἡμέρας
VE | ἄρχεσθαι WA ἔρχεσθαι M ἀπέρχεσθαι VBE    372 φοροῦσιν MWA φορῶσιν VBE
373 ἔμπροσθεν MAVBE ἔμπροσθε W | τὸ MW om. AVBE    374 κατασκέποντες MW καὶ
κατασκεπόντων AVBE    374–375 προσπεπλασμένως MWVE om. AB    375 τὰς MW τάς
τε AVBE | μέχρι…σκέλους MW καὶ τὰ σκέλη AVBE

the depth of the files is reduced, while the width of the battle line is extended and the depth becomes eight men. If he wants to make it four deep, he again says: "March out." In like manner they all march to one side, right or left. This must be observed to make sure that all march in or out to one side.

52. They should march evenly and in good order. When some men step out in front of the line and march in an uneven manner, the command is given: "Straighten out the front." And the front is made straight.

53. They tighten up or close ranks when our battle line gets to about two or three bowshots from the enemy's line and is getting set to charge. The command is: "Close ranks." Joining together, they close in toward the center, keeping their depth and width such that the weapons of the men lined up in front are almost touching those of the men next to them, and the men behind them to the rear are almost glued to one another. This maneuver may be carried out while the battle line is on the march or when it is standing in place. The file closers must be ordered to push forward the men in the rear and to straighten their line when necessary, so they will not, as may be likely, hesitate or act in a cowardly manner.

54. They are said to march in a foulkon when the two lines, ours and the enemy's, are getting close and the archers are about to open fire and the front-rank men are not wearing coats of mail or body armor. The command is: "Close ranks." The men in the front ranks close in on one another until their shields are almost touching, completely covering their midsections down to their shins, also called the shank. The men standing behind them hold their shields above

τες εἰς τοὺς ἔμπροσθεν σκέπουσι τὰ στήθη καὶ τὰς ὄψεις αὐτῶν καὶ οὕτως συμβάλλουσιν.

55. Ὅτ᾽ ἂν δὲ πυκνωθεῖσα καὶ ἡ παράταξις κατὰ λόγον ἀπὸ ἑνὸς σαγιττο-
380 βόλου γένηται τῶν πολεμίων καὶ μέλλει πάντως ἡ συμβολὴ συνάπτεσθαι, παραγγέλλει· "ἕτοιμοι." καὶ ἄλλου διαδεχομένου καὶ κράζοντος· "βοήθει." καὶ πάντων ἀποκρινομένων ἴσως καὶ συμφώνως· "ὁ Θεός." οἱ μὲν ψιλοὶ τοξεύουσιν ὑψηλοτέρως, οἱ δὲ σκουτάτοι, οἱ εἰς τὸ μέτωπον τεταγμένοι, ἔτι ἐγγυτέρω γενομένων τῶν πολεμίων, εἰ μὲν ἔχωσι ματζούκια ἢ τζικούρια ἢ ῥικτάρια, εἰς τὸ
385 ἅμα ῥίπτουσιν αὐτά, εἰ δὲ μήγε, ἀναμένοντες μέχρις οὗ ἐγγὺς ἔλθωσι, τότε ἀκοντίζοντες τὰ κοντάρια ἤτοι ῥικτάρια αὐτῶν, ἐπιλαμβάνονται τῶν σπαθίων αὐτῶν καὶ μάχονται εὐτάκτως ἐν τῇ τάξει αὐτῶν μένοντες καὶ οὐ κατατρέχοντες τῶν, ὡς εἰκός, ὑποχωρούντων αὐτοῖς ἐχθρῶν, οἱ δὲ ὄπισθεν αὐτῶν ἑστῶτες τὰς ἑαυτῶν κεφαλὰς σκέποντες μετὰ τῶν σκουταρίων αὐτῶν ἐπιβοηθοῦσι τοῖς
390 ἔμπροσθεν μετὰ τῶν κονταρίων.

56. Χρεία δέ ἐστιν ἀσφαλῶς τοὺς εἰς <τὸ> μέτωπον τασσομένους προφυ-λάττειν ἑαυτοὺς μέχρις οὗ εἰς χεῖρας ἐκ τοῦ πλησίον ἔλθωσιν ἵνα μὴ κατατοξεύ-ωνται ὑπὸ τῶν πολεμίων, ἐὰν μάλιστα μὴ ἔχωσι ζάβας ἢ χαλκότουβα.

57. Μερίζονται πρὸς διφαλαγγίαν ὅτ᾽ ἂν ἐπ᾽ εὐθείας περιπατούσης τῆς
395 παρατάξεως καὶ ἔμπροσθεν καὶ ὄπισθεν φανῶσιν πολέμιοι. καὶ εἰ μὲν ἀπὸ ις′ ἀνδρῶν ἔχουσιν αἱ ἀκίαι, καὶ ἤγγισαν οἱ δι᾽ ὄψεως ἐρχόμενοι ἐχθροὶ καὶ μέλλου-σιν ἐκ τοῦ πλησίον ἄρχεσθαι τῆς μάχης, παραγγέλλει· "ἀπὸ η′ μερίσθητε," καὶ οἱ μὲν η′ εἰς διφαλαγγίαν ἵστανται, | οἱ δὲ η′ στρεφόμενοι καὶ κινοῦντες πρὸς 307ᵛ διφαλαγγίαν μερίζονται. εἰ δὲ ἢ ἀπὸ η′ ἵστανται τὸ βάθος ἢ ἀπὸ δ′, παραγγέλ-
400 λει· "ἑδραῖοι στῆτε· οἱ δεύτεροι καὶ οἱ τῆς διφαλαγγίας ἐξέλθετε." δεύτεροι δέ

---

377 τοὺς ἔμπροσθεν MW τὰ τοῦ ἔμπροσθεν σκουτάρια A αὐτὰ τὰ τῶν ἔμπροσθεν σκουτάρια B τὰ τῶν ἔμπροσθεν σκουτάρια VE   379–380 σαγιττοβόλου MWA σαγιτοβόλον VBE   380 πάντως MWA πάντων VBE   383 ἔτι WAVBE ἔτι δὲ M   384 ἔχωσι MW ἔχουσι AVBE | ῥικτάρια Va ῥηκτάρια MW ῥιπτάρια AVBE   384–385 εἰς…ἅμα De εἰς τὸ χαμαὶ MW om. AVBE   385 ἐγγὺς ἔλθωσι M ἐγγὺς ἔλθωσιν W ἔλθωσιν ἐγγὺς καὶ AVBE   386 ῥικτάρια Va ῥηκτάρια MW ῥιπτάρια AVBE   387–388 κατατρέχοντες τῶν MW καταδιώκοντες τοὺς AVBE   388 ὑποχωρούντων MW ὑποχωρούντας AVBE | ἐχθρῶν MWVBE ἐχθροὺς A   389 ἑαυτῶν κεφαλὰς MWA κεφαλὰς αὐτῶν VBE   391 ἀσφαλῶς MW om. AVBE | τὸ ci. De om. codd. | τασσομένους MW τασσομένους ἀσφαλῶς AVBE   391–392 προφυλάττειν ἑαυτοὺς MW trsp. AVBE   394 περιπατούσης AVBE περιπατῶσι MW   395 φανῶσιν M φανῶσι WAVBE   396 ἔχουσιν A ἔχωσιν MWVBE | αἱ MWA καὶ VBE   397 η′ MWVBE ὀκτὼ A   397–398 καὶ…διφαλαγγίαν καὶ οἱ μὲν (om. W) η′ (ὀκτὼ A) εἰς διφαλαγγίαν MWA om. VBE   398 η′² MWVBE ὀκτὼ A   399 η′ MWVBE ὀκτὼ A | δ′ MWVBE τεσσάρων A   400 διφαλαγγίας AVBE φαλαγγίας MW

their heads and resting them on those of the men in front, they cover their breasts and faces and in this way engage in battle.

55. When ranks have been properly closed and the line is about one bowshot from the enemy and fighting is definitely just about to begin, the command is given: "Ready." Right after this another officer shouts: "Help <us>." Everyone responds clearly and in unison: "O God." The light-armed troops start shooting their arrows overhead. As the enemy advance even closer, the heavy infantry, drawn up in the front line, if they have lead darts, axes, or missile weapons, they throw them all at once. Otherwise they wait until the enemy gets close, then they hurl their lances or javelins, grasp their swords, and fight in good order, remaining in position and not pursuing the enemy if they happen to fall back before them. The men stationed behind them cover their heads with their shields and with their lances support those in front of them.

56. It is essential for the men drawn up in the first line to keep themselves safe and protected until they come to grips with the enemy. Otherwise they might be shot down by them, especially if they are not wearing body armor or greaves.

57. They are divided into a double phalanx when the battle line is advancing straight ahead and hostile forces appear both in front and to the rear. Assuming that the files are composed of sixteen men, if the enemy force approaching from the front has gotten close and is about to begin fighting up close, give the command: "By eight. Split up." Eight men take their position in a double phalanx. The other eight, facing and marching about, are divided into a double phalanx. If they stand at eight deep or four deep, the command is: "Stand firm. Seconds

εἰσιν οἱ λεγόμενοι πάλαι σεκοῦνδοι ἢ ἐπιστάται. καὶ στρεφόμενοι οἱ σεκοῦνδοι, τοῦτ᾽ ἔστιν, οἱ ὑπὸ τὸν δεκάρχην τεταγμένοι ἐξέρχονται διάστημά τι ἄχρι τριακοσίων βημάτων ἤτοι σκελισμάτων, ὥστε μὴ δύνασθαι τὰς βαλλομένας παρὰ τῶν ἐναντίων σαγίττας ἑκατέρωθεν βλάπτειν τοὺς νώτους τῶν ἀντιβλε-
405 πόντων, ἀλλ᾽ ἐν τῷ εὐκαίρῳ τόπῳ πίπτειν αὐτάς. εἶτα παραγγέλλει· "ὑποστρέ-ψατε." καὶ πάλιν ὑποστρέψαντες, εἰ χρεία γένηται, ἀποκαθίστανται κατὰ τὸ πρότερον σχῆμα.

58. Εἰ δέ, ὡς εἰκός, ἡ μείζων δύναμις τῶν ἐχθρῶν διὰ τοῦ νώτου ἤγουν ὄπισθεν τῆς παρατάξεως ἔρχεται καὶ ἄμαξαι οὐκ ἀκολουθοῦσιν, οἱ σεκοῦνδοι
410 ἤγουν οἱ ἐπιστάται ἵστανται καὶ οἱ πρῖμοι ἤγουν οἱ πρωτοστάται, οἱ καὶ λοχαγοί, ἐξέρχονται.

59. Τὰ δὲ τῆς διφαλαγγίας γίνεται ὅτ᾽ ἂν αἱ ἄμαξαι οὐκ ἀκολουθοῦσιν ἢ ἀκολουθοῦσαι ἐβιάσθησαν ὑπὸ τῶν πολεμίων. ταύτας δὲ χρὴ πάντως ἐπὶ παντὸς ἡτοιμασμένου πεζικοῦ στρατοῦ ἀκολουθεῖν, εἰ μὴ ἄρα καβαλλαρικὸς στρα-
415 τὸς βιασθῇ πεζεῦσαι καὶ ἐν καιρῷ τοιούτῳ ἢ ἁμαξῶν ἢ ἄλλης ὕλης κατὰ τοῦ νώτου ἀπορεῖ.

60. Δεξιᾷ δὲ καὶ ἀριστερᾷ κλίνονται ὅτ᾽ ἂν ἐκ πλαγίου εἰς ἓν μέρος θέλῃ τὴν παράταξιν σῦραι, ἢ διὰ τό, ὡς εἰκός, ἐκτεῖναι τὴν παράταξιν καὶ ὑπερκερᾶσαι ἤγουν κυκλῶσαι τοὺς ἐχθροὺς ἢ μὴ ὑπερκερασθῆναι ἤγουν κυκλωθῆναι παρ᾽
420 αὐτῶν ἢ διὰ τόπου ἐπιτηδειότητα ἢ διὰ παραγωγὴν στενοῦ τόπου. καὶ εἰ μὲν δεξιᾷ θέλει παραγαγεῖν αὐτήν, παραγγέλλει· "ἐπὶ κοντάριν κλῖνον." καὶ στρέ-φονται πάντες οἱ ὁπλῖται ἐκεῖθεν. <"κίνησον," καὶ κινοῦσιν ἕως οὗ χρεία.> εἶτα παραγγέλλει· "ὑπόστρεψον." καὶ ἀποκαθίστανται. εἰ δὲ ἀριστερᾷ θέλει κλῖναι, παραγγέλλει· "ἐπὶ σκουτάριν κλίνας κίνησον." καὶ τὰ ἄλλα ὁμοίως φυλάττονται.

---

401 ἢ MW νῦν δὲ AVBE    402 ὑπὸ MWA ἀπὸ VBE | δεκάρχην MW δέκαρχον AVBE | τεταγμένοι MW τεταγμένοι ἐπιστάται AVBE | διάστημά τι *Strat.* διαστήματα MW διάστημα AVBE    403 βαλλομένας MW ῥιπτομένας AVBE    404 τοὺς νώτους MW τὰς ψύας AVBE    406 κατὰ AVBE εἰς MW    408 διὰ...ἤγουν MW om. AVBE    409–410 τῆς...ἤγουν[1] MWAVE om. B    409 ἔρχεται AVBE ἔρχηται MW    409–410 οἱ...ἤγουν[1] MWB om. AVE    410 οἱ[1] MWVBE om. A | ἵστανται WAVBE ἵστανται δὲ M | οἱ[2]...ἤγουν[2] WVBE om. MA | οἱ[3] MWAB om. VE | πρωτοστάται MWA πρωτοστάτοι VBE | οἱ καὶ A οἱ δὲ MW καὶ VBE    412 διφαλαγγίας AVBE φαλαγγίας MW | ὅτ᾽ ἂν MWA ὅτε VBE | ἀκολουθοῦσιν MWVBE ἀκολουθῶσιν A    413 ἀκολουθοῦσαι VBE ἀκολουθήσασαι MWA | πάντως MWA πάντας VBE    415–416 κατὰ...νώτου MW ἐκ τῶν ὀπίσω AVBE    418 ἢ...ἐκτεῖναι MWVBE ἢ μὴ A | τὴν παράταξιν MW αὐτὴν AVBE    420 παραγωγὴν MWA παραγωγῆς VBE    421 κοντάριν MW κοντάριον AVBE    422 κίνησον...χρεία *Strat.* om. codd.    423–424 ὑπόστρεψον...παραγγέλλει MWAVE om. B    424 σκουτάριν Va κοντάριν MW σκουτάριον AVBE | φυλάττονται MWAVE φυλάττοντα B

and men in the double phalanx, march out." The seconds were formerly called sekoundoi or epistatai. The sekoundoi, that is, those drawn up under the dekarch, face about and march out a distance up to three hundred paces or feet, so that the arrows fired by the enemy from both sides will not cause harm to the rear of those confronting them, but will fall in the clear space <between them>. Then give the command: "Turn around." Again, turning around, if the need arises, they return to their previous formation.

58. If, as is likely, a larger hostile force approaches the rear of our line and the wagons are not following along, the sekoundoi, that is, the epistatai, halt and the primoi, that is, the protostatai, also called group leaders, march out.

59. Adopt the double-phalanx formation when the wagons are not following or if they were following and came under attack by the enemy. It is always necessary for them to follow after every well-prepared infantry army unless perhaps a cavalry army should be forced to go on foot at a time when they are deprived of wagons or other supplies to their rear.

60. They face to the right or to the left when the commander wishes to move the battle line from the flank to one side, either, as would be likely, to extend the line and outflank or encircle the enemy or to avoid being outflanked or encircled by them, or for a more favorable location or for passing through a narrow space. If he wants to lead it to the right, he orders: "To the lance. Face." The heavy-armed troops all turn away from that direction. <"Move." And they move to the designated place.> He then commands: "Turn back." And they return to their original position. If he wants them to face to the left, he commands: "To the shield. Face. Move." And the rest is observed as above.

425　61. Ἀμφίστομος δὲ κίνησις ὅτ᾽ ἂν τῶν ἐχθρῶν, ὡς εἰκός, ἄφνω γυρευόντων
ἔμπροσθεν καὶ ὄπισθεν μὴ φθάσῃ πρὸς διφαλαγγίαν μερισθῆναι ἡ παράταξις.
καὶ παραγγέλλει· "τῶν ἀκιῶν τὴν τάξιν φυλάξατε." καὶ οἱ ἡμίσεις κατὰ τῶν
ἔμπροσθεν ἐρχομένων ἱστάμενοι ἁρμόζονται, οἱ δὲ ἡμίσεις ἐπὶ τὸν νῶτον
ἀντιστρεφόμενοι, | οἱ δὲ ἐν τῷ μέσῳ ἑστῶτες τὰς κεφαλὰς αὐτῶν ἴσως σκέπουσι 308
430　διὰ τῶν σκουταρίων.

62. Μετατίθενται δεξιᾷ καὶ ἀριστερᾷ ὅτ᾽ ἂν ἢ δεξιᾷ ἢ ἀριστερᾷ θέλῃς μετενεγκεῖν τὴν παράταξιν, χρείας, ὡς εἰκός, οὕτω καλούσης. καὶ παραγγέλλει·
"μετάφερε εἰς τὰ δεξιά," ἢ πάλιν· "μετάφερε εἰς τὰ ἀριστερά." καὶ ἑνὸς <ἑνὸς>
τάγματος μετατιθεμένου μεταφέρεται ἡ παράταξις πᾶσα πρὸς τὸ μέρος ἐκεῖνο
435　συντόμως.

63. Ἀραιοῦνται ἤτοι πλατύνονται ὅτ᾽ ἂν πεπυκνωμένοι εἰσι καὶ θέλῃς
μερίσαι ἤτοι λεπτύναι, ὡς εἰκός, τὰς ἀκίας καὶ ἐκτεῖναι τὴν παράταξιν εἰς μῆκος
ἢ διὰ τὸ ἀνετωτέρους αὐτοὺς γενέσθαι. καὶ παραγγέλλει· "πλάτυνον πρὸς τὰ
ἀμφότερα μέρη." καὶ πλατύνονται. τοῦτο δὲ τὸ σχῆμα καὶ περιπατούσης καὶ
440　ἱσταμένης τῆς παρατάξεως δύναται γίνεσθαι τῶν δύο κεράτων ἐπὶ τὰ ἔξω
νευόντων, εἴτε μέρος ἕν ἐστιν εἴτε ἡ παράταξις.

64. Βαθύνονται δὲ ἤτοι διπλοῦνται αἱ ἀκίαι ὅτ᾽ ἂν μὲν ἀπὸ τεσσάρων
ἵστανται καὶ θέλῃς αὐτὰς διπλῶσαι καὶ πρὸς συμβολὴν ἰσχυροποιῆσαι, ἁρμοζόντως τῷ βάθει τῆς παρατάξεως τῶν ἐναντίων. καὶ παραγγέλλει· "εἴσελθε." καὶ
445　γίνονται ὀκτώ. εἰ δὲ θέλεις ις᾽ ποιῆσαι, πάλιν παραγγέλλει· "εἴσελθε." καὶ
εἰσερχόμενοι εἰς τοὺς ἰδίους τόπους εἰς παρ᾽ ἕνα διπλοῦνται καὶ γίνονται ις᾽
πάντες εἰς ἓν μέρος ὡς ἐξῆλθον. εἰ δὲ θέλεις, ὡς εἰκός, ἀπὸ λβ᾽ τὸ βάθος τῶν
ἀκιῶν ποιῆσαι, ὅπερ οὔκ ἐστι χρειῶδες, παραγγέλλει· "ὁ στίχος ὑπὸ τὸν στίχον,"

---

425 γυρευόντων MW περικυκλούντων AVBE　426 καὶ MWA ἢ VBE　427 ἀκιῶν MW
ἀκιῶν ἤτοι τῶν λόχων AVBE　428 ἁρμόζονται MW ἀπαντῶσιν AVBE　428–429 οἱ…
ἀντιστρεφόμενοι MW om. AVBE　429 ἴσως MWA om. VBE | σκέπουσι MA σκέπουσιν
WB σκέπουσιν VE　432 οὕτω καλούσης MW ἀπαιτούσης AVBE　432–433 παραγγέλλει…ἀριστερά MWAVE om. B　433 ἑνὸς² Va om. codd.　435 συντόμως MWA
συντόμως δὲ VBE　436 εἰσι MA εἰσὶν W ὦσι VBE　438 ἀνετωτέρους Strat. ἀνωτέρους
codd.　439 ἀμφότερα AVBE ἀμφίστομα MW　442 ὅτ᾽ ἂν MWA ὅτε VBE | τεσσάρων
MWA δ᾽ VBE　443–444 ἁρμοζόντως MWA ἁρμοζομένης VBE　444 καὶ¹ MW om. AVBE
445 ις᾽ MWVE δεκαὲξ A om. B　445–446 ποιῆσαι…ἰδίους MWAVE om. B　446 ἕνα
Strat. εἰς codd.　447 ὡς¹ MWAVE om. B | λβ᾽ MWVBE τριάκοντα δύο A　448 ἐστι
MAVBE ἐστιν W

61. The two-faced maneuver <is called for> in case the enemy suddenly circles around both front and rear before our battle line has time to divide into the double phalanx. The command is given: "Keep to the formation of the files." Half of the troops stand fast to meet the enemy attacking from the front. The other half turns about to the rear. The middle ranks remain in place covering their heads evenly with their shields.

62. They change front to the right or to the left when you want to transfer the battle line to the right or to the left in order to meet some necessity that may arise. The command is: "Transfer to the right." Or again: "Transfer to the left." By one tagma at a time changing front, the whole line is quickly transferred to that place.

63. The line can be made more open or extended. When the men are in close order and, as is likely, you want to divide or thin out the files and extend the width of the battle line or to give it more slack, give the command: "Extend both sides." And they extend <the line>. This formation may be practiced while the line, whether it be a single meros or the whole line, is marching or has come to a halt, with both flanks heading to the outside.

64. The depth of the files may be increased or doubled. Assume that the troops are standing four deep and you want to double that to correspond to the depth of the enemy's line and to make your own stronger for the charge. The command is: "Enter." And they become eight deep. If you want to make them sixteen deep, give the same command: "Enter." One by one they return to their own positions and the files are doubled, resuming their original depth of one unit of sixteen men. If for some reason you want to make the files thirty-two deep—not a very useful idea—give the command: "File after file." They are

καὶ διπλοῦνται ὁμοίως καὶ βαθύνεται μὲν ἡ παράταξις, συστέλλεται δὲ τὸ μῆκος
450 αὐτῆς.

65. Μεταβάλλονται ὅτ’ ἂν ἐπ’ εὐθείας περιπατούσης τῆς παρατάξεως μηκέτι
δι’ ὄψεως ἔλθωσιν οἱ ἐχθροί, ἀλλὰ ἀπὸ ὄπισθεν αὐτῆς. καὶ ἐὰν μὲν τὸ μέτωπον
ἤτοι τοὺς λοχαγούς, τοὺς καὶ πρωτοστάτας, ὄπισθεν θέλῃς μετενεγκεῖν ἀπὸ ις′
ἀνδρῶν ὄντος τοῦ βάθους, παραγγέλλει· “μετάλλαξον τὸν τόπον.” καὶ διὰ τοῦ
455 βάθους τῶν ἀκιῶν παρερχόμενοι οἱ λοχαγοὶ ἵστανται εἰς παράταξιν συνακολου-
θούντων αὐτοῖς καὶ τῶν λοιπῶν καὶ μεταβάλλονται, τὸ μέτωπον ἐπὶ τοὺς
πολεμίους ποιοῦντες. τοῦτο δὲ πρὸ τῆς πυκνώσεως ἐπιτηδείως γίνεται. εἰ δὲ
πεπύκνωται καὶ οὐ συμφθάζει ἀραιῶσαι, παραγγέλλει· “μετασχημάτισον.” καὶ
στρεφόμενοι, ὡς ἵστανται, ἀντιβλέπουσι | κατὰ τοῦ νώτου ἤγουν τὸ ὀπίσω    308ᵛ
460 μέρος, οὐκέτι τοῦ λοχαγοῦ ἔμπροσθεν εὑρισκομένου, ἀλλὰ τοῦ ἑξκαιδεκάτου
οὐραγοῦ.

66. Αἱ μὲν οὖν γυμνασίαι αὗται δύνανται ἐν καιρῷ πολέμου τὸν στρατιώτην
ἕτοιμον παρασκευάζειν καὶ πρὸ καιροῦ πολέμου ἄνευ σιδήρου διὰ ὅπλων
ἑτέρων τῶν πρὸς γυμνασίαν ἐπιτηδείων ἐθίζειν πρὸς πάντα τὰ σχήματα τῶν
465 κινήσεων καὶ τὰ παραγγέλματα εὐφυῶς καὶ ἄνευ ταραχῆς καὶ θροῖσμοῦ διαγίν-
εσθαι, ὅτ’ ἂν μάλιστα πρὸς ἄλληλα τὰ τάγματα, διαιρούμενα εἰς δύο ἀντιπαρατάξεις, εἴτε καθ’ ἓν τάγμα εἴτε κατὰ πλείονα, ποιεῖται τὴν γυμνασίαν.

67. Οὐκ ἀγνοῶ δὲ ὅτι περ τοῖς ἀρχαίοις καὶ ἕτερά τινα παραδέδοται παραγγέλματα καὶ κινήματα γυμνασίας, ἄλλως τε καὶ Ἀρριανῷ καὶ Αἰλιανῷ, ὥσπερ ἐξ
470 ἑνὸς στόματος περὶ αὐτῶν ὁμοφωνοῦσιν. ἀλλ’ ἵνα μὴ ἐπὶ πλάτος τοσοῦτον
παρεκτείνω τὸν λόγον, ἐν κεφαλαίῳ μόνον μνήμην παραθήσω ἐκείνων καὶ τοῦ
λοιποῦ σιωπήσομαι τὸ πλῆθος, τὸ μὲν διὰ τὴν ἐν αὐτοῖς ἀσάφειάν τε καὶ ἀχρη-

---

468–494 Aelian., 25–31; 36; 42. Arrian., 32.1.

---

449 διπλοῦνται MWA λεπτύνονται VBE | καὶ²…παράταξις MWAVE καὶ βαθείας
περιπατούσης τῆς παρατάξεως B | συστέλλεται MW συσφίγγεται A σφίγγεται VBE
452 ἀλλὰ ἀπὸ MW ἀλλ’ ἐκ τῶν AVBE | μὲν MW μέντοι AVBE    453 τοὺς² MWA om. VBE
456 τῶν MWA τῶν τῶν VBE    457 πρὸ…γίνεται MWA εὐκόλως γίνεται πρὸ τοῦ
πυκνωθῆναι τὴν παράταξιν VBE    458 συμφθάζει MW δύνανται A δύναται VBE | ἀραιῶσαι
Strat. ἁρμόσαι MW ἐξελίξαι AVBE    459 ἀντιβλέπουσι MVBE ἀντιβλέπουσιν WA | κατὰ…
ἤγουν MW εἰς A πρὸς VBE    460 ἑξκαιδεκάτου MW om. AVBE    462 αὗται MWA αὗτῶν
VBE | τὸν WAVBE om. M    464 ἐθίζειν MWA ἐρεθίζειν VBE    465 καὶ θροισμοῦ M om.
AVBE diff. lectu W    466 τὰ MA om. VBE diff. lectu W | δύο MWAB β′ VE    467 εἴτε¹
MWA εἴ τι VBE    468 περ MW om. AVBE    469 ἄλλως Va ἄλλοις codd.    470 ὁμοφωνοῦσιν MWAVE ὁμοφανοῦσιν B    471 τὸν MW τὸν παρόντα AVBE    471–474 τοῦ…
εἰρημένα MW γὰρ τὰ πλείονα καὶ χρησιμώτερα ἀνθολογησάμενοι (ἀνθομολογησάμενοι VBE)
ἐνταῦθα εἰρήκαμεν AVBE

doubled in the above manner and the line is deepened while its width is reduced.

65. When the line is marching on straight ahead and the enemy are not yet approaching from the front but from the rear, the line may be turned around. If you want to transfer the front, that is, the group leaders, also called protostatai, to the rear, the files still being sixteen men deep, the command is: "Change place." The group leaders pass through the depth of the files to the rear and take their stand in a line, while the rest of the men follow behind them and form a new front facing the enemy. It is best to do this before they close ranks; but if they are already closed and there is no time to open them up, the command is given: "About face." Remaining in position they turn around to the rear and, instead of the group leader, the sixteenth man, the file closer, is now stationed in front.

66. These exercises, therefore, can be performed in time of war to prepare the soldier to be ready and before the war begins, without regular iron weapons but with others suitable for drilling, to accustom <the men> to all the forms of maneuvers and to recognize the commands in an orderly manner and without too much noise or confusion. This is especially the case when the tagmata are divided into two battle lines opposed to one another, whether or not the exercise involves one tagma by itself or several.

67. I am not unaware that certain other commands and movements for drill have been handed down by the ancients, especially by Arrian and Aelian, who are in agreement on these matters as though speaking with one voice.[11] But in order not to stretch out the discourse to too great an extent, I shall set forth, albeit only in summary fashion, what we remember of those authorities, and I will pass over most of the rest in silence. One reason is that some of it is not

---

11. Cf. Aelian 25–31; 36; 42; Arrian, 32.1.

στίαν, τὸ δὲ καὶ διὰ τὸ ἐκεῖθεν ἀναληφθῆναι ὥσπερ ἀνθολογηθέντα τὰ παρ᾽
ἡμῶν ἐνταῦθα εἰρημένα μετὰ τῆς τῶν νεωτέρων διὰ πείρας εὑρέσεως, καὶ ἵνα μὴ
475 ἀπειρόκαλοι δόξωμεν εἶναι καὶ δευτερολογεῖν ἀσαφῶς ἐνταῦθα τὰ ἤδη σαφη-
νισθέντα.

68. Παρὰ γὰρ Αἰλιανῷ λέγονται ὀνόματα καὶ κινήσεις αὗται· ἡ μὲν κλίσις
καλουμένη, τὴν δὲ κλίσιν εἰς δύο διαιρεῖ καὶ τὴν μὲν ἐπὶ ἀσπίδα καὶ αὐτὸς κλίσιν
λέγει ἤγουν ἐπὶ σκουτάριν, τὴν δὲ ἐπὶ δόρυ ἤγουν ἐπὶ κοντάριν. ἔστι δέ τις
480 κίνησις καὶ παρ᾽ αὐτῷ καὶ μεταβολὴ καὶ ἐπιστροφὴ καὶ ἀναστροφὴ καὶ περι-
σπασμὸς καὶ ἐκπερισπασμὸς καὶ ζυγεῖν καὶ στοιχεῖν καὶ εἰς ὀρθὸν ἀποδοῦναι καὶ
ἐξελίσσειν καὶ διπλασιάζειν. λέγεται δὲ καὶ ἐπαγωγὴ καὶ δεξιὰ παραγωγὴ καὶ
εὐώνυμος παραγωγὴ καὶ πλαγία φάλαγξ καὶ ὀρθία φάλαγξ καὶ λοξὴ φάλαγξ καὶ
παρεμβολὴ καὶ πρόσταξις καὶ ἔνταξις καὶ ὑπόταξις καὶ ἐπίταξις καὶ προσένταξις
485 καὶ παρένταξις.

69. Αἱ μὲν οὖν ὀνομασίαι τῶν κινήσεων τοσαῦται, τὰ δὲ παραγγέλματα
οὕτως· "ἄγε εἰς τὰ ὅπλα. παράστητε παρὰ τὰ ὅπλα. <ὁ> ὁπλοφόρος μὴ ἀπίτω
τῆς φάλαγγος. ὁ σκευοφόρος ἀποχωρείτω τῆς φάλαγγος. σίγα καὶ πρόσεχε τῷ
παραγγελλομένῳ. ἄνω τὰ δόρατα. κάθες τὰ δόρατα. ὁ οὐραγὸς τὸν λόχον
490 ἀπευθυνέτω. τήρει τὰ διαστήματα. | ἐπὶ δόρυ κλῖνον. ἐπὶ ἀσπίδα κλῖνον. πρόαγε. 309
ἔχ᾽ οὕτως. εἰς ὀρθὸν ἀπόδος. τὸ βάθος διπλασίαζε, ἀποκατάστησον. τὸν
Λάκωνα ἐξέλισσε, <ἀποκατάστησον>. ἐπὶ τὸ δόρυ ἐκπερίσπα, ἀποκατάστησον."
ἀλλὰ ταῦτα διά τε τὸ ἀσαφὲς καὶ τὴν ἀχρηστίαν τέως παρείδομεν, τοῦ
συντόμου καὶ σαφοῦς μάλιστα φροντίζοντες.

---

474–476 καὶ...σαφηνισθέντα MW om. AVBE    478 δύο MWA β′ VBE | καὶ²...κλίσιν² MW
trsp. AVBE    479 ἐπὶ¹ MWA τὸ VBE | σκουτάριν MW σκουτάριον AVBE | κοντάριν MW
κοντάριον AVBE | ἔστι MAVBE ἐστιν W    480 καὶ¹ MW om. AVBE    481 εἰς ὀρθὸν AVBE
ἐπορθὸν MW    483 εὐώνυμος AB ἐξωνύμος VE om. MW | φάλαγξ¹ MWA φάλαξ VE φύλαξ
B | ὀρθία φάλαγξ MW ὀρθὴ φάλαγξ A ὀρθὴ φάλαξ VBE | φάλαγξ³ MWA φάλαξ VBE
484 καὶ πρόσταξις WB πρόταξις M om. VE | προσένταξις Va πρόσταξις codd.
485 παρένταξις Va παράταξις codd.    487 ὅπλα¹ MWA ὅπλα παράτασσε τὰ ὅπλα VBE | ὁ
Va om. codd.    488 ὁ...φάλαγγος² AVBE om. MW | καὶ MW om. AVBE
489 παραγγελλομένῳ MWA παραγγελμένῳ VBE | κάθες MWVE κάτω AB | ὁ AVBE om.
MW | λόχον MWA λόγον VBE    491 ἔχ᾽ Va ex Aelian. ἔχε codd. | ἀποκατάστησον MWA
ἀποκάστησον VBE    491–492 τὸν...ἀποκατάστησον² MWAVE om. B    492 ἐξέλισσε VBE
ἐξέλισσε τὸν χορεῖον ἐξέλισσε τὸν μακεδόνα ἐξέλισσε A om. MW | ἀποκατάστησον¹ Va om.
codd. | τὸ MW om. AVBE | ἀποκατάστησον² MWAB ἀποκάστησον VE    493 τὴν ἀχρηστίαν
MW τὸ ἄχρηστον AVBE

clear or is not useful; another is that what we have taken up from those sources has been gathered into what we have said here, along with what we have derived from the experience of more recent authorities, and that we might not seem foolish repeating here in an unclear way what has already been made clear.

68. Aelian speaks of the following terms and movements. There is the one called turning toward, which he divides into two turnings: he speaks of the turning toward the shield, that is, the large shield. The other is toward the spear, that is, the lance. He also gives names to certain movements. Wheeling about, turning about, turning back, wheeling around, turning out, join, line up, turn back to the front, march out, double up. He also speaks of march in sequence, pass to the right, pass to the left, broad phalanx, straight phalanx, slanted phalanx, parembole, prostaxis, entaxis, hypotaxis, epitaxis, prosentaxis, parentaxis.

69. All the above are the names for the movements. The commands are the following. "Go to the weapons. Stand by the weapons. Let the weapon bearer not depart from the phalanx. Let the skeuophoros remove himself from the phalanx. Be silent and pay attention to the orders. Raise your spears. Lower your spears. Let the file closer straighten out the file. Observe the intervals. Turn toward the spear. Turn toward the shield. Advance. Stay as you are. Go back to the front. Double your depth. Go back to your original position. March out in the Laconian manner.[12] Execute this maneuver toward the spear. Go back to your original position." But we are passing over these because they are not clear or useful today, particularly when our aim is to be brief and clear.

12. The Laconian countermarch is made by file when the rear guard of one of the end files marches out along the rear and is followed by the man who had been in front of him. Cf. Asclepiodotus 10.14; SyrMag 24.

**495**    70. Τὰ μὲν οὖν περὶ γυμνασίας ἡμῖν προειρημένα πεζικῆς τε καὶ ἱππικῆς τῆς τε καθ᾽ ἕνα στρατιώτην καὶ τῆς κατὰ τάγμα καὶ παρατάξεις ὡς ἐν ἐπιτόμῳ ἀρκούντως ἔχει. ἁρμοδίως δὲ τῷ παρόντι συντάγματι καὶ τὰ τοῖς ἁμαρτάνουσι στρατιώταις ἐπιτίμια ἐντάξαι, ἵνα γινώσκωσιν αὐτὰ καὶ μή, ἀγνοοῦντες, ἐμπί-πτωσι ταῖς ἐν αὐτοῖς κειμέναις τιμωρίαις.

---

**495** περὶ…προειρημένα MW εἰρημένα ἡμῖν περὶ γυμνασίας AVBE | τῆς AVBE τῶν MW
**496** τῆς Va τῶν MW om. AVBE | ἐν MWA om. VBE    **498–499** ἐμπίπτωσι MAVBE
ἐμπίπτουσι W    **499** αὐτοῖς MW αὐταῖς AVBE

70. Now therefore, these comments of ours concerning the drilling of the infantry and the cavalry, the individual soldier, the individual tagma, and the whole battle line, must suffice for a summary presentation. It is appropriate to follow the present constitution with a list of punishments for errant soldiers, so they may know them and not, because of ignorance, be subject to the punishments prescribed for them.

# ΠΟΛΕΜΙΚΩΝ ΠΑΡΑΣΚΕΥΩΝ ΔΙΑΤΑΞΙΣ Η′

## Περὶ στρατιωτικῶν ἐπιτιμίων

1. Δεῖ οὖν οὐ μόνον ἐν καιρῷ τῶν ἀληθῶν ἀγώνων, ἀλλὰ καὶ ἐν τῷ καιρῷ τῆς γυμνασίας συνηγμένων ἁπάντων τῶν τε ἀρχόντων καὶ τῶν στρατιωτικῶν
5 ταγμάτων προσκαλεῖσθαι πάντας καὶ ὑπαναγινώσκειν αὐτοῖς τὰ εἰρημένα νόμιμα στρατιωτικὰ ἐπιτίμια, ἔχοντα οὕτως.

2. Ἐὰν στρατιώτης τῷ ἰδίῳ πεντάρχῃ ἢ τετράρχῃ ἐναντιωθῇ, σωφρονιζέσθω. εἰ δὲ τετράρχης ἢ πεντάρχης τῷ ἰδίῳ δεκάρχῳ, ὁμοίως σωφρονιζέσθω. εἰ δὲ δέκαρχος τῷ κεντάρχῳ, ὁμοίως. εἰ δέ τις τῶν τοῦ τάγματος τολμήσει τοῦτο
10 ποιῆσαι εἰς τὸν ἑαυτοῦ κόμητα, κεφαλικῇ τιμωρίᾳ ὑποκείσθω.

3. Εἰ μέντοι ἀδικηθῇ παρά τινος, τῷ ἄρχοντι τοῦ τάγματος προσέλθῃ· εἰ δὲ παρὰ τοῦ ἄρχοντος αὐτοῦ ἀδικηθῇ, τῷ μείζονι ἄρχοντι προσέλθῃ.

4. Ἐάν τις τολμήσῃ βαγεῦσαι ὑπὲρ τὸν χρόνον τοῦ κομεάτου ἤγουν τῆς ἀπολύσεως τῶν στρατιωτῶν εἰς τοὺς ἰδίους οἴκους, εἰς διηνεκῆ ταξατίωνα
15 κατακριθῇ.

5. Εἰ δέ τινες τολμήσωσι συνωμοσίαν ἢ φρατρίαν κατὰ τοῦ ἄρχοντος τοῦ ἰδίου ποιῆσαι ὑπὲρ οἱασδήποτε αἰτίας, κεφαλικῇ τιμωρίᾳ ὑποβληθῶσι, κατεξαίρετον οἱ πρῶτοι τῆς συνωμοσίας ἢ τῆς στάσεως γενόμενοι.

6. Εἴ τις παραφυλακὴν πόλεως ἢ κάστρου πιστευθείς, τοῦτο προδώσει ἢ
20 παρὰ γνώμην τοῦ ἄρχοντος αὐτοῦ ἐκεῖθεν ἀναχωρήσει, ἐσχάτῃ τιμωρίᾳ ὑποβληθήσεται. |

M W (mut.) A V B E    Va    PG 107:764

1–90 Strat., 1.6–8.

1 πολεμικῶν παρασκευῶν M περὶ πολεμικῶν παρασκευῶν A om. WVBE | διάταξις η′ MAVBE om. W   3 ἐν¹ MW ἐν τῷ AVBE   6 νόμιμα MW om. AVBE   7 πεντάρχῃ... τετράρχῃ MWA πεντάρχῳ ἢ τετράρχῳ VBE   9 δέκαρχος MWVBE κέκαρχος A   14 ταξατίωνα A ταξατέωνα MW ταξιῶνα VBE   16 δέ MW om. AVBE | τολμήσωσι M τολμήσωσιν W τολμήσουσιν AVBE | ἢ φρατρίαν MW om. AVBE   16–17 ἄρχοντος...ἰδίου MW trsp. AVBE   17 ὑποβληθῶσι MVBE ὑποβληθῶσιν WA   19 προδώσει Va παραδώσει codd.

# PREPARATION FOR WAR, CONSTITUTION VIII

## About Military Punishments

1. Not only in time of actual combat but also in time of training, when all the officers and their military units have been assembled, it is necessary to address all of them and, in a loud voice, read to them in detail the military punishments decreed by law, as follows.[1]

2. If a soldier disobeys his own pentarch or tetrarch, let him be punished. If a tetrarch or pentarch disobeys his dekarch, let him likewise be punished. In like manner a dekarch who disobeys his kentarch. If anyone of the men in the tagma shall dare to do this to his count, he shall undergo capital punishment.

3. If <a soldier> is unjustly treated by anyone, he should appeal to the commanding officer of the tagma, but if unjustly treated by that officer himself, he should appeal to a superior officer.

4. If anyone should presume to stay beyond the time of his furlough, that is, the dismissal of the soldiers to their own homes, he shall be condemned to continuous garrison duty.

5. If any soldiers dare, for any reason whatsoever, to enter into a conspiracy or mutiny against their commanding officer, they shall undergo capital punishment; this applies particularly to the ringleaders of any such conspiracy or mutiny.

6. If anyone who has been entrusted with the defense of a city or fortress shall betray the same or shall desert his post against the will of his commanding officer, he shall undergo the extreme penalty.

---

1. Cf. *Strat.* 1, 6–8; W. Ashburner, "The Byzantine Mutiny Act," *Journal of Hellenic Studies* 46 (1926): 80–109; E. Korzenszky, *Leges poenales militares e codice Laurentiano LXXV* (Budapest, 1931).

7. Εἴ τις ἐλεγχθῇ θελήσας ἐχθροῖς ἑαυτὸν παραδοῦναι, τῇ ἐσχάτῃ τιμωρίᾳ 309ᵛ
ὑποβληθῇ, οὐ μόνον αὐτός, ἀλλὰ καὶ ὁ τοῦτο συνειδώς, ἐπειδὴ τοῦτο γνοὺς τῷ
ἄρχοντι οὐκ ἐμήνυσεν.

8. Εἴ τις ἀκούσας τὰ μανδάτα τοῦ δεκάρχου μὴ φυλάξῃ, σωφρονιζέσθω· εἰ δὲ
ἀγνοῶν τὰ μανδάτα πταίσει, ὁ δεκάρχης σωφρονιζέσθω, ἐπειδὴ οὐ προεῖπεν
αὐτῷ.

9. Εἴ τις ἄλογον ζῷον ἢ ἄλλο οἱονδήποτε εἶδος μικρὸν ἢ μέγα εὑρὼν μὴ
τοῦτο φανερώσῃ καὶ τῷ ἄρχοντι τῷ ἰδίῳ παραδώσει, σωφρονιζέσθω, οὐ μόνον
αὐτός, ἀλλὰ καὶ ὁ συνειδὼς αὐτῷ, ὡς κλέπται ἀμφότεροι.

10. Εἴ τις ζημιώσει συντελεστὴν καὶ μὴ τοῦτον προαιρέσει ἀποθεραπεῦσαι,
κατὰ τὸ διπλάσιον τὴν ζημίαν αὐτῷ ἀποκαταστήσει.

11. Εἴ τις λαμβάνων ἀπόλυσιν ἐν εὐκαιρίας ἡμέραις τῶν ἑαυτοῦ ὅπλων
περιφρονήσει καὶ μὴ τοῦτον ὁ δεκάρχης ἀναγκάσῃ κτήσασθαι <ταῦτα> ἢ καὶ τῷ
ἰδίῳ ἄρχοντι τοῦτο μὴ φανερώσῃ, καὶ ὁ στρατιώτης αὐτὸς καὶ ὁ δεκάρχης
σωφρονισθῶσιν.

12. Εἴ τις μὴ ὑπακούσῃ τῷ ἰδίῳ ἄρχοντι, σωφρονιζέσθω κατὰ τοὺς νόμους.

13. Εἴ τις ζημιώσει στρατιώτην, ἐν διπλῇ ποσότητι αὐτῷ ἀποκαταστήσει·
ὁμοίως καὶ συντελεστήν.

14. Εἰ δὲ ἐν παραχειμαδίῳ ἐστὶν ὁ στρατὸς ἢ κατὰ πάροδον ὁ ἄρχων ἢ ὁ
στρατιώτης ζημιώσει συντελεστὴν καὶ μὴ τοῦτον δεόντως ἀποθεραπεύσει, ἐν
διπλῇ ποσότητι τοῦτο αὐτῷ ἀποκαταστήσει.

15. Εἴ τις ἐν καιρῷ πολέμου δίχα κομέτου ἤγουν ἀπολύσεως τοῦ στρατηγοῦ στρατιώτην ἀπολῦσαι τολμήσει, τριάκοντα νομισμάτων ποινὴν διδότω· ἐν
καιρῷ δὲ παραχειμαδίου δύο ἢ τρεῖς μῆνας ποιείτω· ἐν καιρῷ δὲ εἰρήνης κατὰ τὸ
διάστημα τῆς ἐπαρχίας ὁ τῆς ἀπολύσεως καιρὸς τῷ στρατιώτῃ διδόσθω.

---

22 ἐχθροῖς ἑαυτὸν MW trsp. AVBE   24 ἐμήνυσεν MWA ἐδήλωσεν VBE   25 μανδάτα
MW παραγγέλματα AVBE   26 μανδάτα MW παραγγέλματα AVBE | δεκάρχης MWA
δέκαρχος VBE   28 ἄλλο MWAVE ἄλλον B   30 συνειδὼς MW συγγινώσκων AVBE
31 προαιρέσει MW ἰδίᾳ προαιρέσει AVBE | ἀποθεραπεῦσαι Μ ἀποθεραπεύσει AVBE
ἀποθεραπεύσῃ W   32 αὐτῷ MW om. AVBE | ἀποκαταστήσει MW ἀποδώσει AVBE
33 λαμβάνων ἀπόλυσιν MW ἀπολυόμενος AVBE | τῶν…ὅπλων MW τὰ ἑαυτοῦ ὅπλα AVBE
34 ταῦτα Va om. codd.   35 τοῦτο MW om. AVBE | δεκάρχης MW δέκαρχος αὐτοῦ AVBE
40 ἢ¹ Μ καὶ WAVBE   41 ad δεόντως scr. mg. πρεπόντως W | ἀποθεραπεύσει MWA
ἀποθεραπεύσειεν VBE   43–44 στρατηγοῦ Strat. στρατοῦ codd.   44 ἀπολῦσαι τολμήσει
MWA trsp. VBE | τριάκοντα MWA λ′ VBE | ποινὴν MW om. AVBE | διδότω MW
ἀπαιτείσθω AVBE   45 δύο…τρεῖς MWA β′ ἢ γ′ VBE   45–46 κατὰ…ἐπαρχίας MWA om.
VBE

7. If anyone be found guilty of wanting to desert to the enemy, he shall undergo the extreme penalty, not only he but also anyone who knew of it, because he knew but did not report it to the commanding officer.

8. If anyone after hearing the orders of his dekarch should not carry them out, he shall be punished. But if he does not do so out of ignorance of the orders, the dekarch shall be punished for not having informed him beforehand.

9. If anyone finds a stray animal or any other object, small or large, and does not report it and turn it over to his commanding officer, he shall be punished, not only he but anyone who knows about it, as thieves both of them.

10. If anyone causes injury to a taxpayer and refuses to make compensation, he shall make restitution for double the amount of the damage.

11. If anyone is granted a leave during some days of leisure but pays no heed to his own weapons and if his dekarch should not force him to hold onto them or should not report this to his own commanding officer, both the soldier himself and the dekarch should be punished.

12. If anyone disobeys his own commanding officer, let him be punished according to the laws.

13. If anyone injures a soldier he shall give restitution for twice the amount, as in the case of injury to a taxpayer.

14. If the army is in winter quarters or on the march and either an officer or a soldier shall cause injury to a taxpayer without making proper restitution, he shall pay him back twice the amount.

15. In time of war, if anyone should presume to release a soldier apart from a furlough, that is, with the permission of the commanding officer, he shall pay a fine of thirty nomismata. While in winter quarters he may take <a furlough for> two or three months. In peacetime the soldier may be granted leave within the borders of the eparchy.

16. Εἴ τις πόλιν ἢ κάστρον πιστευθεὶς εἰς παραφυλακὴν τοῦτο προδώσει ἢ χωρὶς ἀνάγκης εἰς ζωὴν συντεινούσης ἀναχωρήσει, δυνάμενος τοῦτο ἐκδικῆσαι, κεφαλικῇ τιμωρίᾳ ὑποβαλλέσθω.

50    17. Ταῦτα μὲν καὶ ἐν καιρῷ γυμνασίας ὁμοῦ συνηγμένων τῶν στρατιωτῶν ὑπαναγινωσκέσθω τὰ ἐπιτίμια καὶ ἐν ἑτέρῳ οἱῳδήποτε καιρῷ πρὸς εἴδησιν τῶν στρατιωτῶν καὶ τῶν ἀρχόντων αὐτῶν.

18. Δεῖ δὲ συνταγῆναι αὐτοῖς καὶ τὰ λοιπὰ ἐπιτίμια, ὅσα δέον ἐν τῷ καιρῷ τοῦ πολέμου ἀναγκαίως φυλάττεσθαι. |

55    19. Μετὰ οὖν τὸ ταγῆναι τὰ τάγματα ἀναγινώσκεται καὶ ταῦτα οὕτως.    310

20. Ἐὰν στρατιώτης ἐν καιρῷ παρατάξεως καὶ πολέμου τὴν τάξιν ἢ τὸ βάνδον αὐτοῦ ἐάσῃ καὶ ἢ φύγῃ ἢ τοῦ τόπου ἐν ᾧ ἐτάγη προπηδήσῃ ἢ σκυλεύσῃ νεκρὸν ἢ εἰς ἐπιδίωξιν ἐχθρῶν καταδράμῃ ἢ τούλδῳ ἢ φοσσάτῳ ἐχθρῶν ἐπέλθῃ, κελεύομεν καὶ τιμωρεῖσθαι αὐτὸν κεφαλικῶς καὶ πάντα τά, ὡς εἰκός, παρ᾽ αὐτοῦ
60    ἐπαιρόμενα ἀφαιρεῖσθαι καὶ τῷ κοινῷ δίδοσθαι τοῦ τάγματος, ὡς τὴν τάξιν παραλύσαντα καὶ τοῖς ἑταίροις αὐτοῦ ἐπιβουλεύσαντα.

21. Ἐὰν ἐν καιρῷ δημοσίας παρατάξεως ἢ συμβολῆς τροπή, ὅπερ ἀπείη, γένηται ἄνευ τινὸς εὐλόγου καὶ φανερᾶς αἰτίας, κελεύομεν τοὺς στρατιώτας τοῦ πρῶτον φεύγοντος τάγματος καὶ ἀναχωροῦντος τῆς παρατάξεως ἤτοι τοῦ
65    ἰδίου μέρους τοὺς εἰς τὴν μάχην ταγέντας ἀποδεκατοῦσθαι καὶ ὑπὸ τῶν λοιπῶν ταγμάτων κατατοξεύεσθαι, ὡς τὴν τάξιν παραλύσαντας καὶ αἰτίους τῆς τοῦ παντὸς μέρους τροπῆς γενομένους.

22. Εἰ δὲ συμβῇ τινας ἐν αὐτοῖς, ὡς εἰκός, πληγάτους ἐν αὐτῇ τῇ συμβολῇ γενέσθαι, ἐκείνους ἐλευθέρους τοῦ τοιούτου ἐγκλήματος εἶναι.

70    23. Ἐὰν βάνδου ἀφαίρεσις ὑπὸ ἐχθρῶν γένηται, ὅπερ ἀπείη, ἄνευ τινὸς εὐλόγου καὶ φανερᾶς προφάσεως, κελεύομεν τοὺς τὴν φυλακὴν τοῦ βάνδου πιστευθέντας σωφρονίζεσθαι καὶ παντελῶς ἐσχάτους γίνεσθαι τῶν ἀρχομένων ὑπ᾽ αὐτῶν καὶ ἀτίμους. εἰ δὲ συμβῇ τινας αὐτῶν μαχομένους γενέσθαι πληγάτους, τοὺς τοιούτους ἐλευθέρους τοῦ ἐπιτιμίου τούτου φυλάττεσθαι.

---

63 ad αἰτί- des. W (4 foll. desiderantur)

---

47 προδώσει MWA παραδώσει VBE    48 τοῦτο MWVBE om. A    50 καὶ MWA om. VBE |
ὁμοῦ MWA ὁμοίως VBE    51 ὑπαναγινωσκέσθω MWVBE ὑπαναγιγνωσκέσθω A    57 ἐάσῃ
MW καταλίπῃ AVBE    58 τούλδῳ MAVBE τόλδῳ W | ἐπέλθῃ MWAVE ἀπέλθῃ B
61 ἑταίροις Va ἑτέροις codd.    62–63 ὅπερ…γένηται MW γένηται ὃ μὴ γένοιτο AVBE
64 τοῦ πρῶτον MA πρώτου VBE    65 τοὺς…ταγέντας M ἐν ᾧ ἐτάγησαν AVBE    68 ἐν
αὐτοῖς M om. AVBE    68–69 πληγάτους…γενέσθαι M τῇ συμβολῇ πληγῆναι AVBE
70 ἀπείη Va ἀπῇ M μὴ γένοιτο AVBE    72 παντελῶς M om. AVBE | ἐσχάτους MA
ἑκάστους VBE    73–74 γενέσθαι πληγάτους M πληγῆναι AVBE    74 τούτου MVBE om. A

16. If anyone who is entrusted with the defense of a city or a fortress should surrender it or evacuate it while still able to defend it, unless compelled by danger to life, he shall undergo capital punishment.

17. During the period of training, then, with the soldiers assembled together, let these punishments be read aloud and also at any other time so the soldiers and their officers may come to know them.

18. The other punishments as well must be prescribed for them, all those that they are obligated to observe in time of war.

19. After the tagmata have been drawn up, the following should be read to them.

20. If, during the time when the battle line is being formed and in time of combat, a soldier shall abandon his post or his standard and either flee or charge out in front of his assigned place or plunder the dead or race off in pursuit of the enemy or attack the baggage train or camp of the enemy, we order that he be executed and that all the loot he is likely to have taken be confiscated and given to the common fund of his tagma, for he has broken ranks and betrayed his comrades.

21. If, during a general action or pitched battle, <some troops>, who had been lined up for battle, should turn back—may this not happen—without a good and manifest cause, we order that the soldiers of the tagma which first took to flight and withdrew from the line of battle or from their own meros be shot down and decimated by the other tagmata, inasmuch as they broke ranks and are to blame for the rout of the entire meros.

22. But if it should happen that some of them were wounded in the battle, they shall be exempt from such a sentence.

23. If a standard should be captured by the enemy—may this not happen—without a good and manifest excuse, we order that those charged with guarding the banner be punished, disgraced, and reduced to the lowest rank among the enlisted men. Any soldier who may happen to have been wounded in the fighting shall be exempt from such punishment.

75    24. Ἐὰν φοσσάτου ὄντος τροπή, ὅπερ ἀπείη, μέρους ἢ παρατάξεως γένηται καὶ μηδὲ πρὸς διφένσωρας προσδράμωσι, μηδὲ ἐν αὐτῷ τῷ φοσσάτῳ καταφύγωσι <οἱ> τρεπόμενοι, ἀλλὰ περιφρονοῦντες ἐν ἑτέρῳ τόπῳ προσδράμωσι, κελεύομεν τοὺς τοῦτο πράττειν τολμῶντας τιμωρεῖσθαι, ὡς τῶν ἑταίρων περιφρονήσαντας.

80    25. Ἐὰν στρατιώτης τὰ ὅπλα αὐτοῦ ῥίψῃ ἐν πολέμῳ, κελεύομεν αὐτὸν τιμωρεῖσθαι ὡς γυμνώσαντα ἑαυτὸν καὶ τοὺς ἐχθροὺς ὁπλίσαντα.

26. Ἐάν τις τῶν ἀρχόντων παρεμποδίσῃ στρατιώτην ἢ ἐξκουσεύσῃ ἢ μὴ συνελθεῖν ἐν τῷ καιρῷ τοῦ φοσσάτου, ἢ συνελθόντα εἰς οἰκείαν κατάσχῃ δουλείαν, ὥστε τὴν τάξιν αὐτοῦ καταφρονῆσαι καὶ ἀμελῆσαι τῶν ὅπλων, παρεκτὸς | 310ᵛ
85    τῶν τεταγμένων ἀπὸ τοῦ ἡμετέρου σκρινίου, σωφρονιζέσθω καὶ ζημιούσθω, στρατηγὸς μὲν χρυσίου λίτραν α', τουρμάρχης δὲ νομίσματα λϛ', δρουγγάριος δὲ νομίσματα κδ', κόμης δὲ καὶ εἴ τις ἕτερος νομίσματα ιβ'.

27. Τοσαῦτα καὶ περὶ τῶν στρατιωτικῶν ἐπιτιμίων διορισάμενοι, ἑξῆς σοι ὅπως καὶ ὁδοιπορεῖν δέον τόν τε καθόλου στρατὸν καὶ μέρος ἕν τε τῇ ἡμετέρᾳ
90    χώρᾳ καὶ ἐν τῇ τῶν πολεμίων καὶ μετὰ ποίας καταστάσεως ἤδη διαταξόμεθα.

---

75 τροπή MAVE τρόπον B | ἀπείη Va ἀπίη M μὴ γένοιτο AVBE    77 οἱ ci. De om. codd.
82 παρεμποδίσῃ AVBE παροπλίσῃ M | ἐξκουσεύσῃ Va ἐξκουσεύει M ἐκσκουσεύσῃ A ἐκσκουσσεύσῃ VBE    83 συνελθεῖν AVBE εἰσελθεῖν M    84 τὴν τάξιν M τῆς τάξεως AVBE
85 τεταγμένων…σκρινίου M ἀποτεταγμένων καὶ ἀφορισμένων αὐτοῖς AVBE    86 α' M
μίαν AVBE    87 δὲ¹ MA om. VBE    88 ἐπιτιμίων MAVE ἐπιτιμία B | διορισάμενοι MA
δωρισάμενοι VBE | σοι MA σοι καὶ VBE    89 post ὅπως iterantur omnia inde a τοσαῦτα
usque ad finem B

24. If, when the army is encamped, a meros or a whole battle line should be routed—may this not happen—and if the men should not pull back toward the defenders or in their rout should not seek refuge within the camp itself but carelessly run off in some other direction, we order that those who dare to do this be punished for thinking so little of their comrades.

25. If a soldier throws away his weapons in battle, we order that he be punished for disarming himself and arming the enemy.

26. If, when the army is being mustered, one of the officers should put obstacles in the way of a soldier or excuse him from joining in or, having let him join in, retains him for his own service, with the result that he regards his rank with contempt and neglects his weapons, he should be punished. In addition to what has been decreed by our secretariat, he should be fined as follows: for a general one pound of gold, for a tourmarch thirty-six nomismata, for a droungarios twenty-four nomismata, for a count and anyone else twelve nomismata.

27. So much then about military punishments. Next we will provide you with regulations about what is required for the entire army or one meros to march both through our own country and through that of the enemy and in what conditions; this we will now present in an orderly way.

## ΠΟΛΕΜΙΚΩΝ ΠΑΡΑΣΚΕΥΩΝ ΔΙΑΤΑΞΙΣ Θ΄

### Περὶ ὁδοιπορίας

1. Δέον σε τοίνυν, ὦ στρατηγέ, ὅτ᾽ ἂν ὁδοιπορῇς μετὰ τοῦ στρατοῦ, εἰ μὲν ἐν τῇ ἰδίᾳ ἡμῶν γῇ τὴν πορείαν ποιεῖς, ἵνα παραγγέλλῃς τοῖς στρατιώταις ἀπέχ-
5 εσθαι τῆς χώρας καὶ μήτε πραιδεύειν μήτε φθείρειν. πλῆθος γὰρ στρατεύματος, ὅτ᾽ ἂν λάβῃ τοῦ δύνασθαι τὴν ἐξουσίαν, ἀφειδῶς ἐπιπίπτει πρὸς ἅπαντα. δελεά-ζεται γὰρ εἰς πλεονεξίαν, ὅτ᾽ ἂν ὁρᾷ κατ᾽ ὄψιν προκειμένην τὴν χρείαν, καὶ πολλάκις τοὺς ἰδίους διὰ τὴν τοιαύτην αἰτίαν πολεμίους ποιεῖ.

2. Μηδὲ χρόνιζε καθεζόμενος μετὰ τοῦ στρατεύματος ἐν τῇ ἰδίᾳ χώρᾳ, ὅτ᾽
10 ἂν ἤδη ὁρίσῃς εἰσβαλεῖν ἐν τῇ χώρᾳ τῶν πολεμίων. καὶ γὰρ καὶ τοὺς ἰδίους ἀναλώσεις καρπούς, καὶ ζημιώσεις μᾶλλον τοὺς φίλους ἢ τοὺς πολεμίους. ταχέως δὲ μετάφερε τὰς δυνάμεις, μάλιστα ἐὰν εἰς λιπαρὰν καὶ πολύτροφον τῶν πολεμίων γῆν μέλλεις εἰσβαλεῖν.

3. Εἰς ἕνα δὲ τόπον στρατὸν πολὺν μὴ σύναγε, πολεμίων μὴ ἐνοχλούντων,
15 ἵνα μὴ εὐκαιροῦντες οἱ στρατιῶται εἰς στάσεις καὶ ἀκαίρους ἐννοίας ἀσχολοῦν-ται.

4. Εἰ δέ ποτε χρεία καλέσει τοῦτο γενέσθαι χάριν ἀδνουμίου ἢ ἄλλης ἀναγ-καίας αἰτίας ἢ ταχέως τὸν στρατὸν διαμέριζε ἢ γύμναζε καὶ εἰς ἔργα τῶν ὅπλων ἀσχολεῖσθαι παρασκεύαζε, ὡς ἐν τῷ περὶ γυμνασίας ἡμῖν εἴρηται κεφαλαίῳ. ἡ
20 γὰρ ἀργία καινοτέρας μελέτας ἴσως καὶ ἐπιβλαβεῖς ἀπογεννᾷ.

5. Ἐὰν δὲ πόλεμον προσδοκᾷς, μετὰ τάξεως τὸν στρατὸν περιπατεῖν ποίη-σον, κἄν τε κατὰ δρούγγους τὰς ὁδοιπορίας ποιοῦνται, κἄν τε κατὰ τούρμας κἄν τε κατὰ ὅλας παρατάξεις. τὸ γὰρ ἐν τάξει ταύτας γίνεσθαι οὐ μόνον ἐπὶ τῆς

---

M W (mut.) A V (mut.) B E    Va    PG 107:768

3–8 Onas. 6.10.   9–13 Onas. 6.13.   14–96 *Strat.*, 1.9.

1 πολεμικῶν παρασκευῶν ΜΑ om. VBE 2 ὁδοιπορίας ΜΑΒ ὁδοιπορῇς VE 4 παραγγέλλῃς Μ παραγγείλῃς AVBE 4–5 ἀπέχεσθαι VBE ἀπέρχεσθαι ΜΑ 6 ἐπιπίπτει ΜΑVE ἐπίπτει Β 9 καθεζόμενος AVBE καθεξόμενος Μ 10 καὶ² ΜΑ om. VBE 12 πολύτροφον AVBE πολύτροπον Μ 13 εἰσβαλεῖν Μ εἰσβάλλειν AVBE 14 μὴ¹ AVBE om. Μ 15–16 ἀσχολοῦνται Μ ἀσχολῶνται AVBE 20 καινοτέρας De κενοτέρας Μ νεωτέρας AVBE | ἀπογεννᾷ Μ γεννᾷ AVBE 22 ποιοῦνται Μ ποιῶνται AVBE

# PREPARATION FOR WAR, CONSTITUTION IX

## About Marches

1. When you are on the march with your army, O general, and proceeding along in our own land, you must order your troops to keep their hands off the countryside and not to pillage or ravage it. When a large army gets the opportunity to exercise power, it falls upon everything without mercy. Greed takes over whenever it sees something serviceable lying before its eyes. The result is that it frequently turns its own people into enemies.[1]

2. After you have already decided to advance into the enemy's territory, do not settle down for a long time with your army in your own country.[2] You will consume your own crops and do more damage to your friends than to your enemies. Transfer your forces quickly, especially if the hostile territory you intend to invade is fruitful and wealthy.

3. Do not assemble a large army in one place when there is no hostile activity lest, with time on their hands, the soldiers should give themselves to sedition and inappropriate thoughts.[3]

4. If you are compelled to bring all your troops together for the purpose of muster or because of some other pressing reason, then you must quickly divide up the army or drill them or prepare them to devote themselves to working with their weapons, as we have written in the chapter on drills. For idleness easily begets seditious and harmful ways of thinking.

5. If you are expecting combat, have your army march in formation, whether you are proceeding by droungoi or by tourmai or by entire battle lines.

1. Onasander 6.10.
2. Onasander 6.13.
3. Sections 3–21 derive from *Strat.* 1.9.

156    Constitution 9

πολεμίας ἀλλὰ καὶ ἐπὶ τῆς ἰδίας ἀσφαλεστέρους καὶ προγεγυμνασμένους | ποιεῖ  311
25 τοὺς στρατιώτας.

6. Ἕκαστον δὲ δροῦγγον ἐθίζεσθαι ποίησον ὥστε τὴν ἰδίαν ἀποσκευὴν ὄπισθεν ἀκολουθεῖν μετὰ τῶν ἰδίων σημείων καὶ μὴ ἐπιμίγνυσθαι ἑτέρᾳ. ἀναγκαῖον γάρ ἐστιν, ὅτ᾽ ἂν οἱ πολέμιοι οὔτε πάρεισιν οὔτε ἐλπίζονται ἐν τῇ ἡμετέρᾳ γῇ, ἢ κατὰ δρούγγους ἢ κατὰ τούρμας περιπατεῖν καὶ μὴ συνάγειν ἐν ἑνὶ τόπῳ
30 τὸν ἅπαντα στρατὸν διά τε τὸ μὴ λοιμώττειν αὐτὸν εὐχερῶς μηδὲ εὐσύνοπτον τὸ πλῆθος ὅλον τοῖς κατασκόποις τῶν ἐχθρῶν, ὡς εἰκός, γίνεσθαι μηδὲ εἰς βοσκὰς στενοῦσθαι.

7. Ἐγγιζόντων δὲ τῶν ἐχθρῶν ὡς πρὸ ἓξ ἢ ἑπτὰ ἡμερῶν ἢ καὶ δέκα, συνάπτεσθαι καὶ ἐν τῷ ἅμα ἀπληκεύειν. καὶ ἐάν, ὡς εἰκός, ἐν ἀγνώστοις τόποις ἡ ὁδοι-
35 πορία γίνεται καὶ οὐ πάρεισί τινες ἐντόπιοι δουκάτωρες, ἀποστείλῃς τοὺς μινσοράτωρας, ἵνα προλαμβάνωσιν, ἐὰν ἐχθροῦ φόβος οὔκ ἐστι, πρὸ μιᾶς ἡμέρας, οἵτινες ὀφείλουσι τὴν περίμετρον τοῦ παντὸς διαγράφειν στρατοπέδου ἐν ᾧ μέλλεις στρατοπεδεύεσθαι, καὶ τὸ ἐπιβάλλον μέτρον ἀναλόγως ἑκάστῳ μέρει διαμερίσαι.

40 8. Τὰ αὐτὰ δὲ ποιεῖν καὶ τοὺς ἀντικένσωρας. οὗτοι δέ εἰσιν οἱ ὀφείλοντες τῶν ὑδάτων καὶ τῆς νομῆς τὴν χρῆσιν καταμανθάνειν.

9. Ἐὰν δὲ διὰ τραχέων πάνυ τόπων ἡ ὁδοιπορία μέλλῃ γίνεσθαι ἢ κρημνωδῶν ἢ δυσβάτων ἢ δασέων, προευτρέπιζε πλῆθος στρατοῦ καὶ ἀπόστειλον ἐπὶ τοῦτο ὥστε διορθώσασθαι καὶ παρασκευάσαι εὐθείαν γενέσθαι τὴν ὁδὸν κατὰ
45 τὸ δυνατόν, ἵνα μὴ συντρίβηται ἡ ἵππος. τοὺς δὲ ἀφοριζομένους ἐπὶ τούτῳ μὴ ὑποκεῖσθαι βίγλᾳ ἢ ἑτέρᾳ δουλείᾳ.

10. Περιπατοῦντος δὲ τοῦ στρατοῦ ἡγείσθω ἡ σὴ ἐνδοξότης, ὡς τοῦ παντὸς στρατοῦ στρατηγός, προπορευόμενος αὐτοῦ τιμῆς ἕνεκεν καὶ διὰ τὸν φόβον τῶν ἐπιτιμίων, μετὰ τῆς σῆς ἁπάσης προελεύσεως καὶ τῶν μετά σου βάνδων καὶ
50 ὄπισθεν πάντων ἡ περί σε ἀποσκευή.

11. Πρὸς τὸ σχῆμα δὲ τοῦτο καὶ ἕκαστος τουρμάρχης ἢ δρουγγάριος περιπατείτω τὴν αὐτὴν τάξιν φυλάττων, εἴτε ἡνωμένως περιπατοῦσιν εἴτε ἰδίως.

---

26 ἕκαστον...δροῦγγον AVBE ἑκάστῳ δὲ δρούγγῳ M   30 λοιμώττειν αὐτὸν M λοιμικαῖς νόσοις περιπίπτειν AVBE   31 τοῖς κατασκόποις MA τοὺς κατασκόπους VBE | τῶν...εἰκός M trsp. AVBE   33 καὶ MA om. VBE   33–34 συνάπτεσθαι M om. AVBE   35 γίνεται M γίνηται AVE γένηται B | πάρεισί τινες MA παρῶσι τινὲς VBE   36 οὔκ ἐστι MA μὴ ἢ VBE   37 στρατοπέδου Va στρατοῦ codd.   38 ἐπιβάλλον M ἐπιλαγχάνον AVBE   41 νομῆς M βοσκῆς AVBE   43–44 ἐπὶ τοῦτο M om. AVBE   45 συντρίβηται...ἵππος M συντρίβωνται οἱ ἵπποι AVBE   48 τιμῆς MA τιμὴν VBE

Marching in formation, not only in hostile territory but also in your own land, makes it safer for the soldiers and keeps them in practice.

6. Make each droungos accustom its own baggage train to follow behind with its own standards and not to get mixed up with another one. It is essential that, whenever the enemy are not present or are not expected in our country, you should march by droungoi or by tourmai and not bring the whole army together in one place, lest they fall an easy prey to pestilence or, as is likely, the total size of the army may be easily estimated by enemy spies, or fodder may be hard to find.[4]

7. As the enemy approach more closely, six or seven days away, even ten, draw the troops closer together and, at the same time, set up camp. If the march happens to be in unknown places and no local guides are present, then send out surveyors to go ahead a day in advance, if there is no fear of the enemy. Their duty is to survey the perimeter of the entire camping site in which you intend to set up camp and to apportion sections equitably for each meros.

8. The quartering parties should do the same thing; they are charged with reconnoitering the availability of water and forage.

9. If the route of the march is about to pass through very rough, steep, uneven, or heavily wooded terrain, select a large number of men ahead of time and send them off to level the road, as best they can, and to take steps to make it passable, and so prevent the horses from being worn out. The men detailed for this should not be part of a scouting troop or other service unit.

10. When the army is on the march, Your Excellency should be at its head, since you are the general of the entire army. You should march ahead of it as a sign of honor and to instill fear of the penalties. You should be accompanied by your entire retinue and the banda with you. Behind all of them is your baggage train.

11. In similar fashion let each tourmarch or droungarios march along, while preserving his own formation, whether marching together with other units or by himself.

4. Cf. Kekaumenos, 11.18–20 Litavrin = 2.24–25 Spadaro.

12. Ἐν δὲ ταῖς τῶν ποταμῶν διαβάσεσιν ἢ ἄλλων ἀγνώστων χωρίων τοὺς ἀντικένσωρας προλαμβάνειν, ὥστε δοκιμάζειν πρότερον τοὺς τόπους καὶ οὕτως
55 ἀπαγγέλλειν σοι τὰ τοῦ τόπου, ἵνα διὰ τῶν ἐπιτηδείων ἀρχόντων ἀποστέλλῃς καὶ προφυλάττῃς τὴν διάβασιν.

13. Εἰ δὲ πάνυ ἐπισφαλεῖς εἰσιν οἱ τόποι καὶ δύσκολοι, χρή σε αὐτόν, τὸν τοῦ παντὸς στρατηγόν, | ἀπέρχεσθαι καὶ γίνεσθαι κατὰ τὸν τόπον καὶ παραστῆναι   311ᵛ δὲ ἄχρις ἂν πάντες ἀπαθῶς διέλθωσιν.

60 14. Τοῦτο γὰρ καὶ τὸν ἡμέτερον ἀείμνηστον πατέρα καὶ βασιλέα Βασίλειον πεποιηκέναι γινώσκομεν, ὅτε κατὰ Γερμανικείας τῆς ἐν Συρίᾳ τὴν ἐκστρατείαν ἐποιήσατο, προκαταλαβόντα μὲν τὸν Παράδεισον λεγόμενον ποταμόν, παραστάντα δὲ μετὰ λαμπάδων κατὰ τὸ μέσον, καὶ τῇ αὐτοῦ παρουσίᾳ καὶ ἀσφαλείᾳ πάντα τὸν ὑπ᾽ αὐτὸν στρατὸν ἀπαθῶς καὶ εὐκόλως διαβιβάσαντα, ὡς καὶ χεῖρα
65 δοῦναι πολλάκις καὶ δι᾽ ἑαυτοῦ τινας τῶν στρατιωτῶν κινδυνεύοντας ἀνασώσασθαι.

15. Τοῦτο δὲ ποιεῖν σοι κελεύομεν, ὦ στρατηγέ, ἐὰν μὴ ἐγγίζωσιν οἱ πολέμιοι τοῖς τόποις ἐκείνοις. ἐὰν δὲ ἐγγίζωσιν, τότε σε μὲν ἐν τῇ ἰδίᾳ τάξει μένειν, ἕκαστον δὲ ἄρχοντα τοῦ ἰδίου μέρους τὴν χρείαν ἀναπληρῶσαι ἕως ἂν πάντες οἱ
70 ὑπ᾽ αὐτὸν στρατιῶται ἀβλαβῶς διέλθωσιν, ἵνα μὴ σπουδάζοντες πάντες ἄλλος τὸν ἄλλον προλαβεῖν ἀτακτοῦσι καὶ συντρίβωνται. ἴσως τότε καὶ βλάβαι τινὲς γίνονται.

16. Ὅτ᾽ ἂν δὲ ἐν τῇ χώρᾳ τῶν ὑπηκόων ἡμῶν τὴν διάβασιν τοῦ στρατοῦ ποιῇς, φείδεσθαι καὶ ἀποφεύγειν τοὺς γεωργηθέντας τόπους τοῖς στρατιώταις
75 παράγγελλε, εἴτε χωράφιά εἰσιν εἴτε ἀμπελῶνες ἢ κῆποι, καὶ μὴ διαβαίνωσι μέσον αὐτῶν, ἵνα φυλάττῃς τοὺς ὑποτελεῖς ἡμῶν καὶ γεωργοὺς ἀζημίους κατὰ τὸν παρ᾽ ἡμῶν σοι παρεκτεθέντα νόμον.

17. Καί, εἰ μὲν δυνατόν, διὰ τῶν ἀγεωργήτων τόπων μακράν σε διέρχεσθαι. εἰ δὲ ἀνάγκη σε κατεπείγει διὰ τῶν τοιούτων γεωργηθέντων τόπων διελθεῖν,

---

67 ad -τηγέ de novo inc. W

---

57 χρή Va καὶ codd. | τὸν AVBE om. M   58 καὶ γίνεσθαι M om. AVBE   58–59 παραστῆναι...ἄχρις M παρίστασθαι ἐκεῖ μέχρις AVBE   59 διέλθωσιν MA διέλθωσι VBE
61 τὴν MA om. VBE   67 ποιεῖν σοι M trsp. AVBE | ἐγγίζωσιν AVBE ἐγγίζωσι MW
69 τοῦ...μέρους MW τὸ ἴδιον μέρος AVBE | τὴν...ἀναπληρῶσαι MW διαβιβάσαι AVBE |
ἂν MW om. AVBE   70 αὐτὸν MWA αὐτοὺς VBE   71 ἀτακτοῦσι MW ἀτακτῶσι AVBE |
ἴσως MW ἴσως δὲ AVBE   74 ποιῇς MW ποιῆς παράγγελλε τοῖς στρατιώταις AVBE
74–75 τοῖς...παράγγελλε MW om. AVBE   76 ἡμῶν καὶ MW ἡμῖν AVBE   76–77 κατὰ...
νόμον MW om. AVBE   78 διέρχεσθαι MWA συνέρχεσθαι VBE

12. At river crossings or in other unknown regions send quartering parties ahead so they can first investigate the places and thus inform you what the country is like, so you may send out competent officers and safeguard the passage.

13. If the places are unusually precarious and difficult, then you, as supreme commander, should step aside and remain in position at that place until everyone has safely passed through.

14. We recall that our ever-memorable father and emperor Basil did this when he was on campaign against Germanikeia in Syria. He arrived at the river called Paradeisos and stationed himself in the middle of it with lamps, and in his presence and in safety the entire army under his command made the crossing easily and securely.⁵ He frequently gave a hand and, by himself, saved several soldiers from great danger.

15. We order that you do this, O general, if enemy forces are not in the vicinity of those places. If they are getting close, then you should remain in your own formation. But the commanding officer should perform that duty for his own meros until all of the soldiers under his command have crossed over without harm. Otherwise, everyone will rush to get ahead of everyone else, resulting in confusion, with some being trampled, and the likelihood that a number of troops will be injured.

16. Whenever you have your army pass through territory belonging to our subjects, order the soldiers to spare and steer clear of land under cultivation, whether it be a small farm, vineyard, or gardens. They should not pass through them, and so you will preserve the farmers subject to us unharmed, according to the law we laid down to you.

17. If possible, you should make your longer marches through land not under cultivation. But if it is absolutely necessary for you to march through land

---

5. Skylitzes, *Basil.Mak.*, 23 (pp. 141–143); *Kappadokien,* F. Hild and M. Restle, *Tabula imperii Byzantini* 2 (Vienna, 1981), 82–83. For the campaign of 878 see Haldon, *Commentary*.

80 παραγγείλης τοὺς ἑκάστου τάγματος ἄρχοντας, μέχρις ἂν οἱ ὑπ' αὐτοὺς τεταγμένοι στρατιῶται παρέλθωσιν, ἵστασθαι καὶ φυλάττειν καὶ τῷ ἀπ' αὐτοῦ ἐρχομένῳ παραδιδόναι τοὺς τοιούτους τόπους ἀβλαβεῖς καὶ οὕτως ἀναχωρεῖν.

18. Τὸν ὅμοιον δὲ τρόπον ποιεῖν καὶ τὸν ἀπ' ἐκείνου, καὶ ἕκαστος ἄρχων τὸ
αὐτὸ ποιείτω. οὕτως γὰρ καὶ ἡ σὴ εὐταξία καὶ ἡ τῶν ἀρχόντων καὶ ἡ τοῦ στρα-
85 τοῦ καὶ τὸ ἀβλαβὲς τοῦ γεωργοῦ διαφυλαχθήσεται.

19. Ὅτ' ἂν δὲ ἐγγίζῃ καὶ προσδοκᾶται κάματος πολέμου ἢ δυσχερὴς καὶ
ἐπίκοπος διάβασις, ἐὰν ζῷα ἄγρια ἢ ἥμερα κατὰ τὴν ὁδὸν διαναστῶσιν ἢ ὑπ-
αντήσωσι κατὰ πρόσωπον, κωλύῃς ἵνα μὴ διώκωσιν αὐτά, ὅτι δι' αὐτῶν θόρυ-
βος καὶ κραυγὴ γίνεται καὶ οἱ ἵπποι χωρὶς ἀνάγκης συν|τρίβονται.                    312
90 20. Ὅτ' ἂν δὲ καιρός ἐστιν εἰρήνης καὶ οὐδεμία ἀνάγκη ἐλπίζηται, τότε
χρήσιμά εἰσι τὰ κυνήγια τοῖς στρατιώταις.

21. Ἐὰν δὲ ὀλίγον στρατόν, ὡς εἰκός, ἐπιφέρῃ καὶ μέλλῃς ἐπιτηδεύειν κατὰ
τῶν πολεμίων, μὴ διαβιβάζῃς αὐτοὺς διὰ τόπων οἰκουμένων, μηδὲ ἐν τῇ ἡμετέρᾳ
γῇ μηδὲ ἐν τῇ πολεμίᾳ, ἵνα μὴ φανερωθῇς διὰ τῶν κατασκόπων τοῖς ἐχθροῖς,
95 ἀλλὰ δι' ἑτέρων τόπων ἀφανῶν σπούδαζε προέρχεσθαι. καὶ ταῦτα μέν, ὅτ' ἂν ἐν
τῇ ἰδίᾳ χώρᾳ τὸν στρατὸν διαβιβάζῃς, χρή σε διαπράττεσθαι.

22. Ὅτ' ἂν δὲ ἐν τῇ πολεμίᾳ τὴν ὁδοιπορίαν ἐπάγῃς τοῦ στρατοῦ, χρή σε
ταύτην φθείρειν καὶ καίειν καὶ κατατέμνειν. ζημία γὰρ χρημάτων καὶ καρπῶν
ἔνδεια ἐλάττονας ποιεῖ τοὺς πολεμίους καὶ τὸν πόλεμον ἀσθενέστερον, ὥσπερ ἡ
100 τούτων περιουσία μᾶλλον τρέφει τοῦτον καὶ αὐξάνει.

---

97–111 Onas. 6.11–13.

---

80 ἑκάστου MWA ἐκ τοῦ VBE    81 καὶ² MW καὶ ἕκαστος AVBE | ἀπ' αὐτοῦ MW ἀπ' αὐτὸν
A μετ' αὐτὸν VBE    81–82 ἐρχομένῳ MW ἐρχομένῳ ἄρχοντι AVBE    83–84 τὸν...ποιείτω
MW om. AVBE    86–87 ἐγγίζῃ...διάβασις MW πόλεμος προσδοκᾶται ἢ διάβασις δυσχερὴς
καὶ ἐπίκοπος (ἐπίσκοπος B) AVBE    87 ἢ ἥμερα MW om. AVBE    88 δι' αὐτῶν MWA
δυνατῶν VBE    89 καὶ¹...γίνεται MW γίνεται καὶ κραυγὴ AVBE    90 δὲ MWA om. VBE |
ἐστιν MW ἢ AVBE | ἐλπίζηται MAVBE ἐλπίζεται W    91 εἰσι MW ἐστὶ AVBE    92 ὡς εἰκός
MW om. AVBE | ἐπιφέρῃ MW ἔχῃς AVBE | ἐπιτηδεύειν MW ἐπιτίθεσθαι AVBE    93 διὰ
AVBE κατὰ MW | μηδὲ MW μήτε AVE μήτι B    94 μηδὲ MW μήτε AVBE
95 προέρχεσθαι Va παρέρχεσθαι codd.    97 τὴν...στρατοῦ MW ὁδοιπορῆς AVBE    98 καὶ
καίειν MWAVE om. B | κατατέμνειν MW κατακόπτειν AVBE    98–99 ζημία...ἔνδεια MW ἡ
γὰρ τῶν χρημάτων ζημία καὶ ἡ τῶν καρπῶν ὀλίγωσις AVBE    99 ποιεῖ...ἀσθενέστερον MW
καὶ τοὺς πολεμίους ἐλάττονας ποιεῖ καὶ τὸν πόλεμον ὀλιγώτερον AVBE    100 τρέφει τοῦτον
MWA trsp. VBE

under cultivation, you should order the officers of each tagma to remain in place and supervise until the column of soldiers under their command has passed through. They should then hand over those fields in good condition to the next unit approaching and so leave the area.

18. The officer coming after him is to act in like manner and each subsequent commander is to do the same. In this way your good order and that of the officers and of the army will be assured and the farmers will suffer no harm.

19. When the toil of battle is near or is expected or the passage is difficult and laborious, or if wild or domestic animals are startled or encountered on the road ahead of you, forbid <the men> to chase them. This only causes noise and confusion and wears out the horses to no purpose.

20. In time of peace and when no emergency is expected, hunting is a useful exercise for the soldiers.

21. If the army you are leading happens to be small and you intend to engage the enemy in battle, do not march through inhabited areas, either in our country or in that of the enemy, to avoid being observed by enemy spies, but make an effort to proceed through other less obvious places. You must also take such action when you have the army march in its own country.

22. In contrast, when you lead your army marching through hostile territory, you must ruin and burn and thoroughly ravage it.[6] The loss of money and the shortage of crops decrease the strength of the enemy and render them less able to fight, just as the abundance of such things rather nourishes and strengthens their <fighting ability>.

6. Sections 22–24 derive from Onasander 6.11–13.

23. Ἐὰν δὲ πολὺν χρόνον ἐν τῇ πολεμίᾳ γῇ μέλλῃς καταστρατοπεδεύειν, τοσαῦτα καὶ τοιαῦτα φθεῖρον τῆς χώρας, οἵων καὶ ὅσων αὐτὸς οὐχ ἕξεις χρείαν, τὰ δὲ ἀναγκαῖα φύλαττε τοῖς μετά σου στρατεύμασιν εἰς δαπάνην αὐτῶν.

24. Ὅτ᾽ ἂν δὲ τὰς ἁπάσας δυνάμεις ἔχῃς ὁμοῦ, μήτε ἐπὶ τῆς ἡμετέρας χώρας
105 μήτε ἐπ᾽ ἄλλης ὑπηκόου καθεζόμενος ἐγχρόνιζε. καὶ γὰρ τοὺς ἰδίους ἀναλώσεις καρποὺς καὶ ζημιώσεις πλέον τοὺς φίλους μᾶλλον ἢ τοὺς πολεμίους. μετάγαγε δὲ αὐτὰς ταχύ, ἐὰν ἀκίνδυνά ἐστι τὰ τῆς οἰκείας χώρας, καὶ ἐπάγαγε ἐπὶ τὴν πολεμίαν. καὶ γάρ, ἐάν ἐστιν ἡ πολεμία δαψιλὴς καὶ εὔκαρπος καὶ πλουσία, τροφὴν ἕξεις καὶ εὐπορίαν ἄφθονον, ἐὰν δὲ οὔκ ἐστι τοιαύτη, τὴν μὲν ἰδίαν σου
110 καὶ φίλην χώραν οὐκ ἐρημώσεις, πολλὰ δὲ ὅμως καὶ ἀπὸ τῆς πολεμίας, εἰ καὶ μὴ λιπαρά ἐστιν, εὑρήσεις εἰς χρείαν τοῦ ὑπό σε στρατοῦ καὶ ἀναγκαῖα.

25. Ἐν δὲ τῇ πολεμίᾳ γῇ μὴ ἀφίῃς τοὺς στρατιώτας ἀτάκτως φέρεσθαι πρὸς τὰς ὠφελείας. πολλάκις γὰρ ἐπιβουλευόμενοι παρὰ τῶν ἐχθρῶν μεγάλας βλάβας ὑπομένουσιν.

115 26. Φροντίσεις δὲ ἐν τῇ ἰδίᾳ γῇ ὁδοιπορῶν σὺν τῷ στρατεύματι τῆς τε ἀγορᾶς καὶ ἐμπορείας κατά τε γῆν, εἰ τύχοι, καὶ κατὰ θάλασσαν, ἵνα ἀκινδύνου τῆς παρουσίας αὐτοῖς οὔσης ἀόκνως καὶ ἀφόβως κομίζωσι τὸν εἰς τὰ ἐπιτήδεια φόρτον.

27. Ὅτ᾽ ἂν δὲ διὰ στενῶν τόπων μέλλῃς ποιεῖσθαι | τὴν πάροδον ἢ διὰ 312ᵛ
120 ὀρεινῆς καὶ δυσβάτου χώρας πολεμίας παράγειν τὸν στρατόν, ἀναγκαῖον προεκπέμπειν σε μέρος τι τοῦ στρατεύματος καὶ προκαταλαμβάνεσθαι τὰς ὑπερβάσεις καὶ τὰς τῶν στενῶν παρόδους ἤγουν τὰς λεγομένας κλεισούρας, ἵνα μὴ φθάσαντες οἱ πολέμιοι καὶ σταθέντες ἐπὶ τῶν ἄκρων ἢ τῶν στενῶν

---

115-118 Onas. 6.14.    119-129 Onas. 7.1-2.

101 γῇ MWA om. VBE | μέλλῃς MWVBE βούλῃ A    102 φθεῖρον MW φθεῖρε AVBE | οἵων…ὅσων MW οἷα καὶ ὅσα AVBE | οὐχ…χρείαν MW οὐ χρῄζεις AVBE    104 ἁπάσας MW πάσας AVBE    105 ἐγχρόνιζε AVBE χρόνιζε MW    106 πλέον MWA om. VBE | μᾶλλον MW om. AVBE | πολεμίους MW ἐχθροὺς AVBE    107 ἐστι MWA ἢ VBE | οἰκείας MW ἰδίας AVBE    108 ἐστιν MWA ἢ VBE | δαψιλὴς καὶ MW om. AVBE    109 ἐστι MWA ἢ VBE | σου MW σοι AVBE    111 λιπαρά MW πλουσία AVBE    112 ἀφίῃς MW ἀφήσῃς AVBE    113 ὠφελείας MW ἁρπαγὰς AVBE scr. mg. πρὸς κουρὰς προς συναγωγὴν τῶν χρειων W    114 ὑπομένουσιν MWA ὑπομένουσι VBE    116 κατὰ MWA om. VBE    117 αὐτοῖς οὔσης MW οὔσης τοῖς πραγματευταῖς AVBE | κομίζωσι MWVBE κομίζωσιν A    117-118 τὸν…φόρτον MW τὰς χρείας ἐν τῷ στρατῷ AVBE    120 δυσβάτου MW δυσβάτου τόπου AVBE | χώρας πολεμίας MW trsp. AVBE    121 προεκπέμπειν AVBE παρεκπέμπειν MW    123 φθάσαντες MW προλαβόντες AVBE

23. If you intend to encamp for a long time in the enemy's country, you should destroy that amount and that sort of thing in the country that you will not need for yourself. Preserve whatever is needed to supply your own troops.

24. When you have all your forces together, you must not settle down and spend a long time either in our own country or in another one subject to us. For you will consume your own crops and do more damage to your friends than to your enemies. If matters in your home country are not at risk, then lead out your forces quickly and proceed into the country of the enemy. Indeed, if the enemy's country is rich and abounds in a variety of produce, you will have a bounteous source of provisions ready at hand. Even if this is not the case, you will not be laying waste your own land or a friendly one, and you will still find things essential for the use of your army from the enemy country even if it is not prosperous.

25. In hostile territory do not allow the soldiers to search for plunder in an undisciplined manner. When they turn to this they often suffer great harm from the enemy.

26. On the march with your troops in your own country, consider the markets and trade centers on land routes and perhaps also along the coast, so that the <merchants> may be present there without danger and may transport their cargoes for your provisioning without hesitation and without fear.[7]

27. When you intend to make your march through a narrow pass or to lead your army over mountainous and difficult terrain in hostile territory, you must send ahead a detachment of your army to occupy the mountain passes beforehand as well as those through narrow places, the so-called kleisourai.[8] Otherwise the enemy might get there first, take their stand on the summits or in the

---

7. Onasander 6.14.

8. Sections 27–28 derive from Onasander 7.1–2.

κωλύσωσίν σε τὴν διάβασιν ποιήσασθαι ἢ κίνδυνον διὰ τῆς στενοπορίας ἐπαγα-
125 γεῖν τῷ στρατεύματι.

28. Τὸ δὲ αὐτὸ φρόντιζε καὶ ὅτ’ ἂν αὐτὸς πεφόβησαι πολεμίων εἰσβολὴν εἰς
τὴν ἰδίαν χώραν, ἵνα προκαταλάβῃς τὰ στενὰ τῆς ὁδοῦ καὶ κωλύσῃς τῶν πολεμίων τὴν εἴσοδον διά τινος ἀποστελλομένου στρατοῦ ἢ κακῶς διαθήσεις αὐτοὺς
ἐν τῇ τῶν στενῶν διόδῳ.

130 29. Ἐὰν δὲ διὰ μακρᾶς ὁδοῦ μέλλῃς πορεύεσθαι καὶ πολλῶν ἡμερῶν διανύειν πορείαν καὶ ἐν τῇ ἰδίᾳ χώρᾳ καὶ ἐν τῇ πολεμίᾳ, διὰ μὲν τῆς ἰδίας χώρας ἵνα
ἐθίζῃς τὰ στρατεύματα μένειν ἐν τάξει καὶ συμφυλάττειν τοὺς ἰδίους λόχους
ἤγουν τοὺς ὀρδίνους τῆς τάξεως καὶ ἀκολουθεῖν τοῖς ἄρχουσιν ἵνα καὶ ἐν τῇ
πολεμίᾳ πρὸς τάς, ὡς εἰκός, γινομένας ἐξαίφνης ἐπιβουλὰς μὴ ἐν ἀθρόῳ καιρῷ
135 καὶ ὀξέως ἐπιγινομένῳ θορυβοῦνται καὶ ἐπιτρέχουσι καὶ ἄλλοι πρὸς ἄλλους
φέρωνται καὶ διὰ τοῦτο μηδὲν μὲν βοηθεῖν δύνανται, πολλὰ δὲ κακὰ δι’ ἑαυτοῦ
ἢ καὶ διὰ τῶν πολεμίων πάθωσιν, ἀλλ’ ἵνα διὰ τοῦ ἐθισμοῦ τῆς εὐταξίας καὶ εἰς
πορείαν εἰσὶν ἐπιδέξιοι καὶ εἰς μάχην εὐτρεπισμένοι, ἔχοντες καὶ σημεῖόν τι καὶ
ἀλλήλους ἐν τάξει βλέποντες.

140 30. Τὴν δὲ πορείαν τοῦ στρατεύματος ὀλίγην ποιεῖσθαί σε δεῖ, καὶ διὰ
τοιούτων χωρίων διαβίβαζε τὰς τάξεις, δι’ ὧν οὐ συνθλιβήσονται, οὐκ ἔχουσαι
πλάτος, ὥστε ἐκ πλευρᾶς ἐπὶ μῆκος ἐκταθῆναι. εὐεπιβούλευτοι γὰρ γίνονται
πρὸς τὰς αἰφνιδίους τῶν πολεμίων ἐπιφανείας αἱ τοιαῦται καὶ μᾶλλον οὐκ
ἔχουσαι τὸ δραστήριον.

145 31. Ἐὰν γὰρ αὐτοῖς ἀπὸ ἔμπροσθεν ἀπαντήσωσιν οἱ πολέμιοι πλατύτεροι
τεταγμένοι, εὐκόλως αὐτοὺς τρέπονται, καθάπερ οἱ ἐπὶ τῆς μάχης αὐτῆς εὐκαίρως κυκλοῦντες τοὺς ἐναντίους.

---

130–182 Onas. 6.1–8.

---

124 κωλύσωσίν MW κωλύσωσι AVBE　124–125 διὰ…στρατεύματι MW τῶ στρατεύματι
ἐπαγάγωσι διὰ τὴν τοῦ τόπου στενότητα AVBE　126 πεφόβησαι MW om. AVBE
127 χώραν MW χώραν προσδοκᾷς AVBE　129 διόδω MW παρόδω AVBE
130–131 διανύειν πορείαν MW ὁδὸν περιπατεῖν AVBE　132 μένειν…τάξει MW ἐν τάξει
περιπατεῖν AVBE | συμφυλάττειν MWA φυλάττειν VBE　135 ἐπιγινομένῳ MWAVE
ἐπιγενομένω B | θορυβοῦνται MW θορυβῶνται AVBE | ἐπιτρέχουσι M ἐπιτρέχουσιν W
ἐπιτρέχωσι AVBE　136 δύνανται MWA δύνωνται VBE | ἑαυτοῦ MW ἑαυτῶν AVBE
138 εἰσὶν MWA ὦσιν VBE | εὐτρεπισμένοι MW ἕτοιμοι AVBE　141 χωρίων MW τόπων
AVBE　143–144 μᾶλλον…δραστήριον MW ἀνενέργητοι AVBE scr. mg. ἤγουν δια τὰ
στενωματα οὐχέχουσι το κατα τῶν ἐχθρῶν ἐνεργειν W　146 τρέπονται MW κυκλώσαντες
τρέπουσιν AVBE　146–147 αὐτῆς…ἐναντίους MW τὸ τῶν ἐναντίων κέρας κυκλοῦντες
AVBE

defiles, and prevent you from passing through or seriously endanger your army if it does pass through the defile.

28. Be mindful of the same thing when you fear an attack of the enemy against your own country. Before they arrive, have your troops occupy the narrow places on your route. By dispatching some of your troops for this purpose you will prevent enemy incursions or you will inflict serious injury on them in their passage of the defiles.

29. If you plan on a long journey and a march of many days both in your own country and in that of the enemy, first, in passing through your own country, accustom your troops to remain in formation and to keep to their own groups or columns of the formation and to follow their officers; so that, in hostile territory in case of sudden attacks from ambush, perhaps coming very quickly at a critical moment, your men may not be thrown into confusion, run about, and stumble over one another.[9] In such a situation, they will be of no help to themselves, rather they will suffer many evils, some of them self-inflicted and others by the enemy. But by being accustomed to good order they can handle themselves well on the march and be prepared for battle. They should have some kind of watchword among themselves and keep their eyes on each other in formation.

30. You must reduce the size of the marching formation of your army. Have it pass through the kind of terrain in which the troops will not be pressed tightly together because their formations are not wide enough for them to extend their flanks broadly. Such lines are more readily subject to sudden assaults of the enemy and are really not effective at all.

31. For, if the enemy, drawn up in a more extended front, should encounter the head <of your column> they will easily turn it to flight, just as, in the battle itself, they may readily encircle their opponents.

---

9. Sections 29–40 derive from Onasander 6.1–8.

32. Ἐὰν δὲ κατὰ μέσην τὴν δύναμιν ἐκ πλευρᾶς ἐπιβάλωσι, ταχὺ διϊστῶσιν αὐτῶν τὴν πορείαν καὶ διακόπτουσιν. ἐὰν γὰρ ἐπιστρέψωσι πρὸς φάλαγγα οἱ
150 ὁδοιποροῦντες ὥστε ἀντιπαρατάξασθαι, ἀσθενὴς ἡ μάχη γίνεται καὶ οὐκ ἔχουσα πάχος.

33. Ἐὰν δὲ ἀπὸ ὄπισθεν ἐπιφανῶσι, προφανὴς γίνεται ὄλεθρος ὁμοίως τοῖς ἐν τῷ | ἔμπροσθεν τῆς πορείας τεταγμένοις.                                    313

34. Συμβαίνει δὲ καί, ἐάν τις παραβοήθεια γένηται, δυσχερῆ καὶ ἄπρακτον
155 αὐτὴν γενέσθαι. τῶν γὰρ ἀπὸ ὄπισθεν τοῖς ἔμπροσθεν βουλομένων βοηθεῖν ἢ καὶ πάλιν τῶν ἔμπροσθεν τοῖς εἰς τὸ ὄπισθεν, βραδεῖα ἡ ἔλευσις καὶ οὐ κατὰ καιρὸν δύναται γίνεσθαι.

35. Ἡ δὲ συνεσταλμένη πορεία καὶ τετράγωνος, ἡ παραμήκης μέν, μὴ πάνυ δὲ τοῦτο ἔχουσα τὸ σχῆμα ἀλλὰ σύμμετρον, εἰς πάντα καιρὸν ὠφέλιμός ἐστι καὶ
160 εὐμεταχείριστος καὶ ἀσφαλής.

36. Ἐὰν γὰρ εἰς πάνυ στενοὺς τόπους διαβαίνῃ τὸ στράτευμα ἐπὶ πολὺ λεπτυνομένης καὶ ἐπεκτεινομένης τῆς παρατάξεως, πολλάκις γὰρ εἰς ἀμφιβολίαν ἐμπίπτουσιν, ὅταν οἱ πρῶτοι καταβάντες ἀπὸ ὀρεινῶν τόπων εἰς ἐπίπεδα χωρία· θεασάμενοι γὰρ τοὺς ὀπίσω ἐπι<κατα>βαίνοντας ἔδοξαν εἶναι πολεμίων
165 ἐπέλευσιν, ὥστε σπεῦσαι προσβάλλειν ὡς ἐχθροῖς, τινὰς δὲ καὶ εἰς χεῖρας ἐλθεῖν κατ᾽ ἀλλήλων παρὰ μικρόν.

37. Λάμβανε δὲ καὶ τάττε τὸ τοῦλδον ὅλον, τήν τε δουλείαν καὶ τὰ σαγμάρια καὶ τὴν ἀποσκευὴν ἅπασαν ἐν μέσῃ τῇ δυνάμει. ἐὰν δὲ καὶ ἀπὸ ὄπισθεν ὑφ-

---

148 ἐπιβάλωσι Μ ἐπιβάλωσιν W ἐφορμήσωσιν A ἐφορμήσωσι VBE | διιστῶσιν MW διακόπτουσιν AVBE   149 καὶ διακόπτουσιν MW om. AVBE | ἐπιστρέψωσι MAVBE ἐπιστρέψωσιν W   150 ἀντιπαρατάξασθαι MW ἀντιπαρατάξασθαι τοῖς ἐκ πλαγίου ἐπερχομένοις AVBE   150–151 καὶ…πάχος MW διὰ τὸ λεπτὴν εἶναι τὴν παράταξιν καὶ βάθος μὴ ἔχειν AVBE   152 ἐὰν…γίνεται MWAVE om. Β | ἐπιφανῶσι MVBE ἐπιφανῶσιν WA   154 παραβοήθεια MWA παρὰ βοήθειαν VBE | δυσχερῆ καὶ MW om. AVBE   155 αὐτὴν γενέσθαι MW αὐτὸν εἶναι καὶ ἀνενέργητον AVBE | τοῖς WAVBE τῶν Μ   156 καὶ¹ AVBE om. MW   156–157 οὐ…γίνεσθαι MW οὐκ ἐν τῷ ἁρμόζοντι καιρῷ διὰ τὸ ἐπιπολὺ ἐπεκταθῆναι τὴν παράταξιν ὥσπερ εἴρηται AVBE   159 ὠφέλιμός VBE χρήσιμός A om. MW   160 εὐμεταχείριστος MW εὐμετακίνητος AVBE   161–162 ἐὰν…παρατάξεως AVBE om. MW   162 πολλάκις γὰρ Μ πολλάκις γὰρ καὶ W πολλάκις καὶ AVBE   162–163 ἀμφιβολίαν AVBE ἀμφιβολίας MW   163–164 ἐπίπεδα χωρία MW ὁμαλοὺς τόπους AVBE   164 θεασάμενοι γὰρ MW θεάσωνται AVBE | ὀπίσω MW ὀπίσω αὐτῶν AVBE | ἐπικαταβαίνοντας De ἐπιβαίνοντας MW κατερχομένους AVBE | ἔδοξαν MW ἔδοξαν γὰρ AVBE | πολεμίων WAVBE πολεμίαν Μ   165 σπεῦσαι MW σπουδάσαι AVBE   167 τάττε MW τάσσε A κατὰ σε VBE

32. If they attack the center of your force from the flank, they will quickly pierce the column and cut through it. If the marching column wheels about into a phalanx, so as to line up against the foe, their fighting will be without thick ranks and weak.

33. In like manner, if they appear in the rear, it will obviously result in the destruction of the men lined up at the head of the column.

34. It also happens that, even if some assistance can be given, it would be difficult and ineffective. When the men in the rear want to come to the aid of those up front or, in turn, those up front to those in the rear, their arrival is delayed and cannot come in time.

35. A marching formation that is compact and rectangular, shaped <so that its length is> not much longer than its width, but proportionate, is helpful in every contingency and is safe and easy to manage.

36. If the army should march through very narrow defiles with its column extended and very thin, its fate frequently sinks into uncertainty when the first units descend into level terrain from the mountainous area <above>. For they observe the men still descending behind them and mistake them for a hostile attacking force, so that they get set to charge into them as though they were enemies, and they barely avoid coming to blows with one another.

37. Place and draw up your entire baggage train, the service units, the pack animals, and all the equipment in the middle of your force. If you suspect some

168    Constitution 9

ὁρᾶσαι ἔφοδόν τινων, ποίησον καὶ τοὺς νωτοφύλακας ἰσχυροὺς ὁμοίως τῶν
170 ἔμπροσθεν τεταγμένων ἐν τῷ μετώπῳ τῆς πορείας, ὥστε μηδὲν διαφέρειν τοὺς
ὀπίσω τῶν ἔμπροσθεν πρὸς τὰ εἰκὸς συμβαίνοντα.

38. Ἀποστείλῃς δὲ καί τινας καβαλλαρίους, τοὺς μέλλοντας διερευνῆσαι τὰς
ὁδούς, καὶ μάλιστα, ὅτ᾿ ἂν ὑλώδεις καὶ περικεκλεισμένας βουνοῖς ἢ ὄρεσι
διοδεύῃς ἐρημίας. πολλάκις γὰρ ἐγκρύμματα πολεμίων ὑποκαθέζονται καὶ
175 λαθόντα τάχα τὰ ὅλα πράγματα συντρίβουσι τῶν ἐναντίων.

39. Τὴν μὲν γὰρ πεδιάδα γῆν οἱ πάντων ὀφθαλμοὶ περιβλεπόμενοι εὐκόλως
διερευνῶσι. καὶ γὰρ ἐν ἡμέρᾳ κονιορτὸς ἀναφερόμενος πολλάκις μηνύει τὴν
ἐπέλευσιν τῶν πολεμίων καὶ πυρὰ καιόμενα νυκτὸς ὑπέλαμψε καὶ ὑπέδειξε τοὺς
πολεμίους.

180 40. Καὶ ἐὰν μὲν οὐ μέλλῃς ἐκτάσσειν εἰς μάχην τὰς δυνάμεις, ἄγε αὐτὰς ἐν
ἡμέρᾳ μόνον. ἐὰν δὲ ἐπείγεσαι καὶ σπουδάζῃς φθάνειν συντομώτερον, ἄγε
αὐτὰς καὶ ἐν νυκτί, ἐὰν ἄρα ἀσφαλὲς εἶναι τοῦτο νομίζῃς.

41. Καὶ πρὸ μὲν τοῦ καιροῦ τῆς μάχης μετὰ ἀνέσεως καὶ σχολῆς προέρχου.
ἐπὰν δὲ τοῖς πολεμίοις ἐμφανισθῇ, εὐθὺς ἐπιβαλοῦ, καλῶς προεκτάξας τὴν
185 δύναμιν. πολλάκις γὰρ πρὸ τοῦ συμβάλλειν τὸν πόλεμον ὁ περὶ τοῦτον κόπος
εἰς δειλίαν ἄγει καὶ τοὺς ἀνδρείους καὶ δαπανᾷ τῇ μερίμνῃ τὴν δύναμιν τῶν
σωμάτων. |

42. Τοὺς δὲ στενοὺς καὶ δυσβάτους τόπους ἐπὶ πολὺ διάστημα ἐκτεταμένους 313ᵛ
ἐν χώρᾳ ἐχθρῶν κατεξαίρετον οἱ πεζοὶ διαβαίνειν οὐ δυσχερῶς ἔχουσι. περὶ
190 τούτων δὲ μετ᾿ ὀλίγον ἐροῦμεν.

---

**188–254** *Strat.*, 9.4.

---

**169** τινων MW πολεμίων AVBE | ὁμοίως MAVE ὁμοίους WB   **171** πρὸς…συμβαίνοντα
MW κατὰ δύναμιν AVBE   **172** τινας καβαλλαρίους MW trsp. AVBE   **173** ὑλώδεις καὶ
MW δασείας διοδεύῃς ἐρημίας AVBE | περικεκλεισμένας MWA περικεκλεισμένοις VBE |
ὄρεσι MW ὄρεσιν AVBE   **174** διοδεύῃς ἐρημίας MW om. AVBE | ὑποκαθέζονται Onas.
ἐπικαθέζονται codd.   **175** συντρίβουσι MWVBE συντρίβουσιν A | τῶν ἐναντίων MW om.
AVBE   **176** τὴν…γῆν MW τοὺς μὲν ὁμαλοὺς καὶ δένδρα μὴ ἔχοντας τόπους AVBE |
περιβλεπόμενοι MW περιβλέπουσιν A περιβλέπουσι VBE   **177** διερευνῶσι M διερευνῶσιν
W om. AVBE   **178** καιόμενα MW καιομένη AVBE | ὑπέλαμψε MWA ἐπέλαμψε VBE
**180** μέλλῃς MW βούλῃ AVE βούλει B | ἐκτάσσειν MW παρατάσσειν AVBE   **183** σχολῆς
MW ἀργίας AVBE   **184** ἐπὰν MW ἐπειδὰν AVBE   **185** πρὸ τοῦ MW ἐὰν ἐμβραδύνῃς
AVBE | συμβάλλειν MW συμβαλεῖν AVBE | ὁ…κόπος MW om. AVBE | κόπος Va σκοπὸς
MW om. AVBE   **186** ἄγει…δύναμιν MW ἔρχονται οἱ ἀνδρεῖοι καὶ ὁ ἀγὼν καὶ ἡ μέριμνα τὴν
δύναμιν δαπανᾷ AVBE   **188** ἐκτεταμένους MAVBE ἐκτεταμμένους W   **189** ἔχουσι
MVBE ἔχουσιν WA

sort of attack from the rear, make sure your rear guard is as strong as the forces stationed in the front of your column, since there is no difference between the front and the rear with a view to what may happen.

38. Send out some cavalry units to reconnoiter the roads, especially when you are proceeding through deserted areas that are wooded and closed in by hills or mountains. Ambuscades are often set up by the enemy and, when not detected, swiftly bring utter destruction upon their adversaries.

39. On a level plain everyone can look about and easily reconnoiter. By day a cloud of dust often gives warning of the approach of the enemy. By night the light from burning fires points to their location.

40. If you do not intend to draw up your forces for battle, lead them only by day. But if you are in a hurry and anxious to arrive first <at a certain place>, lead your forces at night as well, provided you think it safe to do so.

41. Before the time of battle march along in a relaxed and leisurely manner. But when you come in sight of the enemy, draw up your force in good order and attack immediately. The hard work involved before the actual fighting gets under way frequently causes even courageous men to lose heart, and anxiety saps their bodily strength.

42. Foot soldiers in particular do not find it difficult to traverse long stretches of narrow and difficult places in hostile territory.[10] We will shortly speak about these matters.

10. Sections 42–51 derive from *Strat.* 9.4.

43. Τοὺς δὲ καβαλλαρίους ἐν τῇ χώρᾳ τῶν πολεμίων ἐν καιρῷ θέρους μάλιστα ἀπερισκέπτως καὶ ὡς ἔτυχε διαβαίνειν οὐκ ἐπιτρέπομεν χωρὶς ἀνάγκης. ἐὰν δέ ἐστιν τόπος ἐπ' ὀλίγον ἄχρι ἑνὸς μιλίου ἐκτεταμένος καὶ δύνανται καὶ πεζοὶ διαβαίνειν ἐκεῖ, δυνατόν ἐστι καὶ καβαλλαρίους πεζεύειν ἐν αὐτοῖς ἀσφαλῶς.

195    44. Στενοὺς δὲ καὶ δυσκόλους ἐκείνους λέγω τόπους τοὺς μίαν καὶ μόνην πάροδον ἔχοντας. εἰ γὰρ καὶ ἄλλαι εἰσὶ πάροδοι καὶ ἐπινοηθῆναι δύνανται, ἀνεμποδίστως ἡ πάροδος δύναται γίνεσθαι. ἐὰν οὖν γένηται καιρὸς στενῶν διαβάσεων καὶ διὰ τῶν αὐτῶν πάλιν τόπων μέλλῃ ὑποστρέφειν ὁ στρατός, εἰ μὲν δασεῖς εἰσι καὶ ἐπ' ὀλίγον διάστημα, ὡς εἴρηται, κρατοῦσι, τούτους κατὰ τὸν

200    καιρὸν τῆς ὁδοῦ ἔκκοπτε καὶ πλάτυνε καὶ καθάριζε κατὰ τὸν ἐνδεχόμενον τρόπον. εἰ δὲ στενοὶ καὶ κρημνώδεις, ὥστε μὴ πλατύνεσθαι δύνανται, ὡς ἀνωτέρω ἡμῖν εἴρηται, προκαταλάμβανε αὐτοὺς διά τινος πεζικῆς δυνάμεως καὶ ἐν τοῖς ὑψηλοτέροις αὐτῶν τόποις τὴν ἀρκοῦσαν καταλίμπανε ἀσφαλῶς βοήθειαν ἢ τυχὸν καὶ διὰ καβαλλαρίων μέχρι τῆς ὑποστροφῆς ἢ καὶ τοῦτο κἀκεῖνο ποιεῖν

205    ἐν τοῖς ἀναγκαιοτέροις τόποις, τοῦτ' ἔστιν ἐκκόπτειν ἤγουν καθαρίζειν καὶ βοήθειαν καταλιμπάνειν κατὰ τὸ ἐνδεχόμενον.

45. Τοὺς δὲ τὴν πάροδον διὰ τῶν στενῶν ποιουμένους ἢ μετὰ τούλδου ἢ μετὰ πραίδας εἰς δύο φάλαγγας ἤτοι παρατάξεις γίνεσθαι καὶ ἐπὶ κέρας ἐν ὀρθίᾳ παραγωγῇ περιπατεῖν πεζῇ. ὀρθία δέ ἐστι παραγωγὴ ἡ κατὰ μέτωπον μὲν στενή,

210    κατὰ δὲ τὸ βάθος εἰς μῆκος ἐκτεινομένη. τοῦτο δὲ ποιεῖν πραίδας μάλιστα ἐν χερσὶν οὔσης, εἴτε πεζοί εἰσιν οἷς μᾶλλον εὐχερὴς ἡ τῶν δασέων καὶ δυσβάτων τόπων διάβασις, εἴτε καβαλλάριοι ἐκ τῶν ἵππων καταβαίνοντες καὶ μέσον τὸν τοῦλδον καὶ τὴν ἀποσκευὴν ἔχοντες.

46. Ἐν δὲ τοῖς τοιούτοις καιροῖς καὶ τόποις μετὰ τὴν διφαλαγγίαν, ἥτις ἔχει

215    δυνατὸν τὸν λαὸν ἔμπροσθεν καὶ ὄπισθεν, ὥσπερ στομώματα μαχαίρας, ἣν δέον σε ἀφορίζειν εἰς φυλακὴν τοῦ τούλδου καὶ τῆς πραίδας τῆς, ὡς εἰκός, ἐνούσης

---

193 ἐστιν MW ἐστι A ἢ VBE | ἐπ' MW ἐπὶ AVBE | ἄχρι...ἐκτεταμένος MW ἐκτεταγμένος (ἐκτεταμένος VBE) ἄχρι ἑνὸς μιλίου AVBE | δύνανται MWA δύνονται VBE 194 πεζεύειν...ἀσφαλῶς MW πεζεύοντας διέρχεσθαι AVBE  195–197 στενοὺς...γίνεσθαι MW om. AVBE  199 εἰσὶ MAVBE εἰσὶν W | κρατοῦσι MVBE κρατοῦσιν WA | τούτους MW om. AVBE  201 πλατύνεσθαι MWAB πλατύνασθαι VE  204 ἢ¹ AVBE εἰ MW | κἀκεῖνο MW ἐκεῖνο A καὶ ἐκεῖνο VBE  205 τόποις MW om. AVBE  207 στενῶν MW στενῶν τόπων AVBE | ἢ¹ MWAVE ἢ καὶ B | τούλδου MAVBE τόλδου W | ἢ² MWAVE ἢ καὶ B 208 ἤτοι MW ἤγουν AVBE  209 ἐστι MWA ἐστιν VBE  211 εὐχερὴς MW εὐχερὴς καὶ εὔκολος AVBE  212 τὸν A τὸ MWVBE  215 τὸν MW om. AVBE | στομώματα MW στόματα AVBE  216 τούλδου MAVBE τόλδου W | τῆς² MWA om. VBE | ἐνούσης MW συνούσης AVBE

43. Apart from an emergency, we do not recommend that cavalry, while in hostile territory, especially in summertime, imprudently and without necessity should do that. But if the pass is not very long, extending only a mile or so, and infantry can make their way through it, then the cavalry can pass through on foot.

44. I define narrow and difficult passes as those places that have only one passable road. When other routes exist or can be improvised, the passage can be made without hindrance. Therefore, if the time comes for the army <to pass through> narrow passages with the intention of returning again through the same places, and if it is heavily wooded and, as mentioned, not very long, then, when we first go through it, chop down the trees and level the ground as best fits the situation. If the way is narrow and precipitous, so that it cannot be leveled, as we have said above, have an infantry force go ahead to seize the place and have an auxiliary detachment of sufficient strength take up position on the commanding points, or perhaps also a force of cavalry, until we return. Or take the same steps in more critical locations, that is, cut down <the trees> or clear the ground and leave behind a suitable guard.

45. The troops making their way through the defiles, either accompanied by the baggage train or by plunder, should form into two phalanxes or battle lines marching on foot in columns by the flank. In column means a marching formation narrow in the front but in depth stretched out to a greater extent. Observe this especially when they have plunder in hand. Infantry can traverse wooded and difficult terrain easily enough. But have cavalry dismount and place the baggage train and the equipment in the center.

46. At such times and in such places, in addition to the double phalanx, which has a strong force in front and to the rear, like the hard edges of a sword, it is necessary for you to detail <men> to guard the baggage train and the

αὐτοῖς, πάντως καὶ ἄλλους ἐκπλήκτους ἤγουν ἐπὶ τούτῳ μόνῳ ὄντας, τοὺς | 314
καλλίω καὶ πλείους, ποιεῖν ἐκ περισσοῦ κατὰ τῶν τεσσάρων μερῶν τῆς διφαλαγγίας, ὡς ὁ τόπος παραδέχεται, παρακολουθοῦντας καὶ ἀποσοβοῦντας
220 τοὺς βουλομένους, ὡς εἰκός, ἐκ τῶν ἐχθρῶν ἐπέρχεσθαι καὶ διαταράσσειν
αὐτήν, ἵνα ἀδιάσπαστος καὶ ἀσύγχυτος ἡ πρὸς παραφυλακὴν τοῦ τούλδου καὶ
τῆς πραίδας τάξις φυλάττεται καὶ μηδὲ περισπῶνται οἱ ἐν αὐτῇ διὰ τοὺς ἐπερχομένους. οὐ γὰρ δυνατὸν τοὺς εἰς τὴν διφαλαγγίαν τασσομένους καὶ τὴν πραίδαν μετὰ τάξεως φυλάττειν, καὶ τοῖς, ὡς εἰκός, ἐπερχομένοις τῶν ἐχθρῶν ἁρμό-
225 ζεσθαι. διὰ τοῦτο ἐκ περισσοῦ δεῖ ἔξωθεν τῆς διφαλαγγίας ἔχειν κατὰ τῶν
τεσσάρων μερῶν καὶ κατεξαίρετον ὄπισθεν τοὺς κρείττονας ἀφορίζεσθαι.
οὕτως γὰρ ἄν τις δυνήσεται ἐν παντὶ καιρῷ τοὺς δυσκόλους καὶ τραχεῖς τόπους
διαβαίνειν εὐκόλως.
47. Τοὺς δὲ ἵππους τῶν ἀποβαινόντων καὶ πεζευόντων στρατιωτῶν, ἐὰν
230 πεζοὶ οὐ σύνεισι στρατιῶται, μὴ πλησίον τῶν πεζευόντων ἔχε, ἀλλὰ ἐν μέσῳ
τόπῳ αὐτοὺς ἀσφαλῶς ἄγε, ὥστε μή, ὡς εἰκός, παραλόγου δειλίας γενομένης,
ταρασσόμενοι οἱ πεζεύοντες, ἐὰν πλησίον αὐτοὺς εὕρωσι, προχείρως ἐπιλαμβανόμενοι τῶν ἵππων καταλιμπάνουσι τὴν τάξιν καὶ ἐντεῦθεν βλάβη μεγίστη
γίνεται.
235 48. Εἰ δὲ συμβῇ αἰχμαλωσίαν αὐτοὺς ἢ πραῖδαν ἐπιφέρεσθαι καὶ μέλλουσιν
οἱ ἐχθροὶ ἐπιτηδεύειν ταῦτα, δέον ἢ κατὰ τοῦ ἑνὸς μέρους ἢ κατὰ τῶν δύο, ἔνθα
ἡ πάροδος γίνεται, τοὺς αἰχμαλώτους δεδεμένους ἐξωτέρω τῆς τάξεως παράγειν καὶ ὑπ' αὐτῶν ὡσανεὶ σκουτεύεσθαι, ἵνα αὐτῶν φειδόμενοι οἱ ἐχθροὶ μὴ

217-218 ἐκπλήκτους...πλείους MW ἔχειν δεῖ ἐλαφροὺς καὶ μηδὲν βάρος ἐπιφερομένους
τοὺς καλλίονας καὶ πλείονας AVBE    217 ἐκπλήκτους Va ἐξαπλήκτους codd.    218 ποιεῖν...
περισσοῦ MW om. AVBE    219 παρακολουθοῦντας MWAB παρακαλοῦντας VE |
ἀποσοβοῦντας MW ἀπαντῶντας AVBE    221 ἀσύγχυτος MW ἀτάραχος AVBE | ἡ AVBE ἢ
W om. M | τούλδου AVBE τόλδου MW    222 φυλάττεται MW φυλάττηται AVBE
223 τὴν¹ MWA om. VBE    224 τοῖς...ἐπερχομένοις MW τοὺς...ἐπερχομένους AVBE
224-225 ἁρμόζεσθαι MW ἀπαντᾶν AVBE    225 τοῦτο MW τοῦτο χρὴ AVBE | δεῖ MW om.
AVBE    230 σύνεισι MW συνυπάρχωσι A συνυπάρχουσι VBE | ἀλλὰ MWA ἀλλ' VBE
231 αὐτοὺς ἀσφαλῶς MWA trsp. VBE    232-233 ταρασσόμενοι...ἵππων MW πλησίον
ἔχοντες τοὺς ἵππους αὐτῶν οἱ πεζεύοντες ἐπιβαίνοντες αὐτῶν AVBE    233 καταλιμπάνουσι
MW καταλιμπάνωσι AVBE    234 γίνεται MWAB γίνηται VE    235-236 μέλλουσιν...
ταῦτα MW συμβῇ τοὺς ἐχθροὺς ἐπιτίθεσθαι κατ' αὐτῶν AVBE    236 ταῦτα δέον Va δέον
ταῦτα MW δέον τοὺς αἰχμαλώτους AVBE    237 πάροδος MW ἔφοδος AVBE | τοὺς
αἰχμαλώτους MW om. AVBE

plunder it is likely to be carrying. Over and above this, be sure to assign other light-armed troops, better and more numerous, specifically for this purpose on the four sides of the double phalanx as the terrain permits. They are to march alongside and ward off any hostile parties who might be attempting to harass the column. This provides protection for the formation assigned to guard the baggage train and the plunder without being split up and disordered or the troops drawn off to fight attackers. For it is not possible for the troops stationed in the double phalanx to guard the plunder in an orderly manner and also deal with likely hostile raiding parties. For this reason, it is necessary to have troops that can be spared outside the double phalanx and to post the stronger ones on the four sides and especially to the rear. In this way one will be able at all times to pass through difficult and rugged places easily.

47. If there are no foot soldiers accompanying them, the horses of the soldiers who have dismounted and who are proceeding on foot should not remain close to them but should be led along safely in the center. This is to avoid the likelihood that the men going on foot might break ranks out of reckless fear and, if they find the horses close by, readily take hold of them and abandon their formation. That would lead to the greatest harm.

48. If it should happen that they are transporting prisoners or plunder, and the enemy are about to go after them, you must, either on one side or on both sides of the line of march, lead the prisoners, still bound, to the outside of the column, using them as a sort of shield. Either the enemy will hold their fire out

ἐπιτηδεύωσιν ἀκοντίζειν· εἰ δὲ καὶ ἀκοντίσωσιν, αὐτοὺς μᾶλλον ἀφανίζουσι καὶ
240 μὴ τὸν στρατιώτην.

49. Εἰ δὲ ἄρα ἐν ἀνάγκῃ, ὡς εἰκός, καὶ περιστάσει ἀδοκήτῳ ὁ στρατὸς γένηται καὶ ἐν στενώμασι καταληφθῇ καὶ οὔκ ἐστιν ἀκινδύνως τὴν ἀναχώρησιν
ἐκεῖθεν ποιήσασθαι, τότε κρεῖττόν ἐστιν ἐκ συμφώνου ἢ μέρος τῆς πραίδας ἢ
πᾶσαν παραχωρεῖν τοῖς ἐχθροῖς καὶ ἀβλαβῶς ἐξέρχεσθαι, ἀλλὰ μὴ δι' αὐτὴν
245 κινδυνεύειν.

50. Εἰ δὲ μὴ οὕτω συμβιβασθῆναι βούλονται, διαχρῆσθαι τούτους ἐπ' ὄψεσι
τῶν ἐχθρῶν καὶ ἢ ἐπιμένειν τῇ χώρᾳ αὐτῶν καὶ λυμαίνεσθαι αὐτὴν ἀφειδῶς ἤ,
ὡς δυνατόν ἐστιν, ἑαυτοὺς μετὰ τάξεως περισῴζειν καὶ τῆς ἐξελεύσεως φροντίζειν.

250 51. Καὶ παντοῖός σοι, ὦ στρατηγέ, σκοπὸς ἔστω ἐν τοῖς τοιούτοις στενώμασι
| καὶ μάλιστα τοῖς ἐπὶ πολὺ διάστημα κρατοῦσι μὴ ἐπιτηδεύειν βιάζεσθαι στρα-     314ᵛ
τοῦ πάροδον, ἐξαιρέτως ἐν καιρῷ θέρους, διὰ τὴν τῆς ὕλης δασύτητα πολεμίων
μάλιστα ἐνοχλούντων, πρὶν ἂν ἢ αὐτοὶ ἀποσοβηθῶσι φαινόμενοι ἢ ὑψηλότεροι
τόποι τῆς παρόδου ὑπὸ τοῦ στρατοῦ προκαταληφθῶσιν.

255 52. Καὶ ταῦτα μὲν ἐπὶ τῆς καβαλλαρικῆς ἐκστρατείας. ἐπὶ δὲ τῆς πεζικῆς
ὁδοιπορίας εἰς μὲν ἐπιπέδους τόπους δέον σε καὶ ὄπισθεν αὐτῶν καὶ ἔμπροσθεν
καβαλλαρίους καθιστᾶν εἰς βίγλαν καὶ ἐξωτέρω τῆς βίγλας μηδένα τῶν πεζῶν
φαίνεσθαι. τὰ δὲ ἄπλικτα ἐκ τοῦ πλησίον γίνεσθαι ἵνα μὴ κοποῦνται οἱ πεζοὶ
περιπατοῦντες πολὺ διάστημα.

260 53. Τὰς δὲ μετὰ τῶν πεζῶν ἁμάξας κατὰ τὰ μέρη τῆς παρατάξεως περιπατεῖν
δέον, εἴτε ἐν ὀρδίνῳ εἴτε ἐν παρατάξει, πρὸς τὸν τόπον πρῶτον τοῦ δεξιοῦ

---

255–371 Strat., 12.B.19–20.

---

239 ἐπιτηδεύωσιν MWVBE om. A | ἀκοντίζειν MW ἀκοντίζωσιν ἢ τοξεύωσιν AVBE |
ἀκοντίσωσιν MW ἀκοντίζουσιν AVBE | ἀφανίζουσι M ἀφανίζουσιν A ἀφανίζωσι WVBE
241 στρατὸς MWA στρατηγὸς VBE     243 ἐκεῖθεν MW om. AVBE     246 οὕτω M οὕτως
WAVBE | διαχρῆσθαι…ὄψεσι MW φονεύειν αὐτοὺς βλεπόντων AVBE     247 λυμαίνεσθαι
MW ἀφανίζειν AVBE     248 ἑαυτοὺς MWA αὐτοὺς VBE | ἐξελεύσεως MWA ἐξελάσεως
VBE     250 καὶ…στρατηγέ MW om. AVBE | σκοπὸς MW σκοπὸς δέ σοι AVBE | τοῖς MWA
om. VBE | τοιούτοις στενώμασι MWA trsp. VBE     251 κρατοῦσι MVBE κρατοῦσιν WA
253 ἀποσοβηθῶσι φαινόμενοι MW οἱ φαινόμενοι πολεμίοι ἀποδιωχθῶσιν AVBE
254 προκαταληφθῶσιν MW προκατακρατηθῶσιν AVBE     256 ἐπιπέδους MW ὁμαλοὺς
AVBE     257 βίγλαν M βίγλας WAVBE     258 κοποῦνται AVBE σκοποῦνται MW     260 τὰ
MWA om. VBE

of consideration for them or, if they do shoot, they will kill the prisoners and not our soldiers.

49. If the army, as can easily happen, finds itself in an unexpected critical situation, trapped in narrow passes, and unable to extricate itself without real danger, then it is better to come to an agreement with the enemy, relinquishing part or all of the plunder. The army can thus withdraw without harm and without endangering itself for the sake of the plunder.

50. But if they do not wish to make such an agreement, put the prisoners to death before the eyes of the enemy. Then, either remain in their country and ravage it without mercy or, as best you can, try to save yourselves in an orderly way and concentrate on escape.

51. Above all, O general, when you find yourself in such defiles, especially ones extending a long distance, you must be careful not to have your army try to force its way through, particularly in summer, when the dense foliage enables the enemy to cause a great deal of trouble, before those who appear can be driven off or your own army shall have seized the commanding heights of the passage.

52. So much then about cavalry expeditions.[11] When it comes to infantry marching along in level terrain, you must send out cavalry patrols to the front and to the rear. No infantry man should appear outside the line of patrols. The camp sites should be fairly close, so that the foot soldiers do not become exhausted from marching long distances.

53. The wagons accompanying the infantry should be driven along in accord with the divisions of the battle line, either in column or in a broad formation. In

11. Sections 52–75 derive from *Strat.* 12.B.19–20.

κέρατος, εἶτα τοῦ ἀριστεροῦ, μετ᾽ ἐκείνας δὲ τοῦ μέσου ἀριστεροῦ καὶ τότε τοῦ μέσου δεξιοῦ· καὶ μὴ πεφυρμέναι καὶ ἀναμεμιγμέναι περιπατοῦσιν.

54. Ἐὰν δὲ οἱ ἐχθροὶ πλησίον εἰσίν, δέον τοὺς ὁπλίτας ἕκαστον τὰ ὅπλα
265 αὐτοῦ βαστάζοντα περιπατεῖν καὶ μὴ εἰς τὰς ἁμάξας ταῦτα καταλιμπάνειν, ἵνα ὦσιν ἕτοιμοι πρὸς τὴν μάχην. ἐν δὲ τοῖς ἀναγκαίοις καιροῖς, καθὼς ἐν τῇ παρατάξει τάττονται τὰ τάγματα, οὕτως αὐτὰ δεῖ περιπατεῖν καὶ μὴ συγκεχυμένως ἢ διασπασμένως ἵνα, ἐὰν γένηται χρεία τοῦ παρατάξασθαι, ἑτοίμως εἰς τοῦτο καταστῶσιν.

270 55. Ἐὰν δὲ πολλοί εἰσιν οἱ τῶν ἐχθρῶν καβαλλάριοι, ἐγγιζόντων αὐτῶν τῷ στρατῷ μὴ ἐπιτηδεύειν συνεχῶς τὰ ἄπλικτα ἀλλάσσειν ἢ τὰς ὁδοιπορίας ποιεῖσθαι πρὸ τῆς τοῦ πολέμου ἐκβάσεως, ἀλλὰ πρὸ δύο ἢ τριῶν ἡμερῶν προκαταλαμβάνειν τὸν τόπον, ἔνθα ἡ συμβολὴ μέλλει γίνεσθαι, κἀκεῖσε ἀσφαλῶς ἀπλικεύειν.

275 56. Ἐὰν δὲ μέλλῃς ἔφοδον ποιεῖν κατὰ χώρας ἐχθρῶν μετὰ πεζικοῦ στρατοῦ διὰ δάσεων καὶ δυσβάτων καὶ στενῶν τόπων ἢ καὶ ἐν αὐτοῖς ἐγχειρήσεις κατ᾽ αὐτῶν ποιεῖσθαι, οὐ δεῖ σε πολλοὺς καβαλλαρίους ἔχειν, μήτε ἁμάξας ἔχειν ἢ τοῦλδον πολὺν ἢ ὅπλα πολλὰ <καὶ βαρέα>, οἷον λωρίκια καὶ κασσίδας ἢ κλιβάνια ἢ τι τῶν τοιούτων, ἀλλὰ σκουτάρια μόνον ἔχειν τοὺς σκουτάτους μείζονα,
280 κοντάρια δὲ κοντὰ καὶ τὰ σπαθία καὶ τζικούρια, τοὺς δὲ λεγομένους ψιλοὺς σκουτάρια μικρὰ καὶ ἐλαφρότερα, τοξοφάρετρα, ῥικτάρια, ἀκόντια μικρά, τζικούρια καὶ εἴ τι τοιοῦτον ἐλαφρὸν καὶ | χρήσιμον. ἀξίνας δὲ πάντως περισσὰς 315 χρὴ ἔχειν καὶ ἐν τοῖς σαγμαρίοις ἐπιφέρεσθαι διὰ τὰς χρείας.

57. Τὴν δὲ πεζικὴν τῶν σκουτάτων τάξιν μηδὲ ἐπ᾽ εὐθείας ἤτοι κατὰ μέτωπον
285 τάσσειν χρή, ὡς ἐν τοῖς ὁμαλοῖς καὶ γυμνοῖς τόποις, ἀλλ᾽ εἰς δύο ἢ δ΄ μέρη ἐπὶ β΄ ἢ δ΄ τὸ βάθος τῶν ἀκιῶν πρὸς τὸ ποσὸν τοῦ στρατοῦ ἢ ὡς ἡ χρεία ἀπαιτεῖ. τὰ δὲ μέρη ἴσως κινεῖν καὶ περιπατεῖν ἀφεστῶτα ἀπ᾽ ἀλλήλων, ὡς ἀπὸ λίθου βολῆς.

---

263 ad δεξιοῦ des. W (fol. desideratur)   285 ad μέρη de novo inc. W

262 ἐκείνας MW ἐκείνους AVBE   263 πεφυρμέναι MA περιφυρμέναι VBE | περιπατοῦσιν M περιπατῶσιν AVBE   264 εἰσίν MA ὦσιν VBE   266 ἕτοιμοι MA ἕτοιμα VBE 269 καταστῶσιν AVBE καθιστῶσιν M   270 εἰσιν MA ὦσιν VBE | αὐτῶν MVBE αὐτῶ A 272 ἐκβάσεως AVBE ἐκτάσεως M | δύο…τριῶν MA β΄ ἢ γ΄ VBE   277 μήτε M οὔτε AVBE | ἔχειν² M om. AVBE   278 καὶ βαρέα Va om. codd.   279 τῶν M om. AVBE | μόνον M μόνα AVBE   281 ῥικτάρια Va ῥηκτάρια M ῥιπτάρια AVBE   283 χρὴ MA om. VBE   284 μηδὲ M οὐδὲ AVBE   285 δύο MAB β΄ VE | δ΄ M τέσσαρα A τέσσαρας VBE   285-286 μέρη…δ΄ MWA om. VBE   285 β΄ MW δύο AVBE   286 δ΄ MW τέσσαρας A | τὸ ποσὸν MW τὴν ποσότητα AVBE | ἀπαιτεῖ WAVBE ἀπαντᾷ M   287 ἀφεστῶτα MWA ἐφεστῶτα VBE

first place should be the wagons of the right flank, then those of the left, following them the wagons of the left center and then those of the right center. They should not be in disarray or mixed up with one another as they proceed along.

54. If the enemy are nearby, the heavy-armed troops should march along, each one carrying his weapons, not leaving them in the wagons, but prepared to fight. When they are under pressure, the tagmata line up in the way they form for battle and in that order they march along without any mixing or dispersion of troops in order that, if it becomes necessary to form the battle line, they are in position to do so.

55. If there is a large number of enemy cavalry and they are getting close to our army, we should not immediately get ready to change our campsite or to undertake a march before the battle has ended. Instead, two or three days beforehand, occupy the place where the battle is likely to occur and there set up camp in safety.

56. If you intend to lead an army of infantry on an expedition against hostile territory that is dense, very rugged, and with narrow passes, or to launch assaults on them in such places, you must not have many cavalry or wagons or a large baggage train or much heavy armament, such as body armor, helmets, cuirasses or anything of that sort. The heavy-armed troops should carry only large shields, short spears, swords, and axes. The so-called light-armed troops should have smaller and lighter shields, bows with quivers, throwing spears, short javelins, axes, and anything else light and serviceable like these. They definitely must have extra axes that can be carried by the pack animals until needed.

57. The force of heavy infantry must not be drawn up in a straight line on the front as in flat and open country, but, depending on the size of the army or as the circumstances require, in two or four divisions, two or four ranks deep. Its divisions should move evenly and march along separated from each other by about a stone's throw.

58. Ἐὰν δὲ σύνεισι καβαλλάριοι ἢ τοὖλδος, ὄπισθεν αὐτῶν τὸν τοὖλδον ποιεῖν καὶ μετ᾽ αὐτὸν τοὺς καβαλλαρίους καὶ μετ᾽ αὐτοὺς ὀλίγους σκουτάτους 290 <καὶ> ψιλοὺς νωτοφύλακας διὰ τὰς ἀπὸ ὄπισθεν, ὡς εἰκός, ἐπιγινομένας ἀδοκήτους ἐφόδους.

59. Τοὺς δὲ ψιλοὺς τοὺς μὲν ἐκπορεύεσθαι τῆς παρατάξεως μέχρι ἑνὸς σημείου μετὰ ὀλίγων καβαλλαρίων, τοὺς δὲ ἐκ πλαγίων ἔνθεν κἀκεῖθεν ἀνάγκη περιπατεῖν, ἵνα καὶ σκουλκεύωσι καὶ γινώσκωσι, μήποτε ἐγκρύμματά εἰσιν 295 ἐχθρῶν ἢ δένδρα ἱστάμενα, τὰ ὄπισθεν αὐτῶν πεπρισμένα, ἔχοντα καὶ σχηματικῶς ἱστάμενα, ἅτινα ἀπὸ χειρῶν ὠθούμενα καὶ πίπτοντα κατὰ τῶν παρόδων ἐμφράξεις ποιοῦσιν ἐν τοῖς στενώμασι καὶ ἀγῶνα τοῖς αἰφνιδιαζομένοις παρέχουσιν.

60. Καὶ ταῦτα προερευνᾶν δεῖ διά τε ψιλῶν στρατιωτῶν καὶ ὀλίγων καβαλ- 300 λαρίων, ἅμα δὲ καὶ ἀποσοβεῖν τοὺς κεκρυμμένους ἐχθρούς, εἶθ᾽ οὕτως παρέρχεσθαι τὴν παράταξιν.

61. Καὶ ὅπου μὲν ἀραιότεροί εἰσι τόποι, τοὺς καβαλλαρίους προλαμβάνειν καὶ τὰς βίγλας ποιεῖν, ὅπου δὲ δασεῖς καὶ δυσχερεῖς τόποι, τοὺς ψιλούς.

62. Τοὺς δὲ ψιλοὺς μὴ τάττε ἐπ᾽ εὐθείας καθὼς τοὺς σκουτάτους, ἀλλὰ κατὰ 305 <δρούγγους, τοῦτ᾽ ἔστι,> δύο ἢ τρεῖς ἢ τέσσαρας ψιλοὺς ἀκοντιστὰς τάξεις, ἐπιφερομένους καὶ τὰ σκουτάρια αὐτῶν ἵνα, ἐὰν χρεία γένηται, καὶ σκουτεύσωσι καὶ ἀκοντίσωσιν οἱ αὐτοί· καὶ ἕνα δὲ τοξότην ἔχειν ὅστις καὶ ὑπ᾽ αὐτῶν φυλαχθήσεσθαι δύναται.

63. Τοὺς δὲ τοιούτους δρούγγους μὴ ἐπὶ μιᾶς παρατάξεως ἢ ἐπ᾽ εὐθείας τὴν 310 ὁδοιπορίαν ποιεῖσθαι, ἀλλ᾽ ἐφεξῆς ἐσπαρμένως, ἵνα καὶ τοὺς νώτους ἀλλήλων φυλάττωσιν καί, ἐὰν συμβῇ τοὺς ἔμπροσθεν αὐτῶν ἀντίστασιν ὑπὸ ἐχθρῶν

288 ἐὰν MWA εἰ VBE | σύνεισι MAVBE σύνεισιν W | τοὖλδος AVBE τόλδος MW | τοὖλδον AVBE τόλδον MW   289 μετ᾽ αὐτοὺς MWA μετὰ τοὺς VBE | σκουτάτους MW om. AVBE 290 καὶ Strat. om. codd. | ἐπιγινομένας MW γινομένας AVBE   290–291 ἀδοκήτους ἐφόδους MWA ἐφόδους ἀδοκήτως VBE   294 σκουλκεύωσι W σκουλεύωσι MVBE σκουλκευθῶσι A scr. mg. σκοπευωσι βιγλευωσι W | γινώσκωσι MVBE γινώσκωσιν WA | εἰσιν MWA ὦσιν VBE   295 τὰ...αὐτῶν MW ἅτινα AVBE | πεπρισμένα AVBE περιπρισμένα MW   295–296 ἔχοντα...ἅτινα MW μὲν εἰσὶ (εἰσὶν A) δι᾽ ὅλου τοὺς κορμοὺς ὀλίγον δὲ (δέ τι VBE) μόνον κρατοῦσι (κρατοῦσιν A) καὶ AVBE   296 χειρῶν MW χειρῶν παρὰ τῶν ἐχθρῶν AVBE | ὠθούμενα MWA ὠχούμενα VBE   297 ἐμφράξεις ποιοῦσιν MW ἐμφράσσουσι A ἐμφράττουσι VBE | τοῖς στενώμασι M τοῖς στενώμασιν W τὰ στενώματα AVBE   304 τάττε MW τάττης AVBE   305 δρούγγους...ἔστι Strat. om. codd. | δύο... τρεῖς MWA β΄ ἢ γ΄ VBE   306–307 σκουτεύσωσι MAVBE σκουτεύσωσιν W   308 φυλαχθήσεσθαι AVBE φυλαχθήσεται MW | δύναται A δυνήσεται VBE om. MW   310 τοὺς νώτους MW τὰς ψύας AVBE   311 τοὺς AVBE τοῖς MW

58. If cavalry or a baggage train accompanies them, place the baggage train to their rear, followed by the cavalry, and behind them a few heavy and light infantry as a rear guard because of surprise attacks likely to be launched from the rear.

59. The light infantry, along with a few cavalrymen, should march out about one mile ahead of the main body of troops. Others must march here and there around the flanks to patrol and to discover any enemy ambushes or trees that seem to be standing upright but which have been sawed through in the back so they can be quickly pushed over, fall down, and block the passage in those narrow places, causing serious trouble for those who have been ambushed.

60. The light-armed soldiers, together with a few horsemen, should be looking for such things and, at the same time, should clear out enemy troops in hiding. The main body of troops may then pass through.

61. Where the country is fairly open, the cavalry should ride out in advance and act as scouts, but where it is wooded and difficult the light-armed troops should do that.

62. Do not line up the light-armed infantry in a straight line, as <you do> with the heavy-armed men, but in irregular groups, that is, formations of two, three, or four light-armed soldiers with javelins, carrying their shields, so that, if necessary, they can both protect themselves and hurl the javelins. They should also have one archer who can be protected by them.

63. Irregular groups of this sort must not advance along the route in one solid formation or in a straight line but they should be separated, one following the other, so they may protect each other's rear. If it should happen that the

ὑπομεῖναι καὶ βαρεῖσθαι ὑπὸ δυσχερείας τόπου, ὄπισθεν ἀγνώστως ὑψηλότεροι γενόμενοι κατὰ τοῦ νώτου τῶν ἐχθρῶν ἔρχονται, ὥσπερ ἀναγκαῖόν ἐστιν ἀεὶ σπεύδειν τοὺς ψιλοὺς ἵνα τοὺς ὑψηλοτέρους τόπους κατὰ τῶν ἐχθρῶν προκατα-
315 λαμβάνωσιν.

64. Παραγγείλῃς δὲ καὶ τοὺς ψιλοὺς ἵνα | πλέον τοῦ δύνασθαι αὐτοὺς 315ᵛ ἀκούειν βουκίνου μὴ χωρίζωνται τῆς παρατάξεως ἵνα μὴ γυμνούμενοι βοηθείας, ὡς εἰκός, βαροῦνται.

65. Τῶν δὲ τεσσάρων μερῶν ἐπὶ τὸ ἔμπροσθεν κέρας πορευομένων, ἐὰν
320 στενὸς εὑρεθῇ <ὁ> τόπος, ὥστε μὴ δύνασθαι τὰ τέσσαρα μέρη καθ' ἑαυτὰ παρέρχεσθαι, δύο μέρη ποιεῖν εἰς διφαλαγγίαν. εἰ δὲ μηδὲ δύο χωροῦσιν, κατὰ ἓν μέρος παράγειν ἐπὶ κέρας ὡς μίαν παράταξιν, καὶ τοὺς λοιποὺς ἐφεξῆς, τῶν ψιλῶν, ὡς εἴρηται, ἀεὶ προλαμβανόντων. μετὰ δὲ τὸ παρελθεῖν τὸν στενὸν τόπον πάλιν εἰς τέσσαρας ἀρχὰς ἤγουν μέρη, ὡς ἐτάγησαν, ἐπὶ κέρας ἤγουν
325 πρὸς τὰ ἔμπροσθεν φέρειν αὐτούς.

66. Εἰ δὲ πλῆθος ἐχθρῶν ἐπιφανεῖ ἢ ἔμπροσθεν ἢ ἐκ πλαγίων, <καθ'> οἵου ἂν συνίδῃς μέρους ὅτι πρέπει, κατ' ἐκείνου ποιήσεις ἐπὶ μέτωπον ἤγουν ἐπὶ τὰ ἔμπροσθεν τὴν παράταξιν· τοῦτ' ἔστιν, εἰ μὲν ἀριστερᾷ τῆς παρατάξεως φανῶ-σιν, αὐτοῦ τοῦ ἄκρου μέρους τῆς παρατάξεως ἐν τάξει ἱσταμένου ἔρχονται τὰ
330 ἄλλα τρία μέρη καὶ παρατάσσονται αὐτῷ ἐν τοῖς ἰδίοις τόποις· εἰ δὲ δεξιᾷ φανῶσι, τὸν ὅμοιον τρόπον μεταβαλλόμενοι ποιοῦσι τὰς ὄψεις κατ' ἐκείνου· εἰ δὲ ἔμπροσθεν φανῶσι τῶν μέσων μερῶν ἢ τοῦ ἑνὸς ἢ τῶν β', πρὸς τὸν τόπον δεξιᾷ ἐγκλινομένων καὶ εἰς μέτωπον ἀποκαθισταμένων τὰ ἄλλα δύο μέρη ἐρχόμενα ὁμοίως παρατάσσονται καὶ γίνεται ἡ τάξις πλαγία ἐπὶ μέτωπον.

---

317 ad τῆς des. V

---

313 κατὰ...νώτου MW ὀπίσω AVBE | ὥσπερ MW ὅπερ AVBE    314 σπεύδειν...ψιλοὺς MW σπουδάζειν AVBE | ἵνα MW ἵνα οἱ ψιλοὶ A ἵνα ἵνα οἱ ψιλοὶ VBE    314–315 προκατα-λαμβάνωσιν MWA προκαταλαμβάνωσι VBE    316–318 πλέον...εἰκός MW τοσοῦτον χωρίζωνται ἀπὸ τῆς παρατάξεως ὅσον δύνανται ἀκούειν βουκίνου φωνῆς ἵνα μὴ μακρὰν τῆς παρατάξεως γινόμενοι καὶ βοηθείας στερούμενοι AVBE    318 βαροῦνται MW βαροῦνται ὑπὸ ἐχθρῶν A βαρῶνται BE    320 ὁ Va om. codd. | τέσσαρα MWBE τέσσα A    321 παρέρχεσθαι AE παρέρχεται B πορεύεσθαι MW | χωροῦσιν WABE χωροῦσι M | ἓν MWA τὸ ἓν E τὸ ἕνα B scr. mg. ἐφεξῆς W    326 καθ' Va om. codd.    326–327 οἵου.... μέρους Va οἵον...μέρος codd.    327 πρέπει MW ἁρμόζει ABE | κατ' Va μετ' codd. | ἐπὶ¹ MW εἰς ABE    327–328 ἤγουν...ἔστιν MW om. ABE    328 μὲν MW μὲν οὖν εἰς τὰ ABE    328–329 φανῶσιν MW φανῶσιν οἱ ἐχθροὶ ABE    329 ἱσταμένου MWA ἱσταμένους BE    331 φανῶσι MBE φανῶσιν WA | κατ' Va καὶ MWBE om. A | ἐκείνου Va ἐκεῖνοι codd.    332 ἔμπροσθεν MABE ἔμπροσθε W | β' MW δύο ABE | πρὸς...τόπον Va καὶ τῶν τόπων MW τούτων ABE    333 ἐγκλινομένων MW ἐκκλινομένων ABE

group up front is met by resistance from the enemy or is bogged down in rough terrain, the groups behind may move to higher ground without being observed and come down on the rear of the enemy. So it is always necessary for the light-armed troops to hasten in order to seize the higher places beforehand against the enemy.

64. Order the light-armed troops not to distance themselves from the main body beyond where they can still hear the trumpet, so they may not end up bereft of support and, in all likelihood, be overwhelmed.

65. If the four divisions are marching along on the front flank and they run into a place so narrow that the four divisions cannot pass through by themselves, make two divisions into a double phalanx. But if two will not fit, then lead one at a time through as one battle line by the flank, and have the rest follow, always, as was said, keeping the light-armed troops in front. After passing through the narrow spot they resume their formation of four commands or divisions advancing forward by the flank.

66. If a strong enemy force appears in front of them or off to the side, form the battle line on whatever side you consider appropriate, with its front or its forward units facing that side. That is, if the enemy appears to the left of the battle line, the division on that flank of the line halts in position and the other three divisions come and form up with it in their own positions. If they appear to the right, our men make the corresponding maneuver and make the front in that direction. If they appear in front of either one or both of the center divisions, the other two divisions come and head toward the right and set themselves up as a front, in like manner forming their battle line with their flank as their front.

335     67. Καὶ εἰ μὲν ὁ τόπος ἔχει, συντεταγμένως ἐπέρχεσθαι τοὺς ψιλοὺς τοῖς
ἐχθροῖς ἵνα μετ᾽ αὐτῶν καὶ καβαλλάριοι κατακυκλοῦσι τοὺς ἐναντίους. εἰ δὲ οὐ
χωρεῖ συντεταγμένην αὐτὴν καὶ πεπυκνωμένην διέρχεσθαι, <δεῖ> τὰς δὲ τῶν
ὁπλιτῶν ἤγουν τῶν σκουτάτων ἀκίας βαθείας καὶ ἀραιὰς τάσσεσθαι ἵνα καὶ τὰς
διαβάσεις εὐκόλως διὰ τῶν δένδρων ποιοῦνται καί, ἐὰν χρεία γένηται, πυκνοῦν-
340   ται.

        68. Ἐὰν δὲ οὐ<δὲ οὕτως> χωροῦνται, δεῖ ἵστασθαι τὴν παράταξιν, τοὺς δὲ
ψιλοὺς ἀφίειν εἰς τοὺς ἐχθροὺς καὶ ἐκ τῶν πλησίον ἐπιβοηθεῖν αὐτοῖς διά τε
ὀλίγων σκουτάτων καὶ διὰ καβαλλαρίων.

        69. Παραγγείλῃς δὲ πάντως ἵνα, ὅτ᾽ ἄν, ὡς εἰκός, κραυγὴ γένηται ἐν τῷ
345   ὁδοιπορεῖν ὡς πολεμίων ἐπιφαινομένων, μὴ πάντας φύρεσθαι καὶ κατ᾽ ἐκείνου
τρέχειν τοῦ μέρους, ἀλλὰ τοὺς μὲν σκουτάτους τῆς τάξεως αὐτῶν ἔχεσθαι, τοὺς
δὲ ψιλοὺς ἑκάστου μέρους ἐπὶ τὸν κράζοντα συντρέχειν καὶ μὴ τοὺς ἔμπροσθεν | 316
εἰς τὰ πλάγια προχείρως ἔρχεσθαι ἢ τοὺς τῶν πλαγίων ἐπὶ τὸ ἔμπροσθεν μέρος
ἄνευ τῆς τοῦ ἄρχοντος ἐπιτροπῆς, ἀλλ᾽ ἕκαστον μέρος τοῖς ἰδίοις ἐπιβοηθεῖν ἐν
350   καιρῷ κραυγῆς, ὡς ἡ χρεία καλέσει, καὶ ἵνα, ἐὰν βαροῦνται, ὡς εἰκός, εἰς τὴν
τῶν σκουτάτων παράταξιν τρέχουσι καὶ μὴ βιάζωνται ὑπὸ τῶν ἐχθρῶν.

        70. Ἀσφαλῶς οὖν αἱ ὁδοιπορίαι τῶν πεζῶν καὶ ἁρμοδίως γίνεσθαι δύνανται
ἵνα, ὡς εἴπομεν, ἐν μὲν τοῖς δασυτέροις τόποις καὶ δυσβάτοις ἐπὶ κέρας ἤγουν
στενοεπιμήκη τάσσωνται τάξιν, εἴτε εἰς τέσσαρα μέρη εἴτε εἰς δύο, ὡς οἱ τόποι
355   δέχονται, ἐν δὲ τοῖς ἀραιοτέροις ἐπὶ μέτωπον ἐν πλαγίᾳ τάξει εἰς πλάτος, ἐν
ἀραιοτέραις μὲν κατὰ τὸ πλάτος ἀκίαις, βαθυτέραις δὲ κατὰ τὸ πάχος.

        71. Γίνωσκε δὲ ὅτι ἐν ταῖς δασείαις ὕλαις οἱ ἐκ χειρὸς ἀκοντίζοντες διὰ
ῥικταρίων ἢ μεναύλων ἀναγκαιότεροί εἰσι καὶ τῶν τοξοτῶν καὶ τῶν σφενδονι-

---

336 κατακυκλοῦσι W κατακυκλοῦσιν A κατακυκλῶσι MBE    337 δεῖ Va om. codd.
339 διαβάσεις MWAB om. E | εὐκόλως...δένδρων MW διὰ τῶν δένδρων εὐκόλως ABE |
ποιοῦνται MW ποιῶνται ABE | ἐὰν MWA εἰ E ἢ B    339–340 πυκνοῦνται MW πυκνῶνται
ABE    341 οὐδὲ οὕτως Va οὐ codd. | χωροῦνται MWA χωρῶνται BE | ἵστασθαι MW
ἵστασθαι μὲν ABE    342 ἀφίειν...ἐχθροὺς MW ἐξέρχεσθαι κατὰ τῶν ἐχθρῶν ABE | καὶ
MWA om. BE | τῶν MW τοῦ ABE | πλησίον MWAB πλησίου E    344 πάντως MWA
πάντας BE    345 πάντας ABE πάντως MW    349 ἐπιτροπῆς MW προτροπῆς ABE
350 ὡς¹ MW om. ABE | ἡ...καλέσει MW om. ABE | ἐὰν MWA εἰ BE | βαροῦνται MABE
βαρύνωνται W    351 τρέχουσι M τρέχουσιν W τρέχωσι ABE    353 ἵνα MWA ἵν᾽ BE
354 τάξιν MW τάξει ABE | τέσσαρα MWAE δ᾽ B | δύο MWA β᾽ BE    355 πλαγίᾳ MWAB
πλαγίῳ E    356 ἀραιοτέραις MWA ἀραιοτέροις BE | πάχος MWE βάθος AB    357 ἐκ χειρὸς
MW εὐχερῶς ABE    358 ῥικταρίων Va ῥηκταρίων MW ῥιπταρίων ABE

67. If the terrain permits, the light-armed troops are to advance in close order against the enemy so that both they and the cavalry can encircle the enemy. But if it is not practicable for a formation in compact and close order to pass through, then line up the heavy-armed files (hoplites) in depth and in extended order, so they can easily make their way through wooded areas and, if need be, resume close order.

68. If even this is not feasible, it is necessary to halt the main body and send the light-armed troops against the enemy, closely supported by a few heavy-armed men and cavalry.

69. Most certainly you should give the following order. In the event that, while your men are marching along, the alarm is sounded that the enemy are approaching, everyone must not get excited and rush toward that sector. Rather, the heavy-armed troops should maintain their formation, while the light-armed troops from each division dash toward the man who gave the alarm. The troops in front should not hastily move toward the flanks nor those on the flank to the section in front without the approval of the commanding officer. But each division should support its own troops when the alarm is given, as the situation demands so that, in the event that the men are hard pressed, they hasten back to the main body of heavy infantry to avoid being overwhelmed by the enemy.

70. Infantry, therefore, are capable of undertaking marches safely and in good order, as we have said, in thickly wooded and difficult country if they arrange their formation by the flank, that is, the width being narrow, either in four divisions or in two, depending on the terrain, and in more open country forming the front on the flank more broadly, with the files fairly open according to width but deeper according to thickness.

71. Bear in mind that in thickly wooded country javelin throwers, using short spears or menaula, are needed more than archers or slingers. For this

στῶν. διὰ τοῦτο πρέπον ἐστὶ τοὺς πολλοὺς τῶν ψιλῶν εἰς ῥικτάρια καὶ ἀκόντια
360 ἐκ χειρὸς συμβαλλόμενα γυμνάζεσθαι.

72. Οἱ δὲ τοξόται ἀναγκαῖοί εἰσι τῇ παρατάξει μᾶλλον ὑποτασσόμενοι, καὶ
εἰς τραχεῖς καὶ εἰς κρημνώδεις καὶ εἰς στενοὺς καὶ γυμνοὺς τόπους.

73. Οἱ μέντοι ἀκοντισταὶ καὶ ἔξωθεν τῆς παρατάξεως εἰς τὰς ὕλας τὰς δασεῖς
μάλιστα ἀναγκαῖοί εἰσιν. τοσαῦτα μὲν οὖν καὶ ἐν ταῖς ὁδοιπορίαις παραφυλάτ-
365 τειν σε ἀναγκαῖον, ὦ στρατηγέ.

74. Πρὶν ἢ δὲ πάντας ἀπλικεῦσαι, τὴν παράταξιν μηδέποτε διάλυε, μήτε ἐπὶ
πεζῆς στρατείας μήτε ἐπὶ καβαλλαρικῆς, ἕως ἂν καὶ τὸ φοσσάτον ὀχυρωθῇ καὶ
αἱ βίγλαι ἐξέλθωσιν.

75. Εἰδέναι δὲ πάντας προστάξεις ἵνα τῇ φωνῇ τοῦ κατὰ συνήθειαν βουκί-
370 νου, γνωρίζοντες αὐτό, ἵστανται καὶ πάλιν τῇ συνήθει φωνῇ τοῦ ἑτέρου βουκίνου ἤγουν τοῦ κινήματος κινῶσιν.

76. Οὕτως οὖν ἡμῖν διατετυπωμένων τῶν περὶ ὁδοιπορίας στρατοῦ, ἐφεξῆς
σοι καὶ τὸν περὶ τοῦ λεγομένου τούλδου διαταξόμεθα τύπον. |

---

359 ἐστὶ ΜΒΕ ἐστιν WA | ῥικτάρια Va ῥηκτάρια MW ῥιπτάρια ΑΒΕ    360 συμβαλλόμενα
Μ βαλλόμενα WABE    361 εἰσι ΜΑΒΕ εἰσιν W titulum const. decimae summa pag. scr.
πολεμικῶν παρασκευῶν διάταξις ιʹ W    362 καὶ γυμνοὺς MWA om. ΒΕ    363 δασεῖς MW
δασείας ΑΒΕ    364 εἰσιν MWA εἰσι ΒΕ    367 πεζῆς MW πεζικῆς ΑΒΕ | στρατείας MW
στρατιᾶς ΑΒΕ    368 ἐξέλθωσιν MWA ἐξέλθωσι ΒΕ    369–370 εἰδέναι...αὐτό MW
προστάξεις δὲ πάντας ἀκριβῶς γνωρίζειν τὴν φωνὴν τοῦ βουκίνου ἵνα τῆς συνήθους φωνῆς
τῆς στάσεως ἀκούοντες ΑΒΕ    373 τούλδου ΑΒΕ τόλδου MW

reason, most of the light infantry should be trained in hurling short spears and javelins by hand.

72. Archers, rather, are needed for supporting operations with the main battle line and in rugged, precipitous, narrow, and open country.

73. Javelin throwers, for their part, are needed outside of the main battle line, especially in thickly wooded areas. It is, therefore, necessary for you, O general, to observe all these things when on the march.

74. Never dismiss the main body, whether it is the infantry on campaign or the cavalry, until everyone has settled into camp and it has been fortified and patrols have gone out.

75. Everyone must know the following ordinances. They must come to a halt when they recognize the customary blast of the trumpet and, in turn, at the customary blast of the other trumpet, the one for movement, they move.[12]

76. So then, we have set down the regulations about an army on the march. Next we will set forth ordinances regarding the baggage train, as it is called.

12. Cf. *supra* 7.128–133, 352–354.

# ΠΟΛΕΜΙΚΩΝ ΠΑΡΑΣΚΕΥΩΝ ΔΙΑΤΑΞΙΣ Ι΄

## Περὶ τούλδου

1. Δεῖ οὖν καὶ τοῦ τούλδου ἀναγκαίως σε φροντίζειν καὶ μή, ὡς ἔτυχε, καταλιμπάνειν αὐτό, ἀλλὰ ἀσφαλίζεσθαι, ὅπου ἂν καταληφθῇ. μηδὲ πάλιν
5 ἀπρονοήτως ἐπιφέρεσθαι αὐτὸ ἐν τῇ μάχῃ· συμβαίνει γὰρ καὶ | παλλικάρια εἶναι 316ᵛ ἐν αὐτῷ, χρησίμους τοῖς στρατιώταις, καὶ τέκνα ἢ συγγενεῖς αὐτῶν καί, εἰ μὴ ἐν ἀσφαλείᾳ τυγχάνει, τῷ περισπασμῷ αὐτοῦ οἱ στρατιῶται συνεχόμενοι ἀμφίβολοι καὶ μεριζόμενοι τὰς γνώμας ἐν ταῖς μάχαις γίνονται.

2. Καὶ γὰρ ἑκάστῳ συνετῷ ἀνδρὶ σπουδή ἐστι χωρὶς ἰδίας βλάβης τὰ τοῦ
10 ἐχθροῦ κερδῆσαι· ἐὰν δὲ οἰκείαν ὑφορᾶται βλάβην ἢ ἀπέχεται ἢ ὀκνηρότερος γίνεται.

3. Καὶ πρωτοτύπως μὲν συνεπαγομένου τοῦ τούλδου καὶ συμβυλῆς δημυσίας προσδοκωμένης πλῆθος τῶν λεγομένων παλλικαρίων ἤγουν τῶν δουλευόντων τοῖς τε ἄρχουσι καὶ τοῖς στρατιώταις ἐπιφέρεσθαι οὐ συμβουλεύομεν, οὔτε
15 ἐν τῇ ἰδίᾳ γῇ ἡμῶν τῆς μάχης ἐλπιζομένης οὔτε ἐν τῇ ἀλλοτρίᾳ ἐπερχομένων, ἀλλὰ συμμέτρους εἶναι καὶ τοὺς ἐν δυνάμει ὄντας.

4. Τοσούτους δὲ ἤγουν τοὺς ἐπαρκοῦντας κατὰ τὰ κοντουβέρνια ἀντέχεσθαι καὶ διοικεῖν τὰ ἄλογα αὐτῶν πρὸς τὴν διαφορὰν καὶ τὴν ποιότητα καὶ διάγνωσιν τῶν ταγμάτων ἤτοι τὸ πλῆθος τῶν ἀλόγων, διὰ τὸ μὴ πολλὴν φύρσιν
20 καὶ δαπάνην ἄκαιρον καὶ περισπασμὸν εἰς αὐτοὺς γίνεσθαι.

---

M W (mut.) A B E   Va   PG 107:788

1–70 *Strat.*, 5.

1 πολεμικῶν παρασκευῶν MWA om. BE   2 τούλδου A τόλδου MW τοῦ τούλδου BE   3 τούλδου ABE τόλδους MW   4 καταληφθῇ MW φθασθῇ ABE   5 παλλικάρια MW ἀνθρώπους ABE   7 αὐτοῦ MWA αὐτῷ BE   9 ἐστι MWAE ἐστιν B   10 ἐὰν MWAE εἰ B   12 συνεπαγομένου MWAE συνεχομένου B | τούλδου ABE τόλδου MW   13 τῶν¹...ἤγουν MW om. ABE   15 γῇ ἡμῶν MW trsp. ABE   16 ἐν...ὄντας MW δυνατωτέρους ABE   17 κοντουβέρνια ABE κουτουβέρνια MW   17–18 ἀντέχεσθαι MW om. ABE   18 καὶ διοικεῖν MWA om. BE   18–19 τὴν¹...ἤτοι MW om. ABE   19 ἀλόγων MW ἀλόγων αὐτῶν ABE | μὴ MW μηδὲ ABE   20 εἰς αὐτοὺς ABE om. MW | γίνεσθαι MWA γενέσθαι BE

# PREPARATION FOR WAR, CONSTITUTION X

## About the Baggage Train

1. You must realize that the baggage train is essential and you must never, as has happened, leave it behind.[1] It must be securely guarded, wherever it has been left. On the other hand, it should not be brought carelessly onto the field of battle. For the train happens to include the grooms needed by the soldiers, as well as children and other relatives of theirs. If their safety is not assured, the soldiers become distracted, hesitant, and do not focus their attention on the battle.

2. Every intelligent man indeed makes an effort to profit at the enemy's expense without any harm to himself, but if he suspects harm to himself he stays away or becomes very hesitant.

3. First of all, when you are accompanied by the baggage train and a pitched battle is expected, we advise you not to bring along a large number of the so-called grooms, that is, those in the service of the officers and the soldiers, when we are advancing in expectation of battle, whether in our own country or in a foreign one, but only a moderate number and vigorous men at that.

4. There should be enough of them attached to each squad to take care of its horses and to manage them, making due allowance for their differences, their quality, and the distinction of the units, as well as the number of horses. This will avoid a great deal of confusion, inopportune expense, and distraction among them.

---

1. Sections 1–15 derive from *Strat.* 5. See A. Dain, "'Touldos' et 'touldon' dans les traités militaires," *Mélanges Henri Grégoire* (Brussels, 1950), 2:161–169.

5. Τούτους δὲ ἐν τῷ καιρῷ τῆς μάχης, εἰ μὲν σύνεστι πεζικὸς στρατός, δηλονότι σὺν αὐτῷ μετὰ τῶν ἐπὶ τούτῳ ἀφοριζομένων καταλιμπάνειν ἀρχόντων, εἴτε ἐν τῇ ἰδίᾳ εἴτε ἐν τῇ ἀλλοτρίᾳ ὁ πόλεμος κρίνεται. ἀσφαλῶς δὲ αὐτοὺς εἶναι ἐν τῷ φοσσάτῳ, καθὼς ἐν τῷ περὶ ἀπλίκτων δηλώσομέν σοι τύπῳ.

25    6. Καὶ αὐτὰ δὲ τὰ σαγμάρια καὶ τὴν λοιπὴν ἀποσκευήν, ἅπερ καλεῖται ἀδέστρατα, μετ' αὐτοῦ τοῦ τούλδου καταλιμπάνειν.

7. Καὶ ἐν μὲν τοῖς κούρσοις ἢ ταῖς ἄλλαις ἐφόδοις ἔχειν αὐτὰ τοὺς στρατιώτας τάχα καὶ μέχρι καὶ αὐτῆς τῆς ἡμέρας τῆς συμβολῆς πεφραγμένα καὶ ἐν δυνάμει.

30    8. Ἐν αὐτῇ δὲ τῇ συμβολῇ ἐγγὺς ἔχειν τῆς παρατάξεως ἀδέστρατον οὐκ ἀναγκαῖον κρίνομεν, ἀλλ' ἐν τῷ φοσσάτῳ καταλιμπάνεσθαι. καὶ γὰρ συμβαίνει πολλάκις καὶ ταραχῆς γινομένης εὐκόλως παραπίπτουσι διὰ τὸ ὑπὸ μικρῶν παλλικαρίων κρατεῖσθαι.

9. Εἰ δὲ σύνεστι πεζικὸς στρατός, εἰ μὲν ἐν τῇ ἰδίᾳ χώρᾳ ἢ ἐν αὐτοῖς τοῖς
35    μεθορίοις ἀμφοτέρων τῶν χωρῶν, τῆς τε ἡμετέρας καὶ τῆς πολεμίας, προσδοκᾶται ἡ μάχη εὐθέως γίνεσθαι καὶ οὐκ ἔχει | ὑπέρθεσιν, τότε ἐν ὀχυρῷ τόπῳ, ἔνθα    317
καὶ βοσκαὶ καὶ ὕδατα ἀρκοῦντα εὑρίσκονται, ὡς ἀπὸ τριάκοντα ἢ καὶ πεντήκοντα μιλίων καταλιμπάνειν τὸν πλείονα καὶ ἄχρηστον τοῦλδον καὶ τὰ περισσὰ ἄλογα καὶ ἐργαλεῖα καὶ ἕτερα εἴδη, ὧν χρεία οὐκ ἔστι κατὰ τὴν ἡμέραν τοῦ
40    πολέμου.

10. Ἀφόριζε δὲ καί τινας ἐν τῷ μέσῳ διαστήματι τοῦ τε τούλδου καὶ τῆς μάχης, ἐγνωσμένους πᾶσι καὶ μὴ πονηροὺς καὶ φαύλους ἀνθρώπους, καὶ κατάστησον αὐτοὺς εἰς διάστατα καὶ ὑπόδειξον τούτους τῷ ἄρχοντι τοῦ τούλδου—δεῖ γὰρ αὐτῷ πάντως ἄρχοντα ἴδιον ἔχειν—ὥστε πρὸς τὴν τοῦ πολέμου ἔκβασιν
45    ὀφείλειν αὐτοὺς μηνύσαι τοῖς ἐν τῷ τούλδῳ ἢ μεῖναι ἐν τῷ αὐτῷ τόπῳ ἐν ᾧ

---

22 δηλονότι MW om. ABE    22–23 ἀρχόντων    Va αὐτοὺς codd.    23 ἀλλοτρίᾳ MW ἀλλοτρία χώρα ABE | κρίνεται MW γίνεται ABE    25–26 ἅπερ…ἀδέστρατα MW καὶ τὰ συρτὰ ABE    26 μετ' MW κατ' ABE | τούλδου ABE τόλδου MW    27 ἐφόδοις MW ἐπιδρομαῖς ABE    28 καὶ¹ MW om. ABE | πεφραγμένα MW om. ABE    30 ἀδέστρατον MW συρτὰ ABE    31–33 καὶ…κρατεῖσθαι MW διὰ τὸ ὑπὸ μικρῶν παίδων κρατεῖσθαι αὐτὰ πρὸς ἄλληλα διαμάχεσθαι καὶ ταραχὴν οὐ μικρὰν ἐμποιεῖν ABE    34 σύνεστι MWA σύνεστι καὶ ΒΕ    35 μεθορίοις MW συνόροις ABE | ἀμφοτέρων…χωρῶν MW om. ABE | ἡμετέρας MW ἡμετέρας χώρας ABE | πολεμίας MW τῶν πολεμίων ABE    37 τριάκοντα MW λ' ABE | ἢ καὶ ABE ἢ Μ καὶ W    37–38 πεντήκοντα MW ν' ABE    39 ἔστι ΜΑΒΕ ἐστιν W    41 τοῦ τε MWA τοῦτο ΒΕ | τούλδου WABE τόλδου Μ    42 ἐγνωσμένους MW γνωρίμους ΑΒ γνωρικοὺς Ε    44 αὐτῷ MW om. ABE | πάντως MW πάντως τὸν τοῦλδον ABE    45 ὀφείλειν αὐτοὺς MW om. ABE

5. At the time of battle those servants should be left behind, whether the battle is fought in our own or in foreign territory, and they should be joined by an infantry force, if one is present, with officers assigned to this task. They should find safety in the camp, as we shall make clear in the ordinances about camps.

6. Also leave behind with the baggage train itself the reserve horses, also referred to as spare horses, and the rest of the equipment.

7. For raiding and other offensive actions the soldiers must quickly take possession of the horses <and keep them> well armored and vigorous up to the very day of battle.

8. But once the battle begins, it is our considered judgment that there is no need to keep the spare horses near the battle line, but they should be left behind in the camp. For, as often happens, they may easily fall into confusion when handled by young servants.

9. If an infantry force is present, either in our own country or right on the frontier between both countries, ours and the enemy's, and battle appears imminent with no delay in sight, then, in a strong place, where sufficient fodder and water may be found, about thirty or even fifty miles away, leave most of the nonessential part of the baggage train, the extra horses, tools, and the rest of the equipment that is not needed on the day of battle.

10. In the space between the baggage train and the battle line, detail certain men, not at all ignoble or cowardly, whom everyone recognizes, and station them at intervals. Make them known to the officer in charge of the baggage train—it is absolutely necessary for it to have its own commander—so that, depending on the outcome of the battle, they should advise the troops in the

καταλιμπάνονται ἢ ἐν ἑτέρῳ ἀπελθεῖν τῷ δοκοῦντι τόπῳ ἢ καὶ ἐνέγκαι αὐτοὺς
πρὸς τὸν στρατόν.

11. Ἐκ δὲ τοῦ τούλδου κινοῦντας ἐπὶ τὴν μάχην παραλαβεῖν τὰ ἀδέστρατα
ἤγουν σαγμάρια καὶ ἢ τέντας μικρὰς ἢ σαγία διπλᾶ εἰς τὸ μὲν ἓν σκέπεσθαι,
50 εἴπερ χρεία καλέσει, τὸ δὲ ἕτερον εἰς τένταν ἤτοι τὸ λεγόμενον καμάρδιν ἔχειν.

12. Ἀλλὰ καὶ δαπάνην ἢ παξαματίου ἢ πίστου ἢ ἄλλου τινὸς εἴδους ἐλαφροῦ
εἴκοσι ἢ καὶ τριάκοντα λίτρας καὶ τότε ἀπλικεῦσαι ἐν τῷ φοσσάτῳ, ἐν ᾧ ἂν δόξῃ
γίνεσθαι τόπῳ, ὅτε πρὸς τὴν τῶν ἐχθρῶν μάχην ἀποκινήσουσιν. τοῦτο δὲ τὸ
φοσσάτον ἢ <ἀπὸ ὀρυγμάτων ἢ> ἀπὸ οἰκοδομῆς λίθων ἢ πλίνθων ὀχυρῶσαι,
55 κἂν πρὸς μίαν ἡμέραν συμβῇ μένειν ἐκεῖσε.

13. Ἕκαστον δὲ βάνδον ἀποτίθεσθαι χόρτον ἢ ἄχυρον μιᾶς ἡμέρας ἵνα, ἐάν,
ὡς εἰκός, ἐναντίως τὰ τοῦ πολέμου ἐξέλθῃ, ἐν τῷ ὑποστρέφειν τὸν στρατὸν
μετὰ σπουδῆς ἐν αὐτῷ ἢ μεῖναι ἐν αὐτῷ τῷ φοσσάτῳ ἔχοντα τὴν τῶν ἀλόγων
ἀποτροφὴν μιᾶς ἡμέρας καὶ μὴ ἀναγκάζεσθαι ἐν τοιούτῳ θορύβῳ ἢ βόσκειν ἢ
60 χορτολόγιν ποιεῖν καὶ βλάπτεσθαι ἑτοίμως ὑπὸ τῶν ἐχθρῶν ἢ γυρεύειν ἐν
χωρίοις διὰ δαπάνας τῶν ἐχθρῶν ἐπικειμένων ἢ καὶ παρελθεῖν ἐν τῇ τοιαύτῃ
ἐνδείᾳ αὐτῶν τε καὶ τῶν ἀλόγων καὶ ἐκλυθῆναι.

14. Εἰ δὲ ἄρα καὶ παρέρχονται καὶ οὐκ ἔχουσί τινος χρείαν, ἀφορίσεις τινάς,
ὥστε καίειν τὸν χόρτον καὶ οὕτως ἐπὶ τὰ ἔμπροσθεν περιπατεῖν διὰ τοὺς ἐλπιζο-
65 μένους ὀπίσω ἐπέρχεσθαι πολεμίους.

15. Ἐν δὲ ταῖς ὁδοιπορίαις πολεμίων ἐγγιζόντων ἀναγκαῖόν ἐστιν ἀεὶ μέσον
ἔχειν τὸν τοῦλδον, ἵνα μὴ ἀφύλακτος ὢν ἐπηρεάζηται. τὰς δὲ ὁδοιπορίας, ὡς
ἤδη καὶ ἄνω που εἴπομεν, μὴ ποιεῖσθαι μεμιγμένας μετὰ τούλδου, ἀλλὰ διακε-

---

64 ad ἔμπροσθεν des. W (2 foll. desiderantur)

---

48 τούλδου WABE τόλδου M | παραλαβεῖν MW δεῖ παραλαμβάνειν αὐτοὺς ABE
48–49 τὰ…ἤγουν MW om. ABE   49 ἢ¹ MW om. ABE | τέντας MW τένδας ABE | μικρὰς
Strat. διπλὰς MW om. ABE | εἰς…ἓν MWA τὸ μὲν ἓν εἰς τὸ ABE   50 καλέσει MW καλέσοι
A καλέσαι BE | ἕτερον MW ἕτερον ἔχειν ABE | τένταν MW τένδαν ABE | ἤτοι…ἔχειν MW
om. ABE   52 ἢ ABE om. MW | καὶ¹ WABE om. M | τριάκοντα MWA λ΄ BE   53 τῶν
MWAE om. B | ἀποκινήσουσιν MWA ἀποκινήσουσι BE   54 ἀπὸ¹…ἢ² Va om. codd. |
πλίνθων MW πλίνθου ABE | ὀχυρῶσαι MWA ὠχυρῶσαι χρὴ BE   56 χόρτον MWA χόρτου
BE   57 ἐξέλθη MW συμβῆ ABE   58 ἔχοντα Va ἔχειν codd.   59 ἀποτροφὴν MWAB
ἀποστροφὴν E   60 ποιεῖν MW om. ABE   60–61 ἐν χωρίοις A ἐγχωρίοις MWE ἐγχωρίοις
B   61 τῇ MW om. ABE   62 ἐνδείᾳ MW λείψει ABE | αὐτῶν MW τῶν ἀναγκαίων ABE |
τε…ἐκλυθῆναι MW καὶ ἐκλυθῆναι αὐτούς τε καὶ τὰ ἄλογα αὐτῶν ABE   65 ἐπέρχεσθαι
MAE παρέρχεσθαι B   66 ἐστιν BE ἐστι MA   67 τὸν ABE τὸ M | ἀφύλακτος ὢν ABE
ἀφύλακτον ὂν M   68 που M om. ABE | μετὰ M μετὰ τοῦ ABE   68–69 διακεκριμένας καὶ
M om. ABE

baggage train either to remain in the same place in which they were left, to go off to another suitable place, or to join up with the <main> army.

11. Troops moving from the baggage train up to combat should take with them their spare or reserve horses and small tents or a couple of heavy cloaks, the one for covering if needed and the other as a tent or what is called a canopy.

12. In addition, twenty or thirty pounds of provisions, hardtack, flour, or some other light stuff. They should then set up camp in a place that seems suitable, when they move out to engage the enemy in battle. This camp should be fortified by ditches or by constructions of stone or of brick, even though <the army> might stay there only for one day.

13. Each bandon should store there a day's supply of forage or hay, just in case the battle has an adverse result, and they have to beat a hasty retreat to that place. It may remain in the camp itself with a day's provisions for the horses and not be forced to gather fodder and forage in such great confusion and be easily harmed by the enemy, or to wander around villages <seeking> provisions with the enemy hard upon them, or to march on with so few provisions for themselves and their horses that they come unstrung.

14. But if they should march on and have no need of the supplies, you will detail some men to burn the fodder and then proceed up to the front because the enemy may be expected to attack from the rear.

15. On the march, when the enemy are nearby, it is essential that the baggage train always be in the middle so that it may not be subject to harassment for lack of protection. As we have already said above, troops on the march must not get

κριμένας καὶ κεχωρισμένας, ὥστε ἰδίως τὸν τοῦλδον ὄπισθεν τοῦ ἰδίου μέρους
70 ὁδοιπορεῖν καὶ ἰδίως τοὺς στρατιώτας ἐξπλήκτους.|

16. Δεῖ δὲ τὸν τοῦλδον, ὡς εἴρηται ἡμῖν ἀνωτέρω, καὶ ἡγεμόνα ἔχειν ἴδιον, 317ᵛ
ὥστε αὐτὸν καὶ διατάξει καὶ διευθυνεῖ, καὶ ἄγειν αὐτὸν οὕτως· ἢ πρὸ τῆς παρατάξεως, ἐὰν ἐκ πολεμίας γῆς ὑποστρέφῃς, ὀπίσω δὲ τῆς παρατάξεως, ἐὰν εἰς
πολεμίαν γῆν ἐμβάλλῃς, ἐνθένδε ἢ ἐκεῖθεν, ἐὰν τὰ πλάγια τῆς παρατάξεως
75 φοβούμενος πορεύῃ, ἐντὸς δὲ τῆς φάλαγγος, ἐὰν τὰ πανταχόθεν ὕποπτα ἔχῃς.

17. Τοσαῦτα μὲν οὖν καὶ περὶ τοῦ τούλδου διὰ βραχέων σοι διεξήλθομεν, ὦ
στρατηγέ, εἴτε ἐν ἁμάξαις μετὰ πεζικοῦ στρατοῦ εἴτε ἐν σαγμαρίοις μετὰ καβαλλαρίων εἴτε ἄλλης ἀποσκευῆς τοιαύτης μετὰ συμμίκτου, ὡς ἂν ἐν μηδενί, ὅσον
ἐστὶ τὸ δυνατὸν ἡμῖν, ἐλλίπῃ σοι κεφαλαίῳ ἡ ἡμετέρα παρακέλευσις. ἑπόμενον
80 δὲ τούτοις καὶ τὸν περὶ τῶν λεγομένων ἀπλίκτων διασαφήσομεν τῇ σῇ ἐνδοξότητι τύπον.

---

69 κεχωρισμένας MBE διαχωρισμένας A   69–70 ὄπισθεν…στρατιώτας MABE sed iteravit
B   70 ἐξπλήκτους Va εὐπλίκτους M ἀνενοχλήτους καὶ ἐλεύθερους ABE   71 τὸν ABE τὸ M
| ὡς εἴρηται MAE om. B | ἡμῖν ἀνωτέρω M om. ABE   72 διευθυνεῖ MA διευθυνεῖ αὐτὸν BE |
αὐτὸν² A αὐτὸ M om. BE   72–73 ἢ…παρατάξεως M om. ABE   73 ἐὰν¹ M ἐὰν μὲν ABE |
ὑποστρέφῃς M ὑποστρέφῃς ἔμπροσθεν τῆς παρατάξεως ABE | ὀπίσω…παρατάξεως MA
ὄπισθεν E om. B   74 ἐμβάλλῃς MA ἐμβαλῇς BE | ἐνθένδε MA ἔνθεν BE   75 ἐντὸς M
ἔσωθεν ABE scr. mg. τὰ πανταχόθεν A (alia m.)   78 ἀποσκευῆς M κατασκευῆς ABE
78–79 ὅσον…ἡμῖν M om. ABE   79 ἐλλίπῃ…κεφαλαίῳ M κεφαλαίῳ ἐλλίπῃ σοι ABE |
ἑπόμενον M ἀκολουθῶς (cum quo inc. const. xi) ABE   80 τούτοις ABE τούτων M |
διασαφήσομεν M ἐκθήσομεν ABE

mixed up with the baggage train, but they must be kept apart and separate. The train should proceed by itself behind its own division and the soldiers, unburdened, should travel by themselves.

16. As we have previously remarked, the baggage train must have its own commander, who will draw it up in formation and manage it. He should lead it as follows: ahead of the main body of troops, if you are returning from enemy territory; behind the main body, if you are entering into enemy territory. Proceed on either side if you are worried about the flanks of the main body, but inside the marching column if all sides look suspicious to you.

17. We have, therefore, in summary fashion, gone through all those matters concerning the baggage train, O general, whether it <consists of> wagons with an infantry army or of pack animals with cavalry or any other such <way of carrying> supplies with a mixed force. Thus, to the best of our ability, we have not omitted a single topic in these ordinances we have given you. Following them, now, we shall explain to Your Excellency the rules regarding the so-called encampments.

# ΠΟΛΕΜΙΚΩΝ ΠΑΡΑΣΚΕΥΩΝ ΔΙΑΤΑΞΙΣ ΙΑ΄

## Περὶ ἀπλίκτων

1. Δεῖ οὖν τὰ ἄπλικτα ἤτοι τὰ φοσσάτα—κυρίως γὰρ φοσσάτον τὸ ἄπλικτον τοῦ ὅλου στρατοῦ καλεῖται—ταῦτα οὖν ἀσφαλῶς σε ποιεῖν καί, εἰ μὲν ἐνδέχε-
5 ται, εἰς ἀραιοτέρους τόπους κατασκηνοῦν τὰ στρατιωτικά, εἰ δὲ οὐκ ἀπαντᾷ, μὴ ἀμελῶς ἀλλὰ σφιγκτῶς καὶ ὀχυρῶς ἀπλικεύειν καὶ ἀποφεύγειν τοὺς τόπους ἐκείνους, ὅσοι ἔχουσιν ἐκ τοῦ πλησίον ὑψηλοτέρους αὐτῶν, ἵνα μὴ ἐκείνους οἱ ἐχθροὶ ἀθρόως ἢ ἐν νυκτὶ προκαταλαβόντες κακά τινα διαθήσουσι τῷ φοσσάτῳ.
10 2. Ὅτ᾽ ἂν τοίνυν ἐν τῇ τῶν ἐχθρῶν χώρᾳ στρατοπεδεύῃς, περιβαλοῦ τάφρον βαθεῖαν, κἂν εἰς μίαν μόνην, ὡς εἴρηται, ἡμέραν μέλλῃς ἀπλικεύειν. ἀμετανόητος γὰρ ἡ τοιαύτη στρατοπεδεία καὶ ἀσφαλὴς διὰ τὰς αἰφνιδίους καὶ ἀπροοράτους ἐπιβουλάς. καταστήσεις δὲ καὶ φυλακάς, κἂν μακρὰν εἶναι νομίζῃς τοὺς πολεμίους, ὡς ἐγγὺς ὄντων.
15 3. Ὅπου δὲ μέλλεις ποιεῖσθαι χρόνιον τὸ ἄπλικτον, μὴ ἐχθρῶν ἔφοδον δηλονότι ὑφορώμενος καὶ φθείρειν χώραν ἐναντίαν βουλόμενος, ἐκλέγου χωρία χρήσιμα, μὴ ὑλώδη ἤγουν ὕλας καὶ πηλὰ καὶ βάλτας ἔχοντα καὶ ὕδατα σεσημμένα. τὰ γὰρ τοιαῦτα διὰ τῆς ἀναθυμιάσεως καὶ τὰς ἀπὸ τῶν τόπων δυσωδίας νοσηρά εἰσι καὶ λοιμοὺς καὶ νόσους φθαρτικὰς ἐμ|βάλλει εἰς τὰ   318
20 στρατεύματα. καὶ πολλοὺς μὲν πολλάκις ἐκάκωσε τῇ νόσῳ, πολλοὺς δὲ καὶ ἀπώλεσεν, ὥστε μὴ μόνον ὀλίγον ἐκ τούτου γενέσθαι, ἀλλὰ καὶ ἀσθενὲς τὸ στράτευμα.

---

M W (mut.) A B E   Va   PG 107:792

---

3–9 *Strat.*, 12.20.   10–27 Onas. 8–9.

---

1 πολεμικῶν παρασκευῶν ΜΑ om. ΒΕ   5 εἰς…οὐκ ΜΑΒ om. Ε | ἀπαντᾷ Μ ἐνδέχεται ΑΒ om. Ε   6 σφιγκτῶς ΜΑΕ σφικτῶς Β   7 ἔχουσιν ΜΑΕ ἔχωσιν Β   8 ἀθρόως ΑΒΕ ἀθρόων Μ | κακά τινα Μ κακὸν τι ΑΒΕ   8–9 φοσσά-τω Μ φοσσάτον ἡμῶν ἐμποιήσουσιν ΑΒΕ   10 στρατοπεδεύῃς ΜΑ στρατοπεδεύῃ ΒΕ | τάφρον Μ σούδαν ΑΒΕ   11 κἂν ΜΑΕ καὶ Β | εἰς…μέλλῃς Μ εἰς μίαν μόνην ἡμέραν εἴρηται ὀφείλῃς Α ὡς εἴρηται εἰς μίαν μόνην ἡμέραν ὀφείλῃς Β om. Ε | ἀπλικεύειν Μ ἀπληκεύειν ΑΒ om. Ε   12 ἀπροοράτους ΑΒΕ ἀοράτους Μ   13 κἂν ΜΑ καὶ ΒΕ   15 ποιεῖσθαι χρόνιον ΜΑ trsp. ΒΕ   17 ἤγουν ὕλας Μ μηδὲ δάση ΑΒΕ   18 σεσημμένα Μ διεφθαρμένα ΑΒΕ   19 νοσηρά Va νοσερά codd. | εἰσι ΜΒΕ εἰσὶν Α

# PREPARATION FOR WAR, CONSTITUTION XI

## About Camps

1. You must assure the security of our camps and entrenchments—entrenchment is the specific term used for the camp of the entire army.[1] If possible, the military units should pitch their tents in open country, but if this cannot be done, we should not be careless. Our camps should be strong and tightly guarded. Avoid those places that have higher ground close by, so that the enemy will not occupy them ahead of us and, all of a sudden or at night, cause damage to the entrenchment.

2. When you set up camp in enemy territory, surround it with a deep ditch, even if you intend to camp there only for one day, as has been said.[2] You will not regret setting up a camp of this sort that will be safe from sudden and unexpected attacks. Even if you believe that the enemy are far off, be sure to place guards as though they were in the immediate vicinity.

3. When you intend to camp there for a long time, say, because you do not suspect an enemy attack and you wish to ravage their country, choose beneficial places, not woody areas covered with trees, mud, or swampy ground, all water-soaked. The rising vapors and foul smell of such places are unhealthy and bring pestilence and deadly diseases to the army.[3] The health of many men has often been impaired and many have been taken by death. As a result, not only is the army reduced in numbers but it is also greatly weakened.

1. *Strat.* 12.20. See CampOrg, 1; J. Kulakovskij, "Vizantijskij lager' kontsa X veka," *Vizantijskij Vremennik* 10 (1903): 63–91.

2. Sections 2–4 derive from Onasander 8–9.

3. Cf. *infra*, §§27–28; also Kekaumenos, 11.18–21 Litavrin = 2.29 Spadaro.

4. Χρήσιμον δὲ καὶ σωτήριον τῷ στρατῷ γίνεσθαι, ἐὰν μὴ ἐπὶ τοῦ αὐτοῦ μένῃ ἀπλίκτου πολὺν χρόνον, εἰ μὴ ἄρα χειμάζει καὶ διὰ τὸν καιρὸν ὥσπερ
25 πεπολισμένα ἔχει τὰ ἄπλικτα τὸ στράτευμα. καὶ γὰρ καὶ αἱ σωτηριώδεις ἐκκρί-σεις ἐπὶ τῶν αὐτῶν γινόμεναι τόπων ἀτμοὺς διεφθαρμένους ἀναπέμπουσι καὶ συμμεταβάλλουσιν εἰς νόσον καὶ τὴν τοῦ περιέχοντος ἀέρος εὐεξίαν.

5. Ἐν δὲ ταῖς παραχειμασίαις πάντως, ὡς ἄνω που εἴρηται, γύμναζε τὰ στρα-τόπεδα καὶ πολεμικὰ ποίει, καὶ ἵνα συνεθίζωνται τοῖς πόνοις ἵνα μήτε ἀργῶσι
30 μήτε ῥαθυμῶσιν.

6. Οὐ μόνον δὲ ὑγιεινῶν σε δεῖ φροντίζειν ἀπλίκτων, ὅτ᾽ ἂν ἄδειαν ἔχῃς ἀπὸ τῶν πολεμίων, ἀλλὰ καὶ πολλὰς καὶ διαφόρους ἔχειν αὐτὰ τὰς χορηγίας καὶ μάλιστα ἐν τῷ ἐξπεδίτῳ ἤγουν ἐν τῇ κατὰ καιρὸν τοῦ ὅλου στρατοῦ συναγωγῇ, ἔνθα μάλιστα καὶ χρονίζειν δέον.

35 7. Φροντίζειν δὲ καὶ τῶν ἐμπόρων ἵνα μὴ ἀδικούμενοι λυποῦνται καὶ οὐ φέρουσι τὰς χορηγίας τῶν ἐπιτηδείων.

8. Εἰ δέ τις καὶ ἐλπὶς ἐναντία ἐνοχλεῖ, ἀσφαλίζεσθαι ἢ ὀρύγμασιν ἢ πάλοις ἢ ὁλοκλήρῳ τράφῳ, ὃ λέγουσι φόσσα, ἢ τριβόλοις ἢ οἰκοδομαῖς ἢ ἀπὸ ξύλων ἢ ἀπὸ λίθων ἢ ἄλλως, ὡς δύνασαι ἐπινοῆσαι. ἔχεις δὲ καὶ βίγλας ἔξωθεν, ἀλλὰ καὶ
40 ἁμάξας εἰς χαρακώσεις, ἐάν εἰσιν, λίαν δυνατόν, ἢ χάρακα πήξεις, ὃ λέγεται σταβαρῶσαι, εἴτε ἀραιῶς εἴτε πυκνότερον, ὡς ἡ δύναμις ἔχει, ἤτε διὰ ξύλων τελείων ἢ δένδρων κοπέντων. δεῖ γὰρ πάντως ἀσφάλειαν ἔχειν τὸ ἄπλικτον, εἰ μὴ ἄρα ἐν τῇ ἡμετέρᾳ ἐστὶν χώρᾳ ἢ γυμνασίας χάριν γίνεται ἢ ἄλλου τινὸς χρειώδους τρόπου ἢ τοῦ στρατοῦ κίνησις.

45 9. Μάλιστα δὲ φροντίσεις καὶ τῶν πλησιοχώρων ὑποτελῶν τῆς βασιλείας ἡμῶν, ἵνα μὴ ἀδικοῦνται παρὰ τῶν στρατιωτῶν, καὶ κατεξαίρετον τῶν γεωργῶν. δύο γὰρ ταῦτά μοι δοκοῦσιν ἐπιτηδεύματα λίαν ἀναγκαῖα πρὸς ἔθνους σύστα-

---

34 ad δέον de novo inc. W

---

39–66 *Strat.*, 7.B.13.

23 γίνεσθαι Μ γίνεται ΑΒΕ | μὴ Μ μὴ πολὺν χρόνον ΑΒΕ    24 πολὺν χρόνον Μ om. ΑΒΕ | ὥσπερ Μ ὥσπερ κατησφαλισμένα καὶ ΑΒΕ    25 τὸ στράτευμα Μ om. ΑΒΕ    28 ἄνω που Μ ἀνωτέρω ΑΒΕ    28–29 στρατόπεδα ΜΑ στρατεύματα ΒΕ    29 καὶ² Μ om. ΑΒΕ | ἵνα¹ Μ καὶ ΑΒΕ    31 σε…ἀπλίκτων Μ ἀπλίκτων φροντίζειν δεῖ σε ΑΒΕ    35 ἐμπόρων ΜW πραγματευτῶν ΑΒΕ | λυποῦνται ΜWΒΕ λυπῶνται Α    36 φέρουσι ΜΑΒΕ φέρωσι W    38 τράφῳ ΜW τάφρῳ ΑΒΕ | ὃ…φόσσα Μ ὃ λέγουσι φόσσα W om. ΑΒΕ    39 ἔχεις ΜW ἔχειν ΑΒΕ    40 εἰς…δυνατόν ΜW ἐὰν εἰσιν (ὦσιν ΒΕ) γυρόθεν τοῦ ἀπλήκτου τιθέναι ΑΒΕ | εἰσιν W εἰσι Μ | ἢ ΜW ἢ καὶ ΑΒΕ | πήξεις ΜW πήσσειν ΑΒΕ    42 ἀσφάλειαν ΜW ἀσφαλὲς ΑΕ ἀσφαλῶς Β    43 ἐστὶν ΜW ἐστὶ ΑΒΕ    44 στρατοῦ De στρατηγοῦ codd.    46 ἀδικοῦνται ΜW ἀδικῶνται ΑΒΕ

4. It is advantageous and healthy for the army not to remain in the same camp for a lengthy period, unless it is winter, for at that time of year the soldiers may be billeted in some sort of building. The bodily excretions deposited in the same place will give off harmful vapors and will transform the fresh air surrounding the place into disease-bearing air.

5. As mentioned above, in winter quarters, by all means, continue to drill the army and practice warlike actions to get the men used to hard work, so that they may not become idle or too relaxed.[4]

6. Not only are you to be concerned about healthy encampments when you are free from the enemy, but you should also make sure that the men have plenty of provisions of various kinds, especially on the march and at a time when the whole army is gathered together in a place where you must spend some time.

7. Be concerned too about the merchants. See that they are not unfairly treated and so come to bear a grievance that may lead them to discontinue furnishing the supplies we need.

8. If you are worried about some unexpected opposition, secure your camp by means of ditches, palisades, or by a trench, called fossa, around the whole camp, or by caltrops or some type of construction, whether of wood or stone, or in some other manner that you will be able to devise. Post sentries outside. Wagons, if you have them, make very effective defenses. Or make a wall of pointed stakes, called stabarosai, either spread out or placed more closely together, depending on their strength, either of finished lumber or of trees felled <on the spot>. By all means, the camp must be kept secure, unless perhaps the army may be moving about in our own country, on training exercises or <engaged in> some other useful activity.

9. Take thought especially for the subjects of Our Majesty in neighboring locations so they may not be mistreated by our soldiers. In particular, be concerned about the farmers. It seems to me that these two institutions are truly

4. For example, see Leo the Deacon, 1.9; 2.1 (Talbot and Sullivan trans. pp. 68–70).

σιν καὶ διαμονήν, γεωργικὴ μὲν τρέφουσα καὶ αὔξουσα τοὺς στρατιώτας, στρατιωτικὴ δὲ ἐκδικοῦσα καὶ περιφυλάττουσα τοὺς γεωργούς. αἱ δὲ ἄλλαι ἐπιτη-
50 δεύσεις δεύτεραι τούτων ἐμοὶ καταφαίνονται. διὰ τοῦτο καὶ ἀναγκαῖον ἀεὶ | 318ᵛ
τούτων ἐπιμελεῖσθαι καὶ τὰ ὑπὲρ αὐτῶν φροντίζειν ἑκάστοτε, ὡς ἂν καὶ οἱ
στρατιῶται δικαίως τρεφόμενοι ἀνδραγαθῶσιν καὶ οἱ γεωργοὶ μὴ ἀδικούμενοι
εὐχαῖς αὐτοὺς ταῖς ἁρμοζούσαις προπέμπουσιν.

10. Πολεμίων δὲ ἐγγιζόντων καὶ προσδοκωμένου πολέμου, ἐὰν προλαβὼν
55 ἐν φοσσάτῳ διάγῃς, ὦ στρατηγέ, καὶ τοὺς ἐχθροὺς ἀναμένῃς ἐκεῖσε, δεῖ εὐτρεπίζειν καὶ ἀποτιθέναι χόρτον ἢ ἄχυρον ἢ κριθὴν μιᾶς ἢ δευτέρας ἡμέρας τῶν
ἀλόγων, ὡς ἤδη σοι καὶ ἐν τῷ περὶ ὁδοιπορίας κεφαλαίῳ προδιεθέμεθα. καὶ
πάλιν ἐὰν ἐκεῖθεν βουληθῇς εἰς ἕτερον ἄπλικτον ἀπελθεῖν καὶ ἐκεῖθεν παρατάξασθαι, ἀναγκαῖον χόρτον καὶ ἄχυρον κἂν μιᾶς ἡμέρας βαστάζειν καὶ οὕτως ἐν
60 τῷ γινομένῳ φοσσάτῳ ἀποτίθεσθαι τοῦτον. ἴσως γὰρ οὐ συγχωροῦνται ὑπὸ τῶν
ἐχθρῶν οἱ εἰς δουλείαν ἀφωρισμένοι παῖδες αὐτῇ τῇ ἡμέρᾳ ἐξελθεῖν καὶ χορτολογῆσαι, οὔτε δὲ τὰ ἄλογα εἰς βοσκὴν ἐκβαλεῖν.

11. Εἰ δὲ καὶ πολὺ ἐγγίζουσιν οἱ ἐχθροί, οὐκ ἄτοπον ἐν τῷ περιπατεῖν, ὡς
εἴρηται, ἕκαστον συνάγειν τὸν χόρτον, τὸν ὀφείλοντα ἀποτεθῆναι. οὐδὲ γὰρ
65 μετὰ τὸ ἀπλικεῦσαι πολλάκις συγχωροῦνται οἱ παῖδες ἐξελθεῖν καὶ χορτολογῆσαι, πλειόνων μάλιστα καβαλλαρίων τῶν ἐχθρῶν εὑρισκομένων.

12. Καὶ πῶς γὰρ οὐ δίκαιον καὶ τὰ εἰς δευτέραν τύχην ἀφορᾶν πολλάκις καὶ
τὰς ἐκεῖθεν ἐναντιώσεις σκοπεῖν καὶ προασφαλίζεσθαι τὰ μέλλοντα, μὴ μετα-
μέλλεσθαι ὕστερον καὶ μάλιστα τὰς ἀποτροφὰς ἡμερῶν ὀλίγων τῶν τε στρατιω-
70 τῶν καὶ τῶν ἀλόγων, καὶ φοσσάτα ὀχυρὰ ποιεῖν ἐν ἐπιτηδείοις τόποις ἔνθα
δυνατὸν εἴτε ὕδωρ ποταμοῦ εἴτε τόπος δυσχερὴς εἴτε ἄλλο τι ὀχύρωμα διεκδικεῖν τὸ φοσσάτον ἐν καιρῷ ἀνάγκης;

13. Ἐν δὲ τοῖς ἀναγκαίοις τοῦ πεζικοῦ ἀπλίκτου καὶ τὰς ἁμάξας, ὡς εἴρηται,
περικύκλῳ καθίστα τοῦ ἀπλίκτου, εἴτε ἐν πεζικῷ στρατῷ ἢ καί, ἐὰν εἰσιν, καὶ ἐν
75 καβαλλαρικῷ ἢ συμμίκτῳ, καὶ οἰκοδομεῖν, ὥς μοι εἴρηται, ἐὰν ὁ τόπος ἔχῃ, καὶ

---

67–72 *Strat.*, 7.A.7.    73–115 *Strat.*, 12.B.22.

48 διαμονήν MWBE  διανομὴν A    52 ἀνδραγαθῶσιν MW  ἀνδραγαθῶσι ABE
53 προπέμπουσιν MW  προπέμπωσιν A  προπέμπωσι BE    54 προσδοκωμένου MWA
προσδοκομένου B  προσδοκουμένου E    55–56 δεῖ εὐτρεπίζειν MWA  διευτρεπίζειν BE
58 καὶ MWA om. BE    64 ἕκαστον MWAE  ἔσχατον B    67 τὰ MW om. ABE
68 ἐναντιώσεις MWAE  ἀντιώσεις B  |  τὰ MW  τὸν ABE    68–69 μεταμέλλεσθαι MW
μεταμελεῖσθαι ABE    74 πεζικῷ MWA  πεζῷ BE  |  εἰσιν WA  εἰσὶ M  ὦσιν BE  |  καὶ MWB om.
AE

essential for the constitution and permanence of the nation; farming nourishes and strengthens the soldiers, and the military avenges and protects the farmers. The other institutions impress me as second to these. For this reason it is necessary always to take care and to be concerned for their welfare in both respects, so that the soldiers, properly nourished, will do valiant deeds and the farmers, being fairly treated, will cheer them on their way with appropriate prayers.

10. As the enemy approaches and the time for battle is near and, in anticipation of it, you are spending time in the entrenchments, O commander, and you await the enemy there, you must prepare and set aside one or two days' supply of grass or hay or barley for the animals, as we have already prescribed for you in the chapter on marches.[5] Again, if you should wish to go off from there to another campsite and there line up for battle, it is necessary to transport enough grass and hay for one day and to store it in the new entrenchments. It is unlikely that, on that day, the enemy will permit the servants assigned to this work to go out and gather fodder or to graze the horses.

11. But if the enemy get very close, it would be a good idea, as mentioned, for each man to gather forage on the march and stow away what he needs. Most of the time, after they have set up camp, the servants will not be allowed to go out and gather forage, especially if the enemy cavalry outnumbers ours.

12. Is there anything wrong about frequently considering the possibility of secondary fortune, checking out its adverse effects, and taking measures to guard against future contingencies, so that you will not regret it later, especially when it comes to provisions for a few days for the soldiers and the horses, as well as setting up strong fortified camps in suitable locations where there is the water of a river or difficult terrain or some other obstacle able to provide protection for the camp in emergencies?[6]

13. When the infantry camp comes under heavy pressure, park the wagons, as we said, all around the camp site, whether it be for the infantry army or also, if they are present, for the cavalry or a mixed army.[7] Also construct, as I have

5. Here through §11 derives from *Strat.* 7.B.13. Cf. Skirmishing, 15.
6. *Strat.* 7.A.7.
7. Sections 13–20 derive from *Strat.* 12.B.22.

ἔξωθεν τράφον ποιεῖν πλάτους μὲν ποδῶν εʹ ἢ καὶ ἕξ, βάθους δὲ ἑπτὰ ἢ ὀκτώ,
καὶ τὸ χῶμα ἐν τῇ ἐσωτέρᾳ ὄψει τεθῆναι, ἔξωθεν δὲ ταύτης τριβόλους καὶ
λάκκους μικρούς, ἔχοντες πάλους ἐντὸς πεπηγμένους, οὓς δεῖ ἐν γνώσει ποιεῖν
τοῖς τοῦ στρατοῦ διὰ τὸ μή, ἀγνοοῦντας, ὑπ' αὐτῶν βλάπτεσθαι.

80      14. Ἔχειν δὲ καὶ τὴν περίμετρον τοῦ φοσσάτου τέσσαρας μὲν πόρτας | 319
μεγαλωτέρας καὶ δημοσίας, παραπόρτια δὲ μικρὰ πλείονα, καὶ καθ' ἑκάστην
πόρταν ἤγουν ἔξοδον ἔχειν ἄρχοντα, τὸν πλησίον ἀπλικεύοντα πρὸς παραφυλακὴν αὐτῆς. ἔσω δὲ παρ' αὐτὰς τὰς ἁμάξας <τὰς> τῶν ψιλῶν τέντας ἁπλᾶς
παρακειμένας, ἤγουν τῶν τε ἀκοντιστῶν καὶ τῶν τοξοτῶν, καὶ ἀπ' ἐκείνων
85   εὔκαιρον διάστημα ὡς ποδῶν τριακοσίων ἢ υʹ, καὶ τότε τὰς λοιπὰς ταγῆναι
τέντας, ὥστε ἐν ταῖς τῶν ἐχθρῶν τοξείαις μὴ πλήττεσθαι τὰς ἐν τῷ μέσῳ, ἀλλ'
ἐν τῷ εὐκαίρῳ τόπῳ πίπτειν τὰς σαγίττας.

15. Ἐν τῷ μέσῳ δὲ τοῦ φοσσάτου σταυροειδῆ πλατεῖαν εἶναι στράταν τὸ
πλάτος μʹ ἢ νʹ ποδῶν, καὶ ἔνθεν κἀκεῖθεν παρακεῖσθαι αὐτῇ τὰς τέντας ῥυμο-
90   ειδῶς κατ' ὄρδινον, ἐχούσας αὐτὰς ὀλίγον ἀπ' ἀλλήλων διάστημα.

16. Καὶ ἕκαστον τουρμάρχην μέσον τῶν ὑπ' αὐτὸν ἀπλικεύειν, σὲ δέ, τὸν
στρατηγόν, εἰς ἓν μέρος καὶ μὴ ἐν τῷ μέσῳ τῆς πλατείας, ἵνα μὴ καὶ τῇ μέσῃ
ἐμποδίζῃς πρὸς πάροδον καὶ ὑπὸ τῶν παρερχομένων ὀχλεῖσθαι, τοὺς δὲ καβαλλαρίους, ἐὰν γένηται καιρὸς εἰσελθεῖν, ἐν τῷ μέσῳ τοῦ φοσσάτου ἀπλικεύειν
95   καὶ μὴ ἐν τοῖς ἄκροις.

17. Τοὺς δὲ χρησιμωτέρους τῶν κομήτων μετὰ τῶν ὑπ' αὐτοὺς ταγμάτων εἰς
τὰς πόρτας τοῦ φοσσάτου ἀφορίζεσθαι, ὥστε μετὰ τὰς ἑσπερινὰς μίσσας μηδένα θαρρεῖν μέχρι τοῦ δεδομένου σημείου παρὰ γνώμην τοῦ στρατηγοῦ αὐτῶν

---

76 scr. mg. περὶ τάφρου W | πλάτους MW πλάτος ABE | καὶ ἕξ MBE ἓξ A καὶ ϛʹ W | βάθους
MW βάθος ABE | ὀκτώ MWA ηʹ E καὶ ηʹ B    77 τεθῆναι MW τιθῆναι ABE    78 ἐντὸς MW
ἔσωθεν ABE  79 διὰ τὸ MW ἵνα ABE | ἀγνοοῦντας MWE ἀγνοοῦντες AB
80 τέσσαρας...πόρτας ABE τέσσαρας μὲν παρὰ τὰς M πόρτας (scr. supra lin.) τέσσαρας
παρατὰς W    82 ἤγουν ἔξοδον MW om. ABE    82–83 τὸν...αὐτῆς MW πρὸς παραφυλακὴν
αὐτῆς τὸν πλησίον ἀπλικεύοντα ABE    83 παρ' MW παρὰ ABE | τὰς² Va om. codd. | τέντας
MW τένδας ABE    84 ἤγουν MW om. ABE | τῶν² MW om. ABE    85 τριακοσίων...υʹ M
τριακοσίων ἢ τετρακοσίων A τʹ ἢ υʹ WBE    86 τέντας MW τένδας ABE | ἐν¹ MWA om. BE |
τὰς MW τοὺς ABE    87 τῷ MW τῶ ἀργῶ καὶ ἐν τῷ ABE    88 scr. mg. πῶς ὀφείλει γινεσθαι
τὸ ἄπληκτον W | σταυροειδῆ MWAE σταυροειδῆ καὶ B | στράταν MW ὁδὸν ἔχουσαν ABE
89 μʹ...ποδῶν MW τεσσαράκοντα πόδας ἢ καὶ πεντήκοντα A μʹ πόδας ἢ καὶ νʹ E μʹ ἢ καὶ νʹ
B | τέντας MW τένδας ABE    91 ad τῶν scr. mg. μεσον του ιδίου λαοῦ W | αὐτὸν MWA
αὐτὰ E αὐτὰ νʹ B | δέ MWAE om. B    93 ὀχλεῖσθαι Du ὀχλῆσαι codd.    96 τῶν¹ MWA
τοὺς BE    97 μίσσας MW μίνσας ABE    98 δεδομένου MW διδομένου ABE

written previously, if the ground permits, a trench on the outside. Make it five or six feet wide and seven or eight deep, with the earth thrown up on the inner side. On the outside of the trench put caltrops and small pits with sharp stakes set in them. You must make sure that the troops know their location since, if they do not, they may be injured.

14. Along the perimeter of the camp there should be four really large, public gates and a larger number of small postern gates. The officer who is camped closest to each gate or exit is responsible for guarding it. Inside the line of wagons the simple tents of the light-armed troops, the javelin throwers and the archers, should be pitched. There should be a clear space for a distance of three hundred or four hundred feet from them and then the rest of the tents should be set up. When the enemy start shooting, their arrows will fall in the clear space and not hit the tents in the middle.

15. <Two> broad streets, forty or fifty feet wide, should run through the middle of the camp in the shape of a cross. On both sides of the street the tents should be lined up in rows with a little space between each one.

16. Each tourmarch should camp in the middle of his troops. But you, the commander, should be off to one side, not at the central crossroads, to avoid obstructing the flow of traffic in the middle and to avoid being bothered by troops passing by. If the cavalry have the opportunity to enter the camp, they should pitch their tents in the middle of the camp and not near the edges.

17. The more competent counts, with the units under their command, should be assigned to the gates of the camp, so that from the evening dismissal until the signal is given <in the morning>, nobody shall dare to pass in or out of

εἰσέρχεσθαι ἢ ἐξέρχεσθαι ἐν τῷ φοσσάτῳ. τὰς δὲ νυκτερινὰς βίγλας τῶν καβαλ-
100 λαρίων ἔσωθεν ὄντων ἀσφαλῶς γίνεσθαι.

18. Ἕκαστος δὲ τουρμάρχης ἵνα ἴδιον μανδάτωρα ἀφορίσῃ, ὥστε εἶναι εἰς
τὴν κόρτην τοῦ στρατηγοῦ προσεδρεύοντα. ὁμοίως δὲ καὶ τοὺς δρουγγαρίους
καὶ κόμητας εἰς τὴν τένταν τοῦ τουρμάρχου, ἵνα διὰ τούτων συντόμως γινώσκουσι πάντες τὰ ἐντελλόμενα.

105 19. Ἔχειν δέ σε, ὦ στρατηγέ, περὶ ἑαυτὸν βουκινάτωρας καὶ μικρῶν βουκίνων καὶ μεγάλων. καὶ τοῦ εἰθισμένου βουκίνου σαλπίζοντος περὶ ἑσπέραν
παύεσθαι τῶν πόνων καὶ δειπνοῦντας ψάλλειν τὸν τρισάγιον ὕμνον.

20. Ἀφορίζεσθαι δὲ καί τινας ἰδικούς σου ἀνθρώπους πιστοὺς ἵνα καταμαν-
θάνωσι τὰς βίγλας καὶ πᾶσι παραγγέλλωσι σιωπὴν ἔχειν, ὥστε ἐξ ὀνόματος μὴ
110 θαρρεῖν μετὰ κραυγῆς καλεῖν τὸν ἑταῖρον αὐτοῦ. πολλὰ γὰρ τὰ ἐκ τῆς σιωπῆς
ἀγαθὰ καὶ ὅτι πολλάκις κατάσκοποι πολεμίων ἐκ τούτου τοῦ τρόπου ἐν τῷ
στρατοπέδῳ λανθάνοντες ἐφω|ράθησαν καὶ ἐκρατήθησαν, ὥσπερ καὶ ἐκ τῆς    319ᵛ
κραυγῆς πολλὰ τὰ συμβαίνοντα βλαβερά. κωλύειν δὲ καὶ τὰς ὀρχήσεις καὶ
μάλιστα τὰς ἑσπερινὰς καὶ ἄλλο εἴ τι παίγνιον, ὡς μὴ μόνον ἀκόσμους καὶ
115 θορυβώδεις ποιοῦντα ἀταξίας, ἀλλὰ καὶ κόπους ἀνωφελεῖς παρέχοντα.

21. Ἐὰν δὲ μέλλῃς μεθιστᾶν εἰς ἕτερον τόπον ἀπὸ ἀπλίκτου τὸ στράτευμα
καὶ βούλει λαθεῖν τοὺς πολεμίους, ἢ τόπους ὀχυροὺς προκαταλαβέσθαι προ-
αιρῆσαι ἢ τοὺς μὴ ὄντας τοιούτους φεύγῃς διά τινας ἐκ τῶν πολεμίων βλάβας.
<εἰ> καὶ οὐ βούλει ἐλθεῖν εἰς ἀνάγκην τοῦ μάχεσθαι, πυρὰ πολλὰ καύσας
120 ἀναχώρει. βλέποντες γὰρ οἱ πολέμιοι τὰ φῶτα, δόξουσιν ἔτι ἐν τῷ ἀπλίκτῳ σε
μένειν, καὶ ἐκτελέσεις σου τὸ βούλημα. τοῦτο δὲ καὶ Νικηφόρον ἴσμεν, τὸν
ἡμέτερον στρατηγόν, πεποιηκέναι, ὅτε κατὰ Συρίας ἀπεστάλη παρ' ἡμῶν μετὰ
δυνάμεως ἱκανῆς, πολλήν τε ποιησάμενος λεηλασίαν καὶ οὕτω μετατεθεὶς ἐν

---

107 cant. ἅγιος ὁ Θεός, ἅγιος ἴσχυρος, ἅγιος ἀθάνατος ἐλέησον ἡμᾶς.

103 τένταν MW τένδαν ABE    103–104 γινώσκουσι MBE γινώσκωσι WA    105 ἑαυτὸν
MW σεαυτὸν ABE    106 εἰθισμένου MWA ἐθισμένου BE    109 παραγγέλλωσι ABE
παραγγέλλουσι MW | ἔχειν MWA ἄγειν BE    110 τὰ MWA om. BE    115 θορυβώδεις
WABE θορυβοείδεις M | ποιοῦντα AE ποιοῦντας MW ποιοῦνται B | κόπους MWA σκόπους
BE | παρέχοντα MABE παρέχοντας W    116 μεθιστᾶν…στράτευμα MW ἀπὸ ἀπλήκτον εἰς
ἕτερον τόπον τὸ στράτευμα μεθιστᾶν ABE    117 προκαταλαβέσθαι MW προκαταλαβεῖν
ABE    117–118 προαιρῆσαι MW σπουδάζῃς ABE    118 μὴ ABE om. MW | ὄντας
τοιούτους MW trsp. ABE    119 εἰ Va om. codd. | ἐλθεῖν MW om. ABE | εἰς…τοῦ MW ἐξ
ἀναγκαίου ABE | πυρὰ πολλὰ MW πυρκαιὰς πολλὰς ABE | καύσας MWE ἄψας AB
121 ἴσμεν MW οἴδαμεν ABE    123 τε MWA δὲ BE | λεηλασίαν MW πραῖδαν καὶ ἀφανισμὸν
ABE | μετατεθεὶς MWAB μετατιθεὶς E

the camp without the commander's permission. When the cavalry are safely inside, night patrols are <sent out>.

18. Each tourmarch should assign his own herald to stay in attendance at the pavilion of the general and, in like manner, the droungarioi and the counts should have someone at the tent of the tourmarch. These will expedite the transmission of orders for everyone.

19. Trumpeters, playing both large and small trumpets, should be on duty with you, O general.[8] The customary trumpet should sound in the evening; work should cease and, after supper, the men should chant the Trisagion hymn.[9]

20. Detail some of your own trusted men to inspect the sentries and to proclaim that all should observe silence. Nobody should dare even to shout out the name of his comrade. There are many advantages to keeping silence. Our observance of this has frequently led to the detection and capture of enemy spies lurking in the camp. Likewise, shouting can lead to a great deal of damage. Forbid dancing, especially in the evening, or any other frivolity.[10] Not only are they disorderly, annoying, and destructive of discipline, but they are a waste of energy for the soldiers.

21. If you intend to transfer the army from the camp to another location and you wish to do so without the enemy finding out about it or if you choose to occupy strong points beforehand or if you wish to abandon such places because of damage inflicted by the enemy and if you do not want to be forced into offering battle, light many fires and then withdraw. When the enemy see the lights, they will believe that you are still inside the camp, and you will be able to carry out your plan. We recall that our general, Nikephoros, did just this when he was sent by us to Syria with a fairly large force.[11] His troops severely ravaged <the country> and then moved into the middle of the enemy's land. While his

---

8. Cf. Const. 7, n. 10.

9. "Holy God, Holy Strong One, Holy Immortal One, have mercy on us."

10. Cf. *Strat.* 12.B.22.41–43. While the dancing referred to here was undoubtedly wild, frivolous and, quite possibly, lewd, a more disciplined form of dancing was allowed and even encouraged: see Leo the Deacon, 7.9 (Talbot and Sullivan trans. p. 39). Cf. E. Wheeler, "Hoplomachia and Greek Dances in Arms," *GRBS* 23 (1982): 223–233.

11. The campaign took place about the year 900. This Nikephoros Phokas was the grandfather of the later emperor of the same name. See Skirmishing, 20.

μέση τῇ πολεμίᾳ, τῶν ἐχθρῶν αὐτοῦ που συνηγμένων, οὓς Ἀπουλφέρ, ὁ εὐ-
125 νοῦχος, ὁ τῶν Σαρακηνῶν στρατηγός, ἐπεφέρετο ἤγουν τῶν βαρβαρικῶν
δυνάμεων τήν τε αἰχμαλωσίαν τὴν βαρβαρικὴν καὶ πᾶσαν τὴν ἄλλην πραῖδαν
ἣν εἶχεν ἀβλαβῶς διεσώσατο λεηλατήσας τὴν πολεμίαν.

22. Κατὰ δὲ τὴν Βουλγάρων ἐκστρατείαν καὶ ἕτερον αὐτῷ ἐπενοήθη πρὸς
φυλακὴν ἀπλίκτου χρήσιμον, ὅπερ χρὴ μὴ λήθῃ παραπεμφθῆναι, ὁμοῦ τε γὰρ
130 ἐλαφρὸν εἰς βασταγὴν καὶ ἀναγκαῖον εἰς φυλακὴν ἐγνωρίσθη. ἦν δὲ τοιοῦτον·
κανόνια δύο σύμμετρα λαβὼν ξύλινα ἀνὰ τριῶν που σπιθαμῶν ἢ ὀλίγῳ πλέον
λαβδαραίαν συνέμιξεν, ἕτερον δὲ κανόνιον ὁμοίως, ἔχον σπιθαμὰς πέντε ἢ καὶ
ἕξ, τάξιν μεναύλου ἐν τῇ συμμίξει τοῦ δισκελίου ἐπιθεὶς τρισκέλιον ἐποίησεν,
ἱστάμενον ἰσχυρῶς διὰ τῆς ὑπ' ἀλλήλων τῶν σκελῶν συγκροτήσεως. περὶ δὲ τὸ
135 ἄκρον τοῦ οἷον μεναύλου ξιφάριον μέγα καὶ ἀδρὸν ἐνέβαλεν προκύπτον τοῦ
τρισκελίου, ὡς εἴρηται, σπιθαμὰς δύο ἢ μικρῷ πλέον, καὶ οὕτω τοὺς ξυλίνους
ἐκείνους τριβόλους ὅτε ἐβούλετο συστέλλων, ὅτε ἐβούλετο πάλιν συνίστα, καὶ
εἰς ὀχύρωμα εἶχεν, ὁμοῦ καὶ ὅπλα ἐν ταῖς ἀναγκαίαις χρείαις | τοῦ ἀπλίκτου 320
κατὰ τῶν δυναμένων ἐπέρχεσθαι καβαλλαρίων τῇ τῶν δυνάμεων ἡμῶν τάξει,
140 τιτρωσκομένων ἐν ταῖς προσβολαῖς ὑπὸ τοῦ οἷον χάρακος, εὐκόλως καὶ ἐπαιρό-
μενον καὶ βασταζόμενον καὶ πηγνύμενον, καὶ ὅτε πολλάκις ὀρύγματα οὐκ
ἐγένετο ἕτοιμα, εἶχον ταῦτα εἰς ἀσφάλειαν.

23. Ὅτ' ἂν δὲ μέλλῃς μετὰ ἀδείας κινεῖν ἀπὸ τοῦ ἀπλίκτου, δέον δίδοσθαι
μανδάτα ἀπὸ ἑσπέρας καὶ πάλιν εἰς τὸ αὖγος κατὰ αὐτὴν τὴν ἡμέραν τοῦ
145 κινήματος τὰ βούκινα τρισσάκις σημαίνειν καὶ τότε κινεῖν· καὶ κατὰ τάξιν

---

143–230 Strat., 12.B.22.

---

125–126 ἤγουν…δυνάμεων MW om. ABE   126 τε MWA τε γὰρ BE   127 λεηλατήσας
MW ἀφανίσας ABE   128 βουλγάρων MWA βουλγαρίων BE   131 κανόνια δύο MW trsp.
ABE | σύμμετρα λαβὼν MWA λαβὼν σύμμετρον BE | ἀνὰ ABE om. MW | τριῶν…σπιθαμῶν
MW τριῶν ἔχοντα σπιθαμῶν A τρεῖς ἔχοντα σπιθαμὰς BE | ὀλίγῳ MW καὶ ABE
132 λαβδαραίαν MWA λαβδαρέαν B λαμδαρέαν E | πέντε MWA ε' BE   133 ἕξ MWA ϛ' BE
| τάξιν μεναύλου MW ὥσπερ μεναύλον ABE | δισκελίου MW δισκελίου ἐκείνου A δικελλίου
ἐκείνου BE | τρισκέλιον MWA τρισκέλλιον BE   134 σκελῶν MWAE σκελλῶν B
134–135 τὸ ἄκρον MW τοῦ ἄκρου ἐκείνου ABE   135 μεναύλου MW μεναύλου ὄντος ABE
| ἀδρὸν Va ἀδρὸν MW παχὺ ABE   136 δύο MWA β' BE | ἢ…πλέον MW om. ABE | οὕτω
MW οὕτως ABE   137 συστέλλων MW συνέστελλέ τε καὶ AB συνέστελλε καὶ E
138 ἀπλίκτου M ἀπλήκτου ABE ἀπλήτου W   139 δυναμένων MW βουλομένων ABE | τῇ…
τάξει MW om. ABE   140 χάρακος MW χάρακος τοῦτο δὲ ABE   141 καὶ[3] MW om. ABE
142 ἐγένετο MW ἐγίνετο ABE | εἶχον ταῦτα MW ταῦτα εἶχεν ABE   144 μανδάτα MW τὰ
παραγγέλματα ABE | πάλιν MW om. ABE | αὐτὴν τὴν MW trsp. ABE   145 τρισσάκις
σημαίνειν MW πρῶτον λαλεῖν ABE

adversaries, commanded by Apoulfer,[12] the eunuch general of the Saracens, that is, of the barbarian forces, were gathering together, he held on securely to the barbarian prisoners and all the other booty that he had taken after plundering enemy territory.

22. At the time of the Bulgarian expedition he invented another helpful device for defending the camp that should not lapse into forgetfulness. It is at once light to transport and clearly providing necessary protection. It was like this.[13] He took two lengths of wood of equal size, about three spithamai or a little more,[14] and joined them together to form a lambda. In like manner he then took another length of wood, of five or even six spithamai, and like a menaulon he placed it on the joint of the two-legged device and made it into a three-legged one, which got its strength from the legs being tightly bound to one another. On the tip of the menaulon-like pole he fixed a large and broad sword blade that extended out beyond the three-legged stand, as was reported, two spithamai or a little more. And so he set up those wooden caltrops when he wished and again took them down when he wished, using them for defense. At the same time, they could be used as weapons when the camp came under intense pressure from the <enemy> cavalry. As they advanced to attack the line of our forces, they would be wounded in charging against such a palisade. It could be easily taken up, transported, and set up again. When trenches could not often be gotten ready, these provided security.

23. Whenever you intend to move from the camp in safety, you must give the orders the evening before.[15] Then at dawn on the day designated for moving, the bugles should sound three times to begin the march. The officers march out

---

12. See below, Const. 17 §65.

13. This expedition took place ca. 894. See Skylitzes, *Leon.Phil.*, 12. On the three-legged device see E. McGeer, "Tradition and Reality in the Taktika of Nikephoros Ouranos," *DOP* 45 (1991): 129–140.

14. Ca. 70 cm.

15. Sections 23–40 derive from *Strat.* 12.B.22.

ἐξέρχεσθαι τοὺς ἄρχοντας καὶ πρότερον μὲν τοὺς ὁπλίτας, εἶτα τὰς ἁμάξας, ἐάν
εἰσι, καὶ εἴ τι ἕτερον ἐπιφερόμενον εἰς ὑπηρεσίαν τοῦ στρατοῦ.

24. Ἡ δὲ τῶν τριβόλων χρῆσις ἀναγκαία ἐστὶν ἐν τοῖς ἀπλίκτοις. ἐὰν γὰρ ἢ
πετρώδης ὁ τόπος εὑρεθῇ ἢ μὴ δυνηθῶσιν ὀρύξαι ἢ βραδεία ἡ ὥρα γένηται, τὴν
150 αὐτὴν τῷ στρατῷ παρέχουσι χρείαν ἐν τῇ στρατοπεδείᾳ αἱ τρίβολοι πρεπόντως
ἀποτιθέμεναι ἣν καὶ τὸ ὄρυγμα παρέχει.

25. Οἴδαμεν δὲ ὅτι διαφόρους θέσεις καὶ σχήματα φοσσάτων οἱ ἀρχαῖοι
παραδεδώκασιν ἐν τῇ στρατοπεδείᾳ· ἐπαινετὴ δὲ ἡ παραμήκης τετράγωνος ὡς
εὔτακτος καὶ ἀναγκαία.

155 26. Εἰς δὲ ἐπίδειξιν στρατοῦ καὶ φαντασίαν μᾶλλον τὰ πλάγια καὶ ἐπὶ ὕψος
ἄπλικτα πλείονα τὸν ἐν αὐτοῖς στρατὸν παρὰ τοὺς ἴσους ἢ ἐγκειμένους τόπους
παραδείκνυσιν. ἐὰν οὖν πρὸς ἐπίδειξιν χρεία γένηται, τοὺς πλαγίους δεῖ ἐπιλέγεσθαι τόπους, ἐὰν μάλιστα καὶ τὰ ἐπιτήδεια ἔχωσι τῆς ἀναγκαιοτέρας χρείας.

27. Ἀνόσους δέ, ὡς εἴρηται, ἐπιλέγεσθαι τόπους εἰς ἄπλικτα καὶ μὴ χρόνον
160 πολὺν ἐνδιατρίβειν ἐν ἑνὶ χωρίῳ, εἰ μὴ ἄρα διὰ τοὺς ἀέρας τοὺς καθαροὺς καὶ τὰ
ἐπιτήδεια χρειῶδές ἐστιν καὶ οὐ κατεπείγει τις ἀνάγκη.

28. Ἀλλὰ καὶ τὰς φυσικὰς ἀναγκαίας χρείας τῶν ἀνθρώπων, ὡς εἴρηται, μὴ
γίνεσθαι ἔσωθεν τοῦ φοσσάτου, ἀλλ᾽ ἔξωθεν, διὰ τὴν δυσωδίαν, καὶ μάλιστα ἐὰν
ἐπιμένῃ διά τινα χρόνον τὸ φοσσάτον ἐν ἑνὶ τόπῳ.

165 29. Ἐν δὲ τοῖς ἀναγκαίοις καιροῖς βραχὺν μὲν ἤτοι μικρὸν ὄντα τὸν ποταμὸν
ἐν μέσῳ δεῖ περιλαμβάνειν τοῦ χάρακος τοῦ φοσσάτου ἵνα ἐστὶν εὔβατος τοῖς
τοῦ στρατοῦ. ἐὰν δὲ τραχύς ἐστι καὶ μέγας, ἐκ πλαγίου αὐτὸν ποιεῖν σε χρὴ διὰ
τὸ εἰς ὀχύ|ρωμα γενέσθαι τοῦ στρατοῦ. ποταμοῦ δὲ παρατρέχοντος συμμέτρου    320ᵛ
οὐ δέον τοὺς ἵππους ἐξάγειν εἰς ποτὸν κατὰ τὸ ἄνωθεν μέρος, ἵνα μὴ τῇ κινήσει

150 ad στρατῷ des. W

146 ἐξέρχεσθαι MWA ἔρχεσθαι BE | ἐάν MWA εἴπερ BE    149 πετρώδης...εὑρεθῇ MW ὁ
τόπος εὑρεθῇ πετρώδης ABE    150 χρείαν...τῇ M om. ABE | στρατοπεδείᾳ M
στρατοπεδείαν ABE    151 ἀποτιθέμεναι ABE ἀποτιθέμενοι M    152 διαφόρους M διάφορα
ABE | θέσεις καὶ M om. ABE    153 ἢ MA om. BE    156 στρατὸν M στρατὸν
παραδεικνύουσιν ABE    157 παραδείκνυσιν M om. ABE | δεῖ MAB δὲ E    159 δέ M δὲ χρή
AE χρή B | ὡς εἴρηται M om. ABE | τόπους M τόπους ὡς εἴρηται ABE | καὶ MA om. BE
160 ἐνδιατρίβειν...χωρίῳ M ἐν ἑνὶ χωρίῳ διατρίβειν (ἀδιατρίβειν B) ABE | ἄρα M πολλάκις
ABE | τὰ MAB om. E    161 ἐστιν M ἐστὶ ABE    162 φυσικὰς MB φυσικὰς καὶ AE | ὡς
εἴρηται M om. ABE    163 ἔσωθεν...φοσσάτου ME ἔσω τοῦ φοσσάτου A τοῦ φοσσάτου ἔσω
B    164 χρόνον De χρείαν codd.    165 ἐν...καιροῖς MAB om. E    165–167 βραχὺν...
στρατοῦ M ἐὰν (εἰ BE) μικρός ἐστιν ὁ ποταμὸς ἐν ᾧ μέλλει ἀπληκεύειν χρὴ μέσον αὐτὸν τοῦ
ἀπλήκτου περιλαμβάνειν ABE    167 καὶ MA ἢ BE | σε χρὴ M om. ABE    169 τούς...
ἐξάγειν M trsp. ABE | ἄνωθεν MA ἔσωθεν BE

in order, the heavy-armed infantry first, followed by the wagons if they are present and whatever else might be carried for the service of the army.

24. The employment of caltrops is essential in camping. For if the ground is rocky and impossible to dig or if it is late <in the day>, caltrops properly scattered about provide the same protection to the army on campaign as do entrenchments.

25. We realize that ancient authorities have described various shapes for setting up an expeditionary camp, but we prefer the four-sided, oblong form as basic and making for good order.

26. Camps situated on a broad front and on high ground give the army encamped there a more impressive appearance than those on level or sloping ground. If, therefore, you feel the need to make an impression, you must select sites with a broad front, especially if they have the basic supplies we really need.

27. As mentioned, choose healthy places for camp and do not stay too long in one spot, unless the salubrious air and the availability of supplies are more advantageous and there is no critical pressure.

28. As mentioned, the necessary physical needs of the men should not be taken care of inside the camp but outside, because of the disagreeable odor, especially if the army needs to remain in one place for some time.

29. In critical situations you must choose a site with a small or slow-flowing river in the middle of the army's entrenchment, where it is easily crossed by the soldiers. But if it is large and swift you must keep it on the flank, the better to protect the army. If a good-sized river is flowing <there> the horses must not be watered above the camp. Their trampling around will disturb the water and

170 τῶν ποδῶν ταράσσοντες τὸ ὕδωρ θολερὸν αὐτὸ καὶ ἄχρηστον ποιήσωσιν, ἀλλὰ
κάτωθεν μᾶλλον. ἐὰν δὲ ὀλίγος ἐστὶν ὁ ποταμός, διὰ ἀγγείων αὐτοὺς δέον
ποτίζειν καὶ μὴ ἐπαφιέναι τοὺς ἵππους εἰς τὸ ταράσσειν αὐτόν.

30. Πλησίον δὲ λόφου, εἰς ὃν δύνανται οἱ ἐχθροὶ ἀναβῆναι, τὸ ἄπλικτον μὴ
ποιοῦ, μήπως ἐκεῖθεν τοὺς ἐν τῷ στρατοπέδῳ κατατοξεύσωσιν εὐκόλως.

175 31. Ἐὰν δὲ οὐκ εἰσὶν ἐγγὺς οἱ πολέμιοι ἀλλὰ μακρὰν ἀπὸ ἱκανῶν ἡμερῶν
ὁδοῦ, μὴ ἐπιτήδευε πλησίον ὕδατος τὰ ἄπλικτα ποιεῖν, καὶ μάλιστα τῶν καβαλλαρίων, ἵνα μὴ καὶ τὰ ἄλογα καὶ οἱ ἄνδρες ἐν συνηθείᾳ τῆς πολυποσίας γενόμενοι ἐν καιρῷ λείψεως, ὡς εἰκός, ὕδατος, ὅτε δεῖ καρτερεῖν, μὴ φέροντες ὀλιγω-
ρῶσιν.

180 32. Οὐδὲ τοὺς πεζοὺς μετὰ τῶν καβαλλαρίων δεῖ ἀπλικεύειν, πρὶν ἢ τοὺς
ἐχθροὺς ἐγγίσαι, ἐν τῷ φοσσάτῳ, ἀλλ᾽ ἔξωθεν μὲν πλησίον δὲ τοῦ φοσσάτου,
ἵνα μηδὲ στενοχωροῦνται μηδὲ εὐαρίθμητοι φαίνωνται τοῖς κατασκόποις.
δοκίμαζε δὲ πρὸ ὀλίγων ἡμερῶν εἰς πόσον διάστημα χωροῦνται καὶ πῶς
μέλλουσιν ἀπλικεύειν, ἐὰν γένηται αὐτοῖς καιρὸς εἰσελθεῖν μετὰ τῶν
185 καβαλλαρίων, ἐὰν δὲ οἱ ἐχθροὶ ἐγγίζωσιν, ἵνα συνάπτωνται οἱ καβαλλάριοι τοῖς
πεζοῖς καὶ ἐν τῷ ἅμα ἀπλικεύουσιν ἐν τοῖς τεταγμένοις τόποις.

33. Ἐν δὲ τῷ τοῦ πολέμου καιρῷ δέον σε εἰς ὀχυροὺς τόπους τὰ ἄπλικτα
ἐπινοεῖν καὶ φροντίζειν τῶν ἐπιτηδείων, μὴ μόνον, ὡς εἴρηται, τῆς τῶν ἀνθρώπων ἀποτροφῆς ὀλίγων ἡμερῶν, ἀλλ᾽ εἰ δυνατόν, καὶ τῶν ἀλόγων διὰ τὸ ἄδηλον
190 τοῦ πολέμου· καὶ ἐπιμελεῖσθαι καὶ διασκοπεῖν ἵνα διὰ πάντων δύνασαι τὸ ὕδωρ
ἐκδικεῖν. ἐν καιρῷ γὰρ καὶ τοὺς πολεμίους ἕξεις δεομένους. καὶ ἐὰν μέν ἐστι
κάμπος ἐν ᾧ ἡ συμβολὴ τοῦ πολέμου μέλλει γίνεσθαι, σπουδάζειν μὲν ἔχειν
πάντως εἰς τὰ ὀπίσω ἢ ποταμὸν ἢ λίμνην ἢ ἕτερον τοιοῦτον ὀχύρωμα.

174 ad ἐκεῖθεν de novo inc. W

170 θολερὸν Μ θολὸν ABE   171 ἐὰν Μ εἰ ABE   172 αὐτόν ΒΕ αὐτὸ ΜΑ   173 λόφου Μ
βουνοῦ ABE   174 ἐκεῖθεν MW ἐκεῖθεν εὐκόλως ABE | εὐκόλως MW om. ABE   175 ἐὰν
MWA εἰ ΒΕ | ἱκανῶν ἡμερῶν MW trsp. ABE   176 ὁδοῦ MW om. ABE   177 ἄνδρες MW
ἄνθρωποι ABE   178 ὡς εἰκός MW om. ABE   180–181 πρὶν…ἐγγίσαι MW πρὸ τοῦ
πλησιάσαι τοὺς ἐχθροὺς ABE   182 στενοχωροῦνται MW στενοχωρῶνται ABE |
εὐαρίθμητοι MW ὀλίγοι ABE   184 ἀπλικεύειν ΒΕ ἀπλικεύουσιν MW ἀπληκεύωσιν Α
185 ἐγγίζωσιν MW πλησιάζωσιν ABE   186 ἀπλικεύουσιν MW ἀπλικεύωσιν Α
ἀπληκεύουσιν ΒΕ   189 ἀποτροφῆς MWAE ἀποστροφῆς Β   190 διὰ πάντων MW om.
ABE | δύνασαι MWA δύνη ΒΕ   191 γὰρ MW γὰρ πολλάκις ABE | δεομένους MWA
θεομένους ΒΕ | ἐὰν MWA εἰ ΒΕ   192 σπουδάζειν μὲν MW σπούδαζε μᾶλλον ABE
193 ἕτερον MWAE ἕτερόν τι Β

make it muddy and useless. Water them downstream instead. If it is a small river, you must water them from buckets. Do not allow the horses into the stream since they will stir it up.

30. Do not set up camp near a hill that is accessible to the enemy, since they can easily shoot arrows into the camp from there.

31. If the enemy forces are not nearby but still several days' march distant, do not try to set up camp near water, especially because of our cavalry. The animals and the men will get into the habit of drinking a lot of water and, when there is not much of it or it becomes completely unavailable, just when perseverance is needed, they will not endure it when water is in short supply.

32. Before the enemy gets close, the infantry should not camp together with the cavalry within the entrenchments, but outside although close by. In this way they will not feel cramped for space and may not appear to spies as few in number. A few days beforehand, determine how much room they will require and how they plan to set up camp, if the situation calls for them to enter in with the cavalry. When the enemy approach, the cavalry should join together with the infantry and should camp with them in assigned locations.

33. In time of combat you must plan to situate the camp in a strong location and give thought to supplies for a few days, not only, as said, for provisions for the men but, if possible, also for the animals, for the outcome of battle is uncertain. Above all, give special consideration to the water supply and devise ways of defending it. When the situation arises you will find that the enemy too are in need of it. If the crush of battle is about to take place in an open area, always take care to have a river or lake or some other defense of that sort behind you.

34. Καὶ τὸ μὲν φοσσάτον ποιεῖν ὀχυρὸν καὶ στρατὸν ἐν αὐτῷ καταλιμπάνειν
195 τὸν ἀρκοῦντα, ἵνα μὴ ὁ τῶν πολεμίων στρατηγὸς ἐπιβουλεύσῃ τὸν χάρακα καὶ
διαφθείρῃ τοὺς ἔσωθεν, τὰς δὲ ἁμάξας ἐπακολουθεῖν ἐν τάξει.

35. Εἰ δὲ δύσβατός ἐστιν ὁ τόπος καὶ ἀνώμαλος, τὸν μὲν καραγὸν ἤτοι τὰς
ἁμάξας | καὶ τὰ ὅμοια καὶ τὸν λοιπὸν τοῦλδον ἐν τῷ φοσσάτῳ καταλιμπάνειν 321
μετὰ ὀλίγων τῶν ἁμαξελατῶν εἰς παραφυλακήν, τὴν δὲ παράταξιν πλησίον τοῦ
200 φοσσάτου τάσσειν ἐν ἐπιτηδείῳ τόπῳ.

36. Εἰ γάρ εἰσιν οἱ τόποι δύσβατοι καὶ μάλιστα τῶν ἐχθρῶν ὄντων καβαλλαρίων, ἀρκεῖ τῇ παρατάξει εἰς ὀχύρωμα ἡ τοῦ τόπου δυσχέρεια. ἐὰν γὰρ αἱ
ἅμαξαι ἀκολουθῶσιν ἐν τοῖς τοιούτοις τόποις, ἐπωφελεῖς μὲν τοῖς τασσομένοις
οὐκ εἰσίν, ἀλλὰ καὶ δυσμετάθετοι εὑρίσκονται.

205 37. Ἐπινοήσεις δὲ εἰς τοὺς βόας τῶν ἁμαξῶν ἵνα, ὅτ' ἂν ἀκολουθῶσι τῇ
παρατάξει, ἐὰν χρεία γένηται ἄρα καὶ ἀναμεῖναι τὰς ἁμάξας, ὥστε μὴ διαταράσσεσθαι ὑπὸ τοῦ θορύβου τῶν ἐχθρῶν, ὑπὸ τῶν, ὡς εἰκός, βαλλομένων σαγιττῶν
καὶ ἀτακτεῖν καὶ ἐνοχλεῖν τῇ παρατάξει, ἀλλὰ ἢ πεδικλοῦν ταύτας ἢ δεσμεῖν ἵνα,
ὡς εἴρηται, εἰ καί τινες ἐξ αὐτῶν ὑπὸ σαγιττῶν τιτρώσκωνται, μὴ διαταράσσωσι
210 τοὺς πεζούς. διὸ οὐδὲ χρὴ πολὺ ἐγγὺς τάσσεσθαι αὐτάς.

38. Εἰ δέ, ὡς εἰκός, γένηται χρεία ἐνοχλουμένῳ βοηθῆσαι τόπῳ ὑπὸ ἐχθρῶν
ἢ προκαταλαβεῖν ταχύτερον καὶ οὐ φθάζουσιν αἱ ἅμαξαι, ἵνα μὴ βραδύνωσιν αἱ
χρεῖαι, τὸ μὲν ἄλλο τοῦλδον καὶ τὸ φοσσάτον καταλιμπάνειν ἐν ὀχυρῷ τόπῳ,
παραλαμβάνειν δὲ τοὺς πεζοὺς καὶ τὴν δαπάνην αὐτῶν, εἰ τοιαύτη γένηται
215 χρεία, καὶ παρασκευάζειν βαστάζεσθαι ἢ διὰ σαγμαρίων ἢ ἐπὶ τούτῳ ἀφωρισμένων ἵππων καὶ τὰς τριβόλους, καὶ οὕτως ἀπέρχεσθαι μετὰ τοῦ στρατοῦ.

---

195  τὸν¹ MWA om. BE | τῶν πολεμίων MW στρατηγὸς τῶν πολεμίων λαθραίως ἀποστείλας
ABE | τὸν χάρακα MW om. ABE   196 τοὺς ἔσωθεν MW αὐτὸ ABE   197 δύσβατός A
δυνατός MWBE | τὸν Va τὸ MW om. ABE | μὲν...ἤτοι MW om. ABE | τὰς MW τὰς μὲν
ABE   198 καὶ¹...ὅμοια MW om. ABE | τὸν WABE τὸ M   199 ἁμαξελατῶν MWA
ἁμαξηλατῶν ΒΕ   201–202 ὄντων καβαλλαρίων MW trsp. ABE   202 δυσχέρεια MW
τραχυτὴς ABE   203 μὲν MW om. ABE   | τασσομένοις MW παρατασσομένοις ΑΕ
περιτασσομένοις Β   205–209 ἐπινοήσεις...εἴρηται MW ὅτ' ἂν δὲ ἀκολουθῶσι τῇ παρατάξει
αἱ ἅμαξαι ἐὰν χρεία γένηται ἀναμεῖναι τὰς ἁμάξας προσήκει ἢ πεδικλοῦν ἢ δεσμεῖν τὰς (τοὺς
ΒΕ) βόας ὥστε μὴ διαταράσσεσθαι ὑπὸ τοῦ θορύβου τῶν ἐχθρῶν ἢ ὑπὸ τῶν ῥιπτομένων
σαγιτῶν ἵνα ABE   205 τοὺς MWBE τὰς A   211 βοηθῆσαι MW om. ABE | ἐχθρῶν MW
ἐχθρῶν βοηθῆσαι ABE   212 φθάζουσιν MWAE φθέγξουσιν B   212–213 ἵνα...χρεῖαι MW
om. ABE   214 παραλαμβάνειν MWA προλαμβάνειν ΒΕ   214–215 εἰ...χρεία MW om.
ABE   215–216 καὶ...ἵππων MW ἢ διὰ σαγμαρίων βασταζομένην ἢ διὰ ἵππων ἐπὶ τούτω
ἀφωρισμένων ἀναλαμβάνεσθαι δὲ ABE

34. Make a strong camp and leave a good-sized army behind in it, so that the enemy commander will not plan an attack against the entrenchments and destroy those within. Have the wagons follow in order.

35. If the place is difficult and uneven, leave the trains or the wagons and things like that and the rest of the baggage train in the camp, with a few wagon drivers to guard them, and draw up the battle line in a suitable place near the camp.

36. If the ground is difficult, especially when the enemy are mounted, the difficult ground itself is a good protection for our battle formation. If the wagons follow along in such places, not only will they be of no use to the troops in line, but they will be very much in the way.

37. Take care with the oxen pulling the wagons so that, when they follow the battle formation and it becomes necessary for the wagons to come to a halt, they may not be disturbed by the noise made by the enemy and, as is likely, by the arrows flying about, and panic and throw the line into confusion. They should be hobbled or tied so that, as mentioned, even if some of them are wounded by the arrows they may not cause confusion among the infantry. For this reason they should not be lined up close to them.

38. When the need arises, as is likely, to relieve a position under enemy attack or to seize a place quickly before the wagons should arrive, then, in order not to slow things down, leave the rest of the baggage train and the army behind in a strong place. If such a need does arise, take the foot soldiers and their provisions, as well as the caltrops, and arrange for them to be carried either by pack animals or by horses requisitioned for this purpose, and in this way let them march out with the army.

39. Τότε γάρ, ἐὰν καὶ γένηται καιρὸς ἀπλίκτου, τοῦ ὀρύγματος κατὰ τὸ δέον
γινομένου καὶ τῶν τριβόλων ἀποτιθεμένων ἢ οἰκοδομῆς γινομένης ἔσωθεν ἢ
χάρακος ἀπὸ ξύλων πηγνυμένου, τοιαύτην ἀσφάλειαν ἔχει τὸ φοσσάτον, ἣν
220 ὤφειλεν ἔχειν μετὰ τοῦ καραγοῦ. καραγὸν δὲ λέγομεν τὰς ἁμάξας καὶ τὸν δι᾽
αὐτῶν περιτειχισμὸν τοῦ φοσσάτου.

40. Ἐὰν δὲ τύχῃ ὥστε τοὺς καβαλλαρίους πλείονας εἶναι, ὀλίγους δὲ τοὺς
πεζούς, καὶ οὕτως δόξῃ, ὥστε μεῖναι τὸ τοῦλδον ἐν τῷ φοσσάτῳ, μὴ πάντας
τοὺς πεζοὺς ἵστασθαι ἔσωθεν τοῦ φοσσάτου, ἀλλά τινας μὲν ἐν αὐτῷ τῷ φοσ-
225 σάτῳ παραφυλάττειν, τινὰς δὲ ἔξωθεν τῶν πόρτων καὶ τῶν ὀρυγμάτων τοῦ
φοσσάτου ἐν τάξει ἵστασθαι ἵνα, ἐὰν συμβῇ τῶν καβαλλαρίων τροπὴν γενέσθαι
καὶ μὴ σύνεισιν αὐτοῖς πεζοί, αὐτοὶ δεχόμενοι αὐτοὺς | δύναμιν καὶ ἄδειαν    321ᵛ
αὐτοῖς διδόασιν ἢ ἀντιστραφῆναι κατὰ τῶν ἐχθρῶν ἢ εὐτάκτως ἐπέρχεσθαι εἰς
τὸ φοσσάτον καὶ μὴ στενοχωρεῖσθαι εἰς τὰς πόρτας ἐν τῇ εἰσόδῳ καὶ
230 κινδυνεύειν.

41. Τοὺς δὲ ἄρχοντας τῶν ὑπό σε ταγμάτων δέον σοι παραγγέλλειν ἵνα
διάγνωσιν ποιῶσιν ἐν τῷ καιρῷ τοῦ παραχειμαδίου καὶ διὰ τῶν τουρμαρχῶν
δηλοποιεῖν, πόσων ἵππων καὶ ποίων ὅπλων δέονται οἱ ὑπ᾽ αὐτοῖς τεταγμένοι
στρατιῶται, ἵνα ἀναγκαίως παρασκευάζῃς ἐν τῷ δέοντι καιρῷ ταῦτα εὐτρεπί-
235 ζεσθαι καὶ ἐπιλαμβάνεσθαι αὐτὰ τοὺς στρατιώτας. καὶ μάλιστα τῆς τοξείας ἐπι-
μεληθῇς ὥστε, εἰ δυνατόν, καὶ τοὺς ἀστρατεύτους ἐν τοῖς οἴκοις ἐπιφέρεσθαι
τόξα. ἡ γὰρ τούτου τοῦ κεφαλαίου ἀμέλεια πολλὴν βλάβην καὶ ἀπορίαν τῷ
καθόλου Ῥωμαϊκῷ στρατεύματι ἐνεποίησεν, ὥς μοι καὶ ἄνω που εἴρηται. Τοσαῦτα μὲν οὖν καὶ περὶ ἀπλίκτων ἡμῖν εἰρήσθω. ἀκόλουθον δέ ἐστι καὶ περὶ τῆς εἰς

217 καὶ MW om. ABE | δέον MW πρέπον ABE    218 γινομένου MA γενομένου WBE
219 χάρακος...πηγνυμένου MW σταβάρων πηγνυμένων ABE    220 ὤφειλεν ABE ὀφείλει
M ὀφείλειν W | ἔχειν MW ἔχει ABE | τοῦ καραγοῦ MW τε τῶν ἁμαξῶν καὶ τοῦ λοιποῦ
τούλδου ABE    220–221 δι᾽ αὐτῶν Du δ᾽ αὐτὸν codd.    222 τύχῃ MWA τύχης BE | ὥστε
MW om. ABE    223–224 καὶ...πεζοὺς MWAE om. B    223 οὕτως MW om. ABE | τὸ MW
τὸν AE om. B    225 ἔξωθεν ABE ἔμπροσθεν MW    227 σύνεισιν MW εἰσὶ A ὦσι BE |
αὐτοῖς πεζοί MW πεζοὶ μετ᾽ αὐτῶν ABE    228 διδόασιν MW παρέχωσιν ABE | ἀντιστρα-
φῆναι ABE ἀναστραφῆναι MW | ἐπέρχεσθαι MW εἰσελθεῖν ABE    231 σοι MW σε ABE
232 διάγνωσιν ποιῶσιν MW om. ABE    232–233 καὶ...δηλοποιεῖν MW ἐξετάζωσιν ABE
233 αὐτοῖς MW αὐτοὺς AE αὐτοῦ B    234 στρατιῶται MW στρατιῶται καὶ διὰ τῶν
τουρμαχῶν σοι ταῦτα δηλοποιεῖν (δῆλα ποιεῖν Α) ABE | παρασκευάζῃς...ταῦτα MWA om.
BE    234–235 εὐτρεπίζεσθαι MW ἑτοιμάζεσθαι ABE    236 οἴκοις MABE οἴσκοις W
237 τούτου τοῦ MW τοῦ τοιούτου ABE | ἀπορίαν Va ἀμέλειαν MW ἀπώλειαν ABE
238 καθόλου MW om. ABE | μοι...που MW ἀνωτέρω μοι ABE

39. Then, if the time comes to set up camp, the entrenchments are dug as regulated, the caltrops are scattered about, and on the inside a wooden wall or palisade is constructed and fixed firmly. This will provide the camp with as much security as it would have had with the line of wagons. Karagos is the term we use for the wagons and the defensive wall they form around the camp.

40. If it should happen that there is a very large number of cavalry and only a few infantry and the decision is made to keep the baggage train in the camp, do not have all the infantry stay there. Keep some on guard duty in the camp and station others in formation outside the gates and trenches of the camp. Then, if the cavalry should be driven back, without the foot soldiers, these infantry can cover them and give them the ability and freedom to turn around against the enemy or to withdraw in good order into the camp and not risk being crowded together at the entrance around the gates.

41. You must announce to the officers of the units under your command that they must make their enquiries during winter quarters. Have the tourmarchs make clear how many horses and what sort of weapons the soldiers under their command need. In good time, then, you may make the necessary preparations to get them ready and to allow the soldiers to take charge of them. Show particular concern about archery; have those not registered for military service store bows in their houses, if possible. Neglect of this provision has caused the entire Roman army great harm and rendered it ineffective, as I have indicated somewhere above. Therefore, let us conclude all that we have to say about

240  τὸν πόλεμον προπαρασκευῆς—ἤτοι πρὸ μιᾶς ἢ δύο ἡμερῶν, πολλάκις δὲ καὶ
πρὸ πλειόνων, ὡς ἡ χρεία ἀπαιτεῖ ὀφειλούσης γίνεσθαι—ἤδη σοι διατάξεσθαι,
ὅσα τε ποιεῖν δεῖ καὶ ὅσων ἀπέχεσθαι, καὶ ὅσα τοῖς τε ἄρχουσι καὶ τοῖς στρατιώταις παραγγέλλειν σε πρέπον ἐστίν.

---

240 προπαρασκευῆς MW προπαρασκευῆς ἤδη σοι διατάξεσθαι ABE  241 ὡς MW om.
ABE | ἡ χρεία Μ om. WABE | ἀπαιτεῖ MW om. ABE | ὀφειλούσης MW ὀφείλει ABE | ἤδη…
διατάξεσθαι MW om. ABE  242 ὅσα¹ MWAB ὅσαι Ε  243 σε MW om. ABE

camps. The section following this deals with the immediate preparation for war, that is, one or two days before, even more at times, as need dictates what ought to be done. Now let me give orders to you about what must be done, what must be avoided, and what is appropriate to announce to the officers and the soldiers.

# ΠΟΛΕΜΙΚΩΝ ΠΑΡΑΣΚΕΥΩΝ ΔΙΑΤΑΞΙΣ ΙΒ′

## Περὶ προπαρασκευῆς πολέμου

1. Ὅτ᾽ ἂν μὲν οὖν καιρὸς πολέμου ἐλπίζηταί σοι, ὦ στρατηγέ, καὶ τὸν ἤδη προγυμνασθέντα στρατὸν ἐπισυνάξῃς, καλόν ἐστιν, ἵνα μὴ ἄπαντα ὁμοῦ εἰς
5 μίαν ἐκτάττῃς παράταξιν καὶ μάλιστα πολὺν ὄντα καὶ ἱκανόν, καὶ διὰ τοῦ ἀκαίρου πλήθους συγχέσεις τὴν εὐταξίαν τῆς παρατάξεως, ὡς μὴ δύνασθαι διὰ τὸ μέγεθος καὶ πλῆθος καλῶς πείθεσθαι αὐτὴν πρὸς τὰ κελευόμενα. ἀλλὰ τὸν περισσὸν στρατὸν διαμέρισον καὶ ποίησον καὶ δευτέραν παράταξιν.

2. Ὅτ᾽ ἂν γὰρ δημοσίᾳ μέλλῃ καβαλλαρίων μάχη γίνεσθαι καὶ εἰς μίαν μόνην
10 παραταγήν τις τὸν ὅλον στρατὸν κατ᾽ ὄψιν τῶν πολεμίων παρατάσσῃ καὶ μὴ ἀποβλέπῃ πρὸς ἐναντίαν τύχην, μηδὲ μελετᾷ καὶ ἄλλως ἐπιτηδεύειν κατὰ τῶν ἐχθρῶν ἤγουν | καὶ δι᾽ ἑτέρας παρατάξεως, οὗτος, ὡς ἐμοὶ δοκεῖ, ἀνὴρ ἄπειρός 322 ἐστιν καὶ προφανῶς εἰς κίνδυνον ἑαυτὸν ἐπιρρίπτει.

3. Καὶ γὰρ οὐχὶ τὸ πλῆθος τῶν σωμάτων οὐδὲ ἡ ἄτακτος θρασύτης οὐδὲ ἡ
15 ἁπλῆ προσβολὴ τὸν πόλεμον κρίνουσιν ἢ κατορθοῦσιν, ὥς τινες τῶν ἀπείρων νομίζουσιν, ἀλλὰ μετὰ Θεὸν διὰ τέχνης καὶ φρονημάτων στρατηγικῶν μετὰ τῆς προθυμίας τοῦ στρατοῦ κατορθοῦται ὁ πόλεμος.

4. Διὰ μὲν φρονημάτων καὶ τροπαίων, οἷον εἰς καιροὺς ἤγουν ἡμέρας ἢ νυκτὸς ἢ χειμῶνος ἢ εὐδίας ἢ πάλιν εἰς τόπους ἤγουν δι᾽ ἐγκρυμμάτων ἢ στενω-
20 μάτων καὶ δι᾽ αἰφνιδιασμοῦ ἢ διὰ πολλῶν ἄλλων καὶ διαφόρων τρόπων ἵνα ἀπατᾷς τοὺς ἐχθρούς, ὥστε χωρὶς δημοσίου πολέμου κατορθῶσαι τὴν νίκην

---

M W A B E   Va   PG 107:805

---

18–430 Strat., 2.

---

1 πολεμικῶν…ιβ′ MWA om. BE   5 ἐκτάττῃς W τάττῃς M παρατάξεις AB om. E
5–6 ἀκαίρου MWA εὐκαίρου BE   6 συγχέσεις Va συγχέεις W συγχὴς MABE   7 μέγεθος
καὶ MW om. ABE   9 μέλλη…μάχη MW μάχη καβαλλαρίων μέλλη ABE | γίνεσθαι ABE om.
MW   10 τις MW om. ABE | κατ᾽…παρατάσσῃ MW παρατάσσῃ κατὰ πρόσωπον τῶν
πολεμίων ABE   11 μελετᾷ MW μελετᾶν ABE   13 ἐστιν MWA ἐστὶ BE   15–16 τινες…
νομίζουσιν MW νομίζουσι τινὲς τῶν ἀπείρων ABE   16 μετὰ[1] MW καὶ ABE
18–19 ἤγουν…τόπους MWAE om. B   20 δι᾽ MWBE om. A | τρόπων ABE τόπων MW

# PREPARATION FOR WAR, CONSTITUTION XII

## About Advance Preparation for Battle

1. When you await the hour of battle, O general, and you gather your army together, already well drilled, it is wise not to draw them all up, at the same time, into one battle line, particularly if it is a large and combat-ready army. Such an inconvenient multitude utterly destroys the good order of the battle line. Its size and numbers render it unable to obey the commands properly. Divide an excessively large army and make it into two lines.

2. A man who forms the whole army in just one line facing the enemy when a general cavalry engagement is about to take place, and who does not consider the chance of a reverse or does not consider other ways of dealing with the enemy, say, by a second battle line, strikes me as inexperienced and clearly throwing himself into danger.

3. For it is not, as some inexperienced men imagine, the multitude of bodies or undisciplined boldness or simple assault that determine the outcome of battle or bring it to a successful conclusion but, after God, skill and strategic planning.[1] These, together with the enthusiasm of the troops, lead to victory in battle.

4. It is by means of intelligent planning and changes <in strategy>, with regard to time, that is, day or night, stormy or clear weather, and also place, such as narrow passes, and by ambushes, by surprise attacks, and by a great variety of ways to trick the enemy, that you will achieve victory over them without actual

---

1. Cf. prologue §8. Individual sections through 58 derive from *Strat.* 2. See Haldon, *Commentary* for details.

κατ᾽ αὐτῶν. τοῦτο γάρ ἐστι καὶ σωτήριον καὶ πάνυ ἀναγκαῖον, ἵνα διὰ τῆς σῆς συνέσεως καὶ φρονήσεως καὶ ἀνδρίας καὶ τέχνης νικᾷς τοὺς ἐχθρούς.

5. Καὶ ταῦτα μὲν διὰ τῶν φρονημάτων καὶ τῶν στρατηγημάτων· διὰ δὲ τῆς
25  ἐπιστήμης κατορθώσεις τὸν πόλεμον, ἐὰν μετὰ τάξεως τῆς πρεπούσης διαμερίσῃς ἢ συνάψῃς τὸν στρατόν, ποικίλως καὶ ἀσφαλῶς, καὶ παρατάξῃς μετὰ εὐταξίας πολεμικῆς καὶ οὕτως τὰς τῶν πολέμων ἐγχειρήσεις ποιήσεις. καὶ μὴ μόνον
φυλάξῃς σεαυτὸν ἀπὸ τῶν δόλων καὶ τῶν ἐπιτηδευμάτων ἤγουν φρονημάτων
τῶν ἐναντίων σου, ἀλλ᾽ ἵνα μᾶλλον καὶ σὺ κατ᾽ αὐτῶν ἐπιτηδεύῃς καὶ ἀντιστρα-
30  τεύῃ.

6. Ὅθεν καὶ οἱ παλαιοὶ στρατηγοὶ τοῦτο παρετήρησαν ὡς χρήσιμον ἤγουν
τὴν εὐταξίαν. καὶ διὰ τοῦτο εἰς τούρμας καὶ δρούγγους καὶ κόμητας καὶ κεντάρχους καὶ εἰς ἄλλα μέρη πρὸς τὴν χρείαν τὴν παροῦσαν τὸν ὅλον στρατὸν
διαμερίσαντες οὕτως παρετάσσοντο. οὐ γὰρ πρέπον ἐστὶν εἰς μίαν μόνην πα-
35  ράταξιν ἐκτάσσειν τὸν στρατὸν καὶ ἐν μιᾷ μόνῃ ῥοπῇ κρίσιν καὶ διοίκησιν τοσούτων χιλιάδων καβαλλαρίων πιστεύειν, ἀλλὰ καὶ δευτέραν, πολλάκις καὶ τρίτην,
παράταξιν κατόπισθεν διαιρεῖν καὶ οὕτως τὰς τάξεις ποιεῖν, μάλιστα, ὅτ᾽ ἄν σοί
ἐστιν, καθὼς εἴρηται, πλῆθος στρατιᾶς. καὶ γὰρ οὕτως ποιῶν, ὡς ἄν σοι δόξῃ καὶ
ἀπαιτήσῃ ἡ χρεία, ποικίλως καὶ διαφόρως τὰς ἐγχειρήσεις ποιήσεις.

40  7. Πολλὰ γὰρ τὰ ἐναντία λογιζόμεθα γίνεσθαι, ὅτ᾽ ἄν εἰς μίαν παράταξιν |  322ᵛ
τὸν ὅλον στρατόν τις συναγάγῃ καὶ κατεξαίρετον τοὺς κοντάρια ἔχοντας.
συμβαίνει γάρ, πλήθους ὄντος στρατοῦ καὶ εἰς πολὺ διάστημα ἐξ ἀνάγκης
ἐκτεινομένου, εἶτα καὶ ἀνωμάλων τόπων ὑποπιπτόντων, ἄνισον εὑρίσκεσθαι καὶ
ἀπειθῆ τὴν παράταξιν ὡς μακρὰν οὖσαν καὶ μὴ συμφωνεῖν ἀλλήλοις τὰ μέρη
45  αὐτῆς, καὶ διὰ τοῦτο καὶ πρὸ τῆς συμβολῆς διὰ τὴν ἀταξίαν εὐδιάλυτον αὐτὴν
καὶ πεφυρμένην γίνεσθαι.

8. Εἶτα, ἐάν ποτε συμβῇ τοῖς πολεμίοις ἢ ὑπερεκταθῆναι κατὰ τὸ πλάγιον
ἤγουν ἐπὶ κέρας ἐπεξελθεῖν πρὸς κύκλωσιν αἰφνιδίως, λοιπὸν ἡ παράταξις διά

---

22 σῆς MWA om. BE    24 τῶν² MWBE om. A    27 πολέμων Strat. πολεμίων codd. |
ποιήσεις MW ποιεῖσθαι ABE    31 καὶ MW om. ABE    32–33 κεντάρχους MWA κεντάρχας
BE    34 διαμερίσαντες WABE διαμερίσαντας M | παρετάσσοντο MWA παρατάσσονται BE
35 ἐκτάσσειν…στρατὸν MW τὸν στρατὸν παρατάσσειν ABE    36 χιλιάδων MW om. ABE
38 ἐστιν MW ἐστὶ ABE    40 πολλὰ MWAE πολλάκις B | τὰ MW om. ABE    41 τοὺς MW
τὰ ABE    42 πλήθους MW πλῆθος ABE    43 ἐκτεινομένου ABE ἐκτεινομένους MW
45 διὰ²…ἀταξίαν MWA καὶ διαταξίαν B καὶ διὰ ἀταξίαν E    47 τοῖς πολεμίοις MW τοὺς
πολεμίους ABE

fighting. This is absolutely essential for survival. It is by your intelligence, planning, courage, and skill that you will defeat the enemy.

5. So much for intelligent planning and stratagems. It is through practical knowledge that you will be successful against the enemy, that is, provided that, in various ways, you divide up or unite your army securely and in proper order. After you line it up in good military formation, then launch attacks against the enemy. Not only will you protect yourself against the wiles and machinations or plans of the enemy but, rather, you will turn their machinations and stratagems against them.

6. With this in mind, commanders in the past carefully observed the following as beneficial, namely, good order. This is why they organized the entire army into tourmai and droungoi with counts and kentarchs and into other divisions as conditions required, and so drew it up in this fashion. It is a mistake to draw up the army in only one battle line, staking the management, as well as the fate, of tens of thousands of cavalrymen on only one throw. But behind the main battle line form a second, often a third, and draw up your formation in this way, especially when, as was said, you have a large army. When, in your judgment, the situation requires, you can launch a great variety of attacks.

7. To draw up the whole army in one battle line, especially if it includes lancers, is, in our opinion, to invite a host of evils. For it happens that, if it is a large army, it will have to stretch over a great distance, with part of it located on unfavorable terrain. The length of the line will make it uneven and hard to manage. There will be no coordination between its divisions. It will end up in disarray and, even before contact, will be easily broken up and thrown into confusion.

8. If the enemy should happen to extend their own lines by the flank and launch a sudden encircling movement there, then, without support from the

τε τῶν ὀπίσω καὶ τῶν πλαγίων αὐτῆς ἀποροῦσα βοηθείας καὶ μηδενὸς ὑπάρ-
50 χοντος τοῦ συνηγοροῦντος αὐτὴν ἐξ ἀνάγκης πρὸς τελείαν φυγὴν ὁρμήσει.

9. Ἀλλὰ καὶ ἐν αὐτῇ τῇ τοῦ πολέμου συμβολῇ διὰ τὸ μὴ τὸ μῆκος τῆς
παρατάξεως ἐπιβλέπειν τινὰ ἐκ τῶν ὄπισθεν, πολλάκις τινὲς τῶν ταγμάτων μετὰ
καὶ τῶν βάνδων ἀφανῶς λιποτακτοῦσι. καὶ γίνεται καὶ πᾶσι τοῖς λοιποῖς ἀναχωρήσεως πρόφασις καὶ πρᾶγμα ἐλεεινόν, τρεπομένων <δὲ> αὐτῶν οὐδὲ ἀνακοπὴ
55 τῆς φυγῆς οὐδὲ ὑποστροφὴ οὐδεμία γίνεται. οὐδεὶς γὰρ ἀναφαίνεται ὁ μέλλων
ἀνακαλεῖσθαι ἢ ἐπισυνάγειν αὐτοὺς εἰς τροπήν, ὡς εἴρηται, καὶ φυγὴν ὁρμήσαν-
τας.

10. Ἐὰν δὲ τάχα καὶ νομίσουσιν μετὰ ἐπιτυχίας τὸν πόλεμον ποιεῖν οἱ εἰς
μίαν παράταξιν τασσόμενοι καὶ προωθεῖν ἐν τῇ μάχῃ τοὺς πολεμίους, ὅτ’ ἂν
60 διαλυθῇ πάντως ἡ παράταξις ἐν τῇ συμβολῇ τοῦ πολέμου καὶ ποιοῦσι τὴν
δίωξιν ἀτάκτως οἱ διώκοντες, ἐὰν συμβῇ πολλάκις τοὺς φεύγοντας ἀντιστραφῆναι κατὰ τῶν διωκόντων αὐτοὺς ἢ δύναμιν ἄλλην αἰφνιδίως ἀπὸ ἐγκρύμματος
ἀναφανῆναι, ἀνάγκη πᾶσα, οἱ διώκοντες εἰς φυγὴν ὁρμήσουσι μηδένα ἔχοντες,
ὡς εἴρηται, τὸν δυνάμενον ἀπαντῆσαι ἢ ἀποσοβῆσαι τοὺς διὰ τῆς ὑποστροφῆς
65 ἀπροσδοκήτως ἐπερχομένους.

11. Ἓν δὲ μόνον νομίζω προτέρημα ἔχειν τὸ πάντας εἰς μίαν τάσσεσθαι
παράταξιν, τοῦτ’ ἔστι τὸ φαίνεσθαι τοῖς ἐχθροῖς μήκοθεν τελείαν καὶ ἐξωγκω-
μένην τὴν τάξιν. ἀλλὰ καὶ αὐτὸ μέχρι θεωρίας καὶ μόνης ἔχει τὸ κέρδος. ἔχει δὲ
τάχα καὶ ἕτερον προτέρημα, τὸ δύνασθαι διὰ τῆς μιᾶς παρατάξεως καὶ μεγάλης
70 ποιεῖν κύκλωσιν ἀπὸ ἑνὸς | μέρους καὶ ἀποκλείειν τοὺς πολεμίους, ἐὰν ἄρα καὶ   323
τούτῳ μετὰ τοῦ πρέποντος λόγου καὶ τέχνης τις χρήσεται.

12. Τὸ δὲ διπλᾶς ποιεῖν τὰς παρατάξεις ὥστε εἶναι εἰς ὑποβοήθειαν τῆς
πρώτης παρατάξεως τὴν δευτέραν, κατὰ τὸν ἀνθρώπινον λογισμὸν πολλὰ τὰ
ἐξαίρετα καὶ ἀναγκαῖα νομίζομεν συντρέχειν. καὶ πρῶτον μέν, ὅτι οἱ τῆς πρώτης

---

49 αὐτῆς MW om. ABE   50 συνηγοροῦντος MW συνεργοῦντος ABE | αὐτὴν MW αὐτὴ A
om. BE   50–51 ἐξ…ἐν MWA om. BE   51 μὴ τὸ MABE om. W   52 τινὰ…ὄπισθεν ΛBE
om. MW   53 καὶ¹ MW om. ABE | λιποτακτοῦσι MB λιποτακτοῦσιν WAE   54 δὲ Va om.
codd.   56 καὶ MWAE om. B   58 νομίσουσιν MW νομίσουσι ABE   60 ποιοῦσι MW
ποιῶσι ABE   63 πᾶσα MW πάντα A πάντως BE | οἱ διώκοντες W ἀνδιώκοντες M τοὺς
διώκοντες ABE | ὁρμήσουσι M ὁρμήσουσιν W ὁρμῆσαι ABE | ἔχοντες MW ἔχοντας ABE
64 ἀποσοβῆσαι MW ἀποδιῶξαι ABE   65 ἐπερχομένους MWA ἐπερχομένους πολεμίους
ABE   67 τοῦτ’ ἔστι De τοῦτἔστι M τουτέστιν WA τουτέστι BE | καὶ ABE om. MW
68 αὐτὸ MWA αὐτὸ τὸ BE | καὶ² MW om. ABE | μόνης MWAB μόνης μόνης E | ἔχει¹ MWA
ἔχειν BE   71 καὶ MW καὶ τῆς ABE | χρήσεται W χρήσηται M διαπράξηται ABE
73–74 πολλὰ…συντρέχειν MW κατὰ πολλά ἐστιν ὠφελιμώτερον ABE

rear or from the flanks and without anyone coming to its aid, our line will be forced to rush into headlong flight.

9. In actual combat, furthermore, because nobody has a good view of the long battle line from the rear, frequently some men desert from their units or banda unnoticed and provide the rest of the troops with an excuse to retreat. This is truly pitiable. When they do retreat there is no way of turning back or of checking the flight. None of those present, as was said, is able to call them back or get them to turn around after they have rushed into flight.

10. Sometimes troops drawn up in a single line will seem to be pursuing the battle with success and driving the enemy back in the fighting, but in the melee of battle their formation will surely be broken up and they will continue the pursuit in a disorderly manner. If, perchance, the fleeing enemy should happen to turn around against the men pursuing them or if some other force should suddenly appear out of an ambush, then, without any doubt, the pursuers will be forced to take to flight since, as mentioned above, they have nobody in position to ward off or repel those who have turned about unexpectedly and are charging against them.

11. I think that forming all the troops in one battle line has only one advantage, and that is, from a distance the formation will impress the enemy as very large and imposing. But this advantage is theoretical only. It may, perhaps, have another advantage, namely, because there is one large battle line, it is able to circle around from one side and close in on the enemy, presuming that a person can make use of this maneuver with proper reason and skill.

12. We believe that, as far as human reasoning goes, there are many exceptionally compelling reasons that lead to the conclusion that there should be a twofold battle line, the second of which should be for the support of the

75 παρατάξεως ἔχοντες ὄπισθεν κατὰ τοῦ νώτου αὐτῶν τὴν δευτέραν τάξιν φυλάττουσαν αὐτοὺς προθυμοτέρως μάχονται πρὸς τοὺς πολεμίους, ὁμοίως δὲ καὶ τὰ
ἄκρα ἤγουν τὰ δεξιὰ καὶ τὰ ἀριστερὰ τῆς παρατάξεως διὰ τῶν πλαγιοφυλάκων
φυλαττόμενα ἀφόβως πρὸς τοὺς ἔμπροσθεν πολεμοῦσιν. τὸ δὲ πλέον προτέρημα, ὅτι τῆς δευτέρας παρατάξεως ὄπισθεν οὔσης οἱ πολλάκις λιποτακτοῦντες
80 ἐν τῇ πρώτῃ παρατάξει οὐ τρέπονται, ὡς ἔτυχεν, ὑπὸ τῶν ὄπισθεν αὐτῶν ὑπ-
οπτευόμενοι· τοῦτο γὰρ καὶ μεγάλην ὠφέλειαν ποιεῖ τῇ μάχῃ. καὶ ἐν καιρῷ δὲ
τροπῆς, ὡς πολλάκις συμβαίνει τῇ πρώτῃ τάξει, γίνεται ἡ δευτέρα εἰς ἀντίληψιν
καὶ καταφυγήν, ὅθεν πάλιν δυνατὸν αὐτοὺς ἀνακαλεῖσθαι βοηθουμένους ὑπὸ
τῆς δευτέρας τάξεως καὶ κατὰ τῶν ἐπιπεσόντων ἐχθρῶν πάλιν ἀντιστρέφεσθαι.
85   13. Ἀλλὰ καί, ὅτ᾽ ἂν διώκωσι τοὺς ἐχθρούς, οἱ τῆς πρώτης παρατάξεως
ἀσφαλῶς καὶ μετὰ προθυμίας ποιοῦνται τὴν δίωξιν. ἐὰν γὰρ ἀντιστραφῶσιν, ὡς
πολλάκις γίνεται, φεύγοντες οἱ ἐχθροὶ ἢ ἄλλοθέν ποθεν αἰφνιδίως ἐπέλθωσιν
ἐχθροί, γίνεται ἡ δευτέρα τάξις ἀπαντῶσα καὶ συνάγουσα καὶ φυλάττουσα τοὺς
τῆς πρώτης παρατάξεως. ἀλλὰ καί, ὃ μὴ γένηται, ἐὰν συμβῇ τελείαν τροπὴν
90 γενέσθαι τῆς πρώτης τάξεως καὶ οὐ δύνασαι ἀντιστραφῆναι κατὰ τῶν ἐπελθόν-
των αὐτῇ πολεμίων, εὑρίσκεται ἡ δευτέρα τάξις ἑτοίμη καὶ εὐκόλως πολεμεῖ καὶ
καταγωνίζεται τὴν ἐναντίαν δύναμιν, κἂν τάχα παντελῶς τραπῇ ἡ πρώτη παράταξις.
   14. Καὶ γὰρ ἀνάγκη πᾶσα τὴν τάξιν τῶν ἐχθρῶν ἀπὸ τῆς συγκροτήσεως τοῦ
95 πολέμου ἀκατάστατον γενέσθαι καὶ διαλελυμένην, καὶ τῆς ἡμετέρας δευτέρας
τάξεως εὐτάκτως ἱσταμένης καὶ μετὰ καταστάσεως, τῆς δὲ τῶν ἐχθρῶν πεφυρ-
μένης προτερεῖν μᾶλλον τὴν ἡμετέραν καὶ ἐπιδιώκειν τοὺς | διαλύσαντας τὴν    323ᵛ
τάξιν.

---

75 κατὰ…νώτου MW καὶ κατὰ νῶτον ABE    77 τὰ² MWA om. BE    78 πολεμοῦσιν WA
πολεμοῦσι M πολεμῶσι BE    78-79 πλέον προτέρημα MW μεῖζον ABE    80-81 ὑποπτευ-
όμενοι MW ἐπιβλεπόμενοι ABE    81 τοῦτο MW ὅπερ ABE | γὰρ MWB om. AE | ποιεῖ…
μάχῃ MW ἐν τῇ μάχῃ ποιεῖ ABE | καὶ² MW om. ABE    82 πρώτῃ τάξει MWA παρατάξει B
τάξει E | δευτέρα MW δευτέρα τάξις A β′ τάξις BE    84 δευτέρας MWA β′ BE    85 διώκωσι
MABE διώκουσιν W    87 ἐχθροὶ MW om. ABE    88 γίνεται MW εὑρίσκεται ABE | τάξις
MW παράταξις ABE    89-90 ἀλλὰ…τάξεως MWA om. BE    89 ἐὰν συμβῇ ABE om. MW |
τροπὴν MABE τροπὴν εἰ συμβῇ W (alia m.)    90 δύνασαι MA δύναται W (corr. e δύνασαι)
δύνηται BE    91 καὶ¹ MWA om. BE | εὐκόλως MW μετὰ τάξεως ἱσταμένη καὶ εὐκόλως A
μετὰ τάξεως ἱσταμένη BE | πολεμεῖ MW καταπολεμεῖ A καταπολεμεῖ εὐκόλως BE    92 τὴν
ἐναντίαν MW τῶν ἐναντίων ABE    94 ἐχθρῶν De ἐναντίων ἐχθρῶν codd. | συγκροτήσεως
MABE συγκρούσεως W    96 τάξεως MW παρατάξεως ABE    97 προτερεῖν MW ὑπερέχειν
ABE | τὴν ἡμετέραν MWA τῇ ἡμετέρα BE | ἐπιδιώκειν MWAE ἐπιδιώκει B

first. One reason is that the troops in the first battle line will fight more eagerly against the enemy when they have the second line behind protecting their rear. In like manner, with their flanks, that is, the right and left wings of the battle line, protected by the flank guards, they will fearlessly carry on the battle against those in front of them. There is a further advantage: as has often happened, the soldiers in the first line are not likely to turn and run away while the second line is to their rear, for they will be observed by the troops behind them. In combat this can be extremely important. In the event, a fairly frequent one, that the first line turns back, the second is there as a support and a place of refuge. The support provided by the second line makes it possible to rally the troops once again and gets them to turn back against the attacking enemy.

13. Moreover, when they are pursuing the enemy, the men in the first battle line can safely and in good spirits carry out the pursuit. For if, as often happens, the fleeing enemy should turn back or if they should attack unexpectedly from another quarter, then the second line can confront them, join battle, and protect the troops in the first line. But even if—may this not happen—the first line should be completely routed and cannot turn back into action against the enemy attacking it, the second line is standing there ready. It will easily continue the battle and fight vigorously against the enemy forces, even though the first line may have been completely routed.

14. The enemy's formation will most assuredly be broken up and disordered by the crush of battle while our second line is still standing firmly in good order. The enemy line will be thrown into confusion and ours will gain the advantage and turn to pursue the foe, who will have broken up his formation.

15. Ἀλλὰ καὶ τὸ ἀναγκαιότερον παρὰ πάντα, ὅτι οὐ μόνον πρὸς τὰς ἰσομέτ-
100 ρους δυνάμεις ἤγουν τῶν τε ἡμετέρων καὶ τῶν ἐναντίων ἁρμοδία ἐστὶ καὶ
ἀναγκαία, ὡς εἴρηται, ἡ εἰς δύο παρατάξεις διαίρεσις τοῦ στρατοῦ, ἀλλὰ καὶ
πρὸς τὰς ὑπερεχούσας καὶ πλέον τῶν ἡμετέρων οὔσας δυνάμεις.

16. Ἐὰν δέ τις λέγῃ, ὅτι τί ὄφελος; τῆς γὰρ πρώτης τάξεως ταρασσομένης
καὶ τρεπομένης εὐχέρως καὶ ἡ δευτέρα συναπάγεται αὐτῇ καὶ συντρέπεται·
105 ἀλλὰ ἀκουσάτω ὁ τοιοῦτος ὅτι, ἐὰν δύο παρατάξεων, καθὼς εἰρήκαμεν, γινομένων ἐπισφαλὲς τὸ πρᾶγμα γίνεται, τί ἄν τις ἐλπίσει ὅτ᾽ ἂν καὶ μία μόνη ἐστὶ
παράταξις καὶ ταύτῃ τραπεῖσα οὐκ ἔχει ἑτέραν, δι᾽ ἧς βοηθηθῆναι δύναται καὶ
ἀνακληθῆναι; ἐὰν δὲ πάλιν λέγῃ, ὅτι τῆς δυνάμεως πάσης ἤγουν τοῦ στρατοῦ
μεριζομένου εἰς πρώτην καὶ εἰς δευτέραν παράταξιν ἀσθενεστέρα καὶ ἀδυνατω-
110 τέρα ἡ τάξις εὑρίσκεται, κατανοήσει καὶ τοῦτο, ὅτι, ἐὰν μὲν ἡ δύναμις ἐμερίζετο
καὶ ἐχωρίζετο τοῦ πολέμου, καλῶς ἂν τοῦτο ἠπόρει. ἀλλ᾽ ἡμεῖς οὐ τὴν δύναμιν
κελεύομεν μερισθῆναι, ἀλλὰ μόνον τὸ σχῆμα ἀλλαγῆναι. καὶ γάρ, ὃ πρὸ τοῦ
ἀλλαγῆναι τὸ σχῆμα συνέβαινε γενέσθαι, τὸ πᾶσαν τὴν δύναμιν εἰς μίαν παράταξιν τασσομένην μακρὰν καὶ λεπτὴν εὑρίσκεσθαι, τοῦτο ἐν τῇ διπλῇ τάξει
115 εὐπορήσαμεν συμμέτρους τὰς δύο τάξεις ποιήσαντες διὰ τὸ πλησίον ἀλλήλων
εἶναι, οὐ τῆς μάχης χωρίσαντες, ἀλλὰ τὸ σχῆμα ἐναλλάξαντες καὶ τὴν μὲν
ἔμπροσθεν, τὴν δὲ ὄπισθεν τάξαντες καὶ πλέον τὰς παρατάξεις διὰ τὸν προειρη-
μένον τρόπον κατοχυρώσαντες.

17. Διὰ τοῦτο γὰρ εἰς μέρη διάφορα καλῶς ἂν καὶ πρέπον ἐστὶ τὸ τὸν πάντα
120 καβαλλαρικὸν στρατὸν διαμερίζεσθαι, κἄν τε πολύς ἐστι κἄν τε σύμμετρος.
εὔδηλον γὰρ καὶ πρέπον, ἵνα χρεωστῇς, ὦ στρατηγέ, λόγον ποιεῖσθαι καὶ κατάστασιν, ὡς ἐνδέχεται, ὅτ᾽ ἂν μάλιστα καὶ πρὸς ἔθνη πολεμῇς τάξιν ἔχοντα καὶ
τέχνην πολέμου.

100 ἤγουν…ἐναντίων MW om. ABE | ἐστὶ MABE ἐστιν W    101 ὡς εἴρηται MW om. ABE
| ἡ MWA om. BE    103 τί ὄφελος MW οὐδὲν ὄφελος τῆς δευτέρας παρατάξεως ABE |
ταρασσομένης MW πρώτης γὰρ ταρασσομένης (παρατασσομένης BE) παρατάξεως ABE
104 καὶ τρεπομένης MW om. ABE | συναπάγεται…συντρέπεται MW σὺν αὐτῇ τρέπεται
ABE    105 ἀλλὰ MW om. ABE | καθὼς εἰρήκαμεν MW om. ABE    106 γίνεται MWAB
γίνηται Ε | μόνη MWA μόνον BE | ἐστὶ MWA ὑπάρχη BE    107 ταύτῃ Μ αὕτη WABE |
ἑτέραν MWA δευτέραν BE | δύναται MWAE δύνανται Β    109 εἰς¹ MWA om. ΒΕ
112 ἀλλὰ…ἀλλαγῆναι MWAE om. Β    113 συνέβαινε MWBE συνέβαινεν Α
115 εὐπορήσαμεν MWA ἐμπορήσαμεν ΒΕ | δύο MWA β΄ ΒΕ    117–118 τὸν…τρόπον MW
τῶν προειρημένων τρόπων ABE    119 καλῶς…ἐστὶ MW (ἐστιν) πρέπον ἐστὶ καὶ καλὸν ABE
| τὸ…πάντα Μ τὸ πάντα W τὸ πάντα τὸν Α πάντα τὸν ΒΕ    120 ἐστι MABE ἐστιν W
121 εὔδηλον…ποιεῖσθαι MW πρέπον γάρ ἐστι (ἐστιν Α) φροντίδα ποιεῖσθαί σε ὦ στρατηγέ
ABE

15. The most compelling reason of all is that the division of the army into two battle lines, as said, is appropriate and necessary not only against forces equal in numbers, ours and the enemy's, but also against forces greatly superior to ours.

16. If someone were to ask: What is the advantage of this? If the first line is thrown into confusion or driven back, the second will easily be carried along with it and pushed back. Let such a person listen to this. If, as we have said, the situation is precarious with two battle lines in position, what hope can one have when there is only one battle line? When that one is beaten back, there is no other line capable of providing assistance and rallying the first. Again, if someone should say: By dividing up the entire military force into a first and a second line, the battle line will be weaker and less effective. Let that man consider this. If the force had been divided and kept out of combat, this would surely be open to question. However, we are not ordering the force to be divided but are merely changing its formation. Before the formation came to be changed, the entire force was found to be drawn up in one long, thin battle line. We have now arranged this in a double line and made two equal lines to stand close to one another. We have not taken it out of action but have only altered its formation, drawing it up into a forward line and a rear line and further strengthening the lines by the method noted above.

17. For these reasons it would be well and appropriate to divide every cavalry army, whether large or of average strength, into various divisions. For it is obvious and fitting that you, O commander, be obliged to act in accord with the dictates of reason and adapt to circumstances, as best you can, especially when you are waging war against a nation that is disciplined and skillful in combat.

18. Ἐὰν δὲ δύνασαι, μὴ ποιῇς φανερῶς τὸν πόλεμον, ὅτ᾽ ἂν γινώσκῃς ὅτι
125 πλείους σου εἰσὶν οἱ πολέμιοι. καὶ γὰρ πρέπον σοι πρότερον τὴν δύναμιν τῶν
πολεμίων σου ἀναμαθεῖν καὶ οὕτως ποιήσασθαι τὴν συμβολὴν τοῦ πολέμου.

19. Ἐὰν δὲ | ἔχῃς πεζικὸν στρατόν, ποιήσασθαι τούτου τὴν παράταξιν, ὡς 324
μετὰ ταῦτα δηλώσομεν ἐν τῇ περὶ τῶν πεζῶν καὶ τῶν συμμίκτων τοῖς καβαλλαρίοις διατάξει. ἐὰν δὲ μόνοι καβαλλάριοί εἰσιν καὶ πρὸς καβαλλαρίους ὑπό-
130 κειται ὁ πόλεμος, καὶ εἰς τρεῖς καβαλλαρικὰς τάξεις διαμερίσεις τὸν στρατὸν καὶ
τὴν μὲν πρώτην παράταξιν, ἥτις λέγεται πρόμαχος, εἰς τρία ἴσα μέρη ἐκτάξεις,
ἀπὸ τριῶν μοιρῶν ἔχοντες ἑκάστου μέρους ἤγουν ἀπὸ τριῶν δρούγγων ἑκάστης
τούρμας, καὶ ἐν τῷ μέσῳ μέρει τάξεις τὸν ὑποστράτηγόν σου, ἐν δὲ τοῖς ἑτέροις
δυσίν, ἤγουν τῷ δεξιῷ καὶ τῷ ἀριστερῷ, τοὺς τῶν μερῶν ἄρχοντας, μέσους τῶν
135 ὑποτεταγμένων αὐτοῖς ἀρχόντων ἤγουν τῶν μοιράρχων.

20. Ταῦτα δὲ τὰ τρία μέρη συστήσεις ἀπὸ κουρσώρων ἤγουν τῶν εἰς κοῦρσον τεταγμένων στρατιωτῶν, οὓς νῦν λέγουσι προκλάστας, καὶ διφενσώρων
ἤγουν τῶν ὑποδεχομένων τοὺς εἰς τὸ κοῦρσον ἐλαύνοντας καὶ ἐκδικούντων
αὐτούς, ὥστε ἑκάστου μέρους τὸ τρίτον ποσὸν κουρσάτωρας εἶναι, τούτους δὲ
140 εἶναι καὶ τοξότας, τὸ δὲ δίμοιρον, τὸ ἐν μέσῳ τοῦ στρατοῦ, διφένσωρας ἤγουν
ἐκδίκους, τοὺς ὑποδεχομένους τοὺς κουρσάτωρας.

21. Παρατάξεις δὲ ἐν τῇ πρώτῃ τάξει οὕτως· εἰς μὲν τὸ ἀριστερὸν μέρος, εἰς
ὃ μάλιστα καὶ αἱ κυκλώσεις τῶν ἐναντίων εὐκόλως γίνονται, δύο ἢ τρία βάνδα
ἵνα εἰσὶ πλαγιοφύλακες ἱστάμενοι ἴσοι τοῦ αὐτοῦ μέρους, καὶ βάνδον ἓν ἢ δύο
145 βάνδα τοξότας, τοὺς λεγομένους ὑπερκεραστὰς ἤγουν ἑτοίμους ὄντας εἰς
κύκλωσιν τῶν πολεμίων, τούτους στήσεις εἰς τὸ μέρος τὸ δεξιόν. καὶ τὴν μὲν
πρώτην τάξιν οὕτως παρατάξεις.

22. Τὴν δὲ δευτέραν παράταξιν, τὴν λεγομένην βοηθόν, τάξεις ἵνα ἔχῃ τὸ
τρίτον ποσὸν τοῦ παντὸς στρατοῦ, καὶ ταύτην ποιήσεις εἰς τέσσαρα μέρη, ἵνα
150 ὡς ἀπὸ ἑνὸς σαγιττοβόλου διαστήματος κατὰ τὰς πλευρὰς ἀλλήλων περιπα-

---

124 δύνασαι MWA δύνῃ ΒΕ   125 πλείους MW πλείονες ΑΒΕ | σοι MW σοι ἐστὶν Α σοι
ἐστὶ ΒΕ   127 ἐὰν MWAB εἰ Ε   129 εἰσιν WA εἰσι ΜΒΕ   130 τρεῖς MWA τρεῖς τάχα ΒΕ |
καβαλλαρικὰς ΜWΒΕ καβαλλαρικὰς τάχα Α | τάξεις MW om. ΑΒΕ | τὸν στρατὸν MWE τὸ
στράτευμα ΑΒ   134 τῶ¹ MW τῷ τε ΑΒΕ   135 αὐτοῖς ΑΒΕ αὐτοὺς MW | μοιράρχων
MWΒΕ τουρμάρχων Α   137 στρατιωτῶν De στρατευμάτων codd.   138 ἐκδικούντων
MWA διεκδικούντων ΒΕ   139 κουρσάτωρας ΒΕ κουρσάτορας MW κούσωρας ΑΒΕ
143 καὶ ΑΒΕ om. MW   144 εἰσὶ MWA ὦσι ΒΕ | δύο MWA β′ ΒΕ   145 βάνδα MW om.
ΑΒΕ   146 στήσεις MWA στήσει ΒΕ   149 τέσσαρα MWA δ′ ΒΕ   150 ὡς MWA om. ΒΕ |
ἀπὸ...διαστήματος MW ἀπὸ διαστήματος σαγιττοβόλου ἑνὸς ΑΒΕ | τὰς πλευρὰς MW
πλευρὰν ΑΕ πλευρῶν Β   150–151 περιπατοῦσι W περιπατοῦσιν Μ περιπατῶσι ΑΒΕ

18. If you are able, avoid openly engaging in battle when you know that the enemy force is more numerous than yours. Be sure to ascertain the strength of the enemy before engaging them in pitched battle.

19. If you have an army made up of infantry, you will line them up for battle as we will subsequently explain in the constitution about infantry and mixed formations with cavalry. If they consist only of cavalry and they are to do battle against other cavalry, divide your mounted forces into three lines. Draw up the first line, called promachos, into three equal divisions, with each division having three moirai, that is, each tourma with three droungoi. Station your hypostrategos in the middle division. In the other two divisions, that is, the ones to the right and to the left, post the officers of the divisions in the midst of the officers under their command, that is, the moirarchs.

20. You will organize these three divisions into formations of assault troops, that is, those assigned to assault, whom they now call proklastai, and into defenders, that is, those who provide refuge for the men riding on to assault and who cover for them. One third of each division should consist of assault troops: these are to be archers; and two thirds, in the center of the army, should be defenders or ekdikoi, who provide refuge for the assault troops.

21. Draw up the first line in this manner. Post three banda as flank guards to the side of the left division, where hostile encircling movements may easily occur, their front aligned with that of the division. To the side of the right division post one or two banda of archers, known as outflankers, who should be prepared to encircle the enemy. This is how you shall draw up the first line.

22. Organize the second battle line, referred to as the support line, consisting of a third of the whole army, into four divisions. These divisions should station themselves at about a bowshot's distance from one another's flanks. You will

τοῦσι τὰ τοιαῦτα μέρη. τὰ δὲ ταῦτα μέρη ἀμφίστομα ποιήσεις ἤγουν δίστομα,
ἵνα καὶ οἱ ἔμπροσθεν πρὸς τὸ λεγόμενον μέτωπόν εἰσιν δυνατοὶ καὶ καθωπλισμένοι, ὁμοίως καὶ οἱ ὄπισθεν πρὸς τὴν λεγομένην οὐρὰν δυνατοὶ καὶ καθωπλισμένοι, ἵνα καί, ἐὰν κατὰ τοῦ νώτου ἤγουν ὀπίσω αὐτῶν ποιήσωσι προσβολὴν οἱ
155 ἐχθροί, ἀντιστρέφωνται καὶ εὑρίσκωνται ἀπὸ τῶν δύο μερῶν ἕτοιμοι ἀντιτάσ| 324ᵛ
σεσθαι. ἀλλὰ καὶ ἐν τοῖς ἄλλοις μέρεσιν ὄπισθεν τῆς παρατάξεως ἑκατέρωθεν
ἤγουν ἔνθεν καὶ ἐκεῖθεν ὡς ἀπὸ ἑνὸς σαγιττοβόλου διαστήματος ἐκτάξῃς ἀπὸ
ἑνὸς βάνδου ἐν τάξει νωτοφυλάκων, οἷον εἰς τρίτην τάξιν.
    23. Ἵνα δὲ καὶ τὰ ἐν τῷ μέσῳ χωρία ἤγουν τὰ διαστήματα τῆς δευτέρας
160 τάξεως ἡνωμένα εὑρεθῶσι διὰ παντὸς καὶ ἡ πᾶσα τάξις ὡς ἓν σῶμα φαίνηται
καὶ μὴ διαστρέφηται περιπατοῦσα, ἀναγκαῖόν σοί ἐστιν εἰς ταῦτα τὰ ἐν μέσῳ
διαλείμματα ἀπὸ ἑνὸς βάνδου καταστῆσαι εἰς ὅλον τὸ εὔκαιρον διάστημα,
ἔχοντα τὸ βάθος ἤγουν τὸ πάχος ἢ ἀπὸ δύο καβαλλαρίων ἢ τὸ καλῶς ἔχον ἀπὸ
τεσσάρων, μάλιστα πολλοῦ ὄντος τοῦ στρατοῦ ἵνα, ὅτ᾽ ἂν καιρὸς γένηται τοῦ
165 ὑποδέξασθαι τὰ τρεπόμενα μέρη τῆς πρώτης παρατάξεως, ταῦτα τὰ τρία βάνδα,
τὰ ὄντα ἐν τοῖς εὐκαίροις τόποις, ὑποστελλόμενα καὶ συσφιγγόμενα εὔκαιρα
ποιοῦσι τὰ χωρία πρὸς τὴν ἐκείνων ὑποδοχήν· καὶ ἅμα μὲν ὑποδέχονται τοὺς
τρεπομένους εὔκαιρα χωρία ποιοῦντες, ἅμα δὲ καὶ ἀναστέλλουσι τοὺς θέλοντας
σκορπίζεσθαι ἢ φυγεῖν, ἅμα δὲ καὶ εἰς τρίτην τάξιν συνιστάμενα μετὰ τῶν
170 νωτοφυλάκων ἀποσοβοῦσι πολλάκις τοὺς κατὰ νώτου ἤγουν ὄπισθεν ἐπιφαινομένους καὶ ἐπερχομένους ἐχθροὺς πρὸς τὸ ταράξαι τὴν δευτέραν παράταξιν καὶ

---

151 τὰ²…μέρη² MW τὰ δὲ μέρη ταῦτα ABE | ἀμφίστομα MWA ἀφίστομα BE   152 εἰσιν
MW εἰσὶ A ὦσι BE   153–154 ὁμοίως…καθωπλισμένοι MWAE om. B   154 καί MW om.
ABE | κατὰ…ἤγουν MW om. ABE   155 δύο MWA β′ BE   157 ἑνὸς…διαστήματος MW
διαστήματος ἑνὸς σαγιτοβόλου A διαστήματος σαγιτοβόλου ἑνὸς BE | ἐκτάξῃς MW
παρατάξεις ABE   158 τάξιν MW παράταξιν ABE   159 χωρία…διαστήματα MW
διαχωρίσματα ABE | δευτέρας MWA β′ BE   160 τάξεως MW παρατάξεως ABE | τάξις MW
παράταξις ABE | σῶμα MWA σώματι BE   162 διαλείμματα MW διαχωρίσματα ABE |
καταστῆσαι MW περιβαλεῖν ABE   163 ἔχοντα MW εἶναι δὲ ABE | ἢ¹ MW τῶν
παρεκβαλλομένων (παρεμβαλλομένων BE) εἰς τὰ διαχωρίσματα ABE | δύο MWA β′ BE
164 τεσσάρων MWA δ′ BE   164–165 τοῦ ὑποδέξασθαι ABE om. MW   165 τρεπόμενα
MWAB πρεπόμενα E | πρώτης MWAE om. B   166 τὰ MWA om. BE | συσφιγγόμενα MW
ὑποχωροῦντα ὀπίσω ABE   167 ποιοῦσι MBE ποιοῦσιν W ποιῶσι A   167–168 πρὸς…
χωρία MWAB om. E   168 χωρία MW τὰ διαχωρίσματα AB om. E | ἀναστέλλουσι MA
ἀναστέλλουσιν W ἀναστέλλωσι BE   169 φυγεῖν MW φεύγειν ABE   170 ἀποσοβοῦσι MW
ἀπαντῶσι καὶ ἀποκυκλύουσι (ἀποκυκλύωσι BE) ABE | κατὰ…ἤγουν W κατὰ νῶτον ἤγουν M
om. ABE   170–171 ἐπιφαινομένους καὶ MW om. ABE   171 ἐχθροὺς MWAE πολεμίους B

make these divisions double-fronted, or two-fronted, making sure that those in front, along the so-called front, are strong and well armed and, in like manner, those to the rear, along the so-called tail, are also strong and well armed. Then, if the enemy should launch an attack from the rear or behind, they will turn about and be ready to line up and face them from both sections. In the other divisions behind the main battle line on both sides, here and there, at about a bowshot away, draw up a bandon as a rear guard, that is, as a third line.

23. To make those spaces or intervals in the middle of the second line aligned all the way and to make the entire line appear to be one body and not become disordered when moving about, it is necessary for you to station one bandon in these central intervals along the entire distance of the clear space. They should be two mounted men deep, or thick; four is better, especially if it is a large army. And so, when the time comes to provide refuge for the retreating units of the first battle line, these three banda drawn up in the clear spaces close up and pull back, leaving the clear spaces as a refuge for them. At the same time as they provide refuge in the clear spaces for the retreating troops, they can also turn back men dispersing or trying to run away. Moreover, when they form in the third line with the rear guard, they often take part in repelling enemy forces appearing in the rear or behind and attacking in order to harass the second line,

ἀδιάλυτον αὐτὴν διαφυλάττουσιν. καὶ ταῦτα μέν, ἐὰν πολύς ἐστιν ὁ στρατός, οὕτως ποιήσῃς.

24. Ἐὰν δὲ σύμμετρον ἔχῃς στρατόν, τοῦτ' ἔστιν ἀπὸ ε΄ χιλιάδων ἕως δέκα ἢ
175 δώδεκα, μηκέτι τὴν δευτέραν παράταξιν ἀπὸ δ΄ μερῶν ποιήσῃς, ἀλλὰ ἀπὸ δύο καὶ μόνων, ὥστε ἓν καὶ μόνον χωρίον ἤγουν τόπον ἔχειν εὔκαιρον εἰς ὑποδοχὴν τῶν καταφευγόντων. εἰ δὲ ὀλιγώτερον τῶν ε΄ χιλιάδων ἔχεις στρατόν, τότε τὴν δευτέραν τάξιν ἓν καὶ μόνον μέρος ποιήσεις.

25. Ἐπὶ τούτοις δὲ πᾶσι κελεύομέν σοι ὥστε καὶ τρία ἢ τέσσαρα βάνδα, τοὺς
180 λεγομένους ἐνέδρους ἤγουν ἐγκρύμματα, ἔνθεν καὶ ἐκεῖθεν τῆς παρατάξεως ἀφορίσεις καὶ τάξεις, ἵνα εἰσὶν οἱ μὲν κωλύοντες τὰ ἀπὸ τῶν ἐχθρῶν ἐγχειρού-μενα ἐγκρύμματα κατὰ τῶν ἀριστερῶν τῆς παρατάξεώς σου, οἱ δὲ ἵνα ποιῶσιν ἐγκρύμματα καὶ ἐπιδρομὴν κατὰ τοῦ δεξιοῦ μέρους τῶν ἐχθρῶν, ἐὰν ἄρα καὶ οἱ τόποι εἰσὶν ἁρμόδιοι. |

185    26. Σημείωσαι γάρ, ὅτι αἱ κατὰ τῶν πλαγίων τῆς τῶν ἐχθρῶν παρατάξεως 325 καὶ αἱ κατὰ τοῦ νώτου ἤγουν ἀπὸ ὄπισθεν αὐτῶν γινόμεναι ἐπιδρομαί, ἐὰν καλῶς γίνωνται καὶ εὐκαίρως, μᾶλλον δραστικώτεραί εἰσι καὶ ἀναγκαῖαι παρὰ τὰς γινομένας δι' ὄψεως μόνης συμβολὰς καὶ ὠθήσεις. κἂν τε γὰρ ὀλιγώτεροί εἰσιν οἱ ἐχθροί, ὡς ἐξαίφνης ἐπιλαμβανόμενοι καὶ κυκλούμενοι διὰ τῶν τοιού-
190 των ἐπιδρομῶν, μεγάλην τὴν βλάβην ὑπομενοῦσι μὴ δυναμένων εὐκόλως σώζεσθαι τῶν ἐξ αὐτῶν τρεπομένων, κἂν τε ἰσόμετροί εἰσιν ἢ καὶ πλείονες τοῦ στρατοῦ τοῦ σου, εἰς ἀγῶνα μέγαν εἰσέρχονται καὶ φόβον, νομίζοντες πλῆθος εἶναι πολὺ τοὺς τὴν ἐπιδρομὴν ποιοῦντας.

27. Πρόσεχε δέ, ὅτι οὐ πρέπον ἐστὶ χωρὶς ἀνάγκης ὀλίγον στρατὸν πρὸς
195 πλῆθος πολεμίων εὐτάκτων φανερῶς πρὸς μάχην συμπλέκειν. εἰ δὲ καὶ ἀνάγκη τούτου γένηται, μὴ πάντα φανερῶς καὶ διὰ ὄψεως ἐγχειρεῖν, κἂν τάχα πλείονές

---

172 διαφυλάττουσιν MWA δυαφυλάττουσι BE | ἔστιν MWA ἢ BE    174 ε΄ MWE πέντε AB | δέκα MWA ι΄ BE    175 δώδεκα MWA ιβ΄ BE | δ΄ MWB τεσσάρων AE | ἀλλὰ MWAE ἀλλ' B | δύο MWA β BE    176 καὶ¹ MW om. ABE | χωρίον MW διαχώρισμα ABE | ἤγουν τόπον MW om. ABE    177 ε΄ MWBE πέντε A    178 τάξιν MW παράταξιν ABE    179 τρία MWA γ΄ BE | τέσσαρα MWAE δ΄ B    181 ἀφορίσεις MW ἀφορίσαι A ἀφωρίσαι BE | τάξεις MW τάξαι ABE | εἰσὶν MW om. ABE | κωλύοντες MW κωλύωσι ABE    182 ἵνα MWA om. BE    183 ἐγκρύμματα MW ἔγκρυμα ABE    184 εἰσὶν MWA ὦσιν BE    185 σημείωσαι…ὅτι MW om. ABE | αἱ A οἱ MW αἱ γὰρ BE    186 αἱ MWAE om. B | κατὰ…ἀπὸ MW om. ABE | γινόμεναι MWA γενόμεναι BE    187 γίνωνται…εὐκαίρως (γένωνται M) MW καὶ ἐν ἐπιτηδείῳ καιρῷ γίνωνται ABE    189 εἰσιν MWA ὦσιν BE    190 ὑπομενοῦσι MBE ὑπομενοῦσιν WA    191 εἰσιν MWA ὦσιν BE    192 στρατοῦ…σου MW σοῦ στρατοῦ ABE    194 ἐστὶ MABE ἐστὶν W    196 διὰ ὄψεως MW εἰς πρόσωπον ABE    196–197 πλείονές εἰσιν MW πλείων ἐστὶν A πλείων ἢ BE

and so they keep that sector intact. This is what you should do if you have a large army.

24. If you have an army of medium strength, that is, from five thousand to ten or twelve thousand, you may no longer organize the second line into four divisions but only into two. You will have only one clear space or location to receive the men fleeing for protection. If you have an army of fewer than five thousand, then you will post only one division in the second line.

25. In addition to all of the above, we order you to detail three or four banda, referred to as ambush troops or ambushers, and station them on this side and that side of the battle line. They are to prevent enemy attempts to ambush the left of your battle line and they themselves can set up ambushes and assaults against the right divisions of the enemy, if the terrain is favorable.

26. It should be noted that attacks against the flanks and the rear of the enemy's battle line or behind, if they are well timed and well carried out, are much more effective and decisive than limiting oneself to direct frontal attacks and charges. If the enemy force is smaller, such attacks will catch them by surprise, and by encircling them will subject them to great damage, since the troops driven back will not easily reach safety. If the enemy army is equal to yours or even superior, they will find themselves in a serious struggle and become fearful in the belief that the attacking troops are very numerous.

27. Pay attention to this: unless forced to do so, it is not right for a small army to engage a more numerous and disciplined enemy in open battle. If it should become necessary, though, do not undertake frontal operations only,

εἰσιν ὁ ἡμέτερος στρατός, ἀλλὰ καὶ διὰ τοῦ νώτου ἤγουν ἀπὸ ὄπισθεν τῶν
ἐχθρῶν ἢ διὰ τῶν πλαγίων ἐμβάλλεσθαι εἰς αὐτούς. καὶ γὰρ ἐπισφαλές ἐστι καὶ
ἐπικίνδυνον ἡ δι' ὄψεως μόνον μάχη καὶ πρὸς οἰονδήποτε ἔθνος γινομένη, κἂν
200 τάχα καὶ ὀλιγώτερον πλῆθός ἐστι τὸ ἀντικαθιστάμενον.

28. Οὕτως οὖν ὡς ἐν κεφαλαίῳ κελεύομέν σοι ἵνα πάντα τὰ καβαλλαρικὰ
τάγματα εἰς πρώτην καὶ δευτέραν παράταξιν ἐν καιρῷ πολέμου καταστήσῃς, ὅτ'
ἂν μάλιστα καὶ πολὺν στρατὸν ἔχῃς, καὶ διατάξῃς κατὰ τὸν λεχθέντα σοι τρόπον εἰς κούρσωρας ἤγουν προκλάστας, τοὺς ἔμπροσθεν τῆς παρατάξεως πρὸ
205 τῶν ἄλλων κατὰ τῶν ἐχθρῶν προτρέχοντας καὶ εἰς διφένσωρας ἤγουν τοὺς
εὐτάκτως ἱσταμένους καὶ ὑποδέχεσθαι μέλλοντας τοὺς προδραμόντας κατὰ τῶν
ἐχθρῶν, ἐὰν μὴ τελείως διώξωσιν αὐτούς, ἀλλ' ἀνθυποστρέψουσιν, ἔτι δὲ καὶ εἰς
πλαγιοφύλακας καὶ εἰς ὑπερκεραστὰς ἤγουν τοὺς ἑτοίμους ἱσταμένους εἰς
κύκλωσιν τῶν ἐχθρῶν, ἔτι δὲ καὶ εἰς ἐνέδρους ἤγουν ἐγκρύμματα, ἀλλὰ καὶ εἰς
210 βοηθοὺς ἤγουν τοὺς ὄπισθεν τεταγμένους καὶ ἀναστέλλοντας τοὺς ὅσοι μέλλουσι φεύγειν τὴν ἰδίαν καταλιμπάνοντες τάξιν, ἔτι δὲ καὶ εἰς νωτοφύλακας
ἤγουν τοὺς ὄπισθεν εἰς φυλακὴν τοῦ παντὸς στρατοῦ τεταγμένους.

29. Ἐὰν δὲ πολὺν ἔχωσι στρατὸν καὶ δύνασαι τοιαύτας διπλᾶς παρατάξεις
ποιεῖν εἴτε δύο εἴτε τρεῖς ἢ καὶ πλείονας, | ὥστε μεριζομένην τὴν τῶν ἐχθρῶν   325ᵛ
215 δύναμιν πρὸς αὐτὰς ὀλιγωτέρων ὄντων ἀσθενεῖς γίνεσθαι τὰς ἐκείνων ἢ προσβαλόντων ὁμοῦ πρὸς μίαν τῶν σῶν παρατάξεων ὑπὸ τῶν ἄλλων ἢ διώκεσθαι ἢ
κυκλοῦσθαι. τοῦτό ἐστι τῶν ἀναγκαίων.

30. Τὸ δὲ βάθος ἤγουν τὸ πάχος τῶν παρατάξεων, καθὼς οἱ ἀρχαῖοι διετά-
ξαντο, ἤρκει μὲν ἑκάστῳ τάγματι εἰς τέσσαρας καὶ μόνους καβαλλαρίους
220 γίνεσθαι, ἐπειδὴ τὸ πλέον τούτων ἀργὸν καὶ ἀνωφελὲς δείκνυται ἐπὶ τῶν
καβαλλαρίων, οὔτε γὰρ δύνανται, ὡς ἐπὶ τῆς πεζικῆς τάξεως, ἀπὸ ὄπισθεν διὰ

---

197 διὰ…ἀπὸ MW τῶν ὄπισθεν μερῶν ABE    198 ἐμβάλλεσθαι MW ἐπιτίθεσθαι ABE | εἰς
αὐτούς MW αὐτοῖς ABE | ἐπισφαλές MW ἐπισφαλὴς ABE    199 ἐπικίνδυνον MW
ἐπικίνδυνος ABE    200 ἐστι ΜΑ ἐστὶν W ἢ ΒΕ    201 ἐν MWAE ἐν τῷ Β    204 ἤγουν MW
ἤγουν ἐκδικητὰς ABE    206 προδραμόντας AE προσδραμόντας MWB    207 ἀλλ' MWBE
ἀλλὰ A | ἀνθυποστρέψουσιν MW ἀνθυποστρέψωσιν ABE | εἰς AB om. MWE
208 ἑτοίμους W ἑτοίμως MABE    210–211 ὅσοι μέλλουσι MW βουλομένους ABE
211 φεύγειν MW φεύγειν καὶ ABE | καταλιμπάνοντες τάξιν MW τάξιν καταλιμπάνειν ABE
213 δύνασαι MWA δύνῃ ΒΕ    214 δύο MWA β' ΒΕ | τρεῖς MWA γ' ΒΕ | ὥστε MW ὥστε ἢ
ABE    215 ὀλιγωτέρων ὄντων MW om. ABE | ἀσθενεῖς γίνεσθαι MW ἀσθενῆ γίνεσθαι A
ἀσθενὴς γενέσθαι ΒΕ | τὰς ἐκείνων MW om. ABE    215–216 προσβαλόντων MW
προσβάλλουσαν A προσβαλοῦσαν ΒΕ    217 ἐστι MABE ἐστιν W | τῶν ἀναγκαίων MWA τὸ
ἀναγκαῖον ΒΕ    219 καὶ μόνους MW om. ABE    221 οὔτε MW οὐ ABE | ὄπισθεν WABE
ὄπισθε Μ    221–222 διὰ…πάχους MW om. ABE

even if our army is larger, but carry on attacks against the rear of the enemy, behind them, or against their flanks. For a purely frontal attack against any nation whatsoever is dangerous and full of risk, even if those opposing you may be less numerous.

28. Thus, to sum it up, we order you to form all your cavalry units in a first and a second battle line when engaged in combat, particularly when you have a large army. Organize them, in the manner explained to you, into assault troops or proklastai, those men in front of the battle line who ride out ahead of the others against the enemy, and into defenders, those who position themselves in good order, ready to provide refuge for those troops charging against the enemy in the event that they do not pursue them all the way but have to turn back. Also divide them into flank guards and into outflankers, that is, men lined up ready to encircle the enemy; and further, into ambush troops or ambushers, as well as support troops who are in formation to the rear and who restrain the men who intend to flee and desert their own formation; and finally into rear guards, that is, those stationed behind to protect the whole army.

29. If they have a large army and you are able to form double battle lines of the sort mentioned, whether it be two or three or even more, so that when the smaller enemy force is divided in proportion to these, their force will be weak or, as they charge against one of your lines, they may be pursued or encircled by the others. This is an essential point.

30. For the depth or the thickness of the battle lines, the ancient authorities prescribed that four, all mounted, were sufficient for each tagma. For cavalry greater depth has been shown to be inefficient and useless. Unlike a formation

τοῦ πάχους προωθισμὸν ποιεῖν. τότε γὰρ καὶ μὴ βουλόμενοι οἱ ἔμπροσθεν ἐκ
τῶν ὄπισθεν προωθούμενοι τὴν ὁρμὴν ἐπὶ τὰ ἔμπροσθεν ποιοῦσι. τοῦτο γὰρ ἐπὶ
τῶν πεζῶν γίνεται. οἱ δὲ ἵπποι οὐ δύνανται προωθεῖν τοὺς ἔμπροσθεν αὐτῶν, ὡς
225  οἱ πεζοί, οὐδὲ βοήθειά τις γίνεται ἐκ τῶν περισσοτέρων εἰς τοὺς πρωτοστάτας,
τοῦτ᾽ ἔστιν τοὺς ἐπὶ τὸ μέτωπον τασσομένους, κἄν τε τοξόται εἰσὶ κἄν τε κονταράτοι.

31. Οἱ μὲν γὰρ κονταράτοι, οἱ ὀπίσω τοῦ τετάρτου, οὐ δύνανται φθάζειν εἰς
τὸ ἔμπροσθεν, οἱ δὲ τοξόται εἰς τὸ ἄνω ἀναγκάζονται τοξεύειν διὰ τοὺς ἔμπροσ-
230  θεν αὐτῶν καὶ διὰ τοῦτο ἄπρακτοι κατὰ τῶν ἐχθρῶν ἐν ταῖς συμβολαῖς τῆς
μάχης γίνονται αἱ σαγίτται αὐτῶν, ὡς ἡ πεῖρα διδάσκει καὶ τοὺς ἀμφιβάλλοντας,
ἐὰν βούλωνται.

32. Ἥρκει οὖν, καθὼς εἴπομεν, τὸ πάχος τῶν τεσσάρων καβαλλαρίων, ἀλλ᾽,
ἐπειδὴ συμβαίνει τοὺς ἀνδρείους στρατιώτας ὀλιγωτέρους κατὰ τάγμα εὑρίσκ-
235  εσθαι, τοῦτ᾽ ἔστι τοὺς ἔμπροσθεν ἱσταμένους, τοὺς καὶ τὰς χεῖρας μιγνύειν πρὸς
πόλεμον ὀφείλοντας, διὰ τοῦτο πρέπον ἐστὶ πρὸς τὴν δύναμιν τῶν ταγμάτων
οὕτως ὁρίζειν καὶ τὸ πάχος τῆς παρατάξεως αὐτῶν, οἷον· εἰς τὰ ἀνδρειότερα, τὰ
καὶ μέσον τασσόμενα τάγματα εἰς τὴν τάξιν τὴν πρόμαχον, ἀπὸ ζʹ καβαλλαρίων
ποιεῖν καὶ ἑνὸς παιδὸς ὑπηρέτου αὐτῶν, ἐν δὲ τῇ ἀριστερᾷ τάξει, ἐν ᾗ καὶ ἐκεῖ
240  δεύτεροι κατὰ τὴν ἀνδρίαν τῆς προμάχου τάξεως ὀφείλουσι τάσσεσθαι, ἀπὸ ζʹ
ἀνδρῶν ἑκάστην δεκαρχίαν, πάλιν ἐν δεξιᾷ, ἐν ᾗ καὶ ἐκεῖ ἰσοδύναμοι ἄνδρες τῆς
ἀριστερᾶς ὀφείλουσιν εἶναι, ἀπὸ ἀνδρῶν ηʹ, τὰ δὲ λοιπὰ καὶ ὑποδεέστερα
τάγματα ἀπὸ ηʹ ἢ δέκα ἀνδρῶν γίνεσθαι πρὸς τὰς δεκαρχίας τασσόμενα.

33. Ἐὰν μέντοι συμβῇ ἵνα | ἐκ τῶν ὑποδεεστέρων τούτων ταγμάτων εἰς τὴν  326
245  πρώτην παράταξιν ἐκτάξῃς, ἢ ἀπὸ ηʹ ἢ ἀπὸ ιʹ ποιήσῃς ἀνδρῶν ὡς ἀσθενεστέρων.
τὰ δὲ τάγματα, τὰ ἐν δευτέρᾳ τάξει τασσόμενα καὶ ἐπίλεκτα ὄντα, ἀπὸ πέντε
μὲν στρατιωτῶν καὶ ἑτέρων ὑπηρετῶν εἰς τὰ ἄρματα ποιήσεις, ὥστε δέκα

222 ἔμπροσθεν MWBE ἔμπροσθε A    223 ποιοῦσι MA ποιοῦσιν WBE    226 τοξόται εἰσὶ
M τοξόται εἰσὶν W κονταράτοι εἰσὶ AE κονταράτοι ὦσι B    226–227 κονταράτοι MW
τοξόται ABE    229 τὸ¹ MWA τοὺς BE    231 γίνονται ABE γίνονται ὡς MW | σαγίτται MW
σαγῖται A σαγίτες BE    231–232 καὶ…βούλωνται MW om. ABE    235 ἔστι MABE ἔστιν W
237 οὕτως…αὐτῶν MWAE om. B    238 ζʹ MW ἑπτὰ ABE    240 τάσσεσθαι MW
κατατάσσεσθαι ABE | ζʹ MW ἑπτὰ ABE    241 καὶ ἐκεῖ MW om. ABE    242 εἶναι ABE om.
MW | ηʹ M ὀκτὼ W ἑπτὰ τάσσειν ABE    243 τάγματα WABE πράγματα M | ηʹ MWE ὀκτὼ
AB    244 ἐὰν μέντοι MW πάλιν ἐὰν μὲν ABE    245 ηʹ WE ὀκτὼ MAB | ιʹ MWBE δέκα A
246 τὰ² MWA om. BE | ἐν MW ἐν τῇ ABE | πέντε MWA εʹ BE    247 μὲν MWAE om. B |
δέκα MWAE ιʹ B

of foot, they are unable to apply pressure from the rear because of the thickness, for the men pushing forward from the rear put pressure on those in front who may not wish to go forward. This is what happens with infantry. But horses are not able to push those in front of them forward, as are foot soldiers. The front ranks, that is, those stationed in front, receive no support from additional troops, whether archers or lancers.

31. The lancers behind the fourth rank are unable to reach beyond the front. The archers are forced to shoot up high because of those in front of them, and the result is that their arrows are ineffectual against the enemy in the press of battle. If anyone doubts this, let experience teach him.

32. Therefore, a thickness of four was enough, as we said. Since, however, the number of courageous soldiers, that is, the men stationed in the front ranks who have to engage the enemy in hand-to-hand fighting, is rather limited, it is necessary to regulate the depth of their battle line in accord with the strength of the units. So it is that the more courageous units drawn up in the center of the first line, the promachos, should be composed of seven cavalrymen and one serving boy. In the formation to the left, in which there may be men less noted for courage than those in the promachos line, they ought to be organized with each dekarchy consisting of seven men. The division on the right, in which the men ought to be of equal strength with those on the left, should consist of eight men. The rest of the units, made up of weaker troops, should be formed of eight or ten men to a dekarchy.

33. If it should happen that you station some of these weaker units in the first line, then, because they are weaker, make it eight or ten men. Form the units composed of picked troops drawn up in the second line five regular soldiers <deep>, followed by additional men-at-arms, so that each dekarchy has

ἄνδρας ἑκάστην δεκαρχίαν ἔχειν. οὗτοι δὲ οἱ, ὡς εἴρηται, τεταγμένοι ἵνα κατασταθῶσιν ἐπιτηδείως εἴς τε κούρσωρας καὶ ἐγκρύμματα.

250   34. Οὐκ ἔστιν οὖν πρέπον τῶν η΄ ἢ τὸ πολὺ τῶν δέκα ἀνδρῶν πλείω τὸ πάχος ποιεῖν τῆς παρατάξεως, κἂν τὸ πάνυ εἰσὶν ἀσθενῆ τὰ τάγματα, οὐδὲ τῶν ε΄ ὀλιγώτερον, ὅσον ἄν εἰσιν ἐπίλεκτα, ὥστε πρέπον ἐστὶ κατὰ τὸν εἰρημένον τρόπον καὶ τὴν τοιαύτην διαίρεσιν ἀρκούντως καὶ τὰ βάθη ἤγουν τὰ πάχη τῶν παρατάξεων γίνεσθαι καὶ μηδὲ τὸ μῆκος ἤγουν τὸν ἀριθμὸν τῶν πρωτοστα-
255   τούντων ὀλιγοῦσθαι πολύ. ἐὰν γὰρ ἀπὸ δέκα ἀνδρῶν τὸ πάχος τῶν ταγμάτων ὅλων ἐν ἴσῳ μέτρῳ τάξῃς, εὐχερῶς καὶ συντόμως ὑπὸ τῶν κατασκόπων τῶν ἐχθρῶν ἀριθμεῖσθαι ποιήσεις διὰ τῶν πρωτοστατῶν ὅλον σου τὸν στρατόν, ὅπερ οὐ δέον μανθάνειν τοὺς ἐχθρούς. τῆς δὲ εἰρημένης ἡμῖν ἀναλογίας ἤγουν τοῦ μέτρου φυλαττομένου ἐκ τοῦ περισσεύοντος στρατοῦ τὴν δευτέραν κατα-
260   στήσεις τάξιν.

35. Κελεύομεν δέ σοι καὶ τὰ κοντουβέρνια τῶν στρατιωτῶν ἀπὸ παλαιῶν καὶ νέων γίνεσθαι ἀναλόγως, ἵνα μὴ οἱ παλαιοὶ μόνοι τασσόμενοι καθ᾽ ἑαυτοὺς ἀσθενεῖς εἰσι μηδὲ οἱ νεώτεροι ἄτακτοι εὑρεθῶσιν ὡς ἄπειροι.

36. Ὁπλίσεις δὲ τὴν παράταξιν οὕτως· τὸν μὲν πρωτοστάτην τῆς πρώτης
265   τάξεως καὶ τὸν μετ᾽ ἐκεῖνον ἱστάμενον, τοῦτ᾽ ἔστι τὸν δεύτερον, ἔτι δὲ καὶ τὸν ἑστῶτα ὀπίσω πάντων ἤγουν τὸν οὐραγὸν κονταράτους ποιήσεις μετὰ τῆς λοιπῆς αὐτῶν ἐξοπλίσεως, τοὺς δὲ λοιποὺς πάντας, τοὺς ἐν μέσῳ ἐκείνων τασσομένους, ὅσοι τοξεύειν οἴδασι, χωρὶς κονταρίων εἶναι ποιήσεις. οὐδὲ γὰρ δυνατόν ἐστι δεόντως περιάγειν τινὰ τόξον ἐπάνω ἵππου, ἐὰν ἐν τῇ ἀριστερᾷ
270   αὐτοῦ καὶ τὸ σκουτάριν κατέχῃ καὶ τὸ τόξον. εἰ δὲ γυμνασθῇ ὁ στρατιώτης ὥστε, ἡνίκα τοξεύῃ, ὀπίσω κατὰ τοῦ νώτου εὐφυῶς πέμπῃ τὸ σκουτάριν, οὐδὲ τοῦτο ἄχρηστον ἡμῖν καταφαίνεται.

37. Πρὸς τούτοις κελεύομέν σοι, ὦ στρατηγέ, ἵνα ἀφορίσῃς, καὶ μάλιστα εἰς τὴν πρόμαχον παράταξιν, τοὺς λεγομένους δεποτάτους, τοῦτ᾽ ἔστι τοὺς ἐπι-

248 οἱ MW om. ABE   250 η΄ MWBE ὀκτὼ A | τῶν² MW om. ABE | πλείω MW πλεῖον BE om. A   251 τὸ M om. WABE | εἰσὶν MWA ὦσιν BE   252 ε΄ MWBE πέντε A | ὀλιγώτερον Va ὀλιγωτέρους codd. | εἰσιν MWA εἶεν BE | ἐστὶ MWBE ἐστὶν A   255 ὀλιγοῦσθαι… ταγμάτων MWAE om. B | πολύ MW ἐπιπολὺ AE | δέκα MWA ι΄ E   256 εὐχερῶς MW εὐκόλως ABE | κατασκόπων ABE κατασκόπων καὶ MW   258 δὲ MWAE om. B | ἡμῖν ABE ὑμῖν MW   261 κοντουβέρνια WABE κουτουβέρνια M   263 εἰσι MWA ὦσι BE   265 ἔστι MBE ἔστιν WA   267 αὐτῶν MW αὐτῆς BE om. A   268 οἴδασι MABE οἴδασιν W   269 ἔστι MBE ἔστιν WA   270 σκουτάριν MW σκουτάριον ABE | γυμνασθῇ MWA γεγυμνάσθη E γεγύμνασθαι B   271 ὀπίσω…νώτου ABE om. MW | πέμπῃ MW παραπέμπειν ABE | σκουτάριν Va σκουτάριον codd.   274 δεποτάτους MW διποτάτους ABE | ἔστι MBE ἔστιν WA

ten men. As mentioned, these men should be drawn up so they may conveniently be assigned as assault troops and ambushers.

34. It is wrong, therefore, to make the thickness of the battle line more than eight or at most ten, no matter how weak the units might be, nor should it be less than five, even for the elite units. The depth, or the thickness, of the battle lines made in the above manner and in the proper proportions are correct and adequate. The width, that is, the number of men in the front rank, should not be greatly reduced. If you form all the units in equal measure at ten thick, you will make it easy and quick for enemy spies to estimate the numbers of your entire army <simply by counting> the file leaders. The enemy must not learn this. As we have remarked, maintaining due proportion and measure, you should organize the second line from among the remaining troops.

35. We order you to have the squads made up of veterans and younger men in proper proportion. Otherwise the older men, if formed by themselves, may be weak, and the younger men may turn out to be undisciplined because they lack experience.

36. Arm the battle line in this manner. In the first rank have the file leader and the man standing behind him, that is, the second, and also the one standing behind everyone, that is, the ouragos, all bear lances with the rest of their armament. Have all the others, drawn up in their middle, who know how to shoot, be without lances, for it is not possible to draw the bow effectively on horseback while holding a shield as well as a bow in his left hand. But it seems more useful to train the soldier, while shooting, to shift the shield smoothly behind him, on his back.

37. In addition to the above, we order you, O commander, to assign, especially in the first battle line, men known as deputies, that is, those who take care

275 μελητὰς τῶν τραυματι|ζομένων στρατιωτῶν. καὶ καταστήσεις ὀκτὼ ἢ δέκα 326ᵛ
ἄνδρας καθ' ἕκαστον βάνδον ἐκ τοῦ αὐτοῦ τάγματος ἐλαφροὺς καὶ γοργοὺς
ἄνευ ὅπλων, τοὺς ὀφείλοντας ὄπισθεν ὡς ἀπὸ ἑκατὸν ποδῶν τοῖς ἰδίοις τάγμασιν ἀκολουθεῖν ἵνα τοὺς ἐν ταῖς συμπλοκαῖς τοῦ πολέμου, ὡς πολλάκις γίνεται,
τραυματιζομένους ἐπικινδύνως ἢ ἐκπίπτοντας ἀπὸ τῶν ἵππων καὶ μὴ δυνα-
280 μένους μάχεσθαι ἀναλέγωνται καὶ περιποιῶνται, ἵνα μὴ καταπατῶνται ὑπὸ τῆς
δευτέρας παρατάξεως οἱ ἀληθῶς γενναῖοι στρατιῶται καὶ ἐκ τῆς ὀλιγωρίας τῶν
τραυμάτων διαφθείρωνται. καὶ ἵνα οἱ διασώζοντες αὐτοὺς λαμβάνωσιν ὑπὲρ
μισθοῦ ἀπὸ τοῦ ταμείου τῆς βασιλείας ἡμῶν κατὰ ἕνα ἕκαστον στρατιώτην
διασωζόμενον παρ' αὐτῶν νόμισμα ἕν.

285      38. Εἶτα δὲ οἱ τοιοῦτοι μετὰ τὸ τραπῆναι τοὺς ἐχθροὺς καὶ παρελθεῖν τὴν
δευτέραν παράταξιν τότε τὰ σκῦλα τὰ εὑρισκόμενα ἐν τῷ τόπῳ τῆς πρώτης
συμβολῆς αὐτοὶ συνάγουσι καὶ τοῖς δεκάρχοις ἤγουν τοῖς πρωτοστάταις τοῦ
ἰδίου τάγματος μετὰ τὸ λυθῆναι τὴν μάχην παρέχουσιν αὐτά. λαμβάνουσι δὲ καὶ
αὐτοὶ ὑπὲρ τούτου παρὰ τῶν δεκάρχων εἰς παραμυθίαν αὐτῶν μοῖράν τινα.
290 τοῦτο γὰρ τοῖς πρωτοστάταις ἐν ταῖς μάχαις προνόμιον δίκαιον καὶ ἁρμόδιον ἐν
ταῖς ἐπιτυχίαις ἔχειν κελεύομεν, καθότι πλέον τῶν λοιπῶν τῆς ἀνάγκης μετέ-
χουσιν ἐν τῇ πρώτῃ συμβολῇ τοῦ πολέμου. ἀγαθὸν δὲ καὶ ἕτερον γίνεται, ἵνα μὴ
διὰ τὸ σκυλεῦσαι τοὺς πίπτοντας ἐχθρούς τινες ἐκ τῶν ἵππων κατέρχωνται καὶ
τὴν παράταξιν διαλύουσιν.

295      39. Ἵνα δὲ εὐκόλως ἐπὶ τῶν ἵππων ἀναβαίνωσιν οἵ τε λεγόμενοι δεποτάτοι
καὶ οἱ τραυματιζόμενοι στρατιῶται οἱ ἀπὸ τῶν ἵππων πίπτοντες, πρέπον ἐστὶν
ἵνα ὁ δεποτάτος τὰς δύο σκάλας εἰς τὸ ἀριστερὸν μέρος τῆς σέλλας ἔχῃ, τοῦτ'
ἔστι τὴν μίαν πρὸς τῷ ἐμπροσθοκουρβίῳ καὶ τὴν ἑτέραν πρὸς τῷ ὀπισθοκουρ-
βίῳ, ἵνα ὅτ' ἂν μέλλωσιν οἱ δύο ἐπὶ τοῦ ἵππου ἀνέρχεσθαι, ὅ τε δεποτάτος καὶ ὁ

---

275 ὀκτὼ MWA η′ BE | ἢ MWAE ἢ καὶ B    277 ὅπλων ABE ὅπλου MW | ἑκατὸν MWAB
ἕκαστον E    278 ἀκολουθεῖν MW ἐπακολουθεῖν ABE    280 ἀναλέγωνται MW
ἀναλαμβάνωνται A ἀναλαμβάνονται BE | καταπατῶνται ABE καταπατοῦνται MW
284 διασωζόμενον MWA διασωζόμενοι BE | νόμισμα WAE ν°  MB (sic pro νόμισμα)
285 εἶτα...τοιοῦτοι MW οἱ δὲ αὐτοὶ ABE | καὶ MWAE om. B    286 τὰ σκῦλα MW om. ABE
scr. mg. τὰ τῶν ἐχθρῶν ὅπλα τε καὶ λοιπὰ πράγματα συνάγουσιν W | εὑρισκόμενα MW
εὑρισκόμενα ὅπλα ABE    287 αὐτοὶ συνάγουσι MW συνάγωσι ABE | δεκάρχοις MWA
δεκάρχαις BE    288 παρέχουσιν MW παρέχωσιν ABE | λαμβάνουσι MW λαμβάνωσι ABE
293 σκυλεῦσαι MW ἐκδῦσαι ABE    294 διαλύουσιν MW διαλύωσιν A διαλύωσι BE
295–296 ἵνα...πίπτοντες MW om. ABE    296 οἱ¹ M om. W | πρέπον MW πρέπον δὲ ABE
297 δεποτάτος MW διποτάτος ABE | δύο MWAE β′ B    298 ἔστι MB ἔστιν WAE
298–299 καὶ...ὀπισθοκουρβίῳ MWAE om. B    299 δύο MWAB β′ E    299–300 ὅ...
στρατιώτης Va ὅ τε τραυματιζόμενος στρατιώτης καὶ ὁ διποτάτος ABE om. MW

of the wounded soldiers. You will station eight or ten men to each bandon, from the same unit. They should be nimble, vigorous, and without weapons. Their task is to follow about a hundred feet to the rear of their own units to pick up and give aid to those seriously wounded in the clash of battle, as frequently happens, or who have fallen off their horses and are out of action, so that these truly noble soldiers may not be trampled underfoot by the second line or die through neglect of their wounds. The corpsmen who rescue them should receive one nomisma from Our Majesty's treasury as payment for each soldier rescued by them.

38. Then, when the enemy has been routed and the second line has passed by, these deputies should gather up the spoils found on the site of the first battle and, after the fighting has ceased, they should hand them over to the dekarchs, that is, the file leaders of their own units. They should then receive a share of it from the dekarchs in recompense for their work. We order that it is just and fitting to grant this perquisite to the file leaders for their success in combat, because, more than the rest, they must bear the brunt of fighting in the first onslaught. There is also another good reason: to prevent them from dismounting from their horses and breaking ranks in order to despoil the fallen enemy.

39. To make it easier for the corpsmen and the wounded soldiers who have fallen off their horses to get up onto the rescue horses, the corpsman must put both stirrups on the left side of the saddle, that is, one toward the pommel and the other toward the cantle. Then, when the two of them, the corpsman and the

300 τραυματιζόμενος στρατιώτης, ὁ μὲν διὰ τῆς σκάλας τῆς ἔμπροσθεν, ὁ δὲ διὰ τῆς ἑτέρας σκάλας ἀνέρχεται. ἀναγκαῖον δέ ἐστι τοὺς λεγομένους δεποτάτους εἰς φλασκία ὕδωρ βαστάζειν διὰ τοὺς πολλάκις λιποθυμοῦντας τραυματίας.

40. Ἐν δὲ τῷ καιρῷ τῆς μάχης φλάμουλα τὰ κοντάρια μὴ ἐχέτωσαν. ὅσον γάρ εἰσιν εἰς ἐπίδειξιν καὶ κόμπον ἀναγκαῖα τὰ φλάμουλα, τοσοῦτόν εἰσιν ἐν
305 ταῖς | μάχαις ἄχρηστα. ἐὰν γάρ τις βούληται εὐκαίρως ῥῖψαι ἢ ἀκοντίσαι ἢ 327 τοξεῦσαι, οὐ συγχωρεῖ τὸ φλάμουλον εὐστόχως εἰς ὀρθὸν ἢ εἰς μῆκος βάλλεσθαι τὸ ῥιπτόμενον. ἐὰν δὲ καὶ τοξείας καιρὸς γένηται, παρεμποδίζει τοῖς ὄπισθεν τοξεύουσιν, ἀλλὰ καὶ εἰς τὰς ἐξελασίας καὶ εἰς τὰς ἐπιστροφὰς καὶ εἰς τὰς ἀντιστροφὰς οὐκ ὀλίγον ἐμποδισμὸν ποιοῦσι καὶ διὰ τοῦτο ἐν ταῖς μάχαις
310 ταῦτα χρηματίζειν οὐ πρέπει.

41. Ἀλλὰ διὰ μὲν τὸν κόμπον τῆς παρατάξεως, ὥστε φαίνεσθαι μήκοθεν, ἔχειν μὲν τὰ φλάμουλα εἰς τὰ κοντάρια ἕως ἂν οἱ ἐχθροὶ φθάσωσιν ἀπὸ μιλίου ἑνός, ἀπὸ τότε δὲ ἵνα συστέλλωσιν αὐτὰ καὶ ἐν τοῖς θηκαρίοις αὐτῶν ἀποτιθοῦσιν.

315 42. Πρὸς τούτοις κελεύομέν σοι, ἵνα ἀπὸ τῶν ἰσχυρῶν καὶ δυνατῶν ταγμάτων καθ᾽ ἕκαστον τάγμα, ἀπὸ δὲ τῶν ἄλλων ὑποδεεστέρων καθ᾽ ἑκάστην τοῦρμαν σκουλκάτωρας ἤγουν βιγλεύοντας ἀφορίσῃς, δύο μὲν κατὰ τάγμα, ὀκτὼ δὲ ἢ δώδεκα κατὰ τοῦρμαν, ἀγρύπνους καὶ διεγηγερμένους καὶ γοργούς, οἵτινες καὶ πρὸ τοῦ πολέμου καὶ ἐν αὐτῷ τῷ πολέμῳ, ἐν τοῖς ἰδίοις αὐτῶν μέρε-
320 σιν εἰς οὓς καὶ τάσσονται τόπους ἀπὸ διαστημάτων σκουλκεύειν ὀφείλουσιν ἕως τῆς τελείας τοῦ πολέμου ἐκβάσεως, ἵνα μὴ ἀπὸ ἐγκρύμματος ἐπιδρομὴ ἢ δόλος αὐτοῖς ὑπὸ τῶν ἐχθρῶν γενήσεται.

---

301 ἑτέρας σκάλας MW ὄπισθεν ABE | ἀνέρχεται MW ἀνέρχηται ABE | ἐστι MA ἐστιν W ἐστιν καὶ BE | δεποτάτους MW διποτάτους ABE   302 φλασκία MW ἀγγεῖα ABE | τραυματίας MW τῶν τραυματιζομένων στρατιωτῶν ABE   303 φλάμουλα ABE φλαμουλάτα MW   304 κόμπον MW φαντασίαν ABE scr. mg. οἷον εἰς κομποφάνειαν W   305 ἐὰν MW ἐάν τε ABE | γάρ MABE om. W   306–307 βάλλεσθαι MW ῥίπτεσθαι ABE   307 καιρὸς γένηται MWA trsp. BE   308 καὶ²…ἐπιστροφὰς MWA om. BE   309 ποιοῦσι MBE ποιοῦσιν WA   311 τὸν κόμπον MW τὴν φαντασίαν ABE | ὥστε…μήκοθεν MW om. ABE   313–314 ἀποτιθοῦσιν MW ἀποτίθενται A ἀποτιθῶσιν BE   317 βιγλεύοντας MW βιγλάτωρας ABE   318 ὀκτὼ MWA η′ BE | δώδεκα MWA ιβ′ BE   320 εἰς οὓς MWA om. BE   321 τοῦ…ἐκβάσεως MW συμπληρώσεως τοῦ πολέμου ABE   321–322 ἐπιδρομὴ… δόλος MW ἢ δόλος ἢ ἐπιδρομὴ ABE   322 αὐτοῖς MWA τοῖς B τῶν E | γενήσεται MW γένηται ABE

wounded soldier are ready to mount the horse, the first gets on with the front stirrup and the second with the other stirrup. It is also essential for those assigned as corpsmen to carry flasks of water for the wounded who may well be fainting.

40. The soldiers are not to carry pennons on their lances during combat.[2] Pennons are just as useless in combat as they are important in military demonstrations and displays. For if one should wish to throw properly or hurl or shoot, the pennon will not allow him to hurl his weapon accurately, directly, or for a distance. When the time comes for archery, the pennons interfere with the fire of the archers to the rear. And when it comes to charging, turning movements, and wheeling about, they are no small impediment and, for this reason, they ought not to be used in combat.

41. However, to present a fine appearance of the battle line from a distance, keep the pennons on the lances until the enemy are about a mile away and then furl them and put them back into their cases.

42. In addition to the above, we order you, O general, from among the strong and powerful units to assign spies, that is, scouts for each tagma, and from the weaker units for each tourma, two for the tagma and eight or twelve for the tourma. These men should be alert, wide awake, and vigorous. Both before and during the battle and until its final outcome, in their own locations and in the places in which they are stationed at intervals, their duty is to observe, so the army will not suffer an attack from ambush or some other trick of the enemy.

2. See also *Strat.* 7.B.16–17. S. Dufrenne, "Aux sources des gonfanons," *Byzantion* 43 (1973): 51–60.

43. Καὶ τοὺς μινσοράτωρας δὲ τοσούτους εἶναι, τοὺς ὀφείλοντας προλαμβάνειν καὶ τὰ ἄπλικτα μετρεῖν καὶ τὰς ὁδοὺς προγινώσκειν καὶ πρὸς τὰ ἄπλικτα
325 τὸν στρατὸν ὁδηγεῖν. καὶ περὶ μὲν τούτων τοσαῦτα εἰρήσθω.

44. Χρὴ δὲ τὴν σὴν ἐνδοξότητα τὰ μὲν τῆς πρώτης παρατάξεως μέρη παρασκευάζειν ὥστε πλησίον ἀλλήλων περιπατεῖν καὶ μὴ ἀπὸ πολλοῦ διαστήματος ἤτοι διαλείμματος τὸ μεταξὺ αὐτῶν ἀπὸ μέρους εἰς μέρος, ἀλλὰ ὅσον μὴ συντρίβεσθαι ἐν τῷ περιπατεῖν μηδὲ διακεκριμένα ἀπ' ἀλλήλων φαίνεσθαι.

330 45. Τοὺς δὲ πλαγιοφύλακας μέχρι μὲν τοῦ ἐγγίζειν τοὺς ἐχθροὺς ἐγγὺς εἶναι, ὅτ' ἂν δὲ ἐγγίσωσιν, ὡς ἀπὸ σαγιττοβόλου τοῦ ἀριστεροῦ μέρους παρεκβαίνειν καὶ μὴ πλέον, ἐὰν μάλιστα ὑπερέχῃ εἰς μῆκος ἡ τῶν ἐναντίων παράταξις. ὁμοίως δὲ καὶ τοὺς ὑπερκεραστὰς ἤγουν τοὺς κυκλοῦν τοὺς πολεμίους ὀφείλοντας τάξεις εἰς τὸ δεξιὸν μέρος.

335 46. Τὰ δὲ μέρη τῆς δευτέρας παρατάξεως κατὰ μὲν πλευρὰν ἀλλήλων | ἤτοι 327ᵛ εἰς τὰ πλάγια ἀπὸ ἑνὸς σαγιττοβόλου τάξεις, κατὰ οὐρὰν δὲ ἤγουν κατόπισθεν τῆς πρώτης παρατάξεως περιπατεῖν ὥστε, μέχρι μὲν οἱ πολέμιοι μακρὰν ἀφεστήκασιν, ἀπὸ ἑνὸς ἢ καὶ πλέον μιλίου πρὸς τὴν τοῦ τόπου θέσιν, ὅσον δυνατόν ἐστιν, ἀφανῶς ἐπακολουθεῖν εἰς τὸ μὴ καθορᾶσθαι μήκοθεν ταύτην τοῖς πολεμί-
340 οις καὶ μεθοδεύεσθαι ἢ ἐπιβουλεύεσθαι ὑπ' αὐτῶν. ὅτ' ἂν δὲ οἱ ἐχθροὶ ἐγγίζωσιν καὶ λοιπὸν φαινομένης τῆς δευτέρας οὐ φθάζωσιν ἁρμόσασθαι, τότε ἐπιφαίνεσθαι αὐτὴν καὶ ἕως τεσσάρων σαγιττοβόλων ἐγγίζειν τῇ πρώτῃ καὶ κανονίζειν ἤγουν ἐπισκοπεῖν αὐτήν. οὐδὲ γὰρ μήκοθεν πολὺ ὀφείλει εἶναι ἡ δευτέρα τῆς πρώτης ἐν καιρῷ τῆς συμβολῆς ἵνα μὴ ἀβοήθητον αὐτὴν καταλίπῃ, οὐδὲ πάλιν
345 πολὺ ἐγγύς, ἵνα μὴ συμφύρηται τῇ πρώτῃ ἐν ταῖς συμβολαῖς, κονιορτοῦ μάλι-

---

323 μινσοράτωρας MW μινσουράτωρας ABE   325 στρατὸν MW στρατηγὸν ABE   327 καὶ AE om. MWB   328 διαλείμματος MW om. ABE | αὐτῶν MW αὐτῶν διαχώρισμα ABE | μέρος MW μέρος μὴ ἔστω πολὺ ABE | ἀλλὰ MW ἀλλ' ABE   329 διακεκριμένα MW διακεχωρισμένα ABE   330 μέχρι...εἶναι MW ἕως οὐ πλησιάσωσιν οἱ ἐχθροὶ ἔγγυς περιπατεῖν ABE   331 παρεκβαίνειν MW παρεκβάλλειν αὐτοὺς εἰς πλάγιον ABE   333 ἤγουν...ὀφείλοντας MW om. ABE   334 μέρος MW μέρος ἤγουν τοὺς ὀφείλοντας κυκλῶσαι τοὺς πολεμίους ABE   335 κατὰ MW κατ' ABE   336 εἰς...πλάγια MW ἐκ πλαγίου ABE | κατόπισθεν MW ὄπισθεν ABE   337–338 ἀφεστήκασιν MW εἰσὶν ABE   338 ἢ...μιλίου MW μιλίου ἢ (om. BE) καὶ πλέον ABE   339 μήκοθεν ταύτην MW trsp. ABE   339–340 τοῖς πολεμίοις MW ὑπὸ τῶν πολεμίων ABE   340 ἐγγίζωσιν MW ἐγγίζωσι A ἐγγίσωσι BE   341 φθάζωσιν MW συμφθάζουσιν A συμφθάσωσιν BE   341–342 τότε ἐπιφαίνεσθαι MWA ἢ ἀντιστρατηγῆσαι πρὸς BE   343 ἐπισκοπεῖν MW ἐπιβλέπειν ABE | αὐτήν MW αὐτὴν καὶ πρὸς ἐκείνην περιπατεῖν ABE | δευτέρα MW δευτέρα παράταξις ABE   344 ἐν MW ἐν τῷ ABE

43. There should be an appropriate number of surveyors who are assigned to go ahead and measure the camp sites, reconnoiter the roads and guide the army to the camp. That is enough said about these matters.

44. It is incumbent on Your Excellency to organize the divisions of the first battle line so that they march about close to one another and that the distance or interval between one meros and another is not great, but enough to keep them from crowding together while marching and not to have them appear separated from each other.

45. The flank guards should remain close in until the enemy moves nearer. As they approach, they should move out to the side about a bowshot from the left meros but no further, especially if the battle line of the enemy is longer. In like manner, form the outflankers, that is, those whose task it is to encircle the enemy, on the right side.

46. Line up the divisions of the second battle line about a bowshot from one another's side or flank, moving around to the rear or behind the first battle line. While the enemy are still a good distance away, they are to follow along a mile or more, depending on the terrain and, as much as possible without being noticed, so that the enemy may not observe them from a distance and change their tactics or their plans accordingly. But when the enemy gets close and the second line indeed becomes visible, they have no time to adapt their tactics. Then the second line should make itself seen and move up closely, four bowshots from the first, and observe it and so regulate its moves. During battle, the second line ought not to be so far from the first that it leaves it without support, nor, on the other hand, so close that it gets mixed up with the first in

στα κινουμένου καὶ πρὸ τοῦ διαλυθῆναι τοὺς πολεμίους καταδιώκοντας τὴν πρώτην εὑρεθῇ.

47. Τὰ δὲ τάγματα τὰ ὄπισθεν τῶν ἄκρων τῆς δευτέρας ἑκατέρωθεν τασσό-μενα ἤγουν ἐντεῦθεν καὶ ἐκεῖθεν δεῖ ὡς ἀπὸ ἑνὸς σαγιττοβόλου αὐτῶν εἰς 350 νώτου φυλακὴν ταγῆναι καὶ οὕτως ἀκολουθεῖν.

48. Τὰ δὲ βάνδα ἤγουν τὰ σημεῖα αὐτῶν χρὴ καθ᾽ ἑκάστην τοῦρμαν, τὰ μὲν τῶν ταγμάτων μικρότερα εἶναι καὶ ἐλαφρά, τὰ δὲ τῶν μοιραρχῶν ἤτοι τῶν δρουγγαρίων μεγαλώτερα καὶ ἐξηλλαγμένα· ὁμοίως δὲ καὶ τὰ τῶν τουρμαρχῶν ἐξηλλαγμένα πρὸς τὰ τῶν ὑπ᾽ αὐτοὺς ταττομένων δρουγγαρίων. τὸ δὲ ὑποστρα-355 τήγου βάνδον διαφορὰν ἔχειν παρὰ τὰ τῶν τουρμαρχῶν βάνδα, ὥσπερ οὖν καὶ τὸ τῆς σῆς ἐνδοξότητος ἐνηλλαγμένον ὀφείλει εἶναι καὶ διαφανὲς παρὰ τὰ ἄλλα πάντα καὶ πᾶσιν εὔγνωστον ἐφ᾽ ᾧ, ἐν δευτέρᾳ τύχῃ, πρὸς αὐτὸ βλέποντας εὐκόλως, ὡς εἴρηται, συνάγεσθαι καὶ ἑαυτοὺς ἀνακαλεῖσθαι τούς τε ἄρχοντας καὶ τοὺς στρατιώτας.

360 49. Πάντων δὲ τῶν βάνδων ἰσομετώπων ἐν τάξει ἱσταμένων δέον ἐκ τῶν περὶ αὐτὰ τασσομένων στρατιωτῶν τοὺς γενναιοτέρους, κἂν πεντεκαίδεκα ἢ καὶ εἴκοσι ἄνδρας, ἀφορίσαι ἐπὶ τῇ ἑκάστου αὐτῶν φυλακῇ καὶ διεκδικήσει.

50. Τοὺς δὲ ἄρχοντας τοὺς μείζονας ἀσφαλῶς δεῖ τάσσεσθαι εἰς τὸ μὴ προπετευομένους ἐν ταῖς μάχαις διαπίπτειν καὶ ἐντεῦθεν τοῖς στρατιώταις 365 ὀλιγωρίαν ἐγγίνεσθαι. ἐκ μὲν γὰρ τῶν μικροτέρων ἀρχόντων, εἰ συμβῇ παρα|  328 πεσεῖν τινα, οὐδενὶ εὐκόλως γινώσκεται ἀλλ᾽ ἢ τοῖς τοῦ ἰδίου τάγματος μόνοις,

---

346 κινουμένου MW ἐγειρομένου AE ἐγχειρουμένου B | καταδιώκοντας MW ἐπακολουθοῦσα ABE    346–347 τὴν πρώτην MW τῇ πρώτῃ ABE    348 τὰ² MWA om. BE | δευτέρας MW δευτέρας παρατάξεως ABE  349 ἐντεῦθεν MW ἔνθεν ABE 349–350 αὐτῶν…ταγῆναι MW ταγῆναι αὐτὰ εἰς φυλακὴν τῶν ὀπισθίων μερῶν ABE 353 ἐξηλλαγμένα MW παρηλλαγμένα ABE | τὰ MWA om. BE    354 ἐξηλλαγμένα MW ἐνηλλαγμένα ABE | πρὸς MW παρὰ ABE | ταττομένων MW τεταγμένων ABE | δὲ MW δὲ τοῦ ABE    355 τῶν…βάνδα MW trsp. ABE    356 ἐνηλλαγμένον MWAB ἐνηλλαγμένου E | διαφανὲς MW ἐμφανέστερον ABE  357 πᾶσιν εὔγνωστον MW πᾶσιν εὐδιάγνωστον A εὐδιάγνωστον πᾶσιν B εὐδιάγνωστα πᾶσιν E | ἐφ᾽ ᾧ MW ὥστε ABE    358 ὡς MWA om. BE 361 κἂν ABE καὶ MW | πεντεκαίδεκα MW δεκαπέντε A ιε′ BE    362 εἴκοσι MWA κ′ BE 363 ἄρχοντας…μείζονας MW trsp. ABE    364 διαπίπτειν MW κινδυνεύειν ABE scr. mg. φονεύεσθαι W | ἐντεῦθεν MWA ἐντεῦθεν λοιπὸν BE    364–365 τοῖς…ὀλιγωρίαν (ὀλιγωρίας BE) MWBE ὀλιγωρίαν τοῖς στρατιώταις A    365 ἐγγίνεσθαι ABE ἐγγίγνεσθαι MW | εἰ MW ἐὰν ABE    365–366 παραπεσεῖν τινα MW τινὰ κινδυνεῦσαι ABE    366 οὐδενὶ WABE οὐδὲν M | γινώσκεται MW ἐπιγινώσκεται ABE

the fighting, especially when dust is being kicked up and before the enemy has broken ranks in pursuit of the first line.

47. The units stationed behind the wings on both sides of the second line, that is, here and there, should be drawn up about a bowshot behind to guard the rear and should follow at the same distance.

48. Each tourma must have its flags or standards.[3] Those of the tagmata should be fairly small and light, while those of the moirarchs or the droungarioi should be larger and of a different design. In like manner, those of the tour-marchs should differ from those of the droungarioi under their command. The flag of the lieutenant general should differ from the flags of the tourmarchs. Finally, that of Your Excellency should be clearly distinctive, more conspicuous than all the others, and well known to all, so that in case of adverse fortune both officers and soldiers may easily see it, as said, and rally and regroup themselves.

49. When all the flags have been set up along the length of the line, you must detail fifteen or even twenty men from among the most courageous soldiers in formation around them to guard and defend each flag.

50. Superior officers should be stationed in safe places so they do not dash forward in battle and fall. This greatly weakens the soldiers' resolve. If one of the subordinate officers should happen to fall, it will not easily become known except only to the men of his own unit. But if one of the more prominent officers

3. Cf. Const. 6 §16, n. 6.

εἰ δέ τις τῶν ἐμφανῶν διαπέσῃ ἢ τοῖς πᾶσιν ἢ τοῖς πολλοῖς δηλούμενος ὁ θάνατος αὐτοῦ ὀλιγωρίαν τῷ ὅλῳ στρατῷ εἰσάγει.

51. Διὸ πρέπον ἐστίν, ὦ στρατηγέ, τὸν ὑποστράτηγον καὶ τοὺς τουρμάρχας
370 μέχρι μὲν ἀπὸ ἑνὸς ἢ δευτέρου σαγιττοβόλου τῆς τῶν ἐχθρῶν παρατάξεως ἰσομετώπους τάσσεσθαι μετὰ τῶν βάνδων καὶ ἐπιβλέπειν καὶ ἁρμόζειν τὴν τάξιν. ὅτ᾽ ἂν δὲ μέλλῃ συμβολὴ γίνεσθαι, ἐκ τῶν ἰδικῶν αὐτῶν ἀνθρώπων τοὺς γενναιοτέρους εἰς τὸ πλάγιον αὐτῶν παρατάσσεσθαι καὶ προέρχεσθαι εἰς ὄψιν αὐτῶν καὶ σκέπειν αὐτοὺς καὶ ἐκείνους μᾶλλον χεῖρας μιγνύειν.

375 52. Τὴν δὲ σὴν ἐνδοξότητα κελεύομεν, μέχρι μὲν ὁ καιρὸς τῆς συμβολῆς γένηται, τάσσειν καὶ ἐπιβλέπειν καὶ ἁρμόζεσθαι τῇ τῶν ἐχθρῶν κινήσει, τότε δὲ ἐν τῷ ἰδικῷ σου ἔρχεσθαι τάγματι, ὅπερ οὐ πρὸς μάχην, ἀλλὰ πρὸς σκοπόν τινα καὶ κανόνα τῆς πρώτης καὶ δευτέρας τάξεως τέτακται, τοῦτ᾽ ἔστιν ἐν τῷ μέσῳ χωρίῳ τῆς δευτέρας τάξεως.

380 53. Πολλὰ δὲ βούκινα λαλεῖν ἢ κινεῖν ἐν καιρῷ μάχης, ὡς ἐπιβλαβὲς ὄν, οὐ συμβουλεύομεν ἵνα μὴ ἐκ τούτου θόρυβός τις καὶ σύγχυσις γένηται· καὶ γὰρ διὰ τοῦτο οὐδὲ τὰ παραγγελλόμενα καλῶς ἐξακούεσθαι δύναται. ἀλλ᾽ εἰ μὲν ὁ τόπος ὁμαλὸς εὑρεθῇ, ἀρκεῖ τὸ βούκινον τοῦ μέσου μέρους ἑκατέρᾳ παρατάξει, εἰ δὲ ἀνώμαλός ἐστιν ἢ ἄνεμος, ὡς πολλάκις, ταραχώδης κινεῖται ἢ ἦχος ὕδατος
385 παρεμποδίζῃ τῇ φωνῇ τοῦ καθαρῶς διακούεσθαι, οὐκ ἄτοπον τότε καὶ ἐν τοῖς λοιποῖς μέρεσιν ἓν βούκινον ἐν ἑκάστῳ μέρει λαλεῖν, ὥστε τρία λαλεῖν βούκινα ἐν ὅλῃ τῇ παρατάξει. ὅσον γὰρ ἡσυχία φυλάττεται, τοσοῦτον καὶ οἱ νεώτεροι ἀτάραχοι καὶ τὰ ἄλογα ἄπτυρτα γίνονται καὶ ἡ τάξις φοβερωτέρα τοῖς ἐχθροῖς φαίνεται καὶ τὰ μανδάτα εὐκόλως γινώσκονται.

---

**367** διαπέσῃ MW κινδυνεύσει ABE **368** ὀλιγωρίαν MW ὀλιγωρίαν καὶ ἀθυμίαν ABE | εἰσάγει MW ἐμποιεῖ ABE **370** τῶν MWAE τῶν τῶν B | παρατάξεως MW παρατάξεως οὔσης ABE **372** τάξιν MW παράταξιν ABE | γίνεσθαι MWA γενέσθαι BE | ἰδικῶν MW ἰδίων ABE **373** γενναιοτέρους MW ἰσχυροτέρους ABE | αὐτῶν MWAE om. B **374** αὐτοὺς ABE om. MW **375–376** μέχρι…κινήσει MW πρὸ τῆς συμβολῆς τοῦ πολέμου τάσσειν (στάσιν B) καὶ ἐπιβλέπειν τὸν στρατὸν καὶ πρὸς τὴν κίνησιν τῶν ἐχθρῶν ἁρμόζεσθαι ἡνίκα δὲ ἡ συμβολὴ τοῦ πολέμου γένηται ABE **377** ἔρχεσθαι τάγματι MW trsp. ABE (τάγματα) | σκοπόν MWAE σκοπὴν B **380** λαλεῖν MWA λέγειν BE | ἢ κινεῖν MW om. ABE **380–381** ὡς…συμβουλεύομεν MW οὐ συμβουλεύομεν ἐπιβλαβὲς γὰρ ABE **381** καὶ¹…γένηται MW γένηται καὶ σύγχυσις ABE **382** καλῶς ἐξακούεσθαι MWAB trsp. E | δύναται MW δύνανται ABE **383** ἑκατέρᾳ παρατάξει MW ἀμφοτέραις ταῖς παρατάξεσιν ABE **384** ἔστιν MW ἐστιν ὁ τόπος ABE | ὡς πολλάκις MW om. ABE **385** παρεμποδίζῃ MW παρεμποδίζει AB κίνηται E | διακούεσθαι MW ἐξακούεσθαι ABE | τότε MWAB τε E **388** ἄπτυρτα MW ἄσκυλτα ABE | γίνονται ABE γίνεται MW **389** μανδάτα MW παραγγέλματα ABE

should fall, his death becomes known to all or most of the troops and causes the whole army to lose heart.

51. Therefore, O general, the lieutenant general and the tourmarchs must take their stand on the same line as the flags, there to supervise and regulate the formation until the army is one or two bowshots from the enemy's battle line. When the fighting is just about to begin, the most courageous of our own men are drawn up to the sides <of the flag guards> and should move forward in front of them as a screen and then engage in hand-to-hand combat.

52. We order Your Excellency, up to the moment of the charge, to organize the formation, supervise, and adapt to the movements of the enemy. Then you should join your own tagma that is drawn up, not for battle, but as a sort of landmark and guide for the first and second lines, that is, in the center of the second line.

53. We do not approve of many trumpets being sounded or blown in time of battle, for it is harmful and leads to some disturbance and confusion. It also makes it impossible to hear the commands properly. If the ground is level, one trumpet in the middle meros of each battle line is enough. If the ground is uneven or a violent wind is blowing, as frequently happens, or the noise of water makes it difficult to hear a voice clearly, then it is not a bad idea to have one trumpet sound in each of the other divisions, which means that three trumpets will sound in the whole battle line. The better silence is observed, the less disturbed will the younger men be and the less excited the horses; the line will appear more fearsome to the enemy, and the commands will be more easily understood.

390   54. Διὸ οὐδὲ τὴν οἰανοῦν φωνὴν ἀκαίρως δεῖ ἀκούεσθαι μετὰ τὸ κινεῖσθαι τὴν παράταξιν ἐπὶ πόλεμον, ἀλλὰ ἅμα τοῦ ἐξελθεῖν ἀπὸ τοῦ φοσσάτου ἤγουν τοῦ ἀπλίκτου τὸν στρατὸν ἐπὶ τὴν μάχην παντοίαν ἡσυχίαν ἄγειν καὶ μηδὲν ἀκαίρως φθέγγεσθαι. τοῦτο γὰρ οὐ μόνον τὸν στρατὸν ἀτάραχον φυλάττει, ἀλλὰ καὶ τὰ τῶν ἀρχόντων βάνδα μετὰ προσοχῆς ἀποσκοπεῖσθαι ποιεῖ.

395   55. Τὸ δὲ μέτρον καὶ | τὴν ποιότητα τῆς συμβολῆς αὐτὸ τὸ πρᾶγμα δοκιμάζει  328ᵛ
καὶ ἡ σφίγξις ἡ πρέπουσα καὶ ἡ τῶν ἐχθρῶν παρουσία· καὶ κινοῦντα μὲν πρὸς τὴν συμπλοκὴν τὴν συνήθη Χριστιανοῖς νικητήριον τοῦ σταυροῦ φωνὴν ἀνα-κράζειν δεῖ. ὅτ᾽ ἂν δὲ εἰς χεῖρας ἔλθῃ ὁ στρατός, τότε ἀλαλάζειν ἢ ὠρύᾶσθαι, καὶ μάλιστα τοὺς ὄπισθεν τασσομένους, πρὸς κατάπληξιν τῶν ἐχθρῶν καὶ διανά-
400   στασιν τῶν ἰδίων οὐκ ἄτοπόν ἐστιν.

56. Ἁρμόδιον δὲ ἡμῖν καταφαίνεται ἐν τῷ τῆς συμπλοκῆς καιρῷ καὶ τὸ τῶν λεγομένων καντατώρων ἔργον. οὗτοι δέ εἰσιν οἱ τὸν στρατὸν διὰ λόγων παρο-τρύνοντες καὶ συμβουλεύοντες καὶ κατεπάδοντες καὶ παρακαλοῦντες πρὸς τοὺς ἀγῶνας· καὶ ἵνα, εἰ δυνατόν, ἐξ αὐτῶν ἐκείνων τῶν στρατιωτῶν ἢ τῶν
405   ἀρχόντων τὸ τοιοῦτον ἔργον ποιεῖται. ἐπιλέγονται δὲ τοιούτους λογίους ἄν-δρας οἱ ἄρχοντες καὶ δυνατοὺς διὰ λόγων ὁμιλεῖν τῷ στρατῷ. ἡ γὰρ κοινωνία τοῦ καμάτου καὶ τῶν πόνων εὐπειθεστέρους ποιεῖ τοὺς ἀκούοντας τοῖς παρακο-λουθοῦσι συστρατιώταις.

57. Λέγειν δὲ τοὺς καντάτωρας πρὸς τὸν στρατὸν προτρεπτικά τινα πρὸς
410   τὸν πόλεμον τοιαῦτα· πρῶτον μὲν ἀναμιμνήσκοντας τῶν μισθῶν τῆς εἰς Θεὸν πίστεως καὶ τὰς ἐκ βασιλέων εὐεργεσίας καί τινων ἐπιτυχιῶν προγεγενημένων. καὶ ὅτι ὁ ἀγὼν ὑπὲρ Θεοῦ ἐστι καὶ τῆς εἰς αὐτὸν ἀγάπης καὶ ὑπὲρ ὅλου τοῦ

---

397–398 ὁ σταυρὸς νικᾷ. *vincit crux.*

---

390 δεῖ MWA om. BE | ἀκούεσθαι MWA διακούεσθαι ΒΕ | κινεῖσθαι MW κινῆσαι ΑΒΕ 391 ἀλλὰ MW ἀλλ᾽ ΑΒΕ | τοῦ¹ MW τῷ ΑΕ τὸ Β | τοῦ²…ἤγουν MW om. ΑΒΕ   392 μηδὲν MWA μηδένα ΒΕ   394 ἀποσκοπεῖσθαι MW ἀποβλέπεσθαι ΑΒΕ   395 τὴν ποιότητα MW τὸν τρόπον ΑΒΕ   397 χριστιανοῖς ΑΒΕ om. MW   397–398 ἀνακράζειν MWA ἀναγκάζειν ΒΕ   398 ὠρύᾶσθαι Va ὀρυᾶσθαι MW ὠρύεσθαι ΑΒΕ   399–400 διανάστασιν Va ἀνάστασιν MW διέγερσιν ΑΒΕ   400 ἰδίων MWAB οἰκείων Ε   402 λεγομένων MW om. ΑΒΕ | καντατώρων MW στρατοκηρύκων ΑΒΕ   403 καὶ κατεπάδοντες MW om. ΑΒΕ   404 εἰ MWAE εἰς Β   405 ποιεῖται Va ποιοῦνται MW ποιῶνται ΑΒΕ | λογίους MW περίλογον Α περὶ λόγον ΒΕ   407–408 παρακολουθοῦσι MWE παρακολουθοῦσιν Β παρακαλοῦσι Α (corr. ex παρακολουθοῦσι)   409 δὲ MWBE δὲ καὶ Α | καντάτωρας MW στρατοκήρυκας ΑΒΕ | τινα MW τινα καὶ διεγείροντα ΑΒΕ   410–411 τῶν…πίστεως MW τῆς εἰς θεὸν πίστεως τὸν μισθὸν ΑΒΕ   411 βασιλέων MW βασιλέως ΑΒΕ | ἐπιτυχιῶν MW εὐτυχιῶν ΑΒΕ | προγεγενημένων MWAE προσγεγενημένων Β   412 καὶ¹ MWAB om. Ε | ἐστι MWAB ἐστιν Ε

54. For these reasons, no improper sound of any kind should be heard after the battle line has started to move toward combat.[4] But as the army marches out of the entrenchments, or the camp, to combat, it should keep absolute silence and not utter a word out of order. Not only does this keep the army undisturbed but it also enables the flags of the officers to be observed more attentively.

55. The action itself, the necessary closing up of ranks, and the presence of the enemy dictates the measure and the quality of the charge. As it moves into battle <the men> must loudly shout the victory cry of the cross, customary among Christians.[5] But when the army closes with the enemy, it is not a bad idea for <them> to shout war cries and cheer, especially those in the rear ranks, to unnerve the enemy and encourage our own troops.

56. The function of the so-called heralds in time of battle impresses us as useful. They are the ones who address <the troops> urging them on, exhorting them, stirring them by song, and encouraging them for the struggle. If possible, this task should be performed by the soldiers or the officers themselves. The officers should select men who are eloquent and able to address the army with fitting words. By sharing the toil and the labors, they make their hearers more ready to obey their fellow soldiers who accompany them.

57. The heralds should speak to the army in words exhorting them on to battle. First they should call to mind the reward for their faith in God and the benefactions of the emperor, and some of their previous victories. The struggle is on behalf of God and his love for them and on behalf of the entire nation. It is,

4. See Dennis, "The Byzantines in Battle."

5. Stavros nika (the cross is victorious). On beginning their advance the soldiers were to shout: *Nobiscum Deus* (God is with us): *Strat.* 2.18. Cf. also Vegetius, *Epitoma rei militaris*, 3.5.

ἔθνους. πλέον δὲ ὑπὲρ τῶν ἀδελφῶν τῶν ὁμοπίστων, εἰ τύχοι, καὶ ὑπὲρ γυναι-
κῶν καὶ τέκνων καὶ πατρίδος καὶ ὅτι αἰωνία μένει ἡ μνήμη τῶν ἀριστευόντων
415 κατὰ πολέμους ὑπὲρ τῆς τῶν ἀδελφῶν ἐλευθερίας καὶ ὅτι κατὰ τῶν τοῦ Θεοῦ
ἐχθρῶν ὁ τοσοῦτος ἀγὼν καὶ ὅτι ἡμεῖς μὲν τὸν Θεὸν ἔχομεν φίλον τὸν ἔχοντα
ἐξουσίαν τῆς ῥοπῆς τοῦ πολέμου, ἐκεῖνοι δὲ ἐναντίον αὐτὸν ἔχουσι διὰ τῆς εἰς
αὐτὸν ἀπιστίας καὶ εἴ τι ἕτερον τούτοις ὅμοιον ἐπινοοῦντας ποιεῖσθαι τὴν
προτρεπτικὴν νουθεσίαν. πολλὰ γὰρ ἰσχύει τοιοῦτος λόγος εὐκαίρως γινόμενος
420 διεγεῖραι ψυχὰς μᾶλλον ἢ χρημάτων πλῆθος.

58. Ἔτι δέ σοι καὶ τοῦτο οὐ παραλείψω, ἐπειδὴ γὰρ δυνατόν ἐστι καταστοχά-
σασθαι τοὺς ἐναντίους τῆς ποσότητος τοῦ ἡμετέρου στρατοῦ ὡς ἐπιπολὺ διὰ
τοῦ ἀριθμοῦ τῶν βάνδων, ἀναγκαῖον εἶναι λογιζόμεθα δύο ὅμοια βάνδα καθ᾽
ἕκαστον τάγμα, ἓν μὲν τὸ αὐθεντικόν, τὸ ὀφεῖλον ἐπ᾽ ὀνόματι εἶναι τοῦ κόμη-
425 τος, ἕτερον δὲ τὸ τοῦ κεντάρχου καὶ ἀμφότερα τὰ βάνδα βαστάζεσθαι μέχρι τῆς
ἡμέρας τοῦ πολέμου. κατ᾽ αὐτὴν δὲ | τὴν ἡμέραν τῆς συμβολῆς τὰ αὐθεντικὰ    329
καὶ μόνα βάνδα ὑψοῦσθαι, ὥστε μὴ πολλῶν βάνδων ὑψουμένων φύρειν ἅπαντα
ἢ καὶ ἀνεπίγνωστα γενέσθαι τοῖς ἰδίοις αὐτῶν στρατιώταις. ἐντεῦθεν γὰρ
δυνατόν ἐστι καὶ πολὺν τὸν στρατὸν φαίνεσθαι ἐκ τοῦ ἀριθμοῦ αὐτῶν καὶ τῇ
430 ἡμέρᾳ τοῦ πολέμου τὰ αὐθεντικά, ὡς εὐεπίγνωστα, φαίνεσθαι.

59. Πρὸ δέ τινων ἡμερῶν τοῦ καιροῦ τῆς συμβολῆς, ὅτε μάλιστα καὶ προ-
γυμνασίαν δεῖ γενέσθαι τῶν τε παραγγελμάτων καὶ τῶν μερικῶν κινήσεων, δεῖ
τοὺς ἑκάστης τούρμας ἄρχοντας μετακαλέσασθαι καὶ διαλαλῆσαι πρὸς τοὺς
τοῦ ἰδίου μέρους τὰ ἁρμόδια, οἷον ὅτι· "οὐ μάτην αἱ γυμνασίαι τῶν στρατιωτῶν
435 παρά τε τῶν παλαιῶν καὶ τῶν νέων στρατηγῶν ἐξετέθησαν καὶ αἱ κατὰ τέχνην
παρατάξεις καὶ αἱ ἐπ᾽ εὐθείας καὶ κατὰ κύκλους καὶ τὰ ἄλλα σχήματα κινήσεις.

---

431–582 *Strat.*, 3.11–16.

---

413 τῶν¹ W om. MABE    416 τὸν¹…ἔχομεν MW trsp. ABE    417 ῥοπῆς…πολέμου MW
trsp. ABE    417–418 τῆς²…ἀπιστίας MW τὴν -- ἀπιστίαν ABE    418 τούτοις ὅμοιον MW
trsp. ABE    419 γινόμενος MWA λεγόμενος BE    420 πλῆθος MWA om. BE
421–422 ἔτι…καταστοχάσασθαι MW ἐπειδὴ δὲ δυνατόν ἐστι (ἐστιν A) διὰ τοῦ ἀριθμοῦ τῶν
βάνδων στοχάσασθαι ABE    422–423 ὡς…βάνδων MW om. ABE    423 δύο MWA β′ BE
424 τάγμα MW τάγμα εἶναι ABE | αὐθεντικόν MW κύριον ABE    426 αὐθεντικὰ MW
κύρια ABE    427 καὶ MWA om. BE | βάνδα MWAE βάνδα τοῦ πολέμου B    428 ἢ MW
om. ABE | γενέσθαι MW γίνεσθαι ABE    430 αὐθεντικά MW κύρια ABE | εὐεπίγνωστα
MWAB ἐπίγνωστα E    431 πρὸ MWAE πρὸς B | τινων ἡμερῶν MW trsp. ABE
432 γενέσθαι MWA γίνεσθαι BE    433 μετακαλέσασθαι MW προσκαλέσασθαι ABE
433–434 καὶ…ἁρμόδια MW τοὺς τοῦ ἰδίου μέρους καὶ διαλαλῆσαι πρὸς αὐτοὺς τὰ
ἁρμόζοντα ABE    435 παλαιῶν…νέων MW νέων καὶ τῶν παλαιῶν ABE    436 καὶ²…
κινήσεις MW κινήσεις καὶ τὰ ἄλλα σχήματα ABE

furthermore, on behalf of their brothers and fellow believers and, if it applies, for their wives and children and their fatherland. Eternal indeed remains the memory of those who have valiantly striven against the foe on behalf of the freedom of their brothers, and who have struggled so bravely against the enemies of God. We indeed hold God as our friend who bears the power of balance in war. The foe are the very opposite because of their lack of faith in him. If the heralds think of anything else along these lines, they should make use of it in their exhortations and admonitions. Such words uttered at the right time are very powerful in arousing spirits, more than a large amount of money.

58. Still <addressing> you, I will not omit this. Since it is generally possible for the enemy to estimate the numbers in our army by the number of standards, we consider it necessary for each unit to have two standards, both very similar. One is the authentic standard which ought to be in the name of the count and the other that of the kentarch. Both standards should be carried aloft until the day of battle, but on that day the authentic standard alone should be raised. Flying a large number of standards leads to confusion and they may not be recognized by their own soldiers. In this way, then, it is possible for the army to appear large from the number of standards and on the day of battle to fly the authentic one only and it will be easily recognized.

59. Some days before the day of battle, especially when preparatory drilling in the commands and the maneuvers of divisions is scheduled, the officers of each tourma should be called together and should address appropriate words to the men of their own divisions, along the following lines.[6] It was not in vain that the generals, both ancient and modern, regulated the drills and the skillfully arranged battle lines, as well as maneuvers that are direct, those that are circular,

---

6. Sections 59–80 derive from *Strat.* 3.11–16.

εἰ γὰρ ἄγρια ζῷα διωκόμενα, οἷον ἔλαφοι καὶ λαγωοὶ ἢ ἄλλο τι τῶν εὐτελῶν
ζῴων ἐν τοῖς κυνηγίοις οὐ πάντως ἔξωθεν ἔξω καὶ ἐπ᾽ εὐθείας τὴν φυγὴν ποιοῦνται, ἀλλ᾽ ἀποβλέποντα πρὸς τὸν τόνον καὶ τὴν ὁρμὴν τῶν ἐπιτιθεμένων
440 αὐτοῖς οὕτως καὶ τὰς ὑποχωρήσεις ποιοῦνται, πόσῳ δεῖ μᾶλλον τοὺς ἀνθρώπους ἐν συνέσει ὄντας καὶ ὑπὲρ μεγάλων πραγμάτων ἀγωνιζομένους προσεχόν-
τως καὶ τὰς διώξεις καὶ τὰς ὑποχωρήσεις ποιεῖσθαι ἐν ταῖς μάχαις, καὶ μὴ ὥσπερ
ἐπὶ ὕδατος ἐπὶ τὰ ἔμπροσθεν ἢ ἐπὶ τὰ ὀπίσω ἐκχέεσθαι μικρᾶς, ὡς εἰκός, τινὸς
ὠθήσεως ἢ τοῖς ἐχθροῖς γινομένης ἢ παρ᾽ αὐτῶν ἐπαγομένης, καὶ ἀμέτρως
445 οὕτως ἐλαυνομένους κινδυνεύειν, ἀλλὰ πάντα ὑπομένειν, ὥστε ἐξ οἱουδήποτε
τρόπου σπουδάζειν νικᾶν τὸν ἐχθρόν. οὐδὲ γὰρ τὸ πρὸς ὀλίγον διῶξαι τὸν
ἐναντίον καὶ ἀφεῖναι τελεία νίκη ἐστίν, οὐδὲ τὸ πρὸς μικρὸν ὑποχωρῆσαι καὶ
πάλιν ἀντιστραφῆναι ἧττα, ἀλλὰ ἀπὸ τοῦ πέρατος τοῦ πολέμου ἑκάτερα δείκνυται καὶ πρὸς αὐτὸ δεῖ ἀγωνίζεσθαι." ταῦτα καὶ τούτοις ὅμοια τῷ στρατῷ
450 διαλαλεῖν χρεωστοῦσιν οἱ ἑκάστου μέρους τουρμάρχαι καὶ ἰδίως τοῖς ἰδίοις
στρατιώταις.

60. Σὺ δὲ μετὰ τὴν ἰδιάζουσαν τῶν τουρμαρχῶν καὶ γυμνασίαν καὶ διαλαλιάν, ὦ στρατηγέ, τάξεις εἰς τὸ ἅπαξ ἢ καὶ τὸ πολὺ δεύτερον τὴν ὅλην παράταξιν
καὶ ὁμοίως καταστήσεις αὐτοὺς καὶ διὰ λόγων καὶ δι᾽ ἔργων ἑτοίμους εἶναι καὶ
455 ἐμπείρους πάντοτε πρὸς τοὺς πολεμικοὺς ἀγῶνας.

61. Παραγγείλῃς δὲ τοῖς τῆς πρώτης ἤτοι τῆς προμάχου τάξεως ἄρχουσιν
ὥστε τῷ | μέσῳ πείθεσθαι μέρει, ἔνθα τὸν ὑποστράτηγόν σου συμβαίνει τάσ-   329ᵛ
σεσθαι ἤτοι τὸν λεγόμενον νῦν τοῦ θέματος μεράρχην καὶ ἰσοῦσθαι αὐτῷ καὶ
ἅμα τὴν συμβολὴν ποιεῖσθαι. καὶ ταύτης γενομένης, ἐὰν τραπῶσιν οἱ ἐχθροί,
460 τοὺς μὲν κούρσωρας σὺν ἐλασίᾳ ὁρμᾶν κατ᾽ αὐτῶν εἰς ἐπιδίωξιν ἕως αὐτοῦ τοῦ
φοσσάτου αὐτῶν, τοὺς δὲ διφένσωρας ἐπακολουθεῖν ἐν τάξει καὶ μὴ ἀπομένειν
ἵνα τῶν ἐχθρῶν, ὡς εἰκός, ἀντιστρεφομένων, ἐὰν μὴ δυνηθῶσιν βαστάσαι οἱ

---

437 ζῷα Α   ζῴων MWBE   439–440 ἀλλ᾽…ποιοῦνται MWA om. BE
439–440 ἐπιτιθεμένων αὐτοῖς MW ἐπιδιωκόντων αὐτὰ A om. BE   440 οὕτως MW οὕτω A
om. BE | δεῖ μᾶλλον MW trsp. ABE   443 ἔμπροσθεν MW ἔμπροσθεν μόνον ABE | ἐπὶ³…
ὀπίσω MW ὄπισθεν ABE | ὡς…τινὸς MW τινὸς ὡς εἰκὸς ABE   445 ἐξ οἱουδήποτε MABE
ἐξοιδήποτε W   448 ἀλλὰ MWAE ἀλλ᾽ Β | πέρατος MW τέλους ABE   449 καὶ² MWA καὶ
τὰ BE   450 χρεωστοῦσιν MW ὀφείλουσι τῷ στρατῷ ABE | τοῖς ἰδίοις MWA γυμνάσαι καὶ
διαλαλῆσαι BE   452–453 μετὰ…παράταξιν MW ὦ στράτηγε μετὰ τὸ τοὺς τουρμάρχας
ἰδίως γυμνάσαι καὶ διαλαλῆσαι τοῖς στρατιώταις τάξεις (τάξιν Β) τὴν ὅλην παράταξιν ἅπαξ ἢ
τὸ πολὺ δεύτερον ABE   456 παραγγείλῃς MA παραγγείλεις WE παραγγείλας Β | ἤτοι…
προμάχου MW om. ABE | τάξεως MWA παρατάξεως BE   457 πείθεσθαι μέρει MW trsp.
ABE | ἔνθα MWA ὥστε BE   458 τοῦ MWAE om. Β   459 γενομένης MW γινομένης ABE
| ἐὰν MWA ἂν BE   462 δυνηθῶσιν MWE δυνηθῶσι AB

and those that take other forms. For if wild animals, such as deer, rabbits, and other small animals, when pursued during the hunt, do not utterly abandon themselves to headlong flight, but look back to see the vigor and speed of their attackers and regulate their own running away accordingly, how much more should men possessing intelligence and struggling in the greatest of causes be very attentive to how they conduct their pursuits and their withdrawals in battle. They should not be like water which flows now forward, now backward. With every little advance of the enemy or of their own forces, as likely, they should not charge out without control and endanger themselves, but they ought to be steadfast in everything and strive in every conceivable way to defeat the enemy. To pursue the enemy a short distance and let them go is not a decisive victory. Neither is it a defeat to fall back a little and turn back against them. But it is after the conclusion of the war that both can be determined, and it is toward that goal that one must continue to struggle. The tourmarchs of each division have the obligation of conveying these and similar instructions to the army and individually to their own soldiers.

60. After dealing individually with the tourmarchs and after their drilling and giving instructions, you, O general, will draw up the entire battle line once or at the most twice and, in like manner, you will get them ever ready and always experienced, both by word and deed, for the struggles of battle.

61. Give orders to the officers of the first or promachos line to conform <to the movements of> the center meros, where your lieutenant general, who is now referred to as the merarch of the theme, is usually stationed. They should keep abreast of it and launch their charge at the same time. If the enemy are driven back by the charge, then the assault troops should quickly chase after them, pursuing them right up to the enemy camp. The defenders are to follow in formation and without stopping. Then in case the enemy wheels about and the

κούρσωρες, ἐκ τοῦ πλησίον εἰς τοὺς διφένσωρας καταφεύγοντες πάλιν ἑαυτοὺς
ἀνακαλέσωνται. ἐὰν μέντοι ἐν αὐτῇ τῇ συμβολῇ συμβῇ ἢ ἓν μέρος ἢ τὰ ὅλα
465 τραπῆναι, ὑποχωρεῖν τοὺς κούρσωρας ὡς ἐπὶ τὴν δευτέραν τάξιν ἐπὶ ἓν ἢ
δεύτερον σαγιττόβολον καὶ πάλιν ἀντιστρέφεσθαι κατὰ τῶν ἐχθρῶν, τῶν
συνήθων καὶ ἁρμοδίων φωνῶν ἤτοι παραγγελμάτων λεγομένων.
62. Καί, εἰ μὲν δυνηθῶσιν εἰς φυγὴν τρέψαι τοὺς ἐχθρούς, διώκειν κατ᾽
αὐτῶν, ἐπεί τοί γε ὑποχωρεῖν καὶ πάλιν ἀντιστρέφεσθαι. εἰ δὲ ἅπαξ ἢ δεύτερον
470 ἐγχειροῦντες μὴ ἰσχύσωσιν ἀντωθῆσαι τοὺς ἐχθρούς, τότε τῆς δευτέρας τάξεως
ἐπιφθανούσης καταφεύγειν πρὸς αὐτήν, καὶ διὰ τῶν εὐκαίρων αὐτῆς χωρίων
παρέρχεσθαι καὶ ἐν τῷ μεταξὺ διαστήματι κατὰ οὐρὰν τῆς δευτέρας καὶ τρίτης
ἐξελισσομένης ἅμα τῇ δευτέρᾳ τάξει δρουγγιστὶ ἤγουν ὁμοῦ ἐσφιγμένως τοῖς
ἐχθροῖς ἐπέρχεσθαι καί, ἐὰν τραπῶσιν, ἐπακολουθεῖν αὐτοῖς ὀξέως.
475 63. Παραγγείλῃς δὲ καὶ τοῖς πλαγιοφύλαξιν ὥστε, ἐὰν μὲν μακρότερον
εὑρεθῇ τὸ ἀντὶς κέρας, σπουδάζειν ἐπὶ κέρας, τοῦτ᾽ ἔστιν ἐπὶ σκουτάριν, κλίνοντας συνεκτείνεσθαι αὐτῷ, ἵνα μὴ ὑπ᾽ αὐτοῦ κατακύκλωσις τῷ μέρει γένηται, εἰ
δὲ κοντότερον εὑρεθῇ τὸ ἀντὶς κέρας, σπουδάζειν μηνοειδῶς ἤγουν κατὰ
ἡμικύκλιον ἐπικλίνεσθαι καὶ ἐμπεριλαμβάνειν αὐτὸ ἔσωθεν, πρὶν ἢ τὸ μέρος
480 φθάσῃ συμβαλεῖν, τοῦτ᾽ ἔστιν, ὅτ᾽ ἂν μέλλῃ ἡ φωνὴ τῆς συμβολῆς γίνεσθαι τῆς
μάχης, εἰ δὲ ἴσον ἐστὶ τὸ ἀντίς, μένειν ἐν τῇ ἰδίᾳ τάξει ὡς διφένσωρας καὶ
συμβάλλειν μετὰ τοῦ μέρους.
64. Παραγγείλῃς δὲ καὶ τοῖς ὑπερκερασταῖς ὅτι, μέχρις οὗ γένωνται οἱ
ἐχθροὶ ὡς ἀπὸ δύο σαγιττοβόλων ἢ τριῶν τῆς παρατάξεως, λεληθότως χρὴ
485 παρακολουθεῖν τῷ δεξιῷ κέρατι, τοῦ μὲν ἑνὸς τάγματος ἐπὶ μέτωπον ἤγουν
ἔμπροσθεν ἔχοντος τοὺς δεκάρχας ἢ πεντάρχας—ἀρκοῦσι γὰρ ἀπὸ πέντε μόνων
τὸ βάθος | ἐὰν εἰσὶ χρήσιμοι—τοῦ δὲ ἑτέρου τάγματος δρουγγιστὶ ἤγουν 330
πυκνῶς καὶ ὁμοῦ ὄπισθεν αὐτοῦ ἀκολουθοῦντος.

---

464 συμβῇ MWA om. BE   465 δευτέραν MW δύο A β΄ BE   466 σαγιττόβολον MW
σαγιτόβολα ABE   468–469 κατ᾽ αὐτῶν MW αὐτοὺς ABE   469 ἐπεί…γε MW εἰ δὲ μὴ
ABE   470 ἰσχύσωσιν MWBE ἰσχύσουσιν A   471 εὐκαίρων…χωρίων MW ταύτης
διαχωρισμάτων ABE   472 οὐρὰν MW οὐρὰν ἤγουν ὄπισθεν ABE | καὶ τρίτης MW
παρατάξεως ABE   473 ἐξελισσομένης MW ἐξελισσομένους ABE | δρουγγιστὶ…ὁμοῦ MW
ὁμοῦ καὶ ABE   476 ἀντὶς MW τῶν ἐναντίων ABE | σκουτάριν MW σκουτάριον ABE
476–477 κλίνοντας MWAB κλίνονται E   478 ἀντὶς MW τῶν ἐναντίων ABE
478–479 ἤγουν…ἡμικύκλιον MW ἤτοι σιγματοειδῶς ABE   481 ἐστὶ E ἔστιν MWAB |
ἀντίς MW τῶν ἐναντίων ABE | ἰδίᾳ τάξει MWAB διατάξει E   483 γένωνται ABE γίνονται
MW   484 δύο MWA β΄ BE | λεληθότως χρὴ MW κρυφὰ καὶ λεληθότως ABE
486 ἔχοντος ABE ἔχοντας MW | πέντε MWAE π΄ B(sic)   487 εἰσὶ MWA ὦσι BE
488 πυκνῶς ABE πυκνοὺς MW | ἀκολουθοῦντος Va ἀκολουθοῦντας MW ἀκολουθεῖν ABE

assault troops cannot handle the fighting at close quarters, they can take refuge among the defenders and rally themselves again. If it should happen that in the battle itself one meros, or all of them, are driven back, the assault troops should withdraw a bowshot or two, as though heading for the second line, and again turn around to face the enemy. The usual, appropriate words or commands are shouted out.

62. If they are able to turn the enemy into flight, they should pursue them, then withdraw and wheel about again. If after one or two attempts they do not succeed in pushing the enemy back, the second line should move up and the first seek refuge in it, passing through the clear spaces in it, and in the area between the rear of the second line and the third line it should reform and, together with the second line, attack the enemy in irregular formation, that is, all tightly packed together. If they turn, pursue them sharply.

63. You should give these orders to the flank guards. If the opposite flank is longer, make every effort, inclining to the flank, that is, the shield, to extend our flank <in line with> theirs to prevent its encirclement of the meros. But if the opposite flank is shorter, make every effort to advance in crescent formation, that is, in a semicircle, and envelop it on the inside before the meros is there to attack, that is, just before the signal for the battle charge is given. But if the opposite line is the same length, they should remain in their own position as defenders and join the meros in the charge.

64. You should give these orders to the outflankers. Until the enemy advances to two or three bowshots from our battle line, they are to follow the right wing closely, but under cover. One tagma should have its dekarchs and pentarchs posted forward in the front rank, for a depth of only five is enough if the men are suitable. The other tagma follows along behind the first in irregular order, that is, thickly together.

65. Τὰ δὲ βάνδα ἤγουν τὰς κεφαλὰς αὐτῶν μὴ ὀρθὰς κρατεῖν, ἀλλὰ ἐπικε-
490 κλιμένας ἕως καιρὸς γένηται χρείας τοῦ φαίνεσθαι αὐτά, εἰς τὸ μὴ προφαινό-
μενα τοῖς ἐχθροῖς ἐπιγινώσκεσθαι καὶ μᾶλλον ἐπιβουλεύεσθαι ὑπ' αὐτῶν τοὺς
κρατοῦντας αὐτά.

66. Καὶ ἐὰν μακρότερον τὸ ἀντὶς κέρας εὑρεθῇ, πρότερον ἐπὶ κέρας κλίνεσθαι, τοῦτ' ἔστιν ἐπὶ κοντάριν, καὶ ὀλίγον τοῦ δεξιοῦ μέρους ἐν τῷ περιπατεῖν
495 ἐμβραδύνοντος παρεκτεῖναι μέχρι<ς οὗ> καὶ ἥμισυ σαγιττοβόλου διὰ τὸ ὑπερβάλαι τὸ ἀντὶς κέρας· εἶθ' οὕτως ἐκνεύοντας κατ' αὐτοῦ καὶ κυκλοῦντας παραγγέλλειν τὸ "ἔξελθε" καὶ εὐθέως ἐπιπέμψαι κατὰ τοῦ νώτου αὐτῶν τὸν λανθά-
νοντα δροῦγγον ἄφνω κατὰ ἐλασίας ὀξείας.

67. Τρεπομένων δὲ τῶν ἐχθρῶν μὴ ἐπιδιώκειν τοὺς φεύγοντας, ἀλλὰ εὐθέως
500 κατὰ τοῦ νώτου τῶν ἱσταμένων ἔρχεσθαι ἅμα τῷ ἑτέρῳ τάγματι· εἰ δὲ κοντότε-
ρόν ἐστιν, εὐθέως ἐξέρχεσθαι καὶ μηνοειδῶς ἐμπεριλαμβάνειν αὐτό· εἰ δὲ ἴσον
ἐστίν, ὀλίγον παρεκτείνειν καὶ ὑπερβάλλειν τὸ ἀντίς, εἶτα οὕτως, ὡς εἴρηται,
ὁρμᾶν κατ' αὐτοῦ. ἐὰν μὲν οὖν, ὅτ' ἂν παρεκτείνωνται οἱ ὑπερκερασταί, βουληθῶσιν καὶ οἱ ἀντὶς ὁμοίως παρεκτείνεσθαι, δεῖ καὶ εὐθέως κατ' αὐτῶν ὁρμᾶν, ἐν
505 ὅσῳ ἀκατάστατοι εὑρίσκονται. ἀνάγκη γὰρ στρεφομένων αὐτῶν ἐπὶ κέρας καὶ
τὰ δεξιὰ αὐτῶν γυμνὰ ἔχειν καὶ τὴν σφίγξιν διαλελυμένην.

68. Ταύτας δὲ τὰς κυκλώσεις μὴ μόνον δέον τοὺς ὑπερκερατὰς κανονίζειν
ἤγουν τοὺς τοῦ δεξιοῦ μέρους προμάχους εἰς τὸ μὴ πολὺ ἐμβραδύνειν, μηδὲ
πάλιν πρὸ πολλοῦ ποιεῖν, ἀλλὰ καὶ τὸν τοῦ μέρους ἄρχοντα, εἴτε τουρμάρχης

---

489 ἀλλὰ MW ἀλλ' ABE    489–490 ἐπικεκλιμένας MWAB ἐπικεκλισμένας E
490 φαίνεσθαι MWAB φραίνεσθαι E    493 ἀντὶς MW τῶν ἐναντίων ABE    494 κοντάριν
MW κοντάριον ABE    495 μέχρις οὗ Strat. μέχρι codd. | ἥμισυ MWA ἡμίσεως BE
495–496 ὑπερβάλαι MW περιβαλεῖν ABE    496 ἀντὶς MW ἐξεναντίας ABE    497 κατὰ…
νώτου MW ὀπίσω ABE    498 κατὰ MW μετὰ ABE    499 ἐπιδιώκειν MWA διώκειν BE
499–500 ἀλλὰ…ἔρχεσθαι MW ἀλλ' ἱσταμένους ὀπίσω πολεμεῖν ABE    500 τῶν ἱσταμένων
Va ἱσταμένους codd.    501 ἔστιν MW ἐστιν (ἐστι BE) τὸ ἐξεναντίας κέρας ABE | μηνοειδῶς
MW σιγματοειδῶς ABE | ἐμπεριλαμβάνειν Va ἐπιλαμβάνεσθαι MW περιλαμβάνειν ABE |
αὐτό ABE αὐτοῦ MW    501–502 εἰ…ἀντὶς MWA om. BE    502 τὸ ἀντίς MW αὐτὸ A om.
BE    503 ἐὰν…ἂν MW ὅτ' ἂν μὲν οὖν ABE    503–504 βουληθῶσιν…παρεκτείνεσθαι
MWA om. BE    503–504 βουληθῶσιν MW ἐὰν βουληθῶσι A om. BE    504 ἀντὶς MW
ἐνάντιοι A om. BE | καὶ² MW om. ABE    505 ὅσῳ MWAB ὅσα E    506 σφίγξιν MW σὴν
τάξιν A σύνταξιν BE | διαλελυμένην MW διαλελυμένην καὶ μὴ συνεσφιγμένην ABE
507 μὴ…δέον MW χρὴ μὴ μόνον ABE    508 ἤγουν…προμάχους MW om. ABE
509 πάλιν MWAE om. B

65. The standards, that is, their heads, should not be held straight up but inclined down until the time is right to display them. Otherwise they may be recognized by the enemy, who may then take action against the flag bearers.

66. If the opposite flank is longer, first incline to the flank, that is, the lance, while the right meros slackens its pace a bit, extending itself to about half a bowshot in order to outflank the opposing wing. While they are turning to the side and encircling it, give the command: "Head out." Immediately the concealed droungos should suddenly charge out from behind with great force and speed.

67. If the enemy are turned back in flight we should not pursue them, but straightaway link up with the other tagma and attack the rear of the remaining units. If <the enemy line> is shorter, move out immediately and in crescent formation envelop it. If <the lines> are of the same length, extend the ranks a little to outflank the opposing wing. Then, as instructed, charge against it. If, therefore, while the outflankers are extending their ranks, our opponents want to extend theirs in like manner, then you must immediately charge against them while they are still moving about. As they turn by the flank, they will necessarily have to expose their right, and their tight formation will be broken up.

68. Not only must the outflankers, that is, those in the promachos line of the right meros, regulate these encircling movements so that they are not too far behind or, on the other hand, too much ahead; rather, the commander of the

258    Constitution 12

510 ἐστὶν εἴτε ἕτερός τις, ὥστε ἐγχειρούντων τῶν ὑπερκεραστῶν καὶ ἀρχομένων
τῶν ἀντὶς θορυβεῖσθαι, τότε καὶ αὐτὸν τὸ ὅλον μέρος ἐπάγειν.

69. Λόγος δὲ τῷ ἄρχοντι γίνεσθαι ὀφείλει τοῦ, εἰ μέν ἐστι δυνατὸν αὐτῷ,
ὑπερβάλλειν τὸ ἀντὶς μέρος, ἐπεί τοί γε οὐ, κἂν ἰσοῦσθαι αὐτῷ, ἐὰν καὶ μακρο-
τέρα εὑρεθῇ τῶν ἐναντίων ἡ παράταξις, ὥστε ἐντεῦθεν ἁρμοδίως δύνασθαι
515 τοὺς ὑπερκεραστὰς τὸ ἔργον αὐτῶν ποιεῖν.

70. Γίνωσκε δέ, ὅτι οἱ ὑπερκερασταὶ διὰ τοῦτό εἰσιν ἀναγκαῖοι, καθὸ καὶ ἐν
γυμνοῖς τόποις τὰς ἐπιδρομὰς ποιεῖν ἀσφαλεστέρως δύνανται.

71. Ὁμοίως δὲ καὶ τῇ δευτέρᾳ τάξει παραγγείλῃς, | ὥστε τὸν μέσον τόπον ἐν 330ᵛ
ᾧ συμβαίνει τάσσεσθαι τὴν σὴν ἐνδοξότητα, πείθεσθαί σοι καὶ κανονίζειν ἤγουν
520 στοχάζεσθαι, ὥστε ἐν τῷ καιρῷ τῆς συμβολῆς ἀπὸ τριῶν ἢ τεσσάρων σαγιττοβόλων τῆς πρώτης παρατάξεως εὑρεθῆναι αὐτὴν ἵνα, ἐὰν τραπῶσιν οἱ ἐχθροί,
ὡς διφένσωρ αὐτὴ ἤγουν ἐκδικητὴς καὶ βοηθὸς ἐν τάξει ἐπακολουθῇ καὶ μὴ
ἀπομείνῃ. εἰ δὲ τραπῇ τι τῶν τῆς πρώτης τάξεως ταγμάτων, ὑποδέχεσθαι τὸ
βαρούμενον καὶ ἐρχόμενον μέρος εἰς καταφυγὴν καὶ ἅμα τοῖς τῆς πρώτης
525 τάξεως ἐπέρχεσθαι συντεταγμένως καὶ μὴ διαλύεσθαι μέχρι τελείας ἐκβάσεως
τοῦ πολέμου καὶ τῆς ἐπὶ τὸ φοσσάτον ὑποστροφῆς, ἀλλὰ ἀφιέναι οὕτως συντεταγμένως φυλάττεσθαι καὶ μὴ ἐπιδιώκειν ἀτάκτως τοὺς ἐχθρούς.

72. Ἐὰν δὲ ἀμφίβολος ἡ μάχη τῆς πρώτης τάξεως φαίνηται καὶ διώξεις καὶ
ἀντιδιώξεις γίνονται, χρὴ ἀναμένειν καὶ θεωρεῖν τὴν τοῦ πράγματος ἔκβασιν
530 καὶ ἐπιβάλλειν δεύτερον ἢ τρίτον φωνὰς βρυγμώδεις πρός τε διανάστασιν τῶν
μαχομένων καὶ κατάπληξιν τῶν ἐχθρῶν, μὴ σπουδάζειν δὲ προχείρως συμμίγνυ-
σθαι ἢ ἐγγίζειν πολὺ τῇ πρώτῃ παρατάξει ἵνα μή τις φύρσις καὶ ἀλλόκοτος
τροπὴ ἐν τῇ συμβολῇ τῆς μάχης παρακολουθήσῃ. εἰ δέ, ὡς πολλάκις συμβαίνει,

---

510–511 ἀρχομένων…ἀντὶς MW τῶν ἐναντίων ἀρχομένων ABE   511 αὐτὸν Va αὐτοῖς
MW αὐτοὺς ABE | τὸ…ἐπάγειν MW μετὰ τοῦ ὅλου μέρους ἐπιτίθεσθαι ABE   512 λόγος
MW φροντὶς ABE | γίνεσθαι ὀφείλει MW ἔστω ABE | τοῦ Va ἵνα MW om. ABE | δυνατὸν
MWA δυνατόν ἐστιν BE | αὐτῷ MW om. ABE   513 τὸ ἀντὶς MW τῶν ἐναντίων AB τῶν
ἕναν E | μέρος MW κέρας AE om. B | ἐπεί…οὐ MW εἰ δὲ μὴ AE om. B   513–514 κἂν…
ἐναντίων MWAE om. B   516 καθὸ MW ὅτι ABE   517 ἀσφαλεστέρως MWA
ἀσφαλέστερον BE   520 τριῶν…τεσσάρων MWA γ′ ἢ δ′ BE   521 αὐτὴν Va αὐτὴ codd.
523 ἀπομείνῃ MW ἀπομένῃ ABE | τι τῶν MWA τὸ BE | ταγμάτων MWA τάγμα BE |
ὑποδέχεσθαι MWA ὑποδεχέσθω BE   524 μέρος MW om. ABE | ἅμα MW ἅμα δὲ ABE
525 ἐκβάσεως MW συμπληρώσεως ABE   526 ἀφιέναι οὕτως MW om. ABE
530 βρυγμώδεις MW καὶ ὠρύεσθαι ABE   532–533 ἀλλόκοτος τροπὴ MW τροπὴ
παράλογος ABE

meros, whether a tourmarch or of some other rank, should bring the entire meros into action at the same time that the outflankers make their attack and the enemy are beginning to get confused.

69. That officer ought to be instructed to outflank the opposing meros if he can do so, but if he cannot, he should extend his line to the same length. If the enemy's battle line is longer, he should enable the outflankers to go about their task properly.

70. Note that the outflankers are essential for the reason that they can launch attacks with impunity, even in open country.

71. In like manner give these orders to the second line. It is to obey you and conform, that is, adjust, its movements to the center division in which Your Excellency normally takes your stand. At the moment of engagement it should be three or four bowshots from the first battle line in order that, if the enemy turns back, it should follow along as a support line without any delay and in formation as defenders or ekdikoi. If one of the units of the first line turns back, the second line should receive the division that is under pressure and heading into flight. Together with the soldiers of the first line, the second should advance in good order and not break up until the final outcome of the battle and its return to camp. They must always maintain their formation and not become disordered in pursuing the enemy.

72. If the battle seems to be in doubt as far as the first line is concerned, and there are pursuits and counter-pursuits, then it is necessary to wait and see how things turn out. Let out two or three rousing cheers to encourage our fighters and to frighten the enemy. Be careful not to get into action prematurely or to get too close to the first line, which could result in confusion and a stupid defeat in the heat of battle. But if, as often happens, the second line also turns back, it

καὶ ἡ δευτέρα παράταξις τραπῇ μέχρι τῶν νωτοφυλάκων ἤγουν τῆς τρίτης
535 τάξεως ἐρχομένη, σπουδάζειν ἀναλαμβάνεσθαι αὐτήν.

73. Ἐὰν δὲ ἀπὸ ἐνέδρας τινὸς διὰ νώτου ἤγουν ἀπὸ ὄπισθεν ἔφοδος μηνυθῇ
καὶ ἐπέλευσις ἐχθρῶν, ἐὰν μὲν ὀλίγοι εἰσὶν οἱ μηνυόμενοι καὶ ἀρκοῦσιν οἱ τῆς
τρίτης τάξεως, τότε αὐτὴν κατ᾽ ἐκείνων ἐκπέμπειν· εἰ δὲ μὴ ἀρκοῦσιν, τότε,
καθὼς ἔστιν ἡ τάξις, ἀντιστρεφομένων τῶν προσώπων, ὁμοίως δὲ καὶ τοῦ
540 βάνδου μετὰ τοῦ ἄρχοντος εἰς οὐρὰν ἤγουν ὀπίσω ἐρχομένου, ὡς ἀμφίστομος ἡ
τάξις τὴν συμβολὴν ἁρμοδίως ποιεῖται, καὶ τρεπομένων τῶν ἐχθρῶν τότε τοὺς
νωτοφύλακας, εἴτε ἓν εἴτε δύο βάνδα εὑρεθῶσιν, ὡς κούρσωρας κατ᾽ αὐτῶν
ἐπαφιέναι.

74. Ἐὰν δὲ πολλοί εἰσιν οἱ μηνυόμενοι τὴν ἔξοδον ποιεῖν, τότε παραγγέλλει
545 τὸ "μετάλλαξον" καὶ ἔρχονται οἱ δεκάρχαι ἐπὶ οὐρὰν ἤγουν στρέφονται ὄπισθεν
κατὰ τάγμα ὥστε ἐκεῖνο τὸ μέρος τῆς | οὐρᾶς μέτωπον γίνεσθαι.    331

75. Καὶ ταύτας μὲν τὰς παραγγελίας ποιήσεις πρὸ ὀλίγου καιροῦ τῆς μάχης
καὶ τῶν ἀγώνων, ἵνα γινώσκωσιν οἱ στρατιῶται τὰ ἁρμόζοντα. ὁ γὰρ τῶν
ἀγώνων καιρὸς τὰ τοιαῦτα διδάσκειν τοὺς μήπω τούτων πεῖραν λαβόντας οὐκ
550 ἐπιτρέπει, εἰ μὴ ἄρα μετ᾽ ὀξύτητος τὰ σύντομα παραγγέλματα μόνα.

76. Πάλιν δέ, ἐὰν πρὸ πολλοῦ χρόνου παραγγείλῃς, εἰς λήθην γίνεται τὰ
λεχθέντα. καὶ διὰ τοῦτο χρή σε πρὸ μικροῦ καιροῦ τοῦ πολέμου τὰς ἀναμνήσεις
ποιεῖσθαι. παραγγείλῃς δὲ καὶ καθόλου πᾶσιν ὥστε μηδένα θαρρῆσαι τὴν
δευτέραν τάξιν παρελθεῖν κἄν, ὡς εἰκός, τροπή τις τῇ πρώτῃ τάξει γένηται, ἵνα
555 μὴ πρὸς τὴν ζωὴν κινδυνεύσῃ, εἴτε παρὰ τῶν ἐχθρῶν εἴτε καὶ παρὰ τῶν ἰδίων,
ὡς ἄξιος <θανάτου>, εἰ μὴ ἄρα, ὡς εἴρηται, τοσαύτη ἀπαραίτητος ἀνάγκη
παρακολουθήσῃ.

---

535 ἐρχομένη ΑΒΕ ἐρχομένην MW | σπουδάζειν MW σπουδάζειν προσήκει ΑΒΕ | αὐτήν
MWBE ἑαυτὴν Α    536 ἐνέδρας MW ἐγκρύμματος ΑΒΕ | διὰ…ἤγουν MW om. ΑΒΕ | ἀπὸ²
MW ἀπὸ τῶν ΑΒΕ    536–537 μηνυθῇ…ἐχθρῶν MW καὶ ἐπέλευσις ἐχθρῶν μηνυθῇ ΑΒΕ
537 ἐὰν MWA εἰ BE | ἀρκοῦσιν WAB ἀρκοῦσι ME    540 ἀμφίστομος Va ἀμφιστόμου codd.
541 τότε MWA τοῦ τε BE    542 δύο MWA β′ BE    544 ἐὰν MWA εἰ BE    545 δεκάρχαι
MWA δεκάρχαι καὶ οἱ BE    546 γίνεσθαι MWBE γενέσθαι Α    547 καιροῦ…μάχης MWAE
om. B    548 καὶ…ἀγώνων MW ἀγώνων B om. AE    549 καιρὸς MW καιρὸς οὐ συγχωρεῖ
ΑΒΕ | τὰ τοιαῦτα MW ταῦτα ΑΒΕ | τούτων πεῖραν MW πεῖραν τούτων Α πεῖραν τούτου BE
549–550 οὐκ ἐπιτρέπει MW om. ΑΒΕ    550 μόνα MWBE μόνον Α    552 μικροῦ MW
ὀλίγου ΑΒΕ    554 τάξει MW παρατάξει ΑΒΕ    555 πρὸς MW εἰς ΑΒΕ | ζωὴν MW ζωὴν
αὐτοῦ ΑΒΕ | καὶ MWA om. BE    556 θανάτου ci. De om. codd.

should go as far as the rear guard, that is, the third line, and set about recovering itself.

73. What if you are informed of an enemy attack or assault from some ambush to the rear, that is, from behind? If it is only a small detachment that you have been warned about, then the troops of the third line can deal with it, so send them out against it. But if they cannot deal with it, then <the second> line stays as it is while the individuals turn around. In like manner, the commanding officer with the standard moves to the rear, that is, behind, so the line is facing both ways and easily makes its attack. As the enemy are turned back, then the rear guard, whether one or two banda, should attack them in open order.

74. If the enemy force making the attack is reported to be numerous, give the command: "Countermarch." In each tagma the dekarchs march to the rear, that is, they turn backwards, and that section of the rear becomes the front.

75. You will give these commands a short time before the struggles of battle so that the soldiers may know their duties. The actual moment of combat does not permit those who have not yet had experience of these matters to learn them, except perhaps only those commands which are given rapidly and concisely.

76. Moreover, if you give the commands a long time before <combat>, what you have said will be forgotten. For this reason, you must recall them to mind a short time before actual combat. Issue a standing order to all the troops that nobody should dare to pass beyond the second line even if, as might happen, the first line should be routed, so that they do not put their lives at risk, whether at the hands of the enemy or of their own men, as deserving <of death>, except, as noted, when they encounter a pressing and unavoidable necessity.

77. Ἐπειδὴ δὲ καὶ ἀπὸ ἐνέδρας δέον κατὰ τῆς παρατάξεως τῶν ἐχθρῶν συμβάλλειν, χρὴ τοὺς εἰς τὴν ἐνέδραν ἤγουν ἔγκρυμμα τασσομένους παραγγελ-
560 θῆναι ὥστε πρὸ πάντων βίγλας προπέμπειν ἵνα μὴ ἀπάντημα, ὡς εἰκός, ὑπὸ τῶν ἐχθρῶν ἀθρόως ὑπομείνωσιν ἢ ἐνέδραν ἐκ πλαγίου ἢ καὶ ἀπὸ νώτου ἤγουν ἀπὸ ὄπισθεν τῆς τῶν ἐχθρῶν παρατάξεως.

78. Πολλάκις γὰρ καὶ οἱ ἐχθροὶ εἰς δύο τάσσονται τάξεις καί, ἐὰν μὴ προσ-
εχόντως γίνωνται αἱ κατὰ τῆς πρώτης αὐτῶν παρατάξεως δι᾽ ἐγκρυμμάτων
565 ἐπελεύσεις, ἐνεδρεύονται μᾶλλον ἐκ τοῦ ἐναντίου ὑπ᾽ ἐκείνων. ἐὰν οὖν οἱ ἐχθροὶ ὁμοίως εἰς δύο τάξεις τάσσωνται, οὔκ ἐστι πρέπον τῷ νώτῳ ἤγουν τῷ ὀπισθίῳ μέρει τῆς πρώτης αὐτῶν τάξεως ἐφεδρεύειν, ἀλλὰ τῷ ἄκρῳ αὐτῆς ἤγουν τῷ κέρατι, εἴτε ἐξ ἑνὸς μέρους ἡ ἔφοδος γίνεται εἴτε ἐκ τῶν δύο, ὡς εἴρηται.

570 79. Τὸν δὲ καιρὸν τῆς κατ᾽ αὐτῆς ἐγχειρήσεως κανονίζειν σε χρὴ καὶ στοχάζ-
εσθαι, ὥστε μήτε προλαμβάνειν πολὺ τῆς ἡμετέρας παρατάξεως μήτε ὑστερεῖν, ἀλλ᾽ ὅτ᾽ ἂν ὡς ἀπὸ δύο ἢ τριῶν σαγιττοβόλων αἱ παρατάξεις ἀλλήλων γένωνται, τότε ἐγχειρεῖν κατὰ τῶν ἐχθρῶν τοὺς ἐπὶ τὸ ἔγκρυμμα ἤγουν τὴν ἐνέδραν ἀπερχομένους. ταῦτα δὲ πάντα οὐκ ἐπὶ γυμνασίας, ἀλλ᾽ ἐπὶ τῶν πραγμάτων
575 αὐτῶν παραλαμβάνονται.

80. Ταῦτα μὲν οὖν <οὐ μόνον> τὴν σὴν ἐνδοξότητα καὶ παραγγέλλειν καὶ παρασκευάζειν κελεύομεν, ἀλλὰ καὶ ἑκάστῳ τουρμάρχῃ προστάξαι ἢ καὶ ἐγγρά-
φως | ἀποδοῦναι, ἅπερ καί σοι προειρήκαμεν, ἵνα γινώσκῃ καὶ αὐτὸς τοῦ ἰδίου　331ᵛ
μέρους τὴν κατάστασιν. ὥστε ἕκαστον τουρμάρχην τὸ τρίτον ποσὸν τοῦ ὑπ᾽
580 αὐτὸν ὅλου στρατοῦ ποιῆσαι κούρσωρας ἤγουν προκλάστας καὶ ἔνθεν καὶ ἐκεῖθεν τοῦ μέρους τάσσειν αὐτούς, τὸ δὲ δίμοιρον τοῦ στρατοῦ, τὸ ἐν μέσῳ, τάξαι εἰς διφένσωρας ἤγουν ἐκδικοῦντας.

---

558 ἐπειδὴ MWA ἐπὶ δὲ B ἐπειδὴ δὲ E | ἐνέδρας δέον MW ἐγκρύμματος ABE | παρατάξεως...ἐχθρῶν MW τῶν ἐχθρῶν παρατάξεως δέον ABE　559 τὴν...ἔγκρυμμα MW τὸ ἔγκρυμμα ABE　561 καὶ MWA om. BE | ἀπὸ¹...ἤγουν MW om. ABE　563 δύο MWA β′ BE　565 ὑπ᾽ ἐκείνων ABE om. MW　566 ὁμοίως MW om. ABE | δύο MWA β′ BE | οὔκ ἐστι MW οὐκέτι ABE | πρέπον MW πρέπον ἐστὶν A πρέπον ἐστὶ BE | τῷ¹...ἤγουν MW om. ABE　567 πρώτης MW om. ABE | τάξεως MW παρατάξεως ABE | ἐφεδρεύειν MWE ἐνεδρεύειν AB　568 δύο MWA β′ BE　570 χρὴ MW δεῖ ABE　572 δύο MWAB β′ E　573 ἤγουν...ἐνέδραν MWA om. BE　576 οὐ μόνον Va om. codd.　577 παρασκευάζειν ABE διασκευάζειν MW　578 ἀποδοῦναι MW ἐπιδοῦναι ABE　579 ποσὸν MW μέρος ABE　581 δὲ MWA τε BE | ἐν MW ἐν τῷ ABE　582 ἐκδικοῦντας MW ἐκδικητὰς ABE post ἐκδικοῦντας scr. tit. const. xiii, i.e. πολεμικῶν παρασκευῶν διάταξις ιγ′ M

77. Since it is necessary to lay ambushes against the enemy's battle line, you must issue orders to the men assigned to the ambush or hidden attack that, above all, they should send patrols ahead so that, as is likely, they will not encounter an enemy force unexpectedly and be subjected to an ambush from the flank or from the rear, that is, from the rear of the enemy's battle line.

78. Frequently the enemy draws up in two lines and, unless carefully done, our attacks from ambush against their first battle line may have a very opposite result as our forces are ambushed by theirs. Therefore, if the enemy should also make their formation in two lines, it is not right to launch a raid against their rear, that is, the rear section of their first line, but against a flank or a wing, whether, as noted, the attack takes place from one side or from two.

79. You must regulate, that is, estimate, the time of this attack against their line so that it does not occur too much in advance of our own battle line or too much after. But when the two lines are about two or three bowshots apart, then the detachments sent out on ambuscade, that is, ambush, should assault the enemy. All these things <are not taught> in training, but they are learned from actual practice.

80. We order Your Excellency not only to issue these commands that we have already given to you and to put them into practice, but you should also pass these orders on to each tourmarch or even hand them on in writing, so that he himself will know the situation of his own meros. Each tourmarch should designate one third of the entire army under his command as assault troops, that is, proklastai, and post them here and there about the meros; the other two thirds of the army, those in the center, should be formed as defenders, that is, ekdikoi.

81. Περὶ τῶν ἐν κονταρίοις φλαμούλων.

Καὶ τὰ κοντάρια δὲ αὐτῶν μὴ ἔχειν φλάμουλα ἐν τῷ καιρῷ τῆς τοῦ πολέμου
585 συμβολῆς, ἀλλ᾽ ἵνα ἐπαίρωσι καὶ βάλλωσιν αὐτὰ εἰς τὰ θηκάρια αὐτῶν, ὅτ᾽ ἂν
φθάζωσιν οἱ ἐχθροὶ ἀπὸ ἑνὸς μιλίου. πρότερον δὲ τοῦ καιροῦ τούτου ἔχειν αὐτὰ
πάντως εἰς τὰ κοντάρια.

82. Περὶ διαφορᾶς βάνδων.

Τὰ δὲ βάνδα τῶν ταγμάτων μικρότερα εἶναι ἤτοι τῶν κομήτων, τὰ δὲ τῶν
590 δρουγγαρίων τελειότερα καὶ ἀλλοῖα, ὁμοίως δὲ καὶ τὸ τοῦ τουρμάρχου ἐνηλλαγμένον πρὸς τὰ ἄλλα γίνεσθαι, ὥς μοι εἴρηται.

83. Περὶ τῆς ὥρας τοῦ πολέμου.

Ἐν δὲ τῷ καιρῷ τῆς συμβολῆς τοῦ πολέμου μετὰ τὴν φωνὴν τῆς τοῦ σταυροῦ νίκης ἀλαλάζειν δεῖ καὶ ὠρυᾶσθαι μάλιστα τοὺς ὄπισθεν καὶ προθυμοποιεῖν
595 καὶ ἀλλήλους καὶ τοὺς ἔμπροσθεν. καὶ τὸ μὴ λαλεῖν ἐν καιρῷ μάχης πολλὰ
βούκινα· ἀρκεῖ γὰρ καὶ τὸ τοῦ τουρμάρχου μόνον.

84. <Περὶ στάσεως ἀρχόντων ἐν μάχῃ.>

Τὸν δὲ τουρμάρχην μέσον τοῦ μέρους τάσσεσθαι τῆς ὑπ᾽ αὐτὸν τάξεως,
τοῦτ᾽ ἔστι μέσον τῶν διφενσώρων, τοὺς δὲ δρουγγαρίους εἰς τὰ ἑκατέρωθεν
600 μέρη μέσον τῶν βάνδων τῶν κουρσώρων.

85. Περὶ τοῦ ἐρευνᾶν τοὺς τόπους πρὸ τοῦ πολέμου.

Ἐν δὲ τῷ καιρῷ τῆς παρατάξεως προερευνᾶν δέον διὰ μανδατώρων τοὺς
τῆς συμβολῆς τόπους, τοῦτ᾽ ἔστι τοὺς μέσον τῆς ἰδίας παρατάξεως καὶ τῆς τῶν
ἐχθρῶν, μήποτε λάκκοι εἰσὶν ἢ ὀρύγματα ἢ τέλματα, ἅπερ λέγεται πάλματα, ἢ
605 δόλοι τινές, ὡς εἰκός, παρὰ τῶν ἐχθρῶν μελετώμενοι καί, ἐάν τι τοιοῦτον εὑρε-
θῇ, ἀναμένειν τὴν ἡμετέραν τάξιν ἵνα οἱ ἐχθροὶ αὐτοὺς παρέλθωσι, καὶ τότε ἡ | 332
ἡμετέρα παράταξις ἐν τῷ καθαρῷ κάμπῳ ἀπαντήσῃ.

86. Περὶ βάνδου τοῦ τουρμάρχου.

583–690  Strat., 7.B.16–17.

585 ἐπαίρωσι MAB ἐπαίρουσι W ἐπαίρωσιν E | βάλλωσιν MWBE βάλωσιν A
586 πρότερον MW πρὸ ABE   588 περὶ…βάνδων MWA om. BE   589 τὰ…τῶν¹ Va τῶν
δὲ codd.   590 ἀλλοῖα MWBE παρηλλαγμένα A | τοῦ AE om. MWB   591 ὥς MW καθὼς
ABE   594 ὠρυᾶσθαι Va ὀρυᾶσθαι MW ὠρύεσθαι ABE   595 ἔμπροσθεν Va ἔμπροσθεν
περὶ στάσεως ἀρχόντων ἐν μάχη codd. quod ad 597 trsp. De   596 βούκινα MW βούκινα
καλὸν ABE | τοῦ ABE om. MW   597 περὶ…μάχη De om. codd.   599 τοῦτ᾽ ἔστι M τοῦτ᾽
ἐστιν WABE   603 τοῦτ᾽ ἔστι M τοῦτ᾽ ἔστιν WABE   604 τέλματα…λέγεται MW om. ABE
605 τινές MW τινες ἕτεροι ABE   606 τάξιν MW παράταξιν ABE | παρέλθωσι MA
παρέλθωσιν WBE   607 κάμπῳ MW τόπῳ ABE

81. About the pennons on the lances.[7]

Their lances should not have pennons attached when the time comes for actual fighting in battle. Rather they should be removed and put in their cases when the enemy has come to about a mile away. Before that time they may certainly carry them on their lances.

82. About the difference in standards.

The standards of the tagmata, that is, of the counts, should be rather small, those of the droungarioi larger and of a different pattern and, in like manner, that of the tourmarch should stand out among the others, as I have said.

83. About the moment of battle.

At the moment of contact in battle, after shouting the victory cry of the cross, they should shout the war cry and cheer, especially those in the rear, to encourage one another and the men in front of them. At the moment of combat a number of trumpets should not be sounded; that of the tourmarch is enough by itself.

84. About the post of the officers in battle.

The tourmarch should station himself in the middle of the meros of the line under his command, that is, in the middle of the defenders, whereas the droungarioi should be in the middle of the meros on either side, among the banda of assault troops.

85. About reconnoitering the area before the battle.

When the battle line is being formed, the heralds must reconnoiter the site of the battle, that is, the ground between our own battle line and that of the enemy, in case there are ponds, ditches, swamps, called palmata, or any traps that the enemy may be likely to have planned. If any such are found, our line should stay put, so the enemy may move past them, and then our battle line should encounter them on unobstructed ground.

86. About the standard of the tourmarch.

7. Sections 81–105 derive from *Strat.* 7.B.16–17.

Τὸ δὲ βάνδον τοῦ τουρμάρχου, ὡς εἴρηται, μόνον ἐξηλλαγμένον τὸ εἶδος
610 παρὰ τὰ ἄλλα τὰ ὑπ' αὐτὸν βάνδα ποιῆσαι ἵνα ἐστὶν εὐεπίγνωστον πᾶσι τοῖς ὑπ'
αὐτὸν βανδοφόροις.

87. Περὶ σημείων καὶ κινήσεως βάνδου.

Ἀλλὰ καὶ διὰ κινήσεώς τινος ξένης καὶ διαφόρου χωρίζεσθαι αὐτὸ ἢ ἐν τῷ
ἵστασθαι ἢ ἄνω ἢ κάτω ἢ δεξιᾷ ἢ ἀριστερᾷ, ἢ συνεχῶς ἐπικλίνεσθαι ἢ ἐγείρειν
615 τὴν κεφαλὴν τοῦ βάνδου ἢ πυκνῶς τινάσσειν αὐτὸ ὀρθὸν ὥστε καὶ εἰς τὴν
σύγχυσιν εὐκόλως ὑπὸ τῶν λοιπῶν βάνδων γνωρίζεσθαι.

88. Περὶ τοῦ διαφέρειν τὰ βάνδα τῶν τουρμαρχῶν ἀλλήλων.

Οὐ δεῖ δὲ ὅλων τῶν τουρμαρχῶν τὰ βάνδα ἓν σημεῖον ἔχειν, ἀλλὰ ἐνηλλαγμένα σύμβολα ἑκάστην τοῦρμαν, ἅτινα καὶ ὀφείλουσιν ἐθίζειν τοὺς στρατιώτας
620 <οἱ τουρμάρχαι> διὰ προγυμνασίας γνωρίζειν. οὐ μόνον γὰρ ἐκ τούτου τὰ ὑπὸ
τὸν τουρμάρχην ἕκαστον βάνδα ὠφελοῦνται τὸ μέρος αὐτῶν συντόμως στηρί-
ζοντα, ἀλλὰ καὶ οἱ ἐν αὐτοῖς τεταγμένοι τὸ τοῦ τουρμάρχου βάνδον ἐπιγινώσκοντες δι' αὐτοῦ εὐκόλως καὶ τὰ ἴδια <οἱ>, ὡς εἰκός, πλανώμενοι εὑρίσκουσιν.

89. Περὶ τοῦ βλέπειν τὸν στρατιώτην τὸ βάνδον τοῦ ἄρχοντος.

625 Δεῖ γὰρ ἀεὶ ἐν ἑκάστῃ μάχῃ, ἐὰν καί τι συμβῇ τὸν στρατιώτην ὥστε ἀποχω-
ρισθῆναι μακρὰν τοῦ βάνδου τοῦ ἰδίου τάγματος, παντὶ τρόπῳ σπουδάζειν
ἑνοῦσθαι αὐτῷ, ἵνα ἡ τάξις ἄφυρτος διαμένουσα τὴν σωτηρίαν σημαίνῃ τοῦ
στρατοῦ.

90. Περὶ τοῦ διαχωρίζειν τοὺς ἀλλοφύλους τῆς παρατάξεως.

630 Ἐὰν δὲ συμβῇ εἶναι ἐν τῷ στρατῷ τινας ὁμοφύλους τῶν πολεμίων, δέον πρὸ
τῆς ἡμέρας τοῦ πολέμου χωρίζειν αὐτοὺς καὶ ἐν ἑτέροις τόποις μετὰ εὐλόγου
προφάσεως πέμπειν.

91. Περὶ τοῦ καὶ δρουγγαρίους καὶ κόμητας τὸν στρατὸν παρορμᾶν.

609 τοῦ MWBE om. A | ἐξηλλαγμένον MW παρηλλαγμένον ABE | τὸ εἶδος MW ἐχέτω τὴν
χρόαν ABE   610 ποιῆσαι MW om. ABE | ἐστὶν MWA ἢ BE   612 καὶ MABE om. W |
κινήσεως MWAE κινήσεων B | βάνδου MWA βάνδων BE   614 ἐγείρειν Va ἐγχειρεῖν codd.
615 τινάσσειν MABE τινάσσειν αὐτὸ W   616 λοιπῶν MWAB om. E   617 διαφέρειν MW
διαφέρειν ἀλλήλων ABE | ἀλλήλων MW om. ABE   618 ἀλλὰ MWA ἀλλ' BE   619 καὶ
MWBE om. A   620 οἱ τουρμάρχαι Va om. codd.   621 τὸν…ἕκαστον MWBE ἕκαστον
τουρμάρχην A   622–623 ἐπιγινώσκοντες MWA διαγινώσκοντες BE   623 δι' αὐτοῦ
MWAE διὰ τοῦ B | οἱ Strat. om. codd. | εὑρίσκουσιν MB om. WAE   625 ἀεὶ…μάχῃ MWA
ἐν ἑκάστῃ μάχῃ ἀεὶ BE | καί τι MWBE om. A | τὸν στρατιώτην MWA τῷ στρατιώτῃ BE |
ὥστε MWBE om. A   630 εἶναι…στρατῷ MWA ἐν τῷ στρατῷ εἶναι BE | πρὸ MWA περὶ BE
632 πέμπειν ABE προπέμπειν MW   633 καὶ² MW καὶ τοὺς ABE | παρορμᾶν MABE om. W

The standard of the tourmarch, as noted, should be different in appearance from the other standards in his command, so as to be easily recognized by all the standard-bearers under him.

87. About signals and movement of the standard.

But it must be set apart by some unusual and distinctive motion, either by remaining in place or held high or low or to the right or the left, or by keeping the head of the standard lowered or raised on high or holding it upright and waving it frequently. In this way, even in the confusion, it will be easily recognized by the rest of the standards.

88. About the standards of the tourmarchs differing from one another.

The standards of all the tourmarchs must not have only one way of signaling but each tourma must have its own distinctive way of signaling. It is the duty of the tourmarchs to see that the soldiers become familiar with these signals and get to know them during preparatory training. By this means the standards identifying each tourmarch not only ought to enable them to locate their own meros quickly, but it also makes it easier for any likely stragglers, recognizing the standard of the meros to which they belong, to find their own unit.

89. About the soldier keeping the standard of the commanding officer in sight.

In every action it is always necessary that if something causes a soldier to be separated some distance from the standard of his own unit, he must take every step to join it again, so that the formation will remain free of confusion, <for this> may well signify the salvation of the army.

90. About keeping foreigners away from the battle line.

If it should happen that there are some men of the same race as the enemy in the army, they must be segregated the day before the battle and sent elsewhere on some plausible pretext.

91. About the droungarioi and the counts urging the army on.

Καὶ τοῖς μὲν τουρμάρχαις ταῦτα πράττειν προστάξεις. ἀλλὰ καὶ ἑκάστῳ
635 δρουγγαρίῳ καὶ κόμητι ἅμα αὐτοῖς παρακελεύου καὶ πρόστασσε, ὥστε ἐπιζητεῖν
αὐτοὺς ἐκ παντὸς τὰ δέοντα ἐπιτελεῖν τὸν στρατόν.

92. Περὶ τοῦ πάντως πρωῒ καὶ ἑσπέρας ψάλλειν τὸν στρατὸν τὸν τρισάγιον
ὕμνον.

Χρεὼν γάρ, εἴτε ἐν φοσσάτῳ διάγει ἕκαστον τάγμα ἤτοι τὸ βάνδον εἴτε καὶ | 332ᵛ
640 καθ' ἑαυτὸ ὁπουδήποτε ἀπλικεύει, πρωῒας εἰς αὐτὸν τὸν ὄρθρον πρὸ παντὸς
πράγματος καὶ εἰς ἑσπέραν ὁμοίως μετὰ τὸ δεῖπνον καὶ τὰς μίσσας τὸ τρισάγιον
ψάλλεσθαι καὶ τὰ λοιπὰ κατὰ τὴν συνήθειαν.

93. Περὶ καταστάσεως κοντουβερνίων.

Τὰ δὲ κοντουβέρνια ἤτοι τὰ οἷον μικρὰ βάνδα τῶν ἀκιῶν, καθὼς καί σοι
645 αὐτῷ πρώην ὡρίσαμεν, προστάξαι ἀπὸ παλαιῶν καὶ νέων αὐτοὺς ποιεῖν.

94. Περὶ ὁπλίσεως τῶν ἀκιῶν.

Τὸν δὲ πρῶτον καὶ δεύτερον τῆς ἀκίας καὶ τὸν οὐραγὸν ἤγουν τὸν ὄπισθεν
καὶ τὸν πρὸ αὐτοῦ κονταράτους εἶναι, τὸν δὲ τρίτον καὶ τέταρτον τοξότας καὶ
τοὺς ἐν μέσῳ ὡς ἡ χρεία ἀπαιτεῖ.

650 95. Ὅτι βλάπτει τὰ φλάμουλα ἐν συμβολῇ μάχης.

Τὰ δὲ φλάμουλα τῶν κονταρίων ἐν τῷ καιρῷ τοῦ πολέμου μὴ ἀφίειν, ὡς
εἴρηται, εἰς τὰ κοντάρια ἵνα μὴ τοῖς ὄπισθεν καὶ αὐτοῖς ἔχουσι κοντάρια ἐμποδί-
ζωσιν οὐ μόνον δέ, ἀλλὰ καὶ ταῖς βαλλομέναις παρὰ τῶν τοξοτῶν σαγίτταις.

96. Περὶ τῶν λεγομένων δεποτάτων.

655 Τοὺς δὲ λεγομένους δεποτάτους, καθώς σοι καὶ ἔμπροσθεν διεταξάμεθα,
οὓς εἰς θεραπείαν καὶ πρὸς τὸ ἀνασῴζειν τοὺς πληγάτους στρατιώτας ὡρίσαμεν,
προστάξεις, ἵνα καθ' ἕκαστον αὐτῶν τάγμα ἓξ ἢ ὀκτὼ ἐκ τῶν ὑποδεεστέρων
ἀφορίσωσιν, ἵνα ἐν καιρῷ <πολέμου> περιποιῶνται τοὺς τραυματιζομένους.

97. Περὶ βίγλας καὶ φυλακῆς βάνδου ἐν καιρῷ μάχης.

---

**635** πρόστασσε MWA om. BE | ἐπιζητεῖν MWBE ἀναγκάζειν A    **637** πάντως MWA om.
BE | ψάλλειν MWA om. BE | τὸν στρατὸν MW om. ABE    **638** ὕμνον MWA ὕμνον ἐκτελεῖν
BE    **639** χρεὼν MW χρὴ A χρεῶν BE | γάρ MW δὲ A γὰρ ἵνα BE | τὸ MWBE om. A
**640** ἀπλικεύει MW ἀπληκεύει A ἀπλικεύσει BE | ὄρθρον MWAB ὄρθον E    **641** μίσσας W
μίνσας MABE | τὸ² MW τὸν ABE    **642** ψάλλεσθαι MWA ψάλληται BE
**643** κοντουβερνίων ABE κουτουβερνίων MW    **644** κοντουβέρνια ABE κουτουβέρνια MW
| τὰ...ἀκιῶν (οἷον om BE) MWBE τὰς ἀκίας A    **647** ἀκίας MWBE ἀκίας ἤτοι τοῦ λόχου A
**650** συμβολῇ μάχης MWA τῇ μάχῃ B μάχῃ E    **651** ἀφίειν MW ἔχειν A ἀφιέναι BE
**652** ἔχουσι AE ἔχωσι MWB    **653** σαγίτταις MW σαγίταις AE σαγίτας B    **654** δεποτάτων
MW διποτάτων ABE    **655** δεποτάτους MWB διποτάτους AE    **656** πληγάτους MW
πληττομένους A πλησσομένους BE    **658** πολέμου ci. Va om. codd.    **659** καιρῷ MW ὥρα
ABE

You will command the tourmarchs to do these things. Together with them you will also command and give orders to each droungarios and count to strive in every way so the army may accomplish its objectives.

92. About having the army chant the Trisagion hymn every morning and evening.

Whether each tagma or bandon remains in the main camp or is camping someplace else by itself, early, at the crack of dawn before any other task, and likewise in the evening after supper and the dismissal, the Trisagion must be chanted and the rest of the customary practices observed.[8]

93. About organizing the squads.

You should order the squads, that is, like small banda of the files, as we have prescribed for you earlier, to be composed of both young and older men.

94. About the armament of the files.

The first and second man of the file and the file closer in the rear and the man in front of him should bear lances, while the third and fourth carry bows, and the men in the middle whatever is needed at the time.

95. That pennons are harmful in actual combat.

Lance pennons should not, as noted, be carried on the lances at the time of battle since they get in the way of those in the rear who also carry lances; not only that, but they interfere with the shooting of arrows by the archers.

96. About the so-called deputies.

The so-called deputies, as we prescribed for you earlier, are the men who have been designated by us to take care of and to rescue wounded soldiers. You shall give orders that among the less-qualified men in each tagma six or eight must be set apart to take care of the wounded during combat.

97. About scouts and guarding the standard during battle.

8. Cf. Const. 11 §19.

660 Δύο δὲ σκουλκάτωρας ἤγουν κατασκόπους ἢ βιγλάτωρας χρησίμους καὶ ἀγρύπνους καὶ ἀνδρείους ἐπιλέγεσθαι καὶ δύο μανδάτωρας. ἀφορίζειν δὲ καὶ ἐκ τῶν εἰς τὰς ἀκίας τασσομένων δύο ἄνδρας, χρησίμους εἰς φυλακὴν τοῦ βάνδου ἐν καιρῷ πολέμου.

98. Περὶ τοῦ λεγομένου καντάτωρος.

665 Πάντως δὲ καὶ τὸν λεγόμενον καντάτωρα ἐπιλέγεσθαι ἐπιτήδειον καὶ λόγιον ἕνα στρατιώτην καὶ ἀφορίσαι, ὥστε ἐν αὐτοῖς τοῖς ἀγῶσι περιτρέχοντα κατεπάδειν τοῖς στρατιώταις τοῦ τάγματος καὶ διεγείρειν εἰς προθυμίαν διὰ προτρεπτικῶν λόγων κατὰ τὸν τύπον, ὅνπερ σοι προδιωρισάμεθα.

99. Πότε χρὴ δύο βάνδα ἔχειν καὶ πότε ἕν;

670 Ποιείτωσαν δὲ ἐν τοῖς μεγάλοις τάγμασι καὶ διπλᾶ βάνδα καὶ πρὸ τοῦ πολέμου | τὸ μὲν ἓν τὸν ἄρχοντα ἔχειν τοῦ τάγματος, τὸ δὲ ἄλλο τὸν πρῶτον 333 ἑκατοντάρχην. ἐν δὲ τῇ ἡμέρᾳ τοῦ πολέμου μὴ τὰ δύο βαστάζεσθαι ἤτοι ὀρθοῦ-σθαι, ἀλλὰ τὸ τοῦ ἄρχοντος μόνον.

100. Τί δεῖ ἐπιφέρεσθαι τοὺς στρατιώτας εἰς τροφὴν ἐν καιρῷ μάχης;

675 Χρὴ οὖν καὶ ἐν τῇ ἡμέρᾳ τοῦ πολέμου ἕκαστον στρατιώτην ἐν ταῖς σέλλαις αὐτῶν ἐπιφέρεσθαι ὕδωρ εἰς τὰ λεγόμενα φλασκία καὶ παξαμάτην ἐν τῷ σελλοπουγγίῳ καὶ ἄλευρον μίαν ἢ καὶ δύο λίτρας, ὥστε ἔχειν ἐν ἀνάγκης καιρῷ καὶ ἑαυτοῖς εἰς εὐψυχίαν καὶ παραμυθίαν καὶ ἑτέροις, ὡς εἰκός, εἰς τὴν ἀπὸ ὀλιγωρίας ἀνάκτησιν.

680 101. Περὶ τοῦ μὴ σκυλεύειν τοὺς φονευομένους πρὸ τῆς ἐκβάσεως τοῦ πολέμου.

Ἐν δὲ καιρῷ μάχης ἵνα γινώσκωσιν ὅτι οὐ δεῖ στρατιώτην πρὸ τῆς ἐκβάσεως τοῦ πολέμου σκυλεύειν ἐχθρόν· καὶ τοῦτο πολλάκις αὐτοῖς παραγγέλλειν.

---

661 ἀφορίζειν ABE ἀφορίσωσι MW    662 ἀκίας MWAE ἀκόας B    664 καντάτωρος MW καντάτωρος ἤγουν στρατοκήρυκος ABE    665 καντάτωρα A καντάτορα MW κανδάτωρα BE    666 περιτρέχοντα ABE περιτρέχοντας MW    667 κατεπάδειν MW ἐπιλέγειν ABE | τοῖς στρατιώταις De τῷ στρατῷ codd. | τάγματος MW τάγματος τὰ προτρέποντα A τάγματος τὰ πρέποντα BE | διεγείρειν MWBE διεγείροντα A    667–668 διὰ…λόγων MW om. ABE    668 προδιωρισάμεθα MWA διορισάμεθα BE    669 ἔχειν ABE om. MW    670 δὲ MWBE δὲ καὶ A | τάγμασι MABE τάγμασιν W    672 ἑκατοντάρχην MWA ἑκατόνταρχον BE | δύο MWA β′ BE    674 εἰς MW πρὸς AB πρὸ E    675 τῇ ἡμέρᾳ MWA τῷ καιρῷ BE    676 τὰ… φλασκία MW τὰς λεγομένας ἀσκοδαύλας (ἀσκοδάβλας BE) ABE | παξαμάτην MW παξαμάτιον ABE    677 δύο MWA β′ BE    678–679 καὶ[1]…ἀνάκτησιν MW εἰς παραμυθίαν ἑαυτῶν καὶ (καὶ ἑαυτῶν BE) ἑτέρων ἀνάκτησιν τῶν ὡς εἰκὸς ὀλιγορούντων ABE    680 τοὺς φονευομένους ABE om. MW | ἐκβάσεως MW συμπληρώσεως ABE    682 ἐκβάσεως MW συμπληρώσεως ABE    683 τοῦτο MWAE τοῦ B | παραγγέλλειν MWA προπαραγγέλλεις BE

Select two scouts, that is, spies or watchmen, efficient, alert, and brave, and two heralds. And from the troops formed in files pick out two men to serve as guards for the standard in time of battle.

98. About the so-called cantor.

Be sure to select one soldier, competent and educated, for the position referred to as cantor. Assign him to move about quickly in the midst of the fighting to encourage the troops in the unit and to arouse them to enthusiasm by hortatory words according to the model that we have prescribed for you.

99. When is it necessary to have two standards and when just one?

In the large tagmata let two standards be prepared before the battle; one should be kept by the commander of the tagma, the other by the first hekatontarch. On the day of battle, however, do not carry or raise the two standards but only that of the commander.

100. What must the soldiers carry for nourishment in time of battle?

On the day of battle, then, each soldier must carry on his saddle, in his saddle bags, a flask, as it is called, of water and hardtack and one or two measures of barley meal.[9] In an emergency, then, he can lift up his own spirits and offer comfort to himself and others who are likely to have become downcast.

101. About not plundering the dead before the conclusion of the battle.

They should know that before the end of the battle, while the fighting is still going on, the soldier must not plunder the enemy. Repeat this order to the men frequently.

9. Cf. Const. 6 §23, n. 14.

102. Ποῦ δεῖ τὸν τοῦλδον τάσσεσθαι;

685 Εἰς δὲ τὰς ὁδοιπορίας μὴ συγκαταμιγνύειν μετὰ τοῦ τούλδου τοὺς στρατιώτας καὶ μάλιστα ἐχθρῶν προσδοκωμένων, ἀλλὰ τὸ μὲν βάνδον ἔμπροσθεν ἰδίως, τὸ δὲ τοῦλδον ὄπισθεν ἢ καὶ ὡς ἡ χρεία καλέσοι, καθὼς καὶ ἐν τῷ περὶ τοῦ τούλδου ἡμῖν κεφαλαίῳ εἴρηται. ταῦτα, ἅπερ σοι προδιεταξάμεθα, καὶ αὐτὸς ἑκάστῳ κόμητι καὶ δρουγγαρίῳ, ἀλλὰ καὶ τουρμάρχῃ ἰδίως καὶ προγινώ-
690 σκειν καὶ ἐπιτελεῖν καὶ παραγγελεῖς καὶ παρασκευάσεις.

103. Ὅτι ἐξ ὧν δύναταί τις νικᾶν τοὺς ἐχθρούς, ταῦτα δεῖ φυλάττεσθαι αὐτόν.

Σοὶ δὲ κελεύομεν, ὦ στρατηγέ, ὥστε ἁρμοδίως κεχρῆσθαι τοῖς καιροῖς ἐν ταῖς μάχαις καὶ πρότερον μὲν φυλάττεσθαί σε τὰς ἀφορμάς, δι' ὧν αἱ βλάβαι
695 παρὰ τῶν ἐχθρῶν συμβαίνουσι γίνεσθαι, καὶ τότε διὰ τῶν τοιούτων ἀφορμῶν κατὰ τῶν ἐχθρῶν ἐγχειρεῖν.

104. Περὶ τοῦ μὴ διώκειν ἐχθροὺς ἀτάκτως.

Καὶ πρὸ πάντων δέον σε τὰς παρὰ τῶν ἐναντίων μελετωμένας ἐνέδρας ἐρευνᾶν διὰ βιγλῶν πυκνῶν κατὰ τῶν τεσσάρων μερῶν τοῦ τόπου, ἔνθα ἡ
700 παράταξις γίνεται, καὶ ἀπέχεσθαι τῶν ἀτάκτων καὶ ἐσκορπισμένων διώξεων.

105. Περὶ τοῦ μὴ τὸν στρατηγὸν τὰς προπετεῖς ἐγχειρήσεις ποιεῖν ἀλλὰ διὰ τῶν ἀρχόντων.

Κοῦρσα δὲ ἢ προπετεῖς ἐγχειρήσεις διὰ σεαυτοῦ ποιεῖν οὐκ ἐπιτρέπομέν σοι, ἀλλὰ διὰ | τῶν ἁρμοδίων ἀρχόντων ταῦτα γίνεσθαι. ἐὰν μὲν γὰρ ἐκ τῶν ἄλλων    333ᵛ
705 ἀρχόντων παράπτωμα ἢ ἀστοχία γένηται, ἔστιν ἐλπὶς σύντομος ἐπανορθώσεως, εἰ δὲ ὁ πρῶτος τοῦ στρατοῦ πταίσει, ἀναρχίας πρόφασις ἡ τούτου διάπτωσις γίνεται.

106. Σοφὸς δὲ στρατηγὸς καὶ ἄριστος ὁ πρὸ τοῦ πολέμου τὰ τῶν ἐχθρῶν πολυπραγμονῶν καὶ πρὸς μὲν τὰ πλεονεκτήματα αὐτῶν φυλαττόμενος, πρὸς δὲ
710 τὰ ὑστερήματα ἐπιβαλλόμενος, οἷον, ὡς ἐν κεφαλαίῳ εἰπεῖν. ὑπέρ σε καβαλλα-

---

691-733 *Strat.*, 7.A.praef.

---

**684** τὸν ABE τὸ MW    **685-686** τοῦ…στρατιώτας MW τῶν στρατιωτῶν τὸν τοῦλδον ABE    **686** καὶ MWA om. BE    **687** ἰδίως MW ἰδίως περιπατεῖν ABE    **687-688** τῷ…τοῦ MWA περὶ BE    **688** ἡμῖν MWAE ἡμῖν ἡμῖν B | ταῦτα MW ταῦτα μὲν ABE | προδιεταξάμεθα ABE διεταξάμεθα MW    **689-690** καὶ³…παρασκευάσεις MW παραγγείλεις προγινώσκειν καὶ παρασκευάσεις ἐπιτελεῖν ABE    **695** συμβαίνουσι MWAE συμβαίνουσιν B    **696** ἐγχειρεῖν MWA ἐγείρειν BE    **702** ἀρχόντων MW ἀρχόντων ταῦτα γίνεται BE    **703** κοῦρσα…ἢ A κούρσωρας δὲ ἢ BE om. MW | σοι MWA om. BE    **705** παράπτωμα…γένηται MW συμβῇ τινα ἀστοχῆσαι ἢ κινδυνεῦσαι ABE | σύντομος ἐπανορθώσεως MW trsp. ABE    **707** γίνεται MWA γίνεται περὶ σοφοῦ στρατηγοῦ BE

102. Where should the baggage train be situated?

On the march the soldiers should not get mixed in with the baggage train, especially if the enemy are expected. The bandon goes ahead by itself and the baggage train to the rear or as the situation requires, as we have noted in our chapter about the baggage train. These matters that we have prescribed for you are those about which you will give orders and you will see that each individual count and droungarios, as well as the tourmarch, will know them and carry them out.

103. That a person must observe those things that enable him to defeat the enemy.[10]

We order you, O general, to take advantage of favorable times in engaging the enemy in battle. First, you must be on your guard against enemy assaults that inflict harm <on your troops>, and then you must launch the same sort of assaults against the enemy.

104. About not pursuing the enemy in a disorderly manner.

Above all, you must be on the lookout for ambushes being planned by your opponents, sending out frequent patrols to the four quarters of the area where the battle line is deployed. And refrain from disordered and uncoordinated pursuits.

105. About the general not engaging in headlong attacks but <leaving such> to his subordinate officers.

We do not permit you to take part personally in raids or headlong attacks. These should be carried out by suitable officers. For if one of the subordinate officers blunders or fails, we can hope to straighten out the situation quickly. But if the first in the army fails, his failure can open the way to complete disorder.

106. The best and wisest general is he who, before waging war, carefully studies the enemy and is on his guard against those areas in which <the enemy> is stronger and who takes advantage of those in which he is weaker. To sum it

10. Sections 103–108 derive from *Strat.*, Preface 7.A.

ρίους ἔχει ὁ ἐχθρὸς πλείονας, δέον σε τὰς βοσκὰς ἀφανίζειν διὰ τὸ τοὺς ἵππους δαπάνης ὑστερεῖν. ἐὰν δὲ εἰς πλῆθος ἀνδρῶν πλεονεκτῇ, τὰς τούτων δαπάνας περίστελλε ἢ ἀφάνιζε. ἐὰν δὲ ἀπὸ διαφόρων ἐθνῶν συνέστηκεν, δώροις καὶ χαρίσμασι καὶ ἐπαγγελίαις ὑπονόθευε τοὺς σὺν αὐτῷ. ἐὰν δὲ μάθῃς ὅτι ἐναντίας

715    τὰς γνώμας πρὸς ἀλλήλους ἔχουσιν οἱ ἐχθροί, τοὺς πρώτους αὐτῶν μεταχειρί-ζου. κονταρίοις μάχεται τὸ ἔθνος, εἰς δυσχωρίας αὐτὸ προσκαλοῦ ἐπὶ μάχην. ἐὰν δὲ τοξόται εἰσίν, εἰς κάμπους τάσσεσθαι αὐτοὺς καὶ τὴν ἐκ χειρὸς μάχην ποιεῖ-σθαι. ἐὰν δὲ ἀφυλάκτως ὁδοιποροῦσιν ἢ ἀπλικεύουσιν, ἐν νυκτὶ ἢ ἐν ἡμέρᾳ, τούτοις ἀδοκήτως ἐνέδρευε. ἐὰν δὲ θρασέως καὶ ἀτάκτως τὰς μάχας ποιοῦνται

720    καὶ τοῦ κακοπαθεῖν ἄπειροί εἰσιν, σχηματίζου μὲν αὐτοὺς ὡς πρὸς συμβολήν, ἀναβάλλου δὲ καὶ παράσυρε μέχρις οὗ τὸ ζέον τοῦ θυμοῦ ἐνδώσει καί, ὅτ᾽ ἂν ἀποκνήσωσιν, τότε τὴν συμβολὴν κατ᾽ αὐτῶν ποίησον. ἐὰν δὲ ἐν πλήθει πεζῶν προτερεύῃ, εἰς ὁμαλοὺς τόπους τούτους προτρέπου καὶ μὴ σύνεγγυς, ἀλλὰ μήκοθεν δι᾽ ἀκοντίων τὰς μάχας ποιεῖσθαι.

725    107. Τὰ γὰρ τῶν πολέμων κυνηγίοις εἰσὶν ὅμοια. ὥσπερ γὰρ ἐκεῖ διὰ κατα-σκόπων καὶ ἐγκρυμμάτων καὶ κατακυκλώσεων καὶ τοιούτων σοφισμάτων μᾶλλον ἢ δυνάμει ἡ τούτων θήρα γίνεται, οὕτως δεῖ καὶ ἐπὶ τῶν πολέμων ἁρμόζεσθαι, εἴτε πρὸς πλείονας εἴτε πρὸς ὀλίγους γίνονται.

108. Τὸ γὰρ φανερῶς καὶ χειρὶ δι᾽ ὄψεως μόνον βιάζεσθαι τοὺς ἐναντίους,

730    ὅτε καὶ δόξει τις τούτους νικᾶν μετὰ κινδύνου καὶ ζημίας οὐ τῆς τυχούσης ἡ τοῦ πράγματος ἀπόβασις αὐτῷ συμβαίνει· ὅπερ τῶν ἀλογίστων ἐστὶν ἀνάγκης μεγίστης χωρὶς | μετὰ ζημίας νίκην κτᾶσθαι, κενὴν καὶ ματαίαν ὑπόληψιν μόνην    334 φέρουσαν.

---

711 τὸ MWAE om. B    712 τούτων ABE τούτου MW    713 περίστελλε MW περίκοπτε καὶ ABE | συνέστηκεν W συνέστηκε MA συνεστήκοι BE    714 χαρίσμασι MWA χαρίσμασιν B χαρίσμας E | ὑπονόθευε MW ὑπόκλεπτε A om. BE | αὐτῷ MWA αὐτῶ ὑπόκλεπτε BE    714–716 ἐὰν…μεταχειρίζου MWA om. BE    715 ἀλλήλους Va ἀλλήλας MW ἀλλήλουσιν A om. BE    716 κονταρίοις MWA ἐὰν κονταρίως B εἰ κονταρίως E | δυσχωρίας MW δυσκόλους τόπους ABE | ἐὰν MWA εἰ BE    718 ὁδοιποροῦσιν MW ὁδοιπορῶσιν ABE | ἀπλικεύουσιν MW ἀπλικεύωσιν ABE    719 θρασέως MWA θαρσέως BE | ποιοῦνται MW ποιῶνται ABE    720 ἄπειροί εἰσιν MWAB ὦσιν ἄπειροι E | αὐτοὺς MW αὐτὸς ABE    721 παράσυρε MW παράσυρε τὸν πόλεμον ABE    722 ἀποκνήσωσιν WA ἀποκινήσωσι MBE    724 δι᾽ MWBE διὰ A    725 πολέμων Va πολεμίων codd.    725–726 κατασκόπων MWAE κόπτων B    727 ἢ…θήρα MW ἡ θήρα τούτων ABE | πολέμων W πολεμίων MABE    729 δι᾽ ὄψεως MW εἰς πρόσωπον ABE    731 αὐτῷ MWAE αὐτοῦ B    732 μόνην MW om. ABE

up: if the enemy has more cavalry than you, you must destroy their pasturage so as to reduce the fodder for their horses. If the enemy has more men than you, cut off and destroy their provisions. If the men in his army come from diverse nations, corrupt them with gifts, favors, and promises. If you learn that there is much dissension among the enemy, deal with their leading men. This people relies on the lance, summon them into battle on difficult terrain. If they are archers, have them take their stand in the open and engage them in hand-to-hand combat. If they march or make camp without taking precautions, either at night or during the day, catch them by surprise in an ambush. If they are reckless and undisciplined in combat and are not inured to hardship, make believe you are going to attack but delay and drag things out until their ardor cools and when they begin to hesitate, then launch your attack against them. If the enemy is superior in numbers of infantry, entice them into level areas and, not too close but at a safe distance, fight them with javelins.

107. Warfare is like hunting. Wild animals are taken by scouting, by lying in wait, by circling around, and by other such stratagems rather than by force. And so we must accommodate ourselves to warfare in the same way, whether the enemy be many or few.

108. To try to simply overpower our adversaries in the open, hand-to-hand and face-to-face, even though you might appear to win, is an enterprise fraught with danger and can result in serious harm. Apart from an extreme emergency, it is absolutely ridiculous to try to gain a victory that is so costly and brings only empty and vain glory.

109. Ἐπὶ τούτοις παρακελευόμεθά σοι, ὦ στρατηγέ, καὶ ὅσα χρή σε ποιεῖν
735 πρὸ τῆς τοῦ πολέμου ἡμέρας, ὅτε καὶ ἀνάγκη σε κατεπείγει πρὸς μάχην ἐξελθεῖν
κατὰ τῶν ἐχθρῶν.

---

736 κατὰ τῶν ΑΒΕ κατ' MW

109. These are the orders we issue to you, O general, that you are obliged to carry out before the day of battle, when you are forced to go out and do battle against the foe.

# ΠΟΛΕΜΙΚΩΝ ΠΑΡΑΣΚΕΥΩΝ ΔΙΑΤΑΞΙΣ ΙΓ΄

## Περὶ τῆς πρὸ τοῦ πολέμου ἡμέρας

1. Ὥστε παρασκευάζειν τοὺς τουρμάρχας πρὸ μιᾶς ἢ δευτέρας ἡμέρας τοῦ πολέμου τὰ βάνδα ἁγιάζειν διὰ τῶν ἱερέων καὶ οὕτως ἐπιδιδόναι τοῖς βανδοφό-
5 ροις τῶν ταγμάτων.
2. Τὸν δὲ ἑκάστου τάγματος κόμητα προκαθιστᾶν τὰ κοντουβέρνια καὶ ἀναπληροῦν τὰ λείποντα σώματα.
3. Σπουδάσεις δὲ τὰ κατὰ τοὺς ἐχθροὺς πολυπραγμονῆσαι διὰ βιγλῶν ἀκριβῶς καὶ διὰ κατασκόπων τήν τε κίνησιν αὐτῶν καὶ τὸ ποσὸν τοῦ πλήθους
10 αὐτῶν καὶ τὴν σύνταξιν καὶ οὕτως ἁρμόζεσθαι εἰς τὸ μὴ αἰφνιδιασθῆναι παρ᾽ αὐτῶν.
4. Συντάξεις δὲ ἐπὶ σχολῆς τὸν στρατὸν κατὰ δρούγγους καὶ κατὰ τούρμας καὶ μὴ πάντα ὁμοῦ εἰς ἓν ἐν ἑνὶ τόπῳ καὶ διαλαλήσεις αὐτοῖς τὰ πρέποντα ἢ δι᾽ ἑαυτοῦ ἢ διὰ τῶν ἰδίων ἀρχόντων, παλαιᾶς τε ἀναμιμνήσκων νίκης καὶ προτέ-
15 ρων ἐπιτυχιῶν καὶ διὰ τοιούτων προθυμοποιεῖν αὐτοὺς ἐπαγγείλασθαί τε τὴν ἐκ τῆς βασιλείας ἡμῶν ἀμοιβὴν καὶ εὐεργεσίαν καὶ τὸν ὑπὲρ τῆς εὐνοίας τῆς πολιτείας μισθόν, ἔτι δὲ προσυπομιμνήσκειν καὶ τὰ διδόμενα μανδάτα καὶ τὴν ἄλλην παραγγελίαν, ἣν παρά τέ σου αὐτοῦ καὶ παρὰ τῶν ἰδικῶν αὐτῶν ἀρχόντων ἔλαβον καθ᾽ ἕκαστον τάγμα.

---

M (mut.) W A B E    Va    PG 107:844

---

1–102 *Strat.*, 7.A.1–14.

---

1 πολεμικῶν παρασκευῶν MWA om. BE    2 πρὸ MWA om. BE    3 τουρμάρχας MWAE τουρμάρχους B | ἡμέρας MWAE om. B    6 κόμητα MW ἄρχοντα ABE | κοντουβέρνια AB κουτουβέρνια MW κοντοῦ βέρνια E    7 σώματα MW om. ABE    8 τὰ MWA om. BE | τοὺς ἐχθροὺς ABE τῶν ἐχθρῶν MW    9 τὸ ποσὸν MW τὴν ποσότητα ABE    12 ἐπὶ σχολῆς MW ἐν ἀργίᾳ ABE    13 πάντα MW ὅλον ABE | ὁμοῦ MWAE ἐμοῦ B | εἰς ἓν MW om AB ἓν E    13–14 δι᾽ ἑαυτοῦ MW διὰ σεαυτοῦ ABE    14 ἰδίων MWA om. BE    15 ἐπιτυχιῶν MW εὐτυχιῶν ABE | τε MWA τε καὶ BE    16 τὸν MW τὸν μισθὸν τὸν ABE    16–17 τῆς πολιτείας MW τὴν πρὸς τὴν πολιτείαν ABE    17 μισθόν MW om. ABE    18 παρά τέ MW καὶ παρὰ ABE | ἰδικῶν MW ἰδίων ABE

# PREPARATION FOR WAR, CONSTITUTION XIII

## About the Day before Battle

1. A day or two before combat, the tourmarchs should see that the standards are blessed by the priests and then present them to the standard-bearers of the tagmata.[1]

2. The commanding officer of each tagma should organize it into squads and bring them up to full strength.

3. You will make every effort, employing scouts and spies, to obtain accurate intelligence about the enemy's movements and the number and disposition of their troops. This will allow you to make proper adjustments and not be caught off guard by them.

4. When you are not otherwise occupied, you shall assemble the army by droungoi and by tourmai, but not all at once in one place. Appropriate speeches should be addressed to them, either by yourself or their individual officers. Recall their past victories and their earlier successes to encourage them. Promise rewards and benefactions from Our Majesty and recompense for their loyalty to the state. Remind them, furthermore, of the commands given them and the other orders that they have received from you personally and from their own officers in each unit.

1. Sections 1–17 derive from *Strat.* 7.A.1–14.

20    5. Ἐὰν δέ τινες τῶν ἐχθρῶν συμβῇ κρατηθῆναι ἢ προσρυῆναι, εἰ μὲν γενναῖ-
οί εἰσι τοῖς σώμασι καὶ εὔοπλοι, τούτους μὴ δημοσιεύειν τῷ στρατῷ ἀλλ᾽ ἐν
ἑτέρῳ τόπῳ ἀφανῶς ἐκπέμπειν αὐτούς, εἰ δὲ εὐτελεῖς εἰσι, τοὺς μὲν προσρυομένους ἐπιτηδεύσεις ἐπιδεῖξαι τῷ στρατῷ παντί, τοὺς δὲ κρατουμένους γυμνοὺς
περιάγεις καὶ ὑποθήσεις αὐτοὺς παρακαλεῖν τοὺς στρατιώτας μὴ φονευθῆναι,
25    εἰς τὸ πάντας τοὺς ἐχθροὺς ἐλεεινοὺς εἶναι νομίζεσθαι παρὰ τῶν στρατιωτῶν.
6. Ἐχθρῶν δὲ ἐγγιζόντων καὶ δημοσίου προσδοκωμένου πολέμου παραγγεί-
λης τοῖς ἄρχουσι τῶν | ταγμάτων ὥστε μὴ ποιεῖν ἐν ἐκείναις ταῖς ἡμέραις συνεξ-    334ᵛ
ελεύσεις κατὰ τῶν ἀτακτούντων στρατιωτῶν, φυλάττεσθαι δὲ παντοίως μὴ
κακῶσαι τὸν στρατιώτην, ἀλλὰ καὶ τοὺς ἐν ὑποψίᾳ ὄντας λύπης τινὸς ἕνεκα
30    μεταχειρίζεσθαι εἰς εὐθυμίαν, εἰ δὲ ἀμεταχείριστοι οἱ τοιοῦτοι μένουσιν, χωρίσεις
αὐτοὺς πρὸς μικρὸν καὶ ἑτέρῳ παραπέμψεις τόπῳ μετὰ προφάσεως εὐλόγου
μέχρι τῆς τοῦ πολέμου ἐκβάσεως, ἵνα μὴ τοῖς ἐχθροῖς προσφυγόντες εἴπωσίν τι
ὧν οὐ χρὴ γινώσκειν αὐτούς. τοὺς δὲ ὁμογενεῖς τῶν ἐχθρῶν, ὡς ἤδη προείπομεν,
πρὸ πολλοῦ χωρίζειν καὶ ἐν πολέμῳ τούτους μὴ φέρειν κατὰ τῶν ἰδίων μάχ-
35    εσθαι.
7. Ὅτ᾽ ἂν δὲ μέλλῃς συμβαλεῖν εἰς μάχην, ὦ στρατηγέ, χρή σε καὶ τὰ εἰς
δευτέραν τύχην ἀποσκοπεῖν καὶ τὰς ἐκεῖθεν ἐναντιώσεις προασφαλίζεσθαι καὶ

20 συμβῇ MW συμβῇ εἰς βίγλαν ABE | προσρυῆναι MW προσφυγεῖν ABE    21 εὔοπλοι De
ἔνοπλοι codd.    22 δὲ MWAE δὲ καὶ B | εἰσι MBE εἰσιν WA    22–23 προσρυομένους MW
προσφεύγοντας ABE    23 ἐπιδεῖξαι MW ἐπιδείξεις ABE | τῷ...παντί MW ὅλῳ τῷ στρατῷ
ABE    24 περιάγεις MW περιαγάγεις εἰς ὅλον τὸ στράτευμα ABE | ὑποθήσεις αὐτοὺς MW
παραγγείλης αὐτοῖς ὥστε ABE    25 εἰς...στρατιωτῶν MW ἀλλὰ καὶ ἕτερα ῥήματα λέγειν
ἄξια ἐλέους καὶ συμπαθείας ὡς ἂν τοιούτους ἐλεεινοὺς αὐτοὺς βλέπων ὁ στρατὸς καὶ τοὺς
ἄλλους ἅπαντας ἐχθροὺς τοιούτους, εἶναι ὑπονόηση ABE    27 τοῖς...ταγμάτων MW πᾶσι
τοῖς ὑπό σε ἄρχουσι ABE    27–35 ὥστε...μάχεσθαι MW μηδένα τῶν ὑποχωρίων αὐτῶν
ἐπεξέρχεσθαι (ἐπέρχεσθαι BE) ἐάν τινα ἀταξίαν ποιήσῃ καὶ παντὶ τρόπῳ φυλάττεσθαι ὥστε μὴ
λυπῆσαι τοὺς στρατιώτας ἀλλὰ καὶ τοὺς (τοῖς B) ἐν ὑποψίᾳ ὄντας λύπης τινὸς καὶ ἐκείνους
παραμυθεῖσθαι καὶ εὐθυμοτέρους παρασκευάζειν εἰ δὲ καὶ (καὶ om. BE) οὐ μεταβάλλονται ἐκ
τῆς θλίψεως ἀλλ᾽ ἐπιμένουσι (ἐπιμένουσιν A) σπουδάσεις τοῦ μετὰ εὐλόγου (μετὰ λόγου BE)
προφάσεως ἀποχωρίσαι αὐτοὺς ἐκ τοῦ στρατοῦ μέχρις ἂν ὁ πόλεμος τελειωθῇ πολλάκις γὰρ
οἱ τοιοῦτοι λυπούμενοι προσφεύγουσι τοῖς πολεμίοις καὶ πράγματά τινα αὐτοῖς
ἀποκαλύπτουσιν ἃ οὐκ ἐστι (ἔστιν BE) δέον μαθεῖν αὐτοὺς τοὺς δὲ ὁμογενεῖς καὶ ὁμοφύλους
τῶν πολεμίων πρὸ πολλῶν ἡμερῶν ἀποχωρίζειν καὶ μὴ ἐπάγεσθαι αὐτοὺς ἐν τῇ ἡμέρᾳ τοῦ
πολέμου ABE    30 μένουσιν WA μένουσι MBE    36 συμβαλεῖν MW συμβάλλειν ABE | καὶ
MW καὶ τὰ ἐναντία λογίζεσθαι καὶ ABE | τὰ MW om. ABE    37 ἀποσκοπεῖν MW
ἀποβλέπειν ABE | ἐκεῖθεν MW ἐκ ταύτης ABE

5. If some of the enemy happen to be captured or desert <to us>, then, if they are impressive in bodily appearance and in their armament, do not show them to the army but secretly send them off to some other place. But if they look wretched, make sure to exhibit the deserters to the whole army; strip the prisoners and parade them about and force them to entreat the soldiers not to kill them, so that our soldiers will think that all the enemy are that miserable.

6. When the enemy are approaching and a pitched battle is imminent, you should order the commanders of the tagmata not to pass judgment in those days against soldiers who are disorderly, and not to deal harshly with the soldiers at all. They should, rather, deal with those who are suspected of having some grievance in such a manner as to render them benevolent. But if these men remain intractable, separate them and send them off to some other place for a while, on some plausible pretext, until the battle is over. Otherwise they may go over to the enemy and provide them with information they must not have. Men of the same race as the enemy should, as we have already prescribed, be sent away long before. You should not allow them to fight against their own people.

7. When you are about to engage in battle, O general, you must keep in mind the possibility of second fortune and take steps to guard against its

μάλιστα, ὡς πολλάκις ἡμῖν εἴρηται, τὰς ἀποτροφὰς ἡμερῶν ὀλίγων τῶν τε
στρατιωτῶν καὶ τῶν ἵππων συνάγειν καὶ φοσσάτα ὀχυρώτερα ποιεῖν καὶ ἐν
40 ἐπιτηδείοις τόποις, ἔνθα δυνατὸν τὸ ὕδωρ πάντως ἐκδικεῖσθαι ἐν καιρῷ ἀνάγκης.

8. Μὴ ἀμελήσῃς δὲ τῆς ἀριστοποιΐας τοῦ στρατοῦ. εἰ μὲν γάρ, ὅτε συμβουλευθῇς, ἡ συμβολὴ γίνεται πάντως ἐν ᾧ ἂν δοκιμάσῃς καιρῷ, τὸ ἄριστον τοῦ
στρατοῦ γινέσθω. εἰ δὲ τοῦτο μὴ ἔστιν, μέλλοντος τοῦ πολέμου, πάντως τὸ πρωΐ
45 γίνεσθαι τὸ ἄριστον ἵνα, εἰ τύχοι, καὶ εὔρωστοί εἰσι καὶ δι᾿ ὅλης πολλάκις τῆς
ἡμέρας τοῦ πολέμου κροτουμένου μὴ ἐκλυθῶσιν.

9. Χρὴ δέ σε πάντως, ὦ στρατηγέ, μὴ μόνον ἐν τοῖς ἄλλοις καιροῖς, ἀλλὰ καὶ
ἐν τῷ τοιούτῳ ἐγγὺς τοῦ πολέμου καιρῷ μὴ ἀμελεῖν τοῦ συμβουλεύεσθαι, ἀλλὰ
καὶ τότε μάλιστα συγκαλέσεις τοὺς ὑπό σε τουρμάρχας καὶ εἴ τινα ἕτερον
50 δοκιμάσῃς ἀγχίνουν καὶ φρόνιμον εἰς τὴν κατὰ τὸν καιρὸν ὀφειλομένην γενέσθαι συμβουλήν, καὶ οὕτως βουλεύσασθαί σε δέον τὰ περὶ τοῦ πολέμου.

10. Κατανοεῖν δὲ ἀκριβῶς καὶ τὸν τόπον ἔνθα ἡ συμβολὴ τοῦ πολέμου
μέλλει γίνεσθαι.

11. Προπαραγγείλῃς δὲ τοῖς ἄρχουσιν ἵνα κατὰ τὴν πρώτην φωνὴν τοῦ
55 βουκίνου ἐν τῇ νυκτὶ τῆς τοῦ πολέμου ἡμέρας τοὺς ἵππους ἐπὶ τὸν ποτὸν
παρασκευάσωσιν ἐξαγαγεῖν ἵνα μή, ὡς εἰκός, ἀμελοῦντες τούτου ἐν τῷ καιρῷ
τῆς παρατάξεως ἀπολείπωνται.

12. Προπαραγγείλῃς δέ, καθὼς ἀνωτέρω ἡμῖν εἴρηται, ἵνα καὶ εἷς ἕκαστος | W127
στρατιώτης ἐν τῷ κινεῖν πρὸς παράταξιν ἔχῃ ἐν τῷ σελλοπουγγίῳ αὐτοῦ μίαν ἢ

---

59 ad αὐτοῦ des. M

---

**38** ἀποτροφὰς WABE ἀποστροφὰς M    **38–39** ἡμερῶν…συνάγειν MW συνάγειν τῶν τε
ἵππων καὶ τῶν ἀνδρῶν κἂν ὀλίγων ἡμερῶν ABE    **40** ἐπιτηδείοις τόποις MW trsp. ABE
**42** τῆς ἀριστοποιΐας MW τοῦ γεύματος ABE    **42–43** συμβουλευθῇς MW συμβουληθῇς A
βουληθῇς BE    **43** συμβολὴ MW συμβολὴ τοῦ πολέμου ABE    **44–46** μέλλοντος…
ἐκλυθῶσιν MW ἐν τῇ σῇ ἐξουσίᾳ ἀλλ᾿ ἄδηλός ἐστιν ἡ τοῦ πολέμου συμβολὴ συμφέρον ἐστὶν
ἵνα τὸ πρωὶ ἀριστῶσιν οἱ στρατιῶται συμβαίνῃ γὰρ δι᾿ ὅλης τῆς ἡμέρας συγκροτεῖσθαι τὸν
πόλεμον καὶ ἐὰν τυχῶσι γευσάμενοι ἰσχυρότεροί εἰσι καὶ δύνανται δι᾿ ὅλης τῆς ἡμέρας
ὑπομένειν ABE    **44** πολέμου De στρατοῦ MW om. ABE    **45** τῆς M om. W
**46** κροτουμένου Va κροτοῦντος MW    **48** ἐν…τοιούτῳ MW om. ABE | μὴ…τοῦ² MW καὶ
τότε A om. BE    **48–49** ἀλλὰ…μάλιστα MW om. ABE    **49** συγκαλέσεις MW συγκαλέσεις
δὲ ABE    **50** δοκιμάσῃς…φρόνιμον MW οἶδας εἶναι φρόνιμον καὶ ἐπιτήδειον ABE | καιρὸν
MW καιρὸν ἐκεῖνον ABE    **51** συμβουλήν MW βουλὴν ABE | οὕτως MWA οὕτω BE
**55** τῆς MWAB om. E    **58** προπαραγγείλῃς BE παραγγείλεις MWA | καθὼς MW καθὼς καὶ
ABE    **59** ἔχῃ MWAE ἔχειν B

negative effects.[2] In particular, as we have frequently said, collect food for a few days for both soldiers and horses. Construct strongly fortified camps in suitable locations in which, above all, water may be safely stored for emergencies.

8. Do not neglect the preparation of meals for the army. If, after consultation, fighting is to take place, be sure to schedule the meal for the army at whatever time you think best. If no fighting is anticipated, then by all means, the army should plan to take its main meal very early so that, in case <battle> does take place, the men may be in good physical condition and, while the battle is being waged throughout the day, may not fall apart.

9. By all means, O general, you must, not only at other times, but also in that hour when combat is imminent, not neglect to enter into consultation. Especially at that time, call together the tourmarchs under your command and anyone else you regard as shrewd and thoughtful to seek their advice on what ought to be done at that time. In this way you must make your plans regarding the battle.

10. Make accurate observations about the location in which the battle is to be fought.

11. Issue orders ahead of time to the officers that, at the first sound of the trumpet on the night before battle, they should make sure to lead the horses out to water. If they should neglect this, their horses may fail <them> when it is time to form the battle line.

12. Issue orders ahead of time, as we have previously prescribed, that each soldier, as he moves up to the battle line, should carry in his saddle bags a

2. "Second fortune," a frequent euphemism for ill fortune, i.e., defeat.

60 καὶ δύο λίτρας ἄρτου ἢ ἀλεύρου ἢ πίστου ἑψητοῦ ἢ παξαμάδας ἢ κρέας· ἔχειν δὲ
καὶ φλασκὶν μικρὸν ἐν τῇ ἀργαβίᾳ ὕδατος γέμον καὶ μὴ οἴνου διά τε τὰς τυχηρὰς περιστάσεις καὶ τὰς ἀπαντώσας χρείας. πολλάκις γὰρ τρεπομένων ἐχθρῶν
καὶ ὀχυρώματι προστρεχόντων χρεία παρακαθίσαι αὐτοῖς διὰ νυκτὸς καὶ
ἡμέρας ἢ πάλιν τὴν συμβολὴν μέχρι τῆς ἑσπέρας παρατείνεσθαι. καὶ ἀναγκαῖόν
65 ἐστιν ἐπιφέρεσθαι δαπάνην ἵνα μὴ τῇ ἐλλείψει τῆς δαπάνης τὸ πρακτέον ἐμποδίζηται.

   13. Ἐὰν δὲ πρὸς δυνατὸν ἔθνος ἐστὶν ὁ πόλεμος καὶ ἐκ προλήψεώς τινος ἐν
δειλίᾳ ἐστὶν ὁ στρατός, μὴ σπουδάσῃς συμπλέκεσθαι δημοσίως εὐθύς, ἀλλὰ
πρότερον ἀσφαλῶς ἐπιτήδευε πρὸ τῆς ἡμέρας τοῦ πολέμου μετὰ ἐξπλήκτων καὶ
70 χρησίμων ἀνδρῶν λεληθότως καὶ μὴ φανερῶς | ἐπέρχεσθαί τινι μέρει αὐτῶν. ἐὰν   W127ᵛ
γὰρ φανερῶς φονευθῶσί τινες τῶν ἐναντίων ἢ ζῶντες συλληφθῶσι, νομίσει τὸ
πλῆθος τῶν στρατιωτῶν, ὅτι δυνάμει ἐγένετο τὸ συμβάν, καὶ προθυμότεροι
γίνονται τὴν δειλίαν ἀποβαλλόμενοι· καὶ οὕτως κατὰ μικρὸν ἐθίζονται τολμᾶν
καὶ κατ᾽ αὐτῶν ἐγχειρεῖν.

75   14. Ἐὰν δὲ αἰφνιδιασμὸς γένηται ὑπὸ τῶν ἐχθρῶν καὶ μὴ συμβαίνῃ τῇ τοῦ
πολέμου χρείᾳ ἢ ὁ τόπος ὡς δασὺς καὶ δυσχερὴς ἢ ὁ καιρὸς ἀπρόσφορός ἐστιν,
οἷον πολλοῦ χειμῶνος ἢ ὁμοίως καύματος, μὴ ἐπιτηδεύσῃς συμβαλεῖν αὐτοῖς ἢ
τότε ἢ ἐκεῖσε, ἀλλὰ σπούδαζε μᾶλλον συνάγειν στρατὸν καὶ τόπον ἴδιον κρατεῖν εἰς ἄπλικτον καὶ ὑπερτίθου, μέχρις ἂν καὶ τόπου ἐπιτηδείου καὶ καιροῦ
80 ὁμοίως εὐπορήσῃς, καὶ μὴ ἀκουσίως συμβάλλῃς. τοῦτο γὰρ ποιῶν οὐχὶ τὸν
ἐχθρὸν φεύξῃ ἀλλὰ τὸν ἀνεπιτήδειον καὶ ἀ|σύμφορον τόπον φυλαττόμενος ἔσῃ.   W128

---

60 δύο WAE β′ B | ἑψητοῦ WA ἑψημένου BE | παξαμάδας WA παξαμάτας BE   61 φλασκὶν
μικρὸν W ἀσκοδάβλαν μικρὰν ABE | ἀργαβίᾳ W ἐργαβίᾳ ABE | γέμον W γέμουσαν ABE
61–62 τυχηρὰς Va στυχηρὰς W συμβαινούσας ABE   62 τὰς W τὰς ὡς εἰκὸς ABE
63 παρακαθίσαι αὐτοῖς WA περικαθίσαι αὐτοὺς BE   64 παρατείνεσθαι W κρατεῖν ABE
65 ἐλλείψει W λείψει ABE | τῆς δαπάνης WA ταύτης BE | πρακτέον Va πρακταίον W μέλλον
πραχθῆναι A μέλλον παρεχθῆναι BE   65–66 ἐμποδίζηται W ἐμποδισθῇ ABE   67 ἐστιν...
πόλεμος WA ὁ πόλεμος ἢ BE   68 ἐστὶν WA ὑπάρχῃ BE   69 ἐξπλήκτων W ἐλαφρῶν ABE
71 γὰρ φανερῶς W γὰρ ABE | συλληφθῶσι W κρατηθῶσιν A κρατηθῶσι BE   72 δυνάμει
W ἀπὸ δυνάμεως ABE   73 ἀποβαλλόμενοι A ἀποβαλόμενοι W βαλόμενοι BE
75 συμβαίνῃ W συμβάλληται ABE   76 δυσχερὴς W δύσκολος ABE | ἀπρόσφορός W
ἀσύμφορος ABE | ἐστιν W ὑπάρχῃ ABE   77 ὁμοίως W om. ABE | ἐπιτηδεύσῃς W
ἐπιτηδεύσῃς ὥστε ABE   77–78 ἢ²...ἐκεῖσε W ἢ ἐν ἐκείνῳ τῷ καιρῷ ἢ εἰς ἐκεῖνον τὸν τόπον
ABE   78 στρατὸν De σεαυτὸν codd.   79 ὑπερτίθου W ὑπερτίθου τὸ πόλεμον ABE
79–80 τόπου...εὐπορήσῃς W τόπον καὶ καιρὸν ἐπιτήδειον εὕρῃς ABE   80–81 τὸν ἐχθρὸν
A τῶν ἐχθρῶν W om. BE   81 φεύξῃ W φεύγεις ABE | ἀνεπιτήδειον WAE ἐπιτήδειον B |
φυλαττόμενος ἔσῃ W παραφυλάττῃ ABE

measure or two of bread or barley meal or boiled meal or hardtack or meat. He should also carry a little sack containing a small flask of water but not wine. These may be needed in fortunate circumstances as well as in <other> needs that may occur. For a defeated enemy will often race back to a fortified position, and our men may have to spend the night as well as the day there or even continue the fighting until <the next> evening. It is essential that they carry provisions with them so that the lack of them may not interfere with operations.

13. If we are waging war against a powerful nation, and the army, not knowing what to expect, becomes nervous, do not try to engage in a pitched battle right away. First, before the day of battle, carefully arrange for some lightly armed, capable soldiers to go secretly, without being observed, and attack some detachment of the enemy. If, out in the open, they kill some of our adversaries or take some alive, then most of our soldiers will regard this as evidence of our strength. Their morale will pick up, they will get over their nervousness, and they will gradually become bolder and bolder in fighting against them.

14. If the enemy should launch a surprise attack and conditions are not favorable for battle, either because the area is rugged or thickly wooded or the time is not to our advantage because of heavy storms, say, or scorching heat, do not prepare for combat at that time or in that place. Instead, you should take steps to assemble your army, occupy a place suitable for camp, and delay until you have the luck <to find> a suitable place and time. Do not engage in battle unwillingly. Acting in this manner does not mean you are running away from the enemy, but that you are avoiding an unsuitable and disadvantageous location.

15. Θεοῦ δὲ νίκην παρέχοντος, ἐὰν οἱ πολέμιοι τραπῶσιν, ἀπέχεσθαι τοῖς στρατιώταις παράγγελλε τοῦ σκυλεύειν τοὺς νεκροὺς τῶν ἐχθρῶν· τὸ γὰρ ἢ νεκροὺς σκυλεύειν ἢ τούλδῳ ἢ φοσσάτῳ πολεμίων ἐπέρχεσθαι πρὸ τελείας
85 ἐκβάσεως τοῦ πολέμου πρᾶγμα ὀλέθριον καὶ ἐπικίνδυνόν ἐστι. διὸ χρή σε προπαραγγέλλειν τὸ παντοίως ἀπέχεσθαι τούτων. πολλάκις γὰρ οἱ νικήσαντες διὰ τοιούτων τρόπων οὐ μόνον ἡττήθησαν, ἀλλὰ καὶ ἀπώλοντο σκορπίσαντες ἑαυτοὺς καὶ ὑπὸ τῶν ἐχθρῶν αἰφνιδιασθέντες καὶ οὕτως κινδυνεύσαντες.

16. Ὅπερ δὲ ἡμῖν καὶ πρότερον εἴρηται, δεῖ μάλιστα τῶν πολεμίων ἐγγιζόν-
90 των καὶ προσδοκωμένου πολέμου ἵνα, ἐὰν ἐν φοσσάτῳ διάγει ὁ στρατὸς καὶ τοὺς ἐχθροὺς ἀναμένει ἐκεῖσε, μὴ μόνον εὐτρεπίζειν καὶ ἀποτιθέναι χόρτον ἢ ἄχυρον | μιᾶς ἢ δευτέρας ἡμέρας τῶν ἀλόγων, ἀλλὰ καί, ἐὰν κινήσῃ ὁ στρατὸς    W128ᵛ καὶ βούλεται καὶ ἐν ἑτέρῳ ἀπλίκτῳ ἀπελθεῖν κἀκεῖθεν παρατάξασθαι, ἀναγκαῖ-όν ἐστιν ὥστε χόρτον ἢ ἄχυρον κἂν μιᾶς ἡμέρας βαστάζειν καὶ οὕτως ἐν τῷ
95 γινομένῳ φοσσάτῳ ἀποτίθεσθαι τοῦτον. ἴσως γὰρ οὐ συγχωροῦνται ὑπὸ τῶν ἐχθρῶν οἱ ὑπηρετοῦντες παῖδες αὐτῇ τῇ ἡμέρᾳ ἐξελθεῖν καὶ χορτολογῆσαι οὔτε δὲ τὰ ἄλογα εἰς βοσκὴν ἐκβαλεῖν.

17. Εἰ δὲ οἱ ἐχθροὶ πολὺ ἐγγίζουσιν, οὐκ ἄτοπον ἐν τῷ περιπατεῖν, ὡς καὶ ἀλλαχοῦ ἡμῖν εἴρηται, ἕκαστον συνάγειν τὸν χόρτον, τὸν ὀφείλοντα ἀποτε-
100 θῆναι. οὐδὲ γὰρ μετὰ τὸ ἀπλικεῦσαι πολλάκις συγχωροῦνται οἱ παῖδες ἐξελθεῖν καὶ χορτολογῆσαι, πλειόνων μάλιστα τῶν καβαλλαρίων τῶν ἐχθρῶν εὑρισκο-μένων.

18. Ταῦτα μέν σοι πρὸ τῆς τοῦ πολέμου συμβολῆς τὰ μὲν διατάσσεσθαι, τὰ δὲ διαπράττεσθαι | εἰς ἐντελεστέραν μάθησιν τῶν τε ὑπό σε ἀρχόντων καὶ τῶν    W129
105 στρατιωτῶν παρακελευόμεθα, ἑξῆς δὲ καί, ὅσα χρὴ εἴτε ποιεῖν σε εἴτε παρα-

---

82 τραπῶσιν W τραπῶσι ABE    82–83 ἀπέχεσθαι…τοῦ W παράγγελλε τοὺς στρατιώτας μὴ ἀποδύειν ἢ ABE    83 νεκροὺς…ἐχθρῶν W τοὺς πίπτοντας ἐχθροὺς ABE    83–84 τὸ… σκυλεύειν WE om. AB    84 πρὸ W πρὸ τῆς ABE    85 ἐκβάσεως W συμπληρώσεως ABE | πολέμου W πολέμου τοῦτο γὰρ ABE | καὶ…ἐστι W ἐστι καὶ ἐπικίνδυνον ABE    86 προπαραγγέλλειν W παραγγέλλειν ABE | τὸ W τοῦ ABE | γὰρ WAB γὰρ καὶ E    87 διὰ WA διὰ τῶν BE | καὶ W καὶ τελείως ABE    89 τῶν W om. ABE    90 ἵνα ἐὰν W εἰ μὲν ABE    91 ἀποτιθέναι W ἀποτίθεσθαι ABE    92 ἡμέρας W ἡμέρας λόγου ABE    93 βούλεται W βούληται ABE | καὶ² WA om. BE | κἀκεῖθεν W καὶ ἀπ᾽ ἐκεῖθεν ABE    94 κἂν ABE om. W    96–97 οὔτε δὲ W οὐδὲ ABE    98 οὐκ W οὔκ ἐστιν ABE    98–99 ὡς…εἴρηται W om. ABE    99 τὸν¹ W om. ABE    101 τῶν¹ W om. ABE    103 σοι W σοι παρακελευόμεθα ABE    104 ἐντελεστέραν W τελειοτέραν ABE | τε WA om. BE    105 παρακελευόμεθα W om. ABE | δὲ W δὲ ἐροῦμεν ABE    105–106 παραφυλάττεσθαι W παραφυλάττεσθαι τοῦ μὴ παθεῖν ABE

15. If God grants us the victory and the enemy are routed, order the soldiers to refrain from plundering the enemy dead. Plundering the dead or attacking their baggage train or their camp before the battle is completely finished is fraught with danger and can be disastrous. You must order the soldiers ahead of time, without exception, to refrain from such actions. Often enough, by acting in this fashion, victorious troops have not only suffered defeat but, scattered about and caught by surprise, they have fallen into great danger and have been completely wiped out.

16. We have previously written about the following. Especially as the enemy are approaching and battle is expected and, if the army is to stay within the fortifications and there await the enemy, you must get ready and store enough hay or grass for the horses for one or two days. Not only that, but if the army is to march out with the intention of moving off to another camp and there form its battle line, then it is necessary for it to carry along one day's supply of hay and grass and store it in the new fortification. It is not likely that the enemy will allow the servants who do this work to go out foraging on that day or send out the horses to graze.

17. But if the enemy come very close, it is not a bad idea, as we have remarked somewhere else, while marching along, for each man to gather the fodder he needs to store. Frequently, after they have set up camp, the boys are not allowed to go out and forage, especially if the enemy cavalry is found to outnumber ours.

18. Before engaging in battle, we order you to make the above arrangements and to make sure that the officers and soldiers under your command are more fully instructed in them. Next in order, we will address ourselves, to the best of

φυλάττεσθαι μετὰ τῆς ὑπό σε δυνάμεως ἐν αὐτῇ τῇ ἡμέρᾳ τῆς συμβολῆς τοῦ πολέμου, κατὰ δύναμιν ἤδη ἐροῦμεν.

---

107 κατὰ…ἐροῦμεν W om. ABE

our ability, to the steps you and the force under your command must take and, on the very day of battle, what you must be on your guard against.

# ΠΟΛΕΜΙΚΩΝ ΠΑΡΑΣΚΕΥΩΝ ΔΙΑΤΑΞΙΣ ΙΔ΄

## Περὶ τῆς ἡμέρας τοῦ πολέμου

1. Ὑποτιθέμεθα οὖν σοι, ὦ στρατηγέ, πρό γε πάντων ἐν τῇ ἡμέρᾳ τοῦ πολέμου καθαρὸν εἶναι τὸν στρατὸν καὶ εὐχὴν γενέσθαι διὰ τῆς νυκτὸς ἐκτενῆ διὰ
5 τῶν ἱερέων καὶ ἁγιασθῆναι πάντας καὶ οὕτως καὶ ἔργοις καὶ λόγοις πεισθῆναι ὅτι τὸν Θεὸν ἔχουσι βοηθόν, καὶ ἐπὶ τούτῳ κινῆσαι πρὸς τὸν πόλεμον λαμπροὺς καὶ προθύμους.

2. Σὲ δὲ μὴ πολλὰ πονεῖν ἐν τῇ ἡμέρᾳ τῆς συμβολῆς ἵνα μὴ τῷ πολλῷ κόπῳ καὶ τῇ συντριβῇ τῶν ἀναγκαίων ἐπιλανθάνῃ, μηδὲ κατολιγωρεῖν σε ἀπὸ τῆς
10 φροντίδος, | ἀλλὰ ἀνθηρῶς καὶ εὐθαρσῶς παρέρχεσθαι τὴν παράταξιν καὶ   W129ᵛ προθυμοποιεῖν πάντας διὰ λόγων. |

3. Καὶ μὴ συμπλέκεσθαι τοῖς πολεμίοις διὰ χειρός. στρατιώτου γὰρ μᾶλλον ἢ   335 στρατηγοῦ τοῦτό ἐστιν. ἀλλὰ ποιεῖν σε μὲν τὰ ἁρμόζοντα πάντα, ἐν ἐπιτηδείῳ δὲ ἵστασθαι τόπῳ, ὅθεν ὁρᾶν δύνασαι τούς τε ἀγωνιζομένους καὶ τούς, ὡς
15 εἰκός, ἀμελοῦντας, καὶ ἐπεύχεσθαι τὰ δέοντα καὶ σπουδάζειν διὰ τῶν ἐν ὑποβοηθείᾳ ὄντων συναίρεσθαι τῷ δεομένῳ μέρει, τοῦτ᾽ ἔστι διὰ τῶν πλαγιοφυλάκων καὶ νωτοφυλάκων.

4. Ἐὰν μὲν οὖν ἐν ταῖς παρατάξεσί σου πρὸς τοξότας ἐστὶν ὁ πόλεμος, τοὺς δυσχερεῖς τόπους καὶ τοὺς πρόποδας τῶν ὀρέων ἤγουν τὰς πρώτας ἀναβάσεις
20 ἐπὶ τὰ ὄρη πάντως τούτους φυλάττου καὶ μὴ ἐν αὐτοῖς σύμβαλλε τὴν μάχην. εἴγε δυνατόν σοί ἐστιν, καὶ ἢ ἐν τῷ ὕψει τὴν παράταξιν ἔκτασσε ἢ τελείως

---

M (mut.) W A V (part.) B E  Va (part.)  PG 107:848  **12** ad καὶ de novo inc. M

---

**3–7** *Strat.*, 2.18.  **8–196** *Strat.*, 7.B.1–14.

---

**1** πολεμικῶν παρασκευῶν WA om. BE  **3** γε W om. ABE  **5** ἔργοις…λόγοις WA trsp. BE
**8** πονεῖν W κοποῦσθαι ABE  **9** τῶν…ἐπιλανθάνῃ W trsp. ABE(ἐπιλανθάνειν)  **10** ἀλλὰ
WA ἀλλ᾽ BE  **12** μὴ MWA om. BE  **12–13** στρατιώτου…ἐστιν MW τοῦτο γὰρ
στρατιώτου μᾶλλον ἐστιν οὐ (τοῦ BE) στρατηγοῦ ABE  **14** δύνασαι MW δυνήσῃ ABE
**14–15** ὡς εἰκός MW om. ABE  **15–16** ὑποβοηθείᾳ MWBE ἐπιβοηθεία A
**16** συναίρεσθαι…δεομένῳ MW ἐπιβοηθεῖν τῷ καταπονουμένῳ ABE  **18** ἐὰν MWA εἰ BE |
μὲν MW om. ABE | παρατάξεσί MABE παρατάξεσιν W  **19** δυσχερεῖς τόπους MW
δυσκόλους τόπους ἀπόφευγε ABE  **19–20** τὰς…τούτους MW τὰ κατώτερα μέρη ABE
**20** πάντως M om. WABE | φυλάττου WABE φυλάττε M  **21** εἴγε…ἐστιν MW om. ABE

# PREPARATION FOR WAR, CONSTITUTION XIV

## About the Day of Battle

1. Now then, O general, before all else, we enjoin upon you that on the day of battle your army should be free from sin. The night before, the priests are to offer fervent prayers of intercession. Everyone should be sanctified and so, by words and deeds, they should be convinced that they have the help of God. On this note they are to advance into battle bright and enthusiastic.[1]

2. On the day of battle you should not take on too many tasks.[2] You might exert yourself too much, wear yourself out, and overlook essential matters. Anxiety should not make you <appear> downcast, but ride jauntily and confidently along the battle line, encouraging all by your words.

3. Do not join in hand-to-hand fighting with the enemy; that is the role of the soldier, not of the general. But you are to make all the proper arrangements and then station yourself in a suitable location from which you can observe the troops fighting hard and others, quite possibly, not so hard. You should see to their needs and take steps to call up your reserves, that is, the flank and rear guards, to go to the assistance of a unit in trouble.

4. When you are in formation and have to fight against archers, avoid difficult terrain and, by all means, the lower slopes of mountains, that is, where the mountains first begin to ascend. Do not initiate hostilities there. If you can do so, form your battle line on the heights or else come all the way down the

---

1. Cf. *Strat.* 2.18.

2. Sections 2–29 derive from *Strat.* 7.B.1–14.

ἀπόβαινε τοῦ ὄρους καὶ ἐν ὁμαλωτέρῳ καὶ γυμνῷ τόπῳ παρατάσσου, ἵνα μὴ
τῶν ἐχθρῶν, ὡς εἰκός, ἐκεῖθεν ἐνεδρευόντων ἀπὸ τοῦ ὕψους ἡ παράταξις
ἀθρόως βιάζηται.

25    5. Ἀλλὰ μηδὲ συμπλέκου παρατάξει πολεμίων, μηδὲ τὴν ἰδίαν σου προδείκ-
νυε αὐτοῖς πρὶν ἂν τὴν τάξιν αὐτῶν κατανοήσῃς καὶ τάς, ὡς εἰκός, μελετωμένας
παρ' αὐτῶν ἐνέδρας ἤτοι ἐγκρύμματα πολυπραγμονήσῃς.

6. Ἐὰν δὲ οἱ τόποι ἐν οἷς μέλλεις συμβάλλειν γυμνοί εἰσι καὶ πεδινοὶ καὶ οὐκ
ἔστιν εὐκόλως τὴν δευτέραν σου τάξιν κρύπτειν ἐν αὐτοῖς, εἰς τὸ μὴ τοὺς ἐχ-
30    θροὺς προγινώσκειν ἐν τῷ κινεῖν τὸν στρατὸν εἰς τὴν μάχην, ἐντεῦθεν ἤδη τὴν
δευτέραν τάξιν κατόπισθεν τῆς πρώτης πλησίον συνακολουθεῖν ποίησον, ὥστε
τὰς δύο ὡς μίαν τοῖς ἐναντίοις φαίνεσθαι, ὅτ' ἂν δὲ ἀπὸ ἑνὸς μιλίου τῆς τῶν
πολεμίων γένηται παρατάξεως, τότε τὴν δευτέραν χρεὸν κατ' ὀλίγον ἐμβρα-
δύνουσαν χωρίζειν αὐτὴν ἀπὸ τῆς πρώτης τὸ εἰρημένον διάστημα καὶ εἰς τὸ
35    ἴδιον σχῆμα καθιστᾶν ὥστε εἶναι δευτέραν παράταξιν· ἐντεῦθεν γὰρ τοῖς πολεμίοις οὐκ εὔγνωστος πρὸ πολλοῦ ἡ τάξις γίνεται.

7. Τὰς δὲ ὑποχωρήσεις καὶ φυγὰς τῶν ἐχθρῶν σκέπτου καὶ μὴ ἀκρατῶς
ἐπίτρεχε διὰ τὰ σοφίσματα τά, ὡς εἰκός, γινόμενα, ἀλλὰ μετὰ συντάξεως δίωκε,
ἕως οὗ λάβῃς πληροφορίαν τῆς ἀσφαλείας τῆς νίκης.

40    8. Ἐὰν δὲ ἀπὸ τῶν ἐχθρῶν ἐπέλευσις μηνυθῇ κατὰ τῆς πρώτης παρατάξεως
καὶ οὐκ ἔστι πῶς ἢ διὰ τῶν πλαγιοφυλάκων ἢ διὰ τῶν | εἰς ἐνέδραν κατὰ τῶν    335ᵛ
ἐχθρῶν πεμπομένων βοηθεῖν, τότε δέον ἐκ τῶν εἰς τὰ ἄκρα τῆς δευτέρας παρατάξεως τασσομένων βάνδων μετατίθεσθαι εἰς αὐτούς. εἰ μὲν ἐξ ἑνὸς πλαγίου
ἔρχονται, ἐξ ἐκείνου τοῦ μέρους, εἰ δὲ ἐκ τῶν δύο, ἐξ ἑκατέρωθεν. ὁμοίως δὲ καὶ
45    τοῖς κατὰ νώτου τῆς δευτέρας τάξεως ἐρχομένοις, ἐὰν μὴ ἀρκῶσιν οἱ νωτοφύ-

22 ἀπόβαινε MW ἀπόβαινε ἀπὸ ABE | παρατάσσου MW παράτασσε ABE    25 μηδὲ τὴν
WABE τὴν δὲ M | σου MWA σοι BE    26 τάς MW τὰ AE ταῦτα B | μελετωμένας MW
γινόμενα ABE    27 ἐνέδρας ἤτοι MW om. ABE    30 προγινώσκειν MW προγινώσκειν
αὐτὴν ABE | ἐντεῦθεν ἤδη MW ποίησον ABE    31 δευτέραν MWAE β′ B | τάξιν MW
παράταξιν ABE | πρώτης MW πρώτης καὶ ABE | ποίησον MW om. ABE    32 δύο MWAE β′
B | ὡς ABE εἰς MW    33 γένηται MW γένωνται ABE | τὴν...χρεὸν MW χρὴ τὴν δευτέραν
ABE    34 χωρίζειν αὐτὴν MW χωρίζεσθαι ἀπὸ ABE    35 καθιστᾶν...παράταξιν MW
ἀποκαθίστασθαι ABE    35–36 τοῖς...πολλοῦ MW οὐκ εὔγνωστος πρὸ πολλοῦ τοῖς
πολεμίοις ABE    37 ἀκρατῶς MW ἀκρατῶς καὶ ἀφυλάκτως A ἀκρατῶς καὶ ἀτάκτως BE
38 σοφίσματα MW πανουργεύματα ABE    39 οὗ ABE om. MW    41 ἔστι MABE ἔστιν W |
ἐνέδραν MW ἔγκρυμμα ABE    44 δύο MWA β′ BE | ἐξ ἑκατέρωθεν MW ἐξ ἀμφοτέρων ABE
45 τοῖς...νώτου MW πρὸς τοὺς ὄπισθεν ABE | τάξεως MW παρατάξεως ABE | ἐρχομένοις
MWBE ἐρχομένους A

mountain and draw up on level, open ground. Otherwise there is a chance that your formation may be suddenly overcome by the enemy lying in ambush under cover of the high ground.

5. Do not come to grips with the enemy formation and do not give them a good look at your own before you reconnoiter their lines and take steps to forestall the traps or ambushes they are likely to be setting against us.

6. If the site of the projected battle is in open and flat country, such that you cannot easily hide your second line there, then, to keep the enemy from getting a good idea of the army as it advances to combat, then and there, have the second line follow very closely behind the first so that the two lines will appear to them as one. About a mile away from the enemy battle formation, the second line must slow down a little, separate itself the prescribed distance from the first, and then assume its normal formation as a second battle line. This will prevent the enemy from forming a clear picture, much ahead of time, of the disposition of <our troops>.

7. Be very cautious when you see the enemy withdraw and take flight. Do not race after them intemperately, because they are likely to set traps for you. Rather, pursue them in good order until you receive definitive information that your victory is assured.

8. If it is reported to you that the enemy has attacked the first battle line and there is no way for you to send in their support either the flank guards or the troops assigned to ambush the enemy, then have some of the banda stationed on the wings of the second line move up to join it. If they are attacking from one side, <the support should come> from that sector, if from two sides, then from both sectors. In like manner, if they attack the rear of the second line and its rear

λακες αὐτῆς δι' ἑαυτῶν ἁρμόζεσθαι, τὰ αὐτὰ ποιήσῃς ἵνα οἱ λοιποὶ ἀπερίσπα-
στοι μένωσι πρὸς βοήθειαν τῆς πρώτης παρατάξεως.

9. Ἐὰν δὲ πολύς ἐστιν ὁ τῶν ἐχθρῶν στρατὸς καὶ διὰ πλῆθος ἀλόγων ἢ
ἀνδρῶν κομπὸς ἤγουν ἐξωγκωμένος φαίνηται, μὴ ἐπιτήδευε εὐθὺς εἰς ὑψηλὸν
50  τόπον τὸν στρατὸν τάσσειν μήκοθεν τῶν ἐχθρῶν ὄντων, ἵνα μὴ τῇ θέᾳ τοῦ
πλήθους προκαταλαμβανόμενος δειλιάσῃ προχείρως, ἀλλ' ἐν κοιλοτέρῳ τόπῳ
τάσσε αὐτούς, ὅθεν οὐδὲ κατοπτεύει τοὺς ἐχθρούς, οὐδὲ καθορᾶται ὑπὸ τῶν
ἐχθρῶν· καὶ ὅτ' ἂν ἢ ἀπὸ ἑνὸς ἢ ἀπὸ ἡμίσεως σημείου γένωνται οἱ ἐχθροί, τότε
ἐν τῷ ὕψει φέρειν τὸν στρατὸν ἵνα πρὶν δειλιάσῃ ἡ συμβολὴ γένηται. εἰ δὲ μὴ
55  εὑρίσκεται τόπος τοιοῦτος, ἀλλὰ μήκοθεν οἱ ἐχθροὶ τῷ στρατῷ φαίνονται,
πρόλεγε τῷ στρατῷ ἐν αὐτῇ τῇ παρατάξει ὅτι ἀλόγων ἢ τούλδου πλῆθός ἐστι τὸ
φαινόμενον καὶ οὐκ ἀνθρώπων μόνων.

10. Ἐὰν δέ σοι δυνατόν ἐστι καὶ πρὸ τοῦ παρατάξασθαι τοὺς πολεμίους
συμβαλεῖν αὐτοῖς ἔτι ἀσυστάτοις οὖσιν, μᾶλλον αὐτοὺς βλάψαι ἰσχύσεις.

60  11. Πάντως δὲ ἓν ἢ καὶ δεύτερον βάνδον ἔχε ὡς ἀπὸ ἑνὸς ἢ δευτέρου μιλίου
τῆς παρατάξεως πρὸ τοῦ πολέμου, ἐν ὅσῳ τάσσεται ὁ στρατὸς ἵνα μὴ ἄδειαν
ἔχωσιν οἱ πολέμιοι πρὸ τῆς μάχης κατασκοπεῖν τὴν τάξιν καὶ σοφίζεσθαι κατ'
αὐτῆς.

12. Καί, ἐὰν πεζικὸς οὐκ ἔστι στρατός, τοὺς παῖδας τῶν στρατιωτῶν ἤτοι
65  τοὺς δουλεύοντας αὐτοῖς καταλίμπανε, ὥστε διαμερίζεσθαι δι' ὅλου τοῦ ἐν τῷ

---

48–50 Cf. Schol. in Eurip. *Phoen.*, 600.

---

46 αὐτῆς Va αὐτοὺς MW om. ABE | δι'…ἁρμόζεσθαι MW om. ABE   46–47 ἀπερίσπαστοι
MWA ἀπερίστατοι BE   48 ἐὰν MWA εἰ BE   49 κομπὸς ἤγουν MW om. ABE |
ἐξωγκωμένος MWBE ὑπέρογκος A | φαίνηται MWA φαίνεται BE   50 μήκοθεν…ὄντων
MW om. ABE   51 προχείρως MW om. ABE | κοιλοτέρῳ MW βαθυτέρῳ καὶ χαμηλοτέρῳ
ABE   52 ὅθεν ABE ὁπόθεν MW   52–53 κατοπτεύει…ἐχθρῶν MW τοὺς ἐχθροὺς
καθορᾶν δύνανται οὐδὲ ὑπὸ τῶν ἐχθρῶν καθορᾶσθαι ABE   53 ἢ¹ MWA om. BE | σημείου
MW μιλίου ABE   55 εὑρίσκεται MW εὑρίσκεται ὁ ABE   56 ἐστι MA ἐστιν WBE
57 ἀνθρώπων MWA ἀνδρῶν BE   58 ἐὰν MWAE εἰ B | ἐστι M ἐστιν WABE |
παρατάξασθαι MWA τάξασθαι B προτάξασθαι E   59 συμβαλεῖν MW συμβάλλειν ABE |
οὖσιν MWA οὖσι BE   60 δεύτερον MW δύο AE β' B | βάνδον Va βάνδα ABE om. MW
60–61 ἔχε…παρατάξεως MW ἔχε ἔμπροσθεν τῆς παρατάξεως ὡς ἀπὸ ἑνὸς ἢ δύο μιλίων πρὸ
τοῦ πολέμου AE ἔχει ἀπὸ ἑνὸς ἢ β' μιλίων ἔμπροσθεν τῆς παρατάξεως B   61 τάσσεται MW
παρατάσσεται ABE   62 ἔχωσιν MWAB ἔχειν E | σοφίζεσθαι MWA κατασοφίζεσθαι BE
62–63 κατ' αὐτῆς MWA ταύτῃ BE   64 ἐὰν MWA εἰ BE   65 καταλίμπανε MWA
καταλιμπάνειν BE | τοῦ MWA om. BE

guard is not strong enough to deal with it by itself, take the same action. The rest of the troops can continue to concentrate on supporting the first line.

9. If the enemy's army is large and the multitude of horses and of men makes it appear enormous and formidable, be sure not to draw up your own army on high ground immediately, while the enemy are still at a distance.[3] Apprehensive at the sight of such a multitude, our men may easily become discouraged. Instead, form them on lower ground where they will not see the enemy or be seen by them. When your foe advances within about a mile or half a mile, then bring your army to high ground so that the fighting will begin before your men lose courage. But if such terrain is not found and the enemy can be seen from a distance, then, as the army is drawn up for battle, spread the report that what they are looking at is not just soldiers but a multitude of horses or pack animals.

10. If you are able to do so, launch your attack against the enemy before they form their line for battle, while they are still milling about, and you will be able to inflict serious harm.

11. Always keep one or two banda about a mile or two in front of the main body before combat while the army is moving into formation. In this way the enemy will not have the opportunity to observe our formation before the battle and outmaneuver us.

12. If the army is not composed of infantry, leave the boys, the servants of the soldiers, behind so they may be stationed along the fortifications of the

---

3. Cf. Scholia on Euripides' *Phoenissae*, 600.

φοσσάτῳ ἀπλίκτου ἕκαστον περὶ τὴν ἔσω τράφον μετὰ ὅπλων, εἴτε τοξεύειν δύνανται εἴτε ἀκοντίζειν εἴτε σφενδονᾶν, ἀλλὰ καὶ ἓν βάνδον μετ' αὐτῶν, τὸ ὀφεῖλον βιγλεύειν καὶ τὰς πόρτας τοῦ φοσσάτου φυλάττειν ἤγουν τοῦ περιφραγμένου ἀπλίκτου, καὶ ἄρχοντα δὲ χρήσιμον τοῦ ὅλου τοιούτου φοσσάτου.

70    13. Μηδέποτε τοῦλδον ἐπὶ παρατάξεως περίφερε, | εἰ δυνατόν ἐστι, καὶ γὰρ    336 ἕτοιμον τοῖς ἐχθροῖς βρῶμα γίνεται ἐὰν ἐν μάχῃ εὑρεθῇ. ἐὰν μέντοι, ὡς εἰκός, ὁδοιποροῦντος σοῦ, ἀδοκήτως ἐπέλευσις παρὰ τῶν ἐχθρῶν γένηται καὶ οὐ φθάζῃς ἀπλικεῦσαι καὶ ἀσφαλίσασθαι τὸ τοῦλδον, τότε φέρε αὐτὸ κατὰ τοῦ δεξιοῦ μέρους ἐκ πλαγίου τῆς δευτέρας παρατάξεως καὶ ἐκεῖ τάσσε καὶ ἐν ᾗ
75    δεύτερον βάνδον ἐκ τῶν περισσῶν εἰς παραφυλακὴν αὐτοῦ ἀφόριζε.

14. Ἐὰν δὲ μὴ ἔτυχον, ὡς εἴρηται, προαποθέμενοι χόρτον, καὶ ἐν αὐτῇ τῇ τοῦ πολέμου ἡμέρᾳ, τῶν ἄλλων ὁπλιτῶν ἐπὶ τὴν παράταξιν κινούντων, τὰ παλλικάρια τῶν στρατιωτῶν καὶ τῶν ἀρχόντων ἵνα ἐξέρχωνται εἰς τὸ μέρος τὸ ὀπίσω τῆς παρατάξεως τοῦ ὅλου στρατοῦ μετ' ὀλίγων βιγλατώρων ἐκ τοῦ τῆς παρατά-
80    ξεως μέρους καταλιμπανομένων καὶ συνάγουσι τὸν ἀρκοῦντα χόρτον, ἐν ὅσῳ ὁ πόλεμος γίνεται. τοῖς δὲ χορτολογοῦσιν ὁρίσεις δοθῆναι βάνδα καὶ σημειώσεις ἐν ὑψηλοτέροις τόποις καὶ διαφόροις, ὥστε ἐναντίου τινὸς συμβαίνοντος τὸ ἀνακλητικὸν ἠχεῖν πρὸς συνήθειαν, τότε ἀναχωρεῖν αὐτοὺς δρομαίως καὶ ἐπὶ τὸ φοσσάτον σώζεσθαι ἵνα μὴ ἔξω ἀποκλεισθῶσιν. τοῦτο δὲ ἀναγκαῖόν ἐστι
85    γίνεσθαι διὰ τὸ ἄδηλον τῆς ἐκβάσεως. ἐὰν γὰρ ἐναντίως ἐξέλθῃ τὸ πρᾶγμα, δαπάνην ἔχοντες καὶ ἑαυτῶν καὶ τῶν ἀλόγων οἱ στρατιῶται, ταχέως ἑαυτοὺς πρὸς τὸ ἀναμάχεσθαι ἀνακαλοῦνται ἤγουν καὶ πάλιν πολεμῆσαι καὶ νικῆσαι ἤ, εἰ μὴ τοῦτο, εὐθέως ἀναχωρήσουσιν μετὰ τάξεως ἔτι ἐν δυνάμει τῶν ἵππων

66 φοσσάτω…μετὰ MW ἀπλήκτου φοσσάτω (ἀπλήκτω φοσσάτου BE) περὶ τὸ ἔσωθεν μέρος τῆς σούδας ἕκαστον μετὰ τῶν ἐπιτηδείων ABE    67 δύνανται MW δύναται ABE | τὸ MWA om.    BE    68–69 ἤγουν…ἀπλίκτου    MW om.    ABE    68–69 περιφραγμένου Μ περιπεφραγμένου W om. ABE    69 τοιούτου MWA τοῦτο BE    70 μηδέποτε MW μηδέποτε δὲ ABE    72 ἀδοκήτως MW ἀπροσδοκήτως ABE    73 τὸ MWBE τὸν Α | αὐτὸ MW αὐτὸν ABE    76 ἔτυχον…εἴρηται MW om. ABE | προαποθέμενοι MW προαπέθετο Α προαπευθέντες Β προαπευθέντα Ε    77–78 τὰ παλλικάρια MW οἱ ὑπηρέται ABE    78 καὶ τῶν MWAB καὶ τῶν καὶ τῶν Ε | μέρος…ὀπίσω MW ὀπίσω μέρος ABE    79 τοῦ[1]…στρατοῦ MW om. ABE | μετ' MW μετὰ ABE    79–80 ἐκ…καὶ MW οἵτινες πρὸς τὸ μέρος τῆς παρατάξεως στήσονται· βιγλεύοντες οἱ δὲ ABE    80 συνάγουσι MW συνάξουσι ΑΕ συναύξουσι Β    81 σημειώσεις MW σημεῖα τινα ABE    83 πρὸς συνήθειαν MW καὶ ABE | δρομαίως MWAE δρομαίους Β    84 ἀποκλεισθῶσιν MWA ἀποκλεισθῶσι BE | ἐστι MABE ἐστιν W    85 ἐκβάσεως MW ἐκβάσεως τοῦ πολέμου ABE    86 ἑαυτοὺς ABE αὐτοὺς MW    87 ἀναμάχεσθαι MW ἀναμαχέσασθαι Α ἀνακαλέσεσθαι BE    88 εἰ MWA καὶ BE | ἀναχωρήσουσιν MW ἀναχωρήσουσι ABE

camp, each one along the inner ditch and provided with weapons he can handle: bow, javelin, or sling. One bandon should stay with them under orders to patrol and to guard the gates of the entrenchment, that is, the fortified camp, and place a competent officer over this entire fortification.

13. Never bring the baggage train up to the front line, if it is possible. If discovered in battle, it is an easy prey for the enemy. Now, if it happens that the enemy launches a surprise attack as you are marching along and you do not have time to set up camp and secure the baggage train, then bring it over to the right sector, on the flank of the second battle line, and detail one or two banda from whatever troops are available to guard it.

14. If it has not been possible to gather a supply of fodder ahead of time, as recommended, then, on the very day of battle, as the other heavy-armed troops are moving into formation, the servants of the soldiers should go out to gather it in the area to the rear of the battle line of the whole army. They should be accompanied by a few scouts taken from the men left behind in the area of the battle line. While the battle is in progress, they should gather a sufficient supply of fodder. Instruct those who are out gathering fodder that they will be given signals, <such as by> flags from high, conspicuous places to let them know that a hostile force is approaching and the customary signal for recall is sounded. They are then to return as fast as they can and take refuge in the camp, so they may not be cut off outside. This is essential because the outcome is uncertain. If things turn out adversely, the soldiers will have provisions for themselves and their horses; they can quickly rouse themselves to fight once more, that is, again

αὐτῶν εὑρισκομένων, πρὶν ἢ τά τε τῶν ἀνθρώπων φρονήματα ἐπὶ πλέον κατα-
90 πέσωσι καὶ αἱ τῶν ἵππων δυνάμεις, ὅπερ γενέσθαι δύναται, ἐὰν μή ἐστιν ἐν
ἑτοίμῳ ἡ δαπάνη. μετὰ γὰρ ἧτταν οὐδεὶς θαρρεῖ ἐξέρχεσθαι εἰς συλλογὴν χόρτου καὶ οἱ ἵπποι λιμώττοντες ἀθυμίαν τοῖς στρατιώταις παρέχουσι καὶ βουλὴν
πρὸς συμφέρον οὔκ ἐστι γενέσθαι τῆς ἐνδείας καὶ τοῦ φόβου βιαζομένων αὐτήν.
ἀλλὰ χρὴ πάντως καὶ τὴν τῶν ἀλόγων ἀποτροφὴν παρατίθεσθαι μιᾶς ἢ καὶ
95 δευτέρας ἡμέρας, εἰ δυνατὸν καὶ πλέον, μάλιστα ἐὰν καὶ πλησίον τοῦ φοσσάτου
εἰσὶν αἱ βοσκαί.

　　15. Εἰ δὲ κατὰ τὴν πρώτην ἡμέραν τῆς συμβολῆς τοῦ πολέμου ἐναντία
ἔκβασις παρακολουθήσῃ—ὃ μὴ γένοιτο—ἡμῖν μὲν παντοίως ἀπρόσφορον καὶ
ἀσύμφορον φαίνεται τὸ κατὰ τὰς αὐτὰς ἡμέρας ἤγουν κατὰ τὸν αὐτὸν καιρὸν
100 πάλιν | πρὸς δημόσιον πόλεμον ἐγχειρῆσαι τοὺς ἐκ τῆς παρατάξεως ἡττηθέν- 336ᵛ
τας. διὸ οὐδὲ συμβουλεύσομέν σοι, ὦ στρατηγέ, πρὸς τοῦτο ἐπιτηδεύειν. πᾶσι
γὰρ πάντοτε δυσχερές ἐστι τοῦτο καὶ οὐδεὶς εἴωθεν εὐθέως ἀπὸ τὰς ἥττας
ἀναμάχεσθαι· σπάνιον γὰρ τοῦτο καὶ Ῥωμαίοις ἀνοίκειον. ὥστε, εἰ καὶ σφάλμα
παρακολουθήσει καὶ ἐλπίσει ὁ στρατηγὸς τοῦτο διὰ τῆς δευτέρας μάχης
105 διορθοῦσθαι, οὐκ ἔστιν ἱκανὸν τὸ πλῆθος τὴν αἰτίαν διαγινῶσκον <τοῦ> προαιρέσει εἰς δημοσίαν μάχην εὐθέως ἐλθεῖν. ὡς γὰρ ἐκ θείας ψήφου οὕτως τὸ
ἀποτέλεσμα δεχόμενον ἐν πάσῃ δειλίᾳ γίνεται. διὸ χρή σε ἀνάγκης καὶ περιστάσεως χωρὶς μὴ ἐπιτηδεύειν <κατὰ τὰς αὐτὰς ἡμέρας> φανερῶς συμβάλλειν
μάχην μετὰ δημοσίαν ἧτταν διὰ παρατάξεως, ἀλλὰ δόλῳ καὶ ἀπάτῃ σπούδαζε
110 καιροσκοπῶν, ὅπως αἰφνιδιάσῃς καὶ τὸ δὴ λεγόμενον φυγομαχήσῃς, ἕως ἂν εἰς
λήθην τῆς δειλίας ἐκείνης γενόμενος ὁ στρατὸς θαρρήσῃ τοῦ πάλιν ποιήσασθαι

---

101–103 Cf. Thuc. 7.61.3

---

90 γενέσθαι δύναται MW εὐκόλως δύναται γίνεσθαι ABE | ἐὰν MWA εἰ BE　92 παρέχουσι
MBE παρέχουσιν WA　93 ἐστι MAE ἐστιν W ἔτι B | τῆς ἐνδείας MW τοῦ λιμοῦ AB τοῦ
λοιποῦ E　95 δευτέρας MWA β′ BE | ἐὰν MWA εἰ BE　97–98 ἐναντία…παρακολουθήσῃ
MW ἐναντίον τι συμβῇ ABE　98 ὃ…γένοιτο MW om. ABE | μὲν MWA δὲ BE |
παντοίως…καὶ MW παντελῶς ABE　100 τῆς MW om. ABE　101 συμβουλεύσομέν MBE
συμβουλεύομεν WA　102 πάντοτε MWBE om. A | ἐστι MABE ἐστιν W　103 σπάνιον…
ῥωμαίοις MW τοῦτο δὲ ῥωμαίοις ὡς ἐπὶ τὸ πλεῖστον ABE | σφάλμα MA σφάλματα WBE
105 διαγινῶσκον τοῦ Va διαγιγνῶσκον MW γινῶσκον ἰδίᾳ ABE　106 ἐλθεῖν MW στῆναι
ABE　107 ἐν MWA om. BE | σε MW σε χωρὶς ABE　108 χωρὶς MW om. ABE | κατὰ…
ἡμέρας Va om. codd.　110 καιροσκοπῶν MW ἐπιτηρῶν τὸν καιρὸν A ἐπιτηρεῖν τὸν καιρὸν
BE | δὴ MWAB om. E　111 δειλίας MWAB δουλείας E

enter into combat and be victorious. Or else, if this is not <possible>, they may immediately retreat in an orderly fashion, while their horses are still in good condition, before the men become more dejected and the horses grow weak. This is what can happen if provisions are not available. For after a defeat nobody dares to go out to gather fodder. The horses lose their strength and this destroys the morale of the soldiers. Lack of necessities and fear crush any desire to improve things. Always make sure to keep on hand food for the horses for one or two days, more if possible, especially if there is good grazing near the camp.

15. If the clash of battle on the first day results in an adverse outcome—may such not happen—it is, in our opinion, absolutely undesirable and useless for those troops who have been defeated in the field to undertake actual combat again about the same time or even within a few days. Therefore, O general, we do not advise you to try this. It is always a difficult task for everyone. Nobody makes a habit of immediately retrieving a defeat.[4] This is very rare and foreign to the Romans. Even though the general may understand his mistake and hope to remedy it by means of a second battle, most of the soldiers will be unable to understand his reasons for choosing to go right back into combat. They tend to accept what happened as God's will and completely lose heart. Apart, then, from necessity and special circumstances you must not attempt to fight a pitched battle during those same days after an open, public defeat in the field. Instead, employ tricks and deception, carefully timed surprise moves, and the so-called fighting while fleeing, until the army comes to forget its discouragement and

4. Cf. Thucydides 7.61.3.

συμβολὴν δι᾽ εὐλόγους αἰτίας πολλάκις ἐπισυμβαινούσας, ἃς ἄρτι γράφειν οὐκ
ἔστιν εὔκολον.

16. Ἐὰν δὲ καὶ ἅπαξ θαρρήσῃς συμβαλεῖν μετὰ τὴν ἀποβολὴν τῆς δειλίας,
115 δεῖ τὴν πρόμαχον τάξιν ὡς κατακρουσθεῖσαν εἰς δευτέραν τάξιν ποιεῖν καὶ τὴν
δευτέραν εἰς πρόμαχον μετὰ τῶν ἐπιλέκτων ταγμάτων τῶν ἐν τῇ πρώτῃ· μικρο-
τέρα γὰρ οὖσα τῆς πρώτης καθ᾽ ἑαυτὴν οὐκ ἐπαρκεῖ.

17. Ἀλλ᾽ οὐδὲ ἐμβραδύνειν δεῖ ἀσκόπως ἐπὶ ταῖς ἐναντίαις ἐκβάσεσι τοῦ
πολέμου, εἰ μή που ἐλπὶς συμμαχίας ἢ ἕτερος τρόπος βοηθείας προσδοκᾶται ἤ,
120 ὡς εἰκός, ἀπόκρισις παρὰ τῶν ἐχθρῶν γίνεται, ἥνπερ ἀναγκαῖον μὴ πουβλικίζειν
προχείρως, ἀλλὰ δὴ ἰδίᾳ ταύτην μανθάνειν. καί, ἐὰν τὸ προτεινόμενον παρευθὺ
γίνεσθαι δύναται, μὴ ἀναβάλλεσθαι, ἀλλὰ πράττειν αὐτὸ ἀσφαλῶς δι᾽ ὀψίδων ἢ
ὅρκων. εἰ δὲ ἐπιβλαβές ἐστιν καὶ δι᾽ ὑπέρθεσίν τινος καὶ χαύνωσιν τοῦ ὄχλου
λέγεται, τὰ ἐναντία δεῖ φημίζειν, σκληρότερα τῶν προτεινομένων, ἵνα <τῇ
125 ἀπαγορεύσει τῶν προτεινομένων> μᾶλλον ὁ στρατὸς πρὸς ὀργὴν διανιστά-
μενος τῇ ἀνάγκῃ ἰσχυροτέρως τοῖς ἐχθροῖς ἀντικαταστῇ καὶ ἔτι πειθήνιος τῷ
ἄρχοντι γένηται. ὅσον γὰρ βραδυτὴς γίνεται, τοσοῦτον οἱ ἡττηθέντες δειλό-
τεροι γίνονται καὶ οἱ νικήσαντες τολμηρότεροι.

18. Πρὶν ἢ οὖν εἰς τέλειον τὰ φρονήματα καταπέσωσι, χρή σε, ὦ στρατηγέ,
130 διά τε τῶν ἀρχόντων τῶν ταγμάτων καὶ τῶν δεκάρχων καὶ πεντάρχων προ-
τρέψασθαι τὸν στρατὸν καὶ εἰπεῖν, ὡς οὐκ ἔστι καιρὸς | δειλιάσαι, ἀλλ᾽ ὁρμηθῆ- 337
ναι μᾶλλον κατὰ τῶν ἐχθρῶν καὶ τὸ γενόμενον παρά τινων σφάλμα ἀνδρείως
ἀνακαλέσασθαι. ταῦτα καὶ τὰ ὅμοια δεῖ σε διαλαλῆσαι.

19. Καὶ εἰ μέν ἐστιν ἐλπὶς τοῦ διὰ παρατάξεως δημοσίας τὴν μάχην ἀνακαλέ-
135 σασθαι, τῇ προειρημένῃ μεθόδῳ τῆς τάξεως χρήσῃ. εἰ δὲ τοῦτο οὐ προβαίνει,
δεῖ συμφερόντως τῶν κινδύνων κατατολμᾶν.

20. Καὶ εἰ μὲν πεζοί εἰσιν οἱ νικήσαντες ἐχθροί, σπουδάζειν μετὰ τῶν ἵππων
εὐτάκτως τὰς ἀναχωρήσεις ἤτοι μεταστάσεις τοῦ φοσσάτου ἐκείνου ἀσφαλῶς
ποιεῖσθαι καὶ μὴ ἀναμένειν. εἰ δὲ καβαλλάριοι ὦσιν, μάλιστα τῶν περισσῶν καὶ
140 βαρυτέρων ἀλόγων καὶ πραγμάτων δεῖ περιφρονεῖν καὶ πεζῇ καθίστασθαι καὶ

---

112 συμβολὴν ABE συλλογὴν MW | ἄρτι γράφειν ABE ἀντιγράφειν MW   114 τὴν
ἀποβολὴν MW ἀποβολέσθαι τὴν δειλίαν ABE   119 τρόπος MWA τόπος BE
120 πουβλικίζειν MW δημοσιεύειν ABE   121 προχείρως MW εὐθέως A εὐθὺς BE | ἀλλὰ…
καί MW ἀλλ᾽ ABE | ἐὰν MWA εἰ BE | παρευθὺ MW παρευθὺς ABE   124 δεῖ MW om. ABE
124–125 τῇ…προτεινομένων Va om. codd.   129 ἢ MW om. ABE | εἰς τέλειον MW τελείως
ABE | καταπέσωσι MBE καταπέσωσιν WA   131 ὡς MW ὅτι ABE | ἔστι MABE ἐστιν W
131–132 ὁρμηθῆναι MWA ὁρμῆσαι BE   132 μᾶλλον MWAE om. B   138 ἐκείνου MWE
ἐκείνου καὶ AB   139 ὦσιν MWA εἰσι BE

regains the confidence to engage in battle once more. Good reasons for this may readily be adduced, but it is not convenient to list them here.

16. Provided that you succeed in encouraging <the army> to enter into battle after it has cast aside its discouragement, you must make the shattered promachos line into the second line and make the second into the promachos, retaining selected tagmata of the first line, since the second by itself is smaller than the first and will be too weak.

17. In the event of an adverse outcome in battle, there must be no indecision or delay, unless of course there is reason to expect the arrival of allies or some other form of assistance or, as may well be the case, overtures are made by the enemy. These must not be made public right away, but study them privately. If what is proposed can be done immediately, do not put it off but go along with it, confirming it with hostages or by oath. But if the terms are harsh and proposed for the purpose of delaying and getting the men to drop their guard, you must counter this by spreading rumors making them more unfavorable than the actual proposals, so that in rejecting the actual proposals, the army will rather be moved to anger and feel compelled to resist the enemy more forcefully, and it will be more obedient to its commander. The longer the delay, the more demoralized do the vanquished become and the more confident the victors.

18. Therefore, before the men become utterly depressed, you must, O general, have the tagmatic commanders, including the dekarchs and pentarchs, exhort the army and point out that this is no time for despondency; rather, they should be aroused against the enemy and valiantly make up for the failure of a few. You should address them in these and similar words.

19. If there is some hope that the defeat may be retrieved in the open field, employ the prescribed method of formation. But if this is not the case, it is important to show a bold front in the face of dangers.

20. If the victorious foe consists mostly of infantry, do not remain there but make haste to withdraw in good order with your horses or safely move your camp elsewhere. But if they are horsemen, you must disregard superfluous and cumbersome property and horses. Except for a small mounted force, all should

ἄνευ ὀλίγων καβαλλαρίων πάντας εἰς δύο φάλαγγας ἤτοι τάξεις ἢ καὶ εἰς
ἓν τετράγωνον πλινθίου σχῆμα παρατάξασθαι. καὶ μέσον μὲν τὰ ἄλογα ἢ
τὸν τοῦλδον φέρειν, ἔξωθεν δὲ ἔχειν τοὺς στρατιώτας, ὡς εἴρηται, ἐν τάξει καὶ
τοὺς τοξότας ἐξωτέρω καὶ οὕτως τὰς μεταστάσεις καὶ ἀναχωρήσεις ποιεῖσθαι
145  ἀσφαλῶς.

21. Πάλιν δέ, ἐὰν αἰσίως τὰ τοῦ πολέμου ἐξέλθῃ καὶ Θεοῦ βοηθοῦντος
ἄρξηται ἡ νίκη, οὐ δεῖ τῇ ὠθήσει καὶ μόνῃ ἀρκεῖσθαι ὡς ἀπειροκάλους, μὴ
εἰδότας χρήσασθαι τῷ καιρῷ. ἀλλὰ ἀκαίρως ἀκούειν φιλοῦντας τὸ "νίκα καὶ μὴ
ὑπερνίκα," καὶ ἐνδιδόντας σφαλερῶς καὶ μείζονα διὰ τῆς ἐνδόσεως τοῦ καιροῦ
150  κάματον ἐπισωρεύοντας καὶ ἄδηλον τὴν μέλλουσαν ἔκβασιν ἑαυτοῖς κατασκευάζοντας, ἀλλὰ δεῖ τῇ τοῦ ἐχθροῦ τελείᾳ καταλύσει ἐπιμένειν.

22. Εἰ δὲ ἐν ὀχυρώματι καταφεύγει, σπουδάζειν ἢ χειρὶ ἢ διὰ τῶν λιπόντων
εἰδῶν τοῖς ἀνθρώποις ἢ τοῖς ἀλόγοις διὰ παραφυλακῆς στενοχωρεῖν αὐτὸν
μέχρι τελείας αὐτοῦ καταλύσεως ἢ ἐπωφελῶν ἡμῖν γινομένων συμφώνων καὶ
155  μηδὲ ἐκλύεσθαι τῇ ὀλίγῃ ὠθήσει, μηδὲ ἀμελεῖν τῆς τοῦ πράγματος ἐκβάσεως δι'
ὀλίγην καρτερίαν μετὰ τοσοῦτον πόνον καὶ κάματον καὶ μετὰ τοσοῦτον ἐκ τοῦ
πολέμου κίνδυνον, ἐπεὶ καὶ ἐπὶ τοῦ κυνηγίου τὸ παρὰ μικρὸν ἀντὶ τοῦ μηδενὸς
ἔσται.

23. Μήτε μὴν περιφρονεῖν τῆς τῶν στρατιωτῶν εὐταξίας ἀπὸ τῆς νίκης
160  μάλιστα, ἀλλὰ συντεταγμένους διώκειν καὶ μετὰ ἐπιστήμης καὶ νουνεχίας
ἐπισκοποῦντα τὸν στρατηγὸν τὰ δέοντα. οὐκ ἀρκεῖ γὰρ δύναμις μόνη εἰς
ἀσφάλειαν ἰδίαν ἢ βλάβην τῶν ἐχθρῶν, ἀλλὰ μετὰ τὴν τοῦ Θεοῦ βοή|θειαν καὶ ἡ   337ᵛ
τοῦ στρατηγοῦ διοίκησις ἀναγκαία καὶ πρώτη τυγχάνει.

24. Πρέπον σε οὖν, ὦ στρατηγέ, τοῖς τε καιροῖς καὶ τοῖς τόποις ἁρμοδίως
165  κεχρῆσθαι καί, ἐὰν δοκιμάσῃς τοῦ πάντως γενέσθαι πόλεμον δημόσιον, πάντα

---

148–149 Men. Sent., 419; Strat., 1.B.12.4.   157–158 Arist. Phys., 197a30.

---

141 πάντας MW ἅπαντας ABE | εἰς¹ MWA om. BE | ἢ MW ἢ καὶ ABE   143 τὸν ABE τὸ
MW   146 αἰσίως MW πρεπόντως ABE   147 τῇ MWAE om. B | ἀπειροκάλους MW om.
ABE   148 εἰδότας MW γινώσκοντας ABE   149 καιροῦ MW καιροῦ κόπον καὶ ABE
150 ἐπισωρεύοντας   MW   ὑπομένοντας   ABE   150–151 κατασκευάζοντας   MWA
κατασκευάζοντες BE   152 σπουδάζειν MW σπουδάζειν χρὴ ABE | χειρὶ…λιπόντων MW
διὰ δυνάμεως ἢ διὰ τῶν λειπόντων ABE   155 μηδὲ¹ MWA μὴ BE   155–156 τῇ…ὀλίγην
MWAE om. B   155 τῆς…ἐκβάσεως MW τοῦ τέλους τοῦ πράγματος AE   159 μήτε μὴν
MW μήτε δὲ A μηδὲ BE | περιφρονεῖν MWA καταφρονεῖν BE   160 νουνεχίας MW
φρονήσεως ABE   161 ἐπισκοποῦντα MW ἐπισκοπεῖν ABE   162 τὴν MW τῆς ABE |
βοήθειαν MW βοηθείας ABE   164 σε MW om. ABE | οὖν MWAE οὖν ἔστιν Β
165 κεχρῆσθαι MW κεχρῆσθαι σε ABE | πάντως MW πάλιν ABE

take their stand on foot in two phalanxes or formations or in one four-sided, rectangular formation. Place the horses and the baggage train in the middle with the soldiers lined up on the outside, as described, and the archers in front of them. In this way the army can safely change location.

21. Again, if the outcome of the battle is favorable and, with the help of God, victory is ours, we must not be satisfied with merely driving the enemy back, like inexperienced leaders who do not know how to take advantage of an opportunity. Instead, they have an inordinate love of the saying: "Be victorious but do not press your victory too hard."[5] To their own peril they make concessions and, by surrendering the opportunity, they only heap up more trouble for themselves and place the ultimate results in doubt. You must keep at it until the enemy is utterly destroyed.

22. If they seek refuge behind fortifications, be sure to apply pressure directly or else prevent them from getting more supplies for men and horses until they are completely wiped out or agree to terms advantageous to us. Do not let up after driving them back a short distance. After so much labor and hard work and after so many dangers in battle, do not jeopardize the outcome of the affair because of a lack of persistence. As in hunting, a near miss is still a complete miss.[6]

23. Especially after a victory, do not disregard the good order of the soldiers. They are to maintain formation in pursuit and the general is to use his knowledge and good sense in supervising what has to be done. Strength alone is not sufficient to safeguard oneself and to inflict damage on the enemy but, after the assistance of God, the primary and essential factor is the general's leadership.

24. Therefore, it is incumbent on you, O general, to take advantage of times and places. If you make a definite decision to get into a pitched battle, you must

5. Menander, *Sententiae*, 419; *Strat.* 7.B.12.4; see Attaleiates, *Historia*, ed. I. Bekker (Bonn, 1853), 26.17.

6. Aristotle, *Physics*, 197a30.

σκοπήσῃς καὶ τόπον ἐπιτήδειον γυμνόν τε καὶ ὁμαλὸν διὰ τοὺς κονταράτους
καὶ μὴ μόνον τὰ δεξιὰ καὶ ἀριστερὰ καὶ ὀπίσθια μέρη προερευνᾶν δεῖ καὶ ἀπὸ
δύο καὶ τριῶν ἡμερῶν τῆς παρατάξεως μέχρι τοῦ πέρατος τοῦ πολέμου, ἀλλὰ
καὶ τοὺς προκειμένους τόπους ψηλαφᾶν, μήποτε λάκκοι εἰσὶν ἢ αὐτοφυεῖς ἢ
170  ὠρυγμένοι ἢ δόλος τις ἄλλος πρόκειται.

25. Κατὰ δὲ τὴν τοῦ πολέμου ἡμέραν, ὡς ἄνω εἴπομεν, τῶν βιγλῶν προεξερ-
χομένων ἅμα πρωῒ εἰς τέσσαρα μέρη τοῦ τόπου, ἔνθα ἡ συμβολὴ γίνεται, ἀπὸ
δύο καὶ τριῶν μιλίων ἐν διπλαῖς βίγλαις παραγγέλλειν αὐτοὺς μὴ μόνον πρὸς
τὴν τῶν ἐχθρῶν κίνησιν ἀποβλέπειν καὶ μηνύειν, ἀλλὰ καὶ πρὸς τοὺς θέλοντας
175  προσρυῆναι, ὡς εἰκός, τοῖς ἐχθροῖς ἀποσκοπεῖν καὶ συνέχειν αὐτούς. ἐντεῦθεν
γὰρ καὶ τοὺς ἀποφεύγοντας ἐκ τοῦ στρατοῦ ῥᾳδίως κωλύουσι καὶ τοὺς ἐκ τῶν
ἐχθρῶν βουλομένους προσρυῆναι καὶ ἐπιφερομένους, ὡς εἰκός, εἴδη τινὰ μετὰ
ἀσφαλείας ὑποδέχονται εἰς τὸ μὴ ἐπηρεάζεσθαι αὐτοὺς παρά τινων κακῶν
ἀνθρώπων, ὅπερ καὶ ἀεί σε χρὴ παραφυλάττειν εἰς τοὺς προσφεύγοντας μετὰ
180  τινων πραγμάτων τῇ ἡμετέρᾳ πολιτείᾳ, ὡς ἀναγκαῖον καὶ δίκαιον.

26. Οἱ δὲ κατὰ τὰ ἔμπροσθεν μέρη τῆς παρατάξεως βιγλεύοντες ἄχρι ἑνὸς
σαγιττοβόλου τῆς τῶν ἐχθρῶν παρατάξεως ἔμπροσθεν τῆς ἰδίας περιπατείτω-
σαν καὶ ὁδηγείτωσαν μήπως, ὡς εἴρηται, φόσσαι ἤγουν ὀρύγματά εἰσιν ἢ ἕτερος
δόλος μεμελέτηται παρὰ τῶν ἐχθρῶν καὶ ἀναστέλλειν τοὺς ἰδίους εἰς τὸ μὴ
185  ἀδοκήτως περιπίπτειν.

27. Ἐν γὰρ τοῖς ἀναγκαίοις τόποις καὶ καιροῖς μὴ μόνον, ὡς εἴρηται, ἁπλᾶς
βίγλας κατὰ τῶν αὐτῶν ποιεῖσθαι, ἀλλὰ καὶ διπλᾶς ἵνα τῆς μιᾶς, ὡς εἰκός,
λανθανομένης τὴν ἑτέραν μὴ διαλάθῃ.

168 δύο MWAE β′ B | τοῦ πέρατος MW συμπληρώσεως ABE  169 προκειμένους Va
παρακειμένους codd. | εἰσὶν MWA ὦσιν BE  172 πρωῒ MWA om. BE  173 δύο MWA β′
BE  175 προσρυῆναι MW προσφυγεῖν ABE | συνέχειν MW κατέχειν ABE  176 ῥᾳδίως
MW εὐκόλως ABE | κωλύουσι MBE κωλύουσιν WA  177 προσρυῆναι MW προσφυγεῖν
ABE | εἴδη MW πράγματα ABE  179 σε χρὴ MWBE χρή σε A | παραφυλάττειν MW
παραφυλάττεσθαι ABE  183 φόσσαι ἤγουν MW om. ABE | εἰσιν MWA ὦσιν BE
185 περιπίπτειν MWA περιπίπτειν περὶ βιγλῶν BE  186 μὴ MWBE οὐ A
186–187 εἴρηται…βίγλας MW ἁπλᾶς (ἁπλῶς E) βίγλας ὡς εἴρηται ABE  187 τῶν…
ποιεῖσθαι MW τὸν αὐτὸν τόπον ποιεῖσθαι χρή ABE  187–188 τῆς…λανθανομένης MW
ἐὰν τὴν μίαν ὡς εἰκὸς λαθῶσιν οἱ ἐχθροὶ ABE  188 διαλάθῃ MW διαλάθωσιν A διαλάθωσι
BE

investigate every open and level location suitable for lancers. You must reconnoiter not only the sectors to the right and left and rear for two or three days before forming the line and until the conclusion of the battle, but also closely examine the ground in front in case pools of water, either natural or excavated, or some other trap lies before you.

25. On the day of battle, as we remarked above, patrols, twice the usual number, are to head out early in the morning for two or three miles in the four directions of the area where the battle is to take place. Order them not only to observe and report the movements of the enemy but also to discover and to detain any of our men who, as may happen, want to go over to the enemy. Out there they can easily intercept deserters from our army. Also, in case enemy soldiers want to come over to us bringing with them, as is likely, their equipment, the patrols may receive them in safety so they will not be waylaid by evil men. It is essential and just that you always be protective of those seeking refuge in our nation along with their possessions.

26. The patrols covering the area in front of our battle line should work their way to about a bowshot from the enemy line in front of their own to make sure, as mentioned, that the enemy are not digging any ditches or planning some other trap. This will keep their own men from falling into unexpected trouble.

27. When under pressure because of the terrain and the time, do not send, as prescribed, only one patrol into the area against them but send two, so that if the first one, as can happen, fails to notice <enemy activity>, the second one will be sure to detect it.

28. Καί, ἐὰν ἕτοιμός ἐστιν ἡ τάξις καὶ ὁ τόπος ἐπιτήδειος, μὴ ἀναμένειν τοὺς
190 ἐχθροὺς ἐν τῇ συμβολῇ, ἵνα μὴ κανονίζωσι καὶ μεθοδεύωσι τὴν τάξιν, ἀλλὰ
ἀσφαλῶς ὁρμᾶν καὶ ἐπιτίθεσθαι τοῖς ἐχθροῖς.

29. Ἐὰν δὲ ὑπέρθεσιν ἔχῃ, ὡς εἰκός, τὰ τῆς συμβολῆς διά τινας εὐλόγους
αἰτίας, ἀναγκαῖόν ἐστιν τὴν δευ|τέραν μάλιστα τάξιν ἐν ταῖς εὑρισκομέναις  338
ὕλαις ἢ τοῖς κοιλοτέροις τόποις ὄπισθεν κρύπτειν, ἵνα μὴ πρὸ πολλοῦ τοῖς
195 ἐχθροῖς ἀκαίρως προφαινομένη αὐτὴ μεθοδεύεται καὶ ἐπιβουλεύεται ὑπὸ ἐγκρυμμάτων ἢ καὶ ὑπὸ ἄλλων ἐγχειρήσεων κατασοφίζεται.

30. Ἐπεὶ δὲ περὶ βιγλῶν ἐμνημονεύσαμεν, δεῖ σε αὐτὰς ὀχυρὰς ποιεῖν καὶ
διαιρεῖν τοὺς βιγλεύοντας, ἵνα οἱ μὲν ὑπνοῦσιν, οἱ δὲ ἐγρηγοροῦσιν καὶ οὕτως
ἐναλλάσσοντας ἀλλήλους βιγλεύειν. μὴ γὰρ πιστεύσῃς τινί, κἂν ὑπόσχεσιν
200 ποιεῖται, ὅλην τὴν νύκτα γρηγορῆσαι ἄγρυπνον· καὶ γὰρ ἐνδέχεται καὶ αὐτόμα-
τον ὕπνον ἐπελθεῖν. ἐν δὲ ταῖς ἄλλαις βίγλαις, ὅτε χρεία, πάντως καὶ ὀρθοὺς
ἱσταμένους βιγλεύειν. αἱ γὰρ καθέδραι καὶ αἱ ἀνακλίσεις τὰ σώματα μαραίνουσιν εἰς ὕπνον, ἡ δὲ τῶν σκελῶν στάσις διέγερσιν τῆς διανοίας ποιεῖ.

31. Ἀναγκαῖον δέ σοι μετὰ τὸν πόλεμον, ὦ στρατηγέ, τοὺς πληγωθέντας ἐν
205 αὐτῷ τῶν στρατιωτῶν παραμυθεῖσθαι καὶ τοὺς διαπίπτοντας ἐν τῷ πολέμῳ
ταφῆς ἀξιοῦν καὶ μακαρίζειν διηνεκῶς, ὡς ὑπὲρ τῆς πίστεως καὶ τῶν ἀδελφῶν
μηδὲ τὴν ἑαυτῶν ζωὴν προτιμήσαντας, ἐπειδὴ καὶ ὅσιόν ἐστιν καὶ προθυμίαν
τοῖς ζῶσιν ἐμποιεῖ.

---

204–208 *Strat.*, 7.B.6.

---

189 ἐὰν MWA ἂν BE | ἐστιν…τάξις MWA ἡ τάξις ἢ BE   190 κανονίζωσι καὶ MW om.
ABE | τάξιν MW τάξιν καὶ καταστρατηγῶσιν αὐτὴν (αὐτῆς BE) ABE | ἀλλὰ MWA ἀλλ᾿ BE
192 ὡς εἰκός MW om. ABE | συμβολῆς MW συμβολῆς τοῦ πολέμου ABE   193 ἐστιν
WABE ἐστὶ M   194 κοιλοτέροις MW βαθυτέροις A βαθυτέροις καὶ χαμηλοτέροις BE
195 προφαινομένη MW φαινομένη A φυλαττομένοι BE | αὐτὴ MWE om. AB |
μεθοδεύεται…ἐπιβουλεύεται MW μεθοδεύηται καὶ ἐπιβουλεύται ABE   196 ἢ MWBE om.
A | καὶ MWA om. BE | ἄλλων MWA ἄλλων τινῶν BE | κατασοφίζεται Va κατασοφίζηται
MW om. ABE   197 ἐπεὶ MWA ἐπειδὴ BE | ὀχυρὰς MW ἀσφαλεῖς ABE   198 διαιρεῖν MW
διαμερίζειν ABE | ὑπνοῦσιν MW κοιμῶνται ABE | ἐγρηγοροῦσιν MW γρηγορῶσιν A
γρηγορῶσι BE   199 ἐναλλάσσοντας MWA ἐλλάσσοντας BE | ἀλλήλους MW ἀλλήλους καὶ
διαδεχομένους ABE | κἂν MWA καὶ BE   200 γρηγορῆσαι…καὶ[1] MW ἀγρυπνῆσαι A
ἀγρυπνεῖν BE   202–203 αἱ[1]…ὕπνον MW τὸ γὰρ καθέζεσθαι καὶ (τὸ BE) ἀνακλίνεσθαι εἰς
ὕπνον τὰ σώματα καταφέρει ABE   202–203 μαραίνουσιν W μαραίνουσι M om. ABE
203 ἢ ABE αἱ MW | στάσις ABE στάσεις MW   204 scr. mg. περὶ τοῦ παραμυθεῖσθαι τοὺς
πληγωθέντας καὶ θνήσκοντας θάπτειν καὶ μακαρίζειν E   205 διαπίπτοντας MW
ἀποθνήσκοντας ABE   206 ταφῆς ἀξιοῦν MW θάπτειν ABE   207 ἐστιν MW ἐστὶ τοῦτο
ABE

28. Further, if our lines are ready and the terrain is suitable, do not wait for the enemy to give battle, allowing them to adapt and modify their formation, but in safety charge and fall upon them.

29. In the likely case that the charge is delayed for some good reasons, it is absolutely necessary to hide the second line in the woods that may be found there or on lower ground to the rear. If it is seen by the enemy too soon, they will adapt and deal with it by ambushes or outwit it by other methods.

30. Since we have brought up the subject of patrols, you must make them strong. Divide the scouts in such a way that, while some are sleeping, others are awake, and so they carry out the patrols alternating with one another. Do not trust anyone to be awake and vigilant through the entire night, no matter how much he promises to do so. For it is possible that sleep will come upon him of itself. When other patrols are necessary, always have the scouts stand up straight. Chairs and recliners lull the body into sleep whereas standing on your legs keeps the mind alert.

31. After the battle, O general, you are obliged to see to the comfort of the soldiers wounded in the action, as well as to provide proper burial for those who have fallen.[7] Constantly pronounce them blessed because they have not preferred their own lives over their faith and their brothers. This is a religious act and it greatly helps the morale of the living.

7. *Strat.* 7.B.6.

32. Εἰ δὲ καὶ τέκνα αὐτοῖς εἰσιν ἢ σύμβιος καὶ φανερόν ἐστιν, ὅτι ἀγωνιζό-
210 μενοι προθύμως ἐτελειώθησαν, καὶ ταῦτα παραμυθίας ἀξιοῦν τῆς προσηκούσης.

33. Ἐπειδὴ δὲ εὑρίσκομεν καὶ Ῥωμαίους καὶ πάντας τοὺς ἐθνικούς, ὡς ἐπίπαν
μήκοθεν τὰς ἀλλήλων παρατάξεις ὁρῶντας, ἐπισημαίνεσθαι τὴν στυγνοτέραν
μᾶλλον τῇ ὄψει ἐπιτυγχάνειν ἐν ταῖς μάχαις ἤπερ τὴν ἐν τοῖς ὅπλοις λάμπουσαν,
κἂν τάχα ψευδές ἐστιν τὸ χυδαῖον τοῦτο. μετὰ γὰρ τῆς κρίσεως τοῦ Θεοῦ τῇ
215 τοῦ στρατηγοῦ διοικήσει καὶ προθυμίᾳ τοῦ στρατοῦ ὁ πόλεμος κρίνεται. ἀλλ᾽
οὖν διὰ τοὺς τὰ τοιαῦτα στοχαζομένους δέον ἐστίν, ὥστε εἰ μὲν ὗλαι ἢ κοῖλοι
τόποι πρόκεινται, ἐκεῖσε τὸν στρατὸν ἀποκρύβειν καὶ πρὸ πολλοῦ τοῖς πολεμίοις μὴ ἐπιδεικνύειν, ὥστε μὴ κατασοφίζεσθαι καὶ ἐπιβουλεύειν αὐτῷ, εἰ μήπω
ἔλθωσιν ἀπὸ ἑνὸς ἢ δευτέρου σημείου.

220 34. Εἰ δὲ γυμνὸς ὁ τόπος καὶ καθαρὸς ὁ ἀήρ ἐστιν, τότε τὰς κασσίδας
παρασκευάζειν μὴ πρὸ πολλοῦ φορεῖσθαι, ἀλλὰ ταῖς χερσὶ κατέχεσθαι, μέχρις
ἂν ἐγγίσωσιν οἱ ἐχθροί· ἀλλὰ καὶ τὰ σκουτάρια μικρὰ ὄντα ἔμπροσθεν εἰς τὸ
στῆθος φέρειν καὶ σκέπειν δι᾽ αὐτῶν καὶ τὰ λωρίκια· καὶ τὰς σκαπλίδας ὄπισθεν
| κατὰ τῶν ὠμοπλατῶν φέρειν. εἰ ἔχουσι σιδηρᾶ σκουτάρια λαμπρά, ἀλλὰ καὶ τὰ    338ᵛ
225 σίδηρα τῶν κονταρίων ἀποκρύπτειν εἰς τὸ παντοίως τὰ ὅπλα μήκοθεν <μὴ>
διαλάμπειν διὰ τὸν εἰρημένον τρόπον, ἀλλ᾽ ὥστε καὶ διὰ τοιούτου σημείου, ὅπερ
σημειοῦνται οἱ ἐναντίοι, προκαταλαμβάνεσθαι τὰς γνώμας αὐτῶν, καὶ εἰς
δειλίαν καὶ πρὸ τῆς μάχης μεταπίπτειν.

---

228 ad μεταπίπτειν des. Va

---

211-228 Strat., 7.B.15.

---

209 σύμβιος MWA σύμμιοι B σύμβιοι E    210 ἐτελειώθησαν MW ἀπέθανον ABE |
παραμυθίας…προσηκούσης MW τῆς προσηκούσης παραμυθίας ἀξιοῦν ABE    211 ἐπίπαν
MW ἐπὶ τὸ πλεῖστον A ἐπὶ πλεῖστον BE    212 παρατάξεις MWBE τάξεις A
213 ἐπιτυγχάνειν MW εὐτυχεῖν A ἐντυχεῖν BE    214 ἐστιν…τοῦτο MW ἐστι (ἢ BE) τοῦτο
καὶ χυδαῖον ABE    215 προθυμίᾳ MWAE πολεμία B | τοῦ στρατοῦ MW om. ABE | πόλεμος
MWAE πρόθυμος B    216 ὥστε MW om. ABE | κοῖλοι MW βαθεῖς καὶ (ἢ E) χαμηλοὶ ABE
217 ἀποκρύβειν καὶ MW ἀποκρύπτειν καὶ μὴ ABE    218 μὴ¹ MW om. ABE | αὐτῷ MW
αὐτὸν ABE | μήπω MW μήπου ABE    219 σημείου MW μιλίου ABE    220 ἐστιν MWA ἐστι
BE    221 χερσὶ MABE χερσὶν W    222 ἐγγίσωσιν MWA ἐγγίζωσιν BE    223 σκαπλίδας
Strat. κασσίδας ἢ codd.    223-224 ὄπισθεν…λαμπρά MW εἰ δὲ ἔχωσι σιδηρᾶ σκουτάρια
λάμποντα ὀπίσω εἰς τοὺς ὠμοπλάτας ἀπορρίπτειν ABE    225 παντοίως MW μηδαμῶς ABE
225-226 μήκοθεν…διαλάμπειν MW διαλάμπειν ἀπὸ μάκροθεν ABE    225 μὴ Va om. codd.
226 τὸν…τρόπον MW τὴν εἰρημένην αἰτίαν ABE | διὰ² MW διὰ τοῦ ABE
227 σημειοῦνται…ἐναντίοι MW οἱ ἐχθροὶ παρατηροῦνται καλόν ἐστι (ἐστιν B) ABE |
γνώμας MW διανοίας ABE    227-228 εἰς…μεταπίπτειν MW προκαταπλήττεσθαι καὶ εἰς
δειλίαν ἐμπίπτειν καὶ πρὸ τῆς μάχης ABE

32. If they have children or a wife and it is clear that they met their end struggling valiantly, then provide proper comfort to their children and wives.

33. We are well aware that the Romans and all other peoples, when observing each other's battle lines from a distance, generally pick out the more gloomy-looking one as more likely to win the battle rather than the one in gleaming armor.[8] Although common, this view is clearly wrong. After the judgment of God, war is decided by the leadership of the general and the morale of the army. Be that as it may, following <the report of> those who are attentive to such matters, if woods or hollows are found in the vicinity, the army should be concealed in them and not be visible to the enemy for a long time, until it advances to within a mile or two. This will not allow the enemy to organize countermeasures against it.

34. If the ground is open and the air is clear, then train <the troops> not to wear their helmets during a long wait before <battle> but to hold them in their hands until the enemy gets close. If their shields are small, have them carry them in front on their chests, in this way covering their mail coats, and throw the mail head pieces back over their shoulders. They should conceal bright iron shields, if they have them, and also the iron of the lances. By adopting the above measures, our weapons will not seem to shine at all from a distance. By such indications, which the enemy also make use of, we will frustrate them and, even before the battle, they will fall into dejection.

8. Sections 33–34 derive from *Strat.* 7.B.15.

35. Κελεύομεν δέ σοι, ὦ στρατηγέ, μάλιστα καὶ τὰς ἐνέδρας ἤτοι ἐγκρύμ-
230 ματα ἐν τῇ μάχῃ κατὰ λόγον ποιεῖσθαι ἤτοι κατὰ τὸν πρῴην ἡμῖν διατυπωθέντα
τρόπον. αὐταὶ γὰρ ἐπιτηδείως καὶ πρεπόντως γινόμεναι μεγίστας ὠφελείας ἐν
ταῖς μάχαις ποιοῦσι, καὶ διαφόρως μεγάλας δυνάμεις ὑπὸ ὀλίγων κατέλυσαν,
ὥστε μηδὲ καιρὸν γενέσθαι τὴν ὅλην παράταξιν συμπλακῆναι.

36. Οἱ μὲν γὰρ τόπων ἐπιτηδείων πρὸς ταῦτα εὐπορήσαντες, οἷον ἢ ὕλης
235 δασείας ἢ κοιλάδος ἢ βουνοῦ μεγάλου ἢ φαραγγίων ἢ ὀρέων ἐγγιζόντων, καὶ
μέχρι τῆς τῶν ἐχθρῶν παρατάξεως συνεκτεινομένων, ὥστε δι᾽ αὐτῶν λαθεῖν καὶ
μὴ πόρρωθεν ὁρώμενον τὸ ἔγκρυμμα μεθοδευθῆναι πρὸς ἐπιβουλήν. οὕτως οὖν
τοῖς νώτοις τῶν ἐχθρῶν ὄπισθεν ἄφνω ἐπελθόντες πρὸ τῆς συμπλοκῆς διετάρα-
ξαν καὶ ἔτρεψαν αὐτούς.

240    37. Ἄλλοι δὲ οὐ πλησίον τῶν ἐχθρῶν τῆς παρατάξεως ταύτην ἐποίησαν,
ἐπιτήδειον οὐκ ἔχοντες τόπον, ἀλλὰ ἐκ πλαγίου αὐτῶν μέσον τῆς ἰδίας καὶ τῆς
τῶν ἐχθρῶν τάξεως ποιήσαντες ἢ καὶ ὄπισθεν τῆς ἰδίας ἐκ πλαγίου, καὶ τὴν μὲν
μείζονα δύναμιν εἰς ἐγκρύμματα ἔταξαν, τὴν δὲ ἐλάττονα σχηματικῶς ἔμπροσθεν ἔταξαν.

245    38. Ἄλλοι δὲ μέρος τοῦ στρατοῦ ἔταξαν εἰς ἔγκρυμμα, καὶ οὐ τὸ μεῖζον
μέρος, ἀλλὰ τὸ ὀλιγότερον. τῆς δὲ συμβολῆς γενομένης ἑκουσίως τῶν προταγέντων εἰς φυγὴν ὁρμησάντων, καὶ τῶν ἐχθρῶν τὴν δίωξιν ἀτάκτως ποιουμένων, μετὰ τὸ παρελθεῖν αὐτοὺς τὸν τόπον τῆς ἐνέδρας ἐξελθόντες οἱ τὸ ἔγκρυμμα ποιήσαντες κατὰ τοῦ νώτου ὄπισθεν τῶν ἐχθρῶν ἐπέστησαν. εἶτα καὶ οἱ
250 φυγόντες ἀντίστροφοι γινόμενοι πρὸς τὸ σύνθημα ὅπερ προόρισαν ἐν τῷ μέσῳ

---

250 ad σύνθημα des. W

---

229–407 *Strat.*, 4.

229 δέ ABE om. MW | τὰς…ἤτοι MW τὰ ABE    230–231 ἤτοι…αὐταὶ MW καθώς σοι
προετυπώσαμεν ταῦτα ABE    232 ποιοῦσι MW ποιοῦσιν ABE | διαφόρως MW πολλάκις
ABE | κατέλυσαν MW διὰ τοιούτων τρόπων κατελύθησαν ABE    234 Οἱ De εἰ codd. |
εὐπορήσαντες MW ἐπιτυχόντες ABE    234–235 ὕλης…κοιλάδος MW δάσους ἢ κοιλάδων
ABE  235 φαραγγίων MW φαράγγων ABE | ἐγγιζόντων καὶ MW om. ABE
236 συνεκτεινομένων MW ἐπεκτεινομένων ABE    237 μεθοδευθῆναι…ἐπιβουλήν MW
καταστραταγηθῆναι καὶ ἐπιβουλευθῆναι ABE    238 νώτοις MW ὀπισθίοις μέρεσι ABE |
ὄπισθεν MW om. ABE    240 τῶν…παρατάξεως MW τῆς τῶν ἐχθρῶν παρατάξεως ABE |
ταύτην MW τοῦτο ABE    241 ἐπιτήδειον…τόπον MW μὴ ἔχοντες τόπον ἐπιτήδειον ABE |
ἰδίας MW ἰδίας ἢ ABE    243–244 ἔμπροσθεν ἔταξαν MW προέταξαν ἔμπροσθεν ABE
246–247 προταγέντων MW προτραπέντων ABE    248 τῆς ἐνέδρας MW τοῦ ἐγκρύμματος
ABE    249 κατὰ…ὄπισθεν MW ὀπίσω ABE    250 ἀντίστροφοι γινόμενοι MW
ἀντιστραφέντες ABE | σύνθημα…προόρισαν Μ σημεῖον καὶ τὸ σύνθημα ὃ προώρισαν ABE

35. We order you, O general, to make particular use of ambuscades or ambushes in battle in the prescribed manner, that is, the manner previously set forth by us.[9] When well planned and properly carried out, they are extremely advantageous in warfare. In various ways they have caused large forces to be destroyed by a few men before they had a chance to bring their entire battle line into action.

36. Some commanders have availed themselves of favorable terrain for these purposes, such as dense woods, hollows, steep hills, ravines, or nearby mountains extending up to the enemy battle line. They have used these to conceal themselves and avoid being detected from a distance and so have organized their ambush and gotten it ready. Then, well before battle, they suddenly charged in from behind against the enemy's rear and threw them into disarray and routed them.

37. Others, when the terrain was not to their advantage, would not lay the ambush close to the enemy battle line, but would set it up off to their flanks, between the enemy's line and their own or even to the rear of their own flank. They stationed the larger force in ambush with a smaller force assuming a position out in front.

38. Still others have designated a division of the army for an ambush, not the larger division but a smaller one. When the charge began, those who had been so drawn up quickly rushed into flight and, in disorder, the enemy pursued them. They rode past the site of the ambush and the troops who had set the ambush charged out behind them and struck the enemy in the rear. Then, at the prearranged signal, the men who had been fleeing wheeled about and caught the enemy in the middle. The Northern tribes and the Scythians do this very

---

9. Sections 35–57 derive from *Strat.* 4.

ἀπέλαβον αὐτούς. τοῦτο δὲ ὡς ἐπὶ πολὺ ἐπὶ τῶν βορειοτέρων καὶ Σκυθικῶν ἐθνῶν γίνεται διὰ τὸ ἄτακτα εἶναι, οἷον Τούρκων καὶ τῶν ὁμοίων αὐτοῖς.

39. Ἐὰν δέ τις φόσσαν βαθεῖαν ἤγουν ὄρυγμα ἐπὶ ὀκτὼ ἢ δέκα πόδας τὸ πλάτος ἐπὶ ἱκανὸν διάστημα ὀρύξῃ, καὶ σκεπάσῃ ταύτην ξύλοις λεπτοῖς χόρτῳ
255 τε καὶ χώματι, ὥστε ἠνω|μένην καὶ ὁμοίαν τὴν ἐπιφάνειαν τοῦ ὀρύγματος εἶναι 339
τῇ ἐγγιζούσῃ αὐτῷ γῇ, καὶ κατὰ μηδὲν διαλλάττειν. ἀλλὰ μηδὲ τὸ ἐπαρθὲν χῶμα ἐάσῃ παρακεῖσθαι αὐτῷ, ἵνα μὴ ἐμφαίνῃ τινὰ ξενοπρέπειαν· ἐν τῷ μέσῳ δὲ τοῦ αὐτοῦ ὀρύγματος καταλίπῃ τινὰς τόπους στερεοὺς σεσημειωμένους καὶ ἐγνωσμένους πρὸς τὸ παρὸν τῷ ἰδίῳ στρατῷ. ἑκατέρωθεν δὲ ἤγουν ἔνθεν
260 κἀκεῖθεν ἐκ τοῦ πλησίον τοῦ ὀρύγματος ἔγκρυμμα εἰς ἀφανεῖς τόπους ποιήσῃ, καὶ παρατάξῃ τοὺς λοιποὺς πρὸ τοῦ ὀρύγματος. εἶτα συμβολῆς γενομένης ἑκουσίως οἱ προταγέντες τὴν τροπὴν σχηματισάμενοι αὐτοὶ μὲν διὰ τῶν ἐγνωσ- μένων αὐτοῖς τόπων καὶ στερεῶν ἀκινδύνως παρέλθωσιν. οἱ δὲ ἐναντίοι σφο- δρῶς καὶ ἀσχέτως τὴν δίωξιν ποιησάμενοι ἐμπέσωσιν ἐν τῷ ὀρύγματι, ὑπεξελ-
265 θόντες δὲ ἄνω οἱ τὸ ἔγκρυμμα ποιησάμενοι, εἶτα ἐπαναστρέψαντες καὶ οἱ τὴν ὑποχώρησιν σχηματισάμενοι, τοὺς πλείους τῶν ἐχθρῶν ἀπολέσωσι πάντως, τοὺς μὲν ὡς ἐμπεσόντας εἰς τὸ ὄρυγμα, τοὺς δὲ ὡς τραπέντας ἀτάκτως ἐπὶ τῷ ἀδοκήτῳ συμπτώματι, εἰ μὴ ἄρα παρὰ τῶν ἐχθρῶν προγνωσθῇ ἢ διά τινων προσρυέντων αὐτοῖς καταμηνυθῇ.

270 40. Ἐὰν δὲ τὸν ὅμοιον τρόπον καὶ διὰ πάλων πεπηγμένων τις ποιήσῃ, δύο καὶ ἢ τρεῖς εἰσόδους ἀπαθεῖς ἐπινοήσῃ ἐγνωσμένας τῷ παρατασσομένῳ στρατῷ, εἶτα πρὸ τῶν πάλων ἐκείνων παρατάξηται· καὶ σχηματισάμενος ἐν τῇ συμβολῇ κατὰ τὸν ὅμοιον τρόπον τὴν φυγὴν προτρέψηται τοὺς ἐχθροὺς τοῖς πάλοις περιπεσεῖν. καὶ ἐξαίφνης ἐπελθόντες οἵ τε τὸ ἔγκρυμμα ἔχοντες ἐκ πλαγίου, καὶ

---

251 ἀπέλαβον Μ ἀπέκλεισαν ΑΒΕ | πολὺ Μ τὸ πλεῖστον ΑΒΕ    253 φόσσαν...ὄρυγμα Μ καὶ ὄρυγμα ποιήσας βαθὺ ΑΒΕ    254 ταύτην Μ τοῦτο ΑΒΕ    255 ἐπιφάνειαν Μ ὄψιν ΑΒΕ 256 ἐγγιζούσῃ Μ πλησιαζούσῃ ΑΒΕ | διαλλάττειν ΜΒΕ διαλλάσσειν Α    257 τινὰ Μ τινα παραλλαγὴν καὶ ΑΒΕ    258–259 σεσημειωμένους...ἐγνωσμένους Μ ἀποσημείων τινῶν γνωριζομένους ΑΒΕ    259–260 ἑκατέρωθεν...ἔγκρυμμα Μ ἔνθεν δὲ καὶ ἐκεῖθεν τοῦ ὀρύγματος ἐκ τοῦ πλησίον ἐγκρύμματα ΑΒΕ    260 τόπους Μ τόπους λαθραίως ΑΒΕ 261 καὶ...λοιποὺς Μ τοὺς δὲ λοιποὺς παρατάξῃ ΑΒΕ | παρατάξῃ ΑΒΕ παρατάξει Μ 262 τὴν τροπὴν Μ φυγὴν ΑΒΕ    264 ἀσχέτως Μ ἀκρατῶς ΑΒΕ    265 ἐπαναστρέψαντες Μ ὑποστρέψαντες ΑΒΕ    266 ὑποχώρησιν Μ φυγὴν ΑΒΕ | πλείους Μ πλείστους ΑΒΕ 268 ἀδοκήτῳ Μ ἀπροσδοκήτῳ ΑΒΕ    269 προσρυέντων Μ προσφύγων ΑΒΕ 271 εἰσόδους...ἐγνωσμένας Μ παρόδους καταλείφθη προεγνωσμένας ΑΒΕ    272 πρὸ Μ ἔμπροσθεν ΑΒΕ | σχηματισάμενος Μ σχηματισάμενος φυγὴν ΑΒΕ    273 τὴν φυγὴν Μ om. ΑΒΕ    274 ἐπελθόντες Μ ἐξελθόντες ΑΒΕ | τε Μ om. ΑΒΕ

frequently because they are undisciplined, like the Turks and those similar to them.[10]

39. A commander might dig a deep trench or ditch eight or ten feet wide and extending a good distance and cover it over with light pieces of wood and with hay and earth so it looks uninterrupted and just like the ground around the excavation, so there seems to be no difference at all. He ought then to allow the excavated earth to remain at the site to avoid giving it a strange appearance. In the middle of this trench he might leave several solid spots, well marked and known to his own army. Close to the trench on both sides, that is, here and there, he might lay an ambush in places that cannot be seen and draw up the remaining troops in formation in front of the excavation. When battle is joined, the men stationed in front make believe they are being routed and without harm cross over the solid spots that they know about. The enemy might begin an impetuous and unrestrained pursuit and fall into the trench. Then the soldiers lying in ambush suddenly charge out and the men who had feigned retreat turn back. Most of the enemy will surely perish, some because they will fall into the trench, others because they will be routed in disorder by the unexpected disaster. Of course, this will not work if the enemy learns of it ahead of time or is warned by some men going over to them.

40. If a person were to devise something similar, he could fix stakes in the ground. Plan two or three safe passageways known to the army drawn up in formation. Then draw it up in front of those stakes. In similar fashion, during the fighting it will pretend to take to flight and so cause the enemy to fall upon

10. Cf. Const. 18. Scythian was a general designation for peoples north of the Black Sea. "Northern tribes" probably refers to the Rhos. At this time, "Turks" designated the people known as Magyars or Hungarians.

275 οἱ σχηματισάμενοι τὴν φυγὴν κατὰ κράτος καὶ οὕτως τοὺς ἐχθροὺς ἀπολέσουσιν.

41. Γίνεται δὲ τοιοῦτος δόλος κατὰ τῶν ἐχθρῶν καὶ ἄνευ ὀρύγματος ἢ πάλων, ἐάν τις τριβόλους σιδηρᾶς ἀσυμφανῶς ῥίψῃ πρὸς ὥραν ἐν σφηκώμασιν ὑποδεδεμένας εἰς τὸ ἑτοίμως συστέλλεσθαι μετὰ τὴν χρείαν, τουτέστιν ἐπὶ
280 πλάτος μὲν ρ′ ποδῶν, καὶ πρὸς μῆκος δὲ πρὸς τὸ τῆς παρατάξεως διάστημα. ἐν τῷ μέσῳ δὲ τέσσαρας ἢ πέντε παρόδους καταλείπῃ ἀπὸ τριακοσίων ποδῶν πλάτος ἐγνωσμένας τῷ συμβάλλοντι στρατῷ, καὶ σεσημειωμένας ἀπὸ κλάδων μεγάλων ἢ κονταρίων κεφαλὰς ξενοπρεπεῖς ἐχόντων ἢ γῆς ἀναβολῶν ὡς τυμβίων ἢ λίθων ἀποτιθεμένων ἢ ἕτερον εὔδηλον σημεῖον, οὐ μόνον κατ᾽ αὐτὰς
285 τὰς ἀρχάς, ἤτοι τῶν μετώπων τοῦ μήκους τῶν τριβόλων, ἀλλὰ | καὶ κατὰ τοῦ    339ᵛ
βάθους ἤτοι τοῦ πλάτους παρ᾽ ἑκάτερα τῶν παρόδων, ὥστε τῆς συμβολῆς γενομένης σχηματίσασθαι τροπὴν καὶ μετὰ τὸ παρελθεῖν διὰ τῶν τοιούτων ἐγνωσμένων παρόδων τὸν στρατὸν ἐπαίρεσθαι τὰ τοιαῦτα σημεῖα, ἤτοι καταστρέφεσθαι παρὰ τῶν εἰς τοῦτο ἀφοριζομένων καβαλλαρίων, εἶθ᾽ οὕτως τὴν
290 ἐνέδραν ἐκ τῶν δύο πλαγίων ὑπεξέρχεσθαι ἔνθεν κἀκεῖθεν κατὰ τῶν ἐχθρῶν περιπιπτόντων τοῖς τριβόλοις, καὶ οὐ δυναμένων οὐδὲ πρόσω οὐδὲ ὄπισθεν εὐκόλως ὑποχωρεῖν.

42. Γίνεσθαι δὲ δύναται καὶ κατὰ τὸν ὅμοιον τρόπον καὶ ἄνευ τριβόλων, ἐάν τις στρογγύλα ὀρύγματα, ἃ ἔλεγον οἱ παλαιότεροι ἱπποκλάστας, ὀρύξῃ διε-
295 σπαρμένα ἀπὸ ἑνὸς ποδὸς τὸ διάστημα ἔχοντα, καὶ βάθος δύο ἢ τριῶν ποδῶν, καὶ πάλους ὀξεῖς ἐμπήξῃ ἐν αὐτοῖς. ταῦτα δὲ παρηλλαγμένα ὀρύξει καὶ μὴ ἐπ᾽ εὐθείας ἢ ἀπὸ τριῶν ποδῶν ἀλλήλων κατὰ τὰ τέσσαρα μέρη ἀφεστηκότων, ἐπὶ

---

297 ad τριῶν de novo inc. W

---

293-305 *Strat.*, 4.3.53.

---

278 ἀσυμφανῶς M κρύφα ABE    279 ὑποδεδεμένας M ἀποδεδεμένας ABE |
συστέλλεσθαι...χρείαν M πάλιν μετὰ τὴν χρείαν συστέλλεσθαι ABE    280 ρ′...πρὸς¹ M
ποδῶν ἑκατὸν εἰς ABE    281 παρόδους M ὁδοὺς ABE    281-282 ἀπὸ...ἐγνωσμένας M
πλάτος ἔχουσας ἀπὸ τριακοσίων ποδῶν προεγνωσμένας ABE    282 συμβάλλοντι M om.
ABE    282-283 σεσημειωμένας...μεγάλων M ἀπὸ κλάδων μεγάλων σεσημειωμένας ABE
283 ξενοπρεπεῖς M ξενοπρεπεῖς καὶ παρηλλαγμένας ABE    283-284 ἢ²...τυμβίων M om.
ABE    284 λίθων M λίθων ὡς σωρῶν ABE | ἕτερον...σημεῖον M ἑτέρων σημείων δηλῶν καὶ
φανερῶν ABE    285 τῶν¹ M κατὰ ABE    285-286 τοῦ²...πλάτους M τὸ βάθος ἤτοι τὸ
πλάτος ABE    291 οὐ M οὔτε ἔμπροσθεν ABE | οὐδὲ¹ M οὔτε ABE | πρόσω οὐδὲ M om.
ABE    293 καὶ¹ M om. ABE    294 ὀρύγματα M ὀρύγματα ὀρύξῃ ABE | ὀρύξῃ M om. ABE
295 διάστημα M πλάτος ABE    296-297 παρηλλαγμένα...ἢ M μὴ κατ᾽ εὐθείαν ἀλλήλων
ὀρύξῃ ἀλλὰ παρηλλαγμένα ABE    297 ἀφεστηκότων MW ἀπέχοντα ABE

the stakes. Suddenly the troops in ambush on the flank, together with those who had feigned flight, charge out in force and utterly destroy the enemy.

41. The same sort of trap may be laid for the enemy without a trench or stakes if, in timely fashion and secretly, a person should scatter iron caltrops strung together so they can easily be collected after use. They should extend the whole length of the battle line to a depth of one hundred feet. In the middle section, which would be about three hundred feet wide, one might leave four or five passageways known to our army in combat, marked by large tree branches, spear heads with odd shapes, heaps of earth like burial mounds, piles of stone, or other obvious signs. These could be placed not only at the entrances, that is, the front of the section covered by the caltrops, but also deeply and broadly on both sides of the passages. Then during the battle, after the units feigning flight have passed through these passages known to them, remove the markers or have them overturned by the cavalry men assigned to this task. The men in ambush on both flanks can then charge out here and there while the enemy are tripping over the caltrops and find themselves unable to move forward or backward with ease.

42. It is possible to do something along the same lines, even without caltrops. A person could dig round pits here and there, that the older authorities referred to as horsebreakers.[11] They should be about one foot in diameter and two or three feet deep with sharp stakes set into them. Dig these in alternating rows, not in straight lines, about three feet apart from one another in all four

11. *Strat.* 4.3.53.

πλάτος δὲ πόδας ρν΄, μῆκος δὲ πρὸ τῆς παρατάξεως διάστημα. καὶ τούτου
γενομένου ἐν τῇ συμβολῇ, ὅταν μὲν ἡ πρώτη τάξις προπαρατάσσηται, πρέπον
300  ἵνα ὡς πρὸ ἑνὸς μιλίου τοῦ τοιούτου σοφίσματος ἡ αὐτὴ ἵσταται, ἡ δὲ δευτέρα
ὄπισθεν αὐτοῦ δι᾽ ὅλου τοῦ διαστήματος εἰς τὰ λείμματα τῶν ὀρυγμάτων ὡς
ἀπὸ δύο ἢ τριῶν σαγιττοβόλων ὄπισθεν· ἵνα ἐὰν χρεία γένηται, καὶ οἱ τρεπόμενοι τῆς πρώτης διὰ τῶν ἀκινδύνων παρέρχωνται, καὶ τὴν δευτέραν τάξιν, ἐὰν
χρεία ἐστὶν ἐπιθέσθαι τοῖς ἐχθροῖς, διὰ τῶν αὐτῶν εὐκαίρων διαλειμμάτων
305  διερχομένην καὶ ἀνεμποδίστως οὕτως ἐπιτίθεσθαι τοῖς ἐχθροῖς.

43. Ὅταν δὲ οὐ πρὸ τοῦ σοφίσματος ἡ παράταξις γένηται πᾶσα, ἀλλὰ ὄπισθεν αὐτοῦ, δέον ἀπὸ τῶν τριῶν σαγιττοβόλων τούτου ὄπισθεν τὴν παράταξιν
ἵστασθαι, καὶ ὅταν οἱ ἐχθροὶ παρέλθωσιν ἢ καταλάβωσι τὸ σόφισμα, τότε
ὑπαντιάζειν αὐτοῖς, ἵνα φθάσωσιν οἱ ἵπποι αὐτῶν ἐμπεσόντες ἀφανισθῆναι.
310  ἀλλὰ τότε οὐ χρὴ πολὺ πλατέα τὰ εὔκαιρα χωρία τοῦ σοφίσματος καταλιμπάνειν, ὅταν ἡ παράταξις ὀπίσω αὐτῶν ἐστιν, ὥστε μὴ τοὺς πολλοὺς τῶν ἐχθρῶν
παροδεύοντας ἀκινδύνως τῆς μάχης προσάπτεσθαι.

44. Τὰ δὲ τοιαῦτα ἐγχειρήματα ἤγουν σοφίσματα λανθανόντως σε δεῖ ποιεῖν,
ὦ στρατηγέ, δι᾽ ὀλίγων καὶ πιστῶν ἀνθρώπων ἢ ἐν αὐτῇ τῇ τοῦ πολέμου ἡμέρᾳ
315  ἢ πρὸ μιᾶς αὐτοῦ ἡμέρας περὶ τὰς δειλινὰς αὐτοῦ ὥρας ἢ νυκτός, ἐν ἐκείνῳ
δηλονότι τῷ τόπῳ ἐν ᾧ | ἡ μάχη προσδοκᾶται, κἀκεῖσε τοὺς ἐχθροὺς ἀναμένειν,  340
καὶ πρὸς ὥραν θαρρεῖν τοῖς τοῦ στρατοῦ, καὶ κατ᾽ ἐξαίρετον τοῖς βανδοφόροις

---

298 πρὸ MW πρὸς τὸ ABE | διάστημα MW διάστημα καταλίπη δὲ καὶ ὁδοὺς τέσσαρας ἢ
πέντε προεγνωσμένας τῷ στρατῷ ABE    299 προπαρατάσσηται M προπαρατάσσεται W
ἔμπροσθεν τῶν τοιούτων ὀρυγμάτων παρατάσσεται ABE | πρέπον MW πρέπον ἐστὶν ABE
300 σοφίσματος…αὐτὴ MW πανουργεύματος ABE    301 δι᾽…ὀρυγμάτων MW εἰς τὰ
διαχωρίσματα τῶν ὁδῶν ABE    303 πρώτης MW πρώτης παρατάξεως A om. BE | ἀκινδύνων
MW ἀκινδύνων τόπων καὶ μὴ ἐχόντων ὀρύγματα A om. BE | τὴν…τάξιν MW πάλιν A om.
BE    304 ἐστὶν…ἐχθροῖς MW γένηται ἵνα καὶ ἡ δευτέρα παράταξις ἐφορμήσῃ κατὰ τῶν
ἐχθρῶν εὐκόλως διὰ τῶν τοιούτων διαχωρισμάτων διέλθη καὶ ἀπαρεμποδίστως τοῖς ἐχθροῖς
ἐπιθήσεται ABE    306 οὐ…ἡ MW ἡ πᾶσα ABE    306–307 γένηται…αὐτοῦ MW ὀπίσω τοῦ
τοιούτου σοφίσματος μέλλῃ παρατάσσεσθαι ABE    307 δέον MW δέον ὡς ABE | τῶν MW
om. ABE | τούτου…παράταξιν MW ὄπισθεν τῶν τοιούτων ἐγκρυμμάτων ABE
308–309 παρέλθωσιν…αὐτοῖς MW παρέλθωσι τὰ ὀρύγματα τότε καταπρόσωπον αὐτοὺς
ἀπαντᾶν ABE    309 ἐμπεσόντες MW ἐμπεσόντες εἰς τὰ ὀρύγματα ABE    310 εὔκαιρα…
τοῦ MW διαχωρίσματα τοῦ τοιούτου ABE    311 ὅταν…ἐστιν MW om. ABE
312 παροδεύοντας…προσάπτεσθαι MW ἀκινδύνως δι᾽ αὐτῶν παρελθόντας μάχεσθαι ABE
313 ἐγχειρήματα…σοφίσματα MW σοφίσματα καὶ μηχανήματα ABE    314–316 δι᾽…
προσδοκᾶται MW πρὸ (πρὸς B) μιᾶς ἡμέρας τοῦ πολέμου ἐν τῷ τόπῳ ἐν ᾧ ὁ πόλεμος
προσδοκᾶται μάλιστα δὲ ταῦτα περὶ τὰς δειλινὰς ὥρας ποιεῖν ἢ πρὸς ἑσπέραν δι᾽ ὀλίγων καὶ
πιστῶν ἀνθρώπων ABE    317 ὥραν MW ὥραν τοῦτο ABE

directions and covering an area of 150 feet, extending the length of the battle line. After this has been done and it is time for battle, the first line should draw up in formation, taking its position about a mile in front of these traps. The second line should be two or three bowshots to the rear, that is, behind those traps along the whole distance in the clear spaces between the pits. In an emergency, then, when the troops in the first line are driven back, they can pass through without danger and, if it is necessary to attack the enemy, the second line may safely advance unobstructed through those same clear spaces and fall upon them.

43. When the entire battle line is drawn up, not in front of those traps but to their rear, the line should take its stand about three bowshots behind them. When the enemy advances and encounters the traps, then charge out against them as their horses are falling into the pits and being destroyed. At the same time, when our line is drawn up behind those traps, the clear spaces left between them must not be very wide. This is to prevent large numbers of the enemy from passing through and, having avoided danger, take part in the fighting.

44. You must prepare this sort of operation or artifice secretly, O general, with a few reliable men, either on the very day of battle or late in the evening or at night on the previous day and, of course, in that location in which the battle is expected, and there await the enemy. When the time is right, inform the men in your army, especially the standard-bearers, so they may know and be on their

ἵνα δὲ εἰδότες φυλάξονται καὶ ὄπισθεν τῶν βάνδων σφιγκτοὶ ἀκολουθοῦσιν, ὡς
οἱ εὔκαιροι τόποι ἐπιδέχονται.

320    45. Τοῦτο δὲ πάντες παραγγελθῶσιν, ἵνα τοῖς βάνδοις ἑαυτῶν ἐν τῷ ὑποχωρεῖν μάλιστα ἀκολουθῶσιν, ἵνα μὴ—ὅπερ μὴ γένηται—πλανώμενοι αὐτοὶ
περιπίπτουσι τῇ παγίδι.

46. Πάντων δὲ τῶν εἰρημένων σοφισμάτων, ὡς ἡγούμεθα, ἡ διὰ τῶν τριβόλων ἀπάτη εὐκολωτέρα ὡς καὶ μᾶλλον λεληθότως ἐν ἑκάστῳ τόπῳ δύναται
325    γίνεσθαι. διὰ τοῦτο οὖν χρὴ πρὸς τοὺς τόπους καὶ τὴν τάξιν ἁρμόζεσθαι.

47. Καὶ ἐὰν δόξῃ σοι συμφέρον τὴν ἔφοδον κατὰ τῆς τῶν ἐχθρῶν παρατάξεως γενέσθαι, ὡς ἤδη ἡμῖν εἴρηται, ἀφορίσεις ἀπὸ ἑνὸς ἢ καὶ δευτέρου βάνδου ἢ
πρὸς τὸ ποσὸν τοῦ ὄντος στρατοῦ πλείονας μετὰ ἀρχόντων ἀνδρείων καὶ
τολμηρῶν καὶ φρονίμων καὶ στρατιωτῶν χρησίμων. εἰς μὲν τὸ ἴδιον δεξιὸν
330    μέρος, τοῦ τόπου δηλονότι συμπράττοντος, μίαν ἐνέδραν ὀφείλουσιν κατὰ τῆς
τῶν ἐχθρῶν ἐγχειρῆσαι παρατάξεως, κατὰ δὲ ἀριστερὸν τὴν ἄλλην ἐνέδραν.

48. Καὶ ἐὰν μὲν παρὰ τῶν ἐχθρῶν ἐγχείρηται ταύτην τὴν ἐνέδραν βουλο-
μένην τῶν ἐχθρῶν ἀναστέλλειν, καὶ μὴ δοῦναι καιρὸν ἐλθεῖν καὶ ταράξαι τὴν
παράταξιν. εἰ δὲ μὴ ἐγχειρῆται παρὰ τῶν ἐχθρῶν ἐπέρχεσθαι, ἵνα διὰ τοῦ μέρους
335    ἐκείνου ἢ εἰς τὸ τοῦλδον τῶν ἐχθρῶν, ὡς εἰκός, ἐκεῖσε εὑρισκόμενον ἐπέλθωσιν
ἢ καὶ τοῖς τῶν ἐχθρῶν νώτοις ἢ τῷ κέρατι, ἤγουν τῷ κυκλοῦντι μέρει τῆς τῶν
ἐχθρῶν παρατάξεως ἵνα μή, ὡς εἰκός, καὶ τῶν ἐχθρῶν ἐν δευτέρᾳ τάξει τασσομένων ἢ καὶ αὐτῶν ἔγκρυμμα ὄπισθεν τῆς ἰδίας αὐτῶν τάξεως ἐχόντων εὑρε-

---

318 δὲ εἰδότες MW γινώσκοντες ABE    318–319 καὶ…ἐπιδέχονται MW παραγγείλης δὲ
ἵνα βάνδον τῷ βάνδῳ ἐπακολουθῇ πρὸς τὸ διαχώρισμα καὶ τὸ πλάτος τῶν καταλιμπανομένων
ὁδῶν ἵνα μὴ ἐν τῷ ἅμα σπουδάζοντες παρέρχεσθαι περιπίπτωσι τοῖς ὀρύγμασιν ABE    320 τοῖς…ἑαυτῶν MW om. ABE    321 μάλιστα MW μάλιστα τοῖς βάνδοις αὐτῶν ABE |
ὅπερ…γένηται MW om. ABE    322 περιπίπτουσι MW περιπίπτωσι ABE    323–324 ἡ…ὡς
MW εὐκολωτέρα ἐστὶν ἡ διὰ τῶν τριβόλων ἀπάτη ABE    324–325 δύναται γίνεσθαι MWBE
trsp. A    326 συμφέρον MW συμφέρον εἶναι ABE    326–327 παρατάξεως γενέσθαι MW
trsp. ABE    328 πρὸς…πλείονας MW καὶ πλείονας πρὸς τὴν ποσότητα τοῦ στρατοῦ ABE
330 τοῦ…ὀφείλουσιν MW συμπράττοντος καὶ συνεργοῦντος δηλονότι τοῦ τόπου ἓν (ἐὰν
ΒΕ) ἔγκρυμμα ὀφεῖλον ABE | ἐνέδραν De ἐγχειρεῖν codd.    331 ἐγχειρῆσαι MW ἐπιθέσθαι
ABE | δὲ MW δὲ τὸ ABE    332–334 ἐγχείρηται…παράταξιν MW ἔγκρυμμα γενόμενον
ἐπιθέσθαι (ἐπιτίθεσθαι Β) βούληται τῇ ἡμετέρᾳ παρατάξει ὑπὸ τοῦ εἰς τὸ ἀριστερὸν μέρος
γινομένου ἐγκρύμματος ἀνασταλήσεται καὶ κωλυθήσεται ABE    332 τὴν ἐνέδραν MW
ἕτερον ABE    334 ἵνα MW om. ABE    335 εἰς…τοῦλδον MW κατὰ τοῦ τούλδου ABE | ὡς
MW om. ABE | εὑρισκόμενον MW εὑρισκομένου ABE    336 τοῖς…νώτοις MW εἰς τὰ
ὀπίθια (ὀπίσθια Β) τῶν ἐχθρῶν ABE | ἢ[2] MW ἢ καὶ ABE    336–337 τῶν ἐχθρῶν[2] MW αὐτῆς
ABE    337 παρατάξεως MW παρατάξεως φυλάττεσθαί σε (δὲ Β) χρὴ ABE    338 αὐτῶν
τάξεως MW παρατάξεως ABE    338–339 εὑρεθῶσι MBE εὑρεθῶσιν WA

guard, and the troops will follow behind the standards in close order, as the clear spaces permit.

45. All the soldiers must be ordered to follow their own standards, especially in withdrawing lest—may it not happen—they wander about and themselves fall into the trap.

46. Of all the stratagems described here, it is our opinion that the stratagem of the caltrops can more easily and with greater secrecy be employed on every kind of ground. One must also, of course, form the line in accord with the terrain.

47. If you see an advantage in attacking the enemy battle line, then, as we have prescribed earlier, detail one or two banda, or even more, depending on the size of the army, made up of competent soldiers under intelligent, courageous, and bold officers. If the terrain is favorable, obviously, you should have them undertake one ambush against the enemy battle line on their own right and another one on their left.

48. If the enemy should launch an attack, those units are to repel any attempt planned by the enemy and not allow them the chance to reach and harass our battle line. If the enemy does not attempt any such attack, then those units should attack in that sector or against the enemy's baggage train, if it happens to be in that place, or against the enemy rear or flank, that is, the encircling section of the enemy's battle line. In the likely event that the enemy are drawn up in a second line or have ambushing units behind their own line

θῶσι τὰ σὰ ἐγκρύμματα ἐκ τοῦ ἐναντίου ὑπ᾽ αὐτῶν βλαπτόμενα. δεῖ γὰρ καὶ
340 αὐτοὺς τοὺς εἰς ἔγκρυμμα ἀπερχομένους προσκουλκεύειν ἀσφαλῶς, καὶ οὕτως
ἁρμόζεσθαι τῇ κατὰ τῶν ἐχθρῶν ἐπιθέσει.

49. Τὸν δὲ καιρὸν τοῦ ἐγκρύμματος ἐπιμελῶς κανονίζειν καὶ μηδὲ πρὸ
πολλοῦ τῆς παρατάξεως ἐγχειρεῖν, ἵνα μὴ ὡς ὀλίγους ἔχουσα ἡ ἐνέδρα ὑπὸ τῶν
ἐχθρῶν βαρῆται μηδὲ πάλιν ὑστερεῖν, ἵνα μὴ φθάσῃ ἡ συμβολὴ τῆς παρατάξεως
345 γενέσθαι καὶ ἀνωφελὴς αὐτῇ εὑρεθῇ.

50. Ἀλλὰ πρέπον ἐν τῷ ἅμα μὲν κινεῖν τήν τε παράταξιν καὶ αὐτὰ εἴτε ἓν εἴτε
δύο γίνονται ἐγκρύμματα· μᾶλλον δὲ ὀλίγον | προκινῆσαι τὴν παράταξιν, ἵνα ἡ     340ᵛ
μὲν παράταξις διὰ τῶν φανερῶν τόπων ἐρχομένη ἐκεῖθεν τοὺς ἐχθροὺς ἀντι-
περισπᾷ, ἡ δὲ διὰ τῶν ἀφανῶν ὁμοίως περισπᾷ καὶ ἀλλήλους διὰ σκούλκας καὶ
350 σημείων καὶ εἰκασμοῦ κανονίζειν καὶ τόν, ὡς εἰκός, διὰ συντομίας τοῦ τόπου
προλαμβάνοντα ἐμβραδύνειν καὶ ἀναμένειν τὸν ἄλλον ὥστε, ὡς ἐνδέχεται, ἴσως
τὰς ἀμφοτέρας τήν τε ἐνέδραν ἤγουν τὸ ἔγκρυμμα καὶ τὴν παράταξιν εὑρίσκεσθαι κατὰ τῶν ἐχθρῶν καὶ ὀλίγον τι τὴν ἐνέδραν μᾶλλον προκρούειν ἵνα, ὅταν
ἄρξωνται οἱ ἐχθροὶ ὑπὸ τῆς ἐνέδρας διαταράττεσθαι, τότε ἡ παράταξις ἐγγὺς
355 εὑρισκομένη συμβάλῃ.

51. Διὰ οὖν τοῦτον τὸν τρόπον, ἐὰν οἱ τόποι ἐπιτήδειοί εἰσιν, ἐκ τῶν δύο
μερῶν δεῖ σε τὰ ἐγκρύμματα ἐκπέμπειν, μάλιστα ἐὰν πολὺν καὶ μέγαν στρατὸν
ἔχῃς, ἵνα τὸ μὲν ἓν ἔγκρυμμα τοὺς ἐπερχομένους ἀναστέλλῃ, τὸ δὲ ἕτερον
ἁρμοδίως τοῖς ἐχθροῖς ἐπιχειρῇ.

360 52. Ἐὰν δὲ ἐγχειροῦντες, ὡς εἰκός, μὴ ἐπιτύχωσιν ἢ καὶ τροπὴ τῆς παρατάξεως ἐν τοσούτῳ παρακολουθήσῃ, μηδὲ οὕτως ἐνδιδόναι ἢ ἀφίειν τοὺς ἐχθρούς,
μηδὲ ἐπὶ τὴν δευτέραν τάξιν ἔρχεσθαι καὶ συναπλέκεσθαι τοῖς φεύγουσιν, ἀλλὰ
ἔξωθεν ἀπομένειν καὶ σπουδάζειν αὐτοῖς τῷ νώτῳ τῶν ἐχθρῶν ἤτοι ὄπισθεν
ἐνεδρεύειν καὶ ἐπέρχεσθαι καὶ ἐντεῦθεν ἀνακαλεῖσθαι τὴν τῶν ἰδίων φυγήν.

---

340 ἀπερχομένους MW ἐπερχομένους ABE    342 μηδὲ MW στοχάζεσθαι ὥστε μήτε ABE
343 ἔχουσα...ἐνέδρα MW ἔχον τὸ ἔγκρυμμα ABE    344 μηδὲ MW μήτε ABE | ὑστερεῖν
MW ὑστερῇ ABE    346–347 αὐτὰ...γίνονται MW τὰ ABE    347–348 ἡ...παράταξις MW
αὐτὴ ABE    348–349 ἀντιπερισπᾷ MW περισπῶσιν ABE    349 ἡ MW τὰ ABE | σκούλκας
MW βίγλας ABE    350 σημείων ABE σημείῳ MW | κανονίζειν MW κανονίζωσιν AE
κανονίζειμοι B | συντομίας MW συντομίαν ABE    352 τὰς ἀμφοτέρας MW ἀμφότερα ABE |
ἐνέδραν ἤγουν MW παράταξιν καὶ ABE    353 τὴν ἐνέδραν MW τὸ ἔγκρυμμα ABE
354 τῆς...διαταράττεσθαι MW τοῦ ἐγκρύμματος διαταράσσεται ABE    356 οὖν τοῦτον
MW trsp. ABE    360 μὴ ἐπιτύχωσιν MW om. ABE    361 τοσούτῳ παρακολουθήσῃ MW
ὅσῳ ἐκεῖνοι ἐπιχειροῦσιν ABE    363 αὐτοῖς...νώτῳ MW ὄπισθεν ABE    363–364 ἤτοι...
ἐπέρχεσθαι MW ἐπιτίθεσθαι ABE

assigned to discover and harm your ambushing units opposed to them, our units that have been sent off to set ambushes must keep up careful reconnaissance and adapt their plans as necessary for their assault against the enemy.

49. The time of the ambush should be carefully arranged. Our men should not make their attack too far ahead of the main battle line for, being less numerous, their ambush will be crushed by the enemy. On the other hand, they should not be too far behind so that they show up after the main battle line has gotten into action and they cannot be of any help to it.

50. The units assigned to ambuscades and to the main battle line must move at the same time, whether there is to be one ambush or two. But it is better to have the main battle line move out a bit earlier, because it advances through open spaces where it diverts the enemy's attention; the other likewise distracts the enemy but under cover. They should coordinate <their moves> with one another by scouts, signals, and estimates. If one happens to use a short cut to get ahead, it should slow down and wait for the other one, so that, if possible, both of them, the ambush, that is, the ambuscade, and the main line, should make contact with the enemy at the same time, rather, with the ambush unit pushing ahead just a little. The purpose of this is that when the enemy begins to be thrown into disorder by the ambush, the main battle line moves closer and attacks.

51. In this manner, then, if the ground permits, you must send out ambushes from both sides, especially if you have a large and numerous army. One ambushing party may repel enemy assaults while the other is free to attack them.

52. In the event that the assaults are unsuccessful or, in the meantime, your main battle line is driven back, do not for this reason give in or break off contact with the enemy or fall back on the second line and get mixed in with the fugitives, but remain out in the open and try to ambush and attack the enemy's rear, that is, behind, and in this way rally your own men in flight.

365    53. Ἀσφαλὲς δὲ ὑπολαμβάνομεν ἵνα οἱ πρὸς ἐγκρύμματα πεμπόμενοι εἴτε εἰς
ἐπέλευσιν ἀπὸ ὄπισθεν ἢ ἐκ πλαγίων τινὸς παρατάξεως εἴτε εἰς τούλδου φυλακὴν εἴτε εἰς ὀξεῖαν βοήθειαν μέρους τινός, ὡς εἰκός, βαρουμένου, εἴτε εἰς νώτους παρατάξεως φυλακὴν εἴτε εἰς βίγλαν, ὀλίγοι οἱ τοιοῦτοι, ἁρμόδιόν ἐστιν,
ἵνα μᾶλλον δρουγγιστὶ τάσσωνται, ἤγουν ὁμοῦ ὡς μάζα ἄνευ ὀρδίνων, οὐχὶ δὲ
370    ἐπὶ μακρᾶς παρατάξεως, τουτέστι κατ᾽ ὄρδινον ἀκίας ἢ δεκαρχίας ἢ πενταρχίας.
αὐτὴ γὰρ κομπὴ καὶ ἐξογκωμένη καὶ ἰσχυροτέρα καὶ εὐτακτοτέρα ἐστί, καὶ
ἀσφαλῶς τὰς συμβολὰς ἐν ταῖς μάχαις ποιεῖται· βραδεῖα δὲ καὶ δυσμετάθετός
ἐστι ταῖς χρείαις, ἡ δὲ δρουγγιστὶ τασσομένη τὰ ἐναντία ἔχει καὶ ἐν ταῖς ἐνέδραις μᾶλλον εὐκόλως λανθάνειν δύναται ὀλίγῳ τόπῳ ἀρκουμένη καὶ συν-
375    τόμως μετατίθεται πρὸς τὰς χρείας. διὸ χρὴ μετὰ γυμνασίας δοκιμάσαι εὐκαί-
ρως | καὶ τὸ ἀναγκαιότερον δι᾽ αὐτῆς τῆς πείρας ἐπιλέξασθαι.                          341

54. Ἁρμόζει δὲ καὶ πρὸς τὸ ποσὸν τοῦ στρατοῦ, τοῦ ἐπὶ τούτῳ πεμπομένου,
καὶ πρὸς τὰς τῶν τόπων θέσεις. ἐὰν γὰρ ἡ μείζων δύναμις ἢ ἰσόμετρος τῆς
φανερῶς τασσομένης πέμπηται εἰς ἔγκρυμμα δι᾽ ἑνὸς τόπου ἐγχειρῆσαι προσ-
380    δοκῶσα, τότε δέεται κατὰ δεκαρχίαν τάσσεσθαι. εἰ δὲ ὀλίγοι εἰσὶν οἱ πεμπόμενοι
ἢ κατὰ διαφόρων τόπων, τότε δρουγγιστὶ καὶ ὁμοῦ ἄνευ ὀρδίνων σφιγκτοὺς
τάσσεσθαι.

55. Ἐν τούτοις γάρ ἐστιν ἡ διαφορά, ὡς εἴρηται, ἀμφοτέρων, ὅτι ἡ μὲν ἐν
συντάξει γινομένη ἐνέδρα τὸ ἰσχυρῶς καὶ ἀσφαλῶς μάχεσθαι ἔχει, ἡ δὲ δρουγ-
385    γιστὶ γινομένη τὸ ὀξέως παρέχειν τὰς βοηθείας καὶ τὰς διώξεις καὶ τὰς ἀθρόας
ἐπελεύσεις καὶ ταραχὰς ποιεῖσθαι.

56. Ταύτην οὖν τὴν τάξιν ἐπὶ τῶν καβαλλαρίων ἁρμοδίαν νομίζομεν, ἣν δεῖ
σε κατορθοῦν διὰ συνεχοῦς γυμνασίας, καθ᾽ ὃν εἰρήκαμεν τρόπον, εἴγε μὴ ἐν
πείρᾳ ταύτης προγέγονας. ἐὰν γὰρ αὐτὴ δεόντως κατορθωθῇ, οὐδὲ μανδάτων
390    χρεία ἐν καιρῷ πολέμου, οὐδὲ ἄλλης παραγγελίας. αὐτὴ γὰρ ἡ τάξις καὶ γυμνασία ἕκαστον διδάσκει τὰ δέοντα. ἴσως δέ τινες τῶν ὀκνηροτέρων καὶ ἀσφαλεσ-
τέρων λογίζονται ποικίλην τινὰ καὶ πολυειδῆ τὴν τάξιν ταύτην εἶναι καὶ ἐντεῦ-

---

367–368 νώτους παρατάξεως φυλακὴν MW φυλακὴν τῶν ὄπισθεν τῆς παρατάξεως ABE
371 κομπὴ MW ἐμφανεστέρα μὲν ABE | ἐστί MBE ἐστιν WA    373 ἐστι MBE ἐστιν W
ἐστιν ἐν A    373–374 ταῖς ἐνέδραις MW τοῖς ἐγκρύμμασι ABE    374 δύναται MW δύναται
ἐν AE δύνανται B    377 τὸ ποσὸν MW τὴν ποσότητα ABE    378 ἰσόμετρος BE ἰσόμερος
MWA    380 ὀλίγοι εἰσὶν ABE ὀλίγων MW    383 ὡς εἴρηται MW om. ABE | ἡ² MW τὸ ABE
384 γινομένη ἐνέδρα MW γινόμενον ἔγκρυμμα ABE | ἡ MW τὸ ABE    385 γινομένη MW
τασσόμενον ABE    388–389 εἴγε…προγέγονας MW om. ABE    389 δεόντως MW
πρεπόντως ABE    390 παραγγελίας MWBE παραγγελία A

53. Assuredly, we take it for granted that detachments sent out to lay ambushes or to attack the rear or the flanks of a battle line or to guard the baggage train or to give quick support to a unit which is hard pressed, as is likely, or to guard the rear of the battle line or the small parties sent out for reconnaissance, are more effective if they assume irregular formation, that is, in a mass without regular columns, not as in a large battle formation arranged in files with dekarchies and pentarchies. A battle line is impressive, very full, stronger, and better ordered and it can make its charge more securely in battle, but in emergencies it is slow and not very flexible. The irregular formation has the opposite characteristics. It can be easily concealed when setting up ambushes; it does not require much space, and it can move about quickly in an emergency. For these reasons you must spend time practicing it, and learning its basic elements from experience itself.

54. It should be adapted to the size of the army sent out for this and to the lay of the land. If a very large or even moderate-sized force of the line drawn up in the open is assigned to an ambush with the expectation that it will attack in one place, then it should be organized by dekarchies. But if only a few troops are sent out or they are to attack in different locations, then form them in irregular formation, tight together but not in regular ranks.

55. To repeat, the difference between the two is this: the ambush in regular formation enables one to fight with strength and safety; the irregular one is for quick support, for pursuits, and for sudden raids and harassment.

56. We believe this formation is suitable for cavalry and you must perfect it by constant drilling in the manner we have described, unless you have already learned it from experience. If the skills are acquired properly, there will be no need of instructions in time of battle or of other commands. The formation itself and the drill teach each man what he has to do. Perhaps some people, hesitant and overcautious, might argue that this formation is rather complicated

324   Constitution 14

θεν ἐπὶ κόπον. οὓς εἰδέναι δέον ὅτι οἱ ἀθληταὶ καὶ ἡνίοχοι καὶ ἄλλοι τινὲς τῶν
εἰς παίγνια καὶ τέρψιν ἀγωνιζομένων, ὧν ἡ μὲν ἐπιτυχία ὀλίγων ἐστὶ χρημάτων
395 εὐπορία, ἡ δὲ ἀστοχία ἀζήμιός ἐστι λύπη. οὗτοι οὖν τοσοῦτον μόχθον καὶ
κάματον ὑπομένουσι μετὰ νηστείας βρωμάτων καὶ παραφυλακῆς καὶ ἀνενδότου
γυμνασίας, εἰς τὸ δυνηθῆναι μαθεῖν, ποῖα μέν εἰσι τὰ πρὸς βλάβην τῶν ἀντιπάλων γινόμενα, τίνα δὲ τὰ φυλάττοντα τὴν ἐξ αὐτῶν ἐγχειρουμένην ἐργασίαν.
πόσῳ μᾶλλον ἐνταῦθα χρὴ ἀόκνως καὶ πολυτρόπως καὶ σεσοφισμένως τὰς
400 παρατάξεις καὶ γυμνασίας ποιεῖσθαι, ὅπου τὸ μὲν σφάλμα παρευθὺς ἢ τὸν
θάνατον ἢ τὴν χείρονα θανάτου φυγήν φέρει, ἡ δὲ ἐπιτυχία χαρὰν καὶ κέρδος
καὶ ὑπόληψιν ἀγαθὴν καὶ μνήμην ἔνδοξον ἀληθάργητον.

57. Πῶς γὰρ οὐκ ἄτοπον καὶ ἐπιβλαβὲς καὶ ὀλέθριον, ἑνὶ καὶ τῷ αὐτῷ ἁπλῷ
τρόπῳ τάσσεσθαι καὶ ἐκ τοῦ τυχόντος σφάλματος κρίσιν τοσούτου πλήθους
405 ἀνδρῶν γίνεσθαι, καὶ μηδὲ ἐπιγινώσκεσθαι τὸν ἁμαρτήσαντα; ἀλλὰ τῷ σφάλ-
ματι τοῦ ἑνὸς πάντας ὑπάγεσθαι, | ὁπόταν οὐδὲ πολλά εἰσι τάχα τὰ κεφάλαια τὰ   341ᵛ
ὀφείλοντα γίνεσθαι, ἀλλ᾽ οἱ λογισμοὶ τῶν αἰτίων αὐτῶν ἐμήκυναν τὸν λόγον.

58. Τοσαῦτα μὲν οὖν περὶ τῆς καβαλλαρικῆς τάξεως ἡμῖν εἰρήσθω, περὶ δὲ
τῆς πεζικῆς καὶ τῆς συμμίκτου ἤδη ἐροῦμεν ἅπερ ἀναγκαῖα κατὰ τὸν τοῦ πολέ-
410 μου καιρὸν γενέσθαι νομίζομεν· περὶ ὧν ἀκριβέστερον ἡμῖν καὶ ἐν ἑτέρῳ λόγῳ
προδιώρισται.

59. Τούτων γὰρ οἱ μέν εἰσι σκουτάτοι λεγόμενοι, οὓς καὶ ὁπλίτας καλοῦμεν.
καὶ τοὺς μὲν σκουτάτους ὁρίσεις οὕτως· πρότερον μὲν ποιήσεις τὰς ἀκίας ἤγουν
τοὺς ὀρδίνους τοῦ τάγματος ἑκάστου, τινὲς ἀριστερά, καί τινες δεξιὰ τοῦ
415 βάνδου, ἤγουν τοῦ ἄρχοντος τάσσονται. καὶ προπορευομένου τοῦ ἄρχοντος
ἅμα τῷ βανδοφόρῳ καὶ τῷ βουκινάτωρι καὶ τοῖς λοιποῖς κατὰ συνήθειαν ἐπακολουθοῦσιν ὡς ὡρίσθησαν οἱ λοχαγοί· πρῶτον οἱ τοῦ ἀριστεροῦ μέρους, εἶτα οἱ
τοῦ δεξιοῦ. γινομένων δὲ αὐτῶν ἐν τῷ τῆς παρατάξεως τόπῳ, ἵσταται ὁ ἄρχων

---

412–463 Strat., 12.B.11–13.

---

393 δέον MW προσήκει A χρή BE | οἱ De εἰ codd.   396 κάματον MW κόπον ABE |
ὑπομένουσι MBE ὑπομένουσιν WA scr. mg ὡρ<αῖον> ὅλον W   399 καὶ²...τὰς MW om.
ABE   400 τὸν MW om. ABE   401 θάνατον MW θάνατον ἐπιφέρει ABE | φέρει MW om.
ABE   402 ἀληθάργητον MW ἀνεπίληστον AE ἀνεπίλητον B   403–404 ἁπλῷ τρόπῳ MW
τρόπῳ ἁπλῶς ABE   406–407 ὁπόταν...ὀφείλοντα MW καὶ τότε μηδὲ πολλῶν ὄντων τῶν
κεφαλαίων τῶν ὀφειλόντων ABE   407 ἀλλ᾽ οἱ MW οἱ γὰρ ABE   408 ἡμῖν MW om. ABE
410 γενέσθαι MW γίνεσθαι ABE   412 καλοῦμεν MW καλοῦμεν οἱ δὲ ψιλοὶ οὓς τοξότας καὶ
ῥιπταρίστας ὀνομάζομεν ABE   414 ἑκάστου MW ἑκάστου εἴτα διορίσῃ ABE
415 ἄρχοντος¹ MW ἄρχοντος ὀφείλουσι τάσσεσθαι ABE   416 ἅμα MW σὺν ABE | λοιποῖς
MW λοιποῖς τοῖς ABE

and variable and, consequently, is too much trouble. Those people ought to realize that athletes, charioteers, and others who compete for sport and amusement are rewarded for their success by only a small amount of money, and the only penalty for failure is their own sorrow. They subject themselves to so much hardship and labor; they rigidly restrict their diet and never cease training so they may learn various ways of injuring their adversaries as well as ways of warding off actions attempted by them. How much more, then, ought we to practice those formations and drills tirelessly, with flexibility and with intelligence? In this case, failure brings swift death or flight that is worse than death. Success brings gratification, material gain, good reputation, and a glorious memory that will not be forgotten.

57. How is it not out of place, harmful, and destructive to line up in one and the same simple manner? One accidental mistake decides the fate of such a great multitude of men. The one responsible may never be known, but for the mistake of one man all must suffer. In any case, perhaps, the topics that must <still> be brought up are not many; moreover, listing the reasons themselves has <already> lengthened this book.

58. We have said enough about cavalry formations. We now turn to what we believe is fundamental for the infantry and the mixed formations in time of battle, which we have already set forth in greater detail in another chapter.

59. Among these are those called heavy-armed troops, whom we also refer to as hoplites.[12] This is how you shall organize the heavy-armed troops. First line up the files or columns of each tagma, some to the left and some to the right of the standard, that is, the commanding officer. The commander moves forward together with the standard-bearer, the trumpeter, and the rest as is customary. The group leaders follow in their assigned positions, first those on the left side, then those on the right. On arriving at the site of the battle line, the commander

12. Sections 59–63 derive from *Strat.* 12.B.11–13.

καὶ μετ' αὐτὸν ὁ βανδοφόρος καὶ οἱ πρὸς συνήθειαν. καὶ παρατάσσονται αὐτῷ
420 ἑκατέρωθεν αἱ ἀκίαι ὡς ὡρίσθησαν, πρῶτον ἐν ἀραιοτέρῳ διαστήματι, ἵνα μὴ
συντρίβωνται ὑπ' ἀλλήλων ἀπὸ ἑξκαίδεκα τὸ βάθος ἔχουσαι καὶ τοὺς ψιλοὺς
ὄπισθεν. τὰ δὲ ξίφη τῶν κονταρίων τέως ἄνω βλέποντα, ἵνα μὴ ἐμποδίζωνται ὑπ'
αὐτῶν. ἔμπροσθεν δὲ τοῦ μετώπου περιπατοῦσιν ὁ καμπιδούκτωρ, ἤγουν ὁ τοὺς
τόπους ἐρευνῶν, καὶ ὁ μανδάτωρ, ὁ μὲν ἐπὶ τοὺς τόπους ὁδηγῶν, ὁ δὲ τὰ μαν-
425 δάτα γνώμῃ τοῦ ἄρχοντος διδούς. ὅταν δὲ κατασταθῶσιν τὰ τάγματα, καθὼς
προδιωρισάμεθα, εἰς μοίρας καὶ εἰς μέρη, ἤγουν εἰς τοὺς δρούγγους αὐτῶν καὶ
εἰς τὰς τούρμας καὶ γένηται ἡ πᾶσα παράταξις τῶν σκουτάτων, τότε παρατάξεις
καὶ τοὺς ψιλοὺς λεγομένους κατὰ διαφόρους τόπους.

60. Τοὺς μὲν τοξότας ὄπισθεν ἑκάστης ἀκίας πρὸς τὸ μέτρον τῶν ὄντων,
430 τουτέστιν εἰς τοὺς ἑξκαίδεκα σκουτάτους τέσσαρας ψιλούς, ἵνα καὶ μέχρι
τεσσάρων μεριζομένης τῆς τῶν ὁπλιτῶν, ἤτοι τῶν λεγομένων σκουτάτων ἀκίας
εὑρεθῇ εἷς τοξότης ὄπισθεν αὐτῆς. ἐὰν δὲ ἀπαιτῇ, τάξεις αὐτοὺς εἰς τὸ βάθος
τῶν ἀκιῶν ἕνα παρ' ἕνα σκουτάρατον καὶ τοξότην. ποτὲ δὲ καὶ εἰς τὰς ἀκίας καὶ
εἰς τὰ κέρατα τῆς παρατάξεως, τουτέστιν ἔσωθεν τῶν καβαλλαρίων, πολλάκις
435 δὲ καὶ ἔξωθεν αὐτῶν ἀπὸ μικροῦ διαστήματος, μετὰ | καὶ ὀλίγων σκουταράτων,   342
εἰς τὸ διεκδικεῖν τοὺς ἐξώτερον ἑστῶτας καβαλλαρίους. τοῦτο δὲ ἐὰν πολλοὶ
εἰσιν οἱ ψιλοί. οἱ δὲ ρικτάρια ἢ τζικούρια ἤ τι τοιοῦτον ἔχοντες ἢ ὄπισθεν τῶν
ἀκιῶν τῶν σκουταράτων ἢ εἰς τὰ ἄκρα τῆς παρατάξεως, καὶ οὐκ ἐν τῷ μέσῳ. οἱ
δὲ σφενδοβολισταὶ πάντως εἰς τὰ ἄκρα τῆς παρατάξεως.
440    61. Εἰς δὲ τὰ ἄκρα τῆς πεζικῆς παρατάξεως τάσσεσθαι τοὺς καβαλλαρίους
κελεύομεν. τὰ δὲ μείζονα τάγματα μετὰ τῶν ἀρχόντων αὐτῶν ἐξωτέρω. καὶ ἐὰν
μὲν πολλοί εἰσιν οἱ καβαλλάριοι, τουτέστι πλέον τῶν δώδεκα χιλιάδων, ἀπὸ
δέκα τὸ βάθος ἤγουν τὸ πάχος τῆς ἀκίας τὴν παράταξιν γίνεσθαι. εἰ δὲ καὶ
ὀλιγώτεροι τοῦ μέτρου τούτου, ἀπὸ πέντε εἶναι δὲ ἐκ περισσοῦ τινας ὄπισθεν εἰς
445 ὑποβοήθειαν αὐτῶν ἔξω τῶν ἁμαξῶν ἵνα, ἐὰν μέν τινες τῶν ἐχθρῶν διὰ τοῦ
νώτου ἤγουν τῶν ὄπισθεν φανῶσιν, ἀποσοβήσωσιν αὐτούς. εἰ δὲ μήγε, προστε-

---

419 πρὸς MW ἄλλοι οἱ κατὰ ABE   420 ἀκίαι MW ἀκίαι ἤγουν οἱ λοχαγοὶ ABE
421 ἑξκαίδεκα MW δὲ δεκαὲξ A ις' BE   424–425 μανδάτα γνώμῃ MW ἤτοι τὰ
παραγγέλματα γνώμῃ καὶ προτροπῇ ABE   425 κατασταθῶσιν M κατασταθῶσι WABE
430 τουτέστιν MWBE τουτέστι A | ἑξκαίδεκα MW ις' ABE   431 λεγομένων MW om. ABE
433 σκουτάρατον MW σκουτάτον ABE   435 σκουταράτων MW σκουτάτων ABE
436 ἐξώτερον MW ἔξωθεν ABE   437 ρικτάρια MW ριπτάρια ABE   438 σκουταράτων
MW σκουτάτων ABE   439 σφενδοβολισταὶ MW σφενδονῆται ABE | παρατάξεως MW
παρατάξεως ταχθήσονται ABE   442 δώδεκα MW ιβ' ABE   445–446 διὰ...τῶν MW
ὄπισθεν ABE   446 ἀποσοβήσωσιν MW ἀποκωλύσωσιν ABE

halts with the standard-bearer behind him and the others in the usual manner. The files draw up in formation on both sides of them as they have been ordered, at first far enough apart so they will not bump into each other. They keep the depth at sixteen, with the light-armed troops to the rear. Hold the points of the spears high to avoid any obstructions. The field guide, that is, the one who reconnoiters the sites, and the herald march out in front of the line, the one for guide duty and the other to transmit orders from the commander. When the units have been organized, as we have prescribed, into moirai and divisions, that is, into their droungoi and tourmai, and the entire battle line of the heavy-armed soldiers is in place, then draw up the light-armed troops in different places.

60. The archers are posted in the rear of each file in proportion to the numbers of men, that is, four light-armed men for the sixteen heavy infantry, so that if the hoplites are reduced to four deep, that is, a file of heavy infantry, as they are called, there will be one archer behind it. If called for, station them in the depth of the files alternating one heavy-armed soldier with one archer, at another time, inside the files and on the flanks of the battle line, that is, on the inside of the cavalry. If there is a large number of light-armed troops, <station them> a short distance to the outside, along with a few heavy-armed infantry to provide cover for the cavalry riding along further out. The men with short javelins, axes, or similar weapons should be behind the files of heavy infantry or on the flanks of the line, not in the middle. The slingers always belong on the flanks of the line.

61. We order that the cavalry should be drawn up on the flanks of the battle line, the larger units with their own officers further out. If the cavalry force is large, that is, more than twelve thousand, the line should be ten deep, that is, the thickness of the file. If the force is less than that number, the line should be five deep. An extra force should be posted for their support to the rear, outside the wagons. In case some of the enemy should appear behind, that is, to the rear,

θῶσι τοῖς πλαγίοις καὶ αὐτοί. τάσσονται δὲ καὶ αὐτοὶ εἰς τὸ ἀραιότερον πρότερον διάστημα, ἵνα μὴ ἐμποδίζωνται ὅτε γένηται καὶ καιρὸς καὶ μέλλουσι μεταβάλλεσθαι τὸ σχῆμα τῆς στάσεως αὐτῶν.

450    62. Τοὺς δὲ καβαλλαρίους παραγγείλῃς μὴ κατατρέχειν τῶν ἐχθρῶν μηδὲ
ἀφίστασθαι τῆς πεζικῆς παρατάξεως ἐπὶ πολὺ διάστημα. κἂν τάχα καὶ τραπῶσιν
οἱ ἐχθροί, ἵνα μὴ ἐνέδρας ἤγουν ἐγκρύμματος παρ' αὐτῶν γενομένου, ἐάν περ
ἀπὸ διαστήματός εἰσι γυμνούμενοι τῆς παρατάξεως ἐπηρεασθῶσιν, ὡς ὀλιγώτεροι. ἀλλὰ καὶ ἐὰν βιασθῶσιν, ὡς εἰκός, ὑπὸ τῶν ἐναντίων κατὰ τοῦ νώτου ἤγουν
455    ὄπισθεν τῆς παρατάξεως προσφεύγωσι, καὶ μὴ παρέρχωνται τὰς ἁμάξας. ἐὰν δὲ
μὴ οὕτως ἀντέχωσι κατέρχεσθαι αὐτοὺς ἐκ τῶν ἵππων καὶ οὕτως πεζῇ ἑαυτοὺς
ἐκδικεῖν.

63. Ἐὰν δὲ βουληθῇς παρατάξεσθαι μὲν τὸν στρατόν, μὴ συμβάλλειν δὲ τὴν
μάχην κατὰ τὴν αὐτὴν ἡμέραν, καὶ ὁρμήσουσιν οἱ ἐχθροὶ κατὰ τῶν καβαλλαρί-
460    ων, καὶ μὴ βαστάσωσιν αὐτοὺς ἐκεῖνοι, μὴ ἀναμένειν αὐτοὺς εἰς τὰ κέρατα τῆς
παρατάξεως καὶ τῶν ἁμαξῶν. ἀλλ' εἰ τοῦτο γένηται, τότε χρεία μείζονος τοῦ ἐν
τῷ μέσῳ διαστήματος ἵνα μεταβαλλομένων, ὡς εἰκός, τῶν καβαλλαρίων μὴ
στενοχωρηθῶσιν μηδὲ αἱ τῶν ἐχθρῶν σαγίτται βλάψωσιν αὐτούς.

64. Οὐκ ἀγνοοῦμεν δὲ ὅτι τῶν νῦν εἰρημένων τινὰ καὶ ἐν τῇ περὶ γυμνασίας
465    διατάξει εἰρήκαμεν. ἀλλ' οὐδὲν ἄτοπον καὶ ἐν τῇ περὶ τοῦ πολέμου διατάξει
προσυπο|μνῆσαι περὶ αὐτῶν τοὺς ἐντυγχάνοντας. οὕτω γὰρ σκοποῦμεν ὥστε    342ᵛ
πάντα τῷ πολέμῳ ἁρμόζοντα καὶ ἐν τῇ γυμνασίᾳ δεῖν ἁρμόζειν, πλὴν μόνου τοῦ
ἀσίδηρον γίνεσθαι τὴν ἔκταξιν καὶ ἄμαχον. ὅθεν καὶ πάλιν τοῖς ὁμοίοις ἐμφιλο-
χωρῆσαι οὐκ ὠκνήσαμεν ὑπομνήσεων χάριν ἐκείνων. οὐ γὰρ μικρὸν τὸ παρὰ
470    μικρόν.

469–470 Cf. Arist. Phys., 197a30.

447–448 τὸ...διάστημα MW ἀραιότερον διάστημα πρότερον ABE    448 καὶ¹ MW om.
ABE    448–449 μεταβάλλεσθαι MW μεταλλάξαι ABE    451 καὶ MW om. ABE
452 ἐνέδρας ἤγουν MW om. ABE | γενομένου MW γινομένου ABE    453–454 ὀλιγώτεροι
MW ὀλιγώτεροι μακρόθεν τῆς παρατάξεως εὑρισκόμενοι ABE    455 προσφεύγωσι MBE
προσφεύγωσιν W προσφεύγουσιν A    456 ἀντέχωσι MW ἀντέχωσιν A ἀπαντῶσι BE |
οὕτως² MW om. ABE    457 ἐκδικεῖν MW διεκδικεῖν ABE    459 ὁρμήσουσιν ABE
ὁρμήσωσιν MW    464 περὶ MW om. ABE    466 ὥστε MW om. ABE    467 πάντα MW
πάντα τὰ ABE | δεῖν MW δέον ABE    467–468 μόνου...ἄμαχον MW μόνον τὸ ἄνευ
σιδήρου καὶ μάχης τὴν τοιαύτην γυμνασίαν γίνεσθαι ABE    468–469 καὶ²...ἐμφιλοχωρῆσαι
MW πάλιν τὰ ὅμοια εἰπεῖν ABE    469 ὑπομνήσεων MW ὑπομνήσεως ABE

they can repel them. If such is not the case, they may be assigned to the flanks. They should first line up in a very open formation so they may not be impeded when the time comes for them to change the shape of their position.

62. You should order the cavalry not to race after the enemy or to get too far away from the infantry battle line even if the enemy are routed. They might run into an ambush or ambuscade set by them and, few in numbers, bereft of help and far from the main line, they might be done in. But if, as is likely, they should be driven back by the enemy, they should seek refuge to the rear or behind the battle line, but they should not go further than the wagons. If they still cannot hold out, they should dismount and defend themselves on foot.

63. If you wish to have the army form in line but not engage in battle that same day, and the enemy charges against our cavalry, who may not be able to deal with it, they should not await the enemy on the flanks of the battle line and of the wagons. If this should happen, then the distance between them should be increased, so the cavalry may not be cramped in any maneuvers they may have to make and may not be injured by the enemy's arrows.

64. We are not unaware that, in the constitution on drilling, we have already written about some matters now under discussion in this chapter. But it is not at all out of place, even in this constitution about combat, to speak to our readers about the same topics. It is our aim that everything appropriate to combat must also be appropriate to training except, of course, that those exercises are carried out with blunt weapons and without actual fighting. With this in mind then, we have not hesitated to dwell upon related topics once more to aid in remembering those matters. Missing by a small amount is not a small matter.[13]

13. Cf. Aristotle, *Physics* 197a30.

65. Τάξεις δὲ τὰ μέρη τῆς παρατάξεως ἀπὸ ἑκατὸν ἢ διακοσίων ποδῶν
ἀλλήλων διακεκριμένα, ἵνα μὴ στενοχωροῦνται ὑπ᾽ ἀλλήλων ἐν τῷ περιπατεῖν,
ἐν δὲ τῷ καιρῷ τῆς συμβολῆς ἑνοῦνται καὶ βοηθῶσιν ἑαυτοῖς καὶ παραγγέλλωνται τῷ μέσῳ μέρει πείθεσθαι, ἔνθα τὸ τοῦ στρατηγοῦ ἢ τινος ἑτέρου τεταγμένου
475 ἄρχοντος βάνδον ὀφείλει τάσσεσθαι. τὸν γὰρ μέσον τόπον τῆς παρατάξεως οἱ
ἀρχαῖοι διὰ τοῦτο στόμα ἐκάλεσαν καὶ ὀφθαλμὸν ἵνα αὐτῷ τὰ λοιπὰ μέρη
πείθωνται.

66. Ἐπειδὴ δὲ τὸ σφίγγεσθαι ἤτοι πυκνοῦσθαι πρὸς τὸ ἀραιοῦσθαι καὶ
πλατύνεσθαι συντομώτερον καὶ ἀσφαλέστερόν ἐστιν, οὐ χρὴ ἀπὸ προοιμίων
480 ἑξκαίδεκα τὸ βάθος τῶν ὀρδίνων ἤτοι τῶν ἀκιῶν τάσσεσθαι, ἀλλὰ ἀπὸ τεσσάρων, ἵνα καὶ κομπωδεστέρα φαίνηται τοῖς πολεμίοις ἡ παράταξις, καὶ ἀνετώτεροι γίνωνται οἱ ὁπλῖται ἐν τῷ περιπατεῖν μάλιστα ἐπὶ διάστημα. ἐὰν γὰρ γένηται
χρεία ἢ ἀπὸ ὀκτὼ ἢ ἀπὸ ἑξκαίδεκα γενέσθαι τὸ βάθος ἐν τῷ περιπατεῖν συντόμως γίνεται καὶ σφίγγεται.

485 67. Εἰ μέντοι σφιγκτῆς καὶ κοντῆς οὔσης τῆς παρατάξεως χρεία γένηται
ἐκταθῆναι τὸ μῆκος αὐτῆς, πολλῆς ὥρας δεῖται εἰς τοῦτο, καὶ οὔκ ἐστι χρειῶδες
τῶν πολεμίων ἐγγιζόντων ἐκτείνειν τὴν παράταξιν.

68. Οἱ δὲ βανδοφόροι μέχρι μὲν τῆς παρατάξεως καβαλλάριοι μετὰ τῶν
ἀρχόντων αὐτῶν, ἐν δὲ τῇ παρατάξει καὶ αὐτοὶ πεζοὶ ὀφείλουσιν ἵστασθαι.

490 69. Ὥστε ἀνάγκη μηδὲ τῶν ἑξκαίδεκα πλέον τὸ βάθος τῶν ἀκιῶν γίνεσθαι,
κἂν ᾖ τῶν ἐναντίων βαθυτέρα ἐστίν, μηδὲ τῶν τεσσάρων ἔλαττον, κἂν εἰ λεπτο-
τέρα ἐστὶ τῶν ἐναντίων ἡ παράταξις. ὥστε τὸ μὲν πλέον τῶν ἑξκαίδεκα ἄχρη-

---

489 ad λουσιν de novo inc. V

---

471–532 *Strat.*, 12.B.17–18.   475–477 Cf. Asclepiod., 2.5; Aelian., 7.3; et al.

472 διακεκριμένα MW διακεχωρισμένα ABE | στενοχωροῦνται MW στενοχωρῶνται ABE
473–474 παραγγέλλωνται ABE παραγγέλλονται MW   476 ὀφθαλμὸν MW ὀμφαλὸν ABE
478–479 ἀραιοῦσθαι…πλατύνεσθαι   MW   om.   ABE   479 συντομώτερον   MW
συντομώτερόν ἐστι ABE   479–480 ἐστιν…ἀλλὰ MW παρὰ τὸ ἀραιοῦσθαι καὶ πλατύνεσθαι
οὐ χρὴ ἐξ ἀρχῆς ἀπὸ ις΄ τὸ βάθος τῶν λόχων τάσσεσθαι ἀλλ᾽ ABE   481 κομπωδεστέρα MW
ἐμφανεστέρα ABE   481–482 ἀνετώτεροι   γίνωνται   MW   om.   ABE   482 μάλιστα…
διάστημα MW ἄδειαν ἔχωσιν μὴ ὑπ᾽ ἀλλήλων στενοχωρούμενοι ABE   483 ἑξκαίδεκα MW
δεκαὲξ A ις΄ BE   484 καὶ σφίγγεται MW τοῦτο καὶ σφίγγεται ἡ παράταξις ABE
487 ἐκτείνειν τὴν MW εἰς μῆκος ἐκτείνειν ABE   489 αὐτῶν MW αὐτῶν ὀφείλουσι
περιπατεῖν ABE | ὀφείλουσιν MW ὀφείλουσι AVBE   490 ἑξκαίδεκα MW ις΄ AVBE
491 ἐναντίων MWB ἐναντίων παράταξις AVE | εἰ MW om. AVBE   492 ἐστὶ MVBE ἐστὶν
W ἐστὶν ἡ A | ἤ…ὥστε MW om. AVBE | μὲν MW μὲν γὰρ AVBE | ἑξκαίδεκα MW ις΄ AVBE

65. You will form the divisions of the battle line about one hundred or two hundred feet apart from one another so they will not be crowded all together on the march.[14] But when the time comes for battle, they act in unison and provide mutual support. They should be ordered to use the central meros as a guide, for it is there that the standard of the general, or of another officer posted there, ought to be fixed. For this reason the ancient authorities referred to the middle location as the mouth and the eye because the divisions obey it.[15]

66. Since it is quicker and safer to tighten or close ranks than to open or widen them, the initial formation of the columns or the files does not need to be sixteen deep, but only four. This makes the battle line look more impressive to the enemy and the heavy infantry will be more relaxed while marching, especially if it is for some distance. If, while marching along, it should become necessary to assume a depth of eight or sixteen, they may do this and close ranks quickly.

67. If the battle line is tightly formed and short and the need arises to extend its width, many hours are needed for this. Furthermore, it is not helpful to extend the battle line while the enemy are approaching.

68. The standard-bearers, together with their officers, should remain mounted until the battle line is formed; then they are to take their position in the line on foot.

69. The depth of the files must not be more than sixteen or less than four, even if the battle line of the enemy is deeper than that or not as deep. More than

*14. Sections 65–76 derive from *Strat.* 12.B.17–18.
*15. Cf. Asclepiodotus 2.5; Aelian 7.3; et al.

στον, τὸ δὲ ὀλιγώτερον τῶν τεσσάρων ἀσθενές. μέση δὲ τάξις τῶν ὀκτὼ σκουταράτων λεγομένων ἤγουν ὁπλιτῶν ἐστιν.

495      70. Παραγγείλῃς δὲ ὥστε πᾶσαν ἡσυχίαν γενέσθαι ἐν τῷ στρατῷ. καὶ οἱ
ἑκάστης ἀκίας οὐραγοὶ ἐὰν ἕως ψιθυρισμοῦ ἀκούσωσι παρά τινος τῶν μετ᾽
αὐτῶν, μετὰ τῶν ἀστιλιῶν νύσσουσιν αὐτούς. | καὶ ἐν ταῖς συμβολαῖς δὲ ἤγουν  343
ἐν τῇ μάχῃ ὠθοῦσι τοὺς ἔμπροσθεν αὐτῶν εἰς τὸ μή τινας τῶν ὁπλιτῶν ἐξ
ὀλιγωρίας, ὡς εἰκός, ἀπομένειν.

500      71. Μὴ ἐπιτηδεύῃ δὲ ἐπὶ πολὺ διάστημα τοὺς πεζοὺς ὡπλισμένους περιπατεῖν, ἀλλὰ καὶ ἐὰν ἐμβραδύνωσιν οἱ ἀντιτασσόμενοι καὶ χρεία τοῦ ἀναμεῖναι τὴν
παράταξιν γένηται κατὰ τὸν καιρόν, μὴ ἀναγκάζειν αὐτοὺς ἵστασθαι πολλὰς
ὥρας, ἵνα μὴ ὡς βαρεῖαν ὅπλισιν ἔχοντες ἐν τῇ συμβολῇ κεκοπιωμένοι εὑρεθῶσιν, ἀλλὰ παρασκευάζειν αὐτοὺς καθέζεσθαι καὶ ἀναπαύεσθαι καί, ὅταν ἐκ τοῦ
505  πλησίον ἔλθωσιν, τότε ἐγείρειν αὐτούς, ἵνα ἄκοποι καὶ ἀσύντριπτοι μένωσιν.

72. Μηδὲ ἐν καιρῷ μάχης ἔμπροσθεν τῆς παρατάξεως περιπατεῖν, πλὴν τῶν
τουρμαρχῶν καβαλλαρίων καὶ μανδατώρων δύο καὶ καμπιδουκτώρων δύο καὶ
στράτωρος ἑνὸς καὶ σπαθαρίου ἑνός, ὥς μοι καὶ ἔμπροσθεν εἴρηται, καθ᾽ ἕκαστον ἄρχοντα μέχρις οὗ ἐγγίσωσιν οἱ πολέμιοι. τότε δὲ ἕκαστον ἀσφαλῶς ἐν τῷ
510  ἰδίῳ μέρει ἔρχεσθαι καὶ ἵστασθαι.

73. Ἐὰν δὲ δόξῃ σοι τὸν καραγὸν ἤγουν τὰς ἁμάξας ἀκολουθῆσαι τῇ παρατάξει, τάσσεσθαι αὐτὸ ἀπὸ ἑνὸς τελείου σαγιττοβόλου τῆς παρατάξεως· καὶ
συνακολουθεῖν ἐν τάξει τῷ ἰδίῳ μέρει, τοσοῦτον δὲ διάστημα κρατεῖν τὰς
ἁμάξας ὅσον ἡ παράταξις ἔχει, ἵνα μὴ ἔξωθεν γινόμενοι ταύτης ἀβοήθητοι
515  μείνωσιν.

74. Ἑκάστην δὲ τῶν ἁμαξῶν κιλικίῳ τὸ ὄπισθεν μέρος σκέπεσθαι, ἵνα καὶ οἱ
ἁμαξελάται ἄνω ἱστάμενοι καὶ μαχόμενοι ὡς ἀπὸ προμαχώνων βοηθοῦνται, καὶ
οἱ βόες φυλάττωνται ἀπὸ τῶν βαλλομένων σαγιττῶν, τὰς δὲ βαλιστροφόρους
ἁμάξας, ἤτοι τὰς ἐχούσας τὰς λεγομένας τοξοβολίστρας, καὶ τὰ μαγγανικὰ

---

493–494 σκουταράτων MW σκουτάτων AVBE   494 ἐστιν MW om. AVBE   495 ὥστε
MW om. AVBE   496 ἀκούσωσι MAVBE ἀκούσωσιν W   497 ἀστιλιῶν νύσσουσιν MW
ξύλων τῶν κονταρίων πληττέτωσαν AVBE   498 τῇ…ὠθοῦσι MW (ὠθοῦσιν) ταῖς μάχαις
ὠθείτωσαν AVBE | τινας MW τινα AVBE   500 ἐπιτηδεύῃ MW ἐπιτηδεύῃς AVBE
502 κατὰ…καιρόν MW om. AVBE   502–503 ἵστασθαι…ὥρας MW πολλὰς ὥρας
ἵστασθαι κατὰ τὸν καιρὸν ἐκεῖνον AVBE   505 ἔλθωσιν MW ἐξέλθωσιν AVBE   506 μάχης
MW μάχης ἕτερόν τινα AVBE   511 τὸν…ἤγουν MW om. AVBE   512 αὐτὸ MW αὐτὸς
ABE   514 γινόμενοι ταύτης MW trsp. AVBE   515 μείνωσιν MW καταλειφθῶσιν AVBE
516 ἁμαξῶν MW ἁμαξῶν προσήκει AVBE   517 προμαχώνων MAVBE προμαχώντων W |
βοηθοῦνται MW βοηθῶνται AVBE   518 ἀπὸ AVBE ὑπὸ MW

sixteen is useless and less than four is weak. The middle section consists of eight men referred to as heavy armed, also as hoplites.

70. You shall order absolute silence to be observed by the army. If the file closers of each file hear so much as a whisper from one of their men, they are to poke him with their lance. In combat also, that is, during the fighting they are to push forward the men in front of them so that none of them will lose heart and be likely to fall back.

71. Do not arrange for the foot soldiers to march for long distances in full armor. But, in case their adversaries are slow in coming and the troops on the battle line have to wait in place for some time, they should not be forced to stand there for many hours. When the fighting begins they will already be exhausted because of the heavy armament they are wearing. But arrange for them to sit down and rest so they will not become tired and worn out. Only when the enemy gets close, call them to attention.

72. At the time of combat, nobody should march in front of the battle line except the tourmarchs, mounted, each officer accompanied by two heralds, two field guides, one strator and one spatharios, as I have prescribed earlier. They stay until the enemy gets close, then each should depart safely and take his position in his own meros.

73. If you decide to have the baggage train, that is, the wagons, follow the battle line, station it a full bowshot from that line with each section following its own meros in order. The wagons should cover the same extent of ground as the battle line for, if they go beyond it, they will remain without protection.

74. Each wagon should have its back part covered by heavy cloth so that the drivers can stand up and fight, as though protected by a bulwark, and the oxen are protected from the hail of arrows. The wagons carrying the ballistai, that is, having the so-called toxobolistrai and the alakatia machines, should be distrib-

520 ἀλακάτια, δι' ὅλου μὲν καταμερίζειν τοῦ διαστήματος, τὰς δὲ πλείονας τὰς
χρειώδεις ἐν τοῖς ἄκροις τάσσειν.

75. Τοὺς δὲ ἁμαξηλάτας ἀκοντιστὰς δεῖ εἶναι ἢ σφενδοβόλων ἢ τζικουρίων ἢ
ματζουκίων ἢ σαγιττῶν. ἔσωθεν δὲ τῶν ἁμαξῶν εὐθέως τὸ λοιπὸν τάσσεσθαι
τοῦλδον, ἐφ' ᾧ τὸν μέσον τόπον τῶν ἁμαξῶν καὶ τῆς παρατάξεως εὔκαιρον
525 εἶναι ἵνα, κἂν πρὸς διφαλαγγίαν καιρὸς γένηται, μερισθῆναι τοὺς σκουτάτους
βιαζομένων τῶν ἁμαξῶν, εἴτε τοὺς καβαλλαρίους εἴτε τοὺς πεζούς, μὴ ἔχωσιν
ἐμπόδισμα μηδὲ συγχέωνται.

76. Ἐὰν δὲ πολλὴ δύναμις τῶν ἐναντίων ἐκ τῶν ὄπισθεν ταῖς ἁμάξαις ἐνοχλῇ, καὶ οὐκ ἀντέχωσιν οἱ ἁμαξηλάται ἤ οἱ, ὡς εἰκός, πρὸς διφαλαγγίαν μεριζό-
530 μενοι, τότε ῥίπτεσθαι ὀλίγας τριβόλους. ἀλλ' ἐὰν ῥίπτωνται, παραφυλάττεσθαι | 343ᵛ
χρὴ τοῦ μὴ δι' αὐτῆς τῆς ὁδοῦ ὑποστρέψαι τὸν στρατόν, ἀλλὰ δι' ἑτέρας ἵνα μὴ
βλάβη τις ὑπὸ τῶν τριβόλων γένηται αὐτῷ.

77. Καὶ τοῦτό σοι κελεύομεν, ὦ στρατηγέ, ἵνα κατὰ τὴν ἡμέραν τοῦ πολέμου
τῆς πεζικῆς ἢ καὶ συμμίκτου παρατάξεως, ἐὰν πολλοί εἰσιν οἱ καβαλλάριοι τῶν
535 ἐναντίων, καὶ ὑπὲρ τὸ ἡμέτερόν ἐστι τὸ πλῆθος αὐτῶν, καὶ καραγὸς οὐκ ἀκο-
λουθῇ τοῖς ἡμετέροις, μὴ ἐπιτηδεύῃς εἰς ἴσον καὶ ἐπίπεδον τόπον παρατάσσεσθαι, ἀλλὰ μᾶλλον εἰς τόπους δυσχερεῖς καὶ δυσβάτους, τουτέστιν ἢ ἑλώδεις
καὶ παλματώδεις ἢ πετρώδεις καὶ ἀνωμάλους ἢ δασεῖς.

78. Φροντίσεις δὲ καὶ τάς, ὡς εἰκός, κατὰ τοῦ νώτου καὶ τῶν πλαγίων
540 ἐπελεύσεις, καθὰ πολλάκις εἰρήκαμεν, τὸ ἀσφαλίζεσθαι διὰ βίγλας. ἔχεις δὲ καὶ
ὀλίγους σκουτάτους εἰς τὰ ἄκρα τῶν ἁμαξῶν καὶ εἰς τὸ μέσον αὐτῶν ἵνα, ἐὰν
χρεία γένηται, ἐπιβοηθοῦσιν ἐκ τῶν, ὡς εἰκός, βουλομένων παρενοχλεῖν ἐχθρῶν
ἢ αὐταῖς ἢ τῇ παρατάξει, καὶ τοῖς καβαλλαρίοις αὐτῆς.

79. Ἐὰν δέ ποτε δυνηθῇς, ἀπληκευόντων τῶν πολεμίων καὶ ἔτι ἀκαταστάτων
545 ὄντων, κλέψαι τὸν πόλεμον καὶ τότε συμβαλεῖν αὐτοῖς, πάντως ἂν τὰ μέγιστα
βλάψεις αὐτούς.

---

520 τὰς² MW καὶ AVBE    522 ἢ¹ MW ἢ ἐμπείρους AVBE    524 ἐφ' ᾧ MW ὥστε AVBE
525 σκουτάτους MW σκουτάτους AVBE    529 ἁμαξηλάται AVBE ἁμαξελάται MW
530 ῥίπτεσθαι MW ῥίπτεσθαι προσήκει AVBE    532 ὑπὸ MW ἀπὸ AVBE    534 ἢ καὶ MW
ἤτοι AVBE    535 ἐστι MAVBE ἐστιν W    535–536 καὶ²…ἀκολουθῇ MW αἱ ἅμαξαι δὲ οὐκ
ἀκολουθῶσι AVBE    536 ἐπίπεδον MW ὁμαλὸν AVBE    537 δυσχερεῖς MW τραχεῖς AVBE
| ἑλώδεις MW ὑλώδεις AVBE    538 ἢ² MW καὶ AVBE    539 κατὰ…νώτου MW ἐκ τῶν
ὄπισθεν AVBE    540 τὸ MW τοῦ AVBE | βίγλας MW βιγλῶν AVBE | ἔχεις MW ἔχειν
AVBE    541 σκουτάτους MW σκουτάτους AVBE | ἁμαξιῶν MW ἁμαξῶν AVBE
543 αὐτῆς MW αὐτοῖς AVBE    545 συμβαλεῖν MW συμβάλλειν AVBE

uted along the entire distance with the most useful ones positioned on the flanks.

75. The drivers must be able to throw javelins, slings, axes, metal darts, or arrows. Form the rest of the baggage in a line to the inside of the wagons. The area between the wagons and the battle line must be kept clear so that in case the heavy-armed soldiers, either mounted or on foot, have to split up into the double phalanx because of pressure on the wagons, the wagons will not be an obstacle or cause disorder.

76. If a strong, hostile force harasses the wagons from behind, and the drivers cannot hold them off, and it is not likely that the men making up the double phalanx can do so, then throw out a few caltrops. But if you do throw them out, you must make sure that the army does not return by the same route but by another, so it will not suffer harm from the caltrops.

77. And we enjoin this upon you, O general, that on the day when the infantry or even the mixed formation faces battle, if the enemy has a large cavalry force, more numerous than ours, and the baggage train is not accompanying us, do not draw up your formation in open or level terrain. Line up instead on rugged, impassable ground, that is, swampy, muddy, rocky, uneven, or thickly wooded.

78. Take care, as we have frequently remarked, to protect yourself by means of patrols against likely attacks from the rear and the flanks. Post a few heavy-armed men to the sides of the wagons and in between them, so that, when needed, they may come to assist them against the enemy seeking to harass the wagons or the battle line and its cavalry.

79. If, at some time when the enemy are setting up camp and are still in disarray, you are able to bring about battle by stealth, then charge into them and you will certainly inflict the greatest amount of harm on them.

80. Πολλοὺς δὲ καβαλλαρίους ἐν ταῖς πεζικαῖς μάχαις μὴ βάλλειν, ἀλλ᾿ ὀλίγους κατὰ τῶν ἄκρων τῆς παρατάξεως· ἄχρι τριῶν ἢ τεσσάρων χιλιάδων λωρικάτων καὶ χρησίμους τοὺς ὀφείλοντας, εἰ καιρὸς γένηται, τοὺς τρεπομέν-
550 ους τῶν ἐναντίων ἐπιτίθεσθαι καὶ διώκειν. τὸ γὰρ τούτου πλέον ἐν συμμέτρῳ πεζικῷ οὐκ ἀσφαλές.

81. Ἐὰν δὲ οἱ ἐχθροὶ καβαλλάριοι ὄντες ἐδειλίασαν πρὸς τὴν πεζικὴν μάχην, καὶ πολλοί εἰσιν οἱ καβαλλάριοι ἡμῶν, ὀλίγοι δὲ οἱ πεζοί, τοὺς μὲν καβαλλαρί-ους τάσσειν εἰς τὰ ἔμπροσθεν μέρη, ὄπισθεν δὲ τὴν πεζικὴν παράταξιν ἐπακο-
555 λουθεῖν ἐν τάξει ἀπὸ ἑνὸς ἢ δευτέρου μιλίου τῶν καβαλλαρίων. καὶ παραγγεί-λεις τοῖς καβαλλαρίοις τοῦ διαστήματος τούτου μὴ ἀφίστασθαι τῆς πεζικῆς παρατάξεως. εἰ δὲ καὶ βαρηθῶσιν ὑπὸ τῶν ἐχθρῶν, διὰ τῶν πλαγίων καὶ τοῦ νώτου τῆς παρατάξεως, ἤγουν ὄπισθεν αὐτῆς προτρέχειν, καὶ μὴ διὰ ὄψεως ἵνα μὴ διαλύσωσιν αὐτήν.

560 82. Ἐν δὲ τῇ ἡμέρᾳ τῆς συμβολῆς μὴ σπουδάζειν τὴν πεζικὴν παράταξιν, ὥς μοι καὶ πρόσθεν εἴρηται, ἐπὶ πολὺ διάστημα κινεῖν περαιτέρω δύο μιλίων ἔξωθεν τοῦ φοσσάτου, ἵνα μὴ τῷ βάρει καὶ τῇ ὁπλίσει συντρίβηται, ἀλλ᾿ ἐὰν ὑπερτίθεν-ται οἱ ἐχθροὶ τὴν τοῦ πολέμου συμβολήν, καθέζεσθαι καὶ ἀναπαύεσθαι μέχρις οὗ μέλλωσιν ἐγγίζειν.

565 83. Εἰ δὲ καιρὸς θέρους ἐστὶν καὶ τὰς κασσίδας αὐτῶν ἐπαίρειν ἵνα διαπνέ-ωνται αἱ κεφαλαὶ αὐτῶν. οἴνου δὲ ἐν τοῖς τοιούτοις καιροῖς μεταλαμβάνειν τοὺς στρατιώτας οὐ χρή, ἵνα μὴ ἀναζέων οὗτος σκοτώσῃ αὐτούς, ἀλλὰ ὕδωρ ἐν ταῖς ἁμάξαις βαστάζειν καὶ καθ᾿ ἕνα διδόναι τοῖς δεομένοις ὥς εἰσιν ἐν τῇ παρατάξει αὐτῶν.

570 84. Πρὸ δὲ τοῦ καιροῦ τοῦ πολέμου | δεῖ καὶ αὐτὸν τὸν πεζικὸν στρατὸν 344 ὥσπερ καὶ ἐπὶ τῶν καβαλλαρίων ἐνέγκαι ἐν ἡμέρᾳ μίᾳ ὁμοῦ συνηγμένον. καὶ εἰ μὲν οἴδασιν οἱ στρατιῶται τὰ διὰ τοῦ νόμου μανδάτα, ἤγουν τὰ στρατιωτικὰ ἐπιτίμια, ὑπομνῆσαι αὐτοῖς ἄπαντα· εἰ δὲ μή γε, εἰπεῖν αὐτοῖς διὰ τῶν ἰδικῶν αὐτῶν ἀρχόντων ἰδίως ἑκάστῳ τάγματι, ἅπερ εἴρηται ἡμῖν ἐν τοῖς ἀνωτέρω

---

549–550 τοὺς τρεπομένους MW τοῖς τρεπομένοις AVBE   550 διώκειν MW ἐπιδιώκειν AVBE   551 πεζικῷ MW πεζικῷ στρατῷ AVBE   556 καβαλλαρίοις MW καβαλλαρίοις πλέον τούτου AVBE   557 καὶ¹ MW om. AVBE   557–558 καὶ²…προτρέχειν MW διατρέχοντας ὄπισθεν τῆς πεζικῆς παρατάξεως γίνεσθαι AVBE   560 σπουδάζειν MW σπουδάζειν πλέον τῶν δύο (β′ B) μιλίων περιπατεῖν AVBE   560–561 ὥς…μιλίων MW om. AVBE   562 καὶ WAVBE om. M   563 καθέζεσθαι MW καθέζεσθαι αὐτοὺς AVBE   572 μανδάτα…τὰ² MW om. AVBE   573 αὐτοῖς¹ MW αὐτοὺς AVBE | ἰδικῶν MW ἰδίων AVBE

80. Do not send large numbers of cavalry into an infantry battle, but just a few on the wings of the battle line. There should be no more than three or four thousand well-armed and effective horsemen. If the opportunity presents itself, they are to attack and pursue the enemy who have turned to flight. More than this number in an average-sized infantry force is not safe.

81. If the enemy, although on horseback, are hesitant to engage the infantry in battle and we have a large number of cavalry but few infantry, station the cavalry in the front lines. Have the infantry follow them in formation about one or two miles behind the cavalry. Order the cavalry not to separate itself further than this distance from the infantry formation. Then, if they come under pressure from the enemy, they should ride on through the flanks and the rear of the battle line, that is, behind it, and not through the front so they might not break it up.

82. On the day of battle, as I have previously remarked, do not attempt to have the infantry formation march outside its camp for a long distance, further than two miles, so the men will not be worn out by the weight of their armament. If the enemy puts off attacking in battle, have your men sit down and relax until the enemy are about to draw close.

83. If it is summertime, have them take off their helmets so their heads may breathe a bit. At such a time the soldiers ought not to partake of wine because it might warm them up and make them dizzy. But carry water in the wagons and distribute it to those requesting it as they stand in formation.

84. Before engaging in battle you must, just as you did with the cavalry, bring the infantry army all together on one day. If the soldiers already know what is mandated by law, that is, the military punishments, then remind them of it all. If they do not know them, have each commanding officer announce to the men in his own tagma those prescriptions that we gave earlier in this book

575 κειμένοις, περὶ τῶν τοῖς ἁμαρτάνουσι στρατιώταις κειμένων ἐπιτιμίων ἐν μάχης
καιρῷ. καὶ ταῦτα γινώσκοντας οὕτως ἐλθεῖν ἐπὶ τὴν παράταξιν.

85. Οὐκ ἄχρηστον δέ σοι, ὦ στρατηγέ, ὡς ἐν ἐπιτόμῳ καὶ τὴν τῶν παλαιοτέ-
ρων τακτικῶν ὑποδεῖξαι διατύπωσιν, ἣν ἐν τοῖς πεζικοῖς τε καὶ τοῖς συμμίκτοις
ἐποιοῦντο στρατεύμασιν, ὅτε μάλιστα καὶ πολλοῦ εὐπόρουν στρατοῦ.

580 86. Τὴν γὰρ ἅπασαν πεζικὴν στρατιὰν εἰς δέκα ἓξ χιλιάδας καὶ τριακοσίους
ὀγδοήκοντα τέσσαρας ἄνδρας ἐμέτρουν ὡς τοῦ ἀριθμοῦ τούτου ἐκ πολλῶν
τακτικῶν ἀριθμῶν συνηγμένου καὶ ἀρκοῦντος εἰς τελείαν παράταξιν, καὶ δυναμένου διαιρεῖσθαι καὶ καταμερίζεσθαι ἴσως ἀπὸ τοῦ τοσούτου πλήθους μέχρι
καὶ ἑνός, καὶ τὸ μὲν ὅλον τοῦ στρατοῦ ἐκάλουν τελείαν φάλαγγα. αὕτη δὲ ἡ
585 φάλαγξ παρ' αὐτοῖς εἰς δύο διαιρεῖται μέρη διχοτομουμένη ἐξ ἴσου ἀπὸ τοῦ
μετώπου τῆς φάλαγγος ἤτοι τῆς παρατάξεως μέχρι τῆς οὐρᾶς διὰ τοῦ βάθους,
ἤτοι τοῦ πάχους τῆς τομῆς διερχομένης. καὶ τὸ μὲν ἥμισυ μέρος δεξιὸν καλεῖται
κέρας καὶ κεφαλή, ἐν ᾧ ,ηρθβ´ ἄνδρες εἶναι ὁρίζονται· τὸ δὲ ἕτερον ἥμισυ μέρος
ἀριστερὸν λέγεται κέρας καὶ οὐρά, ἐν ᾧ καὶ αὐτὸ κατὰ τὸ ἴσον μέτρον τοῦ
590 δεξιοῦ τάττονται ὁμοίως ὀκτάκις χίλιοι ἑκατὸν ἐνενήκοντα δύο. ἡ δὲ διὰ μέσου
γινομένη διχοτομία, ἤγουν ὁ κενὸς τόπος, ὀμφαλὸς καλεῖται καὶ στόμα τῆς
φάλαγγος, ἐν ᾧ καὶ ἡ τοῦ στρατηγοῦ γίνεται στάσις, πρὸς τὸ ἐπιβλέπειν τὰ ἐν
τῷ πολέμῳ πραττόμενα, καὶ διακυβερνᾶν, ὡς ἐνδέχεται. αὕτη δὲ ἡ πᾶσα παράταξις ὁπλῖται καλοῦνται, διά τε σκουταρίων τελείων καὶ κονταρίων καὶ σπαθίων
595 καὶ τῶν ἄλλων ὅπλων περιπεφραγμένοι, βαρυτέραν ἔχοντες ὅπλισιν τοῦ ὅλου
στρατοῦ.

87. Ὄπισθεν δὲ ταύτης τῆς διπλῆς τῶν ὁπλιτῶν παρατάξεως τάσσεται ἡ τῶν
ψιλῶν λεγομένων στρατιωτῶν ἐλαφροτέραν ὅπλισιν ἐχόντων τῆς πρώτης
παρατάξεως, διὰ τὸ εὐχερῶς ἔνθα βούλονται τρέχειν, ἐν οἷς εἰσι καὶ ἀκοντισταὶ
600 καὶ τοξόται καὶ σφενδονισταί. τούτων δὲ ἡ παράταξις εἶναι ὀφείλει ἡμίσεια τὸν
ἀριθμὸν τῆς πρώτης παρατάξεως ἤγουν ,ηρθβ´. ἐφεξῆς δὲ ταύτης ὄπισθεν ἡ τῶν
καβαλλαρίων παράταξις τάσσεται καθωπλισμένων καὶ τούτων δὲ ὁ ἀριθμὸς

---

575 τῶν MW τῶν κειμένων AVBE | κειμένων MW om. AVBE   577 ἐπιτόμῳ MW συντόμῳ
AVBE   584 τοῦ AVBE om. MW   585 αὐτοῖς MW αὐτοῦ AVBE   588 ,ηρθβ´ De ,ϛρθβ´ M
χιλιάδες ὀκτὼ καὶ ἑκατὸν ἐνενήκοντα δύο WA   590 ὀκτάκις... δύο M ὀκτάκις χίλιοι ἑκατὸν
ἐνενήκοντα δύο WA   591 ὁ... τόπος MW τὸ διαχώρισμα AVBE   595 ὅλου MW ἄλλου
AVBE   599 εὐχερῶς MW εὐκόλως AVBE | τρέχειν MW διατρέχειν AVBE
600 σφενδονισταί MW σφενδονῆται AVBE   600–601 εἶναι... πρώτης MW τὸν ἥμίση
ἀριθμὸν ἔχειν ὀφείλει τῆς προτέρας AVBE   601 ,ηρθβ´ De χιλιάδες ,ηϛθβ´ M χιλιάδες ὀκτὼ
καὶ ἐνενήκοντα δύο WA

about the punishments decreed for soldiers who commit offenses during combat. When the troops have been informed about these matters, then proceed to form your line.

85. It may not be useless, O general, to present to you, in summary fashion, the regulations laid down by the ancient tactical authors concerning infantry and mixed armies, especially when they had the advantage of a large army.

86. They numbered the entire infantry army at 16,384 men because this number is based on a consensus of the numbers given in many tactical books and is sufficient for a complete battle line.[16] It can be divided and apportioned in equal numbers from such a large multitude down to a single man. The ancients referred to the entirety of the army as a perfect phalanx. This phalanx was divided by them into two sections and was split into two equal parts from the front of the phalanx, that is, the battle line, down to the rear end according to the depth or the thickness of the cut going through it. One half of the division was called the right horn and the head, in which regulations called for 8,192 men. The other half of the division was called the left horn and the tail, in which the same number of men is stationed as in the right division, 8,192. The area of this split down the middle, the empty space, is called the navel and the mouth of the phalanx. This is where the general takes his stand so that he may oversee what is taking place in the battle and manage things as best he can. This entire battle line is <sometimes> referred to as the hoplites because they are armed with full-sized shields, lances, swords, and other weapons, the heaviest arms in the whole army.

87. Behind this double battle line of heavy-armed soldiers is formed that of the troops called light armed, who have lighter armament than those in the first battle line, because their purpose is to move about there rapidly and easily. Among these are javelin hurlers, archers, and slingers. This battle line ought to comprise half the number of the first line, that is, 8,192. Right behind this line

---

16. Cf. Asclepiodotus 2.10; Aelian 8.3 among others. Much of §§86–90 is taken from Aelian. See Haldon, *Commentary.*

ἥμισυ πάλιν ἔχει τῆς τῶν λεγομένων ψιλῶν παρατάξεως, ἤτοι τετρακισχιλίους ἐνενήκοντα ἕξ.

605    88. Καὶ τοὺς μὲν πεζοὺς εἰς τέσσαρα μέρη ἐποίουν συντάσσοντες ἅμα καὶ τοὺς ὁπλίτας καὶ τοὺς ψιλούς, ὡς ἂν ἡ χρεία ἀπήτει, εἴτε παρὰ τὰ πλάγια τῶν ὁπλιτῶν τοὺς ψιλοὺς εἰς δύο ἑτέρας παρατάξεις εἴτε ἔμπροσθεν | ἢ ὡς ἂν ἐδόκει   344ᵛ τῷ στρατηγῷ χρήσιμον.

       89. Τοὺς δὲ καβαλλαρίους εἰς δύο διεμέριζον, ἔνθεν κἀκεῖθεν ἢ ἐπὶ νώτου
610   τῶν πεζῶν ἤγουν ὄπισθεν ἢ εἰς τὰ πλάγια ἢ ὡς ἂν ἡ χρεία ἀπήτει. ὁ γὰρ στρατηγὸς οὐχ ὡς βούλεται, ἀλλὰ μᾶλλον ὡς ἀναγκάζεται, οὕτως καὶ τάσσει τὸ στράτευμα. πρὸς γὰρ τὸ ἀντιπολέμιον καβαλλαρικόν, καὶ τὸ ἴδιον στήσει ἵνα εὐρυ-
χωρίαν ἔχοντες μὴ ἐμποδίζωνται πράττειν ὅσα δεῖ ποιεῖν τοὺς καβαλλαρίους εἰς
τὴν τῶν πεζῶν βοήθειαν, εἴτε κατὰ πρόσωπον εἴτε ἐκ πλαγίου εἴτε ὄπισθεν κατὰ
615   τοῦ νώτου.

       90. Κρεῖττον δὲ ποιήσει τις ἐὰν τῶν λεγομένων ψιλῶν τὴν παράταξιν
πρώτην τάξῃ τῆς τῶν ὁπλιτῶν παρατάξεως, ἢ χρείας οὕτω καλούσης ἐκ πλαγίων. εἰ γὰρ μέσοι ταγῶσιν ἀνενέργητα αὐτῶν τὰ ὅπλα γίνεται· οἱ γὰρ ἀκοντίζοντες ἢ τοξεύοντες ἢ σφενδονοῦντες ἀναγκάζονται εἰς ὕψος πέμπειν καὶ μᾶλλον
620   τοὺς ἰδίους βλάπτουσιν ἢ τοὺς ἐναντίους. καὶ γὰρ τὰ βέλη κατὰ κεφαλῆς
ἐνεχθήσονται τῶν ἔμπροσθεν. οἱ δὲ σφενδονοῦντες ἐμποδισθήσονται τὰς
χεῖρας αὐτῶν μὴ δυνάμενοι τὴν σφενδόνην ἑλίσσειν.

       91. Ἐὰν δὲ οἱ πολέμιοι πλέον ἔχωσι ψιλοὺς ὑπὲρ τοὺς ἡμετέρους, τότε τοὺς
ὁπλίτας ἤγουν τοὺς πρωτοστάτας, ἔμπροσθεν δεῖ τάσσεσθαι ἔχοντας σκουτά-
625   ρια μεγάλα ἐπιμήκη, ἅπερ λέγουσι θυρεούς, ὥστε σκέπειν ὅλα τὰ σώματα,
ἀνδρὸς ἔχοντα μῆκος. οἱ δὲ μετὰ τούτους ὄπισθεν τασσόμενοι καὶ μέχρι τῶν
ὀπίσω ὑπὲρ κεφαλῆς ἄραντες τοὺς θυρεοὺς οὕτως προσερχέσθωσαν, ἕως ἂν
ἐντὸς γένωνται τῶν ῥιπτομένων σαγιττῶν ἢ ῥικταρίων. οὕτως γὰρ ὡς εἰπεῖν
κεραμωθέντες οὐδὲν πάθωσι κακὸν ἀπὸ τῶν ῥιπτομένων παρὰ τῶν πολεμίων
630   βελῶν.

---

603 τετρακισχιλίους MW τετρακισχιλίων AVBE   604 ἐνενήκοντα ἕξ De ἐνενηκονταἑξ
WAVBE τεσσαράκοντα ἕξ M   607 τοὺς ψιλοὺς M τοὺς πεζοὺς W om. AVBE | δύο MW
δύο ἑτέρας AVBE | παρατάξεις MW παρατάξεις διαιροῦντες αὐτοὺς AVBE   609 ἐπὶ νώτου
MW ὄπισθεν AVBE   610 ἤγουν ὄπισθεν MW om. AVBE   612 ἀντιπολέμιον MW
πολέμιον AVBE   617 οὕτω MW om. AVBE   619 ἢ σφενδονοῦντες MW om. AVBE
623 πλέον MW πλείονας AVBE   624 ἤγουν…πρωτοστάτας MW om. AVBE
625 ὥστε…σώματα MW om. AVBE   626 μῆκος MW μήκος ὥστε σκέπειν ὅλον τὸ σῶμα
AVBE   628 ἐντὸς MW ἔσωθεν AVBE | ῥιπτομένων MW βαλλομένων AVBE | ῥικταρίων
MW ῥιπταρίων AVBE

the cavalry units, well armed, take their position. The number of these is again half of that of the line of so-called light-armed troops, that is, 4,096.

88. The ancients divided the foot soldiers into four divisions, drawing up heavy-armed and light-armed troops together, either arranging the light-armed troops in two other battle lines along the flanks of the heavy-armed, as the situation requires, or else in front or wherever the commander thinks is most effective.

89. They also divided the cavalry in two, here and there, to the rear of the infantry, that is, behind them or on the flanks or as need may demand. The general organizes his army, not as he wishes, but as he is compelled to do. When confronted by an enemy cavalry force, he will station his own cavalry so they cover a wide area and will not encounter obstacles in doing what they have to do in support of the infantry, either in front or on the flank or behind to the rear.

90. A person will do better if he positions the so-called light-armed troops for battle in front of the battle line of the heavy-armed troops or, if need calls for it, on their flanks. If they are drawn up in the middle, their weapons are completely ineffective. When hurling javelins or shooting arrows or using their slings, they are forced to shoot on high and are more likely to injure their own men rather than the enemy. Their missiles will land on the heads of the men in front of them, whereas the slingers will not have room for their hands and will be unable to whirl their slings about.

91. If the enemy have more light-armed troops than we do, then you must position the heavy-armed ones, that is, the protostatai, in the front ranks. They should have large, oblong shields, called thyreoi, which cover the entire body, being as tall as a man. The men stationed behind these down to the rear lines should raise these oblong shields over their heads and in this very manner march forward until they come within range of the arrows or other missiles being fired. For with this kind of a roof, so to speak, they will suffer no harm from the missiles fired by the enemy.

92. Εἰ δὲ καὶ ἔνθεν κἀκεῖθεν ἡ παρὰ τῶν ψιλῶν βοήθεια πάρεστιν, οὗτοι πρῶτοι, πρὶν ἢ γένηται ἡ συμβολή, καὶ σαγίττας καὶ ῥικτάρια ῥίψωσι κατὰ τῶν πολεμίων, ἢ καὶ μετὰ τὴν συμβολὴν τῆς μάχης ἐκ πλαγίων τῆς τῶν ἐχθρῶν παρατάξεως ἐπιτιθέντες πεμπέτωσαν τὰ βέλη κατὰ αὐτῶν, ἵνα συνελαυνόμενοι
635 καὶ ἀπὸ τῶν πλαγίων θορυβοῦνται, καὶ ἐλαττοῦνται πρὸς τοὺς ἔμπροσθεν. ἐὰν δὲ παράκειται ὀχύρωμα, τοῦτο μᾶλλον τοὺς ψιλοὺς βοηθήσει· βάλλοντες γὰρ τὰ βέλη κατὰ τῶν πολεμίων καὶ εἰς αὐτὸ κατατρέχοντες ἀφοβώτεροι γίνονται. οἷον εἴτε κρημνώδης τόπος εἴτε ποταμοῦ ὄχθη ἢ καὶ βουνὸς ὑπερανέχων ἢ καὶ ἕτερόν ἐστιν ὀχύρωμα.
640 93. Ὀφείλει δὲ εἶναι διάστημα εἰς τὰς παρατάξεις ἵνα ἐὰν οὕτω συμβῇ καὶ οἱ ψιλοὶ ἐκκενώσωσιν τὰ βέλη αὐτῶν, καὶ οὔπω ἐγένετο ἡ συμβολὴ ἀλλ᾽ ἔτι προάγουσιν οἱ πολέμιοι, τότε ἐπιστρέψωσιν οἱ ψιλοὶ μετὰ εὐταξίας, καὶ διελθόντες μέσην τὴν φάλαγγα ἀταράχως ἐπὶ τὰ ὄπισθεν διασωθῶσιν. οὐ γάρ ἐστιν ἀσφαλὲς κυκλεύειν αὐτοὺς ἔξωθεν τὸ στράτευμα καὶ οὕτω διέρχεσθαι, ἵνα μὴ
645 παρὰ τῶν ἐχθρῶν ἐρχομένων μέσοι γενόμενοι διαπέσωσιν· οὔτε δὲ πάλιν εἰς τὰ ὅπλα μέσους | ἐμπίπτειν, πεπυκνωμένης οὔσης τῆς τάξεως, καὶ οὕτω βιάζεσθαι. 345 ἑτέρας δὲ τάξεις ἔχειν ἐνόπλους καὶ ἑτοίμους ἵνα ὅταν οἱ ψιλοὶ τὰ ὅπλα κενώσωσι, τότε ἐκεῖνοι ἀντεισέλθωσιν καὶ τὴν χρείαν ἐκείνων τελέσωσιν.

94. Ἐπειδὴ δὲ τὸ πάχος τῆς παρατάξεως πρὸς τὰς χρείας ἐκτεινομένης αὐτῆς
650 ἐπὶ μῆκος συστέλλεται καὶ λεπτύνεται, δέον ἐστὶν μὴ ἐκτείνειν τὴν παράταξιν τοσοῦτον, ὥστε πᾶσαν ἀσθενῆ καὶ χωρὶς βάθους ποιῆσαι, ἤγουν κατὰ τὸ πάχος, φοβούμενον τὰς κυκλώσεις. συμβαίνει γὰρ τοὺς πολεμίους ταχὺ διακόψαι αὐτὴν καὶ δίοδον ποιῆσαι, καὶ μηκέτι ἀπὸ ἔμπροσθεν μόνον ἐνεργεῖν τὴν κύκλωσιν, ἀλλὰ καὶ διὰ τοῦ μέσου διελθόντας ἀπὸ ὄπισθεν εὑρεθῆναι, καὶ οὕτω
655 ποιῆσαι τὴν βλάβην. τοῦτο δὲ δεῖ τὸν στρατηγὸν μὴ μόνον φυλάττεσθαι ἵνα μὴ πάθῃ, ἀλλὰ καὶ ζητεῖν ὅπως τοιοῦτον ποιήσῃ κατὰ τῶν πολεμίων.

---

632 ῥικτάρια MW ῥιπτάρια AVBE | ῥίψωσι MW ῥίψουσι AVBE   633 πολεμίων MW ἐναντίων AVBE | συμβολὴν MW συμπλοκὴν AVBE   634 ἐπιτιθέντες De ἐπιτεθέντες MW ἐπιπεσόντων AVBE | κατὰ MW κατ᾽ AVBE   635 θορυβοῦνται MW θορυβῶνται AVBE | ἐλαττοῦνται MW ἐλαττῶνται AVBE   636 τοὺς ψιλοὺς MW τοῖς ψιλοῖς AVBE   639 ἕτερόν MW ἕτερόν τι AVBE   640 οὕτω MW οὕτως AVBE   641 ἐκκενώσωσιν MW ἐκκενώσωσι AVBE   643 ἀταράχως AVBE ταράχως MW   644 οὕτω MW οὕτως AVBE   646 οὕτω MW οὕτως AVBE   647–648 κενώσωσι MVBE κενώσωσιν WA   648 τελέσωσιν MW πληρώσωσιν AVBE   649 ἐκτεινομένης αὐτῆς MW trsp. AVBE   651 κατὰ τὸ MW ἔχουσαν AVBE   653 δίοδον MW πάροδον AVBE   656 τοιοῦτον MW τοιοῦτόν τι AVBE

92. If the light-armed troops provide support here and there, then, before contact is made, these go first and fire arrows and short spears against the enemy. After the enemy have been engaged, moreover, they continue their attack against the enemy's battle line from the flank, firing their missiles against them. Under attack also from the sides, the foe will be confused and less effective against the men in front of them. If there is some kind of fortification nearby, it will be to the advantage of the light-armed troops. They shoot their missiles against the enemy and, without any fear, race right up to the obstacle, whether it be a precipitous place or the banks of a river or a mountain rising up above them or some other obstacle.

93. There must be a distance between the battle lines. If it happens that the light-armed troops have discharged all their missiles and the enemy has not yet been engaged but is still moving forward, then the light-armed troops should turn about in good order and pass undisturbed through the middle of the phalanx to a secure place in the rear. It is not safe for them to circle about outside the main force and so to pass through, for they may be caught in the middle by the advancing enemy and be killed. Then too, the very large number of men in the middle may be so tightly packed together and under such pressure that they may fall upon their own weapons. Have the other formations armed and ready so that, when the light-armed troops have discharged their weapons, then these may march out in their place and perform the task assigned to them.

94. Since the thickness of the battle line, when it is expanded to meet certain contingencies, is reduced and made thinner along its length, it is necessary not to extend it, because of fear of encirclement, to such a degree as to make it extremely weak and without depth, that is, in thickness. It may happen that the enemy will quickly cut through it, making a sort of passageway. They will then put the encirclement into action, not only from the front but also by advancing through the middle and, reaching the rear, they will cause a great deal of damage. The general must not only be on his guard against suffering this but he must also seek ways in which he can do the same sort of thing to the enemy.

95. Πάλιν δὲ μὴ οὕτως πυκνῶσαι τὴν παράταξιν εἰς πάχος, ὥστε εὐκόλως κυκλώσεις παθεῖν παρὰ τῶν πολεμίων, ἀλλὰ μᾶλλον καὶ τοὺς ἐκ πλαγίων καὶ τοὺς εἰς τὸ ὄπισθεν ἑστῶτας στρατιώτας κατὰ τὸ ἴσον ὁπλίσαι τῶν πρωτοστα-
660 τῶν. οὗτοι γὰρ καὶ δύνανται τὰς κυκλώσεις μᾶλλον ἀπαντᾶν τῶν πολεμίων.

96. Σοφοῦ δὲ καὶ φρονίμου στρατηγοῦ τὸ εἰς τοιούτους τόπους παρατάσ-
σεσθαι, ἐὰν ἄρα καὶ ἐπιτύχῃ τοῦ σκοποῦ, ἐν οἷς οὔτε κυκλώσεις οὔτε ἄλλο τι τοιοῦτον δύναται γίνεσθαι, ὡς ἀνωτέρω ἡμῖν δεδήλωται. πολλὰ γὰρ ἰσχύει φρόνησις στρατηγοῦ ἐν καιρῷ πολέμου ἐφευρίσκουσα τὰ συμφέροντα ὅπερ τῆς
665 ἄνωθεν τοῦ Θεοῦ ῥοπῆς καὶ εὐμενείας δῶρον ἐγὼ καλῶ καὶ ἐπίσταμαι τοῖς ἀξίοις τοῦ Θεοῦ διὰ τὴν αὐτῶν ἀρετὴν παρεχόμενον.

97. Καί ποτέ τις ἐν καιρῷ μάχης τῶν πολεμίων προτερευόντων ψεῦδος ἐφήμισε βοήσας· "τέθνηκεν ὁ τῶν πολεμίων στρατηγός." ταύτης δὲ τῆς φωνῆς δοθείσης, ἐπειδὴ ὁ καιρὸς ὀξὺς ὢν οὐκ ἐδίδου ταχέως τὸ δέον πᾶσι νοεῖν, οἱ μὲν
670 πολέμιοι πόρρω τοῦ ἰδίου ὄντες στρατηγοῦ, οἱ μὲν ἀπέγνωσαν, οἱ δὲ τοῦ φημί-
σαντος στρατηγοῦ θάρσος ἀναλαβόντες, ὡς ἀληθοῦς τῆς φήμης, εὐψυχότεροι ἠγωνίζοντο. καὶ οὕτω τῆς σεσοφισμένης φήμης κατισχυσάσης τὴν νίκην ὁ φημίσας ἤρατο. οὕτως ἀγχίνοια ἐπικαίρως τῶν πραγμάτων ἐπιλαμβανομένη πολλάκις κατεστρατήγησε σοφισαμένη τοὺς ἀντιπάλους.

675 98. Εἴρηταί τε τοῖς νεωτέροις περὶ τοῦ μὴ λαμπρὰν φαίνεσθαι τοῖς πολεμίοις τὴν σὴν παράταξιν, ἀλλὰ κρύπτειν τῶν ὅπλων τὴν στίλψιν ἕως αὐτῆς τῆς διὰ χειρῶν συμβολῆς, διὰ τὴν ἐπικρατοῦσαν τοῖς ἔθνεσι φήμην. Ὀνήσανδρος δὲ καὶ αὐτὸς στρατηγικὸν συντάξας λόγον οὐχ οὕτω λέγειν δοκεῖ, ἀλλὰ μᾶλλον λαμπρὰν κελεύει τὴν παράταξιν φαίνεσθαι πρὸς τὴν τῶν πολεμίων παράταξιν.
680 ἐμοὶ δὲ δοκεῖ ἢ ἀγνοεῖν ἐκεῖνον τότε τὴν τοιαύτην φήμην ὡς νεωτέραν γενο-
μένην ἢ τὰ μὲν πρὸ τῆς συμβολῆς ἀφεῖναι, κατ' αὐτὴν δὲ τὴν συμβολήν, καὶ αὐτὸς σὺν τοῖς | νεωτέροις καὶ ἡμῖν ὁμοίως παραγγέλλει λαμπρὰ τὰ ὅπλα 345ᵛ
δεικνύειν ἀθρόως. κατάπληξις γὰρ μᾶλλον γίνεται, οὐχ ὅταν μακρόθεν ἐρχο-

675–680 Onas. 28.

658 κυκλώσεις MW κύκλωσιν AVBE   659 εἰς τὸ MW ἐκ τῶν AVBE   664 τὰ συμφέροντα MW τὸ συμφέρον AVBE   667–668 καί…βοήσας MW πολλάκις δὲ προσήκει καὶ ψεύδη φημίζειν ὅτι AVBE   668–674 ταύτης…ἀντιπάλους MW τοῦτο γὰρ ἀκουόμενον τοῖς μὲν ἡμετέροις προθυμίαν ἐνεποίησεν τοῖς δὲ πολεμίοις δειλίαν ἐνέβαλεν τὸ γὰρ ὀξὺ τοῦ καιροῦ οὐ δίδωσιν αὐτοῖς ἀκριβές τι μανθάνειν περὶ τοῦ αὐτῶν στρατηγοῦ καὶ οὕτως πολλάκις φρόνησις στρατηγοῦ τοὺς ἐναντίους κατεστρατήγησεν AVBE   676 στίλψιν MW λαμπρότητα AVBE   677 χειρῶν AVBE χειρὸς MW | ὀνήσανδρος MW ὀνόσανδρος AVBE   678 συντάξας λόγον MW trsp. AVBE | οὕτω MW οὕτως AVBE   679 παράταξιν¹ MW κατάπληξιν AVBE   681 ἀφεῖναι MW καταλιπεῖν AVBE

95. Again, do not tighten up the thickness of the battle line so that it will easily suffer encirclement by the enemy but rather arm the soldiers on the flanks and those stationed in the rear in the same way as those in the front ranks. These men will be able to deal with any enemy encirclement.

96. It is the mark of a wise and prudent general, if he is to attain his goals, to form his battle lines in such places in which encirclements or anything of that sort cannot be set up, as we have made clear above. In time of war, the prudent discretion of the general is able to discover many things that are beneficial. I call this a gift of the intervention and good disposition of God above and I know that he bestows it upon those whom he deems worthy because of their virtue.

97. Once, during a battle in which the enemy held the advantage, a person made use of falsehood. He cried out: "The enemy general is dead." This cry was made at a critical moment and did not allow everyone to think quickly about what they had to do. Some of the enemy were at a distance from their own general and some of them despaired, whereas those with the general who had shouted the cry took up courage again, <believing> the rumor to be true, and they continued the struggle in excellent spirits. Thus, the man shouted and achieved victory on the strength of a fabricated rumor. By shrewdly taking timely advantage of the situation, a stratagem has frequently out-generaled the adversaries.

98. More recent authorities advise not letting your battle line appear shiny to the enemy but, according to the tradition prevailing among foreign peoples, you should hide the shining of the weapons until you come to close quarters. But Onasander himself, in compiling his book on strategy, does not appear to say this.[17] Rather, he prescribes that the battle line should appear shining in comparison to that of the enemy. But it seems to me that, either he was unaware of such a statement in his day, since it was really of more recent origin, or else <his advice> was to put aside <the shining> of the armament before the battle but, when it comes to the actual battle, he joins the more recent authors, and ourselves as well, in declaring that you should show the weapons in their

17. Onasander 28.

μένων λαμπρῶν τῶν ὁπλιτῶν ἡ θέα συνήθης γίνηται, ἀλλ᾽ ὅταν ἡ δοκοῦσα καὶ
685 φαινομένη στυγνὴ παράταξις ἀθρόον καὶ παρ᾽ εὐθὺ ἀναδειχθῇ ἐξ ἀπροσδοκή-
των λαμπρά. τοῦτο γὰρ μᾶλλον καὶ θείας βοηθείας σημεῖον τάχα ὑπονοήσουσι
καθ᾽ ἑαυτῶν οἱ πολέμιοι. χρήσιμον δέ σοι, ὦ στρατηγέ, καὶ τὸ μὴ πρότερον τὴν
σὴν παράταξιν δεικνύειν τοῖς πολεμίοις ἐν ἡμέρᾳ πολέμου, πρὶν ἂν τὴν ἐκείνων
μάθῃς πῶς καὶ ὁποίῳ σχήματι παρετάξετο.

690    99. Σὲ δὲ χρὴ κατὰ τὸν καιρὸν τῆς μάχης προνοεῖν μᾶλλον τῶν μαχομένων,
καθώς σοι καὶ πρόσθεν ὑπεθέμεθα, ἢ τολμηρότερον ἄλλεσθαι καὶ ταῖς χερσὶ
συμπλέκεσθαι, ὅταν μὴ ἀνάγκης ἐστὶ καιρός· μᾶλλον δὲ τὸ παντελῶς ἀπέχεσθαι διὰ χειρῶν τοῖς πολεμίοις συμπλέκεσθαι, καὶ ἂν ὑπέρβλητον ἀνδρείαν
ἐπιδείξῃς. οὐ τοσοῦτον γὰρ ὠφελήσεις τὸ στράτευμα μαχόμενος, ὅσον ἀποθα-
695 νὼν βλάψεις αὐτό, ὅπερ τοῖς συμπλεκομένοις οὐκ ἀπροσδόκητόν ἐστιν. εἰ γὰρ
διὰ φήμης μόνης ψευδοῦς, ὡς πρὸ μικροῦ ἡμῖν εἴρηται, ὅτι πέπτωκεν ὁ στρατηγός, οἱ τοῦ ἔθνους αὐτοῦ ἀπώλοντο, πόσῳ μᾶλλον, εἰ τῇ ἀληθείᾳ γένηται, τοῦτο
μεγάλη παρακολουθήσει βλάβη τῷ τοῦ πεσόντος ἀληθῶς στρατηγοῦ στρατεύματι.

700    100. Μᾶλλον δὲ ἐν ἀσφαλείᾳ ὀξέως καὶ βλέπε καὶ πρᾶττε τὰ δέοντα. τότε
γὰρ μᾶλλον θαυμάζεται στρατηγός, ὅταν κατὰ τὸ ὀξὺ τῆς ἀνάγκης τὰ πρέποντα
διοικήσῃ, ὅτε ἐν ἀδείᾳ ὢν τὰ εἰκότα προβουλεύσηται.

101. Εἰ δὲ χρὴ τότε καὶ κατὰ τὴν αὐτὴν ὥραν λόγοις παραθαρρύνειν σε τοὺς
στρατιώτας, καὶ ἐπαγγελίαις ταῖς ἀπὸ τῆς βασιλείας ἡμῶν τοῖς ἀριστεύουσιν
705 ἀποκειμέναις, καὶ τὴν ἀπὸ Θεοῦ βοήθειαν παροῦσαν. εἰ δέ τι πλεῖον, καὶ σημεῖα
τινὰ ἐπινοεῖν, καὶ δεικνύειν καὶ ὑποτίθεσθαι φανέντα καὶ τὴν ἡμετέραν σημαίνοντα νίκην, καὶ ἕτερά τινα ποιεῖν ἅπερ τὸ σύνταγμα οὐκ ἐπιδέχεται νῦν, ἐν δὲ
ταῖς συνηγμέναις γνώμαις κατὰ τὸ τέλος τοῦ συντάγματος εὑρίσκων ἀναμάθοις, ὅσα σε δεῖ καὶ πρὸ τοῦ πολέμου καὶ ἐν τῷ πολέμῳ καὶ μετὰ τὸν πόλεμον ἢ
710 λέγειν ἢ πράττειν. καὶ διὰ τούτων καθυπέρτερον τῶν πολεμίων ἀναδείκνυσαι.

---

684 γίνηται MW γένηται AVBE    685 ἀναδειχθῇ MW ἀναφανῇ AVBE    686 ὑπονοήσουσι
MW ὑπονοήσουσιν AVBE    689 ὁποίῳ MW ποίῳ AVBE | παρετάξετο MW παρετάξατο
AVBE    691 πρόσθεν MW ἔμπροσθεν AVBE    691–692 τολμηρότερον…συμπλέκεσθαι
MW τολμηρῶς συμπλέκεσθαι ταῖς χερσὶν AVBE    692 τὸ MW om. AVBE    693–694 καὶ…
ἐπιδείξῃς MW om. AVBE    695 ὅπερ…ἐστιν MW om. AVBE    702 διοικήσῃ ὅτε MW
διοικῇ ἢ ὅταν AVBE    704 καὶ MW καὶ ὑποσχέσεσι καὶ AVBE    705 εἰ…πλεῖον MW om.
AVBE    706 ἐπινοεῖν…δεικνύειν MW φανέντα ὑποδεικνύειν AVBE | καὶ³ MW ὡς AVBE
706–707 σημαίνοντα νίκην MW trsp. AVBE    707 τὸ…νῦν MW λέγεσθαι νῦν οὐκ
ἐνδέχεται AVBE    708–709 συντάγματος…ἀναμάθοις MW βιβλίου ἀναμαθήσῃ AVBE
710 καθυπέρτερον MW ἐπικρατέστερον AVBE | ἀναδείκνυσαι MW ἀναφαίνεσθαι AVBE

brightness very suddenly. For the usual sight of the brilliant heavy-armed men approaching from a distance is not a cause for wonder, but what does cause astonishment is when what appears to be a dull-looking battle line all of a sudden, straightaway, unexpectedly appears brilliantly shining. Perhaps the enemy will look upon this rather as a sign of God's help. It is useful for you, O general, not to be first in showing your battle line to the enemy on the day of battle, before you learn about theirs and how and in what manner they have been organized.

99. At the time of battle you must devote special attention to the men doing the fighting, as we explained to you earlier, rather than very rashly springing into action yourself and engaging in hand-to-hand combat when the situation is not critical. It is better <for you> to refrain completely from close combat with the enemy, even if you could project the image of unlimited bravery. By engaging in combat you will not benefit your army as much as you will harm it by dying, something not unexpected in close combat. For, as we mentioned to you shortly before this, if merely by the false rumor that the general has fallen, the soldiers of that nation were destroyed, how much more, if it should prove to be true, will it cause serious harm to the army of the general who has actually fallen?

100. Rather, in safety keenly observe and carry out your proper task. It is then that the general is admired: when at the critical point of an emergency he arranges for what should be done, when in full freedom he plans ahead for what is likely to happen.

101. If then, at that same time, it is necessary for you to address words of encouragement to your soldiers, <tell them of> the abiding help of God as well as the promised rewards of Our Majesty set aside for those who have distinguished themselves. If anything more <is needed>, contrive certain signs and point to them and suggest that they have appeared and portend victory for us. And there are other things to do that this compilation cannot provide at this time, but which you may find and study in the collected gnomic sayings at the end of this composition, that is, all the things you must do and say before war, during war, and after war, and that will enable you to prove that you are superior

τοιαῦτα καὶ περὶ τῶν ἐν αὐτῷ τῷ πολέμῳ πράξεων ὡς ἐν συντόμῳ ἡμῖν εἴρηται. ταῦτα μὲν οὖν περὶ τῶν πολεμικῶν παρασκευῶν, ὅσαι τε καβαλλαρικαὶ καὶ ὅσαι πεζικαί, εἰρήσθω ἡμῖν ὡς ἐν συνόψει.|

---

711 τοιαῦτα…εἴρηται MW om. AVBE    712 παρασκευῶν MW παρασκευῶν εἰρήσθω AVBE    713 εἰρήσθω ἡμῖν MW om. AVBE

to the enemy. These and other topics dealing with activities during the war itself are summarized by us. These matters, therefore, about military preparations, both for cavalry and for infantry, have been set forth in summary fashion by us.

Περὶ πολιορκίας πόλεων

1. Ἑξῆς δὲ καὶ περὶ πολιορκίας σοι χρεὼν διατάξασθαι, ὦ στρατηγέ, ἅπερ ἔκ τε παλαιῶν καὶ νέων ἀνθολογήσαμεν, καὶ ὅσα δεῖ πράττειν ἢ πολιορκοῦντα
5 πολεμίους, ὡς εἰκός, ἢ πολιορκούμενον ὑπ᾽ αὐτῶν, ὡς ἂν καὶ τούτων μετρίαν πεῖραν ἔχοις, δι᾽ ἧς δυνήσῃ προσεπινοῆσαι λαβόμενος ἀφορμῆς καὶ ὅσα μὴ ἐνταῦθα μὲν εἴρηται, δυνατὰ δὲ γενέσθαι, τῆς χρείας κατά τε καιροὺς καὶ τό- πους διδασκούσης τὰ ἕκαστα.
2. Πολιορκία τοίνυν στρατηγοῦ ἀνδρείαν ἐπιζητεῖ καὶ διάνοιαν ὀξεῖαν καὶ
10 στρατηγικὴν καὶ ἔμφρονα καὶ παρετοιμασίας μηχανημάτων, ἀσφάλειαν δὲ ἐν τῷ παρακαθῆσθαι ἢ πόλει ἢ φρουρίῳ ἢ ὀχυρώματι, καὶ μετὰ πολλῆς προσοχῆς ταύτην γίνεσθαι τὴν ἀσφάλειαν.
3. Χρὴ οὖν σε, ὦ στρατηγέ, παρακαθεζόμενόν τινι τῶν εἰρημένων ἐν ᾧ τόπῳ καθέζῃ φοσσᾶτον ὀχυρὸν ποιεῖν, ἤτοι ἢ τάφρον βαθεῖαν ἢ ἀπὸ κτισμάτων ἢ
15 λίθων ἢ πλίνθων ἢ ξύλων ἢ ὡς ἐπινοήσεις περιφράσσειν σεαυτὸν ἀπὸ τῶν πολεμίων, καὶ βίγλας πολλὰς καὶ ἀκριβεῖς ἔχειν, καὶ μάλιστα εἰς τοὺς ἀνυπονοή- τους τόπους, ἵνα μὴ οἱ πολιορκούμενοι ἢ οἱ ἔξωθεν ὄντες πολέμιοι ἄφνω ἐπερ- χόμενοι, ἢ ἐν νυκτὶ ἢ ἐν ἡμέρᾳ κινδύνους τῷ στρατῷ προσάγουσιν. ὅπερ γέγονε πολλάκις ἐπὶ τῶν πολιορκουμένων πόλεων. οἱ γὰρ ἔξωθεν οὐκ οἴδασι τί μελετῶ-
20 σιν οἱ ἐντός· οἱ δὲ ἔσωθεν ἀπὸ τοῦ τείχους βλέπουσιν ὅπερ ἂν πράττειν μέλλῃς κατ᾽ αὐτῶν. διὸ πρέπον σοι τὸ ἴδιον ἀσφαλίζεσθαι στράτευμα.

---

M W A V B E   PG 107:885

3–405 Cf. Strat., 10.   9–26 Onas. 40–41.

---

1 πολεμικῶν…ιε΄ MW λέοντος ἐν χρίστω βασιλεῖ αἰωνίω βασιλεὺς ρωμαίων A διάταξις ιε΄ VBE   2 πόλεων WAVBE πόλεων πῶς δεῖ ταύτας πολιορκεῖν M   3 χρεὼν MW χρὴ AVBE   4 ἀνθολογήσαμεν MW συνελεξάμεθα AVBE | πράττειν MW ποιεῖν AVBE   5 ὡς εἰκός MW om. AVBE   6 δυνήσῃ MW δυνήσῃ καὶ ἕτερα ἀπό σου AVBE   7 δυνατὰ MWVBE δυνατὸν A   8 τὰ ἕκαστα MW ἅπαντα AVBE   9 στρατηγοῦ…ἐπιζητεῖ MW ἀνδρίαν ἐπιζητεῖ στρατηγοῦ AVBE   14 ἢ¹ M om. WAVBE | τάφρον MW σοῦδαν AVBE   18 προσάγουσιν MW προσφέρωσιν AVE προσφέρουσιν B | γέγονε MWVBE γέγονεν A   20 ὅπερ ἂν AVBE ὅτι ἂν καὶ MW

# PREPARATION FOR WAR, CONSTITUTION XV

## About Besieging a City

1. Next, O general, we are obliged to give you instructions about siege warfare that we have gathered together from ancient and recent authorities, what you must do when you are besieging the enemy and, likely enough, when you are being besieged by them. Even if you have only moderate experience of such matters, this will provide you with a starting point that will enable you to devise further <means>. You will be able to bring matters not mentioned here into being. The needs of time and space will teach you the details.[1]

2. Siege warfare calls for a general who is brave and sharp witted, who has military knowledge, common sense, and who can prepare war machines. He must see to security in encamping about a city or fortress or fortification and he must devote a great deal of attention to such security.

3. Therefore, O general, when you are encamped around one of those places we have mentioned, the site of your camp must be strongly fortified either by a deep ditch or by constructions of stone, brick, wood, or in whatever way you can devise to protect yourself from the enemy. In the most unlikely places, especially, station a large number of sharp-witted scouts to prevent either the besieged or enemy forces on the outside from suddenly attacking, either by day or night, and exposing the army to danger, as has often occurred in cities under siege. The troops outside do not know what the people inside may be planning, but those inside, on the walls, can easily see what operations you are planning to take against them. For this reason you should attend to the security of your own army.

---

1. For Const. 15 cf. *Strat.* 10; for §§2–4 cf. Onasander 40–41. For a more detailed explanation of sources, see Haldon, *Commentary*. See also D. Sullivan, *Siegecraft: Two Tenth Century Instructional Manuals by Heron of Byzantium* (Washington, DC, 2000), including drawings of contemporary siege equipment from cod. Vat. Gr. 1605; H. van den Berg, *Anonymous de obsidione toleranda* (Leiden, 1947).

4. Κρεῖττον δὲ ποιήσεις ἐὰν καὶ παρὰ τὰς πόρτας ἢ εἰς τὰ παραπόρτια τῆς πόλεως ἢ κάστρου ἢ τὰς διεξόδους ἑτέρου ὀχυρώματος παρακαθίσεις τινὰς στρατιώτας, οἵτινες τὰς αἰφνιδίους καταδρομὰς τῶν πολεμίων ἀποκωλῦσαι
25 δύνανται, καὶ μάλιστα ἐν ταῖς νυξί, χρή σε τὴν τοιαύτην ἔχειν ἀσφάλειαν. τότε γὰρ μᾶλλον αἱ τοιαῦται καταδρομαὶ γίνονται.

5. Ἀλλὰ καὶ αὐτὸς ἐὰν ἐν νυκτὶ | ἐπιβάλῃς τὴν πολιορκίαν, φοβερώτερος 389ᵛ γενήσῃ τοῖς ἔσωθεν πολιορκουμένοις· οὐ γὰρ δύνανται ὁρᾶν τὰ γινόμενα διὰ τὸ σκότος, καὶ πλέον ταράσσονται, καὶ τὰ φρονήματα αὐτῶν ὑποχαλῶσιν, καὶ
30 πολλὰ δεινὰ κατὰ τὴν νύκτα γίνεσθαι ὑπονοοῦσι κατ᾽ αὐτῶν, ὅσα πολλάκις οὐδ᾽ αὐτὸς ἐπινοεῖς. πᾶν γὰρ τὸ ἐν νυκτὶ γινόμενον, κἂν μικρόν ἐστι, φοβερώτερον γίνεται τοῖς πολιορκουμένοις· διὸ καὶ ταχύτερον ὑποχαλῶσι καὶ τὴν ὑποταγὴν ἀσπάζονται. εἰ γὰρ ἰσχύσεις ἕνα που ἢ δύο ἐπὶ τὸ τεῖχος ἀναβιβάσαι, νομίσουσιν οἱ ἐντὸς πᾶν στράτευμα ἐπὶ τὰ τείχη ἀναβῆναι, καὶ τραπήσονται καὶ ἔρημα
35 καταλείψουσι τὰ τείχη.

6. Ἐπὶ δὲ τῶν τοιούτων δεῖ τὴν εὐψυχίαν τοῦ στρατηγοῦ καὶ ἀνδρείαν φαίνεσθαι. ἵνα καὶ αὐτὸς τῶν τοιούτων ἐπιπόνων τῆς πολιορκίας ἔργων ἅπτηται χερσὶν οἰκείαις. μᾶλλον γὰρ ὁ στρατὸς ἐντραπήσεται· καὶ οὐκ ἔστιν ὅπως ὡς ἐπιταττόμενοι, ἀλλ᾽ ὡς ἐξ ἴσου φίλῳ συμπονοῦντες ἐπὶ τὰ δυσχερῆ τῶν ἔργων
40 ἐπιδώσωσιν ἑαυτοὺς προθυμότερον.

7. Χρεὼν δέ σε ἀνασκοπῆσαι ἀκριβῶς καὶ τῆς πολιορκίας ἀρχόμενον, πρῶτον μὲν ἐὰν δυνατόν ἐστι στενοχωρεῖν τοὺς ἐντὸς περὶ τῶν ἀναγκαίων εἴσοδον, τοῦτ᾽ ἔστιν, ἢ περὶ τὸ ὕδωρ ἢ περὶ τὴν τροφήν. εἰ δὲ ταῦτα ἀφθόνως ἔχουσι, τότε μηχαναῖς κεχρῆσθαι πολεμικαῖς.

45 8. Καταπλήξεις δὲ αὐτούς, ἐὰν τοὺς ἀρίστους τῶν στρατιωτῶν ἢ ἀρχόντων ἐπιλεξάμενος ἡλικίᾳ καὶ θεωρίᾳ τελείους καὶ ὅπλοις ἀστράπτοντας, τούτους ἐκ τοῦ πλησίον τοῦ τείχους ἢ τοῦ ὀχυρώματος ἐκ παρόδου ὑποδείξῃς τοῖς πολιορ-κουμένοις. τοὺς δὲ ὑποδεεστέρους μετὰ τῆς ἀποσκευῆς μηκόθεν ἐκτάξῃς ἵνα μὴ

25 ad μάλιστα des. W

23 ἢ κάστρου MW om. AVBE    25 νυξί MVBE νυξὶν A    26 καταδρομαὶ γίνονται M trsp. AVBE    27 ἐπιβάλῃς…πολιορκίαν M πολιορκῇς AVBE    30 οὐδ᾽ M οὐδὲ AVBE    32 ὑποχαλῶσι M ἐνδιδοῦσιν AVBE    33 ἀσπάζονται M ἀγαπῶσιν AVBE | που M om. AVBE    34 ἐντὸς M ἔσωθεν τὸ AVBE | ἔρημα M ἔρημα καὶ ἀφύλακτα AVBE    36 καὶ M καὶ τὴν AVBE    37–38 ἅπτηται…οἰκείαις M ταῖς οἰκείαις χερσὶν ἅπτηται AVBE    38 ἐστι ὅπως M ἔτι AVBE    39 φίλῳ M φίλῳ συνεργοῦντες καὶ AVBE | τὰ M τὰ δύσκολα καὶ AVBE    40 ἐπιδώσωσιν M ἐπιδώσουσιν AVBE    41 χρεὼν M χρὴ AVBE | ἀνασκοπῆσαι M κατασκοπῆσαι AVBE    42 περὶ M περὶ τὴν AVBE    44 ἔχουσι MVBE ἔχουσιν A

4. You will do better if you station some soldiers by the gates or at the postern gates of the city or fortress or at the passageways into some other fortification. They should be able to repel sudden assaults of the enemy. You must have this sort of security, especially at night, for such assaults are more commonly made at night.

5. If, however, you carry on your siege operations at night, you will cause more fear among the people inside who come under siege. Darkness prevents them from seeing what is happening and they grow all the more confused, their spirits are cast down, and they imagine that they will suffer many terrible things during the night, even things that you have no intention of doing. For everything that happens at night, even something very minor, causes more fear among people under siege, and so they very quickly become slack and embrace subjection. If you can do so, have one or two men mount the wall and the people inside will think that the whole army has climbed onto the wall. They will run away and leave the walls deserted.

6. These situations call for the general to give evidence of his courageous spirit and bravery. He should take part in the labors and work of the siege with his own hands. Indeed, he will put the soldiers to shame. They will labor together on the difficult tasks not so much because they have been ordered to do so but because it will be on an equal basis with a friend, and they will become more enthusiastic.

7. When you begin the siege, you must make an accurate assessment. First, is it possible to keep the necessities, such as food and water, from getting to the people within? If they possess these in abundance, then resort to siege engines.

8. You will cause great consternation if you select from among your soldiers or officers the most impressive, in the prime of life, very large in appearance, and with bright, shining armor. Show them off to the besieged by having them pass close to the wall or the fortification. Station the less impressive troops

δύνωνται οἱ πολέμιοι διακρίνειν αὐτοὺς ἢ ἄνδρα ἢ ἄλογον. οὕτως γὰρ πάντας
50  τοὺς φαινομένους ἄνδρας εἶναι νομίζουσι καὶ τοιούτους οἵους εἶδον πλησίον
ἐλθόντας.

9. Πάντως δὲ χρήσιμόν ἐστιν τὸ πολλοὺς λωρικάτους καὶ καταφράκτους
φαίνεσθαι τοῖς πολιορκουμένοις, ἀλλὰ καὶ τοὺς μὴ ἔχοντας λωρίκια καὶ κασσίδας δι᾽ ἐπιτηδεύσεως δεικνύειν ὡς λωρικάτους καὶ καταφράκτους ἵνα πάντες
55  τοιοῦτοι φαινόμενοι δειλίαν ἐμποιῶσι τοῖς ἔσωθεν.

10. Καὶ τὰ ἄπλικτα δὲ ἀπὸ μηκόθεν | ποίει, ἵνα πάντα τὰ ὁρώμενα παρὰ τῶν    390
ἐντὸς στρατιῶται φαίνωνται.

11. Καὶ πρότερον μὲν δηλοποιεῖν τοῖς ἐν τῇ πόλει ἢ τῷ φρουρίῳ, καὶ προ-
βάλλεσθαι εἰς ἐπιζήτησιν τῆς διαλύσεως πράγματα εὐχερῆ, ἤτοι ἢ ἄλογα αὐτῶν
60  ἤ τινα ἅρματα ἢ ἕτερά τινα τῶν ὑπαρχόντων αὐτοῖς πραγμάτων φορητά, ἵνα τῇ
εὐχερείᾳ τῶν προτεινομένων καὶ τῇ ἐλπίδι τῆς σωτηρίας εἰς διχόνοιαν ἔλθωσιν,
καὶ χαυνώτεροι γένωνται πρὸς ἀντικατάστασιν καὶ κινδύνους.

12. Τὸ γὰρ εὐθέως ἐκ προοιμίων σκληρὰ καὶ βαρεῖα προτείνειν οὐκ ἔμφρονος κρίνομεν στρατηγοῦ. τῇ γὰρ δυσχερείᾳ καὶ τῷ βάρει τῶν προτεινομένων
65  λόγων ἐλαφρότερον λογίζονται τὸν κίνδυνον οἱ πολιορκούμενοι, καὶ διὰ τοῦτο
εἰς ἕνωσιν καὶ ἀπόνοιαν ἔρχονται.

13. Πρὸ πάντων δὲ πρέπον ἐστί, καὶ μάλιστα ἐν ταῖς μακραῖς πολιορκίαις,
εὐτρεπίζειν σε τὰ ἐπιτήδεια, ἵνα ἀστενοχωρήτως καθέζηται ὁ στρατὸς μηδενὸς
λειπόμενος.

70  14. Ἀφορίσεις δὲ καὶ τοὺς ἀνθρώπους τοὺς ἐπὶ ἑκάστῃ χρείᾳ ἰδιαζόντως
ἐργάζεσθαι καὶ κάμνειν τοῖς πόνοις ὀφείλοντας, καὶ διορίσαι τις ποίαν χρείαν
ποιεῖν ὀφείλει.

15. Ὅταν δὲ ἀπάρξῃ τοῦ προβάλλειν εἰς πολιορκίαν, οὐ χρή σε πάντα τὸν
στρατὸν καθ᾽ ἑκάστην ἡμέραν ἄγειν εἰς πόλεμον, ἵνα μὴ πάντες ὁμοῦ ἀποκάμω-
75  σιν, ἀλλ᾽ εἰς μέρη διάφορα αὐτὸν διαμερίσῃς καὶ ἀφορίσῃς, πόσοι καὶ πόσας
ὥρας τῆς ἡμέρας ὀφείλουσι κάμνειν, καὶ διακρίνῃς τίνες οἱ ἐν τῇ νυκτὶ καὶ τίνες

---

49 ad διακρίνειν de novo inc. W

---

**49** δύνωνται M δύνανται WAVBE    **50** νομίζουσι M νομίζουσιν W νομίσουσιν A νομίσουσι
VBE    **52** ἐστιν M ἐστι WAVBE    **57** ἐντὸς MAVBE ἐκτὸς W    **60** φορητά MW εὐτελῆ
AVBE    **61** εὐχερείᾳ MW εὐτελείᾳ AVBE | προτεινομένων MW ἐπιζητουμένων AVE
ζητουμένων B    **63** ἐκ προοιμίων MW καὶ ἐξ ἀρχῆς AVBE | βαρεῖα MW βαρέα AVBE
**63–64** προτείνειν…ἔμφρονος MW ζητεῖν αὐτοὺς οὐ φρονίμου AVBE    **64** τῇ MW πρὸς
AVBE | δυσχερείᾳ MW δυσχερείαν AVBE | καὶ…βάρει MW om. AVBE    **66** καὶ MW <κα>ὶ
ὁμόνοιαν καὶ AVBE    **67** ἐστί M ἐστὶν WAVBE    **68** καθέζηται MW παρακαθέζεται AVBE
**73** προβάλλειν M προσβάλλειν WAVBE

farther off with the baggage so the enemy will not be able to form any judgment of them, either men or horses. In this way they will believe that all the men are as impressive as those they have seen up close.

9. It is always useful to have a large number of your men be seen by the besieged in coats of mail and full armor. To this end, have those who do not have coats of mail and helmets present themselves as mailed and fully armed. By having all of ours appear in this way, you will instill fear in the people within.

10. Set up your camp a good distance away so that everything in it will look like soldiers to the besieged.

11. First, make clear to the people inside the city or fortress that you are proposing light and bearable terms to seek their surrender, either their horses or some weapons or some of their other moveable possessions. Such moderate proposals and the hope of safety may lead them to differences of opinion and they may become more hesitant to offer resistance and face dangers.

12. In our judgment, an intelligent general does not propose severe and harsh terms at the very beginning. If the terms are severe and harsh, the besieged may think that the risks are more acceptable and this may lead them to unite in rejecting them.

13. Above all, especially in a lengthy siege, you must make sure that your supplies are gotten ready, so the army may undertake the siege fully equipped and with nothing missing.

14. Also assign men who will be obliged to work at each of the necessary tasks and who must work hard at it. You are to designate what kind of duty an individual has to perform.

15. When you begin to get the siege under way, you must not lead the entire army out to combat every day. If you did, all of them would immediately become exhausted. You should divide it into various sections and assign the number of men and how many hours they are obliged to work each day. Sched-

οἱ ἐν τῇ ἡμέρᾳ. δεῖ γὰρ καὶ ἐν ταῖς ἡμέραις ὀχλεῖσθαι τοὺς πολιορκουμένους διὰ
πολέμου ἐκ διαδοχῆς ἀλλήλων, καὶ ἐν ταῖς νυξὶν ὁμοίως διὰ φόβου, ἐπὶ τοῦτο
ἀφοριζομένων τινῶν καὶ ποιούντων διὰ νυκτὸς τοὺς φόβους οἵους καὶ ὅσους
80 ἐπινοήσεις.

16. Εἰ δὲ στρατὸν ἔχεις πολύν, ὥστε δύνασθαι καὶ ἐν νυκτὶ τῆς αὐτῆς ἔχεσθαι πολιορκίας, καλῶς ποιήσεις ἐὰν τοῦτον διέλῃς εἰς ὅσα συνορᾷς μέρη. καὶ
οἱ μὲν αὐτῶν ἐπὶ ὥρας τῆς νυκτὸς ὡρισμένας κοιμῶνται, οἱ δὲ προσβάλλουσιν
καὶ πάλιν οἱ καμόντες τῇ προσβολῇ ὑπνοῦσιν, καὶ οἱ πρῴην ὑπνώσαντες πολι-
85 ορκοῦσιν, καὶ τοῦτο ἐκ διαδοχῆς ἀλλήλων καὶ ἐν νυκτὶ καὶ ἐν ἡμέρᾳ ἀνενδότως
ποιεῖς, ὥστε μὴ ἐᾶσαι κἂν μικρὰν ἄνεσιν τοὺς πολιορκουμένους λαβεῖν. οὕτως
γὰρ ἐκλυόμενοι ὑπό τε τῆς ἀγρυπνίας καὶ τῆς συνοχῆς τοῦ | καμάτου, εὐχερῶς   390ᵛ
διὰ τῶν προσβαλλομένων καὶ μηχανημάτων καὶ λογισμῶν ἢ ἑαυτοὺς ἐπιδώσωσιν ἐθελουσίως ἢ καὶ ἄκοντες ἁλωθήσονται, μικρὸν ἀμελήσαντες διὰ τὸ ἀνέν-
90 δοτον τῶν ἐπερχομένων αὐτοῖς κινδύνων.

17. Ἢ τὸ πολλάκις γινόμενον διὰ προδοτῶν μᾶλλον καὶ εὐχερέστερον
αὐτοὺς παραλάβῃς ἀνυπονοήτου τόπου ἢ τρόπου σοι δι᾽ αὐτῶν ὑποδειχθέντος.

18. Ἐν δὲ ταῖς τοιαύταις ἐκ διαδοχῆς πολιορκίαις καὶ αὐτός, ὦ στρατηγέ,
χρόνον ὀλίγον ἀναπαύου καὶ σύντομον ἵνα νήφῃς πρὸς τὰ ἁρμόζοντά σοι
95 διατάγματα.

19. Ἐὰν δὲ ἀνδρειότερον διακείμενος κελεύσῃς διαμερισθῆναι εἰς πολλὰ
μέρη τὸν στρατόν, καὶ ἕκαστον μέρος προσφέρειν σκάλας εἰς τὸ τεῖχος, κρεῖττον
ποιήσεις. ἐν κύκλῳ γὰρ γινομένης τῆς προσβολῆς ὁμοῦ εἰς ἀμηχανίαν καὶ
ὀλιγωρίαν οἱ πολιορκούμενοι ἐμπεσοῦνται, μάλιστα ὅταν μετὰ τῶν σκαλῶν καὶ
100 τὰ ἕτερα μηχανήματα προσβάλλῃς, οἷον κριοὺς ἢ χελώνας ἢ πύργους ἢ ἕτερόν
τι πολιορκητικὸν ὄργανον. ἐὰν γὰρ ὁμοῦ καὶ τὰ μηχανήματα προσφέρῃς, ὁμοῦ
καὶ τὰς σκάλας ἐπιστήσῃς εἰς τὸ τεῖχος, διὰ πολλῶν μερῶν συνταραχθήσονται
οἱ ἐντός. εἴ τε γὰρ ἀμελήσαντες τῶν ἄλλων μερῶν τοῦ τείχους εἰς τὰς προσβαλ-

82 διέλῃς MW διαχωρίσῃς AVBE   83 προσβάλλουσιν MW προσβαλῶσιν AVBE
84 καμόντες MW κοπιάσαντες ἐν AVBE   85–86 ἐκ...πολιορκουμένους MW καὶ τοῦτο
ποιήσεις ἐν ἡμέρᾳ καὶ ἐν νυκτὶ διαδεχομένων ἀλλήλους τῶν προσβαλλόντων ὥστε μὴ
καταλιπεῖν τοὺς πολιορκουμένους κἂν μικρὰν ἄνεσιν AVBE   87–89 τῆς²...ἐθελουσίως MW
ὑπὸ τοῦ συνεχοῦς καμάτου ἀλλὰ καὶ διὰ τῶν προσβαλόντων μηχανημάτων καὶ τῶν
καταστρατηγήσεων ἢ ἑαυτοὺς ἐπιδώσωσιν (ἐπιδώσουσιν Β) ἑκουσίως AVBE
89 ἁλωθήσονται μικρὸν MW κρατηθήσονται μικρόν τι AVBE   89–90 ἀνένδοτον MW
ἀνένδοτον καὶ ἀδιάπαυστον AVBE   91–92 διὰ...αὐτοὺς MW εὐχερέστερον μᾶλλον αὐτοὺς
διὰ προδοτῶν AVBE   94 ἵνα MW ἵνα ἐγρηγορῇς καὶ AVBE   96 ἀνδρειότερον διακείμενος
MW om. AVBE   101 ὄργανον MW μηχάνημα AVBE   102–103 συνταραχθήσονται...
ἐντός MW οἱ ἔσωθεν περισπώμενοι συνταραχθήσονται AVBE

ule some to work at night and others during the day. For not only must the besieged be harassed by continuous attacks during the day but, in like manner, they should be kept on edge all night by troops designated for this. You will devise what these fears at night should consist of and their duration.

16. If you have an army large enough that you can carry on the same siege at night, you will do well to divide it into as many sections as you judge best. One section sleeps during designated hours of the night, others carry on the attack; again, the men who are weary from <fighting off> the attack sleep, while those who had slept earlier continue the siege. Do this, one following after the other, without let-up both by night and by day, so as not to allow the people under siege even a tiny respite. In this way they easily become unstrung from lack of sleep and constant hard work as well as by the attacks, the siege engines, and stratagems. They will then either willingly surrender themselves or, unwilling, be taken captive, for they will have grown careless because of the unyielding nature of the dangers falling upon them.

17. Or, as frequently happens, you will take them more easily by means of traitors, who may point out to you a place or a way <of attacking> that you had not thought of.

18. In the course of the unrelenting activity of such sieges, you, O general, must take a short and brief rest so you may be wide awake to manage things properly.

19. If you feel more emboldened, you may order the army to be divided into a large number of sections and have each section bring ladders up to the wall. With the assault then being carried on in a circle all at once, the besieged will fall into helplessness and dejection, especially when, along with the ladders, you move the other machines into place, such as rams, tortoises, towers, or other siege engines. If you bring up the siege engines and, at the same time, set the ladders against the wall, the people within will be harassed from many directions. If they neglect the other sections of the wall in order to concentrate

λομένας μηχανὰς ἀντιμάχονται πάντως, οἱ τὰς σκάλας προσφέροντες μηδενὸς
105 ἀποκωλύοντος βιαίως εὐκόλως ἐπὶ τὸ τεῖχος ἀναβήσονται· κἂν τε διαμερίσωσιν
ἑαυτοὺς κατὰ τῶν προσφερόντων τὰς σκάλας, τότε οἱ τὰς μηχανὰς προσάγον-
τες τῶν ὀργάνων σφοδροτέρας αὐτοῖς ποιήσωσι τὰς ἐπιθέσεις καὶ οὐ δυνήσονται τὰ ἐπιφερόμενα κακὰ δι᾽ ἀμφοτέρων τῶν προσβολῶν ἀποκρούσασθαι.
    20. Πολλάκις δὲ ἐπὶ τῆς πολιορκίας οἱ νομιζόμενοι ὀχυρώτατοι καὶ ἀνεπινό-
110 ητοι πρὸς ἅλωσιν τόποι μᾶλλον ἀφορμάς σοι παρέξουσιν ἁλώσεως. οἱ γὰρ
ἐντὸς διὰ τὴν δοκοῦσαν ὀχυρότητα τοὺς τοιούτους τόπους ἀφυλάκτους κατα-
λιμπάνουσιν. σὺ δὲ διὰ τῆς σῆς ἐπινοίας καὶ τῆς ἐπιπόνου ἐργασίας τοὺς τοιούτους τόπους κατανοῶν, τάχα μηχανὴν εὑρήσεις καταλαβεῖν αὐτοὺς ἀφυλάκτους
ὄντας, ἢ διὰ σκαλῶν ἀναβαινόντων ἢ διά τινος βιαίας ἀναβάσεως εὐτόλμων
115 ἀνδρῶν ἐπαγγελίας λαβόντων δωρεῶν καὶ τιμῶν. ἐντεῦθεν γὰρ ἐκ τοῦ ἀπροσ-
δοκήτου θεωρήσαντες οἱ ἐντὸς τοὺς | τοιούτους τόπους καταληφθέντας ἀπο-    391
παύσονται, καὶ τὰ ὅπλα ῥίψαντες, ἢ αἰτήσουσι τὴν σωτηρίαν ἢ κατὰ κράτος
διαφθαρήσονται. οἱ γὰρ ἀναβάντες εἰς τὸ τεῖχος διὰ τῆς δυσχερείας ἐκείνης ἢ
σαλπίσουσι καὶ φόβον ἐμποιήσουσι μέγιστον ὁραθέντες ἢ διαδραμοῦνται μετὰ
120 τὸ εἰσελθεῖν καὶ τὰς πόρτας ἀνοίξουσιν, εἰ τύχοι τοῖς ἔξω στρατιώταις, ἢ διά
τινων ἑτέρων ἐπινοιῶν τὴν ἅλωσιν τῆς πόλεως ἢ τοῦ κάστρου διαθήσουσιν.
    21. Εἰ δὲ τὸ κάστρον ἢ ἡ πόλις πλῆθος ἔχει λαοῦ καὶ δύναμιν, καὶ τολμῶσιν
ὑπαντιάζοντες ἀμύνασθαι τοὺς εἰσελθόντας, δεῖ αὐτοὺς τοὺς ὑψηλωτέρους
τόπους καταλαβεῖν ἢ τὰ ἄκρα τῆς πόλεως, καὶ ἐκεῖθεν πολεμοῦντας κακῶσαι
125 τοὺς ἐν τῇ πόλει ἀλόντας. κηρύξουσι δὲ τότε, ἵνα μηδεὶς κτείνῃ τὸν μὴ ἔχοντα

---

105 βιαίως MAVBE βιαίου W    106 τὰς μηχανὰς MW τὰ πολιορκητικὰ AVBE    107 τῶν
ὀργάνων MW μηχανήματα AVBE | σφοδροτέρας…ἐπιθέσεις MW σφοδροτέρως αὐτοῖς
ἐπιτεθήσονται AVBE    107–108 δυνήσονται MW δυνήσονται αὐτοὶ (οὗτοι B) AVBE
108 δι᾽…τῶν MW διὰ τῶν ἀμφοτέρων AVBE    109–110 καὶ…ἁλώσεως MW τόποι μᾶλλον
ἀφορμάς σοι παρέξουσι (προξένουσι B) πορθήσεως AVBE    112 τῆς² …ἐργασίας MW
φρονήσεως AVBE    113 κατανοῶν MAVBE ἐπινοῶν W | εὑρήσεις MW τινα εὑρήσεις ὥστε
AVBE    114 ἀναβαινόντων MW ἀναβαινόντων τινῶν AVBE | διά MW διὰ ἄλλης AVBE |
βιαίας MW δυσκόλου AVBE | εὐτόλμων MW τολμημῶν AVE τολμηρῶν B    115 ἐπαγγελίας
λαβόντων MW τοῦτο ποιούντων ὑποσχέσεις λαμβανόντων AVBE    116 ἐντὸς MW ἔσωθεν
AVBE | καταληφθέντας MW κατακρατηθέντας AVBE    116–117 ἀποπαύσονται MW
ἀποπαύσονται τῆς μάχης AVBE    118 δυσχερείας MW δυσκολίας AVBE    119 ὁραθέντες
MW θεαθέντες AVBE | διαδραμοῦνται MW διαδράμωσι AVBE    120–121 ἢ…διαθήσουσιν
MW ἢ δι᾽ ἄλλης τινὸς ἐπινοίας τὴν τῆς πόλεως κράτησιν ἢ τοῦ κάστρου ποιήσουσιν AVBE
123 ὑπαντιάζοντες ἀμύνασθαι MW ἀπαντᾶν καὶ ἀμύνεσθαι AVBE    123–126 εἰσελθόντας…φέροντας MW ἔσωθεν συλληφθέντας κηρύξεις δὲ τότε καὶ διαλαλήσεις ἵνα τὸν μὴ
ἔχοντα ὅπλα μηδεὶς φονεύῃ μόνους δὲ ἀποκτείνειν τοὺς τὰ ὅπλα φοροῦντας AVBE

their defense against the engines that have been moved up, the men bringing up the ladders will encounter no strong opposition and will easily climb up onto the wall. Even if they divide their own forces to confront the men bringing up the ladders, then those who are bringing up the machines will make their attacks all the more forcefully. They will not be able to beat off the evils brought upon them by both assaults.

20. Frequently, when it comes to a siege, there are places that are considered extremely well fortified and their capture is inconceivable. Yet, the very fortifications may provide you with the means to take them. The defenders, confident in those fortifications, may leave such places unguarded. Because you are attentive, though, and a diligent worker, you will investigate those places. Since they have been left unprotected, you will soon discover some means of capturing them, such as having some bold men, lured by the promise of gifts and honors, climb ladders and force their way to the top. As a result, when the people inside look upon the completely unexpected capture of those places, they will leave off <fighting> and throw down their weapons. They will beg for their safety or they will be destroyed by force. The men who have climbed up onto the wall in that difficult place will sound the trumpet and the sight of them will cause the greatest fear, or else they will race along as they enter in and will open the gates to our soldiers, who may be outside, or they will think of some other means to bring about the capture of the city or fortress.

21. If the fortress or city is strong and has a large number of men who are bold enough to confront and ward off our troops as they charge in, we must occupy the higher places or the highest points of the city and, fighting from that vantage point, cause serious injury to those caught in the city. Our men will

ὅπλον, μόνους δὲ κτείνειν τοὺς τὰ ὅπλα φέροντας. ταύτην δὲ τὴν φωνὴν κηρύττεσθαι τῇ τῶν πολιτῶν διαλέκτῳ. ἕκαστος γὰρ ἀκούσας, καὶ τῆς ἰδίας προνοού-
μενος σωτηρίας, ἐν τῇ ἀκμῇ τοῦ φόβου ἀπορρίψει τὰ ὅπλα, καὶ τῶν ἀντιπολεμούντων ὀλιγουμένων κατὰ κράτος οἱ πολιορκοῦντες νικήσουσιν. οἱ γὰρ πολι-
130  ορκούμενοι, καὶ οὕτως ἁλισκόμενοι, ὅταν μικρὰν ἐλπίδα τῆς σωτηρίας λάβωσιν,
οἰκέται λοιπὸν ἀντὶ πολεμίων γίνονται.

22. Εἰ δὲ χρόνιος γένηται ἡ πολιορκία καὶ συμβῇ συλλαβεῖν σέ τινας ἔξω τῆς
πόλεως, τοὺς μὲν ἀκμάζοντας ταῖς ἡλικίαις νεωτέρους ὡς ἂν βούλῃ κάτεχε.
γύναια δὲ καὶ παιδάρια καὶ γέροντας καὶ ἀσθενεῖς ἀνθρώπους ἀποπέμπε πρὸς
135  τὴν πόλιν αὐτῶν. οὕτως γὰρ ἡ ἄχρηστος ἡλικία καὶ τὰς τροφὰς δαπανήσει, καὶ
τοὺς πολιορκουμένους οὐδὲν ὠφελήσει, μᾶλλον δὲ καὶ βλάψει. ἔτι δὲ καὶ φιλανθρωπίας ὑπόνοιαν δώσεις τοῖς ἐντός, ὥστε διαιρεθῆναι τὰ φρονήματα αὐτῶν,
καὶ ἀφορμὴν γενέσθαι ἐντεῦθεν τῆς πρός σε ὑποταγῆς αὐτῶν.

23. Ἐπειδὴ δὲ εἴωθεν καὶ θόρυβος γίνεσθαι ἐν ταῖς πολιορκίαις ὑπὸ τῆς
140  κραυγῆς τῶν ἀνθρώπων ἢ ὑπὸ τοῦ ἤχου τῶν σκουταρίων, ἵνα μὴ βαροῦνται καὶ
ἐνοχλοῦνται οἱ τοῦ στρατοῦ πάντες ὁμοῦ, δέον σε ἀπὸ ἑνὸς ἢ δευτέρου μιλίου
ποιεῖν αὐτοὺς ἀπληκεύειν τοῦ ὀχυρώματος, ὁπόθεν οὐκ ἐξακούεται ὁ ἦχος τῶν
θορυβούντων τοὺς πολιορκουμένους.

24. Μὴ ἐπικινδύνως δὲ καὶ ἀσκόπως προστάσσῃς ποιεῖσθαι τὰς προσβολὰς |    391ᵛ
145  ἵνα μή τινων διαπιπτόντων καὶ οἱ τοῦ στρατοῦ δειλιάσωσιν, καὶ οἱ πολιορκούμενοι προθυμότεροι γένωνται—τοῦτο γὰρ πολλάκις ἀνέγνωμεν γενόμενον—
καὶ ὁ κρείττων τῶν ἄλλων στρατιώτης ὑπὸ γυναικὸς οὕτω τύχοι καὶ ἀσθενοῦς ἢ
διὰ λίθου βληθέντος ἢ κεράμου ἢ διὰ ξύλου κατενεχθέντος πληγεὶς ἀπώλετο.

---

146–148 Cf. Leon diac. 3.7; Theoph. Cont., 438.13–14.

---

126–127 κηρύττεσθαι…διαλέκτῳ MW διαλαλεῖσθαι παρακελεύου τῇ ἰδίᾳ διαλέκτῳ καὶ τῇ
γλώσσῃ τῶν πολεμίων AVBE    128 ἐν…φόβου MW om. AVBE    129 νικήσουσιν MAVBE
νικήσουσι W    130 ἁλισκόμενοι MW κατακρατούμενοι AVBE    132 χρόνιος…πολιορκία
MW ἐν ἱκανῷ χρόνῳ ἡ πολιορκία γένηται AVBE    132–133 συμβῇ…βούλῃ MW κρατήσεις
τινὰς τῶν πολεμίων τοὺς μὲν νεωτέρους καὶ ἰσχυροὺς ὡς ἂν βούλει AVBE    134 καὶ³…
ἀνθρώπους MW ἀχρήστους AVBE | πρὸς MW πάλιν εἰς AVBE    135 αὐτῶν οὕτως MW
αὐτὴ AVBE | καὶ¹…καὶ² MW οὔτε AVBE    136 οὐδὲν…βλάψει MW ὠφελήσει τι καὶ τὰς
τροφὰς καταδαπανήσει AVBE    137 ὑπόνοιαν MW ὑπόληψιν AVBE    138 ἐντεῦθεν MW
πρὸ τούτου AVBE    142 ποιεῖν…ὁπόθεν MW τοῦ ὀχυρώματος ποιεῖν αὐτοὺς ἀπλικεύειν
ὅθεν AVBE    145 διαπιπτόντων MW ἀναιρουμένων AVBE | οἱ² MW οἱ λοιποὶ AVBE
147 κρείττων…στρατιώτης MW καλλίων τῶν στρατιωτῶν AVBE | οὕτω…καὶ² MW om.
AVBE | ἀσθενοῦς MW ἀσθενοὺς πολλάκις AVBE    148 βληθέντος MW βληθεὶς ἢ διὰ
AVBE | κατενεχθέντος MW om. AVBE

then proclaim that nobody should kill persons not carrying a weapon but kill only those bearing weapons. Make this proclamation in the language of the citizens. On hearing it, each individual will be concerned for his own safety and, gripped by fear, will throw away his weapons. Armed resistance will then drop off and the besieging forces will win a decisive victory. Those who were under siege and who have been taken in this manner, moreover, when they have small hope of safety, will become your servants rather than your enemies.

22. If the siege proves to be lengthy and you happen to capture some people outside the city, hold on to the younger men in the prime of life as you might wish. But send the women, children, elderly, and infirm individuals back into their city. In this way, people of a useless age will consume the food and will bring no benefit to the besieged, in fact, they will cause them trouble. In addition, you will give the people in the city reason to expect humane treatment. This should instill doubt in their minds and will mark the first steps of their subjection to you.

23. Since a great deal of noise, coming from the shouts of men and the clash of shields, usually accompanies a siege, make sure that all the men in the army together are not unduly disturbed or under stress. Have your men set up camp one or two miles from the fortification, beyond earshot of the noise that is causing confusion to those under siege.

24. Do not order assaults to be made recklessly and without purpose lest, when some losses occur, our troops become discouraged and the people under siege become more defiant. For we have often read about this happening. The strongest soldier might be struck by a stone or tile or piece of wood thrown or hurled down by a weak woman and so perish.[2]

2. In 963, in Constantinople, a woman threw a ceramic flower pot that killed Marianos Argyris, katepano of the West: Leo the Deacon 3.7 (trans. p. 96). Theophanes (Cont.) states that it was a roof tile (438.13–14). Cf. Plutarch, Moralia 3.245C.

25. Ἐὰν δὲ μικρὰ ὀχυρώματα παρακαθίσαι καὶ ἐπιζήμιον ἢ ἐπικίνδυνον
150 νομίζῃς τὴν προσβολήν, καὶ οἶδας ὅτι οὐδὲν τῶν ἐπιτηδείων λείπονται, σπούδαζε διὰ θορύβων αὐτοῖς καὶ ἐν ἡμέρᾳ καὶ ἐν νυκτὶ ἐνοχλεῖν, ἵνα τῇ ὀχλήσει
ἀποκάμωσιν ὀλίγοι ὄντες πρὸς πλῆθος κατὰ διαδοχὴν ἀνενδότως αὐτοῖς
προσβάλλον.

26. Εἰ δὲ καὶ οἶκοι εἰσὶν ἐν τῷ φρουρίῳ ἐπιτήδειοι πρὸς τὸ καῆναι διὰ πυρ-
155 φόρων σαγιττῶν συνεχῶν διὰ πολλῶν τόπων, ἀνέμου μάλιστα σφοδροῦ κινουμένου, πέμπε καὶ ἐμπύριζε, ὕλην πυρὸς προσδεσμῶν τῇ σαγίττῃ διὰ τῶν πετροβόλων μαγγανικῶν τῶν λεγομένων ἀλακατίων ἢ τετραρέων τῶν πετρῶν πυρὸς
πεπληρωμένων δι' ὕλης, καὶ βαλλομένων κατὰ τῶν εὐεμπρήστων οἴκων. καὶ ἐν
ὅσῳ εἰς τὴν τοῦ πυρὸς ἀσχολοῦνται σβέσιν, σκάλας εἰς τοὺς ἐπιδεχομένους
160 τόπους ἱστᾶν καὶ δι' αὐτῶν ἀσφαλῶς ἐπιβαίνειν κέλευε.

27. Εἰσὶ δὲ ὡς ἐπίπαν ἐν ταῖς πολιορκίαις εἴδη μηχανημάτων πολιορκητικὰ
διάφορα, ὅσα οἵ τε παλαιοὶ στρατηγοὶ καὶ οἱ μικρῷ πρὸ ἡμῶν ἐπενόησαν κατὰ
δύναμιν ἕκαστος, καὶ τὴν καλοῦσαν τοῦ καιροῦ καὶ τοῦ τόπου χρείαν. οὐ γὰρ
νῦν ἔστι λέγειν διὰ ποίων ὀργάνων πολιορκήσεις, ἀλλὰ τοῦ καιροῦ ἡ χρεία
165 διδάξει σε ἕκαστα. καὶ γάρ εἰσι καὶ οἱ λεγόμενοι κριοὶ δι' ὧν τὰ τείχη κρουόμενα
συντρίβεται· εἰσὶ δὲ καὶ πύργοι ἀπὸ ξύλων συγκείμενοι καὶ διὰ βυρσῶν ἢ ἑτέρας
ὕλης ἐπισκεπόμενοι, ὥστε διὰ πυρὸς μὴ φθείρεσθαι, οἵτινες καὶ διὰ τροχῶν τοῖς
τείχεσι προσφερόμενοι ἀπὸ ὕψους μάχονται τοῖς ἐν τῷ τείχει· καὶ χελῶναι δὲ
προσφερόμεναι τῷ τείχει καὶ τὰ θεμέλια ἐξορύσσουσιν, καὶ σκάλαι σύνθεται ἢ
170 ἐπιτεθεῖσαι τῷ τείχει ἢ ἐν ὀρθοῖς ξύλοις ἐπικείμεναι καὶ διὰ τροχῶν προσφερόμεναι.

28. Καὶ ὀρύγματα ἔξω μὲν τοῦ τείχους κατὰ γῆν ἀπαρχόμενα, ἐντὸς δὲ διὰ
τῶν θεμελίων εἰσερχόμενα, καὶ ἀνατρυποῦντα τὴν γῆν ἔσωθεν τῆς πόλεως, | 392
εἴγε ἐν ἐπιπέδῳ τόπῳ τύχει κειμένῃ.

---

150 οὐδὲν W οὐδὲ MAVBE | ἐπιτηδείων MW ἐπιτηδείων καὶ ἀναγκαίων AVBE
151 αὐτοῖς MW αὐτοὺς AVBE | ἐνοχλεῖν MW ὀχλεῖν AVBE    152 κατὰ...ἀνενδότως MW
ἐκ διαδοχῆς ἀπαύστως AVBE    153 προσβάλλον AVBE προσβάλλοντος Μ προσβάλλοντες
W    154 φρουρίῳ MW ὀχυρώματι AVBE    155 σφοδροῦ MW om. AVBE    156 σαγίττῃ
MW σαγίττα ἢ AVBE    157 μαγγανικῶν MW μαγγανικῶν ἢ AVBE | ἀλακατίων ἢ MW om.
AVBE    158 εὐεμπρήστων οἴκων MW οἴκων τῶν εὐκόλως ἐμπρησθῆναι δυναμένων AVBE
160 κέλευε MW om. AVBE    161 ἐπίπαν MW ἐπὶ τὸ πλεῖστον AVBE    162 μικρῷ MW
om. AVBE    163 καλοῦσαν MW ἀναγκάζουσαν AVBE    165 εἰσι MW τισὶ AVBE
167 ἐπισκεπόμενοι MAVBE σκεπόμενοι W    169 ἐξορύσσουσαι καὶ MW ἐξορύσσουσιν
AVBE    174 τύχει κειμένῃ Μ κειμένη τύχοι W τύχῃ κειμένη AVBE

25. If you are setting siege to a small fortification, and you believe an assault will be risky and costly and you know that the besieged are not lacking in supplies, concentrate on confusing and harassing them day and night. Such harassment will leave them exhausted, since they are only a few against a multitude of unending attacks, one after the other.

26. If there are houses within the fortified city that can be easily set on fire, shoot a constant barrage of fire-bearing arrows in many directions, especially if there is a strong wind blowing, and set them on fire, affixing inflammable material to the arrows, by means of the stone-throwing machines that are called alakatia or tetrareai, and hurl stones filled with inflammable material against the houses and they will burn easily.[3] While the inhabitants are busy trying to extinguish the fire, put up ladders, where the ground permits, and give the command to climb up on them in safety.

27. In general, when it comes to sieges, there are different kinds of siege engines that have been devised by commanders in the past and by others in recent times, each one according to his ability and the requisite demands of time and place. This is not the time to tell you what machines you should employ in carrying out a siege. The needs of the time will teach you about each one. There are the ones called rams that pound the walls and shatter them. There are also the towers constructed of wood covered with hides or other materials so they will not be destroyed by fire. Wheels are used to bring them close to the walls and from the top soldiers fight against the people on the walls. Tortoises are also brought up to the walls to undermine their foundation. Composite ladders are set up against the walls or placed on rigid wooden beams and brought forward on wheels.

28. Excavation can also begin in the ground outside the walls, continue inside through the foundations, and bore through the earth inside the city, provided that the location is level.

3. See Dennis, "Byzantine Heavy Artillery."

175    29. Καὶ ἁπλῶς εἰπεῖν ἕτεραι μηχαναὶ ὀργάνων, ἅπερ ἔν τε ταῖς ἄλλαις ἱστορίαις, μᾶλλον δὲ ἐν τῷ πλάτει τῶν στρατηγικῶν, ἐρευνῶν εὑρήσεις, καὶ ὅπως
κατασκευάζονται καὶ ὅπως προσάγονται καὶ ἐν ὁποίοις τόποις τῶν πολιορκουμένων. τούτων δὲ τῶν μηχανημάτων αἱ παρασκευαὶ καὶ αἱ ἑτοιμασίαι οὐ μόνον
παρά σου δύνανται γίνεσθαι, ἀλλὰ καὶ δι' ἐπινοίας τῶν συνόντων σοι μαγγανα-
180    ρίων καὶ ἐπιτηδείων ἀνδρῶν πρὸς τὰς τοιαύτας κατασκευάς, ἵνα καὶ αὐτὸς
ἐπινοῇς τὰ δυνατὰ καὶ ἐνδεχόμενα μηχανήματα, κἀκεῖνοι τοῖς διὰ χειρῶν ἔργοις
καὶ ταῖς διὰ τῆς πείρας ἐπινοίαις συμβοηθήσωσί σοι.
       30. Τοὺς δὲ προδότας λεγομένους ἢ πόλεως ἢ ἄλλου τινὸς ὀχυρώματος ἢ
ὁδοῦ τῆς εἰς πολεμίαν εἰσόδου, καὶ ὑποδέχου εὐμενῶς καὶ τὰς πίστεις πρὸς
185    αὐτοὺς καὶ τὰς ἐπαγγελίας φύλαττε, ἐὰν καὶ αὐτοὶ ἀληθεύωσιν, οὐχὶ δι' αὐτούς,
ἀλλὰ διὰ τοὺς μέλλοντας καὶ πάλιν σοι τοιαύτας προξενεῖν χάριτας. ὁ γὰρ
διδούς τι τῷ προδότῃ μᾶλλον λαμβάνει παρ' αὐτοῦ πλέον παρ' ὃ ἐκείνῳ χαρίζε-
ται. οὐ γὰρ κριτὴς τῆς παρὰ τοῦ προδότου ἀδικηθείσης πόλεως ἢ τοῦ ἐχθροῦ
ὑπάρχεις, ἀλλὰ στρατηγός, καὶ διὰ πολλῶν τρόπων ὑπὲρ τοῦ σου λαοῦ λυπεῖν
190    καὶ διαφθείρειν τοὺς πολεμίους σπουδάζων. τὸ γὰρ δοκεῖν τοὺς κακοὺς μὴ
εὐεργετεῖν ἐνταῦθα ἀπειρόκαλόν μοι φαίνεται. πάντα γὰρ καλὰ ἐν καιρῷ αὐτῶν.
ὁ γὰρ προδότης, εἰ καὶ πρὸς τοὺς σοὺς πολεμίους κακὸς γέγονεν, ἀλλ' οὖν πρός
σε καὶ τὸν ὅλον σὸν λαὸν ἀγαθὸς ἀπεδείχθη.
       31. Ἐὰν δὲ Θεοῦ παρέχοντος τὴν χάριν ὑποταγῇ σοι ἢ πόλις ἢ φρούριον ἤτοι
195    κάστρον ἢ διὰ φόβον πολιορκίας ἢ δι' ἄλλην τινὰ αἰτίαν, πράως καὶ εὐμενῶς
διατέθητι πρὸς αὐτούς. καὶ μήτε φόροις αὐτοὺς καταβαρήσῃς μήτε ἀπηνῶς
ἐκφοβήσῃς ἢ ἀπειλήσῃς διά τινος τιμωρίας μήτε ἀδικίαις λυπήσῃς. ἀλλὰ μᾶλλον ἀγαθὸς καὶ ἐπιεικὴς αὐτοῖς γίνου, ἵνα καὶ οἱ λοιποὶ ὁρῶντες τὴν σὴν χρηστότητα εἰς τοὺς ὑποταγέντας σοι μετὰ προθυμίας προσέρχωνταί σοι, μηδὲν
200    κακὸν ὅπερ ὑπενεγκεῖν οὐ δύνανται παρά σου παθεῖν ἐλπίζοντες.

---

192 ad προδότης des. W

---

178 αἱ² MAVBE om. W   179 δύνανται γίνεσθαι MW trsp. AVBE   180 αὐτὸς MW σὺ
AVBE   181 κἀκεῖνοι MW καὶ ἐκεῖνοι AVBE   182 ταῖς MAVBE τοῖς W | συμβοηθήσωσί
AVBE συμβοηθοῦσιν M συμβοηθήσουσιν W   185 ἀληθεύωσιν MAVBE ἀληθεύουσιν W
187 μᾶλλον MW μᾶλλον αὐτὸς AVBE   188 τῆς MWAVBE τοῦ A   190 δοκεῖν MW
δοκεῖν ἐνταῦθα AVBE   191 ἐνταῦθα MW om. AVBE   194 φρούριον M κάστρον AVBE
196 φόροις M πάκτοις AVBE   198 αὐτοῖς γίνου M γένου AVBE   198–199 χρηστότητα
Μ ἀγαθότητα AVBE   200 ὅπερ…δύνανται Μ om. AVBE

29. In a word, there are other machines and engines that, upon investigation, you will find in other historical works and more fully in the expositions of the strategists. How are they constructed? How are they moved forward? In what kind of places under siege? Not only will you be able to bring about the construction and erection on site of these machines but you will be helped by the practical knowledge of the artillerymen with you and of the men familiar with such equipment. You are to figure out what machines are efficient and available and they are to assist you with their craftsmanship and the knowledge they have gained from experience.

30. Be sure to receive kindly those who are called traitors either from a city, some other sort of fortification, or a road leading into enemy territory. Observe the guarantees and promises made to them if they are really telling the truth, not only on their account, but also on account of those who, in return, will present you with certain favors. He who grants something to a traitor actually receives more from him than he has given. For you are not a judge of the city or of the enemy unjustly treated by the traitor, but you are a military commander, employing many means on behalf of your people to injure and destroy the enemy. Giving the impression of not offering favors to wicked men in these circumstances strikes me as foolish. All good things have their time. For the traitor, even if he is wicked as far as your enemies are concerned, yet, as far as you and all your people are concerned, he turns out to be good.

31. If God bestows his grace upon you, and the city or fortress or walled town submits to you, either out of fear of a siege or for some other reason, act gently and kindly toward the population. Do not weigh them down with fiscal impositions or frighten them in a harsh manner or threaten them with some punishment or harass them unjustly. Instead, be good and fair with them. Then, as others see your goodness toward those who have submitted to you, they will eagerly approach you in the hopes that they will not suffer any evil from you that they cannot bear.

366     Constitution 15

32. Τοῦτο γὰρ ἴσμεν καὶ Νικηφόρον τὸν ἡμέτερον στρατηγὸν πρὸς τὸ
Λαγοβάρδων ἔθνος πεποιηκότα, ὅτε πα|ρὰ τῆς βασιλείας ἡμῶν εἰς τὸ ὑποτάξαι   392ᵛ
αὐτοὺς ἐξαπεστάλη. οὐ μόνον γὰρ διὰ πολέμων ἀκριβῶς ἐκτεταγμένων τὸ
τοιοῦτον ὑπήγαγε τὸ ἔθνος, ἀλλὰ καὶ ἀγχινοίᾳ χρησάμενος καὶ δικαιοσύνῃ καὶ
205 χρηστότητι, ἐπιεικῶς τε τοῖς προσερχομένοις προσφερόμενος, καὶ τὴν ἐλευθερίαν αὐτοῖς πάσης τε δουλείας καὶ τῶν ἄλλων φορολογιῶν χαριζόμενος.

33. Οὐ γὰρ κέρδους ἕνεκεν ἡ βασιλεία ἡμῶν τὴν ὑποταγὴν τῶν ἀντικαθ-
ισταμένων ἐπιζητεῖ, ἀλλὰ δόξης μὲν ἰδίας καὶ τιμῆς, σωτηρίας δὲ καὶ εὐεργεσίας
σὺν ἐλευθερίᾳ τῶν ὑπηκόων αὐτῆς.

210 34. Οὕτως οὖν εὐμενῶς τοῖς προσερχομένοις σοι καὶ ὑποτασσομένοις
διακείμενος, δι’ αὐτῶν καὶ τοὺς μήπω προσελθόντας οἰκειώσῃ. ἡ γὰρ τεθηριωμένη γνώμη καὶ ἀπηνὴς καὶ τοὺς ὑποτασσομένους εἰς μετάμελον φέρει, καὶ τοὺς
μήπω ὑποταγέντας ἀναστέλλει καὶ μᾶλλον προθυμοτέρους ποιεῖ κινδυνεύειν
ὑπὲρ τῆς οἰκείας σωτηρίας ἢ ὑπὸ χεῖρας τοιούτου ἀπηνοῦς στρατηγοῦ ἐμπί-
215 πτειν, καὶ ταλαιπωρήσεις πολιορκῶν ἴσως καὶ μηδὲν ἀνύων. εἰ δὲ ἀγαθόν σε
μάθωσιν ὄντα, ταχέως ἐνδώσουσι τῇ ὑποταγῇ.

35. Τῆς γὰρ βασιλείας ἡμῶν τὸ εὐμενὲς καὶ χρηστὸν καὶ εἰρηνικὸν ἀγαπώ-
σης πρὸς τοὺς ὑπηκόους ὁπηνίκα διά σου πρὸς ἡμᾶς προσχωρῆσαι βουληθῇ ἢ
πόλις ἢ φρούριον ἢ ἔθνος τοῖς τῆς ἡμετέρας εὐμενείας σπλάγχνοις σε δεῖ
220 ἀφορᾶν, καὶ τὰς ἡμῶν εὐμενείας καὶ σωτηρίους κελεύσεις περὶ αὐτῶν δέχεσθαι
καὶ κρατεῖν.

36. Οὐκ ἄνευ δὲ σκοποῦ νομίζω καὶ τοῦτο ὥστε γινώσκειν σε ἀκριβῶς
ὥσπερ τὰς ἡμερινὰς ὥρας, οὕτως καὶ τὰς νυκτερινὰς διὰ τῆς τῶν φαινομένων
ἀστέρων καὶ τῆς σελήνης κινήσεων, ἵνα ἐν καιρῷ ὑποσχέσεως ὥρας ἢ παρὰ
225 προδότου προτεινομένης, ἢ παρά σου αὐτοῦ ἐπινοουμένης ἢ ἐν πολιορκίᾳ ἢ ἐν
ὁδοιπορίᾳ ἀσφαλὴς περὶ τὸ σύνθημα τοῦ καιροῦ ἢ τὸν ὁρισμὸν ὑπάρχῃς. τὸ γὰρ

211 ad αὐτῶν de novo inc. W

201–202 Cf. Skylitzes Basil.Mak., 37–38.

201 ἴσμεν M γινώσκομεν AVBE   204 ὑπήγαγε τὸ M ὑπηγάγετο AVBE   206 πάσης…
χαριζόμενος M χαριζόμενος πάσης τε δουλείας καὶ τῶν ἄλλων δημοσίων ἐλευθερῶν AVBE
211–212 τεθηριωμένη…ἀπηνὴς MW τεθηριωμένοι καὶ ἀπηνεῖς AVBE   212 φέρει MW
φέρουσιν AVBE   213 ἀναστέλλει MW ἀναστέλλουσι AVBE | ποιεῖ MW ποιοῦσι AVBE
214 ἀπηνοῦς στρατηγοῦ MW trsp. AVBE   216 ἐνδώσουσι MAVBE ἐνδώσουσιν W
218 προσχωρῆσαι MW προσελθεῖν AVBE   219 τοῖς MW εἰς τὰ AVBE | σπλάγχνοις MW
σπλάγχνα AVBE   220 εὐμενείας MW φιλανθρώπους AVBE   222 οὐκ…ὥστε MW om.
AVBE | ἀκριβῶς MW δὲ δεῖ AVBE   224 κινήσεων MW κινήσεως AVBE

32. We recall that our commander, Nikephoros, acted in this way toward the people of the Lombards when he was sent by Our Majesty to subdue them.[4] For it was not only by well-organized military operations that he subdued that people, but he also displayed shrewdness, justice, and goodness. He presented himself with fairness to those who came to him and he granted them freedom from all servitude and other fiscal exactions.

33. It is not for the sake of gain that Our Majesty seeks the subjection of those who stand against us, but for our glory and honor as well as the security of our subjects and the blessings that accompany freedom.

34. Act, therefore, in an equitable manner to those who approach and submit to you. Through them you will make friends of those who have not yet approached you. A ferocious and harsh manner leads those who have been subjected to change their minds and causes those who have not yet been subjected to resist. It makes them all the more enthusiastic about facing danger on behalf of their own safety rather than falling into the hands of such a harsh commander. You are likely to have a difficult time in carrying out a siege and will accomplish nothing. But if they learn that you are good, they will quickly offer their submission.

35. Seeing that Our Majesty cherishes fairness and goodness and peacefulness toward our subjects, whenever, by your action, a city or fortress or nation should wish to come over to us, you must look to our mercy and kindness and receive and observe our gentle and salutary commands for them.

36. I do not think that even this is without purpose, namely that, just as with the hours of the day, you should have precise knowledge of those at night by following the movements of the visible stars and the moon. Then you appear safely at the opportune hour arranged or proposed by a traitor or devised by you, either during a siege or on the march, according to the time agreed upon or

---

4. This refers to the campaign of Nikephoros Phokas the Elder in Calabria, in 885: Skylitzes, *Basil.Mak.*, 37–38; Theophanes *Cont.* 312–314.

ταχύτερον ἢ βραδύτερον πολλάκις φθάνειν τῆς συνταγῆς ἢ τοῦ ὁρισμοῦ ἄπρακτον ἐποίησε τὸ προκείμενον ἔργον.

37. Ἐξερχόμενος δὲ κατὰ τῆς πολιορκίας, εἴτε διὰ προδότου εἴτε ἄλλως πως,
230 ὅσους κατὰ τὴν ὁδὸν ὑπαντήσεις συλλάμβανε πάντας διά τινων καβαλλαρίων
προαποστελλομένων ἐπ' αὐτῷ τούτῳ ἢ διὰ τῶν μετά σου στρατιωτῶν ἵνα μὴ δι'
αὐτῶν ἡ ἐπέλευσίς σου μηνυθῇ. τὰ γὰρ τοιαῦτα κατὰ τῶν | πολεμίων ἔργα   393
αἰφνιδίως γίνεσθαι δεῖ καὶ ἀνυπονοήτως.

38. Ὅταν γὰρ ἀπροσδοκήτως ἐπέλθῃ κατ' ἐχθρῶν στράτευμα, κἂν ὀλιγώτε-
235 ρόν ἐστι τῶν πολεμίων, διὰ τὴν ἀνυφόρατον ἐπιδρομὴν ἐκπλήττει τοὺς ἐναντίους, κἂν κρείττονές εἰσιν ἐκεῖνοι· καὶ ἐκ τούτου διὰ πολλῶν ἐκφόβων αὐτοὺς
δύνασαι μᾶλλον πρὸ τοῦ θαρρῆσαι αὐτοὺς οἰκειώσασθαι εἰς τὸ σὸν βούλημα.

39. Οὕτως οὖν ἐπειδὰν ἢ πόλιν ἢ κάστρον ἢ ἄλλο τι ὀχύρωμα παραλάβῃς,
καὶ λάβῃ πέρας ὁ πόλεμος, μὴ γενήσῃ βαρὺς διὰ τὴν εὐπραγίαν ἢ τοῖς δυστυχή-
240 σασιν ἢ τοῖς ἅμα σοι ἐκστρατεύουσιν. μηδὲ τῦφον καὶ ἀπήνειαν περιφέρης,
ἀλλὰ εὐμενής, ὡς εἴρηται, καὶ φιλάνθρωπος καὶ ταπεινόφρων γένου· φιλάνθρωπος μὲν περὶ τοὺς ἁλωθέντας καὶ δυστυχήσαντας ἀλλὰ καὶ πρὸς τοὺς μέλλοντας ἔτι παρά σου ἢ πολεμεῖσθαι ἢ πολιορκεῖσθαι, ταπεινόφρων δὲ περὶ τοὺς
πλησίον καὶ φίλους· τοὺς μὲν γὰρ πλησίον καὶ φίλους οὐ μόνον εἰς φθόνον οὐ
245 κινήσεις ἀλλὰ καὶ εἰς ζῆλον τῶν ὁμοίων σου κατορθωμάτων διεγειρεῖς, τοὺς δὲ
πολιορκεῖσθαι μέλλοντας εὐπειθεῖς μᾶλλον καὶ ὑποταττομένους σοι παρασκευάσεις διὰ τὴν ἐλπιζομένην παρά σου εὐμένειαν καὶ ἀγαθότητα. ταῦτα μὲν
παρακελευόμεθά σοι, ὦ στρατηγέ, παραφυλάττειν ὅταν αὐτὸς πολεμίοις ἐπελ-
θὼν πολιορκεῖν τὰ ἐκείνων μέλλῃς.

250 40. Εἰ δ', ὅπερ πολλάκις συμβαίνει, πόλις ἢ κάστρον ἤ τι ἕτερον ὀχύρωμα
ὑπό σε ὑπάρχον μέλλει παρὰ πολεμίων πολιορκεῖσθαι, εἰ μὲν δύνασαι τοὺς
ἐπερχομένους ἐπιτηδεῦσαι, καὶ ἄπρακτον αὐτῶν διὰ τῆς σῆς προσβολῆς τὴν
βουλὴν ἀποδεῖξαι, τῷ Θεῷ χάρις· εἰ δὲ μήγε, πάντως παρασκευάσεις τοὺς
μέλλοντας πολιορκεῖσθαι, εἴτε αὐτὸς μέλλεις ἐξ ἀνάγκης τινὸς ἐκεῖ παρεῖναι
255 εἴτε ἕτερός τις τῶν ὑπό σε ἀρχόντων ἀνὴρ ἐλλόγιμος καὶ ἔμπειρος.

41. Πρῶτον μὲν ἁπάντων χρὴ τῶν ἀναγκαίων εἰς ἀποτροφὴν φροντίσαι τῶν
ἐγκλειομένων ὅσον οἶδας τὸν ἐχθρὸν ἐξαρκεῖν ἐπὶ τῇ πολιορκίᾳ χρόνον, καὶ εἰ

---

228 ἐποίησε MW ἐποίησεν AVBE   229 κατὰ MW διὰ AVBE   230 ὑπαντήσεις MAVBE
ἀπαντήσεις W   233 δεῖ W om. MAVBE | ἀνυπονοήτως MW ἀνυπονοήτως προσήκει AVBE
234 κατ' MW κατὰ τῶν AVBE   239 γενήσῃ MW γένη AVBE   242 ἁλωθέντας MW
κρατηθέντας AVBE   243 πολεμεῖσθαι...πολιορκεῖσθαι MAVBE trsp. W   252 ἐπιτηδεῦσαι
MW καταστρατηγῆσαι AVBE

determined. Often enough, arriving sooner or later than agreed on or determined has rendered the task at hand without effect.

37. When you march out to begin a siege, either with the help of a traitor or in some other way, cavalry units specifically assigned to this duty or the soldiers accompanying you should detain all those you encounter on the road, so they may not give warning of your advance. It is necessary to engage in such actions against the enemy suddenly and unexpectedly.

38. Whenever an army unexpectedly advances against the enemy, even though it is smaller than they are, the unforeseen attack causes panic among its adversaries even though they may be stronger. As a result, you will fill them with fear and, before they regain their confidence, you will be able to win them over to your will.

39. Therefore, whenever you take over a city or walled town or some other fortified place and the war has come to an end, do not become overbearing because of your success either to those who have suffered adverse fortune or to those who campaigned with you. Do not strut around in a cruel and arrogant manner. But act kindly, as has been said, humanely and humbly. Treat in a humane manner those who have been captured and subjected to misfortune, as well as those whom you will still battle or besiege. Act humbly toward your friends and those close to you; not only so you will not make them jealous, but also so you will arouse them to strive for success similar to yours. The people whom you are about to place under siege hope that goodness and kindness will mark your dealings with them and this will render them disposed to obey and submit to you. We command, O general, that you observe these points when you proceed against the enemy with the intention of laying siege to their places.

40. But if, as often happens, a city, walled town, or some other fortified place subject to you is about to come under siege by the enemy, and you are able to deal with them as they approach and your attack nullifies their intention, thanks be to God. But if that is not the case, you are to take all means to prepare the people for what they are soon to face, whether you will be there in person for some necessity or whether one of your officers, prudent and experienced, will be there.

41. First of all, you must take thought for the provisions needed by the people under siege. Find out how much time the enemy has to spend on the

μὲν εὐπορία ἐστὶ τοσαύτης ἀποτροφῆς. εἰ δὲ μὴ τὴν ἄχρηστον ἡλικίαν ἔκβαλε
ἐκ τοῦ ὀχυρώματος πρὸ τῆς τῶν ἐχθρῶν παρουσίας, οἷον γυναῖκας, γέροντας,
260 ἀσθενεῖς, καὶ παιδία, ἵνα τοῖς ἐν δυνάμει οὖσιν ἢ εὑρισκομένοις ἡ δαπάνη ἐξαρ-
κέσῃ, καὶ ἵνα | ὁ μέλλων πολιορκεῖσθαι προευτρεπίσῃ μηχανήματα ἀντικείμενα   393ᵛ
πρὸς τὴν ἀποσοβὴν τῶν πετροβόλων μαγγάνων τῶν ἐχθρῶν.

42. Ἀντίκεινται δὲ ταῖς τοιαύταις βολαῖς κιλίκια κρεμάμενα ἔξωθεν τοῦ
τείχους κατὰ τοὺς προμαχῶνας, ἢ σάρκινα ἢ σχοινία εἰλημένα ἢ πόντιλα ἤτοι
265 ξύλα κρεμάμενα, καὶ πλίνθος δὲ ἐν τοῖς προμαχῶσιν οἰκοδομουμένη, καὶ πρὸς
τοὺς κριοὺς δὲ ἀντίκειται τυλάρια καὶ σακκία γέμοντα ἄχυρα καὶ ψάμμον.

43. Πρὸς δὲ τὰς χελώνας ἅρπαγες ἤτοι ξύλα μεγάλα ἔχοντα ξίφη καὶ ἐμπισ-
σόμενα, ὥστε ἢ ἐκστρέψαι αὐτὴν ἢ ἀνακουφίσαι καὶ γυμνῶσαι τοὺς ἔσωθεν τῆς
χελῶνος καὶ οὕτως κατ' αὐτῶν ἐγχειρεῖν ἄνωθεν.

270 44. Ἀλλὰ καὶ πίσσα, δι' ἧς κενουμένης ἐμπρησθήσονται, καὶ πῦρ καὶ λίθοι
βαρεῖς κατάκεντροι ἀπὸ μαγγάνων ἄφνω χαλώμενοι διὰ σχοινίων ἤτοι ἀλύσεων,
καὶ πάλιν ἀνασπώμενοι δι' ἑτέρων ἀντιβαρημάτων.

45. Πρὸς δὲ τοὺς ἐπαγομένους πύργους πυροβόλα εἴδη καὶ πετροβόλοι, ἢ εἰ
μὴ τοῦτο ἀντισχῇ, ἀντιπύργους ὁμοίως οἰκοδομεῖν, ἢ διὰ ξύλων ἢ δι' ἑτέρας
275 ὕλης τοὺς ἔσωθεν τοῦ τείχους ἄντις ἐκείνων, ἢ ἁπλῶς ὡς ἂν δυνατὸν πρὸς τὴν
μηχανὴν τῶν ἔξωθεν ἀντιμηχανᾶσθαι τοὺς ἔσωθεν, καθὼς ἐν τῷ πλάτει μετὰ
σχολῆς ἐρευνῶν εὑρήσεις πρὸς ἑκάστην μηχανὴν ἀντεξευρημένα. ἀναγκαῖον δέ
ἐστι τοὺς πύργους τοὺς ἐπιμάχους τοῦ τείχους ἀσκεπεῖς εἶναι, ὥστε τοὺς μαχομένους ἀκωλύτως ἐκεῖθεν μάχεσθαι, καὶ τὰ μάγγανα εὐκόπως τίθεσθαι καὶ
280 ἐξεργάζεσθαι. καὶ παραπόρτια δὲ ἐν τοῖς τοιούτοις πύργοις ἐκ πλαγίου στενὰ
ἀνοίγεσθαι κατὰ τοῦ δεξιοῦ μέρους τῶν προσαγομένων μαγγάνων ἐκ τῶν
ἐχθρῶν ἵνα πεζοὶ ἐξερχόμενοι ἐκ τῶν παραπυλῶν, καὶ κατὰ χεῖρα ἁρμοδίως τοῖς
σκουταρίοις σκεπόμενοι, καὶ ὑπὸ τῶν ἄνωθεν βοηθούμενοι δύνανται ἀποσοβεῖν
τὰ μάγγανα. ἔχειν δὲ ταῦτα πύλας δι' ὧν δέον ἀσφαλίζεσθαι ἐν καιρῷ καὶ μὴ
285 μένειν ἠνεῳγμένα.

---

258 εἰ…μὴ AVBE ἐπείτοιγε MW   258–259 ἔκβαλε ἐκ MW ἔκβαλλε AVBE   260 ἢ
εὑρισκομένοις MW om. AVBE   262 τὴν ἀποσοβὴν MW ἀποκώλυσιν AVBE
264 εἰλημένα AVBE εἰλιμμένα MW   265 προμαχῶσιν WAVBE προμαχοῦσιν M
266 ἄχυρα M ἄχυρον WAVBE   267 χελώνας MW χελώνης AVBE   275 ἄντις MW
κατέναντι AVBE | ἂν MW om. AVBE   278 ἐστι M ἐστιν WAVBE   279 εὐκόπως MW
εὐκόλως AVBE   282 παραπυλῶν MW παραπορτίων AVBE

siege and if you are well supplied with a corresponding amount of provisions. Before the arrival of the enemy, be sure to evacuate from the fortified area those who will be useless, such as the women, the elderly, the infirm, and children, so that the provisions will be sufficient for the able fighting men found there and so that the general about to be besieged may get ready devices to defend against the stone-throwing engines of the enemy.

42. As protection against such missiles heavy mats can be hung along the battlements on the outside of the walls. Thick hides, coils of rope, boards, or planks can also be hung there. Brick facing can also be built onto the ramparts. Against battering rams cushions or sacks filled with grain husks and sand are effective.

43. Against the tortoises grappling irons or large pieces of wood with sharp points and covered with pitch so as to overturn the tortoise or uncover it and expose the men inside it to attack from above.

44. Pitch will set the uncovered tortoises on fire. Inflammable objects or heavy, sharpened stones held by ropes or chains can be suddenly dropped from machines and then hauled up again by other counterweights.

45. Against towers that they move up, <use> incendiary missiles or stone throwers. If this does not stop them, construct towers of wood or some other material inside the walls to oppose theirs. To put it simply, do whatever makes it possible for those inside to fight against the machines of those outside. In general, as you take your time in studying the situation, you will discover that you can find the means to confront every machine. The towers of the wall that are exposed to attack must be without roofs so that the fighting men on them can fight unobstructed, and artillery can easily be mounted there and operated. These towers should have small, narrow doorways opening to the side toward the right of the siege engines drawn up by the enemy. Foot soldiers can then go out by these side doorways and engage in hand-to-hand fighting while covered by their shields and supported by the men above, and in this way they will be able to take action against the siege engines. These doorways should have gates so they can be secured when necessary and not remain open.

46. Ἀποκρεμᾶν δὲ κατὰ τῶν προμαχώνων ξύλα βαρέα πάνυ, κορμία, καὶ μύλους λιθίνους διὰ σχοινίων ἵνα, ἐὰν προσάψωσι σκάλας εἰς τὰ τείχη, κοπτομένων τῶν σχοινίων ἐπιπέσωσιν ἐπάνω τῶν ἀναβαινόντων καὶ διαφθείρωσιν | 394 αὐτούς. τοῦτο δὲ ἐν κύκλῳ τοῦ τείχους γενέσθαι κελεύομεν καὶ μηδένα λείπειν
290 προμαχῶνα, εἰ δυνατόν, ὅστις οὐκ ἔχει ἢ λίθον βαρύτατον ἤτοι μύλον ἢ ξύλον μακρὸν καὶ βαρὺ πάνυ, δυνάμενον συντρίψαι καὶ σκάλαν καὶ τοὺς ἐπ᾽ αὐτῆς ἀναβαίνοντας.

47. Χρὴ δὲ καὶ καταμερίσαι τὴν βοήθειαν δι᾽ ὅλου τοῦ τείχους καὶ ἔχειν ἄλλην δύναμιν ἐκ περισσοῦ ἵνα τῷ δεομένῳ μέρει, ἐὰν χρεία γένηται, βοηθῇ, καὶ
295 μὴ ἀναγκάζωνται ἐν καιρῷ ἀνάγκης ἐκ τόπου εἰς τόπον διατρέχειν οἱ πρὸς παραφυλακὴν τοῦ τείχους τεταγμένοι, καὶ ἐκ τούτου γυμνοῦσθαί τινας αὐτοῦ τόπους, ὅπερ ἐστὶν ἐπικίνδυνον.

48. Ἐὰν δὲ καὶ διχοστασία ἐστὶ παρά τινων ἐν τῇ πόλει ἢ τῷ κάστρῳ, δέον ἢ κἀκείνους εἰρηνεῦσαι καὶ συμμίξαι ἐν ταῖς τοῦ τείχους πεδατούραις τοὺς στρατι-
300 ώτας—ἐκ τούτου γὰρ οὐδὲ εὐκαιροῦσι στάσιν μελετῆσαι ἢ κατὰ τοῦ κοινοῦ ἢ καθ᾽ ἑαυτῶν, ἀλλὰ καὶ δοκοῦντες φυλακὴν τῆς πόλεως πιστευθῆναι ἐρυθριῶσιν νεωτερίσαι—ἢ ἐὰν μὴ τοῦτο, πάντως αὐτοὺς προεξαγαγεῖν ἀλλαχοῦ, καὶ μηδὲν ἐξ αὐτῶν ὑφορᾶσθαι παθεῖν στάσεως ἐν τῇ πολιορκίᾳ, ἀλλὰ καὶ τὰς προδοσίας ὑφορᾶσθαι καὶ ἀσφαλίζεσθαι, ὥστε μὴ δύνασθαί τινα τοῖς πολεμίοις ἢ γράφειν
305 ἢ συντυχεῖν ἐκτὸς βουλῆς τοῦ πεπιστευμένου τὴν πόλιν ἢ τὸ κάστρον.

49. Καὶ τὰς πύλας δὲ τῆς πόλεως πιστοῖς ἀνδράσι παραδοθῆναι καὶ μηδ᾽ ὅλως θαρρῆσαί τινας τῶν στρατιωτῶν ἢ πολιτῶν ἐν τοῖς προοιμίοις μάλιστα τῆς πολιορκίας ἐξέρχεσθαι τοῦ τείχους καὶ μάχεσθαι, κἂν συμβῇ πολλοὺς καὶ γενναίους εἰς ἀνδρείαν εἶναι τοὺς ἐγκεκλεισμένους, ἐὰν μήπου καιρὸς γένηται ἢ
310 μάγγανον ἐνοχλοῦν ἐπικινδύνως τῷ τείχει ἀποσοβηθῆναι ἐκ χειρὸς ἤ τις ἑτέρα χρεία ἀναγκαία καὶ κατεπείγουσα τοῦτο, ἀλλὰ πάντας ἄνωθεν ἀμύνασθαι καὶ μὴ ἔξωθεν πληγοῦσθαι ἢ κινδυνεύειν. εἰ γάρ τι τοιοῦτο γένηται, τῶν δυνατωτέρων ἀνδρῶν ἢ ἀποθνησκόντων ἢ πληγουμένων, ὁ λοιπὸς ὄχλος ἐν ὀλιγωρίᾳ

---

286 βαρέα…κορμία M βαρεία πάνυ κορμία W κορμία βαρέα πάνυ AVBE    287 μύλους λιθίνους MW trsp. AVBE | προσάψωσι MW προσάξωσι ABE    288 διαφθείρωσιν MAVBE διαφθείρουσιν W    289 γενέσθαι κελεύομεν MAVBE trsp. W    291 βαρὺ WAVBE βαρὺν M | καὶ³ MW τὴν AVBE    298 ἐστὶ MAVBE ἐστιν W    299–300 τοὺς στρατιώτας M τοῖς στρατιώταις WAVBE    301–302 ἐρυθριῶσιν νεωτερίσαι MW αἰσχύνονται ἀταξίας ποιεῖν AVBE    303 πολιορκία MW πολιορκία γενομένης AVBE    305 συντυχεῖν MW συντυγχάνειν AVBE    307 τοῖς προοιμίοις MW τῇ ἀρχῇ AVBE    310 ἀποσοβηθῆναι MW ἀποκωλυθῆναι AVBE | τις ἑτέρα MW trsp. AVBE    311 ἀμύνασθαι MW ἀμύνεσθαι AVBE    312 τοιοῦτο M τοιοῦτον WAVBE

46. From the battlements be sure to hang heavy timbers, trunks, and mill-stones by ropes. If the ladders are set up against the walls, cut the ropes and they will fall upon the men climbing up and destroy them. We order that you do this along the whole circuit of the walls and, if possible, leave no battlement without either a very heavy stone, a millstone, or a large and very heavy timber, each one of which is able to demolish a ladder and the men climbing up it.

47. You must distribute support groups along the whole length of the walls and hold another force in reserve so they may come to the aid of a threatened sector when necessary. In an emergency the troops assigned to defend the walls will not be forced to dash from place to place, leaving certain spots wide open, a very dangerous thing to do.

48. If there should be dissension among some in the city or the walled town, it is necessary to establish peace among them and have them join the soldiers in the various sections of the wall. In this way they will not find time to plan an uprising either against the commonwealth or against themselves, but by realizing that they have been entrusted with the defense of the city, they will be ashamed to rebel. If this cannot be done, be sure to move them to another location ahead of time and keep an eye on them so you do not have to put up with any dissension during the siege. Also be on the lookout for treachery and guard against it. Nobody should be able to write to or meet with the enemy without permission of the official placed in charge of the city or walled town.

49. The gates of the city should be entrusted to reliable men. Especially in the early stages of the siege, no soldiers or civilians should be so bold as to go outside the walls and fight, even when there are many men of outstanding courage within the city. Make direct contact only if the situation requires that you put some siege engine, posing a serious threat to the walls, out of action or if some other compelling need should arise. Otherwise, everyone should take part in the defense from the top <of the walls> and not endanger themselves or be wounded outside. For when that sort of thing happens, the most capable men are killed or wounded and the rest of them become so discouraged that they are

γίνεται καὶ εὐχείρωτος τοῖς ἐχθροῖς. φανερὸν γάρ ἐστιν ὅτι ἕως ἂν οἱ ἄνδρες
315 σώζωνται καὶ τὸ τεῖχος συνίσταται, ἐκείνων δὲ προδιδομένων τὸ λειπόμενον
κινδυνεύει.

50. Ἐὰν δὲ προτείχισμα ἔχει ἕτερον ἢ ἡ πόλις ἢ τὸ ὀχύρωμα, οὐκ ἄτοπον | 394ᵛ
βίγλας ἐν αὐτῷ γίνεσθαι ἰσχυρὰς καὶ ἀκριβεῖς καὶ μάλιστα εἰς τὰς νύκτας, ὅταν
καὶ προσφεύγειν τινὲς εἰς τοὺς ἐχθροὺς μελετῶσι, καὶ ἐπιβουλαὶ λαθραίως κατὰ
320 τοῦ τείχους δύνανται γίνεσθαι.

51. Ἀλλὰ καὶ τὰ ἀκοντίσματα ἢ διὰ τόξων ἢ διὰ λίθων ἢ διὰ τοξοβολιστρῶν
μὴ ἀκαίρως καὶ μάτην ἐκ τοῦ τείχους ποιεῖν καὶ ἐκ τούτου εἰς καταφρόνησιν
γίνεσθαι αὐτὰ τοῖς ἐναντίοις ὡς μὴ ἐνεργοῦντα.

52. Ἐὰν δὲ ἀπὸ κινστέρνας ἔχωσι τὸ πόσιμον ὕδωρ, καὶ οὐκ ἀπὸ πηγῆς
325 ἀδιάλειπτον ἢ ἀπὸ πλέθρου ὀλιγούμενον τὸ ὕδωρ, μέτρῳ τινὶ καὶ διοικήσει
γίνεσθαι τὴν διανομὴν καὶ μὴ ἔχειν ἐπ' ἐξουσίας τὸν θέλοντα ὡς ἀρέσκει αὐτῷ
δαπανᾶν. ὁμοίως καὶ ἐπὶ τῆς ἄλλης δαπάνης συμμέτρως ἅπαντα γίνεσθαι ἵνα
καὶ ἀρκῇ καὶ εὐρώστους τοὺς πολιορκουμένους φυλάττῃ.

53. Τὰς δὲ βίγλας ἐπιμελῶς κατὰ διαδοχὴν γίνεσθαι καὶ μάλιστα ἐν ταῖς
330 νυξίν. ἐν παραφυλακῇ δὲ τηρεῖσθαι καὶ τὴν δαπάνην εἰς τὸ μὴ εὐκόλως ὑπὸ τῶν
τυχόντων διαρπάζεσθαι.

54. Παραινεῖν δὲ συνεχέστερον τὸν κρατοῦντα τοὺς ἐντὸς διὰ λόγων καὶ
προθυμοποιεῖν πρὸς τὴν ὑπομονὴν ἕως εἴτε διὰ τῆς σῆς δυνάμεως εἴτε δι'
ἑτέρας αἰτίας ὁ καιρὸς τῆς ἀναχωρήσεως τῶν ἐχθρῶν γένηται. ἐπιδρομὰς δὲ
335 ποιεῖν τὸν στρατηγὸν ὅσον ἡ δύναμις ἀπαντᾷ κατὰ τῶν πολιορκούντων διά
τινων διαφόρων προσβολῶν καὶ φήμης, ὡς ἑτέρου πλείστου στρατοῦ
ἐπερχομένου, καὶ ὅσα θροεῖν δύναται τοὺς πολεμίους.

55. Ταῦτα μὲν οὖν ὁ πολιορκούμενος ποιήσει ὅσα μοι εἴρηται, καὶ ἕτερα δέ
τινα προσεπινοήσει τὰ ἐναντία πρὸς ἕκαστον τῶν παρὰ τοῦ πολιορκοῦντος
340 μηχανωμένων, καὶ παρ' ἡμῶν εἰρημένων ἔμπροσθεν, ἀντιτιθεὶς ἐκείνοις τὰ ἴδια
ἐκ τοῦ ἐναντίου. αὐτόθεν γὰρ ἐπινοήσει πῶς δεῖ ἑκάστῳ τῶν ἐπαγομένων
ἀντιμάχεσθαι.

---

318 αὐτῷ MAVBE ἑαυτῷ W   319 μελετῶσι MW μελετῶσιν AVBE   320 δύνανται
γίνεσθαι MW trsp. AVBE   323 γίνεσθαι αὐτὰ MW trsp. AVBE   324 ἔχωσι MAVBE
ἔχουσι W   325 ἀδιάλειπτον MW ἀδιαλείπτου AVBE | ἢ...ὕδωρ MW om. AVBE   326 ἐπ'
ἐξουσίας AVBE ἐπεξουσίως MW   333 δι' De δ' codd.   334 γένηται MAVBE γίνεται W
335–337 ὅσον...δύναται MW κατὰ τῶν πολιορκούντων ὅσον ἡ δύναμις ἀπαντᾷ φημίζειν δὲ
ὅτι καὶ ἕτερον πλῆθος στρατοῦ ἐπέρχεται εἰς βοήθειαν καὶ ἕτερα ὅσα ἐκφοβεῖν καὶ ταράσσειν
δύνανται AVBE   340 παρ' ἡμῶν MAVBE παρὰ τῶν W   341 ἐπινοήσει MW ἐπινοήσεις
AVBE

easily defeated by the enemy. It is obvious that, as long as the men are safe, the wall will also be secure but, when they give up, the rest will be endangered.

50. If the city or the fortified place has another outer wall, it is not a bad idea to post strong and alert sentries on it, especially at night, when some persons may be thinking of deserting to the enemy and attacks against the wall may be prepared in secret.

51. The firing of missiles from the walls, whether by bows, stones, or catapults, must not be ill-timed and ineffective, for the enemy will not take them seriously if they are ineffective.

52. If the drinking water comes from a cistern and does not flow constantly from a spring, or the water in it is less than <would fill a small> pond, it must be distributed by a certain measure and management.[5] No one has the authority to consume as much as he wishes. In like manner all the other provisions are to be evenly distributed so that there will be enough to maintain the besieged in a healthy condition.

53. Be sure to have constant patrols on guard duty, especially at night, to protect the provisions so they cannot easily be stolen by anyone passing by.

54. The person in charge must continuously advise those within <the city> by his words and encourage them to be patient until the time when your forceful action or some other cause brings about the enemy's withdrawal. To the extent possible, the commander must launch attacks against the besiegers in a variety of ways. He should also <spread> rumors that another very large army is approaching or whatever else will terrify the enemy.

55. The man under siege, therefore, will act in the manner I have described and he should devise other means to oppose each stratagem employed by the besieger. Add this also to what we have said above: having set up his own <devices> to oppose them, by himself he will figure out how he must confront each situation he encounters.

---

5. "Small pond": literally, a space less than one hundred feet, πλέθρον. See Schilbach, *Metrologie*, 81–83.

56. Οὐ παραλείψω δὲ καὶ ὅπερ μοι ἐρευνῶντι εὕρηται καὶ ἀνέγνωσται, εἰ καὶ μὴ νῦν ἐστι περισπούδαστον, περὶ τοῦ πῶς δυνατὸν λαθραίως διὰ τάχους κτίζειν
345 φρούριον τὸν βουλόμενον στρατηγὸν ἐν μεθορίῳ πολεμίων ἀλλαχοῦ που λανθάνοντα τοὺς ἐχθρούς. πρότερον μὲν γὰρ δεῖ σε κατασκοπῆσαι τόπον ὀχυρὸν δυνάμενον διὰ δέκα ἢ δώδεκα ἡμερῶν διὰ ξηρᾶς ὕλης περιβληθῆναι ἐν καιρῷ ἐπι|φόβου προσβολῆς τῶν πολεμίων, καὶ ἐάν εἰσιν ὕλαι πλησίον, λίθου ἢ 395 ξύλου ἢ πλίνθου ἑτοίμης, καί ἐστιν ὕδωρ ἢ ἐπινοηθῆναι δυνατόν.
350 57. Καὶ προπαρασκευάσαι τεχνίτας ἱκανοὺς καὶ πόρτας καὶ μάγγανα τείχους καὶ βοήθειαν ἀρκοῦσαν πεζῶν ἐνόπλων καὶ γενναίων μετὰ ἀρχόντων φρονίμων καὶ εὐψύχων, ἅμα καὶ ἁμαξῶν, ὡς εἰς φοσσάτου τάξιν καὶ ἀσφάλειαν αὐτῶν καὶ δαπάνην τριῶν ἢ τεσσάρων μηνῶν. καὶ εἰ καιρός ἐστι θέρους ἐμπρῆσαι τὰς βοσκὰς τὰς πλησίον τοῦ τόπου· εἰ δὲ καῆναι δυσχερεῖς εἰσιν, καταδαπανῆσαι
355 αὐτάς, καὶ διαφημίσαι ὡς ἐν ἑτέρῳ τόπῳ ποιήσεις κατὰ τῶν ἐχθρῶν ἐπέλευσιν, καὶ πέμψεις βοήθειαν ἀσφαλῆ κατὰ τοῦ φημιζομένου τόπου ἵνα ἐκεῖ προσδοκῶντες περισπῶνται οἱ ἐχθροί, καὶ τότε πρὸ μιᾶς ἡμέρας θαρρήσει τοῖς ὀφείλουσιν εἰσελθεῖν ἐν τῷ τόπῳ, καὶ τινὰ μὲν δῶρα δοῦναι εἰς προτροπὴν αὐτῶν, τινὰ δὲ καὶ ἐπαγγέλλεσθαι, καὶ αἰφνίδιον ἐν ἑτέρῳ τόπῳ τῶν ἐχθρῶν ἀσχολουμένων
360 μετὰ παντὸς τοῦ στρατοῦ ἐπιστῇς τῷ ὡρισμένῳ σοι τόπῳ, καὶ στήσεις βίγλας ἀσφαλεῖς καὶ οἱ πεζοὶ ἀπληκεύσουσι κύκλῳ τοῦ ὀχυρώματος καὶ τάφρον βαθυτάτην ποιήσεις, εἰ ἐπιδέχεται ὁ τόπος.

58. Καὶ εἰ μὲν λίθος ἢ πλίνθος εὑρίσκεται, οἰκοδομῆσαι ξηρὸν δεῖ, καὶ δῆσαι διὰ ξύλων ἀσφαλῶς καὶ συνεχῶς· εἰ δὲ ξύλα μόνον εἰσί, δι' αὐτῶν ἀποκλεῖσαι
365 ὀλίγον καὶ ὀχυρὸν τόπον καὶ μὴ μέγαν τέως. μετὰ δὲ τὸ ἀποκλεισθῆναι αὐτὸν κατὰ τὸν λεχθέντα τρόπον, εἰ μὲν ὁρμήσωσιν οἱ ἐχθροὶ κατὰ τοῦ τόπου, καὶ οἶδας ὅτι οὐ δύνασαι πρὸς μάχην ἀντέχειν, τότε ἀναχωρήσεις πρὸ τῆς παρουσίας αὐτῶν, καταλιπὼν ἔσωθεν τοὺς ἱκανούς, καὶ ἀπληκεύσεις πλησίον τοσοῦτον, ὥστε μήτε ἐγγὺς τῶν ἐχθρῶν εἶναι καὶ ἀναγκασθῆναι πολεμῆσαι, μήτε μηκόθεν
370 τῶν ἐν τῷ ὀχυρώματι ἵνα μὴ εὐκαιροῦντες οἱ ἐχθροὶ σφοδρῶς ἐπίκεινται τοῖς ἔσωθεν.

---

343–344 οὐ…πῶς MW ῥητέον καὶ πῶς ἐστι AVBE    345 μεθορίῳ MW συνόρῳ AVBE
345–346 ἀλλαχοῦ…ἐχθρούς MW om. AVBE    348 εἰσιν MAVBE εἰσι W    349 καί MW
καὶ εἰ AVBE    354 εἰσιν MAVBE εἰσι W    357 θαρρήσει MW θαρρήσεις AVBE
359 ἐπαγγέλλεσθαι MW ὑποσχέσθαι AVBE    361 ἀπληκεύσουσι MVBE ἀπληκεύουσιν WA
| τάφρον MW σούδαν AVBE    363 οἰκοδομῆσαι…δεῖ MW δεῖ οἰκοδομῆσαι ξηρὸν AVBE
364 εἰσί M εἰσιν WAVBE    366 τρόπον WAVBE τόπον M | ὁρμήσωσιν MW ὁρμήσουσιν
AVBE

56. I will not leave out what I have discovered and read in my investigations even though it may not be of much concern at present. How it is possible for a general to fulfill his wish to build a fortress at some location on the border with the enemy quickly and without letting them find out? You must first thoroughly scout out a strong site capable of being walled about with dry materials in ten or twelve days, at a time when you fear an enemy attack. Are materials available in the vicinity, stone, wood, or prepared brick? Is there water or can you figure out ways to find it?

57. Get a sufficient force of artisans ready ahead of time, as well as gates and machines for the walls and a good-sized support force of brave and well-armed infantry under intelligent and courageous officers. At the same time, have the wagons form a fortified space for the safety of men and provisions for three or four months. If it is summer, set the pasturelands in the vicinity of the spot on fire. If it proves difficult to burn them, consume them. Spread the rumor that you are going to attack the enemy in some other place. Send a safe support force against the rumored place so that the enemy will expect you there and be diverted. Then, a day ahead, encourage the troops who have been ordered to march into that place, and offer them some gifts to motivate them and promise still others. While the enemy are occupied in that other place, all of a sudden move your whole army to the site you have designated, set up secure sentries, and have the infantry pitch camp in a circle around the fortification and dig a deep ditch, if the ground permits.

58. If stones or bricks are found there, you must construct a dry wall, braced securely along its length with logs. If wood is all there is, use it to enclose a small and strong space, not too large. If the enemy attacks the place, after you have enclosed the area in the prescribed manner, and you know that you are not able to resist them in battle, then withdraw before their approach. Leave a sufficient force inside and pitch camp nearby. Do not camp so close to the enemy that you will be forced to do battle or too far from those in the fortified site, so the enemy may not seize the opportunity to come down hard on those inside it.

378    Constitution 15

59. Δώσεις δὲ σημεῖον τοῖς ἐν αὐτῷ· τί μὲν ἐν τῇ ἡμέρᾳ; τί δὲ ἐν τῇ νυκτὶ ὀφείλουσι ποιεῖν δι᾽ οὗ φανερὸν ἔσται σοι ἐν ποίᾳ εἰσὶν οἱ ἀποκλεισθέντες καταστάσει;

375    60. Εἰ δὲ δυνατὸν διὰ πεζικῆς μάχης ἀποσοβηθῆναι τοὺς ἐχθρούς, ἐὰν ἄρα περίστασις, ὡς εἰκός, συμβῇ τοῖς ἐν τῷ φρουρίῳ, οὐδὲ τοῦτο δεῖ ὑπερτίθεσθαι ἵνα μὴ οἱ ἔσωθεν κινδυνεύωσιν.

61. Ὅταν δὲ ἄδεια γένηται, εὐθέως | κατ᾽ ὀλίγον ἀποτειχίζειν χρὴ τὸ προσ-   395ᵛ
ποιητὸν οἰκοδόμημα καὶ ἐγχορήγῳ ἰσχυρῷ κτίζειν αὐτὸ καὶ ὀχυροποιεῖν, καὶ
380    τῶν ἀναγκαίων ἐν αὐτῷ φροντίζειν.

62. Γίνονται δὲ αἱ τοιαῦται ἐγχειρήσεις ἁρμοδίως κατὰ καβαλλαρικοῦ ἔθνους, περὶ τὸν ἰούλιον ἢ αὔγουστον ἢ σεπτέμβριον μῆνα, ὅταν ἡ βοτάνη εὐκαίρως ξηραινομένη καίεται καὶ οἱ καβαλλάριοι τῶν ἐχθρῶν στενοῦνται παρακαθίσαι χρόνον ἱκανόν.

385    63. Εἰ δὲ ἀπόρως πρὸς τὸ ὕδωρ ὁ τόπος ἔχει, μηδὲ ῥυτοῦ ἐν αὐτῷ ὄντος, μηδ᾽ ἐν ὀρύγματι εὑρισκομένου, δεῖ ἢ πίθους ὀστρακίνους ἢ βουττία τέλεια προευτρεπίζειν, καὶ γεμίζειν ὕδατος καὶ κόχλακας ἐν αὐτῷ ποταμίους ῥίπτειν εἰς τὸ αὐταρκέσαι μέχρι τῆς τοῦ χειμῶνος ὥρας, καὶ φθάσει καὶ κινστέρνα οἰκοδο-
μηθῆναι καὶ ὄμβριον ὑποδέξασθαι ὕδωρ. ἵνα δὲ μή, ὡς εἰκός, ὄζῃ ἀκίνητον
390    μένον τὸ ὕδωρ ἐν τοῖς ἀγγείοις, καὶ δοχεῖα μικρὰ δέον αὐτοῖς παρατίθεσθαι ἵνα κατ᾽ ὀλίγον ἀποστάζον τὸ ὕδωρ ἐν αὐτοῖς κίνησιν δέχεται· ἅμα δὲ τοῦ πληροῦ-
σθαι τὰ δοχεῖα πάλιν ἀποκενοῦμεν τοῖς πίθοις ἢ τοῖς βουττίοις τοῦτο, ἵνα διὰ τῆς κινήσεως ταύτης διαπνέηται τὸ ὕδωρ καὶ μὴ ἀφανίζηται.

64. Χρήσιμον δέ ἐστι καὶ τὸ σανίδας προπαρασκευάσαι παχυτέρας καὶ ἐν
395    κατορύγματι συμπῆξαι αὐτὰς ὡς ἐπὶ σαρπίου, καὶ διὰ πίσσης καὶ στυππίου κατασφαλίσασθαι τὰς ζεύξεις ἤτοι τοὺς ἁρμοὺς αὐτοῦ, καὶ ἐν τάξει ξυλίνης κινστέρνης συμμέτρου κατασκευάσαι, εἴτε μίαν εἴτε πλείους, ἐχούσας εἴκοσι ἐπὶ δέκα πόδας τὸ πλάτος, τὸ δὲ ὕψος ὀκτὼ ἢ δέκα, μέχρις οὗ ἐγχόρηγοι αἱ κινστέρ-
ναι γένωνται. δῆλον γάρ ἐστιν ὡς ἐν τοῖς μειζοτέροις ἀγγείοις πλέον τὸ ὕδωρ
400    διαμένει. κατόχια δὲ ξύλινα ἐν τῷ μέσῳ τῶν κινστερνῶν οἷον συνδέσμους ὡς

375 ἀποσοβηθῆναι MW ἀποδιωχθῆναι AVBE 383 εὐκαίρως ξηραινομένη MW ξηραινομένη εὐκόλως AVBE | στενοῦνται MW στενοῦνται καὶ οὐ δύνανται AVBE 386 μηδ᾽ De μηδὲ codd. | τέλεια MW μεγάλα AVBE 388 τῆς MW om. AVBE | ὥρας… φθάσει MW ἕως οὗ φθάσῃ AVBE 389 ὑποδέξασθαι MAVBE ὑποδέξηται W 391 ἀποστάζον…ὕδωρ MW trsp. AVBE 392 ἀποκενοῦμεν MW ἀποκενοῦν ἐν AVBE | τοῦτο MW om. AVBE 393 ἀφανίζηται MAVBE ἀφανίζεται W 394 ἐστι MW ἐστιν AVBE 397 πλείους MW πλείονας AVBE 398 αἱ MW om. AVBE 399 μειζοτέροις MW μείζοσιν AVBE

59. Give a signal to the men inside. What ought they to use by day? What by night, which will enable the garrison inside to inform you of the situation in which they find themselves.

60. If the infantry is able to engage the enemy and drive them back and if it becomes likely that the situation of those within the fortress is critical, you must not allow any delay so as not to endanger the garrison.

61. When conditions become safe, you must immediately, bit by bit, reinforce the improvised construction, strengthen it with mortar and make it strong. Be concerned also about the necessary provisions for those within.

62. These undertakings are effectively employed against a people relying on horses, about July, August, or September, when the grass is dry and burns easily and the enemy cavalry are hard pressed to stay in one place for any length of time.

63. If the site has no water supply, no flowing source, nothing found by digging, it is necessary to arrange for large earthenware jars or well-built barrels. They should be filled with water and some clean pebbles from a river bed thrown in so the water will last until winter and until cisterns can be constructed to hold rainwater. To prevent the water stored in the casks from becoming stagnant, as is likely, small basins must be placed beside the casks so the water in them may flow drop by drop and be kept in motion. As soon as the small basins are full, we empty the water back into the jars or barrels. By this motion the water is aerated and does not become foul.

64. It is practical to prepare thick planks, put them in a trench and bind them together as a wooden box. Seal the joints and seams with pitch and tow and so prepare a regular, moderate-sized cistern. One or more may be built measuring ten to twenty feet wide and eight or ten feet high. <This will do> until cisterns made with mortar can be gotten ready. It is clear that water keeps better in larger containers. Wooden struts must be placed in the middle of the

τραπεζέα δεῖ βάλλεσθαι καὶ σανίδας παχείας, ἵνα μὴ τῷ πλήθει τοῦ ὕδατος βιαζόμεναι αἱ σανίδες στρέφωνται καὶ τὸ ὕδωρ ἀπολλύωσιν.

65. Οὕτω μὲν οὖν καὶ περὶ τούτου εἰρήσθω, ἴσως ποτὲ καιροῦ καλοῦντος ἕξεις δι᾽ ἑτοίμου καὶ τὴν τοιαύτην διάταξιν. τοσαῦτα μέν σοι καὶ περί τε πολιορ-
405  κίας καὶ τῶν ἄλλων εἰρήσθω.|

---

401 τραπεζέα Μ τραπέζια W τραπεζαία AVBE    402 ἀπολλύωσιν MAVE ἀπολύουσιν WB
404 τε MW om. AVBE

cisterns, like the fastenings of a table, and the planks should be thick so they will not give way because of the water pressure and cause the water to be lost.

65. Let this, therefore, cover these matters, so that, as the situation demands, you may have this exposition in readiness. Let all these words about siege warfare and the other matters be sufficient for you.

Περὶ τῶν μετὰ τὸν πόλεμον

1. Ἐφεξῆς δὲ τούτων καὶ ὅσα μετὰ τὴν πολέμου ἔκβασιν δέον γίνεσθαι ῥητέον. καὶ γὰρ ἐὰν καλῶς ἐκτάξῃς τὸ στράτευμα, μετὰ τῆς τοῦ Θεοῦ βοηθείας,
5 ἐλπίζομεν καὶ τὴν νίκην παρέσεσθαι.

2. Καὶ πρῶτον μὲν ἀποδώσεις κυρίῳ τῷ Θεῷ ἡμῶν Ἰησοῦ Χριστῷ τὴν εὐχαριστίαν καί, εἴ τι ἐπηγγείλω πρὸ τῆς νίκης τοῦ πολέμου ἀποδώσειν μετὰ τὴν νίκην χαριστήριον, μὴ ἀμελήσῃς ἀποδοῦναι.

3. Καὶ εἴθ᾿ οὕτως ἀνερευνήσεις τοὺς ἀριστεύσαντας ἐν τοῖς τῆς μάχης
10 κινδύνοις, καὶ τούτους ἀνευρίσκων, τίμησον αὐτοὺς δωρεαῖς καὶ τιμαῖς ταῖς ἑκάστῳ πρεπούσαις· τοὺς δὲ κακοὺς φανέντας κόλαζε. τιμήσεις δὲ τοὺς ἀριστεύσαντας δωρεαῖς τοιαύταις, οἷον πανοπλίας ἐπιδώσεις ἱερπνὰς καὶ τὰ ἀπὸ τοῦ πολέμου συνηγμένα σκύλα διανεμεῖς αὐτοῖς· τιμήσεις δὲ καὶ εἰς ἀξιώματα κατ᾿ ἀναλογίαν ἁρμοδίως ἕκαστον, οἷον εἰς δρούγγους, εἰς βάνδα, εἰς κενταρχί-
15 ας καὶ εἰς τὰς ἄλλας συνήθεις ὑπὸ τὴν σὴν ἐξουσίαν ἀρχοντικὰς προβολάς, τῶν μὲν λιτῶν στρατιωτῶν τοὺς ἀνδραγαθήσαντας εἰς μικροτέρας τιμάς, τῶν δὲ ἀρχόντων εἰς μείζονας ἀρχάς. οὕτως γὰρ μεγαλόψυχοι καὶ γενναῖοι ἔσονται οἱ ἀγωνιζόμενοι τυγχάνοντες μάλιστα καὶ ὧν ἐπιθυμοῦσιν.

4. Ὅπου δὲ τιμαὶ μὲν καὶ κέρδη ἀποδίδονται τοῖς ἀγαθοῖς, τιμωρίαι δὲ
20 ἐπάγονται τοῖς κακοῖς, ἐνταῦθα καλὰς ἐλπίδας ἔχειν ἐξ ἀνάγκης τὸ στρατόπεδον. οἱ μὲν γὰρ κακοὶ φοβοῦνται ἁμαρτάνειν, οἱ δὲ ἀγαθοὶ σπουδάζουσιν ἀνδραγαθεῖν. καὶ μὴ μόνον κατὰ ἕνα ἄνδρα τὰς ἀμοιβὰς ἀποδίδου, ἀλλὰ καὶ ὅλον τάγμα ἢ δροῦγγον ἢ τούρμαν· ἀνδραγαθήσαντας ἐπίτρεπε διαρπάζειν τὰ τῶν πολεμίων τοὺς στρατιώτας, εἴτε ἀποσκευαί εἰσιν εἴτε τοῦλδον εἴτε πόλις ἢ

---

M W A V B E    PG 107:908

---

6–86 Onas., 34–37. *Strat.*, 7.B.11–12.

1 πολεμικῶν παρασκευῶν WAVBE om. M | διάταξις ις′ WAVBE om. M    2 πόλεμον
WAVBE πόλεμον διάταξις ις′ M    3 ἐφεξῆς MW ἑξῆς AVBE    3–4 τούτων…ῥητέον MW
ῥητέον καὶ ὅσα δέον (δεῖ B) γίνεσθαι μετὰ τὴν τοῦ πολέμου συμπλήρωσιν AVBE
7 ἀποδώσειν VBE ἀποδώσει MWA    14 κατ᾿…ἕκαστον MW ἕκαστον κατὰ τὸ ἀνῆκον τῆς
ἀρετῆς AVBE | κατ᾿ De κατὰ codd. | δρούγγους MW δρουγγαρίους AVBE    20 ἐξ ἀνάγκης
MW ἀνάγκη AVBE    23 ὅλον MWVBE ὅλον τὸ A

# PREPARATION FOR WAR, CONSTITUTION XVI

## About Matters after the War

1. Next in order, we must speak of what has to be done after the conclusion of the war. For if you draw up your army correctly, we hope that, with the help of God, victory will be yours.

2. First, give thanks to the Lord our God, Jesus Christ. If you promised to make some sort of offering before victory in battle, do not neglect to give a thank-offering after the victory.[1]

3. Then search out those who have distinguished themselves in the dangers of battle and, on finding them, honor each one with appropriate gifts and honors. But punish those who performed poorly. Honor those who have distinguished themselves by bestowing gifts upon them, such as a splendid suit of armor, and by giving them a portion of the spoils collected after the war. Also honor them with dignities in proportion to each man's standing, such as in droungoi, in banda, in kentarchiai, and in the other regular units headed by officers under your authority. Treat the ordinary soldiers who have given proof of their valor to lesser honors and the officers to higher commands. By so doing, the men engaged in combat will be brave and in high spirits, especially when they obtain what they have desired.

4. When honors and prizes are granted to the brave and punishments are handed out to those who performed poorly, the troops will certainly be full of good hopes. Those who did poorly are afraid of failing again, while the brave will strive to conduct themselves valiantly. Grant the rewards not only to each individual soldier but to the entire tagma or droungos or tourma. Allow the soldiers who have distinguished themselves to plunder the goods of the enemy, their equipment or their baggage train, or a city or fortified town or something

---

1. From here to §14 cf. Onasander 34–37; *Strat.* 7.B.11–12.

25 κάστρον ἤ τι ἕτερον. ἐὰν ἄρα μὴ βούλῃ χρηστότερόν τι περὶ τῶν ἑαλωκότων καὶ πραγμάτων καὶ αἰχμαλώτων βουλεύσασθαι.

5. Καὶ πῶς γὰρ οὐ δίκαιον τοῖς εἰρημένοις ἀπὸ τῶν πολεμίων σκύλοις τοὺς ἀριστεύσαντας στρατιώτας φιλοτιμεῖσθαι; ὁρῶμεν γὰρ ὅτι καὶ τοὺς κυνηγετικοὺς κύνας οἱ κυνηγοὶ τοῦ θηρευομένου ζῴου τῷ αἵματι, καί ποτε καὶ τοῖς 30 ἐντοσθίοις δελεάζειν ἀναγκαῖον ποιοῦνται, ἵνα προθυμοτέρους καὶ πάλιν εἰς τοὺς ἀγῶνας τῆς θήρας ποιήσωσιν· οὕτως γὰρ μάλιστα, εἰ καὶ μήπω τέλος δέξηται ὁ πόλεμος, προ|θυμότερος ὁ στρατὸς πρὸς τὰς μάχας γενήσεται.    346ᵛ

6. Διαφέρει γὰρ ὁ πόλεμος τῆς μάχης· ὁ μὲν γὰρ πόλεμος ἀπ' ἀρχῆς καὶ μέχρι τέλους καὶ καταπαύσεως τῶν μαχομένων λέγεται, πολλὰς ἐν ἑαυτῷ μάχας 35 περιέχων, ἡ δὲ μάχη μερικὸς λέγεται πόλεμος, πολλάκις γινομένη ἐν τῷ τοῦ καθ' ὅλου πολέμου καιρῷ καὶ ἀπογινομένη, οὐ μὴν δὲ πάντοτε τέλος ἐπάγουσα πολέμου, ἀλλὰ πρὸς τὴν χρείαν καὶ δὶς καὶ τρὶς καὶ πολλάκις ἐν ὅλῳ τῷ τοῦ πολέμου καιρῷ τὰς συμβολὰς ποιουμένη.

7. Τὰς δὲ ἁρπαγὰς οὐκ ἐπὶ πάσης μάχης λέγομεν γίνεσθαι, ἀλλὰ ποτὲ μέν, 40 ποτὲ δὲ οὔ, καθὼς ἂν τὸ συμφέρον ἀπαιτήσῃ τοῦ καιροῦ.

8. Καὶ τὰ μὲν αἰχμάλωτα σώματα πιπράσκειν τὸν στρατόν· εἰ δὲ χρημάτων ἐστὶ χρεία καὶ δαπάνης κοινῆς καὶ μεγάλης, πάντα πρός σε ἀναφέρεσθαι κήρυξον, καὶ πᾶσαν ἐπιθυμίαν καί σου αὐτοῦ καὶ τῶν ὑπό σε ἀρχόντων ἀπὸ τῶν τοιούτων ἐπισωρευομένων χρημάτων χαλίνωσον, καὶ ἀναλογίζου τὴν χρείαν 45 τῶν ἀναγκαίων. καὶ οὕτως δύνασαι τὴν τοῦ κοινοῦ δαπάνην κατὰ τὸ δυνατὸν ἀναλῶσαι καὶ τοὺς ἐν τῇ μάχῃ ἀγωνισαμένους παραμυθήσασθαι, εἰ μὲν δύνασαι διὰ χρημάτων, εἰ δ' οὐκ ἐπαρκεῖ, διὰ τιμῶν καὶ ἀξιωμάτων.

9. Τοὺς δὲ αἰχμαλώτους πρὸ τοῦ τελείως καταπαῦσαι τὸν πόλεμον μὴ κτεῖνε, καὶ μάλιστα τοὺς ἐνδόξους καὶ μεγάλους παρὰ τοῖς πολεμίοις ὄντας· 50 ἐνθυμούμενος τὸ ἄδηλον τῆς τύχης καὶ τὸ παλίντροπον ὡς ἐπὶ τὸ πολὺ τῆς νίκης, ἵν' ἔχῃς, εἴ γε συμβῇ ἢ τῶν ὑπό σέ τινας κρατηθῆναι ἢ κάστρου γενέσθαι

---

33–38 Aelian., pr.6.

---

25–26 ἑαλωκότων…αἰχμαλώτων MW κρατηθέντων αἰχμαλώτων καὶ πραγμάτων AVBE 27 σκύλοις MAVBE σκύλων W (sed οις suprascr.)  29–30 τοῦ…ποιοῦνται MW τῷ αἵματι τοῦ θηρευομένου ζῴου καὶ τοῖς ἐντοσθίοις δελεάζουσιν AVBE  31 τῆς θήρας MW τοὺς κύνας AVBE  32 γενήσεται MAVBE γένεται W (suprascr. ης)  33 ἀπ' ἀρχῆς AVBE ἀπὸ ἀρχῆς MW  36 πολέμου MW πολέμῳ AVBE  39 μέν MW μὲν καὶ AVBE  42–43 κήρυξον MW διαλάλησον AVBE  44 τὴν MW καὶ AVBE  49 κτεῖνε PG κτεῖναι MW φόνευε AVBE  50–51 τό³…νίκης MW τὰς ἐναντίας ἐκβάσεις τοῦ πολέμου AVBE  51 ἵν'…τινας MW ἵνα εἰ συμβῇ τινες τῶν ὑπό σε AVBE | ἔχῃς PG ἔχεις M ἔχοις W om. AVBE | γενέσθαι MW om. AVBE

else, that is, if you do not have more practical plans for the prisoners and the material goods that have been captured.

5. How is it not just to present the soldiers who have distinguished themselves with the spoils of the enemy, as we have mentioned? We observe that hunters deem it necessary to entice their hunting dogs with the blood, sometimes the intestines, of the animal being hunted so they will become more eager to continue the struggle of the chase. Likewise, especially if the war has not yet come to an end, the army will be more enthusiastic for combat.

6. War differs from battle.[2] War is defined as going from the beginning to the end, that is, the cessation of hostilities, and it includes many battles in its course. Battle is defined as a partial war that occurs frequently in the course of the entire war, and its cessation does not always bring about the end of the war but, as need requires, battles can take place two or three times or more often in the course of the entire war.

7. We can say that seizing of booty does not take place in every battle; sometimes it does, sometimes not. It depends on what the occasion calls for.

8. Let the army sell the captives it has taken. But if there is need of money and a large amount of common supplies, issue a proclamation that everything should be brought to you. Curb your own eagerness, and that of the officers under you, for the money that has piled up and calculate what you need for essentials. In this way, you will be able to spend as much as you can on common supplies and you will greatly raise the spirits of those who have struggled in battle. Do this with money, if you can; but if there is not enough, do it with honors and dignities.

9. Do not slay the prisoners before the war has finally come to an end, in particular the important and illustrious men among them. Keep in mind the uncertainty of fortune and the reversals that so often accompany victory. If it should happen that some of your men are taken prisoner or a walled town of

---

2. Aelian, prologue 6.

ἰδίου σου ἅλωσιν, δι᾿ αὐτῶν ἀντικαταλλάττειν καὶ ἀνακαλεῖσθαι τά, ὡς εἰκός, συμβαίνοντα ἡττήματα, καὶ ἀντὶ τῶν πολεμίων αἰχμαλώτων ἀναλάβῃς τοὺς φίλους καὶ συμμάχους. εἰ δὲ μὴ βούλωνται τοῦτο ποιεῖν οἱ πολέμιοι, τότε
55 δικαίως κατὰ τὸ ἴσον ἀμύνου, διαχρώμενος ὡς βούλει ἐπὶ λύπῃ τῶν ἐναντίων.

10. Μετὰ δὲ τὰ κατορθώματα καὶ τοὺς ἀγῶνας, ὦ στρατηγέ, καὶ πρὸς εὐωχίας ἤγουν τραπέζας καὶ ἄριστα προτρέπου καθίστασθαι τούς τε ἄρχοντας καὶ τοὺς συστρατιώτας, τὰ μὲν διά σου αὐτοῦ, τὰ δὲ διὰ τῶν ἀρχόντων, τὰ δὲ διὰ τῶν κοντουβερνίων ἰδίων, καὶ μάλιστα ἐκ τῶν κερδηθέντων ἀπὸ τῶν πολε-
60 μίων. καὶ οὕτως διὰ πολλῶν ἀριστοποιεῖσθαι καὶ ἀναπαύεσθαι τοὺς στρατιώτας παρασκεύαζε, ἵνα εἰδότες οἵων ἀξιοῦνται μετὰ τὸ παρελθεῖν τοὺς πολεμίους ἀγῶνας οἱ ἀριστεύοντες καὶ νικήσαντες, προθυμότεροι γένωνται πρὸς τὸ ὑπομένειν πάντα πρὸ τοῦ νι|κῆσαι, καὶ πρὸς τοὺς πόνους μᾶλλον ἑτοιμότεροι.   347

11. Προνοοῦ δὲ μάλιστα καὶ τῆς τῶν νεκρῶν ταφῆς, μήτε καιρὸν μήτε ὥραν
65 μήτε τόπον μήτε φόβον προφασιζόμενος, κἄν τε νικῶν τύχῃς κἄν τε ἡττώμενος. πάντοτε μὲν γὰρ καλὸν καὶ ὅσιον ἡ πρὸς τοὺς τεθνηκότας εὐσέβεια, ἀναγκαία δὲ μάλιστα ἡ ἐπὶ τοῖς πίπτουσιν ἐν μάχῃ. καὶ γὰρ καὶ ἐν ἐκείνοις τὸ ὅσιον δείκνυται, καὶ πρὸς τοὺς ζῶντας μεγάλης παραμυθίας ἀπόδειξις. ἕκαστος γὰρ τῶν στρατιωτῶν ὁρῶν τὸ γινόμενον, οὕτως ἑαυτὸν νομίσει παθεῖν. εἰ μὲν γὰρ
70 ἀτάφους ἤδη κειμένους ἢ σπαρασσομένους τοὺς πίπτοντας, ἑαυτὸν λογιζόμε-νος, ἐπαχθῶς φέρει τὴν ὕβριν καὶ φεύγει τὸ παθεῖν τι τοιοῦτον, μαχόμενος καὶ ἄταφος καταλειφθῆναι. εἰ δὲ τιμῆς ἀξιοῖτο καὶ μετὰ τὸ πεσεῖν καὶ μνήμης ἀγαθῆς ὁμοίως, ταῦτα συνορῶν οὐ παραιτήσεται προθυμότερον ἀγωνίσασθαι.

12. Εἰ δὲ οὕτω συμβῇ ὥστε ἡττηθῆναι τὸ στράτευμα, μὴ ἀμέλει τοῦ ἀνακτή-
75 σασθαι τοὺς ἀνασωθέντας διὰ λόγων καὶ προθυμοποιῆσαι αὐτούς, ἀλλὰ σπού-

---

66–67 Cf. 2 Macc. 12:43–46.

---

52 ἅλωσιν MW πόρθησιν γενέσθαι AVBE   52–53 ἀντικαταλλάττειν…ἡττήματα MW ἀντικαταλλάξῃς καὶ ἀνακαλέσῃ τὰς συμβαινούσας ἥττας AVBE   53 ἀναλάβῃς MW λάβῃς AVBE   55 διαχρώμενος MW φονεύων αὐτοὺς AVBE   56 τὰ MAVBE om. W   57 εὐωχίας ἤγουν MW om. AVBE   58 συστρατιώτας MW στρατιώτας AVBE | σου αὐτοῦ MW σαυτοῦ AVBE   59 κοντουβερνίων MW κουτουβερνίων MW | ἰδίων MW ἰδίως AVBE   60 πολλῶν MW τελῶν AVBE   61–62 μετὰ…οἱ MW om. AVBE   62 ἀριστεύοντες MW ἀριστεύσαντες AVBE   67 ἐν μάχῃ WAVBE ἐμμάχη M   69 ἑαυτὸν MW καὶ αὐτοὶ AVBE   70–71 ἑαυτὸν λογιζόμενος ἐπαχθῶς MW ὡς αὐτὸς ταῦτα πάσχων AVBE   72 ἀξιοῖτο MW ἀξιοῦται AVBE   74 οὕτω MW om. AVBE | ὥστε MW om. AVBE | τοῦ MW τοῦ διὰ λόγων AVBE   75 ἀνασωθέντας…λόγων MW σωθέντας AVBE

yours suffers capture, then you are able to make use of those prisoners to change matters around again and to recover from the likely effects of a defeat. In exchange for the enemy captives you may receive back your friends and allies. If the enemy are not willing to do this, then, by the same token, you have the right to protect yourself, taking what action you wish to harm the enemy.

10. After your struggles and successes, O general, give the order to the officers and the soldiers under you to set up festive tables and banquets, some arranged by yourself, some by your officers, some by the individual squads, making use especially of what has been acquired from the enemy. In many ways, then, make ready for the soldiers to partake of the festive board and enjoy some relaxation. Knowing the rewards awaiting those who have displayed bravery and have been victorious, after the struggles of war have passed, they will become more enthusiastic to endure everything before victory and will be better prepared for the labors ahead.

11. Show particular concern for the burial of the dead. Whether you are victorious or defeated, do not put forth the time, the hour, the place, or fear as an excuse. Reverence for those who have died is always good and holy.[3] It is especially necessary in the case of those who have fallen in battle, for it is with them that piety must manifest itself. It also provides great consolation for the living. On seeing what transpires, each soldier will think that he will receive the same treatment. If he should observe that the fallen lie unburied or scattered about, he will reflect on his own situation; he will be angry at such an insult and will avoid suffering anything of the sort, that is, fighting and then being left unburied. But if he is deemed worthy of honors and, likewise, after he has fallen, of grateful remembrance, then, considering these things, he will not refrain from engaging in the struggle more enthusiastically.

12. But if it should happen that the army has been defeated, do not neglect to revive the spirits of the survivors by your words and encouragement. But make

3. Cf. 2 Maccabees 12:43–46.

δαζε καὶ ζήτει καιρὸν ὥστε ποτὲ καὶ μᾶλλον ἐπανορθώσασθαι τὴν ἐλάττωσιν διὰ κρυφαίων ἐφόδων ἢ ἐγκρυμμάτων.

13. Εἰώθασι γὰρ πολλάκις οἱ εὐπραγοῦντες ῥαθυμότεροι γίνεσθαι περὶ τὰς φυλακὰς αὐτῶν. καὶ γὰρ ὅταν τῶν ἡττηθέντων καταφρονήσωσι, τῶν ἰδίων
80 καταμελοῦσι. καὶ οὕτως πολλάκις τὰ εὐτυχήματα πλείω βλάπτει τοὺς εὐτυχοῦν-
τας παρ’ ὃ μᾶλλον οἱ δυστυχήσαντες ἐβλάβησαν.

14. Σὺ μὲν γὰρ πταίσας ἐδιδάχθης ἀφ’ ἑαυτοῦ, καὶ ἐφύλαξας ἑαυτὸν πρὸς τὸ μέλλον ἐξ ὧν ἔπαθες. ἐκεῖνος δὲ μηδέπω δυστυχήσας, ὡς ἄπειρος τῆς δυστυχίας, οὐκ ἔχει πρόνοιαν τοῦ φυλάξασθαι μὴ παθεῖν ὅσα οὐκ ἔμαθεν. εἴρηκεν γάρ
85 τίς που παλαιὸς ὅτι φόβος εὔκαιρος μετ’ ἐπιμελείας ἀσφάλεια, καταφρόνησις δὲ ἄκαιρος εὐεπιβούλευτος τόλμα.

15. Ἐὰν δέ ποτε ἀνοχὴν τοῦ πολέμου ποιήσῃς διά τινος λόγου καὶ συνθηκῶν ὁμολογηθέντων, σὺ μὲν τὰς ἰδίας φυλάττων συνθήκας μὴ ἐπιτεθῇς τοῖς ἐναντίοις, ἀφύλακτος δὲ μὴ διαμένῃς ἀλλ’ ἡσύχαζε μὲν πρὸς τοὺς πολεμίους διὰ τὰς
90 σπονδὰς ὡς ἐν εἰρήνῃ, τὸ δὲ ἀσφαλὲς εἰς τὸ μὴ πεσεῖν ἢ παθεῖν τι παρ’ αὐτῶν ὡς ἐπὶ πολέμου οὕτως ἔχε καὶ προνοοῦ. πρέπον γὰρ μήτε ἀφύλακτον ἐν τοιούτῳ καιρῷ σε εἶναι μήτε πάλιν τι ποιεῖν ἀσεβὲς παρὰ τὰς ἐπὶ Θεῷ μάρτυρι τεθειμέ-
νας σπονδάς, ἀλλ’ εἶναι ὕποπτον, ὥστε φυλάττεσθαι τὸ τῶν πολεμίων δολερὸν καὶ ὕπουλον. ἄδηλοι γὰρ αἱ τῶν σπεισαμένων | ἤγουν τῶν εἰρηνευσάντων    347ᵛ
95 ἐναντίων γνῶμαι. καὶ σὺ μὲν ἔχε τὸ βέβαιον ὥστε μὴ ἀδικῆσαι διὰ τὸ εὐσεβές, τῶν δὲ πολεμίων τὸ ἄπιστον ὑπονόου ὥστε μὴ ἀδικηθῆναι διὰ τὸ ἀσεβές. τὸ γὰρ πάντα ἀναφέρειν εἰς τὴν ἀπὸ τοῦ Θεοῦ ἐκδίκησιν οὐκ ἔστιν ἀκεραίου γνώμης. οὐ γὰρ εὐθὺς ἡ θεία δίκη ἐπάγεται, ἀλλ’ ὅτε βούλεται ὁ πάντων προνο-
ητής. τίς γὰρ οἶδεν εἰ ἅμα τῷ ἀσεβῆσαι τοὺς ἐχθροὺς αὐτοὶ μὲν διολεσθῶσιν, σὺ
100 δὲ περισωθήσῃ;

---

84–86 Onas. 36.6.

---

76 ποτὲ…μᾶλλον MW τὸ σφάλμα AVBE 76–77 τὴν…διὰ MW om. AVBE
78 εὐπραγοῦντες MW εὐποροῦντες AVBE 79 καταφρονήσωσι M καταφρονήσωσιν WAVBE 80 καταμελοῦσι MVBE καταμελοῦσιν WA | πλείω MW πλείον AVBE
81 μᾶλλον MW om. AVBE 82 ἀφ’…ἑαυτὸν MW ἀπὸ σεαυτοῦ καὶ σαυτὸν AVBE
83 μέλλον MW μέλλον ἐφύλαξας AVBE 84 εἴρηκεν MW εἴρηκε AVBE 85 που MW om. AVBE 88 ἰδίας MW οἰκείας AVBE 90–91 τὸ¹…προνοοῦ MW ἀσφαλίζου δὲ σεαυτὸν ὡς ἐπὶ πολέμου ὥστε μὴ παρ’ αὐτῶν τι παθεῖν AVBE 92 σε MW om. AVBE | τι MW om. AVBE 99 διολεσθῶσιν MW ἀφανισθῶσι AVBE

an effort to find a time when you can make up for the defeat by covert attacks and ambuscades.

13. Frequently enough, successful persons turn out to be rather lazy about protecting themselves. As they look down upon the defeated, they pay no heed to their own situation. Thus, success often causes more harm to those who have been successful compared to the harm that the unsuccessful have suffered.

14. You, now, have stumbled and have learned from your own experience. Because of what you have suffered, you have been put on guard against suffering the same thing in the future. But that person who has always been successful, since he has no experience of failure, does not have the foresight to defend himself against suffering what he has not come to know. One of the ancients once remarked: a well timed fear accompanied by careful attention makes one secure, but an untimely contempt, leaving one exposed to attack, is reckless.[4]

15. If, <in the course> of a war, you enter upon a truce for some reason and agree to certain conditions, you must observe your part of the treaty and not attack the enemy. But do not leave yourself unprotected in peace time. Act in a peaceful manner toward the enemy according to the treaty. To be on the safe side, though, and to avoid being ruined or suffering something from them, bear yourself as in time of war and think ahead. Be careful not to be unprotected at such a time and also not to do something irreverent, contrary to that treaty you have signed, with God as your witness. Keep an eye out, however, to guard against any treacherous or deceitful act of the enemy. The thoughts of the enemy who have signed a treaty or who have made peace are unclear. You, as a religious person, stick to what is firm and do not act unjustly. Be suspicious, though, of the faithlessness of the enemy so that you may not be treated unjustly because of their irreverence. It is not characteristic of a sincere mind to refer everything to the vengeance of God. The divine judgment is not brought into action immediately, but when the administrator of all things wishes. Who knows if at the same time as the enemy act irreligiously they are destroyed, whereas you are saved?

4. Onasander 36.6.

16. Ἔξεστιν οὖν ἡμῖν μετὰ τῆς τῶν ἡμετέρων πραγμάτων ἀσφαλείας, εἰ οὕτως τύχοι, πεῖραν λαμβάνειν τῆς τῶν πολεμίων ἀσεβείας. οὕτως γὰρ σὺ μὲν διὰ τὴν σὴν πρόνοιαν οὐδὲν κακὸν πάθῃς, οἱ δὲ κακῶσαι βουλευθέντες ἐχθροί, ἀσεβήσουσι μέν, ὡς πράξαντές τι, εἰ ἐδυνήθησαν, σὲ τοῦ Θεοῦ διὰ τὴν πίστιν
105 τῶν ὁμολογηθέντων φυλάξαντος.

17. Πάντα δὲ τὸν βουλόμενόν τι ἀπαγγέλλειν σοι καὶ δοῦλον καὶ ἐλεύθερον, καὶ ἐν νυκτὶ καὶ ἐν ἡμέρᾳ, καὶ ἐν ὁδοιπορίᾳ καὶ ἐν ἀπλήκτῳ, καὶ ἀναπαυόμενον καὶ ὑπνοῦντα, καὶ ἐπὶ λουτροῦ καὶ ἐπὶ τροφῆς, καὶ παντὸς ἑτέρου καιροῦ καὶ τόπου, μὴ ἀποστρέψῃς, ἀλλὰ προσκαλοῦ αὐτόν. οἱ γὰρ ἀναβαλλόμενοι καὶ
110 ἀπρόσιτοι, καὶ τοῖς ὑπηρέταις αὐτῶν κελεύοντες ἀνακόπτειν τοὺς οὕτω προσερχομένους, πολλῶν καὶ μεγάλων εἰκότως διαμαρτάνουσι πραγμάτων. ταῦτά σοι καὶ μετὰ τὸν πόλεμον, καὶ εἴ τι τούτοις παραπλήσιον ἐπινοηθῆναι ἰσχύσεις παραφυλάττειν διαταττόμεθα.|

---

16. It could happen and it is quite possible for us, as well as the security of our affairs, to experience the impiety of the enemy. Your foresight will keep you from suffering any evil. But the enemy, intent on doing evil, may well act in an irreligious manner, getting away with whatever they can. But you have been protected by God because of your fidelity to the agreement you made.

17. Do not turn away anyone who wishes to speak to you about something, whether slave or free, at night or during the day, on the march or in camp, resting or sleeping, bathing or eating, at any other time and place. But summon him. For those who put people off and are not accessible and who order their servants to cut off those who approach them, are likely to miss out on many great matters. We command you to carefully observe these matters also after war as well as whatever else may occur to you along these lines.

Περὶ ἐφόδων ἀδοκήτων

1. Ἑξῆς δὲ καὶ ὅσα σοι δέον ἐν καιρῷ προσήκοντι γενέσθαι δι᾽ ἐπελεύσεων ἀδοκήτων κατὰ τῆς γῆς τῶν πολεμίων καὶ ὅπως αὐτὸς κατὰ τῆς ἐπελεύσεως
5 τῶν πολεμίων ἀντιμηχανεύσῃ ἐν τοῖς ἰδίοις, ὅτε μὴ καιρὸς εἰρήνης ἐπικρατεῖ— πρόδηλος δὲ οὐ συνίσταται πόλεμος—διὰ τὴν τοῦ λόγου συμμετρίαν ἐν ὀλίγοις διεξέλθωμεν.

2. Ἀρχαῖός που διδάσκει λόγος ἡμᾶς, ὅνπερ καὶ οἱ μάλιστα συνετώτεροι τῶν στρατηγῶν καὶ πάλαι παρεφυλάξαντο, καὶ νῦν ὡς ἐπίπαν παραφυλάττοντες
10 εὐδοκιμοῦσι καὶ ἀριστεύουσι, τὸ δίχα ἰδίας βλάβης τὰς κατὰ τῶν πολεμίων ἐφόδους ἤτοι ἐπιδρομὰς ποιεῖσθαι. τοῦτο δὲ γίνεσθαι δυνατόν ἐστιν, ἐὰν μετὰ σοφίας καὶ στρατηγήματος φρονίμου ἀθρόως αἱ κατὰ τῶν ἐχθρῶν γίνωνται ἐπελεύσεις. καὶ γὰρ καὶ πρὸς τὰς ἰσομέτρους δυνάμεις ἐπωφελεῖς εὑρίσκονται αἱ τοιαῦται γινόμεναι καὶ πρὸς τὰς πολὺ τάχα ὑπερβαλλούσας.
15 3. Διὰ τοῦτο οὖν ἀεὶ καὶ πάντοτε καλόν ἐστιν ἁρμοδίας προφάσεις καὶ καιροὺς συμβαλέσθαι δυναμένους τῷ πράγματι ἐπιτηρεῖν, καὶ προκαταλαμβάν- ειν σε τοὺς ἐχθρούς, ὦ στρατηγέ, πρὶν ἢ ἐν ἑτοίμῃ τῆς ἀπαντήσεώς σου γένων- ται, καὶ μάλιστα ἐκείνους ὅσους νομίζεις καὶ πλείονάς σου εἶναι καὶ δυνατωτέ- ρους.
20 4. Δεῖ γὰρ κατὰ τούτων αἰφνιδιασμοῖς μᾶλλον καὶ σοφίσμασι καὶ ἀπάταις, ὡς εἴρηται, κατὰ τὸ δυνατὸν πρότερον ποιεῖσθαι, ἀλλὰ μὴ δημοσίας ἐγχειρή- σεις, ὥστε ἐντεῦθεν εἰς κινδύνους δυσανακλήτους καὶ ἀφεύκτους ἐμπίπτειν. καὶ

---

MWAVBE   PG 107:913

8–11 Cf. Strat., 9.2.   8–570 Strat., 9

1 πολεμικῶν παρασκευῶν WA λέοντος τοῦ ἐν χριστῶ βασιλεῖ αἰωνίω βασιλέως M om. VBE | διάταξις ιζ′ WAVBE om. M   5 ἀντιμηχανεύσῃ W ἀντιμηχανεύσει M ἀντιμηχανήσῃ AVBE 6 διὰ…συμμετρίαν MW om. AVBE | λόγου M λόγου δὲ W om. AVBE   8 που…λόγος MW λόγος διδάσκει AVBE   9 ὡς ἐπίπαν MW om. AVBE   10 ἀριστεύουσι MVBE ἀριστεύουσιν WA   15–16 καὶ καιροὺς MW ἐν καιρῷ AVBE   17–18 ἐν…γένωνται MW ἑτοιμασθῶσι πρὸς ἀπάντησίν σου AVBE   21 ποιεῖσθαι MW χρῆσθαι AVBE   21–22 ἐγχειρήσεις MW ἐγχειρήσεις ποιεῖσθαι AVBE

## PREPARATION FOR WAR, CONSTITUTION XVII

### About Surprise Attacks

1. We will next <turn our attention to> what you must do, when the opportunity presents itself, in launching surprise attacks against the territory of the enemy, as well as how to take countermeasures against attacks by the enemy in your own land. This does not apply, of course, in time of peace and when it is clear that war is not going to be waged. The summary nature of this treatise calls for our exposition here to be brief.[1]

2. An ancient maxim, carefully observed by the more intelligent generals of old and still invariably observed and given the highest priority by our own generals, teaches us to launch attacks and raids against the enemy without causing injury to ourselves. We can achieve this if our assaults against the enemy are intelligently and carefully planned and swiftly carried out. Such assaults have been found to be effective not only against forces of equal strength but also against vastly superior ones.

3. For this reason it is a good idea always to be on the watch for convenient pretexts and opportunities that can prove advantageous. You should strike at the enemy, O general, before they get ready to come out against you, especially if you think that their forces are more numerous and stronger than yours.

4. In such cases it is necessary, as has been said, first to make use of surprise, stratagems, and deception as much as possible rather than engaging in a pitched battle. That may cause you to fall into dangers from which it will be difficult to

---

1. This entire constitution derives from *Strat.* 9.

τῶν τοιούτων σοφισμάτων διαφόρων ὄντων δέον σε τούτοις χρήσασθαι ἁρμοδίως καὶ τοῖς καιροῖς καὶ τοῖς τόποις καὶ τοῖς προσώποις καὶ τοῖς πράγμασιν.

25   5. Καὶ ποτὲ μὲν ἀποκρισιαρίων τῶν ἐχθρῶν πρός σε ἀποσταλέντων ἁπαλά
τε καὶ κολακευτικὰ ῥήματα ἀντιδηλώσας, καὶ μετὰ τιμῆς τοὺς ἀποκρισιαρίους
τῶν ἐχθρῶν ἀπολύσας, εὐθέως ἐπακολουθήσεις αὐτοῖς καὶ ἀδο|κήτως ἐπέλθῃς.   381ᵛ
ποτὲ δὲ ἰδίους πρέσβεις ἤτοι ἀποκρισιαρίους ἀποστείλας μετὰ ῥημάτων ταπει-
νοτέρων, τὴν ἐπέλευσιν ἄφνω ποιήσεις. ποτὲ δὲ καὶ ἐν αὐτοῖς τοῖς τῶν ἐχθρῶν
30   ἀπλίκτοις, εἴτε ἐν τῇ ἰδίᾳ σοῦ εἰσιν γῇ εἴτε ἐν τῇ πολεμίᾳ συνηγμένοι, πολυπραγμονήσεις τὸ πῶς ἀπλικεύουσι. καὶ ἐὰν εὑρίσκηται πρόφασις ἐν νυκτί, τῆς σελήνης λαμπούσης, πρὸ δύο ἢ τριῶν ὡρῶν τῆς ἡμέρας τὴν κατὰ τῶν ἐχθρῶν ἐγχείρησιν ποιήσεις, τοξότας χρησίμους μάλιστα ἔχων· τοιούτων γὰρ χρεία ἐστὶν ἐν
τοῖς τοιούτοις καιροῖς. ποτὲ δὲ μαθὼν ἐν ταῖς πορείαις ἀσυντάκτους καὶ ἐσκορ-
35   πισμένους περιπατεῖν τοὺς ἐχθρούς, ἐν τῷ μέσῳ τῆς ὁδοῦ ἐπέλθεις καὶ βλάψεις,
κρύψας σεαυτόν. ἄλλοτε δὲ ἐν τόποις τισὶ κρύψας ἑαυτὸν μετὰ λαοῦ στρατιωτῶν, ἄφνω τὴν κατὰ τῶν ἐναντίων ἐπέλευσιν ἐργάσῃ. ποτὲ δὲ σχηματισάμενος
ἀναχώρησιν ἐξ ὧν διῆγες τόπων ἄφνω ἐπαναστρέψας τοῖς ἐχθροῖς ἐπιπεσεῖς.

6. Καί τινες δὲ προβαλλόμενοι ἀγέλας ζώων καὶ ἐντεῦθεν τοὺς ἐχθροὺς εἰς
40   τὴν τούτων διαρπαγὴν προτρεψάμενοι, ὡς εἶδον αὐτοὺς ἀτάκτως κατ᾽ αὐτῶν
διασκεδασθέντας, ἐπέθεντο αὐτοῖς.

7. Γίνονται δὲ καὶ φανερῶς ἔφοδοι, ὅταν ἐν τῷ μεταξὺ διαστήματι τῶν
ἐχθρῶν ποταμὸς εὑρεθῇ δύσβατος, καὶ κάλλιστα τοῦτο ποιοῦσιν οἱ καβαλλάριοι. ἐνταῦθα γὰρ συμπηγνύουσι γέφυραν, ἢ διὰ ξύλων μεγάλων, ὥς ἐστιν ἔθος
45   τὰς πολλὰς γεφύρας γίνεσθαι, ἢ διὰ μικρῶν πλοιαρίων, τῶν λεγομένων μονοξύ-
λων. πύργους τε ξυλίνους ἢ ἀπὸ οἰκοδομῆς ἐκ λίθων ξηρῶν ἢ χώματος ἑκατέρωθεν τῶν ἄκρων τῆς γεφύρας ἐγείρουσιν ἵνα, ὅταν χρεία, δι᾽ αὐτῆς ἀσφαλῶς τὴν
διάβασιν ποιήσωσι, καὶ πάλιν ἀναχωρήσωσιν ὅτε βούλονται, ὥστε ἐν τῇ τοῦ

---

42–63  Cf. Polyaen. 1.29.1; 3.9.61.

---

25  ἀποκρισιαρίων MW ἀποκρισιαρίους AVBE | ἀποσταλέντων MW ἀποστελλόντων AVBE
27  ἀπολύσας MAVBE ἀπολύσεις W   29–30 καὶ…εἴτε¹ MW πολυπραγμονήσεις τοὺς
ἐχθροὺς ὅπως ἀπληκεύουσιν (ἀπληκεύουσι VBE) κἂν τε AVBE   30 εἴτε² MW κἂν τε AVBE
30–31 πολεμίᾳ…ἀπλικεύουσι MW ἑαυτῶν AVBE   30 συνηγμένοι PG συνειλεγμένοι MW
om. AVBE   31 ἀπλικεύουσι MVBE ἀπλικεύουσιν WA | εὑρίσκηται MAVBE εὑρίσκεται W
34  πορείαις MW ὁδοιπορίαις AVBE | ἀσυντάκτους MAVBE ἀσυντάκτως W   36 σεαυτόν
WAVBE ἑαυτὸν M   37 σχηματισάμενος MWVBE σχηματισάμενοι A   43 κάλλιστα
MWA μάλιστα VBE   44 συμπηγνύουσι MWVBE συμπηγνύουσιν A   46–47 ἑκατέρωθεν
MW ἐξ ἀμφοτέρων AVBE   47 χρεία MW χρεία γένηται AVBE   48 ποιήσωσι MVBE
ποιήσωσιν WA | ἀναχωρήσωσιν WAVBE ἀναχωρήσουσι M

recover or to extricate yourself. Since there are so many different kinds of stratagems, it is incumbent upon you to make use of those that fit the time, the place, the persons, and the actual situation.

5. When ambassadors from the enemy have been sent to you and you have replied to them in gentle and flattering terms and sent those enemy ambassadors on their way with honors, you will immediately follow along and attack them unexpectedly. At other times you might send your own ambassadors or envoys with submissive words and then suddenly launch an attack. At times you might be conducted into the very camp of the enemy, either in your own country or in theirs. Find out then how they have set up camp. Then, if the opportunity presents itself, on a moonlit night two or three hours before daybreak, make your attack against them. Archers are particularly useful, essential in fact, at times like this. At another time, perhaps, you may learn that the enemy are marching along in disorder and scattered about; hide yourself and then attack them in the middle of their march and you will seriously injure them. At other times, conceal yourself in certain places with a body of soldiers and, suddenly, launch an attack against the enemy. At times, too, pretend to withdraw from the place in which you were spending time, then suddenly wheel around and fall upon the enemy.

6. Some have driven herds of animals ahead of them to lead the enemy to turn aside and round them up. Then, on observing the enemy disordered and scattered they would fall upon them.

7. Some attacks are made out in the open. If, in the area between <us and> the enemy we find a river difficult to cross, we can construct a bridge there—even cavalry are able to do this.[2] It can be made of wooden crossbeams, which is the usual method for building bridges, or on small boats, the ones called monoxyla. At both ends of the bridge they erect towers of wood or of dry masonry or of earth. When necessary, then, they may safely cross over this bridge or again withdraw when they wish. It is left up to the general to decide

---

*2. For §§7–9 cf. Polyaenus 1.29.1; 3.9.61. The translation here is based on the better MSS, MWA, which have κάλλιστα, "very nicely." VBE, however, as well as *Strat.* 9.1, have μάλιστα, "especially."

στρατηγοῦ ἀποκεῖσθαι γνώμῃ, ἢ προσμένειν ὅσον ἐμβαστάζει αὐτῷ χρόνον ἢ
50 συμβάλλειν τοῖς ἐχθροῖς ἀσφαλῶς ἢ ἀναχωρεῖν ἀβλαβῶς τῆς γεφύρας παρ'
αὐτοῦ καταλυομένης.

8. Ἀλλὰ ἐν ταῖς τοιαύταις ἐγχειρήσεσι καὶ ταῖς εἰσόδοις κατὰ τῆς τῶν ἐχθρῶν χώρας, οὐ χρή σε καίειν καὶ ἀφανίζειν τὰς δαπάνας ἐκείνων τῶν χωρίων
δι' ὧν μέλλεις ὑποστρέφειν, ἵνα μὴ ἑαυτὸν στενώσῃς.

55 9. Τὰς δὲ τοιαύτας γεφύρας γίνεσθαι ἀναγκαῖον νομίζω καὶ ἐν καιρῷ | 382
δημοσίας μάχης, καὶ τὰ ἄπλικτα ἐν τοῖς τοιούτοις ποταμοῖς γίνεσθαι. ἐὰν ἄρα
δύσβατος εὑρεθῇ ἐν οἱῳδήποτε μέρει, ἵνα τὴν τοῦ τοιούτου ποταμοῦ ὄχθην
κατεξαίρετον κατὰ τοῦ μέρους τῶν ἐχθρῶν καταλίπῃς, ὥστε ἀνεμποδίστως καὶ
ἀστενοχωρήτως ἐν τῇ ἡμέρᾳ τῆς μάχης τὸν στρατὸν ἐξάγεσθαι. εἶτα καὶ ἐν
60 καιρῷ τροπῆς ἐν τῷ ἀπλίκτῳ μένειν αὐτοὺς ἀσφαλῶς φυλαττομένους καὶ μὴ
ἀναγκάζεσθαι ἐν αὐτῇ τῇ ὥρᾳ, τῶν ἐχθρῶν ἐπικειμένων, τὴν διάβασιν τῆς
γεφύρας ποιεῖσθαι καὶ μὴ βουλομένους. καὶ διὰ τοῦτο δέον εἰς τὴν ὄχθην τὴν
ἐπὶ τὸ μέρος τῶν ἐχθρῶν ἐξ ἐναντίας τὸ ἄπλικτον γίνεσθαι.

10. Νυκτεριναὶ δὲ ἐπελεύσεις διάφοροι παρὰ τῶν παλαιῶν στρατηγῶν
65 ἐπετηδεύθησαν, ἐξ ὧν σοι καὶ ἡμεῖς ταύτας ὑποτιθέμεθα, ἵνα ποτὲ μὲν πλησίον
τῶν ἐναντίων ἀπλικεύσας, ὡς ἀπὸ ἑνὸς ἀπλίκτου πρεσβείαν τε μίαν καὶ δευτέραν εἰρηνικὴν δηλώσας, καὶ ἐλπίδας πρὸς εἰρήνην δεδωκὼς τοῖς ἐναντίοις καὶ
ἀμερίμνους ποιήσας ἀδοκήτως αὐτοῖς ἐπέλθῃς πρὸ ἡμέρας ἐν νυκτὶ τὴν ὁδοιπορίαν ποιησάμενος.

70 11. Ποτὲ δέ, ἐὰν βούλῃ ἐπελθεῖν τοῖς ἐχθροῖς νυκτός, ἡμέρας τινὰς παρατα-
ξάμενος πλησίον τοῦ ἰδίου ἀπλίκτου ὡς ἐπὶ μάχῃ δημοσίᾳ, καὶ σχηματισάμενος
φοβεῖσθαι τοὺς ὑπεναντίους, καὶ διὰ τοῦτο μὴ παρεξέρχεσθαι πλέον τοὺς
τόπους τοῦ ἰδίου ἀπλίκτου, καὶ ἐντεῦθεν αὐτοὺς παραχαυνώσας ἐπέλθῃς ἐν
νυκτί.

75 12. Τοῦτο δὲ γινώσκομεν πεποιηκότα τὸν Χαγάνον τῶν Ἀβάρων ἐπὶ τῶν
χρόνων Ἡρακλείου τοῦ βασιλέως περὶ τὴν Ἡράκλειαν τῆς Θρᾴκης κατὰ τῶν
Ῥωμαίων καβαλλαρίων μὴ βουλομένων ἐν φοσσάτῳ ἀσφαλῶς μετὰ τῶν πεζῶν
ἀπλικεύειν, ἀλλ' ἔξωθεν ἀφυλάκτως.

---

64–69 *Strat.*, 9.2.　75–78 A.D. 592. Cf. Theoph. Simocatta *Historia*, 6.5.

52 ἐγχειρήσεσι MW ἐγχειρήσειν AVBE　53 χρή M δεῖ WAVBE　65 ἐπετηδεύθησαν
MAVBE ἐπενοήθησαν W　67 πρὸς εἰρήνην MW εἰρήνης AVBE　70–71 ἡμέρας...
ἀπλίκτου MW om. AVBE　73 ἐν MAVBE τῇ W　75–76 τῶν χρόνων MW τοὺς χρόνους
AVBE　77 μετὰ...πεζῶν MW om. AVBE

how long to remain in that place, either to attack the enemy in safety or to retreat without injury to himself and then destroy the bridge.

8. In operations of this sort, however, and in incursions into hostile territory, do not burn or destroy supplies in those regions through which you intend to return, so you may not suffer want.

9. I think that the bridges we spoke of may be essential at the time of a pitched battle, when the camps are set up by such rivers. If crossing is found to be difficult at any point, especially on the side where the enemy are, you should abandon that river bank. Then, on the day of battle, you may lead out the army without hindrance and without crowding. In case of a reverse the men may remain safely in the protection of the camp and not be forced against their will to cross over the bridge, at that time, when the enemy are on the offensive. For these reasons it is necessary to pitch camp on the opposite bank, the one on the side of the enemy.

10. The ancient strategists devised a variety of nocturnal attacks, some of which we will now bring to your attention.[3] When you pitch camp close to the enemy, about a day's march away, send a deputation or two to treat of peace. You will have given the enemy hopes of a peaceful settlement and led them to become careless. Then have your army march at night and attack them unexpectedly before daybreak.[4]

11. Sometimes, if you want to attack the enemy at night, for several days draw up your troops close to your own camp as though for a pitched battle. Pretend to be frightened by your adversaries and for this reason do not wander out beyond the area of your own camp, and when you have thus caused them to relax their guard, attack them at night.

12. We recall that, during the reign of the emperor Herakleios, the Khan of the Avars did this at Herakleia in Thrace to the Roman cavalry. They had refused to set up camp safely within the fortified area together with the infantry but stayed outside unprotected.[5]

---

*3. Cf. *Strat.* 9.2; SyrMag 39; Skirmishing, 24.

*4. *Strat.* 9.2 cites the action of the Roman general Lusius, in A.D. 116, probably near Nisibis or Edessa, as reported by Dio Cassius, 68.30.2, et al. See Pauly-Wissowa, *Realencyclopädie der classischen Altertumswissenschaft* (Stuttgart, 1894–1980), 2.13.1874–90.

5. A.D. 592: Theophylact Simocatta, *Historiae*, ed. C. de Boor, rev. P. Wirth (Stuttgart, 1972), 6.5. The emperor was actually Maurice. See Haldon, *Commentary.*

13. Σοφὸν δὲ ποιήσεις ὅταν εὐψύχους καὶ ἀνδρείους μετὰ σεαυτοῦ στρατιώ-
80 τας ἔχῃς, ἐὰν ὑποθήσῃς τινὶ ὥστε προσφυγεῖν τοῖς ἐχθροῖς, καὶ εἰπεῖν ὅτι ἐν
δειλίᾳ ἐστὶν ὁ στρατός. εἶτα πρόφασιν ποιήσῃς ὅτι εἰς τὰ ὀπίσω ὑπαναχωρεῖς,
καὶ ὀλίγον διάστημα τὸ φοσσᾶτον ἤγουν τὸ ἄπλικτον μεταστήσας, αἰφνίδιον ἐν
νυκτὶ ἐπέλθεις τοῖς ἐναντίοις.

14. Ποιήσεις δὲ νυκτερινὰς ἐπελεύσεις κατ᾽ ἐχθρῶν ἁρμοδίως ὑπό τε πεζῶν
85 καὶ καβαλλαρίων καὶ τοξοτῶν μάλιστα καὶ ἀκοντιστῶν κατὰ ἐθνῶν πεζῶν καὶ
καβαλλαρίων τῶν μὴ ἐν φοσσάτῳ καὶ τάξει ἀπλικευόντων, ἀλλὰ ἀτάκτως | καὶ   382ᵛ
ἀφυλάκτως καὶ διεσπαρμένως σκηνούντων.

15. Καὶ κατὰ τῶν μὴ ἐχόντων τόξα ἢ ἀκόντια προχείρως, ἀλλὰ ἐκ χειρὸς
μᾶλλον τὴν μάχην ποιουμένων. οἱ γὰρ τοῖς τόξοις καὶ ῥικταρίοις καὶ τοῖς ἄλλοις
90 ὅπλοις χρώμενοι, δυσεπιχείρητοι πρὸς τὰς τοιαύτας ἐπελεύσεις γίνονται, εἰ μὴ
ἄρα ἀφύλακτοι καὶ διεσπαρμένοι ἀπλικεύσωσιν.

16. Νύκτας δὲ ἐπιλέξαι πρὸς τὰς τοιαύτας ἀπροσδοκήτους ἐφόδους, τουτέστιν, ἢ ὅταν ὁλόνυκτος φαίνῃ ἡ σελήνη ἢ ὅταν οἶδας ὅτι ἀρκεῖ τὸ φέγγος
αὐτῆς τῷ διαστήματι τῆς ὅλης σου ὁδοιπορίας ἢ ὅταν ἐστὶν ἀστερόφωτον, ἵνα
95 μὴ ὁ στρατὸς ἐν σκοτίᾳ περιπατῶν συντρίβεται καὶ πλανᾶται.

17. Ἀεὶ δὲ ἔξπληκτον καὶ παρεσκευασμένον τὸν στρατὸν κίνει, καὶ μηδὲν
περισσὸν ἐπιφερόμενον, καὶ οὕτω κανόνιζε καὶ στοχάζου πρὸς τὰ διαστήματα,
τὰ ἐν τῷ μέσῳ, ὥστε συμμέτρως περιπατεῖν, ἵνα μὴ συντρίβεται ὁ στρατός· καὶ
πρὸ δύο ὡρῶν τῆς ἡμέρας φθάσεις πλησίον ὡς ἀπὸ ἑνὸς ἢ δευτέρου σημείου
100 τοῦ τῶν ἐχθρῶν ἀπλίκτου καὶ ἐκεῖσε λανθανόντως ἀναπαύσεις τὸν στρατόν, καὶ
πρὶν ἢ ἄρξηται αὐγάζειν ἡ ἡμέρα ἐπιτεθῇς τοῖς ἐχθροῖς. εἰς δὲ τὰς τοιαύτας
ὁδοιπορίας, ἵνα ἔχῃς ὁδηγοὺς τοὺς πάνυ ἀκριβῶς εἰδότας τοὺς τόπους εἰς τὸ μὴ
πλανᾶσθαι τὸν στρατόν. παντοίαν δὲ ἡσυχίαν ἐχέτωσαν, καὶ μήτε βούκινον
λαλείτω, μηδὲ οἱαδήποτε κραυγὴ γινέσθω. ἀλλὰ ἐὰν ἐστι δέον τοῦ μεῖναι τὸν
105 στρατόν, ὡς εἰκός, ἢ τοῦ κινῆσαι ἢ διὰ συριγμοῦ ἢ διὰ κτύπου σκουταρίου ἢ διὰ
παραγγέλματος σημαίνειν τὸ κίνημα ἢ τὴν στάσιν.

---

79 εὐψύχους καὶ MW om. AVBE   82 ἤγουν MW ἤτοι AVBE   83 ἐναντίοις MW
πολεμίοις AVBE   84 κατ᾽ MW κατὰ τῶν AVBE   85–86 καὶ¹...ἀτάκτως MW om. AVBE
89 καὶ¹ MW καὶ τοῖς AVBE   91 ἀπλικεύσωσιν MAVBE ἀπλικεύουσιν W   92 νύκτας MW
οὕτως AVBE | ἀπροσδοκήτους MW ἀδοκήτως AVBE   95 συντρίβεται MW συντρίβηται
AVBE   96 ἔξπληκτον MW ἔλαφρον AVBE   97 οὕτω M οὕτως WAVBE   98 συντρίβεται
MW συντρίβηται AVBE   99 σημείου MW μιλίου AVBE   103 παντοίαν WAVBE ἑαντοίαν
M   104 μηδὲ MW μήτε ἄλλη AVBE | ἀλλὰ MW ἀλλ᾽ AVBE | ἐστι MAVBE ἐστιν W | μεῖναι
M εἶναι W στῆναι AVBE   105 ὡς...κινῆσαι M ἢ τοῦ κινῆσαι ὡς εἰκὸς W ὡς εἰκὸς εἴτε
κινῆσαι AVBE   106 σημαίνειν WAVBE ἢ μένειν M

13. You will be wise, when you have good-spirited and brave soldiers with you, if you have one of them pretend to desert to the enemy and inform them that the morale of your army is low. Then make it look as though you are withdrawing to the rear, but go only a short distance and set up your encampment, that is, your camp. Then, suddenly at night attack the enemy.

14. Night assaults against the enemy will be particularly effective if you make use of archers and javelin throwers, both mounted and dismounted. <Employ them> against peoples, whether on foot or on horseback, who do not fortify or set up their camps in an orderly manner but pitch their tents in disorder, unprotected, and scattered all over the place.

15. <They are also effective> against peoples who are not skilled in using the bow and the javelin but prefer to engage in hand-to-hand combat. Those who do make use of bows, throwing weapons, and the other weapons are harder to overcome by such attacks unless they set up camp without protection and scattered about.

16. For surprise attacks of this sort, choose nights when the moon is shining all night or when you know that its light will last as long as the distance of your entire march or when there is enough light from the stars. Otherwise, the army marching along in the darkness may stumble about and get lost.

17. In moving your army, always keep it lightly equipped and ready for action, carrying no unnecessary baggage. Estimate and regulate <your march> proportionate to the distance between the <two camps> in order to arrive two hours before daybreak, someplace about one or two miles from the enemy's camp, marching at a steady pace so the army will not be exhausted. There, the army should stay in hiding and rest and then, before daylight begins, attack the enemy. For expeditions of this sort you should have guides who possess a detailed knowledge of the country, so the army will not be led astray. Absolute silence must be observed, not blowing the bugle and no shouting of any kind. But if it should become necessary, as is likely, for the army to halt or to advance, give the signal for marching or for halting by a whistle, by striking a shield, or by a command.

18. Ἵνα δὲ μὴ θόρυβος τῶν κτύπων γένηται, μηδ' ἐπὶ πολὺ ἐκτεινομένη ἡ παράταξις πλάνην καὶ ἀνισότητα ποιῇ, καὶ διὰ τοῦτο ἐξ ἀνάγκης κραυγὰς καὶ μανδάτα ὥστε καὶ εὔγνωστον τοῖς ἐχθροῖς τὴν παρουσίαν τοῦ στρατοῦ γεν-
110 έσθαι. διὰ τοῦτο χρὴ μὴ ἐπὶ μέτωπον ἤγουν ἐπὶ ἔκταμα πολὺ εἰς πλάτος ἀλλ' ἐπὶ κέρας, τουτέστιν ἐπὶ ὀρθίαν παράταξιν, ὡς ἐπὶ ἀκίας καὶ στίχου κατὰ οὐρὰν ἀλλήλων περιπατεῖν, δηλονότι τοῦ βάθους ἤτοι τοῦ πάχους τῆς τάξεως φυλατ-τομένου.

19. Καὶ ὅταν πλησίον τῶν ἐχθρῶν φθάσῃ ὁ στρατός, τότε λεληθότως καὶ
115 κρυφαίως ἀνάπαυε αὐτοὺς καὶ ὄρθωσον τὴν τάξιν καί, ὡς ὁ τόπος ἐπιδέχεται, εἴτε διὰ δύο εἴτε διὰ τριῶν μερῶν τὴν ἐπέλευσιν ποίησον. | οὐδὲ γὰρ κατὰ τῶν 383
τεσσάρων μερῶν χρεία, ἵνα μὴ περιλαμβανόμενοι πανταχόθεν οἱ ἐχθροὶ ἐκ περιστάσεως συμφράξωνται, ἀλλ' ἵνα ἔχωσιν ἄδειαν δι' ἑνὸς μέρους οἱ θέλοντες φεύγειν.

120 20. Καὶ τότε ἐὰν πλῆθος ἔχῃς στρατοῦ τὸ ἐπερχόμενον, ἐν ᾗ καὶ δεύτερον βούκινον παρασκεύαζε λαλεῖν, ἵνα πρὸς ὀλίγον στρατὸν δοκοῦντες ἔχειν λανθάνωνται οἱ πολέμιοι. εἰ δὲ ὀλίγον στρατὸν ἔχῃς, πλείονα βούκινα λαλείτω-σαν, ἵνα πλῆθος νομίζηται τὸ ἐπερχόμενον.

21. Χρὴ δέ σε πάντως δύναμίν τινα συνιστᾶν στρατοῦ, <μὴ> τὴν μιγνύου-
125 σαν χείρας κατὰ τὴν ὥραν ἐκείνην, ἀλλὰ καὶ εὐκαίρως ἱσταμένην, καὶ ὀφείλου-σαν τούς, ὡς εἰκός, προστρέχοντας ἐκ τῶν ἰδίων προσδέχεσθαι.

22. Τὰς δὲ κατὰ καβαλλαρίων ἐχθρῶν ἐφόδους μάλιστα ἀσφαλῶς ποιοῦ καὶ ὡς ἐπὶ δημοσίας μάχης ἵνα ἐὰν τὰ τῆς ἐφόδου μὴ κατὰ σκοπὸν προέλθῃ, ἀλλ' οἱ πολέμιοι προαισθόμενοι ἀντιπαρατάξωνται, μὴ ἐλαττωθῇς ἐν τῇ κινουμένῃ
130 μάχῃ ὡς ἀπαράσκευος καὶ ἀνέτοιμος.

23. Ἐὰν γὰρ πεζοὶ ὦσιν οἱ ἐναντίοι, καβαλλάριοι δὲ οἱ μετά σου ἐπερχόμε-νοι, πρόδηλόν ἐστιν ὅτι ἢ βλάψεις τοὺς ἐναντίους ἢ ἀβλαβὴς ἀναχωρήσεις, τῶν πεζῶν διώκειν τοὺς καβαλλαρίους οὐ δυναμένων.

24. Εἰ δὲ καβαλλάριοί εἰσιν καὶ οἱ ἐναντίοι, χρή σε πρὸς τὰ συμβαίνοντα
135 πολλάκις ἐναντία ἕτοιμον εἶναι καὶ παρεσκευασμένον.

---

107 γένηται M γένεται W γίνηται AVBE | μηδ' PG μηδὲ MAVBE μὴ W    109 μανδάτα MW μανδάτα γίνεσθαι AVBE | καὶ MAVBE om. W    109–110 γενέσθαι MW συμβαίνειν AVBE
110 ἀλλ' MAVBE ἀλλὰ W    111 ὀρθίαν παράταξιν M ὀρθία παρατάξει WAVBE
115 αὐτοὺς WAVBE ἑαυτοὺς M    121 παρασκεύαζε λαλεῖν MW trsp. AVBE
122 λανθάνωνται…πολέμιοι MW trsp. AVBE    123 νομίζηται MAVBE νομίζεται W
124 μὴ ci. De om. codd.    125 καὶ¹ MW καὶ ἑτέραν AVBE    127 ἐχθρῶν MW om. AVBE
128 σκοπὸν MW βούλησιν AVBE    130 μάχῃ MW τάξει AVBE    134 εἰσιν MW εἰσι AVBE

18. To avoid any noisy confusion or stretching the formation out too much, making for a straggling and uneven line and the consequent necessity of shouting commands, all of which clearly betray the approach of the army to the enemy, it must march not by the front, that is, to a large extent in width, but by the flank, that is, formed in a straight line, marching by files one after the other, maintaining, of course, the depth or thickness of the formation.

19. When the army gets close to the enemy, they should hide and rest under cover, straighten out their line and, depending on the terrain, launch their attack from two or three sides. They must not attack from all four sides, for then, the enemy finding themselves completely surrounded, will be forced to close ranks out of desperation, but one side should be left open for those who wish to flee.

20. If you have a large army moving up to attack, then prepare to sound one or two trumpets so that the enemy will be deceived into thinking they are facing a small army. But if you do have a small army, let more trumpets be sounded so they may believe the approaching army is a large one.

21. You must always hold some units of the army in reserve, taking no part in the action at that time, but opportunely standing by in order to provide cover for their own men who might be charging forth.

22. In particular, make your attacks against enemy cavalry very carefully, as though in a pitched battle, so that, in case the enemy may have been forewarned and lined up in formation to face us, and the attack does not proceed according to plan, you may not suffer defeat in the ensuing battle because you were not ready or prepared.

23. If our opponents consist of infantry and you have your cavalry advance against them, it is obvious that our forces will inflict harm on the enemy or they will themselves withdraw without injury, for infantry are not capable of pursuing cavalry.

24. But if our adversaries are on horseback as well, then you must be ready and prepared for the adverse outcome that frequently occurs.

25. Εἰ δὲ ἐν νυκτὶ ἔφοδος γένηται κατὰ φοσσάτου, εἴτε ἐν ἡμέρᾳ ἢ κατὰ ὁδευόντων ἢ κατὰ τούλδου, δεῖ ἀφωρισμένα τάγματα ἔχειν σε πρὸς διαρπαγὴν τῶν πραγμάτων, ἵνα μὴ εἰς τοῦτο πάντων ἀσχολουμένων, ἐπέλευσις ὑπὸ ἐχθρῶν γένηται καὶ κινδυνεύσῃ ὁ στρατός.

140    26. Τὰς δὲ τοιαύτας ἐφόδους τὰς μείζονας μὲν καὶ τελείας διὰ σεαυτοῦ ποιήσῃς· δυνατὸν δέ σοι μᾶλλον καὶ διὰ τουρμάρχων τῶν ἐπὶ τοιούτοις πράγμασι χρησίμων αὐτὰς γίνεσθαι. οἵτινες ἱκανοί εἰσι τὸν σὸν τόπον ἀναπληρῶσαι διὰ τὴν ἀποδεικνυμένην ἐν αὐτοῖς καὶ ἀνδρείαν καὶ ἀγχίνοιαν.

27. Ἐὰν δὲ ἐν τῇ τῶν πολεμίων χώρᾳ εἰσβάλλων ὁδοιπορεῖν μέλλῃς ἐκεῖσε
145    καὶ πραιδεύειν βλάβης ἰδίας χωρίς, πρῶτον μὲν ἴδιον καὶ ἁρμόδιον καιρὸν ἐπιλεύσσου, οὗτος δέ ἐστιν ὁ ἀσφαλὴς τῆς ἐγχειρήσεως καιρός, ὅτε ἢ συμβαλὼν ἤδη τοῖς ἐχθροῖς μάχῃ ἐκράτησας αὐτῶν ἢ νομίσεις ὅτι οὐκ εἰσὶ δυνατοὶ | 383ᵛ πρὸς τὴν σὴν δύναμιν ἢ ὅταν ἀνετοίμοις αὐτοῖς καὶ ἀπαρασκεύοις οὖσιν, αἰφνιδίως ἐπιτεθῆναι μελετήσῃς, ὡς ἤδη προείπομεν.

150    28. Δέον σε πρὸ πάντων, ὦ στρατηγέ, εἰσβάλλοντα εἰς τὴν πολεμίων γῆν, τῆς ἀποτροφῆς φροντίσαι τοῦ στρατοῦ, καὶ ἢ διὰ βασταγῆς δημοσίας ἢ δι᾽ αὐτῶν τῶν στρατιωτῶν ἢ ἄλλως πως ἐπινοῆσαι βαστάσαι ἀποτροφὴν καὶ ἀλόγων καὶ ἀνθρώπων, ἵνα μὴ περὶ μέσην τὴν χώραν ἄνω τῶν ἐχθρῶν, ὡς εἰκός, ἀφανιζόντων τὰ ἕτοιμα εἴδη στενοχωρηθῇ ὁ στρατός.

155    29. Μὴ ἐπιτηδεύσῃς δὲ νυκτερινὰς ὁδοιπορίας ἐν πολεμίᾳ χώρᾳ ποιεῖσθαι, εἰ μὴ πρὸς ἅπαξ, ἤγουν μίαν καὶ μόνην, καὶ τοῦτο λεληθότως ἴσως χρείας ἀναγκαίας καλούσης εἰς τὸ λαθεῖν τοὺς ἐχθροὺς καὶ τόπον δυσχερῆ προκαταλαβεῖν χάριν ὀχυρώματος ἢ παρελθεῖν ἐν ἑτέρῳ τόπῳ τῶν ἐχθρῶν μὴ γινωσκόντων.

30. Πρότερον δὲ περιεργάσασθαί σε δεῖ καὶ ἐρευνᾶν τὰς ὁδούς, καὶ οὕτως
160    τὰς ὁδοιπορίας ποιεῖσθαι.

31. Πᾶσαν δὲ πάντως ποιεῖσθαι σπουδὴν ἵνα τινὰς τῶν τῆς χώρας ζωγρήσῃς, ὅπως ἐξ αὐτῶν τὴν τῶν ἐχθρῶν μάθῃς δύναμιν καὶ τὰ αὐτῶν βουλεύματα. τί ἄρα σπουδάζουσι ποιῆσαι; τὰς ἐρωτήσεις δὲ τῶν κρατουμένων διὰ σεαυτοῦ ποίει, καὶ μὴ δι᾽ ἑτέρου τινός. καὶ γὰρ πολλάκις ἀναγκαῖά τινα καὶ παρὰ πᾶσαν
165    ὑπόνοιαν διὰ τῶν ἐρωτωμένων ἐφανερώθησαν.

---

140 διὰ σεαυτοῦ A δι᾽ ἑαυτοῦ MWVBE    142 εἰσι MAVBE εἰσίν W    146 ἐπιλεύσσου MW ἐκλέγου AVBE    146–147 συμβαλὼν M συμβάλλων WAVBE    147 εἰσι MAVBE εἰσίν W 152 ἐπινοῆσαι MW ἐπινοῆσαι ὥστε AVBE | καὶ MW om. AVBE    155 ἐπιτηδεύσῃς MW ἐπιτηδεύῃς AVBE    156 ἤγουν…χρείας MW καὶ τοῦτο κρύφα χρείας ἴσως AVBE    159 σε MAVBE om. W    160 ποιεῖσθαι MW ποιήσασθαι AVBE    161 ζωγρήσῃς MW κρατήσῃς AVBE    163 σπουδάζουσι MAVBE σπουδάζουσιν W

25. If the attack is made at night against a fortified camp or in the daytime against marching troops or against the baggage train, you must have certain units assigned to gather plunder. Otherwise, if all the soldiers get involved in this, the enemy might attack and endanger the army.

26. You should personally lead the larger attacks, those made in full force, but they can also be led by the tourmarchs, who have some expertise in these matters. Because of their manifest bravery and shrewdness, they are capable of acting in your place.

27. If, on making an incursion into enemy territory, you intend to march about there and plunder it without any injury to yourself, you must first plan ahead for a proper and suitable time. The safe time for such an undertaking is when you have already attacked and overcome the enemy in battle or when, in comparison with your force, you think they are not so strong, or they are not ready or prepared when you intend to fall upon them suddenly, as we have already explained.

28. Above all, O general, as you enter enemy territory, you must be concerned about supplies for the army. You must arrange for these supplies, both for horses and for men, to be transported in public wagons or by the individual soldiers or in some other way. Otherwise, the enemy are likely to destroy the available supplies and the army may suddenly find itself in critical straits in the middle of a <hostile> country.

29. You should not attempt to undertake marches at night in hostile territory except just once, that is, one time only and secretly. Perhaps such a march might become absolutely necessary to avoid detection by the enemy, or to seize difficult ground ahead of time for the purpose of defense or to pass through to another location without the enemy finding out.

30. But before setting out on any such march, you must take great care to reconnoiter the roads.

31. Be sure to make every effort to take some inhabitants of the country as prisoners in order to obtain information from them about the strength and the plans of the enemy. What is it that they are intent on doing? You should interrogate the prisoners yourself and not have someone else do it. Frequently, extremely important and completely unexpected information has been revealed by such questioning.

32. Ἀλλὰ μηδὲ τοῖς προσφεύγουσί σοι προχείρως πίστευε, ἀλλὰ τοῖς ἐξ
αἰφνιδίου ἐπιδρομῆς κρατουμένοις, ἐπειδὴ συμβαίνει πεπλασμένα καὶ ἐκ τῶν |
προσφευγόντων καὶ ἐκ τῶν κρατουμένων λέγεσθαι. ἀλλὰ μηδὲ τοῖς ἀπὸ ἑνὸς  W185
μόνου λεγομένοις πίστευε ἢ πρόσεχε, ἀλλὰ τῇ ἐκ τῶν πλειόνων συμφωνίᾳ
170 πείθου, μάλιστα δὲ τῶν ἐξ ἐπιδρομῆς ἀθρόας ἁλισκομένων, ὡς εἴπομεν, ἥπερ
τῶν προσφευγόντων σοι. πρὸς δὲ τοὺς προσφεύγοντάς σοι ἀπὸ τῶν ἐχθρῶν, καί
τινα μηνύειν ἐπαγγελλομένους μυστήρια, ἢ ἐν δεσμοῖς φύλαττε τέως ἢ ἄλλως
πως μετὰ ἀσφαλείας ἔχε, καὶ πρόλεγε αὐτοῖς δωρεὰς δώσειν. ἐὰν δὲ ψεύδωνται,
ἀπείλει θάνατον.
175 33. Ἐὰν δὲ συνέστηκεν στρατὸς ἐχθρῶν, καὶ ἔξωθεν ὀχυρωμάτων διάγῃ, μὴ
ἐπαφιῇς τῶν στρατιωτῶν τινας ἐπὶ ἁρπαγὴν ἢ πραίδαν πραγμάτων, ἀλλὰ πρότερον ἐπέρχου κατ᾽ αὐτοῦ. καὶ εἰ μὲν καλῶς ἐξέλθῃ τὸ τοῦ πολέμου πέρας, μὴ
ἀναβάλλου τὸν καιρόν, ἀλλ᾽ ἐν ὅσῳ ἐν φόβῳ καὶ ταραχῇ εἰσιν οἱ ἐχθροὶ ἐπιτί-
θου αὐτοῖς μέχρις τοῦ | τελείως καταλυθῶσι καὶ σκορπισθῶσιν ἢ σύμφωνα  W185ᵛ
180 συμφέροντά σοι γένωνται ἀσφαλῶς.
34. Ἐὰν δὲ οἱ ἐχθροὶ σύστασιν μὲν ποιήσωσιν, ἀναβάλλωνται δὲ συμμίξαι
μάχην, τότε σπούδαζε ἡνωμένως καὶ ἀδιασπάστως περιπατεῖν, καὶ τὰ ἐν ποσὶν
ἀφανίζειν. εἰ δὲ διὰ τῆς τοιαύτης ὁδοῦ ἡ ὑποστροφή σου ἐλπίζεται γενέσθαι, καὶ
οὐκ εἰσὶν ἄλλαι ἀποτροφαὶ ἢ βοσκαί, τότε φείδου τὰς ἐν ποσίν, ἤγουν τὸ ἀφανί-
185 ζειν τὰς δαπάνας· ἐν δὲ τῷ ὑποστρέφειν σε, τότε μᾶλλον ἀφάνιζε ταύτας.
35. Ὥστε δὲ μὴ ἐν τῇ ἀλλοτρίᾳ γῇ πλανᾶσθαί σε εἰς τὰς ὁδούς, δέον σημεῖά
τινα ἐν ταῖς ὁδοῖς καὶ τοῖς ἀμφιβόλοις τίθεσθαι. ἐὰν μὲν ὗλαι εἰσὶν ἐν τοῖς
δένδροις, εἰ δὲ γυμνοί εἰσιν οἱ τόποι, διὰ σωρῶν λίθων ἢ ὑπορυγμάτων μικρῶν
διὰ τὸ ἐπιγινώσκοντας δι᾽ αὐτῶν τοὺς ὑστερίζοντας ἐκ τοῦ στρατοῦ μὴ πλανᾶσ-
190 θαι τὴν ὁδόν.
36. Ὅσους δὲ εἰς πραίδαν ἀφορίσεις καὶ | ἀποστείλεις παράγγελλε μὴ πάν-  W186
τας εἰς τὴν διαρπαγὴν ἀσχολεῖσθαι, ἀλλὰ διῃρημένους εἶναι ἵνα οἱ μὲν αὐτῶν

167 ad ἐκ τῶν des. M

169 ἢ πρόσεχε W om. AVBE    170 ἁλισκομένων W συλλαμβανομένων AVBE    171 πρὸς
δὲ W om. AVBE | τοὺς W τοὺς δὲ AVBE    172 ἐπαγγελλομένους W ὑπισχνουμένους AVBE
175 συνέστηκεν W συνέστηκε AVBE    176 ἁρπαγὴν...πραίδαν W ἁρπαγὴ ἢ πραίδα AVBE
179 καταλυθῶσι AVBE καταλυθῶσιν W    182 ἐν ποσὶν W ἔμπροσθεν εὑρισκόμενα AVBE
184 ἢ βοσκαί W om. AVBE    184–185 τὰς...τὰς W ἀφανίζειν τὰς εὑρισκομένας AVBE
184 τὰς AVBE τὰ W    185 δὲ AVBE om. W    186 δὲ AVBE om. W    186–187 εἰς...ὁδοῖς
AVBE δεῖ ἐν ταῖς διόδοις W    187 ἀμφιβόλοις AVBE ἀμφιβόλοις σημεῖα W
189 ὑστερίζοντας W παραπεμπόμενοντας AVBE    191–192 πάντας AVBE πάντως W

32. Do not, however, be too ready to trust defectors, although you can be-lieve men captured in surprise attacks. It is not uncommon for defectors and prisoners to give false information. Do not believe or pay attention to statements made by one person alone but be convinced only by the agreement of several, especially, as mentioned, persons taken in sudden attacks, rather than defectors. You should place enemy deserters who claim to have some secret information in confinement for a while, or hold them securely in some other way, promising them rewards, but if they are lying threaten them with death.

33. If the enemy army has concentrated its forces and is staying outside fortifications, do not send any of your soldiers to plunder or engage in looting, but they should first advance against the enemy. If the result of the battle is favorable, they should not put off the opportunity but, while the enemy are still very frightened and confused, they should keep after them until they are completely broken up and scattered, or an agreement favorable to you, and with certain safeguards, has been made.

34. But if the enemy has indeed concentrated his forces but avoids getting into action, then make sure that our troops march about, united and without breaking ranks, and lay waste the area around them. But if you hope to return by the same route and there is no other source of food or forage, then spare the supplies in the area rather than destroy them, and only on your return journey should you destroy them.

35. To avoid getting lost while marching in foreign territory, you must set up certain signs on the roads and places where the way is not clear. If the area is wooded, put them on the trees, if barren, piles of rocks or <small pits> dug in the ground will do. These will be recognized by the troops marching along later so they will not lose their way.

36. Order the troops you assign and send out to pillage that not all of them should busy themselves with plundering, but divide them into two groups: the

πραιδεύουσιν, οἱ δὲ πλείους αὐτῶν συντεταγμένοι ἵστανται εἰς φυλακὴν ἢ
παρακολουθοῦσιν, εἴτε κατὰ χωρίου εἴτε κατὰ φοσσάτου ἐχθρῶν εἴτε κατὰ
195 ἀγέλης εἴτε κατὰ τούλδου ἢ ἑτέρου τινὸς ἡ ἐπέλευσις γίνεται. τοῦτο δὲ ποίει καὶ
ὅταν ἡνωμένου ὄντος τοῦ παντὸς στρατοῦ τῆς πραίδας ἐγχειρήσῃς, εἰς τὸ μὴ
πάντας ἐπὶ τῇ ἁρπαγῇ ἀσχολεῖσθαι.

37. Ἀλλ᾽ εἰ καὶ συλλογῆς δαπάνης καιρὸς γένηται, δεῖ τοὺς μὲν συλλέγειν,
τοὺς δὲ συντεταγμένους καὶ παρατεταγμένους ἀκολουθεῖν, ὥστε πάντων εἰς
200 ἁρπαγὴν ἢ συλλογὴν τῶν ἐπιτηδείων χρειῶν ἀσχολουμένων, μὴ αἰφνιδιασμόν
τινα ἢ ἔγκρυμμα ὑπὸ τῶν ἐναντίων συμβῇ γενέσθαι. εἰ γὰρ συμβῇ τοῦτο, μὴ
ὄντων αὐτῶν συντεταγμένων, οὐ δυνήσονται ἑαυτοὺς ἀνακαλέ|σασθαι.   W186ᵛ

38. Ὅταν δὲ χρὴ ἐκ τοῦ αἰφνιδίου τὰς ἐγχειρήσεις κατά τινων Σκυθικῶν ἢ
τινων ὁμοίων ἐθνῶν ποιεῖσθαι, διὰ τὸ μάλιστα ἀνύποπτον, χρὴ μετὰ σκοποῦ τά
205 τε δάση καὶ τὰς δυσχωρίας προσέχειν καὶ διερευνᾶσθαι. καὶ οὕτως προορδινεύ-
ειν χρὴ τὰ βάνδα εἰς τὸ εἰδέναι αὐτά, ποῖον πρῶτον καὶ ποῖον δεύτερον καὶ
ποῖον τρίτον καὶ ἐφεξῆς ὀφείλουσι περιπατεῖν· καὶ μάλιστα ἐὰν διὰ στενῶν
τόπων ἔφοδος γίνεται, καὶ ἵνα μὴ συγχέωνται καὶ βραδέως ἐν τῷ διαμερισμῷ
συνέρχωνται.

210 39. Ἄφνω γὰρ τῆς ἐπελεύσεως γινομένης, εἰ μὲν διὰ δύο τόπων ἐπιτήδειόν
ἐστι τὴν ἐγχείρησιν ποιήσασθαι, δεῖ τὸν στρατὸν εἰς δύο μερίζεσθαι, καὶ τὸ μὲν
ἓν μέρος λαμβάνειν ἢ τὸν μεράρχην, ὃν οἱ παλαιοὶ ὑποστράτηγον ἔλεγον, ἢ τὸν
τουρμάρχην ἢ ὁποῖοι ἂν ἄρχοντες τὴν ἔφοδον ποιοῦνται. δύο πάντως ἄρχοντας
πρῶτον καὶ δεύτερον εἰς τὰ δύο μέρη ἵνα καθ᾽ ἕκαστον ἐπιστῇ|σαι, καὶ τὸ μὲν ἓν   W187
215 μέρος, ὡς εἴρηται, τὸν ἕνα ἄρχοντα ἔξπληκτον ἔχειν, καὶ χωρὶς τούλδου, καὶ
προκόπτοντα ὡς δεκαπέντε ἢ εἴκοσι μιλίων διάστημα διὰ τόπων ἀγνώστων ἐκ
πλαγίου καὶ ἐγγίζοντα τοῖς χωρίοις, ἐκεῖθεν ἄρχεσθαι τῆς πραίδας ὥστε ἐπὶ τὸ
μέρος τοῦ στρατηγοῦ ἔρχεσθαι· τὸν στρατηγὸν δὲ ἔχοντα τὸ ἄλλο μέρος διὰ
τῆς ἑτέρας ἀρχῆς τῶν χωρίων εἰσβάλλειν καὶ πραιδεύειν, καὶ ἀμφοτέρους εἰς
220 ἀπαντὴν ἀλλήλων ἐρχομένους, καὶ πραιδεύοντας τὰ ἐν μέσῳ χωρία, ἐν ᾧ

193 πραιδεύουσιν W πραιδεύωσιν AVBE | πλείους W πλείονες AVBE 199 καὶ
παρατεταγμένους W om. AVBE | ὥστε W ὥστε μὴ AVBE 200 μὴ W om. AVBE
201–202 εἰ…συντεταγμένων W τοῦτο γένηται μὴ ὄντες συντεταγμένοι AVBE
202 ἑαυτοὺς AVBE ἑαυτοῖς W 203 χρὴ W χρεία γένηται AVBE | τινων W καὶ τῶν AVBE
205 δυσχωρίας…καὶ² W δυσκολίας AVBE 206 ποῖον¹ W om. AVBE 208 γίνεται W
γίνηται ΛVBE | καὶ² ΛVBE om. W 211 ἐστι AVBE ἐστιν W 214 ἵνα W ἕνα AVBE |
ἐπιστῆσαι W ἐπιστῆναι AVBE 215 ἔξπληκτον ἔχειν W ἔχειν ἐλαφρὸν AVBE
216 δεκαπέντε…εἴκοσι AVBE δεκακαιπέντε καὶ εἴκοσι W 217 ὥστε W καὶ ὡς AVBE
220 ἐν ᾧ AVBE ἐὰν W

first to do the pillaging and the other, larger group to stand by or follow along in formation to protect them. Observe this whether the attack is directed against a region, a fortified camp of the enemy, a herd of cattle, a baggage train, or anything else. Follow the same procedure when you have the entire army join together in pillaging, although not every individual has to be occupied in the actual plundering.

37. However, if the opportunity for gathering supplies presents itself, some should gather them while others follow in close formation and drawn up for battle. If all the men are busy with plundering and collecting necessary provisions and the enemy happens to catch them unawares or sets up an ambush at a time when they are not lined up for battle, they will not be able to get back into formation.

38. When it is necessary to launch surprise attacks against some Scythians or similar nations, you will avoid any suspicion, if you very carefully study and reconnoiter the wooded and difficult terrain. Make certain ahead of time that the banda know the order in which they are supposed to march, which is first, which second, which third, and so forth, especially if they are to make their attack through narrow places. As they proceed slowly in their separate units, they will not be confused.

39. When it comes to making a sudden attack, if it seems more effective to attack in two places, you must divide your army in two. The merarch, whom the ancient authorities called the lieutenant general, should assume command of one section, or it could be the tourmarch or whatever officers are leading the assault. By all means there must be two officers, a first and a second, for the two divisions, one in command of each of them. The first division, as noted, has one lightly equipped officer and is without a baggage train. It goes ahead to a distance of about fifteen or twenty miles through unknown places, approaching those regions from the side, and begins the pillaging so as to join up with the division led by the general. The general, leading the other division, is to invade through the other entrance to those regions and plunder them. Both divisions then proceed to meet with each other and they pillage the area between them.

συμφθάσωσιν εἰς ἑσπέραν, ἐκεῖσε ἐν τῷ ἅμα ἁπλικεύειν. ἐκ τούτου γὰρ καὶ
ἀσφαλῶς ἡ ἐγχείρησις γίνεται, καὶ οἱ διαφεύγοντες τῶν ἐχθρῶν τὸν ἕνα αὐτῶν
τῷ ἄλλῳ περιπίπτουσιν ἀδοκήτως, μηδ᾽ ἐπισυναχθῆναι δυνάμενοι.

40. Εἰ δὲ μία ἐστιν ἡ ἐπιτηδεία ὁδὸς δι᾽ ἧς τὴν εἰσβολὴν κατὰ τὴν τῶν ἐχ-
225 θρῶν δυνατὸν γενέσθαι, χρὴ καὶ οὕτως τὸν στρατὸν διανεμηθῆναι. καὶ τὸ μὲν
δίμοιρον αὐτοῦ ἢ καὶ τὸ πλέον τούτου ἔξπληκτον καὶ | ἐνδύναμον τὸν ὑποστρά-    W187ᵛ
τηγον λαμβάνειν, καὶ μετὰ τοῦ ἰδίου αὐτοῦ ἐν ᾧ αὐτὸς τάσσεται βάνδου ἔμπροσθεν πάντων προηγήσασθαι, ἔχοντα μεθ᾽ ἑαυτοῦ πάντας τοὺς τῶν ταγμάτων
αὐτοῦ ἄρχοντας, καὶ ὅταν τῷ πρώτῳ χωρίῳ ἐπιστῇ πρὸς τὴν αὐτοῦ δύναμιν,
230 ἀφορίζειν εἴτε ἓν εἴτε δύο βάνδα, ὥστε τοὺς μὲν πραιδεύειν, τοὺς δὲ φυλάττειν
τοὺς πραιδεύοντας.

41. Καλὸν δέ ἐστιν ἐν τοῖς πρώτοις χωρίοις μὴ πολλὰ βάνδα ἀφορίζεσθαι,
κἂν εἰ μεγάλα συμβαίνῃ τὰ χωρία εἶναι. ἐπιφθάζοντος γὰρ ὄπισθεν τοῦ στρατοῦ
οὐ δίδοται καιρὸς ἀντικαταστάσεως τοῖς ἐν αὐτοῖς εὑρισκομένοις. συντόμως δὲ
235 τὸν ὑποστράτηγον ἐπὶ τὰ πρόσω τὴν πάροδον ποιούμενον ὁμοίως καὶ εἰς τὰ
λοιπὰ χωρία ἐφεξῆς, τοῦτο ποιεῖν μέχρις ἂν ἐπαρκέσωσιν τὰ παραδιδόμενα
αὐτῷ τάγματα. αὐτὸν δὲ ὑποστράτηγον ἐξωτέρω πάντων εὑρισκόμενον δεῖ τρία
ἢ τέσσαρα βάνδα ἄχρι χιλίων ἀνδρῶν χρησίμων περὶ αὐτὸν ἔχειν, ἕως τελείας
τοῦ πράγματος ἐκβάσεως, ἤγουν τῆς ἐφόδου, ἵνα βίγλα ἀκριβὴς καὶ ἀσφάλεια
240 τοῖς λοιποῖς γένηται.

42. Τούτων οὖν ἐκ τοῦ ὑποστρατήγου γινομένων δέον σε, ὦ στρατηγέ, ἢ εἴ
τις ἕτερος ὁ τῆς τοιαύτης ἐπελεύσεως τὴν διοίκησιν πεπιστευμένος, ἵνα ἐπακο-
λουθῇς τοῖς κατὰ μέρος πραιδεύουσιν, καὶ ἐπισυνάγῃς καὶ ἐπὶ τὰ ἔμπροσθεν
προκόπτῃς ὡς ἐπὶ τὸν ὑποστράτηγον ἢ τὸν τουρμάρχην. ὁμοίως δὲ καὶ ἐκεῖνον
245 τὸ αὐτὸ ποιεῖν καὶ ἐπισυνάγειν παρερχόμενον τοὺς πραιδεύοντας, καὶ ἐν ᾧ ἂν
τόπῳ ὑπαντήσετε ἀλλήλοις ἁπλικεύετε ἅμα καὶ τὴν αὐτὴν ἡμέραν. διὸ οὐδὲ χρὴ
πλέον τῶν πεντεκαίδεκα ἢ εἴκοσι μιλίων χωρισμένους ποιεῖσθαι τὰς τοιαύτας

---

223 μηδ᾽ W μηδὲ AVBE | δυνάμενοι W δυνάμενον AVBE   224 κατὰ W διὰ AVBE
225 διανεμηθῆναι W διαμερισθῆναι AVBE   226 ἔξπληκτον W ἐλαφρὸν AVBE   227 καὶ
AVBE om. W | αὐτοῦ W αὐτοῦ βάνδου AVBE | βάνδου W om. AVBE   228 προηγήσασθαι
W προηγεῖσθαι AVBE   233 εἰ W om. AVBE | ἐπιφθάζοντος W ἐπιφθάζοντες AVBE
235 πρόσω W ἔμπροσθεν AVBE   236 ἐπαρκέσωσιν W ἐπαρκέσωσι AVBE
241 γινομένων AVBE γινομένου W   243 ἐπισυνάγῃς AVBE συνάγῃς W (ἐπι superscr.)
244 προκόπτῃς W πραιδεύῃς AVBE   245 τὸ…ποιεῖν W om. AVBE   246 ὑπαντήσετε W
ὑπαντήσηται AVBE   247 πεντεκαίδεκα W δεκαπέντε AVBE | ποιεῖσθαι τὰς W εἰς AVBE

They should arrive there by evening and, at the same time, set up camp in that place. As a result, the attack will be carried out safely and in their flight the enemy will unexpectedly fall over one another, unable to reassemble.

40. If there is one suitable road along which it is possible to enter into hostile territory, it is necessary to divide the army as follows. Half of it, even the larger part, should consist of light-armed, but powerful, troops under the command of the lieutenant general. With his own bandon, the one in which he is stationed, he should march in front of all the others, accompanied by all the officers of his units. At his first stop, he should, depending on the strength of his force, assign one or two banda, with some troops to pillage and others to protect them.

41. In the first region <you enter> it is a good idea not to detail many banda, even if that region happens to extend for some distance. With the army coming up behind them, they will have no time to get into formation to oppose the local forces. The lieutenant general up in front quickly moves along and, in like manner, passes through to the other parts of the region in succession. He should do this until the units entrusted to him are sufficient. The lieutenant general himself is located apart from everyone else and must have three or four banda, up to a thousand capable men, with him until the final outcome of the affair, that is, the attack, so that the rest may have alert patrols and security.

42. While these things are being done by the lieutenant general, it is necessary for you, O general, or whoever else you may have entrusted with the conduct of such an assault, to follow the troops taking their turn in pillaging, gather them together, and lead their advance toward the lieutenant general or the tourmarch. That one is to do the same, come up and assemble the pillaging parties. In whatever place you encounter one another, set up camp together that same day. You must not be more than fifteen or twenty miles apart when you

αἰφνιδίους ἐπελεύσεις, ἵνα φθάζετε ἀμφότεροι καὶ τὴν πραίδαν ποιεῖν καὶ κατὰ τὴν αὐτὴν ἡμέραν ἅμα ἀπλικεύειν.

250   43. Ἐν δὲ ταῖς τοιαύταις | ἐπιδρομαῖς οὐ χρὴ τοὺς δυναμένους ἀντικαθ-   W188ᵛ ίστασθαι ἐχθροὺς ζωγρεῖν ἤτοι συλλαμβάνειν, ἀλλὰ πάντας τοὺς παρατυγ-χάνοντας τοιούτους διαχρῆσθαι καὶ παρέρχεσθαι καὶ μὴ εἰς αὐτοὺς ἐμβραδύνειν τοὺς τὴν πάροδον μάλιστα ποιουμένους καὶ τὸν καιρὸν δαπανᾶσθαι.

44. Ἐὰν δέ ποτε βουληθῇς φρούριον ἤτοι κάστρον ἢ ἄκραν τινὰ παραλαβεῖν 255   ἢ ἕτερον τόπον, μὴ πρόλεγε τῷ πλήθει ἄχρις ἂν ἐπὶ τοῦ τόπου γενόμενος ἐγχειρήσῃς τὸ ἔργον.

45. Ἐὰν δὲ καὶ ἀνάγκη ποτὲ γένηται ὥστε ἐκ παντὸς τρόπου τὴν στρατιὰν πλησίον ὀχυρώματος πολεμίων ἢ ἀπλικεῦσαι ἢ πάροδον ποιεῖσθαι, δεῖ σε ἕνα τῶν ἀρχόντων μετὰ ἐξπλήκτων ἀνδρῶν συστῆσαι εἰς τὰς ἐξόδους τοῦ ὀχυρώ- 260   ματος ἵνα τάς, ὡς εἰκός, αἰφνιδίας ἐπιδρομὰς τῶν ἐναντίων κωλύσῃ. τοῦτο δὲ καὶ ἐν τοῖς στενοῖς τόποις γίνεσθαι ἀναγκαῖον.

46. Πλησίον δὲ ὀχυρώματος | ἐχθρῶν ἢ ὕλης μὴ ἐπιτηδεύῃς ἀπλικεύειν τὸν   W189 στρατόν. εἰ δὲ ἀνάγκη πᾶσα ἐκεῖσε ἀπλικεύειν, ἀκριβῶς τὰς παραφυλακὰς ποιοῦ διὰ τὰς τῶν ἐχθρῶν ἐπιθέσεις. καὶ μᾶλλον σπούδαζε ἵνα ἡπλωμένῳ καὶ ὑψηλο- 265   τέρῳ τόπῳ καὶ ὀχυρωτέρῳ ἀπλικεύσῃς.

47. Ὅταν δὲ εἰς τὴν πολεμίαν γῆν εἰσέρχῃ, τὴν ἀποσκευὴν πᾶσαν ἤτοι τὸν τοῦλδον ὄπισθεν ἀκολουθεῖν ποιήσῃς· πλησιαζόντων δὲ τῶν ἐχθρῶν ἐν μέσῳ τοῦ στρατοῦ τὸν τοῦλδον εἶναι παρασκεύασον.

48. Κεχωρισμένην δὲ εἶναι ἀπὸ τῶν ὁπλοφόρων στρατιωτῶν τὴν ἀποσκευὴν 270   καὶ τοὺς αἰχμαλώτους ἐὰν εἰσίν, μήποτε πολεμίων ἀθρόως ἐπιγινομένων τοῖς ἀγωνιζομένοις ἐμπόδισμα γένηται· μὴ μόνον δὲ ἐν τῇ ὁδοιπορίᾳ τοῦτο φύλαττε, ἀλλὰ καὶ ὅταν ἀπλικεύῃς.

49. Ἐπὶ δὲ τῆς πολεμίας γῆς τοὺς μινσουράτωρας ἀπροόπτως μὴ ἀποστέλ-λῃς προλαμβάνειν ἄνευ βοηθείας ἀρκούσης αὐτοῖς, ἀλλὰ μόνον διὰ τῶν αἰχμα|   W189ᵛ 275   λώτων καὶ αὐτομόλων ἀσφαλῶς ἀνερεύνα τὴν τῶν τόπων ποιότητα.

50. Ὅταν δὲ ὁ στρατὸς ἀπλικεύειν μέλλῃ, μὴ ἀναμεμιγμένως καὶ ἀτάκτως ἐπερχέσθωσαν ἐν τῷ τοῦ φοσσάτου ἀπλίκτῳ, ἀλλ' ἐὰν ἐχθροὶ ἐγγίζωσι καὶ συμπάρεισι πεζοὶ τῷ στρατῷ πρότερον τὰς ἁμάξας τιθέτωσαν, καὶ ἐν τάξει τὰ

248 αἰφνιδίους W om. AVBE | φθάζετε W φθάζητε AVBE   252 διαχρῆσθαι W φονεύειν AVBE   255 τοῦ τόπου De τοῦτό που codd.   259 ἐξπλήκτων W ἐλαφρῶν AVBE 260 αἰφνιδίας PG αἰφνιδίους codd. | τῶν AVBE om. W | κωλύσῃ W κωλύσωσιν AVBE 266 τὸν De τὸ codd.   274 μόνον W πρῶτον AVBE   275 αὐτομόλων W προσφυγῶν AVBE   277 ἀλλ' AVBE ἀλλὰ W | ἐγγίζωσι PG ἐγγίζωσιν codd.   278 συμπάρεισι AVBE συμπάρεισιν W

make these surprise attacks, so that both of you may arrive at the same time on that same day to engage in the pillaging and to set up camp.

43. In incursions of this sort it is not necessary to take prisoners from the units of the enemy able to stand up to you, or to capture them, but get rid of all those you happen to encounter, or pass by them, so you will not slow down for them and waste your time, especially when you are in transit.

44. If you want to occupy a fortress, a walled town, some height, or some other place, do not announce it to the troops until you have arrived at the site and then set about your task.

45. If, at some time, it should become absolutely necessary for your army to set up camp or to continue marching along close to a fortification of the enemy, then you must station one of your officers together with some light-armed troops by the gateways of their fortification to forestall any likely, sudden sallies of the enemy. You must follow the same procedure in narrow places.

46. Do not attempt to have your army camp near an enemy fortification or near a wooded area. If it is absolutely necessary to camp there, devote special attention to the guard posts to defend against enemy attacks. It is better to look for unobstructed, high, and defensible ground for a campsite.

47. When you enter hostile territory, have the equipment, that is, the baggage train, follow behind, but, as the enemy get closer, move it up into the middle of the army.

48. The baggage and the prisoners, if there are any, should be kept separated from the weapon-bearing soldiers so that, in case of a sudden enemy attack, they will not get in the way of the fighting men. Observe this not only on the march but also when you are in camp.

49. In hostile territory do not send out surveyors to go on ahead without due precautions and sufficient support. But from prisoners and deserters alone you may safely get information about the nature of the territory.

50. When the army is about to set up camp, it should not march into the fortified enclosure in disorder with its ranks mixed up. If the enemy are drawing near, however, and there are infantry in the army, first park the wagons, then

ὀρύγματα ποιείτωσαν πρεπόντως τοῦ τάφρου. οἱ δὲ ἔξπληκτοι, ἤγουν οἱ εὐπλή-
280 κτως ἄνευ βάρους, περιπατοῦντες πάντες ἀπὸ ὀλίγου διαστήματος ἕτοιμοι
στηκέτωσαν, καὶ τότε τὴν ἀποσκευὴν κατὰ τάξιν εἰσέρχεσθαι καὶ ἀπλικεύειν. καὶ
ὅταν ἀπολύσῃς καὶ τὰς βίγλας, τότε εἰσερχέσθωσαν καὶ αὐτοὶ οἱ ὁπλῖται κατὰ
τάξιν καὶ ἀπλικευέτωσαν, καθώς σοι καὶ ἐν τῷ περὶ ἀπλίκτων λόγῳ διεταξάμεθα. ἐὰν δὲ πλησίον μή εἰσιν οἱ ἐχθροί, ἀρκεῖ καὶ δι᾽ ἑνὸς δρούγγου τοῦτο
285 γίνεσθαι τὸ σχῆμα, καὶ οὕτως ἐκείνων ἱσταμέ|νων τοὺς λοιποὺς ἀπλικεύειν.      W190

51. Ἐχθρῶν δὲ ἐγγιζόντων καὶ σύστασιν ποιούντων, ἢ ὀχυρωμάτων πλησίον
ἢ ὕλης ἢ τόπου δυσχεροῦς, μὴ ἀφίης ὡς ἔτυχεν τινὰς βόσκειν τοὺς ἵππους, ἀλλὰ
καὶ τὰς βίγλας ἀσφαλῶς πέμπε, καὶ ἔχε μὲν τοὺς ἵππους ἐν τῷ χάρακι. σπουδάζειν δὲ ὥστε ἀπὸ χειρῶν συνάγειν ἐκ τῶν εὑρισκομένων καρπῶν ἐν τοῖς πλησίον
290 χωρίοις, τοῦ τε χόρτου καὶ τῶν κριθῶν τὴν συλλογὴν ποιεῖσθαι οὕτως, ὥστε
μετὰ τῶν παλλικαρίων τοῦ τούλδου εὔπληκτοι ἀπὸ ἑκάστου μέρους συνέρχονται ὡπλισμένοι στρατιῶται ἐν τάξει περιπατοῦντες διὰ τὰς αἰφνιδίους τῶν
ἐχθρῶν ἐπελεύσεις.

52. Ἐὰν δὲ χρονίσῃς τῷ τόπῳ, καὶ ὁ καιρὸς ἐπιτήδειός ἐστι, καὶ ὁ τόπος
295 ὁμοίως πρὸς ἀποτροφάς, ἔστι δὲ καὶ τῶν ἐχθρῶν ἡ δύναμις ἀπὸ μακρόθεν, τότε
δυνατόν ἐστι βόσκεσθαι τοὺς ἵππους βίγλας διπλῆς καὶ τριπλῆς πολλάκις |      W190ᵛ
πεμπομένης | ἀπὸ πολλῶν διαστημάτων καὶ ταύτης συχνῶς ἀλλασσομένης.      384

53. Ἐὰν δέ τινας ἐπὶ πραῖδαν τάξῃς, οὗτοι μόνοι ἐξερχέσθωσαν. εἰ δέ τινες
τῶν στρατιωτῶν ἐπιμιχθῶσιν αὐτοῖς ἰδίᾳ αὐθεντίᾳ ποιήσεις γενέσθαι διαλαλιάν,
300 ὥστε μηδένα ἕτερον πλὴν τῶν ὡρισμένων ἐξελθεῖν εἰς τὴν πραῖδαν. καὶ τότε
μετὰ τὸ μανδάτον τοὺς παρακούοντας συνέχεσθαι καὶ παραπέμπεσθαι τοῖς
ἰδίοις αὐτῶν ἄρχουσιν εἰς τὸ σωφρονίζεσθαι, ἵνα μὴ οἱ λοιποὶ λαμβάνοντες
ἄδειαν, καὶ εἰς ἁρπαγὴν ἐκτρέχοντες, γυμνώσωσί σε ἀπὸ στρατοῦ καὶ κινδυνεύσῃ ὅλος ὁ λαός.

---

297 ad ἀπὸ de novo inc. M

279 τοῦ τάφρου W τῆς σούδας AVBE | ἔξπληκτοι ἤγουν W ἐλαφροὶ AVBE
279–280 εὐπλήκτως W om. AVBE    282 βίγλας De βουλὰς codd.    284 οἱ AVBE om. W
286 ὀχυρωμάτων W ὀχυρωμάτων ὄντων AVBE    291 παλλικαρίων W ὑπηρετῶν AVBE
291–292 εὔπληκτοι (-ως)...στρατιῶται W στρατιῶται ἐλαφροὶ ὡπλισμένοι ἀπὸ ἑκάστου
μέρους συνέρχονται AVBE    291 εὔπληκτοι De εὐπλήκτως codd.    294 ἔστι AVBE ἔστιν W
295 ἔστι AVBE ἔστιν W    297 ταύτης MW ταύταις AVBE | ἀλλασσομένης MW
ἀλασσομέναις AVBE    299 ἰδίᾳ...διαλαλιάν MW διαλαλήσεις AVBE    301 τὸ μανδάτον
MW τὴν παραγγελίαν AVBE | συνέχεσθαι MW συλλαμβάνεσθαι AVBE    303 γυμνώσωσί
ΜΑVBE γυμνώσωσιν W

have the men dig the trench in the prescribed manner. All the light-armed troops, that is, those marching quickly without heavy weapons, are to be stationed in readiness a short distance away. The baggage train then enters in good order and takes its place in camp. When you send out the patrols, the hoplites can then enter in formation and set up camp, as we have explained to you in the chapter about camps. But if the enemy are not in the vicinity, it is enough to follow this procedure with a single droungos, so that, while they stand in position, the rest can pitch camp.

51. But if the enemy are approaching, in close formation, or <we> are near a fortified spot or a wooded area or difficult terrain, do not send anyone out to graze the horses but keep them inside the camp. But it is safe to send out scouting parties. Make sure to gather whatever is at hand from the produce found in nearby villages and gather hay and barley as well. In case of sudden attacks by the enemy, though, the boys in the baggage train should be accompanied by light-armed troops from each meros, marching in formation.

52. But if you spend some time in the place, and the time as well as the location seem suitable for foraging, assuming that the enemy forces are a good distance away, then the horses may be allowed to graze. Double, even triple, patrols should be sent frequently to a considerable distance and relieved at regular intervals.

53. If you detail certain men to pillage, only they are to go out. But to prevent other soldiers from mixing in with them on their own authority, issue orders that nobody, other than those assigned, should go out to pillage. After that order has been given, any transgressors should be detained and sent off to their own commanding officers for punishment. This is to prevent the rest from taking leave to go out pillaging and leaving you without an army, and placing all the troops in danger.

305    54. Ἀκρίβειαν δὲ καὶ ἀσφάλειαν ἔχε, ἵνα ἐὰν τύχῃ καὶ εὑρεθῇ ἢ οἶνος ἢ ἄρτος, μὴ τρώγειν αὐτὸν καὶ πίνειν προχείρως πεῖρας, ἐὰν μὴ πρότερον διὰ τῶν αἰχμαλώτων δοκιμάσῃς αὐτόν. καὶ οὕτως εὑρίσκων ἀπαθῆ καὶ ὑγιῆ, τότε ποιήσεις χρήσασθαι αὐτὰ τοὺς στρατιώτας. ἀλλὰ μηδὲ τὸ ἐν τοῖς φρέασιν ὕδωρ ἢ κινστέρναις ἢ λάκκοις ἢ ἐν ἄλλοις ἀγγείοις. πολλάκις γὰρ διὰ φαρμάκων ἀφανί-
310    ζονται καὶ θανατηφόρα γίνεται. εὑρέθησαν γάρ ποτε καὶ κριθαὶ οὕτως φαρμακευθεῖσαι καὶ μὴ ἐχόντων ἄλλοθεν τῶν στρατιωτῶν τοῖς ἀλόγοις ἀποτροφήν, ἠναγκάσθησαν ἐκεῖθεν αὐτοῖς παραλαβεῖν τροφήν, καὶ οὐκ ὀλίγοι διὰ τοῦτο ἵπποι ἀπώλοντο.

55. Παραγγείλῃς δὲ τῷ στρατῷ, καθὼς ἐν τῷ περὶ ὁδοιπορίας ἡμῖν εἴρηται
315    λόγῳ, ἵνα ἐὰν ὡς πολλάκις γένηται ταραχὴ εἰς τὸν λαόν, μὴ ἀλλαχοῦ ὧδε καὶ ἐκεῖσε τρέχειν αὐτοὺς καὶ περιφύρεσθαι, ἀλλ᾽ ἐκεῖ ὁρμᾶν πάντας ὅπου ἡ ταραχὴ γέγονεν· ἐκ τούτου γὰρ καὶ πρὸς τοὺς πολεμίους ἕτοιμοι γίνονται καί, ἐάν τι τοιοῦτον συμβῇ, καὶ οὐ συμφύρονται εἰς ἀλλήλους καὶ οὐ συγχέονται.

56. Τὰς δὲ βίγλας ἡνίκα εἰσβάλλεις εἰς τὴν πολεμίαν γῆν, μὴ μόνον κατὰ τὸ
320    ἔμπρυθεν μέρος ἀποστέλλῃς πάντοτε, καὶ τοῦτο μόνον ἀσφαλίζῃς, ἀλλὰ καὶ κατὰ τοῦ νώτου ὄπισθεν εὐπλήκτους καὶ εὐόπλους στρατιώτας ἤγουν ἱκανὴν δύναμιν μετὰ χρησίμου ἄρχοντος παράτασσε, τοὺς λεγομένους νωτοφύλακας, ὡς ἀπὸ ι′ μιλίων ἢ ιε′, ἢ ὅσον οἶδας διάστημα, μετὰ βίγλας ἀκριβοῦς διὰ τούς, ὡς εἰκός, ὑστερίζοντας ἐκ τοῦ στρατοῦ ἢ δι᾽ ἀρρωστίαν ἢ κατὰ ἑτέραν τινὰ
325    χρείαν, ὅπως μὴ αἰφνιδίως οἱ ἐχθροὶ ἐπιπεσόντες συλλάβωνται αὐτούς.

57. Εἰώθασι γὰρ τότε μάλιστα ποιεῖσθαι τὰς ἐγχειρήσεις οἱ ἐχθροὶ ὅτε καὶ ἀμε|ρίμνως ὁδεύουσιν οἱ στρατιῶται, καὶ οἱ ἔμπροσθεν τοῖς ὄπισθεν εὐκόλως    384ᵛ βοηθεῖν οὐ δύνανται. τοῦτο δὲ καὶ ἐν τῇ ἡμετέρᾳ γῇ ἐὰν ποιήσῃς, οὐκ ἀπρεπές ἐστι διὰ τούς, ὡς εἰκός, ῥεμβομένους ὧδε κἀκεῖσε στρατιώτας, καὶ μὴ καλῶς

---

309-313 Ioan. de Nikiou *Chron.*, 96.

308 χρήσασθαι MW ἐσθίειν AVBE | ἢ MW ἢ ἐν ταῖς AVBE    309 ἢ¹ MW ἢ ἐν AVBE 309-310 ἀφανίζονται καὶ MW om. AVBE    310 γίνεται MW γίνονται AVBE 310-311 φαρμακευθεῖσαι MAVBE φαρκευθεῖσαι W    312 παραλαβεῖν PG παραβαλεῖν codd.    316 ἐκεῖσε MW ἐκεῖ AVBE    317 πολεμίους MW πολέμους AVBE    318 οὐ¹ MW om. AVBE    320 πάντοτε MW πάντοθεν AVBE    321 κατὰ...νώτου MW om. AVBE | εὐπλήκτους MW ἐλαφροὺς AVBE    321-322 ἤγουν...δύναμιν MW ἱκανοὺς AVBE 322 παράτασσε MW om. AVBE    323 ι′ M δέκα WAVBE | ιε′ M δεκαπέντε WAVBE 324 ὑστερίζοντας De ὑποστηρίζοντας M ὑποσκάζοντας W παραπομένοντας AVBE    325 μὴ AVBE om. MW | συλλάβωνται MW κρατήσωσιν AVBE    326 ποιεῖσθαι...ἐγχειρήσεις MAVBE trsp. W    329 ἔστι M ἔστιν WAVBE

54. Be very exacting and cautious. If any wine or bread happens to be found there, do not readily attempt to drink or eat it unless you first test it by giving it to prisoners. If it is found to be uncontaminated and healthy, then you will permit the soldiers to consume it, but water from wells or cisterns or ponds or in any other containers will often have been ruined and rendered lethal by poison. On one occasion even the barley was found to be poisoned and, since the soldiers did not have other access to fodder for their horses, they were forced to provide them with the local fodder and, because of this not a few of the horses perished.[6]

55. Announce to the army, as we have prescribed in the treatise on marches, that if, as often happens, there is a disturbance among the troops, they should not race about here and there and wander around, but all should hurry to that section in which the disturbance occurred. As a result, if something of that sort actually happens, they will be prepared for the enemy and will not get confused and all mixed up with one another.

56. When you enter into hostile territory, you should always send out patrols not only to the front as if protecting that sector alone, but also station lightly but well armed soldiers, that is, a fairly strong force under a competent officer, behind, to the rear. This is called a rear guard and should be about ten or fifteen miles away, or as far as you want. It should send out alert patrols on account of stragglers from the army, who fall behind because of illness or some other need, lest the enemy suddenly fall upon them and take them captive.

57. The enemy are accustomed to launch such attacks particularly when the soldiers are marching along carelessly and the men in front cannot easily come to the support of those behind them. Keep in mind that, if you march along like this, even in our own country, it is quite likely that your soldiers will be wander-

6. *Chronique de Jean de Nikiou*, ed. and trans. H. Zotenberg (Paris, 1883), c. 96, p. 408.

330 διαγινομένους παρὰ γνώμην τοῦ ἄρχοντος αὐτῶν· ἐκ τούτου γὰρ γινώσκεις τίς
ἀμελεῖ τῆς τῶν στρατιωτῶν καταστάσεως.

58. Περὶ δὲ στενῶν τόπων καὶ δυσβάτων διαβάσεων ἐν γῇ πολεμίων μεμνή-
μεθα παρακελευσάμενοι τῇ σῇ ἐνδοξότητι, ὦ στρατηγέ, ὅτε τὴν περὶ τῆς ὁδοιπορίας διάταξιν ἐποιούμεθα. διὸ περὶ τῶν αὐτῶν πάλιν διεξελθεῖν ἀπειρόκαλον
335 ἡγούμεθα, ὡς ἐκεῖθεν ἔχοντός σου ἤδη τὴν περὶ τούτων διάγνωσιν, ὥστε μὴ
ἀπερισκέπτως καὶ ὡς ἔτυχεν ἀνάγκης χωρὶς ἐπιτηδεύειν εἰς δασεῖς καὶ δυσβάτους καὶ δυσχερεῖς τόπους διαβαίνειν. εἰ δέ τις ἀνάγκη τοῦτο γενέσθαι κατεπείγει μετὰ τῆς εἰρημένης, ὡς εἴπομεν ἐν τῇ περὶ ὁδοιπορίας διατάξει, παρατηρήσε-
ως ποιεῖσθαι τὴν τῶν τοιούτων τόπων πάροδον, μάλιστα ἐν γῇ πολεμίᾳ καὶ
340 πολεμίων ἐπικειμένων.

59. Ἐὰν δὲ πολέμιοι εἰς τὴν ἡμετέραν χώραν εἰσβάλλωσιν, σκοπός σοι ἔστω,
ὦ στρατηγέ, μὴ φανερῶς καὶ ἐκ παρατάξεως αὐτοῖς πολεμεῖν, καὶ μάλιστα ἐν τῇ
εἰσόδῳ αὐτῶν, ἐὰν ὑπερέχῃ ἢ καὶ ἰσόμοιρός ἐστιν ἡ δύναμις τοῦ ἐχθροῦ, ἀλλὰ
ἐνεδρεύειν μᾶλλον δι᾽ ἐγκρυμμάτων καὶ ἄλλων ἐπιτηδεύσεων ἢ ἐν ἡμέρᾳ ἢ ἐν
345 νυκτὶ ἀσφαλῶς καὶ τὰς ὁδοὺς ἐμφράσσειν καὶ προκαταλαμβάνειν ὀχυρώματα ἢ
διὰ πεζῶν ἢ διὰ καβαλλαρίων ἢ δι᾽ ἀμφοτέρων, καὶ ἀφανίζειν δαπάνας προκειμένας τῶν ἐχθρῶν.

60. Εἰ δὲ βουληθῇς συμβαλεῖν τῷ πολεμίῳ ὅταν μᾶλλον ἐπανέρχηται ἀπὸ
τῆς πραίδας ἢ ἐξέρχηται τῆς χώρας—τότε γὰρ καὶ εἰς τὴν πραῖδαν περισπᾶται
350 καὶ κοπωμένος ἐστίν, μάλιστα ἐὰν καὶ τοῖς ἰδίοις ἐγγίζῃ—τότε οὖν σύμβαλλε
αὐτῷ, εἰ ἄρα βούλει συμβάλλειν.

61. Ὁ γὰρ ἐν ἰδίᾳ χώρᾳ διάγων, ἀμελέστερον διάκειται περὶ τὴν μάχην,
πολλὰς ἀφορμὰς ἔχων τοῦ σώζεσθαι, καὶ κινδυνεύειν οὐ βουλόμενος. ὁ δὲ τῆς
ἀλλοτρίας γῆς ἐπιβαίνων καὶ κατατρέχων, ὅταν ἐν τοιαύτῃ γένηται ἀνάγκῃ, εἰς
355 ἀπόνοιαν τρέπεται, πάντως λογιζόμενος ὅτι ἡ φυγὴ αὐτῷ εἰς κίνδυνον καὶ
ἀπώλειαν γίνεται.

348–351 Niceph. De velit. belli, 4.

330 αὐτῶν MW αὐτοῦ AVBE   332 διαβάσεων M διαβάσεως WAVBE   333 ὅτε τὴν MW
ὅταν AVBE   333–334 ὁδοιπορίας MW ὁδοιπορίας τὴν AVBE   334 ἀπειρόκαλον MW
ἄκαιρον AVBE   337 καὶ δυσχερεῖς MW om. AVBE   338 ὡς…διατάξει MW om. AVBE
339 τόπων WAVBE τρόπων M   343 ἰσόμοιρός M ἰσόμετρος WAVBE   346–347 δαπάνας
προκειμένας MW τὰς προκειμένας δαπάνας AVBE   347 τῶν ἐχθρῶν M τῷ ἐχθρῷ WAVBE
348 ὅταν MW ὅτε AVBE | ἐπανέρχηται M ἐπανέρχεται W ὑποστρέφει AVBE
349 ἐξέρχηται M ἐξέρχεται WAVBE | καὶ MW om. AVBE   350 κοπωμένος M
κεκοπωμένος WAVBE   351 συμβάλλειν MAVBE συμβαλεῖν W

ing about here and there, acting in a disorderly fashion and ignoring their commanding officers. And so, you will be able to identify anyone who disregards military regulations.

58. We recall that we have already issued orders to Your Excellency, O general, regarding the passage of narrow and difficult places while in hostile territory, when we compiled the constitution on marching.[7] Since that work has already made you cognizant of those matters, we believe it would be foolish to go over the same ground once again. Apart from an emergency, then, do not embark on the passage of thickly wooded, rugged, and difficult areas in a casual manner and without due investigation. But if some emergency forces you to do this, then, as we said in the chapter on marches, observe the precautions we noted and make your way through those places. This is of particular importance in hostile territory with the enemy on the offensive.

59. If the enemy should make an incursion into our country, then, O general, do not plan to fight them out in the open or in battle formation, especially as they enter the country. If the enemy force is superior to ours or even equal, it is better to ambush them by ambuscades and other stratagems safely by day or by night, or fortify the roads, or have infantry or cavalry or both occupy fortified places ahead of time. Also destroy provisions available to the enemy.

60. If you wish to fall upon the enemy when they are returning from a pillaging expedition or making their way out of the country, fall upon them at that time, if indeed you do wish to attack. For it is then that the enemy is scattered about pillaging and is weary from exertion, especially when getting close to their own country.[8]

61. A person spending time in his own country is not concerned about battle, since he has many opportunities to assure his safety and does not want to put himself in danger. But when a person entering and marching through a foreign land finds himself facing an emergency, he gives in to despair for he feels certain that flight will only end in danger and destruction.

7. Const. 9.
8. Skirmishing, 4.

62. Χρεὼν δέ σε, ὦ στρατηγέ, πάντοτε φυλάττειν ἑαυτὸν ἀπαθῆ καὶ ἀπλή-
γωτον ἐν | παντὶ καιρῷ καὶ τόπῳ, μάλιστα ἐχθρῶν παρακειμένων. σοῦ γὰρ 385
φυλαττομένου οὔτε πλατύνονται οἱ ἐχθροὶ εἰς βλάβην τῆς χώρας οὔτε πολιορ-
360 κίας εὐχερῶς τοῖς ὀχυρώμασιν ἐπάγειν δύνανται. ὑφορῶνται γὰρ καὶ ὑποπτεύουσι τὸν στρατὸν συνεστάναι.

63. Καὶ γὰρ εἴγε μὴ δοκεῖ σοι συμβάλλειν δημοσίως τοῖς ἐχθροῖς, ὅμως
οὕτως εὐτρεπίζεσθαί σε δεῖ, καὶ φαίνεσθαι καὶ ὑπόνοιαν πᾶσι τοῖς τοῦ στρατοῦ
παρέχειν, ὡς πάντως συμβάλλειν τοῖς πολεμίοις. τοῦτο γὰρ οἱ ἐναντίοι μαν-
365 θάνοντες καὶ λυποῦνται καὶ συστέλλονται.

64. Ἐὰν δὲ τῶν ἐναντίων εἰς τὴν ἡμετέραν εἰσβαλλόντων, ὁ τόπος καὶ ἡ
θέσις τῆς χώρας ἐπιτηδεία ἐστὶ πρὸς τὴν ἐκείνων ἔφοδον, δι’ ἑτέρου τόπου
μᾶλλον ἐπιτήδευε πέμπειν στρατὸν ἐν αὐτῇ, ἵνα ἐκ τούτου περισπάσῃς τοὺς
ἐχθρούς.

370 65. Πάντως δὲ καὶ τὴν θέσιν, ὡς εἴρηται, κατανοήσεις, καὶ τὰ διαστήματα,
ἵνα εἴπερ γνωσθῇ τοῖς ἐχθροῖς τοῦτο, καὶ ὁρμήσωσι κατὰ τῶν πεμπομένων εἰς
τὴν χώραν αὐτῶν, ὁ ἡμέτερος στρατὸς δι’ ἑτέρου τόπου ἐξέλθῃ ἀπαθής, ὅπως
μὴ ὁρμώντων τῶν ἐχθρῶν ἐκεῖθεν εἰς ὄψιν αὐτῶν περιπέσωσιν. τοιοῦτον
πεποίηκε Νικηφόρος ὁ ἡμέτερος στρατηγός, Ἀπουλφέρου γὰρ τοῦ τῶν Σαρα-
375 κηνῶν ἀμηρᾶ τὴν Καππαδοκίαν καταδραμόντος, αὐτὸς τὴν Ταρσὸν καὶ πᾶσαν
τὴν Κιλικίαν κατελῃΐσατο, πολλὴν Σαρακηνοῖς ἐργασάμενος τὴν βλάβην.

66. Ἐχθρῶν τοίνυν τὴν ὑπό σε χώραν, εἰ οὕτω συμβῇ, κατατρεχόντων, δέον
ἐστὶ πάντα τὰ ἀναγκαιότερα πράγματα ἐν τοῖς ὀχυρωτέροις κάστροις ἢ τόποις
ἀναλώτοις συλλέγειν, φυγαδεύειν δὲ καὶ τὰ ἄλογα τῆς χώρας ἵνα μὴ μᾶλλον
380 συλλαμβανόμενα ἰσχυροτέρους τοὺς ἐχθροὺς ποιήσωσιν.

67. Ἐὰν δὲ ἢ λαὸς ἢ πράγματα εἰς δοκοῦντα μὲν ὀχυρὸν τόπον, μὴ ὄντα δὲ
ἀληθῶς, συνέλθωσιν, πάντως δεῖ αὐτοὺς διὰ τῆς σῆς προνοίας μεθίστασθαι, καὶ

---

370–376  Cf. α′.152–154; Niceph. De velit. belli, 20.

---

360–361 ὑποπτεύουσι Μ ὑποπτεύουσιν WAVBE    361 τὸν…συνεστάναι ΜW συνίστασθαι
τὸν στρατὸν AVBE    362 εἴγε ΜW εἰ AVBE | δημοσίως WAVBE δημοσίῳ Μ
364 συμβάλλειν Μ συμβαλεῖς WAVBE | πολεμίοις ΜW ἐχθροῖς AVBE    367 ἐστὶ ΜAVBE
ἐστιν W | ἐκείνων AVBE om. ΜW    370 θέσιν ΜW θέσιν τοῦ τόπου AVBE    371 ὁρμήσωσι
Μ ὁρμήσωσιν W ὁρμήσουσι AVBE    372 αὐτῶν ΜW om. AVBE    373 ὄψιν ΜW
πρόσωπον AVBE | περιπέσωσιν ΜW περιπέσῃς AVBE    374 ἀπουλφέρου Μ ἀπουλφὲρ W
ἀπελφέρου AVBE · 376 κατελῃΐσατο Μ κατελῃΐζετο W ἠφάνισεν AVBE    377 εἰ…συμβῇ
ΜW om. AVBE    378 ἐστὶ ΜW ἐστιν AVBE    379 συλλέγειν ΜW συνάγειν AVBE
381 δοκοῦντα…τόπον ΜW τόπον συνελθῶσιν δοκοῦντα μὲν εἶναι ὀχυρὰ AVBE
382 συνέλθωσιν ΜW om. AVBE

62. It is necessary for you, O general, to preserve yourself unharmed and unwounded in every time and place, especially when the enemy are in the vicinity. As long as you keep yourself protected, the enemy will not spread out to damage the country; neither will they be able to conduct a siege of a fortified space easily. For they will be suspicious and inclined to believe that your army is standing by.

63. If you do not intend to engage the enemy in the open field, you must nonetheless make preparations for doing so and give all the men in your army the impression and expectation that you are definitely going to attack the enemy. When our adversaries learn about this, they will be gloomy and depressed.

64. If the enemy are invading our country and the location and lay of the land are suitable for them to attack, then, prepare to send your army through another place in the country in order to split up the enemy.

65. You should always, as noted, pay heed to the lay of the land and the distances so that, if these are known to the enemy, they will direct their attack against the forces being sent into their country. Then, our army should exit unharmed by another route so that, while the enemy are advancing, we may not run into them head on in that place. Our general, Nikephoros, once did this sort of thing. While Apoulfer, the emir of the Saracens, was raiding throughout Cappadocia, he set about pillaging Tarsus and all of Cilicia, causing a great deal of damage to the Saracens.[9]

66. If it should happen that the enemy are raiding through the land under your authority, you must gather all essential materials in the stronger walled towns or in places difficult to capture and send away the local horses to prevent the enemy from seizing them and increasing in strength.

67. If the troops or materials are gathered in what seems to be a fortified location, but is not actually so, then you absolutely must have the foresight to

---

9. Skirmishing, 20. Nikephoros Phokas the Elder, grandfather of emperor Nikephoros II, led this campaign in Cappadocia, in 900. The identity of the Saracen emir is less certain; it may have been Abu Gafar. See J. C. Cheynet, "Les Phocas," in *La traité sur la guérilla (De velitatione) de l'Empereur Nicéphore Phocas (963–969)* (Paris, 1986), 293–296. See above, Const. 11 §21.

εἰς ὀχυρωτέρους ἀπελθεῖν τόπους, ἔνθα καὶ ἄφοβος αὐτοῖς ἡ φυλακὴ γενήσεται. ὅσα δὲ μὴ κατὰ φύσιν ὀχυρά εἰσιν ἢ κάστρα ἢ τόποι ἕτεροι, προασφαλίζου αὐτά.

385 καὶ εἴ ποτε οἱ ἐχθροὶ βουληθῶσι παρακαθίσαι αὐτοῖς, μέρος τῆς στρατιᾶς ἀφανῶς καὶ εἰς βοήθειαν καὶ ἐκδίκησιν αὐτῶν ἔκπεμπε, καὶ μὴ ἐᾷς τοὺς ἐχθροὺς ἀδεῶς τὰς ἔξωθεν δαπάνας συλλέγειν, ἀλλὰ περισκόπει καὶ τοὺς ἐπὶ συλλογῇ τῶν δαπανημάτων πεμπομένους ἐνέδρευε | καὶ συλλάμβανε, καὶ ἐντεῦθεν 385ᵛ στενοχώρει τοὺς ἐχθρούς.

390    68. Καὶ ταῦτα μὲν περὶ ἐφόδων σοῦ τε πρὸς τὴν πολεμίαν καὶ τῶν πολεμίων πρὸς τὴν σὴν γινομένων εἴρηται ἡμῖν. χρεὼν δὲ καὶ περὶ τῶν ἄλλων, ὅσα χρήσιμα πρὸς στρατηγίαν δοκοῦσι καὶ ἀσφάλειαν διεξελθεῖν καὶ μάλιστα περὶ τοῦ πῶς δέον κατασκοπεῖν ἐχθρούς, καὶ ὅπως πάλιν τοὺς ἀπ᾽ ἐκείνων πεμπο-μένους κατασκόπους κρατεῖν λανθάνειν θέλοντας ἐν τῷ στρατῷ.

395    69. Δεῖ οὖν σε σκοπεῖν ἀκριβῶς, ὦ στρατηγέ, τὴν ποιότητα τῆς τῶν ἐναντί-ων δυνάμεως πάντως, καὶ πρὸς τοῦτο κανονίζειν καὶ διοικεῖν σε τὰ κατ᾽ αὐτῆς. τὰ γὰρ σχήματα τῶν καβαλλαρικῶν τε καὶ πεζικῶν τάξεων, καὶ αἱ τῶν τόπων θέσεις πολλὴν τῆς ποσότητος τοῦ λαοῦ διαφορὰν ποιοῦνται, καὶ ἀνυπέρβλητον εἰσάγουσιν πλάνην τοῖς ἁπλῶς καὶ ἀπείρως κατανοοῦσιν αὐτά. καὶ ὅτι ὃ λέγω

400 ἀληθές ἐστιν, μαρτυρήσει τάχα τῇ θεωρίᾳ ὁ μέλλων λεχθῆναι τρόπος.

70. Ὑπόθου γὰρ ἑξακοσίους καβαλλαρίους εἰς μῆκος ἐπὶ πεντακοσίοις εἰς πλάτος τάσσεσθαι, ὃ γίνεται τριάκοντα μυριάδες ἤγουν τριακόσιαι χιλιάδες καβαλλαρίων. ἑκάστου δὲ ἵππου εἰς τόπον τασσομένου κρατοῦντος πόδας τρεῖς κατὰ πλάτος, γίνονται πόδες χίλιοι ὀκτακόσιοι· καὶ ἑκάστου ἵππου ἐν τῷ βάθει

405 τασσομένου κρατοῦντος πόδας ὀκτώ, γίνονται πόδες τετρακισχίλιοι, ὥστε γίνεσθαι ἐν τετραπλεύρῳ σχήματι ὑπὸ τοῦ μήκους τῶν χιλίων ὀκτακοσίων, καὶ τοῦ βάθους τῶν τετρακισχιλίων ποδῶν, ἑπτακοσίας εἴκοσι μυριάδας πόδας στερεούς. ἡ δὲ περίμετρος μόνης ἐπιφανείας ἔξωθεν διὰ τῶν τεσσάρων πλευρῶν γίνονται πόδες μύριοι καὶ χίλιοι ἑξακόσιοι, καὶ ἐπειδὴ δὲ οἱ ἓξ πόδες ποιοῦσιν

---

385 βουληθῶσι MAVBE βουληθῶσιν W | αὐτοῖς MW αὐτὰ AVBE    386 καὶ¹...βοήθειαν MW εἰς βοήθειαν αὐτῶν AVBE | αὐτῶν MW om. AVBE    387 ἀδεῶς MW ἀφόβως AVBE | συλλέγειν MW συνάγειν AVBE | περισκόπει MAVBE σκόπει W    390 titulum ins. περὶ κατασκόπων WVBE    391 idem ins. A | χρεὼν M χρεὸν W χρὴ AVBE | ἄλλων MW ἄλλων διεξελθεῖν AVBE    392 δοκοῦσι...διεξελθεῖν MW καὶ ἀσφάλειαν δοκοῦσιν AVBE    393 κατασκοπεῖν MW κατασκοπεῖν τοὺς AVBE    398 ποιοῦνται MW ποιεῖται AVBE    399 εἰσάγουσιν πλάνην M προσάγουσι πλάνην W καὶ πολλὴν πλάνην ἐμποιοῦσιν AVBE    408 στερεούς MW om. AVBE | μόνης ἐπιφανείας M τῆς ἐπιφανείας μόνης W μόνης τῆς ἐπιφανείας AVBE    409 καὶ¹ MW om. AVBE | δὲ MW om. AVBE

transfer them and send them off to a stronger place, where they may be protected and without fear. You must see to the security of the walled towns or other places that are not naturally strong. If, at some time, the enemy should wish to besiege them, send a part of the army covertly to support and protect them. Do not allow the enemy license to gather provisions outside, but carefully observe and ambush those who are sent to collect provisions and seize them. This will reduce the enemy to narrow straits.

68. This is what we have to say about your incursions into hostile territory and those of the enemy into yours. We must now center our discussion on other matters that seem useful for strategy and security, in particular, about how one should spy upon the enemy and, in turn, how to catch the spies sent by them who attempt to hide in our army.

69. You must always investigate in detail, O general, the quality of the force of our adversaries. You are to take appropriate steps and organize measures to counter it. The arrangement of cavalry and infantry formations and the lay of the land cause great differences in the strength of an army. An inexperienced person casually looking at them may be very far off in his estimates. To show the truth of my remarks, the examples to be given here will readily bear witness to the theory.

70. Assume a cavalry formation of six hundred across and five hundred deep. That comes to thirty myriads, that is, three hundred thousand cavalrymen. Each horse in the formation occupies a space three feet wide so the total width is eighteen hundred feet. In depth of formation each horse occupies a space of eight feet, so the total depth is four thousand feet. The rectangular formation thus formed is eighteen hundred feet in width and four thousand feet in depth, that is, seven thousand and twenty myriads of standard feet. The perimeter of what can be seen externally on the four sides amounts to eleven thousand, six hundred feet. Since six feet come to one orguia and a hundred orguiai come to

410 ὀργυιὰν μίαν, αἱ δὲ ἑκατὸν ὀργυιαὶ ποιοῦσι στάδιον ἕν, τὰ δὲ ἑπτὰ καὶ ἥμισυ
στάδια ποιοῦσι μίλιον ἕν, συνάγεται ἡ περίμετρος πᾶσα, ἤτοι οἱ μύριοι καὶ χίλιοι
καὶ ἑξακόσιοι πόδες εἰς μίλια δύο ἥμισυ δέκατον ἔγγιστα. ἐν τούτῳ οὖν τῷ
διαστήματι καὶ σχήματι χωροῦνται αἱ τριάκοντα μυριάδες τῶν καβαλλαρίων
κατὰ τελείαν πύκνωσιν. εἰ δὲ ἀραιότεροι ἵστανται, ἐκ τῆς πυκνώσεως ἐπιλογίζ-
415 εσθαι δεῖ τὴν ἐνοῦσαν ἀραιότητα, καὶ οὕτω συμβάλλειν ἐκ τοῦ μεγέθους τοῦ
τόπου τὸ ποσὸν τοῦ λαοῦ.

71. Τάξομεν δὲ τὰς τριάκοντα μυριάδας ἤγουν τὰς τριακοσίας | χιλιάδας ἐπὶ   386
ἁπλῆς ἀκίας καὶ ἐκτεταμένης. ἑκάστου δὲ ἵππου εἰς μῆκος τασσομένου τῆς
παρατάξεως κρατοῦντος, ὡς εἴρηται, πόδας τρεῖς, γίνονται πόδες μυριάδες
420 ἐνενήκοντα, οἳ ποιοῦσι διάστημα ἐπ' εὐθείας μίλια διακόσια ἔγγιστα. ταῦτα μέν,
ὡς εἴρηται, κατὰ τελείαν πύκνωσιν. εἰ δὲ διεσκεδασμένοι καὶ ἐσκορπισμένοι
κινοῦνται, ὁμολογούμενόν ἐστιν ὅτι πολλαπλάσιονα τοῦ μέτρου τούτου κατ-
έχουσι τόπον καὶ πλείονες τῶν ἐν τῇ τάξει ἑστώτων τῷ ὀφθαλμῷ ὑποπίπτουσιν.
εἰ δὲ ἐν πλαγίῳ τόπῳ καὶ ὑψηλοτέρῳ περιπατοῦσιν, ἔτι πλέον.

425 72. Διὸ καὶ οἱ βουλόμενοι στρατὸν διὰ κόμπον τινὰ ὑποδεῖξαι, ἢ ἐπὶ λεπτο-
τέρου βάθους τάσσουσιν αὐτὸν ἢ κεχυμένον μηκόθεν ἢ διεσκεδασμένον καὶ
διεσπαρμένον. οἱ δὲ παλαιότεροι τῶν τακτικῶν τὴν πεζικὴν τάξιν, ὅταν μέν ἐστι
τεταγμένη, τέσσαρας πήχεις ἱστῶσι τὸν ἕνα ἄνδρα κατέχειν. ὅταν δέ ἐστι
πεπυκνωμένη, εἰς δύο πήχεις· ὅταν δὲ κατὰ συνασπισμὸν ἐν παρατάξει πῆχυν
430 ἕνα κατέχειν τὸν στρατιώτην, ὥστε καὶ ἐκ τούτου τοῦ μέτρου τὸν ἀκριβῆ σκουλ-
κάτορα ἀναλογίζεσθαι ἀπὸ τοῦ μήκους τοῦ τόπου οὐ μόνον τῶν καβαλλαρίων,
ἀλλὰ καὶ πεζῶν τὸ πλῆθος.

73. Τοσαύτης τοίνυν διαφορᾶς οὔσης εἴς τε τὰς τάξεις καὶ εἰς τὰ σχήματα,
οὐ δέον σε, ὦ στρατηγέ, εἰς ἀπείρους τῶν τοιούτων ἀνθρώπους τὰς σκούλκας
435 ἤτοι τὰς διὰ τῶν κατασκόπων τῶν σῶν διακρίσεις καταπιστεύειν ἢ τὰς περὶ
τούτων βίγλας, μηδὲ τοῖς παρ' αὐτῶν, ὡς ἔτυχεν, λεγομένοις πιστεύειν. ἀνείκα-
στον γάρ ἐστιν τοῖς πολλοῖς καὶ ἀκατανόητον, εἴγε ὑπὲρ τὰς εἴκοσι ἢ τριάκοντα

---

419 ad κρατοῦντος des. W

410 ὀργυιὰν A ὀργυὰν MWVBE | ὀργυιαὶ AVBE ὀργυαὶ MW   412 καὶ MW om. AVBE
414 τελείαν πύκνωσιν MW trsp. AVBE   415 οὕτω MW οὕτως AVBE   426 κεχυμένον M
συγκεχυμένον AVBE | διεσκεδασμένον M διεσκορπισμένον AVBE   430–431 σκουλκάτορα
M βιγλάτωρα AVBE   431 τοῦ¹ M τοῦ αὐτοῦ AVBE   432 καὶ M καὶ τῶν AVBE
434 ἀπείρους M ἀπείροις AVBE | ἀνθρώπους M ἀνθρώποις AVBE   434–436 σκούλκας…
βίγλας M βίγλας καταπιστεύειν AVBE   436 ἔτυχεν M ἔτυχε AVBE | πιστεύειν M om.
AVBE   437 εἴγε M εἴτε AVBE

one stadion and seven and a half stadia come to one mile, the entire perimeter, that is, eleven thousand, six hundred feet, equals, in miles, two and a half and very close to a tenth. Within this distance and formation thirty myriads of cavalrymen are accommodated in very close order. If they are spaced further apart, you must reckon the extent of their open order from their close order formation, and so from the extent of the location you estimate the number of troops.

71. We shall draw up the thirty myriads, that is, the three hundred thousand, in a simple, extended file, with each horse taking its position in the battle line to a width, as was noted, of three feet. This comes to ninety myriads of feet, which amounts to a distance in a straight line of close to two hundred miles. This is valid, as noted, when they are in very close order. But if they march in open order and spread about, we must admit that they will occupy a much greater space than this and, to the observer, will appear more numerous than if they were standing in regular formation. All the more so if they are marching on sloping or hilly ground.

72. As a result, if you want to make your army appear more impressive, either have it drawn up in a very thin line or stay at a distance in loose order or scattered or spread about. The ancient tactical authorities position the infantry army, when it is in formation, with each man occupying four pecheis, but in close order two pecheis and, when it is drawn up shield to shield, a soldier takes up only one pechys. Using this measure, an alert scout can estimate from the width of the place not only the number of cavalrymen but also that of the infantry.

73. Since, therefore, there are such great differences in formations and organization, you must not, O general, entrust the scouting to men inexperienced in these matters. Neither should you place confidence in the judgments formed by your spies or the patrols about these matters or have confidence in casual reports from them. Most people are incapable of forming a good estimate if an army numbers more than twenty or thirty thousand men, especially if they

χιλιάδας ἐστί, καὶ μάλιστα ἐπὶ ἐθνῶν, οἵτινες πολλοὺς ἵππους ἐπισύρονται·
διόπερ ἐμπείροις ἀνδράσι τὰ τοιαῦτα χρὴ καταπιστεύειν.

440    74. Μηδὲ προχείρως ἀγωνιᾶν ἐπὶ ταῖς λεπταῖς καὶ μακραῖς παρατάξεσι διὰ
πλήθους ὑπόνοιαν· εἰ γὰρ μή εἰσιν ἀναλόγως ἔχουσαι τὸ βάθος μέγα, ποσὸν
οὐκ ἔχουσιν. τὰς δὲ βαθείας πολυπραγμονείτωσαν οἱ κατάσκοποι, εἰ τὸν τοῦλδον συντέτακται τῇ παρατάξει ὄπισθεν ἢ μόνοι ὁπλῖταί εἰσιν.

75. Τὰ μὲν οὖν περὶ τοῦ ποσοῦ δυνατόν ἐστιν ἀκριβέστερον γινώσκεσθαι διά
445 τε τῶν προσφευγόντων πρὸς ἡμᾶς, καὶ διὰ τῶν κρατουμένων ἐχθρῶν, εἰ βου|    386ᵛ
ληθεῖ δέ τις καὶ διὰ παρόδου στενωτέρων τόπων, ἔτι δὲ καὶ διὰ τῶν ἀπλήκτων, εἰ
συμβῇ αὐτοὺς ἡνωμένως ἀπλικεύειν.

76. Ἐὰν δὲ μή ἐστιν φοσσᾶτον ἐχθρῶν ἐν μὲν τοῖς στενωτέροις τόποις δι᾽
ὀλίγων κατὰ τὰς τῶν τόπων θέσεις ποίει τὰς σκούλκας, εἰς δὲ τοὺς ὁμαλοὺς καὶ
450 γυμνοὺς τόπους ἐν διαφόροις μέρεσι διὰ πλείονας ποιοῦ τὰς σκούλκας, καὶ
κατὰ συνέχειαν καὶ ἀπὸ διαστήματος, καὶ μάλιστα εἰς τὰς νύκτας, ὅταν εὐχέρειαν ἔχῃ ὁ ἐχθρὸς διὰ τοῦ τόπου οὗ ἂν βούληται λαθεῖν καὶ αἰφνιδιάσαι, προκανονίζων τὰς βίγλας, ἐὰν ὀλίγαι εἰσί· καὶ διὰ τοῦτο ἀπὸ διαστήματος τὰς βίγλας δεῖ
γίνεσθαι, καὶ ἀλλεπαλλήλους ἐν διαφόροις τόποις τοῖς ἐπιτηδείοις καὶ συχνῶς
455 ἀλλάσσεσθαι.

77. Γνῶθι δὲ ὅτι ἴδιον ἁρμοδίων κατασκόπων ἐστὶ τὸ φρονήσει καὶ ἀγρυπνίᾳ
τόπους τε καὶ κινήσεις πολεμίων κατασκοπεῖν. τοὺς δὲ τοιούτους ἐλαφρᾷ ὁπλίσει χρῆσθαι δέον, καὶ ἵππους ἔχειν ταχεῖς εἰς τὸ ἀνεμποδίστως ὁδεύειν, καὶ τοὺς
μὲν ἐξπλοράτωρας ἤτοι κατασκόπους δῆθεν ἀφοβώτερον συνδιάγειν τοῖς
460 πολεμίοις, ὥστε ὁμογενεῖς αὐτοὺς εἶναι νομίζεσθαι, τοὺς δὲ βιγλάτορας πιστοὺς
εἶναι καὶ εἴδει σώματος ἀνδρείῳ καὶ ψυχῇ εὐτόλμῳ καὶ ὁπλίσει λαμπροὺς καὶ
τῶν λοιπῶν στρατιωτῶν διαφέρειν, ὥστε ἢ ποιήσαντάς τι γενναῖον ἔργον καὶ
ἀνδρεῖον ἐπανελθεῖν ἢ ζωγρηθέντας παρὰ τοῖς πολεμίοις θαυμάζεσθαι.

---

438 χιλιάδας ἐστί Μ χιλιάδας ἐστὶν τὸ μέτρον AVBE    440 προχείρως Μ ἁπλῶς καὶ ὡς
ἔτυχεν AVBE | ἀγωνιᾶν De ἀγωνία codd. | λεπταῖς…μακραῖς Μ trsp. AVBE    441 ἔχουσαι
Μ ἔχουσαι καὶ AVBE | μέγα ποσὸν Μ πολὺ πλῆθος AVBE    442 τὸν De τὸ codd.    444 τὰ
Μ τὸ AVBE | γινώσκεσθαι Μ ἐπιγινώσκεσθαι AVBE    445 προσφευγόντων…ἡμᾶς Μ trsp.
AVBE    448 ἐστιν Μ ἐστι AVBE    449 κατὰ Μ ποιεῖν τὰς βίγλας πρὸς AVBE | ποίει…
σκούλκας Μ om. AVBE    450 μέρεσι Μ μέρεσιν AVBE    450–451 ποιοῦ…συνέχειαν Μ
ποιεῖν τὰς βίγλας καὶ πυκνὰς AVBE    451–452 εὐχέρειαν Μ εὐκολίαν AVBE
452 βούληται Μ βούλεται AVBE    452–453 προκανονίζων Μ προκανονίζων καὶ
προσκοπῶν AVBE    453 εἰσί Μ εἰσιν AVBE | τὰς βίγλας² Μ ταύτας AVBE
456 ἁρμοδίων…ἐστὶ Μ ἐστι κατασκόπων AVBE    457–458 ἐλαφρᾷ…δέον Μ δέον ἐλαφρᾷ
ὁπλίσει χρῆσθαι AVBE    459 ἐξπλοράτωρας ἤτοι Μ om. AVBE | δῆθεν Μ om. AVBE
461 εἴδει Μ μεγέθει AVBE | ἀνδρείῳ Μ om. AVBE | εὐτόλμῳ Μ τολμηρῷ AVBE

belong to a nation that brings along large herds of horses. Hence it is necessary to entrust such matters to experienced men.

74. You ought not to be easily troubled by a thin, long line of troops, suspecting perhaps that it is a large army. Unless its depth is proportionate, its actual strength will not be great. Have your spies investigate its depth. Is the baggage train drawn up behind the main force or does it consist only of fighting men?

75. More accurate information about the numerical strength may be obtained from defectors to us, from enemy prisoners and, if one wishes, from the passage of narrow defiles and from the camps, if they happen to make camp all together.

76. If there is not a fortified enemy camp, set up patrols in the more narrow locations with a few men, depending on the nature of the ground. In unobstructed and open country set up the patrols with more men, in different places, in touch with one another and further out. This particularly applies at night, when the enemy has the opportunity, in a place of their choosing, to avoid detection and launch a surprise attack, evading the pickets if they are few in number. For this reason, the patrols should be changed frequently and at intervals, one after another, in various suitable locations.

77. Be well aware that it is the specific task of competent scouts, intelligent and alert men, to observe closely the positions and movements of the enemy. These men must make use of light weaponry and possess fast horses to move about without hindrance. Explorers or spies must be truly without fear and move right in with the enemy, so as to pass for belonging to the same people. Men making up the patrols must be reliable and they should be a cut above the other soldiers in projecting a manly, physical appearance, in boldness of spirit, and in brilliance of armament. Thus they will come back to us after having performed a noble, manly task or, if taken captive, they will be admired by the enemy.

78. Τὸν δὲ ἄρχοντα τῆς σκούλκας ἄγρυπνον καὶ φρόνιμον καὶ ἔμπειρον
465 ἐπιλέγου, καὶ μὴ τὸν τυχόντα. οὐδὲ γὰρ τοσοῦτον ἀνδρείας ὅσον φρονήσεως
καὶ ἀγρυπνίας δεῖται ἡ τῶν σκουλκατόρων χρεία.

79. Μόνους δὲ τοὺς κατασκόπους ἀπόστελλε μακρόθεν ἔτι τῶν πολεμίων
ἀπαγγελλομένων, ἡνίκα μάλιστα βούλῃ μαθεῖν ἢ κίνησιν ἐχθρῶν ἢ θέσιν ὁδῶν ἢ
τόπων ὀχύρωσιν.

470    80. Ὅταν δὲ ἐπὶ τῷ κατασχεῖν τινας ἡ ἐπιδρομή ἐστι, τότε ἀναμεμιγμένους
τούτους μετὰ τῶν σκουλκατόρων πρόστασσε εἶναι, καὶ αὐτοὺς μὲν προεκτρέ-
χειν καὶ ἐξ ἀπόπτων ἤγουν ὑψηλῶν χωρίων κατασκοπεῖν, τοὺς δὲ σκουλκάτορας
ἀκολουθεῖν ἐκείνοις καὶ ὁδηγεῖσθαι παρ' αὐτῶν.

81. Τὰς δὲ σκούλκας ἢ βίγλας ἐν τοῖς ἀναγκαίοις καιροῖς μὴ ποιοῦ ἁπλᾶς
475 ἀπὸ ἑνὸς μέρους, ἀλλὰ διαφόρους καὶ ἀλλεπαλλήλους, κατὰ τὴν τοῦ τόπου
θέσιν, καὶ ἀπὸ διαστήματος ἱκανοῦ ἵνα, εἰ συμβῇ τοὺς ἐχθροὺς τὴν μίαν διαλαθ-
εῖν, εἰς | τοὺς ἄλλους περιπίπτοντες μὴ διαλάθωσι. καὶ τοὺς μὲν ἐν τῇ πρώτῃ    387
βίγλᾳ ὄντας ὀλιγωτέρους ποιοῦ, τοὺς δὲ μετ' ἐκείνους ἐν τῇ δευτέρᾳ πλείους,
καὶ τοὺς ἐν τῇ τρίτῃ ἔτι πλείους.

480    82. Μηδὲ καθίζειν μήτε ἀνακλίνεσθαι τοὺς βιγλεύοντας παράγγελλε,
καθάπερ καὶ ἐν ἑτέροις περὶ τούτου σοι παρηγγείλαμεν ἵνα μή, ῥαθυμότερον
τοῦ ἔργου αὐτῶν γινομένου, ἀπόλωνται. καὶ γὰρ ἡ καθέδρα καὶ ἡ ἀνάκλισις
ὕπνον μάλιστα φέρει. καὶ οἱ τοῦτο ποιοῦντες ἀγρυπνεῖν οὐ δύνανται. ἀλλὰ
μηδέ, ἐὰν ἐπαγγέλλωνταί τινες δι' ὅλης τῆς νυκτὸς κρατεῖν, πιστεύσῃς αὐτοῖς· ἡ
485 γὰρ φύσις τὸ ἴδιον ἐπιζητεῖ. καὶ σὺ τὴν ἀσφάλειαν διὰ τῆς τῶν βιγλῶν διαδοχῆς
ποιεῖσθαι μὴ ἀμελῇς, ἵστασθαι δὲ τοὺς βιγλεύοντας πάντως.

83. Ἡ γὰρ ἐπὶ τῆς γῆς στάσις μαραίνει τὸν ὕπνον καὶ μᾶλλον ἐγρηγόρους
τοὺς ἱσταμένους ποιεῖ. ὅταν δὲ χρεία, τότε κοπωθέντας ἀλλάσσεσθαι κατὰ τὰς
δεούσας τῆς νυκτὸς διαμερισθείσας αὐτοῖς ὥρας. εἰ γὰρ μὴ φροντίσωσιν ἐπι-

---

489 ad <ἐπιμε>λῶς de novo inc. W

---

464 σκούλκας Μ βίγλας AVBE    466 σκουλκατόρων Μ βιγλατώρων AVBE    468 θέσιν Μ
θέσεις AVBE    470 ἐστι Μ ἐστιν AVBE    471 σκουλκατόρων Μ βιγλατώρων AVBE
472 ἀπόπτων...χωρίων Μ τόπων ὑψηλοτέρων AVBE | σκουλκάτορας Μ βιγλάτωρας AVBE
474 σκούλκας ἢ Μ om. AVBE    475 ἀλλεπαλλήλους Μ ἐπαλλήλους AVBE
476–477 διαλαθεῖν...ἄλλους Μ τὴν μίαν βίγλαν διαλαθεῖν ἐν τῇ ἄλλῃ AVBE
477 διαλάθωσι Μ διαλάθωσιν AVBE    478 πλείους Μ πλείονας AVBE    480 μηδὲ καθίζειν
Μ μήτε δὲ καθίζεσθαι AVBE    482 ἡ¹ Μ om. AVBE    484 νυκτὸς Μ νυκτὸς τὴν βίγλαν
AVBE | πιστεύσῃς Μ πιστεύσῃς AVBE    487 ἐπὶ...στάσις Μ τῶν ποδῶν τάσις AVBE
489 δεούσας...νυκτὸς Μ ἁρμοζούσας τῆς νυκτὸς ὥρας καὶ AVBE | ὥρας Μ om. AVBE |
φροντίσωσιν Μ φροντίσουσιν AVBE

78. For leader of the patrol select an alert, intelligent, and experienced man, well above average. The work of the men assigned to patrol does not call for bravery as much as it does for intelligence and alertness.

79. While the enemy are still reported to be far off, send out the spies only when you wish to learn particulars about the movements of the enemy, the condition of the roads, or how well fortified are the places.

80. When a raid takes place for the purpose of taking prisoners, then order the spies to mix in with the men on patrol. But they should go on ahead of them to make their observations from concealed positions on heights. The patrols should follow along and be guided by them.

81. In hazardous circumstances do not send out single patrols or scouting parties in only one direction, but in different ones and constantly changing in accord with the nature of the terrain. They should be far enough apart so that, if the enemy happens to elude one, they will run into the others and not be able to hide. Assign only a few men to the first patrol, more to those following them in the second patrol, and still more to the third patrol.

82. Order the men on patrol not to sit or lie down, as we have decreed in other discussions of this topic. If they grow more slack in their duties, they will perish. Sitting and reclining are particularly conducive to sleep and those who do so are unable to stay awake. Even if some of them promise to remain on duty through the entire night, do not rely on them, for nature reclaims what is its own. To assure your security, do not neglect the assigning of patrols, one after the other. But the men on patrol are always to stand.

83. For standing up on the ground quenches sleep and renders those who are standing more alert. But, when necessary, relieve those who are worn out, dividing the night into specific hours of duty for them. If they do not give

490 μελῶς ὅπως ἀγρυπνήσωσι τὴν φύσιν τέως τοῦ ὕπνου χαλινώσαντες, ῥᾳδίως ἂν
παρὰ τῶν ἐχθρῶν ἀπολοῦνται.

84. Διὸ χρή σε καταζητεῖν τὰς βίγλας καὶ ὅπως γίνονται καὶ πέμπειν τοὺς
πιστοτέρους τῶν ἀρχόντων τοὺς ὀφείλοντας αἰφνιδιάσαι, καὶ ἐπιδεῖν πῶς αὗται
γίνονται, καὶ τοὺς ἀμελοῦντας τιμωρεῖσθαι ὡς αἰτίους μεγάλου κινδύνου τῷ
495 στρατῷ γινομένους.

85. Ὑπολαμβάνω δὲ ὅτι ὁ ἔμπειρος σκουλκάτωρ δύναται ἀπό τινων σημείων,
καὶ πρὸ τοῦ ἰδεῖν αὐτὸν τοὺς πολεμίους, κατανοῆσαι τὸ μέτρον τοῦ πλήθους
αὐτῶν ἐκ τῆς τῶν ἵππων αὐτῶν συστάσεως καὶ ἐκ τῶν ἁπλίκτων αὐτῶν. δύναται
δὲ καὶ τὸν χρόνον στοχάσασθαί ποτε διὰ τοῦ τόπου παρελθὼν ἐκ τῆς τῶν
500 ἵππων καὶ τῶν ἀνθρώπων κόπρου.

86. Ἐὰν δὲ φοσσάτον ποιήσῃς ἤγουν χάρακα καὶ ἢ τάφρῳ ἢ οἰκοδομήματι
ὀχυρώσῃς αὐτὸ ἤ τινι ἑτέρᾳ ὕλῃ, δόξῃ σοι δὲ ἔσωθεν εἰσάγειν τοὺς καβαλλαρίους, μὴ πολὺ ἀπὸ διαστημάτων ποιήσῃς τὰς βίγλας, ἵνα μὴ συντρίβωνται ἀκαίρως οἱ ἵπποι.

505 87. Πάντως δὲ τοὺς πεμπομένους ἐπὶ σκούλκαν παραγγέλλῃς ὥστε ζωγρῆσαί τινας καί, ὥσπερ ἐπὶ τῶν κυνηγίων, οὕτως σχολάζειν καὶ σπουδάζειν ὥστε
προσκουλκεύειν, καὶ ἀσυμφανῶς καὶ ἀγνώστως τοὺς μὲν δι' ὄψεως φαίνεσθαι
ὀλίγους | ὄντας καὶ ὑποχωρεῖν, ἄλλους δὲ κεκρυμμένους καὶ ἀφανῶς κατακυ-    387ᵛ
κλοῦν πρὸς τὴν τῶν τόπων ἐπιτηδειότητα· καὶ ἀλλαχοῦ μὲν δεικνύειν ὄψιν
510 ἐπιμόνως, ἑτέρωθεν δὲ ἐπέρχεσθαι μετὰ πλειόνων λεληθότως καὶ διανυκτερεύ-
ειν, μάλιστα ὅταν μακρόθεν δοκοῦσιν εἶναι οἱ πολέμιοι, ὅταν οὐδὲ ὑπόνοιαν
ἔχωσι τούτου τοῦ δράματος.

88. Τὰς δὲ γινομένας βίγλας μὴ μόνον τοὺς ἐναντίους μὴ εἰδέναι καλόν,
ἀλλὰ μηδὲ τοὺς ἰδίους, λανθάνειν δὲ καὶ τὸν σὸν στρατὸν ἵνα, ἐάν τινες, ὡς
515 εἰκός, προσφυγεῖν τοῖς ἐχθροῖς βουληθῶσιν ἐκ τοῦ στρατοῦ, ἀδοκήτως ταύταις
περιπέσωσιν.

---

490 ἀγρυπνήσωσι MVBE ἀγρυπνήσωσιν WA    493 ἐπιδεῖν MW ἰδεῖν AVBE    495 στρατῷ
AVBE στρατηγῷ MW    496 σκουλκάτωρ MW βιγλάτωρ AVBE | τινων σημείων MW trsp.
AVBE    497 αὐτὸν MW om.    AVBE    498 συστάσεως MW στάσεως AVBE
499 παρελθὼν MW παρῆλθον AVBE    501 ἤγουν χάρακα MW om. AVBE | ἢ¹ AVBE om.
MW    502 τινι ἑτέρᾳ MW trsp. AVBE    503 πολὺ…διαστημάτων MW ἀπὸ πολλοῦ
διαστήματος AVBE    505 σκούλκαν MW βίγλαν AVBE    505–506 ζωγρῆσαί MW ζῶντα
κρατῆσαι AVBE    506 σχολάζειν καὶ MW om.    AVBE    507 προσκουλκεύειν MW
προβιγλεύειν AVBE | ἀσυμφανῶς MW ἀφανῶς AVBE    508 κεκρυμμένους MW
κεκρυμμένως AVBE    510 ἐπιμόνως De καὶ μόνως codd.    511 μακρόθεν δοκοῦσιν MW
δοκῶσιν AVBE

careful thought to how they are to stay awake and hold sleep in check, they will easily be finished off by the enemy.

84. You must inspect the patrols to evaluate their performance. Also assign very reliable officers to make surprise visits to observe how they are doing. They are to punish the negligent for seriously endangering the army.

85. I assume that an experienced scout, even before the enemy comes into view, is able to estimate the size of the army from certain indications, such as their campsite and the place where the horses were standing. He should also be able to estimate the time when they passed through the area from the excrement of men and horses.

86. If you set up an encampment, that is, a camp, and fortify it by a ditch or a stone wall or with some other material, and you think it a good idea to have the cavalry enter in, do not send the patrols too far off, to avoid unnecessarily wearing out the horses.

87. By all means, you should order the men sent out on patrol to take some prisoners. They are to go about this just as in hunting and strive to spy on them ahead of time, unseen and undetected. A few men should show themselves and then draw back, while others circle around unseen and concealed, as much as the terrain allows, so that while some are constantly showing themselves in one place, from another the main concealed body attacks, even spending the night <to achieve this>, especially when the enemy are reported to be far off and would not suspect any such activity.

88. It is wise not only to keep the enemy ignorant of the posting of patrols but also our own troops. Keep it secret from your army so that, in the eventuality that some of your troops intend to defect to the enemy, they will unexpectedly run right into the patrols.

89. Ἐὰν δὲ βουληθῇς κατασκόπους κρατῆσαι τῶν ἐχθρῶν, δέον σε θαρρῆσαι τοῖς ἄρχουσι τὸ πρᾶγμα, ἵνα ἕκαστος τοῖς ὑπ᾽ αὐτὸν στρατιώταις καὶ τοῖς λοιποῖς παραγγέλλῃ ὅτι τυχὸν τῇ ἑξῆς περὶ δευτέραν ἢ τρίτην ὥραν τῆς ἡμέρας
520 κατὰ τὴν πρώτην φωνὴν τοῦ βουκίνου, εἴτε στρατιώτης εἴτε παῖς ἐστιν, ἕκαστος εἰς τὴν ἰδίαν τένταν ἵνα εἰσέλθῃ, καὶ μηδεὶς τολμήσῃ ἔξωθεν τῆς τέντας εὑρεθῆναι ἐπεὶ σωφρονίζεται. καὶ μετὰ τὸ πάντας εἰσελθεῖν, αὐτοὺς τοὺς ἄρχοντας μένειν ἔξωθεν τῶν τεντῶν καὶ θεωρεῖν, ἵνα ὅσους ἔξωθεν τῶν τεντῶν εὕρωσιν αὐτοί, κρατήσωσιν αὐτούς. τοὺς δέ, ὡς εἰκός, εἰσερχομένους εἰς τὰς τέντας, οἱ
525 τῶν κοντουβερνίων συλλαμβάνονται καὶ κρατήσουσι καὶ παραδώσουσι τῷ ἰδίῳ ἄρχοντι. ἓν γὰρ γίνεται τῶν δύο εἰς τὸν κατάσκοπον· ἢ γὰρ ἔξωθεν ἱστάμενος συνέχεται ὡς μὴ εἰδὼς ποῦ ἀπελθεῖν ἢ καί, ὡς εἰκός, ἐὰν θαρρήσῃ εἰσελθεῖν ἔν τινι τῶν κοντουβερνίων, ὡς ξένος ἐπιγινώσκεται καὶ παραδίδοται τῷ ἄρχοντι τοῦ κοντουβερνίου. πάντας οὖν τοὺς ὁπωσοῦν κατὰ τοῦτον τὸν τρόπον εὑρι-
530 σκομένους δεῖ κρατεῖσθαι, εἴτε Ῥωμαῖοι δοκοῦσιν εἶναι εἴτε ἀλλογενεῖς, καὶ ἐξετάζεσθαι ὥστε ἐκεῖθεν εὑρίσκεσθαι τὴν ἀλήθειαν. τοῦτο δὲ γίνεται καὶ ἐν φοσσάτῳ συνηγμένου στρατοῦ ἢ πεζικοῦ ἢ καβαλλαρικοῦ ἐπιτηδείως, ὁμοίως δὲ καὶ κατὰ τὸ μέρος μεμερισμένως ἢ πάλιν κατὰ τάγμα ἁπλικευόντων.

90. Γίνεται δὲ καὶ δι᾽ ἑτέρων τοιούτων καὶ ὁμοίων σημείων διαφόρων ἡ
535 ἐπίγνωσις τῶν εἰρημένων κατασκόπων, ἅτινα ἀναγκαῖόν ἐστιν ἐπιτηδεύειν, ὥστε διάφορα | σημεῖα ἤτοι παραγγέλματα ποιεῖν. ἅμα γὰρ καὶ οἱ κατάσκοποι 388 τῶν ἐχθρῶν ἐκ τούτων φανεροῦνται, ἅμα δὲ καὶ οἱ στρατιῶται ἐθίζονται πείθεσθαι τοῖς ἄρχουσιν αὐτῶν καὶ φυλάττειν ἐπιμελῶς τὰ μανδάτα, ἐὰν μάλιστα μετρίως πως σωφρονίζωνται οἱ ἀμελοῦντες περὶ αὐτά. ἐὰν γὰρ τὸ παράγγελμα
540 δοθῇ παρὰ τοῦ ἄρχοντος τοῖς στρατιώταις μυστικώτερον, καὶ τοῦτο ἀγνοεῖ ἐρωτώμενος ὁ κατάσκοπος τοῦ ἐχθροῦ ταχέως εὑρίσκεται, ἀλλότριος ὢν τοῦ συνθήματος, καὶ οὐκ ἔχων τὸ σύσσημον τοῦ φιλίου στρατοῦ. οὐκ ἄτοπον δὲ

---

517–544 Cf. Polyaen. 3.13.1.

---

521 τένταν MW τένδαν AVBE | τέντας MW τένδας AVBE    523 τεντῶν[1] MW τενδῶν AVBE | τεντῶν[2] MW τενδῶν AVBE    524 τέντας MW τένδας AVBE    525 κοντουβερνίων AVBE κουτουβερνίων MW | συλλαμβάνονται καὶ MW om. AVBE | κρατήσουσι MVBE κρατήσουσιν WA | καὶ παραδώσουσι M καὶ παραδώσουσιν W om. AVBE    526 ἄρχοντι MW ἄρχοντι παραδώσουσιν AVBE | γίνεται…δύο MW ἐκ τῶν δύο γίνεται AVBE    527 συνέχεται MW κρατεῖται AVBE    528 κοντουβερνίων AVBE κουτουβερνίων MW    529 κοντουβερνίου AVBE κουτουβερνίου MW    533 τὸ MW om. AVBE | μεμερισμένως MW μεμερισμένου AVBE | ἁπλικευόντων MW ἁπλικεύοντος AVBE    534 δι᾽ MW ἐπὶ AVBE    537 τούτων MW τούτου AVBE    541 ἐρωτώμενος MW om. AVBE

89. If you wish to capture enemy spies, entrust this responsibility to your officers. Have each one announce to the soldiers under his command, and to the rest, that on the next day, probably about the second or third hour of the day, at the first blast of the trumpet, each individual, soldier or serving boy, is to enter his own tent.[10] Anybody who dares to be discovered outside his tent will be punished. After everyone has gone inside, the officers themselves remain outside the tents to observe, so they can arrest anyone found outside the tents. The squad members should seize and hold those who may have entered the tents and hand them over to their own officer. One of two things will happen to the spy. If he stands around outside, he will be caught, since he does not know where to go or, in the likelihood that he is bold enough to enter the tent of one of the squads, he will be recognized as a stranger and handed over to the squad's commander. Every person caught in this manner must be detained, whether they appear to be Romans or foreigners. They should be interrogated to determine their true identity. This may be done in an expeditious manner when the army, either foot or horse, is concentrated in camp or it may also be done separately in camps of a single meros or tagma.

90. The spies we have been discussing may also be detected by other means and, likewise, by a variety of signs, which you must be ready to employ, so as to use different signals or commands. At the same time that the enemy spies are detected by these means, our soldiers also become accustomed to obey their officers and to follow orders carefully, particularly if a reasonable punishment is meted out to those who are careless about such matters. If the command is given secretly by the officer to the soldiers and the enemy spy does not know the password when asked, he is quickly found out, since he is ignorant of it and does not know the sign of the friendly army. It is not a bad idea to give other signs

---

10. For §§89–90 cf. Polyaenus 3.13.1; *Sylloge tacticorum*, 83.2

ἄλλα καὶ σχήματα καὶ μανδάτα διδόναι τοῖς στρατιώταις ὅταν μάλιστα εὐκαιρῶσιν, ἵνα καὶ δοκιμασθῶσιν καὶ ἐν ἔθει γένωνται τοῦ φυλάττειν αὐτά.

545 91. Ἐὰν δέ ποτε συλλάβῃς κατασκόπους, μὴ κέχρησαι εἰς αὐτοὺς μιᾷ καὶ τῇ αὐτῇ γνώμῃ πάντοτε, ἀλλ' ἐὰν μὲν ἀσθενέστερα μᾶλλον τὰ σὰ εἶναι παρὰ τῶν πολεμίων νομίζῃς, τότε κτείνειν τούτους ἢ συνέχειν ἐν ἀσφαλεῖ φρουρᾷ. ἐὰν δὲ καθοπλισμὸν ἔχῃς ἰσχυρὸν καὶ καλὸν καὶ παρασκευὴν ἱκανὴν καὶ δύναμιν πολλὴν καὶ εὐεξίαν ἤτοι μέγεθος καὶ ῥῶσιν σωμάτων καὶ πειθήνιον στράτευμα 550 καὶ ἄρχοντας ἀρίστους καὶ ἀνδρείους καὶ ἐμπειρίαν μεμελετημένους, στῆσον μὲν τὴν στρατειὰν ἐν κόσμῳ καὶ καταστάσει πρὸς κόμπον· παράλαβε δὲ τοὺς κατασκόπους καὶ ταύτην ἐπίδειξον αὐτοῖς. τάχα δέ, εἰ τοῦτο ποιήσας ἀθῴους αὐτοὺς ἀποπέμψεις εἰς τοὺς ἰδίους, οὐκ ἂν ἁμαρτήσῃς. καὶ γὰρ ἀπελθόντες, ἅπερ εἶδον ἀναγγελοῦσι τοῖς ἰδίοις. τὰ μὲν γὰρ πλεονεκτήματα τῶν ἀντιπάλων 555 ἀπαγγελλόμενα πολλάκις ἀναγκάζει φοβεῖσθαι τοὺς ἀκούοντας, τὰ δὲ ἐλαττώματα αὐτῶν θαρρεῖν τοὺς ἀντιτεταγμένους παρεσκεύασεν. ὥστε εἰ μὲν ἐλαττώματα ἔχεις, ἀπολέσθωσαν οἱ κατάσκοποι· εἰ δὲ πλεονεκτήματα, μᾶλλον ἀπολυθέντες καὶ διηγούμενοι τοῖς ὁμοεθνέσιν εἰς δειλίαν αὐτοὺς περιστήσουσιν.

92. Ἐὰν δὲ πρόσφυγες ἀπὸ τῶν ἐχθρῶν πρός σε παραγένωνται, καὶ ἢ ὥραν 560 τινὰ ἐπιθέσεως ἢ ὁδὸν ἐπαγγέλλωνται ὑποδείξειν, καὶ προπορεύεσθαι, καὶ διὰ σκοπῶν ἀοράτων ἐπὶ τοὺς πολεμίους εἰσαγαγεῖν, μὴ ἁπλῶς πίστευε, ἀλλὰ δήσας αὐτοὺς οὕτως ἄγε, παραγγέλλων αὐτοῖς ὅτι, ἐὰν μὲν ἀληθεύσωσιν, καὶ ἐπὶ σωτηρίᾳ καὶ νίκῃ πάντα ποιήσωσι τοῦ στρατεύματος, | ὠφελείας καὶ δωρεᾶς 388ᵛ καταξιωθήσονται. εἰ δὲ ἐξαπατήσωσι καὶ ψεύσωνται εἰς τοὺς ἰδίους ἐπιρρίψαι 565 βουλόμενοι τὸ στράτευμα, γινωσκέτωσαν ὅτι παρ' αὐτὸν ἐκεῖνον τὸν καιρὸν ὄντες ἐν δεσμοῖς, ὑπὸ τῶν κινδυνευόντων κατασφαγήσονται. καὶ γὰρ προσφύ-

---

543 ἄλλα MW om. AVBE    545 συλλάβῃς MW κρατήσῃς AVBE    545–546 μὴ…ἐὰν MW om. AVBE    546 μᾶλλον MW om. AVBE    546–547 παρὰ…νομίζῃς MW νομίζῃς παρὰ τῶν πολεμίων AVBE    547 κτείνειν MW φονεύειν AVBE | συνέχειν…ἀσφαλεῖ MW φυλάττειν ἐν ἀσφαλεστάτῃ AVBE    548–550 καθοπλισμὸν…μεμελετημένους MW καθωπλισμένος ἐστιν ὁ σὸς στρατὸς καὶ ἱκανὸς καὶ πειθόμενός σοι ἔχῃς δὲ καὶ ἄρχοντας ἀνδρείους καὶ ἐμπειρίαν ἱκανὴν κεκτημένους AVBE    550 μεμελετημένους De μεμελετημένην MW    551 κόσμῳ…κόμπον MW τάξει AVBE    552–553 ἀθώους… ἀπελθόντες MW εἰς τοὺς ἰδίους ἀπολύσεις αὐτοὺς οὐχ ἁμαρτήσεις ἀπελθόντες γὰρ AVBE    554 ἀναγγελοῦσι…ἰδίοις MW ἀναγγελοῦσιν αὐτοῖς AVBE    557–558 ἀπολυθέντες καὶ MW ἀπολυθέσθωσαν AVBE    560 ἐπαγγέλλωνται ὑποδείξειν MW ὑπισχνῶνται ὑποδεῖξαι AVBE    562 οὕτως MW om. AVBE | ἀληθεύσωσιν MA ἀληθεύσωσι WVBE    563 πάντα… στρατεύματος MW τοῦ στρατεύματος πάντα ποιήσωσιν AVBE    564 ἐξαπατήσωσι De ἐξαπατήσουσι codd.    566–567 προσφύγου MW πρόσφυγος AVBE

and commands to the soldiers, especially when they are at leisure, to test them and get them used to following orders.

91. Do not always deal in one and the same manner with the spies you may happen to seize. If you believe that your forces are very weak compared to those of the enemy, then kill the spies or hold them in a secure fortress. If, however, you have a strong and impressive armament, fine equipment, great force, all in good condition, large, physically robust, an obedient army, outstanding and brave officers, as well as very experienced, then display your army in its orderly and impressive condition. Invite the spies out to observe it. If you do this and send them back unharmed to their own people, you will surely not make a mistake. After leaving you, they will announce what they have seen to their own people. For when the superiority of one's adversaries is made known, it frequently compels those who hear it to become frightened, whereas their inferiority causes those lined up against them to be bold. And so, if you are inferior, let the spies be done away with, but if you are superior, let them go so they can so inform their compatriots, who will then succumb to cowardice.

92. If fugitives from the enemy present themselves to you and promise to disclose what hour has been fixed for their attack or to show you the road, even to go ahead of you and by unseen signposts to guide you to the enemy, do not blindly trust them. Instead, bind them and deal with them in this way: advise them that if they are telling the truth and they contribute fully to the security and victory of your army, then they will be generously rewarded with benefits and gifts. But if they prove deceitful and lie with the intention of having their own forces fall upon our army, let them know that at that very moment, while still in chains, they will be slaughtered by those whom they tried to endanger.

γου πίστις βεβαιοτάτη, εἴτε πολεμίου πρός σε εἴτε ἀπό σου πρὸς τοὺς πολεμίους, τὸ μὴ εἶναι αὐτὸν κύριον τῆς ἰδίας ψυχῆς, ἀλλὰ τοὺς ἡγουμένους αὐτούς, ἢ
ἐν οἷς προσέφυγεν ἢ ἐξ ὧν ἀπέφυγεν. τοσαῦτα μὲν οὖν εἰρήσθω καὶ περὶ τού-
570   των.|

---

567–568 εἴτε[1]...πολεμίους  MW  om.  AVBE  568 αὐτούς  MW  αὐτοῦ  AVBE
568–569 ἢ...ἀπέφυγεν MW om. AVBE

For the faith to be placed in a fugitive, whether from the enemy to you or from you to the enemy, is most firm when he is not lord of his own soul but is subject to those who have power over him, either among those to whom he has fled or those from whom he has fled. This, therefore, is enough about these matters.

Περὶ μελέτης διαφόρων ἐθνικῶν τε καὶ Ῥωμαϊκῶν παρατάξεων

1. Ἑξῆς δὲ καὶ διαφόρων παρατάξεων μελέτας σοι ὑπαγορεύσω τῶν τε ἄλλων ἐθνικῶν καὶ ὅσαις ἐχρήσαντο κατὰ διαφόρων ἐθνῶν οἱ τῶν Ῥωμαϊκῶν
5 στρατευμάτων κατάρξαντες πάλαι στρατηγοί, ἵνα ταύτας κατανοήσας οὐ μόνον αὐτὸς τοῖς αὐτοῖς χρήσῃ στρατηγήμασιν ἐν τῷ δέοντι καιρῷ, ἀλλὰ καὶ ἕτερα πλείω τούτων προεπινοήσῃς. ἀγχίνοια γὰρ στρατηγοῦ ὅτ' ἂν καὶ ἀφορμῆς τινος δράξηται πραγμάτων στρατηγικῶν, οὐ μέχρις ἐκείνων ἵσταται μόνων, ἀλλὰ καὶ πλείω τούτων προσεφευρίσκειν δύναται.
10 2. Ἡ μὲν οὖν συνεχὴς γυμνασία τῶν τακτικῶν κινήσεων ὠφέλειαν μὲν πολλὴν τῷ στρατιώτῃ ποιεῖ. κατάδηλος δὲ αὐτὴ εὐχερῶς τοῖς ἐχθροῖς γίνεται διά τε κατασκόπων τῶν ἀπὸ τῶν ἐχθρῶν καὶ τῶν, ὡς εἰκός, προσφευγόντων εἰς αὐτούς, καὶ διὰ τοῦτο πολλάκις μεθοδευομένη καὶ κατανοουμένη ἄπρακτος εὑρίσκεται.
15 3. Ἀρκεῖ οὖν ἡ παρ' ἡμῶν ὁρισθεῖσα γυμνασία ἐν τῇ περὶ αὐτῆς ἡμῖν εἰρημένῃ διατάξει, ἁπλῆ οὖσα καὶ δι' αὐτῆς πάσῃ τάξει ἁρμοζομένη καὶ μηδὲ πουβλικίζεσθαι ποιοῦσα τὴν πᾶσαν παράταξιν.
4. Ἐὰν δὲ τύχῃ καὶ εὐκαιρία πολλὴ πρὸς μείζονα γυμνασίαν καὶ μετεωρισμόν, δεῖ τότε διαφόρους μὲν τάξεις καὶ γυμνασίας τὰ μέρη, ἤτοι τὰς τούρμας ἢ
20 δρούγγους ἢ τὰ βάνδα τῶν κομήτων καθ' ἑαυτὰ ἐπιτηδεύειν, τοῦτ' ἔστι, καὶ τὴν λεχθεῖσαν πρὸς τὸ χρειῶδες καὶ ἄλλας ἐκ περισσοῦ, εἰ καὶ οὐκ ἀναγκαίας ἀεί, ἀλλ' οὖν ἔν τινι καιρῷ ποτε χρησίμους.

M W A V B E   Va,Hung.   PG 107:946

10–93 *Strat.*, 6.praef.

1 πολεμικῶν παρασκευῶν MWA om. VBE | ιη' AVBE ιζ' MW   3 μελέτας σοι MW trsp. AVBE   7 πλείω MW πλείονα AVBE | προεπινοήσῃς MW προσεπινοήσῃς AVBE | ὅτ' ἂν De οἳ ἂν M ὅταν WAVBE   8 μόνων MW μόνον AVBE   9 πλείω MW πλείονα AVBE 11 εὐχερῶς... γίνεται MWV τοῖς ἐχθροῖς εὐκόλως γίνεται A τοῖς ἐχθροῖς γίνεται εὐκόλως BE 12 ἀπὸ MWAV ὑπὸ BE   15 ἡμῶν MWV ἡμῖν ABE   16–17 πουβλικίζεσθαι MW φαυλίζεσθαι AVBE   17 ποιοῦσα MWAV ποιουμένη BE   18 καὶ¹ MW om. AVBE 20 ἔστι MBE ἔστιν WAV   22 χρησίμους MW χρησίμως AVBE

## PREPARATION FOR WAR, CONSTITUTION XVIII

## About the Practices of Various Peoples and of the Romans in Their Battle Formations

1. Next, I will teach you about the various battle formations employed by other nations, as well as those that the commanders of Roman armies, going back to ancient times, made use of against different peoples. After getting to know these, not only will you make use of the same stratagems at the proper time but you will be able to devise many more in addition. For the shrewd commander, when he seizes an opportunity for military strategies, will not stop only at those but will be able to invent many more.

2. Constant drilling in tactical movements is of great benefit to the soldier.[1] It is easy, however, for the enemy to learn what is going on through the spies they send out or, as is likely, from our men deserting to them. The result is that, although well observed and correctly done, drills are often found to be without effect.

3. Actually, the drill described by us in the constitution devoted to it is sufficient. Its simplicity by itself makes it adaptable to any formation without disclosing our entire plan of battle.

4. If a good opportunity for more extended drilling and exercises presents itself, then it is necessary for each division, that is, each tourma or droungos or count's bandon, to practice various formations and drills by themselves. There is the one prescribed for actual use and those additional ones which, although not always necessary, may be useful on certain occasions.

---

1. Sections 2–15 derive from *Strat.* 6 preface.

5. Ἵνα τῇ ἑκάστῃ τάξει καὶ γυμνασίᾳ γνώρισμα ἴδιον ἐπιτεθῇ, καὶ οἱ μὲν στρατιῶται τὴν διαφορὰν ἑκάστης παρατάξεως γνωρίζουσιν ἐν συνηθείᾳ τῶν
25 κινήσεων γινόμενοι, καὶ μὴ ξενοφωνοῦσιν ὡς οὐκ εἰδότες, ὅτ' ἂν ἀθρόως αὐτοῖς ἀγγελθῇ τις παράταξις, μὴ οἴδασι δὲ τὴν μέλλουσαν τάξιν ὑπὸ τοῦ στρατηγοῦ γίνεσθαι κατ' αὐτὸν τὸν τοῦ πολέμου καιρόν.

6. Εἰσὶν οὖν διαφοραὶ τῶν τάξεων τῶν κατὰ σχῆμα γινομένων τρεῖς· ὧν μία ἡ χρειώδης, ᾗτινι καὶ Ῥωμαίοις χρῆσθαι σύνηθες. καὶ ἡ μέν ἐστιν ἥτις ἀδιακρί-
30 τως ἔχουσα τὰ τάγματα, τοῦτ' ἔστιν, οὐκ εἰς κούρσορας ἤτοι προκλάστας, καὶ διφένσορας ἤτοι ἐκδίκους διῃρημένη, ἅτινα χρὴ ἐπὶ μιᾶς παρα|τάξεως τάττειν, 348ᵛ καὶ οὐκέτι εἰς τρεῖς, ἀλλὰ εἰς δύο μοίρας διαιρεῖν, ἐφ' ᾧ κινούντων τῶν δύο κεράτων ὡς πρὸς κύκλωσιν, καὶ πρὸς ἄλληλα ἐπικλινομένων καὶ ἐμπεριλαμ-βανόντων εὔκαιρον χωρίον, τὸ μὲν δεξιὸν κέρας ἐξώτερον, τὸ δὲ ἀριστερὸν
35 ἐσώτερον παρερχόμενον κυκλοειδῶς, τὴν ἐναντίαν ἀλλήλων ἐλαύνωσιν, ὃν τρόπον ἐν τῷ μαρτίῳ μηνί ποτε οἱ καβαλλάριοι ἔπαιζον.

7. Ἡ δὲ ἄλλη ἐστὶ παράταξις, ὅτ' ἂν ἐπὶ μιᾶς τάξεως τάσσονται ὑπὸ κούρσο-ρας καὶ διφένσορας, διῃρημένας δὲ τὰς μοίρας ἀπὸ σ' ἢ υ' ποδῶν ἀλλήλων ἀποδιεστώτας, καὶ ἐν τῇ κινήσει σὺν ἐλασίᾳ τῶν κουρσόρων ἐξερχομένων εἰς
40 καταδίωξιν, εἶτα ὑποστρεφόντων, ὅτε μὲν εἰς τὰ διαλείμματα, ἤτοι εἰς τὰ εὔκαι-ρα χωρία αὐτῆς ἐξελίσσεσθαι, καὶ ἅμα τῶν διφενσόρων χωρεῖν κατὰ τῶν ἐχθ-ρῶν, ποτὲ δὲ ὑποστρέφοντας δι' αὐτῶν τῶν διαστημάτων ἀπέρχεσθαι, καὶ ἐπὶ τὰ ἄκρα τοῦ μέρους φαίνεσθαι τοὺς ἐκ τῶν δύο μερῶν κούρσορας, ἕκαστον ὡς ἐτάχθη.

45 8. Ἡ δὲ ἑτέρα παράταξίς ἐστιν ὅτ' ἂν ἐπὶ μιᾶς παρατάξεως τάσσονται, καὶ ἡ μὲν μέση μοῖρα εἰς διφένσορας γίνεται, αἱ δὲ ἑκατέρωθεν αὐτῆς μοῖραι εἰς κούρσορας, εἶτα τῆς ἐλασίας ὡς εἰς ἐπιδίωξιν γινομένης, ἡ μὲν μέση μοῖρα ἐν

---

36 ad μαρτίῳ des. W

28-29 *Strat.*, 6.1.   37-39 *Strat.*, 6.2.   45-47 *Strat.*, 6.3.

---

24 γνωρίζουσιν MW γνωρίζωσιν AVBE   25 ξενοφωνοῦσιν…εἰδότες MW ξενίζωνται AVBE   25-26 ἀθρόως…παράταξις MW αἰφνιδίως αὐτοῖς παράταξίς τις ἀγγελθῇ AVBE   26 οἴδασι MAVBE οἴδασιν W   28 τρεῖς ὧν AVBE τρισσῶν MW   29 ἥτις MW ἡ AVBE   30 ἤτοι MW ἤγουν AVBE   32 ἀλλὰ MWV ἀλλ' ABE | ἐφ' ᾧ MW ὥστε AVBE   34 χωρίον MW τόπον AVBE   35 ἐλαύνωσιν MW ἐλαύνειν AVBE   37 τάξεως MW om. AVBE   38 σ'…υ' MW διακοσίων ἢ τετρακοσίων AVBE   38-39 ἀλλήλων ἀποδιεστώτας Μ ἀπ' ἀλλήλων διεστώτας AVBE   40-41 διαλείμματα…αὐτῆς Μ διαχωρίσματα αὐτῆς AVBE   41 τῶν διφενσόρων Μ τοῖς διφένσορσι AVBE | κατὰ τῶν Μ κατ' αὐτῶν AVBE   46 αὐτῆς Μ αὐτοῖς AVBE

5. Each formation and drill should be identified in a special way so the soldiers who are trained in these movements may recognize the difference between each battle formation. Thus the words will not be strange to them because of ignorance. Whenever a certain battle formation is suddenly announced to them, they will know the plan which the commander intends to implement when the time comes for battle.

6. Now then, there is a threefold division of simulated formations. The first is a useful one that even the Romans were accustomed to use.[2] In this one the units are not split up, that is, not divided into assault troops, also called proklastai, and defenders, also called ekdikoi. They are formed in one battle line, not divided into three moirai as heretofore but into two. The two flanks move out in an encircling maneuver, heading toward each other, and surrounding an open space. They continue along as in a circle, the right wing on the outside and the left on the inside, and thus ride into the opposite section of each other's line. The cavalry used to play at this sort of thing in March.

7. Another formation has them drawn up into a single battle line, some as assault troops and some as defenders.[3] This is divided into moirai separated from each other by about two hundred or four hundred feet. The assault troops charge out in pursuit, riding at a gallop, and then turn back. Sometimes they filter into the intervals, that is, the clear spaces in the line, join together with the defenders, and then charge out against the enemy. At other times, they turn around and march out through those same intervals; the assault troops from both divisions then show up on the flanks of the meros, each man in his original position.

8. Still another battle formation has the troops drawn up in one battle line, with the middle moira composed of defenders and the moirai on both sides composed of assault troops.[4] Maintaining their pace, as though in pursuit, the

2. *Strat.* 6.1.
3. *Strat.* 6.2.
4. *Strat.* 6.3.

τάξει ἐπακολουθεῖ ὡς διφένσορας, αἱ δὲ ἑκατέρωθεν μοῖραι ὡς κούρσορας
ἐξέρχονται. εἶτα ἐν τῷ ὑποστρέφειν ἡ μὲν μία μοῖρα μένει, ἤτοι ἐμβραδύνει ἔξω,
50 ἡ δὲ ἄλλη σὺν ἐλασίᾳ ὑποστρέφει ὡς ἐπὶ τοὺς διφένσορας, καὶ πάλιν κινούσης
τῆς ἀπομεινάσης ὡς πρὸς τοὺς διφένσορας, ἡ ἄλλη ὡς εἰς ἀπάντησιν τρέχουσα
δι᾽ ἑνὸς μέρους ἐπέρχεται, καὶ τῷ τρόπῳ τούτῳ μία παρὰ μίαν αἱ μοῖραι ἀντι-
πρόσωποι ἀλλήλων εὑρίσκονται, μὴ συγκρούουσαι ἑαυταῖς.

9. Ἔστι δὲ καὶ ἄλλη ὁμοιότροπος αὐτῆς εἰς τὸ ἐναντίον τασσομένη, τοῦτ᾽
55 ἔστι, τὴν μὲν μέσην μοῖραν κούρσορας ἔχουσα, τὰς δὲ ἑκατέρωθεν δύο μοίρας
διφένσορας, ἐν ταῖς εἰρημέναις κινήσεσιν.

10. Ἡ μέντοι συνήθης Ῥωμαίοις τάξις καὶ γυμνασία αὕτη πρὸς πᾶν ἔθνος
ἐπιτηδεία ἡμῖν φαίνεται, τοῦτ᾽ ἔστιν, ὅτ᾽ ἂν εἰς δύο τάξεις, εἰς προμάχους καὶ
βοηθοὺς τάσσεται ὑπὸ κούρσορας καὶ διφένσορας, καὶ πλαγιοφύλακάς τε καὶ
60 ὑπερκεραστάς, καὶ ἐνέδρους καὶ νωτοφύλακας, κατὰ τὸν πρώην λεχθέντα ἡμῖν
τρόπον.

11. Χρὴ οὖν ἢ τὰς εἰρημένας διαφορὰς τῶν παρατάξεων ἐθίζειν τὸν στρατόν,
ἵνα μὴ πουβλι|κίζηται ἡ ἀναγκαιοτέρα, ἢ τῆς πρώτης τάξεως γυμναζομένης τὴν  349
δευτέραν τάξιν μὴ φέρειν μετ᾽ αὐτῆς, ἀλλὰ μόνην τὴν πρώτην ἄνευ πλαγιο-
65 φυλάκων καὶ ὑπερκεραστῶν δηλονότι καὶ ἐνέδρων καὶ νωτοφυλάκων, ὅπερ
πλέον ἡμῖν ἁπλούστερον καὶ ἀναγκαιότερον φαίνεται, ἀλλὰ τότε ἀντὶ τῆς
δευτέρας τάξεως ὀλίγους καβαλλαρίους σχηματικῶς ὄπισθεν ἱστᾶν, ἵνα πρὸς τὸ
διάστημα ἐκεῖνο ἐθίζωνται προσφεύγειν οἱ τῆς πρώτης τάξεως. ὁμοίως δὲ ἰδίᾳ
καὶ τὴν δευτέραν τάξιν γυμνάζῃς, καὶ ὀλίγους ἐν τάξει τῆς πρώτης τάξεως
70 ποιῇς, ἤτοι προτάσσῃς ἵνα ἐθίζηται ἡ δευτέρα ὡσαύτως τοὺς τῆς πρώτης τάξεως
καταφεύγοντας εἰς αὐτοὺς δέχεσθαι.

12. Δυνατὸν δὲ ἰδίως καὶ τοὺς πλαγιοφύλακας καὶ τοὺς ὑπερκεραστὰς τὴν
ἰδίαν τάξιν καὶ γυμνασίαν πρὸ τοῦ πολέμου ποιεῖν ἵνα καὶ ἐθίζηται ὁ στρατὸς

---

58 ad <προ>μάχους de novo inc. W

---

48 διφένσορας M διφένσωρ AVBE | ἑκατέρωθεν…κούρσορας M ἐξ ἀμφοτέρων τῶν μερῶν
ὡς κούρσορας AV ἐξ ἑκατέρων τῶν μερῶν BE    52 ἐπέρχεται ME ἐπέρχονται AVB | παρὰ…
μοῖραι De παραμία μοῖρα codd.    53 συγκρούουσαι ἑαυταῖς AV ἐγκρούουσαι ἑαυτοῖς M
συγκρόουσαι BE    54 καὶ M om. AVBE    55 ἔστι MVBE ἔστιν A | ἔχουσα M ἔχουσαν
AVBE    59 τάσσεται ὑπὸ MW τάσσηται πρὸ AVBE | καὶ³ MW om. AVBE
63 πουβλικίζηται MW φαυλίζηται AVBE    65 δηλονότι MW om. AVBE    67 σχηματικῶς
MW ἐν σχήματι AVBE    ⸍68 ἰδίᾳ MW om. AVBE    69 γυμνάζῃς MW ἰδίᾳ γυμνάσεις AVBE
70 ποιῇς MW ποιήσεις AVBE | προτάσσῃς MW προτάξεις AVBE | δευτέρα MVBE δευτέρα
τοῦ WA    71 αὐτοὺς MW αὐτὴν AVBE    72 ἰδίως MW ἡμῖν AVBE    73 τάξιν MW τάξιν τε
AVBE

middle moira follows along in formation as defenders, the moirai of assault troops on both flanks move out. Then, in turning back the one moira stays in position or slows down on the outside while the other turns and races back as though to the defenders. The wing that had halted begins moving again as though toward the defenders. The other quickly moves out as if to meet it, riding off to one side and, in this way, one moira at a time, they end up facing each other but without colliding.

9. There is another one similar to this in which the troops are drawn up in the opposite manner, that is, the middle moira consists of assault troops and the two wings of defenders, but it follows the same movements.

10. Finally, the formation and drill customary for the Romans is, in our opinion, suitable for use against any people.[5] It is formed of two lines, a front battle line and a support line, with assault troops and defenders, flank guards and outflankers, ambushers and rear guards, according to the manner described by us earlier.

11. It is, therefore, necessary to accustom the army to the above-mentioned different types of battle lines, so that the truly essential one may not become known <to outsiders>. If the front line is being drilled, do not bring the second line with it, but just the first line and that without flank guards and outflankers, without ambushers and rear guards. This strikes us as the simplest and most basic plan. Moreover, in place of the second line, station a few cavalrymen to the rear to represent it, so that the troops in the first line may get used to that distance in seeking safety. Likewise, you may drill the second line by itself if you station or put in front a few troops on the site of the first line, so that the second may get used to receiving the men of the first line if they seek refuge among them.

12. It is possible for the flank guards and outflankers to practice their own formations and drills separately before the time of combat, so that the army may

---

5. Cf. *Strat.* 6.4; Const. 7.

442    Constitution 18

πρὸς τὰς κινήσεις, καὶ μὴ πουβλικίζωνται εἰς τοὺς ἐχθροὺς αἱ χρειώδεις παρα-
75 τάξεις, τοῦτ᾽ ἔστιν, ἵνα οἱ ὑπερκερασταί, ἤγουν οἱ ἐπὶ τοῦ δεξιοῦ μέρους πρὸς
τὴν κύκλωσιν τῶν πολεμίων ἑστῶτες, εἴτε ὑποτάσσωνται λανθανόντως τῷ
δεξιῷ κέρατι, εἴτε ἐκ πλαγίου παρατάσσωνται ἰσομετώπως, ὅτ᾽ ἂν καιρὸς γένηται τῆς ὑπερκεράσεως, ἐπὶ δόρυ κλίναντας αὐτούς, εἶτα ὅσον ἀπαιτεῖ ἡ χρεία
διάστημα περιπατοῦντας, οὕτως εἰς ὀρθὸν ἀποκαθισταμένους κινεῖν ἐν τάξει,
80 καὶ σπουδάζειν, ὡσανεὶ τὴν τῶν ἐναντίων τάξιν περιλαμβάνειν.

13. Πάλιν δὲ τοὺς πλαγιοφύλακας τοὺς κατὰ τοῦ ἀριστεροῦ μέρους τασσομένους, ὁμοίως ἐπὶ σκουτάριν κλίναντας. εἶτα ὅσον ἀπαιτεῖ ἡ χρεία διάστημα
περιπατοῦντας, οὕτως εἰς ὀρθὸν ἀποκαθίστασθαι, καὶ σπεύδειν, ὡσανεὶ τῷ
ἐναντίῳ κέρατι τῶν ὑπερκεραστῶν ἐξισοῦσθαι.

85 14. Ταύτας δέ σοι τὰς διαφορὰς τῶν παρατάξεων ὑπεσημάναμεν, ὦ στρατηγέ, ἵνα ἐν καιρῷ εὐκαιρίας ἐθίζῃς καὶ ἐν αὐταῖς γυμνάζεσθαι τὸ στράτευμα, καὶ
ἔχειν πλείονα ἐμπειρίαν τῆς τῶν πολέμων τακτικῆς, ὥστε καὶ ἔν τισι πολλάκις
περιστάσεσι χρειώδεις σοι εὑρίσκεσθαι, ὅτ᾽ ἂν οὕτως ἡ χρεία καλῇ.

15. Καὶ ἑτέρας δὲ διαφόρους παρατάξεις, καὶ ὅσα δέον πράσσειν σε ὑπέρ τε
90 τοῦ οἰκείου στρατοῦ καὶ κατὰ τῶν πολεμίων ὡς ἐν ἐκθέσει διατάξομεν, ὅσας
ἀπὸ διαφόρων ἐθνῶν ἐκ τῆς πείρας Ῥωμαῖοι ἐν γνώσει παρέλαβον, ἵνα γινώσκῃς ταύτας ἐν τῷ δέοντι μὲν καιρῷ χρῆσθαι ὑπὲρ σεαυτοῦ, ἐνίοτε δὲ τῶν
πολεμίων αὐταῖς χρωμένων ὑπὲρ ἑαυτῶν, | ἀντιμηχανᾶσθαι κατ᾽ αὐτῶν.        349ᵛ

16. Ἴσθι οὖν, ὦ στρατηγέ, ὅτι οὐ μόνον σὺ αὐτὸς ὀφείλεις εἶναι σπουδαῖος
95 καὶ φιλῶν τὴν πατρίδα, καὶ ὑπὲρ τῆς ὀρθῆς τῶν Χριστιανῶν πίστεως ἕτοιμος, εἰ
οὕτως τύχει, καὶ αὐτὴν τὴν ψυχὴν τιθέναι, ἀλλὰ καὶ τοὺς ὑπό σε πάντας ἄρχοντας καὶ τῶν στρατιωτῶν ἅπαν τὸ πλῆθος τοιούτους παρασκευάζειν γενέσθαι,
ἵνα οἱ μὲν ὄντες ἐπὶ τοῦ αὐτοῦ καλοῦ τοιοῦτοι μένωσιν, τοὺς δὲ μὴ ὄντας, ὅσον
ἔχεις δυνάμεως, διὰ τῆς σῆς ἐπιμελείας καὶ σπουδῆς γυμναζομένους μὴ ἀμοιρεῖν

74 πουβλικίζωνται…ἐχθροὺς MW φαυλίζωνται τοῖς ἐχθροῖς AVBE   77 ἐκ MW ἐκ τοῦ
AVBE   79 ἀποκαθισταμένους…τάξει   MWVBE   ἀποκαθίστασθαι A   80-83 τὴν…
σπεύδειν MW om. AVBE   85 ὑπεσημάναμεν MW ὑπηγορεύσαμεν AVBE   86 ἐν¹…
εὐκαιρίας MW εὐκαιρία AVBE | αὐταῖς MW ταύταις τὸ στράτευμα πρὸς τὸ AVBE
87 ὥστε…τισι MW om. AVBE   88 περιστάσεσι…καλῇ MW γὰρ ἐν περιστάσει χρειώδεις
αὗται εὑρεθήσονται AVBE   89 πράσσειν MW πράττειν AVBE | τε MW om. AVBE
92 ταύτας MW ταύτας ὥστε AVBE | ἐνίοτε MW πολλάκις AVBE   93 χρωμένων…ἑαυτῶν
MW om. AVBE   94 ἴσθι MW γίνωσκε AVBE   95-96 εἰ…τύχει MW om. AVBE
96 τιθέναι MW τιθέναι εἰ οὕτως τύχη AVBE   97 παρασκευάζειν MW παρασκευάσεις
AVBE   98 ἐπὶ…μένωσιν MW τοιοῦτοι μένουσιν ἐπὶ τῆς αὐτῆς ἀρετῆς AVBE
98-99 ὅσον…δυνάμεως MW om. AVBE   99 γυμναζομένους MW om. AVBE

become accustomed to their movements and that the actual battle line to be used is not made known to the enemy.[6] First, the outflankers, that is, the men stationed by the right meros for the encirclement of the enemy, may either be drawn up under cover behind the right flank or drawn up on the flank even with the line. Whether they are drawn up on the flank or even with the line, when the time comes for their enveloping movement, they incline to the spear and then ride out the necessary distance or as far as is called for. Thus, returning directly to their original position, they move in formation and strive to envelop the enemy line.

13. Again, the flank guards who are drawn up by the left meros should, in like manner, incline to the shield, ride out the required distance as far as necessary, and so return directly to their original position, moving rapidly in order to be on the same line as the opposite wing of the outflankers.

14. We have pointed out these various battle formations to you, O general, so that in time of leisure you may accustom and drill your army in them and acquire a great deal of practical experience of military tactics. Thus, in certain frequently occurring situations, when necessity calls, you will be able to determine what is useful.

15. We will now set forth and propose to you a variety of additional battle formations for you to put in practice, on behalf of your own army and against the enemy. The Romans have come to learn about these formations from experience with various peoples; we hope that you will become familiar with them and make use of them at the proper time on your behalf and that, when the enemy are using them on their behalf, <you will learn> how to devise countermeasures against them.

16. Be well aware, therefore, O general, that it is not you alone who ought to be a serious promoter and lover of the fatherland and defender of the correct faith of Christians, ready, if it so transpires, to lay down your very life, but also all the officers under your command and the entire body of soldiers should be ready to do the same. May those who share the same noble <ideal> remain such. As for those whose training has not led them <to share that ideal>, then, as much as possible, your care and concern <should make sure> that they are not

---

6. *Strat.* 6.5; "incline to the spear" = right, "to the shield" = left.

100 τῆς τοιαύτης ἀρετῆς, ἀλλ' εἶναι αὐτοὺς φιλοπάτριδας καὶ εὐπειθεῖς τοῖς ἄρχουσιν, ἢ δι' ἀγάπην ἢ διὰ φόβον.

17. Εἶναι δὲ αὐτοὺς καὶ καρτερικοὺς πρὸς τοὺς πόνους καὶ ὑπομένειν τοὺς
ὑπὲρ τῆς πατρίδος πολέμους.

18. Καὶ αὐτὸς δὲ βουλῇ τε καὶ στρατηγίᾳ μᾶλλον τὰ πολλὰ τῶν σπουδαζο-
105 μένων σοι κατόρθου καὶ τάξεως ἐπιμελοῦ ἅμα τῷ ὑπό σε στρατῷ, καὶ μὴ θράσους καὶ προπετείας.

19. Καὶ ἐθίζεσθε πάντες ὁμοῦ οἱ διὰ Χριστὸν τὸν Θεὸν ἡμῶν καὶ ὑπὲρ συγγενῶν καὶ φίλων καὶ πατρίδος καὶ τοῦ ὅλου τῶν Χριστιανῶν ἔθνους ἀγωνιζόμενοι εὐκόλως ὑποφέρειν καὶ δίψης ὄχλησιν, καὶ δαπάνης ἔνδειαν, καὶ ψύχους
110 καὶ καύματος ἐπιφοράν, καὶ πρὸς τὰ ἐμπίπτοντα, ὡς εἰκός, δεινὰ γενναίως
ἐγκαρτερεῖν, ἔστι γὰρ τῶν ἀποκειμένων μισθῶν ἔκ τε Θεοῦ αὐτοῦ καὶ ἐκ τῆς ἐξ
αὐτοῦ βασιλείας ἡμῶν παρ' ὑμῶν ἐργασία. καὶ γὰρ καὶ ἡμεῖς διὰ τῆς ὑπὲρ ὑμῶν
ἐπιμόνου μερίμνης συγκακοπαθοῦμεν ὑμῖν.

20. Γενοῦ δὲ ἱκανός, εἴγε τινὰ συμβῇ ἐν καιρῷ λυπηρά, ἐπὶ πολὺ ταῦτα
115 κρύπτειν ἀπὸ τῶν πολεμίων, καὶ γενναίως ἐμμένειν καὶ καρτερεῖν ἐν ταῖς
περιστάσεσι, καὶ ταύτας εἰς τὸ ἐναντίον ἀποδεικνύειν μᾶλλον ἤγουν εἰς εὐθυμίαν καὶ ἀπάθειαν.

21. Ἦσαν γάρ τινα τῶν ἐθνῶν, οἷα τὰ Περσικὰ φῦλά ποτε πρὸς Ῥωμαίους
μαχόμενα ἅπερ, ὅτ' ἂν ἐν τοῖς δεινοῖς ἐνέπιπτεν, μηδὲ τὴν σωτηρίαν, ἣν ηὔχοντο
120 ἑαυτοῖς γενέσθαι, προτείνειν θέλοντα, ἀλλὰ καὶ ταύτην παρὰ τῶν ἐχθρῶν
αὐτῶν προτείνεσθαι ἐκδεχόμενα. τοσοῦτον ἐν αὐτοῖς ἡ τῶν δεινῶν καρτερία.

22. Ἵνα δὲ καὶ πάλιν τὰ πρώην εἰρημένα μετρίως ἀνακεφαλαιώσωμέν σοι,
καθόπλιζε τὸν στρατὸν τοῖς ὅπλοις κατὰ τὸν ἤδη σοι διορισθέντα τύπον, καὶ
μάλιστα τοξαρίοις καὶ σαγίτταις πλείοσι. μέγα γὰρ ὅπλον καὶ δραστήριον ἡ

---

118–132 *Strat.*, 11.1.

---

100 τῆς...ἀρετῆς MW τοῦ τοιούτου καλοῦ AVBE   103 τῆς AVBE om. MW   105 στρατῷ
MW στρατοῦ AVBE   107 καὶ...πάντες MW ἐθίζεσθαι δὲ πάντας AVBE | οἱ MW τοὺς
AVBE   108–109 ἀγωνιζόμενοι MW ἀγωνιζομένους AVBE   110 καύματος MWAVE
χαύματος B   111 ἔκ MW om. AVBE   114 εἴγε MW ἐὰν AVBE | ταῦτα MWA αὐτὰ VBE
116 περιστάσεσι MAVBE περιστάσεσιν W   119 μαχόμενα MWA μαχομένους VBE | μηδὲ
MW οὐδὲ AVBE   120 ἑαυτοῖς MWA αὐτοῖς VBE | θέλοντα MW ἤθελον AVBE
121 ἐκδεχόμενα MW ἐξεδέχοντο AVBE | ἐν MW ἦν AVBE   123 σοι διορισθέντα MW
ῥηθέντά σοι AVBE   124 πλείοσι M πλείοσιν WAVBE | δραστήριον MW ἐνεργέστατον
AVBE

found lacking in this very virtue. Rather, they should become lovers of the fatherland and be very obedient to their officers, either through love or through fear.

17. They should endure heavy labor and bear up well in wars for their fatherland.

18. For you, though, it is by planning and strategy that you will attain most of the goals you are striving for and, at the same time, by your concern for discipline in the army under your command rather than by boldness and headlong haste.

19. Accustom everyone, all together, who are engaged in the struggle for Christ our God and on behalf of relatives and friends and fatherland and for the entire Christian people, to bear readily the distress of thirst, the lack of necessities, the burden of cold and heat, and to endure with courage whatever terrible things may chance to fall upon them. For your labors <gain> the rewards stored up <for you> by God himself and by Our God-given Majesty. Indeed, by our steadfast solicitude on your behalf, we too share in your suffering.

20. Even if at times some harmful things happen, for the most part, do your best to conceal them from the enemy. Remain brave and steadfast in <adverse> situations, even turning them around to the opposite; show yourself in good spirits and not suffering.

21. There were certain peoples, such as the Persian tribes, who fought against the Romans.[7] Whenever they fell into terrible adversity, they did not want to propose means for their salvation that they wished for themselves, but they would receive proposals for it from their enemies. So great was their endurance of adversity.

22. Let us once more briefly recapitulate what we have previously said to you. Provide your army with the weapons according to the regulations already given to you. In particular make sure you have a large number of bows and arrows.

7. For §§21–23 cf. *Strat.* 11.1. On the various ethnic groups, see J. Wiita, "The Ethnika in Byzantine Military Treatises" (Ph.D. diss., University of Minnesota, 1977).

125 τοξεία, καὶ μάλιστα κατὰ τῶν Σαρακηνικῶν ἐθνῶν καὶ Κούρτων, οἷς τὸ πᾶν τῆς
νίκης ἐν ἐλπίδι τῆς παρ' αὐτῶν τοξείας κεῖται.

23. Καὶ γὰρ κατά τε αὐτῶν τῶν τοξοτῶν γυμνουμένων ἐν τῷ βάλλειν τὴν
σαγίτταν, ἀλλὰ καὶ κατὰ τῶν ἵππων τῶν καβαλλαρίων μέγα ἰσχύουσιν αἱ παρὰ
τοῦ ἡμετέρου | στρατοῦ βαλλόμεναι σαγίτται, καὶ πολλὴν τὴν βλάβην τοῖς 350
130 ἐχθροῖς παρέξουσι, τῶν πολυτιμήτων παρ' αὐτοῖς ἵππων διὰ τῆς συνεχοῦς
τοξείας ἀφανιζομένων, καὶ ἐντεῦθεν τοῦ εὐψύχου τῶν εἰς πολέμους ἐξιέναι
προθυμουμένων Σαρακηνῶν ἀνακοπτομένου.

24. Οὐ γὰρ δουλείᾳ καὶ στρατείᾳ ἐκστρατεύουσι Σαρακηνοί, ἀλλὰ φιλοκερ-
δίᾳ μᾶλλον καὶ ἐλευθερίᾳ, ἢ τὸ πλέον εἰπεῖν, λῃστείᾳ καὶ τῆς ἑαυτῶν πίστεως,
135 μᾶλλον δὲ εἰπεῖν ἀπιστίας τῇ δεισιδαιμονίᾳ, ὡς ἐνταῦθα κακὰ πάσχοντες παρ'
ἡμῶν καὶ Θεὸν ἡγοῦνται πολέμιον ἔχειν καὶ τὴν ζημίαν μὴ ὑποφέρειν.

25. Καὶ ὅτ' ἂν μὲν πρὸς πόλεμον κινήσῃς, ἄνευ φοσσάτου μὴ ἀπλικεύῃς
ὀχυροῦ, μάλιστα ἢ καὶ πλησίον ἢ ἐντὸς ὑπάρχῃς τῆς πολεμίας. ὅτ' ἂν δὲ πρὸς
τὸν πόλεμον ἐγγίσῃς τράφον ποίει καὶ ἄλλην ἀσφάλειαν διὰ χάρακος ὡς δύνα-
140 σαι ἀκριβῶς διὰ τὴν ἐκ περιστάσεως ἐν καιρῷ μάχης καταφυγήν.

26. Ὑποδείξω δέ σοι ἑτέρας καὶ τῶν ἐν μάχῃ παρατάξεων διαφορὰς ὡς ἐν
ὀλίγοις. ἔστι μὲν γάρ τις παράταξις μάχης ἐν τρισὶν ἴσοις μέρεσι τασσομένη, ἧς
καὶ ἄνω που ἐμνήσθημεν, τοῦτ' ἔστι, μέσῳ καὶ δεξιῷ καὶ ἀριστερῷ. ἐν δὲ τῷ
μέσῳ μέρει ἔχει ἄχρι τετρακοσίων ἢ πεντακοσίων ἀνδρῶν ἐπιλέκτων κατὰ
145 περίσσειαν, τὰ δὲ βάθη τῆς τοιαύτης τάξεως οὐχ ὡρισμένῳ μέτρῳ γίνεται, ἀλλὰ
μᾶλλον οἱ καβαλλάριοι ἐν ἑκάστῳ τάγματι ἐν τῇ πρώτῃ καὶ δευτέρᾳ τάξει
τάσσονται. καὶ τὸ μέτωπον τῆς τάξεως ἴσον καὶ πεπυκνωμένον ἐστί. τὴν δὲ
ἀποσκευὴν καὶ τὸν τοῦλδον ὄπισθεν κατὰ νώτου τῆς παρατάξεως ἔχει, καὶ ἐὰν
ἐν καιρῷ μάχης ὁ οὕτως παρατασσόμενος ἔχῃ πολεμίους κονταράτους, εἰς
150 δυσχερεῖς καὶ τραχεῖς τόπους τὴν παράταξιν ὀφείλει τάσσειν, καὶ τόξοις κεχρη-

125 κούρτων MW τούρκων AVBE 130 παρέξουσι MWVBE παρέξουσιν A
131-132 τῶν...ἀνακοπτομένου MW ἀνακοπτομένου (ἀνακοπτουμένου E) τῶν εἰς πολέμους
ἐξέρχεσθαι προθυμουμένων σαρακηνῶν AVBE 134-135 μᾶλλον...δεισιδαιμονία MW
δεισιδαιμονία μᾶλλον δὲ εἰπεῖν ἀπιστίας AVBE 135 ἐνταῦθα κακὰ Va,Hung. ἐνταῦθα τάχα
M ἐντεῦθεν τάχα WAVBE 137-138 φοσσάτου...ὀχυροῦ MW ὀχυροῦ ἀπλήκτου μὴ
ἀπλικεύσῃς AVBE 138 ἢ καὶ MW ἐὰν AVBE 139 τὸν MW om. AVBE | τράφον MW
σούδαν AVBE 139-140 χάρακος...ἀκριβῶς MW σταβαρῶν AVBE 141-142 ὡς...
ὀλίγοις MW om. AVBE 143 ἄνω που MW ἀνωτέρω AVBE | ἔστι MVBE ἔστιν WA | καὶ²
MW om. AVBE 145 οὐχ MW οὐχὶ AVBE 147 ἐστί MVBE ἐστιν WA

For archery is a great and effective weapon against the peoples of the Saracens and the Kurds, who place their entire hope of victory in their archery.[8]

23. Indeed, against the archers themselves, defenseless at the moment of loosing the arrow, and against the horses of their cavalry, the arrows shot by our army are extremely effective and will cause severe harm to the enemy. When the horses so highly prized by them are destroyed by the continuous archery, the result is that the morale of the Saracens, who had been so eager to ride out to battle, is completely beaten down.

24. For the Saracens do not go on campaign out of servitude and military service but rather for love of gain and freedom or, to put it better, for robbery and for their own faith, rather, superstitious regard for their non-faith. Because of this, when they suffer evil from us, they think God has become their enemy and they cannot bear the injury.

25. When you march out to war, do not set up your camp unless it is strongly fortified, especially if you are near or within enemy territory. Whenever you approach the enemy, dig a ditch and make it more secure with a palisade, fitted together as tightly as possible so it will be a place of refuge from the difficulties in the time of battle.

26. Let me briefly explain some further differences in battle formations for you. One such formation is drawn up in three equal divisions, as we recalled above, that is, middle, right, and left. In the middle division station up to four hundred or five hundred elite troops, according to availability. There is no determined measure for the depth of such a formation. Rather, the cavalrymen in each tagma are drawn up in a first and a second line, with the front of each line equal and in close order. Put the equipment and the baggage train behind, to the rear of the battle line. If, when you are drawn up in formation and combat has begun, you find yourself facing enemy lancers, then you ought to draw up your battle line in difficult and rugged terrain and make use of archery. Because

8. On archery, see SyrMag 44–47 and p. 4, n. 9. The more reliable MSS, MW, have Kurds (Κοῦρτοι), whereas the later A has Turks (Τοῦρκοι). Both were noted for their ferocity and effective archery, and the Byzantines sometimes got them mixed up. See Moravcsik, *Byzantinoturcica*, 2.169; McGeer, *Dragon's Teeth*, 237–238. Basil I returned from his victorious Eastern campaign of 876–877 with many Kurdish and Saracen captives: Skylitzes, *Basil.Mak.* 13.

σθαι, ἵνα τῇ δυσκολίᾳ τῶν τόπων, διεσπασμένων αὐτῶν, οὐκ εὐλύτως καὶ εὐκόλως αἱ ὁρμαὶ τῶν κονταρίων κατ᾽ αὐτῶν γίνωνται.

27. Καὶ ἐὰν ὁρᾷ ὁ στρατηγὸς ὅτι πρὸς ἔθνος ἔχῃ θερμόψυχον, ὀφείλει οὐ
μόνον πρὸ τῆς ἡμέρας τοῦ πολέμου τὰς ὑπερθέσεις καὶ ἀναβολὰς ποιεῖσθαι τῆς
155 μάχης, ἐὰν μάλιστα γνῷ ὅτι ἕτοιμοί εἰσι καὶ ἀξιόμαχοι οἱ ἐναντίοι, δηλονότι ἐν
δυσβάτοις τόποις ἀφόβως ἀπλικεύων, ἀλλὰ καὶ κατ᾽ αὐτὴν τὴν ἡμέραν τῆς
μάχης ἐν καιρῷ μάλιστα θέρους καὶ περὶ τὴν θερμοτέραν ὥραν τῆς δείλης τότε
τὰς συμβολὰς ποιείτω, ἵνα τῇ τοῦ ἡλίου ζέσει καὶ τῷ τοῦ καιροῦ παρασυρμῷ τὸ
θρασὺ καὶ θυμῶδες τῶν ἀντιταττομένων αὐτῷ παύσηται.

160     28. Ταύτην δὲ τὴν τάξιν, ἣν προδιεγράψαμεν, ἀντιτάττεται ἁρμοδίως πεζικὴ
τάξις ἐπιμελῶς συντεταγμένη καὶ τόπος ὁμαλὸς καὶ γυμνὸς διὰ τὰς τῶν κοντα-
ρίων ὁρμάς, καὶ ἡ κατὰ χεῖρα καὶ ταχέως | συμπλοκὴ χωρὶς ἀναβολῆς, διὰ τὸ   350ᵛ
ἀχρείους ἐκ τοῦ ἐγγὺς τὰς βολὰς τῶν σαγιττῶν γίνεσθαι, καὶ μὴ ἔχειν τοὺς
τοξότας κοντάρια ἢ σκουτάρια.

165     29. Ἐὰν δὲ ἐν τῇ συμπλοκῇ τῆς μάχης καὶ ὤθησις πρὸς αὐτοὺς γένηται, καὶ
πρὸς σύντομον φυγὴν ὁρμήσωσι, βλαβήσονται μεγάλα, ἐὰν μὴ γινώσκωσι τὰς
αἰφνιδίους ὑποστροφὰς κατὰ τῶν ἐπερχομένων αὐτοῖς.

30. Ἀλλὰ καὶ ἐπελεύσεις καὶ κυκλώσεις διὰ τῶν ὑπερκεραστῶν κατὰ τῶν
πλαγίων καὶ τοῦ νώτου τῆς παρατάξεως αὐτῶν γινόμεναι βλάψουσι τὰ μέγιστα
170 αὐτούς, εἰ μὴ ἄρα ἔχωσιν ἐν τῇ παρατάξει πλαγιοφύλακας ἀξίους μεγάλῃ
ἐπελεύσει ἀντικαταστῆναι.

31. Διὰ τοῦτο οὖν, ὡς εἴρηται, χρὴ ἐν ταῖς τοιαύταις μάχαις καὶ παρατάξεσι
τόπους ὁμαλοὺς καὶ ἀνακειμένους καὶ ἴσους ἐπιλέγεσθαι, μὴ ἔχοντας τέλματα ἢ
ὀρύγματα ἢ θάμνους, ἵνα μὴ διασπᾶται ἡ τάξις.

175     32. Ἐμπαρασκεύου δὲ καὶ ἑτοίμου ὄντος καὶ παρατεταγμένου τοῦ στρατοῦ,
μὴ ὑπερτίθεσθαι τὴν συμβολήν, ἐὰν ἄρα καὶ δόξῃ μάχην συγκροῦσαι δημοσίως
κατὰ τὴν ἡμέραν τοῦ πολέμου.

33. Τὰς δὲ συμβολὰς ἤτοι προσκρούσεις ἐν ταῖς μάχαις, πρὸς τὸ μέτρον τῆς
σαγίττας, ἴσας καὶ πυκνὰς κατὰ λόγον καὶ συντόμους δεῖ ποιεῖσθαι, ἵνα μὴ τῇ

---

151 δυσκολίᾳ MW δυσχερείᾳ AVBE    155 εἰσι MVBE εἰσιν WA    160 ταύτην…
ἀντιτάττεται MW ταύτῃ δὲ τῇ τάξει ἀντιτάσσεται AVBE    162 χωρὶς MW χωρὶς ὑπερθέσεως
καὶ AVBE    166 ὁρμήσωσι MVBE ὁρμήσουσιν W ὁρμήσωσιν A    169 βλάψουσι MAVBE
βλάψουσιν W    170 ἔχωσιν MW ἔχουσιν AVBE    171 ἐπελεύσει MW ἐπιδρομῇ AVBE
172 παρατάξεσι MAVBE παρατάξεσιν W    173 τέλματα MW πάλματα AVBE
175 ἐμπαρασκεύου…ἑτοίμου MW ἑτοίμου δὲ AVBE    176–177 συγκροῦσαι…πολέμου
MW συμβαλεῖν δημοσίαν AVBE

of the difficult terrain the lancers will be widely scattered about and it will not be feasible or easy for them to charge with their spears against your line.

27. If the general should see that he has to face a very warlike people, then, before the day of battle, he ought to postpone and delay combat, setting up camp without fear in places difficult of access, especially if he knows that the enemy are prepared and set for battle. Then, on the very day of battle, especially in summer and around the hottest hour of the afternoon, let him initiate hostilities. The heat of the sun and the heaviness of the season will put an end to the boldness and high spirits of his opponents.

28. This formation, which we have previously described, is effectively opposed by an infantry formation carefully drawn up in line, as well as by level and open terrain for the charge of the lancers, also by hand-to-hand fighting and coming to blows swiftly without delay, because shooting arrows in such close quarters achieves nothing, and the archers do not have spears or shields.

29. If the battle is at close quarters and they are forced back and rush into immediate flight, they will suffer the greatest harm if they do not know how to turn back suddenly against their pursuers.

30. Direct attacks and encirclements by the outflankers against the flanks and the rear of their battle line cause them the greatest harm, unless they have flank guards in that line capable of standing up against a very strong attack.

31. For this reason, therefore, as mentioned, to prevent the formation from being scattered about, it is necessary for battle formations of this sort to choose level, flat, even ground where there are no marshes, ditches, or bushes.

32. When the army is all drawn up in formation, well prepared and ready, on the day of battle, do not defer the engagement, if clashing in pitched battle seems to be the correct decision.

33. It is necessary to regulate the engagements or clashing together in battle in proportion to the pressure exerted by the arrows. Are they steady, thick, and

180 βραδύτητι τῆς συμπλοκῆς διὰ τῆς συνεχοῦς τοξείας τῶν ἐναντίων πλείονα τὰ
βέλη καὶ τοῖς στρατιώταις καὶ τοῖς ἵπποις ἐμπέωσιν.

34. Ἐὰν δέ τις ἀνάγκη γένηται, ἵνα ἐν δυσχερεστέρῳ τόπῳ ἡ μάχη γένηται,
καλόν ἐστι τοὺς μὲν ἐν πεζικῇ τάξει καταστῆσαι, τοὺς δὲ ἐπὶ τῶν ἵππων, καὶ μὴ
τὴν πᾶσαν παράταξιν ἐν τοιούτοις ἀνωμάλοις τόποις καβαλλαρίους μόνον
185 ποιοῦντα παρατάσσειν.

35. Αἱ γὰρ τῶν κονταράτων ἐγχειρήσεις κατὰ τῶν τοξοτῶν, ὡς εἴπομεν, ἐὰν
μὴ ἴσοι καὶ ἀδιάσπαστοι ὦσιν, βλάβην πολλὴν ἐκ τῶν σαγιττῶν ὑφίστανται, καὶ
πρὸς τὴν συμβολὴν ἀνακόπτονται. διὸ καὶ ὁμαλωτέρου δέονται τόπου ἐν ταῖς
μάχαις οἱ κονταρίοις χρώμενοι.

190 36. Ἐὰν δὲ κατανοήσῃ ὁ στρατηγὸς ὅτι οὔκ ἐστιν ἀξιόμαχος ὁ στρατὸς
αὐτοῦ πρὸς τοὺς ἐναντίους, οὐ δεῖ αὐτὸν μάχεσθαι πολέμοις δημοσίοις, ἀλλὰ
ἐφόδοις, ἤγουν ἐπελεύσεσι, καὶ κλοπαῖς κατὰ τῶν ἐχθρῶν κεχρῆσθαι ἀσφαλῶς
καὶ εὐσχημόνως διὰ τόπων ἐπιτηδείων εἰς τὸ μὴ δηλοῦσθαι ἢ τοῖς ἐναντίοις ἢ
τοῖς ἰδίοις τὸν σκοπόν, δι’ ὃν γίνεται ἡ ὑπέρθεσις τῆς δημοσίας μάχης, ἵνα μὴ ἐκ
195 τούτου τοῖς μὲν πολεμίοις αὐτοῦ θάρσος, τῷ δὲ λαῷ αὐτοῦ δειλία γένηται.

37. Τὰς δὲ ἐξελίξεις ἤγουν τὰς ἐπιστροφὰς καὶ ἀναστροφὰς ἐν ταῖς ὑποχωρήσεσι μὴ δι’ ὄψεως ποιεῖσθαι τῶν ἐναντίων, ἀλλὰ διὰ τῶν πλαγίων αὐτῶν ἀνα-
στρέφειν, καὶ τοὺς νώτους | αὐτῶν ἀπολαμβάνειν. τινὰ γὰρ τῶν ἐθνῶν, οἷα καὶ  351
τὰ τῶν Περσῶν, ποτὲ μὴ βουλόμενα διαλύειν τὴν τάξιν αὐτῶν, εὐκόλως τοὺς
200 νώτους αὐτῶν προδίδωσι τοῖς κατ’ αὐτῶν ὑποστρέφουσιν οἱονεὶ φυγομαχοῦντες, ἀλλὰ καὶ οἱ ὑποχωροῦντες καὶ ὑποφεύγοντες αὐτούς, εἰ βουληθῶσιν
ἀντιστρεφόμενοι εἰς ὄψιν τῶν διωκόντων αὐτοὺς ἐλθεῖν, βλάπτονται συντεταγμένοις αὐτοῖς περιπίπτοντες.

183 ἐστι MVBE ἐστιν WA | καταστῆσαι MW καταστῆναι AV καταστήσασθαι BE
184 ἀνωμάλοις MW ὁμαλοῖς AVBE    187 ἴσοι…ἀδιάσπαστοι MW ἴσαι καὶ ἀδιάσπατοι
AVBE    188 ἀνακόπτονται AVBE ἀνακόπτωνται MW    189 οἱ MW μὴ AVBE
190–191 ἀξιόμαχος…αὐτοῦ MW ὁ στρατὸς αὐτοῦ ἱκανὸς AVBE    191 μάχεσθαι…
δημοσίοις MW πολέμοις δημοσίοις συμπλέκεσθαι AVBE    192 κεχρῆσθαι MW χρῆσθαι
AVBE    193 καὶ εὐσχημόνως MW om. AVBE    194 μάχης AVBE om. MW    195 αὐτοῦ¹
MWA om. VBE    196–197 ὑποχωρήσεσι MVBE ὑποχωρήσεσιν WA    197 ποιεῖσθαι MW
ποιεῖσθαι    παρὰ    AVBE    200 προδίδωσι Μ    προδίδωσιν W    προδίδουσι AVBE
200–201 φυγομαχοῦντες MW φυγομαχοῦντα AVBE    202 ὄψιν MW πρόσωπον AVBE

rapid? Otherwise, the slow pace of the engagement and the constant archery of the enemy may cause a greater number of arrows to fall upon the soldiers and the horses.

34. If, for compelling reasons, the battle occurs in a fairly difficult location, it is well to station some men in infantry formation and others on horses. In such uneven terrain do not draw up the entire battle line with cavalry only.

35. The assaults of lancers against archers, as we have said, unless they are evenly lined up and not dispersed, will sustain great damage from the arrows, and they will be stopped short of contact in battle, for those who use spears require more level ground in combat.

36. But if the general becomes aware that his army is not ready for combat against his adversaries, he must not engage the enemy in a pitched battle. He should, rather, make use of ambushes, raids, and surprise attacks against the enemy. He should do this in a safe and respectable manner on favorable terrain so as not to reveal, either to the enemy or to his own men, his reason for postponing open battle. That would only make the enemy bolder and his own troops more cowardly.

37. Wheeling or turning about or reversing direction should not be made before the enemy's front but to turn back their flanks and to take their rear. Some peoples, such as the Persians, unwilling to break up their formation, sometimes readily exposed their rear to forces wheeling around against them as though fighting in flight. However, if the forces withdrawing and pretending to flee before them should want to turn about and attack the front lines of their pursuers, they will be hurt on running into their well-ordered lines.

452    Constitution 18

38. Τὰ μὲν γὰρ τῶν ἐθνῶν, οἷον οἱ Τοῦρκοι, ἐν ταῖς διώξεσιν ἀτάκτως ἐπιτί-
205 θενται τοῖς διωκομένοις, ὅθεν καὶ εὐχερέστερον βλάπτονται παρὰ τῶν διωκομένων εὐτάκτως ὑποχωρούντων καὶ ὑποστρεφόντων.

39. Τὰ δὲ πράως καὶ συντεταγμένως διώκουσι, διὸ οὐδὲ χρὴ τοὺς ἀναστρέ-
φοντας κατ' αὐτῶν δι' ὄψεως ἐπιτηδεύειν ἔρχεσθαι, ἀλλὰ καὶ διὰ τῶν πλαγίων
καὶ κατὰ τοῦ νώτου αὐτῶν ποιεῖσθαι τὴν ἐπέλευσιν, ὥς μοι εἴρηται.

210 40. Ἐπεὶ δὲ Τούρκων ἐμνήσθην, οὐκ ἀδόκιμον κρίνομεν καὶ ὅπως αὐτοὶ
παρατάττωνται καὶ ὅπως αὐτοῖς ἀντιπαρατάξασθαι, δέον διασαφῆσαι διὰ
μετρίας πείρας ἀναμαθόντες, ὅτε συμμάχοις αὐτοῖς ἐχρησάμεθα, Βουλγάρων
τὰς εἰρηνικὰς παραβεβηκότων σπονδάς, καὶ τὰ τῆς Θράκης χωρία καταδραμόν-
των, οἷς ἡ δίκη ἐπεξελθοῦσα τῆς εἰς Χριστὸν τὸν Θεὸν παρορκίας, τῶν ὅλων
215 τὸν βασιλέα, τάχος ἔφθασαν ἐπιθεῖναι τὴν τιμωρίαν· καὶ γὰρ τῶν ἡμετέρων
δυνάμεων κατὰ Σαρακηνῶν ἀσχολουμένων Τούρκους ἡ θεία πρόνοια ἀντὶ
Ῥωμαίων κατὰ Βουλγάρων ἐστράτευσε, πλοΐμου στόλου τῆς ἡμῶν βασιλείας
τὸν Ἴστρον αὐτοὺς διαπεράσαντός τε καὶ συμμαχήσαντος, καὶ τὸν κακῶς κατὰ
Χριστιανῶν ὁπλισθέντα Βουλγάρων στρατὸν τρισὶ μάχαις κατὰ κράτος νενικη-
220 κότας, ὡσανεὶ δημίους ἐξαποστείλασα κατ' αὐτῶν, ἵνα μὴ ἑκόντες Ῥωμαῖοι
Χριστιανοὶ Χριστιανῶν Βουλγάρων αἵμασι χραίνοιντο.

41. Τὰ Σκυθικὰ τοίνυν ἔθνη μιᾶς εἰσιν, ὡς εἰπεῖν, ἀναστροφῆς τε καὶ τάξεως,
πολύαρχά τε καὶ ἀπράγμονα, νομαδικῶς ὡς ἐπίπαν βιοῦντα. μόνα δὲ τὰ τῶν
Βουλγάρων, προσέτι δὲ καὶ τὰ τῶν Τούρκων, τῆς ὁμοίας φροντίζουσι τάξεως
225 πολεμικῆς ἰσχυροτέρας τῶν ἄλλων Σκυθικῶν ἐθνῶν τὰς κατὰ σύστασιν μάχας
ποιούμενά τε καὶ μοναρχούμενα.

42. Ἀλλὰ Βουλγάρων τὴν ἐν Χριστῷ εἰρήνην ἀσπαζομένων καὶ κοινωνούν-
των τῆς εἰς αὐτὸν πίστεως Ῥωμαίοις, μετὰ τὴν ἐκ τῆς παρορκίας πεῖραν οὐχ
ἡγούμεθα κατ' αὐτῶν χεῖρας ὁπλίζειν, ἐπὶ τὸ θεῖον ἤδη τὰ κατ' ἐκείνων ἀναρ-

204-359 Strat., 11.2.    210-221 Skylitzes Leon.Phil., 12.

205 εὐχερέστερον MW εὐκόλως AVBE    207 διώκουσι MVBE διώκουσιν WA    208 δι'...
ἐπιτηδεύειν MW εἰς πρόσωπον AVBE    209 κατὰ...νώτου MW ὄπισθεν AVBE | ὥς μοι MW
καθὼς AVBE    210 ἐμνήσθην MW ἐμνήσθημεν AVBE | οὐκ...κρίνομεν MW δέον εἰπεῖν
AVBE    211 αὐτοῖς MW αὐτοῖς χρὴ AVBE | δέον διασαφῆσαι MW om. AVBE
212 ἀναμαθόντες MW τοῦτο μαθόντες AVBE    214 παρορκίας Va,Hung. παροικίας MW
ὕβρεως AVBE    214-215 τῶν...τάχος MW om. AVBE    217 ἐστράτευσε M ἐστράτευσεν
WAVBE    218 διαπεράσαντός τε MW διαπέρασαν τότε AVBE    220 ἐξαποστείλασα
WAVBE ἐξαποστείλας M    221 χραίνοιντο M χραίνωντο W χραίνωνται AVBE    222 εἰσιν
MW ἐστιν AVBE    223 νομαδικῶς...ἐπίπαν MW μοναδικῶς ὡς ἐπὶ τὸ πλεῖστον AVBE
228 παρορκίας MW παροικίας AVBE    229-230 ἀναρτῶντες MW ἀνατιθέντες AVBE

38. When it comes to pursuits, some peoples, such as the Turks, are disorderly in attacking those pursuing them, and so they are very easily harmed by a force pursuing them that withdraws and wheels about in good order.[9]

39. Other peoples carry out pursuits cautiously, maintaining their formation. For this reason, forces turning back against them should be careful not to attack them in front but to make their attacks on the flanks and in the rear, as I have said.

40. Since I have mentioned the Turks, we do not judge it out of place <to describe> how they form up for battle and how one should form up to fight against them. Let us put in writing what we have learned from a certain amount of experience when they were our allies. At that time, the Bulgarians had disregarded the peace treaty and were raiding through the Thracian countryside.[10] Justice pursued them for breaking their oath to Christ our God, the emperor of all, and they quickly met up with their punishment. While our forces were engaged against the Saracens, divine Providence led the Turks, in place of the Romans, to campaign against the Bulgarians. Our Majesty's fleet of ships supported them and ferried them across the Danube. <Providence> sent them out against the army of the Bulgarians that had so wickedly taken up arms against Christians and, as though they were public executioners, they decisively defeated them in three engagements, so that the Christian Romans might not willingly stain themselves with the blood of the Christian Bulgarians.

41. The Scythian nations are one, so to speak, in their manner of life and their organization; they have a multitude of rulers, and they have done nothing of value, living for the most part as nomads.[11] Only the nation of the Bulgarians, and also that of the Turks, give thought to a similar military organization, which makes them stronger than the other Scythian nations as they engage in close combat under one commander.

42. Since the Bulgarians, however, embraced the peace of Christ and share the same faith in him as the Romans, after what they went through as a result of

9. For §§38–73 cf. *Strat.* 11.2. By Turks, Leo means Magyars, who were raiding, and beginning to settle, in a region called Tourkia by the Byzantines, more or less corresponding to modern Hungary. Skylitzes (*Leon.Phil.*, 3) calls them Hungarians, Οὔγγροι.

10. About 894. Skylitzes, *Leon.Phil.*, 12.

11. Scythians: a generic term for the nomadic peoples north of the Black Sea. The *Suda* (Σ 704) calls them Russian (Ῥῶς).

230 τῶντες στρατηγήματα, δι' ὅπερ οὔτε τὴν αὐτῶν καθ' ἡμῶν παράταξιν, οὔτε τὴν
ἡ|μετέραν κατ' ἐκείνων, ἅτε διὰ τῆς μιᾶς πίστεως ἀδελφῶν ὑπαρχόντων καὶ ταῖς  351ᵛ
ἡμετέραις εἴκειν ἐπαγγελλομένων εἰσηγήσεσι, διαγράφειν τέως προθυμούμεθα.

43. Περὶ δὲ τῆς τῶν Τούρκων διαθέσεώς τε καὶ παρατάξεως μικρῷ τῆς
Βουλγάρων ἢ οὐδὲν διαφερούσης ἤδη ἐροῦμεν, ὅτι πολύανδρόν ἐστι καὶ ἐλεύθε-
235 ρον τοῦτο τὸ ἔθνος, μελέτην μόνον ποιούμενον παρὰ τὰς ἄλλας πολυτελείας
καὶ τὴν εὐπορίαν τὸ ἀνδρείως διακεῖσθαι πρὸς τοὺς ἰδίους ἐχθρούς.

44. Τοῦτο τοίνυν ὡς μοναρχούμενον, καὶ ἀπηνεῖς καὶ βαρείας τὰς ποινὰς ἐπὶ
τοῖς ἁμαρτανομένοις παρ' αὐτῶν ἐκ τῶν ἀρχόντων αὐτῶν ὑφιστάμενον, οὐκ
ἀγάπῃ ἀλλὰ φόβῳ κεκρατημένον, τοὺς πόνους καὶ μόχθους γενναίως φέρουσι,
240 πρὸς δὲ καύματα καὶ πρὸς ψῦχος ἀντέχονται, καὶ τῆς λοιπῆς τῶν ἀναγκαίων
ἐνδείας νομαδικὸν ὑπάρχον.

45. Περίεργα δέ εἰσι τὰ Τούρκων φῦλα καὶ κρύπτοντα τὴν βουλὴν αὐτῶν,
ἄφιλα δὲ καὶ ἄπιστα ὄντα, καὶ διὰ τῆς ἀπληστίας τῶν χρημάτων κρατούμενα
ὅρκου περιφρονοῦσι, μήτε συνθήκας φυλάττοντα μήτε δώροις ἀρκούμενα,
245 ἀλλὰ πρὶν τὸ δοθὲν δέξωνται, ἐπιβουλὴν μελετῶσι, καὶ ἀνατροπὴν τῶν συνθηκῶν.

46. Καὶ τοὺς ἐπιτηδείους καιροὺς δεινῶς στοχάζονται καὶ σπουδάζουσιν οὐ
τοσοῦτον χειρὶ καὶ δυνάμει τοὺς ἐχθροὺς καταπολεμῆσαι, ὅσον δι' ἀπάτης καὶ
αἰφνιδιασμοῦ, καὶ διὰ τῆς τῶν ἀναγκαίων στενώσεως.

250 47. Ὁπλίζονται δὲ σπαθίοις καὶ λωρικίοις καὶ τόξοις καὶ κονταρίοις, ὅθεν ἐν
ταῖς μάχαις διπλοῦν ἄρμα οἱ πλείονες αὐτῶν ἐπιφέρονται, ἐν τοῖς ὤμοις τὰ
κοντάρια ἀναβαστάζοντες, καὶ τὰ τόξα ἐν ταῖς χερσὶ κατέχοντες, καὶ ἀμφοτέ-
ροις κατὰ τὴν ἀπαντῶσαν χρείαν κεχρημένοι, διωκόμενοι δὲ μᾶλλον προτεροῦσι τοῖς τόξοις.

255 48. Οὐκ αὐτοὶ δὲ μόνον ὁπλοφοροῦσιν, ἀλλὰ καὶ οἱ ἵπποι τῶν ἐμφανῶν
σιδήρῳ ἢ κενδούκλῳ τὰ ἔμπροσθεν μέρη σκέπονται.

49. Πολλὴν δὲ μελέτην καὶ ἄσκησιν ποιοῦνται περὶ τὴν ἐπὶ τῶν ἵππων
τοξείαν.

---

**231** ἅτε MW ὡς AVBE    **232** εἴκειν (ἥκειν) ἐπαγγελλομένων MW trsp. AVBE | εἰσηγήσεσι
MVBE εἰσηγήσεσιν WA    **233** scr. mg. περὶ τούρκων W    **233–234** μικρῷ…ἐροῦμεν MW
ἤδη ἐροῦμεν μικρὸν ἢ οὐδὲν τῆς τῶν βουλγάρων διαφερούσης AVBE    **236** τὴν εὐπορίαν
MW εὐπορίας AVBE    **239** φέρουσι M φέρουσιν W φέρει A om. VBE    **240** πρὸς¹ MW om.
AVBE | ἀντέχονται MW ἰσχυρῶς ἀντέχει AVBE    **240–241** τῆς…ὑπάρχον MW πρὸς τὴν
λοιπὴν τῶν ἀναγκαίων ἔνδειαν AVBE    **244** περιφρονοῦσι MVBE περιφρονοῦσιν WA
**245** μελετῶσι MAVBE μελετῶσιν W    **249** στενώσεως MWA στενώσεων VBE
**253–254** προτεροῦσι MW χρῶνται AVBE    **256** κενδούκλῳ MW κεντούκλοις AVBE

breaking their oath, we do not think of taking up arms against them.[12] We now refer any military action against them to God. For the present, therefore, inasmuch as we are brothers because of our one faith and because they promise to yield to our advice, we are not eager to describe either their battle formation against ours or ours against theirs.

43. We will now speak about the disposition of the Turks and their battle formation, which differ from the Bulgarians a little or not at all. The Turks are very numerous and independent. More than on wealth and other forms of extravagance, they focus their attention only on conducting themselves bravely against their own enemies.

44. This nation has a monarchical form of government and is subjected to cruel and oppressive punishments by their rulers for their offenses. They are governed not by love but by fear and they steadfastly bear labors and hardships. They bear up under heat and cold, as well as the further lack of necessities, since they are a nomadic people.

45. The Turkish tribes are meddlesome but keep their plans to themselves. They are hostile and faithless. Possessed by an insatiable desire for riches, they scorn their oaths and do not observe agreements they have made. They are not satisfied by gifts; even before they receive the gift, they are making plans to break their agreement.

46. They cleverly estimate suitable opportunities and they strive to defeat their enemies not so much by brute force as by deceit, surprise attacks, and deprivation of necessities.

47. They are armed with swords, body armor, bows, and lances. Thus, in combat most of them bear double arms, carrying the lances high on their shoulders and holding the bows in their hands. They make use of both as need requires, but when pursued they use their bows to great advantage.

48. Not only do they wear armor themselves, but the horses of their illustrious men are covered in front with iron or quilted material.

49. They devote a great deal of attention and training to archery on horseback.

---

12. The Bulgarian Khan Boris was baptized in 864 and, despite some resistance, was followed by his subjects. See "Bulgaria" in *ODB*.

50. Ἀκολουθεῖ δὲ αὐτοῖς καὶ πλῆθος ἀλόγων, ἱππαρίων καὶ φοραδίων, ἅμα
260 μὲν πρὸς ἀποτροφὴν καὶ γαλακτοποσίαν, ἅμα δὲ καὶ διὰ πλήθους φαντασίαν.

51. Ἀπλικεύουσι δὲ οὐκ ἐν φοσσάτῳ, ὥσπερ οἱ Ῥωμαῖοι, ἀλλὰ μέχρι μὲν τῆς
τοῦ πολέμου ἡμέρας διεσπαρμένοι κατὰ γένη καὶ φυλάς, τοὺς ἵππους βόσκον-
τες διηνεκῶς ἐν θέρει καὶ χειμῶνι, ἐν δὲ καιρῷ πολέμου τοὺς ἀναγκαίους ἵππους
κατέχοντες καὶ πεδικλοῦντες πλησίον τῶν Τουρκικῶν τεντῶν φυλάττουσι μέχρι
265 καιροῦ τῆς παρατάξεως, ὑπὸ νύκτα τῆς παρατάξεως ἀπαρχόμενοι.

52. Τὰς δὲ βίγλας αὐτῶν ἀπὸ μακρόθεν ἀλλεπαλ|λήλους ποιοῦσιν, εἰς τὸ μὴ    352
εὐκόλως αὐτοὺς ὑπομένειν αἰφνιδιασμούς.

53. Ἐν δὲ τῇ μάχῃ οὐχ ὡς οἱ Ῥωμαῖοι παρατάσσουσιν ἐν τρισὶ μέρεσιν, ἀλλ᾽
ἐν διαφόροις μοίραις δρουγγιστὶ συνάπτοντες ἀλλήλαις τὰς μοίρας, μικρὸν ἀπ᾽
270 ἀλλήλων διϊσταμένας, ὥστε μίαν φαίνεσθαι παράταξιν.

54. Ἔχουσι δὲ ἔξω τῆς παρατάξεως δύναμίν τινα ἐκ περισσοῦ, ἣν πρὸς ἔγκρυμμα ἐκπέμπουσι κατὰ τῶν ἀμελῶς ἀντιτασσομένων αὐτοῖς, ἢ καὶ εἰς βοήθειαν τοῦ βαρουμένου μέρους φυλάττουσι. τὸν δὲ τοῦλδον αὐτῶν ὄπισθεν τῆς
παρατάξεως ἔχουσι πλησίον ἢ δεξιᾷ ἢ ἀριστερᾷ τῆς παρατάξεως ὡς ἀπὸ ἑνὸς ἢ
275 δευτέρου μιλίου, ἀφιέντες ἐν αὐτῷ καὶ ὀλίγην παραφυλακήν.

55. Πολλάκις δὲ καὶ συζευγνύντες τοὺς περισσοὺς τῶν ἵππων κατὰ νώτου,
ἤγουν ὄπισθεν τῆς παρατάξεως αὐτῶν, ποιοῦσιν εἰς φυλακὴν αὐτῆς. καὶ τὰ μὲν
βάθη τῶν ἀκιῶν τῆς παρατάξεως, ἤγουν τοὺς στίχους, ἀορίστως ποιοῦσι, διὰ τὸ
παχεῖαν εἶναι τὴν παράταξιν βάθους μᾶλλον φροντίζοντες, καὶ ἴσον ποιοῦσι καὶ
280 πυκνὸν τὸ μέτωπον.

56. Χαίρουσι δὲ μᾶλλον ταῖς ἀπὸ μηκόθεν μάχαις καὶ ἐνέδραις καὶ ταῖς
κυκλώσεσι κατὰ τῶν ἐναντίων καὶ ταῖς ἐσχηματισμέναις ὑποχωρήσεσι καὶ
ἀντιστροφαῖς καὶ ταῖς διεσπασμέναις τάξεσιν.

57. Ὅταν δὲ τρέψωσι τοὺς ἐχθροὺς αὐτῶν, πάντα ἐν δευτέρῳ τιθέασι, καὶ
285 ἀφειδῶς ἐπιτίθενται, οὐδὲν ἕτερον λογιζόμενοι ἢ τὸ διώκειν. οὐκ ἀρκοῦνται
γάρ, ὥσπερ οἱ Ῥωμαῖοι καὶ τὰ ἄλλα ἔθνη, τῇ μετρίᾳ καταδιώξει, καὶ τῇ τῶν

---

259 ἀλόγων MW om. AVBE    261 ἐν MW ἔν τε AVBE    264 τεντῶν MW τενδῶν AVBE |
φυλάττουσι MVBE φυλάττουσιν WA    265 ἀπαρχόμενοι MWVE ἀρχόμενοι AB
266 ἀλλεπαλλήλους MW ἀλλεπαλλήλους καὶ πυκνὰς AVBE    271 ἔχουσι MAVBE ἔχουσιν
W    272 ἐκπέμπουσι MAVBE ἐκπέμπουσιν W    273 φυλάττουσι M φυλάττουσιν WA
φράττουσι VBE | ὄπισθεν MW ὄπισθε AVBE    274 ἔχουσι MVBE ἔχουσιν WA | δεξιᾷ…
ἀριστερᾷ MW trsp. AVBE    275 ἀφιέντες MW καταλιμπάνοντες AVBE    276 καὶ MW om.
AVBE    276–277 κατὰ…ἤγουν MWVBE om. A    281 ἐνέδραις MW ἐγκρύμμασιν AVBE
282 κυκλώσεσι MWVBE κυκλώσεσιν A    284 τιθέασι M τιθέασιν W τίθενται AVBE
286 μετρίᾳ MW συμμέτρῳ AVBE

50. A huge herd of horses, ponies and mares, follows them, to provide both food and milk and, at the same time, to give the impression of a multitude.

51. They do not set up camp within entrenchments, as do the Romans, but up until the day of battle they are spread about according to tribes and clans. They graze their horses continually both summer and winter. When time comes for battle, they take the horses they think necessary, hobble them next to the Turkish tents, and guard them until it is time to form for battle, which they begin to do under cover of night.

52. They station their sentries at a good distance one after another so as not to be easily subjected to surprise attacks.

53. In battle they do not line up as do the Romans in three divisions, but in several units of irregular size, linking the divisions close to one another although separated by short distances, so that they give the impression of one battle line.

54. Apart from their battle line, they maintain an additional force that they send out to ambush careless adversaries of theirs or hold in reserve to support a hard-pressed section. They keep their baggage train behind their battle line, to the right or the left of the line about a mile or two away, detailing a small guard for it.

55. Frequently they tie the extra horses together to the rear, that is, behind their battle line, as protection for it. They make the depth of the files, that is, the rows, of their battle line irregular because they consider it more important that the line should be thick than deep, and they make their front even and dense.

56. They prefer battles fought at long range, ambushes, encircling their adversaries, simulated withdrawals and wheeling about, and scattered formations.

57. When they force their enemies to take to flight, they put everything else aside and are ruthless in their onslaught. They think of nothing else except the pursuit. They are not content, as are the Romans and other nations, with pursu-

χρημάτων ἁρπαγῇ, ἀλλὰ μέχρι τοσούτου ἐπίκεινται, ἕως ἂν τελείως τὴν τῶν ἐχθρῶν κατάλυσιν ποιήσωνται, πάσῃ μεθόδῳ εἰς τοῦτο κεχρημένοι.

58. Ἐὰν δέ τινες τῶν ἐχθρῶν αὐτῶν διωκόμενοι εἰς ὀχύρωμα καταφύγωσι,
290 σπουδάζουσιν ἀκριβῶς κατανοοῦντες τὴν τῶν ἀναγκαίων ἔνδειαν, καὶ τῶν ἵππων καὶ τῶν ἀνδρῶν, καὶ προσκαρτεροῦσιν, ἵνα τῇ στενότητι τούτων χειρώσωνται τοὺς ἐχθροὺς ἢ εἰς τὰ ἀρέσκοντα αὐτοῖς σύμφωνα τούτους ἀγάγωσι. πρῶτον μὲν ἐλαφρότερά τινα ἐπιζητοῦντες καὶ τότε, συντιθεμένων αὐτοῖς τῶν ἐχθρῶν, ἕτερα μείζονα προτιθέασιν.

295 59. Ταῦτα μὲν τὰ τῶν Τούρκων ἤθη τοσούτῳ μόνον διαφέροντα τῶν Βουλγάρων, ὅσῳ τὴν Χριστιανῶν οὗτοι ἀσπασάμενοι πίστιν καὶ τοῖς Ῥωμαϊκοῖς ἐπ᾽ ὀλίγον μετεβάλλοντο ἤθεσι, τότε τὸ ἄγριον καὶ νομαδικὸν τῷ ἀπίστῳ συναποβαλόντες.

60. Ἐναντιοῦται δὲ πολεμίοις Τούρκοις ἔνδεια βοσκῆς διὰ τὸ πλῆθος ὧν
300 ἐπιφέρονται ἀλόγων.

61. Καὶ ἐν καιρῷ δὲ συμβολῆς τάξις πεζικὴ συντεταγμένη μάλιστα αὐτοὺς βλάψει, ὡς ἐναντία αὐτῶν καβαλλαρίων ὄντων καὶ μὴ καταβαινόντων ἀπὸ τῶν ἵππων. | οὐδὲ γὰρ στῆναι πεζῇ καρτεροῦσιν, ὡς συντραφέντες ἐποχεῖσθαι τοῖς    352ᵛ ἵπποις.

305 62. Ἐναντιοῦται δὲ αὐτοῖς καὶ τόπος ὁμαλὸς καὶ γεγυμνωμένος, καὶ δὴ καὶ τάξις καβαλλαρικὴ καὶ πεπυκνωμένη καὶ ἀδιαστάτως αὐτοῖς ἀκολουθοῦσα.

63. Ἐναντιοῦται δὲ καὶ ἐκ χειρὸς συμπλοκὴ μετὰ τῶν ὅπλων, καὶ ἔφοδοι νυκτεριναὶ ἀσφαλῶς γινόμεναι, οἷον ἵνα οἱ προσβαλόντες αὐτοῖς ἓν μὲν ἔχουσι μέρος τεταγμένον, τὸ δὲ ἕτερον μέρος ἐγκρυπτόμενον.

310 64. Λυπεῖ δὲ αὐτοὺς σφόδρα καὶ ὅτ᾽ ἄν τινες ἐξ αὐτῶν προσφύγωσι τοῖς Ῥωμαίοις. γινώσκουσι γὰρ ὅτι ἄστατον ἔχει γνώμην τὸ ἔθνος αὐτῶν, καὶ φιλοκερδεῖς εἰσι, καὶ ἐκ πολλῶν φυλῶν συγκείμενοι, καὶ ὅτι διὰ τοῦτο οὐ ποιοῦνται λόγον συγγενῶν καὶ τῆς εἰς ἀλλήλους ὁμονοίας.

---

288 μεθόδῳ MW μηχανῇ AVBE    290 τῶν¹…ἔνδειαν MW λεῖψιν τῶν ἀναγκαίων AVBE
292 ἀγάγωσι MVBE ἀγάγωσιν WA    294 προτιθέασιν MW προστιθέασιν AVBE
295 μόνον MAVBE μόνῳ W    296 καὶ MW om. AVBE    297–298 συναποβαλόντες MW
συμβαλόντες AVBE    301 συμβολῆς MW συμβολῆς μάλιστα αὐτοὺς βλάψει AVBE
301–302 μάλιστα…βλάψει MW om. AVBE    302 ὡς ἐναντία MW ἐναντία οὖσα AVBE
305 γεγυμνωμένος AVBE γεγυμνασμένος MW | δὴ καὶ MW om. AVBE    306 καὶ² MW om.
AVBE    310 προσφύγωσι MWVBE προσφύγωσιν A    312 εἰσι MVBE εἰσίν WA
313 λόγον MW λόγον ἢ φροντίδα AVBE

ing their foes a reasonable distance and plundering their goods, but the Turks press on without respite until they have brought about the complete destruction of their enemies, employing every means to achieve this.

58. If some of the enemy they are pursuing should take refuge in a fortified place, they make careful efforts to discover any shortage of necessities for horses and men. They wait patiently so they can wear down their enemies by the shortage of those items or get them to accept terms favorable to themselves. Their first demands are fairly light, but then, when the enemy agrees to these, they impose others that are heavier.

59. These characteristics of the Turks are different from those of the Bulgarians only inasmuch as the latter have embraced the faith of the Christians and gradually taken on Roman characteristics. At that time they threw off their savage and nomadic way of life along with their faithlessness.

60. Hostile Turks are greatly hurt by a shortage of pasturage, because of the large number of horses they bring along with them.

61. When it comes to battle, an infantry force in close formation opposed to their cavalry will inflict the greatest damage on them. They do not dismount from their horses and, since they have grown up riding on horseback, they do not last long on foot.[13]

62. They are also at a disadvantage on level, unobstructed ground, as well as when a cavalry force follows along after them in a dense, unbroken mass.

63. Hand-to-hand combat with weapons also hurts them, as do attacks made safely at night, in such a way that one section of our attacking force maintains its formation while the other section remains in hiding.

64. They are also seriously hurt when some of them desert to the Romans. They realize that their nation is fickle and they are avaricious and composed of so many tribes and for this reason they set no value on kinship and unity with one another.

13. Cf. *Strat.* 11.2.19. Ammianus Marcellinus (31.2.6), writing about the Huns, notes a similar characteristic: "Their shoes are formed on no last and so prevent their walking with a free step. For this reason they are not at all adapted to battles on foot."

65. Ὀλίγων δὲ τάχα τοῦ προσφυγεῖν ἀπαρχομένων καὶ φιλοφρονουμένων
315 παρ᾽ ἡμῶν πλῆθος αὐτοῖς ἐπακολουθεῖ· διὸ καὶ βαρέως φέρουσιν ἐπὶ τοῖς ἀπ᾽
αὐτῶν ἀναχωροῦσιν.

66. Ὅτ᾽ ἂν οὖν βουληθῇ τις πρὸς αὐτοὺς ἐγγίσαι πρὸς μάχην, πρό γε πάντων
ἔχειν αὐτὸν δέον τὰς βίγλας ἐπιμελῶς καὶ συνεχεῖς ἀπὸ διαστημάτων ὀλίγων,
εἶτα μεριμνῆσαι καὶ προευτρεπίσαι τὰ εἰς δευτέραν τύχην τυγχάνοντα, ἤγουν
320 μήποτε τροπὴ γένηται τῶν ἀντιπολεμούντων αὐτοῖς, ἵνα καὶ ὀχυρὸν τόπον
κατανοήσῃ ἐν καιρῷ περιστάσεως καὶ δαπάνην ἐφεύρῃ ὀλίγων ἡμερῶν, εἰ μὲν
δυνατόν ἐστι καὶ τῶν ἀλόγων, ἐπεὶ πάντως τῶν ἀνδρῶν, καὶ μάλιστα τὴν τοῦ
ὕδατος εὐπορίαν, εἶτα καὶ τὸν τοῦλδον διαθήσῃ, ὡς ἐν τῷ περὶ αὐτοῦ κεφαλαίῳ
ἡμῖν εἴρηται.

325  67. Καὶ ἐὰν μὲν σύνεστι πεζικὸς στρατός, ἐν τῇ πρώτῃ μάλιστα μάχῃ ἐν ὅσῳ
ὁ στρατὸς ἐν συνηθείᾳ τοῦ ἔθνους γίνεται, ἐκτάξαι αὐτὸν κατὰ τὸν δηλωθέντα
ἡμῖν ἐν ἄλλοις τρόπον, τοῦτ᾽ ἔστιν, ὥστε ἔχειν τοὺς καβαλλαρίους ὑποτεταγ-
μένους τοῖς πεζοῖς.

68. Εἰ δὲ μόνον καβαλλάριοί εἰσιν οἱ ἀντιτασσόμενοι αὐτοῖς, καὶ ἀξιόμαχοι
330 πρὸς τὴν ἐκείνων δύναμιν, κατὰ τὸν λεχθέντα τρόπον καὶ αὐτὸν ἐν τῷ περὶ
τάξεως λόγῳ τάξει αὐτούς.

69. Πλείονας δὲ ἐν τοῖς πλαγίοις ἀφορίσει καὶ χρησίμους· ἐν τῷ νώτῳ γὰρ
αὐτῶν ἀρκοῦσιν οἱ λεγόμενοι διφένσορες καβαλλάριοι, ἤτοι οἱ ἔκδικοι. τοὺς δὲ
κούρσορας, ἤτοι προμάχους, μὴ πλέον τριῶν ἢ τεσσάρων σαγιττοβόλων τῆς
335 παρατάξεως τῶν διφενσόρων ἐν ταῖς διώξεσι χωρίζεσθαι, μηδὲ κατατρέχειν
αὐτῶν. πάντως δὲ καὶ σπουδὴν ποιήσηται ἵνα ἐν γυμνῷ καὶ ἴσῳ τόπῳ κατὰ τὸ
δυνατὸν αὐτῷ τὴν παράταξιν ἐκτάξῃ, ἔνθα μήτε ὗλαι εἰσὶ δασεῖαι μήτε πάλματα
μήτε κοιλάδες ἐνοχλοῦσι, διὰ τὰ παρὰ τῶν Τούρκων ἐπινοούμενα ἐγκρύμματα.

70. Καὶ τὰς βίγλας δὲ ἐκ διαστήματος κατὰ τῶν τεσσάρων μερῶν τῆς παρα-
340 τάξεως ποιήσει.

---

314 προσφυγεῖν MW προσφεύγειν AVBE    315–316 ἐπὶ…ἀναχωροῦσιν MW om. AVBE
317 βουληθῇ…ἐγγίσαι MW τις βουληθῇ προσεγγίσαι αὐτοῖς AVBE | γε MW om. AVBE
319 τυγχάνοντα MW    συντείνοντα AVBE    320 αὐτοῖς MW    αὐτοὺς AVBE
327–328 ὥστε…πεζοῖς MW ἵνα ὦσιν οἱ καβαλλάριοι ὄπισθεν τῶν πεζῶν AVBE
329 μόνον MW μόνοι AVBE    332 ἐν² …νώτῳ MW ὄπισθεν AVBE    336 καὶ¹ MW om.
AVBE | ποιήσηται MW ποιήσεται AVBE    338 μήτε MW μήτε δὲ AVBE | ἐνοχλοῦσι
MAVBE ἐνοχλοῦσιν W    340 ποιήσει MW ποιῆσαι AVBE

65. When a few begin to desert and are kindly received by us, a large number will soon follow them. For that reason they bear a grudge against those who depart from them.

66. Now then, when you wish to advance against them for battle, you must, above all, have frequent watches on the alert and not far apart. Then make your plans and advance preparations in the event of second fortune, that is, in case your forces, fighting against them, should be put to flight. Search for a strong position in the event of an emergency and find provisions for a few days, if possible also for the horses and certainly for the men, especially plenty of water. Then, make arrangements for the baggage train, as we have written in the chapter about it.[14]

67. If an infantry force is present, especially in the first engagement, when the army is becoming accustomed to that nation, draw it up according to the method described by us elsewhere, that is, with the cavalry lined up behind the infantry.[15]

68. If the troops drawn up for combat against them consist only of cavalry who are ready for battle against their forces, line them up in the manner described in the book on formations.[16]

69. Set apart a numerous and capable force on the flanks. To their rear, the cavalry called defenders, or ekdikoi, are sufficient. When in pursuit, the assault troops, or promachoi, should not distance themselves more than three or four bowshots from the battle line of the defenders, and they should not outrun them. A concerted effort should be made to draw up the battle line, as much as possible, in an open and even place, free of thick woods, marshes, or hollows that could serve as cover for ambushes prepared by the Turks.

70. Post scouts at some distance from all four sides of the battle line.

14. See above, Const. 10.
15. See above, Const. 7 §§41–45.
16. Probably *Sylloge tacticorum*. See Const. 19, n. 15.

71. Ἐὰν δὲ ἐνδέχεται, καλόν ἐστιν, ἵνα ἢ δύσβατον ποταμὸν ἢ πάλματα ἢ λίμνην κατὰ νώτου τῆς παρατάξεως ἔχῃ, ἵνα ὁ νῶτος ἀσφαλῶς φυλάττεται. |

72. Καὶ ἐὰν καλῶς τὰ τοῦ πολέμου ἐξέλθῃ, μήτε κατατρέχειν αὐτῶν ἀπλή- 353 στως μήτε ἀμελῶς διακεῖσθαι. οὐδὲ γάρ, ὡς τὰ λοιπὰ ἔθνη, τὴν πρώτην ἡττώ-
345 μενα μάχην ἀπολήγουσι τοῦ πολέμου, ἀλλὰ μέχρις ἂν κατὰ κράτος ταπεινωθῶ-
σιν, ἐπιτηδεύουσι διὰ πολλῶν τρόπων κατὰ τῶν ἐχθρῶν αὐτῶν ἐγχειρεῖν. ἐὰν δὲ σύμμικτός ἐστιν ἡ τάξις, καὶ πλείους εἰσὶν οἱ πεζοί, δέον πρόνοιαν ἐν τοῖς τοιούτοις ποιεῖσθαι τῆς ἀποτροφῆς τῶν ἀλόγων. οὐ γὰρ πάντως συγχωροῦνται οἱ καβαλλάριοι ἐγγιζόντων τῶν ἐχθρῶν χορτάσματα τῶν ἀλόγων συνάγειν.
350 73. Αὕτη τοίνυν ἡ πολεμική τε καὶ συνήθης τῶν Τούρκων συνάσκησις διαφέρει τῆς τῶν Βουλγάρων, ὡς εἴρηται, κατά τινα μικρά, τὰ δ' ἄλλα ἐξωμοίω-
ται. ἡμεῖς δὲ τούτου ἕνεκέν σοι ταύτην ὑπεγράψαμεν, οὐχ ὡς Τούρκοις παρα-
τάσσεσθαι μέλλοντι, οὔτε γὰρ γείτονές εἰσιν οὔτε μὴν πολέμιοι νῦν, ἀλλὰ καὶ μᾶλλον ὑπήκοοι Ῥωμαίοις σπουδάζουσιν ἀναδείκνυσθαι, ἀλλ' ἵνα ἔχοις, ὦ
355 στρατηγέ, εἰδέναι τὰ ἕκαστα τῶν διαφόρων παρατάξεων καὶ στρατηγημάτων, καὶ ἐν καιρῷ τῷ προσήκοντι χρῆσθαι αὐτοῖς συντόμως πρὸς ὅ τι ἂν βουληθῇς, καὶ δοκιμάσῃς τὸ χρήσιμον τοῖς ἐκ πολλῆς γυμνασίας παρά τισιν ἐφευρισκο-
μένοις στρατηγήμασί τε καὶ παρατάξεσιν ἢ ὅτε καιρὸς ἀπαιτῇ, καὶ ἀντιστρατεύ-
εσθαι πρὸς αὐτὰ τὸ ἐναντίον διὰ τῆς μελέτης προησκημένος καὶ γυμνασάμενος.
360 74. Εἰσὶ δέ τινα τῶν ἐθνῶν, οἷον Φράγγοι καὶ Λογγίβαρδοι, πάλαι μὲν ἀσεβείᾳ κρατούμενα, νῦν δὲ τὴν ἀληθῆ τῶν Χριστιανῶν πίστιν ἀσπαζόμενα, ὧν τὰ μὲν φίλια, τὰ δὲ ὑπήκοα τῇ ἡμῶν ἐκ Θεοῦ βασιλείᾳ τυγχάνουσι. καὶ τούτοις δέ εἰσι πολεμικὰ ἰδιώματα, τὰ μὲν ἐκ παραδόσεως, τὰ δὲ καὶ αὐτῇ τῇ συνηθείᾳ

---

360–440 *Strat.*, 11.3.

---

342 κατὰ νώτου MW ὄπισθεν AVBE | ἔχῃ MW ἔχειν AVBE | ὁ νῶτος MW τὰ ὄπισθεν μέρη AVBE | φυλάττεται MW φυλάττηται AVBE 343 ἐξέλθῃ MW ἀποβῇ AVBE 345 ἀπολήγουσι MW ἀποπαύουσι AVBE 347 πλείους MW πλείονες AVBE 348 πάντως συγχωροῦνται MW trsp. AVBE 349 ἐγγιζόντων MW πλησιαζόντων AVBE 350 τοίνυν MW om. AVBE | τε MW om. AVBE | συνάσκησις MW γυμνασία AVBE 351 τῶν AVBE om. MW 351–352 κατά…ἐξωμοίωται MW τὰ δὲ ἄλλα ὅμοια εἰσιν AVBE 352–353 παρατάσσεσθαι μέλλοντι MW trsp. AVBE 353 οὔτε¹ MW οὐδὲ AVBE | οὔτε μὴν MW οὐδὲ AVBE 354 ἀναδείκνυσθαι MW εἶναι AVBE 354–356 ἔχοις…τι MW γινώσκῃς ἑκάστου ἔθνους παράταξιν καὶ στρατηγήματα καὶ ἐν τῷ προσήκοντι καιρῷ πολλάκις ἐπιτηδεύειν αὐτὰ πρὸς ὄνπερ AVBE 357–358 τοῖς…ἀπαιτῇ MW ἢ AVBE 359 τὸ… γυμνασάμενος MW ὅτε καιρὸς ἀπαιτεῖ διὰ τῆς μελέτης ταῦτα προγυμνασάμενος AVBE 360 λογγίβαρδοι MW λαγόβαρδοι AVBE 362 ἡμῶν…θεοῦ MW trsp. AVBE | τυγχάνουσι MVBE τυγχάνουσιν WA 363 εἰσὶ MAVBE εἰσιν W | τῇ MW τῇ αὐτῶν AVBE

71. If it can be done, it is good to have a river that is difficult to ford or marshes or a lake behind the battle line so that the rear is securely protected.

72. If the battle turns out well, do not be too hasty in racing after the enemy or behave carelessly. For, unlike other nations, this one does not give up the struggle when worsted in the first battle but, until they are completely beaten down, they try all sorts of ways to assault their enemies. If the formation is mixed, consisting mostly of infantry, you must still be concerned about finding forage for the horses. For when the enemy are getting close, by no means are the cavalry allowed to send out foraging parties.

73. Therefore, these military practices and characteristics of the Turks differ from those of the Bulgarians, as mentioned, in only a few particulars but are similar in others. We have given you this outline, O general, not because you are preparing to face the Turks in battle, for they are neither neighbors nor enemies to us at present, but instead they are eager to show themselves as subjects of the Romans. Still, O general, you should have a good knowledge of each one of the various formations and military practices and, at the proper time, make use of them without delay against anyone you wish. Experiment with what has been useful among those stratagems and battle formations that a great deal of experience has led some individuals to discover. Then, as the situation requires, after carefully practicing the drills and exercises, take the proper military measures to counter theirs.

74. There are some nations, such as the Franks and the Lombards, who had formerly been bound by impiety, but have now embraced the true faith of the Christians.[17] Some are friendly while others are subject to Our God-given Majesty. They have distinctive military practices, some of which are traditional

17. Sections 74–92 derive from *Strat.* 11.3. Franks was a general name for Western Europeans; Lombards meant those in the various principalities of southern Italy, nominally under Byzantine rule.

σύμφωνα, ἅπερ παραθήσομέν σοι, ὦ στρατηγέ, οὐ χάριν τῆς αὐτῶν ἐκστρατείας
365 —πῶς γὰρ τῶν εἰρηνευόντων καὶ συμμάχων καὶ ὁμοθρήσκων καὶ ὑπηκόων;—
ἀλλὰ ἵνα καὶ ἐκ τῶν τοιούτων ἐθίμων καὶ συστάσεων, καὶ εἴ γε δεῖ, καὶ ἐκ τῶν
τοιούτοις ἐναντίων, εἴ τί σοι δόξῃ χρήσιμον ἀναλεξάμενος καὶ ζηλώσῃς καὶ ἔχῃς
ἐν καιρῷ τῷ προσήκοντι γεγυμνασμένον κατὰ τῶν ὁποιωνδήποτέ σοι ἀντιπαραταττομένων πολεμίων.

370   75. Καὶ γὰρ καὶ Σκλάβοι ἦσάν ποτε, ὅτε πέραν κατῴκουν τοῦ Ἴστρου, ὃν καὶ
Δανούβιον καλοῦμεν, οἷς καὶ προσεπολέμουν Ῥωμαῖοι ἐπιτιθέμενοι, νομαδικῶς
καὶ αὐτῶν τότε διαζώντων, πρὶν ἢ περαιωθῆναι τὸν Ἴστρον καὶ ὑπὸ τὸν ζυγὸν
τῆς Ῥωμαϊκῆς ἐξουσίας τὸν ἑαυτῶν αὐχένα ὑποκλῖναι. οὐδὲ τούτῳ δὲ τὰ ἔθιμα
πρὸς τὰς μάχας καὶ τὴν ἄλλην συνήθειαν ἄγνωστά σοι καταλείψω, ἀλλ᾽ ὥσπερ
375 μοι εἴρηται, πάντα συλλέξας διαγράψω, καθ᾽ ὅσον ἡ ἡμῖν δύναμις ἐγχωρεῖ, ἵνα
πανταχόθεν μελίττης δίκην ἐρανίζῃ καὶ συλλέγῃς τὰ χρήσιμα.

76. Φράγγοι τοίνυν καὶ Λογγίβαρδοι λόγον ἐλευθερίας περὶ πολλοῦ ποιοῦνται. ἀλλ᾽ οἱ μὲν Λογγίβαρδοι τὸ πλέον τῆς τοιαύτης ἀρετῆς νῦν ἀπώλεσαν,
πλὴν καὶ οὗτοι καὶ Φράγγοι καὶ μάλιστα θρασεῖς | ἦσαν καὶ ἀκατάπληκτοι, ἐν   353ᵛ
380 τοῖς πολέμοις τολμηροί τε καὶ προπετεῖς, εἰς ὄνειδος ἔχοντες τὴν δειλίαν καὶ
τὴν πρὸς μικρὸν ἀναχώρησιν καὶ ταύτην οἱονεὶ φυγὴν ἡγούμενοι. εὐκόλως δὲ
διὰ τοῦτο θανάτου καταφρονοῦσι τὴν κατὰ χεῖρα μάχην σφοδρῶς καὶ καβαλλάριοι καὶ πεζοὶ μαχόμενοι.

77. Ὅτ᾽ ἂν γάρ, ὡς εἰκός, ἐν ταῖς καβαλλαρικαῖς μάχαις στενωθῶσιν, ἐξ ἑνὸς
385 συνθήματος ἀποκαταβαίνουσι τῶν ἵππων αὐτῶν καὶ πεζῇ παρατάσσονται,
ὀλίγοι τάχα καὶ πρὸς πλείονας καβαλλαρίους μὴ δειλιῶντες ἢ ἀπολέγονται τῆς
μάχης.

---

**364–365** τῆς...ἐκστρατείας MW τοῦ κατ᾽ αὐτῶν ἐκστρατεῦσαι AVBE   **365** ὁμοθρήσκων
MW ὁμοπίστων AVBE   **365–366** ἀλλὰ MW ἀλλ᾽ AVBE   **366–367** ἐθίμων...ἐναντίων
MW om. AVBE   **367** καὶ¹...καὶ² MW om. AVBE   **368** ὁποιωνδήποτέ MW om. AVBE
**368–369** σοι ἀντιπαραταττομένων MW trsp. AVBE   **370** ἦσάν MW om. AVBE | ὅτε MW
om. AVBE   **372** καὶ¹...διαζώντων MW διαζῶσιν AVBE | ἢ περαιωθῆναι MW περάσαι
AVBE   **372–373** ὑπὸ...ὑποκλῖναι MW ὑποταγῆναι ῥωμαίοις AVBE   **375** ἢ AVBE om.
MW   **376** μελίττης MW μελίσσης AVBE | ἐρανίζῃ...συλλέγῃς MW συνάγῃς AVBE
**377** λογγίβαρδοι MW λαγόβαρδοι AVBE | λόγον MW φροντίδα πολλὴν τῆς AVBE | περὶ
πολλοῦ MW om. AVBE   **378** λογγίβαρδοι MW λαγόβαρδοι AVBE   **379** καὶ³ MW om.
AVBE   **382** καταφρονοῦσι MAB καταφρονοῦσιν WVE | κατὰ χεῖρα MW ἀπὸ χειρῶν AVBE
**384** ὡς εἰκός MW om. AVBE   **386–387** ἀπολέγονται...μάχης MW ἀπαγορεύοντες τὴν
μάχην AVBE

among them, while others derive from actual usage. We are transmitting these to you, O general, not because of a military campaign against them—for how <could this be> when they are at peace and are allies, coreligionists, and subjects?—but in order that, from their usages and organization and, if necessary, from their adversaries, you may select whatever might seem useful to you and emulate them. And, when the time comes, you will be well practiced <in facing> absolutely any kind of enemy drawn up in formation against you.

75. Formerly there were the Slavs. When they dwelt across the Ister, which we call the Danube, the Romans attacked them and made war against them. They were then living as nomads, that is, before they crossed the Ister and bent their necks under the yoke of Roman authority. But I will not leave you ignorant of their usual methods in combat and of their other customs. Indeed, as I said, I will gather and explain everything to you, to the best of my ability, so that, like the bee, you may bring together from all sides and collect what is useful.

76. The Franks and the Lombards place great value on freedom. But the Lombards have now lost most of such virtue, although they and the Franks were particularly bold and undaunted, daring and impetuous in battle, regarding any timidity and even a short retreat as a disgrace, considering it just like a rout. For this reason they calmly despise death as they fight violently in hand-to-hand combat either on horseback or on foot.

77. Now, in the event that they are hard pressed in cavalry actions, they dismount from their horses at a single prearranged signal and line up on foot. Although few in number against many horsemen they show no fear and do not shrink from battle.

78. Ὁπλίζονται δὲ σκουταρίοις καὶ κονταρίοις καὶ σπαθίοις κοντοτέροις, ἃ καὶ ἐπὶ τῶν ὤμων αὐτῶν διὰ λωρίων ἀναβαστάζουσιν. ἐνίοτε δέ τινες αὐτῶν καὶ
390 διαζώννυνται αὐτά.

79. Χαίρουσι δὲ μᾶλλον τῇ πεζομαχίᾳ καὶ ταῖς μετ' ἐλασίας καταδρομαῖς. τάσσονται δὲ ἐν ταῖς μάχαις εἴτε πεζοὶ εἴτε καβαλλάριοι οὐκ ἐν μέτρῳ τινὶ ὡρισμένῳ καὶ ἐν τάξει ἢ ἐν μοίραις ἢ ἐν μέρεσι, καθάπερ Ῥωμαῖοι, ἀλλὰ κατὰ φυλὰς καὶ τῇ πρὸς ἀλλήλους συγγενείᾳ τε καὶ προσπαθείᾳ, πολλάκις δὲ καὶ
395 συνωμοσίᾳ. ὅθεν καὶ ἐν καιρῷ περιστάσεως φίλων ἐναπολειφθέντων συνεκινδύνευσαν αὐτοῖς πολλάκις ἐν τῇ μάχῃ τούτους ἐκδικήσαντες.

80. Ἴσον δὲ τὸ μέτωπον τῆς παρατάξεως αὐτῶν ποιοῦνται καὶ πυκνὸν ἐν ταῖς μάχαις.

81. Τὰς δὲ συμβολάς, εἴτε καβαλλάριοι εἴτε πεζοί, σφοδρῶς καὶ ἀκατασχέ-
400 τως ποιοῦσιν, ὡς μονότονοι καὶ πάσης δειλίας ἀπεχόμενοι.

82. Ἀπειθεῖς δέ εἰσι πρὸς τοὺς ἄρχοντας αὐτῶν, καὶ μάλιστα Φράγγοι, ἐλευθερίας ὥσπερ ἀντιποιούμενοι, καὶ ἑκουσίως ἐφ' ὅσον καιρὸν ὁρίσωσιν ἢ παρὰ τῶν ἀρχόντων ὁρισθῶσιν ἐκστρατεύουσι καὶ μόνον, καὶ τούτου παρερχομένου, εἰ τύχοι αὐτοὺς ἐπιμένειν, βαρέως φέροντες τὸν παρασυρμὸν τοῦ χρόνου,
405 λύουσι τὴν σύνταξιν τοῦ ἐξπεδίτου καὶ ἀναχωροῦσιν ἐπὶ τοὺς οἴκους αὐτῶν.

83. Ἀπράγμονες δέ εἰσι καὶ πάσης ποικιλίας καὶ ἀσφαλείας ἐκτὸς καὶ τῆς τοῦ συμφέροντος γνώμης. διὸ καὶ τάξεως περιφρονοῦσι καὶ μάλιστα τῆς καβαλλαρικῆς.

84. Ὑποφθείρονται δὲ διὰ χρημάτων εὐκόλως, φιλοκερδεῖς ὄντες, ἐξ ὧν
410 πείρᾳ μαθόντες, ἴσμεν ἀπὸ τῶν ἐξ Ἰταλίας ἐνταῦθα πολλάκις παραγενομένων ἐπί τισι διοικήσεσιν, ὡς τῇ ἐκείνων ἐπιμιξίᾳ, οἶμαι, καὶ τούτων βαρβαρωθέντων τε καὶ συνεθισθέντων.

85. Λυπεῖ δὲ αὐτοὺς κακοπάθεια καὶ συντριβή. ὅσον γὰρ τὰς ψυχὰς τολμηρὰς καὶ θρασεῖς κέκτηνται, τοσοῦτον τὰ σώματα εὐπαθῆ καὶ ἁπαλὰ καὶ κόπον
415 εὐκόλως φέρειν οὐ δυνάμενα.

---

389 ἐνίοτε MW πολλάκις AVBE   395 ἐναπολειφθέντων MW ἐναπολειφθέντων μέσω τῶν ἐχθρῶν AVBE   399–400 ἀκατασχέτως MW ἀκρατῶς AVBE   400 μονότονοι καὶ MW om. AVBE   402 ὥσπερ MW om. AVBE | ὁρίσωσιν MW ὁρίσουσιν AVBE   404 φέροντες MW φέρουσι AVBE   405 λύουσι MW καὶ λύοντες AVBE | τοῦ ἐξπεδίτου MW τῆς ἐκστρατείας AVBE   406 καὶ ἀσφαλείας MW om. AVBE   407 περιφρονοῦσι MW καταφρονοῦσι AVBE   410 ἴσμεν MW γινώσκομεν AVBE | ἐνταῦθα πολλάκις MW trsp. AVBE   411–412 ὡς…συνεθισθέντων MW καὶ τοσούτων τῆς ἐκείνου γνώμης μεταλαβόντων τῇ πρὸς ἐκείνους συνηθείᾳ καὶ συναναστροφῇ AVBE

78. They are armed with shields and lances and rather short swords slung by straps from their shoulders, although at times some carry them around the waist.

79. They take more pleasure in fighting on foot and in making headlong charges.[18] Whether on foot or on horseback, they draw up for battle not in any fixed measure and formation or in moirai or divisions, as do the Romans, but according to clans, their kinship with one another, or some common bond or often leagued together by oath.[19] As a result, when things are not going well and their friends have fallen, they will often risk their lives fighting to avenge them.

80. In combat they make the front of their battle line even and dense.

81. Either on horseback or on foot their charges are impetuous and uncontrollable, hardheaded as they are without any fear at all.

82. They are disobedient to their leaders, especially the Franks, placing freedom above all else. They willingly go on campaign for as much time as they shall determine or that has been determined by their rulers, and only for that period of time. If it happens that they are to remain <beyond that>, they bear the extension of time grudgingly and break up the formation of the expedition and withdraw to their homes.

83. They are easygoing and avoid anything at all complicated and security measures and planning something beneficial. Thus, they despise good order, especially when it comes to cavalry.

84. They are easily corrupted by money, greedy as they are. This we have learned from experience, and we know from those who have frequently come here from Italy on some business or other that by intermingling with them, I think, even these have adopted their habits and become barbarized.

85. They are hurt by suffering and fatigue. Although they possess bold and daring spirits, their bodies are pampered and soft and unable to bear heavy labor easily.

18. Cf. *Strat.* 11.3.3; Procopius, *Bella*, 6.25.12–14.
19. Cf. Tacitus, *Germania*, 7.2.

86. Προσέτι δὲ λυπεῖ αὐτοὺς καὶ καύσων καὶ ψῦχος καὶ βροχὴ καὶ ἔνδεια δαπανημάτων, καὶ μάλιστα οἴνου, ἔτι δὲ καὶ ὑπέρθεσις πολέμου.

87. Ἐν δὲ τῷ καιρῷ τῆς καβαλλαρικῆς μάχης ἐναντιοῦνται αὐτοῖς τόποι δύσβατοι καὶ δασεῖς διὰ τὸ εἰς ὀξεῖς ἐλασίας ἐπ᾽ εὐθείας μετὰ τῶν κονταρίων
420 αὐτοὺς ἐγγυμνασθῆναι.

88. Ὑπομένουσι δὲ καὶ δι᾽ ἐγκρυμμάτων βλάβας εὐκόλως | κατά τε τῶν 354 πλαγίων καὶ τοῦ νώτου τῆς αὐτῶν παρατάξεως· οὐ γὰρ πάνυ φροντίζουσι βίγλας ἢ τῆς λοιπῆς ἀσφαλείας.

89. Ἐὰν δέ τινες καὶ σχηματίσωνται φυγήν, εὐκόλως διαλύονται, καὶ εἰ ἄφνω
425 κατ᾽ αὐτῶν ἀντιστρέψωσιν, εὐκόλως αὐτοὺς διαφθείρουσι.

90. Πολλάκις δὲ καὶ νυκτεριναὶ ἐπελεύσεις ὑπὸ τοξοτῶν βλάπτουσιν αὐτούς· διεσπασμένοι γὰρ ἀπλικεύουσιν.

91. Εἰ δέ τις αὐτοῖς ἐβουλεύθη ποτὲ προσβαλεῖν οὕτως εἰθισμένοις καὶ διακειμένοις, οὐκ ἔχρητο κατ᾽ αὐτῶν ἐν μάχῃ δημοσίᾳ παρατάξει, καὶ μάλιστα
430 ἐκ προοιμίων, ἀλλ᾽ εὐτάκτως δι᾽ ἐγκρυμμάτων καὶ κλοπῆς κατ᾽ αὐτῶν προσέβαλεν καὶ διὰ σοφισμάτων ἄλλων στρατηγικῶν ἢ διὰ ὑπερθέσεως τῆς μάχης διασύρων τὸν καιρὸν ἢ καὶ σύμφωνα εἰρήνης σχηματιζόμενος πρὸς αὐτούς, ἵνα ἢ τῇ τῶν δαπανημάτων ἐπιλείψει ἢ τῇ τοῦ καύσωνος ἢ καὶ ψύχους τυχὸν ὀχλήσει τὸ θράσος αὐτῶν καὶ τὸ πρόθυμον ἐλαττώσῃ.

435 92. Ἡ δὲ ὑπέρθεσις καὶ τὰ ἄλλα μάλιστα ἐδύνατο πρὸς αὐτοὺς γενέσθαι τότε, ὅτ᾽ ἂν εἰς ὀχυρωτέρους καὶ δυσβάτους τόπους ἠπλίκευεν ὁ πολέμιος ἐκείνων στρατός, ἔνθα, ὡς ἔχοντες κοντάρια, κατὰ τοῦ τόπου ἐγχειρεῖν ἐπιτηδείως οὐκ ἐδύναντο. ἐὰν δὲ διὰ τῶν εἰρημένων οὐκ ἐνήργουν κατ᾽ αὐτῶν, ἀλλὰ

416 προσέτι…λυπεῖ MW λυπεῖ δὲ AVBE | ἔνδεια MW λεῖψις AVBE    417 ὑπέρθεσις πολέμου MW trsp. AVBE    419 ὀξεῖς MW ὀξείας AVBE    421 δὲ MW δὲ βλάβας AVBE | βλάβας MW om. AVBE    422 τοῦ…παρατάξεως MW ὄπισθεν τῆς παρατάξεως αὐτῶν AVBE    423 λοιπῆς MW λοιπῆς αὐτῶν AVBE    424 τινες καὶ MW καὶ οἱ ἀντιτασσόμενοι αὐτοῖς AVBE | διαλύονται MW ἐκεῖνοι τὴν σύνταξιν αὐτῶν διαλύουσιν AVBE    425 ἀντιστρέψωσιν MW ἀντιστρέψωσιν οἱ τὴν φυγὴν σχηματισάμενοι AVBE | διαφθείρουσι MVBE διαφθείρουσιν WA    427 διεσπασμένοι MW διεσπαρμένοι καὶ διεσκορπισμένοι AVBE    428 ἐβουλεύθη MWVE ἐβουλήθη AB    428–429 εἰθισμένοις…διακειμένοις MW trsp. AVBE    429 ἐν μάχῃ MW om. AVBE    430 ἐκ προοιμίων MW ἐξ ἀρχῆς AVBE    430–431 προσέβαλεν MW προσέβαλεν ἢ AVBE    431–432 διὰ¹…καιρὸν MW ἢ ὑπερτιθέμενος καὶ παρασύρων τὸν καιρὸν τῆς μάχης AVBE    433 ἢ³…τυχὸν MW τυχὸν ἢ τῇ τοῦ ψύχους AVBE    435 ὑπέρθεσις MW ὑπέρθεσις τοῦ πολέμου AVBE | ἄλλα MW ἄλλα τότε AVBE    435–436 γενέσθαι τότε MW γίνεσθαι AVBE    436–437 πολέμιος ἐκείνων MW πολέμων ἐκείνους AVBE    437–438 ὡς…ἐδύναντο MW ἐγχειρίζειν καὶ ἐπιτίθεσθαι ἐπιτηδείως οὐκ ἐδύναντο ὡς ἔχοντες κοντάρια AVBE

86. Moreover, they are hurt by heat, cold, rain, and lack of provisions, especially of wine, as well as postponement of battle.

87. When it comes to a cavalry battle, they are hindered by difficult and wooded terrain because they have been trained to charge swiftly with their lances on level ground.

88. They are easily subject to serious damage from ambushes along the flanks and to the rear of their battle line, for they pay no attention whatever to scouts and other security measures.

89. Their ranks are easily broken by a simulated flight, and a sudden turning back against them easily wipes them out.

90. Attacks at night by archers often inflict damage on them since they set up camp all scattered about.

91. In the past, individuals who wanted to assault these people, with their customs and manner of doing things, did not line <their own troops> up for a pitched battle against them, especially in the early stages. Instead, they proceeded against them with well-planned ambushes and sneak attacks, as well as by other clever military actions, or else they delayed combat and kept putting it off. Or they pretended to make an agreement about peace with them, so that the shortage of provisions or else the likely discomforts of heat or cold might put a damper on their boldness and high spirits.

92. Delays and other actions against them could best be carried out at a time when the army opposed to them pitched camp on rugged and difficult ground. Because the Franks relied on lances, they were unable to launch an effective attack against such a place. If <the army opposed to them> did not carry out any

πρὸς μάχην πάντως ἑώρων, τότε παρετάσσοντο πρὸς αὐτούς, ὡς ἐν τῷ περὶ
440 παρατάξεως ἐδηλώσαμεν κεφαλαίῳ.

93. Καὶ τὰ Σκλαβικὰ δὲ ἔθνη ὁμοδίαιτά τε ἦσαν καὶ ὁμότροπα ἀλλήλοις, καὶ
ἐλεύθερα, μηδαμῶς δουλοῦσθαι ἢ ἄρχεσθαι πειθόμενα, καὶ μάλιστα ὅτε πέραν
τοῦ Δανουβίου κατῴκουν ἐν τῇ ἰδίᾳ χώρᾳ. ὅθεν καὶ ἐνταῦθα περαιωθέντα καὶ
οἱονεὶ βιασθέντα δέξασθαι τὴν δουλείαν, οὐχ ἑτέρῳ ἡδέως πείθεσθαι ἤθελον,
445 ἀλλὰ τρόπον τινὰ ἑαυτοῖς. κρεῖττον γὰρ ἡγοῦντο ἀπὸ τοῦ ἄρχοντος τῆς αὐτῶν
φυλῆς φθείρεσθαι ἢ τοῖς Ῥωμαϊκοῖς δουλεύειν καὶ ὑποκλίνεσθαι νόμοις, οὐδὲ
τοῦ σωτηρίου βαπτίσματος τὸν ἁγιασμὸν καταδεξάμενα ἄχρι τῶν ἡμετέρων
χρόνων, τοῦτο ὅσον κατ᾽ αὐτοὺς εἰς ἀρχαίας ἐλευθερίας συνήθειαν διατηροῦν-
τες.

450 94. Πολύανδρά τε ἦσαν καὶ κακοπαθείας ὑπομένοντα, εὐκόλως δὲ πρὸς
καύσωνα καὶ ψῦχος καὶ βροχὴν καὶ σώματος γυμνότητα καὶ τὴν τῶν δαπανημάτων ἔνδειαν καρτεροῦντα.

95. Ταῦτα δὲ ὁ ἡμέτερος ἐν θείᾳ τῇ λήξει γενόμενος πατὴρ καὶ Ῥωμαίων
αὐτοκράτωρ Βασίλειος τῶν ἀρχαίων ἐθῶν ἔπεισε μεταστῆναι καί, γραικώσας,
455 καὶ ἄρχουσι κατὰ τὸν Ῥωμαϊκὸν τύπον ὑποτάξας, καὶ βαπτίσματι τιμήσας, τῆς τε
δουλείας ἠλευθέρωσε τῶν ἑαυτῶν ἀρχόντων, καὶ στρατεύεσθαι κατὰ τῶν
Ῥωμαίοις πολεμούντων ἐθνῶν ἐξεπαίδευσεν, οὕτω πως ἐπιμελῶς περὶ τὰ
τοιαῦτα διακείμενος, διὸ καὶ ἀμερίμνους Ῥωμαίους ἐκ τῆς πολλάκις ἀπὸ Σκλά-
βων γενομένης ἀνταρσίας | ἐποίησεν, πολλὰς ὑπ᾽ ἐκείνων ὀχλήσεις καὶ πολέ- 354ᵛ
460 μους τοῖς πάλαι χρόνοις ὑπομείναντας.

96. Ἦσαν δέ, οὐκ οἶδ᾽ ὅπως εἰπεῖν, τῇ φιλοξενίᾳ κατακόρως χρώμενα τὰ τῶν
Σκλάβων φῦλα, ἣν οὐδὲ νῦν καταλιπεῖν ἐδικαίωσαν, ἀλλ᾽ ἔχουσιν ὁμοίως. τοῖς

441–492  Strat., 11.4.

439 ἑώρων MW ἀπέβλεπον AVBE   440 παρατάξεως MW περιτάξεως AVBE   441 τε…
ὁμότροπα MW καὶ ὁμότροπα ἦσαν AVBE   442 δουλοῦσθαι…πειθόμενα MW πειθόμενα
δουλοῦσθαι ἢ ἄρχεσθαι AVBE   443 περαιωθέντα MW διαπεράσαντα AVBE   444 οἱονεὶ
MW om. AVBE   444–445 ἑτέρῳ…τινὰ MW ἤθελον ἑτέρῳ πείθεσθαι ἀλλ AVBE
446 δουλεύειν…νόμοις MW νόμοις δουλεύειν καὶ ὑποκλίνεσθαι AVBE   447 τοῦ…
ἁγιασμὸν MW τὸ σωτήριον βάπτισμα AVBE | ἄχρι MW μέχρι AVBE   448 ὅσον MW ὅσον
τὸ AVBE   448–449 ἀρχαίας…διατηροῦντες MW συνήθειαν τηροῦντες ἀρχαίας ἐλευθερίας
AVBE   450 τε MW δὲ AVBE   452 ἔνδειαν MW λεῖψιν AVBE   453 ἐν…γενόμενος MW
μακαριώτατος AVBE   454 αὐτοκράτωρ MW βασιλεὺς AVBE   456 στρατεύεσθαι MW om.
AVBE   457 ἐθνῶν MW ἐθνῶν στρατεύεσθαι AVBE   458–459 πολλάκις…γενομένης
MW γενομένης πολλάκις ἀπὸ σκλαβῶν AVBE   461–462 οὐκ…ἦν MW φιλόξενα εἰς
ὑπερβολὴν τὰ τῶν σκλαβῶν φῦλα τὴν δὲ τοιαύτην φιλοξενίαν AVBE   462 ἐδικαίωσαν MW
ἠθέλησαν AVBE

of the above operations against them, but was intent on fighting, it would form its battle line against them, as we explained in the chapter on formations.

93. The Slavic nations have shared the same customs and way of life with each other.[20] They were independent, absolutely refusing to be enslaved or governed, especially when they dwelled across the Danube in their own country. And when they crossed over from there to here and, as it were, were forced to accept slavery, they still did not want to obey another person meekly but in some manner only themselves. For they deemed it better to be destroyed by a ruler of their own race than to serve and to submit themselves to the laws of the Romans. Even after they received the sacrament of salvific baptism, up to our own times, they just as strongly retained their ancient and customary independence.

94. They were always a populous and hardy people, readily bearing up under heat, cold, rain, nakedness, and scarcity of provisions.

95. Our father, autokrator of the Romans, Basil, now in the divine dwelling, persuaded these peoples to abandon their ancient ways and, having made them Greek, subjected them to rulers according to the Roman model, and having graced them with baptism, he liberated them from slavery to their own rulers and trained them to take part in warfare against those nations warring against the Romans.[21] By these means he very carefully arranged matters for those peoples. As a result, he enabled the Romans to feel relaxed after the frequent uprisings by the Slavs in the past and the many disturbances and wars they had suffered from them in ancient times.

96. The tribes of the Slavs—I am not sure how to say this—practiced hospitality[22] to an extreme, and even now they judge it wrong to abandon it, but

---

20. Sections 93–102 derive from *Strat.* 11.4.

21. The conversion of the Slavs, as a whole, is dated to the 860s. See F. Dvornik, *Byzantine Missions among the Slavs* (New Brunswick, NJ, 1970); A. P. Vlasto, *The Entry of the Slavs into Christendom* (Cambridge, 1970). "Made them Greek," γραικώσας: apparently, they had to adopt Greek customs, including, perhaps, the language, as did the orphans, who came from various ethnic groups. Anna Komnene employs a more classical word to describe the same process: ἐλληνίζω (15.7.9). See T. Miller, *The Orphans of Byzantium* (Washington, DC, 2003).

22. Hospitality toward strangers, φιλοξενία, an aspect of philanthropy praised and practiced by religious Byzantines. See *ODB*, s.v. "hospitality."

γὰρ ἐπιξενουμένοις ἐν αὐτοῖς ἤπιοι καὶ πρᾶοι ἐγίνοντο φιλοφρονούμενοί τε
αὐτοὺς καὶ δεξιούμενοι διασῴζοντες, καὶ κατὰ διαδοχὴν ἐκ τόπου εἰς τόπον
465 παραπέμποντες καὶ ἀβλαβεῖς διατηρεῖσθαι καὶ ἀδιαλείπτους δαπάνης ἀλλήλους
παρεγγυώμενοι, ὡς εἴ γε δι᾽ ἀμέλειαν τοῦ ὑποδεχομένου συμβαίη τὸν ξενὸν
βλαβῆναι, πόλεμον κατ᾽ ἐκείνου ὁ τοῦτον παραθέμενος ἐκίνει, ἀντὶ πίστεως
σεβασμίας ἡγούμενος τοῦ ξένου τὴν ἐκδίκησιν.

97. Ἐδόκει δὲ αὐτοῖς καὶ ἕτερον συμπαθέστερόν ποτε εἶναι· τοὺς γὰρ ἐν
470 αἰχμαλωσίᾳ παρ᾽ αὐτῶν λαμβανομένους οὐκ ἀορίστως, ἕως ἂν βούλωνται, πρὸς
δουλείαν κατεῖχον, ἀλλὰ μᾶλλον ἐν τῇ γνώμῃ τῶν αἰχμαλώτων ἐποίουν, ὁρίζον-
τες αὐτοῖς ῥητόν τινα τῆς δουλείας χρόνον ἵνα, μετὰ τοῦτον τὸν ὁρισθέντα
χρόνον, ἐὰν θέλωσιν ἐν τοῖς ἰδίοις ἀναχωρῆσαι μετά τινος ὡρισμένου μισθοῦ ἤ,
ἐὰν βούλωνται παρ᾽ αὐτοῖς εἶναι, μένειν ἐλευθέρους καὶ φίλους.

475 98. Ἐσωφρόνουν δὲ καὶ αἱ θήλειαι αὐτῶν μάλιστα κραταιῶς, ὥστε τὰς
πολλὰς αὐτῶν τὴν τῶν ἰδίων ἀνδρῶν τελευτὴν ἰδίαν ἡγεῖσθαι καὶ ἀποπνίγειν
ἑαυτάς, μὴ δυναμένας φέρειν τὴν ἐν χηρείᾳ ζωήν.

99. Ἐχρῶντο δὲ δαπάνῃ κέγχρῳ, μάλιστα ἐφίλουν δὲ καὶ ὀλιγαρκίαν, δυσχερῶς φέροντες τοὺς ἄλλους τῆς γεωργίας πόνους, διὰ τὸ ἐλευθεριωτέραν μᾶλ-
480 λον φιλεῖν αὐτὰ τὴν διαγωγὴν ποιεῖσθαι καὶ ἄπονον, ἢ σὺν πολλῷ κόπῳ πολυτέλειαν βρωμάτων ἢ χρημάτων ἐπικτίζεσθαι.

100. Ὡπλίζοντο δέ ποτε μικροῖς ἀκοντίοις ἤγουν ῥηκταρίοις, δυσὶν ἕκαστος
ἀνήρ, τινὲς δὲ καὶ σκουταρίοις μεγάλοις ἐπιμήκεσιν, οἷον θυρεοῖς. ἐκέχρηντο δὲ
καὶ τόξοις ξυλίνοις, καὶ σαγίττας εἶχον κεχρισμένας φαρμάκῳ, ὅπερ ἐστὶν

---

463 ἐν MW om. AVBE | ἤπιοι καὶ MW om. AVBE    464 διασώζοντες MW om. AVBE
465–466 καὶ¹...παρεγγυώμενοι MW τε καὶ διασώζοντες καὶ ἀδιαλείπτους δαπάνας
παρατρέχοντες ἀλλήλους τε παρεγγυώμενοι καὶ παραινοῦντες ἀβλαβῆ τὸν ξενοδοχούμενον
διασῶσαι AVBE    466–467 συμβαίη...βλαβῆναι MW τὸν ξένον βλαβῆναι συνέβη AVBE
467 ἐκείνου...ἐκίνει MW πόλεμον ἐκίνει κατὰ τοῦ προλαβόντος αὐτὸν ὁ τοῦτον παραδοὺς
AVBE    468 ἡγούμενος...ἐκδίκησιν MW τὴν τοῦ ξένου ἐκδίκησιν λογιζόμενος AVBE
469 ποτε MW om. AVBE    470 λαμβανομένους MW κρατουμένους AVBE | ἕως...
βούλωνται MW om. AVBE    471–472 ἐποίουν...ῥητόν MW ἀνετίθουν ὡρισμένον AVBE
472 τῆς...χρόνον MW χρόνον τῆς δουλείας τιθέντες αὐτοῖς AVBE | τοῦτον MW τὸ
παρελθεῖν AVBE    473 ὡρισμένου MW συμφωνηθέντος AVBE    475 θήλειαι MW
γυναῖκες AVBE | μάλιστα κραταιῶς MW ὑπερβαλλόντως AVBE    476 ἰδίων MW om.
AVBE | τελευτὴν...ἡγεῖσθαι MW ἴδιον λογίζεσθαι θάνατον AVBE    478–479 δυσχερῶς
MW δυσκόλως AVBE    479–480 τὸ...ἢ MW τὸ ἀγαπᾶν αὐτοὺς τὴν ἐλευθεριωτέραν
διαγωγὴν καὶ ἄπονον οὐ γὰρ ἤθελον AVBE    482 ἀκοντίοις...ῥηκταρίοις MW ῥιπταρίοις
AVBE    483 μεγάλοις MW μεγάλοις καὶ AVBE | οἷον θυρεοῖς MW om. AVBE

hold on to it as formerly. They were kind and gentle to travelers in their land, and were favorably disposed to them. They conducted them safely from one place to another in sequence and preserved them free from harm and always well supplied, commending them to one another. Indeed, if the stranger happened to suffer some harm because of his host's negligence, the one who had commended him would commence hostilities against that host, regarding vengeance for the stranger as a sacred pledge.

97. From former times they held on to another very sympathetic custom. They did not keep those whom they had taken into captivity for an indefinite period, as long as they wished. Rather, they set a definite period of time for their enslavement, and then gave the prisoners a choice: after this set period, if they so desired, they could return to their own homes with a certain assigned recompense or, if they wished to stay with them, they could remain there as free men and friends.

98. Their women manifested particularly strong feelings. Many of them regarded the death of their husbands as their own and would have themselves suffocated, <finding it> unbearable to keep on living as widows.

99. For food they made use of millet. They were truly happy and content with very little and grudgingly bore the labors involved in farming. They far preferred to have a much more independent way of life without any work than to acquire a wide variety of food or money with a great deal of toil.

100. Formerly they were armed with short javelins, or throwing weapons, two to each man, while others had large, thick shields, similar to thyreoi. They also used wooden bows and they had arrows smeared with a drug that was very

485 ἐνεργητικόν. ἐὰν μὴ ὁ λαβὼν τὴν πληγὴν ἢ θηριακὴν πίη ἢ καὶ ἕτερον βοήθημα
ἀντιφάρμακον ἢ καὶ παρευθὺ περικόψῃ τὴν πληγήν, πρὸς τὸ μὴ διαδραμεῖν,
πάντως γὰρ ἂν καὶ τὸ ὅλον σῶμα ἀπόλλυται.

101. Καὶ δάσεσι δὲ καὶ δυσβάτοις οἰκεῖν καὶ καταφεύγειν φιλοῦσιν.

102. Ὅπως δὲ κατ᾽ αὐτῶν ἐποιοῦντο τὰς ἐπιδρομὰς καὶ ἐφόδους Ῥωμαῖοι,
490 τότε διηγησάμην ἔμπροσθεν ἐν τῇ περὶ ἀδοκήτων ἐφόδων διατάξει, ἵνα καὶ
αὐτός, ὦ στρατηγέ, εἰ καὶ μὴ κατ᾽ αὐτῶν νῦν, ἀλλ᾽ ἢ κατὰ τῶν ὁμοίων αὐτῶν ἢ
κατὰ ἑτέρων βαρβάρων ποιούμενος ἀδοκήτους ἐφόδους, εἴ γε ἄρα χρήσιμόν τι
ἐκ τῆς διατυπώσεως ἐκείνης εὑρεθῇ, ἔχῃς καὶ τοῦτο ἐξ ἑτοίμου πρὸς τὴν δέουσαν χρείαν, ὡς προγεγυμνασμένον.

495 103. Ἐπειδὴ δὲ διαφόρων ἐθνικῶν παρατάξεών | τε καὶ διαθέσεων ἐμνημο- 355
νεύσαμεν, φέρε λοιπὸν καὶ τοῦ νῦν ἐνοχλοῦντος τῇ Ῥωμαϊκῇ ἡμῶν πολιτείᾳ
ἔθνους τῶν Σαρακηνῶν ἐπιμνησθῶμεν κατὰ δύναμιν, ὅπως τε ἔχουσι φύσεως
καὶ ὅπως τοῖς τε ὅπλοις ἐν ταῖς ἐκστρατείαις χρῶνται καὶ τοῖς ἐπιτηδεύμασι, καὶ
ὡς ἂν εἴη δέον κατ᾽ αὐτῶν ἀνθοπλίζεσθαί τε καὶ ἀντιστρατεύεσθαι, καὶ τὰς ἐκ
500 τούτων ἐγχειρήσεις ποιεῖσθαι.

104. Σαρακηνοὶ μὲν οὖν Ἄραβές εἰσι τὸ γένος παρὰ τὴν εἴσοδον τῆς Εὐδαί-
μονος Ἀραβίας ποτὲ κείμενον, τῷ χρόνῳ δὲ καὶ πρὸς τὴν Συρίαν καὶ Παλαιστί-
νην διασπαρέν, πρῶτα μὲν οἷον μετοικίας χάριν, ὕστερον δέ, ὅτε τῆς αὐτῶν
δεισιδαιμονίας ἐγένετο ἀρχηγὸς Μουχούμετ, καὶ ὅπλοις κρατοῦντες τῶν τε
505 εἰρημένων ἐπαρχιῶν, καὶ δὴ καὶ Μεσοποταμίας καὶ Αἰγύπτου καὶ τῶν ἄλλων
χωρῶν, ἅπερ αὐτοῖς ὁ καιρὸς τῆς Ῥωμαϊκῆς ἀπὸ Περσῶν ἐρημώσεως χώραν
ἔδωκε κατασχεῖν.

495  M: ff. 401–403 versionem praebent aliam cui signum damus M¹ et cuius lectiones, ubi ab M
divergunt, notamus. inc. λέοντος ἐν χριστῷ βασιλεῖ αἰωνίῳ βασιλέως ῥωμαίων πῶς δεῖ σαρακηνοῖς
μάχεσθαι. ἐπειδὴ δὲ κτλ.

485 ἐνεργητικόν MW ἀναιρετικὸν AVBE | λαβὼν…πληγὴν MW πληγεῖς AVBE
485–486 καὶ…περικόψῃ MW ἕτερον ἀντιφάρμακον ἢ παρευθὺ γύροθεν διακόψῃ AVBE
487 πάντως…ἀπόλλυται MW τὸ φάρμακον AVBE    488 καὶ δάσεσι MW ἀγαπῶσι AVBE |
δυσβάτοις MW δυσβάτοις τόποις καὶ δάσεσι AVBE | φιλοῦσιν MW om. AVBE    489 δὲ
MW δὲ καὶ AVBE    492 ἄρα MW ἄρα εὑρεθῇ AVBE    493 εὑρεθῇ MW om. AVBE
493–494 δέουσαν MW ἀπαιτοῦσαν AVBE    495 δὲ MWAVBE om. M¹ | τε MW om. AVBE
| διαθέσεων MW ἐθῶν AVBE    498 ἐπιτηδεύμασι MW ἐπιτηδεύμασιν AVBE    499 ὡς…
δέον MW πῶς ἐστι πρέπον AVBE | ἀνθοπλίζεσθαί…ἀντιστρατεύεσθαι MW trsp. AVBE
501 scr. mg. περὶ σαρακηνῶν W | γένος MW γένος ἔθνος AVBE    502 κείμενον AVBE
κειμένου MW    503 οἷον…χάριν MW ὡς μέτοικος AVBE    503–504 τῆς…μουχούμετ MW
ἀρχηγὸς ἐγένετο τῆς αὐτῶν κακοδαιμονίας μουχούμετ AVBE    506 ἐρημώσεως AVBE om.
MW

effective. If the wounded man did not drink an antidote or take some other remedy to counteract the drug or immediately cut around the wound to keep <the poison> from spreading, it would assuredly destroy the whole body.

101. They love to make their homes in overgrown and difficult land and to take refuge there.

102. Previously, in the constitution dealing with unexpected ambushes, we explained the manner in which the Romans made their attacks and ambushes against them. Now you, O general, even if you are not setting up surprise ambushes against them but against peoples like them or against other barbarians, if indeed you should find something useful in that ordinance, then you will have something right at hand to meet any contingency, as though you had been drilled in it beforehand.

103. Since we have recalled the various foreign battle formations and dispositions, then permit us now to call to mind as best we can the nation of the Saracens that is presently troubling our Roman commonwealth.[23] What are they really like? What weapons do they make use of in military campaigns? What are their practices? How does one arm himself and campaign against them and thus carry out operations against them?

104. The Saracens, therefore, are Arabs by race, who formerly lived near the entrance to Blessed Arabia, but in time came to be scattered about toward Syria and Palestine.[24] <They came> originally to find a place to live, but later, when Muhammad founded their superstition, they took possession of those provinces by force of arms. In fact, <they took> Mesopotamia, Egypt, and the other lands at that time when the devastation of the Roman land by the Persians allowed them to occupy those lands.

23. Saracens (Arabic: East) is a generic term for Arabs, implying Muslims.

24. Arabia: the southwest section of the Arabian peninsula, known as Felix Arabia, Εὐδαίμων Ἀραβία, present day Yemen. Cf. DAI, 25.65.

105. Εἰσὶ δὲ περὶ μὲν τὸ θεῖον δοκοῦντες εὐσεβεῖν, βλασφημίαν δὲ τὴν αὐτῶν δοκοῦσαν εὐσέβειαν ἀποδεικνύντες, οἷς Χριστὸν μὲν τὸν ἀληθινὸν Θεὸν καὶ
510 τοῦ κόσμου σωτῆρα καλεῖν Θεὸν οὐκ ἀνέχονται, παντὸς δὲ καὶ κακοῦ ἔργου τὸν Θεὸν εἶναι αἴτιον ὑποτίθενται, καὶ πολέμοις χαίρειν λέγουσι τὸν Θεόν, τὸν διασκορπίζοντα ἔθνη τὰ τοὺς πολέμους θέλοντα· καὶ τοὺς οἰκείους δὲ νόμους ἀπαραβάτους φυλάττουσι, τὴν σάρκα λιπαίνοντες καὶ ψυχὴν ἀτιμάζοντες. τῇ οὖν τοιαύτῃ δυσσεβείᾳ διὰ τῆς ἡμῶν εὐσεβείας τε καὶ ὀρθοδόξου πίστεως
515 ἀντιμαχόμενοι καὶ τοὺς θείους νόμους καὶ τοὺς πολιτικοὺς πολλῷ μᾶλλον ἀπαραβάτους διαφυλάττοντες κατ᾽ αὐτῶν ἀντιστρατευόμεθα.

106. Χρῶνται δὲ καμήλοις, τοῖς ἀχθοφόροις αὐτῶν, ἀντὶ ἁμαξῶν καὶ ὑπο- ζυγίων, ὄνοις καὶ ἡμιόνοις, καὶ τυμπάνοις τε καὶ κυμβάλοις ἐν ταῖς παρατάξεσιν, ἐν οἷς τοὺς οἰκείους ἵππους ἐθίζουσι. διὰ δὲ τοιούτων κτύπων καὶ ἤχων τοὺς
520 ἵππους τῶν ἀντιπολεμούντων αὐτοῖς ταράσσοντες τρέπουσιν εἰς φυγήν. ἀλλὰ καὶ τῶν καμήλων ἡ θέα ὁμοίως τοὺς ἀσυνήθεις ἵππους ἐκφοβεῖ καὶ ταράττει, καὶ πρόσω βαίνειν οὐκ ἐᾷ.

107. Τὰς δὲ τοιαύτας τῶν τε καμήλων καὶ τῶν ὑποζυγίων ἀποσκευὰς καὶ εἰς πλήθους πολλάκις φαντασίαν χρῶνται, μέσον μὲν τοῦ στρατιωτικοῦ πλήθους
525 αὐτὰς καθιστῶντες, πυκνὰ δὲ φλάμουλα ἄνωθεν αὐτῶν ἐφιστῶντες, ὡς δοκεῖν στρατιωτῶν εἶναι πλῆθος τῶν ἐκείνων ὄχλον.

108. Θερμοὶ δέ εἰσι τὴν κρᾶσιν ἐν τοιούτῳ κλίματι θερμῷ κατοικοῦντες.

109. Χρῶνται δὲ καὶ πεζικῇ στρατιᾷ, Αἰθίοπί φασι, γυμνοῖς ὅπλων ἔμ- προσθεν τῶν καβαλλαρίων παραταττομένοις, οἱονεὶ ψιλοῖς. τόξα γὰρ φέροντες,
530 καὶ τούτοις χρώμενοι, δυσάντητοι δοκοῦσι τοῖς ἐπερχομένοις.

110. Τοὺς δὲ πεζοὺς αὐτῶν φέρουσιν ἢ ἐφ᾽ ἵππων ἰδίων ὀχουμένους ἢ ὄπισ- θεν τῶν καβαλλαρίων καθημένους, ὅτε πλησίον τῆς αὐτῶν χώρας ἐστὶν ἡ ἐκστρατεία αὐτῶν. χρῶνται δὲ ὅπλοις | καὶ οἱ καβαλλάριοι τόξοις καὶ σπαθίοις,  355ᵛ κονταρίοις καὶ σκουταρίοις καὶ πελέκεσι· καὶ πανοπλίαν γὰρ φοροῦσιν, οἷον
535 λωρίκια καὶ κλιβάνια καὶ κασσίδας καὶ ποδόψελλα καὶ χειρόψελλα καὶ εἴ τι

---

508–509 εἰσὶ…οἷς MW δοκοῦσι δὲ εὐσεβεῖν μὲν περὶ τὸ θεῖον βλασφημίαν δὲ ἀποδεικνύουσιν τὴν δοκοῦσαν αὐτῶν εὐσέβειαν δι᾽ ὅτι AVBE   511 ὑποτίθενται MW λέγουσιν AVBE | λέγουσι MW ὑποτίθενται AVBE   513 φυλάττουσι MWVBE φυλάττουσιν A   517 τοῖς…αὐτῶν MW ἐν ταῖς ὑπηρεσίαις αὐτῶν καὶ AVBE   518 τε De δὲ codd. 519 ἐθίζουσι MVBE ἐθίζουσιν WA   522 πρόσω…ἐᾷ MW ἔμπροσθεν προβαίνει οὐ συγχωρεῖ AVBE   528 αἰθίοψί φασι MW αἰθίοψιν AVBE   530 δυσάντητοι MW δυσαπάνητοι AVBE   534 πελέκεσι MW πελέκεσιν AVBE | καὶ³…γὰρ MW om. AVBE | οἷον MW om. AVBE

105. As far as the divinity is concerned, they appear to show proper reverence, but their apparent reverence must be recognized as blasphemy. They cannot bear to call Christ God, <although he is indeed> true God and savior of the world. They argue that God is the cause of every evil deed and they claim that God rejoices in war and scatters abroad the peoples that want to fight. They observe their own laws as inviolable, fattening their flesh and bringing dishonor on their souls. Fighting, therefore, against such impiety by means of our own piety and orthodox faith and observing divine and civil laws as all the more inviolate, we wage war against them.

106. They make use of camels, asses, and mules to bear their baggage, instead of wagons and pack animals. They use drums and cymbals in their battle formations, to which their own horses become accustomed. Such great din and noise disturbs the horses of their adversaries, causing them to turn to flight. Moreover, the sight of the camels likewise frightens and confuses horses not used to them, preventing them from advancing.

107. Such hordes of camels and pack animals are often used to give the impression of a great number. They place these in the middle of the multitude of soldiers and raise a thick array of pennants above them to give the appearance of a very large crowd of soldiers.

108. Their temperament is hot because they dwell in such a hot climate.

109. They make use of foot soldiers, Ethiopians they say, drawn up in front of the cavalry, without armament, like light-armed troops.[25] They carry bows and, when they shoot, they seem irresistible to their opponents.

110. They transport their infantry either riding on their own horses or sitting behind the cavalrymen, when the campaign takes place near their country. They make use of armament, and their cavalry uses bows, swords, lances, shields, and axes. They wear full armor, including body armor, cuirasses,

25. Ethiopians: a generic term for dark-skinned Africans, from Sudan or elsewhere, who appear in Muslim armies on the borders of Syria and Cilicia in the 2nd half of the 9th century. See Dagron, *Guérilla*, 179. The *Suda* (Αι 129) defines Ethiopian simply as "the black man" (ὁ μέλας).

ἕτερον κατὰ τὸν Ῥωμαϊκὸν τρόπον. τὰς δὲ ζώνας αὐτῶν καὶ τοὺς χαλίνους καὶ τὰ σπαθία ἀργύρῳ ποικίλλουσι φιλοτιμότερον.

111. Οὔτε δὲ διώκοντες οὔτε διωκόμενοι λύουσι τὴν τάξιν αὐτῶν. εἰ δὲ συμβῇ αὐτὴν λυθῆναι δι᾽ ἑαυτῶν, ἀσύστατοι καὶ ἀνεπίστροφοι γινόμενοι μόνῳ

540 τῷ σωθῆναι ἐλαύνουσιν.

112. Θρασεῖς μὲν γάρ εἰσι νικᾶν ἐλπίζοντες, δειλοὶ δὲ λίαν ἀπειπόντες τῆς νίκης. ὡς ἀπὸ Θεοῦ γὰρ τὸ πᾶν, εἰ καὶ κακὸν εἴη, λέγοντες εἶναι· εἰ συμβῇ αὐτοὺς ἐναντίον τι παθεῖν, ὡς ἀπὸ θεοῦ ὁριζομένου οὐκ ἀντιπίπτουσιν, ἀλλὰ τῇ προσβολῇ σφαλέντες χαλῶσι τὸν τόνον. ὑπηλοὶ δέ εἰσι, καὶ διὰ τοῦτο τὰς

545 νυκτομαχίας φοβούμενοι καὶ τὰ ἐν αὐταῖς ἐπιτηδεύματα, μάλιστα ὅτ᾽ ἂν ἐν ἀλλοτρίᾳ ἑαυτῶν γῇ κατατρέχουσι. διόπερ ἢ εἰς ὀχυροὺς τόπους ἀναχωροῦσι, κἀκεῖ τῆς νυκτὸς ποιοῦνται τὴν φυλακήν, ἢ περιφράττουσιν ἀσφαλῶς τὸ στρατόπεδον αὐτῶν, ὥστε μὴ ἐπιβουλεύεσθαι ταῖς νυκτεριναῖς τῶν ἐναντίων προσβολαῖς.

550    113. Τετράγωνον δὲ καὶ ἐπιμήκη ποιοῦνται τὴν οἰκείαν παράταξιν ὡς ἀσφαλεστέραν καὶ ῥᾳδίως λυθῆναι μὴ δυναμένην ἐν ταῖς τῶν ἀντιπαραταττομένων προσβολαῖς.

114. Ταύτῃ δὲ <τῇ παρατάξει> χρῶνται καὶ ἐν ταῖς πορείαις καὶ ἐν ταῖς συστάσεσι τῆς μάχης, ὡς ἐπὶ πολὺ δὲ Ῥωμαίους μιμοῦνται, καὶ κατὰ τὰ ἄλλα

555 σχήματα τῶν παρατάξεων τῇ πείρᾳ τῶν προσβολῶν οἷον ἐγγεγυμνασμένοι, καὶ ἐξ ὧν ἔπαθον παρὰ Ῥωμαίων δρᾶν κατ᾽ αὐτῶν ἐπιτηδεύοντες.

---

537 ποικίλλουσι MW κατακοσμοῦσι AVBE  539 δι᾽ ἑαυτῶν MW om. AVBE
540 ἐλαύνουσιν MA ἐλαύνουσι WVBE  541–542 ἀπειπόντες…νίκης MW τὴν νίκην ἀπελπίσαντες AVBE  542 τὸ…λέγοντες MW καὶ τὰ κακὰ κρίνοντες AVBE  543 ὡς… ἀλλὰ MW οὐκ ἀντιπίπτουσιν ὡς ἀπὸ θεοῦ ὀργιζομένου ἀλλ᾽ ἐν AVBE  544 χαλῶσι… ὑπηλοὶ MW τὴν ὁρμὴν αὐτῶν ὑποχαλῶσιν ὑπνώδεις AVBE  545 φοβούμενοι MW φοβοῦνται AVBE  546 κατατρέχουσι M κατατρέχουσιν WM¹ κατατρέχωσιν A κατατρέχωσι VBE | ἀναχωροῦσι MVBE ἀναχωροῦσιν WA  547 κἀκεῖ MW καὶ ἐκεῖ AVBE  547–548 περιφράττουσιν…αὐτῶν MW τὸ στρατόπεδον αὐτῶν ἀσφαλῶς περιφράττουσιν AVBE  550 οἰκείαν MW ἰδίαν AVBE | ὡς AVBE om. MW  551–552 ῥᾳδίως… ἀντιπαραταττομένων MW μὴ δυναμένων εὐκόλως διαλυθῆναι ἐν ταῖς τῶν ἀντιπαρατασσομένων AVBE  553 τῇ παρατάξει ci. De om. codd.  554 συστάσεσι…μάχης MW μάχαις AVBE | πολὺ MW τὸ πλεῖστον AVBE  555 προσβολῶν οἷον MW πολέμων τῶν πρὸς τοὺς ῥωμαίους AVBE  556 δρᾶν MW ποιεῖν AVBE

helmets, shin guards, gauntlets, and all the rest in the Roman manner. They decorate their belts and bridles and swords very richly with silver.

111. Neither when they are pursuing nor are being pursued do they break their formation. But if it should happen that they do so, they lose their cohesion and are unable to return, only racing on to save themselves.

112. They are bold at the expectation of victory but very cowardly when victory is denied them. They say that everything comes from God, even if it should be evil. If it happens that they suffer a setback, they do not resist since it has been decreed by God. Overthrown by the onslaught, they are completely undone. They are given to sleep and for this reason have a fear of battle at night and all that is connected with it, especially when they are raiding in a country foreign to them. And so they withdraw to strong places and there set up a guard for the night or else they will securely fortify their camp so as not to be subjected to night attacks by their adversaries.

113. Their native battle formations are both square and oblong and so are very secure and not easily broken up by the attacks of their opponents.

114. They employ this formation while marching and in forming up for battle. They also imitate the Romans in many respects. It is as though they have been trained by experience in the other models of battle formations, so the very things they suffered from the Romans they are now busily putting into practice against them.

115. Ἐν δὲ ταῖς παρατάξεσιν αὐτῶν εὐμήχανοι καὶ σταθεροί <εἰσι>, μηδὲ διὰ τάχος προσβολῆς πτοούμενοι τοὺς ἐπερχομένους μήτε διὰ προσποιητὴν ἀναβολὴν ἐκλυόμενοι.

560   116. Προσμένουσι δὲ τῇ παρατάξει φέροντες καὶ τὰς βολὰς μακροθύμως πρὸς τοὺς θρασέως αὐτοῖς ἐπερχομένους, καὶ ὅτ᾽ ἂν τὸν τόνον χαλάσαντα ἴδωσι τῶν ἀντιπολεμίων, τότε διαναστάντες εὐτόνως μάχονται. τοῦτο δὲ ποιοῦσιν οὐ μόνον ἐν πεζομαχίᾳ, ἀλλὰ καὶ ἐν ταῖς κατὰ θάλασσαν μάχαις, ἐκ χειρὸς ἀπὸ τῶν πλοίων μαχόμενοι, καὶ μετὰ τὴν τῶν βαλλομένων κατ᾽ αὐτῶν ἀποπλή-
565   ρωσιν, ἃ σύσκουτα ποιοῦντες καρτεροῦσι, δεχόμενοι εὐθέως ἀνίστανται ἀθρόοι καὶ ἐκ χειρὸς τῆς μάχης ἀπάρχονται, πρὸς οὓς εὐμηχάνως δεῖ προσβάλλειν ἀεί.

117. Χρῶνται δὲ εὐβουλίᾳ καὶ καταστάσει πρὸς τὰς πολεμικὰς μεθόδους τῶν ἄλλων ἁπάντων ἐθνῶν δοκιμώτερον, ὡς παρά τε τῶν ὑποστρατήγων ἡμῶν πολλάκις αὐτοῖς προσβαλλόντων ἐρευνήσαντες ἀνεμάθομεν. καὶ δὴ καὶ ἐκ τῶν
570   ἀνενεχθέντων διηγήσεων τοῖς πρὸ ἡμῶν βασιλεῦσιν ἀνέγνωμεν καὶ μάλιστα παρὰ τοῦ ἡμετέρου θειοτάτου | πατρὸς πολλάκις κατ᾽ αὐτῶν ἐκστρατεύσαντος   356 ἀκηκόαμεν.

118. Λυπεῖ δὲ τοῦτο τὸ ἔθνος ψῦξις καὶ χειμὼν καὶ ὑετῶν ἐπιφοραί, διὸ καὶ ἐν τοῖς τοιούτοις καιροῖς χρὴ τὰς κατ᾽ αὐτῶν συμπλοκὰς ποιεῖσθαι μᾶλλον ἢ ἐν
575   εὐδίαις. καὶ γὰρ καὶ τὰ τόξα αὐτῶν ἀσθενῆ διὰ τὴν ὑγρότητα, καὶ τὸ ὅλον τοῦ σώματος αὐτῶν νωθρὸν διὰ τὸ ψῦχος εὑρεθήσεται. πολλάκις γὰρ ἐν ταῖς κατὰ τοὺς τοιούτους καιροὺς καταδρομαῖς αὐτῶν καὶ λῃστείαις καταληφθέντες ὑπὸ τῶν Ῥωμαίων διεφθάρησαν.

119. Χαίροντες οὖν ταῖς εὐδίαις καὶ ταῖς θερμοτέραις ὥραις τότε συλλέγον-
580   ται, καὶ μάλιστα θέρους, καὶ κατὰ τὴν Ταρσὸν τῆς Κιλικίας τοῖς ἐγχωρίοις ἐνούμενοι τὴν ἐκστρατείαν ποιοῦνται. τοὺς δ᾽ ἄλλους καιροὺς μόνοι οἱ ἐκ

---

557 σταθεροὶ μηδὲ MW γενναῖοι μήτε AVBE | εἰσι De om. codd.   557–558 μηδὲ…τάχος MWA μήτε διὰ τάχους VBEM¹   558 πτοούμενοι MW om. AVBE | ἐπερχομένους MW ἐπερχομένους φοβούμενοι AVBE   558–559 προσποιητὴν ἀναβολὴν MW ἐσχηματισμένην ἀναβολὴν καὶ ὑπέρθεσιν πολέμου AVBE   560 προσμένουσι δὲ MW ὑπομένουσι δὲ ἐν AVBE | φέροντες…μακροθύμως MW μακροθύμως φέροντες τὰς βολὰς AVBE   561–562 τὸν…ἀντιπολεμίων MW τὴν ὁρμὴν αὐτῶν χαλάσασαν ἴδωσιν AVBE   562 εὐτόνως MW εὐτόνως καὶ γενναίως AVBE   565 ἃ MW ἅτινα AVBE | καρτεροῦσι δεχόμενοι MW δέχονται AVBE   570 ἀνέγνωμεν MW om. AVBE   574 τοῖς AVBE om. MW   575 ὑγρότητα MW ὑγρότητα εὑρεθήσεται AVBE   575–576 τοῦ σώματος MW σῶμα AVBE   576 εὑρεθήσεται MW om. AVBE   578 τῶν AVBE om. MW   580 τὴν ταρσὸν MWAVB τέταρσον E   581 οἱ AVBE om. MW

115. In their battle formations they are inventive and steadfast and are not frightened by the rapid onslaught of their attackers nor do they become too relaxed by simulated delays.

116. They stand steadfast in their formation, bearing up valiantly under the missiles fired by the forces boldly attacking them. When they observe that their adversaries' energies are drooping, then they rise up and fight strenuously. They do this not only in battles on foot but also in those on the sea, fighting at close quarters on the ships. After those who had been shooting against them have discharged <their arrows>, which they endure by forming a wall of shields, they quickly come together and in a body rise up and start fighting hand-to-hand. In attacking these people it is always necessary to be ready for anything.

117. They are more notable than all other peoples in relying on good counsel and firm adherence to methods of warfare, as we have learned from our subordinate commanders who have often discovered this in launching attacks against them. Indeed, we have read this in the accounts attributed to the emperors before us and, in particular, we have heard it from our most holy father <Basil> who had frequently campaigned against them.

118. This people is hurt by cold, by winter, and by heavy rain. It is best, therefore, to launch attacks against them at such times rather than in good weather. Their bow strings become slack when it is wet and because of the cold their whole body will become sluggish. Often while making their incursions and plundering raids at such times, they have been overcome by the Romans and destroyed.

119. They flourish, therefore, in good weather and in the warmer seasons, mustering their forces, especially in summer, when they join up with the inhabitants of Tarsus in Cilicia and set out on campaign.[26] At other times of the year

---

26. See Skirmishing, 7: "In that month [August] large numbers would come from Egypt, Palestine, Phoenicia, and southern Syria to Cilicia, to the country around Antioch and to Aleppo and, adding some Arabs to their force, they would invade Roman territory in September."

Ταρσοῦ καὶ Ἀδάνων καὶ τῶν ἄλλων τῆς Κιλικίας πολισμάτων τὰς κατὰ Ῥωμαίων ποιοῦνται καταδρομάς.

120. Χρὴ οὖν αὐτοῖς τότε προσβάλλειν, καὶ μάλιστα κατὰ τὸν χειμῶνα ἐπὶ
585 πραῖδαν ἐξερχομένοις. τοῦτο δὲ γενήσεται ἐὰν τὰ στρατεύματα παραμείναντά που πλησίον ἀσυμφανῶς καὶ τὴν ἔξοδον αὐτῶν ἐπισκοπήσαντα τὴν κατ᾽ αὐτῶν προσβολὴν ποιήσωνται. οὕτως γὰρ διαφθεροῦσιν αὐτούς· ἢ ὅτ᾽ ἂν ὁμοῦ πάντες συνέλθωσιν ἐν πολυπληθίᾳ καὶ καταστάσει πολέμου ἐξηρτισμένοι.

121. Σφαλερὸν γάρ, ὡς πολλάκις ἡμῖν εἴρηται, τὸ πρὸς δημόσιον πόλεμον
590 ἀποκινδυνεύειν τινάς, κἂν πάνυ δοκοῦσι τῶν ἐχθρῶν περιττεύειν τῷ πλήθει· τὸ γὰρ τῆς τύχης ἀόρατον.

122. Συνάγονται δὲ οὐχὶ ἀπὸ καταγραφῆς στρατευόμενοι, ἀλλ᾽ ἕκαστος γνώμῃ ἑκουσίᾳ συντρέχοντες πανοικεί, πλούσιοι μὲν ὥστε ὑπὲρ τοῦ ἰδίου ἔθνους μισθῷ ἀποθανεῖν, πένητες δὲ ἵνα τι τῆς πραίδας κερδήσωσιν. ἀλλὰ καὶ
595 ὅπλα αὐτοῖς οἱ συμφυλέται χορηγοῦσι, καὶ γυναῖκες μάλιστα καὶ ἄνδρες, ὥσπερ διὰ τούτου κοινωνοῦντες αὐτοῖς τῆς ἐκστρατείας, καὶ μισθὸν ἡγούμενοι τὸ καθοπλίσαι στρατιώτας οἱ ὁπλισθῆναι δι᾽ ἀσθένειαν σώματος μὴ δυνάμενοι. καὶ ταῦτα μὲν Σαρακηνοί, ἔθνος βάρβαρόν τε καὶ ἄπιστον.

123. Ῥωμαίους δὲ χρή, οὐ μόνον ταῦτα ἐπιτηδεύειν καὶ εὐψύχους τῇ προαι-
600 ρέσει καὶ στρατιώτας καὶ τοὺς οὔπω στρατευσαμένους συνεκστρατεύειν κατὰ τῶν βλασφημούντων τὸν πάντων βασιλέα Χριστὸν τὸν Θεὸν ἡμῶν καὶ δι᾽ ἁπάντων ἐνδυναμοῦν τοὺς ὑπὲρ αὐτοῦ στρατευομένους κατὰ τῶν ἐθνῶν, καὶ ὅπλοις καὶ δώροις καὶ ταῖς προπεμπτηρίοις εὐχαῖς, ἀλλὰ καὶ πλέον τι τούτων πράττειν, τὸ καὶ τοὺς οἴκους τῶν σὺν προθυμίᾳ καὶ ἀνδρίᾳ στρατευομένων
605 φιλοφρονεῖσθαι, καὶ εἴ τι ἐνδέον τοῖς στρατεύμασιν, ἢ ἵπποι ἢ ἀναλώματα ἢ πανοπλίαι, καὶ ταῦτα χορηγεῖν διὰ κοινωνίας καὶ συγκροτήσεως.

124. Εἰ γὰρ οὕτω γένηται, πάντως πολυπλασίων ὑπάρχων ὁ τῶν Ῥωμαίων στρατός, καὶ καλῶς τε καὶ ὡς προσῆκεν καθωπλισμένος καὶ μάλιστα ὁπόσοι ἐπίλεκτοι | δι᾽ ἀνδρείαν καὶ γενναιότητα τυγχάνουσι, μηδὲν τῶν δεόντων ἐν 356ᵛ

---

584 18.– 20.942 hic om. VBE; v. *Comment.* p. 58.

582 ἀδάνων MW ἀδάλας A ἀδάνας VBE   586 ἀσυμφανῶς MW λαθραίως A |
ἐπισκοπήσαντα MW κατασκοπήσαντα A   588 ἐξηρτισμένοι MW ἡτοιμασμένοι A
590 ἀποκινδυνεύειν MW κινδυνεύειν A | κἂν MW καὶ A | δοκοῦσι MW δοκῶσιν A | ἐχθρῶν
De χειρῶν codd. | περιττεύειν MW περισσεύειν A   590–591 τὸ…ἀόρατον MW ἄδηλον γὰρ
τὸ τῆς τύχης A   595 χορηγοῦσι MW χορηγοῦσιν A   598 τε MW om. A
600 στρατευσαμένους MWA στρατευομένους M¹   602 ἐνδυναμοῦ A ἐνδυναμοῦντα MW
607 οὕτω MW οὕτως A   608 καὶ¹…τε MW om. A   609 τυγχάνουσι M τυγχάνουσιν WA

only the men from Tarsus, Adana, and other cities of Cilicia launch raids against the Romans.

120. Therefore, it is necessary to attack them as they are marching out to pillage, especially in winter. This can be accomplished if <our> armies remain in a location out of sight somewhere nearby. When our men observe them marching out, they can launch an attack against them and so wipe them out. <We can also attack> when all of our troops have come together at the same time in large numbers, fully equipped for battle.

121. It is very dangerous, as we have frequently said, for anyone to run the risk of a pitched battle, even when it seems perfectly clear that <our forces> far outnumber the enemy. The result of fortune is unseen.

122. They are not assembled for military service from a muster list, but they come together, each man of his own free will and with his whole household. The wealthy <consider it> recompense enough to die on behalf of their own nation, the poor for the sake of acquiring booty. Their fellow tribesmen, men and especially women, provide them with weapons, as if sharing with them in the expedition. Because their physical weakness does not enable them to bear arms themselves, they consider it a reward to provide armament for the soldiers. These, then, are the Saracens, a barbaric and faithless people.

123. The Romans, of course, must not only take care of these things, but the soldiers too must be resolute in purpose and those <citizens> who have not actually gone off to war must campaign along with them against those people who blaspheme the emperor of all, Christ our God, and they must strengthen those waging war on his behalf against the nations by every means, by arms, gifts, and processional prayers, even doing more than this, kindly looking after the households of the men who eagerly and bravely march off to war and, if the armies are lacking something such as horses, expenses, or suits of armor, providing these through communal solidarity and collaboration.

124. If this is how everything goes, the army of the Romans, well and properly armed, will greatly increase, especially with a large number of men chosen for

610 αὐτοῖς ὑστερούμενοι, ῥᾳδίως σὺν Θεῷ τὴν κατὰ τῶν βαρβάρων Σαρακηνῶν
ἀναδήσονται νίκην.

125. Εἰ γὰρ τῇ τε ὁπλίσει καὶ μάλιστα τόξοις καὶ βέλεσι πλείστοις, καὶ δὴ καὶ
τῷ πλήθει καὶ τῇ ἀνδρείᾳ καὶ τοῖς προσήκουσι στρατηγήμασί τε καὶ μηχανήμασι
πλεονεκτήσομεν Ῥωμαῖοι μάλιστα κατὰ βαρβάρων, καὶ τὴν θείαν ἐπὶ πᾶσιν
615 ἕξωμεν συμμαχίαν, καὶ εὐκόλως τὴν κατ᾽ ἐκείνων κατορθώσωμεν νίκην.

126. Τοῦτο γὰρ τὸ ἔθνος διὰ τήν, ὡς εἰκός, ἐλπιζομένην πραῖδαν καὶ τὸ μὴ
φοβεῖσθαι κινδύνους πολέμου, εὐκόλως εἰς πολυπληθίαν συνάγεται ἀπὸ τῆς
ἐντὸς Συρίας καὶ Παλαιστίνης ἁπάσης, καὶ τῶν ἀνάνδρων τάχα διὰ τὰς τοιαύτας ἐλπίδας συνερχομένων ἑκουσίως τοῖς ἐκστρατεύουσιν.

620 127. Εἰ δέ, τῆς τοῦ Θεοῦ ἡμῖν συμμαχούσης βοηθείας, καλῶς ὁπλισάμενοι
καὶ παραταξάμενοι, καὶ καλῶς καὶ εὐψύχως προσβαλόντες αὐτοῖς ὑπὲρ τῆς
ψυχικῆς ἡμῶν σωτηρίας, ὡς καὶ ὑπὲρ Θεοῦ αὐτοῦ καὶ συγγενῶν καὶ τῶν ἄλλων
Χριστιανῶν ἀδελφῶν ἡμῶν ἀγωνιζόμενοι ἀνενδοιάστως τὰς εἰς Θεὸν ἐλπίδας
ἔχομεν. οὐκ ἀποτευξόμεθα, ἀλλὰ καὶ ἐπιτευξόμεθα τῶν κατ᾽ ἐκείνων πάντως
625 νικητηρίων.

128. Δεῖ δέ σε, εἴ ποτε καὶ λῃστείας χάριν καταδράμωσι τοῦ Ταύρου ἐντός,
ἐπιτηδεύειν αὐτοὺς καὶ ἐν ταῖς στεναῖς τοῦ ὄρους τούτου διεξόδοις, ὅτ᾽ ἂν
ὑποστρέφωσι μάλιστα κεκοπωμένοι, ἴσως καὶ πραίδας τινὰς ζῷων ἢ πραγμάτων
ἐπιφερόμενοι. ἐπιβιβάζειν γὰρ δεῖ ἐφ᾽ ὑψηλῶν τινων τόπων τοξότας καὶ σφεν-
630 δονήτας καὶ βάλλειν κατ᾽ αὐτῶν, καὶ οὕτως ποιεῖσθαι καὶ τὰς διὰ καβαλλαρίων
προσβολάς, ἢ ὡς ἂν ἡ χρεία καλέσοι ἢ δι᾽ ἐγκρυμμάτων ἢ δι᾽ ἑτέρων ἐπιτηδευμάτων ἢ πετρῶν κατὰ κρημνῶν κυλιομένων ἢ ἀναφραγῆς ὁδοῦ ἀπὸ δένδρων
καὶ ἀδιεξοδεύτου γινομένης, ὡς ἄνω που ἡμῖν εἴρηται, ἢ ὡς ἂν δυνατόν σοι, ὦ
στρατηγέ, κατὰ τὸν τότε καιρὸν τὴν τοῦ πράγματος διάθεσιν κατανοῆσαι.

635 129. Ἐν δὲ ταῖς παρατάξεσιν αὐτῶν οὐ λύουσι τὴν τάξιν, κἂν τις ἐπέλθῃ
αὐτοῖς ἢ δύο ἢ τρεῖς, ἄχρις οὗ ἢ θαρρήσουσι κινήσαντες διῶξαι ἢ δειλιάσουσι
καὶ ὁρμήσουσι πρὸς φυγήν. διὸ χρὴ βαστάξαι τὴν ἔφοδον αὐτῶν πρότερον διὰ
τοξείας τῆς κατ᾽ αὐτῶν τοὺς ἔμπροσθέν τε καὶ μικρὸν ὄπισθεν ἑστῶτας βάλλοντας κατ᾽ αὐτῶν. οὕτως γὰρ τῶν ἵππων αὐτῶν τοξευομένων, τῶν λεγομένων

---

614 ad βαρβάρων des. W

---

610 ῥᾳδίως MW εὐκόλως A   617 πολυπληθίαν M πολὺ πλῆθος A   620 ἡμῖν M ἡμῶν A
621 καὶ καλῶς M γενναίως A   623 ἀνενδοιάστως M ἀδιστάκτους A   624 οὐκ...πάντως
M  ὡς  οὐκ  ἀποτύχωμεν  ἀλλὰ  καὶ  ἐπιτύχωμεν  πάντως  τῶν  κατ᾽  ἐκείνων  A
626–627 καταδράμωσι...καὶ M δράμωσιν ἐντὸς τοῦ ταύρου ἐπιτίθεσθαι αὐτοῖς A
631 καλέσοι M καλέσῃ A   632 κυλιομένων A κυλωμένων M   633 ὡς[1]...που M καθὼς
ἀνωτέρω A   636 ἢ[1]...τρεῖς M om. A   637 βαστάξαι M βαστάσαι A

their courage and nobility, and lacking nothing of what is needed, it will easily, with God's help, be crowned with victory over the barbarian Saracens.

125. If, in our weaponry, especially our great supply of bows and arrows, our numbers and courage, and our requisite stratagems and machines, we Romans are far superior to the barbarians, and if we have the divinity as our ally in everything, we will easily achieve victory over those peoples.

126. Because of the booty they have reason to expect, and because they do not fear the perils of war, this nation is easily gathered together in large numbers from inner Syria and all of Palestine. Because of such expectations, even the cowardly quickly choose to join up with those marching off to war.

127. If we are well armed and drawn up in formation, with God fighting along beside us, we charge against them bravely and in good spirits on behalf of the salvation of our souls, and we carry on the struggle without hesitation on behalf of God himself, our kinsmen, and our brothers the other Christians, then we place our hopes in God. We shall not fail to achieve, rather, we shall certainly achieve the glory of victory over them.

128. If they ever raid inside the Taurus in order to pillage <the area>, it is necessary for you to deal with them in the narrow passes of that mountainous region, when they are on their return journey and are particularly exhausted, perhaps bearing along some booty of animals or objects.[27] Then you must station archers and slingers on some of the high places to shoot at them and thus have the cavalry attack. Or, as the situation requires, lay ambushes or <make use of> other means such as rolling rocks over cliffs or barricading the road with trees and making it impassable, as we have described above. Or make whatever arrangements you deem possible, O general, to deal with the situation at that moment.

129. When they are drawn up for battle, they do not break ranks, even if you charge against them two or three times, up to the point when they either become bold enough to move out in pursuit or become timid enough and rush to escape. It is, therefore, necessary for you to withstand their attack first by archery, with our men stationed in front and those a little behind shooting against them. For in this manner, with their horses, the so-called pharia, being

27. Skirmishing, 20–23.

640 φαρίων, καὶ τῶν Αἰθιόπων ἢ καὶ ἄλλων τοξοτῶν αὐτῶν διὰ τὴν γύμνωσιν αὐτῶν
πληγωμένων, ῥαδίως εἰς φυγὴν ὁρμήσουσι δυοῖν ἕνεκεν· καὶ τοὺς ἵππους
περισῴζειν βουλόμενοι, πολυτίμους ὄντας καὶ οὐκ εὐκόλως ποριζομένους, καὶ
διὰ τῆς τῶν ἵππων σωτηρίας καὶ αὐτοὶ συμπερισῳζόμενοι. τῶν γὰρ ἵππων
ἀπολλυμένων διὰ τῶν βελῶν, καὶ μάλιστα τῶν πεφαρμακευμένων, συναπόλλυν-
645 ται καὶ οἱ ἐποχούμενοι αὐτοῖς ἢ καὶ γνόντες τοῦ φαρμάκου τὴν δύναμιν καὶ πρὸ
τοῦ βληθῆναι | φεύξονται.

357

130. Οὐ τοσοῦτον γὰρ δόξης ὀρεγόμενοι καὶ ὀνόματος ἐκστρατεύονται οἱ
πλεῖστοι Σαρακηνῶν, ὅσον εὐπορίας χάριν καὶ τοῦ τῶν ἐπιτηδείων κέρδους· οὐ
γὰρ γεωργεῖν οἴδασιν, ἵν᾿ ἐντεῦθεν οἱ πένητες διαζῶσιν, ἀλλ᾿ ἐν τῇ μαχαίρᾳ
650 αὐτῶν καὶ μόνῃ ἢ ζῆν ἢ θνήσκειν ἐκ νέου παιδεύονται· ὅθεν ἡ ἅπαξ κατ᾿ αὐτῶν
νίκη πολλῶν ἐλευθερώσει κινδύνων Ῥωμαίους, μηκέτι τολμώντων ἀπερισκέπτως ἐξέρχεσθαι τῶν θεωμένων τοὺς ἐξελθόντας μὴ ὑποστρέψαντας, ἀλλὰ
θρηνουμένους ὑπὸ τῶν ἰδίων.

131. Δοκεῖ δὲ τοῖς Κίλιξι Σαρακηνοῖς, ὅσον ἔχουσι πεζικὸν πρὸς ἀμφοτέρας
655 ἐκπαιδεύειν τὰς μάχας, πρός τε τὴν κατὰ γῆν διὰ τῆς ἐξόδου τῆς διὰ τοῦ Ταύρου
ὄρους καὶ τὴν κατὰ θάλασσαν διὰ τῶν παρ᾿ αὐτοῖς πλοίων, τῶν λεγομένων
κουμβαρίων· καὶ ὅτε μὴ πρὸς τὴν ἤπειρον ἐκστρατεύουσι, διὰ τῆς θαλάσσης
ἐξέρχονται, πραίδας τε ποιοῦντες κατὰ τῶν παραθαλασσίων χωρίων. πολλάκις
δέ, εἰ οὕτω τύχῃ, καὶ ναυμαχοῦντες. ὅτε δὲ μὴ κατὰ θάλασσαν ἐξέλθωσι, διὰ τῆς
660 ἠπείρου κατὰ τῶν Ῥωμαϊκῶν χωρίων ἐκστρατεύουσι.

132. Δεῖ οὖν ἐπιτηρεῖν σε, ὦ στρατηγέ, διὰ κατασκόπων ἀληθῶν καὶ μανθάνειν τὰ κατ᾿ αὐτοὺς ἀκριβῶς καὶ ἑτοιμάζεσθαι σὺν τῷ ἀρκοῦντι στρατῷ, ἵν᾿
ὅτ᾿ ἂν διὰ θαλάσσης ἐκστρατεύσωσιν, αὐτὸς κατὰ γῆν, εἰ δυνατόν, ἐν τῇ ἰδίᾳ
αὐτῶν προσβάλῃς αὐτοῖς. ὅτ᾿ ἂν δὲ ἐπὶ τῆς γῆς ἐκστρατεύειν μέλλωσι, μηνύσῃς
665 τῷ Κιβυρραιώτῃ τοῦ πλοΐμου στρατηγῷ, καὶ μετὰ τῶν ὑπ᾿ αὐτὸν δρομώνων εἰσ-
πιπτέτω κατὰ τῶν Ταρσέων καὶ Ἀδανέων χωρίων, ὅσα κεῖται κατὰ θάλασσαν. οὐ

641 πληγωμένων Μ πληττομένων Α | ῥαδίως Μ συντόμως Α | ὁρμήσουσι…ἕνεκεν Μ
ὁρμήσουσιν Α   642–643 οὐκ…διὰ Μ μετὰ Α   643 αὐτοὶ συμπερισῳζόμενοι Μ ἑαυτοὺς
περισῴζειν ἐθέλοντες Α | τῶν² Α om. Μ   645 ἐποχούμενοι αὐτοῖς Μ ἐπιβαίνοντες αὐτοὺς Α
646 φεύξονται Μ εἰς φυγὴν τραπήσονται Α   647 ὀρεγόμενοι Μ ἐπιθυμοῦντες Α |
ἐκστρατεύονται Μ ἐκστρατεύουσιν Α   648 καὶ…ἐπιτηδείων Μ om. Α   651 ἐλευθερώσει
κινδύνων Μ trsp. Α   654 κίλιξι Μ ἐν κιλικίᾳ Α   655 ἐκπαιδεύειν…μάχας Μ trsp. Α
656 θάλασσαν Μ θάλατταν Α   657 κουμβαρίων Μ κομβαρίων Α | μὴ…ἐκστρατεύουσι Μ
δὲ μὴ κατὰ γῆς ἐκστρατεύουσιν Α   659 εἰ Μ ἐὰν Α | ἐξέλθωσι Μ ἐξέλθωσιν Α
660 ἠπείρου Μ γῆς Α | χωρίων ἐκστρατεύουσι Μ χωρῶν ἐκστρατεύουσιν Α   663 ἰδίᾳ Μ
χώρᾳ Α   664 αὐτοῖς Μ om. Α | μέλλωσι Μ μέλλωσιν Α   666 ἀδανέων Μ ἀδανίων Α

shot at, as well as the Ethiopians or other archers being wounded because they do not wear armor, they will quickly rush off in flight.[28] They will do this for two reasons, namely because of their desire to save their horses, which are highly prized and not easily procured, and because they want to save themselves as well through saving the horses. For when the horses are wiped out by missile fire, especially by poisoned arrows, their riders perish at the same time or, because they know the strength of the poison, they will flee before being hit.

130. The majority of the Saracens do not go on campaign so much to attain glory and fame as for the sake of providing for themselves and gaining material goods. For they do not know how to farm in order to save themselves from poverty, but they are trained from childhood to live or die by the sword alone. And so, just one victory over them will free the Romans from a multitude of dangers. They will no longer be so bold and thoughtless as to march out <against us> again, when they observe that those men who had marched out have not returned, but are being mourned by their own people.

131. The Saracens in Cilicia place great value on thoroughly training all their infantry forces to engage in battle on two fronts, that is, on land along the road leading out from the Taurus mountains and on sea by means of their ships, called koumbaria.[29] When they do not campaign on dry land, they sail out to sea, pillaging the towns along the coast and often, if it so happens, engaging in naval battles. When they do not go out to sea, they campaign against the Roman territories on land.

132. You, therefore, O general, must keep an eye on them by means of trusted spies. Find out exactly what is going on with them and be prepared with a strong enough army. When they campaign by sea, you go by land and, if possible, launch an attack against them in their own territory. But if the spies report that it is their intention to campaign on land, then you should advise the commander of the Kibyrraiotai fleet so that, with the dromons under his command he may fall upon the Tarseote and Adanan territories that lie along

28. Pharia, from a Semitic root, designated the so-called Arabian horses, originally bred by the Bedouins, and highly prized in the medieval and modern worlds. Cf. Theophanes *Cont.*, 480.

29. κουμβάρια. Large ships; see *infra* Const. 19; *LBG*, s.v.

γὰρ πολυπληθία στρατοῦ τοῖς Κίλιξι βαρβάροις ἐστίν, ἐπεί περ οἱ αὐτοὶ καὶ κατὰ
γῆν καὶ κατὰ θάλατταν ἐκστρατεύονται.

133. Τὸ δὲ κεφάλαιον τῆς ἐκείνων καταπτώσεώς ἐστιν, ἵνα ὁμοῦ καὶ διὰ
670 πλοΐμου στόλου τοῦ ἱκανοῦ καὶ διὰ πεζικοῦ στρατοῦ διὰ τοῦ Ταύρου, ἅμα καὶ
ἑτέροις συστρατήγοις τοῖς ἀρκοῦσι ποιήσῃς τὴν κατ’ αὐτῶν προσβολὴν καὶ
ἐπέλευσιν, καὶ οὕτω τῶν λῃστῶν ἐκείνων καταλήσῃ τὴν χώραν, οἷόν ποτε ὁ
ἡμέτερος μακαριώτατος πατὴρ καὶ Ῥωμαίων αὐτοκράτωρ ἐν τοῖς αὐτοῦ χρόνοις
διὰ κελεύσεως αὐτοῦ θείας πεποίηκε.

675 134. Τοὺς δὲ πλησιάζοντας τῇ Μεσοποταμίᾳ Συρίας Σαρακηνοὺς δι’ ἐπιτηδευμάτων καταπολεμήσεις, οἷς ἐχρήσατο ὁ κατὰ τὸν μικρῷ παρελθόντα καιρὸν
τὴν Θεοδοσιούπολιν ὑπ’ ἐκείνων κατεχομένην ἀφελόμενος στρατηγός, καὶ τῇ
ἡμετέρᾳ αὐτὴν ὑποτάξας βασιλείᾳ. ἐπειδὴ δὲ οἱ Ῥωμαϊκοὶ ἵπποι ἀήθως ἔχοντες
πρός τε τὰς καμήλους, καὶ πολλῷ μᾶλλον πρὸς τὰ τύμπανα ἠχοῦντα καὶ τὰ
680 κύμβαλα πτύρονται, καὶ ἀποστρέφονται εἰς τὰ ὀπίσω, ὥστε καὶ εἰς φυγὴν διὰ
τοῦ τοιούτου τρόπου πολλάκις ὁρμᾶν Ῥωμαίους, δεῖ ἐθίζεσθαι τοὺς τῶν στρατι-
ωτῶν ἵππους, καὶ μάλιστα | τῶν πρωτοστατῶν καὶ τῶν ἀρχόντων, εἴς τε τοὺς    357ᵛ
κτύπους τῶν τυμπάνων καὶ τῶν κυμβάλων διὰ τοιαύτης γυμνασίας, καὶ δὴ καὶ
εἰς τὸ συνεῖναι καμήλοις καὶ μὴ ξενίζεσθαι τῇ θέᾳ αὐτῶν. εἰσὶ δὲ καὶ ἕτερα, ἅπερ
685 ἄν τις ἐπινοήσοι πρὸς τὰ παρόντα διασκοπούμενος.

135. Συνελόντα δὲ εἰπεῖν, ἅπαντα τὰ προειρημένα περὶ τῆς τακτικῆς θεωρίας
ἀπ’ ἀρχῆς ἄχρι τέλους, ὅσα τε διά τε τὰ ὅπλα καὶ τὰς ὁπλίσεις καὶ τὰς γυμνασίας καὶ τὰς παρατάξεις τὰς πολεμικὰς καὶ τὰς ἄλλας στρατηγικὰς μεθόδους
εἴρηται, ἕνεκεν τοῦ Σαρακηνῶν ἔθνους ἡμῖν καὶ παρηγγέλθη καὶ διατέτακται.
690 τοῦτο γὰρ γειτονεῦον τῇ ἡμετέρᾳ πολιτείᾳ, οὐδὲν ἧττον τοῦ πάλαι Περσικοῦ
ἔθνους τοῖς ἀρχαίοις βασιλεῦσι, τὰ νῦν ἡμῖν ἐνοχλεῖ καὶ παραλυπεῖ τοὺς
ἡμετέρους ὑπηκόους τὸ καθεκάστην, οὗ χάριν καὶ τὸν παρόντα τῆς πολεμικῆς
διατάξεως ἀνεδεξάμεθα πόνον. εὕρηνται δὲ ἡμῖν πρὸς τοῖς εἰρημένοις καὶ ἕτερα
παρατάξεων σχήματα, οἷς χρησάμενος, ὦ στρατηγέ, κατὰ τοῦ τοιούτου βαρβα-
695 ρικοῦ ἔθνους εὐδοκιμήσεις. εἰσὶ δὲ ταῦτα.

136. Ποιήσεις παράταξιν ποικίλην, ὡς ἐν τύπῳ εἰπεῖν, ἀπὸ ἀνδρῶν ,δ’ ἐπιλέκτων οὕτως· πρώτη μὲν ἔστω παράταξις, ἡ λεγομένη πρόμαχος, ἀνδρῶν ,αφ’,

---

668 θάλατταν Μ θάλασσαν Α   671 ἀρκοῦσι Μ ἀρκοῦσιν Α   672 οὕτω Μ οὕτως Α |
καταλήσῃ…χώραν Μ τὴν χώραν ἐξαφανίσῃς Α   674 πεποίηκε Μ πεποίηκεν Α   681 τοῦ
Α om. Μ   684 καμήλοις Μ καμήλους Α   689 σαρακηνῶν ἔθνους Μ ἔθνους τῶν
σαρακηνῶν Α   690–691 οὐδὲν…βασιλεῦσι Μ om. Α   692 οὖ Μ οὕτινος Α   693 πόνον
Α μόνον Μ | πρὸς Μ σὺν Α   696 ,δ’ Μ τετρακισχιλίων Α   697 ,αφ’ Μ χιλίων φ’ Α

the coast.[30] For the army of the Cilician barbarians is not very numerous, since the same men are campaigning both on land and on the sea.

133. What most contributes to the downfall of those people is the simultaneous assault of a strong battle fleet and of an infantry force through the Taurus. Together with a good number of your subcommanders, launch your attack against them. In this way you will plunder the land of those bandits, as our most blessed father and autokrator of the Romans once did in his days by his sacred command.[31]

134. In waging war against the Saracens of Syria dwelling near Mesopotamia, adopt the methods employed by the commander, who, a short time ago, recaptured Theodosioupolis, which had been occupied by them, and returned it to our dominion.[32] The horses of the Romans are unaccustomed to camels and are even more frightened by the noise of drums and cymbals and they turn around <and move> to the rear. This tactic has often caused the Romans to rush into flight. It is necessary, then, to accustom the horses of the soldiers, especially those of the front line troops and their officers, to the din of the drums and cymbals by using them in drills and also to have camels among them so they will not be scared by the sight of them. There are also other considerations that one could discover by careful investigation of present conditions.

135. To sum it up, all that we have written about tactical theory from the beginning to the end, all that was said about weapons, armament, drills, battle formations, and other military methods in connection with the Saracen people has been transmitted and set forth by us. This people that borders on our commonwealth causes us no less trouble now than the Persian people of old did to former emperors. They cause harm to our subjects every day. It is for this reason that we have undertaken the present task of formulating instructions for war. In addition to what we have already said, we have found other models of battle formations that you may well consider employing, O general, against this barbaric people. They are the following.

136. Vary your battle formation. To give an example, <take> about four thousand picked troops. Let the first battle line, called promachos, consist of one

30. The Kibyrraiotai theme, in southwest Asia Minor, furnished a large number of ships and crews for the imperial navy.

31. This probably refers to the expedition of Basil I in 876–877.

32. Theodosioupolis (Arm.: Karin; Turk.: Erzurum), in Armenia, was taken from the Arabs for a brief period in 754, then retaken by the Byzantines in 949. This note must refer to the campaign led by the magister Leo Katakalon, in 902. See *DAI*, 45; *Commentary*, 173.

ἢν εἰς τρία διαιρήσεις ἴσα μέρη, δεξιόν, ἀριστερόν, μέσον, ὥστε εἶναι καὶ ταῦτα
ἀπὸ ἀνδρῶν φ΄, ἔγγιστα ἀλλήλων, τῶν τριῶν τούτων τάξεων παρατεταγμένων,
700 ὡς δοκεῖν μίαν εἶναι τὴν τάξιν. τὴν δὲ δευτέραν τάξιν ποιήσεις ἀπὸ ἀνδρῶν ͵α΄,
ἢν εἰς δ΄ διαιρήσεις μέρη ἀπὸ ἑνὸς σαγιττοβόλου ἀλλήλων διϊστάμενα, ὥστε
εἶναι αὐτὰ ἀπὸ ἀνδρῶν σν΄, ὀπίσω τῆς πρώτης παρατάξεως ἱσταμένων ὥστε, εἴ
γε τοῦτο συμβῇ, τὴν πρώτην ὑποποδίσαι τάξιν, ὑποδέχεσθαι αὐτὴν ἐν τοῖς
κενοῖς αὐτῶν τῆς διαιρέσεως τόποις, καὶ οἷον μίαν σὺν αὐτοῖς γίνεσθαι παρά-
705 ταξιν. τὰ γὰρ δ΄ μέρη τῆς δευτέρας τάξεως τρία ποιεῖ κενὰ χωρία, εἰς ἅπερ οἱ τῆς
πρώτης τάξεως ἐλθόντες συστήσονται τῇ δευτέρᾳ. ἐπὶ ταύταις δὲ ποιήσεις καὶ
νωτοφύλακας ἄνδρας φ΄, οὓς διαιρήσεις εἰς μέρη β΄ κατὰ οὐράν, ἤτοι δεξιὸν καὶ
ἀριστερόν· ἵστασθαι δὲ αὐτοὺς ὀπίσω τῆς δευτέρας παρατάξεως εἰς τρίτην τάξιν,
ἔχοντας ἕκαστον μέρος ἀνὰ σν΄, ὥστε καὶ ἐν καιρῷ χρείας αὐτοὺς προερχο-
710 μένους ἑνοῦσθαι πρὸς βοήθειαν τῇ δευτέρᾳ παρατάξει, ὑποδεχομένη τὴν
πρώτην. ταύτας μέντοι τὰς τρεῖς τάξεις, εἰ καὶ διῃρημένας διὰ τὴν χρείαν ὡρίσαμεν, ἀλλ᾽ οὖν ἡνωμένας τῇ ἐγγύτητι καὶ τοῖς ὑπὲρ ἀλλήλων ἀγωνίσμασι κατανοοῦμεν, διὰ τὸ τοῦ σχήματος εὔθετον· ἐπὶ τούτοις στήσεις καὶ τὰ λεγόμενα
κέρατα κατὰ χεῖρα, καὶ ἔμπροσθεν τῆς πρώτης τάξεως τοὺς μὲν λεγομένους
715 ὑπερκεραστὰς κατὰ τὸ δεξιὸν | μέρος, τοὺς δὲ πλαγιοφύλακας κατὰ τὸ εὐώνυ- 358
μον· καὶ ταῦτα ἔστωσαν ἀπὸ σ΄ ἀνδρῶν, ὥστε εἶναι ἑτοίμους εἰς τὸ κυκλῶσαι
τὴν ἐπερχομένην τῶν πολεμίων παράταξιν τοὺς ὑπερκεραστάς, εἰς δὲ τὸ κωλῦ-
σαι τὴν ἀπ᾽ ἐκείνων κατὰ τῆς σῆς τάξεως κύκλωσιν τοὺς εὐωνύμους πλαγιοφύλακας, ἢ τάχα καὶ αὐτοὺς εἰς κύκλωσιν ἑτοίμους. καὶ πρὸς τούτοις ποιήσεις ἐν
720 ἑκατέρᾳ πλευρᾷ μακρόθεν τάγματα β΄ ἀπὸ ἀνδρῶν σ΄, ὥστε εἰς ἐγκρύμματα
γενέσθαι, ἔνθεν κἀκεῖθεν τῆς παρατάξεως εἰς τόπους κρυπτοὺς ἐγκαθημένους,
ἢ ὀπίσω μὲν τῆς παρατάξεως ἑστῶτας, ἀθρόως δὲ καὶ τὸ δὴ λεγόμενον δρουγγιστὶ ἐκπηδῶντας, καὶ κατὰ τῶν πλευρῶν τῶν πολεμίων ἐπερχομένους.

---

702 ad ἱσταμένων de novo inc. W

---

698 ἢν A καὶ M   699 φ΄ M πεντακοσίων A | τάξεων M παρατάξεων A   700 ͵α΄ M χιλίων A
701 δ΄ M τέσσαρα A   702 σν΄ M διακοσίων πεντήκοντα A   703 ὑποποδίσαι MW
ὀπισθοποδίσαι A   704 κενοῖς...τόποις MW διαχωρίσμασιν αὐτῶν A   705 δ΄ M τέσσαρα
WA | κενὰ χωρία MW διαχωρίσματα A   706 τάξεως MW παρατάξεως A   707 φ΄ M
πεντακοσίους WA | β΄ M δύο WA | κατὰ οὐράν MW om. A   708 ὀπίσω MW ὄπισθεν A
709 ἔχοντας...μέρος MW ἔχοντα ἑκάστου μέρους A | σν΄ MW διακοσίων πεντήκοντα A |
καὶ MW om. A | χρείας MW χρείας καὶ A   712 ἀγωνίσμασι MA ἀγωνίσμασιν W
715–716 εὐώνυμον MW ἀριστερὸν A   716 σ΄ ἀνδρῶν MW ἀνδρῶν διακοσίων A | ἑτοίμους
MW ἑτοίμους τοὺς ὑπερκεραστὰς A   717 τοὺς ὑπερκεραστὰς MW om. A   720 β΄ M δύο
WA | σ΄ MW διακοσίων A   721 παρατάξεως A om. MW   723 καὶ MW om. A

thousand five hundred men; divide them into three equal divisions, very close to one another, that is, right, left, middle, so each will have five hundred men. When drawn up in formation, these three lines will appear as one line. You will make the second line of one thousand men, and divide it into four divisions separated from one another by one bowshot; these will thus consist of two hundred fifty men. Station them behind the first battle line, so that if the first line happens to retreat, it may find refuge in the empty spaces between the divisions, and with them it will seem to form one battle line. For the four divisions of the second line make three empty spaces in which the men of the first line may take their stand and receive the support of the second line. In addition to these, post five hundred men as rear guards and divide them into two divisions in the rear: right and left. Post them behind the second battle line as a third line, with each section having two hundred fifty men. In time of need have these sections join together and move forward to support the second battle line, which has already received the first. These three lines, then, though we defined them as separate by necessity, nonetheless we still consider them to be united by their closeness and their struggles on behalf of one another, on account of the good arrangement of the model. In addition to these, station the so-called horns close by and, in front of the first line, the so-called outflankers by the right division and the flank guards by the left. These should amount to two hundred men. The outflankers should be prepared to encircle the advancing line of the enemy, while the flank guards on the left are to prevent the encirclement of your line by the enemy, or perhaps they too should be ready to take part in the encircling <of the enemy>. In addition to these, also post two tagmata of two hundred men on each side at a distance to set up ambushes, lying in wait in hidden places on this side and that of your battle line. Or they may be stationed behind the battle line ready to charge out all at once, in what is called a droungos, and attack the flanks of the enemy.

137. Ἔστωσαν δὲ καὶ ἐν τοῖς τρισὶ κενοῖς μέρεσι τῆς δευτέρας παρατάξεως
725 τάγματα ἀπὸ ἀνδρῶν ρ′ ἤγουν ἄνδρες τ′, ὥστε δοκεῖν συνημμένην εἶναι καὶ
αὐτὴν τὴν τάξιν. οὗτοι δέ, εἰ ἄρα χρεία καλέσοι ὑποχωρῆσαι τοὺς τῆς πρώτης
τάξεως εἰς τὰ εἰρημένα τρία κενὰ <χωρία>, ὑποχωρήσουσιν ὀπίσω, ὁμοῦ δὲ καὶ
ἀναστελοῦσι τοὺς ὁρμῶντας πρὸς φυγήν, καὶ ἐπιστρέψουσιν εἰς τὴν οἰκείαν
αὐτῶν τάξιν, τοῖς νωτοφύλαξιν ἅμα γινόμενοι διὰ τῆς ὀπίσω ὑποχωρήσεως,
730 ὅπερ οὐ μικρὰν ῥοπὴν ποιήσει τοῖς ἀγωνιζομένοις ὠφέλιμον.

138. Οἱ δὲ λοιποὶ ρ′ ἄνδρες ἔστωσαν ἅμα τῷ στρατηγῷ μετὰ τῆς ἰδίας αὐτοῦ
προελεύσεως ἵνα, ὁπότ᾽ ἂν συμβῇ χρείαν γενέσθαι βοηθῆσαί τινι βαρουμένῳ
μέρει, ἀποστελλόμενοι ἱκανὴν ῥοπὴν παρέχωσιν αὐτῷ καὶ ἀναψυχὴν διὰ τῆς
αὐτῶν ἱκανότητος.

735 139. Καὶ οὕτως μὲν ἡ πᾶσα πρώτη τε καὶ δευτέρα καὶ τρίτη τάξις τῆς παρατάξεως, καὶ δὴ καὶ οἱ πλαγιοφύλακες καὶ ὑπερκερασταὶ καὶ νωτοφύλακές τε καὶ
ἔνεδροι καὶ οἱ μέσοι τῶν κενῶν τόπων, καὶ δὴ καὶ οἱ ἐν ὑποβοηθείᾳ μετὰ τοῦ
στρατηγοῦ τεταγμένοι, ἐν ὅλοις ‚δ′ ἀνδράσι πάντες ὁμοῦ ταττέσθωσαν.

140. Ὁ δὲ στρατηγὸς τὴν μέσην ἐχέτω τάξιν τῆς πρώτης παρατάξεως, καὶ
740 διατατττέτω καὶ ὁράτω τὰ δέοντα, καὶ ταύτην ἐχέτω πρὸς βοήθειαν, εἴ που καὶ
δέοι μείζονος δυνάμεως, ἐκπέμπων ἅμα τοῦ σὺν αὐτῷ ἑστῶτος τουρμάρχου,
ἤτοι τοῦ πάλαι μὲν ὑποστρατήγου νῦν δὲ μεράρχου καλουμένου. καὶ γὰρ καθ᾽
ἕκαστον μέρος ἔμπροσθεν τουρμάρχης ὀφείλει προτάττεσθαι, καὶ ἐπὶ πάντων
τούτων ὁ στρατηγός.

745 141. Ἐχέτωσαν δὲ τὰ μέρη καὶ τοὺς ἰδίους δρουγγαρίους καὶ τοὺς ὑπ᾽ ἐκείνους κόμητας καὶ τοὺς λοιποὺς ἄρχοντας κατ᾽ ἀρετὴν ἕκαστον συνεστῶτας, καὶ
ἰθύνοντας τοὺς στρατιώτας καὶ διεγείροντας πρὸς τὴν προκειμένην μάχην.

---

724 κενοῖς μέρεσι MW διαχωρίσμασι A   725 τάγματα A om. MW | ρ′ MW ἑκατὸν A | τ′
MW τριακόσιοι A | συνημμένην MW μίαν καὶ ἠνωμένην A   726 τὴν A om. MW |
ὑποχωρῆσαι MW om. A   727 τάξεως MW τάξεως ὀπισθοποδήσαντες A | κενὰ MW χωρία
ci. De διαχωρίσματα εἰσελθεῖν A   727–730 ὁμοῦ…ὠφέλιμον MW καὶ ἐνωθήσονται τοῖς
νωτοφύλαξιν καὶ ἅμα μὲν εἰς τρίτην παράταξιν σὺν αὐτοῖς γενήσονται ἅμα δὲ καὶ τοὺς φεύγειν
βουλομένους ἀποκωλύσουσιν ἅπερ οὐ μικρῶς τοὺς ἀγωνιζομένους ὠφελήσουσιν A
728 ἀναστελοῦσι M ἀναστείλουσιν W om. A   731 ρ′ M ἑκατὸν WA   733 ῥοπὴν MW
βοήθειαν A   733–734 διὰ…ἱκανότητος MW om. A   735 καὶ τρίτη MW om. A
736–737 τε…ἔνεδροι MW καὶ οἱ τῶν ἐγκρυμμάτων A   737 κενῶν τόπων MW
διαχωρισμάτων A | τοῦ MW τῶ A   738 ‚δ′ MW τετρακισχιλίοις A   741 ἑστῶτος
τουρμάρχου MW ἑστῶτι τουρμάρχη A   742 τοῦ MW τῶ A | ὑποστρατήγου MW
ὑποστρατήγω A | μεράρχου καλουμένου MW μεράρχη καλουμένω A

137. In the three empty spaces of the second battle line station between one hundred and three hundred men so that it appears to be one continuous line. If it becomes necessary for the soldiers in the first line to retreat into those three empty spaces, then the men <stationed there> will draw back and, at the same time, restrain the men rushing into flight and make them turn back to their own line. In withdrawing to the rear, they join up with the rear guard. This will be beneficial and of no small importance to the men who are struggling.

138. Station the rest of the one hundred men with the general and his own retinue. Whenever the need arises, they can assist any division under pressure. Because of their numbers, when they are sent out, they may well bring sufficient strength and a respite to such a unit.

139. And so the entire first, second, and third lines of the battle formation, as well as the flank guards, the outflankers, the rear guards, the ambushers, and the men in the middle of the empty spaces, together with the support troops stationed with the general, all these together add up to four thousand men in formation.

140. Let the general have the middle position of the first battle line, where he can see and make arrangements for what is needed. Let him have this support unit so that, if ever a greater force is needed, he may dispatch it together with the tourmarch stationed with him, or the officer formerly called lieutenant general, now known as merarch. A tourmarch ought to take his place in front of each division and the general over all of these.

141. The divisions should have their own droungarioi. The counts under their command and the rest of the officers, each one according to his valor, should be stationed with him to strengthen the soldiers and to arouse them for the impending battle.

142. Τὸ δὲ ποσὸν τῆς πρώτης τάξεως διαιρήσεις, καὶ τὸ μὲν αὐτοῦ, ἤγουν τὸ τρίτον μέρος, ἀφορίσεις εἰς τοὺς λεγομένους κούρσορας, ὅσους μάλιστα γινώ-
750 σκεις ἀνδρείους καὶ εὐτόλμους, τὸ δὲ δίμοιρον μέρος τάξεις εἰς τοὺς λεγομέ-νους διφένσορας, ἵνα οἱ μὲν κατὰ πρόσωπον πεμπόμενοι ὡς πρόμαχοι ἐπέλθωσι κατὰ τῶν πολεμίων | δρουγγιστί, ὅ ἐστιν ὁμοῦ ἄνευ τάξεως, καὶ εἰ μὲν τρέψωσιν 358ᵛ αὐτούς, ἀκολουθήσωσι καὶ οἱ διφένσορες, ἤγουν οἱ βοηθοὶ καὶ ἔκδικοι, μὴ λύοντες τὴν τάξιν αὐτῶν, ἀλλ' εὐτάκτως περιπατοῦντες, εἰ δὲ βαρηθῶσιν οἱ
755 κούρσορες, ἤγουν οἱ λεγόμενοι καὶ προκλάσται, εἶτα ὑποστρέψωσιν, ἵνα ὑπο-δέχωνται αὐτοὺς οἱ διφένσορες μετὰ τάξεως καὶ ἀναστέλλωσι τοὺς πολεμίους. εἰ δέ τι καὶ πλέον καὶ οἱ τῆς δευτέρας τάξεως ὑποβοηθήσουσι, καὶ προσέτι οἱ νωτοφύλακες, καὶ οὕτως διώξουσι τοὺς πολεμίους, ἐκ διαδοχῆς τὴν βοήθειαν παρὰ πολλῶν ὑποδεχόμενοι· οὐ γάρ μοι δοκεῖ ἐν μιᾷ μόνῃ παρατάξει ἀποκιν-
760 δυνεύειν ἀσφαλές, ὁμοῦ γὰρ πονοῦσα ἡ μία ὁμοῦ καὶ φεύγει. ἐνταῦθα δέ, εἰ καὶ ἡ πρώτη πονήσει, ἀλλ' ἡ δευτέρα ἑστῶσα ῥωμαλαιότερον βοηθήσει· εἰ δὲ καὶ αὐτὴ πονήσει, ἀλλ' ἡ τρίτη ἀπαθῶς ἐπέλθῃ, καὶ οὕτως πρὸς τρεῖς ἀπαθεῖς παρατάξεις ἡ μία τῶν πολεμίων πονοῦσα εὐκαταγώνιστος γίνεται, καὶ ταχέως λυθήσεται, καὶ εἰς φυγὴν ὁρμήσει, συμπνεόντων δηλονότι κατὰ τὸ ἐνδεχόμενον
765 καὶ τῶν πλαγιοφυλάκων καὶ τῶν ὑπερκεραστῶν, μάλιστα τῶν εἰρημένων τετρα-κισχιλίων ἀνδρῶν ἐπιλέκτων ὄντων, καὶ διαφερόντων τῇ ἀνδρίᾳ καὶ τῇ περὶ τοὺς πολέμους ἀρετῇ, ὅπερ ὀφείλει. οὐ γὰρ πρὸς ἀνδραποδώδη στρατὸν ἡμῖν πρόκειται ἡ διάταξις, ἀλλὰ πρὸς ἱκανὸν μεταχειρίσασθαι ὅπλον καὶ ἐκθύμως ἀγωνίσασθαι.

770 143. Τὰς δὲ ἀκίας τῆς τοιαύτης παρατάξεως ποιήσεις ἀπὸ ἀνδρῶν δέκα τὸ βάθος, ἤτοι τὸ πάχος αὐτῶν, ὥστε εἶναι καθ' ἑκάστην ἀκίαν ἄρχοντας δύο, τόν τε λεγόμενον λοχαγόν, ἤγουν δέκαρχον ἢ πρωτοστάτην ἢ πρόμαχον, καὶ τὸν οὐραγόν, ὅς ἐστιν ἔσχατος τοῦ στίχου καὶ καλεῖται πεντάρχης, οὓς καὶ μάλιστα ἱκανοὺς εἶναι χρὴ καὶ ἀνδρείους καὶ καταφράκτους τοῖς ἁρμόζουσιν ὅπλοις· καὶ
775 οὕτως τοῦ βάθους τῶν ἀκιῶν τεταγμένου, τὸ ἐπὶ μέτωπον ἔκταμα πρὸς πλάτος κατὰ ζυγόν, ὅσον ἂν ἀπαντήσῃ, τάττεσθαι καὶ κατὰ πλευράν.

---

748 ad τάξεως des. W

755 καὶ M om. A    757 ὑποβοηθήσουσι M ἐπιβοηθήσουσιν A    759 οὐ A οἱ M
759–760 μοι…ἀσφαλές M δοκεῖ μοι ἀσφαλὲς ἐν μιᾷ μόνῃ παρατάξει ἀποκινδυνεύειν A
761 ῥωμαλαιότερον M ἰσχυρότερον A    764 συμπνεόντων M συμπνούντων A    765 τῶν¹
M συνεργούντων A    767 ὅπερ M ὥσπερ δὴ καὶ A | ἀνδραποδώδη M ἀνδραποδώδη καὶ
χυδαῖον A    767–768 ἡμῖν πρόκειται M trsp. A    768 ἐκθύμως M προθύμως A    776 κατὰ²
M παρὰ A

142. Divide the number <of men> in the first line, assigning part of it, that is, a third, into the so-called assault troops, men whom you know to be especially brave and courageous. Designate the second part as the so-called defenders. The assault troops are sent against the front. As promachoi they should attack the enemy in irregular order, that is, all together without any formation. If they force them to flee, the defenders, that is, the support troops and ekdikoi, will pursue them without breaking their formation, but riding along in good order. But if the assault troops, also known as proklastai, come under pressure, they will then withdraw so that the defenders may receive them in order and hold back the enemy. But if there is something more, the men in the second line shall move to help, and the rear guard as well, and in this manner they will pursue the enemy, continuously receiving help from many sources. I do not think it is safe to take such great risks with only one battle line. When the first finds itself in difficulties, at that time it also turns to flight. But here <in our scheme> even if the first finds itself in difficulty, the second line is standing there, ready to assist it most vigorously. If this line is in difficulty, the third, still unharmed, will move up. In this way, against three unharmed battle lines the one line of the enemy will be in difficulty, will be easily overcome, quickly break ranks, and turn to flight. The flank guards and the outflankers, of course, must cooperate in this operation, especially in unison with the above-mentioned four thousand men, all elite troops, as they should be, outstanding for bravery and valor in warfare. For this constitution of ours is not intended for an army of slaves but for one that will take weapons in hand and enthusiastically engage in combat.

143. Make the files of such a battle line ten men deep, or thick, so that in each file there shall be two officers, the one called group leader, also dekarch, protostates, or promachos, and the ouragos, who is the last of the row and is called pentarch. It is necessary that these men be particularly qualified and brave, and equipped with the appropriate armor and weapons. With the depth of the files formed in this way, arrange the extent along the front according to width, line by line, as much as is called for, and also by the flank.

496    Constitution 18

144. Ἐπὶ δὲ τῆς νῦν ὑποθέσεως ἡ μὲν πρώτη τάξις, ἥτις καὶ εἰς τρία μέρη διαιρεθήσεται, καθ᾽ ἕκαστον μέρος ἕξει ἀκίας πεντήκοντα, ἀνὰ δέκα ἔχουσαν τὸ βάθος κατὰ στίχον, ἀπὸ τοῦ λοχαγοῦ καὶ πρωτοστάτου ἕως τοῦ ἐσχάτου οὐρα-
780 γοῦ, ὡς εἶναι τὰς ὅλας ἀκίας τῶν τριῶν μερῶν τῆς πρώτης τάξεως ρν΄, ἤτοι ἄνδρας χιλίους καὶ πεντακοσίους. ἡ δὲ δευτέρα τάξις ἐχέτω διὰ τῶν τεσσάρων αὐτῆς μερῶν ἀκίας ἀνὰ εἴκοσι καὶ πέντε, τὰς πάσας ἀκίας ἑκατὸν ἄνδρας χιλί-ους. <οἱ δὲ νωτοφύλακες, ἤγουν ἡ τρίτη τάξις ἐχέτω ἀκίας ἀνὰ εἴκοσι καὶ πέντε, ὁμοῦ ἄνδρας πεντακοσίους.> οἱ δὲ πλαγιοφύλακες ἕξουσιν ἀκίας δέκα, ἄνδρας
785 ἑκατόν· ὁμοίως καὶ οἱ ὑπερκερασταὶ ἀκίας δέκα, ἄνδρας ἑκατόν, προσέτι δὲ καὶ οἱ ἔνεδροι, ἤγουν τὰ ἐγκρύμματα, ἔνθεν κἀκεῖθεν τῶν δύο μερῶν τῆς παρατά-ξεως ἀνὰ ἀκιῶν εἴκοσιν, ἀκίας τεσσαράκοντα, ἀνὰ ἀνδρῶν διακοσίων, ὁμοῦ δὲ ἄνδρας τετρακοσίους. καὶ οἱ ἐν τοῖς κενοῖς <τόποις> διεστῶτες τῆς δευτέρας παρατάξεως, οἵτινες, ὡς εἴρηται, καὶ τοὺς φεύγοντας ἀναστέλλουσιν, ἔσονται τὰ
790 τρία μέρη ἀπὸ ἀκιῶν δέκα ἤγουν ἀνδρῶν ἑκατόν, ὁμοῦ ἀνδρῶν τριακοσίων, καὶ οἱ τῷ στρατηγῷ παρεστῶτες ἄνδρες ἑκατόν.

145. Ἀλλ᾽ αἱ μὲν τρεῖς παρατάξεις, | ἐξηρημένων τῶν κουρσόρων, ὑπὸ ἀκίας 359 ταχθήσονται, τὰ δὲ λοιπὰ τάγματα, ἤγουν οἱ πλαγιοφύλακες καὶ οἱ ὑπερκε-ρασταί, ἤτοι οἱ πρὸς τὴν κύκλωσιν ταγέντες, καὶ δὴ καὶ οἱ ἐκ τῶν ἐγκρυμμάτων
795 ἤτοι οἱ ἔνεδροι, καὶ οἱ λοιποὶ οὐκ ἀεὶ συντεταγμένοι στήσονται, ἀλλὰ πρὸς τὴν χρείαν ποτὲ μὲν οὕτως, ποτὲ δὲ δρουγγιστὶ ἐπελεύσονται ἢ ὡς ἀπαιτεῖ ἡ τοῦ πολέμου περίστασις.

146. Συναχθήσονται τοίνυν ἀπὸ τῶν οὕτω τεταγμένων δ΄ χιλιάδων ἀνδρῶν οἱ πάντες ἄρχοντες κατὰ τὴν αὐτῶν τάξιν ἄνδρες ἐπίλεκτοι ‚ατμς΄ οὕτως· πεν-
800 τάρχαι μὲν ω΄, δεκάρχαι δὲ υ΄, πεντηκοντάρχαι δὲ οἱ καὶ τριβοῦνοι καλούμενοι π΄, κένταρχοι ἤγουν ἑκατοντάρχαι μ΄, κόμητες κ΄, δρουγγάριοι καὶ χιλίαρχοι δ΄, τουρμάρχαι β΄, ὁμοῦ ἄρχοντες μικροὶ <καὶ> μεγάλοι ‚ατμς΄. καὶ οὕτως μὲν ἐπὶ τοῦ ἑνὸς θέματος ἐπιλεγέσθωσαν ἀνδρεῖοι στρατιῶται καὶ πληρούτωσαν τὸ

780 ρν΄ M ἑκατὸν πεντήκοντα A   783–784 οἱ…πεντακοσίους Va,Hung. om. MA
784 δέκα M εἴκοσι A   785 ἑκατόν¹ M διακοσίους A | δέκα M εἴκοσι A | ἑκατόν² M
διακοσίους A   786 οἱ…ἤγουν M om. A   787 εἴκοσιν M εἴκοσι A   788 κενοῖς…
διεστῶτες M διαχωρίσμασι δὲ ἐστῶτες A | τόποις ci. De om. codd.   790 δέκα…ἑκατόν A
ἑκατὸν M   792–793 ἐξηρημένων…ταχθήσονται M ὑπὸ ἀκίας ταχθήσονται παρεκτὸς τῶν
κουρσώρων A   793 ἤγουν M om. A | οἱ¹ M οἵ τε A | οἱ² M om. A   795 ἤτοι…ἔνεδροι M
om. A   798 οὕτω M οὕτως A | δ΄ M τεσσάρων A   799 ἄνδρες A om. M | ‚ατμς΄ M χίλιοι
τριακόσιοι τεσσαράκοντα ἒξ A   800 ω΄ M ὀκτακόσιοι A | υ΄ M τετρακόσιοι A | καλούμενοι
M λεγόμενοι A   801 π΄ M ὀγδοήκοντα A | μ΄ M τεσσαράκοντα A | κ΄ M εἴκοσι A | δ΄ M
τέσσαρες A   802 β΄ M δύο A | καὶ¹ ci. De om. MA | ‚ατμς΄ M χίλιοι τριακόσιοι τεσσαράκοντα
ἓξ A

144. In this present proposition the first line, divided into three divisions, will have in each division fifty files, ten deep for each row, from the group leader or protostates to the ouragos at the end. Thus, all the files of the three divisions of the first line come to one hundred fifty, totaling one thousand five hundred men. Let the second line have in its four divisions some twenty-five files each, so all the hundred files will total a thousand men. <Let the rear guard, that is, the third line, have some twenty-five files, for a total of five hundred men.> The flank guards will have ten files, one hundred men. Likewise the outflankers ten files, one hundred men. Furthermore, the ambuscades, or ambushes, on this side and that of the two divisions of the battle line <should have> some twenty files: so, forty files or two hundred men. All together, four hundred men. The troops stationed in the empty spaces of the second battle line, who, as said, restrain those who are fleeing, will make up three divisions of ten files, that is, one hundred men, or three hundred all together, as well the one hundred men stationed with the general.

145. With the exception of the assault troops, the three battle lines will be formed by files; the rest of the units, that is, the flank guards and the outflankers who are designated for the encircling movements, as well as those for the ambushes, the ambushers, and the others, will not always take their place in strict formation, but will advance according to need, sometimes in this fashion and sometimes in irregular formation, or as the circumstances of combat require.

146. From these four thousand men in formation all the officers, elite men, will be selected according to their rank, 1,346 in the following manner: 800 pentarchs, 400 dekarchs, 80 pentekontarchs, also called tribunes, 40 kentarchs or hekatontarchs, 20 counts, 4 droungarioi and chiliarchoi, 2 tourmarchs, altogether 1,346 major and minor officers. And in this way, for one theme let brave

λεγόμενον στρατιωτικὸν θέμα, ἤτοι τῶν τετρακισχιλίων τὸν ἀριθμὸν ἐπιλέκτων
805 καὶ ἐνόπλων καβαλλαρίων καὶ γενναίων ταῖς ἀρεταῖς. τὸ δ᾽ ἄλλο πλῆθος ἐκ τοῦ
θέματος εἰς ἑτέρας τάξεις καὶ χρείας καταμεριζέσθω, ὡς ἄν σοι δοκῇ, ὦ στρατηγέ, τὸ λυσιτελοῦν πρὸς τὸν ἑκάστοτε καιρόν.

147. Καὶ ταῦτα μὲν εἴρηται, ἐὰν ἄρα ὀλίγος ἐστὶν ὁ τῶν πολεμίων στρατὸς
<ἢ> ὑπὲρ τὸν σὸν ἢ ἴσος. εἰ δὲ πολυπληθίᾳ πλεονεκτεῖ ὁ ἐναντίος, τότε κατὰ
810 τὸν ὁρισθέντα σοι τύπον ἐν τῇ προδηλωθείσῃ παρατάξει, ἢ διπλώσεις τὸ
στράτευμα ἀπὸ ἑτέρων θεμάτων τῶν συστρατήγων σου, ὥστε γενέσθαι τὴν
πᾶσαν παράταξιν χιλιάδων ὀκτώ, δηλονότι κατὰ τὸν εἰρημένον τύπον μεριζομένου τοῦ ὅλου στρατοῦ, πλὴν μόνου τοῦ ποσοῦ καθ᾽ ἕκαστον τάγμα τῆς τάξεως
προστιθεμένου. εἰ δὲ μὴ διπλῶσαι μόνον ἀρκῇ, καὶ τριπλώσεις συντάσσων καὶ
815 ἑτέρους δύο στρατηγοὺς ἅμα τοῖς ὑπ᾽ αὐτοὺς στρατιώταις οὕτως ἐπιλέκτοις καὶ
καταφράκτοις, ὥστε δύο καὶ δέκα γενέσθαι χιλιάδας. καὶ οὕτως κατὰ τὸν
εἰρημένον ἄνωθεν τύπον διαμερισθήσεται ὅλος ὁ στρατός, τριπλουμένων
δηλονότι τῶν ἐφ᾽ ἑκάστῃ τάξει στρατιωτῶν κατὰ τὸ ἄνω που ὡρισμένον ποσόν.

148. Καὶ εἰ μὲν πρὸς ὀλίγους καὶ ἀνδρείους πολεμίους ἔχεις τὸν ἀγῶνα, καὶ
820 δοκεῖ σοι χρήσιμον, κατὰ ἓν θέμα ἐκτάξας τρεῖς ποιήσεις παρατάξεις ἀνὰ χιλιάδων τεσσάρων κατὰ τὸν ῥηθέντα τύπον, ἢ καὶ πλειόνων χιλιάδων κατὰ τὸ
ποσὸν τῆς τοῦ στρατοῦ εὐπορίας· καὶ τῇ μὲν μιᾷ προσβαλεῖς αὐτοῖς, ἢ προσβάλλοντας ὑποδέξῃ αὐτούς· καὶ ἐπὶ ταύτῃ ἐκείνων ἀσχολουμένων, εἰ μὲν
τραπῶσι, καὶ οὕτως διώξεις ἀσφαλῶς· εἰ δὲ ἀντιστῶσι, τότε καὶ ἡ ἑτέρα ποιήσε-
825 ται προσβολὴν ἐξόπισθεν αὐτῶν ἐπελθοῦσα, καὶ οὕτως κατεργασθήσονται οἱ
πολέμιοι. εἰ δὲ καὶ πρὸς ταύτην | ἀντίσχωσιν, ἀλλ᾽ ἡ τρίτη ἐπελθοῦσα ἢ ὄπισθεν    359ᵛ
ἢ ἐκ πλαγίου, καὶ ἅμα ταῖς ἄλλαις κυκλώσασα τοὺς ἐναντίους πάντως αἱρήσει
αὐτούς. οὐ γὰρ ἄσαρκοί εἰσιν οἱ πολέμιοι, κἂν τὸ θράσος αὐτοῖς ὥσπερ χρῶμα
περίκειται.

830    149. Εἰ δὲ πρὸς πλῆθος πολεμίων διαγωνίζεσθαι μέλλεις, τὰς τρεῖς παρατάξεις τὰς ἀπὸ δ′ χιλιάδων εἰς μίαν, ὡς εἴρηται, συνάξεις καὶ τριπλασιάσεις τὸ
ποσὸν τῆς προειρημένης ἐκτάξεως, διαμερίζων κατὰ λόγον, ὡς πρόκειται, εἴς τε
πρώτην καὶ δευτέραν παράταξιν, καὶ εἰς νωτοφύλακας καὶ εἰς πλαγιοφύλακας

---

819 ad καὶ de novo inc. W

807 τὸ λυσιτελοῦν Μ ὠφέλιμον εἶναι Α    809 ἢ¹ ci. De om. codd. | πολυπληθίᾳ Μ πολλῷ
πλήθει Α    815–816 δύο…χιλιάδας Μ δώδεκα χιλιάδας γενέσθαι Α    818 ἄνω…ὡρισμένον
Μ ἀνωτέρω εἰρημένον Α    824 ἀντιστῶσι Μ ἀντίστωσιν WA    825 ἐξόπισθεν ΜW ὄπισθεν
Α    826 ἀντίσχωσιν ΜW ἀπαντήσουσιν Α    827 αἱρήσει ΜW πορθήσει Α    831 τὰς Α om.
ΜW | δ′ ΜW τεσσάρων Α | εἰς ΜW ὡς Α

soldiers be selected and let what is called the military theme be filled by elite and armed cavalrymen, four thousand in number and noble in their qualities. The other troops from the theme should be divided up among other formations and needs, as appears most useful to you, O general, for each situation.

147. These prescriptions stand whether the enemy's army is small, larger than yours, or equal to it. If your adversary is greatly superior in numbers, then <act> in line with the model set forth for you in the battle line just explained, double your army with your fellow commanders from other themes, so that the entire battle line will total eight thousand. The whole army, of course, should be divided according to the prescribed model, except only for the numbers added according to each tagma of the line. But if doubling alone should not be enough, then triple the number, lining up with yourself the two other generals with elite, armed soldiers under them. This results in twelve thousand. In this way, the entire army will be divided according to the above-mentioned model, that is, tripling the soldiers in each line according to the number prescribed above.

148. If you face combat against a small but brave enemy force, then, if this seems helpful to you, draw up one theme and make three battle lines of up to four thousand, as in the model given, or even more thousands according to the quantity <required> for easily provisioning the army. Have one line charge against them or, if they charge, receive them. If they turn away, you will pursue them in safety, but if they resist, then the other line will launch a charge against them, coming from their rear. In this way, the enemy will be overpowered. Even if they hold up against this, the third line can attack either from the rear or the flank and, together with the other lines, having encircled them, they will utterly destroy them. After all, the enemy are not without flesh even though they wear their boldness like their skin.

149. If you are preparing to engage a large enemy force in battle, join together the three battle lines of four thousand men into one, as said, and you will triple the number of the aforementioned formation. Divide it in the regular manner, as laid down, into the first and the second battle lines, into rear guards,

καὶ εἰς ὑπερκεραστὰς καὶ εἰς ἐνέδρους, ἤτοι ἐγκρύμματα, καὶ εἰς τὰ ἄλλα, ὡς
835 προείρηται, τάγματα, καὶ οὕτως μετὰ εὐταξίας καὶ συντάσεως ποιήσεις τὴν
προσβολὴν διὰ τῶν λεγομένων κουρσόρων, ἤτοι τῶν προμάχων τῆς πρώτης
τάξεως, ἢ καὶ τῶν ὑπερκεραστῶν ἢ ὡς ἂν ἡ χρεία καλέσοι, καθώς σοι καὶ ἐν τῇ
περὶ τοῦ πολέμου διατάξει διωρισάμεθα. εἰ δὲ καὶ ἔτι πλείονές εἰσιν οἱ πολέμιοι,
καὶ χρεία πολλῷ πλείονος στρατοῦ, ἔστωσαν καὶ οἱ λοιποὶ τῶν ἀνατολικῶν
840 θεμάτων στρατηγοὶ πρὸς τὴν τοιαύτην χρείαν ἕτοιμοι, ὁμοίως τὸν οἰκεῖον
στρατὸν ἐπιλεξάμενοι καὶ διακρίναντες τοὺς χρησίμους ἀπὸ τῶν ἀχρείων, ὡς
ἄχρι τεσσάρων χιλιάδων, ὡς εἴρηται, ἐφ' ἑκάστῳ θέματι διὰ τὴν νῦν ἐπικρατη-
σάντων τῶν στρατιωτῶν ἀγυμνασίαν τε καὶ ἀμέλειαν καὶ ὀλιγότητα. καὶ οὗτοι
πάντες πλῆθος δοκίμων στρατιωτῶν συλλέξουσι, καὶ παραστήσουσιν ἅμα σοι
845 κατὰ τῶν πολεμίων, ὥστε καὶ ὑπὲρ τὰς τριάκοντα χιλιάδας καταστῆναι τοὺς
ὀφείλοντας ἀνδρείως καὶ εὐψύχως ἐκστρατεύειν κατὰ τῶν ἐχθρῶν.

150. Καὶ ταῦτα μὲν διωρισάμεθα τῇ ὑμῶν ἐνδοξότητι, τάχα οὐδὲ καινόν τι ἢ
παρὰ τὴν δόξαν ἔχοντα, ἀλλ' ἐξ ὧν, ὡς εἴρηται, τοῖς παλαιοτέροις ἐντυχόντες
ἠνθολογήσαμεν, καὶ μετρίαν πεῖραν ἐκεῖθεν συλλέξαντες συμφώνως ἐκείνοις
850 διεταξάμεθα. καὶ ἕτερα δὲ πλεῖστα δυνήσῃ ἐφευρεῖν ἐντεῦθεν λαμβάνων τὰς
ἀφορμάς, ἅπερ, ὡς εἴρηται, οὔτε γράφειν καθ' ἓν δυνατὸν οὔτε τῷ παρόντι
συντάγματι διὰ τὴν συντομίαν ἐντάξαι ἁρμόδιον. ἐξὸν δέ σοι φιλοπονοῦντι καὶ
τῷ πλάτει τῶν τακτικῶν ἐμμελετήσαντι καὶ τοιαῦτα καὶ τούτων ἔτι δραστικώ-
τερα καὶ προσεπινοῆσαι καὶ διαπράξασθαι Θεὸν ἔχοντι βοηθὸν διά τε τῆς εἰς
855 αὐτὸν πίστεως καὶ τῆς εἰς τὴν ἡμετέραν βασιλείαν ἀγάπης καὶ διαθέσεως.|

---

837 καλέσοι MW καλέσῃ A | σοι A om. MW    844 συλλέξουσι MW συλλέξουσιν A
848 δόξαν MW δόκησιν A    850 πλεῖστα MW πλεῖστα τοιουτότροπα A    852 ἐξὸν MW
ἔξεστι A    853 τῷ πλάτει MA τῷ πολεμικῶν παρασκευῶν διάταξις ιθ' περὶ ναυμαχίας πλάτει
W | ἐμμελετήσαντι MW ἐμμελετῶντι A | καὶ² MW καὶ ἔτι A

flank guards, outflankers, ambushers or ambushes, and the rest of the units, as already explained. Thus, with good order and a united front, you will have the assault troops, as they are called, or the promachoi of the first line launch their attack, or even the outflankers, or do as need requires, as we have prescribed in the constitution concerning battle. But if the enemy are even more numerous and you need a much larger army, have the remaining generals of the eastern themes stand ready for such a necessity. In like manner, each one should muster his own army of four thousand men from each theme, after having separated the useful troops from the useless, as we said. <This condition> has been brought about by the prevailing lack of training, by carelessness, and by the small number of soldiers these days. All of these <commanders> will stand together by your side against the enemy and will assemble a multitude of trustworthy soldiers, so that those who are obliged to wage war bravely and in good spirits against the enemy add up to more than thirty thousand men.

150. We have presented Your Excellency with these regulations. Perhaps they contain nothing new or extraordinary. As noted above, however, we have gathered together what we came across in older authorities and thence, having harmoniously brought together ordinary experience with those authorities, we have issued <these regulations>. Taking these as your starting point, you will be able to discover many other things in this <book>, things that, as we said, owing to the limitations of space, it is not possible to write about individually or to include conveniently in this present constitution. But it is possible for you, dedicated to this task and reflecting on the broad field of tactics, to devise and put into action such practices, as well as those still more effective than these, with God as your support, because of your faith in him and your love and good disposition toward Our Majesty.

Περὶ ναυμαχίας

α΄. Ἤδη δὲ περὶ ναυμαχίας διαταξόμεθα, οὐδὲν μὲν ἐν τοῖς παλαιοῖς τακτικοῖς περὶ αὐτῆς κεκανονισμένον εὑρόντες· ἀφ᾽ ὧν δὲ σποράδην ἀνέγνωμεν καὶ
5 διὰ μετρίας πείρας τοῦ νῦν καιροῦ παρὰ τῶν πλωΐμων στρατηγῶν ἡμῶν ἀνεμάθομεν, τὰ μὲν πεποιηκότων, τὰ δὲ πεπονθότων, ἀναλεξάμενοι μικρά τινα καὶ
ὅσον ἔμφασιν δοῦναι τοῖς καὶ ἐπὶ θαλάσσης μάχεσθαι διὰ τῶν ποτε λεγομένων
τριηρῶν, νῦν δὲ δρομώνων καλουμένων, μέλλουσι ἐν ὀλίγοις διορισώμεθα.

β΄. Πρῶτον μὲν οὖν, ὦ τῆς ναυτικῆς δυνάμεως στρατηγέ—ἤδη γὰρ καὶ πρὸς
10 σὲ δέον τὸν λόγον ποιήσασθαι—τῆς ναυμαχικῆς ἐμπειρίας καὶ τάξεως ἐπιστή-
μονά σε εἶναι χρεών, καὶ τὰς τῶν ἀέρων καὶ τῶν πνευμάτων κινήσεις προσκοπεῖν τε καὶ προειδέναι διὰ τῆς τῶν φαινομένων ἀστέρων καὶ ἐν ἄστροις σημείων
πείρας, καὶ τῶν καθ᾽ ἥλιόν τε καὶ σελήνην γινομένων σημασιῶν, καὶ δὴ καὶ τῆς
τῶν καιρῶν ἐναλλαγῆς τὴν ἀκρίβειαν ἐπιγινώσκειν, ὡς ἂν ἔχων περὶ ταῦτ᾽
15 ἐμπείρως ἀσφαλὴς καὶ ἀκίνδυνος ἀπὸ τῶν τῆς θαλάσσης διαφυλάττῃ χειμώνων.

γ΄. Κατασκευασθῆναι δὲ καὶ δρόμωνας δεῖ ἀρκοῦντας πρὸς ναυμαχίαν κατὰ
τῶν ἀντιστρατευομένων πλωΐμων πολεμίων, καὶ πρὸς τὴν ἐκείνων διάθεσίν τε
καὶ κατάστασιν, καὶ τῶν σῶν ποιήσασθαι τὴν κατασκευὴν δυνατὴν πρὸς ἅπαντα, ἐκείνοις ἀντιμάχεσθαι.

---

M W A    Dain    PG 107:989

1 πολεμικῶν...ιθ′ W λέοντος ἐν χριστῷ βασιλεῖ αἰωνίῳ ῥωμαίων στρατηγικά Μ ναυμαχία
λέοντος βασιλέως Α    2 περὶ ναυμαχίας MW om. A    3 ἤδη δὲ Μ ἐφεξῆς δὲ τούτων ἤδη W
om. A | διαταξόμεθα MW βουλόμεθα διατάξασθαι περὶ ἧς A    4 περὶ αὐτῆς MW om. A |
εὑρόντες MW εὕρομεν Α    5 μετρίας MW ὀλίγης Α | στρατηγῶν ἡμῶν MW trsp. Α
6 πεπονθότων MW παθόντων Α    7 ἔμφασιν MW ἀφορμὴν Α | μάχεσθαι MW μάχεσθαι
μέλλουσιν Α    8 μέλλουσι Μ μέλλουσιν W om. Α    9 τῆς...στρατηγέ MW στρατηγὲ τῆς
ναυτικῆς δυνάμεως Α    9–10 ἤδη...ποιήσασθαι MW om. Α    10–11 τῆς...καὶ¹ MW δεῖ
εἶναί σε ἐπιστήμονα τῆς ναυμαχίας ἐμπειρίας κατατάξεως καὶ προσκοπεῖν καὶ προγινώσκειν Α
11–12 προσκοπεῖν...προειδέναι MW om. Α    13 καθ᾽ MW κατὰ τὸν Α | καὶ² MW καὶ τὴν Α
| σημασιῶν Μ σημείων W ἐπισημειώσεων Α | καὶ δὴ MW ἐπιγινώσκειν δὲ Α    14 ἐπι-
γινώσκειν Μ γινώσκειν W om. Α | ταῦτ᾽ Μ ταῦτα WA    15 ἀσφαλής...διαφυλάττῃ MW
διαφυλάττῃ ἀσφαλὴς καὶ ἀκίνδυνος ἀπὸ τῶν τῆς θαλάσσης Α    16 δὲ MW δὲ δεῖ Α | δεῖ MW
καὶ Α    17–18 διάθεσίν...καὶ¹ MW om. Α

# PREPARATION FOR WAR, CONSTITUTION XIX

## About Naval Warfare

1. We will now set down ordinances for naval warfare. While we found no regulations about it in the older tactical books, still from what we have read here and there and what we have learned from the ordinary experience of our fleet commanders at the present time, their successes as well as their failures, we have selected a few examples, enough to give this presentation to those who intend to do battle at sea on what were once called triremes but are now called dromons.[1] We will present these regulations in a few words.

2. First, therefore, O commander of our naval force—for we must now address this treatise to you—you ought to be skilled and experienced in naval tactics and combat. You should <know how> to make allowance for the movements of air and the winds and to anticipate them by examining the visible stars, the stellar signs, and also the indications relating to the sun and the moon. Indeed, you must have an exact knowledge of the change of the seasons. And so, experienced in these matters, you may safely and without danger guard against the sea's storms.

3. It is necessary to outfit the dromons in numbers sufficient to engage the enemy fleet drawn up against you, according to its disposition and condition. You must equip your own fleet, making it ready in every respect to fight against them.

---

1. Const. 19, as it appears in A, has been edited by A. Dain, together with other writings on naval warfare: *Naumachica* (Paris, 1943). See H. Ahrweiler, *Byzance et la mer* (Paris, 1966); E. Eickhof, *Seekrieg und Seepolitik zwischen Islam und Abendland* (Berlin, 1966). On dromon ("runner"), see Ahrweiler, 409–418; Eickhoff, 135–148. The most detailed work on the dromon and the Byzantine navy is J. Pryor and E. Jeffreys, *The Age of the Dromon: The Byzantine Navy ca. 500–1204* (Leiden–Boston, 2006); this includes texts and translations of Greek and Arabic sources.

20 δʹ. Ἡ δὲ τῶν δρομώνων κατασκευὴ μήτε ἄγαν ἔστω παχεῖα, ἵνα μὴ ἀργοὶ
γένωνται ἐν ταῖς ἐλασίαις, μήτε λίαν εἰς λεπτότητα ἐξειργασμένη, ἵνα μὴ ἀσθενὴς οὖσα καὶ σαθρὰ ῥᾳδίως ὑπὸ τῶν κυμάτων καὶ τῆς τῶν ἐναντίων συναράξεώς τε καὶ κρούσεως διαλύεται. ἀλλὰ σύμμετρον ἐχέτω τὴν ἐργασίαν ὁ δρόμων, ἵνα καὶ ἐλαυνόμενος μὴ λίαν ἀργός ἐστιν, καὶ κλυδωνιζόμενος ἢ παρὰ τῶν
25 ἐχθρῶν συγκρουόμενος ἰσχυρότερος διαμένῃ καὶ ἄρρηκτος.

εʹ. Ἐχέτωσαν δὲ καὶ πάντα τὰ πρὸς ἐξαρτισμὸν δρόμωνος ἀπαράλειπτα καὶ
διπλᾶ, οἷον αὐχένας, κώ|πας, σκαρμούς, σχοινία, κάρυα, καὶ τὰ ἄρμενα δὲ　396ᵛ
αὐτῶν καὶ κερατάρια, καὶ κατάρτια, καὶ ὁπόσα ἄλλα ἡ ναυτικὴ τέχνη πρὸς
χρείαν ἀπαιτεῖ. ἐχέτω δὲ καὶ ἐκ περισσοῦ ξύλα τινὰ ἐγκοίλια, καὶ σανίδας, καὶ
30 στυππία, καὶ πίσσαν, καὶ ὑγρόπισσαν, καὶ ναυπηγὸν μετὰ πάντων τῶν ἐργαλείων αὐτοῦ, ἕνα τῶν ἐλατῶν οἷον σκεπάρνου, τελέτρου, πρίονος, καὶ τῶν ὁμοίων.

ςʹ. Ἐχέτω δὲ πάντως τὸν σίφωνα κατὰ τὴν πρώραν ἔμπροσθεν χαλκῷ ἠμφι-
εσμένον, ὡς ἔθος, δι᾽ οὗ τὸ ἐσκευασμένον πῦρ κατὰ τῶν ἐναντίων ἀκοντίσαι.
καὶ ἄνωθεν δὲ τοῦ τοιούτου σίφωνος ψευδοπάτιον ἀπὸ σανίδων καὶ αὐτὸ
35 περιτετειχισμένον σανίσιν, ἐν ᾧ στήσονται ἄνδρες πολεμισταὶ τοῖς ἐπερχομένοις
ἀπὸ τῆς πρώρας τῶν πολεμίων ἀντιμαχόμενοι, ἢ κατὰ τῆς πολεμίας νηὸς ὅλης
βάλλοντες δι᾽ ὅσων ἂν ἐπινοήσωσιν ὅπλων.

ζʹ. Ἀλλὰ καὶ τὰ λεγόμενα ξυλόκαστρα περὶ τὸ μέσον που τοῦ καταρτίου ἐν
τοῖς μεγίστοις δρόμωσιν ἐπιστήσουσι περιτετειχισμένα σανίσιν, ἐξ ὧν ἄνδρες
40 τινὲς τὸ μέσον τῆς πολεμίας νηὸς ἀκοντίσουσιν ἢ λίθους μυλικοὺς ἢ σίδηρα
βαρεῖα, οἷον μάζας ξιφοειδεῖς, δι᾽ ὧν ἢ τὴν ναῦν διαθρύψουσιν ἢ τοὺς ὑποκει-
μένους συνθλάσουσιν σφοδρῶς καταφερόμενα ἤ τι ἕτερον ἐπιχύσουσιν ἢ
ἐμπρῆσαι δυνάμενον τὴν ναῦν τῶν ἐναντίων ἢ τοὺς ἐν αὐτῇ πολεμίους θανατῶ-
σαι.

45 ηʹ. Ἕκαστος δὲ τῶν δρομώνων εὐμήκης ἔστω καὶ σύμμετρος, ἔχων μὲν τὰς
λεγομένας ἐλασίας δύο, τήν τε κάτω καὶ τὴν ἄνω. ἑκάστη δὲ ἐλασία ἐχέτω
ζυγοὺς τὸ ἐλάχιστον πέντε καὶ εἴκοσι ἐν οἷς οἱ κωπηλάται καθεσθήσονται· ὡς
εἶναι ζυγοὺς τοὺς ἅπαντας κάτω μὲν εἴκοσι καὶ πέντε, ἄνω δὲ ὁμοίως εἴκοσι καὶ

20 ἄγαν MW πάνυ A　22 ῥᾳδίως MW ταχέως A　22–23 συναράξεώς…κρούσεως MW
συγκρούσεως A　24 ἀργός ἐστιν MW trsp. A　28 κερατάρια MA κεράτια W　31 τελέτρου
MW τυμπάνου A　33 ἀκοντίσαι PG ἀκοντίσοι MW ἀκοντίσει A　38 που MW om. A
39 ἐπιστήσουσι MA ἐπιστήσουσιν W　40 τινὲς MW τινες εἰς A　41 βαρεῖα MW βαρέα A |
μάζας MW μαζία A　42 συνθλάσουσιν MW συνθλάσουσι A | τι ἕτερον MW trsp. A
43 ἐναντίων MW πολεμίων A | πολεμίους MW om. A　45 ηʹ MW om.A　46 ἑκάστη…
ἐλασία MW ἡ ἑκάστη A　47 πέντε…εἴκοσι M εʹ καὶ εἴκοσι W κεʹ A　48–49 εἴκοσι²…πέντε
MW κεʹ A

4. The equipment of the dromon should not be too massive, which would make it slow in maneuvering, nor should it be too lightly outfitted, which would make it weak and easily shaken by the waves and broken up when the enemy ships dash against it and crush it. But let the dromon be outfitted in a balanced manner so that it may not be too slow in sailing and, when buffeted by the waves or rammed by the enemy, it may remain stronger and unbreakable.

5. Nothing required for the outfitting of the dromon should be omitted, and there should be two of each item. This includes tillers, oars, pegs for oars, ropes, pulleys and their sails and their yardarms and furnishings, and as many other items as are required for the exercise of the naval art. There should also be some extra lumber for the belly of the ship, and planks, hemp, pitch, and liquid pitch. A shipwright should be on board with all his tools, some of forged metal such as an adze, a drill, a saw, and the like.

6. By all means, it should have a siphon, bound in bronze, and placed up front on the prow, as is customary, so that it can project the prepared fire against the enemy.[2] Above this particular siphon there should be a sort of platform made of planks and walled around by planks. Station combat troops there to ward off attacks coming from the prow of the enemy ships or to shoot whatever weapons they may choose against the whole enemy ship.

7. On the largest dromons erect the so-called wooden castles with their wall of planks somewhere around the middle of the mast.[3] From these <vantage points> our men will shoot millstones or heavy pieces of iron such as those shaped like swords. These will either break up the enemy ship or, landing with great force, crush those on whom they fall. The men may also hurl other things capable of setting the enemy ships on fire or of killing the troops on board.

8. Let each dromon be of good length and proper size with two oarbanks, as they are called, one below and one above. Let each row have at least twenty-five benches for the rowers to sit on. All told, therefore, there should be twenty-five benches below and, likewise, twenty-five above, making a total of fifty. On each

2. Prepared fire, also known as liquid or Greek fire, was a petroleum-based substance, put under pressure, ignited, and discharged through bronze tubes, called siphons, engulfing the enemy in roaring flames and thick black smoke. See R. Partington, *A History of Greek Fire and Gunpowder* (Cambridge, 1960), 1–41; Pryor-Jeffreys, 607–631; J. Haldon and F. Byrne, "A Possible Solution to the Problem of Greek Fire," *BZ* 70 (1977): 91–99; J. Haldon, "Greek Fire Revisited: Recent and Current Research," in *Byzantine Style, Religion, and Civilization: In Honour of Sir Steven Runciman*, ed. E. Jeffreys (Cambridge, 2006).

3. On the location of this fort or fighting platform see Pryor-Jeffreys, 229–238.

πέντε, ὁμοῦ ν'. καθ' ἕνα δὲ αὐτῶν δύο καθεζέσθωσαν οἱ κωπηλατοῦντες, εἷς μὲν
50 δεξιά, εἷς δὲ ἀριστερά· ὡς εἶναι τοὺς ἅπαντας κωπηλάτας ὁμοῦ καὶ τοὺς αὐτοὺς
καὶ στρατιώτας τούς τε ἄνω καὶ τοὺς κάτω ἄνδρας ρ'. ἔξω δὲ τούτων τὸν κέν-
ταρχον τοῦ δρόμωνος καὶ τὸν τὸ φλάμουλον κατέχοντα, καὶ τοὺς δύο κυβερνή-
τας τῶν τοῦ δρόμωνος αὐχένων, οὓς καλοῦσι καὶ πρωτοκαράβους, καὶ εἴ τινα
ἕτερον δέον εἰς τὴν τοῦ κεντάρχου ὑπηρεσίαν. τῶν δὲ πρωρέων ἐλατῶν οἱ
55 τελευταῖοι δύο ὁ μὲν ἔστω σιφωνάτωρ, ὁ δὲ ἕτερος ὁ τὰς ἀγκύρας βάλλων κατὰ
θάλασσαν. ἔστω δὲ καὶ ὁ πρωρεὺς ἄνω που τῆς πρώρας | καθήμενος ἔνοπλος, 397
καὶ ὁ τοῦ ναυάρχου δέ, ἤτοι τοῦ κεντάρχου, κράββατος ἐπὶ τῆς πρύμνης γινέσθω, ὁμοῦ μὲν ἀφορισμένον δεικνύων τὸν ἄρχοντα ὁμοῦ δὲ καὶ φυλάττων ἐν
καιρῷ συμβολῆς ἀπὸ τῶν ῥιπτομένων βελῶν παρὰ τῶν ἐναντίων, ἐξ οὗ καὶ τὰ
60 ἕκαστα βλέπων πρὸς τὴν χρείαν ἄγεσθαι κελεύσοι ὁ ἄρχων τὸν δρόμωνα.
θ'. Καὶ ἕτεροι δὲ δρόμωνες κατασκευαζέσθωσάν σοι τούτων μείζονες ἀπὸ
διακοσίων χωροῦντες ἀνδρῶν ἢ πλείω τούτων ἢ ἐλάττω, κατὰ τὴν χρείαν τὴν
δέουσαν ἐπὶ καιροῦ κατὰ τῶν ἐναντίων· ὧν οἱ μὲν πεντήκοντα εἰς τὴν κάτω
ἐλασίαν ὑπουργήσουσιν, οἱ δὲ ἑκατὸν καὶ πεντήκοντα ἄνω ἑστῶτες ἅπαντες
65 ἔνοπλοι μαχήσονται τοῖς πολεμίοις.
ι'. Καὶ ἔτι δὲ κατασκευάσεις δρόμωνας ἐλάττους δρομικωτάτους οἱονεὶ
γαλαίας ἢ μονήρεις λεγομένους, ταχινοὺς καὶ ἐλαφρούς, οἷσπερ χρήσῃ ἔν τε
ταῖς βίγλαις καὶ ταῖς ἄλλαις ταχιναῖς χρείαις.
ια'. Καὶ ἑτέρας δὲ ναῦς ποιήσεις φορτηγοὺς καὶ ἱππαγωγούς, οἱονεὶ τούλδου
70 δίκην, αἵτινες τὴν ἀποσκευὴν ἅπασαν τῶν στρατιωτῶν βαστάσωσιν ἵνα μὴ δι'
αὐτὴν βαροῦνται οἱ δρόμωνες, καὶ μάλιστα ἐν ἀγῶνος καιρῷ. ὅτε δὲ χρεία
μικρᾶς δαπάνης ἢ ὅπλων ἢ ἄλλης ὕλης, ἐκεῖθεν ἀναλαμβάνωσι τὰς διοικήσεις.
ιβ'. Τὸν δὲ τῶν δρομώνων ἀριθμὸν καὶ τῶν ἐν αὐτοῖς στρατιωτῶν ἀνείκα-
στόν ἐστι καὶ ἄδηλον διορίσασθαι. ἡ γὰρ κατὰ τὸν καιρὸν χρεία πρὸς τὴν τῶν
75 ἀντιμαχομένων πολεμίων δύναμιν, ὡς ἂν ἀπαιτήσῃ καὶ τὸ πλῆθος τῶν δρομώ-

---

49 ν' ΜΑ πεντήκοντα W    50 καὶ MW om. A    51 ρ' ΜΑ ἑκατὸν W    55 ὁ³ ΜΑ om. W
56 θάλασσαν MW θάλασσαν ἤγουν τὰ σίδηρα A | που MW om. A    57 κράββατος WA
ῥάβος Μ    59 τὰ MW om. A    60 ἄγεσθαι κελεύσοι MW μάλιστα κελεύσει A    62 πλείω
MW πλέον A | ἐλάττω MW ἔλαττον A    63 πεντήκοντα MW ν' A | εἰς A om. MW
64 ἑκατὸν…πεντήκοντα MW ρ' καὶ ν' A    66 καὶ…δὲ MW ἔτι δὲ καὶ A | ἐλάττους
δρομικωτάτους MW μικροτέρους γοργωτάτους A    68 ταχιναῖς MW σπουδαίαις A
69 οἱονεὶ MW om. A    70 βαστάσωσιν Μ βαστάσουσιν WA    74 ἔστι Μ ἐστιν WA

one of them let two oarsmen be seated, one on the right and one on the left, so that all the oarsmen, who also serve as soldiers, those above and those below, come to one hundred men. In addition to these are the centurion of the dromon and the standard-bearer and the two pilots at the tillers of the dromon, whom they also call steersmen, and whoever may be needed to assist the centurion. Finally come the two officers in command at the bow; let one operate the siphon and the other be responsible for dropping anchor at sea. Let the commander at the bow be armed and stationed somewhere above the prow. The pallet of the ship's commander, or of the centurion, should be at the stern, making the commander visible by himself and at the same time protecting him during battle from the missiles hurled by the enemy.[4] From there the commander of the dromon can observe everything and give orders to meet any contingency.

9. You should also outfit other dromons larger than these with space for two hundred men, more or less, depending on what is needed against the enemy at the time. Fifty men will serve on the lower row of benches and one hundred fifty, armed and stationed above, will fight against the enemy.

10. In addition, you will outfit smaller dromons, very fast ones, like those called galleys or monoremes, swift and light, which you can use for scouting and other operations requiring speed.[5]

11. You shall also build other ships for transport of material and horses. Much like a baggage train, they will carry all the equipment of the soldiers so as not to weigh down the dromons, especially in time of battle. When a small outlay of weapons or other supplies is needed, they may distribute them from those vessels.

12. To determine the number of dromons and the soldiers on board is uncertain and well-nigh impossible. For, in addition to the strength of the enemy arrayed against you, the needs of the moment are what should set the requirements for the number of dromons as well as for the number of troops on

---

4. Centurion's pallet: κράββατος generally means a bed or couch (see *ImpEx*, C 504, and p. 234). It was also called the commander's tent (σκηνή), and was probably a small platform under an awning in the ship's stern (Dain, *Naumachica*, 5.5). See Pryor-Jeffreys, 215–216.

5. A galley, in Leo's time, designated a smaller, faster ship, intended primarily for scouting. See Pryor-Jeffreys, index, s.v. In March 949, for example, galleys were sent to Syria to find out what the Saracens were up to (*De cerimoniis*, Bonn ed. 2, p. 657). Vegetius (4.37) calls them *liburnii* and recommends a form of camouflage, coloring the ships and the sails blue, with the sailors wearing blue clothing.

νων. καὶ πάλιν τὸν ἀριθμὸν τοῦ ἐν αὐτοῖς λαοῦ κατὰ τὸ μέγεθος τῶν πλοίων καὶ τὴν δέουσαν ἐν αὐτοῖς πολεμικὴν ὅπλισιν οὕτω καὶ ποιήσεις.

ιγ΄. Προσέτι δὲ καὶ τὰ σκευοφόρα καὶ ἱππαγωγὰ πλοῖα τοὺς ἐν αὐτοῖς ἀρκοῦντας ἕξουσι ναύτας, οὐδὲ αὐτοὺς ἀνόπλους, ἀλλὰ καὶ τόξα ἔχοντας καὶ
80 σαγίττας καὶ ῥικτάρια καὶ εἴ τι χρειῶδες πρὸς πόλεμον ἕτερον, διὰ τὰς ἀναγκαί-ας περιστάσεις. ἐπιφερέσθωσαν δὲ καὶ περιττὰ ὅπλα· ποτὲ γὰρ καὶ λειπόντων ὅπλων, ἐκεῖθεν οἱ στρατιῶται πορίσονται. τὰ δὲ τοιαῦτα πλοῖα καὶ ἅρματα ἐχέτωσαν καὶ μάγγανα καὶ τὰ ἄλλα ὅπλα πρὸς χρείαν, εἰ τύχοι, μήποτε ἐπιλεί-πουσι διὰ τὸ ὀλιγοῦσθαι αὐτὰ ἐν ταῖς μάχαις.

85 ιδ΄. Ἐκτὸς δὲ τῶν στρατιωτῶν, ἤτοι τῶν ἄνω ἐλατῶν, ὅσοι ἄν εἰσιν ἀπό τε τοῦ κεντάρχου καὶ ἐφεξῆς | ἕως τοῦ ἐσχάτου, κατάφρακτοι ἔσονται ὅπλα ἔχον- 397ᵛ τες οἷον σκουτάρια, μέναυλα, τόξα, σαγίττας ἐκ περισσοῦ, σπαθία, ῥικτάρια, λωρίκια, κλιβάνια, εἰ καὶ μὴ ὄπισθεν ἀλλὰ πάντως ἔμπροσθεν, κασσίδας, χειρόψελα, καὶ μάλιστα οἱ ἔμπροσθεν ἐν τῇ προσβολῇ τῆς μάχης κατὰ χεῖρας
90 συμπλεκόμενοι καὶ ἀγωνιζόμενοι. οἱ δὲ μὴ ἔχοντες λωρίκια ἢ κλιβάνια πάντως φορείτωσαν τὰ λεγόμενα νευρικά, ἅπερ ἀπὸ διπλῶν κενδούκλων γίνεται. καὶ οὗτοι ὄπισθεν τῶν ἄλλων σκεπόμενοι τόξοις χρήσονται, καὶ λίθους δὲ χειρο-πληθεῖς πλείστους ἐχέτωσαν ἤτοι κόχλακας ἐν τοῖς δρομωνίοις, οὕσπερ κατὰ τῶν πολεμίων βάλλοντες οὐδὲν ἧττω τῶν ἄλλων ὅπλων ἀνοίσουσιν. ὅπλα γὰρ
95 εἰσιν οἱ λίθοι εὐπόριστα καὶ ἀνελλιπῆ.

ιε΄. Μὴ μέντοι οὕτω βαλλέτωσαν τοὺς λίθους μόνον, ὥστε τὴν ἀκμὴν τῆς αὐτῶν δυνάμεως ἐν τούτοις ἐκδαπανῆσαι, καὶ στῆναι τοῦ λοιποῦ, ἢ καὶ τὰ ὅπλα τὰ βαλλόμενα ἀποκενῶσαι, μήποτε οἱ ἐναντίοι σύσκουτα ποιήσαντες καὶ τὰς βολὰς ὁπωσοῦν δεξάμενοι, εἶτα τούτων πληρωθέντων καὶ τῶν βαλλόντων
100 ἀποκαμόντων, ἀθρόοι ἀναστάντες ἀπάρξωνται ταῖς σπάθαις καὶ τοῖς μεναύλοις ἀμύνασθαι. καὶ ὥσπερ ἀκμαιότεροι τῇ ἀθρόᾳ κινήσει ἀναφανέντες καὶ τοῖς κεκμηκόσι στρατιώταις ἐπιτεθέντες ἰσχυρότεροι γένωνται, καὶ ῥαδίως αὐτοὺς καταπολεμήσωσι. φιλεῖ γὰρ τὰ τοιαῦτα τὸ βάρβαρον.

---

80 ῥικτάρια MW ῥιπτάρια A    81 περιττὰ MW περισσὰ A    82 πορίσονται MW λάβωσιν A
83–84 ἐπιλείπουσι...αὐτὰ  MW  ἐπιλείπωσιν  καταδαπανώμενά A    87 ῥικτάρια  MW
ῥιπτάρια A    88 ἔμπροσθεν MW ἔμπροσθεν πέταλα ἔχοντα A    89 κατὰ MA κατὰ τὰς W
91 ἅπερ MW ἅπερ καὶ A    92–93 χειροπληθεῖς MW δυναμένους ἀπὸ χειρῶν ῥίπτεσθαι A
94 τῶν¹ MW om. A | ἧττω MW ἔλαττον A | ἀνοίσουσιν MW αὐτοὺς καταβλάψουσιν A
96 οὕτω MW οὕτως A    96–97 ἀκμὴν...δυνάμεως MW δύναμιν αὐτῶν A    99 τούτων MW
τῶν βελῶν A    101 ὥσπερ ἀκμαιότεροι MW ἀκόπατοι A    102 κεκμηκόσι MW κεκοπιάκοσι
A | ῥαδίως MW εὐκόλως A    103 καταπολεμήσωσι M καταπολεμήσουσιν WA

board, to be determined by the size of the ships, and by the combat armament required for them. And so you shall do this.

13. Furthermore, the ships transporting equipment and horses shall have a sufficient number of sailors, who should not be without weapons, but equipped with bows and arrows, javelins, and whatever else may be useful in battle, depending on the press of circumstances. Let the ships carry extra weapons, so that when the soldiers run out of them, they may be provided on the spot. Ships of this sort should have heavy weapons and artillery as well as the other weapons that may be needed, so they will not fail if they run short of them during combat.

14. Besides the soldiers on the upper bank of oarsmen, all present, from the centurion right down to the lowest private, shall wear armor. They shall have weapons such as shields, heavy spears, bows, arrows in abundance, swords, javelins. They shall have coats of mail and plate armor, if not in back, then certainly in front; also helmets and iron gloves, especially those fighting in the front ranks caught up in battle and struggling in hand-to-hand combat. Those who do not have coats of mail or plate armor should, by all means, wear the surcoats, as they are called, made of a double layer of quilted material. These men will find cover behind the others and use bows. Also they should have a very large supply of rocks or stones that can be held in their hands on the dromons. Hurling these stones at the enemy will be no less effective than other weapons. For stones make weapons that are never lacking and are easy to find.

15. Nonetheless, do not let them restrict themselves only to throwing stones. They will expend the best part of their force in doing that and will end up standing idle and run out of weapons to throw. The enemy might then join shields and be barely affected by the missiles. Then, when these <stones> have all been discharged, the enemy may rise up in a body and begin to defend themselves with swords and spears. As they join together they find new energy and attack the exhausted soldiers and may well prove stronger and easily overpower them. Barbarian peoples delight in this sort of thing.

ιϛʹ. Ὑπομένουσι γὰρ Σαρακηνοὶ τὴν βίαν τῆς προσβολῆς. καὶ ὅταν ἀποκα-
105 μόντας ἴδωσι καὶ τῶν ὅπλων κενωθέντας, ἢ σαγιττῶν ἢ λίθων ἤ τινων ἑτέρων,
τότε ἀναπηδῶντες ὁμοῦ τε καταπλήττουσι, καὶ ταῖς ἐκ χειρὸς ἀπὸ σπαθίων καὶ
μεναύλων προσβολαῖς εὐρώστως καὶ ἀκμαιότερον ἐπέρχονται.

ιζʹ. Διὸ φυλάττεσθαι χρὴ τὰ τοιαῦτα, καὶ μετὰ τοῦ δέοντος σκοποῦ ποιεῖσθαι τὴν προσβολὴν ἵνα μᾶλλον οἱ πολέμιοι πάθωσι τὰ πρὸς βλάβην γινόμενα ἢ
110 οἱ ἡμέτεροι στρατιῶται. δεῖ γὰρ αὐτοὺς τὴν οἰκείαν ἀκμὴν καὶ τὰς βολὰς φυλάττειν ἀπʼ ἀρχῆς ἄχρι τέλους τῆς μάχης, καὶ μετρεῖν τῶν ἐναντίων τὴν διάθεσιν,
καὶ οὕτως τὴν μάχην διασκευάζειν.

ιηʹ. Πρὸς τούτοις φροντίσεις, ὦ στρατηγέ, καὶ τῆς δεούσης τῶν στρατιωτῶν
δαπάνης, ὥστε ἔχειν αὐτοὺς τὰ ἀναγκαῖα· ἵνα μὴ τούτων λει|πόμενοι ἢ στασιά- 398
115 σωσιν ἢ ἐν τῇ ἰδίᾳ χώρᾳ ὄντες τοὺς συντελεστὰς καὶ ὑπηκόους ἡμῶν τυραννοῦσι καὶ ἀδικοῦσι ὑπὸ τῆς σπάνης τῶν ἀναγκαίων συνελαυνόμενοι, ἀλλʼ εἴ γε
δυνατόν, ἐν τάχει τὴν πολεμίαν καταλάβῃς γῆν, καὶ ἐξ αὐτῆς ἅπαντα τὰ ἐπιτήδεια πορίσῃ.

ιθʹ. Παραγγείλεις δὲ καὶ τοῖς ἄρχουσι μηδένα τῶν ὑπʼ αὐτοὺς στρατιωτῶν
120 ἀδικεῖν, ἢ τὸ οἱονοῦν δῶρον παρʼ αὐτῶν λαμβάνειν ἢ τὰς λεγομένας συνηθείας.
περὶ γὰρ τῆς σῆς ἐνδοξότητος, τί χρὴ λέγειν ὡς οὐδʼ ἐνθυμηθῆναί τι τοιοῦτον
δέον, μή τί γε διαπράξασθαι, μήτε δῶρον τὸ οἷον δήποτε ἀπὸ μικροῦ ἢ μεγάλου
ἀνθρώπου τοῦ ὑπό σε τελοῦντος λαμβάνειν τὸ σύνολον;

κʹ. Τοὺς δὲ στρατιώτας ἀνδρείους ἐπίλεγου καὶ ῥωμαλέους καὶ εὐπρο-
125 θύμους, καὶ μάλιστα τοὺς εἰς τὰ ἄνω τοῦ δρόμωνος ταττομένους, οἵτινες καὶ
ἀπὸ χειρὸς τοῖς πολεμίοις συμπλέκονται. εἰ δέ τινας τῶν στρατιωτῶν ἀνάνδρους ἐπιγνῷς, τούτους εἰς τὴν κάτω ἐλασίαν τέως παράπεμπε, καὶ εἴ ποτέ τις
πλήγῃ ἢ πέσῃ τῶν στρατιωτῶν, τὸν ἐκείνου τόπον ἐκ τῶν κάτω ἐξ ἀνάγκης
ἀναπληρώσεις.

130 καʹ. Χρὴ γάρ σε πάντως εἰδέναι τὴν ἑκάστου τῶν ὑπό σε στρατιωτῶν ἕξιν
καὶ διάθεσιν καὶ τὴν ἄλλην πρὸς ἀνδρείαν ποιότητα. ὥσπερ οἱ κυνηγέται τῶν

---

104–105 ἀποκαμόντας ΜΑ ἀποκαμόντες W    105 ἴδωσι ΜW ἴδωσιν Α | τινων ἑτέρων MW
trsp. Α    106 καταπλήττουσι ΜW καταπλήττουσιν Α    107 προσβολαῖς ΜΑ συμπλοκαῖς W
108 διὸ φυλάττεσθαι MW διαφυλάττεσθαι Α    110 ἀκμὴν ΜW δύναμιν Α | βολὰς ΜW
βουλὰς Α    115–116 τυραννοῦσι…σπάνης ΜW τυραννῶσιν καὶ ἀδικῶσιν τῇ σπάνει Α
116 συνελαυνόμενοι MW ἀναγκαζόμενοι Α    117 πολεμίαν Α om. MW    118 πορίσῃ MW
προσλάβῃς Α    121 οὐδʼ MW οὐδὲ Α    122 δέον ΜΑ om. W    124–125 ῥωμαλέους…
εὐπροθύμους MW προθύμους Α    125 ταττομένους MW τασσομένους Α    128 ἐκ…κάτω
WΑ om. Μ | ἀνάγκης ΜΑ om. W

16. The Saracens bear up under the force of such a barrage and when they see that their opponents are getting weary and running out of weapons, whether arrows, stones, or other things, then, all together they leap up and striking hard they charge vigorously and with great force, attacking with swords and heavy spears in their hands.

17. Therefore, it is necessary to be on your guard against such things and to carry out the shooting with the proper goal: the enemy, rather than our own soldiers, should suffer the harmful effects. It is necessary to conserve our own strength and <regulate> the shooting from the beginning to the end of the battle, taking note of the disposition of our opponents. In this manner we should prepare for combat.

18. In addition to the above, you will also take thought, O general, for the required supplies for the soldiers so they will have what they need. Otherwise, deprived of these things, they might rebel while still in their own country and, impelled by the scarcity of necessities, lord it over our subjects and taxpayers and do them harm. But, if it is possible, get to the enemy's territory swiftly and provide for all your needs from it.

19. Announce to your officers that they should not treat any of the soldiers under their command unjustly. They should not accept a gift of any sort from them, including the so-called customary gratuities. As far as Your Excellency is concerned, why is it necessary to say that one should not even think about such a thing, let alone do it? Without exception, you must not accept any kind of gift from any man under your command, whether of high or low rank.

20. Select brave and robust soldiers, highly motivated, especially those stationed on the upper deck of the dromon, who are to engage the enemy in hand-to-hand combat. If you find out that some of the soldiers are cowardly, assign them temporarily to the lower bank of oars. If one of the soldiers should be wounded or should fall, you can, when necessary, fill his place from among the men below.

21. It is essential for you to know the condition and disposition of each soldier under your command. What qualities does he possess that give promise

κυνῶν ἑκάστου τὰς ἐπιτηδειότητας ἐπιγινώσκοντες ἔχουσιν εὐκαίρως αὐτοὺς πρὸς ὃ βούλονται.

κβ΄. Οὕτως οὖν διαθήσεις ἕκαστα, καθὼς ἂν συνίδῃς ἀρκοῦντα πρὸς τὴν
135 προκειμένην ἐκστρατείαν τούς τε δρόμωνας καὶ τοὺς ἐν αὐτοῖς στρατιώτας, τά τε ὅπλα καὶ τὰς δαπάνας καὶ τὴν ἄλλην ἐν ἑτέροις πλοίοις ἀποσκευήν· ἥντινα οἱονεὶ τοὔλδον ἐν ἀσφαλέσι τόποις σε χρὴ καθιστᾶν, ὅταν καιρὸς ἐλπίζεταί σοι μάχης.

κγ΄. Καὶ προσέτι, εἴ γε χρεία τοιαύτη καλέσοι, ὥστε καὶ ἵππους ἐν τοῖς
140 ἱππαγωγοῖς πλοίοις πρὸς ἐπιρριφὴν κατὰ τῆς πολεμίας ἔχειν τινῶν καβαλλαρίων. καὶ ἁπλῶς πάντα ἐξαρτύσας ὁδοιπορήσεις δεόντως.

κδ΄. Καὶ πρῶτον μὲν πρὸ τοῦ ἀποκινῆσαι ἁγιασθήτωσαν ἅπαντα τὰ φλάμουλα τῶν δρομώνων ἑκάστου διὰ θείας τῶν ἱερέων ἱερουργίας καὶ εὐχῆς ἐκτενοῦς πρὸς τὸν τῶν ὅλων Θεὸν ὑπὲρ εὐοδώσεως τοῦ στρατοῦ κατὰ τῶν
145 πολεμίων. ἔπειτα καὶ διαλαλήσεις πρὸς ἅπαντα τὸν λαὸν καὶ πρὸς τοὺς ἄρχοντας ἰδίως τὰ δέοντα καὶ ἁρμόζοντα | τῷ καιρῷ. καὶ οὕτως προθυμοποιήσας τὸν   398ᵛ στρατὸν ἀποκινήσεις, αἰσίου πνεύματος συμπνέοντός σοι καὶ μὴ ἐναντίου.

κε΄. Οὐχ ὡς ἔτυχεν πάντων τῶν δρομώνων πορευομένων, ἀλλ' ἐπιστήσεις αὐτοῖς ἄρχοντας, ἢ κατὰ πέντε ἢ κατὰ τρεῖς δρόμωνας ἕνα τὸν λεγόμενον
150 κόμητα, ὅστις ναύαρχός τε καὶ ἡγεμὼν τῶν ὑπ' αὐτὸν δρομώνων ὑπάρχων, φροντίσει προσεχέστερον περὶ πάντων εὐκόλως, καὶ διατάξει πρὸς ἕκαστα.

κϛ΄. Οἱ δὲ εἰρημένοι ἄρχοντες ὑπό σε τελοῦντες ἀπὸ σοῦ καὶ τὰ παραγγέλματα δέξονται, καὶ τοῖς ὑπ' αὐτοὺς μεταδώσουσι. καὶ ταῦτα μὲν ἐπὶ τοῦ βασιλικοῦ λεγομένου πλωΐμου· ἐπὶ δὲ τῶν θεματικῶν δρομώνων καὶ δρουγγάριοι
155 ἐπιστήσονται, καὶ τουρμάρχαι, καὶ αὐτοὶ τῷ στρατηγῷ ὑποταγήσονται, καὶ τοῖς ἐκείνου παραγγέλμασιν εἴξουσιν.

κζ΄. Οὐκ ἀγνοῶ δὲ ὅτι περ κατὰ τὴν ὁμοίωσιν τοῦ βασιλικοῦ πλωΐμου καὶ οἱ τῶν ἄλλων θεμάτων πλώϊμοι στρατηγοὶ δρουγγάριοι ἐκαλοῦντό ποτε τοῖς ἄνω χρόνοις, καὶ οἱ ὑπ' αὐτοὺς κόμητες μόνον καὶ κένταρχοι. ἀλλὰ νῦν εἰς στρατηγί-
160 δα ἡ ἑκάστου τῶν δρουγγαρίων ἀρχὴ ἀναβέβηκεν, καὶ οὕτω καλουμένη ταῖς στρατηγικαῖς καταμερίζεται τάξεσιν.

---

143 ad θείας des. W

---

132 ἔχουσιν Α ἔχουσι Μ ἔχωσιν W   139 καλέσοι MW καλέσει Α   140 ἐπιρριφὴν MW ἐπιρρίπτειν ὥστε Α   140–141 τινῶν καβαλλαρίων MW καβαλλαρίους Α   141 ἐξαρτύσας MW ἀπαρτίσας Α   143 ἑκάστου MW om. Α   147 αἰσίου…σοι Μ ἐπιτηδείου ἀνέμου πνεύσαντος Α   148 πάντων Μ ἁπάντων Α   149 αὐτοῖς Μ αὐτοὺς Α   153 μεταδώσουσι Μ μεταδώσουσιν Α   153–154 ἐπὶ…δρομώνων Μ om. Α   156 εἴξουσιν Μ ὑπακούσουσιν Α   157 περ Μ om. Α   158 ἄνω Μ πρώην Α

of bravery? Do not hunters find out what each one of their dogs is best suited for so they can make use of it to attain their goal?

22. You will, therefore, arrange everything according to what you consider sufficient for the expedition you are undertaking. This means the dromons and the soldiers on board, as well as the weapons and supplies. You must locate the rest of the equipment in the other ships, like a baggage train, in safe places whenever the time of battle approaches.

23. Moreover, if such a need arises, see that you have horses in the horse transports for a cavalry assault on enemy territory. Finally, after having made all the preparations, you will set out in proper fashion.

24. First, before moving out, let all the standards of each dromon be blessed by the sacred rites of the priests, together with prayers of intercession to the God of all things for the safe voyage of the army against the enemy. After that you should address all the troops, and the officers separately, saying what is necessary and suitable for the occasion. Thus, arousing the courage of the army, you will sail out with a favorable wind accompanying you, not an adverse one.

25. The fleet of dromons should not sail on in a haphazard way. Set officers over them, one called count for <each group of> either three or five dromons. As ship captain and leader of the dromons under his command, he will bear responsibility for all the details and will make arrangements for everything.

26. The aforementioned officers serving under you will receive their orders from you and will transmit them to the men under them. This applies to the so-called imperial fleet.[6] In the case of the thematic dromons, both droungarioi and tourmarchs will be put in charge; they will be ranked below the general and will obey his commands.

27. I am not unaware that, after the manner of the imperial fleet, the fleet commanders of the other themes were, some time ago, called droungarioi and their subordinates only counts and kentarchs. But now the command of each of the droungarioi has been elevated to the level of general and this title now has its place among the ranks of general officers.

---

6. The imperial fleet was stationed in Constantinople and always ready for service; the thematic fleet was provided, when needed, by themes such as that of the Aegean Sea and Kibyrraiotai.

κη΄. Γυμνάσεις δὲ διαφόρως τούς τε πλωΐμους στρατιώτας καὶ αὐτοὺς τοὺς
δρόμωνας, ποτὲ μὲν καθ᾽ ἕνα ἕκαστον ἄνδρα, ποτὲ δὲ καὶ κατὰ πλείους, ὥστε
ἄντις ἀλλήλων ἐπέρχεσθαι σπαθίοις καὶ σκουταρίοις χρωμένους. καὶ αὐτοὺς δὲ
165 ὅλους δρόμωνας κατ᾽ ἀλλήλων ὡς ἐπὶ παρατάξεως ἐπερχομένους καὶ ποτὲ
δεσμοῦντας, ποτὲ δὲ ἀπολύοντας καὶ διαφόρως κατ᾽ ἀλλήλων προσβάλλοντας,
ποτὲ δὲ ἀκοντίοις ὠθοῦντας τὰ πλοῖα τῶν ἐναντίων, ὥστε μὴ πλησιάζοντας
δεσμεῖν. οὐ γὰρ ἀεὶ τὸ διὰ καμάκων σιδηρῶν δεσμεῖν ἀλλήλους τοὺς ἀντιπολε-
μοῦντας χρήσιμον διὰ τοὺς ἀφύκτους καὶ ἀναγκαίους κινδύνους.
170 κθ΄. Καὶ ἑτέρως δὲ γυμναζέσθωσαν ὡς ἂν ἐπιβάλῃ ἡ σὴ ἐνδοξότης τὰς κατὰ
τῶν ἀντιπάλων ἐνδεχομένας ἐπινοίας, ὡς ἂν ἐντεῦθεν ἐθίζωνται πρὸς τοὺς
κτύπους καὶ τὰς βοὰς καὶ τὴν ἄλλην κίνησιν τοῦ πολέμου, καὶ μὴ θροῶνται ὡς
ἀγυμνάστως καὶ ἀθρόον καὶ παρὰ δόξαν ἐπὶ ταῦτα ἐρχόμενοι.
λ΄. Οὕτως οὖν γυμνασθέντες καὶ διατεθέντες πλεύσουσιν ἐν τάξει συνηγ-
175 μένοι τοσοῦτον, ἐφ᾽ ὅσον ἀλλήλοις μὴ ἐμποδίζειν ἔν τε ταῖς ἐλασίαις καὶ ἐν ταῖς,
ὡς εἰκός, κατὰ θάλασσαν ὑπὸ | τῶν ἀνέμων βίαις. ἀλλ᾽, οἱονεί τις παράταξις   399
γεγυμνασμένη, οὕτω πορευέσθωσαν καὶ ἐν ταῖς ὁρμησίαις δὲ τῶν ἀπλίκτων
<καὶ> εὐτάκτως τὸν κατάπλουν ποιείτωσαν, καὶ καταγέτωσαν ἐνορδίνως ἐξορ-
μῶντες πρὸς τὴν ξηρὰν ἢ εἰς λιμένα πάντως ἢ εἰς ὕφορμον τόπον, ἐν ᾧ ζάλης
180 συμβαινούσης οὐ κλυσθήσονται.
λα΄. Δεῖ δέ σε καὶ τοῦ ἀνέμου τὴν ἐπιφορὰν προειδέναι διὰ τῶν σημείων
κατὰ τὸν καιρόν. καὶ πρὸς ταύτην καὶ τὸν τόπον τῆς ὁρμησίας ἐκλέξασθαι. καὶ
εἰ μή τις κατεπείγει ἀνάγκη, μὴ ἄνευ πνεύματος αἰσίου καὶ γαλήνης, καὶ ἀσφα-
λοῦς ἐλπίδος σωτηρίας ἐπιρρίπτειν σεαυτὸν εἰς ἀνεπιτήδειον πλοῦν. ἀλλ᾽
185 ὑφορᾶσθαι καὶ τὰς λεγομένας παρὰ τῶν ναυτικῶν παρασημασίας τῶν ἄστρων
καὶ ὅσα ἄλλα συμφέροντα, καὶ οὕτω ποιεῖσθαι τὴν πορείαν.
λβ΄. Ἐν δὲ τοῖς ἀπλίκτοις, εἰ μὲν ἐν τῇ ἰδίᾳ ὁρμεῖς χώρᾳ, καὶ μηδένα φόβον
ἔχεις ἀπὸ τῶν πολεμίων, καὶ οὕτω μετ᾽ εὐταξίας ἀναπαύεσθαι τὸν στρατὸν καὶ
ἐν νυκτὶ καὶ ἐν ἡμέρᾳ μηδένα τῶν ἐπιχωρίων βλάπτοντας ἢ ἀδικοῦντας ἢ καρ-
190 ποὺς ἁρπάζοντας ἢ φθείροντας.

---

189 ad τῶν de novo inc. W

---

162 δὲ M om. A   163 καὶ M om. A | πλείους M πλείονας A   164 ἄντις M κατενάντια A
169 ἀφύκτους M ἀφεύκτους A | ἀναγκαίους A ἀναγκαίουσιν M   170 ἐπιβάλῃ M νοήσῃ A
172 θροῶνται M ταράσσωνται A   173 παρὰ δόξαν M παραδόξῃ A   178 καὶ¹ ci. De om.
codd.   181 τὴν M om. A   183 ἀνάγκη M ἀνάγκην A   185 παρὰ M om. A   188 οὕτω
μετ᾽ M οὕτως μετὰ A

28. You shall exercise the soldiers of the fleet and the dromons themselves in different ways, sometimes each man by himself, sometimes in larger groups, so they may confront one another using swords and shields. Also exercise entire dromons by themselves in attacking one another and in pretending to attack in battle formation, sometimes closing tightly, sometimes breaking away, and setting upon one another in various ways, and sometimes repelling enemy ships with spears to avoid getting close and linking up. It is not always helpful for adversaries to use iron shafts to link up with one another because of unavoidable and compelling dangers.

29. Let them also be exercised in other ways, by putting plans that seem feasible, such as Your Excellency might devise, into action against the foe. As a result, they will become accustomed to the noise and the shouting and the rest of the turbulence of war and they will not be terrified as though they had no training but suddenly and unexpectedly ran into all this.

30. Therefore, after they have been so trained and equipped, have them sail in formation, in unison, just far enough apart to avoid getting in each other's way, as they set out and face the likely force of the winds at sea. Let them advance like a well-trained battle line as they sail forth from their bases and let them make the return voyage in good order. Let them also put into shore in good order, sailing toward land or, at least, toward a harbor or anchorage, so that, if a storm should arise, they will not be swamped.

31. You must be able to forecast the direction of the wind by certain seasonal signs and, depending on <what you learn>, select your place to anchor. Unless there is some compelling urgency, do not launch yourself into sailing when conditions are not right, that is, without a favorable wind, a calm sea, and a secure hope of safety. Study carefully what sailors call the indications of the stars, as well as other helpful elements. Then begin your voyage accordingly.

32. If you drop anchor at a base in your own country and you have no fear of enemy activity, then you may rest your army in good order night and day, not harming any of the inhabitants or treating them unjustly or seizing or destroying their crops.

516    Constitution 19

λγ′. Εἰ δὲ ἐν τῇ πολεμίᾳ γῇ πλησιάζεις ἢ πολεμίους παρεῖναί που ἐλπίζεις,
πάντως χρεών σε καὶ βίγλας ἔχειν μακρόθεν καὶ κατὰ γῆν καὶ κατὰ θάλασσαν.
καὶ ἀγρύπνως διατελεῖν καὶ κατησφαλισμένον καὶ ἕτοιμον εἶναι πρὸς παράταξιν.
πολλαὶ γὰρ αἱ τῶν πολεμίων ἐπιβουλαί, καὶ γὰρ ἢ κατὰ γῆς εὑρόντες σε ὁρ-
195  μοῦντα βιάσονται, εἰ τύχοι δὲ εὐπορήσαντες, καὶ τὰς ναῦς ἐμπρήσουσιν· ἢ διὰ
θαλάσσης ἀναφανέντες, προσβολὴν ποιήσονται νυκτὸς καὶ ἡμέρας. καὶ ἐὰν
ἀνέτοιμος ἐν ἑτοίμοις εὑρεθῇς, προτερήσουσιν οἱ ἐναντίοι κατὰ σοῦ. εἰ δέ σε
ἕτοιμον εὑρήσουσιν, ἄπρακτος αὐτοῖς ἡ ἐπιβουλὴ γενήσεται.
λδ′. Ἐπεὶ δὲ τούτων συμμέτρως ἐμνήσθημέν τε καὶ διεταξάμεθα, φέρε λοιπὸν
200  καὶ ὅπως παρατάξεις καὶ τὰς προσβολὰς τὰς ἐν ταῖς μάχαις ποιήσεις, ὡς ἐν
συνόψει διορισώμεθα· καθ᾽ ὃν τρόπον καὶ ἐν ταῖς κατὰ γῆν πολεμικαῖς προσβολαῖς ἄνω που διεταξάμεθα.
λε′. Ὅταν τοίνυν ἐλπίζεταί σοι πολέμου καιρός, ὦ στρατηγέ, συνελθόντων
τῶν στρατιωτῶν κατὰ τὰς τάξεις, ἑκάστων διῃρημένων ὑπαναγνωσθήσεται
205  αὐτοῖς τὰ στρατιωτικὰ ἐπιτίμια, ἅπερ ἡμῖν | ἐν τῷ περὶ τῆς κατὰ γῆν στρατιωτι-   399ᵛ
κῆς γυμνασίας εἴρηται· καὶ ἐπιρρώσεις αὐτοὺς λόγοις προσήκουσι παρορμῶν
καὶ ἐπαλείφων πρὸς τοὺς ἀγῶνας ἵνα, τὸ μὲν διὰ τὸν φόβον τῶν ἐπιτιμίων, τὸ δὲ
διὰ τὴν τῆς σῆς ἐνδοξότητος παραίνεσιν, ἀνδρεῖοι καὶ εὔτολμοι γένωνται, καὶ ἐν
τοῖς μέλλουσι πολεμικοῖς κινδύνοις ἐκ χειρὸς ἀγωνιζόμενοι.
210  λς′. Χρὴ δέ σε μᾶλλον δι᾽ ἐφόδων μὲν καὶ ἄλλων ἐπιτηδευμάτων τε καὶ
στρατηγημάτων μεθοδεύειν κατὰ τῶν πολεμίων ἢ δι᾽ ὅλου τοῦ ὑπό σε πλωΐμου
στόλου ἢ διὰ μέρους αὐτοῦ. μὴ μέντοι χωρὶς ἀνάγκης μεγάλης ἐπὶ τοῦτο κατ-
επειγούσης εἰς δημόσιον πόλεμον σεαυτὸν ἐπιρρίπτειν. πολλὰ γὰρ τὰ τῆς λεγο-
μένης τύχης ἀντίρροπα καὶ τὰ τοῦ πολέμου παράδοξα.
215  λζ′. Διὰ τοῦτο χρή σε ἀεὶ παραφυλάττεσθαι καὶ μὴ πρὸς δημοσίας, ὡς
εἴρηται, παρατάξεις ἀποθρασύνεσθαι, μάλιστα ἐν πλοίοις. ὅπου δεσμούντων ἀλλήλους ἄφυκτος ἡ ἐκ χειρὸς γίνεται καὶ βιαία ἡ μάχη, καὶ οὐκ ἔστι δυνατὸν τοῦ
συμφέροντος ἐπιλήψεσθαι.

---

191 δὲ MA δ᾽ W   192 χρεών MW χρὴ A | θάλασσαν M θάλατταν WA   193 πρὸς MW εἰς
A   195 εὐπορήσαντες MW om. A   196 ποιήσονται MW ποιήσουσιν A | καὶ¹ M ἢ WA
197 ἀνέτοιμος WA ἕτοιμος M   202 ἄνω που MW om. A   204 ἑκάστων διῃρημένων A
ἑκάστην διῃρημένως MW   206 αὐτοὺς MW αὐτοὺς καὶ ἐνισχύσεις A   210 χρὴ MW δεῖ A
212 μέρους MW μέρος A   214 ἀντίρροπα MW ἐναντιώματα A   217 ἄφυκτος…μάχη
MW ἄφευκτος καὶ βιαία ἡ ἐκ χειρὸς μάχη γίνεται A   218 ἐπιλήψεσθαι MW ἐπιλαβέσθαι A

33. But if you approach enemy territory or if you expect the enemy to be in the vicinity, it is absolutely necessary for you to station scouts at some distance, both on land and on sea. You must persevere in your vigilance, remain secure, and be ready to get into formation. For the schemes of the enemy are many. If they are on land and find you lying at anchor, they will overpower you and, if they find the opportunity, they will burn your ships. If they should appear at sea, they will launch an attack by night or day. If the enemy finds that you are not as well prepared as you should be, they will have the advantage over you. But if they find you prepared, their scheme will end up accomplishing nothing.

34. Now that we have done our duty in reminding you of these things and have set down the above regulations, we come to prescribe, in summary fashion, the manner in which you should form the battle line and launch attacks in combat. We will do this as we did earlier when giving orders about combat operations on land.

35. Well then, general, when you expect that the time has come for battle, assemble the soldiers by ranks and have the military punishments read clause by clause to each rank separately, just as we have stated in the section about military training on land.[7] With appropriate words you will then encourage them, arousing and stimulating them for their struggles. Thus, both because of fear of punishment and because of the encouragement given by Your Excellency, they will be brave and courageous, even as they face the dangers of fighting hand-to-hand.

36. It is necessary for you to take action against the enemy more by sudden attacks and by other methods and stratagems, whether with the entire naval force under you or only with part of it. Certainly, apart from some urgent necessity forcing you to do so, you should not throw yourself into a pitched battle. For many are the reversals of so-called fortune. What happens in battle is not what one expects.

37. For this reason, you must always be on your guard. Do not be so absolutely daring, as has been said, to form up for a pitched battle, especially in ships.[8] When they become linked together, a fierce hand-to-hand battle is inevitable and it is not possible to obtain any real advantage.

7. See Const. 8.
8. Demosthenes 61.20.

λη′. Καὶ ταῦτα μὲν φυλάττεσθαι εἰ μὴ ἄρα θαρρεῖς καὶ τῷ πλήθει τῶν
220 δρομώνων, καὶ τῇ ἀνδρείᾳ καὶ ὁπλίσει καὶ προθυμίᾳ τῶν στρατιωτῶν καθυπέρτερος εἶναι τῶν πολεμίων.

λθ′. Οὔτε γὰρ πλῆθος πλοίων οὔτε μέγεθος κατορθώσει πόλεμον εἰ μὴ τοὺς
ἐν αὐτοῖς πολεμοῦντας ἔχουσιν εὐψύχους καὶ ῥωμαλέους καὶ προθύμους εἰς τὴν
κατὰ τῶν ἐναντίων ἐγχείρησιν, καὶ πρό γε τούτων εἰ μὴ τὴν θείαν εὐμένειαν καὶ
225 συμμαχίαν ἔχωσι διὰ καθαρότητος βίου καὶ δικαιοσύνης πρός τε τοὺς συντελεστὰς καὶ πρὸς τοὺς πολεμίους, ἥτις ἐστί, τὸ μηδὲν ἀνόσιον ἐν τοῖς αἰχμαλώτοις
διαπράττεσθαι ἢ αἰσχρὸν ἢ ἀφιλάνθρωπον. καὶ τὸ μὴ ἀδικούμενον μὴ ἀδικεῖν,
τοὺς δὲ ἀδικοῦντας μετὰ τῆς τοῦ Θεοῦ βοηθείας ἀνταμύνεσθαι.

μ′. Ἐὰν δὲ πάντως ἀπαιτεῖται καὶ μάχης καιρός, διατάξεις τοὺς δρόμωνας
230 ποικίλως καὶ διαφόρως, καθὼς ἂν ὅ τε καιρὸς καὶ ὁ τόπος ἀπαιτῇ. ὥστε ἐὰν
θαρρῇς καθυπέρτερος εἶναι τῶν πολεμίων, ὥς μοι εἴρηται, καὶ διὰ τοῦτο πρὸς
μάχην συμβαλεῖν, ὡς ἐλπίζων αἱρήσειν αὐτούς, μὴ ἐν τῇ ἰδίᾳ σου γῇ πλησίον
ποιήσῃς τὴν μάχην ἐν ᾗ ἐλπίσουσιν οἱ στρατιῶται, τὸ δὴ λεγόμενον, καταξυλώ-
σαντες σωθῆναι, ἀλλὰ | μᾶλλον πλησίον τῆς τῶν ἐναντίων γῆς, ἵνα αὐτοὶ τὴν    400
235 σωτηρίαν ἐλπίσαντες ἐν τῇ ἰδίᾳ γῇ τὴν φυγὴν παρὰ τοὺς ἀγῶνας προτιμήσων-
ται. στρατιώτης γὰρ εἰς δειλίαν ἐν ἀνάγκῃ πολέμου περιπίπτων τὴν σωτηρίαν
διὰ τῆς φυγῆς ἐλπίσει, καὶ ταχέως ῥίψει τὰ ὅπλα καὶ οὐδὲν αὐτῆς προτιμήσεται.
ὀλίγοι γὰρ οἱ ἐν καιρῷ παρατάξεως τὸ ἀποθανεῖν ὑπὲρ τοῦ ἀδόξως φυγεῖν
προκρίνοντες, εἴτε ἐν τοῖς βαρβάροις εἴπῃς εἴτε ἐν τοῖς Ῥωμαίοις.

240 μα′. Πρὸ δὲ τῆς τοῦ πολέμου ἡμέρας χρή σε βουλεύεσθαι μετὰ τῶν ὑπό σε
ἀρχόντων τί δεῖ πρᾶξαι. καὶ ὅπερ ἀναφανῇ διὰ τῆς κοινῆς γνώμης χρήσιμον,
τοῦτο στοιχῆσαι καὶ παραγγεῖλαι τοῖς ἄρχουσι τῶν δρομώνων, ὥστε αὐτοὺς
εἶναι ἑτοίμους ἐκτελέσαι τὰ βουλευθέντα. εἴ γε ἄρα μὴ ἀπαντήσῃ γνώμη ἐναντία ἐκ τῆς ἐφόδου τῶν πολεμίων, ἀλλὰ καὶ τότε ἑτοίμους εἶναι πάντας ἀφορῶν-
245 τας εἰς τὸν σὸν δρόμωνα, ὥστε ἐξ αὐτοῦ λαβεῖν σημεῖόν τι, εἰ ἄρα πρᾶξαι δεῖ,
καὶ τούτου δοθέντος ὀξέως γενέσθαι τὸ ὑποδειχθέν.

μβ′. Πάντως γὰρ δεῖ σε, ὦ στρατηγέ, δρόμωνα ἔχειν τὸν ἴδιον ἐξ ἅπαντος
τοῦ στρατοῦ ἐπιλέκτους ἔχοντα τοὺς στρατιώτας, μεγέθει καὶ ἀνδρείᾳ καὶ ἀρετῇ

---

220 ὁπλίσει Dain κλίσει codd.    223 ῥωμαλέους MW γενναίους A    224 γε MW om. A
225 ἔχωσι MW ἔχουσι A    226 ἐστί MA ἐστιν W    230 ποικίλως MW ποικίλους A
231 καθυπέρτερος MW ἐπικρατέστερος A    236 περιπίπτων MA περιπίπτων εἰ W
238 ὑπὲρ MW om. A    243 ἐκτελέσαι MW ἐκπληρῶσαι A    243–244 γε…ἐναντία MW περ
μὴ ἐναντίον τι ἀπαντήσει A    244–245 ἀφορῶντας MW ἀποβλέποντας A    245 εἰ MW om.
A | πρᾶξαι δεῖ MW ποιῆσαι προσήκει A    246 δοθέντος MA δειχθέντος W

38. You must indeed observe this unless you are confident that the number of your dromons as well as the bravery, condition, and eagerness of your soldiers are vastly superior to those of the enemy.

39. For neither the number of ships nor their size will assure success in battle unless they carry fighting men who are robust, stout of heart, and eager to engage the enemy. Above all this, they must have the divine benevolence and alliance. That depends on their purity of life and their justice in relating to property owners, as well as to the enemy, that is, doing nothing unholy, shameful, or inhumane to the prisoners. If you have not been treated unjustly, do not act unjustly; with the help of God, ward off those acting unjustly.

40. If the time for battle is definitely upon you, line up the dromons in a varied and diverse manner, as both the time and the place may call for. Thus, if you are confident that you are far superior to the enemy, as I have said, and, for this reason, ready to advance into battle in the hope of overpowering them, do not engage in fighting close to your own country. There the soldiers will hope to be saved by making wooden rafts, as they say. Instead, do battle close to the country of the enemy. Soldiers who had hoped for safety in their own country will prefer flight to combat. A soldier who, under pressure of battle, falls into cowardice will hope for safety in flight and he will quickly toss away his arms and value nothing more than flight. When the time comes for forming up for battle, few judge it better to die than to flee ingloriously, whether you are speaking of the barbarians or of the Romans.

41. Before the day of battle you, together with the officers under you, must make plans about what you have to do. Whatever this common counsel judges advantageous should be presented in detail and announced to the officers of the dromons so they may be prepared to put those plans into action. In the event of an enemy attack, of course, a contrary plan may have to be adopted. Everyone will then be prepared to look toward your dromon in order to receive a signal about what they must do. When this has been given, they will promptly carry out your orders.

42. By all means, O general, it is necessary for you to have your own dromon. The soldiers on board are to be the elite from among the entire army, men

καὶ τῇ ἄλλῃ πανοπλίᾳ διέχοντας· καὶ τὸν δρόμωνα δὲ μεγέθει καὶ ταχύτητι τῶν
250 ἄλλων ἁπάντων διαφέροντα, ὡς ἅτε κεφαλήν τινα τῆς παρατάξεως ἁπάσης· καὶ
καταστῆσαι τὸν τῆς σῆς ἐνδοξότητος τοιοῦτον δρόμωνα, τὸ δὲ λεγόμενον
πάμφυλον.

μγʹ. Ὁμοίως δὲ καὶ τοὺς ἄλλους ὑπό σε ἄρχοντας, ὅσοι ἔχουσιν ὑπ᾽ αὐτούς
τινας δρόμωνας, ἐξ αὐτῶν ἐπιλέξασθαι ἄνδρας, καὶ ἔχειν ἐν τοῖς οἰκείοις, ὥστε
255 καὶ αὐτοὺς διαφέρειν τῶν ἄλλων. καὶ τούτους δὲ πάντας καὶ τοὺς λοιποὺς πρὸς
τὸν σὸν ἀποβλέπειν δρόμωνα, καὶ παρ᾽ αὐτοῦ ῥυθμίζεσθαι κατὰ τὸν τοῦ πολέμου καιρόν, εἰ μή γε ἄρα ἕτερόν τι παράδοξον τῶν βεβουλευμένων ἀναφανῇ,
καὶ δέηται μεθόδου ἑτέρας.

μδʹ. Εἶναι δὲ σημεῖον ἱστάμενον ἐν τῷ σῷ δρόμωνι, εἴτε βάνδον εἴτε φλάμου-
260 λον εἴτε τι ἕτερον, εἰς τόπον περίοπτον, ἵνα δι᾽ αὐτοῦ σημαίνοντός σου τί δεῖ
πράττειν, εὐθέως ἐπιλαμβάνωνται τοῦ δόξαντος ἔργου οἱ λοιποί, εἴτε συμβάλλειν εἰς πόλεμον χρὴ εἴτε ἀναχωρεῖν ἀπὸ πολέμου εἴτε ἐξελίσσειν εἰς κύκλωσιν
κατὰ τῶν πολεμίων εἴτε εἰς βοήθειαν καταπονουμένου μέρους συνδραμεῖν εἴτε
ἀργῆσαι τὴν ἐλασίαν εἴτε | ἐπιδοῦναι εἰς τάχος τὴν κίνησιν εἴτε ἔγκρυμμα δέον 400ᵛ
265 γενέσθαι εἴτε ἀπὸ ἐγκρύμματος ἐξελθεῖν ἢ ἄλλα τινὰ καθ᾽ ἕκαστα ἀπὸ σημείων
τοῦ σοῦ δρόμωνος ἅπαντα ὑποδέχεσθαι ἀφορῶντας ὅπως δέον ποιεῖν.

μεʹ. Οὐ γὰρ δύναταί τις ἐν τοιούτῳ καιρῷ ἀπὸ φωνῆς ἢ βουκίνου παραγγέλλειν τὰ δέοντα διά τε τὸν θροῦν καὶ τὸν τάραχον καὶ τὸν τῆς θαλάσσης ἦχον
καὶ τὸν ἄλλον κτύπον τῆς τε συγκρούσεως καὶ κωπηλασίας τῶν δρομώνων, καὶ
270 πολλῷ μᾶλλον τῆς βοῆς τῶν πολεμούντων.

μϛʹ. Τὸ δὲ σημεῖον ὑποσημαινέτω ἢ ὀρθὸν ἱστάμενον ἢ ἐπὶ δεξιὰ ἢ ἐπὶ
ἀριστερὰ κλινόμενον καὶ ἐπὶ δεξιὰ πάλιν ἢ ἐπὶ ἀριστερὰ μεταφερόμενον ἢ
τινασσόμενον ἢ ὑψούμενον ἢ ταπεινούμενον ἢ ὅλως ἀφαιρούμενον ἢ μετατιθέ-
μενον ἢ διὰ τῆς ἐν αὐτῷ κεφαλῆς ἄλλοτε ἄλλως φαινομένης ἀλλασσόμενον ἢ
275 διὰ σχημάτων ἢ διὰ χρωμάτων.

---

249 διέχοντας MW διαφέροντας A | ταχύτητι MW γοργότητι A    250 ἅτε MW om. A
253 ἔχουσιν MA ἔχωσιν W    256 ῥυθμίζεσθαι MW ῥυθμίζεται καὶ κανονίζεσθαι A
258 δέηται MW δέεται A    260 περίοπτον MW ὑψηλὸν A    264 ἐπιδοῦναι…κίνησιν MW
ταχύτερον ἐλαύνειν A    265–266 σημείων…δρόμωνος MA τοῦ σου δρόμωνος καὶ τῶν ἀπ᾽
αὐτοῦ σημείων ἅπαντα W    266 δέον MW δεῖ A    268 θροῦν MW θόρβιον A    269 τὸν…
κτύπον MA τῶν ἄλλων κτύπων W    270 μᾶλλον MW πλέον A    271–272 ἢ³…κλινόμενον
MW κλινόμενον ἢ ἐπ᾽ ἀριστερὰ A    272 πάλιν MW πάλιν μεταφερόμενον A |
μεταφερόμενον M om. WA    273 ταπεινούμενον…ἀφαιρούμενον MW χαμηλούμενον ἢ
παντελῶς ἐπαιρούμενον A

outstanding for their size, bravery, virtue, and special armament. The dromon should be superior to all the others in its size and speed as a sort of head of the entire battle line. You should make ready such a dromon, called pamphylian, for Your Excellency.[9]

43. Your subordinate officers, who also have some dromons under their command, should do likewise. They should select men from those dromons and enroll them among their personal troops, different from the others. All of these and all the rest should look toward your dromon and pattern their movements on it in time of battle, unless, of course, something else, quite different from what had been planned, should impose itself, and require another way of proceeding.

44. A standard that can be seen all around should be flown on your dromon: a flag, a pennant, or something else, so that when you give the signal for each action that needs to be taken, the other ships may quickly carry out the order, whether it be to engage in battle, to retreat from battle, to form a circle around the enemy, to hasten to assist a section that is hard pressed, to slow down their movement, to increase their speed, to set up an ambush or charge out from an ambush, or to take some other action. Looking to all of the signals from your dromon, they find out how they are to proceed.

45. At such a time it is impossible for a person to issue the necessary commands by voice or by trumpet because of the shouting, the confusion, the roaring of the sea, the rest of the din caused by the collision and movement of oars on the dromons and, much more, the cries of the combatants.

46. Let signals be given by raising the standard up straight or inclined to the right or to the left, transferred again to the right or to the left, shaken or raised high or lowered, completely taken down, or altered by making its head appear different at different times by changing its shape or its colors.

---

9. Leo defined the pamphylian as a larger, faster ship for the commander of the entire fleet. They soon became more plentiful and smaller. On the expedition to Crete, in 949, the imperial fleet included sixty dromons with 230 rowers each and forty pamphylians, twenty with 160 men and twenty with 130 men. The thematic fleets had the same number of men per ship. Ouranos, reflecting the word's etymology, πᾶν φύλον, uses it in the sense of a ship's full complement: ποιῆσαι τὸν πάμφυλον, παμφυλεύση τὸν δρόμωνα (*Taktika*, 6.41). Its relationship with the Asian province of Pamphylia is not clear. See Pryor-Jeffreys, index, s.v.

μζ΄. Οἷόν ποτε τοῖς παλαιοῖς ἐπράττετο. ἐν γὰρ πολέμου καιρῷ σημεῖον εἶχον τῆς συμβολῆς αἴροντες τὴν λεγομένην φοινικίδα. ἦν δὲ τὸ λεγόμενον καμελαύκιον, ἐπὶ κονταρίου ὑψούμενον, μέλαν τὴν χροιάν, καὶ ἄλλα τινὰ ὁμοιοτρόπως ὑποδεικνύμενα. ἀσφαλέστερον δὲ τάχα διὰ τῆς σεαυτοῦ χειρὸς τὰ
280 σημεῖα ὑποδειχθήσεται.

μη΄. Καὶ οὕτως ἔστω σοι ἡ ἐνέργεια, ὦ στρατηγέ, τῶν τοιούτων σημείων γεγυμνασμένη, ὥστε πάντας τοὺς ὑπό σε ἄρχοντας, ὅσοι δρομώνων ἡγοῦνται, ἔχειν τὴν πεῖραν ἀσφαλῆ τῶν τοιούτων ὑποδειγμάτων, καὶ διὰ τί γίνεται ἕκαστον καὶ ποτὲ καὶ πῶς καὶ μὴ διασφάλλεσθαι ἵνα, περὶ ταῦτα καλῶς ἐγγυμνασά-
285 μενοι, ἐν καιρῷ χρείας ἕτοιμοι γένωνται πρὸς τὸ διαγινώσκειν αὐτὰ καὶ πράττειν τὰ δι᾽ αὐτῶν κελευόμενα.

μθ΄. Τὴν δὲ τῶν δρομώνων παράταξιν ἐν καιρῷ προσβολῆς, εἴ γε ἄρα, ὡς εἴρηται, τοσαύτη πάρεστιν ἀνάγκη ἢ κατὰ χεῖρας τὴν νίκην ἐλπίζεις, ποιήσεις καθὼς ἂν συνείδης ἁρμόδιον τῷ καιρῷ καὶ τῷ τόπῳ πρὸς τὴν τῶν πολεμίων
290 παρασκευὴν καὶ παράταξιν. οὐ γὰρ νῦν ἐστι λέγειν ἀσφαλῶς περὶ τῶν τότε μελλόντων ἀπαντήσεσθαι.

ν΄. Ποτὲ μὲν μηνοειδῶς οἷον ἡμικυκλίου τάξιν, τοὺς μὲν ἄλλους δρόμωνας ἔνθεν κἀκεῖθεν, οἷόν τινα κέρατα ἢ χεῖρας καὶ μάλιστα ἐν τῷ ἄκρῳ προάγοντας τοὺς ἀλκιμωτέρους καὶ μείζονας. ἐν δὲ τῷ κοίλῳ τοῦ ἡμικυκλίου, οἱονεί τινα
295 κεφαλήν, τὴν σὴν ἐνδοξότητα, ὥστε πάντα | περισκοπεῖν καὶ διατάττειν καὶ 401 διοικεῖν καί, εἴ που δεῖ καὶ βοηθείας, ἐπικουρεῖν μεθ᾽ ὧν ἂν βούλῃ ἐπὶ τούτῳ εὐκαιρούντων. τὸ δὲ σχῆμα τὸ μηνοειδὲς γινέσθω ὥστε τοὺς ἐμπίπτοντας πολεμίους ἐντὸς ἀποκλείεσθαι τῆς κυκλώσεως.

να΄. Ποτὲ δὲ παρατάξεις κατὰ μέτωπον ἐπ᾽ εὐθείας ὥστε, χρείας καλούσης,
300 ἐπιπίπτειν τοῖς πολεμίοις κατὰ πρώραν, καὶ διὰ τοῦ πυρὸς τῶν σιφώνων ἐμπρήζειν τὰς ἐκείνων ναῦς.

276 ἐπράττετο MW ἐγίνετο A | πολέμου A πολέμῳ MW    277 αἴροντες MW αἴροντες εἰς ὕψος A    278 μέλαν A ἐρυθρὸν MW | χροιάν MA χρόαν W    278–279 ὁμοιοτρόπως MW κατὰ τὸν ὅμοιον τρόπον A    279 σεαυτοῦ MW σῆς A    280 ὑποδειχθήσεται WA ὑποδεχθήσεται M    284 διασφάλλεσθαι MW σφάλλεσθαι A    285 διαγινώσκειν MW γνωρίζειν A    285–286 πράττειν MW πράττειν συντόμως A    287 εἴ… ἄρα MW εἴπερ A    288 ἢ MA καὶ W | κατὰ χεῖρας MW εὐκόλως A    289 καιρῷ… τόπῳ MW εἶναι πρός τε τὸν καιρὸν καὶ τὸν τόπον καὶ A    291 ἀπαντήσεσθαι MW συμβήσεσθαι A    292 οἷον MW οἷον σιγματοειδῶς εἰς A    293 τινα κέρατα MW trsp. A    294 ἀλκιμωτέρους MW ἰσχυροτέρους A | κοίλῳ MW βάθει A    296 εἴ W ἢ M ὃ A | καὶ M om. WA | βοηθείας MA ἐπικουρίας W | ἐπικουρεῖν M καὶ βοηθείας W ἐπιβοηθεῖν A | ἐπὶ τούτῳ MW εἰς τοῦτο αὐτὸ A    298 ἐντὸς MW ἔσωθεν A    299 κατὰ μέτωπον MW ἰσομετώπους τὰς ναῦς A    300 ἐπιπίπτειν MW ἐμπίπτειν A    300–301 ἐμπρήζειν MW κατακαίειν A

47. This sort of thing was sometimes done by the ancients. For in the time of combat they used to raise the signal for battle, called the red flag. There was also the so-called kamelavkion, black in color and raised on a spear.[10] And there were other <ways of signaling> of that sort. The signals will quickly and more securely be transmitted <when given> by your own hand.

48. You should devote yourself, O general, to being proficient in the use of such signals, so that all your officers in command of dromons may become thoroughly acquainted with signals of this type. What does each one mean? When and how <are they to be used>? And so they will not be led astray. Thus, they should be very well practiced in using these signals and, in time of need, be prepared to recognize them and to carry out the orders transmitted by them.

49. If indeed, as was said, you are under very great pressure or you expect that victory is at hand, then you will line up the dromons in time of battle as you deem appropriate to the time and place, and corresponding to the armament and battle line of the enemy. At this moment, it is not possible to speak with any assurance about what one may run up against at some future date.

50. Sometimes <adopt> a crescent-shaped or semicircular formation, with the dromons on one side and on the other, somewhat like horns or hands, with the stronger and better dromons leading them, especially at the extremes. But in the concave space of the semicircle, as a sort of head, should be Your Excellency, so that you may carefully observe, arrange, and manage everything. If there should be need of assistance somewhere you may attend to it with whatever means you think most opportune. The crescent-shaped line should be formed so as to cut off the enemy who have fallen into the encirclement.

51. Sometimes <you will form> the front in a straight line so that, when necessary, you may fall upon the enemy with your prow first. Then, with the fire from the siphons, you can set their ships ablaze.

10. The kamelavkion originally meant a head covering, a turban perhaps, so that, unrolled, it resembled a flag. Although black, it incorporated various colors and designs to make it effective in giving signals. The Arabic adaptation of ibn Mankali (ed. A. Shboul, in Pryor-Jeffreys, 653) suggests changing red to blue or some other color. See Pryor-Jeffreys, 397–399; E. Piltz, *Kamelavkion und Mitra* (Stockholm, 1977).

νβ΄. Ποτὲ δὲ καὶ εἰς διαφόρους μερίζεσθαι παρατάξεις, ἤτοι δύο ἢ τρεῖς, κατὰ τὴν ποσότητα τῶν ὑπό σε δρομώνων. καὶ τῆς μιᾶς παρατάξεως συμβαλλούσης, ἡ ἄλλη εἰσπεσεῖται κατὰ τῶν πολεμίων ἤδη ἐμπεπλεγμένων, ἢ ὄπισθεν
305 ἢ κατὰ πλευράν, καὶ διὰ τῆς βοηθείας τῆς ἐπελθούσης κατ᾽ αὐτῶν ἀπείπωσιν οἱ πολέμιοι τοῦ τόνου.

νγ΄. Ποτὲ δὲ καὶ δι᾽ ἐγκρύμματος. ἀποπλανωμένων γὰρ τῶν πολεμίων καὶ ἐμπιπτόντων, ὡς ὀλίγοις ἀναφανὲν ἀθρόως τὸ ἔγκρυμμα καὶ θροῆσαν αὐτούς, ἐκλύσει τὸν τόνον τῆς ἐνστάσεως.

310 νδ΄. Ἄλλοτε δὲ δι᾽ ἐλαφρῶν καὶ ταχινῶν δρομώνων συμβαλλόντων αὐτοῖς καὶ προσποιουμένων φυγεῖν· κἀκείνων ἐν τῇ διώξει κοπουμένων καὶ βιαζομένων μέν, μὴ καταλαμβανόντων δὲ τοὺς φεύγοντας, ἢ καί τινων τῆς συνεχείας ἀποτεμνομένων, ἕτεροί σου δρόμωνες ἄκοποι καὶ ἀναπεπαυμένοι κατὰ τῶν κεκοπωμένων ὁρμήσαντες αἱρήσουσιν αὐτοὺς ἤ, εἰ καὶ τὰ δυνατὰ τῶν ἐχθρῶν
315 πλοῖα παρελθεῖν ἰσχύσας τις τοῖς ἀσθενεστέροις ἐπιτεθῇ.

νε΄. Ποτὲ δὲ συμβαλὼν καὶ ἱκανῶς ἐκ χειρὸς πολεμήσας ταῖς ἐναντίαις ναυσὶ μέχρι ἄκρας κοπώσεως, ἀπολύσεις μὲν τοὺς δρόμωνας, ἑτέρους δὲ πάλιν ἐπαφήσεις τοῖς πολεμίοις εὐρώστους τοῖς κεκοπωμένοις καὶ ἐκλυθεῖσι τὸν τόνον ἀπὸ τῆς μάχης, καὶ οὕτως τὴν κατ᾽ αὐτῶν νίκην περιποιήσῃ· μάλιστα δὲ
320 τοῦτο γίνεται ὅταν περιττεύῃς αὐτὸς τῷ πλήθει τῶν δρομώνων ὑπὲρ τοὺς πολεμίους.

νς΄. Ποτὲ δὲ φυγὴν προσποιούμενος μετὰ δρομώνων ταχινῶν πρὸς δίωξιν ἐκκαλέσῃ τοὺς πολεμίους κατὰ πρύμναν ἔχων αὐτούς. κἀκεῖνοι ὁρμήσαντες διώκειν διαλύσουσι τὴν τάξιν αὐτῶν. καὶ οὕτως ἀνθυποστρέψας τάχος διεσπαρ-
325 μένοις τοῖς διώκουσι, μάλιστα καὶ πλέον ἐκείνων δρόμωνας ἔχων, ἐπέλθῃς

---

308 ad ὡς des. W

---

304 εἰσπεσεῖται MW ἐμπεσεῖται A | ἐμπεπλεγμένων MA πεπληγμένων W    305 κατὰ πλευράν MW ἐκ πλαγίου A | ἀπείπωσιν MW ἀπαγορεύουσιν A    306 τόνου MW μάχεσθαι A    308 ὀλίγοις M πρὸς ὀλίγους A | θροῆσαν M ταράξαι A    309 ἐνστάσεως M ἐνστάσεως αὐτῶν A    310 ταχινῶν M ταχυτάτων A    311 προσποιουμένων…κἀκείνων M σχηματιζομένων φυγὴν ἐκείνων δὲ A    312–313 τῆς…ἀποτεμνομένων M ἀποκοπουμένων ἀλλήλων τῆς συνεχείας A    314 κεκοπωμένων A κατασκοπῶν M | αἱρήσουσιν M νικήσουσιν A    317 ἄκρας κοπώσεως M τοῦ τελείως κοπωθῆναι τοὺς ἐναντίους A | ἀπολύσεις Du ἀποπλήξεις codd.    318 ἐπαφήσεις M ἐπιπέμψεις A | εὐρώστους M ἀκοπιάτους A    318–319 ἐκλυθεῖσι…τόνον M ἐκλυθεῖσιν A    319 περιποιήσῃ M ἐργάσῃ A    320 περιττεύῃς…δρομώνων M περισσοτέρους αὐτὸς ἔχῃς δρόμωνας A    324 οὕτως M οὕτως συντόμως A | τάχος M om. A    325 πλέον M πλείονας A

52. At times, divide your formations in different ways, either two or three, depending on the number of dromons under your command, and while one battle line is attacking, the other will fall upon the enemy, already heavily engaged, either from the rear or from the side. Such an auxiliary force coming upon them will cause the enemy to lose their fighting spirit.

53. Also sometimes <you will arrange them> into ambushes. When the enemy are attacking and in some disorder, the ambush suddenly appears before a few and confuses them. This will cause the force of the enemy impact to slacken.

54. At other times, have light and fast dromons attack them and then pretend to flee. As the enemy pursue, they will grow weary and feel the pressure because they are failing to overtake the fleeing ships; some will also be cut off from the rest <of their fleet>. Other dromons of yours, then, whose <crews> are rested and not weary, will charge out against the exhausted foe and overpower them. Or, if one <of your dromons> has been able to slip past the more powerful enemy ships, it should then set upon the weaker ones.

55. At other times, when you have attacked and for some time engaged the enemy ships at close quarters until you are absolutely worn out, have your dromons sail away and, in turn, set other strong ones upon the enemy, now exhausted and whose eagerness for battle has slackened. In this way you will be victorious over them. This will surely come about when you have more dromons than the enemy.

56. Sometimes, in pretending to flee with your swift dromons, you will provoke the enemy at your stern and, as they charge out in pursuit, they will break up their formation. In this case, especially if you have a larger number of dromons, you will quickly turn around against your pursuers, who will be in

αὐτοῖς κατὰ πρώραν καί, ἢ καθ᾽ ἕνα ἢ κατὰ δύο, ἐπάγων τοὺς σοὺς δρόμωνας τῷ ἑνὶ πλοίῳ τῶν πολεμίων, αἱρήσεις | τὴν νίκην κατ᾽ αὐτῶν.    401ᵛ

νζ΄. Προσβάλλειν δὲ πολεμίοις χρεὼν ἐν ναυμαχίᾳ, καὶ ὅταν τύχῃ αὐτοὺς ναυαγῆσαι καὶ ὅταν ἀπὸ ζάλης διαταραχθέντες ἀτονήσουσιν, ἢ ἐν νυκτὶ ἐπελ-
330 θόντα ἐμπρῆσαι τὰς ἐκείνων ναῦς ἢ ἐν τῇ χέρσῳ ἀσχολουμένων ἢ ὡς ἂν ἡ χρεία καλέσοι, καὶ αὐτὸς ἐπινοήσεις καὶ ποιήσεις τὰς προσβολάς.

νη΄. Ποικίλης γὰρ οὔσης τῆς τῶν ἀνθρώπων γνώμης, ἀδύνατόν τινα τὰ μέλλοντα ἐμπίπτειν ἐν ταῖς τοιαύταις παρατάξεσιν ἢ προγινώσκειν ἢ προλέγειν ἅπαντα. διὸ οὐδὲ τὰς κατ᾽ αὐτῶν μεθοδεύειν ἀντιπαρατάξεις ἐν τῷ παρόντι
335 λόγῳ δυνατόν, ἀλλὰ τῆς θείας ἅπαντα ταῦτα προνοίας ἀναρτᾶν, καὶ δέεσθαι τοῦ Θεοῦ ἵνα ἐν τοῖς τοιούτοις ὀξέσι καιροῖς καὶ βουλεύεσθαι καὶ διανοεῖσθαι δύναταί τις καὶ πράττειν τὰ δέοντα.

νθ΄. Πολλὰ δὲ καὶ ἐπιτηδεύματα τοῖς παλαιοῖς καὶ δὴ καὶ τοῖς νεωτέροις ἐπενοήθη κατὰ τῶν πολεμικῶν πλοίων καὶ τῶν ἐν αὐτοῖς πολεμούντων. οἷον τό
340 τε ἐσκευασμένον πῦρ μετὰ βροντῆς καὶ καπνοῦ προπύρου διὰ τῶν σιφώνων πεμπόμενον, καὶ καπνίζον αὐτά.

ξ΄. Καὶ τοξοβολίστραι δὲ ἔν τε ταῖς πρύμναις καὶ ταῖς πρώραις καὶ κατὰ τῶν δύο πλευρῶν τοῦ δρόμωνος ἐκπέμπουσαι σαγίττας μικρὰς τὰς λεγομένας μυίας. καὶ θηρία ἕτεροι ἐπενόησαν ἐν χύτραις κεκλεισμένα, καὶ κατὰ τῶν πλοίων τῶν
345 πολεμίων ῥιπτόμενα, οἷον ὄφεις καὶ ἐχίδνας καὶ σαύρας καὶ σκορπίους καὶ τὰ ὅμοια τούτων ἰοβόλα, ὧν συντριβομένων τὰ θηρία δάκνουσι καὶ συμφθείρουσι διὰ τοῦ ἰοῦ τοὺς πολεμίους ἔσωθεν τῶν πλοίων.

ξα΄. Καὶ χύτρας δὲ ἄλλας ἀσβέστου πλήρεις, ὧν ῥιπτομένων καὶ συντριβο-μένων, ὁ τῆς ἀσβέστου ἀτμὸς συμπνίγει καὶ σκοτίζει τοὺς πολεμίους, καὶ μέγα
350 ἐμπόδιον γίνεται.

ξβ΄. Καὶ τρίβολοι δὲ σιδηραῖ ῥιπτόμεναι ἐν τοῖς πλοίοις τῶν πολεμίων οὐ μικρὰ λυπήσουσιν αὐτούς, καὶ ἐμποδίσουσιν πρὸς τὸν κατὰ τὴν ὥραν ὀφείλον-τα ἀγῶνα.

---

327 αἱρήσεις…αὐτῶν Μ νικήσεις αὐτοὺς Α    328 χρεὼν Μ χρὴ Α    331 καὶ ποιήσεις Α
ποιήσῃ Μ    334 μεθοδεύειν Μ om. Α    335 ἀλλὰ…ἀναρτᾶν Μ μεθοδεύειν ἀλλ᾽ εἰς τὴν
θείαν πρόνοιαν ἅπαντα ταῦτα ἀνατιθέναι Α    336 καιροῖς Μ καιροῖς δύναταί τις Α
337 δύναταί τις Μ om. Α    338 νεωτέροις Μ νέοις Α    340 ἐσκευασμένον Μ ἐσκευαστὸν Α
| προπύρου Dain προσπείρου Μ προπείρου Α    341 καπνίζον Μ κατακαίοντα Α
352 ἐμποδίσουσιν Μ ἐμποδίσουσι Α

disarray. Attack them from the prow, positioning one or two of your ships against one of the enemy's, and you will achieve victory over them.

57. It is necessary to move forward against the enemy in naval battle when they happen to have suffered shipwreck and when, after having been tossed about by a storm, they will have lost their effectiveness. Or come upon them by night and set their ships on fire, or <attack> when they are occupied on shore, or you yourself will devise and carry out the assaults as the situation demands.

58. The human mind is very complex. It is impossible for a person to discover what will happen in these battle formations or to foresee or foretell everything. In the present treatise, therefore, it is not possible to devise a way for our battle lines to counteract theirs, but to make all these things dependent on divine providence and to pray to God that in such critical moments one is able to take counsel, to think things through, and to accomplish what is needed.

59. The ancients, as well as more recent authorities, devised many weapons for use against enemy ships and against the fighting men in them, such as prepared fire with thunder and fiery smoke discharged through the siphons, blackening them with smoke.

60. Or catapults <placed> in both the prow and the stern and on the two sides of the dromon, discharging small arrows that are called flies.[11] Still others conceived of animals shut up in pots to be hurled against the enemy ships. Among these would be snakes, vipers, lizards, scorpions, and other such venomous creatures. When the pots are shattered, the animals bite and by their poison wipe out the enemy on board the ships.

61. And other pots filled with unslaked lime. When these are hurled and shattered, the vapor from the asbestos chokes and blinds the enemy and proves to be a huge annoyance.

62. Iron caltrops hurled onto the enemy ships will cause them no little annoyance and will keep them from dutifully engaging in the battle at hand.

---

11. See *supra*, Const. 5, n. 3.

ξγ'. Ἡμεῖς δὲ κελεύομεν καὶ πυρὸς ἐσκευασμένου πλήρεις ἀκοντίζεσθαι καὶ
355 χύτρας κατὰ τὴν ὑποδειχθεῖσαν μέθοδον τῆς αὐτῶν σκευασίας. ὧν συντριβο-
μένων ἐμπρησθήσεσθαι ῥᾳδίως τὰ πλοῖα τῶν πολεμίων.

ξδ'. Χρήσασθαι δὲ καὶ τῇ ἄλλῃ μεθόδῳ τῶν διὰ χειρὸς βαλλομένων μικρῶν
σιφώνων ὄπισθεν τῶν σιδηρῶν σκουταρίων παρὰ τῶν στρατιωτῶν | κρατου-    402
μένων, ἅπερ χειροσίφωνα λέγεται, παρὰ τῆς ἡμῶν βασιλείας ἄρτι κατεσκευασ-
360 μένα. ῥίψουσι γὰρ καὶ αὐτὰ τοῦ ἐσκευασμένου πυρὸς κατὰ τῶν προσώπων τῶν
πολεμίων.

ξε'. Καὶ τρίβολοι δὲ μείζονες σιδηραῖ ἢ ἐν σφαιρίοις ξυλίνοις ἧλοι ὀξεῖς
ἐμπεπηγμένοι, στυππίοις δὲ καὶ ἑτέρᾳ ὕλῃ ἐνειλημμένοι ἐμπυρισθέντα καὶ κατὰ
τῶν πολεμίων βαλλόμενα, εἶτα πίπτοντα ἐν τοῖς πλοίοις διὰ πολλῶν μερῶν
365 ἐμπρήσουσιν αὐτά.

ξϛ'. Ἀλλὰ εἰ καὶ διὰ τὸ σβέσαι οἱ πολέμιοι πατήσουσι τὴν αὐτῶν φλόγα οἱ
πλεῖστοι τοὺς πόδας πληγήσονται κατ' αὐτὴν τὴν ἀκμὴν τοῦ πολέμου, καὶ οὐ
μικρὸν ἔσται τοῖς ἐναντίοις ἐμπόδιον.

ξζ'. Δυνατὸν δὲ καὶ διά τινων γερανίων λεγομένων, ἤ τινων ὁμοίων ἐπιτη-
370 δευμάτων γαμματοειδῶν κύκλῳ περιστρεφομένων ἢ πίσσαν ὑγρὰν πεπυρω-
μένην ἢ σκευὴν ἤ τινα ἑτέραν ὕλην ἐπιχύσαι τοῖς πολεμικοῖς πλοίοις διὰ τῶν
δρομώνων δεσμουμένοις, καὶ τοῦ μαγγάνου στρεφομένου κατ' αὐτῶν.

ξη'. Δυνατὸν δὲ καὶ ἀνατρέψαι ὁλόκληρον τὴν ναῦν τῶν πολεμίων, ἐὰν
πλευρὰν παρὰ πλευρὰν δήσας αὐτὴν τῷ δρόμωνι, καὶ τῶν πολεμίων ἐφ' ἓν
375 μέρος, ὡς εἰώθασι, πρὸς τὴν ἐκ χειρὸς μάχην συνδραμόντων, καὶ δοκούντων
ἐπερείδεσθαι τὴν ἑαυτῶν ναῦν τῷ δρόμωνι, ἐπέλθη μὲν ἕτερος δρόμων κατὰ τῆς
πλευρᾶς ἐν τῇ πρύμνῃ τῆς πολεμίας καὶ ταύτην ὠθήσῃ σφοδρῶς τῇ συγκρού-
σει, καὶ ὁ μὲν δρόμων δυνηθῇ λύσας ἑαυτὸν τοῦ δεσμοῦ ὑποχωρῆσαι μικρόν,
ὥστε μὴ εἶναι ὡς ἔρεισμα τῆς πολεμίας, βαρήσῃ δὲ ὁ ἕτερος δρόμων πάσῃ
380 δυνάμει <καὶ> πάντως ἀνατρέψει αὔτανδρον τὴν πολεμίαν ναῦν. δεῖ δὲ
κανονίσαι τὸν δεσμὸν μὴ πάντως κατ' ἰσότητα γενέσθαι, ἀλλὰ μικρὸν ἀφεῖναι

---

354–355 ἐσκευασμένου...χύτρας Μ σκευαστοῦ γεγεμισμένας χύτρας ἐπιρρίπτεσθαι κατ'
αὐτῶν Α  356 ἐμπρησθήσεσθαι...πολεμίων Μ εὐκόλως τὰ πλοῖα τῶν πολεμίων
κατακαήσεται Α  362 ξε' Α ξϛ' Μ  363 ἐνειλημμένοι Dain ἐνειλημμένη codd.  366 ξϛ' Α
ξζ' Μ | πατήσουσι...φλόγα Μ τὴν αὐτῶν φλόγα πατήσουσι Α  367 ἀκμὴν Μ συμβολὴν Α
369 ξζ' Α ξη' Μ  370 γαμματοειδῶν Μ γαμματοειδῶς Α  371 ἑτέραν ὕλην Μ trsp. Α
372 καὶ Μ om. Α  373 ξη' Α ξθ' Μ | ἀνατρέψαι...ναῦν Μ ὁλόκληρον τὸν ναῦν ἀνατρέψαι Α
374–375 ἐφ'...εἰώθασι Μ ἐπὶ ἓν μέρος ὡς ἔθος ἔχουσι Α  376 ἐπερείδεσθαι...ναῦν Μ
ἐπακουμβίζειν τὸ ἑαυτῶν πλοῖον Α  377 πλευρᾶς ·Μ πλευρᾶς τῆς Α  378 δυνηθῇ Α
συνηθῇ Μ  379 ἔρεισμα Μ ἀκούμβισμα Α  380 αὔτανδρον Μ σὺν αὐτοῖς τοῖς ἀνδράσι Α

63. But we command that pots full of the prepared fire, according to the prescribed method of their preparation, should be hurled; on shattering they easily burn up the ships of the enemy.

64. Make use also of the other method, that is, of the small siphons thrown by hand from behind the iron shields held by the soldiers.[12] These are called hand siphons and have been fabricated recently by Our Majesty. These too will throw the prepared fire into the face of the enemy.

65. Also larger iron caltrops or sharp nails hammered into wooden spheres, then wrapped in hemp or some other substance, set on fire, and thrown against the enemy. Falling in various places, they will set the ships aflame.

66. However, in order to extinguish the flames, the enemy will stamp on them and very many will injure their feet at the very height of battle and this will be no small hindrance to the enemy.

67. It is possible to use the so-called cranes or similar gamma-shaped contrivances that revolve in a circle. When the enemy ships are bound to your dromons, turn the machine around against them and pour on them either burning liquid pitch or a net or some other material.

68. It is possible to overturn an enemy ship completely if you tie it up side-by-side to your dromon. The enemy will race to one side, as they usually do, to engage in hand-to-hand fighting and they will seem to pit the whole force of their own ship against the dromon. Then another dromon should come up against the side of the enemy ship toward the stern and crash into it, giving it a strong push. <Our first> dromon then, having gotten itself loose from the chain, will be able to pull back a little, so it will not provide support for the enemy ship. The other dromon will then bear down with all its might and completely overturn the enemy ship with all hands. It is necessary to make sure that the chains are not absolutely equal but should allow for a little more space on the

12. A hand siphon is illustrated in cod. Vat. Gr. 1605, fol. 36, reproduced in Sullivan, *Siegecraft*, and Pryor-Jeffreys.

γυμνά τινα πλευρὰ κατὰ πρύμναν τῆς πολεμίας, δι' ὧν ἐμπεσὼν ὁ δρόμων
ὠθήσει πρὸς τὴν ἀνατροπὴν τῶν πολεμίων τὴν ναῦν.

ξθ΄. Πρὸς τούτοις, καὶ τὸ νῦν ἐπινοηθέν, μήτε ἀπὸ τῆς κάτω τοῦ δρόμωνος
385 ἐλασίας διὰ τῶν ὀπῶν τῶν κωπίων ἐξαγόμενα μέναυλα κατασφάττειν τοὺς
πολεμίους τῶν λίαν μοι ἀναγκαίων δοκεῖ.

ο΄. Ἀλλὰ καὶ ἕτερον τούτων ἀναγκαιότερον, εἴ γε χειρῶν εὐφυῶν ἐπιτύχοι·
τὸ διὰ τῆς κάτωθεν τοῦ δρόμωνος ἐλασίας τῇ ὑποδειχθείσῃ μεθόδῳ, δι' ὀπῆς
παρασκευάσει πλησθῆναι ὕδατος τὴν ναῦν τῶν πολεμίων.

390 οα΄. Εἰσὶ δὲ καὶ ἕτερα τοῖς | ἀρχαίοις ἐπινοηθέντα ἐν τῷ πλωΐμῳ πολέμῳ  402ᵛ
ἐπιτηδεύματα, καὶ ἔτι δὲ ἐπινοηθῆναι δυνάμενα· ἅπερ ἐν τῷ παρόντι τεύχει
γράφειν διὰ τὴν συντομίαν ἀνοίκειον. τινὰ δὲ καὶ ἀσύμφορον διὰ τὸ μὴ πουβλικίζεσθαι τοῖς πολεμίοις καὶ μᾶλλον ἐκείνους αὐτοῖς χρῆσθαι καθ' ἡμῶν. τὰ γὰρ
στρατηγήματα ἅπαξ κατανοηθέντα, ἀντιστρατηγεῖσθαι καὶ καταμεθοδεύεσθαι
395 παρὰ τῶν πολεμίων δύναται· ἀλλ' ἕκαστον τὸ ἐπινοηθὲν μέχρι τῆς πράξεως
ἔχειν ἐν μυστηρίῳ.

οβ΄. Ἐν δὲ τῷ συνειλημμένῳ τῶν τε ἀρχαίων τακτικῶν καὶ στρατηγημάτων
βιβλίῳ ζητῶν τις εὑρήσει καὶ τὰ τούτων πλείονα. οὐ γὰρ δυνατόν, ὡς εἴρηται,
πρὸς ἕκαστα τὰ ἐμπίπτειν μέλλοντα διὰ τὸ ἄπειρον αὐτῶν γράφειν τὰ ἱκανά.

400 ογ΄. Πλὴν κεφάλαιον εἰπεῖν, ἔστωσαν οἱ δρόμωνες ἐξωπλισμένοι τελείως
ἀπό τε στρατιωτῶν ἀνδρείων καὶ ἐκ χειρὸς μάχεσθαι δυναμένων, καὶ τῷ τῆς
ψυχῆς παραστήματι τολμηρῶν, καὶ πεπαιδευμένων καὶ γεγυμνασμένων. οὗτοι
δὲ ἔστωσαν καθωπλισμένοι ὅπλοις ὁποίοις καὶ ὁ ἐν τῇ ξηρᾷ στρατιώτης ὁπλισθῆναι διώρισται, δηλονότι κατάφρακτος. καὶ οὕτω πάντες οἱ τῆς ἄνω ἐλασίας
405 ὁπλισθήσονται.

οδ΄. Πρὸς δὲ τὴν τῶν ἐχθρῶν ποιότητα καὶ ποσότητα τῶν πλοίων, καὶ αὐτός,
ὦ στρατηγέ, διασκευάσεις τοὺς δρόμωνας, ὡς ἂν μὴ ἐλάττονα στρατὸν ἔχῃ ὁ
ἡμέτερος δρόμων τοῦ πολεμίου, ὅστις μάλιστα εἰς ἰσόπαλον ἐλθεῖν εὐτρεπίζεται

---

400 ad πλὴν de novo inc. W

---

384 ξθ΄ A om. M | μήτε Ṁ ὥστε A    385 ὀπῶν M ὀπῶν ἤτοι τρυπημάτων A | ἐξαγόμενα M
ἐκφερόμενα A    386 λίαν M πάνυ A    387 ο΄ A om. M | τούτων M τούτου A    390 οα΄ A
οβ΄ M    391 τεύχει M om. A    392–393 πουβλικίζεσθαι M φαυλίζεσθαι A    393 ἐκείνους…
χρῆσθαι M ἐκείνοις χρῆσθαι αὐτοῖς A    394 κατανοηθέντα M κατανοηθέντα δύνανται A
395 δύναται M om. A    397 οβ΄ A ογ΄ M | συνειλημμένῳ…τε M om. A    399 γράφειν M
γράφειν ἀλλὰ A    400 ογ΄ A οδ΄ M    406 οδ΄ A οε΄ M om. W    407 ὡς ἂν MW καὶ
καθοπλίσεις ὅπως A    408 ἰσόπαλον MW ἴσην μάχην A | εὐτρεπίζεται MW ἑτοιμάζεται A

side of the enemy ship toward the rear so the dromon can make its impact in that place and capsize the enemy ship.[13]

69. In addition to these, it strikes me as very important—this is how we think about it nowadays—not to stick large spears out through the holes for the oars in the lower rowing bench to kill off the enemy.[14]

70. There is, however, something else that may prove more effective. If you come upon men with natural manual dexterity, follow the prescribed method in preparing to fill the enemy ship with water through the holes for the oars in the lower rowing bench of the dromon.

71. There are also other contrivances devised by the ancients to use in naval warfare and still more possibilities are conceivable. But it is not practical to write about these in the present volume because of its summary nature. It may, moreover, be harmful, for some matters should not be made known to the enemy lest they turn around and employ them against us. Once stratagems have been invented, it is possible for the enemy to take countermeasures and strategies against them. Each invention, then, should be kept secret until put into action.

72. If one searches through the encyclopedic volume of ancient tactics and stratagems, he will find more than these.[15] Because of their unlimited number, as already noted, it is not possible to address fully in writing each one of the future eventualities.

73. Nonetheless, to sum it up, let the dromons be arrayed completely armed, with brave soldiers, able to engage in close combat, emboldened by courage of soul, well-instructed and well-trained. Arm them with weapons similar to those prescribed for soldiers on land, that is, they should be heavily armed. All those in the upper bank of rowers should be armed in this way.

74. You should personally see, O general, to the arrangement of the dromons, with a view to the quality and number of enemy ships. Our dromon should not have fewer fighting men than that of the enemy, but more if possible,

---

13. On the impracticality of this maneuver see Pryor-Jeffreys, 204–208.

14. The meaning of this and the following paragraph is not clear. M writes: "important ... not to" (μήτε), whereas A has "important ... to" (ὥστε). See Pryor-Jeffreys, 405–406.

15. "Encyclopedic volume" must refer to the *Sylloge tacticorum*. See *supra*, Const. 18, n. 16, and Pryor-Jeffreys, 176.

μάχην, διὰ τοῦ εἰς ἀλλήλους δεσμοῦ, ἀλλ᾽ εἰ δυνατὸν καὶ πλείονα. ἀμφοτέρων
410 γὰρ ἀνδρείως, εἰ τύχοι, μαχομένων, οἱ πλείονες προτερήσουσιν.

οε΄. Ἐὰν γὰρ συνορᾷς ἔχειν τοὺς πολεμίους πολυανδρούμενα πλοῖα καὶ
πλείονα στρατὸν ὑποδεχόμενα, οὓς ἰσώσεις καὶ αὐτὸς τοὺς σοὺς δρόμωνας ἐν
πλήθει. ἐκλέξῃ δὲ ἀπὸ πάντων τοὺς ἀρίστους, καὶ ἐξ αὐτῶν ἐξοπλίσεις τὴν
ἀρκοῦσαν δύναμιν διὰ δρομώνων τελείων καὶ ἀλκιμωτάτων ὥστε, εἰ οὕτω
415 τύχοι, ἢ τῶν δύο τὸν στρατὸν εἰς ἕνα ἐμβιβάσεις ἢ ἐκ πάντων ἐπιλέξῃ τοὺς
ἀρίστους, ὡς εἴρηται, καὶ γενήσονται ἄχρι καὶ διακοσίων στρατιωτῶν ἢ καὶ
πλείω κατὰ δρόμωνα ἕνα, ὡς ἂν καὶ τῷ πλήθει καὶ τῷ μεγέθει καὶ τῇ εὐψυχίᾳ
τῶν τε δρομώνων καὶ τῶν στρατιωτῶν καθυπέρτερος τῶν πολεμικῶν πλοίων
γενόμενος, σὺν Θεῷ τὴν κατ᾽ αὐτῶν ἀπολήψῃ νίκην.

420 ος΄. Δεῖ δέ σε καὶ μικροτέρους ἐξοπλίζειν δρόμωνας καὶ ἐλαφροτέρους τῶν | W239ᵛ
συνήθων, ὥστε καὶ διώκοντας καταλαμβάνειν τοὺς πολεμίους, καὶ διωκομένους
μὴ καταλαμβάνεσθαι, | καὶ τούτους ἔχειν ἐν καιρῷ τῆς ἁρμοζούσης αὐτοῖς W240
χρείας, ὥστε δύνασθαι αὐτούς, ἢ δρᾶσαί κακόν τι τοῖς ἐχθροῖς ἢ μὴ παθεῖν
κακόν τι παρ᾽ αὐτῶν.

425 οζ΄. Μικροὺς δὲ καὶ μεγάλους δρόμωνας κατὰ τὴν ποιότητα τῶν πολεμίων
ἐθνῶν κατασκευάσεις. οὐ γὰρ ὁ αὐτός ἐστιν στόλος τῶν πλοίων τῶν τε Σαρακηνῶν βαρβάρων καὶ τῶν λεγομένων Βορείων Σκυθῶν. οἱ μὲν γὰρ Σαρακηνοὶ
κουμβαρίοις χρῶνται μείζοσι καὶ ἀργοτέροις, οἱ δὲ οἷον ἀκατίοις ἐλάττοσι καὶ
ἐλαφροτέροις καὶ ταχίνοις οἱ Σκύθαι. διὰ ποταμῶν γὰρ εἰς τὸν Εὔξεινον ἐμ-
430 πίπτοντες πόντον οὐ δύνανται μείζοσι χρήσασθαι πλοίοις. καὶ ταῦτα μὲν περὶ
παρατάξεων εἰρήσθω.

οη΄. Ὅταν δὲ ἀπαλλαγῆναι βούλῃ τῆς μάχης, μηνοειδῶς, ὡς εἴρηται, τὴν
παράταξιν τῶν δρομώνων ποιήσας, οὕτως ὑποχωρήσεις διὰ τὸ ἀσφαλὲς εἶναι τὸ

---

420 ad τῶν des. M

409 δεσμοῦ MW δεσμοὺς A 410 εἰ τύχοι MW om. A | προτερήσουσιν MW
ὑπερνικήσουσιν A 411 οε΄ A ος΄ M | πολυανδρούμενα…καὶ MW om. A 412 οὓς ἰσώσεις
De οὐσιάσεις codd. 413 ἐξοπλίσεις MA καταστήσεις W 414 ἀλκιμωτάτων MW
ὀχυροτάτων A 415 τὸν στρατὸν MA τῶν στρατῶν W 417 πλείω MW πλείονες A | ἕνα A
om. MW 417–418 καὶ³…καθυπέρτερος MW τῶν δρομώνων καὶ τῇ εὐψυχίᾳ τῶν
στρατιωτῶν ἐπικρατέστερος A 419 ἀπολήψῃ νίκην MW νίκην ἀπολάβῃς A 420 ος΄ A οζ΄
MW 423 δρᾶσαί…ἐχθροῖς W κακόν τι ποιῆσαι τοὺς ἐχθροὺς A 423–424 παθεῖν…τι W
παθεῖν τι κακὸν A 425 οζ΄ A om. W 426 ἐστιν W ἐστι A 427 βαρβάρων W om. A |
λεγομένων W λεγομένων ῥῶς ἤγουν A | σαρακηνοὶ A om. W 428 οἱ δὲ A οἱ βάρβαροι οἱ δὲ
W | ἐλάττοσι W μικροῖς A 429 ταχίνοις W γοργοῖς A 430 μείζοσι…πλοίοις W μείζονα
ἔχειν πλοῖα A 431 παρατάξεων W τάξεων A 432 οη΄ A om. W

especially if one is getting set for an evenly matched battle with <the ships> bound to one another. When both forces are brave, if it comes to fighting, the more numerous will prevail.

75. Now if you should observe that the enemy has ships with a large number of men and a larger army on board, you should make your dromons equal in number. Select the best from among all of your men and arm a sufficient force of them on fully equipped and strong dromons. In such a situation, either put the soldiers from two ships aboard one or else, as was said, from your whole force select the very best so they will add up to two hundred soldiers or more for one dromon. The result will be that, in the number and size and enthusiasm of the dromons and of the soldiers you will be superior to the ships of the enemy. With God's help you will gain victory over them.

76. You must also equip smaller and lighter dromons than usual that can pursue the enemy and catch up to them but if pursued themselves will not be caught. You should have these at a time when they are particularly useful either to cause some harm to the enemy or not to suffer any harm from them.

77. Get large and small dromons ready that match the kind used by hostile ethnic forces. For the fleet of ships of the barbarian Saracens is not the same as that of those called Northern Scythians.[16] For the Saracens make use of larger and slower <ships called> koumbaria, whereas the Scythians use ships that are smaller, lighter, and faster. Because they come into the Euxine Sea from rivers, they cannot use larger vessels. These are enough remarks about battle formations.

78. When you wish to withdraw from battle, form the line of your dromons in a crescent shape, as we said. Make your retreat in this manner because such a

16. Saracens: see *supra*, Const. 18. Koumbaria is from the Arabic; see Pryor-Jeffreys, 513, n. 61. Northern Scythians, in this case, designates the people known as Rhos who sailed down the Dnieper to the Black Sea in small ships. The later manuscript, A, as well as the paraphrase of Ouranos, specifically calls them Rhos (Ῥῶς). Their route is recorded in *DAI*, 9, pp. 56–62; see *DAI Commentary*, 16–31. Cf. Const. 14, n. 10.

τοιοῦτον σχῆμα ἐν ταῖς τοιαύταις | καὶ προόδοις καὶ ὑποχωρήσεσιν, ὥς τινες　W240ᵛ
435　τῶν παλαιῶν μαρτυροῦσι τῷ τρόπῳ τούτῳ χρησάμενοι.

οθ΄. Μετὰ δὲ τὴν λύσιν τοῦ πολέμου δέον σε, ὦ στρατηγέ, τά, ὡς εἰκός,
κερδηθέντα ἀπὸ τῶν πολεμίων λάφυρα ἐξ ἴσου διαμερίζειν τοῖς στρατιώταις καὶ
ἀριστοποιεῖν καὶ φιλοφρονεῖσθαι αὐτοὺς καὶ πανδαισίαν ποιεῖσθαι καὶ εὐωχίαν
εἰς αὐτούς, καὶ τοὺς μὲν ἀριστεύσαντας καὶ δωρεῶν καὶ τιμῶν ἀξιῶσαι, τοὺς δέ
440　τι ἀνάξιον στρατιώτου ποιήσαντας ἐπιτιμῆσαι δεόντως.

π΄. Ἴσθι δέ, ὦ στρατηγέ, ὅτι πλῆθος δρομώνων ἀνάνδρους ἐχόντων στρατιώτας οὐδὲν ἰσχύει, οὐδ᾽ ἂν καὶ πρὸς ὀλίγους μαχήσονται τοὺς ἐναντίους ἀνδρείους καὶ εὐψύχους. οὔτε γὰρ πολυπληθία ἀνδρῶν κατὰ ὀλίγων ἰσχύει, εἰ μὴ καὶ
τῇ προθυμίᾳ καὶ τῇ ὁπλίσει στρατιῶται ἀληθεῖς ἀποδείκνυνται. τί γὰρ οὐκ
445　ἐργάσονται δεινὸν καὶ ὀλίγοι λύκοι πρὸς πολλὰς | χιλιάδας ποιμνίου;　W241

πα΄. Διὸ χρή σε ὁρᾶν ἅπαντα μετὰ ἀκριβείας ἁπάσης τὰ τῶν ἐχθρῶν, ὡς
διάκεινται, καὶ οὕτως τήν τε τῶν δρομώνων κατασκευὴν καὶ τὴν τῶν στρατιωτῶν ὅπλισιν καὶ τὸ πλῆθος αὐτῶν καὶ τὸ μέγεθος καὶ τὰ ἄλλα ἐπιτηδεύματα
ἁρμοδίως κατὰ τῶν ἐναντίων παρασκευάζειν. ἔχειν δὲ καὶ μικροὺς δρόμωνας
450　καὶ ταχεῖς, οὐ πρὸς πόλεμον ἐξωπλισμένους, ἀλλὰ πρὸς τὰς βίγλας καὶ τὰ
μανδάτα καὶ τὰς ἄλλας ἀπαντώσας ὁμοίως χρείας, καὶ ἔτι τά τε μονήρια λεγόμενα καὶ τὰς γαλαίας, πλὴν καὶ αὐτοὺς ἐνόπλους διὰ τὰ τυχηρῶς συμπίπτοντα.

πβ΄. Καί σε δὲ αὐτὸν διὰ πάντων εἶναι δεῖ σπουδαῖον καὶ γενναῖον καὶ
ἀτάραχον καὶ ὀξὺν ἐν ταῖς ἀναγκαίαις μάλιστα τῶν πραγμάτων ἐγχειρήσεσί τε
455　καὶ πράξεσιν ἵνα καὶ Θεῷ εὐάρεστος καὶ τῇ ἡμετέρᾳ ἐκ Θεοῦ βασιλείᾳ | εὔχρη-　W241ᵛ
στός τε καὶ δόκιμος ἀναφανεὶς στρατηγός, ἀμφοτέρωθεν κερδήσῃς τὰς ἀξίας
τῶν πόνων ἀμοιβάς, ἐκ Θεοῦ μὲν μισθοὺς ἀθανάτους ὑπὲρ τῆς αὐτοῦ κληρο-
νομίας ἀγωνιζόμενος, ἐξ ἡμῶν δὲ καὶ δωρεὰς καὶ τιμὰς τὰς προσηκούσας, μὴ
ψευδόμενος τὴν κλῆσιν, ἀλλ᾽ ἀληθὴς στρατηγὸς καὶ ὢν καὶ καλούμενος.
460　<πγ΄.> Τοσαῦτα καὶ περὶ ναυμαχίας ὡς ἐν συνόψει μετρίως εἰρήσθω.

---

434–435 τινες…τούτῳ W μαρτυροῦσί τινες τῶν παλαιῶν τούτῳ τῷ τρόπῳ A　436 οθ΄ A
om. W　437 διαμερίζειν W διαμερίζειν ἐν A　438–439 καὶ²…καὶ¹ W om. A　440 τι
ἀνάξιον W trsp. A　441 π΄ A om. W | ἴσθι W γίνωσκε A　443 πολυπληθία W πλῆθος A
446 πα΄ A om. W | ὁρᾶν W συνορᾶν A | ἁπάσης W πάσης A　449–450 δρόμωνας…ταχεῖς
W καὶ ταχεῖς δρόμωνας A　450–451 τὰ μανδάτα A τὰς δαπανὰς W　452 τυχηρῶς
συμπίπτοντα W ὡς εἰκὸς καὶ κατὰ τύχην ἐμπίπτοντα A　453 πβ΄ A om. W ante
455–456 εὔχρηστός scr. titulum const. xx W　458 δωρεὰς…τιμὰς W trsp. A　459 ἀληθὴς
A ἀληθῶς W　460 πγ΄ ci. De om. codd.

formation is safe in these circumstances both for advancing and retreating, according to the testimony of the ancients who have made use of this method.

79. After the conclusion of the battle, it is necessary for you, O general, to divide up the spoils likely to be taken from the enemy equally among the soldiers. Provide special dinners for them, give them favors, prepare a banquet and festivities for them. Bestow honors and gifts on those who have distinguished themselves and inflict the appropriate punishment on those who have acted in a way unworthy of a soldier.

80. Realize, O general, that a large number of dromons with unmanly soldiers on board accomplishes nothing, not even if they should be fighting against a small number of the enemy who are brave and courageous. Nor will a large number of men against a few accomplish anything unless they show themselves by their enthusiasm and armament to be true soldiers. What terrible things will a few wolves not wreak against many thousands of sheep?

81. Therefore, it is necessary for you to observe with total accuracy the disposition of the enemy, and so prepare the outfitting of your dromons and the armamaent of your soldiers, their number and size and the rest of the equipment in proper fashion against the enemy. Also have small and fast dromons, not equipped for battle, but for scouting, <conveying> orders, and other needs that may occur, and still others called monoremes and galleys, which are armed for situations that arise by chance.

82. In everything you yourself must be serious, high-minded, calm, and sharp-witted in your endeavors and actions, especially under the pressure of events, in order that, having shown yourself to be well pleasing before God and having shown yourself before Our God-given Majesty as a most capable and proven general, you may gain from both the deserved rewards of your labors: from God immortal rewards for your struggles on behalf of his inheritance, and from us appropriate honors and gifts, because you have not made false your title, but you are a true general and are called such.

<83.> As in a summary, let this be enough said about naval warfare.

Περὶ διαφόρων γνωμικῶν κεφαλαίων

α΄. Μετὰ δὲ τὰς εἰρημένας παραγγελίας τε καὶ διατάξεις, ὦ στρατηγέ, χρεὸν τῇ σῇ ἐνδοξότητι καὶ ταῖς ἤδη ῥηθησομέναις ἐγκύψαι γνώμαις, ἃς ἐκ πολλῶν
5 παλαιῶν καὶ στρατηγικῶν συνταγμάτων ἀναλεξάμενοι, συνόψεως χάριν τῶν εἰρημένων ἐνταῦθα παρατεθείκαμεν. ἐκ τούτων γὰρ καὶ ἐπὶ τὰς μείζονας πράξεις τῆς τακτικῆς θεωρίας ἀναβῆναι δυνήσῃ, κατὰ τὸν σοφὸν παροιμιαστὴν βασι-λέα· σοφῷ γὰρ ἀνδρὶ ἀφορμὴ διδομένη σοφώτερον ἀπεργάζεται.

β΄. Ἐν πρώτοις μὲν ἐγχειρεῖν μέλλων ἀναγκαίων πραγμάτων, ὦ στρατηγέ, μὴ
10 χώριζε σεαυτὸν τοῦ πλήθους τῶν ἐν τοῖς ἔργοις πονούντων, ἀλλὰ καὶ αὐτὸς ἀπάρχου τῶν τοιούτων ἐγχειρήσεων καὶ συμπόνει τοῖς ἔργοις κατὰ τὸ δυνατόν σοι, εἴτε τράφους ὀρύσσεις εἴτε προσχωννύεις εἴτε πολιορκίαις ἐπιβάλλεις εἴτε ὅπλων κατασκευαῖς εἴτε μηχανημάτων εἴτε φρουρίων ἁλώσεσι, πρὸς εἴ τι ἔργον χρειῶδες ἐπινοήσεις καὶ κοινωφελὲς ἢ πόλει ἢ στρατεύματι πραχθησόμενον,
15 τούτου χερσὶν ἰδίαις πρῶτος ἀπάρχου. ἐκ τούτου γὰρ ὥσπερ αἰδούμενοι καὶ οἱ στρατιῶται θερμότερόν σοι ὑπακούσονται καὶ τὸ πραττόμενον εὐχερέστερον τελεσθήσεται. εἰ δέ τις καὶ τῶν ἐπιτηδείων σπάνις ἐνοχλήσει, πρῶτος αὐτὸς τῆς ἐγκρατείας τὴν καρτερίαν ἐπίδειξον, ἵνα καὶ τοῖς ὑπὸ χεῖρα κούφην καὶ εὐκολω-τέραν τὴν ὑπομονὴν τῆς ἀνάγκης ἐργάσῃ. ἐν δὲ ταῖς κατὰ τὰς μάχας παραβού-
20 λοις ἐκ χειρὸς συμπλοκαῖς φύλασσε σεαυτόν, ἵνα τῇ μὲν γνώμῃ καὶ τῇ διατάξει καὶ ταῖς ἄλλαις διευθετήσεσιν ἐν αὐτῷ τῷ ὀξεῖ τοῦ καιροῦ συμπαρῇς μέν, καὶ τῶν τοιούτων ἀγώνων ἐφάπτῃ, μὴ μέντοι ἀφυλάκτως οὕτω καὶ ἐπικινδύνως, ὅτε μὴ τούτου χρεία καλή, διὰ χειρῶν ἐμπλέκῃ τοὺς πολεμίους. οὐ τοσοῦτον γάρ,

M W A   PG 107:1013 **1** ad πολεμικῶν de novo inc. M

**8** Prov. 1:5.   **9–29** Strat., 8.1.1; cf. Polyaen. 4.3.3.

**1** κ΄ W ιη΄ M ιθ΄ A   **3–4** χρεὸν...ἐνδοξότητι MW χρὴ τὴν σὴν ἐνδοξότητα A   **9** ἀναγκαίων πραγμάτων MW ἀναγκαίοις πράγμασιν A   **13** ἁλώσεσι M ἁλώσεσιν WA   **13–14** ἔργον χρειῶδες MW trsp. A   **16** θερμότερόν MW εὐκολώτερον A   **17** ἐπιτηδείων MW χρείων A   **18** ἐπίδειξον MW ἐπίδειξαι A   **19–20** παραβούλοις MW παραβόλοις A   **21** αὐτῷ...ὀξεῖ MW αὐτῇ τῇ ὀξύτητι A | συμπαρῇς MW συνυπάρχῃς A | μέν MW om. A   **22** ἐφάπτῃ MW μετέχῃς A | οὕτω MW οὕτως A   **22–23** ὅτε...καλή MW om. A   **23** ἐμπλέκῃ MW συμπλέκῃ A | τοὺς πολεμίους MW τοῖς πολεμίοις ὅτε μὴ τούτου χρεία καλεῖ A

# PREPARATION FOR WAR, CONSTITUTION XX

## About Various Concise Sayings

1.[1] After the commands and the constitutions given above, O general, Your Excellency ought to familiarize yourself with the sayings presented here, which we have gathered from many ancient authorities and military treatises. We lay these before you as a way of summarizing what is written in this book. These will enable you to move on to greater applications of tactical theory. According to the wise king, compiler of proverbs: a starting point given to a wise man results in his becoming more wise.[2]

2. First, if you intend to carry out critical operations, O general, do not set yourself apart from the multitude of men laboring at their tasks. But you should take the lead in such operations and toil along with them in the work as best you can, whether you are digging trenches or piling up mounds of earth or undertaking siege operations or preparing weapons or machines or capturing forts. Moreover, if you think that some work that is useful and beneficial to the city or the army should be done, then, with your own hands, be the first to get it started. The soldiers, as though put to shame, will end up obeying you more fervently and will complete the project more readily. If a scarcity of supplies causes a problem, you be the first to show your patient endurance and self-control, in order that you may bring the men under your command to deal

---

1. Among the many forms of word play enjoyed by the Byzantines was the acrostic. In a literary composition the initial letters of each paragraph or verse were combined to form a phrase or epigram. By taking the first letter of each of the 221 paragraphs (except the first) in Const. 20, J. Grosdidier de Matons ("Trois études sur Léon VI," *TM* 5 [1973], 181–242) has deciphered the following: ἐν ὀνόματι τοῦ πατρὸς καὶ τοῦ υἱοῦ καὶ τοῦ ἁγίου πνεύματος τῆς ἁγίας καὶ ὁμοουσίου καὶ προσκυνητῆς τριάδος τοῦ ἑνὸς καὶ μόνου ἀληθινοῦ θεοῦ ἡμῶν λέων ὁ εἰρηνικὸς ἐν χριστῶ αὐτοκράτωρ πιστὸς εὐσεβὴς εὐμενὴς ἀεισέβαστος αὔγουστος καὶ <u>τοοθπνυιοα</u> βασιλεὺς ῥωμαίων. (In the name of the Father and of the Son and of the Holy Spirit, the holy, consubstantial, and worshipful Trinity, our one and only true God, Leo, peaceful autokrator in Christ, faithful, pious, kindly, ever revered Augustus and ********** emperor of the Romans.) He has shown that the underlined letters, which make no sense, replaced the name of Leo's brother and co-emperor, Alexander, ἀλέξανδρος, by order of Leo's son, Constantine VII, whom Alexander had tried to have castrated.

2. Proverbs 1:5.

ὥς μοι καὶ ἄνω που εἴρηται, συμπλεκόμενος ὡς εἷς τῶν στρατιωτῶν ὠφελήσεις,
25 ὅσον εἴγε συμβῇ τι τοιοῦτον πεσὼν βλάψεις. τὸ γὰρ μέλλον ἀόρατον.

γ΄. Νόμος γινέσθω τοῖς στρατιώταις, ὦ στρατηγέ, ὁ τρόπος ὁ σὸς καὶ ἡ περὶ
τὰ πρακτέα σπουδή σου. οὕτως γὰρ τῆς τοῦ οἰκείου ἄρχοντος ἀρετῆς ὁ ὑποχεί-
ριος μεμνημένος καὶ τὸν Θεὸν θεραπεύσει καὶ τοῖς κελευομένοις ὑπακούσεται
καὶ ὡς ἀπὸ Θεοῦ ταῦτα δεχόμενος τελέσει.

30 δ΄. Ὅταν τὸ πλῆθος τῶν στρατιωτῶν ἐπὶ ἕνα τόπον συναχθῇ, τότε δεῖ σε τὰ
παρ᾽ αὐτῶν ἁμαρτανόμενα μακροθύμως φέρειν καὶ μὴ τὰς ἐπεξε|λεύσεις καὶ   360ᵛ
κατακρίσεις ἀπαραιτήτους ποιεῖσθαι, ἵνα μὴ ἡ κοινὴ λύπη εἰς σύναρσιν καὶ
ἀταξίαν συνάψῃ αὐτούς, ἀλλὰ κατ᾽ ὀλίγον μᾶλλον κατὰ τῶν προκαταρξάντων
τῶν τοιούτων ἁμαρτημάτων ποιεῖσθαι τὴν παίδευσιν.

35 ε΄. Νήφειν καὶ ἐγρηγορεῖν καὶ πρὸς τὰ ἄλλα πάντα κελεύομέν σοι, ὦ στρατηγέ, τὸ δὲ πλέον, ὥστε σε εἶναι ἁπλοῦν ἐν τῇ διαγωγῇ καὶ κοινὸν ἐν τῇ διαίτῃ
μετὰ τῶν ὑπό σε στρατιωτῶν. καὶ πατρικήν σε ἔχειν στοργὴν πρὸς αὐτοὺς μετὰ
πραότητος καὶ τὰ πράγματα καὶ τοὺς λόγους ποιούμενον, εἰ μή τις ἀναγκαία
χρεία καὶ συμφέρουσα πρὸς τραχύτητά σε καλέσῃ. χρὴ δὲ καὶ συνεχῶς διὰ
40 σεαυτοῦ τὰ περὶ τῶν ἀναγκαίων αὐτοῖς παραινεῖν καὶ διαλέγεσθαι. φροντίσεις
δὲ καὶ τῆς ἀπαθείας αὐτῶν καὶ τῆς ἄλλης διοικήσεως καὶ ἀποτροφῆς. ἐκτὸς γὰρ
τούτων οὐ δυνατόν ἐστι κρατῆσαι στρατοῦ κατὰ στάσεως. ἐν δὲ ταῖς δικαίαις
ἐπεξελεύσεσι κατὰ τῶν ἁμαρτανόντων δέον σε φοβερὸν εἶναι καὶ τὰς ἀρχάς,
μάλιστα τῶν ἀταξιῶν, ἐκκόπτειν καὶ μὴ ἀναμένειν, ὥστε ἐπὶ μείζονα ταύτας
45 προκόπτειν. καὶ γὰρ στρατηγοῦ προτέρημά ἐστι τὸ ἀκατάπληκτον αὐτὸν τοῖς
στρατιώταις φαίνεσθαι καὶ δίκαιον, καὶ τὴν ἀδικίαν ἅπασαν ἀπὸ τῆς ἑαυτοῦ
ἐνορίας ἐκκόπτειν, καὶ τοὺς ἀδικοῦντας ἀμύνασθαι καὶ ἀνεπηρεάστους τούς τε
στρατιώτας καὶ τοὺς συντελεστὰς ἐν πᾶσι διατηρεῖν.

ς΄. Οὔτε τὸ φιλάνθρωπον ἀκαίρως οὔτε τὸ ἀπηνὲς ἄξιόν ἐστι στρατηγοῦ,
50 ἀλλὰ τὸ σταθμίζειν ἐν καιρῷ τὰ πάντα, καὶ οὕτως ἐπὶ τοῖς ἁμαρτανομένοις
ἐπάγειν τὰς τιμωρίας, ἐπιβλέποντα καὶ τὴν τοῦ πράξαντος διάνοιαν καὶ τὸν
καιρὸν καὶ τὸν τόπον καὶ διὰ ποίου τρόπου ἐπράχθη καὶ διὰ ποίαν αἰτίαν καὶ

---

**25** Isoc. *Ad Demonicum*, 29.3.   **30–34** *Strat.*, 8.1.2.   **35–48** *Strat.*, 8.1.3.   **35–54** Onas. 1.4.

---

**34** παίδευσιν MW ἐπεξέλευσιν A   **35** πάντα A om. MW   **37** σε² MW om. A   **42** ἐστι M ἐστιν WA   **43** ἐπεξελεύσεσι MA ἐπεξελεύσεσιν W   **45** ἐστι M ἐστὶν WA   **50** τὰ A om. MW

more readily and easily with the crisis. But in the hazardous hand-to-hand engagements of battle, protect yourself so that, while you, at the height of the crisis, are standing by with your mind intent on managing and setting the other things in order, and you are focused on such struggles, you do not leave yourself unprotected and subject to danger by engaging the enemy in close combat (as long as there is no compelling need). For, as I remarked earlier, you will not so much help matters by engaging in close fighting, as one of the soldiers, as you will cause harm, if something such as your falling should happen. For what is to come is unseen.[3]

3. Let your manner, O general, as well as your zeal for the task at hand, be as a law to the soldiers. The subordinate is thus mindful of the good qualities of his officer and he will reverence God and obey orders and he will carry them out as though he had received them from God.

4. When the multitude of soldiers has been assembled in one place, then you must be magnanimous in dealing with their offenses.[4] Do not be unmerciful in your judgments and punishments. Widespread resentment might draw them all together and discipline would suffer. Be more lenient, rather, and punish <only> the men who have initiated such crimes.

5. In addition to everything else, we order you to be sober and alert, O general. Even more, let your way of life be simple; share the life of the soldiers under you. Show a fatherly affection toward them. Be mild in manner when you speak and when you take action, unless expediency and compelling need require you to act more harshly. You must always make sure to give advice and to discuss essential matters with your men in person. You must be concerned about keeping them from harm, about other administrative matters, and about their food. Without these it is impossible to maintain discipline in an army. In justly punishing offenders you must inspire fear. At the first sign of a disciplinary problem, put an end to it without delay before it becomes more serious. The superiority of a general is shown by his appearing to his soldiers unshakeable and just, by eliminating injustice from his territory, turning away persons who act unjustly, and keeping the soldiers and the taxpayers free from all harm.[5]

6. It does not become the general to be tenderhearted in dealing with the men when it is not appropriate; neither should he be harsh with them. But he

3. *Strat.* 8.1.1; cf. Polyaenus 4.3.3; Isocrates, *Ad Demonicum*, 29.3.

4. *Strat.* 8.1.1–2. For clarifications of sources for this constitution, see Haldon, *Commentary*.

5. *Strat.* 8.1.3.

αὐτοῦ τοῦ πράγματος τὴν ποιότητα, καὶ οὕτως ἐπὶ τὰς δεούσας τιμωρίας ἔρχεσθαι.

55 ζ΄. Μέγα προτέρημα στρατηγοῦ τὸ συμμέτρως διαιτᾶσθαι καὶ ἀγρυπνεῖν καὶ ἐν ταῖς νυξὶ μᾶλλον βουλεύεσθαι τὰ περὶ τῶν ἀναγκαίων. καὶ γὰρ εὐχερῶς ἐν νυκτὶ τελειοῦται βουλή, ὅταν ἡ ψυχὴ ἐκ τῶν ἔξωθεν θορύβων ἠρεμῇ.

η΄. Ἀλλὰ φήμιζε τοῖς ἐχθροῖς καὶ ἕτερα πράττε, καὶ τὰ περὶ τῶν ἀναγκαίων κρύπτεσθαι δέοντα μὴ πολλοῖς ἀνατίθου, ἀλλ᾽ ὀλίγοις καὶ τοῖς γνησιωτέροις 60 σου μᾶλλον. τὸ γὰρ οὕτως ἐξαπατᾶν τοὺς ἐχθροὺς ἀναγκαῖον ἀπεδείχθη πολλάκις.

θ΄. Τὸ βουλεύεσθαι βραδέως καὶ ἀσφαλῶς καὶ ὅσα δόξει τῇ βουλῇ μὴ ἀναβάλλεσθαι τοὺς καιροὺς διά τινα ὄκνον ἢ δειλίαν ἀναγκαιότατόν ἐστιν. ἡ γὰρ δειλία οὐ μόνον οὐκ ἀσφαλές πρᾶγμά ἐστιν, ἀλλὰ καὶ τῆς τοῦ καλοῦ ἐναντιώ-65 σεως ἐπίνοια.|

ι΄. Ἴσθι ὅτι τὸ μήτ᾽ ἐπαίρεσθαι ἐν ταῖς εὐτυχίαις μήτε πάλιν καταπίπτειν ἐν 361 ταῖς δυστυχίαις ἐρρωμένου ἐστὶ λογισμοῦ καὶ ψυχῆς ἀνδρείας, καὶ δυναμένης ἀσφαλῶς ἐν τοῖς ἀναγκαίοις πάντοτε πράγμασιν ἐπιβάλλειν.

ια΄. Τὸ διὰ βουλῆς μᾶλλον καὶ στρατηγίας κρατεῖν τῶν ἐχθρῶν ἀσφαλὲς ἐμοῖ 70 δοκεῖ καὶ ὠφέλιμον ἢ τὸ χειρὶ βιάζεσθαι καὶ δυνάμει καὶ πρὸς τὰς κατὰ πρόσωπον μάχας ἀποκινδυνεύειν. τὸ μὲν γὰρ μεθ᾽ ἑκουσίου γνώμης γίνεται, καὶ ὡς ἂν ὁ προσβαλὼν τὸ συμφέρον γινώσκῃ, τὸ δὲ μετά τινος ζημίας πάντως ἔχειν τὴν ἔκβασιν.

ιβ΄. Οὐκ ἀναγκαῖόν ἐστιν, ὡς ἡ πεῖρα δείκνυσι, τὸ ταῖς αὐταῖς ἐγχειρήσεσι 75 κατὰ τῶν ἐχθρῶν συνεχῶς κεχρῆσθαι, κἂν πολλάκις δόξῃς ἐν αὐταῖς εὐτυχεῖν. διὰ γὰρ τῆς συνεχείας προσεπινοοῦντες οἱ ἐχθροὶ τὰ ἐναντία καὶ κανονίζοντες συμφορὰς πολλάκις προσάγουσι ταῖς τοιαύταις κατ᾽ αὐτῶν ἐπιβολαῖς.

ιγ΄. Ὑπερτίθεσθαι ἢ ἀναβάλλεσθαι πρὸς τὰ φημιζόμενα κακὰ ἢ δολερὰ καὶ ἐπίβουλα οὐ δίκαιον οὐδὲ πρέπον οὐδὲ καταφρονεῖν αὐτῶν κἂν τε περὶ τῶν 80 ἐχθρῶν λέγωνται κἂν τε περὶ ἰδίων. ἀλλὰ μᾶλλον σπουδάζειν σε χρή, ὦ στρατη-

---

69 paragr. ια΄ et ιβ΄ trsp. M

---

**55–57** Strat., 8.1.4.   **58–61** Strat.,   8.1.8.   **62–65** Strat.,   8.1.5.   **66–68** Strat.,   8.1.6.
**69–73** Strat., 8.1.7.   **74–77** Strat., 8.1.9.   **78–82** Strat., 8.1.10.

---

**53** αὐτοῦ…ποιότητα MW αὐτὸ τὸ πράγμα ὁποῖόν ἐστι A   **56** ταῖς νυξὶ MW νυκτὶ A
**62–63** ὅσα…καιροὺς MW ἀδόξαντα εἶναι συμφέροντα μὴ ὑπερτίθεσθαι καὶ παρακμάζειν A
**66** μήτε A μηδὲ MW   **69** paragr. ια΄ et ιβ΄ trsp. M   **71** μεθ᾽ A μετ᾽ MW   **74** δείκνυσι MA
δείκνυσιν W   **79** τῶν A om. MW

ought to take into account the proper time for everything. Thus, he should inflict punishment upon malefactors after considering the attitude of the offender, as well as the occasion, the place, and the manner in which he did the deed. What caused him to do it? How serious was the offense? Then, he may proceed to a fitting punishment.

7. That general is truly outstanding who is temperate in his way of life and vigilant. He prefers to deliberate about critical problems at night, for it is more productive to finalize plans during the night when one's soul is free of external disturbances.[6]

8. Spread rumors among the enemy <about one thing>, then do something else. When it comes to essential matters, share what ought to be kept secret not with many but rather with your more intimate circle. It has often proved necessary to deceive the enemy in this way.[7]

9. It is essential to be cautious and to take your time in making plans and, once you have come to a decision, it is even more essential not to put it off to another time because of hesitation or timidity. Timidity, after all, not only is not a safe way of acting but also brings about the opposite of the good.[8]

10. Be aware that a healthy mind is not unduly elated by good fortune or overly depressed by ill fortune, and that a valiant spirit is always able to engage safely in critical activities.

11. I believe that it is safer and more advantageous to overcome the enemy by planning and generalship than by physical force and power and the hazards of a face-to-face battle. One engages in the first of his own volition and, on taking the initiative, knows what is to his advantage, whereas the other always results in something harmful.

12. It is not necessary, as experience shows, always to employ the same modes of operation against the enemy, even though they frequently appear to be successful. Because they are used constantly, the enemy will adapt to them and devise contrary measures and, in return for such attacks against them, they will often bring misfortune upon us.[9]

13. When it comes to rumors of impending evil or traps or treachery, it is not right to postpone or defer action—but it is wrong to pay no heed to such rumors, whether they relate to the enemy or to our own forces. Instead, you

*6. Onasander 1.4, *Strat.* 8.1.4.

*7. *Strat.* 8.1.8.

*8. For §§9–11 see *Strat.* 8.1.5–7.

*9. *Strat.* 8.1.9.

γέ, μεθοδεύειν καὶ καταπαύειν αὐτὰ πρὶν εἰς ἔργον ἔλθωσιν, ὅτε τάχα οὐδὲ ἀναστέλλειν ταῦτα δύνασαι.

ιδ΄. Ποιήσει θάρσος τοῖς στρατιώταις ἐν καιρῷ πολέμου ἀγγελία ἐρχομένη ὅτι ἐν ἄλλοις τόποις τοὺς πολεμίους νενικήκαμεν. οὕτως γὰρ καὶ τὰ δειλὰ
85 φρονήματα διαναστήσονται, καὶ τὰ ἀνδρεῖα μᾶλλον θαρσήσουσιν, ἀγαθὸν σύμβολον τὸ τῆς νίκης ὄνομα καὶ τὴν πρᾶξιν ὡς ἐκ Θεοῦ δεξάμενοι.

ιε΄. Ἀπατήσεις μᾶλλον τοὺς πολεμίους, ἐὰν διὰ προσφύγων ἀπό σου πρὸς αὐτοὺς ἐναντία φημίσης ὧν σὺ βουλεύῃ ποιῆσαι κατὰ τῶν ἐχθρῶν· ἢ γὰρ ἀπιστήσαντες ἀμελήσουσιν ἢ πιστεύσαντες ἀστοχήσουσιν. καὶ τὰ μὲν σὰ βου-
90 λεύματα τελεσθήσονται, τὰ δὲ ἐκείνων ἄπρακτα ἀποβήσονται.

ις΄. Τὸ κρύπτειν τὰ ἀπαγγελλόμενα ἀτυχήματα ὅσα συμβαίνειν εἴωθεν, ὡς εἰκός, ἐν πλήθει στρατοῦ καὶ τὰ ἐναντία τῶν ἀληθῶν ποιεῖν ἀπαγγέλλεσθαι, στρατήγημά ἐστιν ἀνδρὸς ἔμφρονος καὶ ἀνιστᾶν φρονήματα στρατιωτῶν καταπίπτοντα δυναμένου.

95 ιζ΄. Ῥώμην ἐντίθησι στρατηγὸς ἡττηθέντι στρατῷ, ἐὰν ποικίλοις τρόποις καὶ ἐλπίσιν ἀγαθαῖς διά τε λόγων καὶ δι᾽ ἔργων μεθοδεύσῃ αὐτούς· τὸ γὰρ κατονει-δίζειν καὶ ἐπικεῖσθαι τῶν ἡττωμένων τῷ πλήθει καὶ διὰ τούτων εἰς ἀπόνοιαν αὐτοὺς ἄγειν σφαλερόν μοι δοκεῖ καὶ λίαν ἐπιβλαβές.

ιη΄. Ὅταν ἐν καιρῷ πολέμου παρὰ τῶν στρατιωτῶν ἁμαρτήματα γίνωνται,
100 δέον προσποιεῖσθαί σε ἄγνοιαν αὐτῶν καὶ τέως αὐτὰ παρορᾶν. | μετὰ δὲ τὸν   361ᵛ
καιρὸν τῆς τοῦ πολέμου λύσεως τοὺς αἰτίους τῶν στάσεων ὡς ἂν συγγινώσκῃς τὸ δίκαιον ὑπεξέρχου.

ιθ΄. Συγκαλύπτειν σοι προσήκει τὰς δειλίας τῶν στρατιωτῶν καὶ μὴ προχεί-ρως ἐλέγχειν, ἵνα μὴ καταπίπτῃ τὰ φρονήματα αὐτῶν παντελῶς καὶ ταπεινότε-
105 ροι ἑαυτῶν ἀποδειχθῶσιν.

κ΄. Κατασκευάσεις ἀθυμίαν τοῖς πολεμίοις ὅταν ἐν καιρῷ μετὰ τὸν πόλεμον ποιῆσαι δυνηθῇς τὴν ταφὴν ἀφανῶς τῶν ἀπὸ τοῦ σου στρατοῦ πεσόντων, τὰ δὲ σώματα τῶν πεσόντων πολεμίων ἐάσῃς.

---

83–86 *Strat.*, 8.1.12; Onas. 23.1.   **87–90** *Strat.*, 8.1.11.   **91–94** *Strat.*, 8.1.13; cf. Polyaen. 2.1.3.   **95–98** *Strat.*,   8.1.14.   **99–102** *Strat.*,   8.1.15.   **103–105** *Strat.*,   8.1.18. **106–108** *Strat.*, 8.1.16.

---

86 σύμβολον MW ἔργον A   93 ἔμφρονος MW συνετοῦ A   97 τῶν…πλήθει MW trsp. A | τούτων MW τοῦτο A   100 παρορᾶν MW παραβλέπειν A   101 τῆς MW τῆς συμπληρώσεως A | λύσεως MW om. A | στάσεων MW πταισμάτων A | ὡς ἂν MW καθὼς ἂν A   101–102 ἂν…δίκαιον   MW   trsp.   A   102 ὑπεξέρχου   MW   ἐπεξέρχου   A 103–104 προχείρως MW προφανῶς A   104 καταπίπτῃ MW καταπίπτωσι A

must take steps to deal with them, O general, and put a stop to them before they become realities, when you may not be able to hold them in check.[10]

14. During combat, spreading the report that we have defeated the enemy in some other place will arouse courage in the soldiers. They will dispel cowardly thoughts and will stir up manly ones, taking the very word, victory, as a good omen, and expecting to receive the reality from God.[11]

15. You will successfully deceive the enemy if you make use of defectors from you to them, for they can report just the opposite of what you are planning to do against the enemy. Either they will not believe it and become careless or they will believe it and take the wrong action. Your intentions, therefore, will be accomplished, whereas theirs will end up achieving nothing.[12]

16. While reverses are quite likely to occur, an intelligent man employs the stratagem of keeping reports of them secret from the multitude of the army and causes reports stating the opposite of the truth to be circulated. Thus, he is able to raise the low morale of the soldiers.[13]

17. The general instills strength in a defeated army by handling them in various ways and with good hopes both in words and in deeds. To reproach and threaten the multitude of the defeated will cause them to fall further into despair, and strikes me as dangerous and extremely harmful.

18. When offenses are committed by the soldiers in time of combat, you must pretend ignorance of them and overlook them for the time being. But after the conclusion of the battle, subject to justice those whom you know to be guilty of sedition.

19. It behooves you to keep quiet about the cowardice of our soldiers and not condemn them publicly so they may not become utterly dejected and their morale sink even lower.[14]

20. You will contribute to poor morale among the enemy if, in the period after battle, you are able to provide burial secretly for the fallen in your own army, but leave the bodies of the fallen enemy <without burial>.[15]

10. *Strat.* 8.1.10.

11. *Strat.* 8.1.12; Onasander 23.1.

12. *Strat.* 8.1.11.

13. Cf. Polyaenus 2.1.3. For §§16–18 see *Strat.* 8.1.13–15.

14. *Strat.* 8.1.18.

15. *Strat.* 8.1.16.

κα΄. Ἀκινδύνως φεύξῃ, εἴ ποτε καιρός σοι τοιοῦτος γένηται τοὺς πολεμίους
110 λαθεῖν, ἐὰν πυρὰ πολλὰ ἀλλαχοῦ ἀνακαύσῃς καὶ ἐν ἄλλῳ τόπῳ ἡσυχάσῃς. οἱ
γὰρ πολέμιοι ἐπὶ τὰ πυρὰ χωρήσαντες ἀπατηθήσονται, καὶ σὺ τὸ πρακτέον
διανύσεις, καθώς σοι καὶ ἐν ἄλλοις ὑπεθέμεθα.

κβ΄. Ἵνα δὲ διχόνοιαν καὶ ὑπόνοιαν κατασκευάσῃς κατὰ τῶν ἐπισήμων
ἀνδρῶν ἐν τοῖς πολεμίοις, ὅταν κατατρέχῃς τὴν πολεμίαν σου χώραν, τὰ ἐκεί-
115 νων χωρία μὴ ἐμπύριζε, ἀλλὰ καί τινα σημεῖα φιλίας τῆς πρὸς αὐτοὺς ἢ διὰ
γραμμάτων ἢ δι᾽ ἑτέρου τρόπου καταλίμπανε. τὸ αὐτὸ δὲ ποιήσεις καὶ ἐὰν διὰ
τῶν κρατουμένων παρά σου αἰχμαλώτων κρυφαίως αὐτοῖς ἐπιτηδεύσῃς δηλοποιεῖν περί τινων ἀπορρήτων. εἰ γὰρ καὶ πολλάκις τὰ τοιαῦτα γεγονότα φανε-
ρὰν ἀπάτην δοκεῖ τοῖς πολεμίοις καὶ δόλον γίνεσθαι, ἀλλ᾽ οὖν εἰς ὑποψίαν καὶ
120 διχόνοιαν τὴν περὶ τῶν ἀνδρῶν ἐκείνων πάντως ἐμπέσωσιν.

κγ΄. Τρόπον εὐπειθείας ὑποδείξω σοι ὥστε τοῖς πολιορκουμένοις διὰ βελῶν
τῶν ἀπὸ τόξου πεμπομένων ἐπιστολὰς ἐκπέμπειν, καὶ δι᾽ αὐτῶν ἐλευθερίαν καὶ
ἀπάθειαν αὐτοῖς ἐπαγγέλλεσθαι. τὸ αὐτὸ δὲ ποιήσεις δηλοποιῶν αὐτοῖς καὶ δι᾽
αἰχμαλώτων ἀφέσεως.

125 κδ΄. Οὔτε ταῖς φιλανθρωπίαις τῶν πολεμίων ἐξαπατᾶσθαί σε δέον οὔτε ἐάν
ποτε προσποιοῦνται ἀναχώρησιν· δολερὰ γὰρ ἀεὶ τῶν ἐχθρῶν τὰ βουλεύματα,
καὶ πρὸς τὸ οἰκεῖον συμφέρον ὁ ἐναντίος τὰ πάντα ἐπινοεῖ, ὥστε τὸ ἐκείνου
συμφέρον ἀσύμφορόν σοι ἀποδειχθῆναι, καὶ διὰ τῆς ἐναντίας ἀπάτης ἐμποιήσει
σοι βλάβην.

130 κε΄. Ὑφορᾶσθαί σε προσήκει τὰς διώξεις τὰς ἀγούσας εἰς χωρία ἐπιτήδεια
πρὸς ἐγκρύμματα. διὸ καὶ τὸ ἀναχωρεῖν εὐκαίρως τὸν στρατηγὸν καὶ πάλιν
σφοδροτέραν ποιεῖσθαι τὴν ἐπέλευσιν κατὰ τῶν πολεμίων μάλιστά ἐστι στρατηγικόν.

κς΄. Ὑπόνοια δειλίας ἐστὶν ὄκνος καὶ ὠχρίασις. ὅταν οὖν τοιούτους ἴδῃς
135 τινὰς τῶν στρατιωτῶν, καὶ πρὸ τῆς ἐρωτήσεως, χώριζε αὐτοὺς τῆς ἀναγκαίας

---

122 ad πεμπομένων des. W

---

**109–112** *Strat.*, 8.1.27; Onas. 10.13; cf. ια΄.118.   **113–120** *Strat.*, 8.1.20.   **121–124** *Strat.*,
8.1.21.   **125–129** *Strat.*, 8.1.23.   **130–133** *Strat.*, 8.1.22.   **134–137** *Strat.*, 8.1.24.

**109** φεύξῃ MW φύγῃς A   **110** πυρὰ πολλὰ MW πυρκαίας πολλὰς A   **111** τὰ πυρὰ MW
τὰς πυρκαίας A   **112** διανύσεις MW τελειώσεις A   **114** κατατρέχῃς MW κατατρέχῃς καὶ
πραιδεύσῃς A   **114–115** ἐκείνων MW ἐκείνων καὶ μεγάλων A   **115** ἐμπύριζε MW κατακαῖε
A   **119** δοκεῖ...γίνεσθαι MW καὶ δόλον γίνεσθαι τοῖς πολεμίοις A   **120** ἐμπέσωσιν A
ἐμπέσωσι MW   **134** οὖν M οὖν τινας A   **135** τινὰς M om. A | τῆς[1] A om. M

21. Whenever the time is right for you to elude the enemy, you may escape without danger by setting many fires in one place and by lying low in another place. The enemy will be deceived and head toward the fires and so, as we explained to you elsewhere, you will attain your objective.[16]

22. You may sow dissension and suspicion against the distinguished men among the enemy. When you conduct raids in enemy territory, do not burn the estates of those men; instead, leave behind some sign of friendship with them, either in writing or in some other way. You will obtain the same results if you secretly make use of captives held by you to make known certain secret matters to those men. For if this sort of thing happens frequently, the enemy will look upon it as obvious deception and trickery, with the result that they will certainly fall into dissension and become suspicious of those men.[17]

23. I will show you a way of convincing <them>. Send letters to the people under siege, by arrows shot from bows, promising them freedom and immunity. You can also convey the same messages to them by releasing captives.[18]

24. You ought not to be deceived by humane acts of the enemy, not even when they pretend to retreat. The intentions of the enemy are always treacherous. Your adversary devises everything for his own benefit. What benefits him does not benefit you, and by contrary deceit he will cause you harm.[19]

25. You ought to be cautious about pursuits leading to locations suitable for ambushes. It is a particular characteristic of a good general to turn back at the right moment so he can come back and attack the enemy more effectively.[20]

26. Hesitation and a pale countenance are indications of cowardice. Whenever you see soldiers like this, even before interrogation, remove them from the

16. *Strat.* 8.1.27; Onasander 10.13; cf. Const. 11 §21.
17. *Strat.* 8.1.20.
18. *Strat.* 8.1.21.
19. *Strat.* 8.1.23.
20. *Strat.* 8.1.22.

ἐγχειρήσεως τοῦ πολέμου, καὶ δεόντως αὐτοῖς ἐπίτρεπε τὰ ἁρμόζοντα | πράτ-   362
τειν τῷ τοιούτῳ καιρῷ.

κζ΄. Ἴσθι λίαν ἀσφαλὲς καὶ ἐν καιρῷ τάχα φιλίας ἔνθα ἂν ὑπάρχῃς πλησίον
πολεμίων στρατοπεδεύων περιβάλλειν φοσσάτον δι᾿ ὀρύγματος ἢ κτίσματος
140 λίθου ἢ πλίνθου ἢ χάρακα διὰ ξύλων καὶ οὕτως πέριξ ὀχυροποιῆσαι τὸν στρατόν. ἐὰν γάρ τι συμβῇ τῶν ἐναντίων καὶ λέγῃς ὅτι "τοῦτο οὐχ ὑπενόουν," οὔκ
ἐστι στρατηγικόν.

κη΄. Ὅταν, Θεοῦ διδόντος, πόλις παρά σου τῶν πολεμίων ἁλίσκεται, ἀνοίγεσθαι συγχώρει τὰς πύλας ὥστε φεύγειν τοὺς πολλοὺς καὶ μὴ χωρεῖν εἰς ἀπό-
145 γνωσιν. τὸ αὐτὸ δὲ καὶ φοσσάτου ἁλισκομένου τῶν ἐχθρῶν παρά σου ποιήσεις·
ἀναγκαῖα γὰρ εἶναι ταῦτα καὶ ἀκινδυνότερα πρὸς τὴν τῶν ἁλισκομένων κατα-
κράτησιν.

κθ΄. Ὑφόρασιν προδοσίας καὶ ὑπόνοιαν δώσεις τοῖς πολεμίοις κατὰ τῶν
προσφευγόντων ἀπὸ σοῦ πρὸς αὐτούς, ὥστε αὐτοῖς ἢ ἀπιστεῖν ἢ ἀποκτείνειν,
150 ἐὰν γράμματα πέμπῃς καὶ ὡς δῆθεν ἐκπεσόντα ἀπὸ τῶν διακομιζόντων τοῖς
πολεμίοις ἐγχειρισθῶσιν· ἐν οἷς ὡς ἐν τάξει ὑπομιμνήσκεις τοῖς προσφύγοις
καιροῦ προδοσίας συντεθειμένου καὶ πραγμάτων τινῶν πιθανῶν. ἐντεῦθεν γὰρ
ἢ κατασχεθήσονται οἱ προσφυγόντες ἢ ἀπιστηθήσονται, καὶ φοβηθέντες πάλιν
ὑποστρέψουσι πρὸς τὰ ἴδια.

155 λ΄. Καὶ ἑτέρως δὲ τὴν τῶν δειλῶν διάκρισιν ἐν τοῖς ἀναγκαίοις καὶ αἰφνιδίοις
ἐγχειρήμασι ποιήσεις, ἐὰν τοὺς ἀρρώστους ἢ τοὺς κεκτημένους ἵππους ἀδυνά-
τους προστάξεις χωρίζεσθαι ἰδίως. οἱ γὰρ δειλοὶ ἢ ἀρρωστίαν προσποιούμενοι ἢ
τῶν ἵππων ἀσθένειαν, εὐθέως χωρισθήσονται τῶν ἀναγκαίων τοῦ πολέμου
ἐγχειρήσεων. τοὺς δὲ τοιούτους ἢ εἰς παραφυλακὴν κάστρου, ὡς ἄνω που
160 εἴρηται ἡμῖν, ἢ εἰς ἄλλων ὀχυρωμάτων ἢ εἰς ἑτέρας ἀκινδύνους χρείας διατάξας
ἐκπέμψεις, ἵνα μὴ τῇ δειλίᾳ καὶ τοὺς ἀνδρείους μολύνωσιν. εἰ δέ, τῆς παρατάξεως ἱσταμένης πρὸς μάχην παραυτά, κηρύξεις· "ὁ βουλόμενος πρωτοστάτης
ὑποχωρείτω καὶ ὁ βουλόμενος ἀντ᾿ ἐκείνου εἰσίτω," οὐ μόνον τοὺς δειλοὺς τότε

---

138–142 *Strat.*, 8.1.26; cf. Polyaen. 3.9.17; Polyb. *Hist.*, 10.32.11–12; et al.   143–147 *Strat.*,
8.1.25.   148–154 *Strat.*, 8.1.28.   155–166 *Strat.*, 8.1.29.

140 πέριξ M κύκλω A   143 ἁλίσκεται M κρατηθῇ A   144 χωρεῖν M om. A
144–145 ἀπόγνωσιν M ἀπόγνωσιν ὁρμᾶν A   145 καὶ…ποιήσεις M ποιήσεις καὶ φοσσάτου
τῶν ἐχθρῶν κρατουμένου A   146–147 τῶν…κατακράτησιν M trsp. A   148 ὑφόρασιν M
ὑποψίας A   149 ἀποκτείνειν M φονεύειν A   150 ἀπὸ A om. M   150–151 τοῖς πολεμίοις
M εἰς τὰς χεῖρας ἐκπέσωσιν τῶν πολεμίων A   151 ὑπομιμνήσκεις…προσφύγοις M
ὑπομνήσκεις τοὺς πρόσφυγας A   156 κεκτημένους M ἔχοντας A   160 εἴρηται ἡμῖν M trsp.
A

essential tasks of combat and assign them to engage in more suitable chores at that time.[21]

27. Be aware that, even during a period of friendship, security is paramount. If you happen to be encamping in the vicinity of the enemy, construct a fortification of earth or one built with stones or brick or a wooden palisade. In this way, make the army secure all around. For, if the enemy attempts something, you may <find yourself> saying: "I did not expect that." But that is not the mark of a general.[22]

28. When, with God's favor, an enemy city is taken by you, allow the gates to be left open so that most of the people can escape and not be driven to desperation. Be sure to do the same when you take a fortified camp of the enemy. In occupying captured places this is essential and less dangerous.[23]

29. You will furnish the enemy with cause to suspect betrayal and to distrust deserters from you to them so they will either not believe them or will kill them, if you send letters by such conveyance that they will fall into the enemy's hands. In those letters you will, as though it is all set, remind the defectors of the prearranged time for the betrayal and of some other plausible matters. As a result, either the defectors will be caught or they will not be believed. They will be frightened and return to their own people.[24]

30. When it comes to critical and surprise operations, you will, in another way, form a judgment about cowards. Give an order that the sick or those whose horses are too weak are to go off separately. The cowards will then pretend to be sick or claim that their horses are weak. You can then easily keep them away from the essential operations of combat. Send such men off to garrison a fortified town, as we have suggested some time earlier, or some other fortification or you can assign them to other less hazardous duties. In this way, the brave soldiers will not be contaminated by their cowardice. Just before combat, as the battle line is forming, if you proclaim: "Any man who wishes may withdraw from the front ranks," and, "Anyone who wishes may move up in his place," not

---

21. *Strat.* 8.1.24.
22. *Strat.* 8.1.26; cf. Polyaenus 3.9.17; Polybius, *Histories* 10.32.11–12; et al.
23. *Strat.* 8.1.25.
24. For §§29–31 see *Strat.* 8.1.28–30.

νοήσεις, ἀλλὰ καὶ τοὺς ἀνδρείους ἀναμάθῃς. οἱ μὲν γὰρ δειλοὶ καὶ τὸ ἄρχειν
165 προδώσουσιν ὑπὲρ τοῦ μὴ κινδυνεύειν, οἱ δὲ ἀνδρεῖοι μετὰ τοῦ ἄρχειν καὶ τὸ
συγκινδυνεύειν αἱρήσονται.

λαʹ. Ἀκμὴν καιροῦ ἐπιτηρεῖν σε δέον μὴ παρούσης ἀνάγκης, καὶ οὕτως
ἐκστρατεύειν κατὰ τῶν πολεμίων, ἵνα καὶ σὺ περὶ τὴν δαπάνην μὴ στενοῦσαι,
καὶ οἱ πολέμιοι πλέον λυποῦνται τῶν καμάτων αὐτῶν ληϊζομένων.

170 λβʹ. Ἱκανήν σε χρὴ φυλακὴν περιποιεῖσθαι καὶ μετὰ τὴν τῶν πολεμίων σου
νίκην καὶ μὴ ἀμελῶς ἔχειν, ἀλλὰ φυλάττεσθαι τὰς αἰφνιδίους ἐπελεύσεις τῶν
ἡττηθέντων. οὐ γὰρ ἠρεμεῖ τὸ | ἀντίπαλον ἀεί, ἀλλὰ τὴν οἰκείαν ἧτταν πολλά-  362ᵛ
κις ἀναμαχήσασθαι προθυμότερον γίνεται.

λγʹ. Τῶν ἐναντίων τοὺς πρεσβευτὰς ὑβρίζειν οὐ δίκαιον, οὐδ᾽ ἂν πολὺ προ-
175 έχωμεν τῇ δυνάμει. φιλίας γὰρ τρόπῳ παραγίνονται, καὶ λόγῳ ἀτρέπτῳ ὑπὸ τὰς
χεῖρας ἑαυτοὺς τὰς σὰς καταπιστεύουσιν, εἰ καὶ παρὰ πολεμίων ἀποστέλλονται.
τὰ οὖν ὅσια ἐπὶ ἑκάστῳ καὶ πρέποντα παραφυλακτέον. εἰ μὴ γὰρ τοῦτο φυλάτ-
τηται, ἀπιστοῦντες οἱ πρέσβεις ἑκάστου ἔθνους τὴν ἑαυτῶν σωτηρίαν οὐδέποτε
ἡρεσβεύσουσιν καὶ πολλῶν τῶν ἐκ τῆς πρεσβείας ἀγαθῶν τοῖς ἔθνεσι γινομέ-
180 νων ἑκάστοις ἀποστέρησις ἔσεται.

λδʹ. Ὅταν πολλῇ δυνάμει πόλιν ἢ φρούριον πολιορκῇς, οὐ δεῖ σε ποιεῖν
ἀφύλακτον τὴν στρατοπέδειαν, οὐδὲ μόνῳ τῷ χάρακι ἢ ταῖς φόσσαις ἀρκεῖσθαι
εἰς ἀσφάλειαν, ἀλλὰ καὶ βίγλας ἔχειν ἀσφαλεῖς, καὶ παρὰ τὰς πόρτας τῆς
πόλεως στρατὸν ἐγκαθίζειν διὰ τὰς ἀπ᾽ αὐτῆς ἐκ τῶν πορτῶν καταδρομάς,
185 μάλιστα δὲ καὶ τὰς ἀπὸ τῶν ἔξωθέν ποθεν ὑφορωμένας προσβολάς.

λεʹ. Ὑποπτεύονταί τινες προδόται καὶ παρὰ σοὶ πολλάκις ὄντες. ἵνα δὲ καὶ ἐκ
τῶν τοιούτων ὠφέλειαν σεαυτῷ περιποιήσῃ, τὰ ἐναντία ὧν βουλεύῃ λέγε πρὸς
αὐτούς, ὥστε δι᾽ αὐτῶν ἐξαπατωμένων τῶν πολεμίων εὐχερέστερον κατορθοῦν-
ται τὰ σὰ βουλεύματα.

---

172 ad ἠρεμεῖ de novo inc. W | fol. 363 et 364 trsp. M

167–169 Strat., 8.1.30.    170–173 Strat., 8.1.32.    174–180 Strat., 8.1.33.    181–185 Strat.,
8.1.34.    186–189 Strat., 8.1.35.

165 τοῦ¹ Du τὸ codd.    169 ληϊζομένων M ἀφανιζομένων A    170 περιποιεῖσθαι M
ποιεῖσθαι A    172 ἀντίπαλον MW πολέμιον A    174 ὑβρίζειν…δίκαιον MW trsp. A
177 οὖν ὅσια MW trsp. A | ἐπὶ…πρέποντα MW trsp. A    180 ἔσεται MW ἔσται A
182 μόνῳ…φόσσαις MW μόνοις τοῖς σταβάροις ἢ τοῖς ὀρύγμασιν A    185 ποθεν MW om.
A    186 καὶ¹…πολλάκις MW πολλάκις καὶ παρά σοι A    188 εὐχερέστερον MW
εὐκολότερον A

only will you then see who are the cowards but you will also find out who are the brave men. For the cowardly will surrender the first place in order to avoid danger, whereas the brave will choose to be in the forefront and to face danger.

31. When there is no urgency, you ought to observe the most convenient time to go on campaign against the enemy to avoid running short of provisions. And the enemy will suffer more damage as their possessions are plundered.

32. You must take sufficient measures to protect yourself, even after a victory over the enemy, and do not become careless. Be on your guard against surprise attacks by the defeated army. Your adversary is not always without resources but often enough he becomes more eager to make good his own defeat.[25]

33. It is wrong to be disrespectful to envoys from our adversary, even when our forces are much stronger. They come in the guise of friendship and with unwavering assurance entrust themselves to your hands, even though they have been sent by the enemy. What is sacred and proper must be observed in each case. Unless this is observed, the envoys of each nation will not be assured of their own safety and will never come as ambassadors, and each nation will be deprived of the many good results brought about by embassies.

34. Whenever you besiege a city or a fortified place with a strong force, you must not leave your encampment unguarded. Do not rely on a palisade only or a ditch to protect it, but also arrange for secure patrols and have some troops take up positions at the gates of the city to guard against any sallies from within, especially against any suspected attacks from outside forces.

35. Be suspicious of traitors who may frequently be in your company. In order to make use of them to acquire some advantage for yourself, tell them the opposite of what you intend to do so that, by means of them, the enemy will be more easily deceived and you will have achieved what you intended.

25. For §§32–35 see *Strat.* 8.1.32–35.

190   λϛ΄. Ἄνευ ὠφελείας ἢ ἀνάγκης ἐπί τινι πράγματι οὐ δέον παρακινδυνεύειν. οἱ γὰρ τοιούτοις ἐπιχειροῦντες κινδύνοις οὐδὲν διαφέρουσιν ἀνθρώπων τῶν ἀπάτῃ χρυσοῦ δελεαζομένων, καὶ διὰ τὸ τὴν εὔχροιαν μόνον ὁρᾶν τὴν κτῆσιν αὐτοῦ ἔχειν ἀγωνιζομένων.

λζ΄. Γίνου πάντοτε νήφων καὶ ἐγρηγορὼς πρὸς τὰς τῶν πολεμίων ἀντικατα-
195   στάσεις, ὥστε μηδὲ τὸν τῆς ἀνοχῆς τοῦ πολέμου καιρὸν ποιεῖσθαι ἀμελείας καιρόν, μηδὲ πρὸ καιροῦ εἰρήνης βεβαίας γενομένης καταμελήσῃς, ἀλλὰ πάν-τοτε τὰς τῶν ἐχθρῶν ἐπιβουλὰς φυλάττου, καὶ ἀσφαλῶς κατανόει τὸ τούτων ἄπιστον. μετὰ γὰρ τὸ παθεῖν ἡ μεταμέλεια οὐδεμίαν τίκτει ὠφέλειαν.

λη΄. Ἱκανοὶ μὲν ἴσως καὶ οἱ προσφεύγοντες ἀπὸ τῶν πολεμίων παρασχεῖν σοι
200   πίστιν περὶ τῶν ἐρωτωμένων αὐτοῖς. ἀλλὰ μᾶλλον ἀσφαλέστερον ἀναμάθοις τὰ παρὰ τῶν ἐξ ἐπιδρομῆς ἀθρόως κρατουμένων λεγόμενα, καὶ γὰρ ὅταν ἀμφότε-ρα τά τε παρὰ τῶν αὐτομόλων καὶ τὰ παρὰ τῶν αἰχμαλώτων λεγόμενα συμβα-λὼν διακρίνῃς, τότε τὸ ἀληθὲς μᾶλλον γνώσῃ περὶ ὧν ἐπιζητεῖς.

λθ΄. Οὐδενὶ τρόπῳ οὐδὲ οἱαδήποτε προφάσει τὸν πρὸς τοὺς πολεμίους
205   ὅρκον παραβήῃ ποτέ. μέγα γὰρ κακὸν ἐπιορκίας ἔγκλημα. ἐν οἷς γὰρ Θεὸς μεσιτεύει, βέβαια χρὴ μένειν | τὰ συντιθέμενα. αἰσχύνη γὰρ Ῥωμαίοις καὶ μάλι-   364 στα Χριστιανοῖς, τῶν ἄλλων ἐθνῶν τὰς οἰκείας πίστεις τηρούντων, τούτους ἀπίστους περὶ τὰ συμφωνούμενα ὑπὸ Θεῷ μεσίτῃ ἐλέγχεσθαι.

μ΄. Ὑπὸ χάρακός ποτε ἢ φοσσάτου περιφρουρούμενος, ὅτε καλέσει καιρός,
210   μὴ τῷ τοιούτῳ μόνον ὀχυρώματι τὰς ἐλπίδας τῆς σωτηρίας καταπίστευε, ὡς ἑτοίμῳ ὄντι πρὸς παράληψιν, ἀλλὰ μετὰ Θεὸν καὶ ἐν τοῖς ὅπλοις ἔχε τὴν πεποί-θησιν, καὶ μὴ τούτων ἀμέλει διὰ τὴν ἄλλην φρουράν, εἴγε Ῥωμαῖος ὑπάρχεις ἀληθής. πρώτη γὰρ σωτηρία καὶ τελευταία τῷ ἀληθινῷ στρατιώτῃ ἡ τῶν ὅπλων ἐστὶν ἐπιμέλεια καὶ μεταχείρισις, τὰ δὲ ἄλλα καὶ τοῖς χυδαίοις τῶν ὄχλων

190–193 Strat., 8.1.40.   194–198 Strat., 8.1.32.   199–203 Strat., 8.1.36.   204–208 Strat., 8.1.37.   209–216 Strat., 8.1.38.

190 δέον MW χρὴ A   192 ἀπάτῃ   MW ὄψει A   194 ἐγρηγορὼς MW ἐγρηγορῶν A   195–196 ποιεῖσθαι…καιρόν MW ἐν ἀμελείᾳ διάγειν A   198 ἡ…ὠφέλειαν MW οὐδεμίαν τίκτει ὠφέλειαν ἡ μεταμέλεια A   199 πολεμίων MW πολεμίων πίστιν A   200 πίστιν MW om. A | ἀναμάθοις τὰ MW μάθῃ ἐξετάζων τὰ λεγόμενα A   201 ἀθρόως MW καὶ αἰφνιδίως A | λεγόμενα…ὅταν MW ὅταν δὲ A   202 αὐτομόλων MW προφύγων A   203 διακρίνῃς MW συγκρίνῃς A | μᾶλλον MW om. A   206 συντιθέμενα MW συμφωνούμενα A   206–207 ῥωμαίοις…μάλιστα MW om. A   208 μεσίτῃ MW μάρτυρι A   209 χάρακός… φοσσάτου MW σταβάρων ποτὲ ἢ σούδας A   210–211 ὡς…παράληψιν MW εὐκόλως γὰρ τοῦτο ὑπὸ τῶν πολεμίων χειροῦται ἀπαιτεῖ A

36. Unless there is some advantage or urgency in taking some action, you must not place yourself at risk. Those who undertake such dangers do not differ from men who are caught when gold is used as bait; looking only at the beautiful color, they struggle to gain possession of it.[26]

37. Always be vigilant and alert against confrontations with the enemy. Do not let a period when hostilities have ceased lull you into a period of carelessness. Do not become negligent before the conclusion of a firm peace. Always be on guard against the machinations of the enemy. Be careful and watch out for their unfaithfulness. After you have been injured, regret is not of much help.[27]

38. Perhaps you are able to place some trust in the answers given to your questions by defectors from the enemy, but it is much safer to obtain such information from prisoners taken in raids. Form your judgment after you have checked both reports, that from the defectors and that from the prisoners. In this way you will learn the truth of what you are seeking.[28]

39. By no means and on no pretext whatever should you ever break a sworn agreement with the enemy. The crime of breaking an oath is a great evil. Inasmuch as God has been invoked, it is essential that what has been agreed on should remain firm. When other nations keep their own promises, it would be shameful for the Romans, especially for Christians, to be accused of being unfaithful to what they have agreed to with God as their witness.

40. When you are protected round about by a palisade or fortification, as the occasion may require, do not entrust your hopes of safety to such a fortification alone, for it may readily be taken. But, after God, place your confidence in your weapons. Just because you have that other protection, do not neglect these, if indeed you are a true Roman. For the genuine soldier safety is found first and last in the care and handling of his weapons, even though ordinary people attribute it to other things. Instead of a wall, the ancient Romans are said to have

26. *Strat.* 8.1.40.
27. *Strat.* 8.1.32.
28. For §§38–41 see *Strat.* 8.1.36–39.

215 ἐπινοεῖται πολλάκις. καὶ γὰρ καὶ τοῖς πάλαι Ῥωμαίοις κατ᾽ ἀρχὰς ἀντὶ τειχῶν τῇ
Ῥώμῃ φόσσαν καὶ τὰ ὅπλα χρηματίζειν λέγεται. καὶ Λακεδαιμονίῳ ποτὲ στρατιώτῃ ἐρωτωμένῳ· "ποῦ οἱ τῆς γῆς ὑμῶν ὅροι;" λέγεται εἰπεῖν· "ὧδε," δείξας τὸ ἐν
τῇ χειρὶ κατεχόμενον δόρυ.

μα΄. Παρακελεύου τοίνυν τοῖς στρατιώταις, οὕτως εἶναι παρεσκευασμένους
220 ἀεὶ ὡς καὶ ἐν ἑορτῇ καὶ ἐν ὄμβρῳ καὶ ἐν νυκτὶ καὶ ἐν ἡμέρᾳ καὶ ὅταν ἡ χρεία
καλέσῃ, μέλλειν αὐτοὺς ἐξιέναι κατὰ τῶν πολεμίων. διὰ τοῦτο γὰρ ἐπὶ τὸν
τοιοῦτον καιρὸν οὐδ᾽ ἡμέραν αὐτοὺς δεῖ προλέγειν ὡρισμένην, διὰ τὸ ἑτοίμους
αὐτοὺς εἶναι διὰ παντός.

μβ΄. Νίκης σοι παρὰ Θεοῦ ἐν δημοσίᾳ μάχῃ παρεχομένης, ἐὰν συμβῇ τοὺς
225 ἀντιπάλους ἢ ἐν χάρακι ἢ ἐν ἑτέρῳ ὀχυρῷ τόπῳ καταφυγεῖν, μὴ ἐνδώσῃς αὐτοῖς
καιρὸν ἀνέσεως, ἀλλὰ τοῦ φόβου νεάζοντος αὐτοῖς ἐπέρχου καὶ ἐπιτίθου, ἵνα μὴ
τῇ ἐνδόσει ἀσφαλέστεροι γενόμενοι θαρρήσωσι τὴν ἧτταν αὐτῶν ἀναμαχήσασθαι.

μγ΄. Ἐάν τινες ἱκέται προσφεύγωσιν ἀπὸ τῶν πολεμίων πρός σε, μὴ ὡς ἔτυχε
230 τούτους προσδέχου· πολλάκις γὰρ ὑπὸ τῶν ἐχθρῶν πέμπονται δόλῳ ὡς ἱκέται
καί τινων δεόμενοι, καὶ οὕτως τοῖς δεξαμένοις ἐπιβουλεύουσιν.

μδ΄. Ὑπονοεῖν δεῖ καὶ παραφυλάττειν ἀσφαλῶς τοὺς προσρυομένους ταῖς
πολιορκουμέναις ἡμῶν πόλεσι παρὰ τῶν ἐχθρῶν διὰ τὸ μὴ παρ᾽ αὐτῶν τινα
βλάβην ὑποστῆναι· πολλάκις γὰρ ἐμπρησμοὺς ποιοῦσιν, καὶ τῶν ἔσωθεν ἀνθρώ-
235 πων περὶ τοὺς ἐμπρησμοὺς ἀσχολουμένων, ἔξωθεν οἱ πολέμιοι ἀδεέστερον
ἐπιτίθενται.

με΄. Μάχης προκειμένης ἐὰν ἄρα δοκιμάζῃς ἀξιόμαχος εἶναι τῶν ἐχθρῶν, ὦ
στρατηγέ, ἐν τῇ ἐκείνων χώρᾳ τὴν μάχην ἐπιτηδεύσῃς. τοῦτο γὰρ μᾶλλον
ἁρμόδιον ἤπερ ἐν τῇ ἰδίᾳ. τῶν γὰρ ἐν τῇ πολεμίᾳ γῇ μαχομένων καὶ τὰ φρονή-
240 ματα μείζονα γίνονται, καὶ ὁ ἀγὼν οὐκ ἔστι ὡς ὑπὲρ τοῦ ἰδίου ἔθνους μόνου
πρόκειται αὐτοῖς ὁ τοῦ πολέμου, ἀλλὰ καὶ ὑπὲρ τῆς αὐτῶν σωτηρίας. καὶ γὰρ

---

216–218 Plut. *Mor.*, 201E (*Apophthegm. Lac.*).    219–223 *Strat.*, 8.1.39.    224–228 *Strat.*,
8.1.43.    229–231 *Strat.*, 8.1.41.    232–236 *Strat.*, 8.1.42.    237–247 *Strat.*, 8.1.44.

215 ἐπινοεῖται πολλάκις MW trsp. A    215–216 τῇ…λακεδαιμονίῳ MW ὀρύγματα καὶ τὰ
ὅπλα εἰς ἀσφάλειαν τῇ ῥώμῃ ὑπάρχειν A    219 παρεσκευασμένους MW παρασκευασμένους
καὶ ἑτοίμους A    221 μέλλειν MW om. A | αὐτοὺς De αὐτὸν MW om. A    222 οὐδ᾽ A οὐδὲ
MW    225 ἀντιπάλους…χάρακι MW ἐναντίους ἢ ἐν φοσσάτῳ σταβαρωμένῳ A
226 ἀνέσεως MW μηδὲ ἄνεσιν A | αὐτοῖς MW καὶ ἐγκειμένου αὐτοῦ τῇ ψυχῇ A    229 ἔτυχε
A ἔτυχεν MW    232 προσρυομένους MW προσφεύγοντας A    233 πόλεσι A πόλεσιν MW
235 ἀδεέστερον MW ἀδεῶς A    237 ἀξιόμαχος…ἐχθρῶν MW ἀπαντᾶν τοὺς ἐχθροὺς A

originally made use of a ditch and their arms to <protect> Rome. When a Lacedemonian soldier was asked: "Where are the borders of your land?" he is said to have replied: "Here." And he showed the spear he was holding in his hand.[29]

41. Give orders to the soldiers that they should at all times be prepared to march out against the enemy: on a holiday, in the rain, by day or by night, and whenever it is necessary. For this reason on such occasions you must not tell them the scheduled day beforehand, so they may always be prepared.

42. When God has granted you victory in open battle and your adversaries manage to find refuge within a palisade or some other fortified place, do not allow them a moment of relaxation, but while their fear is still fresh, move up and fall upon them. If you allow them <to relax> they might feel more secure and gain enough confidence to reverse their defeat.[30]

43. If some suppliants from the enemy seek refuge with you, do not receive them casually. Often enough they are sent by the enemy deceptively as suppliants and begging certain favors. In this way, they conspire against their hosts.[31]

44. You ought to be suspicious and very much on your guard against deserters approaching one of our cities under enemy siege, so you will sustain no damage from them. Frequently they set fires and, when the men on the inside are busy extinguishing them, the enemy more readily attack from the outside.[32]

45. When battle is imminent, if you believe, O general, that you are prepared to face the enemy in combat, get set to do the fighting in their country. This is more advantageous than in your own. Men waging war in a foreign land become more aggressive. The struggle of war no longer lies before them as though it were only on behalf of their nation but also of their own safety. They are aware

29. Plutarch, *Moralia* 210E (*Sayings of the Spartans*).

30. *Strat.* 8.1.43.

31. *Strat.* 8.1.41.

32. *Strat.* 8.1.42.

οἴδασιν ὡς, ἐὰν μὴ στερρῶς ἀντικατα|στάντες εἰς φυγὴν ἐν τῇ πολεμίᾳ γῇ 364ᵛ
τραπῶσιν, ἀνέλπιστος αὐτοῖς ἡ σωτηρία γίνεται, ὅπερ ἐν τῇ ἰδίᾳ γῇ πολεμούντων αὐτῶν γενέσθαι οὐκ ἀναγκαῖον. καὶ γὰρ καὶ φυγόντες ἐλπίζουσιν ἀκινδύ-
245 νως σωθῆναι καὶ ὀχυρωμάτων ἐπιλαβέσθαι ἐν οἷς σωθήσονται· καὶ διὰ τοῦτο
γενναίως ἀντιστῆναι τοῖς πολεμίοις οἱ στρατιῶται, μὴ συγχωρούμενοι εἰς φυγὴν
ἀκίνδυνον συνωθοῦνται ἐλθεῖν.

μς΄. Ἀεί τι πραττέτωσαν οἱ στρατιῶται, ὅταν μὴ ὁ πόλεμος ἐνοχλῇ, καὶ μὴ
ἀργείτωσαν· ἡ γὰρ ἀργία στρατιώταις συντρεφομένη ταραχῆς ὑπάρχει γεννη-
250 τική.

μζ΄. Τὸ θεραπεύειν τὸ θεῖον διὰ παντὸς χρεών ἐστιν. μάλιστα δὲ τοῦτο
θεραπεύσεις, ὦ στρατηγέ, τῶν πολεμικῶν κινδύνων ἀπάρχεσθαι μέλλων. ἐὰν
γὰρ γνησίως τότε τὸν Θεὸν θεραπεύσῃς, τάχα θαρρήσεις ἐν τοῖς δεινοῖς ὡς
πρὸς φίλον σοι τοῦτον τὰς ἱκεσίας ποιεῖσθαι, καὶ τὴν σωτηρίαν μετὰ παρρησίας
255 ἐπιζητεῖν.

μη΄. Ὁ συναγρυπνῶν τῷ στρατεύματι στρατηγὸς καὶ πλέον πονῶν ἐν τῷ
γυμνάζευθαι τοὺς στρατιώτας, ἥττονα κινδυνεύσει κατὰ τὸν πόλεμον.

μθ΄. Στρατιώτας ἐξάγειν ἐπὶ τὴν μάχην ἐκείνους οὐ δέον, ὧν μὴ πρότερον
εἴληφας τὴν πεῖραν ἱκανὴν ἐπὶ ἀνδρείαν τυγχάνουσαν. ἀλλὰ δεῖ σε γινώσκειν εἰ
260 δυνατὸν ἕκαστον τῶν στρατιωτῶν ἐν ποίῳ πράγματι καὶ ἐν ποίῳ τάγματί ἐστιν
ἁρμόδιος, καὶ οὕτως αὐτοὺς διατάττειν.

ν΄. Ταῦτα μόνα καλῶς βουλευσόμεθα κατὰ τῶν πολεμίων ὅσα πρὶν ἢ πράξο-
μεν ἠγνόησαν ἐκεῖνοι. ἐὰν δὲ τούτων τὴν γνῶσιν λάβωσιν, ταχέως κατὰ τῶν
βουλευμάτων ἡμῶν μεθοδεύσουσιν.

265 να΄. Ἢ δόλοις ἢ ἐπιδρομαῖς ἢ λιμῷ τοὺς πολεμίους βλάπτειν καλόν ἐστιν, καὶ
λυπεῖν αὐτοὺς κατὰ μακρὸν διὰ συχνοτέρων ἐπαγωγῶν καὶ ἐπιτηδεύσεων. οὐχὶ
δὲ πάντως ἐπὶ δημόσιον ἐγκαλεῖσθαι πόλεμον, ἔνθα πολλάκις τὸ πλέον ὁρῶμεν
τῆς τύχης προτέρημα ἢ τῆς ἐπιδεικνυμένης ἀνδρείας.

---

242 ad ἀντι- des. W

248–250 Strat., 8.2.15; Polyaen. 3.9.35.    251–255 Strat., 8.2.1; Onas. 5.1.    256–257 Strat.,
8.2.2.    258–261 Strat., 8.2.3.    262–264 Strat., 8.2.5.    265–268 Strat., 8.2.4.

249–250 στρατιώταις… γεννητική Μ ταραχῆς ὑπάρχει γεννητική στρατιώταις συντρεφομένη
Α    251 χρεών Α χρέος Μ    252 θεραπεύσεις Μ θεραπεύεις Α    257 ἥττονα Μ ὀλίγα Α
258 τὴν Α om. Μ    259 εἴληφας Μ ἔλαβε Α    266 ἐπαγωγῶν Μ ἐπιθέσεων Α

that, unless they put up a stiff resistance, they will turn to flight in a foreign land and will have no hope of saving themselves. When waging war in their own land, though, this is not critical. If they turn to flight, they still hope to avoid danger and be saved by reaching some fortified place in which they will be secure. The soldiers bravely stand up to the foe and, without yielding, they rush into a flight without risk.[33]

46. Whenever war does not intrude let the soldiers always be doing something. Let them not be idle. Idleness nurtured among soldiers gives birth to confusion.[34]

47. It is necessary to worship the Divinity at all times. Especially, O general, should you offer worship when you plan to enter upon the dangers of war. If, at that time, you genuinely worship God, then, when the time is full of terror, you will be confident that you can offer your prayers to him as to a friend and you can seek your salvation with utter confidence.[35]

48. The general who remains vigilant together with his army, and who works harder in drilling his troops, runs fewer risks <in fighting> the enemy.[36]

49. You must not lead into battle those soldiers of whose courage you have not previously had sufficient experience. You must know what duty each one of the soldiers can perform and what unit he best fits into, and you should so assign him.[37]

50. Our plans against the enemy will be successful only if they are unaware of them before we put them into action. If they come to know our plans, they will quickly take steps to counter them.[38]

51. It is well to harm the enemy by deceit, by raids, by hunger, and to hurt them for a long time by means of very frequent assaults and other actions. You should never be enticed into a pitched battle. For the most part, we observe that success is a matter of luck rather than of proven courage.[39]

33. *Strat.* 8.1.44.
34. *Strat.* 8.2.15; Polyaenus, 3.9.35.
35. *Strat.* 8.2.1; Onasander 5.1.
36. *Strat.* 8.2.2.
37. *Strat.* 8.2.3.
38. *Strat.* 8.2.5.
39. *Strat.* 8.2.4.

νβ′. Στρατιῶται πρὸς πόνους γυμναζόμενοι προκόπτουσιν εἰς ἀνδρείαν.
270 ἀργοῦντες δὲ νωθροὶ καὶ ἀσθενεῖς μᾶλλον γίνονται. διὸ φροντίσεις μὴ ἀργεῖν
αὐτούς, ἀλλὰ πρὸς τὰς γυμνασίας πονεῖν, καθώς σοι καὶ ἐν ἑτέροις διεταξάμεθα.

νγ′. Ἄδολον μὲν ἐν τοῖς ἄλλοις ἅπασι διαζῆν σε παρακελευόμεθα, ἐν δὲ τοῖς
κατὰ πόλεμον στρατηγήμασι μόνοις καὶ δόλος ὠφελήσει πολλάκις, ὅταν τοὺς
ἐχθροὺς καὶ πολεμίους ἐξαπατᾶν μέλλῃς δι’ αὐτοῦ.

275 νδ′. Γίνωσκε καὶ σύγκρινε τάς τε σὰς δυνάμεις καὶ τὰς τῶν πολεμίων ὅπως
ἔχουσι. τοῦτο γὰρ ποιῶν στρατηγὸς καὶ ἀνακρίνων κατὰ μέρος τάς τε τῶν
οἰκείων καὶ τὰς τῶν πολεμίων ἀρετάς, δυσκόλως ἐν τοῖς κατὰ πόλεμον ἔργοις
σφαλήσεται.

νε′. Ἴσθι ἀκριβῶς, ὦ στρατηγέ, ὅτι ἀνδρεία μᾶλλον | καὶ τάξις στρατηγικὴ 363
280 οἴδασιν ἐν πολέμῳ εὐεργετεῖν ἢ πλῆθος τῶν μαχομένων ἄνανδρον καὶ ἄτακτον.

νς′. Αἱ τῶν τόπων θέσεις πολλάκις μεγάλα τοὺς μαχομένους ὠφέλησαν· καὶ
γὰρ ἐνίοτε καὶ τοὺς ἀσθενεστέρους καλλίονας ἔδειξαν· διὸ χρή σε μάλιστα
τοιούτοις τόποις ἁρμόζεσθαι πρὸς μάχην, ἐν οἷς ἂν γινώσκῃς τὸν μὲν σὸν
στρατὸν προτερῆσαι, τὸν δὲ τῶν πολεμίων ἐλαττωθῆναι.

285 νζ′. Στρατηγοῦ ἀγχίνοια γενναίους τοὺς στρατιώτας ποιεῖ. ἡ μὲν γὰρ φύσις
ὀλίγους ἀνδρείους ἀπογεννᾷ, ἡ δὲ ἐπιμέλεια καὶ γυμνασία μετὰ στρατηγοῦ
φρονήσεως γινομένη πολλοὺς χρησίμους ἀποδεικνύει.

νη′. Καλόν μοι δοκεῖ δικαίαν εἶναι τὴν ἀρχὴν τοῦ πολέμου. ὁ γὰρ τοῖς
ἀδικήσασιν ἀνταμυνόμενος οὗτος δίκαιός ἐστιν καὶ τὴν θείαν ἔχει δικαιοσύνην
290 βοηθόν τε καὶ σύμμαχον κατὰ τῶν ἀδίκων ἐκστρατευόμενος. ὁ δὲ πρῶτος
κατάρξας ἀδικίας παρ’ αὐτῆς τῆς θείας δίκης ἀφαιρεῖται τὴν νίκην.

νθ′. Ἀσφαλῶς δίωκε τοὺς πολεμίους μετὰ νίκην, ὦ στρατηγέ, καὶ μὴ διεσπαρμένως ἐπέρχου, μάλιστα συντεταγμένοις ἐκείνοις. ὁ γὰρ τοῦτο ποιῶν τὴν
ἑαυτοῦ νίκην τοῖς πολεμίοις προδίδωσι. καὶ γὰρ ἀντιστρέψαντες μετὰ συντάξε-
295 ως οἱ ἐχθροὶ κατὰ σοῦ ἀσυντάκτως καὶ διεσπαρμένως διώκοντος, ῥᾳδίως σου
περιγένωνται καὶ πρὸς τὸ ἐναντίον ἀντιπνεύσουσι τὴν κατ’ αὐτῶν μάχην.

---

269–271 Strat., 8.2.9; Polyaen. 3.9.35.   272–274 Strat., 8.2.6.   275–278 Strat., 8.2.7.
279–280 Strat., 8.2.8.   281–284 Strat., 8.2.8.   285–287 Strat., 8.2.9.   288–291 Strat.,
8.2.12.   292–296 Strat., 8.2.11.

276 ἔχουσι M ἔχουσιν A   286–287 στρατηγοῦ φρονήσεως M trsp. A   289 ἀδικήσασιν
ἀνταμυνόμενος M ἀδικήσοντας ἀμυνόμενος A   295 ῥᾳδίως M εὐκόλως A

52. Soldiers who become habituated to work improve in courage, whereas the idle ones become sluggish and weak. For this reason, you must take care that they are not idle. Make them work at their exercises, as we have prescribed elsewhere.[40]

53. We enjoin upon you to lead a guileless life in every other respect, but with the sole exception of the stratagems of war. Deception is often very advantageous when you intend to use it to trick the foe and the enemy.[41]

54. Know and evaluate the condition of your own forces and those of the enemy. The general who does this and who analyzes in detail the strong points of his own men and those of the enemy will not be tripped up by the actions of war.

55. Know for a certainty, O general, that courage and military discipline contribute more to success in war than does an unmanly and undisciplined multitude of warriors.

56. The condition of the terrain has often proved greatly advantageous to the men engaged in combat. There have been times when it enabled the weaker side to become the stronger. For this reason, you must accommodate your battle plans to such terrain in which you know that your army has an advantage and the enemy are at a loss.

57. A shrewd general makes for brave soldiers. Nature produces but few brave men, whereas care and training, as well as the general's intelligence, result in many efficient soldiers.

58. I feel strongly that the initiation of hostilities must be just. A person defending himself against others who are acting unjustly is truly just himself. He has divine justice for support and as an ally in campaigning against the unjust. The person who first begins injustice has his victory taken away by divine justice itself.[42]

59. After victory, O general, pursue the enemy in a safe manner. Do not advance in a scattered fashion, especially if they have maintained their formation. A man acting in this way surrenders the victory that should be his to the enemy. If, while you are pursuing in a disorderly and scattered manner, the enemy wheels about in good order, they will easily overcome you and, like the wind changing direction, they turn the assault against them to the opposite.[43]

40. *Strat.* 8.2.9; Polyaenus 3.9.35.
41. For §§53–57 see *Strat.* 8.2.6–9.
42. *Strat.* 8.2.12.
43. *Strat.* 8.2.11.

ξ΄. Ἰσχύσεις μᾶλλον, ὦ στρατηγέ, κατὰ τῶν σῶν πολεμίων, ὅταν ἀφορᾷς πρὸς τὴν ποιότητα τῶν καιρῶν καὶ τῶν τόπων καὶ τῶν ἀντιμαχομένων ἐχθρῶν. καὶ οὕτως πρὸς τὴν ἑκάστου χρείαν ταῖς οἰκείαις τέχναις καὶ μεθόδοις συγκέ-
300 χρησαι.

ξα΄. Οὔτε συνάγειν ὁμοῦ βουλῆς ἕνεκα τὸ στράτευμα πρέπον ἐστὶν οὔτε συνεχῶς καλεῖν τὸν στρατηγὸν πρὸς ἑαυτὸν ἀργοῦντας καὶ πρὸς μηδὲν ἀσχολουμένους ἕτερον· ταῦτα γὰρ ἀκαίρου μελέτης καὶ στάσεως αἴτια τοῖς στρατεύμασι γίνεται.

305 ξβ΄. Μεγάλη σύνεσις στρατηγοῦ, ὅταν χρῆται μὲν συμμάχοις μετρίοις εἰς τὴν ἑαυτοῦ χώραν, ἀλλὰ μὴ πλέον τῆς οἰκείας δυνάμεως, τούτους εἰσάγων μάλιστα, δυσμενεῖς ποτε τοὺς τοιούτους ἔσεσθαι ἐλπιζομένους, μήποτε συμφρονήσαντες ἀντάρωσι καὶ τῆς χώρας κρατήσωσιν, δι᾽ ἣν εἰς συμμαχίαν ἐκλήθησαν. οἱ γὰρ ἕνεκεν χρημάτων ὑπέρ σου κινδυνεύειν ἑλόμενοι, τάχα καὶ πλειόνων χρημάτων
310 πορισμοῦ ἕνεκεν καὶ κατὰ σοῦ παρακινδυνεύσουσιν.

ξγ΄. Ὅταν μὴ τοῖς στρατεύμασι τὰ ἐπιτήδεια καὶ τὰς ἀναγκαίας τροφὰς προευτρεπίσῃς, τότε καὶ πολεμίων χωρὶς ἡττηθήσῃ· ἡ γὰρ σπάνις καὶ ἔνδεια τῆς δαπάνης καὶ τοὺς στρατιώτας καὶ τοὺς ἵππους | ἐκλυθῆναι παρασκευάσει.                    363ᵛ

ξδ΄. Ὅταν τοῖς ἰδίοις καβαλλαρίοις θαρρῇς καὶ μάλιστα τοῖς μετὰ κονταρίων
315 πολεμοῦσιν, τοὺς στενοὺς καὶ ἀνωμάλους τόπους ἔκφευγε, ἐπιζητεῖ δὲ τόπους ὁμαλοὺς καὶ ἴσους· οὗτοι γάρ εἰσι τοῖς οὕτω παρατασσομένοις ἁρμόδιοι, καὶ ἐνταῦθα συγκρότει τὸν πόλεμον. εἰ δὲ πεζικαῖς θαρρεῖς δυνάμεσιν, ἀνωμάλους καὶ δασεῖς καὶ τραχυτέρους ἐπιλέγου τόπους, καὶ ἐν τούτοις ἐπιτέλει τὴν μάχην.

ξε΄. Ὑπὲρ σεαυτοῦ καὶ τοῦ σοῦ λαοῦ ἄν τι βουλεύσῃ κατὰ τῶν πολεμίων, καὶ
320 τὴν τοιαύτην βουλὴν ἀκούσῃς προδεδομένην αὐτοῖς, καθόλου τὰ βεβουλευμένα, εἴτε ἐν παρατάξει εἴτε ἐν ἄλλαις παραγγελίαις ἢ σχήμασιν ἐναλλάσσειν ὀφείλεις.

ξϛ΄. Σὺν πλείοσι μὲν περὶ ὧν μέλλεις πράττειν βουλεύου, τί δὲ πράξεις σὺν ὀλίγοις καὶ τούτοις πιστοῖς. τὸ δὲ συμφέρον σου ἤγουν τὴν πασῶν καλλίονα
325 βουλὴν κατὰ σεαυτὸν ἐπιλεξάμενος κάτεχε.

---

297–300 Strat., 8.2.13.   301–304 Strat., 8.2.14.   305–310 Strat., 8.2.16.   311–313 Strat., 8.2.19.   314–318 Strat., 8.2.20–21.   319–322 Strat., 8.2.22.   323–325 Strat., 8.2.23.

---

299 τέχναις…μεθόδοις M trsp. A   299–300 συγκέχρησαι M κέχρησαι A   305 μετρίοις M συμμετρίοις A   307 δυσμενεῖς M ἐχθροὺς A | ἔσεσθαι M γενέσθαι A | συμφρονήσαντες M συμφρονήσαντες καὶ ὁμονοήσαντες A   309–310 πλειόνων…ἕνεκεν M πορισμοῦ ἕνεκεν πλειόνων χρημάτων A

60. You will be stronger, O general, against your enemies if you carefully observe the nature of the seasons and the places and the enemy you are fighting. In doing this, you apply your own skill and methodology to deal with each situation.[44]

61. It does not help to assemble the army together in council or for the general constantly to invite into his presence men who are idle and not occupied with anything else. This is evidence of misplaced concern and can cause discord among the troops.[45]

62. The general <must> display great prudence when employing an allied force in his own country; it must be of moderate size, no larger than his own army. In particular, one may expect the forces he brings in to be ill disposed at times, and conspire, rise up, and occupy the country into which they were invited as allies. Such men have chosen to endure dangers on your behalf for the sake of money. For the sake of more money, they will quickly face dangers in fighting against you.[46]

63. When you do not provide your army with necessary supplies and food, then, even without the enemy <attacking>, you have been defeated. Scarcity and lack of food prepares both soldiers and horses to fall apart.[47]

64. When you rely on your own cavalry, especially lancers, steer clear of narrow and uneven locations. Seek out level and even places—for these are more suitable for formations of that sort—and there force the battle. If you rely on infantry, select uneven, wooded, and rugged places and there engage in battle.[48]

65. If you make some plans for yourself and your troops against the enemy and you hear that those plans have been betrayed to them, you absolutely ought to make changes in your battle formation or in other commands or signals.[49]

66. For what you intend to do seek the advice of many, but for what you will actually do take counsel with only a few, trustworthy people. For the most helpful plan, better than all the others, make your decision by yourself and keep it to yourself.

44. *Strat.* 8.2.13.
45. *Strat.* 8.2.14.
46. *Strat.* 8.2.16.
47. *Strat.* 8.2.19.
48. *Strat.* 8.2.20–21.
49. For §§65–68 see *Strat.* 8.2.22–25.

ξζ΄. Ἵνα δέ σοι ἡ ἐκστρατεία ἄλυπος διατηρῆται καὶ ἐρρωμένη, δέον σε ἢ πρὸς τὰ ἐπιτήδεια τῆς χρείας τὸ στράτευμα ἀπάγειν ἢ αὐτὰ τὰ ἐπιτήδεια πρὸς τὸ στράτευμα μετακομίζειν.

ξη΄. Οὐ διὰ σκοπῶν δεῖ μόνον προερευνᾶν τὰς ὁδούς, ἀλλὰ καὶ αὐτόν, εἰ
330 δυνατόν, τὸν στρατηγὸν λαθραίως τοῖς οἰκείοις ὀφθαλμοῖς μετὰ ἀκριβείας ταύτας κατανοεῖν, καὶ οὐ μόνον τὰς ὁδούς, ἀλλ᾽ εἴγε δυνατὸν καὶ τὸ πλῆθος τῶν ἐπερχομένων πολεμίων καὶ τὴν τάξιν αὐτῶν, ὡς ἂν ἐντεῦθεν διδασκόμενος δύναται καὶ κατ᾽ αὐτῶν καὶ ὑπὲρ ἑαυτοῦ ἀσφαλῶς τὰ ἐνδεχόμενα ἐπινοεῖν καὶ μεθοδεύειν.

335 ξθ΄. Ὑψηλῇ διανοίᾳ τὴν ἐμπεσουμένην ποτὲ δειλίαν τοῖς στρατιώταις ἀνακαλοῦ, καὶ τέχναις διαφόροις εἰς θάρσος τούτους ἐπάναγε, ποτὲ μὲν λόγοις, ποτὲ δὲ δώροις, ἀνακτώμενος, καὶ πρὸς εὐθυμίαν μεθέλκων τὴν ἀθυμίαν.

ο΄. Καλὸν ἐν παντὶ καιρῷ τιμᾶν καὶ σέβεσθαι τοὺς ἱεροὺς τοῦ Θεοῦ ναούς, μάλιστα δὲ καὶ ἐν τῷ ἀσύλους αὐτοὺς διατηρεῖσθαι εἰς τοὺς ἐν αὐτοῖς προσφεύ-
340 γοντας. διὰ τοῦτο παραφύλαττε, ὦ στρατηγέ, καὶ μήτε σὺ αὐτὸς μήτε εἷς τινα ἕτερον καταδέξῃ ἀπὸ θείου ναοῦ ἀποσπᾶσαί τινα ἱκέτην καθήμενον ἕως ἂν τοῦ δικαίου αὐτοῦ ἐπιτύχῃ. τοὺς δέ τι τοιοῦτον τολμῶντας ὡς ἀσεβεῖς κόλαζε, ἵνα μὴ τὰ θεῖα καταφρονοῦνται.

οα΄. Ἀγγαρείας ἁπάσης ἰδιωτικῆς καὶ ἀδικίας ἐλεύθερον φύλαττε τὸν ὑπό σε
345 τεταγμένον λαόν, ὅσοι τοῦ στρατοῦ εἰσι καὶ ὅσοι τῆς λεγομένης ἐξατορίας. ἀρκεῖ γὰρ αὐτοῖς τελεῖν τούς τε δημοσίους φόρους καὶ τὰ ἐπικείμενα αὐτοῖς ἀερικὰ καὶ μηδὲν πλέον καταβαρεῖσθαι. ἐὰν δὲ ἡ καστροκτισία γένηται ἢ καραβοποιΐα ἢ γεφύρας | ἀνάκτισις ἢ ὁδοῦ κατάστασις ἢ ἀνάγκη τις ἑτέρα τῶν    365 δημοσίων διοικήσεων, καὶ οὐκ ἐπαρκῇ τὸ κατὰ τὸν τόπον δημόσιον διὰ μισθοῦ
350 ταῦτα ἐργάζεσθαι, τότε μετὰ τοῦ δικαίου λόγου καὶ τῆς ἰσότητος ἅπαντες δουλευέτωσαν, καὶ μηδεὶς παρά τινος ἐξκουσευέσθω, μήτε διὰ δώρων μήτε διὰ φιλίαν τῆς τοιαύτης δουλείας ἀπολιμπανέσθω, ἀλλὰ κατὰ ἀναλογίαν τῆς δυνάμεως αὐτοῦ ἕκαστος, καὶ πλούσιος καὶ πένης, τὴν δημοσίαν δουλείαν ἐπιτελείτωσαν.

355 οβ΄. Ἱερά εἰσι τὰ τῶν τελευτώντων ἐν πολέμῳ στρατιωτῶν σώματα, καὶ μάλιστα τῶν ἀριστευσάντων ἐν τῇ ὑπὲρ τῶν Χριστιανῶν μάχῃ. καὶ ταῦτα χρεὸν ἐκ παντὸς τρόπου τιμᾶν ὁσίως καὶ ταφῆς ἀξιοῦν καὶ μνήμης ἀειμνήστου. ἀλλὰ

326–328 Strat., 8.2.24.   329–334 Strat., 8.2.25.   335–337 Strat., 8.2.30.   355–362 Cf. ιδ΄.204–208; Onas. 3.6.

331 εἴγε Μ εἰ Α   335 ἐμπεσουμένην ποτὲ Μ ἐμπίπτουσαν πολλάκις Α   339 εἰς Μ om. A
342 τι…τολμῶντας Μ trsp. A   355 εἰσι Μ ἐστιν Α   356 χρεὸν Μ χρὴ Α

67. To preserve your expeditionary force in good condition and free from harm, you must either lead the army to the supplies they need or transport the supplies to the army.

68. Do not rely only on scouts to reconnoiter the roads but the general himself, if he can do so, should, under cover, carefully observe them with his own eyes, not only the roads but, if possible, the size of the approaching enemy force and its formation. With this information he will be able to figure out what actions he can safely take against them as well as protect himself.

69. Whenever the morale of the soldiers sinks, raise them up again to lofty thoughts and restore them to courage by various arts, winning them over sometimes by words, sometimes by gifts, thus converting their poor spirits to good spirits.[50]

70. At all times, it is good to honor and revere the holy temples of God, especially to preserve them inviolate for those taking refuge in them. For this reason, O general, be on your guard and do not allow yourself or any other person to expel from the holy temple any suppliant staying there until he obtains justice. Punish those bold enough to do such an impious thing, and keep them from contemning divine things.[51]

71. Keep the troops serving under your command free of all individual impressments and injustice.[52] It is sufficient for those who belong to the army, as well as those exempt from military service, to pay both the public taxes and the aerikon imposed on them, and not to be burdened with anything more. But if a fortress is to be constructed, a ship to be built, bridges to be raised, a road to be laid out, or something else required by the state administration, and the public funds of that locality do not cover the payments to complete the work, then let everyone contribute his services on a fair and equal basis. Let nobody be excused and let nobody be released from such service because of gifts or friendship, but let each person, in proportion to his abilities, rich and poor, carry out that public service.[53]

72. The bodies of the soldiers who have been killed in battle are sacred, especially those who have been most valiant in the fight on behalf of Christians.

50. *Strat.* 8.2.30.

51. See E. Herman, "Zum Asylsrecht im byzantinischen Reich," *OCP* 1 (1935): 204–238; R. Macrides, "Killing, Asylum and the Law in Byzantium," *Speculum* 63 (1988): 509–538.

52. On mistreatment of soldiers by imperial officials, see Skirmishing, 216–17; CampOrg, 318–23.

53. See *ODB*, s.v. "taxation," "aerikon."

καὶ τὰ τέκνα τούτων καὶ τὰς γαμετὰς καὶ τοὺς ὅλους οἴκους αὐτῶν δέον τῆς
παρά σου προνοίας ἀπολαύειν, ὦ στρατηγέ, καὶ ἐπιμελείας καὶ ἀντιλήψεως.
360 οὕτως γὰρ οἱ στρατιῶται καὶ εὔψυχοι καὶ πρόθυμοι πρὸς τοὺς πολεμικοὺς
κινδύνους γενήσονται, ἐν ἐκείνοις βλέποντες τί αὐτοῖς συμβήσεται μετὰ τὸ
τέλος, ἐὰν προθύμως ἀριστεύσαντες ἀγωνίζωνται.

ογ'. Παρασκευῆς τῆς ἐν πολέμοις ὀφειλούσης μὴ ἀμέλει, ὦ στρατηγέ, κατὰ
τὸν καιρὸν τοῦ χειμῶνος, ἵνα τοῦ ἔαρος ἐπιγινομένου ἀνυστερήτως καὶ ἀνεμπο-
365 δίστως τὴν στρατείαν ἐξάγῃς.

οδ'. Ῥήμασι πειθηνίοις ὁμίλει συνεχῶς τῷ πλήθει τῶν στρατιωτῶν, ὥστε
ὁμονοεῖν αὐτοὺς ἐν τῷ καιρῷ τῆς μάχης, καὶ φιλικῶς αὐτοὺς διακεῖσθαι ἐπιτήδευε, ἵνα ἡδέως ὑπὲρ ἀλλήλων συναγωνίζωνται.

οε'. Ὅταν δημοσίως παρατάξῃς σύμμικτον στρατόν, ἤγουν πεζῶν ὁμοῦ καὶ
370 καβαλλαρίων, τοὺς μὲν πεζοὺς δέκα πλασίον κατὰ τὸ βάθος ἤγουν ἐπὶ δέκα τὸ
πάχος ποιήσεις τοὺς ὀρδίνους· τοὺς δὲ καβαλλαρίους ἐκτάξεις ὥσπερ δύο
κέρατα ἔνθεν κἀκεῖθεν πρὸ τῆς παρατάξεως.

ος'. Στρατιωτῶν γενναίων δοκιμασία γίνεται, ἐὰν ἀγνοούντων αὐτῶν
ἀθρόον κτύπον τινὰ ἤτοι ἦχον μέγαν ἢ τυμπάνου ἢ ἑτέρου τινὸς ἐξαισίου
375 προσφέρῃς ἀπροσδοκήτως. τότε γὰρ τοὺς μὴ καταπλησσομένους, ἀλλ' ἀτρε-
μοῦντας πρὸς τὸν ἐξαίσιον κτύπον, ἐκλέγου ὡς σταθεροὺς καὶ ἀνδρείους, ἐξ ὧν
καὶ ἄρχοντας καταστήσεις.

οζ'. Κατὰ τὸν καιρὸν τοῦ πολέμου δεῖ μὲν εὐχὰς πρὸς Θεὸν καταβαλέσθαι
καὶ σύμμαχον ἐκεῖνον καλεῖν, μὴ μέντοι τῶν προκειμένων ἀγώνων καταμελεῖν ἢ
380 τῶν ὀφειλομένων πράξεων κατολιγωρεῖν. σὺν Θεῷ γὰρ δεῖ καὶ τὰς χεῖρας
σαλεύειν καὶ ὡς ὄργανα παρέχειν ὑπηρετοῦντα. οὔτε γὰρ τοξότης, ἐὰν μὴ ῥίψῃ
τὸ βέλος, εὐστοχήσει ποτέ οὔτε ὁ μὴ μένων, ἀλλὰ φεύγων, κρατήσει τῶν ἐχ-
θρῶν, οὔτε ὅλως ὁ μὴ πράξεως ἀρξάμενος εὐπραγήσει· ἀλλ' εὔχεσθαι μὲν δεῖ | 365ᵛ
τὴν νίκην λαβεῖν τοῦ πολέμου παρὰ Θεοῦ, ὁμοῦ δὲ καὶ τὰ ὅπλα κατέχειν, καὶ
385 μαχόμενον σύμμαχον ἐπικαλεῖσθαι τὸ θεῖον.

οη'. Ὑπό τινος συνηθείας πολλάκις ὁ στρατὸς ἀπὸ συμβόλων ἢ σημείων
τινῶν εἰς δειλίαν εἴωθε τρέπεσθαι, ἀλλ' εἴποτε τοιοῦτόν τι γένηται, ἀναζητήσεις
αὐτός, καὶ εὑρὼν ἀντιμεταλλάξεις αὐτῶν τὴν διάνοιαν διὰ τῆς σῆς ἀγχινοίας

386–390 Cf. ιδ'.703–709.

366 ῥήμασι M ῥήμασιν A | στρατιωτῶν M στρατιωτῶν τοῖς δυναμένοις πείθειν αὐτοὺς A
368 συναγωνίζωνται M ἀγωνίζωνται A    370 πλασίον κατὰ M πλασίονα κατὰ τὸ πάχος
ἤγουν ἐπὶ δέκα A    370–371 ἤγουν…πάχος M om. A    378 καταβαλέσθαι M ποιεῖσθαι A

By all means, it is necessary to honor them reverently and to dignify them with burial and eternal memory. You must, moreover, O general, by your foresight, your concern, and your support, provide assistance to their children, their wives, and their whole household. The soldiers will thus be in good spirits and eager to face the dangers of war, as they look upon the treatment of the dead as something that will happen to themselves after their end, if they are courageous and valiant in the struggle.[54]

73. During the period spent in winter quarters, O general, do not neglect the preparation of the things needed in combat, so that, with the arrival of spring, you may lead your army out without delay and without obstacles.

74. On a regular basis, address the assembled soldiers with words conducive to obedience so they will all be of the same mind at the time of battle. Deal with them in such a manner that they will be kindly disposed and will gladly support one another in combat.

75. When you draw up a mixed army, that is, infantry and cavalry together, for a pitched battle, make the infantry columns ten deep to ten thick and form the cavalry as two horns on either side in front of the battle line.

76. One test of a brave soldier is this. If, without their knowledge, you unexpectedly produce some sort of sudden crashing sound or the heavy beating of a drum or some other unusually loud instrument, then <notice> which men are not struck dumb with fear but are unperturbed by the unusual banging, and from their number select those men as solid and brave and commission them as officers.

77. In time of war it is necessary to offer prayers to God and to invoke him as an ally. Nevertheless, do not completely neglect the struggles before you and do not think lightly of the tasks incumbent on you. With God, you must move your hands and offer them as instruments in his service. The archer will never hit the target if he does not shoot the arrow nor will that man ever overcome the enemy who does not stay in position, but runs away. To sum it up, a person who does not begin a task will not be successful at it. It is certainly necessary to pray to God to obtain victory in battle, but, at the same time, hold on to your weapons and, while you fight, invoke the Divinity as an ally.

78. Under the influence of certain customary practices, the army frequently used to succumb to cowardice because of symbols or certain signs. If something of the sort ever occurs, however, you will personally look into it. After investi-

---

54. Cf. Const. 14 §31; Onasander 3.6.

μεθερμηνεύων τὰ σύμβολα ὡς ἐνδέχεται, ἵνα δι᾽ ὧν εἰς δειλίαν κατέπεσον, διὰ
390  τούτων εἰς θάρσος αὐτοὺς καὶ ἐλπίδας ἀγαθὰς διαναστήσεις.

οθ΄. Νίκης φημιζομένης προθυμότερον πρὸς τὰς μάχας τὸ στράτευμα
γίνεται. ἐὰν τοίνυν διὰ μὲν τοιαύτης φήμης θάρσος ἐμποιήσῃς τοῖς στρατιώταις,
μετ᾽ εὐψυχίας δὲ καὶ ἀνδρείας ἐπιμελῶς ἐγχειρήσῃς τῆς μάχης, ἔλπιζε σὺν Θεῷ
τὴν φημιζομένην νίκην παρέσεσθαι.

395  π΄. Ἦν ποτε καιρὸς ὅτε Σκιπίων Ῥωμαίων ᾑρέθη ἀπὸ ψήφου κοινῆς στρατηγὸς καὶ ἡλικίας ἦν ἐτῶν τῶν ὀκτωκαίδεκα στρατηγικῶν ἀπαρχόμενος ἔργων.
παρευθὺ δὲ τῆς ἀρχῆς ἐκέλευσεν ἀποπέμπεσθαι ἐκ τοῦ στρατοῦ κραββάτους
καὶ τὰς τραπέζας καὶ διάφορα ἐκπώματα καὶ τὰ ἄλλα σκεύη πάντα, πλὴν χύτρας
χαλκῆς καὶ σουβλίου σιδηροῦ καὶ ποτηρίου, τοῖς ἄρχουσι μὲν ἀργύρου, τοῖς δ᾽
400  ἄλλοις ξυλίνου. μὴ λούεσθαι δέ τινα μήτε ἀλείφεσθαι μύρον ἐκέλευσε τὸ
οἱονοῦν. ἀριστᾶν δὲ ὄρθρου ἄπυρον βρῶσιν, δειπνοῦντας δὲ προσφέρεσθαι
κρέας ἢ ὀπτὸν ἢ ἑψητόν, ἀνακλίνεσθαι δὲ ἐπὶ μικρᾶς σκέπης τοὺς ἄρχοντας. καὶ
οὕτως τὸν ὅλον χρόνον τῆς αὐτοῦ στρατηγίας διανύσας, περιβόητος ἐν ταῖς
στρατηγίαις καὶ ταῖς νίκαις ἐγένετο. ἀπεσείετο δὲ καὶ ἀστρολογίας καὶ μαντείας
405  καὶ τὰς ἀπὸ συμβόλων ἢ σημείων δηλώσεις καὶ ὀρνεοσκοπίας καὶ δι᾽ ὀνείρων
μαντείας καὶ τὰς ἄλλας τοιαύτας προγνώσεις τε καὶ κρίσεις καὶ τὰ ἄλλα ὅσα τῆς
ὀφειλομένης προνοίας τὸν στρατηγὸν ἀναστέλλουσι. τοῦτον οὖν ἐὰν μιμήσῃ, ὦ
στρατηγέ, καὶ αὐτὸς τῆς ὁμοίας δόξης ἐκείνῳ καὶ τῶν νικητικῶν ἐπιτεύξῃ
τροπαίων.

410  πα΄. Τὰ τόξα ὅπλα εἰσὶν εὐπόριστα, ἐν καιρῷ δὲ χρείας μεγάλην ἔχει τὴν
ὠφέλειαν. παρακελευόμεθα οὖν σοι διατάξασθαι πᾶσι τοῖς ὑπό σε καὶ κάστροις
καὶ χωρίοις καὶ κωμοπόλεσι καὶ ἁπλῶς ἅπασιν ὥστε, εἰ δυνατόν, ἕκαστον ἄνδρα
ἴδιον τόξον ἔχειν· εἰ δὲ μήγε κατ᾽ οἶκον ἓν τόξον καὶ σαγίττας μέχρι τεσσαράκοντα, καὶ γυμνάζεσθαι ἐν αὐτοῖς καὶ εἰς δυσχωρίας καὶ εἰς ὁμαλοὺς τόπους καὶ
415  εἰς κλεισούρας καὶ εἰς δάση. οἱ μὲν γὰρ στρατιῶται ἐν τοῖς πολέμοις τούτοις
χρήσονται, οἱ δὲ λοιποὶ ἐν τοῖς ἰδίοις τόποις, εἰ ἄρα τύχῃ τῶν ἐχθρῶν αἰφνίδιος
ἐπιδρομὴ κατ᾽ αὐτῶν. καὶ γὰρ καὶ κατὰ πετρῶν ἀκροτόμων ἱστάμενοι ἄνδρες καὶ

---

395–409 Polyaen. 8.16.1–2.

395 ᾑρέθη…κοινῆς Μ προεκρίθη Α    396 καὶ…ὀκτωκαίδεκα Μ ἀπὸ ψήφου κοινῆς καὶ ἐτῶν
ἦν ὀκτωκαίδεκα τῶν Α    397 ἀποπέμπεσθαι ἐκ Μ ἐκβάλλεσθαι Α | στρατοῦ Μ στρατοῦ τούς
τε Α    398 τὰς Α om. Μ    399 ἄρχουσι Μ ἔχουσι Α    400–401 ἐκέλευσε…οἰονοῦν Μ
ἐκελεύσεν οἰοδήποτε Α    401 ἄπυρον…προσφέρεσθαι Μ βρῶμα ἐσθίων μὴ δεόμενον πυρός
πρὸς ἔψησιν δειπνοῦντας δὲ ἐσθίειν Α    407 ἀναστέλλουσι Μ ἀναστέλλουσιν Α
410 εὐπόριστα Μ εὐπορίας ταῦτα δὲ Α    413 ἓν Α ἕνα Μ

gating it, bring the minds of your men around to the opposite, as best you can, by a clever interpretation of the symbols. By taking the very thing that caused them to fall into cowardice, you will raise them up again to courage and good hopes.[55]

79. The rumor of victory makes the army more enthusiastic in fighting. By making use of such a rumor, you can instill courage in your soldiers. In good spirits and with bravery, you will carefully enter into combat. With God's help, you must hope that the rumor of victory will become a reality.

80. There was once a time when Scipio was chosen by common vote of the Romans as general. He was eighteen years old when he began his service as general. As soon as he took office, he ordered that the army should get rid of beds and tables, the variety of drinking cups, and all other such utensils except for bronze pots and iron spits. The officers could have silver drinking cups and the others wooden ones. He gave orders that nobody at all should bathe or anoint himself with perfumed oil. They should breakfast on cold food in the morning, although for dinner they could be served roasted or boiled meat. And the officers could recline under small shelters. He spent the entire term of his generalship in this manner and became very famous because of his strategy and his victories. He rejected astrology and divination and the meanings of symbols and signs and the auguries from birds and divination through dreams and other such modes of prophecy and judgments, as well as all those other things that distract a person from the foresight incumbent on a general. If you imitate him, O general, you too will obtain a glory similar to his, as well as the trophies of victory.[56]

81. Bows are weapons that are easily obtained and are extremely helpful in critical moments. We command you, therefore, to issue orders that, in the fortresses, towns, villages, and, in general, every place under your command, every single man, if possible, should possess a bow, but if not, then one per household and up to forty arrows. He should practice with them in difficult country as well as in level places, in defiles, and in wooded areas. For the soldiers will make use of these in combat and the other men in their own localities, if they happen to be subject to a sudden attack by the enemy. Men stationed amid rocky cliffs,

---

55. Cf. Const. 14 §101.
56. Polyaenus 8.16.1–2.

ἐν στενοῖς τόποις καὶ εἰς δάση ὕλης, πολλὴν ἐμποιήσουσι | τὴν βλάβην τοῖς   A301ᵛ
ἐχθροῖς τοξεύοντες, καὶ οὐ ταχέως θαρρήσουσιν αὐτοῖς ἀδέως ἐπελθεῖν οἱ
420 πολέμιοι, καὶ ἐντεῦθεν ἀνάλωτα τὰ τοιαῦτα χωρία καὶ ἀβλαβῆ διαφυλαχθήσον-
ται, φοβουμένων τῶν πολεμίων τὰς ἐκ τῶν βελῶν πληγάς.

πβ΄. Ἡνίκα Θεὸς παράσχῃ σοι μαχομένῳ τρέψασθαι τοὺς ἐχθρούς, μὴ ἐάσῃς
τοὺς στρατιώτας λύσαντας τὴν τάξιν διαρπάζειν ἢ τὰ ὅπλα ἢ τὰ σκεύη τῶν
πολεμίων, ἵνα μὴ ἀντιστραφέντες βλάβην ποιήσωσι κατὰ τῶν διωκόντων οἱ
425 διωκόμενοι. ἡττηθέντες μὲν γὰρ οὐδὲ τὰ ἴδια σκεύη κερδήσομεν, νικήσαντες δὲ
καὶ τὰ ἡμέτερα καὶ τὰ τῶν πολεμίων ἕξομεν.|

πγ΄. Στρατηγὸς δωρολήπτης πρᾶγμα δεινὸν καὶ ὀλέθριον τῷ στρατεύματι.   A302
δύο γὰρ τὰ μέγιστα ἐντεῦθεν συμβαίνει κακά· καὶ γὰρ καὶ οἱ στρατιῶται πλε-
ονέκτοι ἄποροι γίνονται, καὶ οἱ ἄρχοντες ἄνανδροι προχειρίζονται, ἀπὸ τῶν
430 πρώτων ἕως τῶν ἐσχάτων ἀφορίζοντος τοῦ τῆς δωροληψίας κακοῦ, ἐξ οὗ
στράτευμα κατ’ ἐχθρῶν ἀνδραγαθεῖν οὐ δύναται.

πδ΄. Τοὺς κατασκόπους ἐπιλέγου σταθεροὺς καὶ ὀξεῖς καὶ πιστοὺς καὶ
σπουδαίους, δόξαν μᾶλλον καὶ τιμὴν ἢ χρήματα ἀγαπῶντας. οἱ γὰρ τοιοῦτοι
ὄντες μηνύουσι τὴν ἀλήθειαν, οἱ δὲ ἐλαφροὶ τὴν γνώμην, καὶ δειλοὶ καὶ ὅσοι
435 περὶ τὴν κτῆσιν τῶν χρημάτων σπουδάζουσιν, οὐ δύνανται ἀπαγγέλλειν τὴν
ἀλήθειαν. διὸ καὶ κινδύνου πολλάκις αἴτιοι καὶ αὐτῷ τῷ στρατηγῷ καὶ τῷ στρατεύματι γίνονται.

πε΄. Ῥᾳδίως οἱ στρατιῶται ἐν ταῖς ἐκστρατείαις διὰ δώρων μὲν ἀγαθῶν
καλλίονες γίνονται· ἐν δὲ καιρῷ εἰρήνης ἢ διὰ φόβου ἢ διὰ κολάσεως ἐπὶ τοῖς,
440 ὡς εἰκός, ἁμαρτανομένοις γινομένης ἀνορθοῦνται.

πϛ΄. Ἴσθι ὅτι μᾶλλον κατορθώσεις, ὦ στρατηγέ, λιμῷ καὶ συχναῖς ἐπιδρομαῖς
τὴν τῶν πολεμίων δύναμιν καταλύειν ἢ τοῖς ὅπλοις αὐτὴν πειρώμενος κατα-
στρέφειν.

πζ΄. Ἀσφαλῆ καὶ ἰσχυρὰ καὶ ἀπαθῆ ὄντα τὰ ἡμέτερα κατανοῶν, ἐὰν ἐπ’
445 αὐτοῖς κατάσκοπον κρατήσεις ἐν πολέμου καιρῷ, μὴ κατάσχῃς τοῦτον, ἀλλ’
ἔασον ὡς ἂν ἀπαγγείλας τοῖς πολεμίοις τὰ περὶ τῆς σῆς καταστάσεως κατα-
πλήξῃ τὰ τούτων φρονήματα. ἐὰν δέ τι παρά σοι γινώσκεις ἀσθενές, κόλαζε
τοῦτον, ἵνα τῶν πολεμίων ἐξείποι τὰ μυστήρια, καὶ τελευταῖον ἢ διάφθειρε ἢ
ἀσφαλῶς ἀλλαχοῦ τοῦτον ἔκπεμπε.

---

418 ad ἐμποιήσουσι des. M

432–437 Strat., 8.2.26.   438–440 Strat., 8.2.27.   441–443 Strat., 8.2.28.   444–449 Strat.,
8.2.29.

narrow defiles, and thick woods and shooting their arrows will wreak great damage on the enemy, who will not quickly regain their courage and will not be eager to continue their attack. And so, those areas will not be taken and will be preserved unharmed, for the enemy will fear being wounded by the arrows.[57]

82. When God grants you the favor of routing the enemy in battle, do not permit your soldiers to break formation to plunder the arms and equipment of the enemy lest those who are being pursued wheel around and inflict serious harm on their pursuers. In defeat we will not even hold on to our own equipment, but in victory we will possess our own and that of the enemy.

83. A general who takes bribes is a terrible thing and can bring destruction down on his army. Two of the greatest evils may result from this. The soldiers, as victims of his greed, are left without resources and become greedy themselves, and cowardly men are promoted to be officers. From the first to the last, they are marked by the evil of bribe-taking and, as a result, the army is unable to face the enemy with courage.

84. Choose scouts who are steady, keen-eyed, reliable, serious, and fonder of their reputation than of honors or money. Such men will make accurate reports. But the lighthearted, the timid, and those looking for material gain are not capable of providing accurate information, and so they frequently bring danger upon the general and the army.[58]

85. While on campaign, generous gifts make the soldiers better but, in time of peace, fear and punishment meted out to offenders is more likely to keep them in line.

86. Be aware, O general, that you will be more successful in destroying the enemy's force by hunger and frequent raids than by attempting to overturn them with weapons.

87. If, in time of war, you capture a spy from the enemy among us, and you are sure that our forces are secure, strong, and unharmed, then do not hold him but let him go so that, when he reports to the enemy that you are in such good shape, they will be utterly dismayed. On the other hand, if you know that our forces are weak, treat him roughly to get him to disclose enemy secrets and, finally, put him to death or send him off elsewhere under guard.

57. Cf. *Strat.* 1.1.2–34.
58. For §§84–87 see *Strat.* 8.2.26–29.

450    πη'. Δυνατὰ γενέσθαι καὶ μεγάλα βουλόμενος, ἐμβράδυνε μικρὸν τῇ βουλῇ
ἐρευνῶν τὸ χρήσιμον. ἐπὰν δὲ τὴν πρέπουσαν βεβαιώσῃς γνώμην, ἐπιτέλει τὰ
βουλευθέντα χωρὶς ὑπερθέσεως, μάλιστα ἐν πολέμου καιρῷ. καὶ γὰρ καὶ
Ἀλέξανδρόν ποτε τὸν βασιλέα ἐρωτώμενον, πῶς ἐν ὀλίγοις ἔτεσι τοσαῦτα καὶ
τηλικαῦτα μεγάλα κατώρθωσε πράγματα, λέγεται εἰπεῖν | ὅτι· "οὐδὲν δεόμενον    A302ᵛ
455    τῇ σήμερον ὑπερεθέμην εἰς τὴν αὔριον."

πθ'. Ὅταν χρεία σοι γενήσεται συμμάχων, οὐ δεῖ σε τούτους μετὰ τοῦ οἰκείου συμμιγνύειν στρατοῦ, μάλιστα ἑτέρας ὑπάρχοντας πίστεως. ἀλλὰ καὶ τὰ
ἄπληκτα αὐτῶν καὶ τὰς ὁδοιπορίας ἰδίᾳ καὶ χωρὶς γίνεσθαι παρασκεύαζε, καὶ
παντοίως αὐτῶν ἀπόκρυβε τὰ στρατηγήματα τῆς σῆς παρατάξεως, ἵνα μὴ ταῦτα
460    γινώσκοντες, ἐν καιρῷ ἔχθρας εὐμηχανώτεροι γένωνται ἐν ταῖς κατά σου
πολεμικαῖς συμπλοκαῖς. ἀλλὰ μηδὲ πλείονα στρατὸν ἐπάγου τῶν σῶν δυνάμεων, ἵνα μή, καθὼς καὶ ἐν ἄλλοις ἡμῖν εἴρηται, ἢ εὐκόλως παρ' αὐτῶν ἐπιβουλευ-
θῇς ἢ τῆς σῆς γῆς ἐγκρατεῖς γένωνται.

ϟ'. Στρατηγὸς εἰρήνης ἐπιθυμῶν εὐτρεπὴς ἔστω πρὸς τὸν πόλεμον. ἐὰν οὖν
465    βούλει πτοῆσαι τοὺς πολεμίους καὶ εἰρήνην αἰτεῖσθαι παρά σου, ἕτοιμον ἀεὶ
πρὸς τὸν κατ' αὐτῶν πόλεμον σεαυτὸν ἀποδείκνυε. οὕτως γὰρ δειλιάσουσιν καὶ
τὴν εἰρήνην ἀσπάσονται.

ϟα'. Τρυφὴν μηδέποτε ἀγαπήσεις, ὦ στρατηγέ, μάλιστα δὲ σὺν τῷ στρατῷ
διάγων· κοινὸς ὄλεθρος αὕτη καὶ τῷ στρατηγῷ καὶ τῷ στρατεύματι γίνεται.

470    ϟβ'. Οὔτε ἐν ταῖς εὐπραγίαις ἐπαίρεσθαί σε χρεὼν οὔτε ἐν ταῖς δυσπραγίαις
καταπίπτειν. οὐδὲ γὰρ δεῖ σε τοιοῦτον τῷ στρατεύματι φαίνεσθαι, ἀλλὰ σταθε-
ρὸν ἀεὶ καὶ πρὸς τὰ τοιαῦτα ἀνεπίγνωστον. τὸ γὰρ ταχέως πρὸς χαρὰν ἐπαίρεσθαι φανερῶς καὶ πρὸς λύπην πάλιν προδήλως καταπίπτειν, χαύνης ἐστὶν ψυχῆς
καὶ ἀναξίας στρατηγοῦ.

475    ϟγ'. Ὑπερβολὴ παντὸς πράγματος οὐκ ἀπόδεκτόν ἐστι, διὸ μήτε λίαν φοβερὸς τοῖς ὑπηκόοις ὑπάρχῃς, ὦ στρατηγέ, μήτε λίαν ἐπιεικής· ἀμφότερα γὰρ
ἀνάρμοστα τῷ στρατηγῷ πρὸς τὸ στράτευμα γίνεται. ὁ μὲν γὰρ πολὺς φόβος
μῖσος ἀπογεννᾷ, ἡ δὲ πολλὴ ἐπιείκεια καταφρόνησιν ἐργάζεται. ἀρίστη δὲ ἡ τοῦ
μέσου διάθεσις, ὥστε σύμμετρόν σε εἶναι πρὸς ἀμφότερα καὶ μήτε τὰς ἐπεξελεύ-
480    σεις τῶν ἁμαρτανομένων μετὰ ἀπονοίας ποιεῖσθαι καὶ ἀμέτρου ὀργῆς μήτε

---

450–455 *Strat.*, 8.2.31.  456–463 *Strat.*, 8.2.80.  464–467 *Strat.*,  8.2.60; Arist. *Pol.*,
7.1333A35.  468–469 *Strat.*, 8.2.58.  470–474 *Strat.*, 8.2.32.  475–482 *Strat.*, 8.2.35.

88. In considering what is important and what is possible, take your time as you turn your mind to discerning what is to your advantage, but once you have reached a firm and fitting decision, without any delay put your plans into action, especially in time of war. Alexander the emperor was once asked: "How have you managed to accomplish so many great deeds in a few years?" He is said to have replied: "Nothing that ought to be done today did I put off until tomorrow."[59]

89. When you are in need of allies, you must not mix them in with your own troops, especially if they are of another faith. Make sure that they set up their own camp and that they march by themselves apart from us. By all means hide the tactical plans for your formations from them. If a period of hostilities ensues, they may use such knowledge to great advantage in military engagements against you. Do not invite an army larger than your own. Otherwise, as we noted elsewhere, they might easily conspire against you or take possession of your land.[60]

90. A general who desires peace must be ready for war. If, therefore, you wish to scare the enemy and have them seek either conflict or peace with you, always show yourself prepared to wage war against them. This will make them so nervous that they will embrace peace.[61]

91. Never be a lover of luxury, O general, especially when you are staying with your army. This results in wholesale destruction, both of the general and of his army.[62]

92. You must not be unduly elated by success or utterly cast down by failure. You must not give any such impression to the army, but always appear steady and inscrutable when it comes to such things. To be quickly and obviously exalted by joy and clearly to be cast down again into sorrow is the mark of a frivolous spirit and unworthy of a general.[63]

93. Doing anything to excess is unacceptable. You should not be too frightening to your subjects, O general, nor should you be too lenient. Both make the general unfit to command the army. Great fear gives birth to hatred and great leniency results in being despised. It is best to take the middle course.

59. *Strat.* 8.2.31.

60. *Strat.* 8.2.80.

61. *Strat.* 8.2.60; Aristotle, *Politics* 7.1333A35; Cf. Anna Komnene, *Alexiad.* 12.5.4; Veg. 3.praef.8.

62. *Strat.* 8.2.58.

63. For §§92–94 see *Strat.* 8.2.32, 35, 34.

πάλιν παντελῶς ἀφιέναι | ἀτιμώρητα, ὥστε εἰς ἀναρχίαν δοκεῖν περιΐστασθαί A303
σου τὴν ἀρχήν.

ϟδ΄. Ἐν πολέμου καιρῷ βουλεύου μὲν ἐν νυκτὶ τὸ πρακτέον, τὰ δὲ δόξαντα
τῇ βουλῇ ἐπιτέλει μεθ' ἡμέραν. οὐ γὰρ ὁ αὐτὸς ὀφείλει καιρὸς εἶναι βουλῆς τε
485  καὶ πράξεως.

ϟε΄. Νικητὴς καὶ φοβερὸς τοῖς πολεμίοις λογισθήσεται ὁ στρατηγός, οὐχ ὁ
ἐν τῷ λέγειν μόνον καὶ ἐγκαυχᾶσθαι κατ' αὐτῶν δυνατός, ἀλλ' ὁ ταῖς πράξεσιν
αὐτοῦ τοὺς λόγους βεβαίους ἀποδεικνύς.

ϟϛ΄. Ὅταν ὀλίγον ἔχῃς στράτευμα, τὸ τῶν πολεμίων δὲ εἰς πλῆθός ἐστιν,
490  σπεῦδε καταλαβεῖν μικρότερον χωρίον καὶ στενώτερον καὶ σύμμετρον τῷ σῷ
στρατεύματι. τὸ γὰρ περισσὸν τῶν πολεμίων πλῆθος | ἄχρηστον γενήσεται, τοῦ  366
τόπου μὴ ἐπιδεχομένου τὸ πλέον.

ϟζ΄. Συνθήκας καὶ ἀνοχὰς πολέμου πρὸς τοὺς πολεμίους ποιούμενος, μὴ διὰ
ταύτας ἐν ἀμελείᾳ διατελῇς, ἀλλὰ μᾶλλον μείζοσι καὶ ἀκριβεστέραις περιλάμ-
495  βανε ταῖς φυλακαῖς τὸ στρατόπεδον ἢ τὴν χώραν. ἐὰν γὰρ παρασπονδῆσαι
βουληθῶσιν οἱ πολέμιοι, ἐκεῖνοι μὲν μετὰ τῆς τοῦ Θεοῦ δυσμενείας καὶ ἀπειλῆς
ἕξουσι τὸ ἄπιστον, σὺ δὲ μετὰ τῆς ἀσφαλείας εὑρισκόμενος ἕξεις τὸ πιστὸν μετὰ
τῆς τοῦ Θεοῦ βοηθείας. ἀνάξιον γὰρ στρατηγοῦ τὸ λέγειν· "τοῦτο οὐ προσεδό-
κων."

500      ϟη΄. Καὶ τοῦτο δέ σοι ἀναγκαῖον, ὦ στρατηγέ, πρὸς στρατηγικὴν τελειότητα,
τὸ συλλογίζεσθαι καὶ γινώσκειν ἀκριβῶς ἐκ τῆς πείρας τὸ τῶν πολεμίων στρατόπεδον πόσον ἐστίν. τοῦτο δὲ γίνεται, ἐὰν προγυμνασάμενος γινώσκῃς πόσος
τόπος καὶ ποῖος πόσους στρατιώτας ἐπιδέχεσθαι δύναται, καὶ ὡς ἐν ἄλλοις ἡμῖν
προδιώρισται.

505      ϟθ΄. Ἄξιον δέ σοι, ὦ στρατηγέ, ὥσπερ τὴν εἰρημένην γνῶσιν τῆς τῶν πολεμίων στρατείας ὀφείλεις ἔχειν, οὕτως καὶ τοὺς πολεμίους λανθάνειν τὸ πλῆθος
τῶν σῶν στρατευμάτων. ὅταν δὲ βούλῃ λαθεῖν τοὺς ἐχθροὺς τῆς σῆς δυνάμεως
τὸ πλῆθος, πυκνοὺς περιπατεῖν ἢ ἑστάναι παράγγελλε τοὺς στρατιώτας. ἡ γὰρ
συνέχεια καὶ σφίγξις σφάλλειν ποιεῖ τὴν ὅρασιν τῶν πολεμίων, καὶ ἀκριβῶς
510  εἰκάζειν τὸν ἀριθμὸν τῆς σῆς δυνάμεως οὐκ ἐᾷ. ὁμοίως καὶ ἐπὶ τοῦ ἐναντίου, εἰ
βούλῃ παραδεῖξαι τὴν σὴν δύναμιν πολλήν, ὀλίγην οὖσαν, ἀραιοτέρους καὶ

---

491 ad ἄχρηστον de novo inc. M

---

483–485 Strat., 8.2.34.   486–488 Strat., 8.2.33.   489–492 Strat., 8.2.37.   493–499 Strat.,
8.2.36; cf. supra, 138–142.   500–504 Strat., 8.2.37.   505–514 Strat., 8.2.38.

---

494–495 περιλάμβανε ταῖς M κατασφάλιζε A   505 ὦ στρατηγέ M om. A   508 πυκνοὺς…
παράγγελλε M παράγγελλε πυκνοὺς περιπατεῖν ἢ ἵστασθαι A   510 ἐᾷ M συγχωρεῖ A

You should show moderation in both respects, not inflicting punishment on offenders senselessly and with immeasurable anger, nor, at the same time, should you dismiss them totally unpunished. Otherwise, your command will devolve into anarchy.

94. In time of war, during the night, plan what you have to do and, during the day, carry out what you have decided. For the same time is not suitable both for planning and for taking action.

95. The general who gains the reputation of being victorious is not the one who is powerful in words only and in boasting against the enemy, but the one who shows by his actions that he means what he says.[64]

96. When you have a small army and the enemy has a large one, make haste to occupy a smaller space, more narrow and a better fit for the size of your army. The superior numbers of the enemy will prove useless, for the space will not accommodate the great number.[65]

97. After having agreed to a treaty or a truce with the enemy, do not for that reason become careless. Rather, surround your camp or location with stronger and more alert guards. If the enemy decides to break the agreement, they will incur, along with disfavor and threats from God, <the reputation> of faithlessness. You, however, will remain safe and, with the help of God, will enjoy <the reputation> of being true to your word. It is unworthy of a general to say: "I did not expect that."[66]

98. This too is essential for you, O general, if you are to become expert in military matters, namely, from experience to calculate and reach an accurate knowledge of the strength of the enemy's army. This can be done if you train yourself ahead of time to recognize how much space and what kind of space is able to accommodate a certain number of soldiers, as we have prescribed for you elsewhere.[67]

99. It is very important for you, O general, to acquire a good knowledge of the enemy's army, as we have noted, and by the same token, to conceal from the enemy the size of your own armed forces. When you want to hide the size of your force from the enemy, order the soldiers to march or to stand in place in close formation. Their compact and tight formation leads the enemy observers to make mistakes and keeps them from estimating the number of your troops

64. *Strat.* 8.2.33.
65. *Strat.* 8.2.37.
66. *Strat.* 8.2.36; cf. *supra*, §27.
67. *Strat.* 8.2.37.

περιπατεῖν καὶ ἵστασθαι τοὺς στρατιώτας ποιήσεις, ὡς ἂν καὶ πλείονα τοῦ
συμμέτρου τόπον περιλαμβάνωσιν. ἀμφότερα γὰρ ἐν καιρῷ ἰδίῳ γενόμενα καὶ
χρείᾳ χρήσιμα πρὸς ἀπάτην τῶν ἐχθρῶν εὑρίσκεται.

515 ρ΄. Ἴσης καὶ ὁμοίας οὔσης τῆς τε τῶν πολεμίων παρασκευῆς καὶ τῆς ἡμετέρας, ὁ κάλλιον παρατασσόμενος στρατηγός, εἴτε σὺ εἴτε ὁ πολέμιος, μᾶλλον
πλεονεκτήσει, περιττὴν ἔχων τῆς δυνάμεως τὴν ἐκ τῶν στρατηγημάτων ἢ
τάξεων ἰσχύν.

ρα΄. Μὴ πρώτους ἐάσῃς παρά σε τὴν οἰκείαν δύναμιν τοὺς ἐναντίους ἐκτά-
520 ξαι, ἀλλὰ σπεῦδε πρότερος ἐκείνων τὴν παράταξίν σου διατάξαι. ἐὰν γὰρ πρότερος φθάσῃς παρατάξασθαι, σὺ μὲν ὃ βούλῃ κατ᾽ ἐξουσίαν ὡς ἕτοιμος πράξεις, ὁ
δὲ πολέμιος οὐδὲ τοῦ καθοπλισθῆναι τάχα λάβοι καιρόν, τὴν σὴν ταχεῖαν
φοβούμενος ἐπέλευσιν.

ρβ΄. Οὕτως οὖν ἐὰν προεκτάξῃς καὶ κατὰ τὴν συμβολὴν ἐξ ἑτοίμου τοῖς
525 ἐναντίοις ἐγχειρήσῃς ἀσφαλῶς, θάρσος μὲν τῷ σῷ στρατεύματι ἐμποιήσεις,
δειλίαν δὲ τοῖς πολεμίοις ἐνθήσεις.

ργ΄. Νόμον ἔχε | ἀπαράβατον, τὸ πολλὴν ποιεῖσθαι τῶν πληγάτων στρατιω- 366ᵛ
τῶν τὴν πρόνοιαν. ἐὰν γὰρ ἀμελήσῃς αὐτῶν, τοὺς λοιποὺς στρατιώτας ἐθελοκα-
κοῦντας ἐν ταῖς μάχαις καὶ λυπουμένους εὑρήσεις. καὶ οὐ μόνον τοῦτο, ἀλλὰ
530 καὶ αὐτοὺς τοὺς τραυματισθέντας, καὶ δι᾽ ἐπιμελείας δυναμένους ἀνασωθῆναι,
διὰ ῥαθυμίαν ἀπολέσεις.

ρδ΄. Ὅταν εἰς φυγὴν τρέψῃς τοὺς πολεμίους, ἀπέχεσθαι τῆς πραίδας παράγγελλε τοῖς στρατιώταις, ἵνα μὴ περὶ ταύτην διασπειρομένους καὶ ἐν αὐτῇ ἀσχολουμένους, εὑρόντες οἱ πολέμιοι ἐπιβουλεύσουσιν αὐτοῖς καὶ διαφθείρουσιν.
535 ἀλλ᾽ οἱ μὲν στρατιῶται ἐχέσθωσαν τῆς διώξεως μετὰ ἀσφαλείας, οἱ δὲ ἐπὶ τῇ
συλλογῇ τῆς πραίδας τεταγμένοι, οἵτινες καὶ τοὺς τραυματίας στρατιώτας ἐν
αὐτῇ τῇ μάχῃ ἀναλέξονται καὶ θεραπεύσουσιν, αὐτοὶ καὶ τὰ τῶν τεθνηκότων
πολεμίων σκῦλα συλλέγοντες, καὶ τοῖς δεκάρχαις παραδιδόντες, ὡς καὶ ἐν

---

515–518 Strat., 8.2.73. 519–523 Strat., 8.2.40. 524–526 Strat., 8.2.41. 527–531 Strat.,
8.2.43. 532–540 Strat., 8.2.44.

---

513 ἰδίῳ M ἰδίῳ καὶ χρεία A 514 χρείᾳ M om. A 517 περιττὴν M περισσὴν A
519 τὴν...ἐναντίους M trsp. A 519–520 ἐκτάξαι M παρατάξαι A 520 σπεῦδε M
σπούδαζε A 520–521 πρότερος φθάσῃς M προλάβῃς A 521 ἕτοιμος πράξεις M trsp. A
527 πληγάτων M πληττομένων A 529 ἐν...λυπουμένους M trsp. A 532 πολεμίους
ἀπέχεσθαι M πολεμίους παράγγελλε τοῖς στρατιώταις ἀντέχεσθαι A 532–533 παράγ-
γελλε...στρατιώταις M om. A 535 ἐχέσθωσαν...διώξεως M διωκέτωσαν A | ἐπὶ M περὶ A
536 τραυματίας M τραυματιζομένους A 538 σκῦλα M ὅπλα A

with any accuracy. In like manner, do the opposite. If you want to demonstrate that your force is a large one, when in reality it is small, have the soldiers march and stand in open order, so they will take up more space than is proportionately theirs. Both of these, done at the right time and as the situation requires, will be found useful in deceiving the enemy.[68]

100. When the armament of both the enemy and ourselves are equal and of the same quality, that general who is better at forming for battle, either you or the enemy general, is more likely to prevail—<especially> if he has additional capability, the strength <that comes> from stratagems or tactics.[69]

101. You should not allow your adversaries to assume their formation before you line up your own force. Make haste to establish your battle line before they do theirs. If you are the first to get your troops into formation, then, since you are ready, you are free to take what action you want. The enemy, though, may not even have time to arm themselves, fearful of a sudden attack by you.[70]

102. If, therefore, you have gotten into formation first and are ready for the charge, you may safely launch your attack against the enemy. You will instill confidence in your army, and cowardice in that of the enemy.[71]

103. Keep this law inviolate: devote great care to wounded soldiers. If you neglect them, you will note that the rest of the troops will be distressed and deliberately will not fight well in battle. Even more so, because of your indifference, you may lose the wounded men themselves who, with some care, could have been saved.[72]

104. When you have put the enemy to flight, order your soldiers to refrain from plundering, so that the enemy may not come upon them all caught up in this, and set traps and destroy them. But let the soldiers carry on the pursuit in a safe manner. <The deputies> are the men detailed for the collection of plunder, who are also to pick up the soldiers wounded in the battle and care for them. They are to gather the spoils from the enemy dead and hand them over to the dekarchs, as we have mentioned elsewhere, who should hold on to them so they

68. *Strat.* 8.2.38.
69. *Strat.* 8.2.73.
70. *Strat.* 8.2.40.
71. *Strat.* 8.2.41.
72. *Strat.* 8.2.43.

ἄλλοις ἡμῖν εἴρηται, παραφυλάξουσιν αὐτά, ὥστε διαμερισθῆναι ἐξ ἴσου κατὰ
540  τὸν περὶ αὐτῶν ὁρισθέντα τύπον.

ρε΄. Ὑποπτεύων στρατηγὸς συχνότερον τὰ τῶν πολεμίων ἐπιτηδεύματα
ἀσφαλής μοι δοκεῖ κατά τε τὸν πόλεμον καὶ τὴν ἄλλην αὐτοῦ διαγωγὴν ἀναδειχθῆναι.

ρς΄. Ἁμάρτημα στρατηγοῦ μέγιστον οἶδα τὸ μιᾷ μάχῃ φθαρῆναι τὸ πολὺ τοῦ
545  στρατεύματος. ἐὰν γὰρ νουνεχῶς τὴν κατὰ τῶν πολεμίων ποιήσηται παράταξιν
καὶ μετὰ φρονήσεως περιστρέφηται, κἂν συμβῇ τι πταῖσμα περὶ τὸν ἑαυτοῦ
στρατόν, ἢ εὐτάκτως ἀναχωρήσῃ ἢ ταχέως τὴν ἧτταν ἀναμαχέσηται.

ρζ΄. Λυπήσει τοὺς πολεμίους ἡ μετὰ εὐταξίας καὶ ἁρμοδία παρά σου γινομένη παράταξις καὶ οὕτως φυλαττομένη ἐν ὅλῳ τῷ τῆς μάχης καιρῷ· μέγιστον
550  γὰρ ἐν παρατάξει κεφάλαιον καὶ πρὸς σωτηρίαν βέβαιον τὸ φυλάττειν τοὺς
μαχομένους τήν τε τάξιν αὐτῶν καὶ τὰ μεταξὺ διαστήματα.

ρη΄. Ἥλιον καὶ ἄνεμον καὶ κονιορτὸν ὄπισθεν μὲν ποίει τοῦ σοῦ στρατεύματος, κατὰ πρόσωπον δὲ τῶν πολεμίων. τοῦτο γὰρ πάνυ συμφέρον εὑρήσεις· οἱ
γὰρ πολέμιοι τὴν ὅρασιν συσχεθέντες, ἢ τὴν ἀναπνοὴν ἐπεχόμενοι καὶ κρατού-
555  μενοι ἢ παρὰ τοῦ ἀνέμου τυπτόμενοι, ταχεῖάν σοι παραδώσουσι τὴν νίκην.

ρθ΄. Θρασὺν ὄντα τὸν πολέμιον, ὦ στρατηγέ, εἰς ἄκαιρον προπέτειαν ἐκκάλει καὶ ματαίας κινήσεις. ἐὰν δέ ἐστιν δειλός, ἐν ταχείαις αὐτὸν ἐπελεύσεσι καὶ
συνεχέσι κατάπληττε. δεῖ γάρ σε γινώσκειν τοῦ στρατηγοῦ τῶν πολεμίων τὴν
διάθεσιν, καὶ πρὸς ταύτην κεχρῆσθαι τοῖς σοῖς στρατηγήμασιν.

560  ρι΄. Ἱκανὸς ὢν ἐν τῷ λέγειν, ὦ στρατηγέ, καὶ τοὺς δειλιῶντας πολλάκις εἰς
μάχην ἀναστήσεις, καὶ τὰς ἐν τοῖς στρατοπέδοις συμφορὰς εὐκόλως παραμυ-
θήσῃ, | καὶ τοὺς ἀνδρείους μᾶλλον ἐπιρρώσεις, καὶ πολλῶν ἀγαθῶν διὰ τῆς σῆς  367
ἔμφρονος δημηγορίας τὸν ὑπήκοον στρατὸν ἀναπλήσεις.

ρια΄. Νήφειν ὀφείλεις καὶ λίαν ὑπάρχειν ἐγρήγορος καὶ μᾶλλον τῶν ἄλλων
565  στρατιωτῶν τῶν πολεμικῶν μετέχειν πόνων, ὦ στρατηγέ, ὀλίγου δὲ τοῦ κέρ-

---

544–547 *Strat.*, 8.2.45.  548–551 *Strat.*, 8.2.42.  552–555 *Strat.*, 8.2.39.  556–559 *Strat.*,
8.2.49.  560–563 *Strat.*, 8.2.74; Onas. 1.13.  564–567 *Strat.*, 8.2.51.

---

547 ἀναμαχέσηται Μ ἀνακαλέσεται Α   548 ἁρμοδία Μ ἁρμοδίως Α   556–557 ἐκκάλει…
κινήσεις Μ ματαίας κινήσεις ἐγκαλοῦ Α   558 συνεχέσι κατάπληττε Μ πυκναῖς κατάπληττε
αὐτὸν Α   559 κεχρῆσθαι…στρατηγήμασιν Μ ἐπιτηδεύειν τὰ στρατηγήματα Α
562 ἐπιρρώσεις Μ ἐνισχύσεις Α   563 ἔμφρονος Μ ἔμφρονος καὶ συνετῆς Α | ἀναπλήσεις Μ
ἐμπλήσεις Α   564 καὶ μᾶλλον Μ ὦ στρατηγὲ καὶ πλέον Α | ἄλλων Μ om. Α   565 τῶν…
στρατηγέ Μ μετέχειν τῶν πόνων τῶν πολεμικῶν καὶ Α

can be distributed on an equal basis, according to the regulations prescribed for them.[73]

105. A general who is constantly suspicious of the preparations of the enemy impresses me as giving proof that he is secure in war and in the rest of his conduct.

106. The greatest failing in a general that I know of is to have most of his army destroyed in one battle. If he forms his battle line against the enemy in an intelligent manner and maneuvers it with prudence, then, even if something unfortunate happens to his army, he may withdraw in good order or quickly retrieve the defeat.[74]

107. You will hurt the enemy by drawing up a suitable battle line in good order and keeping it as such during the entire period of battle. In the battle line the most important point and the one that assures safety is for the fighting men to maintain their formation and the intervals between the lines.[75]

108. See that the sun, wind, and dust are behind your army but in the face of the enemy. You will find this extremely helpful. When the enemy's vision is obscured, his breathing is constrained and difficult, and he is buffeted by the wind, all this will quickly present you with victory.[76]

109. General, when the enemy acts boldly, entice him into premature, reckless action and useless maneuvers. If he is on the timid side, hit him hard with constant and rapid attacks. You must know the disposition of the enemy general and employ your own stratagems accordingly.[77]

110. With some skill in speaking, O general, you will often arouse the faint-hearted to battle and readily counteract despondency in the army and offer even more strength to the brave and, by your intelligence and public speaking, you will present the army under your command with many benefits.[78]

111. You ought to be watchful and very alert and, more than the other soldiers, do your share of the wartime tasks, O general, but with little recom-

---

73. *Strat.* 8.2.44.
74. *Strat.* 8.2.45.
75. *Strat.* 8.2.42.
76. *Strat.* 8.2.39.
77. *Strat.* 8.2.49.
78. *Strat.* 8.2.74; Onasander 1.13.

δους. οὕτως γὰρ καὶ τὴν παρὰ πάντων εὔνοιαν μετὰ δόξης κτήσῃ καὶ φιλούμενος ὑπ' αὐτῶν συναγωνιζομένους σοι προθύμως ἐν τοῖς κινδύνοις ἕξεις.

ριβ'. Ὅταν, μετὰ νίκην ἣν ὁ Θεός σοι παράσχῃ, ἐπιζητῇ ὁ πολέμιος εἰρήνην
ἐπωφελῆ, μὴ γίνου ἀκαμπής, ἀλλ' ὑπάκουε τούτῳ καὶ εἰρήνευε, ἐννοῶν τὸ τῶν
570   πολέμων καὶ τῆς τύχης ἄδηλον.

ριγ'. Ὑπομιμνήσκου ἀεὶ καὶ τῶν πάλαι σοι εἰρημένων παρὰ τῆς ἡμῶν βασιλείας, ὦ στρατηγέ, ὅτι μᾶλλον τὴν ἐπιμέλειάν τε καὶ πρόνοιαν τῶν ὅπλων
χρεωστεῖς ποιεῖσθαι ἤπερ τῶν ἐπιτηδείων περὶ τὰ ὅπλα. οἶδας γὰρ ὅτι τὰ
ἐπιτήδεια μὲν οἷον διατροφὰς καὶ τὰ ἄλλα ἀπὸ τῆς χώρας τῶν πολεμίων πορίζε-
575   σθαι δυνατόν ἐστιν, ὅπλων δὲ χωρὶς ἢ τούτων ἐπιλιπόντων τοῖς χρῄζουσιν οὐ
κρατήσεις τῶν δυσμενῶν.

ριδ'. Θαρσαλέως ἀναφωνῆσαν μεγαλόφωνον στράτευμα καὶ ἐπιτήδειον
πρὸς ἀλαλαγμὸν καταπλήξει πάντως τὴν τῶν πολεμίων παράταξιν.

ριε'. Ἐὰν ἐν πλήθει τοξοτῶν οἱ πολέμιοι πεποίθασιν, ὑγροτέρους ἀέρας
580   ἐπιτηρεῖ διὰ τὸ ἁπαλώτερα γίνεσθαι τὰ τόξα. οὕτως γὰρ τὴν πρὸς τοὺς ἐναντίους ποιούμενος συμπλοκὴν εὐκαταφρόνητα αὐτῶν καταστήσεις τὰ βέλη.

ρις'. Ὁ ταῖς οἰκείαις καλλωπιζόμενος πράξεσι στρατηγὸς ἐκεῖνός ἐστιν
ἄριστος, ἀλλ' οὐχ ὁ ἀπὸ τοῦ γένους λαμπρός, ὥσπερ οὐδὲ χρυσέα λόγχη
χρησίμη πρὸς πόλεμον, ἀλλὰ σιδηρέα καὶ ἄκρως ἠκονημένη.

585   ριζ'. Ὑψηλὸς τὴν διάνοιαν λογισθήσῃ ὅταν οὐ τὰ παρόντα μόνον καὶ προσ-
πίπτοντα διοικῇς ὀρθῶς, ὦ στρατηγέ, ἀλλ' ὅταν τοῦ μέλλοντος τὴν δέουσαν
ποιήσῃ καὶ φροντίδα καὶ πρόνοιαν.

ριη'. Ἡδονῆς κρατεῖν καὶ ἐν παντὶ καιρῷ ἄριστόν ἐστιν· στρατηγῷ δὲ μάλιστα ἐν πολέμου καιρῷ λίαν ὑπάρχει τοῦτο χρησιμώτατον.

590   ριθ'. Μήτε μάχης ἐπικινδύνου καὶ πολλὴν ἐχούσης ἀδηλίαν ἑκουσίως ἀπάρχου, μήτε τοὺς παραβούλως μᾶλλον δ' ἐπιβούλως χρησαμένους ποτὲ τοῖς

---

566–567 φιλούμενος M ἀγαπώμενος A   569 τούτῳ M αὐτῷ A   573 ἤπερ…τὰ² M ἢ τὴν
τῶν ἐπιτηδείων τὰ μὲν γὰρ A   574 μὲν M om. A   574–576 ἀπὸ…δυσμενῶν M δυνατόν
ἐστιν τῆς τῶν πολεμίων χώρας ἀναλαμβάνεσθαι χωρὶς δὲ πολεμικῶν ὅπλων οὐ δυνήσῃ
πολεμίων κρατῆσαι A   577 ἀναφωνῆσαν M καὶ τολμηρῶς ἀναβοῆσαν A   578 ἀλαλαγμὸν
M τὸ ῥύεσθαι καὶ ἀλαλάζειν A   579 πεποίθασιν M θαρρῶσιν A   581 συμπλοκὴν M μάχην
A | καταστήσεις…βέλη M τὰ βέλη ποιήσεις A   583 ὥσπερ M κἂν γὰρ A   585 μόνον M
μόνα A   586 ὅταν M ὅταν καὶ A   587 καὶ¹ M om. A   589 τοῦτο M om. A   590 καὶ…
ἐχούσης M πολλὴν A   591 τοὺς…χρησαμένους A τοῖς … χρησαμένοις M

pense. In this way you will enhance your reputation and gain the goodwill of all; you will be loved by them and you will have them eagerly fighting along with you in time of danger.[79]

112. When the enemy, after God has granted you victory, should seek terms of peace, do not be rigid, but listen graciously to them and make peace. Keep in mind the uncertainties of war and of fortune.

113. Always bear in mind what Our Majesty said to you a long time ago, O general, namely, that you are obliged to devote greater attention and forethought to the weapons than to equipment only. You know that it is possible to procure equipment such as food, supplies, and other things in enemy territory. But without weapons, or if there is a shortage of them for those who want them, you will not overcome your adversary.

114. An army that boldly shouts out its war cries loud and clear is able to strike great terror into the enemy battle line.[80]

115. If the enemy relies on a large force of archers, watch for fairly wet weather because it weakens the bows. Then, when you launch your charge against the enemy, you will nullify the effect of their missiles.[81]

116. That general is best who has distinguished himself by his own deeds, not the one who is illustrious because of his family. A golden lance is not useful in combat, but an iron one, perfectly sharpened, is.[82]

117. You will be considered highly intelligent when you correctly manage not only matters of immediate concern, O general, but also when you show proper concern and forethought for the future.[83]

118. To keep pleasure under control is best at all times, but for a general it is extremely expedient in wartime.[84]

119. Do not willingly enter upon a hazardous and highly uncertain battle. Refrain from emulating those who once engaged in such hazardous, not to say

79. For §§111–113 see *Strat.* 8.2.51–53.

80. *Strat.* 8.2.46.

81. *Strat.* 8.2.48.

82. *Strat.* 8.2.54.

83. *Strat.* 8.2.55.

84. *Strat.* 8.2.66.

πράγμασι καὶ θαυμασθέντας διὰ τύχην μηδὲ τούτους ζηλοῦν καταδέχου. ἀλλ᾽ ὅταν χρεία γένηται πολέμου, τοὺς μὲν πολεμίους ὑποδέχου μετὰ ἀσφαλείας, ταῖς δὲ οἰκείαις ἐπιβολαῖς ὡς ἂν δοκιμάσῃς εἶναί σοι τὸ χρήσιμον καὶ συμφέρον
595 ἑκάστοτε κέχρησο. τύχη μὲν γὰρ ἅπαξ ἐνίκησεν καὶ πολλάκις ἔπταισεν, στρατη- γία δὲ διαφόροις τέχναις κε|χρημένη πολλάκις μὲν ἐνίκησεν, πρὸς ἅπαξ δ᾽ ἴσως   367ᵛ ἔπταισεν.

ρκʹ. Ὀλέσεις σου τοὺς ὑποχειρίους, ὦ στρατηγέ, ἐὰν ὑπάρξεις χρημάτων ἐραστής, καὶ οὐ μόνον τοῖς οἰκείοις ὀλέθριος ὑπάρχεις φιλοχρήματος ὤν, ἀλλὰ
600 καὶ τοῖς πολεμίοις γενήσῃ εὐκαταφρόνητος.

ρκαʹ. Νουνεχῶς ἐπίβαλλε καὶ μετὰ πολλῆς συζητήσεως τοῖς πολεμικοῖς ἔργοις. ἐὰν γὰρ τοῖς λοιποῖς πράγμασι πταίσας τις, μετ᾽ ὀλίγον ἴσως τὸ πταῖσμα ἐπανορθώσασθαι δύναται. ἐν δὲ τοῖς κατὰ πόλεμον ἁμαρτήμασιν ἡ βλάβη μένει· οἱ γὰρ τεθνηκότες διεφθάρησαν.

605 ρκβʹ. Λογίζου καὶ κατανόει τοῦ ἀπλίκτου τὸ χωρίον, ὦ στρατηγέ, ἐάν ἐστιν ὑγιεινὸν καὶ σωτήριον ἢ νοσερὸν καὶ τοῖς οἰκείοις πολέμιον, καὶ αὐτὰς δὲ τὰς ἐπιτηδείους χρείας, ὕδωρ καὶ ξύλα καὶ χόρτον, ἐὰν πλησίον εἰσίν. εἰ γὰρ πόρρω- θέν εἰσιν, δυσχερής ἐστι καὶ ἐπικίνδυνος ἡ τούτων συγκομιδή, καὶ μάλιστα πολεμίων ἐπικειμένων. καὶ βουνὸν δέ τινα δέον παρακεῖσθαι ἵνα, εἰ οὕτω τύχῃ
610 ἐπὶ τοῦτον ἀνέλθῃς, πρὸ τοῦ φθάσαντες καταλάβωσιν αὐτὸν οἱ πολέμιοι.

ρκγʹ. Ἐὰν πολέμιοι παράκεινταί σοι, ὦ στρατηγέ, καὶ προσποιηθῇς πρὸς αὐτοὺς ἐναντία ὧν ἐλπίζουσιν, οὐ μικρὰ ὠφελήσεις. δόξας γὰρ ἐνίοτε χάρακα πηγνύειν ἢ ἕτερόν τι κυκλοῦν ὀχύρωμα, καὶ διὰ τοιαύτης δόξης εἰς ὁμοίαν πρᾶξιν τοὺς ἐναντίους παρορμήσας, δύνασαι συντεταγμένος αὐτὸς διασκεδασ-
615 μένοις ἐκείνοις εἰς τὰ ἐπιτήδεια συντόμως ἐπιπεσεῖν ἢ ἐὰν καὶ τοῦτο συμβῇ ἐκ τόπων δυσχερῶν ἀκινδύνως ἀπαγάγῃς τὸ στράτευμα.

ρκδʹ. Ὥσπερ ἀγαθὸν παλαιστὴν οὕτως δεῖ ἐν ταῖς πράξεσι τὸν στρατηγὸν δεικνύειν μὲν ἕτερα, καὶ διὰ τούτων πειρᾶσθαι τοὺς ἐναντίους ἐξαπατᾶν, κεχρή- σθαι δὲ τοῖς ἁρμόζουσι τῷ καιρῷ καὶ οἷς ἂν τῶν μαχομένων πολεμίων κρατή-
620 σῃς.

---

598–600 *Strat.*, 8.2.57.   601–604 *Strat.*, 8.2.61.   605–610 *Strat.*, 8.2.75.   611–616 *Strat.*, 8.2.76.   617–620 *Strat.*, 8.2.77.

---

592 πράγμασι Μ πράγμασιν Α   594 τὸ Μ om. Α   595–596 στρατηγία δὲ Μ om. Α
598 ὑπάρξεις Μ ὑπάρχῃς Α   601 ἐπίβαλλε Μ om. Α   602 ἔργοις ἐὰν Μ ἔργοις ἐπίβαλλε ἐν Α | πράγμασι Α πράγμασιν Μ   605 τὸ χωρίον Μ τὸν τόπον Α   606 ὑγιεινὸν...πολέμιον Μ ὑγιεινὸς καὶ σωτήριος ἢ νοσερὸς καὶ τοῖς οἰκείοις πολέμιος Α   607–608 πόρρωθέν Μ μακρόθεν Α   610 πρὸ τοῦ Μ πρὶν Α   612 ἐνίοτε Μ πολλάκις Α | χάρακα Μ σταβαρὰ περὶ τὸ φοσσάτον Α   613 δόξης Μ ἐλπίδος Α   619 οἷς ἂν Μ δι᾽ ὧν Α

treacherous, operations and were admired because of their good luck. But, when it is necessary to wage war, remain secure in dealing with the enemy and follow your own designs as in each instance you think useful and helpful for you. For fortune has gained victory once but has been defeated many times. Strategy, however, making use of various skills, has led to defeat perhaps once but has been victorious many times.[85]

120. You will bring ruin on your subjects, O general, if you are a lover of money. Not only do you cause the destruction of your own people if you are a money lover but you will also be viewed with contempt by the enemy.[86]

121. Undertake military operations with intelligence and extensive investigation. If some mistake is made in other matters, in a little while, perhaps, the mistake can be rectified, but errors made in war cause lasting harm, for the dead are gone for good.[87]

122. Study and carefully observe the location of the camp, O general. Is it healthy and safe or is it inhospitable and unhealthy for your troops? Are the necessary supplies, water, wood, forage, nearby? If these are at a distance, it will be difficult and dangerous to procure them, especially in the presence of the enemy. Try to locate some hill in the vicinity and, if you find one, ascend it before the enemy arrives and occupies it.[88]

123. If the enemy are nearby, O general, you will gain no small advantage if you pretend to do the opposite of what they expect. At one time, give the impression that you are going to set up camp or encircle some other fortified place and, by appearing to do so, you may lure the enemy into like activity. While they are scattered about getting things organized, you remain in formation and suddenly fall upon them. Even if this happens to take place in difficult terrain, you may lead your army out without risk.

124. The general must carry out operations like a good wrestler, feinting in one direction in an effort to deceive his opponent. You must make use of suitable opportunities and other ways by which you can overpower the enemy's fighting men.

85. *Strat.* 8.2.56.
86. *Strat.* 8.2.57.
87. *Strat.* 8.2.61.
88. For §§122–124 see *Strat.* 8.2.75–77.

ρκε΄. Νίκης καὶ ἥττης ἀμφοτέρων ἐν ἀδήλῳ κειμένων, ἄριστος καὶ σοφὸς λογισθήσῃ στρατηγὸς καὶ ἐν πολέμοις καὶ ἐν πάσῃ σου κατ᾽ ἐχθρῶν ἐγχειρήσει, ἐὰν πρὸς δευτέραν τύχην καὶ ἐναντίαν ἔκβασιν ἀποβλέπῃς, καὶ ὡς αὐτῆς παρούσης τὰ δέοντα περὶ αὐτῆς προνοήσῃς. εἰ γάρ τι συμβῇ ἐναντίον, ἕτοιμος
625 πρὸς τὴν σωτηρίαν εὑρεθήσῃ.

ρκϛ΄. Ὁ ἀσφαλὴς στρατηγὸς οὐ μόνον τὰ εἰκότα γενέσθαι ἐν τοῖς κινδύνοις εὖ διαθῇ, ἀλλὰ καὶ τὰ παράδοξα λογιζόμενος τὴν περὶ αὐτῶν ποιήσεται πρόνοιαν.

ρκζ΄. Εἰ δέ τις τῶν περί σε ἀρχόντων πολλὰ πράττων ἀνάξια καὶ φαῦλα
630 εὑρεθῇ, μηδὲ περὶ μικρῶν καὶ τῶν τυχόντων πραγμάτων αὐτῷ καταπιστεύσῃς.

ρκη΄. Ἴσθι γὰρ | ὅτι τοιούτους ὀφείλεις προβάλλεσθαι ἄρχοντας, οἵτινες τῶν 368
ὑποχειρίων αὐτῶν κρείττονες ἔσονται· φιλοῦσι γὰρ ἀεὶ τὰ φρονήματα τῶν
ἀρχομένων συνδιατίθεσθαι τοῖς ἄρχουσιν. οὕτως γὰρ ὁ ἀρχαῖος πληρωθήσεται
λόγος, μὴ ἐλάφους ἄρχειν λεόντων, ἀλλὰ λέοντας ἐλάφων.

635 ρκθ΄. Ῥωμαλέον κατασκευάσεις τὸ στράτευμα, ἐὰν τὸν τῆς ἀνοχῆς τοῦ
πολέμου καιρὸν εἰς ἄσκησιν καὶ γυμνασίαν τῶν κατὰ πόλεμον ἔργων ἀφοσιώ-
σῃς. τότε γὰρ ἐν καιρῷ πολεμικῶν ἀγώνων οὔκ ἐστι μελέτην, ἀλλ᾽ ἐπίδειξιν τῆς
ἀνδραγαθίας παραστήσεις.

ρλ΄. Ἡ μελέτη σοι τῶν ἀναγκαίων πραγμάτων ἠρεμοῦντι γινέσθω, καὶ μὴ
640 πρότερον εἰς ὕπνον τρέπου πρὶν ἂν κατανοήσῃς τί μὲν ἔδει πραχθῆναι καὶ τοῦτο
παρέλιπες· τί δὲ εἰς τὴν αὔριον πραχθῆναι καλὸν καὶ τούτου ταχέως ἀπάρξῃ.

ρλα΄. Νομισθήσῃ κωφὸς καὶ εὐκαταφρόνητος τοῖς ἐντυγχάνουσιν, ἐὰν
προχείρως πιστεύῃς τοῖς ὑποσχομένοις σοί τι πράξειν. ἐὰν δὲ ἐξετάζων καὶ
γυμνάζων τὸ πρᾶγμα φανῇς, αἰδούμενος ἕκαστος τῶν φαύλων τὴν σὴν ἀκρί-
645 βειαν καὶ ἀγχίνοιαν, οὐδέν σοι πρὸς ἀπάτην εἰπεῖν τολμήσει, ἀλλὰ καὶ θαυμά-
σονταί σου τῆς στερρότητος οἱ ὑποχείριοι, καὶ τῆς ἀληθείας οὐκ ἀστοχήσεις.

---

621–625 Strat., 8.2.78.  626–628 Strat., 8.2.63.  629–630 Strat., 8.2.62.  631–634 Strat.,
8.2.79; cf. β΄.220–221.  635–638 Strat., 8.2.64.  639–641 Strat., 8.2.65.  642–646 Strat.,
8.2.67.

---

621 ἐν M om. A  623 ἐὰν M εἰ A  627 εὖ διαθῇ M καλῶς διαθήσει A | παράδοξα M παρὰ
προσδοκίαν A  632 φιλοῦσι…ἀεὶ M ἀεὶ γὰρ A  633 συνδιατίθεσθαι…ἄρχουσιν M πρὸς
τὰς τῶν ἀρχόντων γνώμας συμμεταβάλλονται A  636–637 ἀφοσιώσης A ἀφοσιώσῃ M
643 προχείρως M εὐκόλως A  646 σου M σε ἕνεκεν A

125. Since both victory and defeat remain uncertain, you will be regarded as a most courageous and wise general, in combat and in every undertaking of yours against the enemy, if you keep in mind second fortune and an adverse outcome. Make plans about how you should deal with them as though they were actually occurring. If the opposite does happen, you will be ready to find safety.[89]

126. The cautious general should not only be good at making arrangements for what is likely to happen in time of danger but he should also consider the unexpected and make plans for it ahead of time.[90]

127. If one of the officers around you is discovered to be engaged in many unworthy and disreputable activities, do not entrust him even with small and ordinary matters.[91]

128. Keep in mind that you ought to promote such officers who are better than the men they will command. The spirit of subordinates always tends to model itself on that of the commander. Thus, the ancient saying will be fulfilled: "The deer is not to rule over the lion, but the lion to rule over the deer."[92]

129. Maintain your army in good condition. If battle is postponed, devote the time to exercise and drill in combat activities. When the time comes to take the field, you will provide, not just a a training exercise in manly valor, but an actual demonstration of it.[93]

130. Deliberate about necessary matters when you are calm. Do not go to sleep before you reflect on what you should have done and may perhaps have neglected. Reflect too on what it would be wise to do tomorrow and quickly get to it.[94]

131. You will be regarded as a lightweight and be despised by all who encounter you if you readily believe those who promise you to do something. But if you are seen investigating and testing the matter, each one of the common men will be in awe at your precision and shrewdness and will not dare to say anything to deceive you. Instead, your subordinates will be amazed at your firmness, and you will not fall short of the truth.[95]

89. *Strat.* 8.2.78; cf. Const. 13 §7, n. 2.

90. *Strat.* 8.2.63.

91. *Strat.* 8.2.62.

92. *Strat.* 8.2.79; cf. Const. 2 §32.

93. *Strat.* 8.2.64.

94. *Strat.* 8.2.65.

95. *Strat.* 8.2.67.

ρλβ΄. Ἴσθι ὅτι ἡ μετὰ λογισμοῦ κατὰ πόλεμον ἔφοδος ἀσφάλειαν ἔχει πολλήν. οἱ γὰρ ὀξεῖς καὶ προπετεῖς στρατηγοί, ὡς ἡ πεῖρα ἔδειξεν, πλεῖστα διαμαρτάνουσι.

650  ρλγ΄. Καλῶς ποιήσεις ὅταν τὰ σὰ βουλεύματα λανθάνειν θέλεις τοὺς πολεμίους, ἐὰν οὐδὲ τοῖς πολλοῖς τῶν οἰκείων ταῦτα θαρρήσῃς. δύσκολον γὰρ κρυβῆναι λαθραίαν βουλὴν πολλοῖς χείλεσι πεπιστευμένην.

ρλδ΄. Ὁρμὴν ἑκάστου καὶ κίνησιν καὶ ἄρχοντος καὶ στρατιώτου δεῖ σε γινώσκειν, ὦ στρατηγέ, καὶ εἰς ὁποίαν ἕκαστος πρᾶξιν ἁρμόδιός ἐστιν, ἵνα ἕκαστον
655  δεόντως ἐκτάξῃς. ὡς ἔοικε γάρ, τὸ ἀγνοεῖν ταῦτα ἀνωμάλους ποιεῖται τὰς παρατάξεις.

ρλε΄. Στρατηγὸς ἀγαθὸς εἰκὼν γίνεται τῶν πρακτέων τοῖς ὑποχειρίοις αὐτοῦ καὶ ὁ φαῦλος ὁμοίως. σὺ οὖν τῆς ἡμετέρας βασιλείας δεχόμενος τὴν παραίνεσιν, ὦ στραγηγέ, ἀγαθὴ γενοῦ τοῖς ὑπηκόοις εἰκών, καὶ ἄριστα γυμναζόμενος, καὶ
660  ποιῶν ἅπερ δεῖ, ἀπεχόμενος δέ, ὅσα καὶ τοὺς στρατιώτας καὶ πάντας τοὺς ὑπό σε τεταγμένους ἀπέχεσθαι χρήσιμον.

ρλϛ΄. Ἔνδοξόν τι πρᾶγμα καὶ λίαν ὀνήσιμόν ἐστιν ἡ στρατηγικὴ ἐπιστήμη· καὶ γὰρ ἄνευ μάχης πολλάκις νικᾷ τοὺς πολεμίους. ταύτης οὖν ἐπιμελεῖσθαί σε χρή, καὶ διὰ ταύτης τὰς ἐγχειρήσεις ἄνευ φανεροῦ πολέμου κατὰ τῶν ἐναντίων
665  ποιεῖσθαι. ὅταν δὲ | ἀνάγκη ταύτην μὴ ἐνεργεῖν, τότε διὰ τῆς τῶν σωμάτων    368ᵛ
ῥώμης παρακινδυνεύειν ἀναγκαῖον, καὶ μάχῃ πρὸς τοὺς πολεμίους διαγωνίζεσθαι.

ρλζ΄. Νεάζειν ὀφείλει ὁ στρατηγὸς καὶ τῇ ῥώμῃ τοῦ σώματος. διὰ τῆς στρατηγικῆς τέχνης ὀφείλει θαυμάζεσθαι ἤγουν τῶν ἐπιτηδευμάτων αὐτῆς. ἔθος γάρ
670  ἐστι παλαιὸν ὥστε τοὺς μέλλοντας στρατηγεῖν, οὐ μόνον ἀπὸ ἔθνους καὶ γένους ἕλκειν τὴν συγγένειαν ἐν ταῖς νίκαις λαμπρυνομένου, ἀλλὰ καὶ τοῖς πᾶσι πράγμασιν ἄχρι καὶ αὐτοῦ τοῦ ὀνόματος εἶναι τῆς νίκης σημαντικῆς.

---

647–649 Strat., 8.2.68.    650–652 Strat., 8.2.72.    653–656 Strat., 8.2.71.    657–661 Strat., 8.2.69.    662–667 Onas. 1.17.    668–672 Cf. β΄.93–100.

648–649 διαμαρτάνουσι Μ διαμαρτάνουσιν Α    650–651 πολεμίους Μ πολεμίους τοῦτο δὲ γενήσεται Α    654 ὁποίαν Μ ποίαν Α    655 ὡς…γάρ Μ om. Α    655–656 ποιεῖται… παρατάξεις Μ trsp. Α    657 τῶν πρακτέων Μ om. Α | αὐτοῦ Μ αὐτοῦ τῶν ὀφειλόντων πράττεσθαι Α    659 γενοῦ…εἰκών Μ εἰκὼν τοῖς ὑπηκόοις γενοῦ Α    660 δεῖ Μ προσήκει Α | πάντας τοὺς Μ ἐκ πάντων ὧν Α    662 ὀνήσιμόν Μ ὀφέλιμον Α    665 ποιεῖσθαι Μ ποιήσεις Α    666 ῥώμης…ἀναγκαῖον Μ δυνάμεως ἀναγκαῖόν ἐστι παρακινδυνεύειν Α    668 σώματος Μ σώματος καὶ Α    670–671 γένους…συγγένειαν Μ om. Α    671 λαμπρυνομένου Μ λαμπρυνομένου κατάγειν τὸ γένος Α    672 ἄχρι Μ ἕως Α | σημαντικῆς Μ τὸ σημαντικὸν Α

132. Bear in mind that approaching war with deliberation promises great safety, whereas hasty and impetuous generals, as experience shows, commit many blunders.[96]

133. When you want to conceal your plans from the enemy, you will act correctly if you do not take the rank and file of your men into your confidence. It is difficult to hide a secret plan that has been entrusted to many lips.[97]

134. You must be familiar with the tendencies and inclinations of each officer and soldier, O general, and for what task each one is suited, so you can assign them properly. I believe that paying little heed to these matters results in an uneven battle line.[98]

135. A good general sets an example for his subordinates of how things are to be done, as does also a bad general. Therefore, you, O general, who have received this counsel from Our Majesty, set a good example for your subordinates, training yourself in the highest ideals and doing what is needed, but refraining from those things that the soldiers and everyone under your command should refrain from.[99]

136. Knowledge of strategy is an honorable and extremely useful thing. Frequently it leads to victory over the enemy without battle. You must study this attentively and, by following it, launch assaults against the enemy without getting into a pitched battle. When the situation is such that you cannot act in this manner, then it is necessary to face the dangers with physical force and engage the enemy in battle.[100]

137. The general ought to be youthful in spirit and robust in body. He ought to be admired because of his military skill and the way he puts it into practice. It is an ancient custom for those men who are to embark on a military career to trace their lineage from a tribe and family not only illustrious in their victories, but in all their actions even to the point that their very name signifies victory.[101]

96. *Strat.* 8.2.68.
97. *Strat.* 8.2.72.
98. *Strat.* 8.2.71.
99. *Strat.* 8.2.69.
100. Onasander 1.17.
101. Cf. Const. 2 §15.

ρλη΄. Χρήσιμόν τι στρατήγημα διηγήσομαι, καὶ τοῦτο ὅπερ ἀναγνοὺς ἀνέμα-
θον, ἵνα ἐάν ποτε συμβῇ σοι μέλλειν πρὸς πολεμίους πλείονά σου δύναμιν
675 ἔχοντας διαγωνίζεσθαι, καὶ βούλει πρὸς αὐτοὺς μὴ συνάψαι πόλεμον, ἀλλὰ
ἀκινδύνως ἐπεξελθεῖν, ἐπιτήρησον ἐὰν παράκειται ποταμός, καὶ τοῦτον ἐπιστρέψας ἐπάγαγε τοῖς πολεμίοις κατὰ τοῦ πεδίου ἐν ᾧ ἡ παράταξις πρόκειται, καὶ
οὕτως τὸν μέλλοντα πόλεμον ἀνενέργητον ποιήσεις.

ρλθ΄. Ῥᾳδίως ἀναστείλῃ βουλὴν πολεμίων ὁ στρατηγὸς ἐὰν καὶ αὐτός, καὶ
680 κατὰ γῆν καὶ κατὰ θάλασσαν κρατῇ ὑποχειρίων τινῶν· καὶ οἱ πολέμιοι δὲ γῆς
ἠπείρου κρατοῦντες κατὰ τῶν αὐτοῦ νηῶν ἢ ἑτέρων παραλίων τόπων ἐκστρατεύειν βουλεύωνται. ἐὰν γὰρ φημίσῃ ὅτι αὐτὸς διὰ τῆς ἠπείρου βούλεται κατ᾽
αὐτῶν στρατεῦσαι καταπλήξει αὐτοὺς καὶ ἀναστείλῃ τῆς κατὰ θάλασσαν
ἐγχειρήσεως.

685 ρμ΄. Ἴσθι εὐσεβὲς εἶναι πρᾶγμα, ὦ στρατηγέ, καὶ λίαν ὀνήσιμον τὸ ἐν ταῖς
ἀναγκαίαις καὶ κοιναῖς χρείαις μηδέποτε ἰδίας μιμνήσκεσθαι ἔχθρας μηδὲ δι᾽
ὑπόνοιαν ἰδίαν ἐμποδίζεσθαι τὰ δέοντα γίνεσθαι, ἀλλὰ ἐν ταῖς τῶν κοινῶν
προνοίαις τὰ τοιαῦτα πάντα κατατίθεσθαι καὶ περὶ προσώπων καὶ πραγμάτων,
καὶ πρὸς μόνον τὸ χρήσιμον ἀποβλέπειν, καὶ τοῦτο πράττειν. ἡ γὰρ τοιαύτη
690 αἰτία πολλοῖς παρορωμένη μεγάλας βλάβας πολλάκις ἐποίησεν.

ρμα΄. Σοφιζόμενος, ὦ στρατηγέ, χρείας οὕτω καλούσης, ὠφελήσεις τὰ
μέγιστα. ἐὰν γὰρ διά τινος ἐπινοίας προνοήσῃς τὰ μέλλοντα γίνεσθαι, καὶ
μάλιστα ἐπὶ ἀστέρων ἐπιτολῆς, καὶ ταῦτα προείπῃς, ὅτι ἐπ᾽ ἀγαθῇ σημασίᾳ
μέλλουσι γίνεσθαι, ὑπὲρ τῶν παρά σου ἐγχειρουμένων πραγμάτων ἐπιρρωσθή-
695 σονται οἱ ὑπό σε στρατιῶται, ὥσπερ ἀπὸ οὐρανοῦ ἐπιτολήν τινα σημαίνουσαν
αὐτοῖς ἀγαθὰ ὑποδεχόμενοι, καὶ θαρραλέοι ἔσονται κατὰ τῶν πολεμίων.

ρμβ΄. Τοὺς παρά σου ἐν ὁμαλῷ καὶ πεδινῷ τόπῳ ποτὲ παρατασσομένους
πεζοὺς ἐνόπλους πρὸς καβαλλαρίους ἐχθρῶν μηδέποτε ἐάσῃς, κἂν πολλὴν
ἀνάγκην ὑποστῶσιν, καταλιπόντας τὴν παρά|ταξιν ἐκφυγεῖν. μενόντων γὰρ    369

---

691–696 Cf. ιδ΄.703–707.

---

673 καὶ τοῦτο M om. A    674–675 πλείονά…διαγωνίζεσθαι M διαγωνίζεσθαι πλείονά σου
ἔχοντας δύναμιν A    676–677 ἐπιστρέψας M μετοχετεύσας A    677 πεδίου M τόπου A
679 καὶ¹ M ὁ A    680 θάλασσαν M θάλατταν A    681 παραλίων M παραθαλαττίων A
682 ἠπείρου M γῆς A    685 ὀνήσιμον M ὀφέλιμον A    690 πολλοῖς παρορωμένη M τῶν
πολλῶν παραλειπομένη A    691 οὕτω καλούσης M ἀπαιτούσης A    692 τινος ἐπινοίας M
trsp. A    693 ἐπιτολῆς M ἀνατολῆς καὶ ἐλλείψεως A    693–694 ἐπ᾽…γίνεσθαι M ἀγαθὰ
σημαίνουσιν A    694–695 ἐπιρρωσθήσονται M ἐνδυναμωθήσονται A    695 ἐπιτολήν M
ἐπιστολήν A    695–696 σημαίνουσαν…ὑποδεχόμενοι M ὑποδεχόμενοι ἀγαθὰ αὐτοῖς
σημαίνουσαν A

138. I will tell you about a useful stratagem that I have learned from my reading. If it ever happens that you are about to fight against an enemy whose army is larger than yours and you do not want to face it in battle but to extricate yourself without danger, then be on the lookout for a nearby river, turn it around, and divert it against the enemy onto the plain on which the battle line was being formed. In this way, you will bring it about that the intended battle will not take place.

139. The general can easily confound the plans of the enemy if he has some men under his command on both land and sea. The enemy, who occupy territory on the mainland, may plan to campaign against his ships or other places along the shore. If the general lets it be known that he intends to war against them on land, he will catch them by surprise and turn back their attack by sea.

140. You must know, O general, that it is a religious deed and an extremely useful one, when it involves essential matters and public service, never to keep in mind personal enmity or to let personal suspicions be an obstacle to duty. Rather, in concerns affecting the common good, put all such feelings aside, regarding both persons and things, and look only toward what is beneficial, and do that. In many cases, overlooking this responsibility has resulted in great harm.

141. By acting cleverly, O general, when the situation requires, you will reap the greatest benefits. There may be some means that enable you to foretell future events, especially the rising of the stars. You foretell such events because they will occur under a favorable sign. The soldiers under your command will be strongly encouraged to support the actions you are taking, as though the rising of the star was a sort of sign from heaven that they were to experience good fortune and they will become bolder in facing the enemy.[102]

142. Never allow the infantry, while they are drawn up on even and level ground against the enemy cavalry, to abandon the line of battle and run away, even under heavy pressure. If they remain in place, there are good hopes for

---

102. Cf. Const. 14 §101.

700 αὐτῶν πολλαὶ τοῦ νικᾶν ἐλπίδες, φευγόντων δ᾽ οὐδεμία σωτηρίας ἐλπίς, πεζῶν
διασκορπισθέντων καὶ ὑπὸ καβαλλαρίων διωκομένων.

ρμγ΄. Ὥσπερ τὸ ζῆν ἡδέως ἐπιθυμητόν, οὕτως καὶ τῶν κατὰ πόλεμον κινδύνων τοὺς στρατιώτας προθύμως ἀπάρχεσθαι χρέος ἐστίν· ἐκεῖνοι γάρ εἰσι τοῦ
ζῆν ἡδέως οἱ αἴτιοι. τότε γὰρ τὰ κατορθώματα τῶν πολεμίων ἀληθῶς γινώσκε-
705 ται, ἡνίκα τῇ καρτερίᾳ τῶν πόνων ἐμμένωσιν· ταῦτα δὲ τὸ ζῆν ἡδέως καὶ εἰρηνεύειν ἀπὸ τῶν πολεμίων πορίζουσιν.

ρμδ΄. Ἀπονώτερον διὰ ἐφόδων ἀγρεύσεις καὶ κάστρα ποτὲ καὶ χωρία τῶν
πολεμίων διὰ μὲν τῆς ξηρᾶς, ἐὰν σχηματίσῃς τοὺς σοὺς στρατιώτας ὁμοίως τοῖς
ἐγχωρίοις. διὰ δὲ θαλάσσης, ἐάν ποτε ναυμαχῶν φθάσῃς τὰ πλοῖα τῶν πολεμί-
710 ων κρατῆσαι ἢ ἕτερα ὅμοια ἐκείνων κατασκευάσαι, καὶ τούτοις τοὺς σοὺς
στρατιώτας ἐμβιβάσαι, καὶ τῇ γῇ τῶν πολεμίων σὺν αὐταῖς καταπλεῦσαι. οὕτως
γὰρ ὡς φιλίαις ταῖς ναυσὶ προσχόντες οἱ ἐναντίοι οὐ φεύξονται, καὶ εὐχερέστερον ἁλωθήσονται.

ρμε΄. Ὕλην ἀγρυπνίας σοι διηγήσομαι. ἀκριβὴς γὰρ ἂν γένοιτο καὶ πάννυχος
715 παραφυλακή, εἴτε φοσσάτου ὑπὸ βίγλας φυλαττομένου, ἐὰν εἴπῃς ὅτι "μέλλω
κατὰ διαφόρους οὓς θέλω καιροὺς ἀνάπτειν λαμπτῆρας εἰς τόνδε τὸν περίοπτον τόπον," ἵνα καὶ οἱ φύλακες πρὸς ἕκαστον τῶν παρά σου λαμπτήρων ἀντ-
ανέχωσι καὶ δεικνύωσιν ἰδίους λαμπτῆρας. οὕτως γὰρ τὴν ὥραν τῆς σῆς
ἀναλάμψεως ἀγνοοῦντες καὶ ἐκδεχόμενοι διὰ παντὸς ἐγρηγορήσουσι, καὶ
720 ἀποσκοπεῖν τὰς βίγλας αὐτῶν παρασκευάσουσιν. εἰ δέ τινες ὑστερήσουσιν
εὐθέως γνωσθήσονται.

ρμϛ΄. Τὸ φυλάσσεσθαι τὰς ἐξ ἀπονοίας μάχας τῶν πολεμίων ἐχέφρονός ἐστι
στρατηγοῦ. ἡ γὰρ ἀπόνοια τὴν ἀνάγκην ἔχουσα παροτρύνουσαν, θρασυτάτους
καὶ ἀνδρείους τοὺς μαχομένους ποιεῖ. ἀπόνοια δέ ἐστιν ὅταν τις σωτηρίας
725 ἐλπίδα εὑρεῖν μὴ δυνάμενος ἐνστῇ πρὸς τὸν ἐναντίον, ὥστε ἢ νικῆσαι ἢ ἀποθανεῖν. ἐὰν δὲ στρατοπεδεύῃς κατέναντι πολεμίων, καὶ ὁ ἄνεμός ἐστι πρὸς αὐτοὺς
ἐπερχόμενος, ἐμπύριζε τὸν ἀπὸ τῆς γῆς ἀναφυέντα χόρτον ἵνα πρὸς αὐτοὺς
ἐπερχόμενον τὸ πῦρ τροπῆς αἴτιον γένηται.

ρμζ΄. Ὅταν μέλλῃς κατὰ χωρίου τινὸς τῶν πολεμίων ἔφοδον ποιεῖσθαι περὶ
730 τὸ αὖγος, ἐγκρύμματα διάφορα ἄλλα ἀλλαχοῦ κατάστησον διὰ τῆς νυκτός.
οὕτως γὰρ διαφόρως προσβαλὼν καὶ πλέον θορυβήσῃς καὶ διεσπαρμένους

---

705 ἐμμένωσιν M ἐμμένουσιν A   706 πορίζουσιν M παρέχουσιν A   709 φθάσῃς τὰ M
κρατήσῃς A   710 κατασκευάσαι M κατασκευάσῃς A   711 καὶ…αὐταῖς M ὥστε σὺν αὐτοῖς
τῇ γῇ τῶν πολεμίων A   712 φιλίαις M φιλίας οἱ ἐναντίοι τὰς ναῦς λογιζόμενοι οὐ φυγῶσιν A
713 ἁλωθήσονται M κρατήσονται A   716–717 περίοπτον M ὑψηλὸν A   717–718 ἀντέχωσι καὶ M ἀναστάντες A   722 ἐχέφρονός M φρονίμου A

victory, but if they run away, there is no hope of salvation, for the foot soldiers will be scattered about and pursued by the cavalry.

143. Just as a person desires a pleasant life, so must soldiers eagerly engage in the perils of warfare. Indeed, it is they who assure <us> of a pleasant life. Success over the enemy is truly achieved when the soldiers continually persevere in their labors. And it is success over the enemy that makes for pleasant living and peace.

144. At times, when you assault them on land, you will capture the fortresses and other places held by the enemy with less hard work if you have your soldiers dress like the local inhabitants. If you attack by sea, then, before the naval battle, seize some enemy ships or outfit others similar to those. Have your soldiers go aboard these ships and sail off to the land of the enemy. Your adversaries will look upon them as friendly ships, will not run away, and will be more easily taken.

145. I will discuss the matter of vigilance with you. The guards will remain alert and vigilant all night and the encampment will be well guarded by scouts if you announce: "I intend to light lanterns at different times, whenever I so choose, at this observation post." The guards should then, in response to each one of your lanterns, raise and show their own lanterns. Not knowing the hour of your lantern lighting and always being on the lookout for it, they will stay awake. They will make it easy for you to check on the scouts; those who happen to be late will be recognized immediately.

146. It is the mark of a prudent general to guard against the enemy fighting out of despair. Desperation only makes the emergency more acute and makes the combatants braver and bolder. Desperation sets in when a person takes his stand against his adversary but cannot find any hope of salvation. There is either victory or death. If you lead your army on campaign against the enemy and there is a wind blowing in their direction, set fire to the grass growing in that area so that the fire rushing on them will result in their defeat.

147. When you intend to launch an assault about dawn against some place held by the enemy, then, during the night set up various ambuscades here and there, so that, by attacking in different places, you will disturb them all the more

ἐπισυνάξει τοὺς ἁλισκομένους. καὶ τοῦτο δέ σοι προστίθημι, ἵνα ἐν ταῖς τοιαύταις κατὰ χώρας ἀδοκήτοις ἐπελεύσεσι τριβόλους σιδηροῦς νυκτὸς διαρρίπτεις
ἐν κύκλῳ, τοὺς δὲ πεζοὺς τοῦ σοῦ | στρατεύματος προστάξεις στερεὰ ἤτοι   369ᵛ
735 ξύλινα ἴχνη ἀντὶ κασσυμάτων ἔχειν τὰ ὑποδήματα. οὕτως γάρ, ἐὰν καί τινες
βουληθῶσιν ἢ πεζοὶ ἢ καβαλλάριοι ἀμύνασθαι τοῖς τριβόλοις ἐμπεσόντες
κωλυθήσονται, οἱ δὲ πεζοὶ τὸ οἰκεῖον ἔργον ἀνύσουσιν.

    ρμη΄. Κτῆμα τίμιον ἡ σωφροσύνη καὶ στρατηγῷ καὶ στρατεύματι, ὥσπερ ἡ
πορνεία ἐναντίον καὶ ὀλέθριον, καὶ μάλιστα ἐν αἰχμαλωτίσι γυναιξὶ γινομένη.
740 καὶ μαρτυρεῖ τὰ κατὰ τὸν Φινεὲς εἰς τὴν Μαδιανίτιδα γυναῖκα καὶ τὸν Ζαμβρῆ
γεγονότα. μιᾶς γὰρ γυναικὸς αἰχμαλώτου πορνεία ὅλον τὸ στρατόπεδον τῶν
νενικηκότων μικροῦ διέφθειρεν, εἰ μὴ ἔστη Φινεὲς καὶ ἐκκεντήσας τοὺς ἁμαρτά-
νοντας καὶ θανατώσας ἐξιλάσατο. καὶ ἐκόπασεν ἡ θραῦσις καὶ ἐλογίσθη αὐτῷ
εἰς δικαιοσύνην.

745    ρμθ΄. Ῥώμην ἐνθήσεις τοῖς στρατιώταις ἐν ἡμέρᾳ πολέμου, ἐὰν ἐξαναστὰς
ἕωθεν ὡς ἀπὸ Θεοῦ σοι ὀφθέντα ὄνειρον ἐπιφημίσῃς ἢ ὡς ἀπό τινος ἁγίας
δυνάμεως προτρεπούσης ἐπελθεῖν κατὰ τῶν πολεμίων καὶ ἐπιφανείσης σοι πρὸς
συμμαχίαν.

    ρν΄. Ἀπὸ χρημάτων πολλάκις καὶ ἄνευ πολέμου κατορθώσεις κατὰ πολεμίων
750 σου νίκην, ὅταν ἑτέρων πολεμίων αὐτοῖς που παρακειμένων τούτους χρήμασι
πείσας πολεμεῖν τοῖς σοῖς ἐναντίοις ποιήσεις. ἢ γὰρ ἀλλήλους φθεροῦσιν ἢ τὸ
ἓν μέρος ἐπικρατήσει, πολλοὺς ἀρίστους ἀποβαλὸν ἐν τῷ κατὰ τὴν μάχην
ἀγῶνι. καὶ γὰρ τῶν ἄμφω πολεμίων οὕτως ἡλασσωμένων ὁμοῦ ἀπαθὴς αὐτὸς
καὶ ἰσχυρότερος ἐκείνων ἀναδειχθήσῃ.

755    ρνα΄. Τοῖς βουλομένοις βιαίως ἐν καιρῷ πολέμου τὴν σὴν παράταξιν διαρρῆ-
ξαι καὶ διεκθεῖν, δίοδον ἑκουσίως πάρεχε, καὶ μετὰ ταῦτα ἐπίστρεψον καὶ ὥσπερ
φεύγουσι κατὰ νώτου ἐπιτεθεὶς ῥαδίως καταδιώξεις αὐτούς.

    ρνβ΄. Ὥστε μὴ φόβον εἰσάγεσθαι εἰς τὸ στρατόπεδον διὰ τοὺς ἀκαίρως
λιποτακτοῦντας, ταχέως αὐτοὺς καὶ συντόμως ἀποχωρίσας τῆς παρατάξεως ἐν
760 ἑτέραις χρείαις κατάστησον.

---

**738–744** Num. 25:7–14.

**732** ἁλισκομένους M κρατουμένους A | προστίθημι M παραγγέλλομεν A   **733** χώρας M
χώραν A | διαρρίπτεις M διασπείρῃς A   **734–735** ἤτοι…ἴχνη M trsp. A   **737** ἀνύσουσιν M
πληρώσουσιν A   **742** μικροῦ M παρ' ὀλίγου A   **744** εἰς δικαιοσύνην M ἐν δικαιοσύνῃ A
**746** ἕωθεν M πρωὶ A   **747** κατὰ…πολεμίων M om. A   **753** τῶν ἄμφω M ἀμφοτέρων τῶν
A | ἡλασσωμένων M φθειρωμένων A   **756** δίοδον M πάροδον A   **757** φεύγουσι Du
φεύγωσι M φεύγωσιν A | ῥαδίως M εὐκόλως A

and you will gather in the prisoners as they are scattered about. I will add this for you: in such surprise attacks against places, throw out iron caltrops at night in a circle. Order the foot soldiers in your army to wear shoes with stiff or wooden soles instead of leather ones. In this way, even if some, infantry or cavalry, should wish to protect themselves from falling upon the caltrops, this will prevent them from doing so. The infantry shall complete their special task.

148. Self-control is a valued possession for the general and for the army, just as fornication is adverse and destructive, especially when it occurs with captive women. Evidence of this is what happened in the time of Phinees concerning the Madianite woman and Zambres. The fornication of one captive woman just about destroyed the entire army, even though it was victorious. But Phinees arose and ran his spear through the sinners and, by putting them to death, made atonement. The plague abated and it was accounted to him as righteousness.[103]

149. You will make your soldiers stronger on the day of battle if you get up early and spread it about that you have had a dream ostensibly sent by God or by some holy power that urged you on to attack the enemy and appeared in support of you.

150. You will achieve frequent victories against your enemies without actual war by making use of money. When they have other enemies lying in wait for them somewhere, an offer of money should be persuasive in getting this people to wage war against your adversaries. Either they will destroy one another or one side will conquer, although it will have lost many brave soldiers in the heat of battle. The result will be that both enemies will be weakened while, at the same time, you will be unharmed and end up stronger than those armies.

151. In the course of battle, when the enemy wants to break through by force and run through your battle line, give way willingly and, a bit later, wheel about and fall upon their rear as though they were running away and you will easily pursue them.

152. To keep your army from becoming frightened because some men are deserting at the wrong time, quickly and without formalities separate them from your battle line and assign them to other tasks.

---

103. Numbers 25:7–14.

ρνγ΄. Ῥώμη στρατηγοῦ χερσὶ μὲν συμπλεκομένου πολλάκις οὐδὲν μέγα
ὠφέλησεν, εἰ μὴ ἄρα μικρὸν ἐν δειλίᾳ στρατοῦ ἐπιρρῶσαι τούτους βουλομένου
διὰ τῆς κοινωνίας τῶν κινδύνων· πεσόντος δὲ τὰ μέγιστα ἔβλαψεν. στρατηγίαι
δὲ καὶ ἐπιτηδεύματα, ὅταν σώζηται καὶ διαφυλάττηται ὁ στρατηγός, παρ᾽ αὐτοῦ
765  γινόμενα μεγάλας ὠφελείας ἐν ταῖς μάχαις ἀποτελοῦσιν.

ρνδ΄. Πλήθους φαντασίαν τοῦ σοῦ στρατεύματος ποιήσεις, εἴγε τοῦτο
βουληθῇς, ἐὰν καὶ τοῖς ὑποζυγίοις καὶ τοῖς ὄνοις καὶ ταῖς βουσὶν ἐποχεῖσθαί
τινας καβαλλαρίους ποιήσῃς· ἐνίοτε γὰρ | καὶ τοῦτο ἐπιδεικνύμενον χρήσιμον.    370

ρνε΄. Ἱκανῶς καταπλήξεις τοὺς πολεμίους ἐν παρατάξει ὅταν τοὺς ὁπλίτας
770  τοῦ σοῦ στρατεύματος πρῶτα μὲν κατὰ βῆμα μετὰ εὐταξίας προσάγῃς, ὅταν δὲ
ἔσωθεν σαγιττοβόλου γένωνται, τότε δρομαίως μετ᾽ ὀξύτητος συμπλέκεσθαι
ποιήσῃς. οὐ γὰρ βλαβήσονται ὑπὸ τῶν τοξευομένων βελῶν, καὶ ἀπαθεῖς προσβαλόντες τρέψουσι τοὺς ἐναντίους.

ρνϛ΄. Σοφοῦ στρατηγοῦ ἔργον σοι διηγήσομαι. ποτὲ γὰρ παρατασσομένου
775  αὐτοῦ βροντὴ γέγονε βαρεῖα, καὶ τοῦ στρατοῦ αὐτοῦ δειλιάσαντος, ὡς ἐπὶ κακῷ
αὐτοῖς συμβόλῳ, ἀντεπήνεγκεν εἰπών· "οὐ δι᾽ ἡμᾶς ἡ βροντὴ γέγονεν, ἀλλὰ
τοὺς πολεμίους ὁ Θεὸς ὡς ἐχθροὺς ἐμβροντήτους ποιήσας κατ᾽ αὐτῶν ἡμᾶς
ἐπάγεσθαι κελεύει."

ρνζ΄. Τοὺς πολεμίους εὐκαταφρονήτους ποιήσεις ἐὰν τοὺς ἐκ τοῦ γένους
780  αὐτῶν παρά σοι ὄντας ἐν ταῖς παλαίστραις τῶν παιγνίων ἐλάττους, τοὺς δὲ
σοὺς ὑπερέχειν παρασκευάσῃς.

ρνη΄. Ὅτε βούλῃ κρύψαι τοὺς ἀνηρημένους ἐν τῇ μάχῃ τοῦ σοῦ στρατεύματος, εἴγε καὶ τοῦτο συμβαίη ποτέ, ὡς πολλάκις εἴωθε, μετὰ τὴν λύσιν τῆς μάχης
μὴ συνδειπνεῖν ὁμοῦ τὰ κοντουβέρνια παρακελεύου, ἀλλ᾽ ὡς ἔτυχεν ἕκαστον.
785  οὕτως γὰρ οὐ διαγνόντες τοὺς ἀνηρημένους οὐκ εἰς δειλίαν ἐμπεσοῦνται, ἀλλὰ
θαρσήσουσιν.

ρνθ΄. Στρατηγὸς πολεμίων, ὥσπερ κεφαλὴ ἐχίδνης, οὕτως ἐπὶ τῷ στρατεύματι αὐτοῦ. πᾶσαν οὖν ἐπίνοιαν ποιοῦ, ὥστε αὐτὸν πεσεῖν, ἢ διὰ πλήθους
συμπεφραγμένου καὶ πρὸς αὐτὸν μόνον ὀξέως ἐπιδραμόντος ἢ διὰ βελῶν πρὸς
790  ἕνα σκοπὸν κατ᾽ αὐτοῦ βληθέντων, ἢ δι᾽ ἑτέρου τινὸς ἐπιτηδεύματος. καὶ γὰρ
τῆς ἐχίδνης ἡ κεφαλὴ συντριβεῖσα τὸ λοιπὸν σῶμα κατέλιπεν ἀνενέργητον.

---

761–765 Onas. 33.    774–778 Cf. Polyaen. 2.3.4.    787–791 Cf. Polyaen. 2.3.15.

---

768 ἐνίοτε M πολλάκις A    776 συμβόλῳ M σημείῳ A    780 ἐλάττους M ἐλάττονας A
783 εἴγε M εἰ A | εἴωθε M εἴωθεν A    784 κοντουβέρνια A κουτουβέρνια M

153. A strong general engaging in hand-to-hand combat is usually of no great help. Perhaps, when the army is timid, he may intend to strengthen them a little by sharing in their dangers, but it is disastrous if he falls. Strategy and good management on his part, when the general is safe and protected, result in great benefits in combat.[104]

154. You will give the impression that you have a large army, if this is what you desire, by having some cavalrymen ride on the pack animals, the asses, and the cattle. Sometimes a display of this sort is useful.

155. You will strike the enemy with great amazement if you bring up the heavy-armed troops of your army in good order at a gradual pace and, when they come within a bowshot, have them race quickly forward and engage closely. They will not be injured by the arrows fired at them and, charging forward unharmed, they will rout the foe.

156. I will tell you what a wise general once did. As the army was being drawn up in formation, a loud thunder clap was heard and caused the army to become fearful, as though it were an evil omen. He made a counterargument by saying: "The thunder did not come because of us, but because of the enemy; God has sent the thunder on them, as our enemies, and orders us to march out against them."[105]

157. You will make the enemy into objects of contempt if you show that the men of their nation who are with you are inferior in wrestling matches, whereas you make sure that your own men prove to be superior.

158. When you wish to hide from your army those who have died in battle, if this should indeed happen, as it does frequently, then, after the battle has come to an end, order the squads not to take their meal together but each one wherever it finds itself. In this way, they will not know who has been killed and they will not become discouraged but will take heart.

159. The enemy general is like the head of a viper in relation to his army. Focus your full attention on making him fall, either by a large number of heavy-armed troops charging directly against him alone or by discharging arrows against him as a single target or handle it in some other manner. Once the head of the viper has been cut off, the rest of the body can do nothing.[106]

104. Onasander 33.
105. Cf. Polyaenus 2.3.4.
106. Cf. Polyaenus 2.3.15.

ρξ΄. Ἐν πολέμου καιρῷ τοὺς φιλτάτους καὶ συνήθεις καὶ συγγενεῖς πλησίον συντάττειν ἀλλήλων ἀγαθόν ἐστιν. ἡ γὰρ ἀγάπη συγκινδυνεύειν ἀλλήλοις καὶ ἀριστεύειν παρασκευάζει.

795   ρξα΄. Ὑπόνοιαν κατασκευάσεις ἐν τοῖς πολεμίοις κατὰ ἀλλήλων, ἐὰν τῶν ἐν τοῖς πολεμίοις ὄντων παρ᾽ αὐτοῖς ἐπισήμων τὰ χωρία καταλίπῃς ἀβλαβῆ δηλονότι κατακαίων τὰ πλησιόχωρα.

ρξβ΄. Στρατὸς εἰ μὲν ἔστι σοι ἱκανός, ὦ στρατηγέ, καὶ μόνος αὐτάρκης, ἐπείτοιγε καὶ τοὺς ἀνικάνους πρὸς χρείαν ἐκείνων καὶ δουλείαν καὶ πλήθους
800  φαντασίαν ὅτε καλέσει καιρὸς συμπαραλαβεῖν χρήσιμόν ἐστιν ἢ ἐλασσουμένου τοῦ στρατοῦ καὶ διὰ συμμάχων ἀναπληροῦσθαι αὐτόν, ὥστε ἀρκεῖν πρὸς τὸ καταπολεμῆσαι τοὺς ἐναντίους. εἴρηται γὰρ λόγος παλαιός· ὅτι ἔνθα μὴ ἐξαρκεῖ ἡ λεοντῆ προσράπτειν δεῖ τῆς ἀλωπεκῆς.

ρξγ΄. Ἐὰν συμβῇ σοί ποτε ὑποσύνθημα | γράψαι τινὶ ἐν χώρᾳ ὄντι τῶν 370ᵛ
805  πολεμίων, ἐν ἀκηρώτοις πινακιδίοις ὃ ἂν βούλῃ καταγράψας, ἐπικάλυπτε τῷ κηρῷ τὰ γράμματα, καὶ τότε κατὰ τοῦ κηροῦ γράφε τὰ ἀνύποπτα. οὕτως γὰρ ἀνύσεις τοῦ ὑποσυνθήματος τὴν κρυφαίαν σου δήλωσιν.

ρξδ΄. Βουλὴν ποτέ τις προδοσίας ποιήσας, γνωσθεὶς δὲ καὶ μέλλων ἁλίσκεσθαι τὴν ἐπιβουλὴν τῶν πολεμίων τοῖς ἰδίοις κατεμήνυσεν, καὶ ὅπως δεῖ ταύτην
810  φυλάξασθαι συνεβούλευσεν. ἐμήνυσαν δὲ καὶ οἱ πολέμιοι τούτῳ μὲν τὴν ἐπιβουλήν, τὰ δὲ ἔργα τὰ ἐναντία τῆς ἐπιβουλῆς. τίνι πιστεύσῃς μᾶλλον ἢ πάντως τῷ βουλευθέντι προδότῃ καὶ μηνύσαντι, ἀλλὰ μὴ τοῖς λόγοις τῶν πολεμίων; οὗτος γάρ, εἰ καὶ προδότης, ἀλλὰ καὶ ὁμοδίαιτος πάντοτε καὶ συγγενὴς καὶ χρήμασιν ἴσως ὑποφθαρεὶς ἃ λαβεῖν οὐκ ἔφθασεν ἢ λαβὼν ἠθέτησεν, ἐκεῖνοι δὲ φύσει
815  πολέμιοι καὶ διὰ πάντων ἀλλότριοι.

ρξε΄. Ἡ δειλία τῶν στρατιωτῶν ἐκ τοῦ ὄκνου καὶ τῆς ὠχριάσεως δείκνυται. τοὺς οὖν τοιούτους ἀσυμφανῶς χώριζε τοῦ στρατοῦ καὶ ἀπόστελλε, ὡς δῆθεν κομίσοντας ἃ ἐπελάθοντο. τοῦτο δὲ ποιήσας παρορμήσεις λόγοις τοὺς στρατιώ-

---

792–794 Cf. δ΄.160–167.   798–803 Polyaen. 2.10.5; Plut. *Lys.*, 7.4.   804–807 Polyaen. 2.20.

---

792 καὶ συγγενεῖς M om. A   793 συντάττειν ἀλλήλων M trsp. A   799 ἐπείτοιγε M εὖ ἂν ἔχοι εἰ δὲ μὴ A | δουλείαν M δουλείων A   807 τοῦ ὑποσυνθήματος Du ἀπὸ συνθήματος MA   808–809 ἁλίσκεσθαι M κρατῆσθαι A   810 τούτῳ Du τούτον MA   817 ἀσυμφανῶς M μετὰ εὐλόγου προφάσεως A

160. In combat it is a good idea to line up very close friends, companions, and relatives close to one another. For their love makes them ready to endure dangers by one another's side and to distinguish themselves.[107]

161. You will make the enemy suspicious of one another if you leave undamaged the estates of the important men among them and burn down the neighboring estates.

162. Your army may be large enough, O general, and sufficient by itself, yet when the situation requires, it is useful to take in some people who are unsuited for <combat> to assist with the needs and service of the soldiers and <to create> the impression of a large force. If your army is smaller, expand it by adding allied forces so that it is large enough to overcome its adversaries in battle. An ancient saying goes: "When the lion skin is not sufficient, then it is necessary to sew on that of the fox."[108]

163. If at some time it occurs to you to write a watchword to a person in enemy territory, write down what you wish on an unwaxed tablet, cover over the writing with wax, and then write something on the wax that will not arouse suspicion. In this way, you will manage to communicate your watchword and still keep it secret.[109]

164. A certain person once conceived a plan of betrayal but, on being discovered and about to be arrested, he informed his own people about the plan of the enemy and gave them advice on how they should guard against it. The enemy had indeed informed him of such a plan but their actions were the opposite of the plan. Whom would you trust more completely than the one who planned betrayal and <then> provided information? Surely not the words of the enemy. For this man, albeit a traitor, remains still a fellow countryman and of the same race and was perhaps corrupted by money that he did not actually take or after taking handed it back. They, in contrast, are enemies by nature and in every respect foreign.

165. The cowardice of the soldiers is manifested by their hesitation and pallid color. Secretly separate such men from the army and send them off as though they were to bring back things they had forgotten. After doing this, address the soldiers in stirring words to the effect that, now that they have

---

107. Cf. Const. 4 §41.

108. Polyaenus 2.10.5; Plutarch, *Lysander* 7.4.

109. Polyaenus 2.20.

τας, ὡς τῶν ἀνδραπόδων ἐκείνων ἤδη ἀπηλλαγμένους μόνους τῆς ἀνδραγαθίας

820  ἔχεσθαι, καὶ τῶν τῆς νίκης δωρεῶν ἀξιωθῆναι.

ρξς΄. Στρατιωτῶν δειλίας διάκρισιν καὶ ἑτέρως σοι ὑποδείξω. τοῦ γὰρ στρατοῦ παντὸς ὁμοῦ ὄντος, ἐὰν κινήσῃς σάλπιγγα, ὡς ὅτι οἱ πολέμιοι συμπλέκονται πρὸς μάχην, ταραχῆς γενομένης, οἱ μὲν δειλοὶ φεύξονται, οἱ δὲ ἀνδρεῖοι
παρατάξονται.

825  ρξζ΄. Ἐὰν πρὸς ἀγυμνάστους καὶ ἀπείρους μάχης πολεμίους παρατάσσῃ,
αὐτὸς δὲ γεγυμνασμένους ἔχῃς στρατιώτας, οὐ παρευθὺ τὴν μάχην συνάψεις,
ἀλλὰ συντηρεῖν σε δεῖ τὸν χρόνον ἐν τῇ συστάσει, καὶ προεκλύειν τοὺς πολεμίους ὡς ἐπ᾽ ὀλίγον πονεῖν εἰθισμένους, καὶ τότε ἐπιτεθῇς αὐτοῖς. εἰ δὲ πρὸς
γεγυμνασμένους μάχης πολεμίους μάχεσθαι μέλλῃς, ἀγυμνάστους αὐτὸς ἔχων

830  τοὺς στρατιώτας, ἐκ τοῦ εὐθέως καὶ παραχρῆμα τὴν μάχην σύμβαλλε. ἡ γὰρ
ἀκμὴ τῶν σῶν στρατιωτῶν γενναίως ἀπομαχήσεται πρὸς τοὺς ἐναντίους.

ρξη΄. Ὑπόνοιαν ἐπιμονῆς ἐν τοιαύτῃ καιροῦ χρείᾳ δείξεις τοῖς πολεμίοις, εἰ
ἄρα μέλλεις ὑποχωρῶν ὡς μένων ἐξαπατῆσαι αὐτούς, ἐὰν δένδρα περικόψας ἢ
τούτων μὴ ὄντων ἕτερά τινα ξύλα στήσας ἐνδύσῃς αὐτὰ διὰ σκουταρίων, ὡς

835  μίμημα ἀνδρῶν ἐνόπλων ἤ, ἐὰν τοσαύτη τύχῃ ἀνάγκη, καὶ ἑτέρων ὅπλων
λαμπρῶν. οὕτως γὰρ κρείττονα τῆς τῶν ὅπλων ἀπωλείας τὴν τοῦ στρατοῦ
σωτηρίαν ἡγησάμενος διὰ τὴν κατεπείγουσαν ἴσως χρείαν ἀκινδύνως ὑποχωρήσεις.

ρξθ΄. Μάλιστα μὲν μετὰ δικαιοσύνης | παντὸς ἔργου ἀπάρχεσθαι δεῖ. πλέον   371

840  δὲ τῶν ἄλλων τὰς ἀρχὰς χρὴ τοῦ πολέμου δικαίας εἶναι, καὶ μὴ μόνον δικαίας,
ἀλλὰ καὶ φρονίμως προάγεσθαι τὸν πόλεμον. καὶ γὰρ τότε καὶ Θεὸς συναγωνι-
εῖται τοῖς στρατεύμασιν εὐμενὴς γινόμενος, καὶ οἱ ἄνθρωποι προθυμότεροι
γίνονται τοῦ δικαίου προασπίζοντες καὶ εἰδότες ὡς οὐκ ἄρχουσιν ἀδικίας, ἀλλὰ
ἀμύνονται κατὰ τῶν ἀδικούντων.

845  ρο΄. Ἐπὰν δὲ δικαίως ἀπάρχεσθαι τοῦ πολέμου μέλλῃς, ὦ στρατηγέ, χρή σε
τὴν στρατιὰν διασκευάσαι ἀκριβῶς, καὶ μετὰ ἀσφαλείας ταύτην ἐξαγαγεῖν. ἐὰν
γὰρ ἀσθενεῖς εἰσιν αἱ πολεμικαὶ κινήσεις, ὅταν τὸ βάρος ἀναλάβωσι τοῦ πολέμου, ταχὺ θλίβονται καὶ ὑστεροῦσιν. ὅθεν ὥσπερ ἀγαθὸς κυβερνήτης ἀπὸ

---

839–844 Onas. 4.1; cf. β΄.193–221.

825 καὶ ἀπείρους A om. M   827 συντηρεῖν M διατρίβειν A   830 ἐκ τοῦ M om. A
832 καιροῦ M om. A   833 μένων M μέλλων A   839 δεῖ M χρὴ A   840 χρὴ M δεῖ A
844 ἀμύνονται…ἀδικούντων M τοὺς ἀδικοῦντας ἀμύνονται A   845 ἐπὰν M ἐπεὶ A
846 διασκευάσαι M ἑτοιμάσαι A

gotten rid of those slaves, they alone can lay claim to valor and have proven <themselves> worthy of the rewards of victory.

166. I will show you another way of discerning the cowardice of the soldiers. When the entire army is gathered together, sound the trumpet as though the enemy were advancing into battle. In the confusion the cowardly will run away, whereas the brave will line up in formation.

167. If your soldiers have been well-trained and you line them up against an enemy inexperienced and untrained for battle, do not engage them immediately. Rather, maintain your formation, and wear out the enemy first, in case they are not accustomed to much <hard> work. Then attack them. But if you are about to engage a trained enemy in battle and your own troops are not well-trained, then send yours into battle immediately and without hesitation. For the best of your soldiers will fight it out bravely with the enemy.

168. When need arises, make it appear to the enemy that you are remaining in place. If, indeed, you intend to withdraw but want to trick them into <thinking> that you are remaining, chop down trees or, if there are none, set up pieces of wood and place shields upon them or, if necessary, other shiny weapons to imitate armed men. In this way, considering the safety of your army more important than the loss of the weapons because of the pressing emergency, you will withdraw without risk.[110]

169. Certainly justice must be at the beginning of every action. More than other actions, the beginnings of war must be just. Not only must it be just but the war must be conducted with prudence. For then God will become benevolent and will fight along with our armies. The men will be more enthusiastic, holding the shield of justice before them, with the realization that they are not initiating injustice but are warding off those committing unjust acts.[111]

170. Whenever you intend, O general, to enter into war justly, make sure that your army is thoroughly prepared and lead it out in safety. If your military movements are weak, your men, as they run up against the pressures of war, may be quickly worn out and fail. As a good pilot, then, sail your ship out of the

---

110. Cf. *Sylloge tacticorum*, 99.1.
111. Onasander 4.1; cf. Const. 2 §29.

λιμένος ἐξαρτήσας τὸ σκάφος, καὶ πάντα τὰ ἀναγκαῖα περὶ αὐτὸ ποιήσας, τότε
850 ἐπίτρεπε τῷ Θεῷ τὸ πᾶν τῆς ἐκβάσεως.

ροα΄. Νόμον ἐπίθες σεαυτῷ πρὸς τὸ πέρας ἀποβλέπειν τῆς τοῦ πολέμου
κινήσεως, καὶ οὕτω ταύτης ἀπάρχεσθαι. φαῦλον γὰρ καὶ σφαλερὸν κίνησιν μὲν
ποιήσασθαι πολέμου, αὖθις δὲ ἐπιστραφῆναι τὸ στράτευμα. ἕκαστος μὲν γὰρ
καταγελάσεταί σου τῆς προπετείας· οἱ δὲ ἐχθροὶ καταφρονήσουσί σου τῆς
855 ἀφελείας, οὐχὶ ὡς μὴ βουλομένου, ἀλλ᾿ οὐ δυναμένου δικαίως καὶ πρεπόντως
διαθεῖναι τὰ πράγματα.

ροβ΄. Ἡνίκα δὲ τὰς δυνάμεις ἐξάγειν μέλλεις πρὸς πόλεμον, δεῖ μὲν καθαρὰς
αὐτὰς ἐξ ἁμαρτημάτων εἶναι· φροντίσεις δὲ διὰ τῶν ἱερέων καθαγνίσαι αὐτὰς δι᾿
εὐλογίας, καὶ οὕτως μετὰ θάρσους ἐπὶ τῆς μάχης ἀποκινῆσαι.

860 ρογ΄. Σὺν πάσῃ δὲ τάξει καὶ εὐκοσμίᾳ καὶ τῇ κατὰ πόλεμον ἐμπειρίᾳ δεῖ τὸν
στρατὸν ὁδοιπορεῖν, κἂν μήπω μέλλῃ συμβαλεῖν, ἀλλὰ διὰ μακρᾶς ὁδοῦ πορεύεσθαι, κἂν πολλῶν ἡμερῶν ἀνύειν μέλλῃ ὁδὸν καὶ ἐν τῇ ἰδίᾳ χώρᾳ καὶ ἐν τῇ
πολεμίᾳ. οὕτως γὰρ ἐθισθήσεται τὰ στρατεύματα μένειν ἐν τάξει, καὶ συμφυλάττειν τὰ ἴδια τάγματα καὶ ἀκολουθεῖν τοῖς ἄρχουσιν αὐτῶν, ἀλλὰ καὶ πρὸς τὰς
865 ἐξαίφνης γινομένας ἐπιβουλὰς ἐν τῇ πολεμίᾳ μὴ ἐν ἀθρόῳ καιρῷ θορυβεῖσθαι.

ροδ΄. Ἀσφαλέστερον δὲ τὸ στράτευμα διαβήσεται τὰς προκειμένας ὁδούς,
ἐὰν διά τινων ὀλίγων προαποστείλας ἐρευνᾷς τὰς ἔμπροσθεν τρίβους ἤγουν διὰ
τῶν καλουμένων τῇ ῥωμαίᾳ γλώσσῃ μινσωρατώρων καὶ ἀντικηνσώρων.

ροε΄. Ἐὰν γυμνάζῃς στράτευμα συνεχῶς, ἕξεις αὐτοὺς πρὸς τοὺς πόνους
870 ἑτοίμους, καὶ τὴν τάξιν φυλάττοντας καὶ ῥωμαλέους τὸ σῶμα. ἡ μὲν γὰρ ἀργία
μαλθακὰ καὶ ἀσθενῆ κατασκευάζει τὰ σώματα καὶ ῥαθύμους καὶ ἀνάνδρους καὶ
δειλὰς τὰς ψυχάς· ἡ δὲ γυμνασία καὶ οἱ πόνοι καὶ τὰ σώματα εὔρωστα καὶ τὰς
ψυχὰς ἀνδρείας κατασκευάζουσιν. χρεόν σε οὖν, ὦ στρατηγέ, πρὸ καιροῦ | 371ᵛ
ὀξέως τὰ τοῦ καιροῦ μελετᾶν ἁρμόδια, καὶ τὰ χρήσιμα τότε σκευάζειν, ὅτε οὐ
875 κατεπείγει τῆς παρατάξεως ἡ ἀνάγκη.

ρος΄. Ἴσμεν πολλάκις τοὺς θρασυτέρους τῶν στρατιωτῶν ἐκ τοῦ μὴ πείθεσθαι τοῖς ἄρχουσιν ἀπολλυμένους. διὸ τοὺς βουλομένους τοῦ στρατοῦ ἄνευ τῆς
σῆς ἢ τοῦ ἄρχοντος αὐτῶν ἐντολῆς ἢ πρὸς πραῖδαν ἀπιέναι ἢ τῆς παρατάξεως

---

857–859 Cf. ιδ΄.3–7.

849 ἐξαρτήσας…σκάφος Μ τὸ σκάφος εὐτρεπίσας Α   851 νόμον Α νόμος Μ   
853 ποιήσασθαι…ἐπιστραφῆναι Μ πολέμου ποιήσασθαι πάλιν δὲ κενὸν ὑποστρέψαι Α   
855 οὐχὶ ὡς Du ὡς οὐχὶ ΜΑ   859 τῆς μάχης Μ τὴν μάχην Α   861 μέλλη συμβαλεῖν Μ
μέλλης συμβάλλειν Α   868 τῇ ῥωμαίᾳ Μ om. Α   870 ῥωμαλέους Μ ἰσχύρους Α   
872 εὔρωστα Μ ὑγιῆ Α   873 χρεόν Μ χρὴ Α   874 τοῦ Α om. Μ | σκευάζειν Μ
κατασκευάζειν Α   878 ἀπιέναι Μ ἀπέρχεσθαι Α

harbor after you have made all the necessary preparations. Then entrust the entire undertaking to God.

171. Make a law for yourself to look <first> to the end of the course of the war and only then to begin it. It is despicable and mistaken to make a movement in war and then to have the army turn back again. Everyone will make fun of your impetuosity. The enemy will despise you for your simplicity, not because you were unwilling but because you were unable to arrange matters justly and properly.

172. When you intend to lead your forces out to war, they must be purified from sin and you must take care to have them sanctified by the blessing of the priests. With confidence, then, march out to battle.[112]

173. It is necessary for the army to march in full formation, in good order, and with experience of war, even if you are not yet going to engage in combat, but are marching on a long road, even one that will take many days to complete, both in your own country and in that of the enemy. In this manner, the soldiers will get used to remaining in formation and they will maintain their own units and follow their officers. They will not be thrown into confusion all at once by a surprise attack in hostile territory.

174. The army will proceed more safely along the road before it if you reconnoiter the paths that lie ahead of you by sending out a few men, who are called minsoratores and antikensores in the Roman tongue.

175. If you drill your army continuously, you will find them ready for labor, maintaining their formation, and physically robust. Idleness renders their bodies soft and weak and their spirits lazy, unmanly, and cowardly. But drilling and hard work make their bodies robust and their spirits manly. Therefore, O general, it is necessary for you to consider ahead of time what best fits the occasion, and then to prepare what will be helpful, when there is no immediate pressure on your battle line.

176. We recognize that, frequently, the bolder soldiers are killed because they have not obeyed their officers. Anyone, therefore, who wishes to go off pillaging or who drops out of the battle line without an order from you or their

112. Cf. Const. 14 §1.

παρεξέρχεσθαι, κόλαζε τούτους διὰ μαστίγων καὶ ἀναχαίτιζε τῆς ἀταξίας, ὡς
880 αἰτίους τῆς ἑαυτῶν ἀπωλείας.

ροζʹ. Σοφὸς ἔσται στρατηγὸς φυλαττόμενος ἀπὸ πάντων τῶν μελλόντων
παρὰ τῶν πολεμίων γίνεσθαι στρατηγημάτων. γνώσεται δὲ ταῦτα ἐξ ὧν καὶ
αὐτὸς καταστρατηγεῖν τοὺς ἐχθροὺς μελετᾷ. οἷς γὰρ αὐτὸς γινώσκει τί δέον
κατὰ τῶν πολεμίων ποιεῖν, τούτοις γνώσεται καὶ τί χρὴ παρὰ τῶν πολεμίων μὴ
885 παθεῖν. αἱ γὰρ ἴδιαι πρὸς τὸ λυπεῖν ἄλλους ἐμπειρίαι καὶ τὰς τῶν ἐναντίων
ἐπινοίας καθ’ ἑαυτῶν τεκμαίρονται.

ροηʹ. Ἐάν ποτε λαθεῖν τοὺς πολεμίους βουληθῇς, εἴτε κίνημα ἀπὸ ἀπλίκτου
εἴτε ἄλλην τινὰ πρᾶξιν, μηδενὶ θάρρει ἑτέρῳ πλὴν ἑνί τινι τῶν ἀρχόντων. εἰ γὰρ
εἰς πολλοὺς διαδραμεῖ τὸ βούλευμα, πάντως ἀπὸ τῶν ἀρχόντων τοῖς ὑποχειρί-
890 οις παραδίδοται. οἱ δὲ τοιοῦτοι καιροὶ πολλοὺς εὑρίσκουσι τοὺς δι’ ἐλπίδα
δώρων προδότας γινομένους τῶν σῶν βουλευμάτων τοῖς πολεμίοις.

ροθʹ. Βέβαιον μὲν οὐδέν μοι δοκεῖ τῶν ὀνείρων. πλάττεσθαι δὲ καὶ πείθειν
τοὺς στρατιώτας ὥστε πιστεύειν τοὺς σοὺς ὀνείρους νίκην ἐπαγγελλομένους,
ἐν καιρῷ μάλιστα πολέμου, χρήσιμόν ἐστιν καὶ ἀναγκαῖον. δόξαντες γὰρ ὡς ἀπὸ
895 Θεοῦ χρήσιμον εἶναι τὸν παρά σου ἀφηγούμενον ὄνειρον, θαρσαλέως καὶ
ἀνεπιστρόφως κατὰ τῶν πολεμίων ἐπιχειρήσουσι, καὶ τῇ προθυμίᾳ τὴν ἀνδρείαν
διπλασιάσουσιν.

ρπʹ. Ἀπειροκάλως ἐπακολουθεῖν ταῖς τῶν πολεμίων ὑποχωρήσεσι σφαλερὸν
ἡγοῦμαι καὶ βλάβης αἴτιον πολλάκις. ἐξεπίτηδες γὰρ τοῦτο ποιοῦντες, ἐνίοτε δι’
900 ἐγκρυμμάτων ἢ δι’ ὑποστροφῆς, καὶ ἀσυντάκτοις καὶ διεσκεδασμένοις ἐμπί-
πτοντες τοῖς διώκουσι μεγάλας ποιήσουσι τὰς βλάβας. ὅταν τοίνυν ὑποφευγόν-
των τῶν ἐχθρῶν διώκειν μέλλῃς, μὴ λύε τὴν τάξιν τῆς παρατάξεως μέχρις ἂν
τελείαν λάβῃς πληροφορίαν τῆς τῶν διωκομένων ἀνελπίστου σωτηρίας.

ρπαʹ. Στρατιωτῶν φρονήματα πρὸς δειλίαν καταπεσόντα ἐχέφρων στρατη-
905 γὸς δύναται διεγεῖραι διὰ τῆς οἰκείας ὄψεως, θαρσαλέος αὐτοῖς καὶ περιχαρὴς
φαινόμενος, καὶ πρὸς τούτοις καὶ τοῖς λόγοις ἀλείφων καὶ πιθανώτερος γινό-

904–908 Cf. βʹ.58–70.

886 τεκμαίρονται M στοχάζονται A 890 παραδίδοται M γνωσθήσεται A
890–891 ἐλπίδα δώρων M trsp. A 892–894 καὶ…μάλιστα M ὀνείρατα νίκην
ἐπαγγελλόμενα τοῖς στρατιώταις μάλιστα ἐν καιρῷ A 894 καὶ ἀναγκαῖον M om. A
895 εἶναι A om. M 898 ἀπειροκάλως PG ἀπειροκάλας M ἁπλῶς καὶ ὡς ἔτυχεν A |
ὑποχωρήσεσι M ὑποχειρήσεσιν A 899 πολλάκις M πολλάκις γὰρ A | ἐνίοτε M om. A
901 διώκουσι M διώκουσιν A 902 λύε M λύῃς A 903 τελείαν λάβῃς M trsp. A
904 ἐχέφρων M φρόνιμος A 906 καὶ¹…τούτοις M om. A | πιθανώτερος M προτρεπόμενος
A 906–907 γινόμενος…τὰ M ὥστε μετασχηματίσαι καὶ μεταβαλεῖν τὰ τῶν στρατιωτῶν A

commanding officer, should be punished by flogging, and so bring this disorder to an end. Such men are responsible for their own destruction.

177. A wise general is the one who defends himself against all the stratagems that the enemy may plan to employ. He knows what they are because he himself is thinking about the stratagems he may employ to counter those of the enemy. From his knowledge of what actions he ought to take against the enemy, he will know what steps are necessary to avoid being harmed by them. One's own experience in causing harm to others enables one to estimate the plans of his adversaries against himself.

178. If you wish to conceal from the enemy a movement out of camp or any other activity, do not confide in another person except only one of the officers. For if your intention is spread among a large number of officers, assuredly they will pass it on to their subordinates. This provides an opportunity for many who are ready to betray your plans to the enemy in the hope of gifts.

179. I do not believe that there is anything certain about dreams. But it is useful, even necessary, in time of war, to manipulate and persuade the soldiers to believe that your dreams portend victory. They will think that the dream related by you is something positive, coming from God, and they will engage the enemy more boldly and without relenting and their eagerness will double their bravery.

180. I think that following rashly after the enemy as they withdraw is a mistake and frequently causes harm. They do this on purpose. Sometimes by ambushes and sometimes by wheeling about, they fall upon their disorganized and scattered pursuers and inflict the greatest damage. So, whenever you wish to pursue the enemy as they are running away, do not break up the order of your battle line until you shall have received definite information about the hopelessness of the situation for those being pursued.

181. A sensible general is able to arouse the spirits of those soldiers who are turning into cowards by means of his own appearance, presenting himself as confident and very cheerful before them. In addition, he should be very persua-

μενος, ὥστε συσχηματίσαι τῶν στρατιωτῶν τὰ φρονήματα | πρὸς τὸ τοῦ στρα-    372
τηγοῦ φαινόμενον θάρσος.

ρπβ΄. Τάξις οὐ μία ἐστὶ πολέμου, ἀλλὰ πολλαὶ καὶ διάφοροι, καὶ παρὰ τοὺς
910 ὁπλισμοὺς καὶ παρὰ τοὺς στρατευομένους καὶ παρὰ τοὺς ἀντιπολεμίους καὶ
παρὰ τοὺς τόπους καὶ παρὰ τοὺς καιρούς. τούτων δὲ τὰς διαφοράς, ὦ στρατηγέ,
ἐπὶ αὐτῶν τῶν πραγμάτων μαθήσῃ. οὐ γάρ, ὡς βούλει, παρατάξεις, ἀλλ᾿ ὡς
ἀνάγκη ἀπαιτεῖ οὕτως καὶ ποιήσεις τὴν ἔκταξιν καὶ τοῦ στρατοῦ καὶ τῆς ὁπλίσεως καὶ κατὰ πρόσωπον καὶ ἐκ πλαγίου καὶ ὄπισθεν καὶ ὡς ἡ χρεία τῶν πραγμά-
915 των ἀπαιτήσει.

ρπγ΄. Ὅταν πεζικὴν στρατείαν παρατάξῃς ἢ ὁπλοφόρων ἀνδρῶν τῶν λεγομένων σκουτάτων ἢ τῶν ψιλῶν, ἤγουν τοξοτῶν καὶ σφενδονητῶν, ἀντιπολε-
μοῦντες δὲ αὐτοῖς τινες βάλωσι κατ᾿ αὐτῶν ἢ ρικτάρια ἢ διὰ σφενδοβόλων καὶ
τόξων, δεῖ αὐτοὺς ὑπὸ σκουταρίων τετραγώνων ἐπιμηκῶν τῶν λεγομένων
920 θυρεῶν ἢ ἑτέρων σκουταρίων μεγάλων κεραμῶσαι ἑαυτοὺς ἄνωθεν, καὶ οὕτως
προσβαλεῖν. καὶ γὰρ κεραμωθέντες καὶ σκεπόμενοι οὐδὲν πάθωσι κακὸν ὑπὸ
τῶν πεμπομένων βελῶν κατ᾿ αὐτῶν.

ρπδ΄. Στρατῷ πολεμίων μηνοειδῶς παραταττομένῳ—αὕτη γὰρ ἡ παράταξις
δοκεῖ τάξις ἡμικυκλίου γινομένη ἀσφαλὴς εἶναι καὶ ἄτρεπτος· τοὺς γὰρ ἐμπί-
925 πτοντας ἀντιπολεμίους ἐν τῷ τοῦ σίγματος κοιλώματι ἐκ τῶν ἔνθεν καὶ ἐκεῖθεν
τὰς κεραίας ἁπλοῦντες καὶ περικυκλοῦντες ἐναποκλείουσι καὶ οὕτως δραστικώτερον κατ᾿ αὐτῶν ἀπομάχονται—πρὸς ταύτην οὖν ἀντιπαραταττόμενος τὴν
μηνοειδῆ τάξιν εἰς τρία μέρη τὴν σὴν παράταξιν διαιρήσεις. καὶ τοῖς μὲν δυσὶ
μέρεσι τῷ τε δεξιῷ καὶ τῷ εὐωνύμῳ ποιήσεις τὴν προσβολὴν κατὰ τῶν δύο
930 κεράτων τῶν πολεμίων, τὸ δὲ μέσον μέρος στήσεις μὴ προσβαλὸν τῇ κοιλότητι,
ἀλλ᾿ ἐν ὑποβοηθείᾳ τῶν προσβαλόντων δύο μερῶν ἱστάμενον. οὕτως γὰρ ἢ
ἄπρακτος ὁ ἐν κύκλῳ τῶν πολεμίων στρατὸς ἐναπομείνῃ ἢ κἀκεῖνος προσβαλὼν τὴν μηνοειδῆ τάξιν διαλύσει. εἰ δὲ πλασάμενος αὐτὸς ὑποχώρησιν τοῦ

---

909 οὐ…ἐστὶ M οὔκ ἐστι μία A    913 ἀνάγκη…καὶ¹ A ἀναγκάζει M    916 ὁπλοφόρων M
ὁπλιτῶν A  917 τῶν M om. A  918 βάλωσι A  βάλωσιν M  923 μηνοειδῶς
παρατεττομένῳ M σιγματοειδῶς παρατασσομένῳ A    924 τάξις Du τάξιν M om. A |
ἡμικυκλίου γινομένη M om. A  925–926 ἐν…καὶ¹ M ἐντὸς τοῦ σιγματοειδοῦς ἐκείνου
σχήματος A  926–927 δραστικώτερον M ἰσχυρώτερον A  928 μηνοειδῆ τάξιν M
σιγματοειδῆ παράταξιν A  929 εὐωνύμῳ M ἀριστερῷ A  930 στήσεις M τῆς σῆς
παρατάξεως A | κοιλότητι M κοιλότητι καὶ τῷ βάθει τοῦ σιγματοειδοῦς σχήματος A
932 τῶν…στρατὸς M trsp. A  932–933 προσβαλὼν…τάξιν PG προσβαλὼν τῇ μηνοειδεῖ
τάξει M προσβαλεῖν βουλόμενος τῇ μέσῃ σου παρατάξει τὴν σιγματοειδῆ τάξιν A
933 πλασάμενος M σχηματισάμενος A

sive, encouraging them by his words so as to mould the thoughts of the soldiers by the obvious confidence of the general.[113]

182. There is not only one formation for war, but many and diverse because of the armament, the men in military service, the enemy, and because of time and place. You may learn, O general, these differences from the actual practice itself. You will not form your line just as you wish, but you will so dispose the army and see to the weaponry in accord with what is necessary, facing the front, the flanks, the rear, and whatever the needs of the situation shall require.

183. When you draw up an infantry army, either of men bearing weapons called heavy-armed troops, or of light-armed troops, such as archers and slingers, and the force fighting against them hurl javelins or <make use of> slings and bows, then your men should cover themselves above by oblong, four-sided shields, called thyreoi, or by other large shields, and in this way proceed to attack. So roofed over and covered, they will not suffer any harm from the missiles hurled against them.

184. <Facing> an enemy army drawn up in crescent formation. This formation, shaped like a semicircle, seems safe and unbreakable, for when the adversary falls into the hollow space of the sigma,[114] then those on the flanks here and there spread out, close them in and encircle them and, in this way, fight more effectively against them. Therefore, in drawing up your line to oppose this crescent formation, divide your battle line into three sections. Make two sections, the right and the left, advance against the horns of the enemy. Position the middle section so it does not advance against the hollow space but stands ready to come to the aid of the two sections moving forward. The enemy army then remains in a circle accomplishing nothing, or else it moves to attack and, by doing so, breaks up its crescent formation. If you simulate a withdrawal of your middle section, you will provoke your adversaries into pursuing you. Not

113. Cf. Const. 2 §12.

114. This is the lunate sigma, written in ancient and medieval Greek like the letter C, hence crescent formation.

μέσου μέρους κινήσεις τοὺς ἐναντίους πρὸς δίωξιν, οὐ μόνον λυθήσεται ἡ
935 παράταξις, ἀλλὰ καὶ ἀσυντάκτως διώκουσα τὸ σὸν στράτευμα συντεταγμένον,
δι᾽ ὑποστροφῆς ἀθρόας ἐπιτεθῇς αὐτοῖς, καὶ εὑρεθήσονται πάντως οἵ σε διώκοντες διωκόμενοι παρά σου.

ρπε΄. Ἅπασα μὲν ἐνέδρα ἤτοι ἔγκρυμμα ἐπερχόμενον τοῖς πολεμίοις ἰσχυρο-
τέραν τῶν ἄλλων ἐπιβολῶν ποιεῖται τὴν κατ᾽ αὐτῶν ἐπίθεσιν, μάλιστα δὲ ἡ κατὰ
940 νώτου τῶν πολεμίων. τοιαύτην οὖν ποτε ποιήσας καὶ αὐτὸς ἐνέδραν καὶ ὄπι-
σθεν αὐτῶν ἐπιτεθείς, δραστικωτέραν καὶ | ἐνεργεστέραν αὐτὴν ὄψει γινομένην    372ᵛ
τῶν ἐκ πλαγίου ἐγκρυμμάτων.

ρπς΄. Ὑπὸ τῶν ἄλλων ἀρχόντων τὰ παραγγέλματα πρὸς τὸν στρατὸν δεῖ
γίνεσθαι καὶ τὰ διατάγματα καὶ τὰ συνθήματα, ἀλλὰ μὴ διὰ τῆς σῆς ἐνδοξότη-
945 τος, ὦ στρατηγέ. τὸ γὰρ κηρύττειν σε ταῦτα δι᾽ ἑαυτοῦ ἐν ὀξύτητι καιροῦ
ἰδιώτου ἐστὶ καὶ ἀπείρου λίαν τῶν δεόντων· καὶ γὰρ καὶ χρόνος πολὺς ἐν τῷ
παραγγέλλειν ἀναλωθήσεται καὶ θόρυβος ὁμοῦ πάντων ἀλλήλους ἐρωτώντων,
τάχα δὲ καὶ ὁ μὲν προσθήσει τι πλέον τοῦ παραγγέλματος, ὁ δὲ καὶ παραλείψει.

ρπζ΄. Γνώρισμα γνησίου στρατηγοῦ καὶ θαυμάζεσθαι ἀξίου τὸ τῆς ἀνάγκης
950 ἐπικειμένης ὀξέως νοεῖν τὰ δέοντα μᾶλλον ἤπερ τὸ πρὸ τῆς ἀνάγκης περὶ
τούτων βουλεύσασθαι. οὐ γὰρ δυνατὸν προβουλεύεσθαι, εἰ καὶ τὰ μάλιστα
δέον, ὅσα μέλλει γεννᾶν ἡ τοῦ πολέμου ἐπικειμένη περίστασις.

ρπη΄. Ὅταν ἐν παρατάξει, μάλιστα ἡλίου ἀνταυγάζοντος, προσβάλῃς πρὸ
τοῦ συμπλακῆναι τὴν μάχην, κέλευε τοὺς στρατιώτας ἄνω ἔχειν τὰ ὅπλα καὶ
955 ἀκάλυπτα, ξίφη τε καὶ τὰ σιδηρᾶ σκουτάρια στίλβοντα, καὶ τῶν κονταρίων τὰς
λόγχας. οὕτως γὰρ λαμπρὰ παρὰ τοῖς πολεμίοις φαινόμενα, κατάπληξιν ποιήσει.
ὅταν δὲ εἰς χεῖρας ἤδη συμπλέκεσθαι μέλλεις, μετὰ ἀλαλαγμοῦ σφοδροῦ ἤγουν
μεγάλης φωνῆς καὶ δρόμου πατάσσοντας τὰ ὅπλα οὕτω τὴν προσβολὴν πρὸς
τοὺς πολεμίους ἀπάρχεσθαι.

960 ρπθ΄. Ὑπὸ τῶν πολεμίων διὰ πλῆθος αὐτῶν καβαλλαρίων πλεονεκτούμενος,
τραχέα χωρία ἐκλέγου καὶ στενὰ καὶ παρόρια, ἐν οἷς οὐ δυνατὸν τοὺς ἵππους

---

935 διώκουσα Du διώκουσαν MA   936 ἀθρόας M ἀθρόως A | καὶ εὑρεθήσονται M
εὑρεθήσονται γὰρ A   938 ἐνέδρα ἤτοι M om. A   939–940 ἡ…νώτου M ἐὰν ὄπισθεν
ἐπέλθῃ A   940 ἐνέδραν M ἔγκρυμμα A   941 δραστικωτέραν καὶ M om. A
946 ἀπείρου…δεόντων M πάνυ ἀπείρου τῶν πρεπόντων A   947 ἀναλωθήσεται M
παρελεύσεται A | ὁμοῦ M ὁμοῦ γενήσεται A   948 καὶ¹…προσθήσει M μηδὲ τούτου σάφους
ἀκούοντες καὶ οἱ μὲν προσθήσουσιν A | ὁ²…παραλείψει M οἱ δὲ καὶ παραλείψουσιν A
958–959 τὴν…ἀπάρχεσθαι M τῆς πρὸς τοὺς πολεμίους ἀπάρχεσθαι προσβολῆς A

only will their formation be broken up, but they will be disorganized in chasing after your troops, who are still in formation. Then, suddenly wheel about and attack them. The army pursuing you will swiftly find out that it is they who are being pursued by you.

185. More than any other kind of attack, every ambush or ambuscade set up against the enemy, especially against their rear, gives added strength to your offensive against them. At times, therefore, set up an ambush and attack them in the rear. You will see that this is more efficient and effective than an ambush against their flanks.

186. Commands, orders, and passwords must be given to the army by the officers, not by Your Excellency, O general. For you to make such announcements in person at a critical moment is clearly the mark of an ignorant person who has absolutely no experience of what has to be done. Much time will be wasted in making the announcements along with the confusion as everyone is asking questions of one another. One individual will quickly add something more to the announcement and another will leave something out.

187. The mark of a genuine general and one worthy of admiration lies in perceiving what has to be done at the moment of great emergency rather than the ability to make plans about such matters before the emergency. Even for particularly necessary matters, it is not possible to plan ahead for all that the present circumstances of war are about to engender.

188. Before engaging the enemy in battle, when you are about to begin the charge, while you are still in formation, and with the sun in your eyes, order the soldiers to raise their weapons on high, uncovered, with the swords and the iron on the shields shining, as well as the points of the spears. This will cause them to appear bright to the enemy and will strike them with consternation. When you are about to come to close quarters with them, launch your charge against the enemy with a forceful war cry, shouting loudly and on the run, banging your weapons.

189. When the enemy has the advantage because of his large number of cavalry, choose rough places, narrow and near mountains, in which the horses

τῶν ἐναντίων διώκειν κατὰ δύναμιν· ὅπερ καὶ προσκοπεῖν σε χρὴ πρὸς δευτέραν τύχην ἀεὶ βλέποντα. τοῦτο γάρ ἐστιν ἐχέφρονος μάλιστα στρατηγοῦ.

ρϟ΄. Συμφέρον μᾶλλον γίνωσκε εἶναι, τὸ ἐν ταῖς μάχαις ἐνίστασθαι καὶ
965 κινδυνεύειν ἀνδρείως τὴν παράταξιν μαχομένην ἢ φυγόντας διώκεσθαι· ἐν γὰρ
τῇ ἐνστάσει μᾶλλον τὴν σωτηρίαν ἐλπίζειν χρεόν, ἀλλὰ μὴ τοῖς ἐχθροῖς τὰ νῶτα
διδόντας πιστεύειν τὸ σώζεσθαι.

ρϟα΄. Τῆς μάχης σὺν Θεῷ τὴν νίκην σοι χαρισαμένης, ὦ στρατηγέ, δέον σε
φιλοφρονεῖσθαι τοὺς στρατιώτας τοῖς τῶν πολεμίων λαφύροις—εἴτε ὅπλα εἰσὶν
970 εἴτε ἵπποι εἴτε ἕτερά τινα εἴδη—καὶ εὐωχίας καὶ τραπέζας αὐτοῖς παρασκευάζειν,
καὶ τοὺς μὲν ἀνδρείως ἀγωνισαμένους κατὰ τάξιν προβιβάσαι καὶ δώροις
τιμῆσαι. τοὺς δὲ δειλοὺς καὶ ἀχρήστους ἀναφανέντας ἢ λειποταξίας πεποιηκότας, τοὺς μὲν κόλαζε δεόντως, τοὺς δὲ ὀνείδιζε μέχρις αἰσχύνης. οὕτως γὰρ καὶ
τοὺς δειλοὺς ἀναρρώσεις καὶ διεγερεῖς, καὶ τοὺς ἀνδρείους εὐτολμοτέρους καὶ
975 εὐθαρσεῖς πρὸς τὰς ἐπιούσας μάχας παρασκευάσεις.|

ρϟβ΄. Ὅταν κατὰ πολεμίων τρόπαιον στήσῃς, ὦ στρατηγέ, τότε κατὰ τοὺς    373
ἤδη παρὰ τῆς βασιλείας ἡμῶν τεθέντας νόμους, τῶν, ὡς εἰκός, εὑρισκομένων
σκύλων τὸν διαμερισμὸν οὕτως ποιήσεις, ὥστε τὸ πέμπτον μέρος ἀφορίσεις τῷ
μέρει τοῦ δημοσίου, τὸ δὲ λοιπὸν ἐξ ἴσης μοίρας. οἵ τε ἄρχοντες καὶ οἱ ἀρχόμε-
980 νοι μεριζέσθωσαν, ἐπείπερ κοινοὺς καὶ τοὺς ἀγῶνας ἐν τοῖς κινδύνοις ἀναδέ-
χονται. εἰ δέ τινες εὑρεθῶσιν ἐκ τῶν ἀρχόντων ἢ προμάχων τῆς παρατάξεως ἢ
τις ἕτερος τῶν στρατιωτῶν διαφόρως ἀνδρισάμενοι, τότε ἐκ τοῦ εἰρημένου
μέρους τοῦ δημοσίου ἄδειαν ἕξεις φιλοτιμεῖσθαι αὐτοὺς ἐφ᾽ ὅσον ἡ χρεία καὶ τὸ
δίκαιον ἀπαιτεῖ, κατὰ δὲ τὴν μερίδα τοῦ ἐν τῷ πολέμῳ εὑρισκομένου καὶ οἱ ἐν
985 τῷ τούλδῳ καταλειπόμενοι λήψονται φύλακες.

ρϟγ΄. Στρατοῦ συμμίκτου πεζῶν καὶ καβαλλαρίων παράταξις οἷον θώρακι
ἔοικεν· ἀντὶ μὲν χειρῶν ἔχουσα τοὺς ψιλοὺς ἤγουν τοξότας καὶ ἀκοντιστὰς καὶ
σφενδονήτας, ἀντὶ δὲ ποδῶν τοὺς καβαλλαρίους, ἀντὶ δὲ κεφαλῆς ἐν μέσῳ τῶν
χειρῶν σε τὸν στρατηγόν. ἀντὶ δὲ τοῦ ἄλλου σώματος τοὺς ὁπλίτας ἤγουν τοὺς
990 σκουτάτους, τοὺς καὶ τὴν πανοπλίαν φοροῦντας. διὰ τοῦτο ἐν πᾶσι χρεωστεῖς

---

968–975 Onas. 34.

---

963 ἐστιν ἐχέφρονος M ἐστι φρονίμου A    966 χρεόν M χρὴ A    968 μάχης…χαρισαμένης
M νίκης παρὰ θεοῦ χαρισθείσης A    974 ἀναρρώσεις καὶ M om. A    977 ἡμῶν A om. M
982 διαφόρως M διαφερόντως A    984 τοῦ…εὑρισκομένου M τῶν ἐν τῷ πολέμῳ
εὑρισκομένων A    990 τοὺς…φοροῦντας M om. A

of the enemy are not able to pursue in force. With an eye always toward second fortune, you must search out such places ahead of time. This is a sure sign of a sensible general.

190. Know that it is more beneficial to take a stand in battle and to face danger bravely fighting in the ranks than to flee and be pursued. You must, rather, place your hope of salvation in your resistance. Do not believe you will be saved by showing your back to the enemy.

191. When, with the help of God, you have been favored with victory in battle, O general, you must be generous to your soldiers with the spoils taken from the enemy, weapons, horses, or other items—and you should prepare celebrations and banquets for them. You should promote in rank those who have fought bravely and honor them with gifts. As for those who acquitted themselves in a cowardly fashion, proved useless, or were guilty of desertion, punish some in a fitting manner and reproach others to shame them. In this way, you will give renewed strength to the cowardly and stir them up again, and you will cause the brave soldiers to be even bolder and more courageous in engaging in future battles.[115]

192. When you are victorious over the enemy, O general, then, according to the laws already laid down by Our Majesty, you should arrange for the distribution of the booty likely to be found, as follows. Apportion the fifth part to the division of the public funds and the rest of it in equal portions. Let both the officers and the men under them divide it among themselves inasmuch as they have taken part in the struggle and faced danger together. But if some of the officers or men in the front ranks of the battle line, or any other soldiers, have been outstanding in valor, then, from the aforementioned public division, feel free to be generous to them to the extent that need and justice demand. Even the guards left behind with the baggage train should receive a share of the spoils from battle.

193. The battle line of a mixed army of infantry and cavalry resembles the trunk of a body. In place of hands it has light-armed troops, that is, archers, javelin throwers, and slingers. In place of feet it has the cavalry. In place of a head between the hands it has you, the general. In place of the other parts of the body it has the heavy-armed troops, those in full armament, once called hoplites. In every way, bearing all this in mind, you have an obligation to be concerned for your own safety and for that of the army, just as if <you were> the

---

115. Onasander 34.

καὶ αὐτὸς προνοεῖν τῆς ἑαυτοῦ ἀσφαλείας καὶ τοῦ στρατοῦ ὥσπερ κεφαλὴ
κἀκεῖνοι τῆς σῆς φυλακῆς καὶ σωτηρίας.

ρρδ΄. Καὶ ταῦτα δὲ χρειώδη ἐν καιρῷ αὐτῶν ὥστε, ἐὰν στρατὸν ἔχων πλείονα βούλῃ αὐτὸν διά τινα χρείαν ὀλίγον ὑποδεῖξαι τοῖς πολεμίοις, κοινοποιήσῃς
995  τὰ κοντουβέρνια καὶ εἰς μίαν καμάρδαν λεγομένην ποιήσεις ἀναπαύεσθαι, καὶ
τὰ ὅπλα δὲ ἐπάλληλα θεῖναι κελεύσεις. ὅταν δὲ ὀλίγον ἔχῃς στρατόν, τὸ ἓν
κοντουβέρνιον διαμερίσεις εἰς δύο ἢ καὶ πλείονα κατὰ στρατιώτην, καὶ οὕτως
πλῆθος φανεῖται, ἵνα μὴ διὰ τὴν ὀλιγότητα καταφρονηθείς, ταχέως δὲ τοῦ
ἁπλίκτου μεταστάς, εἰς ἕτερον ἀπελεύσῃ. καὶ οὕτως τοὺς πολεμίους καταμαθὼν
1000  τὸν πόλεμον συνάψῃς.

ρρε΄. Ἀπὸ τῶν πεπλασμένως γινομένων κατ᾽ αὐτῶν προσβολῶν οἱ στρατιῶται ἐθιζόμενοι ἀκατάπληκτοι γίνονται πρὸς τὰ ἀληθῆ, οἷον ψευδοβοηθείας
μέρους τινὸς ἐπελθούσης κατὰ ἑτέρου πάλιν ψευδοπροδοσίας ἢ ψευδοεγκρυμμάτων ἢ ψευδοκτύπων καὶ ἤχων ἢ ψευδοαυτομόλων ἢ ψευδοεφόδων. οὕτως
1005  γὰρ ἐθισθήσονται καὶ οὐκ ἐκπλαγήσονται ἐξαίφνης τούτων καὶ ἀληθῶς γινομένων.

ρρς΄. Ἱστορήσω σοι καὶ ναυτικοῦ στόλου στρατήγημα. ὅταν γὰρ εἰς ἀλιμένους καὶ ψαμμώδεις τόπους τὴν ἀπόβασιν μέλλῃς ἐν καιρῷ ναυτικῆς στρατηγίας, εἰ οὕτω τύχοι, ποιήσασθαι σάκκους πολλοὺς πληρώσας ἄμμου, καὶ τοῖς
1010  σχοινίοις προσδήσας ἀπὸ ἑκάστου | δρόμωνος ἐκκρεμάσεις τοὺς ἀρκοῦντας    373ᵛ
οἱονεὶ σιδηρᾶς ἀγκύρας, καὶ οὕτως τὸν λεγόμενον πελαγολιμένα ποιήσας,
εὐκόλως κατὰ τὸν τόπον νυκτὸς ἐξελθὼν τὴν βεβουλευμένην σοι καταδρομὴν
ποιήσεις.

ρρζ΄. Τόπους ἀνύδρους μέλλων ποτὲ διαβαίνειν, ὕδωρ μὲν ὅσον δυνατὸν
1015  συνεπάγου· νυκτὸς δὲ ποιοῦ τὴν ὁδοιπορίαν ἀπὸ ἑσπέρας ἕως πρωῖ, τὴν δὲ
ἡμέραν καθεύδειν προτρέπου ἀντὶ τῆς νυκτός. οὕτως γὰρ ἧττον διψήσουσι τὰ
ζῷα, καὶ αὐτάρκης σοι γενήσεται ἡ τοῦ ὕδατος χρεία.

ρρη΄. Οἰωνιστικοῖς λόγοις προσέκειτό ποτε στρατὸς καὶ σημείοις. πταρμοῦ
δὲ γενομένου παρά τινος ἠθύμουν οἱ στρατιῶται ὡς ἐπὶ χαλεπῷ οἰωνίσματι.

---

1007–1013 Polyaen. 3.9.38.    1018–1023 Polyaen. 3.10.2.

995 κοντουβέρνια Α κουτουβέρνια Μ | καμάρδαν λεγομένην Μ ἀτεγίαν τῶ δύο Α
997 κοντουβέρνιον Α κουτουβέρνιον Μ  1003–1004 ψευδοεγκρυμμάτων Du ψευδοεγ-
κρύμματα ΜΑ  1004 ψευδοαυτομόλων Μ ψευδοπροφύγων Α  1007–1008 ἀλιμένους…
τόπους Μ τόπους μὴ ἔχοντας λιμένας καὶ ψαμμώδεις Α  1009 εἰ…τύχοι Μ om. Α
1015 συνεπάγου Μ ἐπιφέρου Α  1016 καθεύδειν προτρέπου Μ προτρέπου κοιμᾶσθαι Α |
ἧττον Μ ὀλιγώτερον Α  1018 προσέκειτο ποτε Μ ποτὲ προσεῖχεν Α  1019 οἰωνίσματι Μ
μαντεύματι Α

head, and they \<are likewise\> obliged to be concerned for your protection and safety.

194. These things too are useful on occasion. If you have a large army and, for some reason, you want it to look small to the enemy, have the squads come together and take their rest in one so-called shelter, and order them to place their weapons next to one another. But, when you have a small army, divide the squad in two or more, according to the number of soldiers. It will then seem to be a very large army and you will not be despised because you are few in number. Quickly move out of your campsite, go off to another one and, after closely observing the enemy, join battle with them.

195. Simulated attacks against the soldiers will accustom them to real attacks so they will not be caught by surprise. There may be a simulated support force of some division advancing against another, against a pretended betrayal or a simulated ambush or false clanging and loud noises, or pretended deserters or simulated attacks. In this way, they will become accustomed and will not be struck by surprise on encountering the real thing.

196. I will tell you of a stratagem for the naval fleet. When, in the course of a naval expedition, it happens that you wish to disembark in a sandy place without a harbor, fill a large number of sacks with sand, tie them with ropes, and hang a sufficient number of them from each dromon like iron anchors. Thus, having made what is called a harbor at sea, you will easily disembark at that place at night and make the raid you had planned.[116]

197. At times when you intend to traverse places without water, carry as much water as possible with you. Do your marching at night, from evening until early morning, and give yourself to sleep during the day instead of at night. Thus, the animals will not be as thirsty and you will be able to handle the need for water by yourself.

198. Once there was an army that gave credence to stories about omens and to signs. When an individual sneezed, the soldiers lost courage, as though it

116. Polyaenus 3.9.38.

1020　εἶτα εἶπεν ὁ στρατηγός· "οὐ θαυμαστὸν εἰ τοσούτων περιεστώτων εἷς ἔπταρεν."
καὶ τούτου λεχθέντος, γέλως ἐγένετο· ἔστι δὲ ὁ γέλως σωτηρίας δηλωτικὸς
σημαντικός. καὶ οὕτως ἐχέφρων στρατηγὸς τὸ οἰώνισμα ἐναλλάξας θαρρεῖν
τοὺς στρατιώτας παρεσκεύασεν.

ρθ′. Ὅρα σὺ ἵνα, ἐὰν ἐν ἡμέρᾳ τινὶ τοῦ ἐνιαυτοῦ ἢ μηνὸς γέγονε νίκη,
1025　μέλλεις δὲ πρὸς πόλεμον συμβάλλειν, εἴγε δυνατόν σοι ἐν αὐτῇ τῇ ἡμέρᾳ. καὶ
αὖθις τῆς μάχης ἀπάρξασθαι ἐπιτήδευσον, ὥστε εὐθαρσεῖς εἶναι τοὺς στρατιώτας, καὶ μετὰ ἀγαθῆς ἐλπίδος, ὡς κατ᾽ αὐτὴν ἑορτὴν τῆς νίκης καὶ αὖθις δυναμένους ἔχειν τοὺς προσβαλόντας τὴν θείαν βοήθειαν. ὁμοίως δὲ καὶ ἐπὶ τόπου
ἐν ᾧ νενίκηκάς ποτε.

1030　σ′. Θροείτω δέ σε μηδὲν ὃ μέλλω λέγειν· ὅτι στρατηγὸς ἀληθὴς καὶ ἄριστος
τότε γινώσκεται, ὅταν μὴ τὸ δοκοῦν αὐτῷ ἴδιον συμφέρον ἐργάζεται μόνον,
ἀλλὰ καὶ τὰ κοινὰ καὶ συμφέροντα τοῖς ὑποχειρίοις πραγματεύεται. οὕτως γὰρ
μετὰ τοῦ κοινῇ συμφέροντος καὶ τοῦ ἰδίου τεύξεται. ὅταν γὰρ ὁ ποιμὴν τῆς
ποίμνης ἐπιμελεῖται, τῆς ἑαυτοῦ ὠφελείας παραίτιος γίνεται. εἰ δὲ ταύτης
1035　καταμελήσοι, οὐ μόνον ποιμὴν ἀληθὴς οὐ λογίζεται, ἀλλὰ καὶ τὴν ποίμνην
ζημιούμενος τῆς ἐξ αὐτῆς ὠφελείας στερηθήσεται.

σα′. Πολεμίου ποτὲ ναυτικοῦ στόλου ὄντος μετὰ οἰκείας δυνάμεως ναυτικῆς
ὑποχωρῶν στρατηγὸς μηνοειδῆ παράταξιν ποιούμενος, ὑποστρεφέτω πλέων
κατὰ πρύμναν, καὶ οὕτως ἀποχωρίζεσθαι τῶν πολεμίων βουλευέσθω. καὶ γὰρ οὐ
1040　φεύγων, ἀλλὰ φυγομαχῶν ἑτοίμους ἕξει τὰς ναῦς καὶ αὖθις ἐπελθεῖν τοῖς πολεμίοις κατὰ πρῶραν, εἴγε καὶ τούτου χρεία γένηται, τὰς πρῶρας ἔχων πρὸς αὐτούς. καὶ γὰρ οὐδὲ θαρσήσουσιν ἐν τῷ κοιλώματι εἰσελθεῖν τὴν κύκλωσιν
ὑφορώμενοι.

σβ′. Νίκης σοι παρὰ Θεοῦ διδομένης, μὴ σφαλερῶς καὶ ἀκρατῶς δίωκε τοὺς
1045　πολεμίους. ἀλλὰ φυλάσσου τὰς ὑποστροφὰς αὐτῶν. ἡ γὰρ ἀκρατὴς δίωξις
διαλύουσα τὴν τάξιν | ἐπιβουλευτοὺς ποιήσει τοὺς διώκοντας.　374

σγ′. Νουνεχῶς διέρχου διὰ στενῶν τόπων, καὶ μάλιστα ἀναχωρῶν ἀπὸ τῆς
πολεμίας τοὺς εὐρώστους καὶ ῥωμαλέους τῶν στρατιωτῶν ὄπισθεν ἐν τῇ
οὐραγίᾳ τάσσε, ἵνα καὶ τοὺς ἐπερχομένους πολεμίους ἀμύνωνται ὄπισθεν, καὶ

---

1021 τούτου A τοῦτο M　1022 ἐχέφρων M φρόνιμος A | οἰώνισμα M παρατήρημα A
1026 αὖθις M πάλιν A　1027 αὖθις M πάλιν A　1029 νενίκηκάς ποτε M trsp. A
1030 δέ…μηδὲν M σε μηδὲ ταράσσετω A　1033 τεύξεται M ἐπιτύχῃ A　1035 ποιμὴν…
λογίζεται M trsp. A　1036 ἐξ αὐτῆς codd. an ἑαυτοῦ legendum? (cf. 1034)　1037 ὄντος A
om. M　1040 αὖθις M πάλιν A　1046 ἐπιβουλευτοὺς M εὐεπιβουλευτοὺς A　1048 καὶ
ῥωμαλέους M om. A　1049 καὶ[1] M om. A

were a very bad omen. The general then remarked: "It is no wonder, given the number present, that one person has sneezed." When he had said this, laughter broke out. Laughter, now, is a clear indication of salvation and so, a sensible general changed the omen around and managed to encourage his troops.[117]

199. Be attentive so that, if a victory happened on a certain day of the year or of the month, you plan to advance into battle on that same day, if you can do so. Make ready to enter into battle anew so that the soldiers will be in good spirits and have good hopes that, on the very anniversary of the victory, they will once more, as they attack, have the divine assistance. The same goes for the place in which you had once been victorious.

200. Do not be disturbed by what I am about to say. A true general, indeed, the very best, is recognized when he does not work only for what seems to be for his own benefit, but also takes measures for the common benefit of his subordinates. For in this way, along with the common good, he will achieve what is beneficial for him as well. When the shepherd is concerned about his flock, it redounds to his own benefit, but if he neglects it, not only is he not regarded as a genuine shepherd but, in causing harm to the flock, he will be deprived of its help as well.

201. If at some time there is a naval fleet of the enemy, and <one of our> generals with his own naval force is withdrawing and assuming a crescent-shaped formation, let him turn about and sail toward the stern and, in this way, plan to distance himself from the enemy. He is not fleeing, but by <performing the maneuver called> fighting while fleeing, he will once again have his ships ready to attack the enemy on the bow, if there is need of this, with his bows facing theirs. They will not be bold enough to enter the hollow space because they will suspect encirclement.

202. When God has granted you victory, do not act in a precarious manner by pursuing the enemy without a force under control. Be on your guard against their wheeling about. A pursuit that gets out of control breaks up your formation and it will turn the pursuing troops into objects of attack.

203. Be very attentive in passing through narrow places. In retiring from enemy territory, especially, draw up the physically fit and robust soldiers behind in the rear guard. They will hold off the attacking enemy to the rear, and nobody

117. Polyaenus 3.10.2.

1050  μηδεὶς φεύγῃ ἔμπροσθεν μὴ τολμῶν παρελθεῖν τὴν σὴν ἐνδοξότητα παρατεταγ-
μένην καὶ δι' ἀμφοτέρων τηρεῖται ἡ τάξις ἀσφαλὴς καὶ ἄρρηκτος.

σδ'. Ἵνα ῥώμην κατὰ τῶν πολεμίων ἐνθήσῃς τῷ στρατεύματι παράγγελλε
αὐτούς, ἵνα εἰ μὲν βοῶντες ἐπέρχονται αὐτοῖς οἱ πολέμιοι ἐν τῇ συμβολῇ τῆς
μάχης δέχωνται αὐτοὺς μετὰ σιωπῆς. ἐὰν δὲ ἐκεῖνοι μετὰ σιωπῆς ἐπέρχωνται,
1055  τότε μετὰ βοῆς καὶ κραυγῆς οἱ σοὶ ἀντεξελαύνουσι κατ' αὐτῶν.

σε'. Ὅταν ἀπορῇς ἐξοπλίσεως τῶν στρατιωτῶν, τοῖς εὐπόροις μέν, μὴ στρατευομένοις δέ, κέλευε, ἐὰν μὴ βούλωνται στρατεύεσθαι, παρέχειν ἕκαστον
ἵππον ἀντὶ ἑαυτοῦ καὶ ἄνδρα, καὶ οὕτως οἵ τε πένητες ἀνδρεῖοι ὁπλισθήσονται,
οἵ τε πλούσιοι καὶ ἄνανδροι δουλεύσουσι κατ' ἰσότητα τῶν στρατευομένων.

1060  σϛ'. Ἅμα τοῖς καβαλλαρίοις καὶ πεζικὴν ἐπιφερόμενος στρατιάν, συνεποχεῖ-
σθαι αὐτὴν ἐν τοῖς ἵπποις πολλάκις κέλευε, δηλονότι ἐλαφρὴν ὅπλισιν, ὅπερ
δέον ἔχοντας, καὶ τοῖς ποσὶν ὀξέως τρέχειν δυναμένους. οἵτινες ἐν ἐπικαίροις
τόποις εὔρωστοι καταπηδήσαντες ἀπὸ τῶν ἵππων τόπους ὑψηλοὺς καταλήψον-
ται, καὶ σφενδόναις χρήσονται καὶ τόξοις καὶ ἑτέροις ὅπλοις, ἢ καὶ πρὸς ἄλλο τι
1065  τῶν ἐμπιπτόντων ἀνδρίσονται.

σζ'. Βεβαίως ἐπιστάμενος ἄνδρα τινὰ πολλάκις ἀριστεύσαντα, ἐξαιτούμενον
δὲ περί τινος σωτηρίας ἢ ἑαυτοῦ ἢ φίλου ἢ συγγενοῦς, χρεών σε, ὦ στρατηγέ,
ἀντὶ πολλῶν καὶ μεγάλων παρασχεῖν αὐτῷ δυστυχίαν φίλου ἐπανορθώσασθαι.
καὶ ἐν αὐτῷ γὰρ τὸ ὅσιον ποιήσεις καὶ ἑτέρους ἐπαλείψεις ἀριστεύειν ἐπ' ἐλπίδι
1070  τοιαύτης ἀνταποδόσεως.

ση'. Ἄρχοντος ἀγαθοῦ τεκμήρια καὶ ἀρετῆς ἀπόδειξις ὅταν ἐθελουσίῳ
γνώμῃ πείθωνται αὐτῷ οἱ ὑποχείριοι καὶ ἐν τοῖς προσπίπτουσι πόνοις παρα-
μένειν ἐθέλωσιν. οἱ γὰρ ἀνάγκῃ καὶ βίᾳ ὑποταττόμενοι τοῖς ἀνάξια στρατηγοῦ
πρὸς αὐτοὺς πράττουσιν, ἐπίβουλοι μᾶλλον, ἀλλ' οὐ φίλοι, καὶ φυγάδες, ἀλλ' οὐ
1075  συγκινδυνεύοντες ὀφθήσονται.

σθ'. Στρατηγῷ ἀγαθῷ μηδὲν ἕτερον ἐπιτήδευμα δέον ἐπαινεῖν, ἀλλ' ἢ δύο
ταύτας· τὴν μὲν γεωργικήν, ὡς τρέφουσαν τοὺς στρατιώτας, τὴν δὲ πολεμικήν,
ὡς ἐκδικοῦσαν καὶ φυλάττουσαν τοὺς τρέφοντας γεωργούς. διὸ μᾶλλον καὶ

---

1076–1080 Cf. ια'.45–53.

---

1060 ἐπιφερόμενος M ἐπαγόμενος A  1061–1062 ὅπερ…ἔχοντας M trsp. A
1062–1063 ἐπικαίροις…εὔρωστοι M τοῖς ἁρμόζουσι ἀκόπιατοι A  1063–1064 καταλήψον-
ται M καταλάβωσι A  1067 χρεών M χρὴ A  1069 ὅσιον M πρέπον A  1071 τεκμήρια M
τεκμήριον A | ἐθελουσίῳ M ἑκουσίῳ A  1076 στρατηγῷ…μηδὲν M στρατηγὸν ἀγαθὸν
οὐδὲν A  1078–1079 μᾶλλον…τούτων M trsp. A

will try to escape by the front, not daring to pass Your Excellency positioned there. Thus, in both directions the formation is preserved safe and unbreakable.

204. In order to strengthen the army in facing the enemy, issue the following command. In the heat of battle, if the enemy shout loudly while attacking them, your men should meet them in silence. But if the enemy attack in silence, then your men should charge out against them with shouts and loud cries.

205. When you find yourself without armament for your soldiers, give orders to those who are well provided for but who are not going on campaign that, if they do not wish to go on campaign, they should each provide a horse and a man in their place. In this way, the valiant poor will be armed and the cowardly rich will serve equally with those who actually campaign.

206. When you are leading an infantry army together with cavalry, give the order at frequent intervals for them to ride on the horses. Have them carry light weapons, as is proper, since they are also able to run swiftly on foot. They are of great advantage in certain places where they can leap off the horses and occupy the heights. There they will make good use of their slings, arrows, and other weapons and they will act in manly fashion in whatever situation occurs.

207. If you learn with certainty of a man who has frequently distinguished himself but who is begging for the safety of someone, either himself or a friend or a relative, it is necessary for you, O general, instead of providing him with many great things, to correct the misfortune of a friend. In this regard you will do what is right and you will encourage others to distinguish themselves in the hope of such recompense.

208. The characteristics of a good officer and the manifestation of his virtue are seen when his subordinates obey him with a willing spirit and desire to persevere in the labors that come their way. Those who, because of compulsion and force, are subject to superiors who treat them in a manner unworthy of a general will turn out to be plotters instead of friends and deserters rather than partners in danger.

209. No other enterprise must be commended to a good general than these two: agriculture, inasmuch as it feeds the soldiers, and the military, because it defends and protects the farmers who provide them with food. For this reason,

τούτων τῶν ἐπιτηδευμάτων ἐπιμελεῖσθαί σε χρὴ παρὰ τὰ ἕτερα πάντα. ἐκεῖνα | 374ᵛ
1080 μὲν γάρ εἰσι τάχα καὶ περιττά, ταῦτα δὲ καὶ ἀναγκαιότατα καὶ σωτήρια.

σι΄. Ἵνα δὲ καὶ ἐνδοξότερος καὶ αἰδέσιμος ἀναδείκνυσαι, μᾶλλον τοῦ σοῦ
συμφέροντος τὸ κοινῇ συμφέρον προτίμα, ὡς καὶ ἄνω που ἡμῖν εἴρηται. καὶ γὰρ
ἀγαθὸς στρατηγός ἐστιν, οὐκ ἐὰν τὸν ἑαυτοῦ βίον καλῶς διεξάγῃ, ἀλλ᾽ ἐὰν καὶ
ὧν ἄρχει τούτοις σωτηρίας αἴτιος γίνεται. στρατηγὸς γὰρ προχειρίζεται παρὰ
1085 τῆς ἡμετέρας βασιλείας, οὐχ ἵνα ἑαυτοῦ καλῶς ἐπιμεληθῇ μόνον, ἀλλ᾽ ἵνα καὶ οἱ
ἐπιμελούμενοι παρ᾽ αὐτοῦ καλῶς διεξάγωνται. καὶ γὰρ καὶ στρατεύονται πάντες
ἵνα ὁ βίος αὐτοῖς βελτίων ὑπάρχῃ, καὶ στρατηγοὺς δέχονται τούτου αὐτοῦ
ἕνεκα, ἵνα πρὸς τὰ καλὰ καὶ σωτήρια ἡγεμόνες αὐτοῖς ὑπάρχουσιν.

σια΄. Λύμη στρατοῦ τρυφητὴς στρατηγὸς καὶ ἄτακτος. ἡ γὰρ εὐταξία καὶ ἡ
1090 μετὰ σωφροσύνης ἐγκράτεια μάλιστά ἐστιν τοῖς στρατευομένοις χρήσιμος. χρὴ
γὰρ μηδὲν ἄλλο ἐπιφέρεσθαι πρὸς χρείαν βρώσεως ἢ τῆς ἄλλης διαίτης πλὴν
τῶν ἀναγκαίων. τρυφὴν γὰρ οὔτε πόλεμος οὔτε εἰρήνη δέχεται σωφρονοῦσα.
πῶς γὰρ οὐκ αἰσχρὸν ἄνδρα ἐπὶ ἵππου καπηλεύειν; διαφθείρεται γὰρ ἡ δύναμις
καὶ βλάβη οὐ μικρὰ γίνεται. διὸ πανταχοῦ μὲν τοὺς ἄρχοντας ἀκριβεῖς εἶναι δεῖ
1095 καὶ δικαίους ἄρχειν, μάλιστα δὲ ἐν τοῖς στρατιωτικοῖς. ὀξεῖς δὲ οἱ καιροί, καὶ
ὀξεῖς αἱ πράξεις ὀφείλουσι καὶ ἐπὶ παντὸς πολέμου, μάλιστα δὲ τοῦ κατὰ θάλασσαν διὰ ναυμαχίας εἰς μάχην συνισταμένου.

σιβ΄. Ἐὰν πολεμῇς πρὸς ἀνθρώπους ἐκ πολλῶν τόπων συλλεγομένους, ὦ
στρατηγέ, δέον σε μὴ περιμένειν ἕως εἰς ἓν συναχθῶσιν, ἀλλ᾽ ἔτι ἐσπαρμένοις
1100 αὐτοῖς, ἢ κατὰ τῆς ἰδίας χώρας ἕκαστον ἢ εἰς ἑτέρους τόπους, πρὶν ἢ συνέλθωσιν ἐπιχείρει. καὶ νῦν δὲ τοῖς ἐξ Αἰγύπτου καὶ Συρίας καὶ Κιλικίας ἀθροιζομένοις
βαρβάροις πρὸς τὴν κατὰ Ῥωμαίων ἐκστρατείαν δέον τοὺς πλωΐμους στρατηγοὺς σὺν τῷ ναυτικῷ στόλῳ τὴν Κύπρον καταλαβόντας πρὸ τοῦ συναφθῆναι
τὰς βαρβαρικὰς ναῦς, ἀποστεῖλαι κατ᾽ αὐτῶν πλώϊμον δύναμιν ἱκανὴν καταγω-
1105 νίσασθαι τὴν βαρβαρικὴν ναυμαχίαν ἔτι διῃρημένην, ἢ τὰς ναῦς ἐκείνων ἐμπρῆσαι πρὸ τοῦ ἀποπλεῦσαι τῆς ἰδίας.

σιγ΄. Ὑπολαμβάνω σε ἰατρὸν οἱονεὶ μεγάλου σώματος τοῦ στρατεύματος. καὶ
χρή σε ὥσπερ τῆς νόσου τὰς αἰτίας ἐξελαύνειν τοῦ στρατοῦ, οἷον ἀργίαν, τρυ-

---

1101–1106 καὶ¹...ἰδίας Cf. ιη΄.    1107–1118 Strat., 8.2.58.

---

1081 αἰδέσιμος Μ ἐντιμότερον Α    1082 ἄνω που Μ ἀνωτέρω Α    1100 αὐτοῖς Μ αὐτοῖς
καὶ διεσκορπισμένοις Α    1100–1101 πρὶν...ἐπιχείρει Μ πρὸ τοῦ συνελεῖν αὐτοὺς ἐπιτίθου Α
1101 ἀθροιζομένοις Μ συναγομένοις Α    1102–1103 τοὺς...στρατηγοὺς Α    τοῖς
πλωΐμοις στρατηγοῖς Μ    1103 συναφθῆναι Μ ἑνωθῆναι Α    1108 τῆς νόσου Μ τινα νόσον
Α

it is necessary for you to be concerned about these more than all the others. For other enterprises are perhaps even superfluous, but these are most necessary and salutary.[118]

210. So that you may present yourself as very honorable and respected, you should prefer what is beneficial for the commonwealth above what is beneficial for yourself, as we have remarked somewhere above. A man is a good general, not if he conducts his own life very well, but if he becomes an agent of the safety of those under his command. A man is promoted to general by Our Majesty, not so he can take care of his own well being only, but that those who come under his care may also be well treated. Everyone goes to war in order to improve their lives and they accept generals for this very reason, that they may lead them on to good and salutary things.

211. A general given to luxury and lacking discipline causes harm to the army, whereas good order and self-control, together with common sense, are particularly beneficial to those in military service. It is necessary to bring along nothing more than what is needed for food and other sustenance. Neither war nor peace, which teaches moderation, has a place for luxury. How is it not shameful for a man to drink alcohol while on horseback? His strength is destroyed and no small damage ensues. The officers must be strict and just in exercising command, especially in matters concerning the soldiers. The times are critical and our actions must be critical. This is true of every war but especially when engaging in a naval battle at sea.[119]

212. If you are waging war against men who have come together from many places, O general, you must not wait around until they have managed to form one army, but attack them while they are still scattered about, each one either in his own country or in other places, before they can join forces. Now, as the barbarians are gathering together from Egypt, Syria, and Cilicia to campaign against the Romans, it is necessary for the fleet generals with their naval forces to occupy Cyprus before the barbarian ships can get together. Then dispatch against them a naval force capable of overwhelming the barbarian war fleet while it is still divided or else set their ships on fire before they can sail away from their own country.[120]

213. I picture you as the physician for a large body, that is, the army. It is

118. Cf. Const. 11 §9.
119. *Strat.* 8.2.58.
120. Cf. Const. 18.

φήν, πολυτέλειαν, ἀσωτίαν, ἀλλὰ καὶ μαντείας καὶ σύμβολα καὶ οἰωνισμοὺς καὶ
1110 ὀνείρους· μάλιστα εὐσεβῆ τυγχάνοντα περὶ τὸ θεῖον παρορᾶν σε χρή, εἰ μή τις
ἀνάγκη καὶ τούτων παρεῖναι προσποίησιν. οὐ γὰρ προσήκει ταῦτα στρατηγῷ
οὐδὲ πρὸς νίκην καὶ σωτηρίαν διὰ προνοίας ἰδίας σημεῖα κρίνειν, ἀλλὰ προνοεῖν
ἀσφαλῶς, καὶ πρὸς τὰ προκείμενα μετὰ | ἀγχινοίας καὶ πείρας τὰς ἑαυτοῦ   375
πράξεις διεξάγειν. πάντων δὲ μάλιστα τὴν πορνείαν ἐξορίζειν χρεὼν τοῦ στρα-
1115 τεύματος. ταύτην γὰρ τὰ μέγιστα κακὰ ἐπάγειν καὶ ἐν ταῖς παλαιαῖς ἱστορίαις
καὶ ἐν ταῖς καιναῖς τοῖς στρατεύμασιν ἀνεμάθομεν. ἀλλὰ καὶ σημείοις τινὲς καὶ
ὀνείροις πεποιθότες πολλάκις ἐψεύσθησαν καὶ ἀπώλοντο τῆς ἐκείνων κρίσεως
ἀστοχήσαντες.

σιδ′. Συνεκστρατεύειν μετὰ σεαυτοῦ τούς τε σοὺς υἱοὺς καὶ τῶν ἐπισήμων
1120 ἐπ᾽ ἀνδρείᾳ ἀρχόντων ἢ στρατιωτῶν οὐκ ἀδόκιμον, ἀλλὰ καὶ πρέπον ἡγοῦμαι
θέας ἕνεκα καὶ πείρας στρατιωτικῶν ἔργων καὶ ἡγεμονικῶν. ἀναγκαῖον γὰρ
διδασκαλεῖον ἀναγκαίων μαθημάτων ὁ πόλεμος. διὸ καὶ τοὺς ἀκμάζοντας καὶ
φίλων καὶ οἰκείων παῖδας ὥσπερ εὐγενεῖς σκύλακας, ὦ στρατηγέ, συνεκστρατεύειν σε χρὴ καὶ συνεθίζειν ἀνέχεσθαι καὶ τολμᾶν καὶ νεκρῶν ἁπτομένους καὶ
1125 πληγὰς θεωμένους, καὶ ἐν ταῖς ἐναγωνίοις βοαῖς καὶ τοῖς ἀλαλάγμασι κατὰ τὰ
πρῶτα τῆς μάχης γινομένοις παρατυγχάνοντας ἵστασθαι, ἵνα πρὸς τὰ πολεμικὰ
ἔργα καὶ πάθη ἐκ νέου συνεθιζόμενοι καὶ ἀριστεύειν ἐν αὐτοῖς μάθωσιν.

σιε′. Ῥωμαλέον καὶ ἄριστον ἀναδείξει σε στρατηγὸν ἤ τῆς τόλμης ὀξύτης καὶ
τὸ βούλευμα τὸ χρηστὸν καὶ ὁ τῶν φίλων εὐπρόθυμος συναγωνισμὸς καὶ τὸ
1130 θαρρεῖν ἐν τοῖς κινδύνοις τοῦ πολέμου καὶ τὸ χρῆσθαι τῷ τε σταθηρῷ λογισμῷ
καὶ ἀκαταπλήκτῳ. ταῦτα γὰρ στερροῦ στρατηγοῦ καὶ φιλοτίμου, ἵνα καὶ αὐτὸς
ἐν καιρῷ ἐξ ἑαυτοῦ παρέχῃ τὰ δέοντα, καὶ διὰ τῆς αὐτοῦ ἀγαθῆς γνώμης καὶ
φιλίας συναγωνιστὰς ἔχῃ ὡς φίλους οἰκείους καὶ συγκινδυνεύοντας αὐτῷ ἐν
ἅπασι τοὺς στρατιώτας.

1135 σις′. Ὥσπερ κυνηγέτης ἀγαθὸς τέχνῃ τοὺς λύκους μετερχόμενος ἢ τὰς
ἀλώπεκας ἀγρεύει, οὕτως καὶ αὐτὸς τοὺς ἀπὸ τῶν πολεμίων κατασκόπους διὰ
τέχνης ἀνευρήσεις. ἐὰν γὰρ ἔξωθεν τοῦ σοῦ χάρακος φύλακας τάξῃς, εἶτα
ἐπιλαβέσθαι τοῦ πλησίον ἑκάστῳ κελεύσῃς, καὶ μὴ ἀφεῖναι ἕως ἂν εἴπῃ καὶ τὸν

---

1111 προσποίησιν Μ προσποίησιν σχηματισμὸν Α   1113 ἀγχινοίας Μ φρονήσεως Α
1114 διεξάγειν Μ οἰκονομεῖν Α | χρεὼν Μ χρὴ Α   1117 πεποιθότες…ἐψεύσθησαν Μ
θαρρήσαντες πολλάκις ἠπατήθη Α   1119 ἐπισήμων Μ γνωρίμων Α   1120 ἀρχόντων Μ
ἀνθρώπων Α | οὐκ…καὶ Μ om. Α | πρέπον Α τρόπον Μ | ἡγοῦμαι Μ ἡγούμεθα Α
1125 ταῖς Α τοῖς Μ   1128 ἀναδείξει PG ἀναδείξαι ΜΑ   1129 χρηστὸν Μ ἀγαθὸν Α
1131 στερροῦ Μ γενναίου Α   1138 ἐπιλαβέσθαι…κελεύσῃς Μ ἑκάστῳ κελεύσῃς
ἐπιλαβέσθαι τοῦ πλησίον Α

your responsibility, as it were, to drive away the causes of disease in the army, such as idleness, luxurious living, extravagance, profligacy, and also divination, signs, omens, and dreams. It is particularly incumbent upon you, truly reverent as you are toward the Divinity, to disregard these unless there is some need for <permitting> the pretense of these being present. It is not fitting for a general, by means of his own foresight, to judge whether these signs indicate victory and salvation, but he is to think carefully ahead to what lies before him with shrewdness and experience, and so conduct his own actions. Above everything else you must drive fornication out of the army, for this introduces the greatest evils, as we have learned from both ancient and recent histories. Some individuals, moreover, who have believed in signs and dreams, have frequently been deceived and have perished because their interpretation of them missed the mark.[121]

214. It is not a bad idea for your sons and those of the officers or soldiers distinguished for bravery to accompany you on campaign. Indeed, I think it is fitting because of what they will see and the experience they will have of the work of the soldiers and the officers. War is a basic school of necessary teachings. Because of this, your sons and those of your friends, as they come of age, like pedigreed dogs, O general, ought to go along on campaign with you and become accustomed to bear up and show courage when they come in contact with corpses and gaze upon wounds, to stand and experience the shouts of the fighting men and the war cries in the forefront of the battle. In this way, they will become accustomed to the actions and the suffering of war from their youth and they will learn to take part in them with courage.[122]

215. The high point of daring, excellent planning, enthusiastic fighting alongside one's friends, showing confidence amid the dangers of war, and making use of firm, undaunted reasoning will prove that you are a strong and excellent general. A solid and generous general is one who personally does what is called for at the right time. Because of his fine mind and friendly manner, he has made the soldiers fighting along with him into close friends who share all the dangers with him.

216. As a good hunter skillfully goes after wolves or catches foxes, so you should skillfully search out spies from the enemy. Station guards outside your

---

121. Cf. *Strat.* 8.2.58.

122. For example, Basil I took his oldest son Constantine on his expedition to Syria, in 876–877. Skylitzes, *Basil.Mak.*, 23; Theophanes *Cont.*, 278.

ἄρχοντα καὶ τὸ τάγμα καὶ τὸ κοντουβέρνιον ὅθεν ἐστὶν ἢ ἕτερον σύνθημα. τοὺς
1140 δὲ ταῦτα λέγειν μὴ δυναμένους ἐξετάζῃς, καὶ οὕτως ἀνευρήσεις τοὺς κατασκόπους.

σιζ΄. Μέγα πρᾶγμα καὶ ἀναγκαῖον δημηγορῶν μετὰ φρονήσεως στρατηγός·
πλείονα γὰρ πολλάκις ἐκ τῆς διὰ λόγων ὁμιλίας ἤπερ ἐκ τῶν ὅπλων τὴν ἀνδρείαν παρασκευάσει τῷ στρατεύματι, καὶ μάλιστα προστιθεὶς τῷ λόγῳ, ὅτι πρὸς
1145 ἀντιπάλους ἐστὶ μάχεσθαι σάρκα καὶ αἷμα ἔχοντας καὶ τὰ ἀνθρώπων πάσχοντας
καὶ αὐτούς.

σιη΄. Ἀναγκαῖόν σοι, ὦ στρατηγέ, ὅταν χεῖρας συμμίξωσι πρὸς μάχην κατὰ
τῶν πολεμίων οἱ στρατιῶται, παρατρέχοντα βοᾶν· "ἔτι ἅπαξ προσβαλοῦμεν τοῖς
πολεμίοις καὶ νικήσομεν." καὶ πάλιν ὁμοίως· "ἔτι ἅπαξ προσβαλοῦμεν καὶ νι| 375ᵛ
1150 κήσομεν." καὶ τρίτον δὲ τοῦτο ποιῆσαι παριππεύοντα. οὕτως γὰρ νίκην ὡς
ἀληθῶς ἐκ τῆς προθυμίας ποιήσεις, ἐφεξῆς καὶ συνεχῶς τὰς τρεῖς προσβολὰς
ποιούμενος. τοῦτο δὲ ποιήσεις, ὅταν μετὰ τῆς τοῦ Θεοῦ βοηθείας ὁρᾷς ὅτι κατὰ
τὴν πρώτην συμβολὴν προτερῇς κατὰ τῶν πολεμίων.

σιθ΄. Ἵνα δὲ μνήμων θαυμαζόμενος καὶ τοῖς ἀντιπολεμίοις εἶναι δόξῃς καὶ διὰ
1155 τοῦτο φοβερός, ἐάν σοι πρέσβεις ἀποστείλωσι, δέον σε ἀνερωτῆσαι περὶ αὐτῶν,
ἐάν ποτε ἐπρεσβεύσαντο, καὶ ὑπέρ τινων πραγμάτων καὶ μετά τινων προσώπων
καὶ ἐν ποίῳ καιρῷ καὶ ἐν ποίῳ τόπῳ. ἔτι δὲ καὶ περὶ τῆς προκειμένης πρεσβείας
προμελετῆσαι ἃ δεῖ, καὶ εἴ τι ὅμοιον ἐπράχθη ποτὲ ἢ παρά σοι ἢ παρ᾽ ἑτέρῳ
ἔθνει, ἵνα ἐν ταῖς ἐρωτήσεσι καὶ συντυχίαις ἐκπλήσσῃς αὐτοὺς ὡς πάνυ μνημο-
1160 νικὸς καὶ πολύπειρος.

σκ΄. Ὧν ἕνεκα ἢ τόπων ποτὲ ἢ πόλεων ἐκπέμπειν μέλλεις ναυτικὸν στόλον,
κρύπτειν σε δεῖ καὶ τοὺς τόπους καὶ τὰς πόλεις, ὥστε μηδένα προγνῶναι ποῦ
μέλλει γίνεσθαι ὁ κατάπλους. ἔνταλμα δὲ γράψας, τοῦτο σφραγισάμενος
ἀσφαλῶς ἐπίδος τῷ καθισταμένῳ παρά σου ναυάρχῳ, ἵνα κατὰ τὸ πέλαγος
1165 ἐξελθών, τότε λύσῃ τὴν σφραγίδα καὶ μάθῃ ποῦ μέλλει πορεύεσθαι. οὕτως γὰρ
ποιήσας λάθῃς τοὺς πολεμίους.

σκα΄. Νόμοι στρατηγικοὶ φυλαττόμενοι καὶ τοὺς στρατηγοὺς νικηφόρους
καὶ ἐνδόξους καὶ δὴ καὶ ἀειμνήστους ἀποτελοῦσιν καὶ τοῖς βασιλεύουσι χαρᾶς
καὶ εὐφροσύνης αἴτιοι γίνονται, καὶ πρὸς εἰρήνην καὶ ὑποταγὴν τοὺς πολεμίους
1170 καταναγκάζουσι, καὶ κακῶν ἐλευθερίας παντὶ τῷ ὑπηκόῳ γινόμενοι, μᾶλλον δὲ

---

1139 κοντουβέρνιον A κουτουβέρνιον M | σύνθημα M γνώρισμα A    1140 ἐξετάζῃς M
ἐξετάσεις A    1153 συμβολὴν…κατὰ M προσβολὴν ὑπερέχεις A    1154 μνήμων…
ἀντιπολεμίοις M καὶ τοῖς πολεμίοις καὶ μνημονευτικὸς A    1154–1155 διὰ…φοβερός M
φοβερὸς διὰ τοῦτο καὶ θαυμασθῆναι παρ᾽ αὐτῶν A    1159 ἐκπλήσσῃς M ἐκπλήττῃς A
1161 ναυτικὸν στόλον M om. A    1167 νικηφόρους M νικητὰς A    1168 καὶ δὴ M om. A

campsite, then give the order for each man to take hold of the person next to him and not let him go until he tells him who his officer is and what tagma and squad he belongs to, or some other password. Subject those who are unable to name these to further questioning, and in this way you will uncover the spies.

217. It is a great and even necessary thing for a general to speak sensibly in public. By a reasonable speech he will often incite the army to bravery more than by weapons. This is particularly true if he adds to his speech that they are fighting against opponents who are flesh and blood and who also suffer what all men suffer.

218. When the soldiers are about to engage the enemy in close combat, it is necessary for you, O general, to ride about and shout: "Let us charge against the enemy one more time and we shall be victorious." In like manner again: "Let us charge one more time and we shall be victorious." Do it a third time riding about on horseback. In this way, launching three charges one right after the other, you will truly bring about victory because of their enthusiasm. You will do this when, with God's help, you see that, at the first charge, you gain an advantage over the enemy.

219. In order that you appear to the enemy as having a wonderful memory and, for this reason, as someone to be feared, if they send ambassadors to you, make inquiries about them. Have they previously been sent as ambassadors and about what matters and with what persons and at what time and in what place? Consider, moreover, what must be done concerning the present embassy and whether something similar was ever dealt with, either by you or by another nation. And so, in your meeting and by your questioning you will astound them by your excellent memory and great expertise.

220. Whenever you intend to send out a naval force to some place or city, you must keep the places or cities secret so nobody will know your destination ahead of time. Write the orders, seal them safely, and hand them over to the commander designated by you. Only after sailing out to sea is he to break the seal and find out where he is to proceed. This way of doing things will keep your plan hidden from the enemy.

221. Observance of the military laws will result in victorious generals, illustrious and deserving perpetual memory, and it will also be the cause of happiness and kind thoughts for the emperors, and it will compel the enemy to live in peace and subjection. It will free all our subjects from many evils and

καὶ ἀγαθῶν εὐπορίαν προξενοῦντες αὐτοῖς, τὴν εἰς Θεὸν εὐχαριστίαν αὔξουσι καὶ πρὸς δοξολογίαν αὐτοῦ πᾶσαν εὐσεβῆ ψυχὴν διεγεροῦσι. τούτους οὖν, ὦ στρατηγέ, καθάπερ σωτῆρας μετὰ Θεὸν καὶ εὐεργέτας κοινοὺς τοὺς στρατηγικοὺς νόμους διὰ παντὸς περιφύλαττε. καὶ πρό γε τούτων τοὺς θείους καὶ
1175   παναληθεῖς νόμους, δι᾽ ὧν ἡ εὐσέβεια κρατύνεται, περίθαλπε καὶ ἀνενδοιάστως τούτοις ὑπάκουε. ἐκ τούτων γὰρ ἀρίστη ἀρχὴ γένοιτο, καὶ εὐάρεστος ὀφθήσῃ στρατηγὸς αὐτῷ τε τῷ Θεῷ τῶν ὅλων καὶ βασιλεῖ καὶ κυρίῳ ἡμῶν Ἰησοῦ Χριστῷ, καὶ ἡμῖν τοῖς δι᾽ αὐτοῦ βασιλεύουσιν.

---

1171 αὔξουσι Μ ἔξουσι Α    1173 εὐεργέτας κοινοὺς Μ trsp. Α    1174 γε Μ om. Α
1175 ἀνενδοιάστως Μ ἀδιστάκτως Α

even more it will offer them an abundance of good things. It will increase gratitude toward God and it will stir up every pious soul to glorify him. Always, therefore, observe these military laws, O general, for, after God, they are your saviors and common benefactors. Above these, cherish and without hesitation obey the divine and wholly true laws by which reverence is fortified. It is from these that the best beginning proceeds, and the general will be most pleasing in the sight of the God and emperor of all and to our Lord Jesus Christ and to us who rule through him.

# ΥΠΟΘΕΣΙΣ ΕΝ ΕΠΙΛΟΓΩι

α΄. Ὡς ἐν συνόψει δὲ τὰ προειρημένα ἡμῖν ἅπαντα οἷον ἀνακεφαλαιωσά-
μενοι ἐνταῦθα παρακελευόμεθα καὶ ὑποτιθέμεθα τῇ σῇ ἐνδοξότητι. ἐξ ὧν, ὡς
εἴρηται, καὶ αὐτὸς στρατηγὸς ἀναδειχθεὶς ἀγαθός, καὶ βίον ἀκινδυνότατόν τε
5 καὶ ἀλυπώτατον τοῖς ὑπό σε ἀρχομένοις περιποιήσῃ.

β΄. Καὶ πρῶτον | μὲν πᾶν ὅπερ μέλλεις ἢ λέγειν ἢ πράττειν ἀπὸ Θεοῦ λάμ- 376
βανε τὴν ἀρχήν, καὶ μηδὲν ἄνευ τῆς ἐκείνου μνήμης τε καὶ ἐντεύξεως μήτε
λόγου ἄρξῃ μήτε πράξεως.

γ΄. Οὕτω γὰρ ἐγὼ κρίνω χρεὼν εἶναι ἀπὸ Θεοῦ λαμβάνειν ἅπαντα τὴν
10 ἀρχήν. καὶ γὰρ ὁ Θεὸς πατὴρ ἡμῶν καὶ ποιητὴς καὶ ἐπόπτης καὶ τῶν λόγων
ἡμῶν καὶ τῶν πράξεων· καὶ κριτικός ἐστιν ἐνθυμήσεων καὶ ἐννοιῶν καρδίας, καὶ
οὔκ ἐστι κτίσις ἀφανὴς ἐνώπιον αὐτοῦ· πάντα δὲ γυμνὰ καὶ τετραχηλισμένα
τοῖς ὀφθαλμοῖς αὐτοῦ κατὰ τὸν θεολογικώτατον Παῦλον. διὸ οὐδὲν τῆς αὐτοῦ
γνώμης χωρὶς πράττειν ὀφείλομεν.

15 δ΄. Ἕπεται γάρ τις ἡμῖν οἱονεὶ συγγένεια πρὸς αὐτὸν καὶ σχέσις, ὡς οἵα
γένοιτο παισὶ πρὸς πατέρα. καὶ γὰρ παρ' αὐτοῦ εἰς φῶς καὶ βίον ἤλθομεν, καὶ
ὑπὲρ αὐτοῦ καὶ ζῆν καὶ θνήσκειν ὀφείλομεν. ἐπὶ δώροις γὰρ τοῖς ἐκείνου τρεφό-
μεθα, καὶ ἐν αὐτῷ ζῶμεν καὶ κινούμεθα καὶ ἐσμεν. καὶ τοσοῦτον αὐτῷ πειθό-
μεθα, ὅσον ἰδιῶται ἄρχοντι, καὶ δεσπότῃ ἀγαθῷ δοῦλοι καὶ ἄρχοντες βασιλεῖ.
20 καὶ πάντες αὐτοῦ ἐσμεν, ὡς κατὰ πάντων κεκτημένου τὸ κράτος. καὶ ἡμῖν μὲν ἐξ
ἐκείνου δεδούλωται πάντα τὰ ἔμψυχα καὶ τὰ ἄψυχα. ἡμεῖς δὲ αὐτὸν θεραπεύο-
μεν. καὶ ἡ μὲν ἄλογος πᾶσα ἀγέλη ὑφ' ἡμῶν ποιμαινομένη ἄγεται, ἡμεῖς δὲ ὑπὸ
τοῦ θεοῦ ποιμαινόμεθα τοῦ καλοῦ ποιμένος, καὶ δι' ἡμᾶς φιλανθρώπως φορέ-
σαντος τὸ ἡμέτερον.

---

M A   PG 107:1076

11–13 Hebr. 4:12–13.   18 Acta 17:28.   22–24 Ioan. 10:11.

---

1 ἐν A om. M   2 ἅπαντα οἷον M πάντα A   6 ἢ¹ M om. A   7 μηδὲν M μήτε λόγου ἄρξῃ
μήτε πράξεως A   7–8 μήτε…πράξεως M om. A   9 χρεὼν M πρέπον A   13 παῦλον M
ἀπόστολον παῦλον A   17 ἐπὶ…ἐκείνου M τοῖς γὰρ ἐκείνου δώροις A

# EPILOGUE

1. As a sort of recapitulation, in synoptic form, of everything we have said previously, we here recommend and propose <the following> to Your Excellency. As noted, it is by <observing> these recommendations that you will prove yourself to be an excellent general and you will obtain for yourself and those under your command a life without danger and sorrow.

2. First, everything you intend to say or do should take its beginning from God. Do not begin any word or deed without remembrance of him and conversing with him.

3. Thus, I judge it to be necessary for all things to take their beginning from God. He is our father and creator and watches over our words and our deeds. He is the judge of the desires and thoughts of our hearts and no creature is unseen in his presence. Everything is open and laid bare before his eyes, according to the great theologian Paul.[1] Wherefore, we ought to do nothing apart from his will.

4. For there is a certain sort of relationship and bond between us and him such as that of children to their father. Indeed, it is from him that we have come into light and life and we ought to live and die for him. We are nourished by his gifts and in him we live and move and have our being.[2] We should obey him to the extent that a private soldier obeys his commanding officer, as slaves a good master, and as officials the emperor. We are all his since he possesses power over all things. It is from him that all animate and inanimate beings are in service to us. But we give our service to him. While the entire irrational flock is pastured and led by us, we are pastured by God, the good shepherd, who for our sake out of love for mankind put on our nature.[3]

---

1. Hebrews 4:12–13.
2. Acts 17:28.
3. John 10:11.

25 ε΄. Καὶ οὐδεὶς ἔξαρνός ποτε γένοιτο ὅτι ἔστι Θεός, εἰ μὴ καὶ τὴν ψυχὴν διεφθαρμένος ὑπάρχει. μεστὰ γὰρ τὰ πάντα Θεοῦ καὶ αὐτὸς ἐκ μὴ ὄντων ταῦτα παρήγαγεν καὶ πάντα πληροῖ καὶ πάντα διαπράττει, καὶ προνοεῖται καὶ διοικεῖ.

ϛ΄. Ἔλεγχος δὲ τῆς ἀληθείας τὰ ποιήματα αὐτοῦ· οὐρανὸς καὶ τὰ ἐν αὐτῷ, γῆ καὶ τὰ ὅσα ἐν αὐτῇ, καὶ μέντοι καὶ θάλασσα καὶ τὰ ἐν ἐκείνῃ ἅπαντα, καὶ ὅσα ἐν
30 αὐτοῖς ὠφέλιμα, μαρτύρια τῆς ἐκ Θεοῦ εἰς ἡμᾶς κηδεμονίας τε καὶ προνοίας ἀναδείκνυται.

ζ΄. Καὶ αὐτὸς καὶ βασιλεῖς καθιστᾷ. καὶ γάρ φησι· δι᾽ ἐμοῦ βασιλεῖς βασιλεύουσι. καὶ στρατηγὸς δι᾽ αὐτοῦ προχειρίζεται, ὁ πάσης ἀρχῆς ἀγαθῆς καὶ ἐξουσίας αὐτός ἐστιν αἴτιος. διὸ καὶ χρὴ μὴ πρότερόν τινα τὴν ἀρχὴν ὑποδύεσθαι πρὶν
35 ἢ διὰ τῆς εὐχῆς καὶ ἐντεύξεως πρὸς αὐτὸν ὥσπερ ἑαυτὸν ἀφιερώσει τῷ Θεῷ, καὶ τῇ ἐκείνου προνοίᾳ τὴν ἑαυτοῦ διοίκησιν καταπιστεύεται.

η΄. Διὰ τοῦτο δεῖ σε πάντα τὰ εἰς Θεοῦ θεραπείαν, ὦ στρατηγέ, πρὸ τῶν ἄλλων ἁπάντων ἐπιτηδεύειν καὶ διαφυλάττειν, ἐξαιρέτως τὴν εἰς τοὺς ἱερεῖς τε καὶ ἀρχιερεῖς αὐτοῦ τιμὴν καὶ θεραπείαν, καὶ τοὺς ἁγίους αὐτοῦ ναοὺς ὥστε
40 ἀσύλους εἶναι καὶ μὴ αὐτῶν ἀναρπάζεσθαι τοὺς ἐν αὐτοῖς καταφεύγοντας ἄνευ διαγνώσεως τῆς ἡμετέρας βασιλείας.

θ΄. Καὶ τὰ ἱερὰ δὲ τῶν μοναχῶν ἀσκητήρια καὶ τοὺς ἐν αὐτοῖς τὴν παρθενείαν | ἀσκοῦντας ἀβλαβῆ καὶ ἀβίαστα καὶ σεμνὰ διατηρεῖσθαι. καὶ ἁπλῶς εἰπεῖν, 376ᵛ ὅσα τῷ Θεῷ ἀνάκεινται παραφυλάττειν ἀνεπηρέαστα καὶ τίμια καὶ αἰδέσιμα ὡς
45 ἅγια πάντα καὶ τῷ ἁγίῳ Θεῷ ἀνακείμενα.

ι΄. Καὶ μηδένα βεβήλων ἢ τυραννικῶν χεῖρας ἐπαίρειν κατ᾽ αὐτῶν ἢ ἄλλως ἀποθρασύνεσθαι, μήτε σεαυτὸν μήτε ἄλλον τινὰ τῶν ὑπὸ τὴν σὴν ἐξουσίαν οἵαν δή ποτέ τινα πεπιστευμένον ἀρχὴν ἢ στρατιωτικὴν ἢ πολιτικήν. ἀλλ᾽ εἶναι αὐτοὺς ὡς κτῆμα τοῦ Θεοῦ πάσης βλάβης καὶ ἐπηρείας ἐλευθέρους.

50 ια΄. Καὶ μάλιστα τοὺς ἀρχιερεῖς ὡς πατέρας καὶ ποιμένας τῶν ἀνθρωπίνων ψυχῶν, ὅσαι τε ἀρχόντων καὶ ὅσαι ἀρχομένων, καὶ τὰ πρὸς Θεὸν ἡμῖν μεσιτεύοντας· τούτους διὰ πάσης ἄγειν τιμῆς καὶ αἰδοῦς, καὶ μηδὲν ἐφ᾽ ὕβρει τούτων καταδέχεσθαι.

ιβ΄. Καὶ γὰρ τὰ εἰς αὐτοὺς γινόμενα εἰς τὸν Θεὸν ἀναφέρεται, παρ᾽ οὗ καὶ
55 τὴν ἀρχιερωσύνην εἰλήφασι, δι᾽ ἧς καὶ τὸ ποιμαίνειν τὰς ψυχὰς καὶ τὰ πρὸς Θεὸν αὐταῖς μεσιτεύειν ἀνεδέξαντο. οἱ γὰρ ἱερεῖς ὥσπερ ψυχή τις διεσπαρμένη

---

26–27 Ps. 13 (14): 1.   32–33 Prov. 8:15.   37–41 Cf. κ΄.338–343.

---

25 ἔξαρνός…ὅτι Μ ἀρνήσεται ποτὲ γέγονε ὅτι οὔκ Α   28 τὰ¹ Μ om. Α   32–33 βασιλεύουσι Μ βασιλεύουσιν Α   33 ἀγαθῆς Μ om. Α   36 καταπιστεύεται Μ καταπιστεύσει Α
48 πολιτικήν Α πολεμικήν Μ   55 εἰλήφασι Μ εἰλήφασιν Α | τὰς Μ om. Α

5. Nobody might ever deny the existence of God, except perhaps one who has <already> destroyed his own soul. For everything is full of God and he brings forth all things from nonbeing and completes everything and finishes everything and provides for and manages all.[4]

6. Proof of this truth is what he has made, heaven and all that is in it, the earth and what is in it, indeed, the sea and everything in it. All that is helpful in them bear witness to God's solicitude for us and manifest his providence.

7. He it is who sets up emperors, for he says: It is by me that emperors reign.[5] It is also by him that a general is promoted. He is the cause of every good rule and authority. For this reason a person must not be invested with command before prayer and converse with him, as though he were to consecrate himself to God. And he should entrust the ordering of his own life to his providence.

8. Because of this, it is necessary for you, O general, to handle and observe all things, above everything else, for the service of God. In particular, honor and reverence his priests and bishops, and keep his holy temples as places of asylum and do not seize hold of those who have sought refuge in them without the authorization of Our Majesty.[6]

9. Preserve reverence for the holy monasteries of the monks and those observing virginity in them and keep them free from harm and violence. To put it simply, preserve everything consecrated to God unmolested, honored, and respected, for they are all holy and dedicated to God, who is holy.

10. Nobody is to raise impure or tyrannical hands against them or to act boldly against them in any other way, neither you nor anyone else who comes under your authority and who has been entrusted with some command, military or civil, but all, as belonging to God, must be free from all harm and abuse.

11. Especially toward the bishops, fathers and pastors of human souls, both of rulers and those who are ruled, and who are intermediaries for us with God, you must show all honor and respect and not allow anyone to insult them.

12. What is done to them is referred to God, from whom they have received the high-priestly office, by which they both shepherd souls and undertake to mediate for them to God. For the priests form a sort of soul, spread throughout

---

4. Cf. Psalms 13 (14): 1.
5. Proverbs 8:15.
6. Cf. Const. 20 §70.

καὶ ζωογονοῦσα ὅλον τὸ σῶμα τοῦ Χριστιανικοῦ λαοῦ καὶ ἀρχόντων καὶ ἀρχομένων καθέστηκε, νοῦν καὶ ἡγέμονα τὸν βασιλέα τῶν ἁπάντων Θεὸν κεκτη-
μένη, καὶ ἀπ᾽ αὐτοῦ τὰς τοῦ ὅλου σώματος διοικήσεις διαπορθμεύουσα καὶ
60 κυβερνῶσα καὶ περιάγουσα.

ιγ΄. Οὕτως οὖν περὶ Θεὸν εὐσεβῶς καὶ ὀρθοδόξως καὶ περὶ τοὺς ἐκείνου
θεράποντας διακείμενος, ἐπιμελοῦ μετὰ τοὺς θείους τῆς πίστεως νόμους καὶ
τοὺς βασιλικοὺς διαφυλάττεσθαι νόμους ἀπαραβάτους, ὥστε ποιεῖν σε κρῖμα
καὶ δικαιοσύνην ἐν μέσῳ τῆς γῆς σου.

65 ιδ΄. Ἐπιμελοῦ δὲ καὶ τῶν στρατηγικῶν ἔργων καὶ τῶν πολεμικῶν ὅπλων, οὐχ
ἵνα ἀδικήσῃς ἢ ἀδίκου πολέμου κατάρξῃς ἢ λῃστείας τινὰς καὶ ἀδίκους κατὰ
τῶν οὐδὲν ἠδικηκότων ἐπιδρομὰς ποιήσῃς, ἀλλ᾽ ἵνα σὺν εὐσεβείᾳ ζῶν, ἀλλὰ καὶ
τοῖς πολεμίοις, ὅσον τὸ ἐπί σοι εἰρηνεύων, καὶ οὕτως εὐσεβῶς καὶ θεαρέστως
πολιτευόμενος, ἔχῃς τὰ ὅπλα πρὸς ἄμυναν τῶν ἀδικούντων πολεμίων.

70 ιε΄. Ἡ γὰρ εὐσεβής σου ζωὴ ταῦτα παραλαβοῦσα, εὖ οἶδ᾽ ὅτι καὶ Θεὸν αὐτὸν
μετὰ τῆς δικαιοσύνης ἕξει συνεκστρατεύοντα.

ις΄. Καὶ ἡ πίστις τοῦ μὴ ἀδικεῖν ἀλλ᾽ ἀδικεῖσθαι στρατηγὸν καὶ ἡγέμονα τὸ
θεῖον ἕξει, καὶ ἀνάγκη πιστεύειν ὅτι δικαίῳ πολέμῳ ἀπὸ Θεοῦ ὀφείλεται τὸ
τέλος ἀγαθόν, ὥσπερ τῷ ἀδίκῳ τὸ ἐναντίον.

75 ιζ΄. Ὥσπερ γὰρ τὸν ἀδικοῦντα ἀδύνατον μὴ παθεῖν ποτε τὴν τῆς ἀδικίας
ποινὴν παρά γε Θεῷ κριτῇ, οὕτως ἀδύνατον καὶ τὸν τὴν ἀδικίαν ἀμυνόμενον
καὶ ἀντιπολεμοῦντα, μὴ τῆς παρὰ Θεοῦ νίκης ἐπιτυχεῖν. ὁ γὰρ Θεὸς κριτὴς
δίκαιος καὶ σὺν δίκῃ ἐξάγει τὰ σύμπαντα.

ιη΄. Τούτων τοίνυν χάριν ἀσκεῖν σε δεῖ <δι᾽> ὅπλων καὶ γυμνασίας καὶ τῆς
80 ἄλλης στρατηγικῆς ἐπιμελείας.

ιθ΄. Εἰδέναι δέ σε ἐπὶ | τούτοις βούλομαι, ὅτι δεῖ σε ἐν πολέμου καιρῷ τῶν τε   377
ἀντιπολεμούντων τὴν φύσιν γινώσκειν καὶ τὴν ἄλλην κατάστασιν, καὶ δὴ καὶ τὸ
ἐκείνων στράτευμα πότερον ὀξύτατόν ἐστιν πρὸς τὰς ἐπιχειρήσεις καὶ πρὸς τὰς
πρώτας ὁρμὰς δραστικὸν ἢ πρὸς μακρόθυμα καὶ χρονοτριβῆ ἔργα μᾶλλον
85 ἐγγεγύμνασται.

---

**65–69** β΄.193–216.  **72–78** β΄.193–216.

**58** καθέστηκε νοῦν Α καθέστηκεν οὖν Μ    **62** θείους…νόμους Μ νόμους τῆς θείας πίστεως
Α    **63** διαφυλάττεσθαι…ἀπαραβάτους Μ νόμους ἀπαραβάτους διαφυλάττεσθαι Α
**79** χάριν…καὶ¹ Μ ἔνεκεν δεῖ σε ἀσκεῖν καὶ ὅπλων Α | δι᾽ ci. Du om. codd.    **83** πότερον Μ
ἄρα Α

and giving life to the whole body of the Christian people, both rulers and ruled. It has, therefore, set itself up as the property of the leader and emperor and God of all. From him it carries on, governs, and effects the management of the whole body.

13. In this way, then, be reverent, orthodox, and well disposed toward God and those who serve him. Be concerned to observe inviolate, after the divine laws, also those of the emperor, so as to establish judgment and justice in the midst of your land.

14. Be concerned about the tasks incumbent on a general and about the weapons of your soldiers. Do not act unjustly or initiate an unjust war. Do not launch unjust attacks or pillaging raids against people who have done you no wrong. Live in piety but also, as far as it depends on you, live in peace with your enemy. Thus, you will conduct yourself reverently, in a manner pleasing to God and, by so doing, you will possess the weapons to ward off any unjust foe.[7]

15. Your pious life having encompassed these things, be well assured that, along with righteousness, you will have God himself campaigning along with you.

16. The belief that one is not acting unjustly but is being treated unjustly will bring <you> the Divinity as your general and leader, and you will be compelled to believe that God has obligated himself to bring a just war to a good conclusion, and an unjust one to the contrary.[8]

17. Just as it is impossible for the unjust person not to suffer at some time the penalty for his injustice from God the judge, so it is impossible for one who has warded off and fought against injustice not to obtain victory from God. For God is a just judge and will bring everything about with justice.[9]

18. For these reasons, indeed, you must exercise yourself with weapons and training and the other military concerns.

19. I want you to be aware, in addition to these things, that in time of war you must know the nature of those fighting against you and their condition. Is their army at the height of readiness for what it must attempt? Has it been trained to be effective in its first assaults or rather for more drawn-out and time-consuming operations?

7. Cf. Const. 2 §§29–31.
8. Ibid.
9. Ibid.

κ′. Χρὴ δέ σε διαγινώσκειν καὶ αὐτὸν τὸν πόλεμον, πότερον πολυχρόνιός ἐστιν, καὶ διά τινος δαπάνης χρημάτων, ἢ μᾶλλον ὀξύτητι ῥώμης ὀλιγοχρόνιος καὶ ἐπιχειρητικός.

κα′. Ἐν δὲ τοῖς τοιούτοις πολέμοις ἀντιπαρασκευάζου πρὸς τὰς τῶν ἐναντί-
90 ων ψυχὰς καὶ πρὸς τὸ ὅλον αὐτῶν στράτευμα, ἤτοι πρὸς ἀνδρείας καὶ ὀξύτητας ἢ καὶ πρὸς τὰ τούτων ἐναντία, ἤγουν φόβους καὶ θράση καὶ ὀργὰς καὶ τιμωρίας καὶ φιλοτιμίας καὶ ῥαθυμίας, ὥστε τὰ τοιαῦτα πάθη τῶν τε σῶν στρατευμάτων ἢ καὶ τῶν πολεμίων δύνασθαί σε καὶ αὔξειν καὶ ταπεινοῦν.

κβ′. Καὶ μάλιστα τὰ παρά σοι διὰ παραγγελμάτων ἐντέχνων καὶ προσποιή-
95 σεως προγνωστικῆς καὶ τῆς περὶ τὸ θεῖον ἐπιμελείας καὶ τῆς διὰ λόγων δημηγο-ρίας, ταῦτα δὲ παραφυλάττειν ὥστε γίνεσθαι ἐν τῷ χρόνῳ καθ' ὃν αἱ ψυχαὶ ὑπὸ τοῦ λόγου κινηθεῖσαι διαμένειν δύνανται διὰ τῆς μνήμης πρὸς τὴν διάθεσιν τῆς κινήσεως, ἀλλὰ μὴ παρὰ τὰς ἀνάγκας αὐτάς, ὅτε πρὸς τὸ διαμάχεσθαι παρα-σκευάζονται. συμβαίνει γὰρ ἀπαρασκεύους διαγωνιζομένους τοὺς στρατιώτας
100 ἀτάκτως ἔχειν πρὸς τὸν τῆς μάχης κίνδυνον.

κγ′. Χρὴ οὖν πρὸ τῶν κινδύνων μεθαρμόζειν τὰς ψυχὰς τῶν στρατιωτῶν πρὸς τὰς παρούσας δόξας χρησίμως, ἀλλὰ καὶ τὰς τῶν ἀντιπολεμίων ψυχὰς καταδουλοῦν ἐντέχνως εἴς τε φόβους καὶ ῥαθυμίας καὶ μαλακίας, καὶ τότε ἐπιτίθεσθαι αὐτοῖς καὶ ἄνευ παντὸς ὄκνου διαμάχεσθαι. μηδαμῶς δὲ ἄλλως
105 δυνατόν σε περιγενέσθαι τῶν ἐναντίων, εἰ μὴ πρότερον εἰς ἀνάγκας αὐτοὺς περιστήσεις.

κδ′. Μηδὲ ἄγειν εἰς τοιούτους κινδύνους ἐξ ὧν βελτίονες μᾶλλον ἔσονται οἱ ἐχθροὶ παρ' ὃ βούλονται.

κε′. Εἰ δὲ πίστεις εἰσὶ καὶ ὁμολογίαι, ταύτας χρή σε φυλάττειν ἀπαραβάτους.

110 κϛ′. Ἐν δὲ ταῖς τῶν πραγμάτων ἐκβάσεσι δέον σε μήτε εὐτυχοῦντα καὶ τῆς τῶν πολεμίων ἀτυχίας κρατοῦντα μέγα φρονεῖν διαπράξασθαι, μηδὲ πρὸς τὰ κατεργασθέντα ἐναπομένοντα τῶν πόνων ἀμελεῖν, ἀλλ' εἰς τὰ μακρόθεν καὶ ἔμπροσθεν ἀποβλέπειν καὶ βουλεύεσθαι τί χρὴ ποιεῖν, μήτε δὴ δυστυχῶν φανε-ρὸς γίνου ὡς καταπεπληγμένος μήτε τοῖς στρατιώταις μήτε τοῖς πολεμίοις.

115 κζ′. Ἀλλὰ μηδὲ πρὸς τοὺς πολεμίους διάλυε ἐν οἷς καιροῖς δυνατὸς ὑπάρχεις κατ' αὐτῶν ἀντέχειν καὶ καταγωνίσασθαι, εἰ μὴ βεβαίαν εἰρήνην καὶ ἐπωφελῆ οἱ ἐναντίοι αἰτήσονται. μεγάλαι γὰρ ἐλαττώσεις πολλάκις ἐκ τοῦ τοιούτου τρόπου γίνονται.

---

86 πότερον M κἂν τε A   87 διά τινος M χρήζῃ A   99 ἀπαρασκεύους M ἀνετοίμους A
104 ἄλλως M ἄλλους A   105 περιγενέσθαι M γενέσθαι περὶ A   110 ἐκβάσεσι M
συμπληρώσεσι A   111 ἀτυχίας M δυστυχίας A   111–112 διαπράξασθαι…κατεργασθέντα
M εἰ πρὸς τὰ ἤδη τελειωθέντα A   113 δὴ PG δὲ M om. A

20. You must form an estimate of the war itself, whether it will last for a long time and with what expenditure of money, or, rather, for a short time with hostilities ready to begin because <the army> is at the height of its strength.

21. In such wars you must take counterpreparations that match the spirits of your adversaries and their entire army. Are they brave and sharp or the opposite, that is, fearful, bold, angry, vengeful, ambitious, and lazy? This makes it possible for you to increase or lessen such feelings in your own army, as well as in that of the enemy.

22. You must especially <attend to> your own responsibilities by way of skillful commands, anticipation of what is to be done, concern for the Divinity, and public orations, but make sure that these occur at a time when the souls that have been moved by <your> words are able to keep them in mind as they line up to move, not longer than necessary, but when they are getting ready to fight it out. Soldiers who enter the struggle unprepared are likely to be disorderly in facing the dangers of battle.

23. Before the dangers, therefore, it is necessary, in an effective manner, to bring the souls of the soldiers into harmony with the glory awaiting them. In addition, skillfully subject those of the enemy to fear, laziness, softness. Then attack them and fight them without any hesitation. There is absolutely no other way by which you are able to overcome your adversaries if you do not first bring them under duress.

24. Do not enter into such dangers that result in the enemy obtaining more of an advantage than they actually intended.

25. If pledges have been given or there are terms of truce, these you must observe inviolate.

26. As matters approach a conclusion, you must not, because of your good fortune and the misfortune of the enemy whom you have overcome, bring yourself to think in a haughty manner. Nor, content with what has been achieved, should you neglect the tasks remaining, but you should pay attention to what is still far off and ahead of you and make plans for what you must do. In misfortune you must not present yourself as beaten down, neither to your soldiers nor to the enemy.

27. Do not let up in the face of the enemy at those times when you are able to resist and fight against them, unless your adversaries should request a firm and beneficial peace. Great losses often occur by such a way of acting.

κη΄. Χρεὼν | δέ σε καὶ τὸ στράτευμα εἰς πόλεμον ἐξάγειν μὴ ἀτελὲς διὰ  377ᵛ
120 τὸ πλῆθος μηδὲ τῶν συνεργῶν τεχνῶν καὶ πραγμάτων ἀπολειπόμενον μηδ᾽
ἄλλην μηδεμίαν ἔχον ἐλάττωσιν, ἐξ οὗ μάλιστα τρόπου οἱ κακοὶ στρατηγοὶ
διαβάλλονται.

κθ΄. Χρὴ δέ σε σπουδαῖον ἀναφανῆναι, καὶ μάλιστα ἐν τῇ διοικητικῇ προνοίᾳ τῶν στρατευμάτων.

125 λ΄. Καὶ τὰς δαπάνας εἰς τὸ δυνατὸν ὀλίγας καὶ συνεσταλμένας κελεύειν, καὶ
τὰ ἄλλα τὰ κοινὰ διασῴζειν ἐμπείρως.

λα΄. Καὶ ἐπὶ τούτοις μελετᾶν σε μετὰ πόνου τὰ δέοντα ἔν τε τοῖς ἀρχαίοις
καὶ τοῖς νέοις, ὥστε ἱστορικὸν εἶναι πάντων τῶν κατὰ πόλεμον, καὶ ἔμπειρον
παλαιῶν στρατηγημάτων ὅσα ἀξιάγαστα γεγόνασιν.

130 λβ΄. Καὶ εἴ τις ἐπαγγέλλεταί σοι περὶ στρατηγίας τι εἰπεῖν ἢ τεχνίτης ἢ
ἰδιώτης, πάντων ἄκουε καὶ γίνου τῶν λεγομένων κριτής.

λγ΄. Συμβουλεύεσθαι δέ σε χρὴ μετὰ γερόντων ἅμα ἐμπείρων γενομένων
τῶν κατὰ πόλεμον ἔργων καὶ ἀξιώμασι διαπρεπόντων καὶ μετὰ εὐνοήσας ἐν τοῖς
πράγμασι περὶ ὧν ἂν ᾖ ἡ συμβουλὴ διακειμένων.

135 λδ΄. Δεῖ δέ σε ἐν τοῖς κινδύνοις τῆς μάχης μὴ ἐκ χειρὸς μάχεσθαι, ἀλλὰ
φυλακὴν ἔχειν περὶ σεαυτόν, καὶ ἑρμηνέα γίνεσθαι τοῦ στρατοῦ κατὰ τὴν ὥραν
τῆς μάχης πρὸς τὴν κατεπείγουσαν χρείαν.

λε΄. <Δεῖ δέ σε> ὀξέως ποιητικόν τε εἶναι στρατηγημάτων καὶ ἀγχίνουν ἐν
ταῖς ἐπιχειρήσεσιν ὑπάρχειν, καὶ ὅταν αὐτὸς ἐπιτίθεσθαι βούλει τοῖς πολεμίοις
140 καὶ ὅταν ἐπιβουλεύεσθαι μέλλῃς παρὰ τῶν πολεμίων.

λς΄. Ἔσο δὲ καὶ ἐν τοῖς αἰφνιδίοις φόβοις εὔπορος καὶ πρὸς τὰς τῶν πολεμίων κακουργίας δεινὸς προϊδεῖν καὶ τὸ μέλλον προστοχάσασθαι.

λζ΄. Εἶναι δέ σε χρὴ καὶ πρὸς τὰ συνθήματα, ὅσα κατὰ τῶν πολεμίων ἐπινοήσεις, σύντονον καὶ ἐπιμελέστατον, συνέσει τε καὶ φύσει καὶ ἐπιμελείᾳ διαφέρον-
145 τα τῶν ὑπό σε ἀρχόντων.

λη΄. Καὶ τῷ σώματι δὲ ῥωμαλέον καὶ πρὸς πᾶσαν ὅπλισιν, ὥστε χρῆσθαι
αὐτῇ δυνατῶς καὶ ἀνεμποδίστως, καὶ εὐτρεπῆ δὲ ἐντεῦθεν γίνεσθαι τὴν ἰδέαν,

---

146–157 Cf. β΄.3–10.

---

119 χρεὼν Μ χρὴ Α | πόλεμον Α πολέμους Μ | διὰ Μ κατὰ Α   120 μηδ᾽ PG μηδὲ ΜΑ
123–124 διοικητικῇ προνοίᾳ Μ προνοίᾳ τῆς διοικήσεως Α   125 εἰς Μ κατὰ Α | κελεύειν Μ
κελεύειν ἐπιφέρεσθαι Α   134 πράγμασι Μ πράγμασι διακειμένων Α | ἢ PG om.˙ΜΑ |
διακειμένων Μ om. Α   137 χρείαν Μ χρείαν ὀξέως Α   138 δεῖ...σε ci. De om. codd. |
ὀξέως Μ om. Α | ἀγχίνουν Μ συνετὸν Α   141 ἔσο Μ ὕπαρχε Α   145 τῶν Μ τῶν ἄλλων Α
146 ῥωμαλέον Μ ἰσχυρὸν Α | ὅπλισιν Μ ὅπλισιν ἐπιτήδειον Α   146–149 ὥστε...εὔρωστον
Μ om. Α

28. It is necessary for you to lead the army out to war when it is not below strength, when it is not lacking any of the skills and practices that make it effective, and is not inferior in any way at all. Failure to observe this is the principal reason why bad generals incur blame.

29. You must appear serious, especially in the management and foresight for the armies.

30. Issue orders that, as much as possible, the expenses be few and restricted and, on the basis of your experience, maintain the other public funds.

31. In addition to these matters, you are to reflect diligently on the necessary tasks <as presented> both by the ancient authors and the modern ones. You will then become well informed on everything pertaining to war and an expert on all the admirable stratagems of the ancients.

32. If anyone, whether a specialist or a private person, lets you know that he has something to say about strategy, listen to all he has to say and then, when he has finished, form your judgment.

33. You must make your plans together with older men experienced in the tasks of war and illustrious because of their dignities and well disposed to those matters about which advice is sought.

34. In the perilous conditions of war you must not engage in close fighting, but keep a guard around yourself. In the hour of battle you are the interpreter for the army to deal with its pressing needs.

35. <You ought> to be an inventor of keen stratagems, and shrewd in your undertakings, both when you plan to attack the enemy yourself and when you are about to be attacked by the enemy.

36. Also be ingenious in dealing with sudden fears and clever in foreseeing the evil works of the enemy, and in estimating what is to come.

37. You must also be earnest and most careful regarding passwords that you make up <for use> against the enemy, allowing for differences in intelligence, nature, and concern for the officers under you.

38. <You ought to be> robust in body and able to use every sort of weapon effectively and without being impeded and, as a result, ready to take up any one

καὶ κατεσκευάσθαι τῇ παντευχίᾳ τῶν ὅπλων καλῶς καὶ εὐπρεπῶς καὶ ἀπόνως, ὡς γενναῖον τὴν ἡλικίαν καὶ τὴν ψυχὴν καὶ τὸ σῶμα εὔρωστον.

150    λθ′. Εἶναι δέ σε μάλιστα καὶ ἐγκρατῆ χρημάτων καὶ ἡδονῶν ἁπασῶν, φιλόπονον δὲ πρὸς τὰς καρτερίας, ἀνδρεῖον δὲ πρὸς τοὺς κινδύνους καὶ μὴ ταρασσόμενον ἐν τοῖς ἀγῶσιν, φιλότιμον περὶ τὰς πράξεις τὰς μετὰ δικαιοσύνης, μεγαλόψυχον δὲ ἐν τοῖς ἔργοις τοῖς πρὸς τοὺς στρατιώτας, ἀξίωμα ἔχοντα ἀντὶ πόλεως καὶ γένους καὶ πολιτείας εὐνομουμένης τὴν οἰκείαν ἀρετήν, καὶ τῷ
155    προέχειν ἁπάντων ἐν τῇ κατὰ πόλεμον ἐμπειρίᾳ, εὐνοίᾳ τε καὶ φιλοτιμίᾳ ἐν τοῖς παροῦσιν ἀεὶ πράγμασιν τοὺς ἄλλους νικῶντα, καὶ ὡς ὑπὲρ ἰδίων πραγμάτων τοὺς κοινοὺς κινδύνους ἀναδεχόμενον.

μ′. Προσέτι δὲ δημηγορικόν σε εἶναι χρὴ | καὶ ἀγωνιστὴν καὶ τοῖς ἀληθεστά-   378
τοις τῶν λόγων χρώμενον περὶ τὴν ἀλήθειαν. πλὴν ὅσον συμφέρειν οὐδὲ
160    ἐπιψεύδεσθαι, ὥστε εἰς ἄλλο ἦθος μεταστῆσαι καὶ κινῆσαι τὰς τῶν ἀκουόντων ψυχὰς χρήσιμον καὶ βελτίους ποιῆσαι πρὸς τὸν παρόντα καιρόν.

μα′. Περὶ δὲ τοὺς ἐν ταῖς μάχαις ἀποθνήσκοντας μεγαλοπρεπὴς γενοῦ καὶ φιλότιμος καὶ τιμητικός, μάλιστα περὶ τοὺς ἀγαθοὺς ἄνδρας, δόξαν αὐτοῖς διὰ τοῦ μακαρισμοῦ καὶ τῆς ἐντίμου ταφῆς περιποιούμενος.

165    μβ′. Τῶν νοσούντων θεραπευτικός, περὶ τοὺς ἀπόρους εὔπορος ἐκ τῶν ἰδίων, ἀφιλόδοξος δὲ καὶ ἐλεύθερος ἐν ταῖς ἰδίαις καὶ ἐν ταῖς κοινῇ συνερχομέναις ὁμιλίαις.

μγ′. Μὴ δύσερις ὑπάρχῃς μηδὲ πολυπράγμων μηδὲ πολύλογος, τῇ δὲ ἐσθῆτι μέτριος, καὶ τῷ σχήματι καὶ τῷ βαδίσματι. καὶ μᾶλλον τῶν ἄλλων τὸ ἀνεπίφθο-
170    νον παραφύλαττε, ὥστε μὴ δάκνεσθαι τῷ φθόνῳ περὶ τοὺς συστρατήγους τι κατορθοῦντας, ἀλλὰ ζηλοῦν μᾶλλον καὶ μιμεῖσθαι καὶ συναγωνίζεσθαι τοῖς στρατευομένοις πρὸς ἅπαντα τὰ συμφέροντα.

μδ′. Τῷ δὲ ἀγαθῷ στρατηγῷ χρέος ἐστὶν πρὸς πᾶν ἔθνος ἁρμοζομένῳ, διαφόρους πρὸς ἕκαστον τὰς στρατηγίας ἐπινοεῖσθαι.

175    με′. Εἰ δέ ποτε καὶ ναυαρχίας ἐπιστήσεται, ἀκύμαντον τὴν τοῦ στόλου τάξιν διαφυλάξει, ἐμπείρως ἔχων τῆς τοῦ ἀέρος φορᾶς, καὶ τὰς οὐραγίας δὲ ἤτοι τοὺς

---

150 ἁπασῶν Μ πασῶν Α    152 φιλότιμον Μ σπουδὴν ἔχονται Α    156 πράγμασιν Μ πράγμασι Α    165 εὔπορος…τῶν Μ ἐκ τῶν σῶν εὐπορωτέρους ποιῶν Α    166 ἰδίων Μ om. Α | ἐλεύθερος Α ἐλεύθριος Μ | ἰδίαις Μ κατ' ἰδίαν Α    166–167 καὶ²…ὁμιλίαις Μ ὁμιλίαις καὶ ἐν ταῖς εἰς τὸ κοινὸν συνερχομέναις Α    168 δύσερις Μ φιλόνεικος Α | μηδὲ¹…μηδὲ² Μ μὴ…μὴ Α | τῇ…ἐσθῆτι Μ τοῖς δὲ ἱματίοις Α    169 μέτριος Μ εὐτελέστατος Α    171 ζηλοῦν…μιμεῖσθαι Μ μιμεῖσθαι μᾶλλον Α    175 ναυαρχίας Μ ναυαρχίας καιρὸς Α | ἀκύμαντον Μ ἀκίνδυνον Α    176 διαφυλάξει Μ om. Α | ἔχων Μ ἔχει Α

of them. Equip yourself with the full panoply of weapons nicely, properly, and with ease, as a person noble in age and soul and very strong in body.[10]

39. You <ought> to be particularly restrained when it comes to money and all pleasures, a lover of work in addition to endurance, brave in confronting dangers, not confused during combat, generous in your deeds, righteous, magnanimous in your dealings with the soldiers, possessing your personal virtue as a dignity in place of a city, nation, or well-ordered commonwealth, standing ahead of all in your experience of war, by your goodwill and generosity ever surpassing others in the matters at hand, and placing the common dangers above your own concerns.[11]

40. You ought, moreover, to be a public speaker, as well as a good debater. You are to employ the truest words about the truth, not uttering falsehoods, apart from what may be beneficial, so as to turn <your troops> around to another disposition and to move the spirits of your audience and to make them better able to face the situations that present themselves.

41. Be generous, respectful, and honorable regarding those who have died in battle, especially the men <cited for> bravery, assuring them of glory by blessing and an honorable burial.

42. <See that> the sick receive proper care. For those who have no resources, provide resources from your own possessions. Be free from conceit and bountiful in your own affairs and in the public affairs that devolve upon you.

43. You should not be quarrelsome, meddlesome, or garrulous. Be moderate in your clothing, your appearance, and the way you walk. Preserve yourself from being jealous of others so that you are not bitten by envy regarding your fellow generals when they achieve some success. Rather, emulate, imitate, and struggle along with them on campaign for everything that is beneficial.

44. A good general has to make accommodation for every nation, devising a different strategy for each one.

45. If he will ever be given a naval command, he shall preserve the order of the fleet from being broken up by the waves, with his experience of the move-

10. Cf. Const. 2 §1.
11. Ibid.

ὀπισθοφύλακας εὐτάκτως συνάγειν, ἵνα μὴ ὑπὸ τόπου ἢ ὑπὸ ζάλης θαλαττίας ἢ ὑπὸ πολεμίων ἀναγκαζόμενοι φθείροιντο.

μϛ΄. Δεῖ δέ σε γινώσκειν, ὦ στρατηγέ, καὶ ἐξ ὅσων τρόπων αἱ μάχαι συνά-
180    πτονται, ἢ γὰρ ἐκ παρατάξεως κατὰ πρόσωπον ἢ ἐκ παραλογισμοῦ κατὰ μέθοδον ἢ τόπων ἀποστερίσκοντας ὀχυρῶν ἢ χώρας ἐξ ἐφόδου φθείροντας ἢ δεν-
δροτομίας ἢ σιτοφθορίας ἢ δώματα ἐμπυρίζοντας ἢ λεηλατοῦντας ἢ αἰχμαλωτί-
ζοντας ἢ ὑδάτων ἀποστεροῦντας ἢ ἐξ ἐνέδρας ἐπερχομένους.

μζ΄. Συνάπτονται δὲ αἱ μάχαι καὶ ἐκ τούτων, ὅταν αἰφνιδίως ἐπιστῇ στράτευ-
185    μα στρατεύματι, καὶ ποταμὸν διαβαίνοντι τῷ πολεμίῳ συνάπτειν, καὶ εἰς στενοὺς τόπους ἐξ εὐρυχωρίας μεταλλασσομένῳ, καὶ ἀπὸ στενῶν τόπων εἰς εὐρυ-
χωρίαν καθισταμένῳ, καὶ μήπω συντεταγμένῳ. καὶ ὅταν μεταλλαγὴ ἀθρόα τοῦ
στρατοῦ τῶν πολεμίων γένηται, καὶ ὅταν ἐν τόποις κατακλεισθῶσι δυσδιεξο-
δεύτοις, καὶ ὅταν τῶν ἀναγκαίων ἀπορήσωσιν, καὶ ὅταν εἰς νόσον τὸ στράτευμα
190    τῶν ἐναντίων ἐμπέσῃ, καὶ ὅταν ὑπὸ χειμῶνος παραλόγως ἐνοχληθῶσιν ἢ
ἐναπολειφθῶσι χειμῶνι, καὶ ὅταν ἀπὸ τῶν ἡμερινῶν πόνων τὰ σώματα κατάκοποι γενόμενοι ἄσιτοί εἰσι καὶ νηστεύοντες ἢ πορείας μακρᾶς ἐμπεσούσης καὶ
κόπος τῶν ἀλόγων καὶ | ἀνδρῶν γένηται ἢ ὅταν ἄγρυπνοι γένωνται διά τινας    378ᵛ
αἰτίας. ἐν δὲ τοῖς ναυτικοῖς μάχαι συνάπτονται ἢ ὅταν οἱ πολέμιοι ναυαγήσωσιν
195    ἢ ὅταν ὑπὸ χειμῶνος ταλαιπωρηθῶσιν.

μη΄. Δεῖ δὲ εἰδέναι τὰ τοιαῦτα τὸν στρατηγὸν καὶ τὰ ἐκ τούτων ἐναντία
γινόμενα, προσέτι δὲ καὶ τοὺς καταμερισμοὺς τοῦ στρατοῦ καὶ τὰς παρατάξεις
καὶ τὰς παραγωγὰς τῶν τάξεων, ἵνα δι᾽ ὀλίγων πείθωνται, εἰδέναι δεῖ καὶ τὰ εἴδη
τῶν παραγγελμάτων.

200    μθ΄. Καὶ πρὸς μὲν τὰς ἀπηριθμημένας ἁπάσης τῆς μάχης ἐπιβολὰς νουνεχῶς
ἐπιβάλλειν σε παρακελευόμεθα, ὦ στρατηγέ, καθόσον ἐπινοήσεις ἐνδέχεσθαι
τὰς ἐγχειρήσεις, φυλάττεσθαι δὲ ἀπ᾽ αὐτῶν τὰς τῶν πολεμίων ἐπιθέσεις. καὶ
πρὸς πάντα τὰ τοιαῦτα, εἰ οὕτω τύχοι, ἐμπίπτοντά σε φεύγειν τὰς ἐγχειρήσεις. ἃ
γὰρ ἑτέροις δράσεις δι᾽ αὐτῶν τὰ ὅμοια πάθοις πάλιν ὑφ᾽ ἑτέρων δι᾽ αὐτῶν, εἰ μὴ

---

179 ὅσων Μ πόσων Α    180 ἐκ παραλογισμοῦ Μ ἀπὸ ἀπάτης Α    182 ἐμπυρίζοντας…ἢ⁴ Μ
κατακαίοντας ἢ πραιδεύοντας ἢ Α    183 ἐξ ἐνέδρας Μ ἀπὸ ἐγκρύμματος Α    184 καὶ Α om.
Μ    185 εἰς Α ὡς Μ    186 ἐξ Μ ἀπὸ Α | μεταλλασσομένῳ Μ μεταβαίνοντι Α
187 καθισταμένῳ Μ ἐξερχομένῳ Α | ἀθρόα Μ αἰφνιδία Α    188 στρατοῦ Μ κρατοῦντος Α
188–189 δυσδιεξοδεύτοις Μ διεξοδεύτοις Α    191 ἐναπολειφθῶσι χειμῶνι Μ κλεισθῶσιν Α |
πόνων Μ πόνων ταλαιπωρηθέντες Α    191–192 κατάκοποι…ἄσιτοί Μ ἀγευστοί Α
192 πορείας Μ ὁδοῦ Α    198 δεῖ Du δὲ codd.    200 ἀπηριθμημένας Μ ἠριθμημένας Α |
ἐπιβολὰς Μ ἐγχειρήσεις Α    204 δράσεις Μ ποιήσεις Α

ments of the air. The rear guard, that is, the guard behind, must accompany him in good order so that they will not be destroyed by the location or the storms at sea or the pressure of the enemy.

46. It is necessary for you, O general, to know the number of situations that may entice you to enter into battle: either from a battle line facing to the front or by deceiving <the enemy> in some way or dismantling their fortified places or destroying a region in a raid or chopping down trees or destroying crops or setting houses on fire or pillaging or taking prisoners or cutting off the water supply or attacking from ambush.

47. Battles are joined in the following situations as well. When an army comes upon another army unexpectedly or joins battle as the enemy is crossing a river, or as it is transferring itself from open country into narrow places, or when it exits narrow places and is setting itself up in open country and is not yet drawn up in formation. Also when the enemy army is suddenly transferred or finds itself in closed off spaces difficult to exit, or when it is deprived of necessities, or when the opposing army succumbs to disease, or when it is exceptionally disturbed by stormy weather or left behind by winter, or when the men become physically exhausted because of their daily labors and are without food and starving. Or when they endure a very long march that is hard on the horses and the men or when, for various reasons, they do not get enough sleep. Engage in naval battle when the enemy are suffering shipwreck or when they have been severely battered by storms.

48. The general must know all these things as well as their opposites. He must, moreover, know the divisions of the army and the battle formations and the marching in formation, in order that he might be obeyed quickly. He should also know the various kinds of commands.

49. We order you, O general, to confront intelligently the innumerable offensive acts of every battle to the extent that you think the assaults will allow. Guard yourself against the attacks of the enemy. Confront whatever happens to fall upon you and free yourself from their assaults. The things you will do to others by such assaults, you may in turn suffer from others who also make use

205 λίαν ὀξέως καὶ νουνεχῶς ἐπιβάλῃς τοῖς ἐμπίπτουσι καὶ ἀντιτιθῇς ταῖς ἀνάγκαις
τὰ δέοντα.

ν΄. Ἐν δὲ τούτοις τοῖς χρόνοις τοῦ ἐνιαυτοῦ δέον σε τὰς ἐκστρατείας ποιεῖσθαι ὅταν εἰσὶν οἱ καρποί.

να΄. Ἐν δὲ ταῖς στάσεσι τῶν παρατάξεων τὰ ἐναντία πνεύματα κατὰ νώτου
210 ποιεῖσθαι καὶ τὸν ἥλιον δὲ ὡσαύτως κατὰ τὰς πολεμικὰς ἀγῶνας ἐν ὄψει τῶν
ἐναντίων ποιεῖν.

νβ΄. Εἶναι δέ σε δεῖ μεγαλόφωνον ἐν τοῖς παραγγέλμασι καὶ εὐθαρσὲς καὶ
ἐμμελὲς ἔχειν τὸ φθέγμα.

νγ΄. Συνεργοῦσι δὲ τῇ φύσει τοῦ πολέμου αὗται αἱ τέχναι, οἷον ὁπλιτική,
215 λογιστική, ἀρχιτεκτονική, ἀστρονομική, ἱερατική, ἰατρική.

νδ΄. Ἔργα δὲ τῆς ὁπλιτικῆς, ὥστε περιφράττειν τὰ σώματα ὅπλοις συμμέ-
τροις καὶ ἁρμόζουσι καὶ ἰσχυροῖς καὶ ἀκριβῶς εἰργασμένοις καὶ εὐπρέπειαν
παρέχουσι τῶν φερόντων αὐτὰ σωμάτων. ἐκλέξασθαι δὲ δεῖ καὶ τὰ σώματα, ὅσα
πρὸς πανοπλίαν ἁρμόζουσιν.

220 νε΄. Δεῖ δέ σε ὑποδεικνύναι τοῖς στρατιώταις οἵας καὶ ὅσας εἶναι χρὴ τῶν
ὅπλων τὰς χρήσεις καὶ τὰς μελέτας τούτων καὶ πάσας τὰς ἀγωνίας πρὸς πᾶσαν
συσκευὴν καὶ γυμνασίαν πρὸς τὰς μάχας.

νϛ΄. Φροντίζειν δὲ καὶ τιμῶν καὶ οὐσιῶν καὶ εὐπορίας, ἐξ ὧν αἱ κτήσεις τῶν
ὅπλων καὶ αἱ δαπάναι αἱ περὶ τὰ σώματα ἀρκοῦσαι ἔσονται. ταῦτα μὲν τὰ
225 ὁπλιτικά.

νζ΄. Λογιστικῆς δὲ ἔργον ἐστίν, ὥστε μερίζειν τὸ στράτευμα κατὰ κοντουβέρνια καὶ τάξεις καὶ τούρμας καὶ δρούγγους καὶ βάνδα καὶ κενταρχίας τε καὶ
δεκαρχίας καὶ πενταρχίας καὶ τοὺς ἄλλους ἀριθμοὺς καὶ ὅλας παρατάξεις καὶ
πάντων τούτων ποιεῖσθαι διαίρεσιν. τίνες καὶ ὅσοι τὰ κάστρα φυλάξουσιν; καὶ
230 τίνες καὶ ὅσοι νέοι ἢ γέροντές εἰσιν ἢ ἀνάπηροι τὰ μέλη ἢ διὰ νόσου ἀδύνατοι | 379
καὶ ὅσοι τῆς πολιτικῆς ἀρχῆς ἢ περὶ τὰ δημόσια πράγματα τεταγμένοι; ταῦτα
λογιστικῆς εἰσι. διακρῖναι δὲ καὶ ἐπιλέξασθαι τὸ λοιπὸν τὰ ἀκμάζοντα σώματα
πάσης τῆς στρατιᾶς καὶ τούτων τὸν μερισμόν, ὁπόσοι εἰσὶ κατά τε μέγεθος καὶ
σμικρότητα. καὶ ὅπως ἄρχοντας ἐπὶ τούτοις μεγάλους τὰς ἡλικίας δεῖ ποιεῖσθαι
235 καὶ πῶς τὰ περὶ τὴν στάσιν ἔν τε τῷ μήκει καὶ τῷ βάθει γινόμενοι ταχθήσονται,

---

216-225 Cf. Strat., 5.   226-237 Cf. Strat., 4.

---

205 ἐπιβάλῃς…καὶ² M πρὸς τὰ ἐμπίπτοντα A   209 τὰ…νώτου M τοὺς ἀνέμους ὀπίσω A
210 τὰς…ὄψει M πρόσωπον A   211 ποιεῖν M om. A   218 τῶν…σωμάτων M τοῖς
φέρουσιν αὐτοῖς σώμασιν A   226-227 κοντουβέρνια A κουτουβέρνια M   230 ἀνάπηροι M
παραλελυμένοι A   231 τεταγμένοι M παρατεταγμένοι A

of them, unless you take action, in a very shrewd and intelligent manner, against what falls on you and match what is fitting to the needs.

50. You ought to embark upon your expeditions at that time of the year when the harvest is ready.

51. In positioning your battle line have the contrary winds at your back and, at the time of combat, have the sun in the face of your adversaries.

52. You ought to have a loud voice when giving commands. Your voice should also sound harmonious and should inspire courage.

53. War, by its very nature, needs the work of these skills: armament, logistic, architectonic, astronomic, priestly, medical.

54. The task of armament is to provide protection for the body by means of weapons that are well proportioned, fitting the body, and strong. They should be expertly crafted and make for a nice appearance on the bodies bearing them. One must select the bodies that are suitable for a complete suit of armor.[12]

55. You must instruct the soldiers in the number and kinds of ways in which the weapons are to be used, the ways of practicing with them, and all the hard work involved in every preparation and drilling for battle.[13]

56. You must take thought for the price, the material, and the resources leading to the purchase of the weapons and the expenses that will be sufficient to cover the bodies <of the men>. So much for weaponry.[14]

57. This is what the logistic art is to do. It divides the army into squads and units, tourmai, droungoi, and banda, also kentarchies, dekarchies, pentarchies, and the other units, as well as entire battle lines. It makes a proper division of all these. Which ones and how many will guard fortified towns? Which ones and how many young or old men there are? Which ones are maimed in their limbs or incapacitated by illness? How many have a position in the civil government or one dealing with public affairs? This is what logistics are. To determine and to select, moreover, the bodies in their prime for the whole army and to make divisions among these. Which are larger? Which are smaller? What age must the senior officers over them be? How are they to be assigned a position in the width and depth of the formation? What should be the numbers in each of the

12. Cf. *Strat.* 5.
13. Ibid.
14. Ibid.

καὶ ἐν ποίοις ἀριθμοῖς ἕκαστα τῶν μερῶν καὶ ποῦ καταταγήσονται πρὸς τὰς ἐν ταῖς χρείαις ἀναγκαίας κινήσεις. καὶ ταῦτα μὲν τῆς λογιστικῆς.

νη΄. Τῆς δὲ τακτικῆς ἔργον ἐστίν, ὥστε τὰ σχήματα τῶν ταγμάτων δεῖξαι. ἐν οἷς ἢ ἐγχειρεῖσθαι συμβαίνει, καὶ ποῖα χρήσιμα πρὸς τὸ ὑποδέχεσθαι πολεμίων
240 ἐπιφοράς, καὶ ποῖα πρὸς τὸ ἐπέρχεσθαι ἢ ἀμύνασθαι πέφυκεν, καὶ μετὰ ποίου τρόπου γίνονται ἕκαστα, καὶ ποίας ὁπλίσεις δεῖ ποιεῖσθαι κατὰ τῶν ἐναντίων, καὶ πῶς μετακινεῖσθαι τὰς τάξεις δυνατόν, καὶ ἐν τίνι τόπῳ καὶ πότε χρηστέον. ταῦτα μὲν καὶ τῆς τακτικῆς.

νθ΄. Τῆς δὲ ἀρχιτεκτονικῆς ἐστιν τὰ τῶν στρατοπέδων καὶ φοσσάτων σχή-
245 ματα ἤτοι τῶν ἀπλίκτων, πῶς δεῖ ταῦτα περιλαβεῖν διὰ φοσσάτου ἢ χάρακος, καὶ τὸν ἔσωθεν τόπον διαμερίσαι συμμέτρως καὶ ποιῆσαι διεξόδους τὰς ἁρμο-ζούσας καὶ τὸ δεῖξαι διαστήματα μεγίστου στρατοπέδου διὰ τοῦ μήκους καὶ ἐλαχίστου πάλιν διὰ συστολῆς, ὅτε καιρὸς τῆς ἑκάστου χρείας ἐστίν· ἐκλέγε-σθαι δὲ καὶ τόπους ὅσοι μὴ εὐεπιβούλευτοί εἰσι τοῖς πολεμίοις καὶ ὅσοι εὐαπάλ-
250 λακτοι ἐν ταῖς ὑποστροφαῖς καὶ ταῖς ἀναζεύξεσιν.

ξ΄. Προσέτι δὲ μηχανικῆς ἐστι τειχίσματα πόλεων ἢ ἄλλων φρουρίων πρὸς τὰς τῶν πολεμίων μηχανὰς ἀκαταγώνιστα κατασκευάσαι, καὶ ὑπὸ ὑδάτων ἐπαγωγῆς ἀνάλωτα. καὶ περὶ τὰ τείχη δὲ κατασκευὰς ποιῆσαι καὶ παρασκευάσαι ὅπλισιν, οἷον τὰ λεγόμενα μαγγανικὰ καὶ τοξοβολίστρας καὶ τὰ ἄλλα ὅπλα ὅσα
255 πρὸς τειχομαχίαν ἀντίκειται, καὶ ἕτερα πρὸς τειχομαχίαν ἐπιτήδεια. ταῦτα μὲν καὶ τῆς ἀρχιτεκτονικῆς.

ξα΄. Τῆς δὲ ἀστρονομίας εἰσὶν τοὺς καιροὺς τοῦ ἐνιαυτοῦ προλέγειν, ἐν οἷς χειμώνων ἢ καυμάτων μεταβολαὶ γίνονται, ἢ ὑδάτων ὀμβρίων καταφοραὶ ἢ πνευμάτων ἐξαισίων κινήσεις, ἐξ ὧν στρατεύματα πολλάκις εἰς μεγίστους
260 κινδύνους ἐνέπεσον. καὶ περὶ τὰ μέρη δὲ τῆς ἡμέρας καὶ τῆς νυκτὸς ἀκριβῶς διαιρεῖν τοὺς καιροὺς πρὸς τὰς ὥρας τῶν ἐπιθέσεων καὶ πρὸς τὰς ἀναπαύσεις, ἐν αἷς ἀστοχοῦντες πολλάκις ἄχρηστον τὴν δύναμίν τινες | ἀπεργάζονται. περὶ    379ᵛ
δὲ σεισμῶν καὶ τῶν ἄλλων σημείων τὰ μέλλοντα δηλοποιεῖν ἢ καὶ πρὸς τὸ

---

244-250 Cf. Strat., 11.    257-265 Arist. Meteor., 362b 17.

238-239 ἐν...συμβαίνει M om. A    242 χρηστέον M προσήκει χρῆσθαι A
245 φοσσάτου...χάρακος M ὀρυγμάτων ἢ σταβάρων A    247 μεγίστου M μέχρι τοῦ A | διὰ τοῦ M διά τε A    248 ἐλαχίστου M ἐλαχίστης A | διὰ M om. A    249-250 εὐαπάλλακτοι M ἀνεμποδίστοι καὶ ἀκώλυτοί εἰσιν A    250 καὶ...ἀναζεύξεσιν M om. A    251 φρουρίων M ὀχυρωμάτων A    252 κατασκευάσαι M παρασκευάσαι A    253-254 καὶ²...οἷον M ἤτοι A
254 τὰ² M om. A    258-259 ὑδάτων...πνευμάτων M ὀμβρίοι σφοδροὶ ἢ ἀνέμων A
261 διαιρεῖν M διαιρεῖ A    262 ἀστοχοῦντες M ἀστοχοῦντες τινὲς A | τινες M om. A

divisions? Where should they be lined up for the necessary movements in time of need? These are the functions of logistics.[15]

58. This is the task of tactics. It shows the formations of the units in which they are set to take offensive action as well as the formations that are useful in receiving the attacks of the enemy. What kinds of formations are set for attacking? What kind for defensive action? What manner is appropriate for each one? What sort of armament must be employed against the foe? How is it possible to transfer the units from one place to another and in what place and when is it useful? These are the functions of tactics.

59. The architectonic deals with the forms of army camps and fortified places, in a word, camps. How it is necessary to surround these by a ditch or a palisade, and to divide the interior space proportionately and to make convenient roadways. To show the distances of the largest campsite by its length and, in turn, the smallest by contraction, as the situation calls for each one. Also to select the sites that are not easily subject to enemy assaults, and that are easy to evacuate when it comes to wheeling about and breaking up camp.[16]

60. In addition, it is the task of mechanics to construct the walls of cities and other fortresses that can hold out against the machines of the enemy and withstand the onrush of water. And to make preparations about the walls and prepare armament, such as the so-called manganika and toxobolistrai and all the other weapons available for fighting on the walls, and whatever else is useful for such fighting. These are the functions of architectonics.

61. The task of astronomy is to foretell the seasons of the year. When do the changes of wintry storms or burning heat take place, or the downpours of heavy rain or the movements of favorable winds? All these have often inflicted serious damage upon armies. About the divisions of the day and of the night, to determine accurately the times with a view to the hours of offensive action and of rest. By missing the mark often in these matters, one ends up with a force that proves useless. To make clear what will occur on the basis of earthquakes and

---

15. Cf. *Strat.* 4.
16. Cf. *Strat.* 11.

συμφέρον τὰς ἐπιφανείας ἐντέχνως μεταρυθμίζειν. πάντα ταῦτα τῆς ἀστρονομί-
265 ας εἰσίν.

ξβ′. Τῆς δὲ ἱερατικῆς ἐστιν τὸ καλῶς τὰ θεῖα χρῆσθαι καὶ ταῦτα ἐπιτελεῖν
ἀδιαλείπτως ἐν τῷ στρατεύματι εὐσεβῶς τε καὶ θεαρέστως κατὰ τὸν παραδο-
θέντα θεσμὸν ἄνωθεν τοῖς εὐσεβοῦσι Χριστιανοῖς, διά τε ἱερολογιῶν καὶ
ἱερουργιῶν καὶ τῶν ἄλλων εὐχῶν καὶ δεήσεων πρὸς τὸν Θεὸν ἐκτενῶς γινομέ-
270 νων καὶ πρὸς τὴν πανάχραντον αὐτοῦ μητέρα καὶ Θεοτόκον καὶ τοὺς ἁγίους
αὐτοῦ θεράποντας. ἐξ ὧν ἱλεοῦται τὸ θεῖον καὶ διὰ τὴν πίστιν τῆς σωτηρίας αἱ
ψυχαὶ τῶν στρατιωτῶν εὐρωστότεραι πρὸς τοὺς κινδύνους παρασκευάζονται.

ξγ′. Τῆς δὲ ἰατρικῆς ἐστι περὶ τὰ ἕλκη τὰ ἐκ τῶν τραυμάτων γινόμενα καὶ
περὶ τὰς πληγὰς ὅσαι ἀπὸ λίθων ἢ ἀπὸ βελῶν ἢ ἄλλου τινὸς ὅπλου γίνονται,
275 τούτων πάντων φάρμακα ἔχειν θεραπευτικὰ καὶ ἐπιστήμην ἰατρικήν. ἀλλ᾽ ὅσα
νοσήματα κοινὰ συμβαίνειν εἴωθε διὰ ψύχη καὶ καύματα καὶ πόνους καὶ ὑδάτων
μεταβολὰς καὶ τόπων θέσεις καὶ ἀέρων κράσεις καὶ σωμάτων ἀθεραπευσίαν καὶ
τροφῶν ἀταξίαν, οἷον καρπῶν νέων, καὶ τῶν ὁμοίων, τούτων πάντων ἡ ἰατρική
ἐστι θεραπευτική.

280 ξδ′. Προσέτι δὲ τῆς λογιστικῆς εἰσι διοικήσεως καὶ τὰ ἀναλώματα τῶν
στρατιωτῶν καὶ ὅσα ἀπὸ λαφύρων συναθροίζονται ἢ ἄλλοθεν συνάγματα
χρημάτων καὶ πάλιν ποῦ ἀναλίσκεται, εἰς τὰς ὅπλων καὶ μηχανημάτων κατασκευὰς καὶ εἰς ἑτέρας χρείας, ὡς εἰκός, ἑκάστης ἐκστρατείας. τούτων πάντων
διάκρισις καὶ διοίκησις τῆς λογιστικῆς εἰσι μεθόδου.

285 ξε′. Τέχναι μὲν οὖν τοσαῦται πρός τε κατασκευὴν καὶ σωτηρίαν στρατεύματος, καὶ τεχνῖται δὲ τούτων οἱ ἐπιστημόνως αὐτὰς μεταχειριζόμενοι.

ξϛ′. Τὴν μὲν οὖν ὁπλιτικὴν οἱ περὶ τὴν τῶν ὅπλων ἐργασίαν πονοῦντες
τεχνῖται, τὴν δὲ λογιστικὴν γραμμάτων καὶ ψήφων ἔμπειροι ἄνδρες, τὴν δὲ
τακτικὴν σύ τε αὐτός, ὦ στρατηγέ, καὶ ὅσοι ὑπό σε τεταγμένοι ἄρχοντες.

290 ξζ′. Τὴν δὲ ἀρχιτεκτονικὴν οἱ τέκτονες καὶ μηχανικοὶ καὶ ἐκ πολλοῦ πρὸς τὴν
τοιαύτην γυμνασίαν ἔμπειροι. τὴν δὲ ἀστρονομίαν οἱ περὶ τοῦ οὐρανοῦ σχολά-

---

290-298 Cf. Suda, Π 3033; Α 3745; Γ 131.

---

264-265 ἀστρονομίας De ἀστρολογίας codd.    266 χρῆσθαι...ἐπιτελεῖν Μ ἐπιτελεῖν καὶ
ταῦτα Α    267 ἐν...στρατεύματι Α τὰ στρατεύματα Μ    270-271 ἁγίους αὐτοῦ Μ trsp. Α
272 εὐρωστότεραι Μ γενναιότερον Α    275 θεραπευτικὰ Du θεραπευτικὴν codd. | ἀλλ᾽ Μ
ἀλλὰ καὶ Α    277 ἀθεραπευσίαν Μ κακουχίας Α    278-279 ἡ...θεραπευτική Μ ἐστὶ ἡ
ἰατρικὴ θεραπευτική Α    281-282 ἢ...χρημάτων Μ χρήματα ἢ ἄλλοθεν πόθεν Α    282 τὰς
Α τε Μ    284 διάκρισις Α μὴ εὐκρίνεια Μ | διοίκησις Α οἱ λόγοι Μ    287 πονοῦντες Du
πονοῦσι Μ πονοῦνται Α    289 τεταγμένοι Μ τάσσονται Α    291 τοῦ οὐρανοῦ Du τῷ
οὐρανῷ Α τὰ μετέωρα Μ    291-292 σχολάζοντες Α στοχάζονται Μ

other signs or to skillfully change the manifestations to something beneficial. All these matters are part of astronomy.[17]

62. The priestly task is to deal with divine things properly and incessantly to perform these <rites> in the army piously and in a manner pleasing to God, according to the law handed down from the beginning to pious Christians. They do this by sacred words and sacred actions[18] and by the other prayers and entreaties they fervently address to God and to his wholly immaculate mother and Theotokos, and to his holy servants. As a result the Divinity takes pity and by their faith in salvation the souls of the soldiers are made ready to face dangers more firmly.

63. The medical task is concerned with the wounds resulting from injuries and with those inflicted by stones or missiles or by some other weapon. It provides healing medicines for all these and for medical knowledge to treat all the common illnesses that usually come about because of cold or heat, by hard labor, changes of water, the conditions of places, the mixture of air, the lack of care for the bodies, and irregularity of nourishment (such as with unripe fruit and the like). All these belong to the medical or healing skill.

64. In addition, part of logistics is the management of the expenses of the soldiers and what they have collected as booty or money collected from some other source. In turn, how it is spent for weapons and construction of machines and for other likely needs for each expedition. The division and management of all of these are a function of the art of logistics.

65. These, then, are the skills for the preparation and security of an army and the technicians in each case are those who perform them in a scientific manner.

66. For the skill of armament there are the technicians who labor on the manufacture of weapons. For logistics men experienced in letters and numbers. For tactics yourself, O general, and the officers stationed under you.

67. For architectonics builders and engineers who have a great deal of experience in this sort of activity. For astronomy those who can make estimates about

---

17. Aristotle, *Meteorology* 362b17. In the MSS the last line reads "astrology," probably a mistake for "astronomy." The Byzantines, though, did not always clearly distinguish between the two. See now P. Magdalino, *L'orthodoxie des astrologues: La science entre le dogme et la divination à Byzance* (Paris, 2006).

18. ἱερολογιῶν καὶ ἱερουργιῶν. The *Suda* (I 179) defines ἱερολογία as the Divine Liturgy.

ζοντες, σοφίᾳ τε καὶ ἐπιστήμῃ τῆς τῶν ἀστέρων ψηφοφορίας διαφέροντες, περί
τε τὸν Πτολεμαίου Πρόχειρον Κανόνα καὶ περὶ τὴν αὐτοῦ λεγομένην Τετράβι-
βλον, καὶ περὶ ἕτερά τινα τῶν Χαλδαϊκῶν παρασημειώσεων. προσέτι δὲ καὶ τὴν
295 τοῦ Ἀράτου περὶ τῶν φαινομένων διαγόρευσιν, | Ἰωάννου τοῦ Λυδοῦ καθημερι-    380
νήν τε καὶ μηνιαίαν παρατήρησιν, τὰ δὲ τῆς γενεθλιαλογίας ὅσα ἐν τοῖς εἰρημένοις παρέσπαρται, ὡς ἀπόβλητα τῆς τοῦ Θεοῦ ἐκκλησίας ἡ ἡμετέρα ἀποτρέπε-
ται βασιλεία. καὶ ταῦτα μὲν τῆς ἀστρονομίας.

ξη΄. Τὴν δὲ ἱερατικὴν ἱερεῖς καθαροί, σεμνοὶ τὸν βίον καὶ τὸν τρόπον καὶ
300 καθηγιασμένοι τελεσιουργήσουσιν καὶ αὐτοὶ τὸ τέλος τῆς οἰκείας ἐνεργείας τῷ
Θεῷ ἀναστήσουσιν, ὥσπερ δὴ καὶ ἡμεῖς τὰ πρώην ἡμῖν εἰρημένα ἀνακεφαλαιω-
σάμενοι, τὸ τέλος τῆς στρατηγικῆς ἡμῶν ταύτης ἀφηγήσεως τῷ πάντων ἀγαθῶν δοτῆρι Θεῷ ἀνατίθεμεν.

ξθ΄. Νόμοι μὲν οὖν στρατηγικοὶ καὶ τύποι τοσοῦτοι παρὰ τῆς ἡμετέρας
305 βασιλείας σοί τε αὐτῷ καὶ τῷ ὑπό σε στρατεύματί τε καὶ πολιτεύματι διὰ πείρας
ἐγγεγυμνασμένοι ἔστωσάν τε καὶ φυλαττέσθωσαν, ὦ στρατηγέ, καὶ χρή σε τοῖς
ἐνταῦθα ἐγγεγραμμένοις μετὰ προσοχῆς τε καὶ νήψεως πλείστης ἐμμελετᾶν.
μεγάλα γὰρ κερδήσεις ἐκ τοῦ βιβλίου τούτου, καὶ λίαν ὠφέλιμα· ὅταν γὰρ ἐν
αὐτῷ ἀκριβῶς στρατηγήματά τε καὶ διατάγματα ὑπέρ σου κατανοήσεις, τότε
310 ἄρα καὶ εἴποτε τοῖς αὐτοῖς οἱ πολέμιοι χρήσονται, ῥᾳδίως τὰ ἐναντία τούτων
κατὰ ἐκείνων ἐπινοήσεις.

ο΄. Ταῦτα γὰρ κατὰ τὸ δυνατὸν ἔκ τε τῆς τῶν πολέμων πείρας, ὡς εἴρηται,
καὶ ἐκ τῶν εἰρημένων παρὰ τῶν ἀρχαίων, εἰς κοινὴν ὠφέλειαν προτεθείκαμεν,
οὔτε κάλλους λέξεως φροντίσαντες, ὡς ἐν ἀρχῇ που ἡμῖν εἴρηται τοῦ συντάγμα-
315 τος οὔτε τῆς ἄλλης ἐμπεριέργου συντάξεως, ἀλλ᾽ ἢ μόνον δὲ ἁπλαῖς καὶ κοιναῖς
χρησάμενοι ταῖς λέξεσι καὶ ὁποίαις μᾶλλον ἡ στρατιωτικὴ συνήθεια χρῆσθαι
εἴωθεν.

οα΄. Ὅσα δὲ κεφάλαια ἕτερα τά, ὡς εἰκός, ἀπαντῶντα ἐν ἑκάστῳ πολέμου
καιρῷ ἤ τινος ἐκείνου παρασκευῆς, καὶ μάλιστα ἐν τῷ νῦν ἡμῖν ἐνοχλοῦντι

---

312–317 Cf. praef.63–72.    318–326 Cf. Strat., 11 (fin).

292 διαφέροντες Α διαφέρονται Μ    293 πρόχειρον Α om. Μ    295 περὶ…φαινομένων Α
om. Μ    299 τὸν² Α om. Μ    300 καθηγιασμένοι τελεσιουργήσουσιν Μ καθηγνισμένοι
ἐπιτελέσουσιν Α    301 ἀναστήσουσιν Μ ἀναθήσουσιν Α    303 ἀνατίθεμεν Α ἀνατιθέαμεν
Μ    308–309 ἐν…ἀκριβῶς Μ trsp. Α    310 ἄρα…εἴποτε Μ ἐάν ποτε Α | ῥᾳδίως Μ εὐκόλως
Α    313 ἀρχαίων Μ ἀρχαίων κατανοήσαντες Α    314 που Μ om. Α    315 τῆς…
ἐμπεριέργου Μ τινὸς ἄλλης περιέργου Α | ἀλλ᾽ ἢ Μ ἀλλὰ Α    316 ταῖς Μ om. Α | ὁποίαις
μᾶλλον Μ οἵας ἔχει Α    316–317 χρῆσθαι εἴωθεν Μ om. Α    318 ἑκάστῳ Μ ἑκάστου Α
319 παρασκευῆς Μ παρασκευῆς καὶ ἑτοιμασίας Α

celestial phenomena. They should be distinguished for their wisdom and knowledge of calculation of the stars, about the Handy Table of Ptolemy[19] and about his so-called Tetrabiblos, and about other matters in the observational notes[20] of the Chaldaeans and, in addition, the declaration of Aratos concerning Phenomena,[21] and the daily and monthly observations of John Lydos.[22] But as for the nativities[23] found scattered about in those writings, inasmuch as they are rejected by the church of God, Our Majesty also forbids them. This is the function of astronomy.

68. For the priestly skill pure priests, respected for their life and conduct. Having been sanctified themselves, they are to bring to perfection and offer up the consummation of their own activity to God. As indeed we too, having recapitulated what we have said previously, commend the consummation of this dissertation on strategy to God the giver of all good things.

69. Let these, then, be the laws and models for generals from Our Majesty to you and to the army and the commonwealth under you, which have been thoroughly tested by experience. Let them be observed, O general. It is incumbent on you to meditate on what is written in them with attention and a great deal of sobriety. For you will derive great profit from this book and it will prove very helpful. When you have an accurate understanding of the stratagems and ordinances it contains for your benefit, then, if the enemy ever make use of them, you will easily devise the opposite of these against them.

70. To the best of our ability, then, we have placed before you for the common benefit the experience gained from war, as was said, and what was written by the ancient authors, without regard for fancy language, as we remarked somewhere in the beginning of this composition, or for any other elaborate arrangement. But we have made use only of simple and common expressions and those of the kind that military men are accustomed to use.[24]

71. As for all the other topics that naturally crop up in each period of war or

19. The Byzantines regarded Ptolemy (ca. 130–175) as the greatest authority on astronomy and astrology: *Suda* (Π 3033); *ODB*.

20. Refers to the Chaldaean Oracles, supposed divine revelations, consulted by the Byzantines, ed. E. des Places (Paris, 1971). But see Hippolytus, *Refutatio*, 4.4.4.

21. On Aratos and his *Phenomena*, see *Suda* A 3745.

22. John Lydos, bureaucrat and scholar (490–ca.565), wrote on monthly calendars and feasts: *De mensibus*, ed. R. Wünsch (Leipzig, 1898).

23. Prophecies about birth: *Suda*, Γ 131; Ptolemy, *Tetrabiblos*, 7.

24. Cf. prologue 63–72.

320 Σαρακηνῶν ἔθνει, δι᾿ ὅπερ, ὡς εἴρηταί που ἡμῖν, καὶ τὸ παρὸν συντέτακται
βιβλίον, εἰ καὶ μὴ πάντα συλλαβεῖν ἐδυνήθημεν, ἀλλ᾿ ἔκ τε τῶν γεγραμμένων, ἔκ
τε τῆς προλαβούσης πείρας, καὶ αὐτῆς δὲ τῆς τῶν πραγμάτων φύσεως στοχάζε-
σθαί σε δέον καί, ὡς δυνατόν, ἁρμόζεσθαι τοῖς ἀναφυομένοις. οὐ γὰρ οἶμαι
δυνατόν, οὔτε ἡμᾶς οὔτε τινὰ ἕτερον, ἅπαντα γράφειν πρὸς ἅπαντα τὰ μέλλον-
325 τα ἀναφύεσθαι, ὥστε παραφυλάττεσθαι ἅπαντα ἀπείρων οὐσῶν τῷ μέτρῳ τῶν
ἐμπιπτουσῶν ἑκάστοτε διαφόρων περιστάσεων.

οβ΄. Οὔτε γὰρ ὡσαύτως ἀεὶ οὔτε ὁμοίως ὑπὸ τῶν ἐναντίων τὰ ἐκείνων
ἐγχειροῦνται στρατηγήματα. διὸ οὐδέ δύναταί τις τεκμήρασθαι τὰ | μέλλοντα  380ᵛ
ἀναγκαῖα πρὸς χρῆσιν ἑκάστοτε. ἀλλ᾿ οὐδὲ μιᾷ γνώμῃ στρατηγοῦνται, ἀλλὰ
330 ποικίλης οὔσης τῆς παρὰ τῶν ἐναντίων ἐγχειρήσεως, καὶ διάφοροι οἱ τρόποι
τῶν ἀντεγχειρήσεων ὀφείλουσι γίνεσθαι. πανοῦργος γὰρ καὶ ἀκατάληπτος ἡ
ἀνθρωπεία φύσις ὑπάρχουσα, πολλὰ καὶ βουλεύεσθαι καὶ ἐγχειρεῖν παρ᾿
ἐλπίδας δύναται.

ογ΄. Ὅθεν καὶ ἁρμοδίως καὶ καταχρέως δέον ἀεί σε, ὦ στρατηγέ, τῇ πρὸς
335 Θεὸν δεήσει σχολάζειν καὶ τὰς αὐτοῦ ἐντολὰς φυλάττειν, ἵνα δι᾿ αὐτοῦ δύνασαι
καὶ κατ᾿ ἐχθρῶν σοφίζεσθαι, καὶ αὐτὸς ἀβλαβὴς ἅμα τοῖς ὑπό σε περισῴζεσθαι,
καὶ τὴν ἐν Χριστῷ τῷ ἀληθινῷ Θεῷ καὶ βασιλεῖ τοῦ παντὸς αἰωνίῳ σωτηρίαν
καὶ νίκην ἄνωθεν ὑποδέχεσθαι, ᾧ ἡ δόξα καὶ τὸ κράτος εἰς τοὺς αἰῶνας. ἀμήν.

---

320 που M om. A　324 γράφειν Du γράφειν ἢ codd.　325 ἅπαντα Du ἁπάντων codd. |
οὐσῶν A ὄντων M　327 ὡσαύτως…ὁμοίως M ὁμοίως ἀεὶ τὰ A　330 καὶ διάφοροι M trsp.
A　331 τῶν M τῶν κατ᾿ αὐτῶν A　332 ἀνθρωπεία M ἀνθρωπινὴ A　335 φυλάττειν M
φυλάσσειν A　338 καὶ² … κράτος M om. A

of preparation for it, and especially against the Saracen nation now causing us trouble—on whose account, as we have said, the present book has been compiled—even if we have not been able to take up everything, still, from what has been written, as well as from experience acquired, and from the very nature of things, you must form estimates to the extent possible and accommodate yourself to the situations that arise.[25] I do not think it possible, either for us or for anyone else to write about everything that is likely to happen, so as to be on one's guard against everything, seeing that the diverse circumstances in each case are unlimited in number.

72. Stratagems are not always attempted by our adversaries in a like manner. Thus, nobody can instruct us about what <tactics> to employ in the future each time. The enemy does not go to war with only one plan, but takes the offensive in a variety of ways and so there ought to be many ways of counteracting them. Human nature is very tricky and beyond understanding; it will make many plans and is able to undertake things beyond expectation.

73. And so it is always necessary for you, O general, in a fitting, dutiful way, to devote yourself to prayer to God and to observe his commandments, so that you will be able to outwit the enemy and preserve yourself and those under you safe from harm. By so doing you will receive salvation and victory from above in Christ the true God and eternal emperor of all, to whom be the glory and the power for the ages. Amen.

25. Cf. *Strat.* 11 (*fin*).

Sites discussed in the *Taktika*.

Maps drawn by Kachergis Book Design.
© Dumbarton Oaks, Trustees for Harvard University.

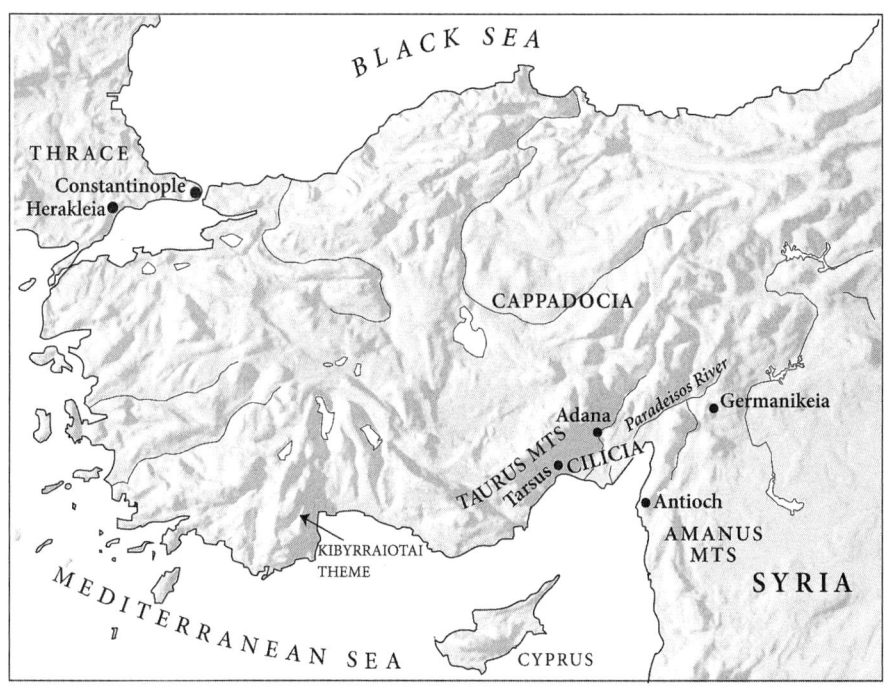

# BYZANTINE MEASUREMENTS

Note: Schilbach = Schilbach, E. *Byzantinische Metrologie*. Munich, 1970.

**bowshot** (σαγιττόβολον): Flight range has been estimated at about 300 m: W. McLeod, "The Range of the Ancient Bow," *Phoenix: The Journal of the Classical Association of Canada* 19 (1965): 1–14. Schilbach, 42, puts it at 328.84 m. A. Bivar limits accurate target range to about 133 m: "Cavalry Equipment and Tactics on the Euphrates Frontier," *DOP* 26 (1972): 283.

**daktylos, pl. daktyloi** (δάκτυλος): 1.95 cm (Schilbach, 16).

**foot** (πούς): 31.23 cm (Schilbach, 13–16).

**liter** (λίτρα): Approximately 320 g (Schilbach, 162).

**mile** (μίλιον): The Roman mile, still standard in the seventh century, came to 1,480 m (Schilbach, 32–36).

**milestone** (σημεῖον): one mile.

**orguia** (ὀργυιά): ca. 2 m; from 187 cm to 210 cm. (Schilbach, 22–23).

**pechys, pl. pecheis** (πῆχυς): 46.8 cm. Another pechys was an agricultural measure of 62.46 cm (Schilbach, 20–21).

**spithame, pl. spithamai** (σπιθαμή): 23.4 cm (Schilbach, 19).

**stadion, pl. stadia** (στάδιον): A term, antiquated in the time of Leo, indicating a mile (Schilbach, 32–33).

# GLOSSARY

Abbreviations. Ger. = Germanic, Gk. = Greek, Lat. = Latin, pl. = plural

**alakation, pl. alakatia**: A stone-throwing machine that revolves in a circle with men pulling on ropes at one end while the other holds the object to be hurled. In the West called trebuchet.

**antikensor, pl. antikensores**: Quartering parties who go ahead of the main body looking for suitable roads and camp sites (cf. Lat. *anticenseo*). By Leo's time they were not distinguished from the **minsoratores**.

**arithmos**: A number of troops, usually meaning a bandon, i.e., about three hundred soldiers (cf. Lat. *numerus*).

**assault troops**: See **koursores**.

**avengers**: See **defenders**.

**ballista**: A general term for torsion-powered artillery.

**bandon, pl. banda**: A flag or standard, also a unit of about 320 soldiers. (cf. Ger. Band, Bänner).

**caltrop**: Metal object with three or four protruding spikes designed to trip up and impale horses.

**chartoularios, pl. chartoularioi**: Official in charge of registering the troops in a **theme**, (cf. Lat. *charta*).

**chiliarchy**: (Gk. χίλιοι = thousand) Division of about one thousand men, equivalent to a **moira** or **droungos**.

**count**: (cf. Lat. comes) Commander of a **bandon**.

**crescent formation**: A half-moon or C-like formation used by troops on land, and by ships at sea.

**defenders**: Troops in close or compact order who were assigned to support assault troops (Lat. *defensores*). Also called **avengers** (ἔκδικοι).

**dekarchy**: Unit of ten or fewer soldiers, commanded by a **dekarch** (δέκα = ten).

**deputies**: Depotatoi, medical corpsmen (cf. Lat. *deputatus*). Also called **skribones**.

**domestic**: Designates a broad range of officials: ecclesiastical, civil, and military. In the *Taktika* it seems to mean an adjutant to the general. Later in the tenth century it designated the supreme army commander. In this last function, more properly **Domestic of the Schools**.

**dromon, pl. dromons**: "Runner"; a large battleship with two banks of oars.

**droungarios, pl. droungarioi**: Commander of a **droungos** or **moira** and, sometimes, of special divisions or a naval command. Later, a position in the civil administration of a **theme**.

**droungos, pl. droungoi**: Troops massed together in irregular formation, made up of three **banda**. Cf. Lat. *globus*, thought to come from Ger. drängen, thronga; but it may have begun as a Gallic word: see Rance, 2004. See also **moira**.

**epistates, pl. epistatai**: Second man in **file** (= **sekoundos**, Lat. *secundus*).

**file**: See **lochos**.

**flank guards**: Troops guarding flanks (sides) of the battle line.

**foulkon**: A body of troops in very close order, sometimes forming a dense mass with shields overlapping and spear points projecting out (cf. Ger. Volk).

**galley**: Small ship employed mostly in scouting (cf. Lat. *galea*).

**group leader**: See **lochagos**.

**general**: See **strategos**.

**Greek fire**: Prepared fire, also known as liquid or Greek fire, was a petroleum-based substance, put under pressure, ignited, and discharged through bronze tubes, called siphons, engulfing the enemy in roaring flames and thick black smoke. See Constitution 19, n. 2.

**hardtack**: Twice-cooked biscuit; staple of the Byzantine soldier.

**hekatontarch**: Commander of a hundred troops (Gk. ἑκατόν = one hundred), (= **kentarch**, after Lat. *centum*. Cf. centurion).

**herald**: Conveys commands of officers to troops.

**hoplite**: Classical Greek term for heavily armed infantryman.

**hypostrategos, pl. hypostrategoi**: Second in command of a **meros**.

**kamelavkion, pl. kamelavkia**: Originally a headcovering, then used as a signal flag.

**kampidouktor**: Field guide who also drilled the soldiers (cf. Lat. *campus*, field; *ductor*, leader).

**kantator, pl. kantatores**: (Lat. *cantator*) Men who exhort and stir up the army before combat.

**karagos, pl. karagoi**: The baggage train when drawn up into a defensive barrier.

**kleisoura, pl. kleisourai**: Small, border province in the mountains (Gk. κλείω, to close).

**klibanon**: (Lat. *clibanum*) Clay container for baking bread. The name was also used for various sorts of thoracic body armor, which retained so much heat, the soldiers compared them to baking ovens.

**kontubernion**: (Lat. *contubernium*) A squad of ten soldiers or fewer.

**koumbarion, pl. koumbaria**: Large ship used by Arabs.

**koursor, pl. koursores**: Troops in open or extended order, assigned to move out ahead of the line and pursue the retreating enemy (cf. Lat. *cursus*).

**lieutenant general**: See **hypostrategos**.

**lochos**: From front to rear, a ten-man line of cavalry, or a sixteen-man line of infantry.

**lochagos, pl. lochagoi**: The first soldier in a file or **lochos** (= **protostates** and **primos**).

**menavlon, pl. menavla**: Heavy spear, pike.

**merarch**: See **meros**.

**meros**: A division of troops, also known as **tourma**, made up of three **moirai**, from three thousand to six thousand men, commanded by a **merarch**. A great deal of flexibility was allowed in making up these divisions. See Constitution 4.

**moira, pl. moirai**: Division of troops made up of three banda, from one thousand to three thousand men, commanded by a **moirarch**.

**moirarch**: see **moira**.

**nomisma, pl. nomismata**: (Lat. *solidus*) The standard gold coin that formed the basis of the Byzantine monetary system.

**ouragos, pl. ouragoi**: Last man in a **file** (Gk. οὐρα = tail). Also called **tetrarch**: "in charge of four men."

**outflankers**: Troops assigned to envelop enemy wings.

**pelta, pl. peltai**: Small round shield carried by light armed troops.

**pentarch**: In charge of five men (Gk. πέντε = five).

**phalanx**: A square or rectangular infantry formation of one thousand men.

**praetor**: Chief legal officer in a **theme**.

**promachos, pl. promachoi**: First line of troops in battle formation. See also **koursores**.

**protonotary**: Official in the civil administration of a **theme**.

**rear guards**: Take up position behind the entire battle line.

**Saracens**: A generic term for Arabs, implying Muslims (Arabic = Eastern).

**Scythians**: A general term for the nomadic peoples north of the Black Sea and throughout central Asia.

**siphon**: Bronze tube through which **Greek fire** was discharged.

**skoutatos, pl. skoutatoi**: Heavily armed foot soldier

**Slavs**: Peoples who lived along the lower Danube.

**squad (kontubernion)**: A basic unit of ten soldiers or fewer.

**strategos, pl. strategoi**: commander of a **theme**.

**strategy**: Generalship; the conduct of a war in its totality, including objectives, alliances, stratagems, and other matters to be decided by the commander.

**stratelates, pl. stratelatai**: Term designating a higher officer, frequently a **tourmarch**.

**tactics**: Orderly arrangement of weaponry, drills, battle formations and movements of troops.

**tagma, pl. tagmata**: A general term for a formation of troops, usually equivalent to a **bandon**.

**theme**: An army, commanded by a general and composed of three divisions or **tourmai**; also the land or province in which that army resided (Gk. θέμα = something put in place; how it came to be applied to an army division is not clear).

**thyreos, pl. thyreoi**: Large oblong shield.

**touldos (also touldon)**: (Lat. *tultum*) Baggage train.

**tourma, pl. tourmai**: Large body of troops, later **meros**. Commanded by a **tourmarch**.

**trireme**: (Lat. *tres*, three; *remi*, oars) Ancient large battleship.

**Trisagion**: A hymn: "Holy God, holy strong one, holy immortal one, have mercy on us" (Gk. Τρισάγιον = Thrice Holy).

**Turks**: In Leo's time this generally designated the Magyars (see map).

# PERSONS MENTIONED

**Aelian** (second century A.D.): Greek author who lived in Rome and compiled treatises about military tactics and drills.

**Alexander the Great** (356–323 B.C.): King of Macedon and conqueror of Greece, Persia, and Egypt. He was regarded as the model of an ideal emperor. Legends about his exploits, real and imaginary, were popular among the Byzantines.

**Arrian** (third century B.C.): Greek historian who wrote about the campaigns of Alexander the Great.

**Asclepiodotus** (ca. 130–71 B.C.): Although a rhetorician, and not a military man, he compiled a lengthy work on tactics.

**Basil I** (r. 867–886): Although of peasant origin, he earned the favor of influential persons. He became a favorite of Michael III, whom he murdered to ascend the throne and found the Macedonian dynasty. He was a strong emperor and successful in his wars. He disliked and even imprisoned his son and heir, Leo, but they were reconciled before his death.

**Nikephoros Phokas** (late ninth century): From a noble family, he rose rapidly to become Domestic of the Schools (supreme army commander) and conducted successful campaigns in Southern Italy, Bulgaria, and Asia Minor. He was greatly admired by Leo.

**Onasander** (first century A.D.): Author of a (lost) commentary on Plato's *Republic*, he wrote a military treatise that centered on the duties of the commander and greatly influenced subsequent authors, including Leo.

**Polyaenus** (second century A.D.): Macedonian rhetorician residing in Rome, who compiled, in Greek, a large collection of military stratagems (*Strategemata*) gleaned from historical sources.

**Scipio** (236–183 B.C.): Roman general, noted for victories in Spain and elsewhere, who defeated the Carthaginians under Hannibal, in 202 B.C.

# GREEK PROPER NAMES

# GREEK TERMS

The asterisk (*) identifies *hapax legomena*.

# INDEX FONTIUM

# GENERAL INDEX

Most entries refer to Constitution (in **boldface**), then section.
*Italic* numerals refer to pages.

into units, 4§34, 60, 65, 67

*See also specific groups/individuals*

divisions, *xiv*, 4§45–46

first in command of, 4§56

during marches, 9§57, 66, 69

doctors, 1§7. *See also* deputies

domestic, 4§32; *650*

dreams, 20§149, 179, 213

drilling. *See* training/drilling

drills (tools), 19§5

dromons, 19§1; *650*

benches and oarsmen for, 19§8

equipment of, 19§4–13, 75–77

*See also* naval warfare

droungarios/droungarioi

defined, 4§11, 44; *650*

in formations, 18§141

during marches, 9§11

in naval warfare, 19§26–27

position of, 4§11

ranking of, 4§6

droungos/droungoi

defined, *650*

in division of army, 4§11, 45

during marches, 9§6

number of men in, 4§47, 49

officers in, 4§3

training for, 7§32

drums

Saracens' use of, 18§106, 134

for test of bravery, 20§76

dust

in face of enemy, 20§108

as warning of enemy approach, 9§39

earthquakes, Ep§61

Egypt, 18§104; 20§212

ekdikoi, 7§23. *See also* defenders

elephants, 1§7

emperors, Ep§7

concern for subjects, Pr§2, 2n; 15§35

generals appointed by, 1§10; 4§8

as supreme general, Pr§6n

enemy

assessment of, 12§106; 13§3; 14§17, 25,
98; 17§69–79, 85; 19§75–77, 81; 20§68,
98–99, 105, 109, 177; Ep§19, 21, 36

breaking agreements with, 20§39

deception of, 20§15, 19–24, 35, 51, 53, 99,
123–124, 144, 168; Ep§46

desertion by, 13§5; 14§25; 17§32; 20§44

different modes of operation against,
20§12

formations secret from, 7§28–29; 14§11

pursuit of, 12§104; 14§7; 18§38, 57–58;
20§25, 59, 180, 202

strength of, Pr§9; 9§22; 12§18; 17§31,
74–75; 20§98

*See also* hostile territory; prisoners; spies

entrenchments, 11§1, 39. *See also* camps

envoys. *See* ambassadors

epigram, 20§1n

epistates/epistatai, *650*. *See also* sekoundoi/
sekoundos

equipment. *See* baggage train

Ethiopians, 18§109, 109n, 129

Euxine Sea, 19§77

excavation, in siege warfare, 15§28

excrement, time determined from, 17§85

exercises. *See* training/drilling

exhortation. *See* speeches

expenses, Ep§30, 56, 64

face-to-face battle (one on two fronts), 7§8

family. *See* ancestry

farmers, 4§1; 9§16–18; 11§9; 20§209

fatherland, love of, 18§16–17, 19

fathers, generals as, 2§1, 11

favorable wind, 19§24, 31

fear

impacts of, 3§16; 17§91; 18§112; 20§76

siege warfare and, 15§5, 9, 15, 20–21, 38

*See also* cowardice

field guides

position of, 14§59, 72

during training, 7§38, 38n, 39, 50

*See also* kampidouktor

fighting units, 1§7

fighting while fleeing (maneuver), 14§15; 20§201

file(s), 4§72

armaments of, 12§94

depth/thickness of, 4§72, 76; 7§64; 14§69;
18§143–144

formation of, 4§39, 66, 71–76; 18§143–145

number in tagmata, 4§58

*See also* lochos; squads

file closers, 7§53, 65, 69; 14§70

file position

army size and, 4§35, 48

of dekarchs, 4§6, 14; 18§142

qualities of men and, 4§36

of tetrarchs, 4§15

files (tools), 5§3; 6§2

fire-bearing arrows, 15§26

fires

burning down estates, 20§161